Analytical Lexicon of New Testament Greek

Analytical Lexicon of New Testament Greek

Revised and Updated

Edited by

Maurice A. Robinson and Mark A. House

HENDRICKSON
PUBLISHERS

Analytical Lexicon of New Testament Greek: Revised and Updated

© 2012 by Hendrickson Publishers Marketing, LLC
P. O. Box 3473
Peabody, Massachusetts 01961-3473
www.hendrickson.com

ISBN: 978-1-59856-701-4

The parsing information in this work is derived from and based upon data that has been revised and edited by Maurice A. Robinson and used in various print and software works and made available in the public domain.

The dictionary entries in this work are from the *Compact Greek-English Lexicon of the New Testament*, revised and edited by Mark A. House.

The various appendices in this work were compiled and edited by Mark A. House.

Printed in the United States of America

Third Printing — September 2017

Library of Congress Cataloging-in-Publication Data

Analytical lexicon of New Testament Greek / Maurice A. Robinson and Mark A. House, editors.—Rev. and updated.
    pages. cm.
   ISBN 978-1-59856-701-4 (alkaline paper)
   1. Greek language, Biblical—Dictionaries. 2. Greek language, Biblical—Grammar.
  I. Robinson, Maurice A. II. House, Mark A.
   PA881.A55 2012
   487′.4—dc23
                 2011053343

Table of Contents

Preface

Analytical lexicons, which provide a comprehensive grammatical analysis of the words of particular texts, have long been available to assist students seeking a better understanding of the Greek of the New Testament. Since George W. Wigram first published his *Analytical Greek Lexicon of the New Testament* (Bagster & Sons, 1852), a number of subsequent editions have sought to refine and expand the database of parsed Greek words that formed the basis for Wigram's edition, particularly as new understandings of the New Testament text have prompted a movement away from the Received Text (or *Textus Receptus*)—the text behind the King James Version—toward the Greek editions that have become the basis for contemporary Bible translations.

This new edition of the *Analytical Lexicon of New Testament Greek* is based on a digitized database of Greek words developed over the course of decades by Maurice A. Robinson. Robinson's database, while seeking to preserve, in corrected form, the content of previous databases of the Received Text, has also kept abreast of later editions of the New Testament text. Thus the database upon which this edition is based contains analyses of several hundred Greek words contained neither in Wigram's original work nor in recent analytical lexicons based solely on the latest editions of the United Bible Society's Greek text.

The dictionary entries in this edition are taken from the *Compact Greek-English Lexicon of the New Testament*, edited by Mark A. House (Hendrickson, 2008), a thorough revision and updating of Alexander Souter's *A Pocket Lexicon to the Greek New Testament* (Oxford: Clarendon, 1916). Souter's succinct yet lucid definitions of the entire New Testament vocabulary, based on insights from Greek papyri and combined with a host of helpful Scripture references, have made his pocket edition one of the most widely-used compact Greek dictionaries. For this edition, the keywords for each dictionary entry have been brought into agreement with the lexical forms found in the analytical lexicon and keyed to the Strong's Greek numbering system.

A unique and helpful feature of Wigram's original work was his comprehensive set of Greek paradigms that illustrated the patterns of word formation inherent in the Greek grammatical system. Wigram also included detailed explanatory notes that highlighted the unique features of each of the paradigms. Unfortunately, many beginning Greek students have found Wigram's notes to be overly detailed and technical, making it difficult to navigate the vast territory of Greek grammar in order to find the information needed to analyze a particular Greek word. Wigram also included many forms and grammatical details relevant to broader Greek, but not particularly relevant to the Greek of the New Testament. A revised but largely unchanged edition of Wigram's paradigms and notes was also included in *The New Analytical Greek Lexicon*, edited by Wesley J. Perschbacher (Hendrickson, 1990).

Replacing Wigram's paradigms and notes in this edition are two appendices designed to provide additional help to students of New Testament Greek seeking to gain a fuller grammatical analysis of New Testament words. The second appendix, the *Glossary of Greek Grammatical Terms,* assists students in deciphering the host of technical terms used in the study of Greek grammar—terms such as "accusative," "deponent," and "reduplication." The glossary includes not only all of the grammatical terms used in abbreviated form throughout the *Analytical Lexicon,* but other terms commonly used in textbooks of basic Greek grammar. The third appendix, the *Greek Word Tables,* provides an overview of Greek word paradigms, with simplified explanatory notes, designed to assist the student in comparing the forms found in the *Analytical Lexicon* with similar forms in the wider system of New Testament Greek grammar. A fourth appendix offers a list of the "principal parts" of the most frequent irregular verbs found in the New Testament.

We wish to thank the editors for their respective contributions as well as their assistance and guidance in the various aspects of preparing and compiling them into this new edition. We also want to especially thank Scott Musser for his programming and helpful computer database processing at many stages of the work.

— The Publisher

Features of the Analytical Lexicon

The *Analytical Lexicon* contains two types of entry—the analytical entry and the dictionary entry. A description of the various features of both types of entry follows:

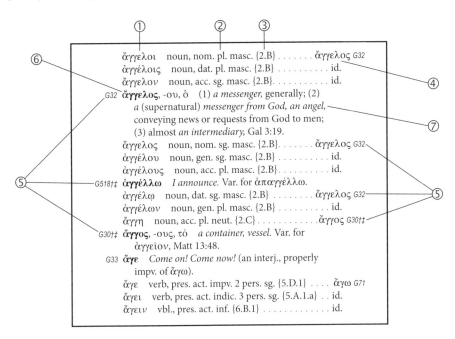

① **Analytical Entry**: Greek words in regular type are the full spellings (inflected forms) that a reader will encounter in the text of the New Testament.

② **Parsing**: The basic information needed to analyze each inflected word's syntactical relationship within its context. Processing this information is the first step in appropriately translating the Greek word. For words with more than one possible analysis, each parsing is listed on a separate line. The full forms of the abbreviated parsing elements may be found in the *Abbreviations* section (page xv). Definitions of the various parsing items may be found in the *Glossary of Greek Grammatical Terms* (Appendix II, page 381).

③ **Table Reference**: The location (in curly braces) of the corresponding word form in the *Greek Word Tables* (Appendix III, page 401). The word tables show the form in the larger context of Greek morphology.

④ **Lexical Form**: Found at the end of an analytical entry, this is the form (spelling) used to look up the word's meaning in a dictionary entry in this work or in another lexicon. When "id." (= *idem*, the same) stands in place of a lexical form, it indicates that the parsed form has the same lexical form as the entry just above it.

⑤ **Strong's Numbering**: The number assigned to the lexical form in the *Greek Dictionary* of the *Strong's Exhaustive Concordance*. This number stands at the end of each analytical entry and at the beginning of the corresponding dictionary entry. This numbering reference system is included to provide a quick and easy way to identify and locate a desired dictionary entry or to gain additional information about the word by using other tools keyed to the Strong's numbering system. **Note:** If the Strong's number is followed by a **dagger symbol** (†), the word in question is a variant Greek word that is either spelled differently from, or was not included in, the original Strong's dictionary. A Strong's number followed by a **double dagger symbol** (‡) indicates that the numerical arrangement of the original Strong's dictionary has been broken such that the corresponding entry is consequently out of position and not located in the regular Strong's numerical order. Appendix I (page 379) gives a complete listing of these Strong's numbers along with the page and column in this book where they can be found.

⑥ **Dictionary Entry**: Greek words in bold type are the lexical form of a word at the beginning of an entry which provides the basic English meanings of the word, often also referred to as a lexical entry.

⑦ **Definition**: The meaning of the word (in italics), with explanatory information provided in regular type. Multiple meanings are numbered.

Using the Analytical Lexicon

The Analytical Lexicon has been designed with four primary purposes in mind:

1. *Identifying and Analyzing Greek Words:* The primary purpose for the Analytical Lexicon is to enable students of the Greek NT to *parse* words—to identify the morphological elements that contribute to the meaning of each word in the NT, including the part of speech that each Greek word represents.

2. *Strengthening Grammatical Understanding:* An important secondary purpose is to assist students of NT Greek to see how each parsed word fits into the larger scheme of Greek grammar. This purpose is accomplished primarily through the *Greek Word Tables* (Appendix III). These tables, while not providing an exhaustive analysis of Greek morphology (word forms), illustrate the basic patterns of formation needed to enable the student to gain an overview of the system of Greek word formation and to see how each word fits in with that system.

3. *Elucidating Word Meanings:* Understanding the meaning of the words of Scripture requires at least three critical steps: 1) grasping the range of lexical significance of each word, 2) decoding the host of morphological elements that impact the meaning of each word, and 3) comprehending how the words of Greek sentences impact each other.

   The Analytical Lexicon provides critical assistance in taking the first two of these steps. The word definitions summarize the basic meanings of each NT word. The analytical entries enable step 2 by giving a complete analysis of each Greek word.

4. *Unlocking Morphological Significance:* Unlike other analytical lexicons, this lexicon takes the student a step farther in unlocking the significance of the various Greek words listed by illustrating how each morphological element contributes to meaning. This purpose is accomplished through the *Glossary of Greek Grammatical Terms* (Appendix II). Using the glossary, the student can look up each morphological element to discover how it contributes to the word's meaning. By combining this information with an understanding of the word's lexical meaning derived from the lexical entries, the student can arrive at a fuller picture of how NT words fit into their context.

The first step in using the Analytical Lexicon is to select the particular word from the Greek text of the NT that you wish to analyze. This will require a working knowledge of the

Greek alphabet so that you can find the alphabetical listing for that particular word. The listing(s) will look similar to the following:

ἀγαπᾶτε verb, pres. act. impv. 2 pers. pl. {5.D.2} . . . . id.
ἀγαπᾶτε verb, pres. act. indic. 2 pers. pl. {5.A.2} . . . . id.
ἀγαπᾶτε verb, pres. act. subjunc. 2 pers. pl. {5.B.2} . . . . . . id.

Many Greek words do not inflect, and thus will have no parsing information. The Greek word ἀγαπᾶτε (from ἀγαπάω, "I love") can be parsed in three different ways, as indicated by the fact that there are three listings of the same form. The context from which the word was drawn must be examined to know which analysis applies best. Sometimes more than one analysis is possible in a given context. Since all forms of ἀγαπᾶτε are verbs, the second listing indicates that the word is present tense, active voice, indicative mood, second person, plural number.

You can find out more about the significance of each of these parsing elements by look-ing them up in the *Glossary of Greek Grammatical Terms*. Taking the elements of the second line of the above example in reverse order, the person and number indicate who is doing the loving: "you" (plural); the indicative mood shows that the loving is actually happening (as opposed to being potential); the active voice indicates that the subject ("you") is doing (as opposed to receiving) the loving; and the present tense indicates: 1) that the loving is happening at the present time, and 2) that it is a process or something that generally occurs. Together these elements suggest the translation, "You are loving," or "You (generally) love."

If one parsing does not seem to fit the context, an alternative analysis may fit better. For example, for the first listing, the person and number indicate "you" (plural); the imperative mood indicates that this is an exhortation or command: "you must ..."; the active voice in-dicates that "you" must do the loving (rather than merely receive it); and the present tense indicates that "you" must love continually or in a general way. Together these parsing ele-ments suggest the translation, "Love!" or "Go on loving!"

All entries list the headword (lexeme), followed by morphological analysis, laid out in one of the following arrangements:

Nouns and Adjectives: *type, case, number, gender*

Pronouns: *type, person, case, number, gender*

Verbs: *tense, voice, mood, person, number*

Participles: *tense, voice, participle, case, number, gender*

Infinitives: *tense, voice, infinitive*

In curly braces {} following the parsing information are references to sections in the *Greek Word Tables* (Appendix III) that illustrate the pattern of inflection followed by the word under consideration. These serve to set the particular word being analyzed within the larger structure of the Greek morphological system. For example, in the second entry for ἀγαπᾶτε above, we find "5.A.2." in curly braces. This refers to section 5 (Verbs), sub-section A (Indicative Mood), and paragraph 2 (Contract, Liquid, and ιζω Verbs) in the Greek

Word Tables resource. By matching the parsing information from the analytical listing with the relevant word table in the indicated section, you should be able to find a word form that corresponds to the form you are investigating. In this case it is the present active indicative, second person plural verb form τιμᾶτε. While the references in curly braces in the analytical listings refer to tables with forms that are generally similar to the listed form, the forms in the tables will normally have a different verb stem from the one you are working with, and other factors in Greek word formation may cause the form in the table to differ slightly in other ways as well.

The final piece of information contained in the analytical listing is the lexical form of the word under investigation—the form you would use to look the word up in a Greek dictionary or lexicon. This form is found at the right margin of the analytical listing. If the form is identical to the one listed above it, "id." will be listed, as in the examples above. All of the sample entries above are from the lexical word ἀγαπάω. Using this lexical form, you can refer to the dictionary entry in this or another lexicon to discover its range of meanings and other pertinent information about the word. The dictionary entry for this lexicon has the following:

> G25 ἀγαπάω   *I love* (never of love between the sexes,
> but nearly always of the love of God or Christ
> to us, and of our love to Him and to our fellow
> creatures, as inspired by His love for us).

In the individual entries, the number that follows the lexical form in parentheses relates to the Strong's numbering system, which is used in a variety of Bible study tools and resources. The Strong's numbers are particularly useful for those who are unfamiliar with the Greek alphabet, since information related to Greek words can be located by using the number system.

In using the Analytical Lexicon, it is important to understand its limitations. This resource can assist you in taking the first steps in understanding the Greek words of the NT. It can help you identify each word's part of speech and provide a basic grammatical analysis of its form. It can also help you gain a basic grasp of each grammatical feature of a particular word and how these features may impact the meaning of a word. However, since a host of contextual factors beyond the individual word can impact meaning, a thorough understanding of Greek grammar and syntax of the phrase, clause, sentence, and discourse levels is important for gaining a more complete understanding.

Abbreviations

General

1	first person
2	second person
3	third person
A.D.	*anno domini* (Common Era)
absol.	absolute(ly)
abstr.	abstract
acc.	accusative case
act.	active voice
adj.	adjective
adv.	adverb(ial)
aor.	aorist tense
Aram.	Aramaic
art.	definite article
AV	Authorized Version (KJV)
B.C.	before Christ (before the Common Era)
c.	century
cf.	compare
cog.	cognate
comp.	comparative
concr.	concrete
cond.	conditional
conj.	conjunction
constr.	construction
correl.	correlative
dat.	dative case
def.	definite
dem.	demonstrative
depon.	deponent (verb)
e.g.	*exempli gratia*, for example

Eng.	English
esp.	especially
etc.	*et cetera*
excl.	exclamation, exclamatory
fem.	feminine gender
fut.	future tense
gen.	genitive case
Gk.	Greek
Heb.	Hebrew
id.	the same as the previous analytical entry
i.e.	*id est,* that is
impers.	impersonal(ly)
impf.	imperfect tense
impv.	imperative mood, imperatival
indecl.	indeclinable
indef.	indefinite
indic.	indicative mood
indir.	indirect
inf.	infinitive
interj.	interjection
interrog.	interrogative
intrans.	intransitive
Lat.	Latin
lit.	literal(ly)
LXX	Septuagint
masc.	masculine
met.	metaphorical(ly)
mid.	middle voice
mod.	modern
mid./pass.	middle or passive voice
MSS	manuscripts
neg.	negative
neut.	neuter gender
nom.	nominative case
NT	New Testament
obj.	object(ive)
opp.	opposite (of)
opt.	optative mood
orig.	original(ly)
OT	Old Testament

part.	particle
pass.	passive voice
perf.	perfect tense
pers.	person(al)
pl.	plural number
plup.	pluperfect tense
pred.	predicate
prep.	preposition(al)
pres.	present tense
pron.	pronoun
prop.	proper
ptc.	participle
q.v.	*quod vide* (which see)
recip.	reciprocal
refl.	reflexive
rel.	relative
sg.	singular number
subj.	subject
subjunc.	subjunctive mood
subs.	substantive
superl.	superlative
temp.	temporal
trans.	transitive
var.	textual variant
vb.	verb
vbl.	verbal
voc.	vocative case

Abbreviations for Appendix III: Greek Word Tables

1P	first person plural
2P	second person plural
3P	third person plural
1S	first person singular
2S	second person singular
3S	third person singular
A	accusative case
AP	accusative plural
APM	accusative plural masculine
APN	accusative plural neuter

AS	accusative singular
ASM	accusative singular masculine
ASN	accusative singular neuter
D	dative case
DP	dative plural
DPM	dative plural masculine
DPN	dative plural neuter
DS	dative singular
DSM	dative singular masculine
F	feminine gender
G	genitive case
GP	genitive plural
GPM	genitive plural masculine
GS	genitive singular
GSM	genitive singular masculine
GSN	genitive singular neuter
M	masculine gender
Mid./Pass.	middle or passive voice
N	neuter gender
NP	nominative plural
NPF	nominative plural feminine
NPM	nominative plural masculine
NS	nominative singular
NSF	nominative singular feminine
NSM	nominative singular masculine
NSN	nominative singular neuter
P	plural
S	singular
V	vocative
VP	vocative plural
VS	vocative singular
VSM	vocative singular masculine
VSN	vocative singular neuter

Biblical Books

Gen	Genesis
Exod	Exodus
Lev	Leviticus
Num	Numbers

Deut	Deuteronomy
1–2 Kgs	1–2 Kings
1–2 Chr	1–2 Chronicles
Neh	Nehemiah
Ps(s)	Psalm(s)
Prov	Proverbs
Isa	Isaiah
Jer	Jeremiah
Ezek	Ezekiel
Dan	Daniel
Zech	Zechariah
Matt	Matthew
Rom	Romans
1–2 Cor	1–2 Corinthians
Gal	Galatians
Eph	Ephesians
Phil	Philippians
Col	Colossians
1–2 Thess	1–2 Thessalonians
1–2 Tim	1–2 Timothy
Phlm	Philemon
Heb	Hebrews
Jas	James
1–2 Pet	1–2 Peter
Rev	Revelation

Analytical Lexicon with Compact Greek-English Dictionary

A α

G1 **A** (1) ἄλφα (*alpha*), the first letter of the Greek
alphabet; (2) the numeral 1; (3) *first*.
α noun, letter . . . . A *G1*
ἅ pron. rel., acc. pl. neut. {4.C} . . . . .ὅς *G3739*
ἅ pron. rel., nom. pl. neut. {4.C} . . . . id.

G2 **Ἀαρών**, ὁ *Aaron*, son of Amram and Jochebed,
younger brother of Moses (Heb.).
Ἀαρών noun prop. . . . . Ἀαρών *G2*

G3 **Ἀβαδδών**, ὁ *Destroyer* (i.e., *Destroying Angel*)
or "*place of destruction*" (personified) (Heb.).
Ἀβαδδών noun prop. . . . . Ἀβαδδών *G3*
ἀβαρῆ adj., acc. sg. masc. {3.E} . . . . ἀβαρής *G4*

G4 **ἀβαρής**, -ές *not burdensome, bringing no*
weight or oppression upon.
Ἀββα noun prop. . . . . .ἀββά *G5*

G5 **ἀββά** (ἀββᾶ), ὁ *Father!* (voc., from Aram.).
ἀββά noun . . . . .ἀββά *G5*
Ἀββά noun prop. . . . . id.
Ἀββά noun prop. . . . . id.
Ἀββαδών noun prop. . . . . Ἀβαδδών *G3*
Ἀβειληνῆς noun prop., gen. sg. fem. {2.A;
2.D} . . . . Ἀβιληνή *G9*
Ἄβελ noun prop. . . . . .Ἄβελ *G6*

G6 **Ἄβελ**, ὁ *Abel*, second son of Adam and Eve,
brother of Cain (Heb.).
Ἄβελ noun prop. . . . . Ἄβελ *G6*

G7 **Ἀβιά**, ὁ *Abijah*, founder of the eighth class of
priests (1 Chr 24:10) (Heb.).
Ἀβιά noun prop. . . . . .Ἀβιά *G7*
Ἀβιαθάρ noun prop. . . . . .Ἀβιαθάρ *G8*

G8 **Ἀβιαθάρ**, ὁ *Abiathar*, a priest in King David's
time (Heb.).
Ἀβιαθάρ noun prop. . . . . Ἀβιαθάρ *G8*

G9 **Ἀβιληνή**, -ῆς, ἡ *Abilene*, the territory surrounding Abila (in Syria), a small principality
in the mountains northwest of Damascus.
Ἀβιληνῆς noun prop., gen. sg. fem. {2.A;
2.D} . . . . Ἀβιληνή *G9*

G10 **Ἀβιούδ**, ὁ *Abiud*, son of Zorobabel and father
of Eliakim (Heb.).
Ἀβιούδ noun prop. . . . . .Ἀβιούδ *G10*

G11 **Ἀβραάμ**, ὁ *Abraham*, progenitor of the
Hebrew race; hence the phrase θυγατέρα
Ἀβραάμ (Luke 13:16) means simply *a woman*
of Hebrew race (Heb.).
Ἀβραάμ noun prop. . . . . .Ἀβραάμ *G11*
ἄβυσσον noun, acc. sg. fem. {2.B} . . . . . . ἄβυσσος *G12*

G12 **ἄβυσσος**, -ου, ἡ *the abyss, the unfathomable*
depth, an esp. Jewish conception, the home of
the dead and of evil spirits.
ἀβύσσου noun, gen. sg. fem. {2.B} . . . . . . ἄβυσσος *G12*
Ἄγαβος noun prop., nom. sg. masc. {2.B;
2.D} . . . . Ἄγαβος *G13*

G13 **Ἄγαβος**, -ου, ὁ *Agabus*, a Christian prophet
(Acts 11:28; 21:10).
Ἄγαβος noun prop., nom. sg. masc. {2.B;
2.D} . . . . .Ἄγαβος *G13*

ἀγαγεῖν vbl., ²aor. act. inf. {6.B.1} . . . . ἄγω *G71*
ἀγάγετε verb, ²aor. act. impv. 2 pers. pl. {5.D.1} . id.
ἀγάγῃ verb, ²aor. act. subjunc. 3 pers. sg. {5.B.1} id.
ἀγαγόντα vbl., ²aor. act. ptc. acc. sg. masc.
{6.A.1.a} . . . . id.
ἀγαγόντες vbl., ²aor. act. ptc. nom. pl. masc.
{6.A.1.a} . . . . id.
ἀγάγωσιν verb, ²aor. act. subjunc. 3 pers. pl.
{5.B.1} . . . . id.
ἀγαθά adj., acc. pl. neut. {3.A} . . . . .ἀγαθός *G18*
ἀγαθά adj., nom. pl. neut. {3.A} . . . . id.
ἀγαθάς adj., acc. pl. fem. {3.A} . . . . id.
ἀγαθέ adj., voc. sg. masc. {3.A} . . . . id.
ἀγαθή adj., nom. sg. fem. {3.A} . . . . id.
ἀγαθῇ adj., dat. sg. fem. {3.A} . . . . id.
ἀγαθήν adj., acc. sg. fem. {3.A} . . . . id.
ἀγαθῆς adj., gen. sg. fem. {3.A} . . . . id.
ἀγαθοεργεῖν vbl., pres. act. inf. {6.B.2} ἀγαθοεργέω *G14*

G14 **ἀγαθοεργέω** (ἀγαθουργέω) *I work that which*
is good, I perform good deeds.
ἀγαθοῖς adj., dat. pl. masc. {3.A} . . . . .ἀγαθός *G18*
ἀγαθοῖς adj., dat. pl. neut. {3.A} . . . . id.
ἀγαθόν adj., acc. sg. masc. {3.A} . . . . id.
ἀγαθόν adj., acc. sg. neut. {3.A} . . . . id.
ἀγαθόν adj., nom. sg. neut. {3.A} . . . . id.
ἀγαθοποιεῖτε verb, pres. act. impv. 2 pers. pl.
{5.D.2} . . . . ἀγαθοποιέω *G15*

G15 **ἀγαθοποιέω** *I do that which is good* (opp.
κακοποιέω).
ἀγαθοποιῆσαι vbl., aor. act. inf.
{6.B.1} . . . . ἀγαθοποιέω *G15*
ἀγαθοποιῆτε verb, pres. act. subjunc. 2 pers.
pl. {5.B.2} . . . . id.

G16 **ἀγαθοποιΐα** (ἀγαθοποιΐα), -ας, ἡ *the doing*
of that which is good.
ἀγαθοποιΐα noun, dat. sg. fem. {2.A} . . ἀγαθοποιΐα *G16*
ἀγαθοποιΐα noun, dat. sg. fem. {2.A} . . . . id.

G17 **ἀγαθοποιός**, -οῦ, ὁ *a doer of that which is*
good, opp. of κακοποιός (subs., ἀγαθοποιῶν
gen. pl. masc., 1 Pet 2:14).
ἀγαθοποιοῦντας vbl., pres. act. ptc. acc. pl. masc.
{6.A.2} . . . . ἀγαθοποιέω *G15*
ἀγαθοποιοῦντες vbl., pres. act. ptc. nom. pl.
masc. {6.A.2} . . . . id.
ἀγαθοποιοῦσαι vbl., pres. act. ptc. nom. pl.
fem. {6.A.2} . . . . id.
ἀγαθοποιῶν adj., gen. pl. masc. {3.A} . .ἀγαθοποιός *G17*
ἀγαθοποιῶν vbl., pres. act. ptc. nom. sg. masc.
{6.A.2} . . . . ἀγαθοποιέω *G15*

G18 **ἀγαθός**, -ή, -όν (1) *good* (intrinsically), *good*
(in nature), *good* (whether it be seen to be
so or not), the widest and most colorless of
all words with this meaning (opp. πονηρός,
κακός); (2) subs. τὰ ἀγαθά, *the goods*, Luke
12:18.
ἀγαθός adj., nom. sg. masc. {3.A} . . . . ἀγαθός *G18*
ἀγαθοῦ adj., gen. sg. masc. {3.A} . . . . id.

ἀγαθοῦ   adj., gen. sg. neut. {3.A} . . . . id.
ἀγαθουργῶν   vbl., pres. act. ptc. nom. sg. masc.
   {6.A.2}. . . . . ἀγαθοεργέω G14
ἀγαθούς   adj., acc. pl. masc. {3.A} . . . . .ἀγαθός G18
ἀγαθῷ   adj., dat. sg. masc. {3.A} . . . . id.
ἀγαθῷ   adj., dat. sg. neut. {3.A}. . . . . id.
ἀγαθῶν   adj., gen. pl. masc. {3.A}. . . . . id.
ἀγαθῶν   adj., gen. pl. neut. {3.A} . . . . id.
G19 **ἀγαθωσύνη**, -ης, ἡ   *goodness* (intrinsic, esp. as
   a personal quality), with stress on the kindly
   (rather than the righteous) side of goodness.
ἀγαθωσύνη   noun, nom. sg. fem. {2.A} .ἀγαθωσύνη G19
ἀγαθωσύνη   noun, dat. sg. fem. {2.A} . . . . id.
ἀγαθωσύνης   noun, gen. sg. fem. {2.A} . . . . . . id.
ἀγαλλιαθῆναι   vbl., aor. pass. inf. {6.B.1} ἀγαλλιάω G21
ἀγαλλιάσει   noun, dat. sg. fem. {2.C} . . ἀγαλλίασις G20
ἀγαλλιάσεως   noun, gen. sg. fem. {2.C} . . . . . id.
ἀγαλλιᾶσθε   verb, pres. mid./pass. impv. 2 pers. pl.
   {5.D.2}. . . . . ἀγαλλιάω G21
ἀγαλλιᾶσθε   verb, pres. mid./pass. indic.
   2 pers. pl. {5.A.2}. . . . . id.
ἀγαλλιασθῆναι   vbl., aor. pass. inf. {6.B.1} . . . . id.
G20 **ἀγαλλίασις**, -εως, ἡ   *wild joy, ecstatic delight,
   exultation, exhilaration.*
ἀγαλλίασις   noun, nom. sg. fem. {2.C} .ἀγαλλίασις G20
ἀγαλλιᾶτε   verb, pres. act. indic. 2 pers. pl.
   {5.A.2}. . . . . ἀγαλλιάω G21
G21 **ἀγαλλιάω**   *I exult, I am full of joy.*
ἀγαλλιώμεθα   verb, pres. mid./pass. subjunc.
   1 pers. pl. {5.B.2} . . . . ἀγαλλιάω G21
ἀγαλλιῶμεν   verb, pres. act. subjunc. 1 pers. pl.
   {5.B.2} . . . . id.
ἀγαλλιώμενοι   vbl., pres. mid./pass. ptc. nom.
   pl. masc. {6.A.2} . . . . id.
ἀγάμοις   noun, dat. pl. masc. {2.B}. . . . . . . ἄγαμος G22
G22 **ἄγαμος**, -ου, ὁ or ἡ   *unmarried, not married,* of
   a person not in a state of wedlock, whether he
   or she has formerly been married or not.
ἄγαμος   noun, nom. sg. fem. {2.B} . . . . ἄγαμος G22
ἄγαμος   noun, nom. sg. masc. {2.B} . . . . id.
ἀγανακτεῖν   vbl., pres. act. inf. {6.B.2} . . ἀγανακτέω G23
G23 **ἀγανακτέω**   *I am angry, I am incensed.*
ἀγανάκτησιν   noun, acc. sg. fem.
   {2.C} . . . . .ἀγανάκτησις G24
G24 **ἀγανάκτησις**, -εως, ἡ   *feeling of anger, vexation.*
ἀγανακτοῦντες   vbl., pres. act. ptc. nom. pl. masc.
   {6.A.2}. . . . . ἀγανακτέω G23
ἀγανακτῶν   vbl., pres. act. ptc. nom. sg. masc.
   {6.A.2}. . . . . id.
ἀγαπᾷ   verb, pres. act. indic. 3 pers. sg.
   {5.A.2}. . . . . ἀγαπάω G25
ἀγαπᾷ   verb, pres. act. subjunc. 3 pers. sg. {5.B.2}id.
ἀγάπαις   noun, dat. pl. fem. {2.A} . . . . ἀγάπη G26
ἀγαπᾶν   vbl., pres. act. inf. {6.B.2} . . . . . . ἀγαπάω G25
ἀγαπᾶν   vbl., pres. act. inf. {6.B.2} . . . . id.
ἀγαπᾷς   verb, pres. act. indic. 2 pers. sg. {5.A.2}. id.
ἀγαπᾶτε   verb, pres. act. impv. 2 pers. pl. {5.D.2} id.
ἀγαπᾶτε   verb, pres. act. indic. 2 pers. pl. {5.A.2} id.
ἀγαπᾶτε   verb, pres. act. subjunc. 2 pers. pl.
   {5.B.2} . . . . id.

ἀγαπάτω   verb, pres. act. impv. 3 pers. sg.
   {5.D.2}. . . . . id.
G25 **ἀγαπάω**   *I love* (never of love between the
   sexes, but nearly always of the love of God or
   Christ to us, and of our love to Him and to
   our fellow creatures, as inspired by His love
   for us).
G26 **ἀγάπη**, -ης, ἡ   (1) *love* (this was the sense of
   the word *charity* in the time of the AV), as
   that of God or Christ to us, and our love to
   Him and to our fellow creatures thus inspired
   (a word exclusively biblical, curtailed from
   ἀγάπησις (from ἀγαπάω); (2) in LXX generally of sexual love; first in higher sense not
   before about 100 B.C.); (3) ἀγάπη τοῦ θεοῦ,
   τοῦ χριστοῦ are sometimes ambiguous,
   when it is doubtful whether God's/Christ's
   love for us, or our love for God/Christ, is
   intended; in most cases the former is probably
   the primary thought; (4) ἀγάπαι pl. concr.,
   of the *love feasts* of the Christians, evening
   meals partaken of by Christians in the early
   Church, either accompanied or followed by
   the Eucharist (Jude 12). Such common meals
   were sacred, and intended to be expressive of
   the union of Christians in their Head.
ἀγάπη   noun, nom. sg. fem. {2.A}. . . . . ἀγάπη G26
ἀγάπη   noun, dat. sg. fem. {2.A}. . . . . id.
ἀγαπηθήσεται   verb, fut. pass. indic. 3 pers. sg.
   {5.A.1}. . . . . .ἀγαπάω G25
ἀγάπην   noun, acc. sg. fem. {2.A}. . . . . ἀγάπη G26
ἀγάπης   noun, gen. sg. fem. {2.A}. . . . . id.
ἀγαπήσαντι   vbl., aor. act. ptc. dat. sg. masc.
   {6.A.2}. . . . . .ἀγαπάω G25
ἀγαπήσαντος   vbl., aor. act. ptc. gen. sg. masc.
   {6.A.2}. . . . . id.
ἀγαπήσας   vbl., aor. act. ptc. nom. sg. masc.
   {6.A.2}. . . . . id.
ἀγαπήσατε   verb, aor. act. impv. 2 pers. pl.
   {5.D.1}. . . . . id.
ἀγαπήσει   verb, fut. act. indic. 3 pers. sg. {5.A.1} id.
ἀγαπήσεις   verb, fut. act. indic. 2 pers. sg.
   {5.A.1}. . . . . id.
ἀγαπήσητε   verb, aor. act. subjunc. 2 pers. pl.
   {5.B.1} . . . . id.
ἀγαπήσω   verb, fut. act. indic. 1 pers. sg. {5.A.1} id.
ἀγαπητά   adj., acc. pl. neut. {3.A}. . . . . . ἀγαπητός G27
ἀγαπητά   adj., nom. pl. neut. {3.A} . . . . id.
ἀγαπητέ   adj., voc. sg. masc. {3.A} . . . . id.
ἀγαπητῇ   adj., dat. sg. fem. {3.A} . . . . id.
ἀγαπητήν   adj., acc. sg. fem. {3.A} . . . . id.
ἀγαπητοί   adj., nom. pl. masc. {3.A} . . . . id.
ἀγαπητοί   adj., voc. pl. masc. {3.A} . . . . id.
ἀγαπητοῖς   adj., dat. pl. masc. {3.A}. . . . . id.
ἀγαπητόν   adj., acc. sg. masc. {3.A} . . . . id.
ἀγαπητόν   adj., nom. sg. neut. {3.A} . . . . id.
G27 **ἀγαπητός**, -ή, -όν   *loved, beloved,* with two
   special applications; (1) ὁ ἀγαπητός, *the
   Beloved,* a title of the Messiah (Christ), as beloved beyond all others by the God who sent

Him; (2) of Christians, as beloved by God, Christ, and one another.

ἀγαπητός   adj., nom. sg. masc. {3.A} . . . . ἀγαπητός *G27*
ἀγαπητοῦ   adj., gen. sg. masc. {3.A} . . . . id.
ἀγαπητῷ   adj., dat. sg. masc. {3.A} . . . . id.
ἀγαπητῷ   adj., dat. sg. neut. {3.A} . . . . id.
ἀγαπῶ   verb, pres. act. indic. 1 pers. sg.
  {5.A.2} . . . . ἀγαπάω *G25*
ἀγαπῶμαι   verb, pres. pass. indic. 1 pers. sg.
  {5.A.2} . . . . id.
ἀγαπῶμεν   verb, pres. act. indic. 1 pers. pl.
  {5.A.2} . . . . id.
ἀγαπῶμεν   verb, pres. act. subjunc. 1 pers. pl.
  {5.B.2} . . . . id.
ἀγαπῶν   vbl., pres. act. ptc. nom. sg. masc.
  {6.A.2} . . . . id.
ἀγαπῶντας   vbl., pres. act. ptc. acc. pl. masc.
  {6.A.2} . . . . id.
ἀγαπῶντι   vbl., pres. act. ptc. dat. sg. masc.
  {6.A.2} . . . . id.
ἀγαπῶντων   vbl., pres. act. ptc. gen. pl. masc.
  {6.A.2} . . . . id.
ἀγαπῶσι   verb, pres. act. indic. 3 pers. pl. {5.A.2} id.
ἀγαπῶσι   vbl., pres. act. ptc. dat. pl. masc.
  {6.A.2} . . . . id.
ἀγαπῶσιν   verb, pres. act. indic. 3 pers. pl.
  {5.A.2} . . . . id.
ἀγαπῶσιν   vbl., pres. act. ptc. dat. pl. masc.
  {6.A.2} . . . . id.

G28 **Ἀγάρ**, ἡ   *Hagar*, the servant of Sarah, wife of Abraham, and interpreted by Rabbinic lore, countenanced by Paul, as a type of Mount Sinai, where the Mosaic Law was given (Gal 4:24–25) (Heb.).

Ἀγάρ   noun prop. . . . . Ἀγάρ *G28*
Ἄγαρ   noun prop. . . . . id.
Ἄγαρ   noun prop. . . . . id.
ἀγγαρεύουσι   verb, pres. act. indic. 3 pers. pl.
  {5.A.1.a} . . . . ἀγγαρεύω *G29*
ἀγγαρεύουσιν   verb, pres. act. indic. 3 pers. pl.
  {5.A.1.a} . . . . id.
ἀγγαρεύσει   verb, fut. act. indic. 3 pers. sg.
  {5.A.1.a} . . . . id.

G29 **ἀγγαρεύω**   *I compel into service, I send* (on an errand); from a Persian word, meaning *to compel into the postal service.*

ἀγγεῖα   noun, acc. pl. neut. {2.B} . . . . ἀγγεῖον *G30*
ἀγγείοις   noun, dat. pl. neut. {2.B} . . . . id.

G30 **ἀγγεῖον**, -ου, τό   *a vessel, flask, can.*

G31 **ἀγγελία**, -ας, ἡ   *a message.*
ἀγγελία   noun, nom. sg. fem. {2.A} . . . . . . ἀγγελία *G31*
ἀγγέλλουσα   vbl., pres. act. ptc. nom. sg. fem.
  {6.A.1} . . . . ἀγγέλλω *G518†‡*
ἀγγέλοι   noun, nom. pl. masc. {2.B} . . . . . . ἄγγελος *G32*
ἀγγέλοις   noun, dat. pl. masc. {2.B} . . . . id.
ἄγγελον   noun, acc. sg. masc. {2.B} . . . . id.

G32 **ἄγγελος**, -ου, ὁ   (1) *a messenger*, generally; (2) *a* (supernatural) *messenger from God, an angel,* conveying news or requests from God to men; (3) almost *an intermediary,* Gal 3:19.

ἄγγελος   noun, nom. sg. masc. {2.B} . . . . . . ἄγγελος *G32*
ἀγγέλου   noun, gen. sg. masc. {2.B} . . . . id.
ἀγγέλους   noun, acc. pl. masc. {2.B} . . . . id.
G518†‡ **ἀγγέλλω**   *I announce.* Var. for ἀπαγγέλλω.
ἀγγέλῳ   noun, dat. sg. masc. {2.B} . . . . . . ἄγγελος *G32*
ἀγγέλων   noun, gen. pl. masc. {2.B} . . . . id.
ἄγγη   noun, acc. pl. neut. {2.C} . . . . ἄγγος *G30†‡*
G30†‡ **ἄγγος**, -ους, τό   *a container, vessel.* Var. for ἀγγεῖον, Matt 13:48.
G33 **ἄγε**   *Come on! Come now!* (an interj., properly impv. of ἄγω).
ἄγε   verb, pres. act. impv. 2 pers. sg. {5.D.1} . . . . ἄγω *G71*
ἄγει   verb, pres. act. indic. 3 pers. sg. {5.A.1.a} . . id.
ἄγειν   vbl., pres. act. inf. {6.B.1} . . . . id.
G34 **ἀγέλη**, -ης, ἡ   *a herd.*
ἀγέλη   noun, nom. sg. fem. {2.A} . . . . ἀγέλη *G34*
ἀγέλην   noun, acc. sg. fem. {2.A} . . . . id.
G35 **ἀγενεαλόγητος**, -ον   *not provided with a genealogy, whose descent cannot be traced.*
ἀγενεαλόγητος   adj., nom. sg. masc.
  {3.C} . . . . ἀγενεαλόγητος *G35*
ἀγενῆ   adj., acc. pl. neut. {3.E} . . . . ἀγενής *G36*
G36 **ἀγενής**, -ές   *ignoble,* lit., *without γένος (family).*
ἄγεσθαι   vbl., pres. pass. inf. {6.B.1} . . . . ἄγω *G71*
ἄγεσθε   verb, pres. pass. indic. 2 pers. pl.
  {5.A.1.d} . . . . id.
ἅγια   adj., acc. pl. neut. {3.A} . . . . ἅγιος *G40*
ἅγια   adj., nom. pl. neut. {3.A} . . . . id.
ἁγία   adj., nom. sg. fem. {3.A} . . . . id.
ἁγίᾳ   adj., dat. sg. fem. {3.A} . . . . id.
ἁγιάζει   verb, pres. act. indic. 3 pers. sg.
  {5.A.1.a} . . . . ἁγιάζω *G37*
ἁγιάζεται   verb, pres. pass. indic. 3 pers. sg.
  {5.A.1.d} . . . . id.
ἁγιαζόμενοι   vbl., pres. pass. ptc. nom. pl.
  masc. {6.A.1} . . . . id.
ἁγιαζομένους   vbl., pres. pass. ptc. acc. pl.
  masc. {6.A.1} . . . . id.
ἁγιάζον   vbl., pres. act. ptc. nom. sg. neut.
  {6.A.1} . . . . id.
G37 **ἁγιάζω**   *I make ἅγιος (set apart, holy);* apparently exclusively biblical.
ἁγιάζω   verb, pres. act. indic. 1 pers. sg.
  {5.A.1.a} . . . . ἁγιάζω *G37*
ἁγιάζων   vbl., pres. act. ptc. nom. sg. masc.
  {6.A.1} . . . . id.
ἅγιαι   adj., nom. pl. fem. {3.A} . . . . ἅγιος *G40*
ἁγίαις   adj., dat. pl. fem. {3.A} . . . . id.
ἁγίαν   adj., acc. sg. fem. {3.A} . . . . id.
ἁγίας   adj., gen. sg. fem. {3.A} . . . . id.
ἁγιάσαι   verb, aor. act. opt. 3 pers. sg. {5.C.1} ἁγιάζω *G37*
ἁγιάσας   vbl., aor. act. ptc. nom. sg. masc.
  {6.A.1.a} . . . . id.
ἁγιάσατε   verb, aor. act. impv. 2 pers. pl. {5.D.1} id.
ἁγιάσῃ   verb, aor. act. subjunc. 3 pers. sg. {5.B.1} id.
ἁγιασθήτω   verb, aor. pass. impv. 3 pers. sg.
  {5.D.1} . . . . id.
ἁγιασμόν   noun, acc. sg. masc. {2.B} . . . . . ἁγιασμός *G38*
G38 **ἁγιασμός**, -οῦ, ὁ   *the process of making or becoming ἅγιος (set apart, holy).*

ἁγιασμός   noun, nom. sg. masc. {2.B} . . . .ἁγιασμός G38
ἁγιασμῷ   noun, dat. sg. masc. {2.B} . . . . id.
ἁγίασον   verb, aor. act. impv. 2 pers. sg.
   {5.D.1} . . . . .ἁγιάζω G37
ἅγιε   adj., voc. sg. masc. {3.A} . . . . ἅγιος G40
ἅγιοι   adj., nom. pl. masc. {3.A} . . . . id.
ἅγιοι   adj., voc. pl. masc. {3.A} . . . . id.
ἁγίοις   adj., dat. pl. masc. {3.A} . . . . id.
G39 **ἅγιον**   neut. subs. of ἅγιος.
ἅγιον   adj., acc. sg. masc. {3.A} . . . . ἅγιος G40
ἅγιον   adj., acc. sg. neut. {3.A} . . . . id.
ἅγιον   adj., nom. sg. neut. {3.A} . . . . id.
G40 **ἅγιος, -α, -ον**   set apart by (or for) the God,
   holy, sacred, e.g., (of Jerusalem) ἁγία πόλις
   (Matt 4:5); τὸ ἅγιον πνεῦμα, practically
   synonymous with τὸ πνεῦμα τοῦ θεοῦ; ὁ
   ἅγιος τοῦ θεοῦ (Mark 1:24) of the Messiah;
   οἱ ἅγιοι, of the Christians as the new people
   of God, taking the place of the Hebrews; neut.
   subs., τὸ ἅγιον, τὰ ἅγια, the temple; τὰ ἅγια
   τῶν ἁγίων, the inmost part of the temple, the
   inner shrine.
ἅγιος   adj., nom. sg. masc. {3.A} . . . . ἅγιος G40
G41 **ἁγιότης, -ητος, ἡ**   holiness (see ἅγιος), as an
   abstr. quality.
ἁγιότητι   noun, dat. sg. fem. {2.C} . . . . ἁγιότης G41
ἁγιότητος   noun, gen. sg. fem. {2.C} . . . . id.
ἁγίου   adj., gen. sg. masc. {3.A} . . . . ἅγιος G40
ἁγίου   adj., gen. sg. neut. {3.A} . . . . id.
ἁγίους   adj., acc. pl. masc. {3.A} . . . . id.
ἁγίῳ   adj., dat. sg. masc. {3.A} . . . . id.
ἁγίῳ   adj., dat. sg. neut. {3.A} . . . . id.
ἁγίων   adj., gen. pl. masc. {3.A} . . . . id.
ἁγίων   adj., gen. pl. neut. {3.A} . . . . id.
G42 **ἁγιωσύνη, -ης, ἡ**   a holy or sanctified state, the
   resulting state of the ἅγιος.
ἁγιωσύνη   noun, dat. sg. fem. {2.A} . . . . ἁγιωσύνη G42
ἁγιωσύνην   noun, acc. sg. fem. {2.A} . . . . id.
ἁγιωσύνης   noun, gen. sg. fem. {2.A} . . . . id.
ἁγιωτάτῃ   adj. superl., dat. sg. fem. {3.A} . . . . ἅγιος G40
ἀγκάλας   noun, acc. pl. fem. {2.A} . . . . ἀγκάλη G43
G43 **ἀγκάλη, -ης, ἡ**   an arm, esp. as bent to receive
   a burden.
G44 **ἄγκιστρον, -ου, τό**   a fishhook.
ἄγκιστρον   noun, acc. sg. neut. {2.B} . . . . ἄγκιστρον G44
G45 **ἄγκυρα, -ας, ἡ**   an anchor.
ἄγκυραν   noun, acc. sg. fem. {2.A} . . . . ἄγκυρα G45
ἀγκύρας   noun, acc. pl. fem. {2.A} . . . . id.
ἁγνά   adj., nom. pl. neut. {3.A} . . . . .ἁγνός G53
ἁγνάς   adj., acc. pl. fem. {3.A} . . . . id.
G46 **ἄγναφος, -ον**   unshrunken (of cloth), unmilled,
   not yet dressed (by the fuller).
ἀγνάφου   adj., gen. sg. neut. {3.C} . . . . ἄγναφος G46
G47 **ἁγνεία, -ας, ἡ**   purity, chastity.
ἁγνείᾳ   noun, dat. sg. fem. {2.A} . . . . ἁγνεία G47
ἁγνή   adj., nom. sg. fem. {3.A} . . . . .ἁγνός G53
ἁγνήν   adj., acc. sg. fem. {3.A} . . . . id.
ἁγνίᾳ   noun, dat. sg. fem. {2.A} . . . . ἁγνεία G47
ἁγνίζει   verb, pres. act. indic. 3 pers. sg.
   {5.A.1.a} . . . . .ἁγνίζω G48

G48 **ἁγνίζω**   I make pure, either (1) ceremonially (e.g.,
   Acts 21:24), or (2) actually (e.g., 1 Pet 1:22).
ἁγνίσατε   verb, aor. act. impv. 2 pers. pl.
   {5.D.1} . . . . .ἁγνίζω G48
ἁγνισθείς   vbl., aor. pass. ptc. nom. sg. masc.
   {6.A.1.a} . . . . id.
ἁγνίσθητι   verb, aor. pass. impv. 2 pers. sg.
   {5.D.1} . . . . id.
G49 **ἁγνισμός, -οῦ, ὁ**   purification (ceremonial).
ἁγνισμοῦ   noun, gen. sg. masc. {2.B} . . . . .ἁγνισμός G49
ἁγνίσωσιν   verb, aor. act. subjunc. 3 pers. pl.
   {5.B.1} . . . . .ἁγνίζω G48
ἀγνοεῖ   verb, pres. act. indic. 3 pers. sg.
   {5.A.2} . . . . .ἀγνοέω G50
ἀγνοεῖν   vbl., pres. act. inf. {6.B.2} . . . . id.
ἀγνοεῖται   verb, pres. pass. indic. 3 pers. sg.
   {5.A.2} . . . . id.
ἀγνοεῖτε   verb, pres. act. indic. 2 pers. pl. {5.A.2} id.
ἀγνοείτω   verb, pres. act. impv. 3 pers. sg.
   {5.D.2} . . . . id.
G50 **ἀγνοέω**   I do not know, I am ignorant of (a person, thing, or fact), sometimes with the idea of
   willful ignorance.
G51 **ἀγνόημα, -ατος, τό**   an offence committed
   through ignorance, an error due to (willful or
   culpable) ignorance.
ἀγνοημάτων   noun, gen. pl. neut. {2.C} . . . . ἀγνόημα G51
ἀγνοήσαντες   vbl., aor. act. ptc. nom. pl. masc.
   {6.A.2} . . . . .ἀγνοέω G50
G52 **ἄγνοια, -ας, ἡ**   ignorance, inadvertence; some-
   times with the idea of willful blindness (Eph
   4:18).
ἀγνοίᾳ   noun, dat. sg. fem. {2.A} . . . . .ἄγνοια G52
ἄγνοιαν   noun, acc. sg. fem. {2.A} . . . . id.
ἀγνοίας   noun, gen. sg. fem. {2.A} . . . . id.
ἀγνόν   adj., acc. sg. masc. {3.A} . . . . .ἁγνός G53
ἀγνοοῦμεν   verb, pres. act. indic. 1 pers. pl.
   {5.A.2} . . . . .ἀγνοέω G50
ἀγνοούμενοι   vbl., pres. pass. ptc. nom. pl.
   masc. {6.A.2} . . . . id.
ἀγνοούμενος   vbl., pres. pass. ptc. nom. sg.
   masc. {6.A.2} . . . . id.
ἀγνοοῦντες   vbl., pres. act. ptc. nom. pl. masc.
   {6.A.2} . . . . id.
ἀγνοοῦσι   verb, pres. act. indic. 3 pers. pl.
   {5.A.2} . . . . id.
ἀγνοοῦσι   vbl., pres. act. ptc. dat. pl. masc.
   {6.A.2} . . . . id.
ἀγνοοῦσιν   verb, pres. act. indic. 3 pers. pl.
   {5.A.2} . . . . id.
ἀγνοοῦσιν   vbl., pres. act. ptc. dat. pl. masc.
   {6.A.2} . . . . id.
G53 **ἁγνός, -ή, -όν**   (1) pure (either ethically, or
   ritually, ceremonially); (2) chaste (orig., in a
   condition prepared for worship).
ἁγνός   adj., nom. sg. masc. {3.A} . . . . .ἁγνός G53
G54 **ἁγνότης, -ητος, ἡ**   purity, chastity.
ἁγνότητι   noun, dat. sg. fem. {2.C} . . . . . . .ἁγνότης G54
ἁγνότητος   noun, gen. sg. fem. {2.C} . . . . id.
ἁγνούς   adj., acc. pl. masc. {3.A} . . . . .ἁγνός G53

ἀγνοῶν   vbl., pres. act. ptc. nom. sg. masc.
{6.A.2}. . . . . ἀγνοέω G50

G55 ἀγνῶς   adv., *purely, with pure motives, honestly.*
ἀγνῶς   adv. {3.F}. . . . . .ἀγνῶς G55

G56 ἀγνωσία, -ας, ἡ   disgraceful *ignorance.*
ἀγνωσίαν   noun, acc. sg. fem. {2.A}. . . . . . ἀγνωσία G56

G57 ἄγνωστος, -ον   *unknown, unknowable.*
ἀγνωστω   adj., dat. sg. masc. {3.C}. . . . . ἄγνωστος G57
ἀγνώστῳ   adj., dat. sg. masc. {3.C}. . . . . id.
ἀγόμενα   vbl., pres. pass. ptc. acc. pl. neut.
{6.A.1}. . . . . ἄγω G71
ἀγομένους   vbl., pres. pass. ptc. acc. pl. masc.
{6.A.1}. . . . . id.
ἀγομένων   vbl., pres. pass. ptc. gen. pl. neut.
{6.A.1}. . . . . id.
ἄγονται   verb, pres. pass. indic. 3 pers. pl.
{5.A.1.d} . . . . id.
ἄγοντες   vbl., pres. act. ptc. nom. pl. masc.
{6.A.1}. . . . . id.

G58 ἀγορά, -ᾶς, ἡ   *marketplace, market.*
ἀγορᾷ   noun, dat. sg. fem. {2.A}. . . . . ἀγορά G58
ἀγοράζει   verb, pres. act. indic. 3 pers. sg.
{5.A.1.a} . . . . ἀγοράζω G59
ἀγοράζοντας   vbl., pres. act. ptc. acc. pl. masc.
{6.A.1}. . . . . id.
ἀγοράζοντες   vbl., pres. act. ptc. nom. pl.
masc. {6.A.1} . . . . id.

G59 ἀγοράζω   *I buy.*
ἀγοραῖοι   adj., nom. pl. fem. {3.C}. . . . . . ἀγοραῖος G60
ἀγοραῖοι   adj., nom. pl. masc. {3.C}. . . . . ἀγοραῖος G60

G60 ἀγοραῖος, -ον   (1) *a lounger in the marketplace,*
perhaps with the idea of *agitator* (Acts 17:5);
(2) pl. fem., ἀγοραῖοι (understand ἡμέραι),
market days; (3) pl. masc. (understand σύνο-
δοι), *judicial inquests.*
ἀγοραῖς   noun, dat. pl. fem. {2.A}. . . . . . . ἀγορά G58
ἀγοραίων   adj., gen. pl. masc. {3.C}. . . . . ἀγοραῖος G60
ἀγοράν   noun, acc. sg. fem. {2.A}. . . . . ἀγορά G58
ἀγορᾶς   noun, gen. sg. fem. {2.A}. . . . . id.
ἀγοράσαι   vbl., aor. act. inf. {6.B.1} . . . . . ἀγοράζω G59
ἀγοράσαντα   vbl., aor. act. ptc. acc. sg. masc.
{6.A.1.a} . . . . id.
ἀγοράσας   vbl., aor. act. ptc. nom. sg. masc.
{6.A.1.a} . . . . id.
ἀγοράσατε   verb, aor. act. impv. 2 pers. pl.
{5.D.1}. . . . . id.
ἀγορασάτω   verb, aor. act. impv. 3 pers. sg.
{5.D.1}. . . . . id.
ἀγοράσει   verb, fut. act. indic. 3 pers. sg.
{5.A.1.a} . . . . id.
ἀγοράσομεν   verb, fut. act. indic. 1 pers. pl.
{5.A.1.a} . . . . id.
ἀγόρασον   verb, aor. act. impv. 2 pers. sg.
{5.D.1}. . . . . id.
ἀγοράσωμεν   verb, aor. act. subjunc. 1 pers. pl.
{5.B.1} . . . . id.
ἀγοράσωσι   verb, aor. act. subjunc. 3 pers. pl.
{5.B.1} . . . . id.
ἀγοράσωσιν   verb, aor. act. subjunc. 3 pers. pl.
{5.B.1} . . . . id.

ἄγουσι   verb, pres. act. indic. 3 pers. pl. {5.A.1.a} ἄγω G71
ἄγουσιν   verb, pres. act. indic. 3 pers. pl.
{5.A.1.a} . . . . id.

G61 ἄγρα, -ας, ἡ   *catching, a catch.*
ἄγρα   noun, dat. sg. fem. {2.A}. . . . . ἄγρα G61
ἀγράμματοι   adj., nom. pl. masc. {3.C} ἀγράμματος G62

G62 ἀγράμματος, -ον   *unlettered, illiterate,*
uneducated, perhaps with the narrower idea,
unacquainted with Rabbinic teaching.
ἄγραν   noun, acc. sg. fem. {2.A}. . . . . ἄγρα G61

G63 ἀγραυλέω   *I spend the night in the open,*
bivouac.
ἀγραυλοῦντες   vbl., pres. act. ptc. nom. pl. masc.
{6.A.2}. . . . . ἀγραυλέω G63
ἀγρεύσωσι   verb, aor. act. subjunc. 3 pers. pl.
{5.B.1} . . . . ἀγρεύω G64
ἀγρεύσωσιν   verb, aor. act. subjunc. 3 pers. pl.
{5.B.1} . . . . id.

G64 ἀγρεύω   *I catch, capture.*
ἄγρια   adj., nom. pl. neut. {3.A} . . . . ἄγριος G66

G65 ἀγριέλαιος, -ου, ἡ   *a wild olive.*
ἀγριέλαιος   noun, nom. sg. fem. {2.B} . . ἀγριέλαιος G65
ἀγριελαίου   noun, gen. sg. fem. {2.B} . . . . id.
ἄγριον   adj., acc. sg. neut. {3.A} . . . . ἄγριος G66
ἄγριον   adj., nom. sg. neut. {3.A} . . . . id.

G66 ἄγριος, -α, -ον   *wild.*
Ἀγρίππα   noun prop., gen. sg. masc. {2.A;
2.D}. . . . . .Ἀγρίππας G67
Ἀγρίππα   noun prop., voc. sg. masc. {2.A; 2.D} . id.

G67 Ἀγρίππας, -α, ὁ   *Agrippa,* i.e., Herod Agrippa
II (M. Iulius Agrippa, 28–c. 93 A.D.), son
of Agrippa I (the Herod of Acts 12), king of
Chalcis (50 A.D.), and afterwards of the old
tetrarchies of Philip and Lysanias also.
Ἀγρίππας   noun prop., nom. sg. masc. {2.A;
2.D}. . . . . .Ἀγρίππας G67
ἀγρόν   noun, acc. sg. masc. {2.B} . . . . .ἀγρός G68

G68 ἀγρός, -οῦ, ὁ   (1) *a field* (a word rare in
papyrus documents, and now obsolete), esp.
as bearing a crop; (2) *the country,* Mark 15:21;
16:12: pl. ἀγροί, *lands, property in land, a*
country estate.
ἀγρός   noun, nom. sg. masc. {2.B} . . . . .ἀγρός G68
ἀγροῦ   noun, gen. sg. masc. {2.B} . . . . id.
ἀγρούς   noun, acc. pl. masc. {2.B} . . . . id.
ἀγρυπνεῖτε   verb, pres. act. impv. 2 pers. pl.
{5.D.2}. . . . . ἀγρυπνέω G69

G69 ἀγρυπνέω   (1) *I am not asleep, I am awake;* (2)
esp. *I am watchful, careful.*

G70 ἀγρυπνία, -ας, ἡ   *the state of being awake* (at
night).
ἀγρυπνίαις   noun, dat. pl. fem. {2.A}. . .ἀγρυπνία G70
ἀγρυπνοῦντες   vbl., pres. act. ptc. nom. pl. masc.
{6.A.2}. . . . . ἀγρυπνέω G69
ἀγρυπνοῦσιν   verb, pres. act. indic. 3 pers. pl.
{5.A.2}. . . . . id.
ἀγρῷ   noun, dat. sg. masc. {2.B} . . . . .ἀγρός G68
ἀγρῶν   noun, gen. pl. masc. {2.B} . . . . id.

G71 ἄγω   (1) *I lead, I lead away, I bring* (a person, or
animal); thus *I bring* before a court of justice;

(2) esp. in first pers. pl. subjunc. ἄγωμεν,
intrans., *let us depart* (e.g., Mark 1:38); (3) *I
hold, keep, celebrate;* ἀγοραῖοι ἄγονται (Acts
19:38), *judicial inquests are held.* See ἄγε G33.

ἄγω   verb, pres. act. indic. 1 pers. sg. {5.A.1.a} .. ἄγω G71

G72 ἀγωγή, -ῆς, ἡ   (1) *leading;* (2) hence, *mode of
life, conduct.*

ἀγωγῇ   noun, dat. sg. fem. {2.A} .... ἀγωγή G72

ἄγωμεν   verb, pres. act. subjunc. 1 pers. pl.
{5.B.1} .... ἄγω G71

G73 ἀγών, -ῶνος, ὁ   (1) *an* (athletic) *contest;* (2)
hence, *a struggle* (in the soul).

ἀγῶνα   noun, acc. sg. masc. {2.C} .... ἀγών G73

ἀγῶνι   noun, dat. sg. masc. {2.C} .... id.

G74 ἀγωνία, -ας, ἡ   (1) *great fear, terror,* of death;
(2) *anxiety* (properly the feeling of the athlete
before a contest).

ἀγωνίᾳ   noun, dat. sg. fem. {2.A} .... ἀγωνία G74

ἀγωνίζεσθε   verb, pres. mid./pass. impv. 2 pers. pl.
{5.D.1} .... ἀγωνίζομαι G75

G75 ἀγωνίζομαι   *I am struggling* (as in an athletic
contest or warfare); sometimes with the obj.
ἀγῶνα expressed.

ἀγωνιζόμεθα   verb, pres. mid./pass. indic. 1 pers.
pl. {5.A.1.d} .... ἀγωνίζομαι G75

ἀγωνιζόμενος   vbl., pres. mid./pass. ptc. nom.
sg. masc. {6.A.1} .... id.

ἀγωνίζου   verb, pres. mid./pass. impv. 2 pers.
sg. {5.D.1} .... id.

ἄγωσιν   verb, pres. act. subjunc. 3 pers. pl.
{5.B.1} .... ἄγω G71

G76 Ἀδάμ, ὁ   *Adam,* the first man, the first parent
of the human race; ὁ ἔσχατος Ἀδάμ (1 Cor
15:45), its latest ideal representative, who
inaugurates the new age, Jesus the Messiah
(Heb.). Var. Ἀδμίν, *Admin,* Luke 3:33.

Ἀδάμ   noun prop. .... Ἀδάμ G76

ἀδάπανον   adj., acc. sg. neut. {3.C} ..... ἀδάπανος G77

G77 ἀδάπανος, -ον   *without expense, for which
nothing has to be paid.*

Ἀδδεί   noun prop. .... Ἀδδί G78

G78 Ἀδδί, ὁ   *Addi,* son of Cosam, and father of
Melchei, one of the ancestors of Jesus (Luke
3:28) (Heb.).

Ἀδδί   noun prop. .... Ἀδδί G78

ἀδελφαί   noun, nom. pl. fem. {2.A} ...... ἀδελφή G79

ἀδελφάς   noun, acc. pl. fem. {2.A} .... id.

ἀδελφέ   noun, voc. sg. masc. {2.B} ...... ἀδελφός G80

G79 ἀδελφή, -ῆς, ἡ   (1) *a sister;* (2) *a woman (fellow) member of a church, a Christian woman*
(Rom 16:1; 1 Cor 7:15, etc.).

ἀδελφή   noun, nom. sg. fem. {2.A} ...... ἀδελφή G79

ἀδελφῇ   noun, dat. sg. fem. {2.A} .... id.

ἀδελφήν   noun, acc. sg. fem. {2.A} .... id.

ἀδελφῆς   noun, gen. sg. fem. {2.A} .... id.

ἀδελφοί   noun, nom. pl. masc. {2.B} ...... ἀδελφός G80

ἀδελφοί   noun, voc. pl. masc. {2.B} .... id.

ἀδελφοῖς   noun, dat. pl. masc. {2.B} .... id.

ἀδελφόν   noun, acc. sg. masc. {2.B} .... id.

G80 ἀδελφός, -οῦ, ὁ   (1) *a brother* (so probably even
in Rom 16:23; 2 Cor 12:18); (2) *a member of the
same religious community,* esp. *a fellow Christian* (particularly in the pl., a use characteristic
of Jewish literature but not confined to it).

ἀδελφός   noun, nom. sg. masc. {2.B} ..... ἀδελφός G80

G81 ἀδελφότης, -ητος, ἡ   *brotherhood* (in the
collective sense), *the members of the Christian
Church, Christendom.*

ἀδελφότητα   noun, acc. sg. fem. {2.C} .. ἀδελφότης G81

ἀδελφότητι   noun, dat. sg. fem. {2.C} .... id.

ἀδελφοῦ   noun, gen. sg. masc. {2.B} ...... ἀδελφός G80

ἀδελφούς   noun, acc. pl. masc. {2.B} .... id.

ἀδελφῷ   noun, dat. sg. masc. {2.B} .... id.

ἀδελφῶν   noun, gen. pl. masc. {2.B} .... id.

Ἅιδη   noun prop., voc. sg. masc. {2.A; 2.D} .... Ἅιδης G86

Ἅιδη   noun prop., dat. sg. masc. {2.A; 2.D} ..... id.

ἄδηλα   adj., nom. pl. neut. {3.C} ...... ἄδηλος G82

ἄδηλον   adj., acc. sg. fem. {3.C} .... id.

G82 ἄδηλος, -ον   *unseen, inconspicuous, indistinct*
(also of sound).

G83 ἀδηλότης, -ητος, ἡ   *the quality of being unseen*
(of disappearing), *indefiniteness, uncertainty.*

ἀδηλότητι   noun, dat. sg. fem. {2.C} .... ἀδηλότης G83

G84 ἀδήλως   adv., (1) *out of sight, obscurely,
inconspicuously;* (2) in 1 Cor 9:26 perhaps =
uncertainly, without certain aim.

ἀδήλως   adv. {3.F} .... ἀδήλως G84

ἀδημονεῖν   vbl., pres. act. inf. {6.B.2} .... ἀδημονέω G85

G85 ἀδημονέω   (1) *I feel fear, I lack courage;* (2) *I
am distressed* (orig., *I am bewildered,* from
δήμων, *knowing, prudent*).

ἀδημονῶν   vbl., pres. act. ptc. nom. sg. masc.
{6.A.2} .... ἀδημονέω G85

Ἅιδην   noun prop., acc. sg. masc. {2.A; 2.D} ... Ἅιδης G86

G86 Ἅιδης (Ἄιδης), -ου, ὁ   *Hades, the unseen world,*
into which the spirits of all persons pass at
death (in LXX = Heb. *šĕôl,* Sheol).

Ἅιδης   noun prop., nom. sg. masc. {2.A; 2.D} .. Ἅιδης G86

G87 ἀδιάκριτος, -ον   *without divisions of mind,
undivided, wholehearted.*

ἀδιάκριτος   adj., nom. sg. fem. {3.C} .. ἀδιάκριτος G87

ἀδιάλειπτον   adj., acc. sg. fem. {3.C} .. ἀδιάλειπτος G88

G88 ἀδιάλειπτος, -ον   *unceasing, unremitting.*

ἀδιάλειπτος   adj., nom. sg. fem. {3.C} .. ἀδιάλειπτος G88

G89 ἀδιαλείπτως   adv., *unceasingly, without
remission.*

ἀδιαλείπτως   adv. {3.F} .... ἀδιαλείπτως G89

G90 ἀδιαφθορία, -ας, ἡ   *sincerity.*

ἀδιαφθορίαν   noun, acc. sg. fem. {2.A} ἀδιαφθορία G90

ἀδικεῖσθε   verb, pres. pass. indic. 2 pers. pl.
{5.A.2} .... ἀδικέω G91

ἀδικεῖτε   verb, pres. act. indic. 2 pers. pl. {5.A.2} id.

G91 ἀδικέω   *I act unjustly towards, I injure, I harm*
(animate or inanimate).

ἀδικηθέντος   vbl., aor. pass. ptc. gen. sg. masc.
{6.A.1.a.} .... ἀδικέω G91

ἀδικηθῇ   verb, aor. pass. subjunc. 3 pers. sg.
{5.B.1} .... id.

G92 **ἀδίκημα**, -ατος, τό   (1) *a legal wrong, a crime* (with which one is charged), *a misdeed;* (2) *a crime against God, a sin* (Rev 18:5).

ἀδίκημα   noun, acc. sg. neut. {2.C} . . . . . ἀδίκημα G92
ἀδίκημα   noun, nom. sg. neut. {2.C} . . . . id.
ἀδικήματα   noun, acc. pl. neut. {2.C} . . . . id.
ἀδικῆσαι   vbl., aor. act. inf. {6.B.1} . . . . ἀδικέω G91
ἀδικήσαντος   vbl., aor. act. ptc. gen. sg. masc.
   {6.A.2} . . . . id.
ἀδικησάτω   verb, aor. act. impv. 3 pers. sg.
   {5.D.1} . . . . id.
ἀδικήσει   verb, fut. act. indic. 3 pers. sg. {5.A.1} id.
ἀδικήσῃ   verb, aor. act. subjunc. 3 pers. sg.
   {5.B.1} . . . . id.
ἀδικήσῃς   verb, aor. act. subjunc. 2 pers. sg.
   {5.B.1} . . . . id.
ἀδικήσητε   verb, aor. act. subjunc. 2 pers. pl.
   {5.B.1} . . . . id.
ἀδικήσουσιν   verb, fut. act. indic. 3 pers. pl.
   {5.A.1} . . . . id.
ἀδικήσωσι   verb, aor. act. subjunc. 3 pers. pl.
   {5.B.1} . . . . id.
ἀδικήσωσιν   verb, aor. act. subjunc. 3 pers. pl.
   {5.B.1} . . . . id.

G93 **ἀδικία**, -ας, ἡ   *injustice, unrighteousness, hurt;* sometimes in a Hebraistic gen., equivalent to the adj. ἄδικος (e.g., Luke 16:8; 18:6).

ἀδικία   noun, nom. sg. fem. {2.A} . . . . ἀδικία G93
ἀδικίᾳ   noun, dat. sg. fem. {2.A} . . . . id.
ἀδικίαις   noun, dat. pl. fem. {2.A} . . . . id.
ἀδικίαν   noun, acc. sg. fem. {2.A} . . . . id.
ἀδικίας   noun, gen. sg. fem. {2.A} . . . . id.
ἄδικοι   adj., nom. pl. masc. {3.C} . . . . ἄδικος G94

G94 **ἄδικος**, -ον   *unjust, unrighteous* (opp. δίκαιος).

ἄδικος   adj., nom. sg. masc. {3.C} . . . . ἄδικος G94
ἀδικούμενοι   vbl., pres. pass. ptc. nom. pl. masc.
   {6.A.2} . . . . ἀδικέω G91
ἀδικούμενον   vbl., pres. pass. ptc. acc. sg.
   masc. {6.A.2} . . . . id.
ἀδίκους   adj., acc. pl. masc. {3.C} . . . . ἄδικος G94
ἀδικοῦσι   verb, pres. act. indic. 3 pers. pl.
   {5.A.2} . . . . ἀδικέω G91
ἀδικοῦσιν   verb, pres. act. indic. 3 pers. pl.
   {5.A.2} . . . . ἀδικέω G91
ἀδικῶ   verb, pres. act. indic. 1 pers. sg. {5.A.2} . . id.
ἀδίκῳ   adj., dat. sg. masc. {3.C} . . . . ἄδικος G94
ἀδικῶν   vbl., pres. act. ptc. nom. sg. masc.
   {6.A.2} . . . . ἀδικέω G91
ἀδίκων   adj., gen. pl. masc. {3.C} . . . . ἄδικος G94

G95 **ἀδίκως**   adv., *unjustly.*

ἀδίκως   adv. {3.F} . . . . ἀδίκως G95
Ἀδμείν   noun prop. . . . . Ἀδμίν G76†‡

G76†‡ **Ἀδμίν** (Ἀδμείν), ὁ   *Admin,* son of Arnei, father of Naasson, one of the ancestors of Jesus. Var. for Ἀδάμ, Luke 3:33 (Heb.).

Ἀδμίν   noun prop. . . . . Ἀδμίν G76†‡
ἀδόκιμοι   adj., nom. pl. masc. {3.C} . . . . . ἀδόκιμος G96
ἀδόκιμον   adj., acc. sg. masc. {3.C} . . . . id.

G96 **ἀδόκιμος**, -ον   *failing to pass the test, unapproved, counterfeit.*

ἀδόκιμος   adj., nom. sg. fem. {3.C} . . . . . . ἀδόκιμος G96
ἀδόκιμος   adj., nom. sg. masc. {3.C} . . . . id.
ἄδολον   adj., acc. sg. neut. {3.C} . . . . ἄδολος G97

G97 **ἄδολος**, -ον   *unadulterated, pure.*

ᾄδοντες   vbl., pres. act. ptc. nom. pl. masc.
   {6.A.1} . . . . ᾄδω G103
Ἅιδου   noun prop., gen. sg. masc. {2.A; 2.D} . . . Ἅιδης G86
ᾄδουσι   verb, pres. act. indic. 3 pers. pl.
   {5.A.1.a} . . . . ᾄδω G103
Ἀδραμυττηνῷ   adj. prop., dat. sg. neut.
   {3.A} . . . . Ἀδραμυττηνός G98

G98 **Ἀδραμυττηνός** (Ἀδραμυντηνός), -ή, -όν   *belonging to Adramyttium,* a port in Mysia, northwest Asia Minor.

Ἀδραμυττηνῷ   adj. prop., dat. sg. neut.
   {3.A} . . . . Ἀδραμυττηνός G98
Ἀδρίᾳ   noun prop., dat. sg. masc. {2.A; 2.D} . Ἀδρίας G99
Ἀδρίᾳ   noun prop., dat. sg. masc. {2.A; 2.D} . . . . id.

G99 **Ἀδρίας**, -ου, ὁ   *the Adria,* a name given by sailors not merely to the Adriatic Sea, to which it properly belonged, but also to the open Mediterranean to the southeast of Italy, to the sea that lay between Malta, Italy, Greece, and Crete.

G100 **ἁδρότης**, -ητος, ἡ   *lavishness, lavish generosity.*

ἁδρότητι   noun, dat. sg. fem. {2.C} . . . . . . ἁδρότης G100
ἀδύνατα   adj., nom. pl. neut. {3.C} . . . . . ἀδύνατος G102

G101 **ἀδυνατέω**   of things, *to be impossible.*

ἀδυνατήσει   verb, fut. act. indic. 3 pers. sg.
   {5.A.1} . . . . ἀδυνατέω G101
ἀδύνατον   adj., nom. sg. neut. {3.C} . . . . ἀδύνατος G102
ἀδύνατον   adj., acc. sg. neut. {3.C} . . . . id.

G102 **ἀδύνατος**, -ον   (1) of persons, *incapable* (Acts 14:8; Rom 15:1); (2) of things, *impossible;* τὸ ἀδύνατον, either *the inability,* or *that which is impossible* (Rom 8:3).

ἀδύνατος   adj., nom. sg. masc. {3.C} . . . ἀδύνατος G102
ἀδυνάτων   adj., gen. pl. masc. {3.C} . . . . id.

G103 **ᾄδω** (ἄδω)   *I sing.*

G104 **ἀεί**   adv., *always* (rare in colloquial Gk.).

ἀεί   adv. . . . . ἀεί G104
ἀέρα   noun, acc. sg. masc. {2.C} . . . . ἀήρ G109
ἀέρος   noun, gen. sg. masc. {2.C} . . . . id.
ἀετοί   noun, nom. pl. masc. {2.B} . . . . ἀετός G105

G105 **ἀετός**, -οῦ, ὁ   *an eagle.*

ἀετοῦ   noun, gen. sg. masc. {2.B} . . . . ἀετός G105
ἀετῷ   noun, dat. sg. masc. {2.B} . . . . id.
ἄζυμα   adj., nom. pl. neut. {3.C} . . . . ἄζυμος G106
ἄζυμοι   adj., nom. pl. masc. {3.C} . . . . id.
ἀζύμοις   adj., dat. pl. neut. {3.C} . . . . id.

G106 **ἄζυμος**, -ον   (1) *unleavened,* esp. in the neut. pl., τὰ ἄζυμα, *the unleavened bread,* a festival of the Hebrews, held from 15 to 21 Nisan, in commemoration of their deliverance from Egypt; (2) in a moral sense, 1 Cor 5:7–8.

ἀζύμων   adj., gen. pl. neut. {3.C} . . . . ἄζυμος G106

G107 **Ἀζώρ**, ὁ   *Azor,* son of Eliakim and father of Zadok, an ancestor of Jesus (Heb.).

Ἀζώρ   noun prop. . . . . Ἀζώρ G107
Ἄζωτον   noun prop., acc. sg. fem. {2.B; 2.D} Ἄζωτος G108
G108 **Ἄζωτος**, -ου, ἡ   *Azotus, Ashdod*, a coast town of Palestine belonging to the ancient Philistia, and part of Herod's kingdom.
G109 **ἀήρ**, -έρος, ὁ   *air*, the lower air we breathe.
ἀήρ   noun, nom. sg. masc. {2.C}. . . . . .ἀήρ G109
ἀθά   Aram. .μαρὰν ἀθά G3134
G110 **ἀθανασία**, -ας, ἡ   *immortality, imperishability, freedom from death.*
ἀθανασίαν   noun, acc. sg. fem. {2.A} . . ἀθανασία G110
ἀθεμίτοις   adj., dat. pl. fem. {3.C}. . . . . . ἀθέμιτος G111
ἀθέμιτον   adj., nom. sg. neut. {3.C} . . . . id.
G111 **ἀθέμιτος**, -ον   (1) *illegal, unlawful;* (2) thus *abominable.*
ἄθεοι   adj., nom. pl. masc. {3.C}. . . . . ἄθεος G112
G112 **ἄθεος**, -ον   *without god, without (the only true) god, godless.*
G113 **ἄθεσμος**, -ον   *lawless, ignoring the* (divine) *ordinances.*
ἀθέσμων   adj., gen. pl. masc. {3.C}. . . . . . ἄθεσμος G113
ἀθετεῖ   verb, pres. act. indic. 3 pers. sg. {5.A.2}. . . . . ἀθετέω G114
ἀθετεῖτε   verb, pres. act. indic. 2 pers. pl. {5.A.2} id.
G114 **ἀθετέω**   (1) *I annul, make of no effect, set aside, ignore, slight;* (2) *I break faith with,* Mark 6:26.
ἀθετῆσαι   vbl., aor. act. inf. {6.B.1} . . . . . . ἀθετέω G114
ἀθετήσας   vbl., aor. act. ptc. nom. sg. masc. {6.A.2} . . . . id.
ἀθέτησιν   noun, acc. sg. fem. {2.C} . . . . ἀθέτησις G115
G115 **ἀθέτησις**, -εως, ἡ   *annulment.*
ἀθέτησις   noun, nom. sg. fem. {2.C} . . . . ἀθέτησις G115
ἀθετήσω   verb, fut. act. indic. 1 pers. sg. {5.A.1}. . . . . ἀθετέω G114
ἀθετοῦσι   verb, pres. act. indic. 3 pers. pl. {5.A.2}. . . . . id.
ἀθετοῦσιν   verb, pres. act. indic. 3 pers. pl. {5.A.2}. . . . . id.
ἀθετῶ   verb, pres. act. indic. 1 pers. sg. {5.A.2}. . id.
ἀθετῶν   vbl., pres. act. ptc. nom. sg. masc. {6.A.2} . . . . id.
G116 **Ἀθῆναι**, -ῶν, ἡ   *Athens,* the intellectual capital of Greece.
Ἀθηναῖοι   adj. prop., nom. pl. masc. {3.A}Ἀθηναῖος G117
Ἀθηναῖοι   adj. prop., voc. pl. masc. {3.A}. . . . . id.
G117 **Ἀθηναῖος**, -α, -ον   *Athenian, belonging to Athens.*
Ἀθήναις   noun prop., dat. pl. fem. {2.A; 2.D}. . . . . .Ἀθῆναι G116
Ἀθηνῶν   noun prop., gen. pl. fem. {2.A; 2.D} . . . id.
G118 **ἀθλέω**   *I engage, compete, in an* (athletic) *contest.*
ἀθλῇ   verb, pres. act. subjunc. 3 pers. sg. {5.B.2}. . . . . .ἀθλέω G118
ἀθλήσῃ   verb, aor. act. subjunc. 3 pers. sg. {5.B.1}. . . . . id.
ἄθλησιν   noun, acc. sg. fem. {2.C}. . . . . . ἄθλησις G119
G119 **ἄθλησις**, -εως, ἡ   *a struggling* (as in an athletic contest).
G4867‡ **ἀθροίζω**   *I gather together, collect.* Var. for συναθροίζω, Luke 24:33.

G120 **ἀθυμέω**   *I lose heart., am despondent.*
ἀθυμῶσιν   verb, pres. act. subjunc. 3 pers. pl. {5.B.2}. . . . . ἀθυμέω G120
ἄθφον   adj., acc. sg. neut. {3.C} . . . . .ἄθφος G121
ἄθφος   adj., nom. sg. masc. {3.C}. . . . . id.
G121 **ἄθφος**, -ον   *guiltless, innocent* (sometimes, *unpunished*).
ἄθφος   adj., nom. sg. masc. {3.C} . . . . .ἄθφος G121
αἱ   art., nom. pl. fem. {1}. . . . . ὁ G3588
αἵ   art., nom. pl. fem. {1}. . . . . id.
αἵ   pron. rel., nom. pl. fem. {4.C}. . . . . .ὅς G3739
αἰγείοις   adj., dat. pl. neut. {3.A}. . . . . .αἴγειος G122
G122 **αἴγειος**, -α, -ον   *of a goat.*
αἰγιαλόν   noun, acc. sg. masc. {2.B}. . . . .αἰγιαλός G123
G123 **αἰγιαλός**, -οῦ, ὁ   (1) *sea coast,* (sandy) *beach;* (2) *shore* (of sea or lake), *land.*
αἰγίοις   adj., dat. pl. neut. {3.A} . . . . .αἴγειος G122
Αἰγύπτιοι   adj. prop., nom. pl. masc. {3.A}. . . . . .Αἰγύπτιος G124
Αἰγύπτιον   adj. prop., acc. sg. masc. {3.A} . . . . id.
G124 **Αἰγύπτιος**, -α, -ον   *Egyptian.*
Αἰγύπτιος   adj. prop., nom. sg. masc. {3.A}. . . . . .Αἰγύπτιος G124
Αἰγυπτίων   adj. prop., gen. pl. masc. {3.A} . . . . id.
Αἴγυπτον   noun prop., acc. sg. fem. {2.B; 2.D}. . . . . Αἴγυπτος G125
G125 **Αἴγυπτος**, -ου, ἡ   *Egypt.*
Αἴγυπτος   noun prop., nom. sg. fem. {2.B; 2.D}. . . . . Αἴγυπτος G125
Αἰγύπτου   noun prop., gen. sg. fem. {2.B; 2.D}. . id.
Αἰγύπτῳ   noun prop., dat. sg. fem. {2.B; 2.D} . . . id.
ἀϊδίοις   adj., dat. pl. masc. {3.C}. . . . . .ἀΐδιος G126
G126 **ἀΐδιος**, -ον   *lasting forever.*
ἀΐδιος   adj., nom. sg. fem. {3.C}. . . . . .ἀΐδιος G126
αἰδοῦς   noun, gen. sg. fem. {2.C}. . . . . αἰδώς G127
G127 **αἰδώς**, -οῦς, ἡ   *shame, modesty.*
Αἰθιόπων   noun prop., gen. pl. masc. {2.C; 2.D}. . . . . Αἰθίοψ G128
G128 **Αἰθίοψ**, -οπος, ὁ   *Ethiopian, Abyssinian* (apparently absent from papyri).
Αἰθίοψ   noun prop., nom. sg. masc. {2.C; 2.D}. . . . . Αἰθίοψ G128
G129 **αἷμα**, -ατος, τό   *blood* (esp. as shed); σὰρξ καὶ αἷμα (αἷμα καὶ σὰρξ), a Hebraistic expression for *a human being, human beings, human nature.*
αἷμα   noun, acc. sg. neut. {2.C}. . . . . αἷμα G129
αἷμα   noun, nom. sg. neut. {2.C} . . . . id.
αἷματα   noun, nom. pl. neut. {2.C} . . . . id.
G130 **αἱματεκχυσία**, -ας, ἡ   *a shedding* or *pouring forth of blood* (in sacrifice).
αἱματεκχυσίας   noun, gen. sg. fem. {2.A} . . . . .αἱματεκχυσία G130
αἵματι   noun, dat. sg. neut. {2.C}. . . . . αἷμα G129
αἵματος   noun, gen. sg. neut. {2.C} . . . . id.
αἱμάτων   noun, gen. pl. neut. {2.C} . . . . id.
G131 **αἱμορροέω**   *I suffer from a continual flow* (oozing) *of blood.*
αἱμορροοῦσα   vbl., pres. act. ptc. nom. sg. fem. {6.A.2}. . . . . .αἱμορροέω G131

Αἰνέα   noun prop., voc. sg. masc. {2.A; 2.D}. Αἰνέας G132
Αἰνέαν   noun prop., acc. sg. masc. {2.A; 2.D}... id.

G132 **Αἰνέας**, -ου, ὁ   *Aeneas, a citizen of Lydda.*
αἰνεῖν   vbl., pres. act. inf. {6.B.2} .... αἰνέω G134
αἰνεῖτε   verb, pres. act. impv. 2 pers. pl. {5.D.2} . id.
αἰνέσεως   noun, gen. sg. fem. {2.C} ...... αἴνεσις G133

G133 **αἴνεσις**, -εως, ἡ   *praise, commendation.*

G134 **αἰνέω**   *I praise.*

G135 **αἴνιγμα**, -ατος, τό   *a riddle.*
αἰνίγματι   noun, dat. sg. neut. {2.C}...... αἴνιγμα G135
αἶνον   noun, acc. sg. masc. {2.B} .... αἶνος G136

G136 **αἶνος**, -ου, ὁ   *praise.*
αἰνοῦντα   vbl., pres. act. ptc. acc. sg. masc.
   {6.A.2}............................ αἰνέω G134
αἰνοῦντες   vbl., pres. act. ptc. nom. pl. masc.
   {6.A.2}................................ id.
αἰνούντων   vbl., pres. act. ptc. gen. pl. masc.
   {6.A.2}................................ id.

G137 **Αἰνών**, ἡ   *Aenon. Eusebius and Jerome*
   place this site eight (Roman) miles south of
   Scythopolis near the Jordan.
Αἰνών   noun prop..................... Αἰνών G137
αἰνῶν   vbl., pres. act. ptc. nom. sg. masc.
   {6.A.2}............................ αἰνέω G134
αἶρε   verb, pres. act. impv. 2 pers. sg. {5.D.1} .. αἴρω G142
αἴρει   verb, pres. act. indic. 3 pers. sg. {5.A.1.a} . id.
αἴρεις   verb, pres. act. indic. 2 pers. sg. {5.A.1.a}. id.
αἱρέσεις   noun, acc. pl. fem. {2.C} .... αἵρεσις G139
αἱρέσεις   noun, nom. pl. fem. {2.C} .... id.
αἱρέσεως   noun, gen. sg. fem. {2.C} ...... id.
αἵρεσιν   noun, acc. sg. fem. {2.C}......... id.

G139 **αἵρεσις**, -εως, ἡ   (1) *a self-chosen opinion;* (2) *a*
   religious or philosophical sect (orig., *choosing,*
   choice).
αἵρεσις   noun, nom. sg. fem. {2.C}...... αἵρεσις G139
αἵρεται   verb, pres. pass. indic. 3 pers. sg.
   {5.A.1.d} .... αἴρω G142
αἴρετε   verb, pres. act. impv. 2 pers. pl. {5.D.1} .. id.

G140 **αἱρετίζω**   *I choose.*
αἱρετικόν   adj., acc. sg. masc. {3.A} ..... αἱρετικός G141

G141 **αἱρετικός**, -ή, -όν   *disposed to form sects,*
   sectarian, factious.

G138‡ **αἱρέω**   mid. *I choose.*
αἱρήσομαι   verb, fut. mid. indic. 1 pers. sg.
   {5.A.1}.......................... αἱρέω G138‡
αἱρόμενον   vbl., pres. pass. ptc. acc. sg. masc.
   {6.A.1}........................... αἴρω G142
αἴροντος   vbl., pres. act. ptc. gen. sg. masc.
   {6.A.1}............................ id.

G142 **αἴρω**   (1) *I raise, lift up;* (2) *I take away, remove.*
αἴρων   vbl., pres. act. ptc. nom. sg. masc.
   {6.A.1}............................. αἴρω G142
αἴρωσιν   verb, pres. act. subjunc. 3 pers. pl.
   {5.B.1}............................. id.
αἷς   pron. rel., dat. pl. fem. {4.C}......... ὅς G3739

G143 **αἰσθάνομαι**   *I perceive.*
αἰσθήσει   noun, dat. sg. fem. {2.C} ..... αἴσθησις G144

G144 **αἴσθησις**, -εως, ἡ   *perception.*
αἰσθητήρια   noun, acc. pl. neut. {2.B} αἰσθητήριον G145

G145 **αἰσθητήριον**, -ου, τό   *perceptive faculty.*

αἴσθωνται   verb, ²aor. mid. subjunc. 3 pers. pl.
   {5.B.1}......................... αἰσθάνομαι G143
αἰσχροκερδεῖς   adj., acc. pl. masc.
   {3.E} .... αἰσχροκερδής G146
αἰσχροκερδῆ   adj., acc. sg. masc. {3.E} ...... id.

G146 **αἰσχροκερδής**, -ές   *fond of base gain.*

G147 **αἰσχροκερδῶς**   adv., *in a spirit of eagerness for*
   base gain.
αἰσχροκερδῶς   adv. {3.F}......... αἰσχροκερδῶς G147

G148 **αἰσχρολογία**, -ας, ἡ   *filthy, obscene speech.*
αἰσχρολογίαν   noun, acc. sg. fem.
   {2.A} .... αἰσχρολογία G148

G149 **αἰσχρόν**   neut. subs. of αἰσχρός, *a disgraceful*
   thing.
αἰσχρόν   adj., nom. sg. neut. {3.A}...... αἰσχρός G150

G150 **αἰσχρός**, -ά, -όν   *base, disgraceful.*

G151 **αἰσχρότης**, -ητος, ἡ   *baseness.*
αἰσχρότης   noun, nom. sg. fem. {2.C} .. αἰσχρότης G151
αἰσχροῦ   adj., gen. sg. neut. {3.A} .... αἰσχρός G150
αἰσχύνας   noun, acc. pl. fem. {2.A} ...... αἰσχύνη G152
αἰσχυνέσθω   verb, pres. pass. impv. 3 pers. sg.
   {5.D.1}......................... αἰσχύνω G153

G152 **αἰσχύνη**, -ης, ἡ   (1) *shame;* (2)
   shamefacedness.
αἰσχύνη   noun, nom. sg. fem. {2.A}.... αἰσχύνη G152
αἰσχύνῃ   noun, dat. sg. fem. {2.A} .... id.
αἰσχύνης   noun, gen. sg. fem. {2.A} ...... id.
αἰσχυνθήσομαι   verb, fut. pass. indic. 1 pers. sg.
   {5.A.1.d} .... αἰσχύνω G153
αἰσχυνθῶμεν   verb, aor. pass. subjunc. 1 pers.
   pl. {5.B.1}........................ id.
αἰσχύνομαι   verb, pres. mid. indic. 1 pers. sg.
   {5.A.1.d} .... id.

G153 **αἰσχύνω**   pass., *I am ashamed.*
αἰτεῖν   vbl., pres. act. inf. {6.B.2}.......... αἰτέω G154
αἰτεῖς   verb, pres. act. indic. 2 pers. sg. {5.A.2} .. id.
αἰτεῖσθαι   vbl., pres. mid. inf. {6.B.2}........ id.
αἰτεῖσθε   verb, pres. mid. indic. 2 pers. pl.
   {5.A.2}............................. id.
αἰτεῖτε   verb, pres. act. impv. 2 pers. pl. {5.D.2} . id.
αἰτεῖτε   verb, pres. act. indic. 2 pers. pl. {5.A.2} . id.
αἰτείτω   verb, pres. act. impv. 3 pers. sg. {5.D.2}. id.

G154 **αἰτέω**   *I ask, request, beg, petition;* mid. voice
   αἰτέομαι, *I ask for myself* (perhaps with
   entreaty).

G155 **αἴτημα**, -ατος, τό   *a request.*
αἴτημα   noun, acc. sg. neut. {2.C}........ αἴτημα G155
αἰτήματα   noun, acc. pl. neut. {2.C}.......... id.
αἰτήματα   noun, nom. pl. neut. {2.C} .... id.
αἰτῆσαι   vbl., aor. act. inf. {6.B.1} .... αἰτέω G154
αἰτήσας   vbl., aor. act. ptc. nom. sg. masc.
   {6.A.2}............................. id.
αἰτήσασθε   verb, aor. mid. impv. 2 pers. pl.
   {5.D.1}............................. id.
αἰτήσει   verb, fut. act. indic. 3 pers. sg. {5.A.1}.. id.
αἰτήσεσθε   verb, fut. mid. indic. 2 pers. pl.
   {5.A.1}............................. id.
αἰτήσῃ   verb, aor. act. subjunc. 3 pers. sg. {5.B.1} id.
αἰτήσῃ   verb, aor. mid. subjunc. 2 pers. sg.
   {5.B.1} .... id.

αἰτήσῃς   verb, aor. act. subjunc. 2 pers. sg.
{5.B.1}............................id.
αἰτήσηται   verb, aor. mid. subjunc. 3 pers. sg.
{5.B.1}............................id.
αἰτήσητε   verb, aor. act. subjunc. 2 pers. pl.
{5.B.1}............................id.
αἰτῆσθε   verb, pres. pass. subjunc. 2 pers. pl.
{5.B.2}............................id.
αἰτήσομαι   verb, fut. mid. indic. 1 pers. sg.
{5.A.1}............................id.
αἴτησον   verb, aor. act. impv. 2 pers. sg. {5.D.1}. id.
αἰτήσουσιν   verb, fut. act. indic. 3 pers. pl.
{5.A.1}............................id.
αἰτήσωμαι   verb, aor. mid. subjunc. 1 pers. sg.
{5.B.1}............................id.
αἰτήσωμεν   verb, aor. act. subjunc. 1 pers. pl.
{5.B.1}............................id.
αἰτήσωνται   verb, aor. mid. subjunc. 3 pers. pl.
{5.B.1}............................id.
G156 **αἰτία**, -ας, ἡ   (1) a cause, reason; excuse; (2) a
charge, accusation; (3) guilt; (4) relationship,
matter, circumstances, case, Matt 19:10.
αἰτία   noun, nom. sg. fem. {2.A}..........αἰτία G156
αἰτιάματα   noun, acc. pl. neut. {2.C}.... αἰτίωμα G157‡
αἰτίαν   noun, acc. sg. fem. {2.A}..........αἰτία G156
αἰτίας   noun, acc. pl. fem. {2.A}............id.
αἰτίας   noun, gen. sg. fem. {2.A}...........id.
αἵτινες   pron. indef. rel., nom. pl. fem. {4.C}. ὅστις G3748
G158 **αἴτιον**   neut. subs. of αἴτιος.
αἴτιον   adj., acc. sg. neut. {3.A}..........αἴτιος G159
G159 **αἴτιος**, -ία, -ον   (1) neut. subs., cause shading
into crime, the originator of; (2) neut. subs.,
guilt, criminality; (3) adj., responsible for.
αἴτιος   adj., nom. sg. masc. {3.A}........αἴτιος G159
αἰτίου   adj., gen. sg. neut. {3.A}...........id.
G157‡ **αἰτίωμα**, -ατος, τό   a charge, accusation.
αἰτιώματα   noun, acc. pl. neut. {2.C}.... αἰτίωμα G157‡
αἰτοῦμαι   verb, pres. mid. indic. 1 pers. sg.
{5.A.2}.........................αἰτέω G154
αἰτούμεθα   verb, pres. mid. indic. 1 pers. pl.
{5.A.2}............................id.
αἰτούμενοι   vbl., pres. mid. ptc. nom. pl. masc.
{6.A.2}............................id.
αἰτοῦντι   vbl., pres. act. ptc. dat. sg. masc.
{6.A.2}............................id.
αἰτοῦσα   vbl., pres. act. ptc. nom. sg. fem.
{6.A.2}............................id.
αἰτοῦσι   verb, pres. act. indic. 3 pers. pl. {5.A.2} id.
αἰτοῦσιν   verb, pres. act. indic. 3 pers. pl.
{5.A.2}............................id.
αἰτοῦσιν   vbl., pres. act. ptc. dat. pl. masc.
{6.A.2}............................id.
αἰτώμεθα   verb, pres. mid. subjunc. 1 pers. pl.
{5.B.2}............................id.
αἰτῶμεν   verb, pres. act. subjunc. 1 pers. pl.
{5.B.2}............................id.
αἰτῶν   vbl., pres. act. ptc. nom. sg. masc. {6.A.2} id.
G160 **αἰφνίδιος**, -ον   sudden.
αἰφνίδιος   adj., nom. sg. fem. {3.C} .... αἰφνίδιος G160
αἰφνίδιος   adj., nom. sg. masc. {3.C} .... id.

G161 **αἰχμαλωσία**, -ας, ἡ   (1) captivity; (2) Hebraistically = captives, Eph 4:8.
αἰχμαλωσίαν   noun, acc. sg. fem.
{2.A}.................... αἰχμαλωσία G161
αἰχμαλωτεύοντες   vbl., pres. act. ptc. nom. pl.
masc. {6.A.1}................. αἰχμαλωτεύω G162
G162 **αἰχμαλωτεύω**   I take captive (in war).
αἰχμαλωτίζοντα   vbl., pres. act. ptc. acc. sg. masc.
{6.A.1}......................αἰχμαλωτίζω G163
αἰχμαλωτίζοντες   vbl., pres. act. ptc. nom. pl.
masc. {6.A.1}........................ id.
G163 **αἰχμαλωτίζω**   I take captive (in war), I subdue,
I ensnare.
αἰχμαλωτισθήσονται   verb, fut. pass. indic.
3 pers. pl. {5.A.1.d} ....αἰχμαλωτίζω G163
αἰχμαλώτοις   noun, dat. pl. masc.
{2.B} ....αἰχμάλωτος G164
G164 **αἰχμάλωτος**, -ου, ὁ   a captive (in war), hence
generally.
G165 **αἰών**, -ῶνος, ὁ   an age, a cycle (of time), esp. of
the present age as contrasted with the future
age, and of one of a series of ages stretching
to infinity; ἀπ᾽ αἰῶνος, from the beginning
of the present age, from the beginning of time,
Luke 1:70, etc.; εἰς αἰῶνα for eternity; αἰῶνες
αἰώνων, a Hebraistic expression, more
emphatic than the simple αἰῶνες, Gal 1:5, etc.
(From a root meaning life, esp. long life, old
age.).
αἰῶνα   noun, acc. sg. masc. {2.C}..........αἰών G165
αἰῶνας   noun, acc. pl. masc. {2.C} ....id.
αἰῶνι   noun, dat. sg. masc. {2.C} ....id.
αἰώνια   adj., nom. pl. neut. {3.C} ...... αἰώνιος G166
αἰωνίαν   adj., acc. sg. fem. {3.C}..........id.
αἰωνίοις   adj., dat. pl. masc. {3.C} ....id.
αἰώνιον   adj., acc. sg. fem. {3.C}...........id.
αἰώνιον   adj., acc. sg. masc. {3.C} ....id.
αἰώνιον   adj., acc. sg. neut. {3.C} ....id.
αἰώνιον   adj., nom. sg. neut. {3.C} ....id.
G166 **αἰώνιος**, -ον   (1) age-long, and, therefore,
practically eternal, unending; (2) partaking of
the character of that which lasts for an age,
as contrasted with that which is brief and
fleeting.
αἰώνιος   adj., nom. sg. fem. {3.C}....... αἰώνιος G166
αἰωνίου   adj., gen. sg. fem. {3.C} ....id.
αἰωνίου   adj., gen. sg. masc. {3.C} ....id.
αἰωνίου   adj., gen. sg. neut. {3.C}..........id.
αἰωνίους   adj., acc. pl. fem. {3.C} ....id.
αἰωνίων   adj., gen. pl. masc. {3.C} ....id.
αἰῶνος   noun, gen. sg. masc. {2.C}........αἰών G165
αἰώνων   noun, gen. pl. masc. {2.C}..........id.
αἰῶσι   noun, dat. pl. masc. {2.C} ....id.
αἰῶσιν   noun, dat. pl. masc. {2.C} ....id.
G167 **ἀκαθαρσία**, -ας, ἡ   uncleanness, impurity.
ἀκαθαρσία   noun, nom. sg. fem. {2.A} ἀκαθαρσία G167
ἀκαθαρσίᾳ   noun, dat. sg. fem. {2.A} ....id.
ἀκαθαρσίαν   noun, acc. sg. fem. {2.A} ....id.
ἀκαθαρσίας   noun, gen. sg. fem. {2.A} ....id.
ἀκάθαρτα   adj., acc. pl. neut. {3.C} ... ἀκάθαρτος G169

ἀκάθαρτα   adj., nom. pl. neut. {3.C} . . . . id.

G168 **ἀκαθάρτης**, -ητος, ἡ   *impurity (moral).*
ἀκαθάρτητος   noun, gen. sg. fem.
{2.C} . . . . ἀκαθάρτης G168
ἀκαθάρτοις   adj., dat. pl. neut. {3.C} . . ἀκάθαρτος G169
ἀκάθαρτον   adj., acc. sg. masc. {3.C} . . . . id.
ἀκάθαρτον   adj., acc. sg. neut. {3.C} . . . . id.
ἀκάθαρτον   adj., nom. sg. neut. {3.C} . . . . id.
ἀκάθαρτον   adj., voc. sg. neut. {3.C} . . . . id.

G169 **ἀκάθαρτος**, -ον   *unclean, impure;* in reference
to dem., spirits, Matt 10:1, etc.
ἀκάθαρτος   adj., nom. sg. masc. {3.C} . ἀκάθαρτος G169
ἀκαθάρτου   adj., gen. sg. neut. {3.C} . . . . id.
ἀκαθάρτῳ   adj., dat. sg. neut. {3.C} . . . . id.
ἀκαθάρτων   adj., gen. pl. neut. {3.C} . . . . id.

G170 **ἀκαιρέομαι**   *I am without a suitable opportunity* (to effect something).

G171 **ἀκαίρως**   adv., *unseasonably, out of due season,
inopportunely.*
ἀκαίρως   adv. {3.F} . . . . ἀκαίρως G171

G172 **ἄκακος**, -ον   (1) *innocent, guileless;* (2) *simple,*
Rom 16:18.
ἄκακος   adj., nom. sg. masc. {3.C} . . . . . . ἄκακος G172
ἀκάκων   adj., gen. pl. masc. {3.C} . . . . id.

G173 **ἄκανθα**, -ης, ἡ   *a thorn bush.*
ἄκανθαι   noun, nom. pl. fem. {2.A} . . . . . ἄκανθα G173
ἀκάνθας   noun, acc. pl. fem. {2.A} . . . . id.
ἀκάνθινον   adj., acc. sg. masc. {3.A} . . . ἀκάνθινος G174

G174 **ἀκάνθινος**, -η, -ον   *made of thorns.*
ἀκανθῶν   noun, gen. pl. fem. {2.A} . . . . . . ἄκανθα G173
ἄκαρπα   adj., nom. pl. neut. {3.C} . . . . . . ἄκαρπος G175
ἄκαρποι   adj., nom. pl. masc. {3.C} . . . . id.
ἀκάρποις   adj., dat. pl. neut. {3.C} . . . . id.

G175 **ἄκαρπος**, -ον   *fruitless, profitless.*
ἄκαρπος   adj., nom. sg. masc. {3.C} . . . . ἄκαρπος G175
ἀκάρπους   adj., acc. pl. masc. {3.C} . . . . id.
ἀκατάγνωστον   adj., acc. sg. masc.
{3.C} . . . . ἀκατάγνωστος G176

G176 **ἀκατάγνωστος**, -ον   *uncondemned,
unimpeachable.*
ἀκατακάλυπτον   adj., acc. sg. fem.
{3.C} . . . . ἀκατακάλυπτος G177

G177 **ἀκατακάλυπτος**, -ον   *not veiled, unveiled.*
ἀκατακαλύπτῳ   adj., dat. sg. fem.
{3.C} . . . . ἀκατακάλυπτος G177
ἀκατάκριτον   adj., acc. sg. masc.
{3.C} . . . . ἀκατάκριτος G178

G178 **ἀκατάκριτος**, -ον   *uncondemned* (probably
an attempt to translate the Lat. *re incognita*
or *causâ indictâ,* "one's case not having been
tried").
ἀκατακρίτους   adj., acc. pl. masc.
{3.C} . . . . ἀκατάκριτος G178

G179 **ἀκατάλυτος**, -ον   *indissoluble, that cannot be
broken up.*
ἀκαταλύτου   adj., gen. sg. fem. {3.C} . ἀκατάλυτος G179
ἀκαταπάστους   adj., acc. pl. masc.
{3.C} . . . . ἀκατάπαυστος G180

G180 **ἀκατάπαυστος** (ἀκατάπαστος), -ον   *not ceas-
ing from, not abandoning (giving up),* with gen.

ἀκαταπαύστους   adj., acc. pl. masc.
{3.C} . . . . ἀκατάπαυστος G180

G181 **ἀκαταστασία**, -ας, ἡ   *disturbance, upheaval,
revolution,* almost *anarchy,* first in the political, and thence in the moral sphere.
ἀκαταστασία   noun, nom. sg. fem.
{2.A} . . . . ἀκαταστασία G181
ἀκαταστασίαι   noun, nom. pl. fem. {2.A} . . . . id.
ἀκαταστασίαις   noun, dat. pl. fem. {2.A} . . . . id.
ἀκαταστασίας   noun, acc. pl. fem. {2.A} . . . . . id.
ἀκαταστασίας   noun, gen. sg. fem. {2.A} . . . . id.
ἀκατάστατον   adj., nom. sg. neut.
{3.C} . . . . ἀκατάστατος G182

G182 **ἀκατάστατος**, -ον   *unsettled, unstable* (though
these are hardly strong enough equivalents),
almost *anarchic;* (in LXX *staggering, reeling*).
ἀκατάστατος   adj., nom. sg. masc.
{3.C} . . . . ἀκατάστατος G182
ἀκατάσχετον   adj., nom. sg. neut.
{3.C} . . . . ἀκατάσχετος G183

G183 **ἀκατάσχετος**, -ον   *uncontrollable.*
Ἀκελδαμά   noun prop. . . . . Ἀκελδαμάχ G184

G184 **Ἀκελδαμάχ** (Ἀκελδαμά)   *Akeldama,* the place
where Judas Iscariot committed suicide (Aram.).
Ἀκελδαμάχ   noun prop. . . . . Ἀκελδαμάχ G184
ἀκέραιοι   adj., nom. pl. masc. {3.C} . . . . . ἀκέραιος G185

G185 **ἀκέραιος**, -ον   *simple, unsophisticated* (lit.
unmixed).
ἀκεραίους   adj., acc. pl. masc. {3.C} . . . . . ἀκέραιος G185
ἀκήκοα   verb, ²perf. act. indic. 1 pers. sg.
{5.A.1.c} . . . . ἀκούω G191
ἀκηκόαμεν   verb, ²perf. act. indic. 1 pers. pl.
{5.A.1.c} . . . . id.
ἀκηκόασι   verb, ²perf. act. indic. 3 pers. pl.
{5.A.1.c} . . . . id.
ἀκηκόασιν   verb, ²perf. act. indic. 3 pers. pl.
{5.A.1.c} . . . . id.
ἀκηκόατε   verb, ²perf. act. indic. 2 pers. pl.
{5.A.1.c} . . . . id.
ἀκηκοότας   vbl., ²perf. act. ptc. acc. pl. masc.
{6.A.1} . . . . id.
ἀκλινῆ   adj., acc. sg. fem. {3.E} . . . . ἀκλινής G186

G186 **ἀκλινής**, -ές   *unbent, unyielding, resolute.*

G187 **ἀκμάζω**   (1) *I reach maturity, become ripe;* (2) *I
am in full vigor.*

G188 **ἀκμήν**   adv., *thus* (properly adv. acc. of ἀκμή,
full term, maturity, and meaning *just now*), Matt
15:16 where the parallel in Mark 7:18 has οὕτως).
ἀκμήν   adv. . . . . ἀκμήν G188
ἀκοαί   noun, nom. pl. fem. {2.A} . . . . ἀκοή G189
ἀκοαῖς   noun, dat. pl. fem. {2.A} . . . . id.
ἀκοάς   noun, acc. pl. fem. {2.A} . . . . id.

G189 **ἀκοή**, -ῆς, ἡ   (1) *hearing, faculty of hearing,
ear;* in ἀκοῇ ἀκούειν (Matt 13:14, etc.), a He-
braistic(?) expression, the ἀκοή is emphatic;
(2) *report, rumor.*
ἀκοή   noun, nom. sg. fem. {2.A} . . . . ἀκοή G189
ἀκοή   noun, dat. sg. fem. {2.A} . . . . id.
ἀκοήν   noun, acc. sg. fem. {2.A} . . . . id.
ἀκοῆς   noun, gen. sg. fem. {2.A} . . . . id.

ἀκολούθει   verb, pres. act. impv. 2 pers. sg.
{5.D.2}. ἀκολουθέω *G190*
ἀκολουθεῖ   verb, pres. act. indic. 3 pers. sg.
{5.A.2}. . . . . id.
ἀκολουθεῖν   vbl., pres. act. inf. {6.B.2}. . . . . . . id.
ἀκολουθείτω   verb, pres. act. impv. 3 pers. sg.
{5.D.2}. . . . . id.
G190 **ἀκολουθέω**   *I accompany, attend* (takes the
     place of the old ἕπομαι).
ἀκολουθῆσαι   vbl., aor. act. inf. {6.B.1} ἀκολουθέω *G190*
ἀκολουθήσαντες   vbl., aor. act. ptc. nom. pl.
     masc. {6.A.2}. . . . . id.
ἀκολουθησάντων   vbl., aor. act. ptc. gen. pl.
     masc. {6.A.2}. . . . . id.
ἀκολουθήσατε   verb, aor. act. impv. 2 pers. pl.
{5.D.1}. . . . . id.
ἀκολουθήσει   verb, fut. act. indic. 3 pers. sg.
{5.A.1}. . . . . id.
ἀκολουθήσεις   verb, fut. act. indic. 2 pers. sg.
{5.A.1}. . . . . id.
ἀκολουθήσουσιν   verb, fut. act. indic. 3 pers.
     pl. {5.A.1}. id.
ἀκολουθήσω   verb, fut. act. indic. 1 pers. sg.
{5.A.1}. . . . . id.
ἀκολουθήσωσιν   verb, aor. act. subjunc.
     3 pers. pl. {5.B.1}. . . . . id.
ἀκολουθοῦντα   vbl., pres. act. ptc. acc. sg.
     masc. {6.A.2}. . . . . id.
ἀκολουθοῦντας   vbl., pres. act. ptc. acc. pl.
     masc. {6.A.2}. . . . . id.
ἀκολουθοῦντες   vbl., pres. act. ptc. nom. pl.
     masc. {6.A.2}. . . . . id.
ἀκολουθοῦντι   vbl., pres. act. ptc. dat. sg.
     masc. {6.A.2}. . . . . id.
ἀκολουθούσης   vbl., pres. act. ptc. gen. sg.
     fem. {6.A.2}. . . . . id.
ἀκολουθοῦσι   verb, pres. act. indic. 3 pers. pl.
{5.A.2}. . . . . id.
ἀκολουθοῦσιν   verb, pres. act. indic. 3 pers. pl.
{5.A.2}. . . . . id.
ἀκολουθοῦσιν   vbl., pres. act. ptc. dat. pl.
     masc. {6.A.2}. . . . . id.
ἀκολουθῶν   vbl., pres. act. ptc. nom. sg. masc.
     {6.A.2}. . . . . id.
ἄκουε   verb, pres. act. impv. 2 pers. sg.
{5.D.1}. ἀκούω *G191*
ἀκούει   verb, pres. act. indic. 3 pers. sg. {5.A.1.a} id.
ἀκούειν   vbl., pres. act. inf. {6.B.1}. . . . . id.
ἀκούεις   verb, pres. act. indic. 2 pers. sg.
{5.A.1.a}. . . . . id.
ἀκούεται   verb, pres. pass. indic. 3 pers. sg.
{5.A.1.d}. . . . . id.
ἀκούετε   verb, pres. act. impv. 2 pers. pl. {5.D.1} id.
ἀκούετε   verb, pres. act. indic. 2 pers. pl.
{5.A.1.a}. . . . . id.
ἀκουέτω   verb, pres. act. impv. 3 pers. sg. {5.D.1} id.
ἀκούομεν   verb, pres. act. indic. 1 pers. pl.
{5.A.1.a}. . . . . id.
ἀκούοντα   vbl., pres. act. ptc. acc. sg. masc.
     {6.A.1}. . . . . id.

ἀκούοντα   vbl., pres. act. ptc. nom. pl. neut.
     {6.A.1}. . . . . id.
ἀκούοντας   vbl., pres. act. ptc. acc. pl. masc.
     {6.A.1}. . . . . id.
ἀκούοντες   vbl., pres. act. ptc. nom. pl. masc.
     {6.A.1}. . . . . id.
ἀκούοντι   vbl., pres. act. ptc. dat. sg. masc.
     {6.A.1}. . . . . id.
ἀκούοντος   vbl., pres. act. ptc. gen. sg. masc.
     {6.A.1}. . . . . id.
ἀκουόντων   vbl., pres. act. ptc. gen. pl. masc.
     {6.A.1}. . . . . id.
ἀκούουσι   verb, pres. act. indic. 3 pers. pl.
{5.A.1.a}. . . . . id.
ἀκούουσι   vbl., pres. act. ptc. dat. pl. masc.
     {6.A.1}. . . . . id.
ἀκούουσιν   verb, pres. act. indic. 3 pers. pl.
{5.A.1.a}. . . . . id.
ἀκούουσιν   vbl., pres. act. ptc. dat. pl. masc.
     {6.A.1}. . . . . id.
ἀκοῦσαι   vbl., aor. act. inf. {6.B.1}. . . . . id.
ἀκούσαντες   vbl., aor. act. ptc. nom. pl. masc.
     {6.A.1.a}. . . . . id.
ἀκουσάντων   vbl., aor. act. ptc. gen. pl. masc.
     {6.A.1.a}. . . . . id.
ἀκούσας   vbl., aor. act. ptc. nom. sg. masc.
     {6.A.1.a}. . . . . id.
ἀκούσασα   vbl., aor. act. ptc. nom. sg. fem.
     {6.A.1.a}. . . . . id.
ἀκούσασιν   vbl., aor. act. ptc. dat. pl. masc.
     {6.A.1.a}. . . . . id.
ἀκούσατε   verb, aor. act. impv. 2 pers. pl. {5.D.1} id.
ἀκουσάτω   verb, aor. act. impv. 3 pers. sg.
{5.D.1}. . . . . id.
ἀκουσάτωσαν   verb, aor. act. impv. 3 pers. pl.
{5.D.1}. . . . . id.
ἀκούσει   verb, fut. act. indic. 3 pers. sg. {5.A.1.a} id.
ἀκούσεσθε   verb, fut. mid. indic. 2 pers. pl.
{5.A.1.d}. . . . . id.
ἀκούσετε   verb, fut. act. indic. 2 pers. pl.
{5.A.1.a}. . . . . id.
ἀκούσῃ   verb, aor. act. subjunc. 3 pers. sg.
{5.B.1}. . . . . id.
ἀκούσῃ   verb, fut. mid. indic. 2 pers. sg.
{5.A.1.d}. . . . . id.
ἀκούσητε   verb, aor. act. subjunc. 2 pers. pl.
{5.B.1}. . . . . id.
ἀκουσθεῖσι   vbl., aor. pass. ptc. dat. pl. neut.
     {6.A.1.a}. . . . . id.
ἀκουσθεῖσιν   vbl., aor. pass. ptc. dat. pl. neut.
     {6.A.1.a}. . . . . id.
ἀκουσθῇ   verb, aor. pass. subjunc. 3 pers. sg.
{5.B.1}. . . . . id.
ἀκουσθήσεται   verb, fut. pass. indic. 3 pers.
     sg. {5.A.1.d}. . . . . id.
ἀκουσόμεθα   verb, fut. mid. indic. 1 pers. pl.
{5.A.1.d}. . . . . id.
ἀκούσονται   verb, fut. mid. indic. 3 pers. pl.
{5.A.1.d}. . . . . id.

ἀκούσουσι verb, fut. act. indic. 3 pers. pl.
{5.A.1.a} . . . . id.
ἀκούσουσιν verb, fut. act. indic. 3 pers. pl.
{5.A.1.a} . . . . id.
ἀκούσω verb, aor. act. subjunc. 1 pers. sg.
{5.B.1} . . . . id.
ἀκούσωσι verb, aor. act. subjunc. 3 pers. pl.
{5.B.1} . . . . id.
ἀκούσωσιν verb, aor. act. subjunc. 3 pers. pl.
{5.B.1} . . . . id.
G191 **ἀκούω** *I hear, listen;* pass., *is heard, is reported;*
ἀκοῇ ἀκούειν, see ἀκοή.
ἀκούω verb, pres. act. indic. 1 pers. sg.
{5.A.1.a} . . . . ἀκούω G191
ἀκούω verb, pres. act. subjunc. 1 pers. sg.
{5.B.1} . . . . id.
ἀκούων vbl., pres. act. ptc. nom. sg. masc.
{6.A.1} . . . . id.
ἀκούωσι verb, pres. act. subjunc. 3 pers. pl.
{5.B.1} . . . . id.
ἀκούωσιν verb, pres. act. subjunc. 3 pers. pl.
{5.B.1} . . . . id.
G192 **ἀκρασία** (= ἀκράτεια), -ας, ἡ *incontinence,*
intemperance (in wide sense).
ἀκρασίαν noun, acc. sg. fem. {2.A} . . . . .ἀκρασία G192
ἀκρασίας noun, gen. sg. fem. {2.A} . . . . id.
ἀκρατεῖς adj., nom. pl. masc. {3.E} . . . . .ἀκρατής G193
G193 **ἀκρατής**, -ές (*impotent*), hence, *lacking self*
control, inclined to excess.
G194 **ἄκρατος**, -ον *unmixed, undiluted* (from
κεράννυμι).
ἀκράτου adj., gen. sg. masc. {3.C} . . . . . .ἄκρατος G194
G195 **ἀκρίβεια**, -ας, ἡ *accuracy, exactness, attention*
to detail, scrupulousness.
ἀκρίβειαν noun, acc. sg. fem. {2.A} . . . . ἀκρίβεια G195
ἀκριβεστάτην adj. superl., acc. sg. fem.
{3.A} . . . . ἀκριβής G197
G196 **ἀκριβέστατος**, -η, -ον superl. of ἀκρίβης; see
ἀκριβής.
ἀκριβέστερον adv. comp. {3.F; 3.G} . . . . . ἀκριβής G197
G197 **ἀκριβής**, -ές *careful, accurate, exact, strict,*
scrupulous, precise. careful, accurate, exact,
strict, scrupulous, precise. Neut. comp.
ἀκριβέστερον as adv., *more precisely, more*
accurately; superl. adj. ἀκριβέστατος, *strict-*
est, most precise.
G198 **ἀκριβόω** *I examine carefully, inquire strictly.*
G199 **ἀκριβῶς** adv., *carefully, exactly, strictly.*
ἀκριβῶς adv. {3.F} . . . . ἀκριβῶς G199
ἀκρίδας noun, acc. pl. fem. {2.C} . . . . ἀκρίς G200
ἀκρίδες noun, nom. pl. fem. {2.C} . . . . id.
ἀκρίδων noun, gen. pl. fem. {2.C} . . . . id.
G200 **ἀκρίς**, -ίδος, ἡ *a locust.*
ἀκροαταί noun, nom. pl. masc. {2.A} . . .ἀκροατής G202
G201 **ἀκροατήριον**, -ου, τό (1) *auditorium, recita-*
tion hall; (2) *court room* (for hearing cases).
ἀκροατήριον noun, acc. sg. neut.
{2.B} .ἀκροατήριον G201
G202 **ἀκροατής**, -οῦ, ὁ *a hearer of, a listener to.*
ἀκροατής noun, nom. sg. masc. {2.A} . . .ἀκροατής G202

G203 **ἀκροβυστία**, -ας, ἡ *foreskin, prepuce* (a technical word of Jewish use, perhaps adapted from
ἀκροποσθία); *uncircumcision,* a slang term
used by Jews to refer to Gentiles (Eph 2:11).
ἀκροβυστία noun, nom. sg. fem.
{2.A} . . . . .ἀκροβυστία G203
ἀκροβυστίᾳ noun, dat. sg. fem. {2.A} . . . . id.
ἀκροβυστίαν noun, acc. sg. fem. {2.A} . . . . . . id.
ἀκροβυστίας noun, gen. sg. fem. {2.A} . . . . . . id.
ἀκρογωνιαῖον adj., acc. sg. masc.
{3.A} . . . . ἀκρογωνιαῖος G204
G204 **ἀκρογωνιαῖος**, -α, -ον adj., *in the corner* (of a
building), *corner*(stone) (= Attic γωνιαῖος).
ἀκρογωνιαίου adj., gen. sg. masc.
{3.A} . . . . ἀκρογωνιαῖος G204
G205 **ἀκροθίνιον**, -ου, τό *spoil, treasure* (taken in
war); lit. *top of a heap.*
ἀκροθινίων noun, gen. pl. neut. {2.B} . ἀκροθίνιον G205
G206 **ἄκρον**, -ου, τό *edge, tip* (neut. of adj. ἄκρος).
ἄκρον noun, acc. sg. neut. {2.B} . . . . . . .ἄκρον G206
ἄκρου noun, gen. sg. neut. {2.B} . . . . id.
ἄκρων noun, gen. pl. neut. {2.B} . . . . id.
Ἀκύλαν noun prop., acc. sg. masc. {2.A;
2.D} . . . . Ἀκύλας G207
G207 **Ἀκύλας**, acc. -αν, ὁ the Gk. way of writing the
Latin name *Aquila,* a male proper name; the
husband of Priscilla (Prisca), and a Jew, of a
family belonging to (Sinope in) Pontus.
Ἀκύλας noun prop., nom. sg. masc. {2.A;
2.D} . . . . Ἀκύλας G207
ἀκυροῖ verb, pres. act. indic. 3 pers. sg.
{5.A.2} . . . . ἀκυρόω G208
ἀκυροῦντες vbl., pres. act. ptc. nom. pl. masc.
{6.A.2} . . . . id.
G208 **ἀκυρόω** *I annul, make of no eject, cancel.*
G209 **ἀκωλύτως** adv., *without let or hindrance* (characteristic of legal documents).
ἀκωλύτως adv. {3.F} . . . . ἀκωλύτως G209
G210 **ἄκων** adj., *unwilling,* generally used where
Eng. would express by an adv., *unwillingly.*
ἄκων adj., nom. sg. masc. {3.D} . . . . ἄκων G210
ἅλα noun, acc. sg. neut. {2.C} . . . . .ἅλας G217
ἀλάβαστρον noun, acc. sg. neut.
{2.B} . . . . ἀλάβαστρος G211
G211 **ἀλάβαστρος** (-ον), -ου, ὁ or τό *an alabaster*
phial or *bottle.*
ἀλαζόνας noun, acc. pl. masc. {2.C} . . . . . ἀλαζών G213
G212 **ἀλαζονεία**, -ας, ἡ (1) *arrogant display, osten-*
tation; (2) pl. = *occasions of ostentation.*
ἀλαζονεία noun, nom. sg. fem. {2.A} . . ἀλαζονεία G212
ἀλαζονείαις noun, dat. pl. fem. {2.A} . . . . id.
ἀλαζόνες noun, nom. pl. masc. {2.C} . . . ἀλαζών G213
ἀλαζονία noun, nom. sg. fem. {2.A} . . .ἀλαζονεία G212
ἀλαζονίαις noun, dat. pl. fem. {2.A} . . . . id.
G213 **ἀλαζών**, -όνος, ὁ *boastful,* giving one's self
airs in a loud and flaunting way.
ἀλαλάζον vbl., pres. act. ptc. nom. sg. neut.
{6.A.1} . . . . ἀλαλάζω G214
ἀλαλάζοντας vbl., pres. act. ptc. acc. pl. masc.
{6.A.1} . . . . id.

G214 **ἀλαλάζω** (1) *I cry aloud,* generally of persons
(in Mark 5:38 from sorrow); (2) κύμβαλον
ἀλαλάζον, a *clanging* or *clashing* cymbal
(1 Cor 13:1); onomatopoeic, cf. Heb.
ἀλαλήτοις adj., dat. pl. masc. {3.C}. . . . .ἀλάλητος G215

G215 **ἀλάλητος,** -ον *unutterable, that baffles words.*
ἄλαλον adj., acc. sg. neut. {3.C} . . . . .ἄλαλος G216
ἄλαλον adj., nom. sg. neut. {3.C} . . . . id.
ἄλαλον adj., voc. sg. neut. {3.C} . . . . id.

G216 **ἄλαλος,** -ον *dumb.*
ἀλάλους adj., acc. pl. masc. {3.C} . . . . . . .ἄλαλος G216

G217 **ἅλας,** -ατος, τό *salt.*
ἅλας noun, acc. sg. neut. {2.C} . . . . .ἅλας G217
ἅλας noun, nom. sg. neut. {2.C} . . . . id.
ἅλατι noun, dat. sg. neut. {2.C}. . . . . id.
ἁλεεῖς noun, acc. pl. masc. {2.C} . . . . ἁλιεύς G231
ἁλεεῖς noun, nom. pl. masc. {2.C}. . . . . id.

G218 **ἀλείφω** *I anoint.*
ἄλειψαι verb, aor. mid. impv. 2 pers. sg.
{5.D.1}. . . . . .ἀλείφω G218
ἀλείψαντες vbl., aor. act. ptc. nom. pl. masc.
{6.A.1.a} . . . . id.
ἀλείψασα vbl., aor. act. ptc. nom. sg. fem.
{6.A.1.a} . . . . id.
ἀλείψωσιν verb, aor. act. subjunc. 3 pers. pl.
{5.B.1} . . . . id.
ἀλέκτορα noun, acc. sg. masc. {2.C} . . . . .ἀλέκτωρ G220

G219 **ἀλεκτοροφωνία,** -ας, ἡ *cockcrow,* as a period
of time, between midnight and 3 a.m.
ἀλεκτοροφωνίας noun, gen. sg. fem.
{2.A} . . . . ἀλεκτοροφωνία G219

G220 **ἀλέκτωρ,** -ορος, ὁ *a cock.*
ἀλέκτωρ noun, nom. sg. masc. {2.C} . . . . .ἀλέκτωρ G220

G221 **Ἀλεξανδρεύς,** -έως, ὁ *an Alexandrian,* a native (or resident) of Alexandria in Egypt.
Ἀλεξανδρεύς noun prop., nom. sg. masc. {2.C;
2.D}. . . . . .Ἀλεξανδρεύς G221
Ἀλεξανδρέων noun prop., gen. pl. masc. {2.C;
2.D}. . . . . id.
Ἀλεξανδρινόν adj. prop., acc. sg. neut.
{3.A} . . . . .Ἀλεξανδρῖνος G222
Ἀλεξανδρινον adj. prop., acc. sg. neut. {3.A} . . id.

G222 **Ἀλεξανδρῖνος,** -η, -ον *Alexandrian, belonging
to Alexandria* in Egypt.
Ἀλεξανδρινῷ adj. prop., dat. sg. neut.
{3.A} . . . . .Ἀλεξανδρῖνος G222
Ἀλεξανδρίνῳ adj. prop., dat. sg. neut. {3.A} . . . id.
Ἀλέξανδρον noun prop., acc. sg. masc. {2.B;
2.D}. . . . . .Ἀλέξανδρος G223

G223 **Ἀλέξανδρος,** -ου, ὁ *Alexander,* a proper name
of Gk. origin, borne by four, possibly five,
persons in the NT: (1) an early Christian, son
of Simon of Cyrene, who carried the Cross,
Mark 15:21; (2) a leading non-Christian Jew
in Jerusalem, Acts 4:6; (3) an Ephesian Jew,
Acts 19:33; (4) a renegade Christian at Rome
(1 Tim 1:20), probably to be identified with
Alexander the coppersmith (2 Tim 4:14).
Ἀλέξανδρος noun prop., nom. sg. masc. {2.B;
2.D}. . . . . .Ἀλέξανδρος G223

Ἀλεξάνδρου noun prop., gen. sg. masc. {2.B;
2.D}. . . . . id.

G224 **ἄλευρον,** -ου, τό *meal.*
ἀλεύρου noun, gen. sg. neut. {2.B} . . . . .ἄλευρον G224

G225 **ἀλήθεια,** -ας, ἡ *truth,* but not merely truth as
spoken; truth of idea, reality, sincerity, truth
in the moral sphere, straightforwardness; ἐπʼ
ἀληθείας, *really, truly.*
ἀλήθεια noun, nom. sg. fem. {2.A} . . . . .ἀλήθεια G225
ἀληθείᾳ noun, dat. sg. fem. {2.A} . . . . id.
ἀλήθειαν noun, acc. sg. fem. {2.A} . . . . id.
ἀληθείας noun, gen. sg. fem. {2.A} . . . . id.
ἀληθεῖς adj., nom. pl. masc. {3.E} . . . . . . .ἀληθής G227
ἀληθές adj., acc. sg. neut. {3.E} . . . . id.
ἀληθές adj., nom. sg. neut. {3.E} . . . . id.
ἀληθεύοντες vbl., pres. act. ptc. nom. pl. masc.
{6.A.1}. . . . . .ἀληθεύω G226

G226 **ἀληθεύω** (1) *I say (speak) truth,* Gal 4:16; (2)
I do truth, I maintain truth (the truth); see
ἀλήθεια for the sense of "truth."
ἀληθεύων vbl., pres. act. ptc. nom. sg. masc.
{6.A.1}. . . . . .ἀληθεύω G226
ἀληθῆ adj., acc. pl. neut. {3.E} . . . . .ἀληθής G227
ἀληθῆ adj., acc. sg. fem. {3.E} . . . . id.
ἀληθῆ adj., nom. pl. neut. {3.E} . . . . id.

G227 **ἀληθής,** -ές *true* in fact; hence more widely
(see ἀλήθεια).
ἀληθής adj., nom. sg. fem. {3.E} . . . . . . .ἀληθής G227
ἀληθής adj., nom. sg. masc. {3.E} . . . . id.
ἀληθιναί adj., nom. pl. fem. {3.A}. . . . .ἀληθινός G228
ἀληθινή adj., nom. sg. fem. {3.A} . . . . id.
ἀληθινῆς adj., gen. sg. fem. {3.A} . . . . id.
ἀληθινοί adj., nom. pl. masc. {3.A} . . . . id.
ἀληθινόν adj., acc. sg. masc. {3.A} . . . . id.
ἀληθινόν adj., acc. sg. neut. {3.A} . . . . id.
ἀληθινόν adj., nom. sg. neut. {3.A} . . . . id.

G228 **ἀληθινός,** -ή, -όν *true* (lit., *made of truth*),
real, genuine (less common than ἀληθής).
ἀληθινός adj., nom. sg. masc. {3.A} . . . .ἀληθινός G228
ἀληθινῷ adj., dat. sg. masc. {3.A} . . . . id.
ἀληθινῶν adj., gen. pl. neut. {3.A} . . . . id.
ἀληθοῦς adj., gen. sg. fem. {3.E} . . . . .ἀληθής G227
ἀλήθουσαι vbl., pres. act. ptc. nom. pl. fem.
{6.A.1}. .ἀλήθω G229

G229 **ἀλήθω** *I grind.*

G230 **ἀληθῶς** adv., *truly, verily.*
ἀληθῶς adv. {3.F} . . . . .ἀληθῶς G230
ἁλί noun, dat. sg. masc. {2.C} . . . . .ἅλς G251
ἁλιεῖς noun, acc. pl. masc. {2.C} . . . . ἁλιεύς G231
ἁλιεῖς noun, nom. pl. masc. {2.C} . . . . id.
ἁλιεύειν vbl., pres. act. inf. {6.B.1} . . . . . .ἁλιεύω G232

G231 **ἁλιεύς** (ἀλεεύς), -έως, ὁ *a fisherman.*

G232 **ἁλιεύω** *I fish.*

G233 **ἁλίζω** *I salt, sprinkle with salt* (of sacrifices or
of those who offer sacrifice), *keep fresh and
sound,* and so acceptable to God.

G234 **ἁλίσγημα,** -ατος, τό *pollution,* perhaps *a pol-
luted thing* (esp. of food); from ἀλισγέω, read
in Freer manuscript at Mark 9:49.
ἀλισγημάτων noun, gen. pl. neut. {2.C} .ἁλίσγημα G234

ἀλισθήσεται   verb, fut. pass. indic. 3 pers. sg.
    {5.A.1.d} . . . . .ἁλίζω G233
ἀλλ᾽   conj.. . . . . .ἀλλά G235
ἄλλα   adj., acc. pl. neut. {3.A}. . . . . .ἄλλος G243
ἄλλα   adj., nom. pl. neut. {3.A} . . . . id.
G235 ἀλλά   (1) *but*; (2) *except* (used very like πλήν),
    Mark 4:22; Matt 20:23; ἀλλ᾽ ἤ, *except,* 2 Cor
    1:13; in Mark 6:9 ἀλλά is probably a misren-
    dering of an Aram. word meaning *and not.*
ἀλλά   conj.. . . . . .ἀλλά G235
ἀλλαγησόμεθα   verb, ²fut. pass. indic. 1 pers. pl.
    {5.A.1.d} . . . . .ἀλλάσσω G236
ἀλλαγήσονται   verb, ²fut. pass. indic. 3 pers.
    pl. {5.A.1.d} . . . . id.
ἄλλαι   adj., nom. pl. fem. {3.A} . . . . .ἄλλος G243
ἀλλάξαι   vbl., aor. act. inf. {6.B.1} . . . . .ἀλλάσσω G236
ἀλλάξει   verb, fut. act. indic. 3 pers. sg. {5.A.1.a} id.
ἄλλας   adj., acc. pl. fem. {3.A} . . . . .ἄλλος G243
G236 ἀλλάσσω   trans., *I change, alter.*
G237 ἀλλαχόθεν   adv., *from another quarter,* practi-
    cally *by another way.*
ἀλλαχόθεν   adv. . . . . ἀλλαχόθεν G237
G237† ἀλλαχοῦ   adv., *elsewhere, to another place,*
    Mark 1:38.
ἀλλαχοῦ   adv. {3.F} . . . . .ἀλλαχοῦ G237†
ἄλλη   adj., nom. sg. fem. {3.A} . . . . .ἄλλος G243
G238 ἀλληγορέω   *I allegorize, I interpret as an*
    allegory.
ἀλληγορούμενα   vbl., pres. pass. ptc. nom. pl.
    neut. {6.A.2} . . . . ἀλληγορέω G238
ἀλλήλοις   pron. recip., dat. pl. masc.
    {4.G} . . . . .ἀλλήλων G240
ἀλλήλοις   pron. recip., dat. pl. neut. {4.G} . . . . . id.
ἀλληλούϊα   interj, Heb.. . . . . ἀλληλούϊα G239
ἀλληλούϊα   interj, Heb.. . . . . id.
G239 ἀλληλούϊα   (ἀλληλουϊά)   *Hallelujah, Praise*
    the Lord (Heb.).
ἀλληλούϊα   interj, Heb. . . . . ἀλληλούϊα G239
ἀλληλούϊα   interj, Heb.. . . . . id.
ἀλλήλους   pron. recip., acc. pl. masc.
    {4.G} . . . . .ἀλλήλων G240
G240 ἀλλήλων, -ους   *one another* (a reciprocal
    word).
ἀλλήλων   pron. recip., gen. pl. masc.
    {4.G} . . . . .ἀλλήλων G240
ἀλλήλων   pron. recip., gen. pl. neut. {4.G} . . . . id.
ἄλλην   adj., acc. sg. fem. {3.A} . . . . .ἄλλος G243
ἄλλης   adj., gen. sg. fem. {3.A} . . . . id.
ἄλλο   adj., acc. sg. neut. {3.A}. . . . . id.
ἄλλο   adj., nom. sg. neut. {3.A} . . . . id.
G241 ἀλλογενής, -οῦς, ὁ   *a man of another race, a*
    foreigner.
ἀλλογενής   adj., nom. sg. masc. {3.E}. . . ἀλλογενής G241
ἄλλοι   adj., nom. pl. masc. {3.A}. . . . . .ἄλλος G243
ἄλλοις   adj., dat. pl. masc. {3.A} . . . . id.
G242 ἅλλομαι   *I leap, leap up.*
ἁλλόμενος   vbl., pres. mid./pass. ptc. nom. sg.
    masc. {6.A.1} .ἅλλομαι G242
ἁλλομένου   vbl., pres. mid./pass. ptc. gen. sg.
    neut. {6.A.1} . . . . id.

ἄλλον   adj., acc. sg. masc. {3.A} . . . . .ἄλλος G243
G243 ἄλλος, -η, -ο   (1) *other, another* (of more than
    two), *different;* (2) see under ἕτερος; ὁ ἄλλος,
    the other (of two only), Matt 5:39, etc.; ἄλλοι
    . . . ἄλλο τι . . . *some . . . one thing, some . . .*
    another thing.
ἄλλος   adj., nom. sg. masc. {3.A} . . . . .ἄλλος G243
ἀλλοτρίᾳ   adj., dat. sg. fem. {3.A} . . . . ἀλλότριος G245
ἀλλοτρίαις   adj., dat. pl. fem. {3.A} . . . . id.
ἀλλοτρίαν   adj., acc. sg. fem. {3.A} . . . . id.
G244 ἀλλοτριεπίσκοπος   (ἀλλοτριοεπίσκοπος),
    -ου, ὁ   *one who pries into other men's affairs*
    by means of soothsayers, astrologers, etc. (a
    word of uncertain application).
ἀλλοτριεπίσκοπος   noun, nom. sg. masc.
    {2.B} . . . . .ἀλλοτριεπίσκοπος G244
ἀλλοτριοεπίσκοπος   noun, nom. sg. masc.
    {2.B} . . . . id.
ἀλλοτρίοις   adj., dat. pl. masc. {3.A} . . . ἀλλότριος G245
ἀλλότριον   adj., acc. sg. masc. {3.A} . . . . id.
G245 ἀλλότριος, -α, -ον   *belonging to another per-*
    son, belonging to others.
ἀλλοτρίῳ   adj., dat. sg. masc. {3.A} . . . ἀλλότριος G245
ἀλλοτρίῳ   adj., dat. sg. neut. {3.A}. . . . . id.
ἀλλοτρίων   adj., gen. pl. masc. {3.A} . . . . id.
ἄλλου   adj., gen. sg. masc. {3.A} . . . . .ἄλλος G243
ἄλλους   adj., acc. pl. masc. {3.A} . . . . id.
G246 ἀλλόφυλος, -ον   *a foreigner.*
ἀλλοφύλῳ   adj., dat. sg. masc. {3.C}. . . ἀλλόφυλος G246
ἄλλῳ   adj., dat. sg. masc. {3.A} . . . . .ἄλλος G243
ἄλλων   adj., gen. pl. masc. {3.A}. . . . . id.
G247 ἄλλως   *otherwise;* τὰ ἄλλως ἔχοντα, *things*
    that are other wise.
ἄλλως   adv. {3.F} . . . . .ἄλλως G247
G248 ἀλοάω   *I thresh* (corn).
ἄλογα   adj., nom. pl. neut. {3.C} . . . . ἄλογος G249
ἄλογον   adj., nom. sg. neut. {3.C}. . . . . id.
G249 ἄλογος, -ον   (1) *without (devoid of) human*
    reason; (2) *unreasonable, senseless.*
G250 ἀλόη, -ης, ἡ   *aloes,* the powdered fragrant aloe
    wood.
ἀλόης   noun, gen. sg. fem. {2.A}. . . . . .ἀλόη G250
ἀλοῶν   vbl., pres. act. ptc. nom. sg. masc.
    {6.A.2} . . . . .ἀλοάω G248
ἀλοῶντα   vbl., pres. act. ptc. acc. sg. masc.
    {6.A.2}. . . . . id.
G251 ἅλς, ἁλός, ὁ   *salt.*
ἁλυκόν   adj., nom. sg. neut. {3.A}. . . . . .ἁλυκός G252
ἁλυκόν   adj., acc. sg. neut. {3.A}. . . . . id.
G252 ἁλυκός, -ή, -όν   *salty, saline.*
G253 ἄλυπος, -η, -όν   *free from pain (grief, trouble),*
    comp. in Phil 2:28.
ἀλυπότερος   adj. comp., nom. sg. masc. {3.A;
    3.G} . . . . .ἄλυπος G253
ἁλύσει   noun, dat. sg. fem. {2.C} . . . . .ἅλυσις G254
ἁλύσεις   noun, acc. pl. fem. {2.C} . . . . id.
ἁλύσεις   noun, nom. pl. fem. {2.C} . . . . id.
ἁλύσεσι   noun, dat. pl. fem. {2.C} . . . . id.
ἁλύσεσιν   noun, dat. pl. fem. {2.C} . . . . id.
ἅλυσιν   noun, acc. sg. fem. {2.C} . . . . id.

G254 **ἅλυσις**, -εως, ἡ   *a (light) chain.*
ἀλυσιτελές   adj., nom. sg. neut. {3.E} . ἀλυσιτελής G255
G255 **ἀλυσιτελής**, -ές   *profitless, unprofitable.*
ἄλφα   noun, letter . . . . A G1
G256 **Ἀλφαῖος**, -ου, ὁ   *Alphaeus,* apparently two
persons: (1) father of Levi (Mark 2:14); and (2)
father of James (Mark 3:18, etc.). (Some say
= Aram. Chalphai, and identify with Clopas,
John 19:25.).
Ἀλφαίου   noun prop., gen. sg. masc. {2.B;
2.D} . . . . .Ἀλφαῖος G256
Ἀλφαίου   noun prop., gen. sg. masc. {2.B; 2.D} . id.
G257 **ἅλων**, -ωνος, ἡ   *a threshing floor* (= ἅλως).
ἅλωνα   noun, acc. sg. fem. {2.C} . . . . ἅλων G257
ἀλώπεκες   noun, nom. pl. fem. {2.C} . . . . ἀλώπηξ G258
ἀλώπεκι   noun, dat. sg. fem. {2.C} . . . . id.
G258 **ἀλώπηξ**, -εκος, ἡ   *a fox.*
ἅλωσιν   noun, acc. sg. fem. {2.C} . . . . ἅλωσις G259
G259 **ἅλωσις**, -εως, ἡ   *capture, capturing.*
G260 **ἅμα**   (1) adv., *at the same time, therewith;* (2)
prep. with dat., *along with, together with.*
ἅμα   adv. and prep. . . . . .ἅμα G260
ἀμαθεῖς   adj., nom. pl. masc. {3.E} . . . . ἀμαθής G261
G261 **ἀμαθής**, -ές   *unlearned* (very rare in Hellenistic
period).
ἀμαράντινον   adj., acc. sg. masc.
{3.A} . . . . .ἀμαράντινος G262
G262 **ἀμαράντινος**, -η, -ον   *unfading, fadeless.*
ἀμάραντον   adj., acc. sg. fem. {3.C} . . . ἀμάραντος G263
G263 **ἀμάραντος**, -ον   *unfading.*
ἁμάρτανε   verb, pres. act. impv. 2 pers. sg.
{5.D.1} . . . . .ἁμαρτάνω G264
ἁμαρτάνει   verb, pres. act. indic. 3 pers. sg.
{5.A.1.a} . . . . id.
ἁμαρτάνειν   vbl., pres. act. inf. {6.B.1} . . . . id.
ἁμαρτάνετε   verb, pres. act. impv. 2 pers. pl.
{5.D.1} . . . . id.
ἁμαρτάνετε   verb, pres. act. indic. 2 pers. pl.
{5.A.1.a} . . . . id.
ἁμαρτάνοντα   vbl., pres. act. ptc. acc. sg.
masc. {6.A.1} . . . . id.
ἁμαρτάνοντας   vbl., pres. act. ptc. acc. pl.
masc. {6.A.1} . . . . id.
ἁμαρτάνοντες   vbl., pres. act. ptc. nom. pl.
masc. {6.A.1} . . . . id.
ἁμαρτανόντων   vbl., pres. act. ptc. gen. pl.
masc. {6.A.1} . . . . id.
ἁμαρτάνουσι   vbl., pres. act. ptc. dat. pl. masc.
{6.A.1} . . . . id.
ἁμαρτάνουσιν   vbl., pres. act. ptc. dat. pl.
masc. {6.A.1} . . . . id.
G264 **ἁμαρτάνω**   orig., *I miss the mark;* hence, (1)
I make a mistake; (2) *I sin, I commit a sin*
(against God); sometimes (Luke 17:4; Acts
25:8, etc.) the idea of sinning against a fellow
creature is present.
ἁμαρτάνων   vbl., pres. act. ptc. nom. sg. masc.
{6.A.1} . . . . .ἁμαρτάνω G264
ἁμάρτῃ   verb, ²aor. act. subjunc. 3 pers. sg. {5.B.1} id.
G265 **ἁμάρτημα**, -ατος, τό   *a fault, a sin.*

ἁμάρτημα   noun, nom. sg. neut. {2.C}. . ἁμάρτημα G265
ἁμαρτήματα   noun, nom. pl. neut. {2.C}. . . . . id.
ἁμαρτήματος   noun, gen. sg. neut. {2.C}. . . . . id.
ἁμαρτημάτων   noun, gen. pl. neut. {2.C} . . . . id.
ἁμαρτήσαντας   vbl., aor. act. ptc. acc. pl. masc.
{6.A.1.a} . . . . ἁμαρτάνω G264
ἁμαρτήσαντος   vbl., aor. act. ptc. gen. sg.
masc. {6.A.1.a}. . . . . id.
ἁμαρτησάντων   vbl., aor. act. ptc. gen. pl.
masc. {6.A.1.a}. . . . . id.
ἁμαρτήσασιν   vbl., aor. act. ptc. dat. pl. masc.
{6.A.1.a} . . . . id.
ἁμαρτήσει   verb, fut. act. indic. 3 pers. sg.
{5.A.1.a} . . . . id.
ἁμαρτήσῃ   verb, aor. act. subjunc. 3 pers. sg.
{5.B.1} . . . . id.
ἁμαρτήσομεν   verb, fut. act. indic. 1 pers. pl.
{5.A.1.a} . . . . id.
ἁμαρτήσωμεν   verb, aor. act. subjunc. 1 pers.
pl. {5.B.1}. . . . . id.
ἁμάρτητε   verb, ²aor. act. subjunc. 2 pers. pl.
{5.B.1} . . . . id.
G266 **ἁμαρτία**, -ας, ἡ   *a sin* (i.e., *an error, a wrong
state of mind* or *soul*).
ἁμαρτία   noun, nom. sg. fem. {2.A}. . . . .ἁμαρτία G266
ἁμαρτίᾳ   noun, dat. sg. fem. {2.A} . . . . id.
ἁμαρτίαι   noun, nom. pl. fem. {2.A} . . . . id.
ἁμαρτίαις   noun, dat. pl. fem. {2.A} . . . . id.
ἁμαρτίαν   noun, acc. sg. fem. {2.A} . . . . id.
ἁμαρτίας   noun, acc. pl. fem. {2.A} . . . . id.
ἁμαρτίας   noun, gen. sg. fem. {2.A} . . . . id.
ἁμαρτιῶν   noun, gen. pl. fem. {2.A}. . . . . id.
ἀμάρτυρον   adj., acc. sg. masc. {3.C} . . ἀμάρτυρος G267
G267 **ἀμάρτυρος**, -ον   *unwitnessed, untestified to.*
ἁμαρτωλοί   adj., nom. pl. masc. {3.C} ἁμαρτωλός G268
ἁμαρτωλοί   adj., voc. pl. masc. {3.C} . . . . id.
ἁμαρτωλοῖς   adj., dat. pl. masc. {3.C} . . . . . . id.
ἁμαρτωλόν   adj., acc. sg. masc. {3.C}. . . . . . . id.
G268 **ἁμαρτωλός**, -όν   (1) *sinning, sinful;* (2)
frequent as a translation of a contemptuous
Aram. word, with reference to particular
classes despised by strict Jews, *a sinner.*
ἁμαρτωλός   adj., nom. sg. fem. {3.C}. . ἁμαρτωλός G268
ἁμαρτωλός   adj., nom. sg. masc. {3.C}. . . . . . id.
ἁμαρτωλούς   adj., acc. pl. masc. {3.C} . . . . . . id.
ἁμαρτωλῷ   adj., dat. sg. fem. {3.C} . . . . id.
ἁμαρτωλῷ   adj., dat. sg. masc. {3.C} . . . . id.
ἁμαρτωλῶν   adj., gen. pl. masc. {3.C} . . . . . . id.
ἄμαχον   adj., acc. sg. masc. {3.C} . . . . .ἄμαχος G269
G269 **ἄμαχος**, -ον   *not quarrelsome, peaceable* (orig.
a military word).
ἀμάχους   adj., acc. pl. masc. {3.C} . . . . . . .ἄμαχος G269
G270 **ἀμάω**   *I mow, reap.*
ἀμέθυσος   noun, nom. sg. fem. {2.B}. . .ἀμέθυστος G271
G271 **ἀμέθυστος**, -ου, ἡ   *amethyst* (a kind of rock
crystal; the best specimens are the color of
unmixed wine, whence perhaps the name).
ἀμέθυστος   noun, nom. sg. fem. {2.B} . .ἀμέθυστος G271
ἀμέλει   verb, pres. act. impv. 2 pers. sg.
{5.D.2}. . . . . .ἀμελέω G272

G272 **ἀμελέω**   *I neglect.*
  ἀμελήσαντες   vbl., aor. act. ptc. nom. pl. masc.
    {6.A.2} . . . . .ἀμελέω *G272*
  ἀμελήσω   verb, fut. act. indic. 1 pers. sg. {5.A.1} id.
  ἄμεμπτοι   adj., nom. pl. masc. {3.C} . . . . ἄμεμπτος *G273*
G273 **ἄμεμπτος**, -ον   *blameless.*
  ἄμεμπτος   adj., nom. sg. fem. {3.C} . . . . ἄμεμπτος *G273*
  ἄμεμπτος   adj., nom. sg. masc. {3.C} . . . . id.
  ἀμέμπτους   adj., acc. pl. fem. {3.C} . . . . id.
G274 **ἀμέμπτως**   adv., *blamelessly.*
  ἀμέμπτως   adv. {3.F} . . . . .ἀμέμπτως *G274*
G275 **ἀμέριμνος**, -ον   *free from anxiety* (though
    "anxiety" is rather too strong a word).
  ἀμερίμνους   adj., acc. pl. masc. {3.C} . . ἀμέριμνος *G275*
  ἀμετάθετον   adj., acc. sg. neut. {3.C} . . ἀμετάθετος *G276*
G276 **ἀμετάθετος**, -ον   *unchanged, unchangeable.*
  ἀμεταθέτων   adj., gen. pl. neut. {3.C} . . ἀμετάθετος *G276*
  ἀμετακίνητοι   adj., nom. pl. masc.
    {3.C} . . . . ἀμετακίνητος *G277*
G277 **ἀμετακίνητος**, -ον   *immovable.*
  ἀμεταμέλητα   adj., nom. pl. neut.
    {3.C} .ἀμεταμέλητος *G278*
  ἀμεταμέλητον   adj., acc. sg. fem. {3.C} . . . . id.
G278 **ἀμεταμέλητος**, -ον   *not to be repented of,*
    about which no change of mind can take place,
    not affected by change of mind.
  ἀμετανόητον   adj., acc. sg. fem. {3.C}ἀμετανόητος *G279*
G279 **ἀμετανόητος**, -ον   *unrepentant.*
  ἄμετρα   adj., acc. pl. neut. {3.C} . . . . ἄμετρος *G280*
G280 **ἄμετρος**, -ον   *unmeasurable, immeasurable;* εἰς
    τὰ ἄμετρα, *to a limitless degree.*
G281 **ἀμήν**   *verily, truly;* at the end of sentences may
    be paraphrased by *So let it be!* (Heb.).
  ἀμήν   interj, Heb. . . . . .ἀμήν *G281*
  ἀμησάντων   vbl., aor. act. ptc. gen. pl. masc.
    {6.A.2} . . . . ἀμάω *G270*
G282 **ἀμήτωρ**, -ορος   *whose mother's name is not*
    recorded (or *known*); lit., *motherless.*
  ἀμήτωρ   adj., nom. sg. masc. {3.C} . . . . . . ἀμήτωρ *G282*
  ἀμίαντον   adj., acc. sg. fem. {3.C} . . . . . ἀμίαντος *G283*
G283 **ἀμίαντος**, -ον   *undefiled, untainted.*
  ἀμίαντος   adj., nom. sg. fem. {3.C} . . . . ἀμίαντος *G283*
  ἀμίαντος   adj., nom. sg. masc. {3.C} . . . . id.
G284 **Ἀμιναδάβ**, ὁ   *Aminadab,* son of Aram. and
    father of Naasson, one of the ancestors of Jesus
    (Heb.).
  Ἀμιναδάβ   noun prop. . . . . Ἀμιναδάβ *G284*
  ἄμμον   noun, acc. sg. fem. {2.B} . . . . .ἄμμος *G285*
G285 **ἄμμος**, -ου, ἡ   *sand.*
  ἄμμος   noun, nom. sg. fem. {2.B} . . . . ἄμμος *G285*
G286 **ἀμνός**, -οῦ, ὁ   *a lamb* (as a type of innocence,
    and with sacrificial connotation).
  ἀμνός   noun, nom. sg. masc. {2.B} . . . . .ἀμνός *G286*
  ἀμνοῦ   noun, gen. sg. masc. {2.B} . . . . id.
  ἀμοιβάς   noun, acc. pl. fem. {2.A} . . . . . ἀμοιβή *G287*
G287 **ἀμοιβή**, -ῆς, ἡ   (1) a *change, an exchange;* (2)
    hence, pl. *reciprocal good deeds* (services), *a*
    fitting requital.
  ἄμπελον   noun, acc. sg. fem. {2.B} . . . . . .ἄμπελος *G288*
G288 **ἄμπελος**, -ου, ἡ   *a vine.*

  ἄμπελος   noun, nom. sg. fem. {2.B} . . . . .ἄμπελος *G288*
  ἀμπέλου   noun, gen. sg. fem. {2.B} . . . . id.
  ἀμπελουργόν   noun, acc. sg. masc.
    {2.B} . . . . .ἀμπελουργός *G289*
G289 **ἀμπελουργός**, -οῦ, ὁ   *a vinedresser.*
  ἀμπέλῳ   noun, dat. sg. fem. {2.B} . . . . . . .ἄμπελος *G288*
G290 **ἀμπελών**, -ῶνος, ὁ   *a vineyard* (-ών indicates
    "plantation of," cf. ἐλαιών).
  ἀμπελῶνα   noun, acc. sg. masc. {2.C} . . . ἀμπελών *G290*
  ἀμπελῶνι   noun, dat. sg. masc. {2.C} . . . . id.
  ἀμπελῶνος   noun, gen. sg. masc. {2.C} . . . . id.
  Ἀμπλίαν   noun prop., acc. sg. masc. {2.B;
    2.D} . . . . .Ἀμπλιᾶτος *G291*
  Ἀμπλιᾶτον   noun prop., acc. sg. masc. {2.B; 2.D}id.
G291 **Ἀμπλιᾶτος**, -ου, ὁ   *Ampliatus,* a male member
    of the church at Rome, probably of the impe-
    rial household (pet form Ἀμπλίας).
G292 **ἀμύνομαι**   *I attack in defense, I defend* (by
    force); (very rare in the colloquial language).
  ἀμφιάζει   verb, pres. act. indic. 3 pers. sg.
    {5.A.1.a} . . . . ἀμφιάζω *G294†‡*
G294†‡ **ἀμφιάζω** (-εζω)   *I clothe, I put clothing (cover-*
    ing) on (over). Var. for ἀμφιέννυμι, Luke 12:28.
  ἀμφιβάλλοντας   vbl., pres. act. ptc. acc. pl. masc.
    {6.A.1} . . . . .ἀμφιβάλλω *G906†‡*
G906†‡ **ἀμφιβάλλω**   *I cast (a fishing net), I fish.* Var. for
    βάλλω, Mark 1:16.
G293 **ἀμφίβληστρον**, -ου, τό   *a* (casting) *net.*
  ἀμφίβληστρον   noun, acc. sg. neut.
    {2.B} . . . . .ἀμφίβληστρον *G293*
  ἀμφιέζει   verb, pres. act. indic. 3 pers. sg.
    {5.A.1.a} . . . . ἀμφιάζω *G294†‡*
G294 **ἀμφιέννυμι**   *I clothe* (a survival of literary
    language).
  ἀμφιέννυσι   verb, pres. act. indic. 3 pers. sg.
    {5.A.3.a} . . . . ἀμφιάζω *G294†‡*
  ἀμφιέννυσιν   verb, pres. act. indic. 3 pers. sg.
    {5.A.3.a} . . . . id.
  Ἀμφίπολιν   noun prop., acc. sg. fem. {2.C;
    2.D} . . . . Ἀμφίπολις *G295*
G295 **Ἀμφίπολις**, -εως, ἡ   *Amphipolis,* a leading city
    of Macedonia.
G296 **ἄμφοδον**, -ου, τό   *a street,* or rather *a quarter*
    or *block* of a city.
  ἀμφόδου   noun, gen. sg. neut. {2.B} . . . . . ἄμφοδον *G296*
  ἀμφότερα   adj., acc. pl. neut. {3.A} . . . . ἀμφότεροι *G297*
G297 **ἀμφότεροι**, -αι, -α   *both* (of two); in Acts
    19:16; 23:8, perhaps = *all* (of more than two);
    so in common speech and in Byzantine Gk.
  ἀμφότεροι   adj., nom. pl. masc. {3.A} . . ἀμφότεροι *G297*
  ἀμφοτέροις   adj., dat. pl. masc. {3.A} . . . . id.
  ἀμφοτέρους   adj., acc. pl. masc. {3.A} . . . . id.
  ἀμφοτέρων   adj., gen. pl. masc. {3.A} . . . . id.
  ἄμωμα   adj., nom. pl. neut. {3.C} . . . . . ἄμωμος *G299*
  ἀμώμητα   adj., nom. pl. neut. {3.C} . . . . ἀμώμητος *G298*
  ἀμώμητοι   adj., nom. pl. masc. {3.C} . . . . id.
G298 **ἀμώμητος**, -ον   *unblemished* (a literary word;
    the Gk. properly means *not to be blamed,* but
    under the influence of Heb. the other sense
    has come into prominence).

ἄμωμοι   adj., nom. pl. masc. {3.C} . . . . . . ἄμωμος G299
ἄμωμον   noun, acc. sg. neut. {2.B} . . . . id.
ἄμωμον   adj., acc. sg. masc. {3.C} . . . . id.
G299 ἄμωμος, -ον   (1) *blameless,* the original sense,
        which may be that in Eph 1:4; 5:27, etc.; (2)
        without blemish, unblemished, a sense almost
        invariable in the LXX, of sacrificial animals,
        and possibly the only sense intended in NT
        (cf. ἀμώμητος). (3) Noun, ἄμωμον, -ου, τό,
        a spice, an odorous unguent derived from an
        Eastern plant with fruit like grapes, Rev 18:13.
ἄμωμος   adj., nom. sg. fem. {3.C} . . . . ἄμωμος G299
ἀμώμου   adj., gen. sg. masc. {3.C} . . . . id.
ἀμώμους   adj., acc. pl. masc. {3.C} . . . . id.
G300 Ἀμών, ὁ   *Amon,* son of Manasseh and father of
        Josiah. Var. spelling of Ἀμώς.
Ἀμών   noun prop. . . . . Ἀμών G300
G301 Ἀμώς, ὁ   (1) *Amos,* son of Manasseh and
        father of Josiah, an ancestor of Jesus (Heb. =
        ʾamon); (2) *Amos,* son of Nahum and father of
        Mattathias.
Ἀμώς   noun prop. . . . . Ἀμώς G301
G302 ἄν   (1) an untranslatable particle *(under the
        circumstances, in that case, anyhow),* the
        general effect of which is to make a statement
        contingent, which would be otherwise be defi-
        nite; it is thus regularly used with the subjunc.
        mood; cf. ἕως ἄν, *until such time as,* ὃς ἄν,
        ὅστις ἄν, *whosoever,* ὅσοι ἄν, *as many as . . .
        may,* ὅπως ἄν, ὡς ἄν (1 Cor 11:34, etc., not
        in 1 Cor 12:2), *that so;* so, with the indic. past,
        in the apodosis of a cond. sentence, e.g., Matt
        11:21 ἄν . . . μετενόησαν, "*would have re-
        pented,*" where μετενόησαν alone would have
        meant "repented"; cf. also Mark 7:11 (reading
        ὃ ἄν . . . ὠφεληθῇς); and with the opt. (rare
        in NT), e.g., τί ἄν θέλοι, "how he *would* like"
        (Luke 1:62), where τί θέλοι would be "how he
        might like"; (2) *if* (= Attic ἤν, ἐάν), e.g., John
        12:32 (var.), 13:20.
ἄν   part. . . . . ἄν G302
G303 ἀνά   prep. with acc., (1) *up;* hence, *up along;*
        (2) ἀνὰ μέσον, *in the middle;* (3) most com-
        monly with a distributive force, e.g., ἀνὰ
        δηνάριον (Matt 20:9), "a denarius *each,*" ἀνὰ
        δύο χιτῶνας (Luke 9:3), "two tunics *each,*"
        ἀνὰ πεντήκοντα (Luke 9:14), "in fifties," "in
        groups of fifty," ἀνὰ δύο (Luke 10:1), "two by
        two" (where perhaps ἀνὰ δύο δύο, a mixed
        distributive, ought to be read).
ἀνά   adv. and prep. ἀνά G303
ἀνάβα   verb, ²aor. act. impv. 2 pers. sg.
        {5.D.1} . . . . ἀναβαίνω G305
G304 ἀναβαθμός, -οῦ, ὁ   (1) *a step;* (2) pl. *a flight
        of steps,* the well known "stairs" leading up
        from the temple to the tower of Antonia at
        Jerusalem.
ἀναβαθμούς   noun, acc. pl. masc. {2.B} ἀναβαθμός G304
ἀναβαθμῶν   noun, gen. pl. masc. {2.B} . . . . id.

ἀναβαίνει   verb, pres. act. indic. 3 pers. sg.
        {5.A.1.a} . . . . ἀναβαίνω G305
ἀναβαίνειν   vbl., pres. act. inf. {6.B.1} . . . . id.
ἀναβαίνομεν   verb, pres. act. indic. 1 pers. pl.
        {5.A.1.a} . . . . id.
ἀναβαῖνον   vbl., pres. act. ptc. acc. sg. neut.
        {6.A.1} . . . . id.
ἀναβαῖνον   vbl., pres. act. ptc. nom. sg. neut.
        {6.A.1} . . . . id.
ἀναβαίνοντα   vbl., pres. act. ptc. acc. sg. masc.
        {6.A.1} . . . . id.
ἀναβαίνοντα   vbl., pres. act. ptc. nom. pl.
        neut. {6.A.1} . . . . id.
ἀναβαίνοντας   vbl., pres. act. ptc. acc. pl.
        masc. {6.A.1} . . . . id.
ἀναβαίνοντες   vbl., pres. act. ptc. nom. pl.
        masc. {6.A.1} . . . . id.
ἀναβαινόντων   vbl., pres. act. ptc. gen. pl.
        masc. {6.A.1} . . . . id.
ἀναβαίνουσιν   verb, pres. act. indic. 3 pers. pl.
        {5.A.1.a} . . . . id.
G305 ἀναβαίνω   *I go up, mount, ascend.*
ἀναβαίνω   verb, pres. act. indic. 1 pers. sg.
        {5.A.1.a} . . . . ἀναβαίνω G305
ἀναβαίνων   vbl., pres. act. ptc. nom. sg. masc.
        {6.A.1} . . . . id.
G306 ἀναβάλλω   mid., *I postpone,* esp. *I postpone the
        trial of,* with acc. of the person affected.
ἀναβάντα   vbl., ²aor. act. ptc. acc. sg. masc.
        {6.A.1.a} . . . . ἀναβαίνω G305
ἀναβάντες   vbl., ²aor. act. ptc. nom. pl. masc.
        {6.A.1.a} . . . . id.
ἀναβάντων   vbl., ²aor. act. ptc. gen. pl. masc.
        {6.A.1.a} . . . . id.
ἀναβάς   vbl., ²aor. act. ptc. nom. sg. masc.
        {6.A.1.a} . . . . id.
ἀνάβατε   verb, ²aor. act. impv. 2 pers. pl. {5.D.1} id.
ἀναβέβηκα   verb, perf. act. indic. 1 pers. sg.
        {5.A.1.c} . . . . id.
ἀναβέβηκεν   verb, perf. act. indic. 3 pers. sg.
        {5.A.1.c} . . . . id.
ἀναβήσεται   verb, fut. mid. indic. 3 pers. sg.
        {5.A.1.d} . . . . id.
ἀνάβητε   verb, ²aor. act. impv. 2 pers. pl. {5.D.1} id.
G307 ἀναβιβάζω   *I cause to come up, bring up,* regu-
        larly from sea to land.
ἀναβιβάσαντες   vbl., aor. act. ptc. nom. pl. masc.
        {6.A.1.a} . . . . ἀναβιβάζω G307
ἀναβλέπουσι   verb, pres. act. indic. 3 pers. pl.
        {5.A.1.a} . . . . ἀναβλέπω G308
ἀναβλέπουσιν   verb, pres. act. indic. 3 pers. pl.
        {5.A.1.a} . . . . id.
G308 ἀναβλέπω   (1) *I look up,* e.g., Matt 14:19; (2) *I
        recover my sight,* e.g., Matt 11:5.
ἀναβλέψαι   vbl., aor. act. inf. {6.B.1} . . . ἀναβλέπω G308
ἀναβλέψαντος   vbl., aor. act. ptc. gen. sg.
        masc. {6.A.1.a} . . . . id.
ἀναβλέψας   vbl., aor. act. ptc. nom. sg. masc.
        {6.A.1.a} . . . . id.

ἀναβλέψασαι   vbl., aor. act. ptc. nom. pl. fem.
 {6.A.1.a} . . . . id.
ἀναβλέψῃ   verb, aor. act. subjunc. 3 pers. sg.
 {5.B.1} . . . . id.
ἀναβλέψῃς   verb, aor. act. subjunc. 2 pers. sg.
 {5.B.1} . . . . id.
ἀνάβλεψιν   noun, acc. sg. fem. {2.C} . . .ἀνάβλεψις G309
G309 ἀνάβλεψις, -εως, ἡ   recovery of sight.
ἀνάβλεψον   verb, aor. act. impv. 2 pers. sg.
 {5.D.1} . . . . .ἀναβλέπω G308
ἀναβλέψω   verb, aor. act. subjunc. 1 pers. sg.
 {5.B.1} . . . . id.
G310 ἀναβοάω   I shout upwards, cry out, raise my
 voice, Matt 27:46 (var.).
ἀναβοήσας   vbl., aor. act. ptc. nom. sg. masc.
 {6.A.2} . . . . .ἀναβοάω G310
G311 ἀναβολή, -ῆς, ἡ   postponement, delay, putting off.
ἀναβολήν   noun, acc. sg. fem. {2.A} . . . ἀναβολή G311
ἀναγαγεῖν   vbl., ²aor. act. inf. {6.B.1} . . . . . ἀνάγω G321
ἀναγαγών   vbl., ²aor. act. ptc. nom. sg. masc.
 {6.A.1.a} . . . . id.
G508†‡ ἀνάγαιον, -ου, τό   an upper room; alternate
 spellings: ἀνώγεον, ἀνώγαιον.
ἀνάγαιον   noun, acc. sg. neut. {2.B} . . .ἀνάγαιον G508†‡
ἀναγγεῖλαι   vbl., aor. act. inf. {6.B.1} . . .ἀναγγέλλω G312
ἀνάγγειλον   verb, aor. act. impv. 2 pers. sg.
 {5.D.1} . . . . id.
ἀναγγελεῖ   verb, fut. act. indic. 3 pers. sg. {5.A.2}id.
ἀναγγέλλομεν   verb, pres. act. indic. 1 pers. pl.
 {5.A.1.a} . . . . id.
ἀναγγέλλοντες   vbl., pres. act. ptc. nom. pl.
 masc. {6.A.1} . . . . id.
G312 ἀναγγέλλω   I announce, report.
ἀναγγέλλων   vbl., pres. act. ptc. nom. sg. masc.
 {6.A.1} . . . . .ἀναγγέλλω G312
ἀναγγελῶ   verb, fut. act. indic. 1 pers. sg. {5.A.2}id.
ἀναγεγεννημένοι   vbl., perf. pass. ptc. nom. pl.
 masc. {6.A.2} . . . . .ἀναγεννάω G313
G313 ἀναγεννάω   I beget again, I beget into a new life.
ἀναγεννήσας   vbl., aor. act. ptc. nom. sg. masc.
 {6.A.2} . . . . .ἀναγεννάω G313
ἀνάγεσθαι   vbl., pres. pass. inf. {6.B.1} . . . . ἀνάγω G321
ἀναγινώσκεις   verb, pres. act. indic. 2 pers. sg.
 {5.A.1.a} . . . . ἀναγινώσκω G314
ἀναγινώσκεται   verb, pres. pass. indic. 3 pers.
 sg. {5.A.1.d} . . . . id.
ἀναγινώσκετε   verb, pres. act. indic. 2 pers. pl.
 {5.A.1.a} . . . . id.
ἀναγινώσκηται   verb, pres. pass. subjunc.
 3 pers. sg. {5.B.1} . . . . id.
ἀναγινωσκομένας   vbl., pres. pass. ptc. acc. pl.
 fem. {6.A.1} . . . . id.
ἀναγινωσκομένη   vbl., pres. pass. ptc. nom.
 sg. fem. {6.A.1} . . . . id.
ἀναγινωσκόμενος   vbl., pres. pass. ptc. nom.
 sg. masc. {6.A.1} . . . . id.
ἀναγινώσκοντες   vbl., pres. act. ptc. nom. pl.
 masc. {6.A.1} . . . . id.
ἀναγινώσκοντος   vbl., pres. act. ptc. gen. sg.
 masc. {6.A.1} . . . . id.

G314 ἀναγινώσκω   I read aloud (in the scriptures,
 i.e., the OT).
ἀναγινώσκων   vbl., pres. act. ptc. nom. sg. masc.
 {6.A.1} . . . . ἀναγινώσκω G314
ἀναγκάζεις   verb, pres. act. indic. 2 pers. sg.
 {5.A.1.a} . . . . ἀναγκάζω G315
ἀναγκάζουσιν   verb, pres. act. indic. 3 pers. pl.
 {5.A.1.a} . . . . id.
G315 ἀναγκάζω   I compel, I constrain.
ἀναγκαῖα   adj., nom. pl. neut. {3.A} . . . .ἀναγκαῖος G316
ἀναγκαίας   adj., acc. pl. fem. {3.A} . . . . id.
ἀναγκαῖον   adj., acc. sg. neut. {3.A} . . . . id.
ἀναγκαῖον   adj., nom. sg. neut. {3.A} . . . . id.
G316 ἀναγκαῖος, -α, -ον   (1) necessary, essential; (2)
 intimate, Acts 10:24.
ἀναγκαιότερον   adj. comp., nom. sg. neut. {3.A;
 3.G} . . . . .ἀναγκαῖος G316
ἀναγκαίους   adj., acc. pl. masc. {3.A} . . . . id.
ἀνάγκαις   noun, dat. pl. fem. {2.A} . . . . . .ἀνάγκη G318
ἀνάγκασον   verb, aor. act. impv. 2 pers. sg.
 {5.D.1} . . . . .ἀναγκάζω G315
G317 ἀναγκαστῶς   adv., by way of compulsion, by
 force.
ἀναγκαστῶς   adv. {3.F} . . . . ἀναγκαστῶς G317
G318 ἀνάγκη, -ης, ἡ   necessity, constraint, compulsion; ἔχω ἀνάγκη, I am obliged.
ἀνάγκη   noun, nom. sg. fem. {2.A} . . . . . . .ἀνάγκη G318
ἀνάγκη   noun, dat. sg. fem. {2.A} . . . . id.
ἀνάγκην   noun, acc. sg. fem. {2.A} . . . . id.
ἀνάγκης   noun, gen. sg. fem. {2.A} . . . . id.
ἀναγνόντες   vbl., ²aor. act. ptc. nom. pl. masc.
 {6.A.1.a} . . . . ἀναγινώσκω G314
ἀναγνούς   vbl., ²aor. act. ptc. nom. sg. masc.
 {6.A.1.a} . . . . id.
ἀναγνῶναι   vbl., ²aor. act. inf. {6.B.1} . . . . id.
G319 ἀναγνωρίζω   I make known to again, I make to
 be recognized (var. in Acts 7:13).
ἀναγνώσει   noun, dat. sg. fem. {2.C} . . .ἀνάγνωσις G320
ἀναγνωσθῇ   verb, aor. pass. subjunc. 3 pers. sg.
 {5.B.1} . . . . ἀναγινώσκω G314
ἀναγνωσθῆναι   vbl., aor. pass. inf. {6.B.1} . . . . . id.
ἀνάγνωσιν   noun, acc. sg. fem. {2.C} . . .ἀνάγνωσις G320
G320 ἀνάγνωσις, -εως, ἡ   public reading (of the law
 and prophets in synagogue or church).
ἀναγνῶτε   verb, ²aor. act. subjunc. 2 pers. pl.
 {5.B.1} . . . . ἀναγινώσκω G314
ἀναγομένοις   vbl., pres. pass. ptc. dat. pl. masc.
 {6.A.1} . . . . ἀνάγω G321
G321 ἀνάγω   (1) I lead up; (2) mid. and pass. I put to
 sea, set sail.
G322 ἀναδείκνυμι   (1) I show forth or clearly; (2)
 hence, I proclaim (a person's appointment to
 an office), I appoint.
ἀναδείξεως   noun, gen. sg. fem. {2.C} . . .ἀνάδειξις G323
G323 ἀνάδειξις, -εως, ἡ   (1) the proclamation of an
 appointment (to an office); (2) perhaps rather
 admission to membership of a society.
ἀνάδειξον   verb, aor. act. impv. 2 pers. sg.
 {5.D.3} . . . . ἀναδείκνυμι G322

ἀναδεξάμενος vbl., aor. mid. ptc. nom. sg. masc.
{6.A.1.b} . . . . ἀναδέχομαι G324

G324 **ἀναδέχομαι** (1) *I welcome, receive kindly;* (2)
in Heb 11:17 perhaps *I undertake, I assume the
responsibility of.*

G325 **ἀναδίδωμι** *I send up, deliver, hand over.*
ἀναδόντες vbl., ²aor. act. ptc. nom. pl. masc.
{6.A.3} . . . . ἀναδίδωμι G325

G326 **ἀναζάω** *I come to life again, I revive* (var. in
Luke 15:24).

G327 **ἀναζητέω** *I seek out, search for* (implying the
difficulty of the task).
ἀναζητῆσαι vbl., aor. act. inf. {6.B.1} . . ἀναζητέω G327
ἀναζητοῦντες vbl., pres. act. ptc. nom. pl.
masc. {6.A.2} . . . . id.

G328 **ἀναζώννυμι** *I gird up, brace up* (with a view
to active exertion). A metaphor from the gird-
ing of the flowing tunic, to prevent its hamper-
ing one in active work.
ἀναζωπυρεῖν vbl., pres. act. inf.
{6.B.2} . . . . ἀναζωπυρέω G329

G329 **ἀναζωπυρέω** *I stir up the fire, fan the flame of.*
ἀναζωσάμενοι vbl., aor. mid. ptc. nom. pl. masc.
{6.A.3} . . . . ἀναζώννυμι G328

G330 **ἀναθάλλω** *I cause to bloom again.*
ἀναθεμα noun, nom. sg. neut. {2.C} . . . . ἀνάθεμα G331

G331 **ἀνάθεμα**, -ατος, τό *a curse, a cursed thing*
(properly, a devoting to the vengeance of
the infernal goddesses). Distinguish from
ἀνάθημα, q.v.
ἀνάθεμα noun, nom. sg. neut. {2.C} . . . . ἀνάθεμα G331
ἀναθέματι noun, dat. sg. neut. {2.C} . . . . id.
ἀναθεματίζειν vbl., pres. act. inf.
{6.B.1} . . . . ἀναθεματίζω G332

G332 **ἀναθεματίζω** *I curse, I invoke curses.*

G333 **ἀναθεωρέω** *I look up at, I gaze up at.*
ἀναθεωροῦντες vbl., pres. act. ptc. nom. pl. masc.
{6.A.2} . . . . ἀναθεωρέω G333
ἀναθεωρῶν vbl., pres. act. ptc. nom. sg. masc.
{6.A.2} . . . . id.

G334 **ἀνάθημα**, -ατος, τό *an offering dedicated*
(hung up in a temple) by a worshipper to a
god, in return for a favor received, Luke 21:5.
ἀναθήμασι noun, dat. pl. neut. {2.C} . . . ἀνάθημα G334
ἀναθήμασιν noun, dat. pl. neut. {2.C} . . . . . . id.

G335 **ἀναίδεια**, -ας, ἡ *shamelessness, shameless
persistence* (e.g., in greed).
ἀναίδειαν noun, acc. sg. fem. {2.A} . . . . ἀναίδεια G335
ἀναιδίαν noun, acc. sg. fem. {2.A} . . . . id.
ἀναιρεθῆναι vbl., aor. pass. inf. {6.B.1} . . ἀναιρέω G337
ἀναιρεῖ verb, pres. act. indic. 3 pers. sg. {5.A.2} id.
ἀναιρεῖν vbl., pres. act. inf. {6.B.2} . . . . id.
ἀναιρεῖσθαι vbl., pres. pass. inf. {6.B.2} . . . . . . id.
ἀναιρέσει noun, dat. sg. fem. {2.C} . . . . ἀναίρεσις G336

G336 **ἀναίρεσις**, -εως, ἡ *taking away* (of life), *kill-
ing, slaying, murder.*

G337 **ἀναιρέω** (1) *I take up,* e.g., Acts 7:21; more
often (2) *I take away the life of, murder*
(2 Thess 2:8, var.).

ἀναιρουμένων vbl., pres. pass. ptc. gen. pl. masc.
{6.A.2} . . . . ἀναιρέω G337
ἀναιρούντων vbl., pres. act. ptc. gen. pl. masc.
{6.A.2} . . . . id.
ἀναίτιοι adj., nom. pl. masc. {3.C} . . . . . ἀναίτιος G338

G338 **ἀναίτιος**, -ον *guiltless.*
ἀναιτίους adj., acc. pl. masc. {3.C} . . . . . ἀναίτιος G338

G339 **ἀνακαθίζω** *I sit up* (var. in Luke 7:15; in classical Gk. *I cause to sit up*).
ἀνακαινίζειν vbl., pres. act. inf.
{6.B.1} . . . . ἀνακαινίζω G340

G340 **ἀνακαινίζω** *I make fresh again, I make fresh
as at the first.*
ἀνακαινούμενον vbl., pres. pass. ptc. acc. sg.
masc. {6.A.2} . . . . ἀνακαινόω G341
ἀνακαινοῦται verb, pres. pass. indic. 3 pers.
sg. {5.A.2} . . . . id.

G341 **ἀνακαινόω** *I renew, I make new again* (cf.
ἀνακαινίζω); not cited before Paul.
ἀνακαινώσει noun, dat. sg. fem.
{2.C} . . . . ἀνακαίνωσις G342
ἀνακαινώσεως noun, gen. sg. fem. {2.C} . . . . . id.

G342 **ἀνακαίνωσις**, -εως, ἡ *renewing* (not cited earlier).
ἀνακαλυπτόμενον vbl., pres. pass. ptc. nom. sg.
neut. {6.A.1} . . . . ἀνακαλύπτω G343

G343 **ἀνακαλύπτω** *I unveil.*

G344 **ἀνακάμπτω** *I return.* Var. ἐπανακάμπτω
I return; Luke 10:6
ἀνακάμψαι vbl., aor. act. inf. {6.B.1} . . ἀνακάμπτω G344
ἀνακάμψει verb, fut. act. indic. 3 pers. sg.
{5.A.1.a} . . . . id.
ἀνακάμψω verb, fut. act. indic. 1 pers. sg.
{5.A.1.a} . . . . id.

G345 **ἀνάκειμαι** *I recline* (esp. at a dinner table).
ἀνακειμένοις vbl., pres. mid./pass. ptc. dat. pl.
masc. {6.A.3} . . . . ἀνάκειμαι G345
ἀνακείμενον vbl., pres. mid./pass. ptc. nom.
sg. neut. {6.A.3} . . . . id.
ἀνακείμενος vbl., pres. mid./pass. ptc. nom.
sg. masc. {6.A.3} . . . . id.
ἀνακειμένου vbl., pres. mid./pass. ptc. gen. sg.
masc. {6.A.3} . . . . id.
ἀνακειμένους vbl., pres. mid./pass. ptc. acc.
pl. masc. {6.A.3} . . . . id.
ἀνακειμένων vbl., pres. mid./pass. ptc. gen. pl.
masc. {6.A.3} . . . . id.
ἀνάκειται verb, pres. mid./pass. indic. 3 pers.
sg. {5.A.3.a} . . . . id.
ἀνακεκαλυμμένῳ vbl., perf. pass. ptc. dat. sg.
neut. {6.A.1.b} . . . . ἀνακαλύπτω G343
ἀνακεκύλισται verb, perf. pass. indic. 3 pers.
{5.A.1.f} . . . . ἀνακυλίω G617†‡
ἀνακεφαλαιοῦται verb, pres. pass. indic. 3 pers.
sg. {5.A.2} . . . . ἀνακεφαλαιόω G346

G346 **ἀνακεφαλαιόω** (1) *I sum up, summarize, reca-
pitulate;* (2) in Eph 1:10 *gather up in one* (a literary word, from κεφάλαιον, *chapter, section*).
ἀνακεφαλαιώσασθαι vbl., aor. mid. inf.
{6.B.1} . . . . ἀνακεφαλαιόω G346
ἀνακλιθῆναι vbl., aor. pass. inf. {6.B.1} ἀνακλίνω G347

ἀνακλιθήσονται   verb, fut. pass. indic. 3 pers. pl. {5.A.1.d} . . . . id.

ἀνακλῖναι   vbl., aor. act. inf. {6.B.1} . . . . id.

ἀνακλινεῖ   verb, fut. act. indic. 3 pers. sg. {5.A.2} . . . . id.

G347   **ἀνακλίνω**   (1) *I make to recline* (esp. at a dinner table); (2) mid. and pass. *I recline at a table.*

G348   **ἀνακόπτω**   *I restrain, I hinder.*

G349   **ἀνακράζω**   *I shout* (aloud); colloquial.

ἀνακράξας   vbl., aor. act. ptc. nom. sg. masc. {6.A.1.a} . . . . ἀνακράζω G349

ἀνακριθῶ   verb, aor. pass. subjunc. 1 pers. sg. {5.B.1} . . . . .ἀνακρίνω G350

ἀνακρίναντες   vbl., aor. act. ptc. nom. pl. masc. {6.A.1.a} . . . . id.

ἀνακρίνας   vbl., aor. act. ptc. nom. sg. masc. {6.A.1.a} . . . . id.

ἀνακρίνει   verb, pres. act. indic. 3 pers. sg. {5.A.1.a} . . . . id.

ἀνακρίνεται   verb, pres. pass. indic. 3 pers. sg. {5.A.1.d} . . . . id.

ἀνακρινόμεθα   verb, pres. pass. indic. 1 pers. pl. {5.A.1.d} . . . . id.

ἀνακρίνοντες   vbl., pres. act. ptc. nom. pl. masc. {6.A.1} . . . . id.

ἀνακρίνουσιν   vbl., pres. act. ptc. dat. pl. masc. {6.A.1} . . . . id.

G350   **ἀνακρίνω**   *I examine, inquire into* (judicially; see ἀνάκρισις); of the preliminary examination, preceding the trial proper; hence with derived applications.

ἀνακρίνω   verb, pres. act. indic. 1 pers. sg. {5.A.1.a} . . . . ἀνακρίνω G350

ἀνακρίνων   vbl., pres. act. ptc. nom. sg. masc. {6.A.1} . . . . id.

ἀνακρίσεως   noun, gen. sg. fem. {2.C} . ἀνάκρισις G351

G351   **ἀνάκρισις**, -εως, ἡ   *judicial examination, preliminary inquiry.*

G617†‡   **ἀνακυλίω**   *I roll back.* Var. for ἀποκυλίω, Mark 16:4.

G352   **ἀνακύπτω**   (1) *I raise myself, become erect* (Luke 13:11); (2) *I look up* (Luke 21:28).

ἀνακύψαι   vbl., aor. act. inf. {6.B.1} . . . . ἀνακύπτω G352

ἀνακύψας   vbl., aor. act. ptc. nom. sg. masc. {6.A.1.a} . . . . id.

ἀνακύψατε   verb, aor. act. impv. 2 pers. pl. {5.D.1} . . . . id.

ἀναλάβετε   verb, ²aor. act. impv. 2 pers. pl. {5.D.1} .ἀναλαμβάνω G353

ἀναλαβόντες   vbl., ²aor. act. ptc. nom. pl. masc. {6.A.1.a} . . . . id.

ἀναλαβών   vbl., ²aor. act. ptc. nom. sg. masc. {6.A.1.a} . . . . id.

ἀναλαμβάνειν   vbl., pres. act. inf. {6.B.1} . . . . id.

G353   **ἀναλαμβάνω**   (1) *I take up, raise*; (2) *I pick up*, 2 Tim 4:11, or *take on board*, Acts 20:13, 14; (3) *I carry off, lead away*, Acts 23:31.

ἀναλημφθείς   vbl., aor. pass. ptc. nom. sg. masc. {6.A.1.a} .ἀναλαμβάνω G353

ἀναλήμψεως   noun, gen. sg. fem. {2.C} ἀνάλημψις G354

G354   **ἀνάλημψις**, -εως, ἡ   *a taking up, lifting up* (of the Ascension); lit. *Assumption.*

ἀναληφθείς   vbl., aor. pass. ptc. nom. sg. masc. {6.A.1.a} . . . . .ἀναλαμβάνω G353

ἀναλήψεως   noun, gen. sg. fem. {2.C} . ἀνάλημψις G354

G355   **ἀναλίσκω**   *I destroy, annihilate* (var. ἀναλόω, 2 Thess 2:8).

G356   **ἀναλογία**, -ας, ἡ   *proportion, measure.*

ἀναλογίαν   noun, acc. sg. fem. {2.A} . . . .ἀναλογία G356

G357   **ἀναλογίζομαι**   *I reckon up, count over* (from λόγος = *account*).

ἀναλογίσασθε   verb, aor. mid. impv. 2 pers. pl. {5.D.1} . . . . .ἀναλογίζομαι G357

ἄναλον   adj., nom. sg. neut. {3.C} . . . . . . .ἄναλος G358

G358   **ἄναλος**, -ον   *saltless, tasteless, flat.*

ἀναλῦσαι   vbl., aor. act. inf. {6.B.1} . . . . . ἀναλύω G360

ἀναλύσει   verb, fut. act. indic. 3 pers. sg. {5.A.1.a} . . . . id.

ἀναλύσεως   noun, gen. sg. fem. {2.C} . . .ἀνάλυσις G359

ἀναλύσῃ   verb, aor. act. subjunc. 3 pers. sg. {5.B.1} . . . . ἀναλύω G360

G359   **ἀνάλυσις**, -εως, ἡ   *departing, departure* (from this life, probably a metaphor from the yoking and unyoking of transport animals).

G360   **ἀναλύω**   (1) *I depart*, Phil 1:23; (2) perhaps, *I return*, Luke 12:36 (see ἀνάλυσις).

ἀναλωθῆτε   verb, aor. pass. subjunc. 2 pers. pl. {5.B.1} . . . . ἀναλίσκω G355

ἀναλῶσαι   vbl., aor. act. inf. {6.B.1} . . . . id.

ἀναλώσει   verb, fut. act. indic. 3 pers. sg. {5.A.1.a} . . . . id.

G361   **ἀναμάρτητος**, -ον   *sinless.*

ἀναμάρτητος   adj., nom. sg. masc. {3.C} . . . . ἀναμάρτητος G361

ἀναμένειν   vbl., pres. act. inf. {6.B.1} . . . . ἀναμένω G362

G362   **ἀναμένω**   *I await* (one whose coming is expected).

ἀναμιμνήσκεσθε   verb, pres. mid. impv. 2 pers. pl. {5.D.1} . . . . .ἀναμιμνήσκω G363

ἀναμιμνήσκεσθε   verb, pres. mid. impv. 2 pers. pl. {5.D.1} . . . . id.

ἀναμιμνησκομένου   vbl., pres. mid. ptc. gen. sg. masc. {6.A.1} . . . . id.

ἀναμιμνησκομένου   vbl., pres. mid. ptc. gen. sg. masc. {6.A.1} . . . . id.

ἀναμιμνήσκω   verb, pres. act. indic. 1 pers. sg. {5.A.1.a} . . . . id.

G363   **ἀναμιμνήσκω**   (1) act. *I remind*; (2) mid. or pass. *I am reminded, remind myself, remember, recall.*

ἀναμιμνήσκω   verb, pres. act. indic. 1 pers. sg. {5.A.1.a} .ἀναμιμνήσκω G363

ἀναμνήσει   verb, fut. act. indic. 3 pers. sg. {5.A.1.a} . . . . id.

ἀναμνησθείς   vbl., aor. pass. ptc. nom. sg. masc. {6.A.1.a} . . . . id.

ἀνάμνησιν   noun, acc. sg. fem. {2.C} . .ἀνάμνησις G364

G364   **ἀνάμνησις**, -εως, ἡ   *a recalling, remembrance, memory.*

ἀνάμνησις   noun, nom. sg. fem. {2.C} . .ἀνάμνησις G364

ἀνανεοῦσθαι vbl., pres. pass. inf. {6.B.2} ἀνανεόω G365

G365 ἀνανεόω pass. *I am renewed* (regularly a legal word).

G366 ἀνανήφω *I become sober again, I recover sound sense.*

ἀνανήψωσιν verb, aor. act. subjunc. 3 pers. pl. {5.B.1} . . . . ἀνανήφω G366

Ἀνανία noun prop., voc. sg. masc. {2.A; 2.D} . . . . Ἀνανίας G367

Ἀνανία noun prop., voc. sg. masc. {2.A; 2.D} . . id.

Ἀνανίαν noun prop., acc. sg. masc. {2.A; 2.D} . id.

Ἀνανίαν noun prop., acc. sg. masc. {2.A; 2.D} . id.

Ἀνανίας noun prop., nom. sg. masc. {2.A; 2.D} id.

G367 Ἀνανίας (Ἀνανίας), -ου, ὁ *Ananias*, (1) husband of Sapphira, a member of the early church at Jerusalem, Acts 5; (2) a member of the church at Damascus, Acts 9:10, etc.; (3) the high priest at Jerusalem, Acts 23:2; 24:1.

Ἀνανίας noun prop., nom. sg. masc. {2.A; 2.D} . . . . Ἀνανίας G367

ἀναντιρήτων adj., gen. pl. masc. {3.C} . . . . ἀναντίρρητος G368

ἀναντιρήτως adv. {3.F} . . . . ἀναντιρρήτως G369

G368 ἀναντίρρητος (ἀναντίρητος), -ον *that cannot be gainsaid, undeniable.*

ἀναντιρρήτων adj., gen. pl. neut. {3.C} . . . . ἀναντίρρητος G368

G369 ἀναντιρρήτως (ἀναντιρήτως) adv., *without saying anything against* (the request), *unquestioningly.*

ἀναντιρρήτως adv. {3.F} . . . . ἀναντιρρήτως G369

ἀνάξιοι adj., nom. pl. masc. {3.C} . . . . . . ἀνάξιος G370

G370 ἀνάξιος, -ον *unworthy.*

G371 ἀναξίως adv., *unworthily, in an unworthy manner.*

ἀναξίως adv. {3.F} . . . . ἀναξίως G371

ἀναπαήσονται verb, ²fut. pass. indic. 3 pers. pl. {5.A.1.d} . . . . ἀναπαύω G373

ἀναπαύεσθε verb, pres. mid. impv. 2 pers. pl. {5.D.1} . . . . id.

ἀναπαύεσθε verb, pres. mid. indic. 2 pers. pl. {5.A.1.d} . . . . id.

ἀναπαύεται verb, pres. mid. indic. 3 pers. sg. {5.A.1.d} . . . . id.

ἀναπαύου verb, pres. mid. impv. 2 pers. sg. {5.D.1} . . . . id.

ἀναπαύσασθε verb, aor. mid. impv. 2 pers. pl. {5.D.1} . . . . id.

ἀνάπαυσιν noun, acc. sg. fem. {2.C} ἀνάπαυσις G372

G372 ἀνάπαυσις, -εως, ἡ *a resting, rest,* esp. *a respite* or *temporary rest* as a preparation for future toil.

ἀνάπαυσον verb, aor. act. impv. 2 pers. sg. {5.D.1} . . . . ἀναπαύω G373

ἀναπαύσονται verb, fut. mid. indic. 3 pers. pl. {5.A.1.d} . . . . id.

ἀναπαύσω verb, fut. act. indic. 1 pers. sg. {5.A.1.a} . . . . id.

ἀναπαύσωνται verb, aor. mid. subjunc. 3 pers. pl. {5.B.1} . . . . id.

G373 ἀναπαύω (1) act. *I make to rest, I give rest to;* (2) mid. and pass. *I rest, take my ease* (see ἀνάπαυσις).

ἀναπείθει verb, pres. act. indic. 3 pers. sg. {5.A.1.a} . . . . ἀναπείθω G374

G374 ἀναπείθω *I urge by* (evil) *persuasion, I tempt.*

ἀναπείρους adj., acc. pl. masc. {3.C} . . ἀνάπειρος G376†‡

G376†‡ ἀνάπειρος *maimed, disabled.* Var. for ἀνάπηρος, Luke 14:13.

G375 ἀναπέμπω (1) *I send up* (to a higher tribunal), Luke 23:7; Acts 25:21, etc.; (2) *I send back,* Phlm 12, etc.

ἀναπέμψω verb, aor. act. subjunc. 1 pers. sg. {5.B.1} . . . . ἀναπέμπω G375

ἀναπέπαυται verb, perf. pass. indic. 3 pers. sg. {5.A.1.f} . . . . ἀναπαύω G373

ἀνάπεσαι verb, aor. mid. impv. 2 pers. sg. {5.D.1} . . . . ἀναπίπτω G377

ἀνάπεσε verb, ²aor. act. impv. 2 pers. sg. {5.D.1} id.

ἀναπεσεῖν vbl., ²aor. act. inf. {6.B.1} . . . . id.

ἀνάπεσον verb, aor. act. impv. 2 pers. sg. {5.D.1} . . . . id.

ἀναπεσών vbl., ²aor. act. ptc. nom. sg. masc. {6.A.1.a} . . . . id.

G450†‡ ἀναπηδάω *I leap up.* Var. for ἀνίστημι, Mark 10:50.

ἀναπηδήσας vbl., aor. act. ptc. nom. sg. masc. {6.A.2} . . . . ἀναπηδάω G450†‡

G376 ἀνάπηρος, -όν *maimed.*

ἀναπήρους adj., acc. pl. masc. {3.C} . . . ἀνάπηρος G376

G377 ἀναπίπτω (1) *I lie down, recline* (at a dinner table); (2) *I fall back upon* (the breast of another person reclining at dinner).

ἀναπληροῦται verb, pres. pass. indic. 3 pers. sg. {5.A.2} . . . . ἀναπληρόω G378

G378 ἀναπληρόω (1) *I fill up, make up, complete the measure of,* Phil 2:30; (2) *I fulfill, I carry out the commands* (provisions, etc.) *of,* Matt 13:14; Gal 6:2, etc.

ἀναπληρῶν vbl., pres. act. ptc. nom. sg. masc. {6.A.2} . . . . ἀναπληρόω G378

ἀναπληρῶσαι vbl., aor. act. inf. {6.B.2} . . . . . id.

ἀναπληρώσατε verb, aor. act. impv. 2 pers. pl. {5.D.1} . . . . id.

ἀναπληρώσετε verb, fut. act. indic. 2 pers. pl. {5.A.1} . . . . id.

ἀναπληρώσῃ verb, aor. act. subjunc. 3 pers. sg. {5.B.1} . . . . id.

G379 ἀναπολόγητος, -ον *without* (ground of) *defense, indefensible, inexcusable.*

ἀναπολόγητος adj., nom. sg. masc. {3.C} . . . . ἀναπολόγητος G379

ἀναπολογήτους adj., acc. pl. masc. {3.C} . . . . id.

ἀνάπτει verb, pres. act. indic. 3 pers. sg. {5.A.1.a} . . . . ἀνάπτω G381

ἀναπτύξας vbl., aor. act. ptc. nom. sg. masc. {6.A.1.a} . . . . ἀναπτύσσω G380

G380 ἀναπτύσσω *I unroll* (reading uncertain).

G381 ἀνάπτω *I kindle.*

G382 **ἀναρίθμητος**, -ον   *uncountable, innumerable,*
    that cannot be numbered.
ἀναρίθμητος   adj., nom. sg. fem.
    {3.C} . . . . ἀναρίθμητος G382
ἀνασείει   verb, pres. act. indic. 3 pers. sg.
    {5.A.1.a} . . . . ἀνασείω G383
G383 **ἀνασείω**   *I shake up, stir up, excite.*
ἀνασκευάζοντες   vbl., pres. act. ptc. nom. pl.
    masc. {6.A.1} . . . . ἀνασκευάζω G384
G384 **ἀνασκευάζω**   (1) *I pack up*; (2) hence, *I carry*
    away, or *dismantle*; (3) hence, *I upset, destroy,*
    overthrow, subvert (lit. and met.).
ἀνασπάσει   verb, fut. act. indic. 3 pers. sg.
    {5.A.1} . . . . ἀνασπάω G385
G385 **ἀνασπάω**   *I drag up, pull up.*
ἀνάστα   verb, ²aor. act. impv. 2 pers. sg.
    {5.D.3} . . . . ἀνίστημι G450
ἀναστάν   vbl., ²aor. act. ptc. nom. sg. neut.
    {6.A.3} . . . . id.
ἀναστάντες   vbl., ²aor. act. ptc. nom. pl. masc.
    {6.A.3} . . . . id.
ἀναστάς   vbl., ²aor. act. ptc. nom. sg. masc.
    {6.A.3} . . . . id.
ἀναστᾶσα   vbl., ²aor. act. ptc. nom. sg. fem.
    {6.A.3} . . . . id.
ἀναστάσει   noun, dat. sg. fem. {2.C} . . ἀνάστασις G386
ἀναστάσεως   noun, gen. sg. fem. {2.C} . . . . . . id.
ἀνάστασιν   noun, acc. sg. fem. {2.C} . . . . id.
G386 **ἀνάστασις**, -εως, ἡ   *a rising again,*
    resurrection.
ἀνάστασις   noun, nom. sg. fem. {2.C} . . ἀνάστασις G386
ἀναστατοῦντες   vbl., pres. act. ptc. nom. pl. masc.
    {6.A.2} . . . . ἀναστατόω G387
G387 **ἀναστατόω**   *I turn upside dawn, upset, unsettle*
    (perhaps a political metaphor).
ἀναστατώσαντες   vbl., aor. act. ptc. nom. pl.
    masc. {6.A.2} . . . . ἀναστατόω G387
ἀναστατώσας   vbl., aor. act. ptc. nom. sg.
    masc. {6.A.2} . . . . id.
ἀνασταυροῦντας   vbl., pres. act. ptc. acc. pl.
    masc. {6.A.2} . . . . ἀνασταυρόω G388
G388 **ἀνασταυρόω**   *I crucify again* (so the sense
    seems to require, but elsewhere simply =
    σταυρόω, *I crucify*).
G389 **ἀναστενάζω**   *I groan.*
ἀναστενάξας   vbl., aor. act. ptc. nom. sg. masc.
    {6.A.1.a} . . . . ἀναστενάζω G389
ἀναστῇ   verb, ²aor. act. subjunc. 3 pers. sg.
    {5.B.3} . . . . ἀνίστημι G450
ἀνάστηθι   verb, ²aor. act. impv. 2 pers. sg.
    {5.D.3} . . . . id.
ἀναστῆναι   vbl., ²aor. act. inf. {6.B.3} . . . . id.
ἀναστήσας   vbl., aor. act. ptc. nom. sg. masc.
    {6.A.3} . . . . id.
ἀναστήσει   verb, fut. act. indic. 3 pers. sg.
    {5.A.1} . . . . id.
ἀναστήσειν   vbl., fut. act. inf. {6.B.1} . . . . id.
ἀναστήσεται   verb, fut. mid. indic. 3 pers. sg.
    {5.A.1} . . . . id.

ἀναστήσονται   verb, fut. mid. indic. 3 pers. pl.
    {5.A.1} . . . . id.
ἀναστήσω   verb, aor. act. subjunc. 1 pers. sg.
    {5.B.1} . . . . id.
ἀναστήσω   verb, fut. act. indic. 1 pers. sg.
    {5.A.1} . . . . id.
ἀναστράφητε   verb, ²aor. pass. impv. 2 pers. pl.
    {5.D.1} . . . . ἀναστρέφω G390
ἀναστρέφεσθαι   vbl., pres. pass. inf. {6.B.1} . . . id.
ἀναστρεφομένους   vbl., pres. pass. ptc. acc. pl.
    masc. {6.A.1} . . . . id.
ἀναστρεφομένων   vbl., pres. pass. ptc. gen. pl.
    masc. {6.A.1} . . . . id.
G390 **ἀναστρέφω**   (1) *I overturn, turn upside down,*
    John 2:15 (var.); (2) *I return,* Acts 5:22; 15:16 (in
    a Hebraistic idiom, where the verb means little
    more than the adv. *again*); (3) mid. and pass. *I*
    conduct (behave) myself, live (w. reference to the
    manner of life, esp. in a moral and religious as-
    pect), Matt 17:22 (var.), etc., often with ἐν and a
    noun indicating condition or circumstances.
ἀναστρέψαντες   vbl., aor. act. ptc. nom. pl. masc.
    {6.A.1.a} . . . . ἀναστρέφω G390
ἀναστρέψω   verb, fut. act. indic. 1 pers. sg.
    {5.A.1.a} . . . . id.
ἀναστροφαῖς   noun, dat. pl. fem. {2.A} ἀναστροφή G391
G391 **ἀναστροφή**, -ῆς, ἡ   *dealing with* other men,
    going up and down among men, *life, manner of*
    life (not in papyri, common in inscriptions).
ἀναστροφῇ   noun, dat. sg. fem. {2.A}   ἀναστροφή G391
ἀναστροφήν   noun, acc. sg. fem. {2.A} . . . . . . id.
ἀναστροφῆς   noun, gen. sg. fem. {2.A} . . . . . . id.
ἀναστῶσι   verb, ²aor. act. subjunc. 3 pers. pl.
    {5.B.3} . . . . ἀνίστημι G450
ἀναστῶσιν   verb, ²aor. act. subjunc. 3 pers. pl.
    {5.B.3} . . . . id.
ἀνατάξασθαι   vbl., aor. mid. inf.
    {6.B.1} . . . . ἀνατάσσομαι G392
G392 **ἀνατάσσομαι**   *I arrange, draw up,* but
    perhaps, as Blass thought, *I set down from*
    memory, I restore from memory, Luke 1:1.
ἀνατεθραμμένος   vbl., perf. pass. ptc. nom. sg.
    masc. {6.A.1.b} . . . . ἀνατρέφω G397
ἀνατείλαντος   vbl., aor. act. ptc. gen. sg. masc.
    {6.A.1.a} . . . . ἀνατέλλω G393
ἀνατείλῃ   verb, aor. act. subjunc. 3 pers. sg.
    {5.B.1} . . . . id.
ἀνατέλλει   verb, pres. act. indic. 3 pers. sg.
    {5.A.1.a} . . . . id.
ἀνατέλλουσαν   vbl., pres. act. ptc. acc. sg.
    fem. {6.A.1} . . . . id.
G393 **ἀνατέλλω**   (1) *I make to rise,* Matt 5:45; (2)
    I rise, shine (generally of the sun, and hence
    met.).
ἀνατέταλκεν   verb, perf. act. indic. 3 pers. sg.
    {5.A.1.c} . . . . ἀνατέλλω G393
G394 **ἀνατίθημι**   mid. *I lay* (a case) *before, I impart,*
    I communicate, I relate (with a view to
    consulting).

G395 **ἀνατολή**, -ῆς, ἡ   (1) *rising* of the sun; (2)
    hence, the quarter whence the sun rises, *the*
    east (sg. and pl.).
ἀνατολή   noun, nom. sg. fem. {2.A} . . . . ἀνατολή G395
ἀνατολῇ   noun, dat. sg. fem. {2.A}. . . . . id.
ἀνατολῆς   noun, gen. sg. fem. {2.A} . . . . id.
ἀνατολῶν   noun, gen. pl. fem. {2.A} . . . . id.
ἀνατρέπουσι   verb, pres. act. indic. 3 pers. pl.
    {5.A.1.a} . . . . ἀνατρέπω G396
ἀνατρέπουσιν   verb, pres. act. indic. 3 pers. pl.
    {5.A.1.a} . . . . id.
G396 **ἀνατρέπω**   *I overturn* (lit. or met.; var. in John
    2:15).
G397 **ἀνατρέφω**   *I rear, bring up* (var. in Luke 4:16).
ἀναφαίνεσθαι   vbl., pres. pass. inf.
    {6.B.1} . . . . ἀναφαίνω G398
G398 **ἀναφαίνω**   (1) *I sight* (a place); (2) mid. *I appear*
    (as it were, out of the unseen); a nautical term.
ἀναφάναντες   vbl., aor. act. ptc. nom. pl. masc.
    {6.A.1.a} . . . . ἀναφαίνω G398
ἀναφανέντες   vbl., aor. pass. ptc. nom. pl.
    masc. {6.A.1.a}. id.
ἀναφέρει   verb, pres. act. indic. 3 pers. sg.
    {5.A.1.a} . . . . ἀναφέρω G399
ἀναφέρειν   vbl., pres. act. inf. {6.B.1} . . . . id.
G399 **ἀναφέρω**   (1) *I carry up, lead up;* (2) *I offer up*
    (on a high altar) as a sacrifice, *I offer up* to
    God on high.
ἀναφέρωμεν   verb, pres. act. subjunc. 1 pers. pl.
    {5.B.1} . . . . ἀναφέρω G399
G400 **ἀναφωνέω**   *I call out, shout.*
ἀναχθέντες   vbl., aor. pass. ptc. nom. pl. masc.
    {6.A.1.a} . . . . ἀνάγω G321
ἀναχθῆναι   vbl., aor. pass. inf. {6.B.1} . . . . id.
ἀνάχυσιν   noun, acc. sg. fem. {2.C} . . . . ἀνάχυσις G401
G401 **ἀνάχυσις**, -εως, ἡ   *outpouring, excess* (prob-
    ably literary).
ἀναχωρεῖτε   verb, pres. act. impv. 2 pers. pl.
    {5.D.2} . . . . ἀναχωρέω G402
G402 **ἀναχωρέω**   (1) *I return,* Matt 2:12; (2) *I retire,*
    depart (underlying idea perhaps of taking ref-
    uge from danger or of going into retirement).
ἀναχωρήσαντες   vbl., aor. act. ptc. nom. pl. masc.
    {6.A.2} . . . . ἀναχωρέω G402
ἀναχωρησάντων   vbl., aor. act. ptc. gen. pl.
    masc. {6.A.2} . . . . id.
ἀναχωρήσας   vbl., aor. act. ptc. nom. sg. masc.
    {6.A.2} . . . . id.
ἀνάψαντες   vbl., aor. act. ptc. nom. pl. masc.
    {6.A.1.a} . . . . ἀνάπτω G381
ἀναψύξεως   noun, gen. sg. fem. {2.C} . . ἀνάψυξις G403
G403 **ἀνάψυξις**, -εως, ἡ   *refreshing, refreshment.*
G404 **ἀναψύχω**   *I refresh, revive, comfort.*
ἄνδρα   noun, acc. sg. masc. {2.C} . . . . ἀνήρ G435
ἀνδραποδισταῖς   noun, dat. pl. masc.
    {2.A} . . . . ἀνδραποδιστής G405
G405 **ἀνδραποδιστής**, -οῦ, ὁ   *an enslaver,* one who
    forcibly enslaves, *a kidnapper.*
ἄνδρας   noun, acc. pl. masc. {2.C} . . . . ἀνήρ G435
ἀνδράσι   noun, dat. pl. masc. {2.C} . . . . id.

ἀνδράσιν   noun, dat. pl. masc. {2.C} . . . . id.
Ἀνδρέᾳ   noun prop., dat. sg. masc. {2.A;
    2.D} . . . . Ἀνδρέας G406
Ἀνδρέαν   noun prop., acc. sg. masc. {2.A; 2.D} . id.
G406 **Ἀνδρέας**, -ου, ὁ   *Andrew* (a Gk. name), brother
    of Simon Peter, and one of the disciples of
    Jesus, belonging to Bethsaida (John 1:44).
Ἀνδρέας   noun prop., nom. sg. masc. {2.A;
    2.D} . . . . Ἀνδρέας G406
Ἀνδρέου   noun prop., gen. sg. masc. {2.A; 2.D} . id.
ἄνδρες   noun, nom. pl. masc. {2.C} . . . . ἀνήρ G435
ἄνδρες   noun, voc. pl. masc. {2.C} . . . . id.
ἀνδρί   noun, dat. sg. masc. {2.C} . . . . id.
ἀνδρίζεσθε   verb, pres. mid./pass. impv. 2 pers. pl.
    {5.D.1} . . . . ἀνδρίζομαι G407
G407 **ἀνδρίζομαι**   *I act in manly fashion, I play the*
    man, I display manly qualities.
Ἀνδρόνικον   noun prop., acc. sg. masc. {2.B;
    2.D} . . . . Ἀνδρόνικος G408
G408 **Ἀνδρόνικος**, -ου, ὁ   *Andronicus,* a member of
    the Roman church, probably husband of Junia,
    and a kinsman or fellow tribesman of Paul.
ἀνδρός   noun, gen. sg. masc. {2.C} . . . . ἀνήρ G435
ἀνδροφόνοις   noun, dat. pl. masc.
    {2.B} . . . . ἀνδροφόνος G409
G409 **ἀνδροφόνος**, -ου, ὁ   *a murderer.*
ἀνδρῶν   noun, gen. pl. masc. {2.C} . . . . ἀνήρ G435
ἀνεβαίνομεν   verb, impf. act. indic. 1 pers. pl.
    {5.A.1.b} . . . . ἀναβαίνω G305
ἀνέβαινεν   verb, impf. act. indic. 3 pers. pl.
    {5.A.1.b} . . . . id.
ἀνεβάλετο   verb, ²aor. mid. indic. 3 pers. sg.
    {5.A.1.e} . . . . ἀναβάλλω G306
ἀνέβη   verb, ²aor. act. indic. 3 pers. sg.
    {5.A.1.b} . . . . ἀναβαίνω G305
ἀνέβημεν   verb, ²aor. act. indic. 1 pers. pl.
    {5.A.1.b} . . . . id.
ἀνέβην   verb, ²aor. act. indic. 1 pers. sg. {5.A.1.b}id.
ἀνέβησαν   verb, ²aor. act. indic. 3 pers. pl.
    {5.A.1.b} . . . . id.
ἀνέβλεψα   verb, aor. act. indic. 1 pers. sg.
    {5.A.1.b} . . . . ἀναβλέπω G308
ἀνέβλεψαν   verb, aor. act. indic. 3 pers. pl.
    {5.A.1.b} . . . . id.
ἀνέβλεψε   verb, aor. act. indic. 3 pers. sg.
    {5.A.1.b} . . . . id.
ἀνέβλεψεν   verb, aor. act. indic. 3 pers. sg.
    {5.A.1.b} . . . . id.
ἀνεβόησε   verb, aor. act. indic. 3 pers. sg.
    {5.A.1} . . . . ἀναβοάω G310
ἀνεβόησεν   verb, aor. act. indic. 3 pers. sg.
    {5.A.1} . . . . id.
ἀνεγίνωσκε   verb, impf. act. indic. 3 pers. sg.
    {5.A.1.b} . . . . ἀναγινώσκω G314
ἀνεγίνωσκεν   verb, impf. act. indic. 3 pers. sg.
    {5.A.1.b} . . . . id.
ἀνέγκλητοι   adj., nom. pl. masc. {3.C} . ἀνέγκλητος G410
ἀνέγκλητον   adj., acc. sg. masc. {3.C} . . . . id.
G410 **ἀνέγκλητος**, -ον   *irreproachable* (esp. in pri-
    vate life), *blameless.*

ἀνέγκλητος   adj., nom. sg. masc. {3.C}. ἀνέγκλητος *G410*
ἀνεγκλήτους   adj., acc. pl. masc. {3.C} . . . . id.
ἀνεγνωρίσθη   verb, aor. pass. indic. 3 pers. sg.
   {5.A.1.b} . . . . ἀναγνωρίζω *G319*
ἀνέγνωσαν   verb, ²aor. act. indic. 3 pers. pl.
   {5.A.1.b} . . . . ἀναγινώσκω *G314*
ἀνέγνωτε   verb, ²aor. act. indic. 2 pers. pl.
   {5.A.1.b} . . . . id.
ἀνέδειξεν   verb, aor. act. indic. 3 pers. sg.
   {5.A.3.b} . . . . ἀναδείκνυμι *G322*
ἀνέζησαν   verb, aor. act. indic. 3 pers. pl.
   {5.A.1} . . . . ἀναζάω *G326*
ἀνέζησε   verb, aor. act. indic. 3 pers. sg. {5.A.1}. id.
ἀνέζησεν   verb, aor. act. indic. 3 pers. sg. {5.A.1}id.
ἀνεζήτουν   verb, impf. act. indic. 3 pers. pl.
   {5.A.2} . . . . ἀναζητέω *G327*
ἀνεθάλετε   verb, ²aor. act. indic. 2 pers. pl.
   {5.A.1.b} . . . . ἀναθάλλω *G330*
ἀνεθεματίσαμεν   verb, aor. act. indic. 1 pers. pl.
   {5.A.1.b} . . . . ἀναθεματίζω *G332*
ἀνεθεμάτισαν   verb, aor. act. indic. 3 pers. pl.
   {5.A.1.b} . . . . id.
ἀνεθέμην   verb, ²aor. mid. indic. 1 pers. sg.
   {5.A.3.b} . . . . ἀνατίθημι *G394*
ἀνέθετο   verb, ²aor. mid. indic. 3 pers. sg.
   {5.A.3.b} . . . . id.
ἀνέθη   verb, aor. pass. indic. 3 pers. sg.
   {5.A.1} . . . . ἀνίημι *G447*
ἀνεθρέψατο   verb, aor. mid. indic. 3 pers. sg.
   {5.A.1.e} . . . . ἀνατρέφω *G397*
ἀνεῖλαν   verb, ²aor. act. indic. 3 pers. pl.
   {5.A.1.b} . . . . ἀναιρέω *G337*
ἀνείλατε   verb, aor. act. indic. 2 pers. pl. {5.A.1} id.
ἀνείλατο   verb, aor. mid. indic. 3 pers. sg.
   {5.A.1} . . . . id.
ἀνεῖλε   verb, ²aor. act. indic. 3 pers. sg. {5.A.1.b} id.
ἀνεῖλεν   verb, ²aor. act. indic. 3 pers. sg.
   {5.A.1.b} . . . . id.
ἀνεῖλες   verb, ²aor. act. indic. 2 pers. sg.
   {5.A.1.b} . . . . id.
ἀνείλετε   verb, ²aor. act. indic. 2 pers. pl.
   {5.A.1.b} . . . . id.
ἀνείλετο   verb, ²aor. mid. indic. 3 pers. sg.
   {5.A.1.e} . . . . id.
ἀνεῖλον   verb, ²aor. act. indic. 3 pers. pl.
   {5.A.1.b} . . . . id.
ἀνείχεσθε   verb, impf. mid./pass. indic. 2 pers. pl.
   {5.A.1.e} . . . . ἀνέχω *G430*
ἀνεκάθισε   verb, aor. act. indic. 3 pers. sg.
   {5.A.1.b} . . . . ἀνακαθίζω *G339*
ἀνεκάθισεν   verb, aor. act. indic. 3 pers. sg.
   {5.A.1.b} . . . . id.
G411 **ἀνεκδιήγητος**, -ον   *indescribable, that cannot*
   be thoroughly, related.
ἀνεκδιηγήτῳ   adj., dat. sg. fem. {3.C} ἀνεκδιήγητος *G411*
ἀνέκειτο   verb, impf. mid./pass. indic. 3 pers. sg.
   {5.A.3.a} . . . . ἀνάκειμαι *G345*
G412 **ἀνεκλάλητος**, -ον   *incapable of expression in*
   speech.
ἀνεκλαλήτῳ   adj., dat. sg. fem. {3.C} ἀνεκλάλητος *G412*

ἀνέκλειπτον   adj., acc. sg. masc. {3.C} ἀνέκλειπτος *G413*
G413 **ἀνέκλειπτος** (ἀνέγλειπτος), -ον   *unfailing.*
ἀνεκλίθη   verb, aor. pass. indic. 3 pers. sg.
   {5.A.1.b} . . . . ἀνακλίνω *G347*
ἀνέκλιναν   verb, aor. act. indic. 3 pers. pl.
   {5.A.1.b} . . . . id.
ἀνέκλινεν   verb, aor. act. indic. 3 pers. sg.
   {5.A.1.b} . . . . id.
ἀνέκοψε   verb, aor. act. indic. 3 pers. sg.
   {5.A.1.b} . . . . ἀνακόπτω *G348*
ἀνέκραγον   verb, ²aor. act. indic. 3 pers. pl.
   {5.A.1.b} . . . . ἀνακράζω *G349*
ἀνέκραξαν   verb, aor. act. indic. 3 pers. pl.
   {5.A.1.b} . . . . id.
ἀνέκραξε   verb, aor. act. indic. 3 pers. sg.
   {5.A.1.b} . . . . id.
ἀνέκραξεν   verb, aor. act. indic. 3 pers. sg.
   {5.A.1.b} . . . . id.
G414 **ἀνεκτός**, -όν   *endurable, tolerable.*
ἀνεκτότερον   adj. comp., nom. sg. neut. {3.A;
   3.G} . . . . ἀνεκτός *G414*
ἀνέκυψεν   verb, aor. act. indic. 3 pers. sg.
   {5.A.1.b} . . . . ἀνακύπτω *G352*
ἀνελάβετε   verb, ²aor. act. indic. 2 pers. pl.
   {5.A.1.b} . . . . ἀναλαμβάνω *G353*
ἀνελεήμονας   adj., acc. pl. masc. {3.E} ἀνελεήμων *G415*
G415 **ἀνελεήμων**, -ον   *unpitying, unmerciful.*
ἀνελεῖ   verb, fut. act. indic. 3 pers. sg.
   {5.A.1} . . . . ἀναιρέω *G337*
ἀνελεῖν   vbl., ²aor. act. inf. {6.B.1} . . . . id.
G448†‡ **ἀνέλεος**, -ον   *unmerciful.* Another form is
   ἀνίλεως.
ἀνέλεος   adj., nom. sg. fem. {3.C} . . . . ἀνέλεος *G448†‡*
ἀνελήμφθη   verb, aor. pass. indic. 3 pers. sg.
   {5.A.1.b} . . . . ἀναλαμβάνω *G353*
ἀνελήφθη   verb, aor. pass. indic. 3 pers. sg.
   {5.A.1.b} . . . . id.
ἀνέλωσι   verb, ²aor. act. subjunc. 3 pers. pl.
   {5.B.1} . . . . ἀναιρέω *G337*
ἀνέλωσιν   verb, ²aor. act. subjunc. 3 pers. pl.
   {5.B.1} . . . . id.
ἀνεμιζομένῳ   vbl., pres. pass. ptc. dat. sg. masc.
   {6.A.1} . . . . ἀνεμίζω *G416*
G416 **ἀνεμίζω**   pass. *I am blown with the wind*
   (referring to the gentler motions of the air).
ἀνεμνήσθη   verb, aor. pass. indic. 3 pers. sg.
   {5.A.1.b} . . . . ἀναμιμνήσκω *G363*
ἄνεμοι   noun, nom. pl. masc. {2.B} . . . . ἄνεμος *G417*
ἀνέμοις   noun, dat. pl. masc. {2.B} . . . . id.
ἄνεμον   noun, acc. sg. masc. {2.B} . . . . id.
G417 **ἄνεμος**, -ου, ὁ   (1) *wind* (lit., and in Eph 4:14
   met.); (2) in the sense *quarter of the heaven,*
   cardinal point, as both Greeks and Romans
   habitually defined the quarters of the heaven
   by the winds which came from those quarters,
   Matt 24:31 (Mark 13:27).
ἄνεμος   noun, nom. sg. masc. {2.B} . . . . . . ἄνεμος *G417*
ἀνέμου   noun, gen. sg. masc. {2.B} . . . . id.
ἀνέμους   noun, acc. pl. masc. {2.B} . . . . id.
ἀνέμῳ   noun, dat. sg. masc. {2.B} . . . . id.

ἀνέμων   noun, gen. pl. masc. {2.B}. . . . . id.
ἀνένδεκτον   adj., nom. sg. neut. {3.C} . ἀνένδεκτος G418
G418 **ἀνένδεκτος**, -ον   impossible.
ἀνενέγκαι   vbl., aor. act. inf. {6.B.1}. . . . . ἀναφέρω G399
ἀνενέγκας   vbl., aor. act. ptc. nom. sg. masc.
   {6.A.1.a} . . . . id.
ἀνενεγκεῖν   vbl., aor. act. inf. {6.B.1} . . . . id.
ἀνέντες   vbl., ²aor. act. ptc. nom. pl. masc.
   {6.A.3}. . . . . ἀνίημι G447
ἀνεξεραύνητα   adj., nom. pl. neut.
   {3.C}. . . . . .ἀνεξεραύνητος G419
G419 **ἀνεξεραύνητος**, -ον   that cannot be searched
   into, inscrutable.
ἀνεξερεύνητα   adj., nom. pl. neut.
   {3.C} . . . . .ἀνεξεραύνητος G419
ἀνεξίκακον   adj., acc. sg. masc. {3.C} . ἀνεξίκακος G420
G420 **ἀνεξίκακος**, -ον   enduring evil, patient of evil.
ἀνεξιχνίαστοι   adj., nom. pl. fem.
   {3.C} . . . . ἀνεξιχνίαστος G421
ἀνεξιχνίαστον   adj., acc. sg. masc. {3.C}. . . . . id.
ἀνεξιχνίαστον   adj., acc. sg. neut. {3.C}. . . . . id.
G421 **ἀνεξιχνίαστος**, -ον   that cannot be tracked
   out, unexplorable, unsearchable (perhaps from
   Job, LXX).
ἀνέξομαι   verb, fut. mid. indic. 1 pers. sg.
   {5.A.1.d} . . . . .ἀνέχω G430
ἀνέξονται   verb, fut. mid. indic. 3 pers. pl.
   {5.A.1.d} . . . . id.
ἀνεπαίσχυντον   adj., acc. sg. masc.
   {3.C} .ἀνεπαίσχυντος G422
G422 **ἀνεπαίσχυντος**, -ον   not ashamed (of his
   work).
ἀνέπαυσαν   verb, aor. act. indic. 3 pers. pl.
   {5.A.1.b} . . . . .ἀναπαύω G373
ἀνέπεμψα   verb, aor. act. indic. 1 pers. sg.
   {5.A.1.b} .ἀναπέμπω G375
ἀνέπεμψεν   verb, aor. act. indic. 3 pers. sg.
   {5.A.1.b} . . . . id.
ἀνέπεσαν   verb, ²aor. act. indic. 3 pers. pl.
   {5.A.1.b} .ἀναπίπτω G377
ἀνέπεσε   verb, ²aor. act. indic. 3 pers. sg.
   {5.A.1.b} . . . . id.
ἀνέπεσεν   verb, ²aor. act. indic. 3 pers. sg.
   {5.A.1.b} . . . . id.
ἀνέπεσον   verb, ²aor. act. indic. 3 pers. pl.
   {5.A.1.b} . . . . id.
ἀνεπίλημπτοι   adj., nom. pl. masc.
   {3.C} . . . . .ἀνεπίλημπτος G423
ἀνεπίλημπτον   adj., acc. sg. fem. {3.C} . . . . . . id.
ἀνεπίλημπτον   adj., acc. sg. masc. {3.C} . . . . . . id.
G423 **ἀνεπίλημπτος** (ἀνεπίληπτος), -ον   giving no
   cause for accusation.
ἀνεπίληπτοι   adj., nom. pl. masc.
   {3.C} . . . . .ἀνεπίλημπτος G423
ἀνεπίληπτον   adj., acc. sg. fem. {3.C}. . . . . id.
ἀνεπίληπτον   adj., acc. sg. masc. {3.C}. . . . . . . id.
ἀνεπλήρωσαν   verb, aor. act. indic. 3 pers. pl.
   {5.A.1}. . . . . .ἀναπληρόω G378
ἄνερ   noun, voc. sg. masc. {2.C}. . . . . .ἀνήρ G435
G424 **ἀνέρχομαι**   I go up (to the capital).

ἀνέσεισαν   verb, aor. act. indic. 3 pers. pl.
   {5.A.1.b} . . . . .ἀνασείω G383
ἄνεσιν   noun, acc. sg. fem. {2.C} . . . . ἄνεσις G425
G425 **ἄνεσις**, -εως, ἡ   (1) relief, remission, indulgence, freedom, Acts 24:23; (2) rest (opp.
   θλῖψις, lit., loosening, relaxing).
ἄνεσις   noun, nom. sg. fem. {2.C} . . . . ἄνεσις G425
ἀνεσπάσθη   verb, aor. pass. indic. 3 pers. sg.
   {5.A.1}. . . . . .ἀνασπάω G385
ἀνέστη   verb, ²aor. act. indic. 3 pers. sg.
   {5.A.3.b} . . . . ἀνίστημι G450
ἀνέστησαν   verb, aor. act. indic. 3 pers. pl.
   {5.A.3.b} . . . . id.
ἀνέστησε   verb, aor. act. indic. 3 pers. sg.
   {5.A.3.b} . . . . id.
ἀνέστησεν   verb, aor. act. indic. 3 pers. sg.
   {5.A.3.b} . . . . id.
ἀνεστράφημεν   verb, ²aor. pass. indic. 1 pers. pl.
   {5.A.1.e} .ἀναστρέφω G390
ἀνέστρεψε   verb, aor. act. indic. 3 pers. sg.
   {5.A.1.b} . . . . id.
ἀνέστρεψεν   verb, aor. act. indic. 3 pers. sg.
   {5.A.1.b} . . . . id.
ἀνεσχόμην   verb, ²aor. mid. indic. 1 pers. sg.
   {5.A.1.e} . . . . .ἀνέχω G430
ἀνετάζειν   vbl., pres. act. inf. {6.B.1} . . . .ἀνετάζω G426
ἀνετάζεσθαι   vbl., pres. pass. inf. {6.B.1}. . . . . id.
G426 **ἀνετάζω**   I examine (a person on trial, a
   witness) judicially (frequently by the aid of
   torture).
ἀνέτειλε   verb, aor. act. indic. 3 pers. sg.
   {5.A.1.b} . . . . .ἀνατέλλω G393
ἀνέτειλεν   verb, aor. act. indic. 3 pers. sg.
   {5.A.1.b} . . . . id.
ἀνετράφη   verb, ²aor. pass. indic. 3 pers. sg.
   {5.A.1.e} . . . . .ἀνατρέφω G397
ἀνέτρεψεν   verb, aor. act. indic. 3 pers. sg.
   {5.A.1.b} . . . . .ἀνατρέπω G396
G427 **ἄνευ**   prep. with gen., without, without the
   cooperation (or knowledge) of (Matt 10:29).
ἄνευ   prep. . . . . .ἄνευ G427
G428 **ἀνεύθετος**, -ον   unfitted, unsuitable.
ἀνευθέτου   adj., gen. sg. masc. {3.C} . . . ἀνεύθετος G428
ἀνεῦραν   verb, ²aor. act. indic. 3 pers. pl.
   {5.A.1.b} . . . . .ἀνευρίσκω G429
G429 **ἀνευρίσκω**   I find by seeking out.
ἀνεῦρον   verb, ²aor. act. indic. 3 pers. pl.
   {5.A.1.b} . . . . .ἀνευρίσκω G429
ἀνευρόντες   vbl., ²aor. act. ptc. nom. pl. masc.
   {6.A.1.a} . . . . id.
ἀνεφέρετο   verb, impf. pass. indic. 3 pers. sg.
   {5.A.1.e} . . . . .ἀναφέρω G399
ἀνεφώνησε   verb, aor. act. indic. 3 pers. sg.
   {5.A.1}. .ἀναφωνέω G400
ἀνεφώνησεν   verb, aor. act. indic. 3 pers. sg.
   {5.A.1}. . . . . id.
ἀνέχεσθε   verb, pres. mid./pass. impv. 2 pers. pl.
   {5.D.1}. . . . . .ἀνέχω G430
ἀνέχεσθε   verb, pres. mid./pass. indic. 2 pers.
   pl. {5.A.1.d} . . . . id.

ἀνεχόμεθα   verb, pres. mid./pass. indic. 1 pers.
pl. {5.A.1.d} . . . . id.
ἀνεχόμενοι   vbl., pres. mid./pass. ptc. nom. pl.
masc. {6.A.1} . . . . id.
G430 ἀνέχω   mid. *I endure,* Matt 6:24 (= Luke 16:13);
2 Thess 1:4 (var.).
ἀνεχώρησαν   verb, aor. act. indic. 3 pers. pl.
{5.A.1} . . . . ἀναχωρέω G402
ἀνεχώρησε   verb, aor. act. indic. 3 pers. sg.
{5.A.1} . . . . id.
ἀνεχώρησεν   verb, aor. act. indic. 3 pers. sg.
{5.A.1} . . . . id.
G431 ἀνεψιός, -οῦ, ὁ   *cousin* (male), whether on the
father's or on the mother's side.
ἀνεψιός   noun, nom. sg. masc. {2.B} . . . . . ἀνεψιός G431
ἀνέψυξε   verb, aor. act. indic. 3 pers. sg.
{5.A.1.b} . . . . ἀναψύχω G404
ἀνέψυξεν   verb, aor. act. indic. 3 pers. sg.
{5.A.1.b} . . . . id.
ἀνέῳγε   verb, ²perf. act. indic. 3 pers. sg.
{5.A.1.c} . . . . ἀνοίγω G455
ἀνέῳγεν   verb, ²perf. act. indic. 3 pers. sg.
{5.A.1.c} . . . . id.
ἀνεῳγμένας   vbl., perf. pass. ptc. acc. pl. fem.
{6.A.1.b} . . . . id.
ἀνεῳγμένη   vbl., perf. pass. ptc. nom. sg. fem.
{6.A.1.b} . . . . id.
ἀνεῳγμένην   vbl., perf. pass. ptc. acc. sg. fem.
{6.A.1.b} . . . . id.
ἀνεῳγμένης   vbl., perf. pass. ptc. gen. sg. fem.
{6.A.1.b} . . . . id.
ἀνεῳγμένον   vbl., perf. pass. ptc. acc. sg. masc.
{6.A.1.b} . . . . id.
ἀνεῳγμένον   vbl., perf. pass. ptc. acc. sg. neut.
{6.A.1.b} . . . . id.
ἀνεῳγμένος   vbl., perf. pass. ptc. nom. sg.
masc. {6.A.1.b} . . . . id.
ἀνεῳγμένους   vbl., perf. pass. ptc. acc. pl.
masc. {6.A.1.b} . . . . id.
ἀνεῳγμένων   vbl., perf. pass. ptc. gen. pl. masc.
{6.A.1.b} . . . . id.
ἀνεῳγότα   vbl., ²perf. act. ptc. acc. sg. masc.
{6.A.1} . . . . id.
ἀνέῳξε   verb, aor. act. indic. 3 pers. sg. {5.A.1.b} id.
ἀνέῳξεν   verb, aor. act. indic. 3 pers. sg.
{5.A.1.b} . . . . id.
ἀνεῴχθη   verb, aor. pass. indic. 3 pers. sg.
{5.A.1.b} . . . . id.
ἀνεῳχθῆναι   vbl., aor. pass. inf. {6.B.1} . . . . . . id.
ἀνεῴχθησαν   verb, aor. pass. indic. 3 pers. pl.
{5.A.1.b} . . . . id.
ἀνήγαγον   verb, ²aor. act. indic. 3 pers. pl.
{5.A.1.b} . . . . ἀνάγω G321
ἀνήγγειλαν   verb, aor. act. indic. 3 pers. pl.
{5.A.1.b} . . . . ἀναγγέλλω G312
ἀνήγγειλε   verb, aor. act. indic. 3 pers. sg.
{5.A.1.b} . . . . id.
ἀνήγγειλεν   verb, aor. act. indic. 3 pers. sg.
{5.A.1.b} . . . . id.

ἀνηγγέλη   verb, ²aor. pass. indic. 3 pers. sg.
{5.A.1.e} . . . . id.
ἀνήγγελλον   verb, impf. act. indic. 3 pers. pl.
{5.A.1.b} . . . . id.
G432 ἄνηθον, -ου, τό   *dill (anethum graveolens).*
ἄνηθον   noun, acc. sg. neut. {2.B} . . . . ἄνηθον G432
ἀνῆκεν   verb, impf. act. indic. 3 pers. sg.
{5.A.1.b} . . . . ἀνήκω G433
ἀνῆκον   vbl., pres. act. ptc. acc. sg. neut. {6.A.1} id.
ἀνήκοντα   vbl., pres. act. ptc. nom. pl. neut.
{6.A.1} . . . . id.
G433 ἀνήκω   *is due, becoming, suitable, proper;* in
third pers., esp. of impf. (cf. Eng. *ought* =
owed).
ἀνῆλθε   verb, ²aor. act. indic. 3 pers. sg.
{5.A.1.b} . . . . ἀνέρχομαι G424
ἀνῆλθεν   verb, ²aor. act. indic. 3 pers. sg.
{5.A.1.b} . . . . id.
ἀνῆλθον   verb, ²aor. act. indic. 1 pers. sg.
{5.A.1.b} . . . . id.
ἀνήμεροι   adj., nom. pl. masc. {3.C} . . . . ἀνήμερος G434
G434 ἀνήμερος, -ον   (1) *ungentle;* (2) *untamed.*
ἀνήνεγκεν   verb, aor. act. indic. 3 pers. sg.
{5.A.1.b} . . . . ἀναφέρω G399
G435 ἀνήρ, ἀνδρός, ὁ   (1) *a male human being, a
man* (contrast ἄνθρωπος); (2) often in ad-
dresses, at the beginning of speeches, *Gentle-
men;* (3) *a husband.*
ἀνήρ   noun, nom. sg. masc. {2.C} . . . . ἀνήρ G435
ἀνῃρέθη   verb, aor. pass. indic. 3 pers. sg.
{5.A.1} . . . . ἀναιρέω G337
ἀνήφθη   verb, aor. pass. indic. 3 pers. sg.
{5.A.1.b} . . . . ἀνάπτω G381
ἀνήχθη   verb, aor. pass. indic. 3 pers. sg.
{5.A.1.b} . . . . ἀνάγω G321
ἀνήχθημεν   verb, aor. pass. indic. 1 pers. pl.
{5.A.1.b} . . . . id.
ἀνήχθησαν   verb, aor. pass. indic. 3 pers. pl.
{5.A.1.b} . . . . id.
ἀνθ᾽   prep. . . . . ἀντί G473
ἀνθέξεται   verb, fut. mid. indic. 3 pers. sg.
{5.A.1.d} . . . . ἀντέχω G472
ἀνθέστηκε   verb, perf. act. indic. 3 pers. sg.
{5.A.1} . . . . ἀνθίστημι G436
ἀνθέστηκεν   verb, perf. act. indic. 3 pers. sg.
{5.A.1} . . . . id.
ἀνθεστηκότες   vbl., perf. act. ptc. nom. pl.
masc. {6.A.3} . . . . id.
ἀνθίστανται   verb, pres. mid. indic. 3 pers. pl.
{5.A.3.a} . . . . id.
ἀνθίστατο   verb, impf. mid. indic. 3 pers. sg.
{5.A.3.a} . . . . id.
G436 ἀνθίστημι   *I take a stand against, oppose, resist;*
only in intrans. tenses of act., and in all tenses
of the mid. or pass.
G437 ἀνθομολογέομαι   *I confess* (so e.g., the Latin
and Sahidic versions), (1) *I acknowledge,
formally admit;* (2) *I give thanks* (so e.g., the
Peshitta Syriac and the Bohairic versions, and
moderns generally; the senses *I agree, I answer*

to, I come to an understanding with, appear in
papyri).

G438 **ἄνθος**, -ους, τό   *bloom,* possibly a reference to
the bright flowers, such as poppies (among the
grass).

ἄνθος   noun, nom. sg. neut. {2.C} . . . . ἄνθος G438
ἄνθρακας   noun, acc. pl. masc. {2.C}. . . . . ἄνθραξ G440
G439 **ἀνθρακιά**, -ᾶς, ἡ   *a coal fire.*
ἀνθρακιάν   noun, acc. sg. fem. {2.A} . . . . ἀνθρακιά G439
G440 **ἄνθραξ**, -ακος, ὁ   *a coal.*
ἀνθρωπάρεσκοι   adj., nom. pl. masc.
   {3.C} . . . . ἀνθρωπάρεσκος G441
G441 **ἀνθρωπάρεσκος**, -ον   *a men-pleaser, one who
renders service to human beings* (as opposed to
God).
ἄνθρωπε   noun, voc. sg. masc. {2.B} . . . . ἄνθρωπος G444
ἀνθρωπίνη   adj., dat. sg. fem. {3.A} . . . ἀνθρώπινος G442
ἀνθρωπίνης   adj., gen. sg. fem. {3.A} . . . . id.
ἀνθρωπίνων   adj., acc. sg. neut. {3.A} . . . . id.
G442 **ἀνθρώπινος**, -η, -ον   (1) *belonging to human
beings* (esp. as contrasted with God), *human*
(as contrasted with divine); (2) perhaps *mod-
erate,* Rom 6:19; 1 Cor 10:13.
ἀνθρώπινος   adj., nom. sg. masc. {3.A} ἀνθρώπινος G442
ἀνθρωπίνων   adj., gen. pl. fem. {3.A} . . . . id.
ἄνθρωποι   noun, nom. pl. masc. {2.B} . . ἄνθρωπος G444
ἀνθρώποις   noun, dat. pl. masc. {2.B} . . . . id.
G443 **ἀνθρωποκτόνος**, -ου, ὁ   *a murderer* (borrowed from poetry).
ἀνθρωποκτόνος   noun, nom. sg. masc.
   {3.C} . . . . ἀνθρωποκτόνος G443
ἄνθρωπον   noun, acc. sg. masc. {2.B} . . ἄνθρωπος G444
G444 **ἄνθρωπος**, -ου, ὁ   *a human being;* υἱὸς
ἀνθρώπου, notable because of the sg. (rather
than the pl. ἀνθρώπων), a Hebraistic expression of a somewhat frequent type (see under
υἱός), indicating *a human being with all the
characteristics of a human being* (ὁ υἱὸς τοῦ
ἀνθρώπου, a Messianic title esp. favored by
our Lord for this very reason).
ἄνθρωπος   noun, nom. sg. masc. {2.B} . . ἄνθρωπος G444
ἀνθρώπου   noun, gen. sg. masc. {2.B} . . . . id.
ἀνθρώπους   noun, acc. pl. masc. {2.B} . . . . id.
ἀνθρώπῳ   noun, dat. sg. masc. {2.B} . . . . id.
ἀνθρώπων   noun, gen. pl. masc. {2.B} . . . . id.
ἀνθυπατεύοντος   vbl., pres. act. ptc. gen. sg. masc.
   {6.A.1} . . . . ἀνθυπατεύω G445
G445 **ἀνθυπατεύω**   *to be proconsul* (a governor of a
Roman senatorial province).
ἀνθύπατοι   noun, nom. pl. masc. {2.B} . ἀνθύπατος G446
ἀνθύπατον   noun, acc. sg. masc. {2.B} . . . . id.
G446 **ἀνθύπατος**, -ου, ὁ   *a proconsul,* a title applied
to the governor of a senatorial province under
the Empire, such as Cyprus (Acts 13:7, 8, 12),
Achaia (Acts 18:12), and Asia (Acts 19:38,
where the pl. is general and does not mean
that there were more than one at a time).
The word means orig. *one with the rank and
insignia of a consul* (i.e., the chief Roman
magistrate), but was later applied to those who

had not yet held the office of consul as well as
to those who had.

ἀνθύπατος   noun, nom. sg. masc. {2.B} . ἀνθύπατος G446
ἀνθυπάτου   noun, gen. sg. masc. {2.B} . . . . id.
ἀνθυπάτῳ   noun, dat. sg. masc. {2.B} . . . . id.
ἀνθωμολογεῖτο   verb, impf. mid./pass. indic.
   3 pers. sg. {5.A.2} . . . . ἀνθομολογέομαι G437
ἀνιέντες   vbl., pres. act. ptc. nom. pl. masc.
   {6.A.3} . . . . ἀνίημι G447
G447 **ἀνίημι**   *I let go, loosen, release, give up.*
ἀνίλεως   adj., nom. sg. fem. {3.C} . . . . . . ἀνέλεος G448†‡
ἀνίπτοις   adj., dat. pl. fem. {3.C} . . . . ἄνιπτος G449
G449 **ἄνιπτος**, -ον   *unwashed.*
ἀνιστάμενος   vbl., pres. mid. ptc. nom. sg. masc.
   {6.A.3} . . . . ἀνίστημι G450
ἀνίστασθαι   vbl., pres. mid. inf. {6.B.3} . . . . . . id.
ἀνίσταται   verb, pres. mid. indic. 3 pers. sg.
   {5.A.3.a} . . . . id.
G450 **ἀνίστημι**   (1) *I raise up, set up;* only the fut.
ἀναστήσω and the 1aor. ἀνέστησα are used
in this trans. sense in the NT; (2) much more
frequent are the mid. voice and the ²aor. of
the act. in the intrans. sense, *I rise,* esp. ἐκ
νεκρῶν, *from among (the) dead bodies, dead
persons, the dead.*
Ἄννα   noun prop., nom. sg. fem. {2.A; 2.D} . . Ἄννα G451
Ἄννα   noun prop., gen. sg. masc. {2.A; 2.D} . . Ἄννας G452
G451 **Ἄννα**, -ας, ἡ   *Anna,* a prophetess, who visited
the infant Jesus. (The aspirated form Ἅννα, fa-
vored by WH, is contradicted by the evidence
of the versions.).
Ἄννα   noun prop., nom. sg. fem. {2.A; 2.D} . . Ἄννα G451
Ἄννα   noun prop., gen. sg. masc. {2.A; 2.D} . . Ἄννας G452
Ἄνναν   noun prop., acc. sg. masc. {2.A; 2.D} . . . id.
Ἄνναν   noun prop., acc. sg. masc. {2.A; 2.D} . . . id.
Ἄννας   noun prop., nom. sg. masc. {2.A; 2.D} . . . id.
G452 **Ἄννας** (Ἅννας), -α, ὁ   *Annas,* high priest at
Jerusalem.
Ἄννας   noun prop., nom. sg. masc. {2.A; 2.D} Ἄννας G452
ἀνόητοι   adj., nom. pl. masc. {3.C} . . . . . . ἀνόητος G453
ἀνόητοι   adj., voc. pl. masc. {3.C} . . . . id.
ἀνοήτοις   adj., dat. pl. masc. {3.C} . . . . id.
G453 **ἀνόητος**, -ον   *senseless* (in Gal 3:1 pathos
is behind the use of the word, according to
Ramsay, *Historical Commentary,* pp. 308 ff.,
and it describes a state of culture unworthy of
the Romanized Galatians).
ἀνοήτους   adj., acc. pl. fem. {3.C} . . . . . . ἀνόητος G453
G454 **ἄνοια**, -ας, ἡ   *senselessness.*
ἄνοια   noun, nom. sg. fem. {2.A} . . . . ἄνοια G454
ἀνοίας   noun, gen. sg. fem. {2.A} . . . . id.
ἀνοίγει   verb, pres. act. indic. 3 pers. sg.
   {5.A.1.a} . . . . ἀνοίγω G455
ἀνοίγειν   vbl., pres. act. inf. {6.B.1} . . . . id.
ἀνοιγήσεται   verb, ²fut. pass. indic. 3 pers. sg.
   {5.A.1.d} . . . . id.
G455 **ἀνοίγω**   *I open.*
ἀνοίγων   vbl., pres. act. ptc. nom. sg. masc.
   {6.A.1} . . . . ἀνοίγω G455

ἀνοιγῶσιν   verb, ²aor. pass. subjunc. 3 pers. pl.
{5.B.1} . . . . id.
G456 **ἀνοικοδομέω**   (1) *I rebuild, build up* (what
has fallen or been razed to the ground); (2)
sometimes merely *I build.*
ἀνοικοδομήσω   verb, fut. act. indic. 1 pers. sg.
{5.A.1} . . . . ἀνοικοδομέω G456
ἀνοῖξαι   vbl., aor. act. inf. {6.B.1} . . . . ἀνοίγω G455
ἀνοίξαντες   vbl., aor. act. ptc. nom. pl. masc.
{6.A.1.a} . . . . id.
ἀνοίξας   vbl., aor. act. ptc. nom. sg. masc. {6.A.1.a} id.
ἀνοίξει   noun, dat. sg. fem. {2.C} . . . . ἄνοιξις G457
ἀνοίξει   verb, fut. act. indic. 3 pers. sg.
{5.A.1.a} . . . . ἀνοίγω G455
ἀνοίξῃ   verb, aor. act. subjunc. 3 pers. sg. {5.B.1} id.
G457 **ἄνοιξις**, -εως, ἡ   *opening* (abstr.).
ἄνοιξον   verb, aor. act. impv. 2 pers. sg.
{5.D.1} . . . . ἀνοίγω G455
ἀνοίξω   verb, fut. act. indic. 1 pers. sg. {5.A.1.a}. id.
ἀνοίξωσιν   verb, aor. act. subjunc. 3 pers. pl.
{5.B.1} . . . . id.
ἀνοιχθήσεσται   verb, fut. pass. indic. 3 pers.
sg. {5.A.1.d} . . . . id.
ἀνοιχθῶσιν   verb, aor. pass. subjunc. 3 pers. pl.
{5.B.1} . . . . id.
G458 **ἀνομία**, -ας, ἡ   (1) *lawlessness;* (2) esp. *disobedience to the* divine *law, sin.*
ἀνομία   noun, nom. sg. fem. {2.A} . . . . . ἀνομία G458
ἀνομίᾳ   noun, dat. sg. fem. {2.A} . . . . id.
ἀνομίαι   noun, nom. pl. fem. {2.A} . . . . id.
ἀνομίαν   noun, acc. sg. fem. {2.A} . . . . id.
ἀνομίας   noun, gen. sg. fem. {2.A} . . . . id.
ἀνομιῶν   noun, gen. pl. fem. {2.A} . . . . id.
ἀνόμοις   adj., dat. pl. masc. {3.C} . . . . ἄνομος G459
ἀνόμοις   adj., dat. pl. neut. {3.C} . . . . id.
G459 **ἄνομος**, -ον   (1) *lawless, disobedient to the law*
of God, *sinful;* (2) *illegal;* ἄνομος θεοῦ =
ἄνευ νόμου θεοῦ (1 Cor 9:21).
ἄνομος   adj., nom. sg. masc. {3.C} . . . . . . ἄνομος G459
ἀνόμους   adj., acc. pl. masc. {3.C} . . . . id.
ἀνόμων   adj., gen. pl. masc. {3.C} . . . . id.
G460 **ἀνόμως**   adv., *without law.*
ἀνόμως   adv. {3.F} . . . . ἀνόμως G460
G461 **ἀνορθόω**   *I make upright (straight) again, I rear
again, restore.*
ἀνορθώσατε   verb, aor. act. impv. 2 pers. pl.
{5.D.1} . . . . ἀνορθόω G461
ἀνορθώσω   verb, fut. act. indic. 1 pers. sg. {5.A.1}. id.
ἀνόσιοι   adj., nom. pl. masc. {3.C} . . . . . . ἀνόσιος G462
ἀνοσίοις   adj., dat. pl. masc. {3.C} . . . . id.
G462 **ἀνόσιος**, -ον   *regarding nothing as holy.*
G463 **ἀνοχή**, -ῆς, ἡ   (1) *forbearance;* (2) *suspense* or
delay (of punishment).
ἀνοχῇ   noun, dat. sg. fem. {2.A} . . . . ἀνοχή G463
ἀνοχῆς   noun, gen. sg. fem. {2.A} . . . . id.
G464 **ἀνταγωνίζομαι**   *I struggle against.*
ἀνταγωνιζόμενοι   vbl., pres. mid./pass. ptc. nom.
pl. masc. {6.A.1} . . . . ἀνταγωνίζομαι G464
G465 **ἀντάλλαγμα**, -ατος, τό   *an exchange, purchasing price.*

ἀντάλλαγμα   noun, acc. sg. neut.
{2.C} . . . . ἀντάλλαγμα G465
G466 **ἀνταναπληρόω**   *I fill up in place of someone else.*
ἀνταναπληρῶ   verb, pres. act. indic. 1 pers. sg.
{5.A.2} . . . . ἀνταναπληρόω G466
G467 **ἀνταποδίδωμι**   *I give in return.*
ἀνταποδοθήσεται   verb, fut. pass. indic. 3 pers.
sg. {5.A.1} . . . . ἀνταποδίδωμι G467
G468 **ἀνταπόδομα**, -ατος, τό   *a gift in return* (for
another), *a return, a recompense.*
ἀνταπόδομα   noun, acc. sg. neut.
{2.C} . . . . ἀνταπόδομα G468
ἀνταπόδομα   noun, nom. sg. neut. {2.C} . . . . . id.
ἀνταπόδοσιν   noun, acc. sg. fem.
{2.C} . . . . ἀνταπόδοσις G469
G469 **ἀνταπόδοσις**, -εως, ἡ   orig. abstr., *giving in return,* but in Col 3:24 practically =
ἀνταπόδομα.
ἀνταποδοῦναι   vbl., ²aor. act. inf.
{6.B.3} . . . . ἀνταποδίδωμι G467
ἀνταποδώσω   verb, fut. act. indic. 1 pers. sg.
{5.A.1} . . . . id.
ἀνταποκριθῆναι   vbl., aor. pass. inf.
{6.B.1} . . . . ἀνταποκρίνομαι G470
G470 **ἀνταποκρίνομαι**   *I give a hostile answer.*
ἀνταποκρινόμενος   vbl., pres. mid./pass. ptc.
nom. sg. masc. {6.A.1} . . . . ἀνταποκρίνομαι G470
ἀντειπεῖν   vbl., ²aor. act. inf. {6.B.1} . . . . . ἀντιλέγω G483
G471 **ἀντεῖπον**   ²aor. of ἀντιλέγω.
ἀντελάβετο   verb, ²aor. mid. indic. 3 pers. sg.
{5.A.1.e} . . . . ἀντιλαμβάνω G482
ἀντέλεγον   verb, impf. act. indic. 3 pers. pl.
{5.A.1.b} . . . . ἀντιλέγω G483
ἀντελοιδόρει   verb, impf. act. indic. 3 pers. sg.
{5.A.2} . . . . ἀντιλοιδορέω G486
ἀντέστη   verb, ²aor. act. indic. 3 pers. sg.
{5.A.3.b} . . . . ἀνθίστημι G436
ἀντέστην   verb, ²aor. act. indic. 1 pers. sg.
{5.A.3.b} . . . . id.
ἀντέστησαν   verb, aor. act. indic. 3 pers. pl.
{5.A.3.b} . . . . id.
ἀντέχεσθε   verb, pres. mid./pass. impv. 2 pers. pl.
{5.D.1} . . . . ἀντέχω G472
ἀντεχόμενον   vbl., pres. mid./pass. ptc. acc. sg.
masc. {6.A.1} . . . . id.
G472 **ἀντέχω**   mid., *I hold fast (firmly) to.*
G473 **ἀντί**   prep. with gen. (1) *instead of, in return
for, in exchange for, as a substitute for;* λύτρον
ἀντὶ πολλῶν Mark 10:45 (= Matt 20:28), *a
ransom to buy the many, for the many;* cf. Heb
12:16 and ἀντίλυτρον; (2) ἀντὶ ἐμοῦ, *on my
behalf,* Matt 17:27; (3) ἀνθ' ὧν (lit., *in return
for which things*) has become a conj., *wherefore, because;* (orig. local, *in front of, opposite*).
ἀντί   prep.. . . . . ἀντί G473
ἀντιβάλλετε   verb, pres. act. indic. 2 pers. pl.
{5.A.1.a} . . . . ἀντιβάλλω G474
G474 **ἀντιβάλλω**   (1) *I throw at in opposition* (or
quasi-opposition), *I exchange* (words) *with;*
(2) perhaps, *I compare.*

ἀντιδιατιθεμένους vbl., pres. mid. ptc. acc. pl.
masc. {6.A.3} . . . . ἀντιδιατίθημι *G475*

G475 **ἀντιδιατίθημι** mid. *I am adversely affected*
against, I oppose.

G476 **ἀντίδικος**, -ου, ὁ *an opponent* (in a lawsuit);
probably so even in 1 Pet 5:8.
ἀντίδικος noun, nom. sg. masc. {2.B} . . . ἀντίδικος *G476*
ἀντιδίκου noun, gen. sg. masc. {2.B} . . . . id.
ἀντιδίκῳ noun, dat. sg. masc. {2.B} . . . . id.
ἀντιθέσεις noun, acc. pl. fem. {2.C} . . . ἀντίθεσις *G477*

G477 **ἀντίθεσις**, -εως, ἡ *a proposition, tenet, opinion*
advanced by one party *against* another.

G478 **ἀντικαθίστημι** *I stoutly resist.*
ἀντικαλέσωσι verb, aor. act. subjunc. 3 pers. pl.
{5.B.1} . . . . ἀντικαλέω *G479*
ἀντικαλέσωσιν verb, aor. act. subjunc. 3 pers.
pl. {5.B.1} . . . . id.

G479 **ἀντικαλέω** *I invite in return.*
ἀντικατέστητε verb, ²aor. act. indic. 2 pers. pl.
{5.A.3.b} . . . . ἀντικαθίστημι *G478*

G480 **ἀντίκειμαι** *I resist, oppose* (used as a pass.
for ἀντιτίθημι, just as κεῖμαι is a pass. for
τίθημι).
ἀντικείμενοι vbl., pres. mid./pass. ptc. nom. pl.
masc. {6.A.3} . . . . ἀντίκειμαι *G480*
ἀντικείμενος vbl., pres. mid./pass. ptc. nom.
sg. masc. {6.A.3} . . . . id.
ἀντικειμένῳ vbl., pres. mid./pass. ptc. dat. sg.
masc. {6.A.3} . . . . id.
ἀντικειμένων vbl., pres. mid./pass. ptc. gen.
pl. masc. {6.A.3} . . . . id.
ἀντίκειται verb, pres. mid./pass. indic. 3 pers.
sg. {5.A.3.a} . . . . id.
ἀντικρύ adv. and prep. . . . . ἄντικρυς *G481*

G481 **ἄντικρυς** adv. and prep. with gen., *right opposite, off* (nautical sense).
ἄντικρυς adv. and prep. . . . . ἄντικρυς *G481*
ἀντιλαμβάνεσθαι vbl., pres. mid./pass. inf.
{6.B.1} . . . . ἀντιλαμβάνω *G482*
ἀντιλαμβανόμενοι vbl., pres. mid./pass. ptc.
nom. pl. masc. {6.A.1} . . . . id.

G482 **ἀντιλαμβάνω** mid. (1) *I lay hold of* (in order to
help), *I aid* (succor); (2) *I take in hand* (lit. and
met.), *I undertake*; (3) *I partake of, enjoy*, 1 Tim 6:2.
ἀντιλέγει verb, pres. act. indic. 3 pers. sg.
{5.A.1.a} . . . . ἀντιλέγω *G483*
ἀντιλέγεται verb, pres. pass. indic. 3 pers. sg.
{5.A.1.d} . . . . id.
ἀντιλεγόμενον vbl., pres. pass. ptc. acc. sg.
neut. {6.A.1} . . . . id.
ἀντιλέγοντα vbl., pres. act. ptc. acc. sg. masc.
{6.A.1} . . . . id.
ἀντιλέγοντας vbl., pres. act. ptc. acc. pl. masc.
{6.A.1} . . . . id.
ἀντιλέγοντες vbl., pres. act. ptc. nom. pl.
masc. {6.A.1} . . . . id.
ἀντιλεγόντων vbl., pres. act. ptc. gen. pl.
masc. {6.A.1} . . . . id.

G483 **ἀντιλέγω** *I speak* or *say in opposition, I contra-
dict* (oppose, resist); σημεῖον ἀντιλεγόμενον,

a disputed sign, a sign that is debated about.
Aor. ἀντεῖπον.
ἀντιλήμψεις noun, acc. pl. fem. {2.C}. ἀντίλημψις *G484*

G484 **ἀντίλημψις**, -εως, ἡ *a lending a hand to, a
helping* (cf. ἀντιλαμβάνομαι, both being
often used in petitions).
ἀντιλήψεις noun, acc. pl. fem. {2.C} . . ἀντίλημψις *G484*

G485 **ἀντιλογία**, -ας, ἡ *contradiction, dispute.*
ἀντιλογίᾳ noun, dat. sg. fem. {2.A} . . . . .ἀντιλογία *G485*
ἀντιλογίαν noun, acc. sg. fem. {2.A} . . . . id.
ἀντιλογίας noun, gen. sg. fem. {2.A} . . . . id.

G486 **ἀντιλοιδορέω** *I abuse in return, I give abuse
for abuse.*

G487 **ἀντίλυτρον**, -ου, τό *a stronger form of
λύτρον, a ransom.*
ἀντίλυτρον noun, acc. sg. neut. {2.B} . ἀντίλυτρον *G487*

G488 **ἀντιμετρέω** *I measure in return, I give equivalent measure*, Luke 6:38 (var.).
ἀντιμετρηθήσεται verb, fut. pass. indic. 3 pers.
sg. {5.A.1} . . . . ἀντιμετρέω *G488*

G489 **ἀντιμισθία**, -ας, ἡ *a reward, recompense* (a
more emphatic expression than the simple
μισθός).
ἀντιμισθίαν noun, acc. sg. fem. {2.A}. ἀντιμισθία *G489*
Ἀντιοχέα noun prop., acc. sg. masc. {2.C;
2.D} . . . . Ἀντιοχεύς *G491*

G490 **Ἀντιόχεια**, -ας, ἡ *Antioch* (derived from
Antiochus, a king of the Seleucid dynasty),
(1) *Antioch* on the river Orontes, capital of
the Province Syria; (2) "Pisidian" *Antioch*,
not in Pisidia, but near Pisidia, in the Roman
Province Galatia, where was a Roman colony
founded by Augustus, Acts 13:14; 14:19, 21;
2 Tim 3:11.
Ἀντιοχεία noun prop., dat. sg. fem. {2.A;
2.D} . . . . Ἀντιόχεια *G490*
Ἀντιόχειαν noun prop., acc. sg. fem. {2.A; 2.D} id.
Ἀντιοχείας noun prop., gen. sg. fem. {2.A; 2.D} id.

G491 **Ἀντιοχεύς**, -έως, ὁ *an Antiochian, an inhabitant of* (Syrian) *Antioch.*

G492 **ἀντιπαρέρχομαι** *I pass opposite, on the opposite side of the road.*
ἀντιπαρῆλθε verb, ²aor. act. indic. 3 pers. sg.
{5.A.1.b} . . . . ἀντιπαρέρχομαι *G492*
ἀντιπαρῆλθεν verb, ²aor. act. indic. 3 pers. sg.
{5.A.1.b} . . . . id.

G493 **Ἀντιπᾶς**, -α, ὁ *Antipas*, a Christian martyr of
Pergamum (a pet form of Ἀντίπατρος).
Ἀντιπᾶς noun prop., nom. sg. masc. {2.A;
2.D} . . . . Ἀντιπᾶς *G493*
Ἀντίπας noun prop., nom. sg. masc. {2.A; 2.D}. id.
Ἀντιπατρίδα noun prop., acc. sg. fem. {2.C;
2.D} . . . . Ἀντιπατρίς *G494*

G494 **Ἀντιπατρίς**, -ίδος, ἡ *Antipatris*, a town, where
was a Roman colony, on the road between
Caesarea and Jerusalem.

G495 **ἀντιπέρα** adv. and prep. with gen., *opposite.*
ἀντιπέρα adv. and prep. . . . . ἀντιπέρα *G495*
ἀντίπερα adv. and prep. . . . . id.
ἀντιπέραν adv. . . . . id.

ἀντιπίπτετε   verb, pres. act. indic. 2 pers. pl.
  {5.A.1.a} . . . . ἀντιπίπτω G496
G496 **ἀντιπίπτω**   (1) *I fall foul of;* (2) *I resist, oppose.*
ἀντιστῆναι   vbl., ²aor. act. inf. {6.B.3} . . ἀνθίστημι G436
ἀντίστητε   verb, ²aor. act. impv. 2 pers. pl.
  {5.D.3} . . . . id.
G497 **ἀντιστρατεύομαι**   *I campaign against, war against.*
ἀντιστρατευόμενον   vbl., pres. mid./pass. ptc.
  acc. sg. masc. {6.A.1} . . . . ἀντιστρατεύομαι G497
ἀντιτάσσεται   verb, pres. mid. indic. 3 pers. sg.
  {5.A.1.d} . . . . ἀντιτάσσω G498
ἀντιτασσόμενος   vbl., pres. mid. ptc. nom. sg.
  masc. {6.A.1} . . . . id.
ἀντιτασσομένων   vbl., pres. mid. ptc. gen. pl.
  masc. {6.A.1} . . . . id.
G498 **ἀντιτάσσω**   mid. *I range myself against, resist* (the attack of).
ἀντίτυπα   adj., acc. pl. neut. {3.C} . . . . ἀντίτυπος G499
ἀντίτυπον   adj., nom. sg. neut. {3.C} . . . . id.
G499 **ἀντίτυπος**, -ον   (1) *typical of, representing by type* (or *pattern*), *corresponding to;* (2) neut., as noun, *an image* (from τύπος, *impress, impression left by a die*).
ἀντίχριστοι   noun, nom. pl. masc.
  {2.B} . . . . ἀντίχριστος G500
G500 **ἀντίχριστος**, -ου, ὁ   *antichrist,* either *one who puts himself in the place of* or *the enemy (opponent) of the Messiah,* a figure first appearing in the NT, identified with various historical persons; the pl., of many such, in 1 John 2:18.
ἀντίχριστος   noun, nom. sg. masc.
  {2.B} . . . . ἀντίχριστος G500
ἀντιχρίστου   noun, gen. sg. masc. {2.B} . . . . . . id.
ἀντλεῖν   vbl., pres. act. inf. {6.B.2} . . . . ἀντλέω G501
G501 **ἀντλέω**   (1) *I draw* (generally water from a deep well in the ground); (2) perhaps, *I draw out,* John 2:9.
G502 **ἄντλημα**, -ατος, τό   *a pail* attached to a rope, by which it is let down into a well.
ἄντλημα   noun, acc. sg. neut. {2.C} . . . . ἄντλημα G502
ἀντλῆσαι   vbl., aor. act. inf. {6.B.1} . . . . . . ἀντλέω G501
ἀντλήσατε   verb, aor. act. impv. 2 pers. pl.
  {5.D.1} . . . . id.
ἀντοφθαλμεῖν   vbl., pres. act. inf.
  {6.B.2} . . . . ἀντοφθαλμέω G503
G503 **ἀντοφθαλμέω**   (1) *I face* (lit. "I present my eye to"); (2) *I resist.*
ἄνυδροι   adj., nom. pl. fem. {3.C} . . . . ἄνυδρος G504
G504 **ἄνυδρος**, -ον   *waterless.*
ἀνύδρων   adj., gen. pl. masc. {3.C} . . . . . . ἄνυδρος G504
ἀνυπόκριτον   adj., acc. sg. fem. {3.C} ἀνυπόκριτος G505
G505 **ἀνυπόκριτος**, -ον   *unfeigned, genuine* (literary).
ἀνυπόκριτος   adj., nom. sg. fem.
  {3.C} . . . . ἀνυπόκριτος G505
ἀνυποκρίτου   adj., gen. sg. fem. {3.C} . . . . id.
ἀνυποκρίτῳ   adj., dat. sg. fem. {3.C} . . . . id.
ἀνυπότακτα   adj., acc. pl. neut. {3.C}.ἀνυπότακτος G506
ἀνυπότακτοι   adj., nom. pl. masc. {3.C} . . . . . . id.

ἀνυποτάκτοις   adj., dat. pl. masc. {3.C} . . . . . . id.
ἀνυπότακτον   adj., acc. sg. neut. {3.C} . . . . id.
G506 **ἀνυπότακτος**, -ον   *disorderly, unruly.*
ἄνω   adv. . . . . ἄνω G507
G507 **ἄνω**   adv., *up, above;* ἕως ἄνω, *up to the top, up to the brim,* John 2:7; τὰ ἄνω, *things above, heaven, the heavenly region;* see ἀνώτερον.
ἀνῶ   verb, ²aor. act. subjunc. 1 pers. sg. {5.B.3} . ἀνίημι G447
ἀνώγαιον   noun, acc. sg. neut. {2.B} . . . .ἀνάγαιον G508†‡
ἀνώγεον   noun, acc. sg. neut. {2.B} . . . . id.
G509 **ἄνωθεν**   adv. (1) *from above,* sometimes strengthened by ἀπό, *from heaven* (locally and spiritually); (2) *from the beginning, from their origin (source), from of old,* Luke 1:3; Acts 26:5; Gal 4:9; Jas 1:17; (3) *again* (the meaning taken out of Jesus' words by Nicodemus, John 3:4, where δεύτερον is his paraphrase of ἄνωθεν, John 3:3).
ἄνωθεν   adv. ἄνωθεν G509
ἀνωρθώθη   verb, aor. pass. indic. 3 pers. sg.
  {5.A.1} . . . . ἀνορθόω G461
ἀνωτερικά   adj., acc. pl. neut. {3.C} . . ἀνωτερικός G510
G510 **ἀνωτερικός**, -ή, -όν   *upper, higher-lying* (the high central plateau of Asia Minor in contrast to the road through the valley).
ἀνώτερον   adv. comp. {3.F; 3.G} . . . . ἀνώτερος G511
G511 **ἀνώτερος**   neut. comp. of ἄνω, as adv. (1) *higher, to a more honorable place* (at the dinner table), Luke 14:10; (2) *previously, in an earlier passage* (of the book); (3) *above.*
ἀνωφελεῖς   adj., nom. pl. fem. {3.E} . . . . ἀνωφελής G512
ἀνωφελές   adj., acc. sg. neut. {3.E} . . . . id.
G512 **ἀνωφελής**, -ές   *useless, unprofitable* (perhaps also with the further idea, *harmful,* as in Plato).
ἄξει   verb, fut. act. indic. 3 pers. sg. {5.A.1.a} . . . ἄγω G71
ἄξια   adj., acc. pl. neut. {3.A} . . . . ἄξιος G514
ἄξια   adj., nom. pl. neut. {3.A} . . . . id.
ἄξια   adj., nom. sg. fem. {3.A} . . . . id.
ἄξια   adj., acc. sg. fem. {3.A} . . . . id.
G513 **ἀξίνη**, -ης, ἡ   *axe.*
ἀξίνη   noun, nom. sg. fem. {2.A} . . . . ἀξίνη G513
ἄξιοι   adj., nom. pl. masc. {3.A} . . . . ἄξιος G514
ἄξιον   adj., acc. sg. masc. {3.A} . . . . id.
ἄξιον   adj., acc. sg. neut. {3.A} . . . . id.
ἄξιον   adj., nom. sg. neut. {3.A} . . . . id.
G514 **ἄξιος**, -α, -ον   (1) *worthy;* (2) *worthy of, deserving.*
ἄξιος   adj., nom. sg. masc. {3.A} . . . . ἄξιος G514
ἀξιοῦμεν   verb, pres. act. indic. 1 pers. pl.
  {5.A.2} . . . . ἀξιόω G515
ἀξίους   adj., acc. pl. masc. {3.A} . . . . ἄξιος G514
ἀξιούσθωσαν   verb, pres. pass. impv. 3 pers. pl.
  {5.D.2} . . . . ἀξιόω G515
G515 **ἀξιόω**   *I account* or *treat as worthy.*
ἀξιωθήσεται   verb, fut. pass. indic. 3 pers. sg.
  {5.A.1} . . . . ἀξιόω G515
G516 **ἀξίως**   adv., *worthily, in a manner worthy of.*
ἀξίως   adv. {3.F} . . . . ἀξίως G516
ἀξιώσῃ   verb, aor. act. subjunc. 3 pers. sg.
  {5.B.1} . . . . ἀξιόω G515

ἄξων vbl., fut. act. ptc. nom. sg. masc. {6.A.1.a}. ἄγω *G71*
ἀόρατα adj., nom. pl. neut. {3.C} . . . . . .ἀόρατος *G517*
ἀόρατον adj., acc. sg. masc. {3.C} . . . . id.
G517 **ἀόρατος**, -ον *unseen, invisible.*
ἀοράτου adj., gen. sg. masc. {3.C}. . . . . .ἀόρατος *G517*
ἀοράτῳ adj., dat. sg. masc. {3.C}. . . . . id.
ἀπ᾽ prep.. . . . . .ἀπό *G575*
ἀπάγαγε verb, ²aor. act. impv. 2 pers. sg.
  {5.D.1}. . . . . ἀπάγω *G520*
ἀπαγάγετε verb, ²aor. act. impv. 2 pers. pl. {5.D.1}. id.
ἀπαγαγών vbl., ²aor. act. ptc. nom. sg. masc.
  {6.A.1.a} . . . . id.
ἀπαγγεῖλαι vbl., aor. act. inf. {6.B.1} . .ἀπαγγέλλω *G518*
ἀπαγγείλατε verb, aor. act. impv. 2 pers. pl.
  {5.D.1}. . . . . id.
ἀπάγγειλον verb, aor. act. impv. 2 pers. sg.
  {5.D.1}. . . . . id.
ἀπαγγελεῖ verb, fut. act. indic. 3 pers. sg. {5.A.2}id.
ἀπαγγέλλει verb, pres. act. indic. 3 pers. sg.
  {5.A.1.a} . . . . id.
ἀπαγγέλλομεν verb, pres. act. indic. 1 pers. pl.
  {5.A.1.a} . . . . id.
ἀπαγγέλλοντας vbl., pres. act. ptc. acc. pl.
  masc. {6.A.1}. . . . . id.
ἀπαγγέλλοντες vbl., pres. act. ptc. nom. pl.
  masc. {6.A.1}. . . . . id.
ἀπαγγέλλουσα vbl., pres. act. ptc. nom. sg.
  fem. {6.A.1}. . . . . id.
ἀπαγγέλλουσιν verb, pres. act. indic. 3 pers.
  pl. {5.A.1.a} . . . . id.
G518 **ἀπαγγέλλω** *I report* (from one place to another), *I bring a report, I announce.*
ἀπαγγέλλω verb, pres. act. indic. 1 pers. sg.
  {5.A.1}. . . . . .ἀπαγγέλλω *G518*
ἀπαγγέλλων vbl., pres. act. ptc. nom. sg. masc.
  {6.A.1}. . . . . id.
ἀπαγγελῶ verb, fut. act. indic. 1 pers. sg. {5.A.2}id.
ἄπαγε verb, pres. act. impv. 2 pers. sg.
  {5.D.1}. . . . . ἀπάγω *G520*
ἀπάγει verb, pres. act. indic. 3 pers. sg. {5.A.1} . id.
ἀπάγετε verb, pres. act. impv. 2 pers. pl. {5.D.1} id.
ἀπαγόμενοι vbl., pres. pass. ptc. nom. pl.
  masc. {6.A.1}. . . . . id.
ἀπαγομένους vbl., pres. pass. ptc. acc. pl.
  masc. {6.A.1}. . . . . id.
ἀπάγουσα vbl., pres. act. ptc. nom. sg. fem.
  {6.A.1}. . . . . id.
G519 **ἀπάγχω** mid. *I choke, strangle, hang myself.*
G520 **ἀπάγω** (1) *I lead away* (e.g., *I lead away* to
  execution, Acts 12:19); (2) hence, in the moral
  sphere, 1 Cor 12:2; also, (3) of a road *leading*
  to a place.
ἀπάγων vbl., pres. act. ptc. nom. sg. masc.
  {6.A.1}. . . . . ἀπάγω *G520*
G521 **ἀπαίδευτος**, -ον *untrained, uneducated, showing a want of training or education.*
ἀπαιδεύτους adj., acc. pl. fem. {3.C}. .ἀπαίδευτος *G521*
G522 **ἀπαίρω** *I take away, remove.*
ἀπαίτει verb, pres. act. impv. 2 pers. sg.
  {5.D.2}. . . . . .ἀπαιτέω *G523*

G523 **ἀπαιτέω** *I ask back,* or *I ask what is my due.*
ἀπαιτοῦσιν verb, pres. act. indic. 3 pers. pl.
  {5.A.2}. . . . . .ἀπαιτέω *G523*
G524 **ἀπαλγέω** *I am past feeling, cease to care*
  (suggesting sometimes despair, sometimes
  recklessness), *I become callous;* (lit. *I cease to
  feel pain*).
ἀπαλλάξῃ verb, aor. act. subjunc. 3 pers. sg.
  {5.B.1}. .ἀπαλλάσσω *G525*
ἀπαλλάσσεσθαι vbl., pres. pass. inf. {6.B.1}. . . id.
G525 **ἀπαλλάσσω** (1) *I free* (a person) *from*
  (anything); (2) oftener in the mid. voice, *I am
  released from, I am rid of* (a person or thing).
G526 **ἀπαλλοτριόω** pass. (1) lit. *I am being alien-
  ated from;* (2) the perf. pass. ptc. is practically
  a noun, *aliens.*
G527 **ἀπαλός**, -ή, -όν *tender.*
ἀπαλός adj., nom. sg. masc. {3.C} . . . . . . .ἀπαλός *G527*
ἅπαν adj., nom. sg. neut. {3.D} . . . . .ἅπας *G537*
ἅπαντα adj., acc. pl. neut. {3.D}. . . . . id.
ἅπαντα adj., acc. sg. masc. {3.D}. . . . . id.
ἅπαντα adj., nom. pl. neut. {3.D} . . . . id.
ἅπαντας adj., acc. pl. masc. {3.D} . . . . id.
G528 **ἀπαντάω** *I meet.*
ἅπαντες adj., nom. pl. masc. {3.D} . . . . .ἅπας *G537*
ἀπαντῆσαι vbl., aor. act. inf. {6.B.1} . . . .ἀπαντάω *G528*
ἀπαντήσει verb, fut. act. indic. 3 pers. sg.
  {5.A.1}. . . . . id.
ἀπάντησιν noun, acc. sg. fem. {2.C} . . .ἀπάντησις *G529*
G529 **ἀπάντησις**, -εως, ἡ the act of *meeting;* εἰς
  ἀπάντησιν, *to meet* (a phrase seemingly
  almost technical for the reception of a newly
  arrived official).
ἁπάντων adj., gen. pl. neut. {3.D} . . . . .ἅπας *G537*
G530 **ἅπαξ** adv., (1) *once;* (2) *once for all.*
ἅπαξ adv.. . . . . .ἅπαξ *G530*
ἀπαράβατον adj., acc. sg. fem. {3.C} ἀπαράβατος *G531*
G531 **ἀπαράβατος**, -ον *inviolate, inviolable.*
G532 **ἀπαρασκεύαστος**, -ον *unprepared.*
ἀπαρασκευάστους adj., acc. pl. masc.
  {3.C} .ἀπαρασκεύαστος *G532*
ἀπαρθῇ verb, aor. pass. subjunc. 3 pers. sg.
  {5.B.1}. . . . . ἀπαίρω *G522*
G533 **ἀπαρνέομαι** *I deny, disown, repudiate* (either
  another person or myself).
ἀπαρνηθήσεται verb, fut. pass. indic. 3 pers. sg.
  {5.A.1}. . . . . .ἀπαρνέομαι *G533*
ἀπαρνησάσθω verb, aor. mid. impv. 3 pers.
  sg. {5.D.1} . . . . id.
ἀπαρνήσῃ verb, fut. mid. indic. 2 pers. sg.
  {5.A.1}. . . . . id.
ἀπαρνήσομαι verb, fut. mid. indic. 1 pers. sg.
  {5.A.1}. . . . . id.
ἀπαρνήσωμαι verb, aor. mid. subjunc. 1 pers.
  sg. {5.B.1} . . . . id.
G534 **ἀπαρτί** (1) *henceforth;* (2) *even now* (properly
  ἀπ᾽ ἄρτι, lit., *from now*).
ἀπαρτί adv.. . . . . .ἀπαρτί *G534*
ἀπαρτισμόν noun, acc. sg. masc.
  {2.B} . . . . .ἀπαρτισμός *G535*

G535 **ἀπαρτισμός**, -οῦ, ὁ   (1) *setting up, erection;* (2) hence, *completion.*

G536 **ἀπαρχή**, -ῆς, ἡ   (1) *firstfruits, the earliest crop* of the year; (2) hence also met., e.g., of the earliest converts in a district. There is evidence in favor of rendering in some passages merely by *sacrifice, gift.*

ἀπαρχή   noun, nom. sg. fem. {2.A} . . . . . ἀπαρχή G536
ἀπαρχήν   noun, acc. sg. fem. {2.A} . . . . id.

G537 **ἅπας**, -ασα, -αν *all, whole* (cf. πᾶς). It is rather a literary word and is used by preference after consonants.

ἅπας   adj., nom. sg. masc. {3.D} . . . . .ἅπας G537
ἅπασαν   adj., acc. sg. fem. {3.D} . . . . id.
ἅπασι   adj., dat. pl. masc. {3.D} . . . . id.
ἅπασιν   adj., dat. pl. masc. {3.D} . . . . id.

G782†‡ **ἀπασπάζομαι** *I give parting greetings to.* Var. for ἀσπάζομαι, Acts 21:6.

ἀπάταις   noun, dat. pl. fem. {2.A} . . . . .ἀπάτη G539
ἀπατάτω   verb, pres. act. impv. 3 pers. sg. {5.D.2} . . . . .ἀπατάω G538

G538 **ἀπατάω** *I deceive, cheat* (becoming obsolete in most countries).

G539 **ἀπάτη**, -ης, ἡ   (1) *deceit, deception;* (2) (more probably, according to a Hellenistic sense) *pleasure* in Mark 4:19 (= Matt 13:22, cf. Luke 8:14); 2 Pet 2:13.

ἀπάτη   noun, nom. sg. fem. {2.A}. . . . . .ἀπάτη G539
ἀπάτῃ   noun, dat. sg. fem. {2.A}. . . . . id.
ἀπατηθεῖσα   vbl., aor. pass. ptc. nom. sg. fem. {6.A.1.a} . . . . .ἀπατάω G538
ἀπάτης   noun, gen. sg. fem. {2.A}. . . . . .ἀπάτη G539
ἀπατῶν   vbl., pres. act. ptc. nom. sg. masc. {6.A.2}. . . . . .ἀπατάω G538

G540 **ἀπάτωρ**, -ορος *without* (recorded) *father, of unknown father.*

ἀπάτωρ   adj., nom. sg. masc. {3.E} . . . . . . ἀπάτωρ G540

G541 **ἀπαύγασμα**, -ατος, τό *a light flashing forth* (from), *radiation, gleam.*

ἀπαύγασμα   noun, nom. sg. neut. {2.C} . . . . .ἀπαύγασμα G541
ἀπαχθῆναι   vbl., aor. pass. inf. {6.B.1} . . . . . ἀπάγω G520
ἀπέβησαν   verb, ²aor. act. indic. 3 pers. pl. {5.A.1} . . . . .ἀποβαίνω G576
ἀπέβλεπε   verb, impf. act. indic. 3 pers. sg. {5.A.1.b} .ἀποβλέπω G578
ἀπέβλεπεν   verb, impf. act. indic. 3 pers. sg. {5.A.1.b} . . . . id.
ἀπέδειξεν   verb, aor. act. indic. 3 pers. sg. {5.A.3.b} . . . . .ἀποδείκνυμι G584
ἀπεδέξαντο   verb, aor. mid. indic. 3 pers. pl. {5.A.1.e} . . . . ἀποδέχομαι G588
ἀπεδέξατο   verb, aor. mid. indic. 3 pers. sg. {5.A.1.e} . . . . id.
ἀπέδετο   verb, ²aor. mid. indic. 3 pers. sg. {5.A.3.b} .ἀποδίδωμι G591
ἀπεδέχετο   verb, impf. mid./pass. indic. 3 pers. sg. {5.A.1.e} . . . . .ἀποδέχομαι G588
ἀπεδέχθησαν   verb, aor. pass. indic. 3 pers. pl. {5.A.1.b} . . . . id.

ἀπεδήμησε   verb, aor. act. indic. 3 pers. sg. {5.A.1} . . . . .ἀποδημέω G589
ἀπεδήμησεν   verb, aor. act. indic. 3 pers. sg. {5.A.1} . . . . id.
ἀπεδίδουν   verb, impf. act. indic. 3 pers. pl. {5.A.3.a} .ἀποδίδωμι G591
ἀπεδοκίμασαν   verb, aor. act. indic. 3 pers. pl. {5.A.1.b} . . . . .ἀποδοκιμάζω G593
ἀπεδοκιμάσθη   verb, aor. pass. indic. 3 pers. sg. {5.A.1.b} . . . . id.
ἀπέδοντο   verb, ²aor. mid. indic. 3 pers. pl. {5.A.3.b} .ἀποδίδωμι G591
ἀπέδοσθε   verb, ²aor. mid. indic. 2 pers. pl. {5.A.3.b} . . . . id.
ἀπέδοτο   verb, ²aor. mid. indic. 3 pers. sg. {5.A.3.b} . . . . id.
ἀπέδωκεν   verb, aor. act. indic. 3 pers. sg. {5.A.3.b} . . . . id.
ἀπέθανε   verb, ²aor. act. indic. 3 pers. sg. {5.A.1.b} .ἀποθνήσκω G599
ἀπέθανεν   verb, ²aor. act. indic. 3 pers. sg. {5.A.1.b} . . . . id.
ἀπεθάνετε   verb, ²aor. act. indic. 2 pers. pl. {5.A.1.b} . . . . id.
ἀπεθάνομεν   verb, ²aor. act. indic. 1 pers. pl. {5.A.1.b} . . . . id.
ἀπέθανον   verb, ²aor. act. indic. 1 pers. sg. {5.A.1.b} . . . . id.
ἀπέθανον   verb, ²aor. act. indic. 3 pers. pl. {5.A.1.b} . . . . id.
ἀπέθεντο   verb, ²aor. mid. indic. 3 pers. pl. {5.A.3.b} .ἀποτίθημι G659
ἀπέθετο   verb, ²aor. mid. indic. 3 pers. sg. {5.A.3.b} . . . . id.
ἀπέθνησκεν   verb, impf. act. indic. 3 pers. sg. {5.A.1.b} .ἀποθνήσκω G599
ἀπέθνῃσκεν   verb, impf. act. indic. 3 pers. sg. {5.A.1.b} . . . . id.

G542 **ἀπεῖδον** ²aor. of ἀφοράω.

G543 **ἀπείθεια**, -ας, ἡ *disobedience, rebellion, contumacy;* for υἱοὶ τῆς ἀπειθείας, see υἱός.

ἀπειθείᾳ   noun, dat. sg. fem. {2.A} . . . . . . ἀπείθεια G543
ἀπείθειαν   noun, acc. sg. fem. {2.A} . . . . id.
ἀπειθείας   noun, gen. sg. fem. {2.A}. . . . . id.
ἀπειθεῖς   adj., acc. pl. masc. {3.E} . . . . ἀπειθής G545
ἀπειθεῖς   adj., nom. pl. masc. {3.E}. . . . . id.

G544 **ἀπειθέω** *I disobey, I rebel, I am disloyal.*

G545 **ἀπειθής**, -ές *disobedient.*

ἀπειθής   adj., nom. sg. masc. {3.E} . . . . ἀπειθής G545
ἀπειθήσαντες   vbl., aor. act. ptc. nom. pl. masc. {6.A.2}. . . . . .ἀπειθέω G544
ἀπειθήσασι   vbl., aor. act. ptc. dat. pl. masc. {6.A.2}. . . . . id.
ἀπειθήσασιν   vbl., aor. act. ptc. dat. pl. masc. {6.A.2}. . . . . id.
ἀπειθίᾳ   noun, dat. sg. fem. {2.A} . . . . . . ἀπείθεια G543
ἀπειθίαν   noun, acc. sg. fem. {2.A}. . . . . id.
ἀπειθίας   noun, gen. sg. fem. {2.A} . . . . id.
ἀπειθοῦντα   vbl., pres. act. ptc. acc. sg. masc. {6.A.2}. . . . . .ἀπειθέω G544

ἀπειθοῦντες   vbl., pres. act. ptc. nom. pl. masc.
{6.A.2}. . . . . id.
ἀπειθούντων   vbl., pres. act. ptc. gen. pl. masc.
{6.A.2}. . . . . id.
ἀπειθοῦσι   verb, pres. act. indic. 3 pers. pl.
{5.A.2}. . . . . id.
ἀπειθοῦσι   vbl., pres. act. ptc. dat. pl. masc.
{6.A.2}. . . . . id.
ἀπειθοῦσιν   verb, pres. act. indic. 3 pers. pl.
{5.A.2}. . . . . id.
ἀπειθοῦσιν   vbl., pres. act. ptc. dat. pl. masc.
{6.A.2}. . . . . id.
ἀπειθῶν   vbl., pres. act. ptc. nom. sg. masc.
{6.A.2}. . . . . id.
ἀπειλάς   noun, acc. pl. fem. {2.A} . . . . ἀπειλή G547
G546 **ἀπειλέω**   I threaten (apparently going out of popular speech).
G547 **ἀπειλή**, -ῆς, ἡ   threatening, a threat.
ἀπειλῇ   noun, dat. sg. fem. {2.A} . . . . ἀπειλή G547
ἀπειλήν   noun, acc. sg. fem. {2.A} . . . . id.
ἀπειλῆς   noun, gen. sg. fem. {2.A} . . . . id.
ἀπειλησόμεθα   verb, fut. mid. indic. 1 pers. pl.
{5.A.1}. . . . . ἀπειλέω G546
ἀπειλησώμεθα   verb, aor. mid. subjunc. 1 pers. pl. {5.B.1}. . . . . id.
ἄπειμι   verb, pres. act. indic. 1 pers. sg. {7.A} ἄπειμι¹ G548
G548 **ἄπειμι**¹ (from εἰμί)   I am absent.
G549 **ἄπειμι**² (from εἶμι)   I shall go away, I go away (only in Acts 17:10).
ἀπειπάμεθα   verb, ²aor. mid. indic. 1 pers. pl.
{5.A.1.e}. . . . . ἀπεῖπον G550
G550 **ἀπεῖπον**   mid., ἀπειπάμην, I have renounced.
G551 **ἀπείραστος**, -ον   (1) untried, inexperienced (w. gen. = in); (2) or untempted (w. gen. = to).
ἀπείραστος   adj., nom. sg. masc. {3.C} ἀπείραστος G551
G552 **ἄπειρος**, -ον   inexperienced (in), without experience (of), unacquainted (with); from πεῖρα.
ἄπειρος   adj., nom. sg. masc. {3.C} . . . . . . ἄπειρος G552
ἀπεῖχεν   verb, impf. act. indic. 3 pers. sg.
{5.A.1.b}. . . . . ἀπέχω G568
ἀπεκαλύφθη   verb, aor. pass. indic. 3 pers. sg.
{5.A.1.b}. . . . . ἀποκαλύπτω G601
ἀπεκάλυψας   verb, aor. act. indic. 2 pers. sg.
{5.A.1.b}. . . . . id.
ἀπεκάλυψε   verb, aor. act. indic. 3 pers. sg.
{5.A.1.b}. . . . . id.
ἀπεκάλυψεν   verb, aor. act. indic. 3 pers. sg.
{5.A.1.b}. . . . . id.
ἀπεκατεστάθη   verb, aor. pass. indic. 3 pers. sg.
{5.A.1}. . . . . ἀποκαθίστημι G600
ἀπεκατέστη   verb, ²aor. act. indic. 3 pers. sg.
{5.A.3.b}. . . . . id.
ἀπεκδέχεται   verb, pres. mid./pass. indic. 3 pers. sg. {5.A.1.d}. . . . . ἀπεκδέχομαι G553
G553 **ἀπεκδέχομαι**   I expect eagerly, I wait for eagerly (rare).
ἀπεκδεχόμεθα   verb, pres. mid./pass. indic. 1 pers. pl. {5.A.1.d}. . . . . ἀπεκδέχομαι G553
ἀπεκδεχόμενοι   vbl., pres. mid./pass. ptc. nom. pl. masc. {6.A.1} . . . . id.

ἀπεκδεχομένοις   vbl., pres. mid./pass. ptc. dat. pl. masc. {6.A.1} . . . . id.
ἀπεκδεχομένους   vbl., pres. mid./pass. ptc. acc. pl. masc. {6.A.1} . . . . id.
G554 **ἀπεκδύομαι**   I put off (as a garment) from myself, I throw off (probably coined by Paul).
ἀπεκδυσάμενοι   vbl., aor. mid. ptc. nom. pl. masc.
{6.A.1.b} . . . . ἀπεκδύομαι G554
ἀπεκδυσάμενος   vbl., aor. mid. ptc. nom. sg.
masc. {6.A.1.b} . . . . id.
ἀπεκδύσει   noun, dat. sg. fem. {2.C} . . . ἀπέκδυσις G555
G555 **ἀπέκδυσις**, -εως, ἡ   a putting off (as of a garment), a casting off (probably coined by Paul).
ἀπεκεφάλισα   verb, aor. act. indic. 1 pers. sg.
{5.A.1.b} . . . . ἀποκεφαλίζω G607
ἀπεκεφάλισε   verb, aor. act. indic. 3 pers. sg.
{5.A.1.b} . . . . id.
ἀπεκεφάλισεν   verb, aor. act. indic. 3 pers. sg.
{5.A.1.b} . . . . id.
ἀπέκοψαν   verb, aor. act. indic. 3 pers. pl.
{5.A.1.b} . . . . ἀποκόπτω G609
ἀπέκοψε   verb, aor. act. indic. 3 pers. sg.
{5.A.1.b} . . . . id.
ἀπέκοψεν   verb, aor. act. indic. 3 pers. sg.
{5.A.1.b} . . . . id.
ἀπεκρίθη   verb, aor. pass. indic. 3 pers. sg.
{5.A.1.e} . . . . ἀποκρίνομαι G611
ἀπεκρίθην   verb, aor. pass. indic. 1 pers. sg.
{5.A.1.e} . . . . id.
ἀπεκρίθης   verb, aor. pass. indic. 2 pers. sg.
{5.A.1.e} . . . . id.
ἀπεκρίθησαν   verb, aor. pass. indic. 3 pers. pl.
{5.A.1.e} . . . . id.
ἀπεκρίνατο   verb, aor. mid. indic. 3 pers. sg.
{5.A.1.e} . . . . id.
ἀπέκρυψας   verb, aor. act. indic. 2 pers. sg.
{5.A.1.b} . . . . ἀποκρύπτω G613
ἀπέκρυψε   verb, aor. act. indic. 3 pers. sg.
{5.A.1.b} . . . . id.
ἀπέκρυψεν   verb, aor. act. indic. 3 pers. sg.
{5.A.1.b} . . . . id.
ἀπεκτάνθη   verb, aor. pass. indic. 3 pers. sg.
{5.A.1.b} . . . . ἀποκτείνω G615
ἀπεκτάνθησαν   verb, aor. pass. indic. 3 pers. pl. {5.A.1.b} . . . . id.
ἀπέκτειναν   verb, aor. act. indic. 3 pers. pl.
{5.A.1.b} . . . . id.
ἀπεκτείνατε   verb, aor. act. indic. 2 pers. pl.
{5.A.1.b} . . . . id.
ἀπέκτεινεν   verb, aor. act. indic. 3 pers. sg.
{5.A.1.b} . . . . id.
ἀπεκύησεν   verb, aor. act. indic. 3 pers. sg.
{5.A.1} . . . . ἀποκυέω G616
ἀπεκύλισε   verb, aor. act. indic. 3 pers. sg.
{5.A.1.b} . . . . ἀποκυλίω G617
ἀπεκύλισεν   verb, aor. act. indic. 3 pers. sg.
{5.A.1.b} . . . . id.
ἀπέλαβεν   verb, ²aor. act. indic. 3 pers. sg.
{5.A.1.b} . . . . ἀπολαμβάνω G618

ἀπέλαβες   verb, ²aor. act. indic. 2 pers. sg.
{5.A.1.b} . . . . id.

G556 ἀπελαύνω   *I drive away.*

ἀπελεγμόν   noun, acc. sg. masc. {2.B} . . ἀπελεγμός G557

G557 ἀπελεγμός, -οῦ, ὁ   (1) *refutation, rejection;* (2)
hence, *disrepute.*

ἀπέλειπον   verb, impf. act. indic. 1 pers. sg.
{5.A.1.b} . . . . ἀπολείπω G620

ἀπέλειχον   verb, impf. act. indic. 3 pers. pl.
{5.A.1.b} . . . . ἀπολείχω G621

G558 ἀπελεύθερος, -ου, ὁ   *a freedman,* one who has
been a slave but has been manumitted by his
master.

ἀπελεύθερος   noun, nom. sg. masc.
{2.B} . . . . ἀπελεύθερος G558

ἀπελεύσομαι   verb, fut. mid. indic. 1 pers. sg.
{5.A.1.d} . . . . ἀπέρχομαι G565

ἀπελευσόμεθα   verb, fut. mid. indic. 1 pers. pl.
{5.A.1.d} . . . . id.

ἀπελεύσονται   verb, fut. mid. indic. 3 pers. pl.
{5.A.1.d} . . . . id.

ἀπελήλυθε   verb, ²perf. act. indic. 3 pers. sg.
{5.A.1.c} . . . . id.

ἀπεληλύθεισαν   verb, plu. act. indic. 3 pers.
pl. {5.A.1.b} . . . . id.

ἀπελήλυθεν   verb, ²perf. act. indic. 3 pers. sg.
{5.A.1.c} . . . . id.

ἀπελθεῖν   vbl., ²aor. act. inf. {6.B.1} . . . . id.

ἀπέλθη   verb, ²aor. act. subjunc. 3 pers. sg.
{5.B.1} . . . . id.

ἀπέλθητε   verb, ²aor. act. subjunc. 2 pers. pl.
{5.B.1} . . . . id.

ἀπελθόντες   vbl., ²aor. act. ptc. nom. pl. masc.
{6.A.1.a} . . . . id.

ἀπελθόντι   vbl., ²aor. act. ptc. dat. sg. masc.
{6.A.1.a} . . . . id.

ἀπελθόντων   vbl., ²aor. act. ptc. gen. pl. masc.
{6.A.1.a} . . . . id.

ἀπελθοῦσα   vbl., ²aor. act. ptc. nom. sg. fem.
{6.A.1.a} . . . . id.

ἀπελθοῦσαι   vbl., ²aor. act. ptc. nom. pl. fem.
{6.A.1.a} . . . . id.

ἀπέλθω   verb, ²aor. act. subjunc. 1 pers. sg.
{5.B.1} . . . . id.

ἀπελθών   vbl., ²aor. act. ptc. nom. sg. masc.
{6.A.1.a} . . . . id.

ἀπέλθωσιν   verb, ²aor. act. subjunc. 3 pers. pl.
{5.B.1} . . . . id.

ἀπέλιπον   verb, ²aor. act. indic. 1 pers. sg.
{5.A.1.b} . . . . ἀπολείπω G620

Ἀπελλῆν   noun prop., acc. sg. masc. {2.A;
2.D} . . . . Ἀπελλῆς G559

G559 Ἀπελλῆς, -οῦ, ὁ   *Apelles,* a Christian (man) in
Rome.

ἀπελογεῖτο   verb, impf. mid./pass. indic. 3 pers. sg.
{5.A.2} . . . . ἀπολογέομαι G626

ἀπελούσασθε   verb, aor. mid. indic. 2 pers. pl.
{5.A.1.e} . . . . ἀπολούω G628

ἀπελπίζοντες   vbl., pres. act. ptc. nom. pl. masc.
{6.A.1} . . . . ἀπελπίζω G560

G560 ἀπελπίζω   *I despair;* in Luke 6:35, if μηδέν is
the correct reading, μηδὲν ἀπελπίζοντες
must be translated *despairing not at all;* if
μηδένα ἀφ., *despairing of no one.*

ἀπέλυεν   verb, impf. act. indic. 3 pers. sg.
{5.A.1.b} . . . . ἀπολύω G630

ἀπελύθησαν   verb, aor. pass. indic. 3 pers. pl.
{5.A.1.b} . . . . id.

ἀπελύοντο   verb, impf. mid. indic. 3 pers. pl.
{5.A.1.e} . . . . id.

ἀπέλυσαν   verb, aor. act. indic. 3 pers. pl.
{5.A.1.b} . . . . id.

ἀπέλυσε   verb, aor. act. indic. 3 pers. sg.
{5.A.1.b} . . . . id.

ἀπέλυσεν   verb, aor. act. indic. 3 pers. sg.
{5.A.1.b} . . . . id.

G561 ἀπέναντι   adv. and prep. with gen., (1) *over
against, opposite;* (2) *in view of, in presence of.*

ἀπέναντι   adv. and prep. . . . . ἀπέναντι G561

ἀπενεγκεῖν   vbl., ²aor. act. inf. {6.B.1} . . . . ἀποφέρω G667

ἀπενεχθῆναι   vbl., aor. pass. inf. {6.B.1} . . . . . . id.

ἀπενίψατο   verb, aor. mid. indic. 3 pers. sg.
{5.A.1.e} . . . . ἀπονίπτω G633

ἀπεξεδέχετο   verb, impf. mid./pass. indic. 3 pers.
sg. {5.A.1.e} . . . . ἀπεκδέχομαι G553

ἀπέπεσαν   verb, ²aor. act. indic. 3 pers. pl.
{5.A.1.b} . . . . ἀποπίπτω G634

ἀπέπεσον   verb, ²aor. act. indic. 3 pers. pl.
{5.A.1.b} . . . . id.

ἀπεπλανήθησαν   verb, aor. pass. indic. 3 pers. pl.
{5.A.1} . . . . ἀποπλανάω G635

ἀπέπλευσαν   verb, aor. act. indic. 3 pers. pl.
{5.A.1} . . . . ἀποπλέω G636

ἀπέπλυναν   verb, aor. act. indic. 3 pers. pl.
{5.A.1.b} . . . . ἀποπλύνω G637

ἀπεπνίγη   verb, ²aor. pass. indic. 3 pers. sg.
{5.A.1.e} . . . . ἀποπνίγω G638

ἀπέπνιξαν   verb, aor. act. indic. 3 pers. pl.
{5.A.1.b} . . . . id.

ἀπεράντοις   adj., dat. pl. fem. {3.C} . . . . ἀπέραντος G562

G562 ἀπέραντος, -ον   *unaccomplished, unending,
endless.*

G563 ἀπερισπάστως   adv., *without distraction,
without being distracted.*

ἀπερισπάστως   adv. {3.F} . . . . ἀπερισπάστως G563

ἀπερίτμητοι   adj., voc. pl. masc. {3.C} ἀπερίτμητος G564

G564 ἀπερίτμητος, -ον   (1) *uncircumcised;* (2) hence
practically, *unclean;* (3) met, used of rankness,
want of restraint.

ἀπέρχεσθαι   vbl., pres. mid./pass. inf.
{6.B.1} . . . . ἀπέρχομαι G565

ἀπέρχη   verb, pres. mid./pass. subjunc. 2 pers.
sg. {5.B.1} . . . . id.

G565 ἀπέρχομαι   *I go away from* (a place).

ἀπερχομένων   vbl., pres. mid./pass. ptc. gen. pl.
fem. {6.A.1} . . . . ἀπέρχομαι G565

ἀπέσπασε   verb, aor. act. indic. 3 pers. sg.
{5.A.1} . . . . ἀποσπάω G645

ἀπέσπασεν   verb, aor. act. indic. 3 pers. sg.
{5.A.1} . . . . id.

ἀπεσπάσθη   verb, aor. pass. indic. 3 pers. sg.
{5.A.1}. . . . . id.
ἀπεστάλη   verb, [2]aor. pass. indic. 3 pers. sg.
{5.A.1.e} . . . . ἀποστέλλω G649
ἀπεστάλην   verb, [2]aor. pass. indic. 1 pers. sg.
{5.A.1.e} . . . . id.
ἀπέσταλκα   verb, perf. act. indic. 1 pers. sg.
{5.A.1.c} . . . . id.
ἀπεστάλκαμεν   verb, perf. act. indic. 1 pers.
pl. {5.A.1.c} . . . . id.
ἀπέσταλκαν   verb, perf. act. indic. 3 pers. pl.
{5.A.1.c} . . . . id.
ἀπεστάλκασιν   verb, perf. act. indic. 3 pers. pl.
{5.A.1.c} . . . . id.
ἀπεστάλκατε   verb, perf. act. indic. 2 pers. pl.
{5.A.1.c} . . . . id.
ἀπέσταλκε   verb, perf. act. indic. 3 pers. sg.
{5.A.1.c} . . . . id.
ἀπέσταλκεν   verb, perf. act. indic. 3 pers. sg.
{5.A.1.c} . . . . id.
ἀπέσταλμαι   verb, perf. pass. indic. 1 pers. sg.
{5.A.1.f}. . . . . id.
ἀπεσταλμένα   vbl., perf. pass. ptc. nom. pl.
neut. {6.A.1.b} . . . . id.
ἀπεσταλμένοι   vbl., perf. pass. ptc. nom. pl.
masc. {6.A.1.b} . . . . id.
ἀπεσταλμένος   vbl., perf. pass. ptc. nom. sg.
masc. {6.A.1.b} . . . . id.
ἀπεσταλμένους   vbl., perf. pass. ptc. acc. pl.
masc. {6.A.1.b} . . . . id.
ἀπεστέγασαν   verb, aor. act. indic. 3 pers. pl.
{5.A.1.b} . . . . ἀποστεγάζω G648
ἀπέστειλα   verb, aor. act. indic. 1 pers. sg.
{5.A.1.b} . . . . ἀποστέλλω G649
ἀπεστείλαμεν   verb, aor. act. indic. 1 pers. pl.
{5.A.1.b} . . . . id.
ἀπέστειλαν   verb, aor. act. indic. 3 pers. pl.
{5.A.1.b} . . . . id.
ἀπέστειλας   verb, aor. act. indic. 2 pers. sg.
{5.A.1.b} . . . . id.
ἀπέστειλε   verb, aor. act. indic. 3 pers. sg.
{5.A.1.b} . . . . id.
ἀπέστειλεν   verb, aor. act. indic. 3 pers. sg.
{5.A.1.b} . . . . id.
ἀπεστερημένος   vbl., perf. pass. ptc. nom. sg.
masc. {6.A.2}. . . . . ἀποστερέω G650
ἀπεστερημένων   vbl., perf. pass. ptc. gen. pl.
masc. {6.A.2}. . . . . id.
ἀπέστη   verb, [2]aor. act. indic. 3 pers. sg.
{5.A.3.b} . . . . ἀφίστημι G868
ἀπέστησαν   verb, [2]aor. act. indic. 3 pers. pl.
{5.A.3.b} . . . . id.
ἀπέστησε   verb, aor. act. indic. 3 pers. sg.
{5.A.3.b} . . . . id.
ἀπέστησεν   verb, aor. act. indic. 3 pers. sg.
{5.A.3.b} . . . . id.
ἀπεστράφησαν   verb, [2]aor. pass. indic. 3 pers. pl.
{5.A.1.e} . . . . ἀποστρέφω G654
ἀπέστρεψε   verb, aor. act. indic. 3 pers. sg.
{5.A.1.b} . . . . id.

ἀπέστρεψεν   verb, aor. act. indic. 3 pers. sg.
{5.A.1.b} . . . . id.
ἀπετάξατο   verb, aor. mid. indic. 3 pers. sg.
{5.A.1.e} . . . . ἀποτάσσω G657
ἀπεφθέγξατο   verb, aor. mid. indic. 3 pers. sg.
{5.A.1.e} . . . . ἀποφθέγγομαι G669
G566 **ἀπέχει**   impers. form of ἀπέχω.
ἀπέχει   verb, pres. act. indic. 3 pers. sg.
{5.A.1.a} . . . . ἀπέχω G568
ἀπέχεσθαι   vbl., pres. mid. inf. {6.B.1} . . . . id.
ἀπέχεσθε   verb, pres. mid. impv. 2 pers. pl.
{5.D.1}. . . . . id.
ἀπέχετε   verb, pres. act. indic. 2 pers. pl.
{5.A.1.a} . . . . id.
ἀπέχῃς   verb, pres. act. subjunc. 2 pers. sg.
{5.B.1} . . . . id.
G567 **ἀπέχομαι**   mid. form of ἀπέχω.
ἀπέχοντος   vbl., pres. act. ptc. gen. sg. masc.
{6.A.1}. . . . . ἀπέχω G568
ἀπέχουσαν   vbl., pres. act. ptc. acc. sg. fem.
{6.A.1}. . . . . id.
ἀπέχουσι   verb, pres. act. indic. 3 pers. pl.
{5.A.1.a} . . . . id.
ἀπέχουσιν   verb, pres. act. indic. 3 pers. pl.
{5.A.1.a} . . . . id.
G568 **ἀπέχω**   (1) trans., *I have received* (payment),
a formula of receipts; so prob. also in Mark
14:41, ὁ Ἰούδας being understood as subj.
(there is hardly any other example in Gk. of
the meaning *it is sufficient*); (2) intrans., *I
am away (from, distant from)*, of places and
objects; (3) mid., *I keep myself away* (from), *I
refrain* (from), *I abstain* (from).
ἀπέχω   verb, pres. act. indic. 1 pers. sg.
{5.A.1.a} . . . . ἀπέχω G568
ἀπεχωρίσθη   verb, aor. pass. indic. 3 pers. sg.
{5.A.1.b} . . . . ἀποχωρίζω G673
ἀπήγαγε   verb, [2]aor. act. indic. 3 pers. sg.
{5.A.1.b} . . . . ἀπάγω G520
ἀπήγαγον   verb, [2]aor. act. indic. 3 pers. pl.
{5.A.1.b} . . . . id.
ἀπήγγειλαν   verb, aor. act. indic. 3 pers. pl.
{5.A.1.b} . . . . ἀπαγγέλλω G518
ἀπήγγειλε   verb, aor. act. indic. 3 pers. sg.
{5.A.1.b} . . . . id.
ἀπήγγειλεν   verb, aor. act. indic. 3 pers. sg.
{5.A.1.b} . . . . id.
ἀπηγγέλη   verb, [2]aor. pass. indic. 3 pers. sg.
{5.A.1.e} . . . . id.
ἀπήγγελλον   verb, impf. act. indic. 1 pers. sg.
{5.A.1.b} . . . . id.
ἀπήγξατο   verb, aor. mid. indic. 3 pers. sg.
{5.A.1.e} . . . . ἀπάγχω G519
ἀπῆεσαν   verb, impf. act. indic. 3 pers. pl.
{7.A} . . . . ἄπειμι[2] G549
ἀπήλασεν   verb, aor. act. indic. 3 pers. sg.
{5.A.1.b} . . . . ἀπελαύνω G556
ἀπηλγηκότες   vbl., perf. act. ptc. nom. pl. masc.
{6.A.2}. . . . . ἀπαλγέω G524

ἀπῆλθα   verb, ²aor. act. indic. 1 pers. sg.
   {5.A.1.b} . . . . ἀπέρχομαι G565
ἀπῆλθαν   verb, ²aor. act. indic. 3 pers. pl.
   {5.A.1.b} . . . . id.
ἀπῆλθε   verb, ²aor. act. indic. 3 pers. sg. {5.A.1.b}id.
ἀπῆλθεν   verb, ²aor. act. indic. 3 pers. sg.
   {5.A.1.b} . . . . id.
ἀπῆλθον   verb, ²aor. act. indic. 1 pers. sg.
   {5.A.1.b} . . . . id.
ἀπῆλθον   verb, ²aor. act. indic. 3 pers. pl.
   {5.A.1.b} . . . . id.
ἀπηλλάχθαι   vbl., perf. pass. inf.
   {6.B.1} . . . . ἀπαλλάσσω G525
ἀπηλλοτριωμένοι   vbl., perf. pass. ptc. nom. pl.
   masc. {6.A.2} . . . . ἀπαλλοτριόω G526
ἀπηλλοτριωμένους   vbl., perf. pass. ptc. acc.
   pl. masc. {6.A.2} . . . . id.
ἀπήνεγκαν   verb, aor. act. indic. 3 pers. pl.
   {5.A.1.b} . . . . ἀποφέρω G667
ἀπήνεγκε   verb, aor. act. indic. 3 pers. sg.
   {5.A.1.b} . . . . id.
ἀπήνεγκεν   verb, aor. act. indic. 3 pers. sg.
   {5.A.1.b} . . . . id.
ἀπήντησαν   verb, aor. act. indic. 3 pers. pl.
   {5.A.1} . . . . ἀπαντάω G528
ἀπήντησεν   verb, aor. act. indic. 3 pers. sg.
   {5.A.1} . . . . id.
ἀπησπασάμεθα   verb, aor. mid. indic. 1 pers. pl.
   {5.A.1.e} . . . . ἀπασπάζομαι G782†‡
ἀπίδω   verb, ²aor. act. subjunc. 1 pers. sg.
   {5.B.1} . . . . ἀφοράω G872
G569 ἀπιστέω   (1) I am unfaithful; (2) I disbelieve.
ἀπιστήσας   vbl., aor. act. ptc. nom. sg. masc.
   {6.A.2} . . . . ἀπιστέω G569
G570 ἀπιστία, -ας, ἡ   unbelief.
ἀπιστία   noun, nom. sg. fem. {2.A} . . . . . . ἀπιστία G570
ἀπιστία   noun, dat. sg. fem. {2.A} . . . . id.
ἀπιστίαν   noun, acc. sg. fem. {2.A} . . . . id.
ἀπιστίας   noun, gen. sg. fem. {2.A} . . . . id.
ἄπιστοι   adj., nom. pl. masc. {3.C} . . . . ἄπιστος G571
ἀπίστοις   adj., dat. pl. masc. {3.C} . . . . id.
ἄπιστον   adj., acc. sg. fem. {3.C} . . . . id.
ἄπιστον   adj., acc. sg. masc. {3.C} . . . . id.
ἄπιστον   adj., nom. sg. neut. {3.C} . . . . id.
G571 ἄπιστος, -ον   (1) unbelieving, incredulous;
   (2) unchristian; some times substantivally,
   unbeliever.
ἄπιστος   adj., nom. sg. fem. {3.C} . . . . . ἄπιστος G571
ἄπιστος   adj., nom. sg. masc. {3.C} . . . . id.
ἄπιστος   adj., voc. sg. fem. {3.C} . . . . id.
ἀπίστου   adj., gen. sg. masc. {3.C} . . . . id.
ἀπιστοῦμεν   verb, pres. act. indic. 1 pers. pl.
   {5.A.2} . . . . ἀπιστέω G569
ἀπιστούντων   vbl., pres. act. ptc. gen. pl. masc.
   {6.A.2} . . . . id.
ἀπιστοῦσιν   vbl., pres. act. ptc. dat. pl. masc.
   {6.A.2} . . . . id.
ἀπίστων   adj., gen. pl. masc. {3.C} . . . . . . ἄπιστος G571
G572 ἁπλότης, -ητος, ἡ   singleness of mind, sincerity.
ἁπλότητα   noun, acc. sg. fem. {2.C} . . . . . ἁπλότης G572

ἁπλότητι   noun, dat. sg. fem. {2.C} . . . . id.
ἁπλότητος   noun, gen. sg. fem. {2.C} . . . . id.
G573 ἁπλοῦς, ἡ, -οῦν   (1) single; (2) of the eye,
   directed towards one object.
ἁπλοῦς   adj., nom. sg. masc. {3.A} . . . . ἁπλοῦς G573
G574 ἁπλῶς   adv., (1) singly, simply; (2) in Jas 1:5 either graciously or unreservedly, without reserve.
ἁπλῶς   adv. {3.F} . . . . ἁπλῶς G574
G575 ἀπό   prep. with gen., with nouns or advs., from
   (as distinguished from ἐκ) = from the outside
   of, away from; (1) ἀπ᾿ ἀγορᾶς, fresh from
   market, Mark 7:4; ἀπ᾿ ἀγροῦ, fresh from the
   country, Mark 15:21; Rev 1:4, constr. is pecu-
   liar; (2) οἱ ἀπὸ τῆς Ἰταλίας, those who are
   in(?) Italy, Heb 13:24; (3) φοβεῖσθαι ἀπό, see
   φοβέομαι; (4) by (expressing agent), e.g., Luke
   8:43; (5) = gen. of material, Matt 3:4; 27:21.
ἀπό   prep. . . . . ἀπό G575
G576 ἀποβαίνω   (1) I disembark; (2) ἀποβαίνειν
   εἰς, to result in, to end in (lit. I go away).
ἀποβάλητε   verb, ²aor. act. subjunc. 2 pers. pl.
   {5.B.1} . . . . ἀποβάλλω G577
ἀποβάλλειν   vbl., pres. act. inf. {6.B.1} . . . . id.
G577 ἀποβάλλω   (1) I cast away, I cast off; (2) I lose,
   Heb 10:35.
ἀποβαλών   vbl., ²aor. act. ptc. nom. sg. masc.
   {6.A.1.a} . . . . ἀποβάλλω G577
ἀποβάντες   vbl., ²aor. act. ptc. nom. pl. masc.
   {6.A.1.a} . . . . ἀποβαίνω G576
ἀποβήσεται   verb, fut. mid. indic. 3 pers. sg.
   {5.A.1.d} . . . . id.
G578 ἀποβλέπω   I look away from one thing to
   another, I turn my attention to.
ἀπόβλητον   adj., nom. sg. neut. {3.C} . . ἀπόβλητος G579
G579 ἀπόβλητος, -ον   worthy to be cast away,
   worthless.
G580 ἀποβολή, -ῆς, ἡ   a casting away, a loss.
ἀποβολή   noun, nom. sg. fem. {2.A} . . . . ἀποβολή G580
ἀπογεγραμμένων   vbl., perf. pass. ptc. gen. pl.
   masc. {6.A.1.b} . . . . ἀπογράφω G583
ἀπογενόμενοι   vbl., ²aor. mid. ptc. nom. pl. masc.
   {6.A.1.b} . . . . ἀπογίνομαι G581
G581 ἀπογίνομαι   w. the dat., I die away from (opp.
   γίνομαι; therefore, I go out of being, I cease to
   be).
ἀπογράφεσθαι   vbl., pres. mid./pass. inf.
   {6.B.1} . . . . ἀπογράφω G583
ἀπογράφεσθαι   vbl., pres. pass. inf. {6.B.1} . . . . id.
G582 ἀπογραφή, -ῆς, ἡ   an enrollment, a census
   taking, in which particulars not only of the
   persons but also of their property were generally given on the census papers. The system
   began 10–9 B.C., and such an enrollment took
   place every fourteen years.
ἀπογραφή   noun, nom. sg. fem. {2.A} . . ἀπογραφή G582
ἀπογραφῆς   noun, gen. sg. fem. {2.A} . . . . id.
G583 ἀπογράφω   mid. I enroll myself (for the census); hence Heb 12:23, in another connection.
ἀπογράψασθαι   vbl., aor. mid. inf.
   {6.B.1} . . . . ἀπογράφω G583

ἀποδεδειγμένον   vbl., perf. pass. ptc. acc. sg. masc.
{6.A.3}. ἀποδείκνυμι G584
ἀποδεδοκιμασμένον   vbl., perf. pass. ptc. acc. sg.
masc. {6.A.1.b} . . . . ἀποδοκιμάζω G593
G584 **ἀποδείκνυμι**   (1) *I show off, display, exhibit,*
1 Cor 4:9; (2) *I make good, demonstrate,* Acts
25:7; (3) *I make out* (to be so and so), *proclaim*
(to be), 2 Thess 2:4; (4) *I designate, nominate,*
appoint, Acts 2:22.
ἀποδεικνύντα   vbl., pres. act. ptc. acc. sg. masc.
{6.A.3}. ἀποδείκνυμι G584
ἀποδείξαι   vbl., aor. act. inf. {6.B.3} . . . . id.
ἀποδείξει   noun, dat. sg. fem. {2.C} . . . . ἀπόδειξις G585
G585 **ἀπόδειξις**, -εως, ἡ   (1) *display, exhibition*
(abstr.); (2) the ordinary sense is *proof.*
G586† **ἀποδεκατεύω**   *I tithe, I pay a tenth.* Var. for
ἀποδεκατόω, Luke 18:12.
ἀποδεκατεύω   verb, pres. act. indic. 1 pers. sg.
{5.A.1.a} . . . . .ἀποδεκατεύω G586†
ἀποδεκατοῖν   vbl., pres. act. inf. {6.B.2} . . . . . . id.
ἀποδεκατοῦν   vbl., pres. act. inf.
{6.B.2} . . . . ἀποδεκατόω G586
ἀποδεκατοῦτε   verb, pres. act. indic. 2 pers. pl.
{5.A.2}. . . . . id.
G586 **ἀποδεκατόω**   (1) *I take off (deduct) a tenth part*
(of my property to give away), *I pay tithe;* (2)
with acc. pers. *I take a tenth part from.*
ἀποδεκατῶ   verb, pres. act. indic. 1 pers. sg.
{5.A.2}. . . . . ἀποδεκατόω G586
ἀπόδεκτον   adj., nom. sg. neut. {3.C} . . . ἀπόδεκτος G587
G587 **ἀπόδεκτος**, -ον   *worthy to be received (wel-
comed), acceptable, welcome.*
ἀποδεξάμενοι   vbl., aor. mid. ptc. nom. pl. masc.
{6.A.1.b} . . . . .ἀποδέχομαι G588
ἀποδεξάμενος   vbl., aor. mid. ptc. nom. sg.
masc. {6.A.1.b} . . . . id.
ἀποδέξασθαι   vbl., aor. mid. inf. {6.B.1} . . . . . . id.
G588 **ἀποδέχομαι**   (1) *I receive, welcome, entertain*
(with hospitality); (2) hence, met. Acts 2:41;
24:3.
ἀποδεχόμεθα   verb, pres. mid./pass. indic. 1 pers.
pl. {5.A.1.d} . . . . .ἀποδέχομαι G588
G589 **ἀποδημέω**   *I am away from my parish, I am
away from home, I am absent* (ἀπό *from,*
δῆμος *parish*).
G590 **ἀπόδημος**, -ον   *away from home* (see
ἀποδημέω).
ἀπόδημος   adj., nom. sg. masc. {3.C} . . . .ἀπόδημος G590
ἀποδημῶν   vbl., pres. act. ptc. nom. sg. masc.
{6.A.2}. . . . . ἀποδημέω G589
ἀποδιδόναι   vbl., pres. act. inf. {6.B.3} . . ἀποδίδωμι G591
ἀποδιδόντες   vbl., pres. act. ptc. nom. pl. masc.
{6.A.3}. . . . . id.
ἀποδιδότω   verb, pres. act. impv. 3 pers. sg.
{5.D.3}. . . . . id.
ἀποδιδοῦν   vbl., pres. act. ptc. nom. sg. neut.
{6.A.3}. . . . . id.
ἀποδιδούς   vbl., pres. act. ptc. nom. sg. masc.
{6.A.3}. . . . . id.

G591 **ἀποδίδωμι**   (1) *I give back, return, restore;* (2)
I give, render, as due; (3) mid., *I sell,* Acts 5:8,
etc.
ἀποδίδωμι   verb, pres. act. indic. 1 pers. sg.
{5.A.3.a} . . . . .ἀποδίδωμι G591
ἀποδίδωσι   verb, pres. act. indic. 3 pers. sg.
{5.A.3.a} . . . . id.
ἀποδίδωσιν   verb, pres. act. indic. 3 pers. sg.
{5.A.3.a} . . . . id.
ἀποδιορίζοντες   vbl., pres. act. ptc. nom. pl. masc.
{6.A.1}. . . . . ἀποδιορίζω G592
G592 **ἀποδιορίζω**   *I make separate, I cause division.*
ἀποδοθῆναι   vbl., aor. pass. inf. {6.B.1} . ἀποδίδωμι G591
G593 **ἀποδοκιμάζω**   *I reject after testing (examination), I disqualify.*
ἀποδοκιμασθῆναι   vbl., aor. pass. inf.
{6.B.1}. ἀποδοκιμάζω G593
ἀπόδος   verb, ²aor. act. impv. 2 pers. sg.
{5.D.3}. .ἀποδίδωμι G591
ἀπόδοτε   verb, ²aor. act. impv. 2 pers. pl. {5.D.3} id.
ἀποδοῦναι   vbl., ²aor. act. inf. {6.B.3}. . . . . id.
ἀποδούς   vbl., ²aor. act. ptc. nom. sg. masc.
{6.A.3}. . . . . id.
G594 **ἀποδοχή**, -ῆς, ἡ   *acceptance, appreciation,
approbation* (properly *reception, welcome,* of
guests).
ἀποδοχῆς   noun, gen. sg. fem. {2.A} . . . . ἀποδοχή G594
ἀποδῷ   verb, ²aor. act. subjunc. 3 pers. sg.
{5.B.3}. .ἀποδίδωμι G591
ἀποδῴη   verb, ²aor. act. opt. 3 pers. sg. {5.C.3} . . id.
ἀποδῷς   verb, ²aor. act. subjunc. 2 pers. sg.
{5.B.3}. . . . . id.
ἀποδώσει   verb, fut. act. indic. 3 pers. sg. {5.A.1} id.
ἀποδώσεις   verb, fut. act. indic. 2 pers. sg.
{5.A.1}. . . . . id.
ἀποδώσοντες   vbl., fut. act. ptc. nom. pl. masc.
{6.A.3}. . . . . id.
ἀποδώσουσι   verb, fut. act. indic. 3 pers. pl.
{5.A.1}. . . . . id.
ἀποδώσουσιν   verb, fut. act. indic. 3 pers. pl.
{5.A.1}. . . . . id.
ἀποδώσω   verb, fut. act. indic. 1 pers. sg. {5.A.1} id.
ἀποθανεῖν   vbl., ²aor. act. inf. {6.B.1} . . ἀποθνήσκω G599
ἀποθανεῖσθε   verb, fut. mid. indic. 2 pers. pl.
{5.A.2}. . . . . id.
ἀποθανεῖται   verb, fut. mid. indic. 3 pers. sg.
{5.A.2}. . . . . id.
ἀποθάνῃ   verb, ²aor. act. subjunc. 3 pers. sg.
{5.B.1}. . . . . id.
ἀποθανόντα   vbl., ²aor. act. ptc. nom. pl. neut.
{6.A.1.a} . . . . id.
ἀποθανόντες   vbl., ²aor. act. ptc. nom. pl.
masc. {6.A.1.a}. . . . . id.
ἀποθανόντι   vbl., ²aor. act. ptc. dat. sg. masc.
{6.A.1.a} . . . . id.
ἀποθανόντος   vbl., ²aor. act. ptc. gen. sg. masc.
{6.A.1.a} . . . . id.
ἀποθανοῦνται   verb, fut. mid. indic. 3 pers. pl.
{5.A.2}. . . . . id.

ἀποθάνωμεν   verb, ²aor. act. subjunc. 1 pers.
   pl. {5.B.1} . . . . id.
ἀποθανών   vbl., ²aor. act. ptc. nom. sg. masc.
   {6.A.1.a} . . . . id.
ἀποθέμενοι   vbl., ²aor. mid. ptc. nom. pl. masc.
   {6.A.3} . . . . ἀποτίθημι G659
ἀποθέσθαι   vbl., ²aor. mid. inf. {6.B.3} . . . . id.
ἀπόθεσθε   verb, ²aor. mid. impv. 2 pers. pl.
   {5.D.3} . . . . id.
G595 **ἀπόθεσις**, -εως, ἡ   *a putting off, a laying down.*
   ἀπόθεσις   noun, nom. sg. fem. {2.C} . . . . ἀπόθεσις G595
   ἀποθήκας   noun, acc. pl. fem. {2.A} . . . . . ἀποθήκη G596
G596 **ἀποθήκη**, -ης, ἡ   *a storehouse, storeroom* for
   foodstuffs, *a barn.*
   ἀποθήκη   noun, nom. sg. fem. {2.A} . . . . ἀποθήκη G596
   ἀποθήκην   noun, acc. sg. fem. {2.A} . . . . id.
   ἀποθησαυρίζοντας   vbl., pres. act. ptc. acc. pl.
   masc. {6.A.1} . . . . ἀποθησαυρίζω G597
G597 **ἀποθησαυρίζω**   *I store up, treasure up.*
   ἀποθλίβουσι   verb, pres. act. indic. 3 pers. pl.
   {5.A.1.a} . . . . ἀποθλίβω G598
   ἀποθλίβουσιν   verb, pres. act. indic. 3 pers. pl.
   {5.A.1.a} . . . . id.
G598 **ἀποθλίβω**   *I jostle;* (lit. *I rub*).
   ἀποθνήσκει   verb, pres. act. indic. 3 pers. sg.
   {5.A.1.a} . . . . ἀποθνήσκω G599
   ἀποθνήσκει   verb, pres. act. indic. 3 pers. sg.
   {5.A.1.a} . . . . id.
   ἀποθνήσκειν   vbl., pres. act. inf. {6.B.1} . . . . . . id.
   ἀποθνήσκειν   vbl., pres. act. inf. {6.B.1} . . . . . . id.
   ἀποθνήσκομεν   verb, pres. act. indic. 1 pers.
   pl. {5.A.1.a} . . . . id.
   ἀποθνήσκομεν   verb, pres. act. indic. 1 pers.
   pl. {5.A.1.a} . . . . id.
   ἀποθνήσκοντες   vbl., pres. act. ptc. nom. pl.
   masc. {6.A.1} . . . . id.
   ἀποθνήσκοντες   vbl., pres. act. ptc. nom. pl.
   masc. {6.A.1} . . . . id.
   ἀποθνήσκουσιν   verb, pres. act. indic. 3 pers.
   pl. {5.A.1.a} . . . . id.
   ἀποθνήσκουσιν   verb, pres. act. indic. 3 pers.
   pl. {5.A.1.a} . . . . id.
   ἀποθνήσκω   verb, pres. act. indic. 1 pers. sg.
   {5.A.1.a} . . . . id.
G599 **ἀποθνήσκω**   *I am dying* (= obsolete θνήσκω),
   Luke 8:42; 2 Cor 6:9; Heb 11:21; aor. ἀποθανεῖν, *to die;* the pres. is frequentative in 1 Cor
   15:22; Heb 7:8; 10:28; Rev 14:13 (different
   individuals), iterative in 1 Cor 15:31 (same
   person), equivalent to the fut., John 21:23;
   1 Cor 15:32.
   ἀποθνήσκω   verb, pres. act. indic. 1 pers. sg.
   {5.A.1.a} . . . . ἀποθνήσκω G599
   ἀποθνήσκωμεν   verb, pres. act. subjunc.
   1 pers. pl. {5.B.1} . . . . id.
   ἀποθνήσκωμεν   verb, pres. act. subjunc.
   1 pers. pl. {5.B.1} . . . . id.
   ἀποθνήσκων   vbl., pres. act. ptc. nom. sg.
   masc. {6.A.1} . . . . id.

ἀποθνήσκων   vbl., pres. act. ptc. nom. sg.
   masc. {6.A.1} . . . . id.
ἀποθώμεθα   verb, ²aor. mid. subjunc. 1 pers. pl.
   {5.B.1} . . . . ἀποτίθημι G659
ἀποκαθιστᾷ   verb, pres. act. indic. 3 pers. sg.
   {5.A.3.a} . . . . ἀποκαθίστημι G600
ἀποκαθιστάνει   verb, pres. act. indic. 3 pers.
   sg. {5.A.3.a} . . . . id.
ἀποκαθιστάνεις   verb, pres. act. indic. 2 pers.
   sg. {5.A.3.a} . . . . id.
G600 **ἀποκαθίστημι** (ἀποκαθιστάνω)   (1) *I set up*
   again, I restore to its original position or *condi-*
   tion; (2) hence, *I restore, give back.*
   ἀποκαλύπτεσθαι   vbl., pres. pass. inf.
   {6.B.1} . . . . ἀποκαλύπτω G601
   ἀποκαλύπτεται   verb, pres. pass. indic. 3 pers.
   sg. {5.A.1.d} . . . . id.
G601 **ἀποκαλύπτω**   *I unveil, reveal* (correlative to
   μυστήριον, *secret*).
   ἀποκαλυφθῇ   verb, aor. pass. subjunc. 3 pers. sg.
   {5.B.1} . . . . ἀποκαλύπτω G601
   ἀποκαλυφθῆναι   vbl., aor. pass. inf. {6.B.1} . . . id.
   ἀποκαλυφθήσεται   verb, fut. pass. indic.
   3 pers. sg. {5.A.1.d} . . . . id.
   ἀποκαλυφθῶσιν   verb, aor. pass. subjunc.
   3 pers. pl. {5.B.1} . . . . id.
   ἀποκαλύψαι   vbl., aor. act. inf. {6.B.1} . . . . . . id.
   ἀποκαλύψει   noun, dat. sg. fem. {2.C} ἀποκάλυψις G602
   ἀποκαλύψει   verb, fut. act. indic. 3 pers. sg.
   {5.A.1.a} . . . . ἀποκαλύπτω G601
   ἀποκαλύψεις   noun, acc. pl. fem.
   {2.C} . . . . ἀποκάλυψις G602
   ἀποκαλύψεων   noun, gen. pl. fem. {2.C} . . . . . id.
   ἀποκαλύψεως   noun, gen. sg. fem. {2.C} . . . . . id.
   ἀποκάλυψιν   noun, acc. sg. fem. {2.C} . . . . id.
G602 **ἀποκάλυψις**, -εως, ἡ   *an unveiling, uncover-*
   ing, revealing.
   ἀποκάλυψις   noun, nom. sg. fem.
   {2.C} . . . . ἀποκάλυψις G602
G603 **ἀποκαραδοκία**, -ας, ἡ   *eager expectation*
   (perhaps coined by Paul).
   ἀποκαραδοκία   noun, nom. sg. fem.
   {2.A} . . . . ἀποκαραδοκία G603
   ἀποκαραδοκίαν   noun, acc. sg. fem. {2.A} . . . . id.
   ἀποκαταλλάξαι   vbl., aor. act. inf.
   {6.B.1} . . . . ἀποκαταλλάσσω G604
   ἀποκαταλλάξῃ   verb, aor. act. subjunc. 3 pers.
   sg. {5.B.1} . . . . id.
G604 **ἀποκαταλλάσσω**   *I reconcile.*
   ἀποκατασταθῶ   verb, aor. pass. subjunc. 1 pers.
   sg. {5.B.3} . . . . ἀποκαθίστημι G600
   ἀποκαταστάσεως   noun, gen. sg. fem.
   {2.C} . . . . ἀποκατάστασις G605
G605 **ἀποκατάστασις**, -εως, ἡ   *reestablishment,*
   restoration.
   ἀποκαταστήσει   verb, fut. act. indic. 3 pers. sg.
   {5.A.1} . . . . ἀποκαθίστημι G600
   ἀποκατεστάθη   verb, aor. pass. indic. 3 pers.
   sg. {5.A.1} . . . . id.

ἀποκατήλλαξεν verb, aor. act. indic. 3 pers. sg.
{5.A.1.b} . . . . ἀποκαταλλάσσω G604
ἀποκατιστάνει verb, pres. act. indic. 3 pers. sg.
{5.A.3.a} . . . . ἀποκαθίστημι G600
G606 ἀπόκειμαι I have been put away, I am stored.
ἀποκειμένην vbl., pres. mid./pass. ptc. acc. sg.
fem. {6.A.3} . . . . ἀπόκειμαι G606
ἀπόκειται verb, pres. mid./pass. indic. 3 pers.
sg. {5.A.3.a} . . . . id.
ἀποκεκρυμμένην vbl., perf. pass. ptc. acc. sg. fem.
{6.A.1.b} . . . . ἀποκρύπτω G613
ἀποκεκρυμμένον vbl., perf. pass. ptc. acc. sg.
neut. {6.A.1.b} . . . . id.
ἀποκεκρυμμένου vbl., perf. pass. ptc. gen. sg.
neut. {6.A.1.b} . . . . id.
ἀποκεκυλισμένον vbl., perf. pass. ptc. acc. sg.
masc. {6.A.1.b} . . . . ἀποκυλίω G617
ἀποκεκύλισται verb, perf. pass. indic. 3 pers.
sg. {5.A.1.f} . . . . id.
G607 ἀποκεφαλίζω I behead.
ἀποκλείσῃ verb, aor. act. subjunc. 3 pers. sg.
{5.B.1} . . . . ἀποκλείω G608
G608 ἀποκλείω I shut.
G609 ἀποκόπτω (1) I cut of, I cut loose; (2) I emasculate, castrate (Gal 5:12, where mid. = pass.,
probably).
ἀπόκοψον verb, aor. act. impv. 2 pers. sg.
{5.D.1} . . . . ἀποκόπτω G609
ἀποκόψονται verb, fut. mid. indic. 3 pers. pl.
{5.A.1.d} . . . . id.
ἀποκριθείς vbl., aor. pass. ptc. nom. sg. masc.
{6.A.1.a} . . . . ἀποκρίνομαι G611
ἀποκριθεῖσα vbl., aor. pass. ptc. nom. sg. fem.
{6.A.1.a} . . . . id.
ἀποκριθέν vbl., aor. pass. ptc. nom. sg. neut.
{6.A.1.a} . . . . id.
ἀποκριθέντες vbl., aor. pass. ptc. nom. pl.
masc. {6.A.1.a} . . . . id.
ἀποκριθῇ verb, aor. pass. subjunc. 3 pers. sg.
{5.B.1} . . . . id.
ἀποκριθῆναι vbl., aor. pass. inf. {6.B.1} . . . . . id.
ἀποκριθήσεται verb, fut. pass. indic. 3 pers.
sg. {5.A.1.d} . . . . id.
ἀποκριθήσονται verb, fut. pass. indic. 3 pers.
pl. {5.A.1.d} . . . . id.
ἀποκρίθητε verb, aor. pass. impv. 2 pers. pl.
{5.D.1} . . . . id.
ἀποκριθῆτε verb, aor. pass. subjunc. 2 pers. pl.
{5.B.1} . . . . id.
ἀποκριθῶσι verb, aor. pass. subjunc. 3 pers. pl.
{5.B.1} . . . . id.
ἀποκριθῶσιν verb, aor. pass. subjunc. 3 pers.
pl. {5.B.1} . . . . id.
G610 ἀπόκριμα, -ατος, τό an answer (of God to the
apostle's appeal, preserved in his heart).
ἀπόκριμα noun, acc. sg. neut. {2.C} . . . . ἀπόκριμα G610
ἀποκρίνεσθαι vbl., pres. mid./pass. inf.
{6.B.1} . . . . ἀποκρίνομαι G611
ἀποκρίνεται verb, pres. mid./pass. indic.
3 pers. sg. {5.A.1.d} . . . . id.

ἀποκρίνῃ verb, pres. mid./pass. indic. 2 pers.
sg. {5.A.1.d} . . . . id.
G611 ἀποκρίνομαι (1) I answer (either a spoken or
an unspoken question), ἀπεκρίθην, etc. (absent from papyri after second c. B.C.), are borrowed by NT from LXX; (2) ἀπεκρινάμην, I
uttered solemnly, Luke 3:16; John 5:17, 19; Acts
3:12; (3) I replied in a court of law, Matt 27:12;
Mark 14:61; Luke 23:9 (cf. John 5:11 var.).
ἀποκρίσει noun, dat. sg. fem. {2.C} . . . . ἀπόκρισις G612
ἀποκρίσεσιν noun, dat. pl. fem. {2.C} . . . . . . id.
ἀπόκρισιν noun, acc. sg. fem. {2.C} . . . . id.
G612 ἀπόκρισις, -εως, ἡ answering, answer (rare in
NT times).
G613 ἀποκρύπτω I hide away, conceal.
ἀπόκρυφοι adj., nom. pl. masc. {3.C} . ἀπόκρυφος G614
ἀπόκρυφον adj., nom. sg. neut. {3.C} . . . . id.
G614 ἀπόκρυφος, -ον hidden away, secret.
ἀποκτανθείς vbl., aor. pass. ptc. nom. sg. masc.
{6.A.1.a} . . . . ἀποκτείνω G615
ἀποκτανθῆναι vbl., aor. pass. inf. {6.B.1} . . . . id.
ἀποκτανθῶσι verb, aor. pass. subjunc. 3 pers.
pl. {5.B.1} . . . . id.
ἀποκτανθῶσιν verb, aor. pass. subjunc. 3 pers.
pl. {5.B.1} . . . . id.
ἀποκτεῖναι vbl., aor. act. inf. {6.B.1} . . . . id.
ἀποκτεινάντων vbl., aor. act. ptc. gen. pl.
masc. {6.A.1.a} . . . . id.
ἀποκτείνας vbl., aor. act. ptc. nom. sg. masc.
{6.A.1.a} . . . . id.
ἀποκτείνει verb, pres. act. indic. 3 pers. sg.
{5.A.1.a} . . . . id.
ἀποκτείνεσθαι vbl., pres. pass. inf. {6.B.1} . . . . id.
ἀποκτείνοντες vbl., pres. act. ptc. nom. pl.
masc. {6.A.1} . . . . id.
ἀποκτεινόντων vbl., pres. act. ptc. gen. pl.
masc. {6.A.1} . . . . id.
ἀποκτείνουσα vbl., pres. act. ptc. nom. sg.
fem. {6.A.1} . . . . id.
G615 ἀποκτείνω (ἀποκτέννω, ἀποκτεννύω) I kill.
ἀποκτείνωμεν verb, aor. act. subjunc. 1 pers. pl.
{5.B.1} . . . . ἀποκτείνω G615
ἀποκτείνωσι verb, aor. act. subjunc. 3 pers. pl.
{5.B.1} . . . . id.
ἀποκτείνωσιν verb, aor. act. subjunc. 3 pers.
pl. {5.B.1} . . . . id.
ἀποκτενεῖ verb, fut. act. indic. 3 pers. sg. {5.A.2}id.
ἀποκτένει verb, pres. act. indic. 3 pers. sg.
{5.A.1.a} . . . . id.
ἀποκτενεῖτε verb, fut. act. indic. 2 pers. pl. {5.A.2}. id.
ἀποκτένεσθαι vbl., pres. pass. inf. {6.B.1} . . . . . id.
ἀποκτέννει verb, pres. act. indic. 3 pers. sg.
{5.A.1.a} . . . . id.
ἀποκτέννεσθαι vbl., pres. pass. inf. {6.B.1} . . . . id.
ἀποκτέννοντες vbl., pres. act. ptc. nom. pl.
masc. {6.A.1} . . . . id.
ἀποκτεννόντων vbl., pres. act. ptc. gen. pl.
masc. {6.A.1} . . . . id.
ἀποκτέννουσα vbl., pres. act. ptc. nom. sg.
fem. {6.A.1} . . . . id.

ἀποκτέννυντες   vbl., pres. act. ptc. nom. pl.
  masc. {6.A.1} . . . . id.
ἀποκτένοντες   vbl., pres. act. ptc. nom. pl.
  masc. {6.A.1} . . . . id.
ἀποκτενόντων   vbl., pres. act. ptc. gen. pl.
  masc. {6.A.1} . . . . id.
ἀποκτένουσα   vbl., pres. act. ptc. nom. sg. fem.
  {6.A.1} . . . . id.
ἀποκτενοῦσι   verb, fut. act. indic. 3 pers. pl.
  {5.A.2} . . . . id.
ἀποκτενοῦσιν   verb, fut. act. indic. 3 pers. pl.
  {5.A.2} . . . . id.
ἀποκτενῶ   verb, fut. act. indic. 1 pers. sg. {5.A.2} id.
ἀποκυεῖ   verb, pres. act. indic. 3 pers. sg.
  {5.A.2} . . . . ἀποκυέω G616
ἀποκύει   verb, pres. act. indic. 3 pers. sg. {5.A.2} id.
G616 **ἀποκυέω**   *I bring forth, give birth to* (a child), a
  medical or physical word, marking the close of
  pregnancy.
ἀποκυλίσει   verb, fut. act. indic. 3 pers. sg.
  {5.A.1.a} . . . . ἀποκυλίω G617
G617 **ἀποκυλίω**   trans., *I roll away from.*
ἀπολαβεῖν   vbl., ²aor. act. inf. {6.B.1} .ἀπολαμβάνω G618
ἀπολάβῃ   verb, ²aor. act. subjunc. 3 pers. sg.
  {5.B.1} . . . . id.
ἀπολάβητε   verb, ²aor. act. subjunc. 2 pers. pl.
  {5.B.1} . . . . id.
ἀπολαβόμενος   vbl., ²aor. mid. ptc. nom. sg.
  masc. {6.A.1.b} . . . . id.
ἀπολάβωμεν   verb, ²aor. act. subjunc. 1 pers.
  pl. {5.B.1} . . . . id.
ἀπολάβωσι   verb, ²aor. act. subjunc. 3 pers. pl.
  {5.B.1} . . . . id.
ἀπολάβωσιν   verb, ²aor. act. subjunc. 3 pers.
  pl. {5.B.1} . . . . id.
ἀπολαμβάνειν   vbl., pres. act. inf. {6.B.1} . . . . id.
ἀπολαμβάνομεν   verb, pres. act. indic. 1 pers.
  pl. {5.A.1.a} . . . . id.
ἀπολαμβάνοντες   vbl., pres. act. ptc. nom. pl.
  masc. {6.A.1} . . . . id.
G618 **ἀπολαμβάνω**   (1) *I get back, I receive back;*
  (2) *I get (receive) as due (deserved);* (3) mid., *I
  draw aside, separate,* Mark 7:33.
ἀπόλαυσιν   noun, acc. sg. fem. {2.C}. . .ἀπόλαυσις G619
G619 **ἀπόλαυσις**, -εως, ἡ   *the faculty* or *experience of
  enjoyment.*
ἀπολείπεται   verb, pres. pass. indic. 3 pers. sg.
  {5.A.1.d} . . . . .ἀπολείπω G620
G620 **ἀπολείπω**   *I leave behind;* in Heb 4:6 ἀπολείπεται is impers., *it remains.*
ἀπολεῖσθε   verb, fut. mid. indic. 2 pers. pl.
  {5.A.1} . . . . .ἀπόλλυμι G622
ἀπολεῖται   verb, ²fut. mid. indic. 3 pers. sg.
  {5.A.2} . . . . id.
G621 **ἀπολείχω**   *I lick off.*
ἀπολελυμένην   vbl., perf. pass. ptc. acc. sg. fem.
  {6.A.1.b} .ἀπολύω G630
ἀπολελυμένον   vbl., perf. pass. ptc. acc. sg.
  masc. {6.A.1.b} . . . . id.

ἀπολέλυσαι   verb, perf. pass. indic. 2 pers. sg.
  {5.A.1.f} . . . . id.
ἀπολελύσθαι   vbl., perf. pass. inf. {6.B.1} . . . . . id.
ἀπολέσαι   vbl., aor. act. inf. {6.B.3} . . . . ἀπόλλυμι G622
ἀπολέσας   vbl., aor. act. ptc. nom. sg. masc.
  {6.A.3} . . . . id.
ἀπολέσει   verb, fut. act. indic. 3 pers. sg. {5.A.1} id.
ἀπολέσῃ   verb, aor. act. subjunc. 3 pers. sg.
  {5.B.3} . . . . id.
ἀπολέσητε   verb, aor. act. subjunc. 2 pers. pl.
  {5.B.3} . . . . id.
ἀπολέσθαι   vbl., ²aor. mid. inf. {6.B.3} . . . . id.
ἀπολέσουσιν   verb, fut. act. indic. 3 pers. pl.
  {5.A.1} . . . . id.
ἀπολέσω   verb, aor. act. subjunc. 1 pers. sg.
  {5.B.3} . . . . id.
ἀπολέσωμεν   verb, aor. act. subjunc. 1 pers. pl.
  {5.B.3} . . . . id.
ἀπολέσωσι   verb, aor. act. subjunc. 3 pers. pl.
  {5.B.3} . . . . id.
ἀπολέσωσιν   verb, aor. act. subjunc. 3 pers. pl.
  {5.B.3} . . . . id.
ἀπολήμψεσθε   verb, fut. mid. indic. 2 pers. pl.
  {5.A.1.d} . . . . .ἀπολαμβάνω G618
ἀπόληται   verb, ²aor. mid. subjunc. 3 pers. sg.
  {5.B.1} . . . . .ἀπόλλυμι G622
ἀπολήψεσθε   verb, fut. mid. indic. 2 pers. pl.
  {5.A.1.d} . . . . .ἀπολαμβάνω G618
ἀπολιπόντας   vbl., ²aor. act. ptc. acc. pl. masc.
  {6.A.1.a} . . . . .ἀπολείπω G620
ἀπόλλυε   verb, pres. act. impv. 2 pers. sg.
  {5.D.3} . . . . .ἀπόλλυμι G622
ἀπολλύει   verb, pres. act. indic. 3 pers. sg.
  {5.A.3.a} . . . . id.
ἀπόλλυμαι   verb, pres. mid. indic. 1 pers. sg.
  {5.A.3.a} . . . . id.
ἀπολλύμεθα   verb, pres. mid. indic. 1 pers. pl.
  {5.A.3.a} . . . . id.
ἀπολλυμένην   vbl., pres. mid. ptc. acc. sg. fem.
  {6.A.3} . . . . id.
ἀπολλύμενοι   vbl., pres. mid./pass. ptc. nom.
  pl. masc. {6.A.3} . . . . id.
ἀπολλυμένοις   vbl., pres. mid./pass. ptc. dat.
  pl. masc. {6.A.3} . . . . id.
ἀπολλυμένου   vbl., pres. mid. ptc. gen. sg.
  neut. {6.A.3} . . . . id.
G622 **ἀπόλλυμι**   (1) *I destroy;* (2) *I lose;* (3) mid., *I
  am perishing* (the resultant death being viewed
  as certain).
ἀπόλλυνται   verb, pres. pass. indic. 3 pers. pl.
  {5.A.3.a} .ἀπόλλυμι G622
ἀπόλλυται   verb, pres. pass. indic. 3 pers. sg.
  {5.A.3.a} . . . . id.
G623 **Ἀπολλύων**, -ονος, ὁ   *The Destroying One*, a
  Gk. translation of the Heb. ʾ*Abaddôn* (properly
  pres. ptc. of ἀπολλύω, cf. ἀπόλλυμι).
Ἀπολλύων   noun prop., nom. sg. masc. {2.B;
  2.D} . . . . .Ἀπολλύων G623
Ἀπολλώ   noun prop., acc. sg. masc. {2.B;
  2.D} . . . . .Ἀπολλῶς G625

Ἀπολλώ   noun prop., gen. sg. masc. {2.B; 2.D} . . id.
Ἀπολλῶ   noun prop., acc. sg. masc. {2.B; 2.D} . . id.
Ἀπολλῶ   noun prop., gen. sg. masc. {2.B; 2.D} . . id.
Ἀπολλών   noun prop., acc. sg. masc. {2.B; 2.D} . id.
Ἀπολλών   noun prop., acc. sg. masc. {2.B; 2.D} . id.
G624 **Ἀπολλωνία**, -ας, ἡ   *Apollonia*, a city of
      Macedonia.
Ἀπολλωνίαν   noun prop., acc. sg. fem. {2.A;
      2.D} . . . . Ἀπολλωνία G624
Ἀπολλώς   noun prop., nom. sg. masc. {2.B;
      2.D} . . . . Ἀπολλῶς G625
G625 **Ἀπολλῶς**, -ῶ, ὁ   *Apollos*, a Jew of Alexandria (a
      pet, familiar form of Ἀπολλώνιος).
Ἀπολλῶς   noun prop., nom. sg. masc. {2.B;
      2.D} . . . . Ἀπολλῶς G625
ἀπολογεῖσθαι   vbl., pres. mid./pass. inf.
      {6.B.2} . . . . ἀπολογέομαι G626
G626 **ἀπολογέομαι**   *I give a defense, I defend myself*
      (esp. in a law court); it can take an obj. of what
      is said in defense.
ἀπολογηθῆναι   vbl., aor. pass. inf.
      {6.B.1} . . . . ἀπολογέομαι G626
ἀπολογήσησθε   verb, aor. mid. subjunc. 2 pers.
      pl. {5.B.1} . . . . id.
G627 **ἀπολογία**, -ας, ἡ   *a defense* (particularly in a
      law court).
ἀπολογία   noun, nom. sg. fem. {2.A} . . . . ἀπολογία G627
ἀπολογίᾳ   noun, dat. sg. fem. {2.A} . . . . id.
ἀπολογίαν   noun, acc. sg. fem. {2.A} . . . . id.
ἀπολογίας   noun, gen. sg. fem. {2.A} . . . . id.
ἀπολογοῦμαι   verb, pres. mid./pass. indic. 1 pers.
      sg. {5.A.2} . . . . ἀπολογέομαι G626
ἀπολογούμεθα   verb, pres. mid./pass. indic.
      1 pers. pl. {5.A.2} . . . . id.
ἀπολογουμένου   vbl., pres. mid./pass. ptc. gen.
      sg. masc. {6.A.2} . . . . id.
ἀπολογουμένων   vbl., pres. mid./pass. ptc.
      gen. pl. masc. {6.A.2} . . . . id.
ἀπολομένου   vbl., ²aor. mid. ptc. gen. sg. masc.
      {6.A.3} . . . . ἀπόλλυμι G622
ἀπολοῦνται   verb, fut. mid. indic. 3 pers. pl.
      {5.A.2} . . . . id.
ἀπόλουσαι   verb, aor. mid. impv. 2 pers. sg.
      {5.D.1} . . . . ἀπολούω G628
G628 **ἀπολούω**   (1) *I wash off*; (2) mid. *I wash away*
      (my sins, in baptism).
ἀπολύει   verb, pres. act. indic. 3 pers. sg.
      {5.A.1.a} . . . . ἀπολύω G630
ἀπολύειν   vbl., pres. act. inf. {6.B.1} . . . . id.
ἀπολύεις   verb, pres. act. indic. 2 pers. sg.
      {5.A.1.a} . . . . id.
ἀπολύετε   verb, pres. act. impv. 2 pers. pl.
      {5.D.1} . . . . id.
ἀπολυθέντες   vbl., aor. pass. ptc. nom. pl.
      masc. {6.A.1.a} . . . . id.
ἀπολυθήσεσθε   verb, fut. pass. indic. 2 pers.
      pl. {5.A.1.d} . . . . id.
ἀπολυθῆτε   verb, aor. pass. subjunc. 2 pers. pl.
      {5.B.1} . . . . id.
ἀπολῦσαι   vbl., aor. act. inf. {6.B.1} . . . . id.

ἀπολύσας   vbl., aor. act. ptc. nom. sg. masc.
      {6.A.1.a} . . . . id.
ἀπολύσασα   vbl., aor. act. ptc. nom. sg. fem.
      {6.A.1.a} . . . . id.
ἀπολύσῃ   verb, aor. act. subjunc. 3 pers. sg.
      {5.B.1} . . . . id.
ἀπολύσῃς   verb, aor. act. subjunc. 2 pers. sg.
      {5.B.1} . . . . id.
ἀπολύσητε   verb, aor. act. subjunc. 2 pers. pl.
      {5.B.1} . . . . id.
ἀπόλυσον   verb, aor. act. impv. 2 pers. sg.
      {5.D.1} . . . . id.
ἀπολύσω   verb, aor. act. subjunc. 1 pers. sg.
      {5.B.1} . . . . id.
ἀπολύσω   verb, fut. act. indic. 1 pers. sg.
      {5.A.1.a} . . . . id.
ἀπολυτρώσεως   noun, gen. sg. fem.
      {2.C} . . . . ἀπολύτρωσις G629
ἀπολύτρωσιν   noun, acc. sg. fem. {2.C} . . . . . . id.
G629 **ἀπολύτρωσις**, -εως, ἡ   *ransoming, deliverance,
      liberation* (from captivity), *ransoming away,
      emancipation, manumission* (of a slave by his
      master); the idea of payment, though orig.
      present, seems wholly to have disappeared in
      NT.
ἀπολύτρωσις   noun, nom. sg. fem.
      {2.C} . . . . ἀπολύτρωσις G629
G630 **ἀπολύω**   (1) *I let loose, set free, release, permit
      to depart*; (2) mid., *I withdraw myself, depart*,
      Acts 28:25.
ἀπολύων   vbl., pres. act. ptc. nom. sg. masc.
      {6.A.1} . . . . ἀπολύω G630
ἀπολῶ   verb, fut. act. indic. 1 pers. sg.
      {5.A.1} . . . . ἀπόλλυμι G622
ἀπολωλός   vbl., ²perf. act. ptc. acc. sg. neut.
      {6.A.3} . . . . id.
ἀπολωλότα   vbl., ²perf. act. ptc. acc. pl. neut.
      {6.A.3} . . . . id.
ἀπολωλώς   vbl., ²perf. act. ptc. nom. sg. masc.
      {6.A.3} . . . . id.
ἀπόλωνται   verb, ²aor. mid. subjunc. 3 pers. pl.
      {5.B.1} . . . . id.
ἀπομασσόμεθα   verb, pres. mid. indic. 1 pers. pl.
      {5.A.1.d} . . . . ἀπομάσσω G631
G631 **ἀπομάσσω**   mid. *I wipe off myself* (on to
      another).
ἀπονέμοντες   vbl., pres. act. ptc. nom. pl. masc.
      {6.A.1} . . . . ἀπονέμω G632
G632 **ἀπονέμω**   *I apportion, render* (as due).
G633 **ἀπονίπτω** (ἀπονίζω)   *I wash dirt off.*
ἀπόντες   vbl., pres. act. ptc. nom. pl. masc.
      {7.C.1} . . . . ἄπειμι¹ G548
G634 **ἀποπίπτω**   *I fall away* (from), *I fall off.*
ἀποπλανᾶν   vbl., pres. act. inf. {6.B.2}. ἀποπλανάω G635
ἀποπλανᾶν   vbl., pres. act. inf. {6.B.2} . . . . id.
G635 **ἀποπλανάω**   *I cause to wander astray*; 1 Tim
      6:10 (aor. pass.), *I have wandered away.*
ἀποπλεῖν   vbl., pres. act. inf. {6.B.2} . . . . ἀποπλέω G636
ἀποπλεύσαντες   vbl., aor. act. ptc. nom. pl.
      masc. {6.A.2} . . . . id.

G636 **ἀποπλέω**   *I sail away.*

G378†‡ **ἀποπληρόω**   *I fulfill.* Var. for ἀναπληρόω, Gal. 6:2.

G637 **ἀποπλύνω**   *I wash off or out.*

G638 **ἀποπνίγω**   (1) *I choke, drown;* (2) *I stop the growth of.*
ἀπορεῖσθαι   vbl., pres. mid. inf. {6.B.2} . . . ἀπορέω *G639*

G639 **ἀπορέω**   esp. mid., *I am in difficulties, I am at my wits' end* (lit. *I lose the way*).

G640 **ἀπορία**, -ας, ἡ   *state of difficulty, distress.*
ἀπορία   noun, dat. sg. fem. {2.A} . . . . ἀπορία *G640*

G641 **ἀπορίπτω** (ἀπορρίπτω)   *I throw away* from, *I throw overboard.*
ἀπορίψαντας   vbl., aor. act. ptc. acc. pl. masc. {6.A.1.a} . . . . ἀπορίπτω *G641*
ἀποροῦμαι   verb, pres. mid. indic. 1 pers. sg. {5.A.2} . . . . ἀπορέω *G639*
ἀπορούμενοι   vbl., pres. mid. ptc. nom. pl. masc. {6.A.2} . . . . id.
ἀπορούμενος   vbl., pres. mid. ptc. nom. sg. masc. {6.A.2} . . . . id.
ἀπορρίψαντας   vbl., aor. act. ptc. acc. pl. masc. {6.A.1.a} . . . . ἀπορίπτω *G641*

G642 **ἀπορφανίζω**   *I separate from* someone.
ἀπορφανισθέντες   vbl., aor. pass. ptc. nom. pl. masc. {6.A.1.a} . . . . ἀπορφανίζω *G642*

G643 **ἀποσκευάζω**   mid., *I pack up baggage.*
ἀποσκευασάμενοι   vbl., aor. mid. ptc. nom. pl. masc. {6.A.1.b} . . . . ἀποσκευάζω *G643*

G644 **ἀποσκίασμα**, -ατος, τό   either *a shadow cast* by an object, or *a faint image* or *copy* of an object.
ἀποσκίασμα   noun, nom. sg. neut. {2.C} . . . . ἀποσκίασμα *G644*
ἀποσπᾶν   vbl., pres. act. inf. {6.B.2} . . . . ἀποσπάω *G645*
ἀποσπᾶν   vbl., pres. act. inf. {6.B.2} . . . . id.
ἀποσπασθέντας   vbl., aor. pass. ptc. acc. pl. masc. {6.A.1.a} . . . . id.

G645 **ἀποσπάω**   (1) lit. *I wrench away from, I drag away;* (2) but perhaps sometimes in the well attested weakened sense, *I withdraw.*
ἀποσταλέντι   vbl., ²aor. pass. ptc. dat. sg. neut. {6.A.1.a} . . . . ἀποστέλλω *G649*
ἀπεσταλῶσι   verb, ²aor. pass. subjunc. 3 pers. pl. {5.B.1} . . . . id.
ἀπεσταλῶσιν   verb, ²aor. pass. subjunc. 3 pers. pl. {5.B.1} . . . . id.
ἀποστάντα   vbl., ²aor. act. ptc. acc. sg. masc. {6.A.3} . . . . ἀφίστημι *G868*
ἀποστάς   vbl., ²aor. act. ptc. nom. sg. masc. {6.A.3} . . . . id.

G646 **ἀποστασία**, -ας, ἡ   *a revolting, revolt,* esp. religious *apostasy.*
ἀποστασία   noun, nom. sg. fem. {2.A}   ἀποστασία *G646*
ἀποστασίαν   noun, acc. sg. fem. {2.A} . . . . . . id.

G647 **ἀποστάσιον**, -ου, τό   *divorce.*
ἀποστάσιον   noun, acc. sg. neut. {2.B} ἀποστάσιον *G647*
ἀποστασίου   noun, gen. sg. neut. {2.B} . . . . . . id.

G648 **ἀποστεγάζω**   *I unroof, take the roof off.*
ἀποστεῖλαι   vbl., aor. act. inf. {6.B.1} . . ἀποστέλλω *G649*

ἀποστείλαντα   vbl., aor. act. ptc. acc. sg. masc. {6.A.1.a} . . . . id.
ἀποστείλαντας   vbl., aor. act. ptc. acc. pl. masc. {6.A.1.a} . . . . id.
ἀποστείλαντες   vbl., aor. act. ptc. nom. pl. masc. {6.A.1.a} . . . . id.
ἀποστείλας   vbl., aor. act. ptc. nom. sg. masc. {6.A.1.a} . . . . id.
ἀποστείλῃ   verb, aor. act. subjunc. 3 pers. sg. {5.B.1} . . . . id.
ἀπόστειλον   verb, aor. act. impv. 2 pers. sg. {5.D.1} . . . . id.
ἀποστείλω   verb, aor. act. subjunc. 1 pers. sg. {5.B.1} . . . . id.
ἀποστελεῖ   verb, fut. act. indic. 3 pers. sg. {5.A.2} . . . . id.
ἀποστέλλει   verb, pres. act. indic. 3 pers. sg. {5.A.1.a} . . . . id.
ἀποστέλλειν   vbl., pres. act. inf. {6.B.1} . . . . . . id.
ἀποστέλλῃ   verb, pres. act. subjunc. 3 pers. sg. {5.B.1} . . . . id.
ἀποστελλόμενα   vbl., pres. pass. ptc. nom. pl. neut. {6.A.1} . . . . id.
ἀποστέλλουσι   verb, pres. act. indic. 3 pers. pl. {5.A.1.a} . . . . id.
ἀποστέλλουσιν   verb, pres. act. indic. 3 pers. pl. {5.A.1.a} . . . . id.

G649 **ἀποστέλλω**   (1) *I send away, commission;* (2) *I put forth,* Mark 4:29.
ἀποστέλλω   verb, pres. act. indic. 1 pers. sg. {5.A.1.a} . . . . ἀποστέλλω *G649*
ἀποστελῶ   verb, fut. act. indic. 1 pers. sg. {5.A.2} . . . . id.
ἀποστερεῖσθε   verb, pres. pass. indic. 2 pers. pl. {5.A.2} . . . . ἀποστερέω *G650*
ἀποστερεῖτε   verb, pres. act. impv. 2 pers. pl. {5.D.2} . . . . id.
ἀποστερεῖτε   verb, pres. act. indic. 2 pers. pl. {5.A.2} . . . . id.

G650 **ἀποστερέω**   *I deprive one of something, I rob;* absol. in Mark 10:19; 1 Cor 7:5 (var.).
ἀποστερήσῃς   verb, aor. act. subjunc. 2 pers. sg. {5.B.1} . . . . ἀποστερέω *G650*
ἀποστῇ   verb, ²aor. act. subjunc. 3 pers. sg. {5.B.3} . . . . ἀφίστημι *G868*
ἀποστῆναι   vbl., ²aor. act. inf. {6.B.3} . . . . . . id.
ἀποστήσονται   verb, fut. mid. indic. 3 pers. pl. {5.A.1} . . . . id.
ἀπόστητε   verb, ²aor. act. impv. 2 pers. pl. {5.D.3} . . . . id.
ἀποστήτω   verb, ²aor. act. impv. 3 pers. sg. {5.D.3} . . . . id.

G651 **ἀποστολή**, -ῆς, ἡ   *commission, duty of* ἀπόστολος (apostle), apostle ship.
ἀποστολήν   noun, acc. sg. fem. {2.A} . . ἀποστολή *G651*
ἀποστολῆς   noun, gen. sg. fem. {2.A} . . . . id.
ἀπόστολοι   noun, nom. pl. masc. {2.B} .ἀπόστολος *G652*
ἀπόστολοι   noun, voc. pl. masc. {2.B} .ἀπόστολος *G652*
ἀποστόλοις   noun, dat. pl. masc. {2.B} . . . . . . id.
ἀπόστολον   noun, acc. sg. masc. {2.B} . . . . id.

G652 **ἀπόστολος**, -ου, ὁ *a messenger, an envoy, a delegate,* one commissioned by another to represent him in some way, esp. a man sent out by Jesus Christ Himself to preach the Gospel, *an apostle.*
ἀπόστολος noun, nom. sg. masc. {2.B}.ἀπόστολος G652
ἀποστόλου noun, gen. sg. masc. {2.B} . . . . id.
ἀποστόλους noun, acc. pl. masc. {2.B} . . . . id.
ἀποστόλων noun, gen. pl. masc. {2.B} . . . . id.
ἀποστοματίζειν vbl., pres. act. inf.
    {6.B.1} . . . . ἀποστοματίζω G653
G653 **ἀποστοματίζω** *I draw out* by questioning (literary, from ἀπὸ στόματος).
ἀποστραφῇς verb, ²aor. pass. subjunc. 2 pers. sg.
    {5.B.1} . . . . ἀποστρέφω G654
ἀποστρέφειν vbl., pres. act. inf. {6.B.1} . . . . . . id.
ἀποστρεφόμενοι vbl., pres. mid. ptc. nom. pl.
    masc. {6.A.1} . . . . id.
ἀποστρεφομένων vbl., pres. mid. ptc. gen. pl.
    masc. {6.A.1} . . . . id.
ἀποστρέφοντα vbl., pres. act. ptc. acc. sg.
    masc. {6.A.1} . . . . id.
G654 **ἀποστρέφω** (1) *I turn away (from);* (2) mid., *I turn myself away from;* (3) met., *I pervert,* Luke 23:14; (trans., seems mostly literary).
ἀποστρέψει verb, fut. act. indic. 3 pers. sg.
    {5.A.1.a} . . . . ἀποστρέφω G654
ἀπόστρεψον verb, aor. act. impv. 2 pers. sg.
    {5.D.1} . . . . id.
ἀποστρέψουσιν verb, fut. act. indic. 3 pers.
    pl. {5.A.1.a} . . . . id.
G655 **ἀποστυγέω** *I shrink from* (with horror).
ἀποστυγοῦντες vbl., pres. act. ptc. nom. pl. masc.
    {6.A.2} . . . . .ἀποστυγέω G655
ἀποσυνάγωγοι adj., nom. pl. masc.
    {3.C} . . . . ἀποσυνάγωγος G656
G656 **ἀποσυνάγωγος**, -ον *away from the synagogue, expelled the synagogue, excommunicated.*
ἀποσυνάγωγος adj., nom. sg. masc.
    {3.C} . . . . ἀποσυνάγωγος G656
ἀποσυναγώγους adj., acc. pl. masc. {3.C} . . . . . id.
ἀποταξάμενος vbl., aor. mid. ptc. nom. sg. masc.
    {6.A.1.b} . . . . ἀποτάσσω G657
ἀποτάξασθαι vbl., aor. mid. inf. {6.B.1} . . . . . . id.
ἀποτάσσεται verb, pres. mid. indic. 3 pers. sg.
    {5.A.1.d} . . . . id.
G657 **ἀποτάσσω** mid. (1) *I give parting instructions;* (2) *I say farewell (good bye), I take leave;* (3) *renounce*
ἀποτελεσθεῖσα vbl., aor. pass. ptc. nom. sg. fem.
    {6.A.1.a} . . . . .ἀποτελέω G658
G658 **ἀποτελέω** (1) *I complete, accomplish,* Luke 13:32; (2) *I form fully,* Jas 1:15.
ἀποτελῶ verb, pres. act. indic. 1 pers. sg.
    {5.A.2} . . . . .ἀποτελέω G658
G659 **ἀποτίθημι** mid. (1) *I put off (away), cast off (away) from myself;* (2) hence, *I put, store (in).*
ἀποτινάξας vbl., aor. act. ptc. nom. sg. masc.
    {6.A.1.a} . . . . ἀποτινάσσω G660

ἀποτινάξατε verb, aor. act. impv. 2 pers. pl.
    {5.D.1} . . . . id.
ἀποτινάσσετε verb, pres. act. impv. 2 pers. pl.
    {5.D.1} . . . . id.
G660 **ἀποτινάσσω** *I shake off.*
G661 **ἀποτίνω** *I repay, pay what is due* (by way of punishment or fine).
ἀποτίσω verb, fut. act. indic. 1 pers. sg.
    {5.A.1.a} . . . . .ἀποτίνω G661
ἀποτολμᾷ verb, pres. act. indic. 3 pers. sg.
    {5.A.2} . . . . .ἀποτολμάω G662
G662 **ἀποτολμάω** *I break out boldly* (literary).
G663 **ἀποτομία**, -ας, ἡ *peremptoriness, inexorableness, harshness, severity* (lit. *sheerness,* of a rock).
ἀποτομία noun, nom. sg. fem. {2.A} . . . .ἀποτομία G663
ἀποτομίαν noun, acc. sg. fem. {2.A} . . . . id.
G664 **ἀποτόμως** adv., *sharply, severely.*
ἀποτόμως adv. {3.F} . . . . ἀποτόμως G664
ἀποτρέπου verb, pres. mid. impv. 2 pers. sg.
    {5.D.1} . . . . ἀποτρέπω G665
G665 **ἀποτρέπω** mid. *I turn myself away from.*
G666 **ἀπουσία**, -ας, ἡ *absence.*
ἀπουσίᾳ noun, dat. sg. fem. {2.A} . . . . . . ἀπουσία G666
ἀποφέρεσθαι vbl., pres. pass. inf. {6.B.1} ἀποφέρω G667
G667 **ἀποφέρω** *I carry, bear away* (sometimes with violence, as Mark 15:1).
ἀποφεύγοντας vbl., pres. act. ptc. acc. pl. masc.
    {6.A.1} . . . . ἀποφεύγω G668
G668 **ἀποφεύγω** *I flee from.*
ἀποφθέγγεσθαι vbl., pres. mid./pass. inf.
    {6.B.1} . . . . ἀποφθέγγομαι G669
G669 **ἀποφθέγγομαι** *I utter forth, speak out.*
ἀποφθέγγομαι verb, pres. mid./pass. indic. 1 pers.
    sg. {5.A.1.d} . . . . .ἀποφθέγγομαι G669
G670 **ἀποφορτίζομαι** *I discharge my cargo.*
ἀποφορτιζόμενον vbl., pres. mid./pass. ptc. nom.
    sg. neut. {6.A.1} . . . . .ἀποφορτίζομαι G670
ἀποφυγόντας vbl., ²aor. act. ptc. acc. pl. masc.
    {6.A.1.a} . . . . ἀποφεύγω G668
ἀποφυγόντες vbl., ²aor. act. ptc. nom. pl. masc.
    {6.A.1.a} . . . . id.
ἀποχρήσει noun, dat. sg. fem. {2.C} . . .ἀπόχρησις G671
G671 **ἀπόχρησις**, -εως, ἡ *using up.*
ἀποχωρεῖ verb, pres. act. indic. 3 pers. sg.
    {5.A.2} . . . . .ἀποχωρέω G672
ἀποχωρεῖτε verb, pres. act. impv. 2 pers. pl.
    {5.D.2} . . . . id.
G672 **ἀποχωρέω** *I go away, depart.*
ἀποχωρήσας vbl., aor. act. ptc. nom. sg. masc.
    {6.A.2} . . . . .ἀποχωρέω G672
G673 **ἀποχωρίζω** mid. *I separate myself from.*
ἀποχωρισθῆναι vbl., aor. pass. inf.
    {6.B.1} . . . . ἀποχωρίζω G673
ἀποψυχόντων vbl., pres. act. ptc. gen. pl. masc.
    {6.A.1} . . . . ἀποψύχω G674
G674 **ἀποψύχω** *I faint* or *I die.*
G675 **Ἄππιος** *Appius* (censor 312 B.C.), after whom the township *Appi Forum* (Ἀππίου Φόρον) on the Appian Way, 43 Roman miles from Rome, was named (Acts 28:15).

Ἀππίου   noun prop., gen. sg. masc. {2.B;
  2.D}. . . . . .Ἄππιος G675
ἀπρόσιτον   adj., acc. sg. neut. {3.C} . . . . ἀπρόσιτος G676
G676 ἀπρόσιτος, -ον   unapproachable.
ἀπρόσκοποι   adj., nom. pl. masc.
  {3.C} . . . . ἀπρόσκοπος G677
ἀπρόσκοπον   adj., acc. sg. fem. {3.C}. . . . . id.
G677 ἀπρόσκοπος, -ον   (free from hurt or harm),
  hence, not offending, not causing offence,
  blameless.
G678 ἀπροσωπολήμπτως   adv., without any preference (undue favor, partiality) for a person
  (literary and Jewish).
ἀπροσωπολήμπτως   adv. {3.F}ἀπροσωπολήμπτως G678
ἀπροσωπολήπτως   adv. {3.F} . . . . id.
G679 ἄπταιστος, -ον   not stumbling (literary and
  rare).
ἀπταίστους   adj., acc. pl. masc. {3.C}. . . ἄπταιστος G679
ἅπτει   verb, pres. act. indic. 3 pers. sg. {5.A.1.a}ἅπτω G681
ἅπτεσθαι   vbl., pres. mid. inf. {6.B.1} . . . . ἅπτομαι G680
ἅπτεσθε   verb, pres. mid. impv. 2 pers. pl.
  {5.D.1}. . . . . id.
ἅπτεται   verb, pres. mid. indic. 3 pers. sg.
  {5.A.1.d} . . . . id.
ἅπτηται   verb, pres. mid. subjunc. 3 pers. sg.
  {5.B.1} . . . . id.
G680 ἅπτομαι   mid. of ἅπτω, with gen. I lay hold of,
  I cling to (eagerly).
ἅπτου   verb, pres. mid. impv. 2 pers. sg.
  {5.D.1}. . . . . .ἅπτομαι G680
G681 ἅπτω   act. I light, kindle.
G682 Ἀπφία, -ας, ἡ   Apphia, a Christian lady of
  Colossae, either wife or sister of Philemon.
Ἀπφία   noun prop., dat. sg. fem. {2.A; 2.D} . .Ἀπφία G682
ἀπωθεῖσθε   verb, pres. mid./pass. indic. 2 pers. pl.
  {5.A.2}. . . . . ἀπωθέω G683
G683 ἀπωθέω   mid. I push (thrust) away from myself.
G684 ἀπώλεια, -ας, ἡ   destruction, ruin, loss.
ἀπώλεια   noun, nom. sg. fem. {2.A}. . . . .ἀπώλεια G684
ἀπωλείαις   noun, dat. pl. fem. {2.A} . . . . id.
ἀπώλειαν   noun, acc. sg. fem. {2.A} . . . . id.
ἀπωλείας   noun, gen. sg. fem. {2.A}. . . . . id.
ἀπώλεσα   verb, aor. act. indic. 1 pers. sg.
  {5.A.3.b} .ἀπόλλυμι G622
ἀπώλεσε   verb, aor. act. indic. 3 pers. sg.
  {5.A.3.b} . . . . id.
ἀπώλεσεν   verb, aor. act. indic. 3 pers. sg.
  {5.A.3.b} . . . . id.
ἀπώλετο   verb, ²aor. mid. indic. 3 pers. sg.
  {5.A.3.b} . . . . id.
ἀπώλλυντο   verb, impf. mid. indic. 3 pers. pl.
  {5.A.3.a} . . . . id.
ἀπώλοντο   verb, ²aor. mid. indic. 3 pers. pl.
  {5.A.3.b} . . . . id.
ἀπών   vbl., pres. act. ptc. nom. sg. masc.
  {7.C.1}. . . . . ἄπειμι¹ G548
ἀπωσάμενοι   vbl., aor. mid. ptc. nom. pl. masc.
  {6.A.2}. . . . . ἀπωθέω G683
ἀπώσαντο   verb, aor. mid. indic. 3 pers. pl.
  {5.A.1}. . . . . id.

ἀπώσατο   verb, aor. mid. indic. 3 pers. sg.
  {5.A.1}. . . . . id.
Ἄρ   noun prop. . . . . Ἁρμαγεδών G717
G685 ἀρά, -ᾶς, ἡ   cursing, a curse.
G686 ἄρα   an inferential particle, then, therefore;
  found also in combination with other
  particles, such as γε and οὖν, etc.; εἰ ἄρα, if
  perchance, Mark 11:13, etc.
ἄρα   part. . . . . .ἄρα G686
G687 ἆρα   a particle asking a question, to which a
  neg. answer is expected.
ἆρα   part., interrog. . . . . .ἆρα G687
Ἄραβες   noun prop., nom. pl. masc. {2.C;
  2.D}. . . . . Ἄραψ G690
G688 Ἀραβία, -ας   Arabia, the district south of
  Palestine.
Ἀραβίᾳ   noun prop., dat. sg. fem. {2.A; 2.D}Ἀραβία G688
Ἀραβίαν   noun prop., acc. sg. fem. {2.A; 2.D} . . id.
ἄραγε   part. . . . . .ἄρα G686
ἆραι   vbl., aor. act. inf. {6.B.1} . . . . .αἴρω G142
G689 Ἀράμ, ὁ   Aram., son of Esrom and father of
  Aminadab (Heb.).
Ἀράμ   noun prop. . . . . Ἀράμ G689
ἄραντες   vbl., aor. act. ptc. nom. pl. masc.
  {6.A.1.a} . . . . .αἴρω G142
ἀρᾶς   noun, gen. sg. fem. {2.A}. . . . . .ἀρά G685
ἄρας   vbl., aor. act. ptc. nom. sg. masc.
  {6.A.1.a} . . . . .αἴρω G142
ἄρατε   verb, aor. act. impv. 2 pers. pl. {5.D.1} . . . id.
ἀράτω   verb, aor. act. impv. 3 pers. sg. {5.D.1} . . id.
ἄραφος   adj., nom. sg. masc. {3.C} . . . . . ἄρραφος G729
G690 Ἄραψ, βος, ὁ   an Arabian.
ἀργαί   adj., nom. pl. fem. {3.A}. . . . . .ἀργός G692
ἀργεῖ   verb, pres. act. indic. 3 pers. sg. {5.A.2}.ἀργέω G691
G691 ἀργέω   I am idle (unemployed, without occupa-
  tion); generally, outside NT, of necessity, and
  not blame worthily.
ἀργή   adj., nom. sg. fem. {3.A} . . . . .ἀργός G692
ἀργοί   adj., nom. pl. masc. {3.A}. . . . . id.
ἀργόν   adj., acc. sg. neut. {3.A}. . . . . id.
ἀργόν   adj., nom. sg. neut. {3.A}. . . . . id.
G692 ἀργός, -ή, -όν   (1) idle, lazy; (2) thoughtless,
  Matt 12:36.
ἀργούς   adj., acc. pl. masc. {3.A}. . . . . .ἀργός G692
ἀργυρᾶ   adj., acc. pl. neut. {3.A}. . . . . . ἀργυροῦς G693‡
ἀργυρᾶ   adj., nom. pl. neut. {3.A}. . . . . id.
ἀργύρια   noun, acc. pl. neut. {2.B} . . . . . ἀργύριον G694
G694 ἀργύριον, -ου, τό   a piece of silver money
  (except 1 Cor 3:12, where silver).
ἀργύριον   noun, acc. sg. neut. {2.B} . . . . . ἀργύριον G694
ἀργύριον   noun, nom. sg. neut. {2.B} . . . . id.
ἀργυρίου   noun, gen. sg. neut. {2.B}. . . . . id.
ἀργυρίῳ   noun, dat. sg. neut. {2.B}. . . . . id.
G695 ἀργυροκόπος, -ου, ὁ   a silversmith (lit., silver
  cutter).
ἀργυροκόπος   noun, nom. sg. masc.
  {2.B} . . . . ἀργυροκόπος G695
ἄργυρον   noun, acc. sg. masc. {2.B} . . . . . ἄργυρος G696
G696 ἄργυρος, -ου, ὁ   silver as a metal (except Matt
  10:9, where silver used as money); rare in papyri.

ἄργυρος   noun, nom. sg. masc. {2.B} . . . . . ἄργυρος *G696*
ἀργύρου   noun, gen. sg. masc. {2.B} . . . . id.
G693‡ **ἀργυροῦς** (ἀργύρεος), -ᾶ, -οῦν *made of silver, silver.*
ἀργυροῦς   adj., acc. pl. masc. {3.A} . . . ἀργυροῦς *G693‡*
ἀργύρῳ   noun, dat. sg. masc. {2.B} . . . . . . ἄργυρος *G696*
ἀρεῖ   verb, fut. act. indic. 3 pers. sg. {5.A.2} . . . αἴρω *G142*
Ἄρειον   noun prop., acc. sg. masc. {2.B; 2.D} . . . . Ἄρειος Πάγος *G697*
G697 **Ἄρειος Πάγος,** ὁ *the Aeropagus,* a hill in Athens (lit. *Hill of Ares,* the Athenian war god, corresponding to Mars). As on this hill the Council of the Areopagus (ἡ ἐξ Ἀρείου Πάγου βουλή), the supreme court of Athens, had met in early times, the expression ὁ Ἄρειος Πάγος came to be used (as in Acts 17:19, 22) for the *Council of the Aeropagus,* wherever it met.
Ἀρείου   noun prop., gen. sg. masc. {2.B; 2.D} . . . . Ἄρειος Πάγος *G697*
G698 **Ἀρεοπαγίτης,** -ου, ὁ *member of the Council of the Aeropagus, an Areopagite.*
Ἀρεοπαγίτης   noun prop., nom. sg. masc. {2.A; 2.D} . . . . Ἀρεοπαγίτης *G698*
ἀρέσαι   vbl., aor. act. inf. {6.B.1} . . . . . . ἀρέσκω *G700*
ἀρεσάσης   vbl., aor. act. ptc. gen. sg. fem. {6.A.1.a} . . . . id.
ἀρέσει   verb, fut. act. indic. 3 pers. sg. {5.A.1.a} . id.
ἀρέσῃ   verb, aor. act. subjunc. 3 pers. sg. {5.B.1}. id.
G699 **ἀρεσκεία** (ἀρέσκεια), -ας, ἡ *pleasing, willing service.*
ἀρεσκείαν   noun, acc. sg. fem. {2.A} . . . . ἀρεσκεία *G699*
ἀρεσκειαν   noun, acc. sg. fem. {2.A} . . . . id.
ἀρέσκειν   vbl., pres. act. inf. {6.B.1} . . . . . . ἀρέσκω *G700*
ἀρεσκέτω   verb, pres. act. impv. 3 pers. sg. {5.D.1} . . . . id.
ἀρεσκίαν   noun, acc. sg. fem. {2.A} . . . ἀρεσκεία *G699*
ἀρέσκοντες   vbl., pres. act. ptc. nom. pl. masc. {6.A.1} . . . . ἀρέσκω *G700*
ἀρεσκόντων   vbl., pres. act. ptc. gen. pl. masc. {6.A.1} . . . . id.
G700 **ἀρέσκω** (1) *I please,* with the idea of willing service rendered to others; (2) hence almost, *I serve.*
ἀρέσκω   verb, pres. act. indic. 1 pers. sg. {5.A.1.a} . . . . ἀρέσκω *G700*
ἀρεστά   adj., acc. pl. neut. {3.A} . . . . ἀρεστός *G701*
ἀρεστόν   adj., nom. sg. neut. {3.A} . . . . id.
G701 **ἀρεστός,** -ή, -όν *pleasing, satisfactory, acceptable.*
Ἀρέτα   noun prop., gen. sg. masc. {2.A; 2.D} Ἀρέτας *G702*
Ἀρέτα   noun prop., gen. sg. masc. {2.A; 2.D} . . . id.
ἀρετάς   noun, acc. pl. fem. {2.A} . . . . ἀρετή *G703*
G702 **Ἀρέτας,** -α, ὁ *Aretas,* Aretas IV, King of the Nabataeans (Arabic *Hāritā*).
G703 **ἀρετή,** -ῆς, ἡ (1) *excellence,* particularly *moral excellence;* (2) *manifestation of power,* 2 Pet 1:3 (a word of wide significance in non-Christian ethics).
ἀρετή   noun, nom. sg. fem. {2.A} . . . . ἀρετή *G703*
ἀρετῇ   noun, dat. sg. fem. {2.A} . . . . id.

ἀρετήν   noun, acc. sg. fem. {2.A} . . . . id.
ἀρετῆς   noun, gen. sg. fem. {2.A} . . . . id.
ἄρῃ   verb, aor. act. subjunc. 3 pers. sg. {5.B.1} . . αἴρω *G142*
G704 **ἀρήν,** ἀρνός, ὁ *a lamb;* acc. pl. ἄρνας (Luke 10:3); the nom. is found only in early times, and its place is taken by ἀρνίον.
ἄρης   verb, aor. act. subjunc. 2 pers. sg. {5.B.1}. αἴρω *G142*
ἀρθῇ   verb, aor. pass. subjunc. 3 pers. sg. {5.B.1}. id.
ἀρθήσεται   verb, fut. pass. indic. 3 pers. sg. {5.A.1.d} . . . . id.
ἄρθητι   verb, aor. pass. impv. 2 pers. sg. {5.D.1} . id.
ἀρθήτω   verb, aor. pass. impv. 3 pers. sg. {5.D.1} id.
ἀρθῶσιν   verb, aor. pass. subjunc. 3 pers. pl. {5.B.1} . . . . id.
G705 **ἀριθμέω** *I number, count.*
ἀριθμῆσαι   vbl., aor. act. inf. {6.B.1} . . . . . ἀριθμέω *G705*
ἀριθμόν   noun, acc. sg. masc. {2.B} . . . . . . ἀριθμός *G706*
G706 **ἀριθμός,** -οῦ, ὁ *a number, total.*
ἀριθμός   noun, nom. sg. masc. {2.B} . . . . ἀριθμός *G706*
ἀριθμοῦ   noun, gen. sg. masc. {2.B} . . . . id.
ἀριθμῷ   noun, dat. sg. masc. {2.B} . . . . id.
G707 **Ἀριμαθαία,** -ας, ἡ *Arimathaea,* a place in Palestine, identical with Ramathaim, the birthplace of Samuel. Orig. part of Samaria, it with its surrounding district was united to Judaea under the Maccabees.
Ἀριμαθαίας   noun prop., gen. sg. fem. {2.A; 2.D} . . . . Ἀριμαθαία *G707*
Ἀριμαθαίας   noun prop., gen. sg. fem. {2.A; 2.D} . . . . id.
Ἀρίσταρχον   noun prop., acc. sg. masc. {2.B; 2.D} . . . . Ἀρίσταρχος *G708*
G708 **Ἀρίσταρχος,** -ου, ὁ *Aristarchus,* a Christian, belonging to Thessalonica in Macedonia.
Ἀρίσταρχος   noun prop., nom. sg. masc. {2.B; 2.D} . . . . Ἀρίσταρχος *G708*
Ἀριστάρχου   noun prop., gen. sg. masc. {2.B; 2.D} . . . . id.
G709 **ἀριστάω** *I breakfast.*
ἀριστερά   adj., nom. sg. fem. {3.A} . . . . ἀριστερός *G710*
G710 **ἀριστερός,** -ά, -όν *on the left hand;* ἡ ἀριστερά (understand χείρ), Matt 6:3; ἐξ ἀριστερῶν, *on the left hand.*
ἀριστερῶν   adj., gen. pl. fem. {3.A} . . . . ἀριστερός *G710*
ἀριστερῶν   adj., gen. pl. masc. {3.A} . . . . id.
ἀριστερῶν   adj., gen. pl. neut. {3.A} . . . . id.
ἀριστήσατε   verb, aor. act. impv. 2 pers. pl. {5.D.1} . . . . ἀριστάω *G709*
ἀριστήσῃ   verb, aor. act. subjunc. 3 pers. sg. {5.B.1} . . . . id.
G711 **Ἀριστόβουλος,** -ου, ὁ *Aristobulus,* a Christian in Rome.
Ἀριστοβούλου   noun prop., gen. sg. masc. {2.B; 2.D} . . . . Ἀριστόβουλος *G711*
G712 **ἄριστον,** -ου, τό *breakfast.*
ἄριστον   noun, acc. sg. neut. {2.B} . . . . . . ἄριστον *G712*
ἀρίστου   noun, gen. sg. neut. {2.B} . . . . id.
ἀρκεῖ   verb, pres. act. indic. 3 pers. sg. {5.A.2} ἀρκέω *G714*
ἀρκεῖσθε   verb, pres. pass. impv. 2 pers. pl. {5.D.2} . id.
ἀρκέσει   verb, fut. act. indic. 3 pers. sg. {5.A.1} . id.

ἀρκέσῃ   verb, aor. act. subjunc. 3 pers. sg. {5.B.1}id.
ἀρκεσθησόμεθα   verb, fut. pass. indic. 1 pers.
   pl. {5.A.1} . . . . id.
ἀρκετόν   adj., nom. sg. neut. {3.A} . . . . . . ἀρκετός G713
G713 ἀρκετός, -ή, -όν   sufficient (rare).
   ἀρκετός   adj., nom. sg. masc. {3.A} . . . . . . ἀρκετός G713
G714 ἀρκέω   (1) act. I am sufficient, I suffice; impers.
   John 14:8; (2) mid. with dat. I am content,
   satisfied (with).
G715 ἄρκος, -ου, ὁ   a bear (a later form of ἄρκτος).
   ἄρκου   noun, gen. sg. fem. {2.B} . . . . ἄρκος G715
   ἀρκούμενοι   vbl., pres. pass. ptc. nom. pl. masc.
   {6.A.2} . . . . ἀρκέω G714
   ἀρκούμενος   vbl., pres. pass. ptc. nom. sg.
   masc. {6.A.2} . . . . id.
   ἀρκοῦσιν   verb, pres. act. indic. 3 pers. pl.
   {5.A.2} . . . . id.
   ἄρκτου   noun, gen. sg. fem. {2.B} . . . . ἄρκος G715
G716 ἅρμα, -ατος, τό   a chariot.
   ἅρμα   noun, acc. sg. neut. {2.C} . . . . ἅρμα G716
   Ἁρμαγεδδών   noun prop. . . . . Ἁρμαγεδών G717
G717 Ἁρμαγεδών (Ἁρμαγεδδών, Ἁρ Μα-
   γεδών)   Armageddon. In the neighborhood
   of Megiddo the sovereignty of Palestine was
   often decided by battle. Hence, the name was
   transferred to the place of the decisive battle
   on the Day of Judgment. (Heb. har măgiddôn,
   "the hill of Megiddo.")
   Ἁρμαγεδών   noun prop. . . . . Ἁρμαγεδών G717
   ἅρματι   noun, dat. sg. neut. {2.C} . . . . ἅρμα G716
   ἅρματος   noun, gen. sg. neut. {2.C} . . . . id.
   ἁρμάτων   noun, gen. pl. neut. {2.C} . . . . id.
G718 ἁρμόζω   mid. I fit, join (the mid. indicating
   deep personal interest).
G719 ἁρμός, -οῦ, ὁ   a joint of the body.
   ἁρμῶν   noun, gen. pl. masc. {2.B} . . . . ἁρμός G719
   ἄρνας   noun, acc. pl. masc. {2.C} . . . . ἀρήν G704
   Ἀρνεί   noun prop. . . . . Ἀρνεί G689†‡
   ἀρνεῖσθαι   vbl., pres. mid./pass. inf.
   {6.B.2} . . . . ἀρνέομαι G720
G720 ἀρνέομαι   (1) I deny (a statement); (2) I repu-
   diate (a person, or belief).
   ἀρνησάμενοι   vbl., aor. mid. ptc. nom. pl. masc.
   {6.A.2} . . . . ἀρνέομαι G720
   ἀρνησάμενος   vbl., aor. mid. ptc. nom. sg.
   masc. {6.A.2} . . . . id.
   ἀρνήσασθαι   vbl., aor. mid. inf. {6.B.1} . . . . . . id.
   ἀρνησάσθω   verb, aor. mid. impv. 3 pers. sg.
   {5.D.1} . . . . id.
   ἀρνήσεται   verb, fut. mid. indic. 3 pers. sg.
   {5.A.1} . . . . id.
   ἀρνήσῃ   verb, fut. mid. indic. 2 pers. sg. {5.B.2} id.
   ἀρνήσηται   verb, aor. mid. subjunc. 3 pers. sg.
   {5.B.1} . . . . id.
   ἀρνήσομαι   verb, fut. mid. indic. 1 pers. sg.
   {5.A.1} . . . . id.
   ἀρνησόμεθα   verb, fut. mid. indic. 1 pers. pl.
   {5.A.1} . . . . id.
G689†‡ Ἀρνί (Ἀρνεί), Arni. Var. for Ἀράμ, Luke 3:33.
   Ἀρνί   noun prop. . . . . Ἀρνί G689†‡

ἀρνία   noun, acc. pl. neut. {2.B} . . . . ἀρνίον G721
G721 ἀρνίον, -ου, τό   a lamb (orig., a little lamb, but
   diminutive force was lost), see ἀρήν.
   ἀρνίον   noun, acc. sg. neut. {2.B} . . . . ἀρνίον G721
   ἀρνίον   noun, nom. sg. neut. {2.B} . . . . id.
   ἀρνίου   noun, gen. sg. neut. {2.B} . . . . id.
   ἀρνίῳ   noun, dat. sg. neut. {2.B} . . . . id.
   ἀρνούμεθα   verb, pres. mid./pass. indic. 1 pers. pl.
   {5.A.2} . . . . ἀρνέομαι G720
   ἀρνούμενοι   vbl., pres. mid./pass. ptc. nom. pl.
   masc. {6.A.2} . . . . id.
   ἀρνούμενος   vbl., pres. mid./pass. ptc. nom. sg.
   masc. {6.A.2} . . . . id.
   ἀρνουμένων   vbl., pres. mid./pass. ptc. gen. pl.
   masc. {6.A.2} . . . . id.
   ἀρνοῦνται   verb, pres. mid./pass. indic. 3 pers.
   pl. {5.A.2} . . . . id.
   ἀρξάμενοι   vbl., aor. mid. ptc. nom. pl. masc.
   {6.A.1.b} . . . . ἄρχομαι G756
   ἀρξάμενον   vbl., aor. mid. ptc. acc. sg. neut.
   {6.A.1.b} . . . . id.
   ἀρξάμενον   vbl., aor. mid. ptc. nom. sg. neut.
   {6.A.1.b} . . . . id.
   ἀρξάμενος   vbl., aor. mid. ptc. nom. sg. masc.
   {6.A.1.b} . . . . id.
   ἀρξαμένου   vbl., aor. mid. ptc. gen. sg. masc.
   {6.A.1.b} . . . . id.
   ἄρξασθαι   vbl., aor. mid. inf. {6.B.1} . . . . id.
   ἄρξεσθε   verb, fut. mid. indic. 2 pers. pl.
   {5.A.1.d} . . . . id.
   ἄρξῃ   verb, fut. mid. indic. 2 pers. sg. {5.B.1} . . id.
   ἄρξησθε   verb, aor. mid. subjunc. 2 pers. pl.
   {5.B.1} . . . . id.
   ἄρξηται   verb, aor. mid. subjunc. 3 pers. sg.
   {5.B.1} . . . . id.
   ἄρξονται   verb, fut. mid. indic. 3 pers. pl.
   {5.A.1.d} . . . . id.
   ἄρξωνται   verb, aor. mid. subjunc. 3 pers. pl.
   {5.B.1} . . . . id.
   ἆρον   verb, aor. act. impv. 2 pers. sg. {5.D.1} . . . αἴρω G142
   ἀροτριᾶν   vbl., pres. act. inf. {6.B.2} . . . . . ἀροτριάω G722
   ἀροτριᾶν   vbl., pres. act. inf. {6.B.2} . . . . id.
G722 ἀροτριάω   I plough.
   ἀροτριῶν   vbl., pres. act. ptc. nom. sg. masc.
   {6.A.2} . . . . ἀροτριάω G722
   ἀροτριῶντα   vbl., pres. act. ptc. acc. sg. masc.
   {6.A.2} . . . . id.
G723 ἄροτρον, -ου, τό   a plough.
   ἄροτρον   noun, acc. sg. neut. {2.B} . . . . . . ἄροτρον G723
   ἀροῦσι   verb, fut. act. indic. 3 pers. pl. {5.A.2} . αἴρω G142
   ἀροῦσιν   verb, fut. act. indic. 3 pers. pl. {5.A.2} . id.
   ἁρπαγέντα   vbl., ²aor. pass. ptc. acc. sg. masc.
   {6.A.1.a} . . . . ἁρπάζω G726
   ἅρπαγες   adj., nom. pl. masc. {3.E} . . . . ἅρπαξ G727
G724 ἁρπαγή, -ῆς, ἡ   robbery, robbing.
   ἁρπαγήν   noun, acc. sg. fem. {2.A} . . . . . . ἁρπαγή G724
   ἁρπαγῆς   noun, gen. sg. fem. {2.A} . . . . id.
   ἁρπαγησόμεθα   verb, ²fut. pass. indic. 1 pers. pl.
   {5.A.1.d} . . . . ἁρπάζω G726
   ἁρπαγμόν   noun, acc. sg. masc. {2.B} . . . . ἁρπαγμός G725

G725 **ἁρπαγμός**, -οῦ, ὁ   either (1) *snatching, robbery, the action of plundering, rapacity, self-aggrandizement*, or (2) *a thing to be snatched, plunder, prey, booty, a prize, spoil.*
ἁρπάζει   verb, pres. act. indic. 3 pers. sg. {5.A.1.a} . . . . ἁρπάζω G726
ἁρπάζειν   vbl., pres. act. inf. {6.B.1} . . . . id.
ἁρπάζοντες   vbl., pres. act. ptc. nom. pl. masc. {6.A.1} . . . . id.
ἁρπάζουσιν   verb, pres. act. indic. 3 pers. pl. {5.A.1.a} . . . . id.

G726 **ἁρπάζω**   *I seize, snatch, obtain by robbery.*
G727 **ἅρπαξ**, -αγος   (1) *snatching, robbing, greedy*; (2) subs. *swindler, extortioner,* 1 Cor 5:10.
ἅρπαξ   adj., nom. sg. masc. {3.E} . . . . ἅρπαξ G727
ἅρπαξιν   adj., dat. pl. masc. {3.E} . . . . id.
ἁρπάσαι   vbl., aor. act. inf. {6.B.1} . . . . . . ἁρπάζω G726
ἁρπάσει   verb, fut. act. indic. 3 pers. sg. {5.A.1.a} id.

G728 **ἀρραβών** (ἀραβών), -ῶνος, ὁ   *an earnest, earnest money,* a large part of the payment, given in advance as a security that the whole will be paid afterwards (a word of Semitic origin).
ἀρραβών   noun, nom. sg. masc. {2.C} . . . ἀρραβών G728
ἀρραβῶνα   noun, acc. sg. masc. {2.C} . . . . . . id.

G729 **ἄρραφος** (ἄραφος), -ον   *without seam* (Heb.).
ἄρραφος   adj., nom. sg. masc. {3.C} . . . ἄρραφος G729
ἄρρενα   adj., acc. sg. masc. {3.E} . . . . ἄρσην G730‡
ἄρρενες   adj., nom. pl. masc. {3.E} . . . . id.
ἄρρητα   adj., acc. pl. neut. {3.C} . . . . ἄρρητος G731

G731 **ἄρρητος**, -ον   *not to be uttered* (because too sacred), secret.
ἄρρωστοι   adj., nom. pl. masc. {3.C} . . . ἄρρωστος G732
ἀρρώστοις   adj., dat. pl. masc. {3.C} . . . . id.

G732 **ἄρρωστος**, -ον   (1) *infirm;* (2) *sick, ill.*
ἀρρώστους   adj., acc. pl. masc. {3.C} . . . ἄρρωστος G732
ἄρσεν   adj., acc. sg. neut. {3.E} . . . . ἄρσην G730‡
ἄρσεν   adj., nom. sg. neut. {3.E} . . . . id.
ἄρσενα   adj., acc. sg. masc. {3.E} . . . . id.
ἄρσενες   adj., nom. pl. masc. {3.E} . . . . id.
ἀρσενοκοῖται   noun, nom. pl. masc. {2.A} . . . . ἀρσενοκοίτης G733
ἀρσενοκοίταις   noun, dat. pl. masc. {2.A} . . . . . id.

G733 **ἀρσενοκοίτης**, -ου, ὁ   *a pederast.*
ἄρσεσι   adj., dat. pl. masc. {3.E} . . . . ἄρσην G730‡
ἄρσεσιν   adj., dat. pl. masc. {3.E} . . . . id.

G730‡ **ἄρσην** (ἄρρην), -εν, gen. ενος   *male.*
Ἀρτεμᾶν   noun prop., acc. sg. masc. {2.A; 2.D} . . . . Ἀρτεμᾶς G734

G734 **Ἀρτεμᾶς**, -ᾶ, ὁ   *Artemas,* a Christian in Rome (a pet form of Ἀρτεμίδωρος).
Ἀρτέμιδος   noun prop., gen. sg. fem. {2.C; 2.D} . . . . Ἄρτεμις G735

G735 **Ἄρτεμις**, -ιδος, ἡ   *Artemis,* a goddess, worshipped principally at Ephesus, typifying fertility (she had no relation with the other Artemis, the maiden huntress, to whom corresponded the Lat. *Diana*).
Ἄρτεμις   noun prop., nom. sg. fem. {2.C; 2.D} . . . . Ἄρτεμις G735
ἀρτέμονα   noun, acc. sg. masc. {2.C} . . . . ἀρτέμων G736

G736 **ἀρτέμων**, -ωνος, ὁ   *a foresail,* set on the bow.
ἀρτέμωνα   noun, acc. sg. masc. {2.C} . . . . ἀρτέμων G736
G737 **ἄρτι**   adv., *now, just now* (of present time).
ἄρτι   adv. . . . . ἄρτι G737
ἀρτιγέννητα   adj., nom. pl. neut. {3.C} . . . . ἀρτιγέννητος G738

G738 **ἀρτιγέννητος**, -ον   *newly begotten, newly born.*
G739 **ἄρτιος**, -α, -ον   *perfect.*
ἄρτιος   adj., nom. sg. masc. {3.A} . . . . ἄρτιος G739
ἄρτοι   noun, nom. pl. masc. {2.B} . . . . ἄρτος G740
ἄρτοις   noun, dat. pl. masc. {2.B} . . . . id.
ἄρτον   noun, acc. sg. masc. {2.B} . . . . id.

G740 **ἄρτος**, -ου, ὁ   *bread, a loaf.*
ἄρτος   noun, nom. sg. masc. {2.B} . . . . ἄρτος G740
ἄρτου   noun, gen. sg. masc. {2.B} . . . . id.
ἄρτους   noun, acc. pl. masc. {2.B} . . . . id.
ἀρτυθήσεται   verb, fut. pass. indic. 3 pers. sg. {5.A.1.d} . . . . ἀρτύω G741
ἀρτύσετε   verb, fut. act. indic. 2 pers. pl. {5.A.1.a} . . . . id.

G741 **ἀρτύω**   *I season.*
ἄρτῳ   noun, dat. sg. masc. {2.B} . . . . ἄρτος G740
ἄρτων   noun, gen. pl. masc. {2.B} . . . . id.

G742 **Ἀρφαξάδ**, ὁ   *Arphaxad,* son of Shem, and father of Cainam (Heb.).
Ἀρφαξάδ   noun prop. . . . . Ἀρφαξάδ G742

G743 **ἀρχάγγελος**, -ου, ὁ   *a ruler of angels, a superior angel, an archangel.*
ἀρχάγγελος   noun, nom. sg. masc. {2.B} ἀρχάγγελος G743
ἀρχαγγέλου   noun, gen. sg. masc. {2.B} . . . . id.
ἀρχαί   noun, nom. pl. fem. {2.A} . . . . ἀρχή G746
ἀρχαῖα   adj., nom. pl. neut. {3.A} . . . . . . ἀρχαῖος G744
ἀρχαίοις   adj., dat. pl. masc. {3.A} . . . . id.
ἀρχαῖον   adj., acc. sg. masc. {3.A} . . . . id.

G744 **ἀρχαῖος**, -α, -ον   (1) *original, primitive;* (2) *ancient,* Matt 5:21, etc.
ἀρχαῖος   adj., nom. sg. masc. {3.A} . . . . . . ἀρχαῖος G744
ἀρχαίου   adj., gen. sg. masc. {3.A} . . . . id.
ἀρχαῖς   noun, dat. pl. fem. {2.A} . . . . ἀρχή G746
ἀρχαίῳ   adj., dat. sg. masc. {3.A} . . . . ἀρχαῖος G744
ἀρχαίων   adj., gen. pl. fem. {3.A} . . . . id.
ἀρχαίων   adj., gen. pl. masc. {3.A} . . . . id.
ἀρχάς   noun, acc. pl. fem. {2.A} . . . . ἀρχή G746
ἄρχειν   vbl., pres. act. inf. {6.B.1} . . . . ἄρχω G757

G745 **Ἀρχέλαος**, -ου, ὁ   *Archelaus,* Herod Archelaus, son and successor of Herod I, reigned over Judaea from 4 B.C. to 6 A.D. and died before 18 A.D.
Ἀρχέλαος   noun prop., nom. sg. masc. {2.B; 2.D} . . . . Ἀρχέλαος G745

G746 **ἀρχή**, -ῆς, ἡ   (1) *rule* (kingly or magisterial); (2) pl., in a quasi-personal sense, almost *rulers, magistrates,* Titus 3:1; (3) *beginning.* In the very difficult John 8:25 τὴν ἀρχήν would naturally mean *originally,* but the passage is not yet explained.
ἀρχή   noun, nom. sg. fem. {2.A} . . . . ἀρχή G746
ἀρχῇ   noun, dat. sg. fem. {2.A} . . . . id.
ἀρχηγόν   noun, acc. sg. masc. {2.B} . . . . . ἀρχηγός G747

G747 **ἀρχηγός**, -οῦ, ὁ   *originator, author, founder.*

ἀρχήν noun, acc. sg. fem. {2.A}. . . . . .ἀρχή G746
ἀρχῆς noun, gen. sg. fem. {2.A}. . . . . id.
G748 **ἀρχιερατικός**, -όν *high priestly, to which the chief priest belongs.*
ἀρχιερατικοῦ adj., gen. sg. neut.
{3.C}. . . . . .ἀρχιερατικός G748
ἀρχιερέα noun, acc. sg. masc. {2.C} . . . ἀρχιερεύς G749
ἀρχιερεῖ noun, dat. sg. masc. {2.C}. . . . . id.
ἀρχιερεῖς noun, acc. pl. masc. {2.C} . . . . id.
ἀρχιερεῖς noun, nom. pl. masc. {2.C} . . . . id.
G749 **ἀρχιερεύς**, -έως, ὁ *high priest, chief priest.*
ἀρχιερεύς noun, nom. sg. masc. {2.C} . ἀρχιερεύς G749
ἀρχιερεῦσι noun, dat. pl. masc. {2.C}. . . . . id.
ἀρχιερεῦσιν noun, dat. pl. masc. {2.C} . . . . id.
ἀρχιερέων noun, gen. pl. masc. {2.C} . . . . id.
ἀρχιερέως noun, gen. sg. masc. {2.C} . . . . id.
ἀρχιποίμενος noun, gen. sg. masc.
{2.C} . . . . .ἀρχιποίμην G750
G750 **ἀρχιποίμην**, -ενος, ὁ *chief shepherd.*
G751 **Ἄρχιππος**, -ου, ὁ *Archippus,* a Christian of Colossae.
Ἀρχίππῳ noun prop., dat. sg. masc. {2.B; 2.D}. . . . . .Ἄρχιππος G751
ἀρχισυνάγωγοι noun, nom. pl. masc.
{2.B} . . . . .ἀρχισυνάγωγος G752
ἀρχισυνάγωγον noun, acc. sg. masc. {2.B} . . . . id.
G752 **ἀρχισυνάγωγος**, -ου, ὁ *a leader of the synagogue,* a leading man (or woman) connected with the synagogue; some times there was only one, and the name was in some cases merely honorary.
ἀρχισυνάγωγος noun, nom. sg. masc.
{2.B} . . . . .ἀρχισυνάγωγος G752
ἀρχισυναγώγου noun, gen. sg. masc. {2.B} . . . id.
ἀρχισυναγώγῳ noun, dat. sg. masc. {2.B}. . . . . id.
ἀρχισυναγώγων noun, gen. pl. masc. {2.B} . . . id.
G753 **ἀρχιτέκτων**, -ονος, ὁ *master builder.*
ἀρχιτέκτων noun, nom. sg. masc.
{2.C} . . . . ἀρχιτέκτων G753
G754 **ἀρχιτελώνης**, -ου, ὁ *head of a custom house, chief tax gatherer.*
ἀρχιτελώνης noun, nom. sg. masc.
{2.A} . . . . ἀρχιτελώνης G754
G755 **ἀρχιτρίκλινος**, -ου, ὁ *master of ceremonies* at a dinner, *master of the feast.*
ἀρχιτρίκλινος noun, nom. sg. masc.
{2.B} . . . . ἀρχιτρίκλινος G755
ἀρχιτρικλίνῳ noun, dat. sg. masc. {2.B}. . . . . . id.
G756 **ἄρχομαι** mid. of ἄρχω, *I begin.*
ἀρχόμεθα verb, pres. mid. indic. 1 pers. pl.
{5.A.1.d} . . . . .ἄρχομαι G756
ἀρχόμενος vbl., pres. mid. ptc. nom. sg. masc.
{6.A.1}. . . . . id.
ἀρχομένων vbl., pres. mid. ptc. gen. pl. neut.
{6.A.1}. . . . . id.
ἄρχοντα noun, acc. sg. masc. {2.C} . . . ἄρχων G758
ἄρχοντας noun, acc. pl. masc. {2.C} . . . . id.
ἄρχοντες noun, nom. pl. masc. {2.C} . . . . id.
ἄρχοντες noun, voc. pl. masc. {2.C} . . . . id.
ἄρχοντι noun, dat. sg. masc. {2.C}. . . . . id.

ἄρχοντος noun, gen. sg. masc. {2.C}. . . . . id.
ἀρχόντων noun, gen. pl. masc. {2.C} . . . . id.
ἄρχουσιν noun, dat. pl. masc. {2.C} . . . . id.
G757 **ἄρχω** act. with gen. *I rule.*
G758 **ἄρχων**, -οντος, ὁ (1) *a ruler, governor, leader, leading man;* (2) with the Jews, *an official member (a member of the executive)* of the γερουσία.
ἄρχων noun, nom. sg. masc. {2.C}. . . . . . .ἄρχων G758
ἀρῶ verb, fut. act. indic. 1 pers. sg. {5.A.2}. . . .αἴρω G142
G759 **ἄρωμα**, -ατος, τό *spice.*
ἀρώματα noun, acc. pl. neut. {2.C} . . . . . . ἄρωμα G759
ἀρωμάτων noun, gen. pl. neut. {2.C} . . . . id.
ἅς pron. rel., acc. pl. fem. {4.C} . . . . .ὅς G3739
G760 **Ἀσά** (Ἀσάφ) *Asa* or *Asaph,* son of Abijah and father of Jehoshaphat, king of Judah about 900 B.C. for 41 years (Heb.).
Ἀσά noun prop.. . . . . Ἀσά G760
ἀσάλευτον adj., acc. sg. fem. {3.C} . . . .ἀσάλευτος G761
G761 **ἀσάλευτος**, -ον *unshaken, immovable.*
ἀσάλευτος adj., nom. sg. fem. {3.C} . . .ἀσάλευτος G761
Ἀσάφ noun prop.. . . . . Ἀσά G760
ἄσβεστον adj., acc. sg. neut. {3.C}. . . . . .ἄσβεστος G762
G762 **ἄσβεστος**, -ον *inextinguishable, unquenchable.*
ἀσβέστῳ adj., dat. sg. neut. {3.C} . . . . .ἄσβεστος G762
G763 **ἀσέβεια**, -ας, ἡ *impiety, irreverence.*
ἀσέβειαν noun, acc. sg. fem. {2.A} . . . . . ἀσέβεια G763
ἀσεβείας noun, acc. pl. fem. {2.A} . . . . id.
ἀσεβείας noun, gen. sg. fem. {2.A} . . . . id.
ἀσεβεῖν vbl., pres. act. inf. {6.B.2} . . . . . .ἀσεβέω G764
ἀσεβεῖς adj., nom. pl. masc. {3.E} . . . . . . ἀσεβής G765
ἀσεβειῶν noun, gen. pl. fem. {2.A} . . . . . .ἀσέβεια G763
ἀσεβέσι adj., dat. pl. masc. {3.E} . . . . ἀσεβής G765
ἀσεβέσιν adj., dat. pl. masc. {3.E} . . . . id.
G764 **ἀσεβέω** (1) intrans., *I am impious, irreverent;* (2) trans., *I do impiously.*
ἀσεβῆ adj., acc. sg. masc. {3.E} . . . . .ἀσεβής G765
G765 **ἀσεβής**, -ές *impious, irreverent, irreligious.*
ἀσεβής adj., nom. sg. masc. {3.E} . . . . . . ἀσεβής G765
ἀσεβῶν adj., gen. pl. masc. {3.E} . . . . id.
G766 **ἀσέλγεια**, -ας, ἡ *wantonness, lewdness,(outrageous conduct; conduct shocking to public decency; a wanton violence).*
ἀσέλγεια noun, nom. sg. fem. {2.A} . . . . ἀσέλγεια G766
ἀσελγείᾳ noun, dat. sg. fem. {2.A} . . . . id.
ἀσελγείαις noun, dat. pl. fem. {2.A} . . . . id.
ἀσέλγειαν noun, acc. sg. fem. {2.A} . . . . id.
G767 **ἄσημος**, -ον *undistinguished, obscure* (lit., *unmarked, unstamped).*
ἀσήμου adj., gen. sg. fem. {3.C} . . . . ἄσημος G767
G768 **Ἀσήρ**, ὁ *Asher,* one of the sons of Jacob, and founder of one of the Twelve Tribes (Heb.).
Ἀσήρ noun prop.. . . . . .Ἀσήρ G768
ἀσθενεῖ verb, pres. act. indic. 3 pers. sg.
{5.A.2}. . . . . .ἀσθενέω G770
G769 **ἀσθένεια**, -ας, ἡ *want of strength, weakness, illness.*
ἀσθένεια noun, nom. sg. fem. {2.A} . . . ἀσθένεια G769
ἀσθενείᾳ noun, dat. sg. fem. {2.A} . . . . id.
ἀσθενείαις noun, dat. pl. fem. {2.A} . . . . id.

ἀσθένειαν   noun, acc. sg. fem. {2.A} . . . . id.
ἀσθενείας   noun, acc. pl. fem. {2.A} . . . . id.
ἀσθενείας   noun, gen. sg. fem. {2.A} . . . . id.
ἀσθενεῖς   adj., acc. pl. masc. {3.E} . . . . . . ἀσθενής *G772*
ἀσθενεῖς   adj., nom. pl. masc. {3.E} . . . . id.
ἀσθενειῶν   noun, gen. pl. fem. {2.A} . . . ἀσθένεια *G769*
ἀσθενές   adj., acc. sg. neut. {3.E} . . . . ἀσθενής *G772*
ἀσθενές   adj., nom. sg. neut. {3.E} . . . . id.
ἀσθενέσιν   adj., dat. pl. masc. {3.E} . . . . id.
ἀσθενέστερα   adj. comp., nom. pl. neut. {3.E;
     3.G} . . . . id.
ἀσθενεστέρῳ   adj. comp., dat. sg. neut. {3.E;
     3.G} . . . . id.
G770 **ἀσθενέω**   (1) (physically) *I am weak;* (2) (then
     morally) *I am sick.*
ἀσθενῆ   adj., acc. pl. neut. {3.E} . . . . ἀσθενής *G772*
ἀσθενῆ   adj., acc. sg. masc. {3.E} . . . . id.
G771 **ἀσθένημα**, -ατος, τό   *weakness.*
ἀσθενήματα   noun, acc. pl. neut. {2.C} . ἀσθένημα *G771*
G772 **ἀσθενής**, -ές   lit. *not strong;* (1) *weak* (physi-
     cally or morally); (2) *ill.*
ἀσθενής   adj., nom. sg. fem. {3.E} . . . . . . ἀσθενής *G772*
ἀσθενής   adj., nom. sg. masc. {3.E} . . . . id.
ἀσθενήσας   vbl., aor. act. ptc. nom. sg. masc.
     {6.A.2} . . . . ἀσθενέω *G770*
ἀσθενήσασαν   vbl., aor. act. ptc. acc. sg. fem.
     {6.A.2} . . . . id.
ἀσθενοῦμεν   verb, pres. act. indic. 1 pers. pl.
     {5.A.2} . . . . id.
ἀσθενοῦντα   vbl., pres. act. ptc. acc. sg. masc.
     {6.A.2} . . . . id.
ἀσθενοῦντας   vbl., pres. act. ptc. acc. pl. masc.
     {6.A.2} . . . . id.
ἀσθενούντων   vbl., pres. act. ptc. gen. pl. masc.
     {6.A.2} . . . . id.
ἀσθενοῦς   adj., gen. sg. masc. {3.E} . . . . . ἀσθενής *G772*
ἀσθενοῦσαν   vbl., pres. act. ptc. acc. sg. fem.
     {6.A.2} . . . . ἀσθενέω *G770*
ἀσθενοῦσιν   vbl., pres. act. ptc. dat. pl. masc.
     {6.A.2} . . . . id.
ἀσθενῶ   verb, pres. act. indic. 1 pers. sg. {5.A.2} id.
ἀσθενῶ   verb, pres. act. subjunc. 1 pers. sg.
     {5.B.2} . . . . id.
ἀσθενῶμεν   verb, pres. act. subjunc. 1 pers. pl.
     {5.B.2} . . . . id.
ἀσθενῶν   adj., gen. pl. masc. {3.E} . . . . . ἀσθενής *G772*
ἀσθενῶν   vbl., pres. act. ptc. nom. sg. masc.
     {6.A.2} . . . . ἀσθενέω *G770*
G773 **Ἀσία**, -ας, ἡ   *the Roman province Asia,* roughly
     the western third of Asia Minor.
Ἀσία   noun prop., nom. sg. fem. {2.A; 2.D} . . . Ἀσία *G773*
Ἀσίᾳ   noun prop., dat. sg. fem. {2.A; 2.D} . . . . . id.
Ἀσίαν   noun prop., acc. sg. fem. {2.A; 2.D} . . . . . id.
Ἀσιανοί   noun prop., nom. pl. masc. {2.B;
     2.D} . . . . Ἀσιανός *G774*
G774 **Ἀσιανός**, -οῦ, ὁ   *belonging to the Roman prov-
     ince Asia.*
G775 **Ἀσιάρχης**, -ου, ὁ   *Asiarch,* an official con-
     nected with the worship of Rome and the
     Emperor in the Roman province Asia.

Ἀσιαρχῶν   noun prop., gen. pl. masc. {2.A;
     2.D} . . . . Ἀσιάρχης *G775*
Ἀσίας   noun prop., gen. sg. fem. {2.A; 2.D} . . . Ἀσία *G773*
G776 **ἀσιτία**, -ας, ἡ   either *lack of corn, lack of food*
     (the lit. meaning), or *abstinence from food,
     loss of appetite, seasickness* (the extended
     meaning).
ἀσιτίας   noun, gen. sg. fem. {2.A} . . . . ἀσιτία *G776*
ἄσιτοι   adj., nom. pl. masc. {3.C} . . . . ἄσιτος *G777*
G777 **ἄσιτος**, -ον   either *without corn, without food,*
     or *seasick.*
G778 **ἀσκέω**   *I train, practice, exercise.*
ἀσκοί   noun, nom. pl. masc. {2.B} . . . . ἀσκός *G779*
G779 **ἀσκός**, -οῦ, ὁ   *a wineskin.*
ἀσκούς   noun, acc. pl. masc. {2.B} . . . . ἀσκός *G779*
ἀσκῶ   verb, pres. act. indic. 1 pers. sg. {5.A.2} ἀσκέω *G778*
G780 **ἀσμένως**   adv., *joyfully, with delight.*
ἀσμένως   adv. {3.F} . . . . ἀσμένως *G780*
ἄσοφοι   adj., nom. pl. masc. {3.C} . . . . ἄσοφος *G781*
G781 **ἄσοφος**, -ον   *unskilled, unwise, foolish.*
ἀσπάζεσθαι   vbl., pres. mid./pass. inf.
     {6.B.1} . . . . ἀσπάζομαι *G782*
ἀσπάζεται   verb, pres. mid./pass. indic. 3 pers.
     sg. {5.A.1.d} . . . . id.
G782 **ἀσπάζομαι**   (1) *I greet, salute;* (2) *I pay my
     respects to* (a term regularly used at the end of
     a letter), Acts 25:13.
ἀσπάζομαι   verb, pres. mid./pass. indic. 1 pers. sg.
     {5.A.1.d} . . . . ἀσπάζομαι *G782*
ἀσπάζονται   verb, pres. mid./pass. indic.
     3 pers. pl. {5.A.1.d} . . . . id.
ἀσπάζου   verb, pres. mid./pass. impv. 2 pers.
     sg. {5.D.1} . . . . id.
ἄσπασαι   verb, aor. mid. impv. 2 pers. sg.
     {5.D.1} . . . . id.
ἀσπασάμενοι   vbl., aor. mid. ptc. nom. pl.
     masc. {6.A.1.b} . . . . id.
ἀσπασάμενος   vbl., aor. mid. ptc. nom. sg.
     masc. {6.A.1.b} . . . . id.
ἀσπάσασθε   verb, aor. mid. impv. 2 pers. pl.
     {5.D.1} . . . . id.
ἀσπάσησθε   verb, aor. mid. subjunc. 2 pers. pl.
     {5.B.1} . . . . id.
ἀσπασμόν   noun, acc. sg. masc. {2.B} . . ἀσπασμός *G783*
G783 **ἀσπασμός**, -οῦ, ὁ   *a greeting, salutation* (very
     rare in papyri).
ἀσπασμός   noun, nom. sg. masc. {2.B} . ἀσπασμός *G783*
ἀσπασμοῦ   noun, gen. sg. masc. {2.B} . . . . id.
ἀσπασμούς   noun, acc. pl. masc. {2.B} . . . . id.
ἀσπασόμενοι   vbl., fut. mid. ptc. nom. pl. masc.
     {6.A.1.b} . . . . ἀσπάζομαι *G782*
ἀσπίδων   noun, gen. pl. fem. {2.C} . . . . ἀσπίς *G785*
ἄσπιλοι   adj., nom. pl. masc. {3.C} . . . . ἄσπιλος *G784*
ἄσπιλον   adj., acc. sg. fem. {3.C} . . . . id.
ἄσπιλον   adj., acc. sg. masc. {3.C} . . . . id.
G784 **ἄσπιλος**, -ον   *unstained, undefiled.*
ἀσπίλου   adj., gen. sg. masc. {3.C} . . . . . . ἄσπιλος *G784*
G785 **ἀσπίς**, -ίδος, ἡ   *an asp* (hooded snake, cobra da
     capello).
ἄσπονδοι   adj., nom. pl. masc. {3.C} . . . . ἄσπονδος *G786*

G786 **ἄσπονδος**, -ον   *untrue to one's promise.*
     ἀσπόνδους   adj., acc. pl. masc. {3.C} . . . .ἄσπονδος *G786*

G787 **ἀσσάριον**, -ου, τό   *a penny (one sixteenth of a*
     denarius and one tenth of a drachma).
     ἀσσαρίου   noun, gen. sg. neut. {2.B} . . . ἀσσάριον *G787*
     ἀσσαρίων   noun, gen. pl. neut. {2.B} . . . . id.
     Ἀσσάρωνα   noun prop., acc. pl. masc. {2.C;
        2.D} . . . . Σαρών *G4565*
     Ἄσσον   noun prop., acc. sg. fem. {2.B; 2.D} . Ἄσσος *G789*

G788 **ἆσσον**   adv., *nearer* (comp. of ἄγχι).
     ἆσσον   adv. comp. {3.F; 3.G} . . . . ἆσσον *G788*
     Ἄσσον   noun prop., acc. sg. fem. {2.B; 2.D} . Ἄσσος *G789*

G789 **Ἄσσος**, -ου, ἡ   *Assos,* a port of Mysia, in the
     Roman province Asia.

G790 **ἀστατέω**   *I am unsettled, have no place of*
     abode, lead a vagabond life.
     ἀστατοῦμεν   verb, pres. act. indic. 1 pers. pl.
        {5.A.2} . . . . .ἀστατέω *G790*
     ἀστεῖον   adj., acc. sg. neut. {3.A} . . . . ἀστεῖος *G791*

G791 **ἀστεῖος**, -α, -ον   *elegant, pretty, fair, fine* (lit.
     belonging to the city; then *witty, clever).*
     ἀστεῖος   adj., nom. sg. masc. {3.A} . . . . . . ἀστεῖος *G791*
     ἀστέρα   noun, acc. sg. masc. {2.C} . . . . .ἀστήρ *G792*
     ἀστέρας   noun, acc. pl. masc. {2.C} . . . . id.
     ἀστέρες   noun, nom. pl. masc. {2.C} . . . . id.
     ἀστέρος   noun, gen. sg. masc. {2.C} . . . . id.
     ἀστέρων   noun, gen. pl. masc. {2.C} . . . . id.

G792 **ἀστήρ**, -έρος, ὁ   *a star.*
     ἀστήρ   noun, nom. sg. masc. {2.C} . . . . .ἀστήρ *G792*
     ἀστήρικτοι   adj., nom. pl. masc. {3.C} . ἀστήρικτος *G793*

G793 **ἀστήρικτος**, -ον   *unsteady, unstable* (rather
     literary, lit. *unpropped).*
     ἀστηρίκτους   adj., acc. pl. fem. {3.C} . . ἀστήρικτος *G793*
     ἄστοργοι   adj., nom. pl. masc. {3.C} . . . . ἄστοργος *G794*

G794 **ἄστοργος**, -ον   *unloving, devoid of affection.*
     ἀστόργους   adj., acc. pl. masc. {3.C} . . . . ἄστοργος *G794*

G795 **ἀστοχέω**   *I miss the mark, miss my aim, make a*
     false aim.
     ἀστοχήσαντες   vbl., aor. act. ptc. nom. pl. masc.
        {6.A.2} . . . . .ἀστοχέω *G795*
     ἄστρα   noun, nom. pl. neut. {2.B} . . . . .ἄστρον *G798*
     ἀστραπαί   noun, nom. pl. fem. {2.A} . . . ἀστραπή *G796*

G796 **ἀστραπή**, -ῆς, ἡ   *a flash of lightning.*
     ἀστραπή   noun, nom. sg. fem. {2.A} . . . . . ἀστραπή *G796*
     ἀστραπῇ   noun, dat. sg. fem. {2.A} . . . . id.
     ἀστραπήν   noun, acc. sg. fem. {2.A} . . . . id.
     ἀστράπτουσα   vbl., pres. act. ptc. nom. sg. fem.
        {6.A.1} . . . . .ἀστράπτω *G797*
     ἀστραπούσαις   vbl., pres. act. ptc. dat. pl.
        fem. {6.A.1} . . . . id.
     ἀστραπούσῃ   vbl., pres. act. ptc. dat. sg. fem.
        {6.A.1} . . . . id.

G797 **ἀστράπτω**   *I flash* (with, then like, lightning).
     ἄστροις   noun, dat. pl. neut. {2.B} . . . . . . .ἄστρον *G798*

G798 **ἄστρον**, -ου, τό   *a star.*
     ἄστρον   noun, acc. sg. neut. {2.B} . . . . .ἄστρον *G798*
     ἄστρων   noun, gen. pl. neut. {2.B} . . . . id.
     Ἀσύγκριτον   noun prop., acc. sg. masc. {2.B;
        2.D} . . . . Ἀσύγκριτος *G799*

G799 **Ἀσύγκριτος**, -ου, ὁ   *Asyncritus,* a Christian in
     Rome.
     ἀσύμφωνοι   adj., nom. pl. masc. {3.C}. ἀσύμφωνος *G800*

G800 **ἀσύμφωνος**, -ον   *inharmonious, disagreeing.*
     ἀσύνετοι   adj., nom. pl. masc. {3.C} . . . . ἀσύνετος *G801*

G801 **ἀσύνετος**, -ον   *unintelligent, without wisdom,*
     unwise, undiscerning (implying probably
     moral defect, like ἀμαθής sometimes in clas-
     sical Gk.).
     ἀσύνετος   adj., nom. sg. fem. {3.C} . . . . . ἀσύνετος *G801*
     ἀσυνέτους   adj., acc. pl. masc. {3.C} . . . . id.
     ἀσυνέτῳ   adj., dat. sg. neut. {3.C} . . . . id.

G802 **ἀσύνθετος**, -ον   *not covenanting, untrue to an*
     agreement, treacherous.
     ἀσυνθέτους   adj., acc. pl. masc. {3.C} . . ἀσύνθετος *G802*
     Ἀσύνκριτον   noun prop., acc. sg. masc. {2.B;
        2.D} . . . . Ἀσύγκριτος *G799*

G803 **ἀσφάλεια**, -ας, ἡ   (1) *safety;* (2) *security, reli-*
     ability, Luke 1:4.
     ἀσφάλεια   noun, nom. sg. fem. {2.A} . . ἀσφάλεια *G803*
     ἀσφαλείᾳ   noun, dat. sg. fem. {2.A} . . . . id.
     ἀσφάλειαν   noun, acc. sg. fem. {2.A} . . . . id.
     ἀσφαλές   adj., acc. sg. neut. {3.E} . . . . . . .ἀσφαλής *G804*
     ἀσφαλές   adj., nom. sg. neut. {3.E} . . . . id.
     ἀσφαλῆ   adj., acc. sg. fem. {3.E} . . . . id.

G804 **ἀσφαλής**, -ές   *safe, reliable, trustworthy* (lit.,
     unfailing).

G805 **ἀσφαλίζω**   *I make safe (secure, fast).*
     ἀσφαλίσασθε   verb, aor. mid. impv. 2 pers. pl.
        {5.D.1} . . . . .ἀσφαλίζω *G805*
     ἀσφαλισθῆναι   vbl., aor. pass. inf. {6.B.1} . . . . id.

G806 **ἀσφαλῶς**   adv., *securely.*
     ἀσφαλῶς   adv. {3.F} . . . . ἀσφαλῶς *G806*
     ἀσχήμονα   adj., nom. pl. neut. {3.E} . . . . ἀσχήμων *G809*
     ἀσχημονεῖ   verb, pres. act. indic. 3 pers. sg.
        {5.A.2} . . . . .ἀσχημονέω *G807*
     ἀσχημονεῖν   vbl., pres. act. inf. {6.B.2} . . . . id.

G807 **ἀσχημονέω**   (1) *I am unseemly, I behave unbe-*
     comingly (or even *dishonorably);* (2) perhaps, *I*
     consider (something) *unseemly.*

G808 **ἀσχημοσύνη**, -ης, ἡ   *unseemly behavior,*
     indecency, or concr., *an indecent (lewd) act.*
     ἀσχημοσύνην   noun, acc. sg. fem.
        {2.A} . . . . ἀσχημοσύνη *G808*

G809 **ἀσχήμων**, -ον   *unseemly, indecent.*

G810 **ἀσωτία**, -ας, ἡ   *wantonness, profligacy.*
     ἀσωτία   noun, nom. sg. fem. {2.A} . . . . . . .ἀσωτία *G810*
     ἀσωτίας   noun, gen. sg. fem. {2.A} . . . . id.

G811 **ἀσώτως**   adv., *prodigally;* ζῶν ἀσώτως, *with*
     prodigal living.
     ἀσώτως   adv. {3.F} . . . . .ἀσώτως *G811*

G812 **ἀτακτέω**   *I am disorderly, I neglect my duty, I*
     am careless (or *idle) in habits* (lit. *I march out*
     of order; then *I riot, I rebel).*

G813 **ἄτακτος**, -ον   *disorderly, slack* (in performance
     of duty; lit. *out of order).*
     ἀτάκτους   adj., acc. pl. masc. {3.C} . . . . . . ἄτακτος *G813*

G814 **ἀτάκτως**   adv., *in a disorderly manner* (see
     ἄτακτος, ἀτακτέω).
     ἀτάκτως   adv. {3.F} . . . . .ἀτάκτως *G814*

G815 **ἄτεκνος**, -ον *childless.*
ἄτεκνος adj., nom. sg. masc. {3.C}. . . . . . ἄτεκνος *G815*
ἀτενίζετε verb, pres. act. indic. 2 pers. pl.
{5.A.1.a} . . . . ἀτενίζω *G816*
ἀτενίζοντες vbl., pres. act. ptc. nom. pl. masc.
{6.A.1}. . . . . id.

G816 **ἀτενίζω** *I direct my gaze, I look steadily.*
ἀτενίσαι vbl., aor. act. inf. {6.B.1} . . . . . . ἀτενίζω *G816*
ἀτενίσαντες vbl., aor. act. ptc. nom. pl. masc.
{6.A.1.a} . . . . id.
ἀτενίσας vbl., aor. act. ptc. nom. sg. masc.
{6.A.1.a} . . . . id.
ἀτενίσασα vbl., aor. act. ptc. nom. sg. fem.
{6.A.1.a} . . . . id.

G817 **ἄτερ** prep., *apart from, without* (orig. poetic).
ἄτερ prep. . . . . ἄτερ *G817*
ἀτιμάζεις verb, pres. act. indic. 2 pers. sg.
{5.A.1.a} . . . . .ἀτιμάζω *G818*
ἀτιμάζεσθαι vbl., pres. mid./pass. inf. {6.B.1}. . id.
ἀτιμάζετε verb, pres. act. indic. 2 pers. pl.
{5.A.1.a} . . . . id.

G818 **ἀτιμάζω** (ἀτιμάω) (1) *I disgrace, treat dis-*
gracefully, dishonor, insult; (2) *I despise.*
ἀτιμάσαντες vbl., aor. act. ptc. nom. pl. masc.
{6.A.1.a} . . . . .ἀτιμάζω *G818*
ἀτιμασθῆναι vbl., aor. pass. inf. {6.B.1} . . . . . . id.

G819 **ἀτιμία**, -ας, ἡ *disgrace, dishonor.*
ἀτιμία noun, nom. sg. fem. {2.A} . . . . ἀτιμία *G819*
ἀτιμίᾳ noun, dat. sg. fem. {2.A}. . . . . id.
ἀτιμίαν noun, acc. sg. fem. {2.A} . . . . id.
ἀτιμίας noun, gen. sg. fem. {2.A} . . . . id.
ἄτιμοι adj., nom. pl. masc. {3.C} . . . . ἄτιμος *G820*

G820 **ἄτιμος**, -ον *unhonored, without honor,*
unesteemed.
ἄτιμος adj., nom. sg. masc. {3.C}. . . . . ἄτιμος *G820*
ἀτιμότερα adj. comp., acc. pl. neut. {3.C; 3.G} . id.

G821 **ἀτιμόω** Var. spelling of ἀτιμάζω.
ἄτινα pron. indef. rel., nom. pl. neut. {4.C} . .ὅστις *G3748*
ἀτμίδα noun, acc. sg. fem. {2.C} . . . . ἀτμίς *G822*

G822 **ἀτμίς**, -ίδος, ἡ (1) *breath;* (2) *steam, vapor.*
ἀτμίς noun, nom. sg. fem. {2.C} . . . . ἀτμίς *G822*

G823 **ἄτομος**, -ον *an indivisible part of time, a*
second (lit., *that cannot be cut*).
ἀτόμῳ adj., dat. sg. neut. {3.C}. . . . . .ἄτομος *G823*
ἄτοπον adj., acc. sg. neut. {3.C}. . . . . .ἄτοπος *G824*
ἄτοπον adj., nom. sg. neut. {3.C}. . . . . id.

G824 **ἄτοπος**, -ον (1) *improper, unrighteous, per-*
verse, froward; (2) almost = *evil*, Acts 28:6 (lit.,
out of place, unusual, unbecoming).
ἀτόπων adj., gen. pl. masc. {3.C}. . . . . . . .ἄτοπος *G824*

G825 **Ἀττάλεια**, -ας, ἡ *Attalia,* the port of Perga in
Pamphylia.
Ἀττάλειαν noun prop., acc. sg. fem. {2.A;
2.D}. . . . . .Ἀττάλεια *G825*
Ἀτταλίαν noun prop., acc. sg. fem. {2.A; 2.D}. . id.

G826 **αὐγάζω** *I flash, gleam, appear white, bright* (as
in LXX), but perhaps, *I see, I see clearly* (as in
classical poetry).
αὐγάσαι vbl., aor. act. inf. {6.B.1} . . . . . . αὐγάζω *G826*

G827 **αὐγή**, -ῆς, ἡ *light (of day).*

αὐγῆς noun, gen. sg. fem. {2.A}. . . . . .αὐγή *G827*

G828 **Αὔγουστος**, -ου, ὁ *Augustus,* a title conferred
on the first Roman Emperor, C. Iulius Oc-
tauianus, denoting sanctity (almost divinity);
Graecized as Σεβαστός (q.v.).
Αὐγούστου noun prop., gen. sg. masc. {2.B;
2.D}. . . . . .Αὔγουστος *G828*
αὐθάδεις adj., nom. pl. masc. {3.E} . . . . .αὐθάδης *G829*
αὐθάδη adj., acc. sg. masc. {3.E} . . . . id.

G829 **αὐθάδης**, -ες *self-satisfied;* hence, *arrogant.*
αὐθαίρετοι adj., nom. pl. masc. {3.C} . αὐθαίρετος *G830*

G830 **αὐθαίρετος**, -ον *of one's own accord.*
αὐθαίρετος adj., nom. sg. masc. {3.C} αὐθαίρετος *G830*
αὐθεντεῖν vbl., pres. act. inf. {6.B.2} . . .αὐθεντέω *G831*

G831 **αὐθεντέω** *I domineer over* (a colloquial word,
from αὐθέντης, "master," "autocrat").

G832 **αὐλέω** *I play the flute.*

G833 **αὐλή**, -ῆς, ἡ (1) *courtyard, forecourt;* (2) but it
may be understood as *palace, house,* e.g., Matt
26:3.
αὐλῇ noun, dat. sg. fem. {2.A}. . . . . .αὐλή *G833*
αὐλήν noun, acc. sg. fem. {2.A}. . . . . id.
αὐλῆς noun, gen. sg. fem. {2.A} . . . . id.
αὐλητάς noun, acc. pl. masc. {2.A} . . . . .αὐλητής *G834*

G834 **αὐλητής**, -οῦ, ὁ *a flute player.*
αὐλητῶν noun, gen. pl. masc. {2.A} . . . . αὐλητής *G834*

G835 **αὐλίζομαι** *I bivouac, I pass the night.*

G836 **αὐλός**, -οῦ, ὁ *a flute.*
αὐλός noun, nom. sg. masc. {2.B} . . . . . . .αὐλός *G836*
αὐλούμενον vbl., pres. pass. ptc. nom. sg. neut.
{6.A.2}. . . . . αὐλέω *G832*
αὐξάνει verb, pres. act. indic. 3 pers. sg.
{5.A.1.a} . . . . αὐξάνω *G837*
αὐξάνειν vbl., pres. act. inf. {6.B.1}. . . . . id.
αὐξάνετε verb, pres. act. impv. 2 pers. pl.
{5.D.1}. . . . . id.
αὐξανόμενα vbl., pres. pass. ptc. nom. pl.
neut. {6.A.1} . . . . id.
αὐξανομένης vbl., pres. pass. ptc. gen. sg.
fem. {6.A.1} . . . . id.
αὐξανόμενοι vbl., pres. pass. ptc. nom. pl.
masc. {6.A.1}. . . . . id.
αὐξανόμενον vbl., pres. pass. ptc. nom. sg.
neut. {6.A.1} . . . . id.
αὐξάνοντα vbl., pres. act. ptc. acc. sg. masc.
{6.A.1}. . . . . id.
αὐξάνουσιν verb, pres. act. indic. 3 pers. pl.
{5.A.1.a} . . . . id.

G837 **αὐξάνω** (αὔξω) (1) trans., *I cause to increase;*
(2) intrans., *I increase, grow;* with cog. acc. Col
2:19.
αὐξάνων vbl., pres. act. ptc. nom. sg. masc.
{6.A.1}. . . . . .αὐξάνω *G837*
αὔξει verb, pres. act. indic. 3 pers. sg. {5.A.1.a} . id.
αὐξηθῇ verb, aor. pass. subjunc. 3 pers. sg.
{5.B.1}. . . . . id.
αὐξηθῆτε verb, aor. pass. subjunc. 2 pers. pl.
{5.B.1}. . . . . id.
αὐξῆσαι verb, aor. act. opt. 3 pers. sg. {5.C.1}. . id.

αὐξήσει   verb, fut. act. indic. 3 pers. sg. {5.A.1.a} id.

αὔξησιν   noun, acc. sg. fem. {2.C} . . . . . . αὔξησις *G838*

G838 **αὔξησις**, -εως, ἡ   *increasing, increase, growth.*

αὐξήσωμεν   verb, aor. act. subjunc. 1 pers. pl.
{5.B.1} . . . . αὐξάνω *G837*

G839 **αὔριον**   adv. *tomorrow.*

αὔριον   adv. {3.F} . . . . αὔριον *G839*

G840 **αὐστηρός**, -ά, -όν   (1) *grim, severe;* (2) *strict, exacting.*

αὐστηρός   adj., nom. sg. masc. {3.A} . . .αὐστηρός *G840*

αὐτά   pron. pers., acc. pl. neut. {4.A} . . . . αὐτός *G846*

αὐτά   pron. pers., nom. pl. neut. {4.A} . . . . id.

αὗται   pron. dem., nom. pl. fem. {4.B} . . . . οὗτος *G3778*

αὐταῖς   pron. pers., dat. pl. fem. {4.A} . . . . . αὐτός *G846*

G841 **αὐτάρκεια**, -ας, ἡ   *self-sufficiency, independence.*

αὐτάρκειαν   noun, acc. sg. fem. {2.A} . . αὐτάρκεια *G841*

αὐταρκείας   noun, gen. sg. fem. {2.A} . . . . id.

G842 **αὐτάρκης**, -ες   *self-sufficient, independent, contented* (a literary use).

αὐτάρκης   adj., nom. sg. masc. {3.E} . . .αὐτάρκης *G842*

αὐτάς   pron. pers., acc. pl. fem. {4.A} . . . . αὐτός *G846*

αὐτή   pron. pers., nom. sg. fem. {4.A} . . . . id.

αὐτῇ   pron. pers., dat. sg. fem. {4.A} . . . . id.

αὕτη   pron. dem., nom. sg. fem. {4.B} . . . . οὗτος *G3778*

αὐτήν   pron. pers., acc. sg. fem. {4.A} . . . . αὐτός *G846*

αὐτήν   pron. refl., 3 pers. acc. sg. fem. {4.F} . .αὑτοῦ *G848*

αὐτῆς   pron. pers., gen. sg. fem. {4.A} . . . . αὐτός *G846*

αὐτῆς   pron. refl., 3 pers. gen. sg. fem. {4.F} . .αὑτοῦ *G848*

αὐτό   pron. pers., acc. sg. neut. {4.A} . . . . αὐτός *G846*

αὐτό   pron. pers., nom. sg. neut. {4.A} . . . . id.

αὐτοί   pron. pers., nom. pl. masc. {4.A} . . . . id.

αὐτοῖς   pron. pers., dat. pl. masc. {4.A} . . . . id.

αὐτοῖς   pron. pers., dat. pl. neut. {4.A} . . . . id.

αὑτοῖς   pron. refl., dat. pl. masc. {4.F} . . . . .αὑτοῦ *G848*

G843 **αὐτοκατάκριτος**, -ον   *self-condemned* (per-haps a new coinage).

αὐτοκατάκριτος   adj., nom. sg. masc.
{3.C} . . . . αὐτοκατάκριτος *G843*

αὐτομάτη   adj., nom. sg. fem. {3.A} . . . .αὐτόματος *G844*

G844 **αὐτόματος**, -η, -ον   *of its own accord.*

αὐτόν   pron. pers., acc. sg. masc. {4.A} . . . . .αὐτός *G846*

αὑτόν   pron. refl., 3 pers. acc. sg. masc. {4.F} .αὑτοῦ *G848*

αὐτόπται   noun, nom. pl. masc. {2.A} . . .αὐτόπτης *G845*

G845 **αὐτόπτης**, -ου, ὁ   *eyewitness.*

G846 **αὐτός**, -ή, -ό   (1) *he,* etc.; (2) *self;* e.g., αὐτός ὁ, etc., *the very,* but often weakened to mean simply *that;* αὐτός = αὐτόματος, *of his own accord,* John 16:27; (3) ὁ αὐτός, etc., *the same.* Parts of αὐτός are sometimes added pleonas-tically to the rel. pron. (colloquial; where the usage is not due to inferior culture, it is due to translation Gk.), cf. Mark 7:25; (4) αὐτοῦ, adv., *there;* (5) ἐπὶ τὸ αὐτό, κατὰ τὸ αὐτό, *together.*

αὐτός   pron. pers., nom. sg. masc. {4.A} . . . . .αὐτός *G846*

G847 **αὐτοῦ**   adv. *there; see* αὐτός (4).

αὐτοῦ   adv. . . . . .αὐτοῦ *G847*

αὐτοῦ   pron. pers., gen. sg. masc. {4.A} . . . . αὐτός *G846*

αὐτοῦ   pron. pers., gen. sg. neut. {4.A} . . . . id.

G848 **αὑτοῦ**   contracted form of ἑαυτοῦ.

αὐτούς   pron. pers., acc. pl. masc. {4.A} . . . . αὐτός *G846*

αὑτούς   pron. refl., acc. pl. masc. {4.F} . . . . .αὑτοῦ *G848*

αὐτοφόρῳ   adj., dat. sg. neut. {3.A} . ἐπαυτοφώρῳ *G1888*

αὐτοφώρῳ   adj., dat. sg. neut. {3.A} . . . . id.

G849 **αὐτόχειρ**, -ος   *with one's own hand* (probably exclusively literary).

αὐτόχειρες   adj., nom. pl. masc. {3.E} . . . αὐτόχειρ *G849*

αὐτῷ   pron. pers., dat. sg. masc. {4.A} . . . . . αὐτός *G846*

αὐτῷ   pron. pers., dat. sg. neut. {4.A} . . . . id.

αὑτῷ   pron. refl., 3 pers. dat. sg. masc. {4.F} .αὑτοῦ *G848*

αὐτῶν   pron. pers., gen. pl. fem. {4.A} . . . . αὐτός *G846*

αὐτῶν   pron. pers., gen. pl. masc. {4.A} . . . . id.

αὐτῶν   pron. pers., gen. pl. neut. {4.A} . . . . id.

αὑτῶν   pron. refl., gen. pl. masc. {4.F} . . . . .αὑτοῦ *G848*

αὐχεῖ   verb, pres. act. indic. 3 pers. sg.
{5.A.2} . . . . αὐχέω *G3166†‡*

G3166†‡ **αὐχέω**, *I boast.* Var. for μεγαλαυχέω, James 3:5.

G850 **αὐχμηρός**, -α, -όν   *dingy, dusky, obscure, dark, funereal* (poetic, lit. *dry and parched;* then *squalid and rough*).

αὐχμηρῷ   adj., dat. sg. masc. {3.A} . . . . αὐχμηρός *G850*

ἀφ'   prep. . . . . .ἀπό *G575*

ἀφαιρεθήσεται   verb, fut. pass. indic. 3 pers. sg.
{5.A.1} . . . . .ἀφαιρέω *G851*

ἀφαιρεῖν   vbl., pres. act. inf. {6.B.2} . . . . id.

ἀφαιρεῖται   verb, pres. mid. indic. 3 pers. sg.
{5.A.2} . . . . id.

G851 **ἀφαιρέω**   *I take away.*

ἀφαιρῇ   verb, pres. act. subjunc. 3 pers. sg.
{5.B.2} . . . . .ἀφαιρέω *G851*

ἀφαιρήσει   verb, fut. act. indic. 3 pers. sg.
{5.A.1} . . . . id.

G852 **ἀφανής**, -ές   *invisible.*

ἀφανής   adj., nom. sg. fem. {3.E} . . . . ἀφανής *G852*

ἀφανίζει   verb, pres. act. indic. 3 pers. sg.
{5.A.1.a} . . . . .ἀφανίζω *G853*

ἀφανιζομένη   vbl., pres. pass. ptc. nom. sg.
fem. {6.A.1} . . . . id.

ἀφανίζουσι   verb, pres. act. indic. 3 pers. pl.
{5.A.1.a} . . . . id.

ἀφανίζουσιν   verb, pres. act. indic. 3 pers. pl.
{5.A.1.a} . . . . id.

G853 **ἀφανίζω**   (1) *I cause to disappear, hide, remove;* (2) *I disfigure* (probably by leaving unwashed for a long period), Matt 6:16.

ἀφανίσθητε   verb, aor. pass. impv. 2 pers. pl.
{5.D.1} . . . . .ἀφανίζω *G853*

G854 **ἀφανισμός**, -οῦ, ὁ   *disappearing, disappearance.*

ἀφανισμοῦ   noun, gen. sg. masc. {2.B} .ἀφανισμός *G854*

G855 **ἄφαντος**, -ον   *disappearing, invisible, hidden* (orig. poetic).

ἄφαντος   adj., nom. sg. masc. {3.C} . . . . .ἄφαντος *G855*

G856 **ἀφεδρών**, -ῶνος, ὁ   *a drain, latrine.*

ἀφεδρῶνα   noun, acc. sg. masc. {2.C} . . . ἀφεδρών *G856*

ἀφεθῇ   verb, aor. pass. subjunc. 3 pers. sg.
{5.B.3} . . . . .ἀφίημι *G863*

ἀφέθησαν   verb, aor. pass. indic. 3 pers. pl.
{5.A.1} . . . . id.

ἀφεθήσεται verb, fut. pass. indic. 3 pers. sg.
{5.A.1} . . . . id.
G857 **ἀφειδία**, -ας, ἡ *severe treatment* (lit. *unsparingness*).
ἀφειδίᾳ noun, dat. sg. fem. {2.A} . . . . ἀφειδία G857
ἀφεῖλεν verb, ²aor. act. indic. 3 pers. sg.
{5.A.1.b} .ἀφαιρέω G851
ἀφεῖναι vbl., aor. act. inf. {6.B.3} . . . . ἀφίημι G863
ἀφείς vbl., ²aor. act. ptc. nom. sg. masc. {6.A.3} . id.
ἀφεῖς verb, pres. act. indic. 2 pers. sg. {5.A.2} . . id.
ἀφελεῖ verb, ²fut. act. indic. 3 pers. sg.
{5.A.1} . . . . .ἀφαιρέω G851
ἀφελεῖν vbl., ²aor. act. inf. {6.B.1} . . . . id.
ἀφέλῃ verb, ²aor. act. subjunc. 3 pers. sg. {5.B.1} id.
ἀφέλοι verb, aor. act. opt. 3 pers. sg. {5.C.1} . . id.
G858 **ἀφελότης**, -ητος, ἡ *simplicity*.
ἀφελότητι noun, dat. sg. fem. {2.C} . . . .ἀφελότης G858
ἀφέλωμαι verb, ²aor. mid. subjunc. 1 pers. sg.
{5.B.1} . . . . .ἀφαιρέω G851
ἀφέντες vbl., ²aor. act. ptc. nom. pl. masc.
{6.A.3} . . . . ἀφίημι G863
ἄφες verb, ²aor. act. impv. 2 pers. sg. {5.D.3} . . . id.
ἀφέσει noun, dat. sg. fem. {2.C} . . . . . .ἄφεσις G859
ἄφεσιν noun, acc. sg. fem. {2.C} . . . . id.
G859 **ἄφεσις**, -εως, ἡ (1) a *sending away, a letting go, release*; (2) hence, *remission, forgiveness* (cf. in inscriptions, *remission* from debt or punishment; from ἀφίημι).
ἄφεσις noun, nom. sg. fem. {2.C} . . . . ἄφεσις G859
ἄφετε verb, ²aor. act. impv. 2 pers. pl. {5.D.3}ἀφίημι G863
ἀφέωνται verb, perf. pass. indic. 3 pers. pl.
{5.A.1} . . . . id.
ἀφῇ verb, ²aor. act. subjunc. 3 pers. sg. {5.B.3} . . id.
G860 **ἀφή**, -ῆς, ἡ a *band, fastening* (hence, possibly, *a ligament*).
ἀφῆκα verb, aor. act. indic. 1 pers. sg.
{5.A.3.b} . . . . ἀφίημι G863
ἀφήκαμεν verb, aor. act. indic. 1 pers. pl.
{5.A.3.b} . . . . id.
ἀφῆκαν verb, aor. act. indic. 3 pers. pl. {5.A.3.b}id.
ἀφῆκας verb, aor. act. indic. 2 pers. sg. {5.A.3.b}id.
ἀφήκατε verb, aor. act. indic. 2 pers. pl.
{5.A.3.b} . . . . id.
ἀφῆκε verb, aor. act. indic. 3 pers. sg. {5.A.3.b} . id.
ἀφῆκεν verb, aor. act. indic. 3 pers. sg. {5.A.3.b} id.
ἀφῆκες verb, aor. act. indic. 2 pers. sg. {5.A.3.b} id.
ἀφῆς noun, gen. sg. fem. {2.A} . . . . .ἀφή G860
ἀφήσει verb, fut. act. indic. 3 pers. sg.
{5.A.1} . . . . ἀφίημι G863
ἀφήσεις verb, fut. act. indic. 2 pers. sg. {5.A.1} . . id.
ἀφήσουσι verb, fut. act. indic. 3 pers. pl. {5.A.1}id.
ἀφήσουσιν verb, fut. act. indic. 3 pers. pl.
{5.A.1} . . . . id.
ἀφήσω verb, fut. act. indic. 1 pers. sg. {5.A.1} . . id.
ἀφῆτε verb, ²aor. act. subjunc. 2 pers. pl. {5.B.3} id.
G861 **ἀφθαρσία**, -ας, ἡ (1) *indestructibility, incorruptibility*; (2) hence, *immortality*.
ἀφθαρσίᾳ noun, dat. sg. fem. {2.A} . . . . ἀφθαρσία G861
ἀφθαρσίαν noun, acc. sg. fem. {2.A} . . . . id.
ἄφθαρτοι adj., nom. pl. masc. {3.C} . . .ἄφθαρτος G862

ἄφθαρτον adj., acc. sg. fem. {3.C} . . . . id.
ἄφθαρτον adj., acc. sg. masc. {3.C} . . . . id.
ἄφθαρτον adj., acc. sg. neut. {3.C} . . . . id.
G862 **ἄφθαρτος**, -ον (1) *indestructible, imperishable, incorruptible*; (2) hence, *immortal*.
ἀφθάρτου adj., gen. sg. fem. {3.C} . . . .ἄφθαρτος G862
ἀφθάρτου adj., gen. sg. masc. {3.C} . . . . id.
ἀφθάρτῳ adj., dat. sg. masc. {3.C} . . . . id.
ἀφθάρτῳ adj., dat. sg. neut. {3.C} . . . . id.
G901‡ **ἀφθορία**, -ας, ἡ *(moral) incorruptness, incorruption, purity, freedom from taint*. Var. for ἀδιαφθορία, Titus 2:7.
ἀφθορίαν noun, acc. sg. fem. {2.A} . . . . . ἀφθορία G901‡
ἀφίδω verb, ²aor. act. subjunc. 1 pers. sg.
{5.B.1} . . . . ἀφοράω G872
ἀφίεμεν verb, pres. act. indic. 1 pers. pl.
{5.A.3.a} . . . . ἀφίημι G863
ἀφιέναι vbl., pres. act. inf. {6.B.3} . . . . id.
ἀφίενται verb, pres. pass. indic. 3 pers. pl.
{5.A.3.a} . . . . id.
ἀφίεται verb, pres. pass. indic. 3 pers. sg.
{5.A.3.a} . . . . id.
ἀφίετε verb, pres. act. impv. 2 pers. pl. {5.D.3} . . id.
ἀφίετε verb, pres. act. indic. 2 pers. pl. {5.A.3.a} id.
ἀφιέτω verb, pres. act. impv. 3 pers. sg. {5.D.3} . id.
G863 **ἀφίημι** (1) *I send away*; (2) *I let go* or *away, release, permit to depart*; (3) *I remit, forgive*; (4) *I permit*, followed by the subjunc. with (or without) ἵνα, or with acc. obj. and inf.; ἄφες ἐκβάλω (Matt 7:4 = Luke 6:42), *let me (allow me to) cast out*; so also Matt 27:49 = Mark 15:36; John 12:7.
ἀφίημι verb, pres. act. indic. 1 pers. sg.
{5.A.3.a} . . . . ἀφίημι G863
ἀφίησι verb, pres. act. indic. 3 pers. sg. {5.A.3.a}id.
ἀφίησιν verb, pres. act. indic. 3 pers. sg.
{5.A.3.a} . . . . id.
ἀφίκετο verb, ²aor. mid. indic. 3 pers. sg.
{5.A.1.e} . . . . ἀφικνέομαι G864
G864 **ἀφικνέομαι** *I arrive, reach* (in ordinary use very rare at this time).
ἀφιλάγαθοι adj., nom. pl. masc. {3.C} ἀφιλάγαθος G865
G865 **ἀφιλάγαθος**, -ον *not loving that which is good*.
ἀφιλάργυρον adj., acc. sg. masc.
{3.C} . . . . .ἀφιλάργυρος G866
G866 **ἀφιλάργυρος**, -ον *not loving money, not avaricious*.
ἀφιλάργυρος adj., nom. sg. masc.
{3.C} . . . . .ἀφιλάργυρος G866
ἄφιξιν noun, acc. sg. fem. {2.C} . . . . .ἄφιξις G867
G867 **ἄφιξις**, -εως, ἡ *departure*. (This is the sense required by Acts 20:29, but as the word comes from ἀφικνέομαι, it ought to mean *arrival*.)
ἀφίομεν verb, pres. act. indic. 1 pers. pl.
{5.A.3.a} . . . . ἀφίημι G863
ἀφίουσιν verb, pres. act. indic. 3 pers. pl.
{5.A.3.a} . . . . id.
ἀφίστανται verb, pres. mid./pass. indic. 3 pers. pl.
{5.A.3.a} . . . . ἀφίστημι G868

ἀφίστασο   verb, pres. mid./pass. impv. 2 pers.
    sg. {5.D.3} . . . . id.
ἀφίστατο   verb, impf. mid./pass. indic. 3 pers.
    sg. {5.A.3.a} . . . . id.
G868 **ἀφίστημι**   (1) 1aor. trans., *I made to stand
    away, I drew away,* Acts 5:37; *I repelled;* (2)
    other tenses of act. and mid., *I take up a posi-
    tion away from, I withdraw from, I leave.*
G869 **ἄφνω**   adv., *suddenly.*
    ἄφνω   adv. . . . . ἄφνω G869
G870 **ἀφόβως**   adv., *fearlessly* (literary).
    ἀφόβως   adv. {3.F} . . . . ἀφόβως G870
G871 **ἀφομοιόω**   *I make like to.*
G872 **ἀφοράω**   *I look away from (something else) to;*
    ἀφίδω, Phil 2:23, aspirated from ἀπίδω by
    analogy with ἀφοράω; (cf. ἀποβλέπω).
    ἀφοριεῖ   verb, fut. act. indic. 3 pers. sg.
    {5.A.2} . . . . ἀφορίζω G873
    ἀφορίζει   verb, pres. act. indic. 3 pers. sg.
    {5.A.1.a} . . . . id.
G873 **ἀφορίζω**   *I rail off, I separate, I place apart.*
    ἀφοριοῦσι   verb, fut. act. indic. 3 pers. pl.
    {5.A.2} . . . . ἀφορίζω G873
    ἀφοριοῦσιν   verb, fut. act. indic. 3 pers. pl.
    {5.A.2} . . . . id.
    ἀφορίσας   vbl., aor. act. ptc. nom. sg. masc.
    {6.A.1.a} . . . . id.
    ἀφορίσατε   verb, aor. act. impv. 2 pers. pl.
    {5.D.1} . . . . id.
    ἀφορίσει   verb, fut. act. indic. 3 pers. sg.
    {5.A.1.a} . . . . id.
    ἀφορίσθητε   verb, aor. pass. impv. 2 pers. pl.
    {5.D.1} . . . . id.
    ἀφορίσωσιν   verb, aor. act. subjunc. 3 pers. pl.
    {5.B.1} . . . . id.
G874 **ἀφορμή**, -ῆς, ἡ   (1) *a starting, a start;* (2) *cause,
    occasion, opportunity.*
    ἀφορμήν   noun, acc. sg. fem. {2.A} . . . . . . ἀφορμή G874
    ἀφορῶντες   vbl., pres. act. ptc. nom. pl. masc.
    {6.A.2} . . . . ἀφοράω G872
    ἀφρίζει   verb, pres. act. indic. 3 pers. sg.
    {5.A.1.a} . . . . ἀφρίζω G875
G875 **ἀφρίζω**   *I foam* (at the mouth).
    ἀφρίζων   vbl., pres. act. ptc. nom. sg. masc.
    {6.A.1} . . . . ἀφρίζω G875
    ἄφρον   adj., voc. sg. masc. {3.E} . . . . ἄφρων G878
    ἄφρονα   adj., acc. sg. masc. {3.E} . . . . id.
    ἄφρονες   adj., nom. pl. masc. {3.E} . . . . id.
    ἄφρονες   adj., voc. pl. masc. {3.E} . . . . id.
    ἀφρόνων   adj., gen. pl. masc. {3.E} . . . . id.
G876 **ἀφρός**, -οῦ, ὁ   *foam* (at the mouth).
G877 **ἀφροσύνη**, -ης, ἡ   *want of sense, foolishness.*
    ἀφροσύνη   noun, nom. sg. fem. {2.A} . ἀφροσύνη G877
    ἀφροσύνη   noun, dat. sg. fem. {2.A} . . . . id.
    ἀφροσύνης   noun, gen. sg. fem. {2.A} . . . . id.
    ἀφροῦ   noun, gen. sg. masc. {2.B} . . . . ἀφρός G876
G878 **ἄφρων**, -ον   *senseless, foolish, inconsiderate.*
    ἄφρων   adj., nom. sg. masc. {3.E} . . . . ἄφρων G878
    ἄφρων   adj., voc. sg. masc. {3.E} . . . . id.
G879 **ἀφυπνόω**   *I fall asleep* (very rare).

ἀφύπνωσε   verb, aor. act. indic. 3 pers. sg.
    {5.A.1} . . . . ἀφυπνόω G879
    ἀφύπνωσεν   verb, aor. act. indic. 3 pers. sg.
    {5.A.1} . . . . id.
G650†‡ **ἀφυστερέω**   *I withdraw, take away.* Var. for
    ἀποστερέω, Jas 5:4.
    ἀφυστερημένος   vbl., perf. pass. ptc. nom. sg.
    masc. {6.A.2} . . . . ἀφυστερέω G650†‡
    ἀφῶμεν   verb, ²aor. act. subjunc. 1 pers. pl.
    {5.B.3} . . . . ἀφίημι G863
    ἀφωμοιωμένος   vbl., perf. pass. ptc. nom. sg.
    masc. {6.A.2} . . . . ἀφομοιόω G871
    ἀφῶν   noun, gen. pl. fem. {2.A} . . . . ἀφή G860
    ἄφωνα   adj., acc. pl. neut. {3.C} . . . . ἄφωνος G880
    ἄφωνον   adj., nom. sg. neut. {3.C} . . . . id.
G880 **ἄφωνος**, -ον   *soundless, voiceless, speechless,
    dumb.*
    ἄφωνος   adj., nom. sg. masc. {3.C} . . . . ἄφωνος G880
    ἀφωριζεν   verb, impf. act. indic. 3 pers. sg.
    {5.A.1.b} . . . . ἀφορίζω G873
    ἀφώρισε   verb, aor. act. indic. 3 pers. sg.
    {5.A.1.b} . . . . id.
    ἀφώρισεν   verb, aor. act. indic. 3 pers. sg.
    {5.A.1.b} . . . . id.
    ἀφωρισμένος   vbl., perf. pass. ptc. nom. sg.
    masc. {6.A.1.b} . . . . id.
G881 **Ἀχάζ**, ὁ   *Ahaz,* son of Joatham and father of
    Hezekiah (Heb.).
    Ἀχάζ   noun prop. . . . . Ἀχάζ G881
    Ἀχάζ   noun prop. . . . .
    Ἀχαΐα   noun prop., nom. sg. fem. {2.A; 2.D} . .Ἀχαΐα G882
    Ἀχαΐᾳ   noun prop., dat. sg. fem. {2.A; 2.D} . . . . id.
G882 **Ἀχαΐα**, -ας, ἡ   *the Roman Province Achaia,*
    governed by a proconsul, and practically
    conterminous with mod. Greece before 1912.
    Ἀχαΐα   noun prop., nom. sg. fem. {2.A; 2.D} . .Ἀχαΐα G882
    Ἀχαΐᾳ   noun prop., dat. sg. fem. {2.A; 2.D} . . . . id.
    Ἀχαΐαν   noun prop., acc. sg. fem. {2.A; 2.D} . . . . id.
    Ἀχαΐαν   noun prop., acc. sg. fem. {2.A; 2.D} . . . . id.
    Ἀχαΐας   noun prop., gen. sg. fem. {2.A; 2.D} . . . . id.
    Ἀχαΐας   noun prop., gen. sg. fem. {2.A; 2.D} . . . . id.
G883 **Ἀχαϊκός**, -οῦ, ὁ   *Achaicus,* a Corinthian
    Christian.
    Ἀχαϊκοῦ   noun prop., gen. sg. masc. {2.B;
    2.D} . . . . Ἀχαϊκός G883
    ἀχάριστοι   adj., nom. pl. masc. {3.C} . . ἀχάριστος G884
G884 **ἀχάριστος**, -ον   *ungrateful.*
    ἀχαρίστους   adj., acc. pl. masc. {3.C} . . ἀχάριστος G884
    Ἄχας   noun prop. . . . . Ἀχάζ G881
    Ἀχείμ   noun prop. . . . . Ἀχίμ G885
    ἀχειροποίητον   adj., acc. sg. fem.
    {3.C} . . . . ἀχειροποίητος G886‡
    ἀχειροποίητον   adj., acc. sg. masc. {3.C} . . . . id.
G886‡ **ἀχειροποίητος**, -ον   *not made by hand, not
    handmade* (unknown outside NT).
    ἀχειροποιήτῳ   adj., dat. sg. fem.
    {3.C} . . . . ἀχειροποίητος G886‡
    ἀχθῆναι   vbl., aor. pass. inf. {6.B.1} . . . . ἄγω G71
    ἀχθήσεσθε   verb, fut. pass. indic. 2 pers. pl.
    {5.A.1.d} . . . . id.

G885 **Ἀχίμ**, ὁ   *Achim,* son of Zadok and father of
    Eliud (Heb.).
    Ἀχίμ   noun prop. . . . . Ἀχίμ *G885*

G887 **ἀχλύς**, -ύος, ἡ   *mist.*
    ἀχλύς   noun, nom. sg. fem. {2.C} . . . . ἀχλύς *G887*
    ἀχρεῖοι   adj., nom. pl. masc. {3.C} . . . . . . ἀχρεῖος *G888*
    ἀχρεῖον   adj., acc. sg. masc. {3.C} . . . . id.

G888 **ἀχρεῖος**, -ον   *unprofitable, useless, unworthy.*

G889 **ἀχρειόω** (ἀχρεόω)   pass. *I am good for nothing*
    (lit. *I become sour, I turn,* of milk).
    ἀχρηστον   adj., acc. sg. masc. {3.C} . . . . ἀχρηστος *G890*

G890 **ἄχρηστος**, -ον   *unprofitable, useless* (a play
    upon words, with ὀνήσιμος).

G891 **ἄχρι** (ἄχρις)   prep. with gen., *as far as, up to,*
    conj. *until;* ἄχρι τοῦ νῦν = *until now;* ἄχρι οὗ
    (with or without ἄν) with the subjunc., *until.*
    ἄχρι   prep. . . . . ἄχρι *G891*
    ἄχρις   prep. . . . . id.

G892 **ἄχυρον**, -ου, τό   *chaff.*
    ἄχυρον   noun, acc. sg. neut. {2.B} . . . . ἄχυρον *G892*
    ἀψάμενος   vbl., aor. mid. ptc. nom. sg. masc.
    {6.A.1.b} . . . . ἅπτομαι *G680*

    ἅψαντες   vbl., aor. act. ptc. nom. pl. masc.
    {6.A.1.a} . . . . .ἅπτω *G681*
    ἁψάντων   vbl., aor. act. ptc. gen. pl. masc.
    {6.A.1.a} . . . . id.
    ἅψας   vbl., aor. act. ptc. nom. sg. masc. {6.A.1.a} id.

G893 **ἀψευδής**, -ές   *not guilty of falsehood, truthful.*
    ἀψευδής   adj., nom. sg. masc. {3.E} . . . . . ἀψευδής *G893*
    ἅψῃ   verb, aor. mid. subjunc. 2 pers. sg.
    {5.B.1} . . . . ἅπτομαι *G680*
    ἅψηται   verb, aor. mid. subjunc. 3 pers. sg.
    {5.B.1} . . . . id.
    ἄψινθον   noun, acc. sg. fem. {2.B} . . . . . . ἄψινθος *G894*

G894 **ἄψινθος**, -ου, ὁ   *wormwood;* ὁ Ἄψινθος, a star.
    Ἄψινθος   noun prop., nom. sg. fem. {2.B;
    2.D} . . . . Ἄψινθος *G894*
    Ἄψινθος   noun prop., nom. sg. masc. {2.B; 2.D}. id.
    ἄψυχα   adj., nom. pl. neut. {3.C} . . . . ἄψυχος *G895*

G895 **ἄψυχος**, -ον   *lifeless.*
    ἅψωμαι   verb, aor. mid. subjunc. 1 pers. sg.
    {5.B.1} . . . . ἅπτομαι *G680*
    ἅψωνται   verb, aor. mid. subjunc. 3 pers. pl.
    {5.B.1} . . . . id.

B β

G896 **Βάαλ**, ὁ   *Baal,* a god worshipped by the
    Hebrews (in Rom 11:4 fem., because Jews in
    reading substituted αἰσχύνη), being the high-
    est god of all the West Semitic peoples. (Bahal,
    properly = *Lord,* and so not a proper name).
    Βάαλ   noun prop. . . . . Βάαλ *G896*
    Βαβυλων   noun prop., nom. sg. fem. {2.C;
    2.D} . . . . Βαβυλών *G897*

G897 **Βαβυλών**, -ῶνος, ἡ   (1) *Babylon,* the ancient
    city on the Euphrates, to which the people of
    Jerusalem, etc., were transported; (2) hence
    allegorically of Rome, from the point of view of
    the Christian people, Rev (6 times), 1 Pet 5:13
    (probably).
    Βαβυλών   noun prop., nom. sg. fem. {2.C;
    2.D} . . . . Βαβυλών *G897*
    Βαβυλῶνι   noun prop., dat. sg. fem. {2.C; 2.D} . id.
    Βαβυλῶνος   noun prop., gen. sg. fem. {2.C; 2.D}id.
    βαθέα   adj., acc. pl. neut. {3.D} . . . . βαθύς *G901*
    βαθεῖ   adj., dat. sg. masc. {3.D} . . . . id.
    βαθέος   adj., gen. sg. masc. {3.D} . . . . id.
    βαθέως   adj., gen. sg. masc. {3.D} . . . . id.
    βάθη   noun, acc. pl. neut. {2.C} . . . . βάθος *G899*
    βαθμόν   noun, acc. sg. masc. {2.B} . . . . βαθμός *G898*

G898 **βαθμός**, -οῦ, ὁ   (1) *a step* (of a stairway); (2)
    hence, *a stage* in a career, *a position.*

G899 **βάθος**, -ους, τό   (1) *depth;* (2) *a depth, a deep*
    (also met.).
    βάθος   noun, acc. sg. neut. {2.C} . . . . βάθος *G899*
    βάθος   noun, nom. sg. neut. {2.C} . . . . id.
    βάθους   noun, gen. sg. neut. {2.C} . . . . id.
    βαθύ   adj., nom. sg. neut. {3.D} . . . . βαθύς *G901*

G900 **βαθύνω**   *I deepen.*

G901 **βαθύς**, -εῖα, -ύ   *deep* (lit., and met.); ὄρθρου
    βαθέως, *in the depths of the early morning,*
    while still very early.
    βαῖα   noun, acc. pl. neut. {2.B} . . . . βάϊον *G902*

G902 **βάϊον**, -ου, τό   *a palm branch.*

G903 **Βαλαάμ**, ὁ   *Balaam* (Balaham), son of Beor of
    Pethor on the Euphrates, a soothsayer in the
    OT (Heb.).
    Βαλαάμ   noun prop. . . . . Βαλαάμ *G903*

G904 **Βαλάκ**, ὁ   *Balac, Balak,* son of Zippor, King of
    Moab (Heb.).
    Βαλάκ   noun prop. Βαλάκ *G904*
    βαλάντια   noun, acc. pl. neut. {2.B} . . βαλλάντιον *G905*
    βαλάντιον   noun, acc. sg. neut. {2.B} . . . . id.
    βαλαντίου   noun, gen. sg. neut. {2.B} . . . . id.
    βάλε   verb, ²aor. act. impv. 2 pers. sg. {5.D.1} βάλλω *G906*
    βαλεῖ   verb, fut. act. indic. 3 pers. sg. {5.A.2} . . id.
    βαλεῖν   vbl., ²aor. act. inf. {6.B.1} . . . . id.
    βάλετε   verb, ²aor. act. impv. 2 pers. pl. {5.D.1} . . id.
    βαλέτω   verb, ²aor. act. impv. 3 pers. sg. {5.D.1} . id.
    βάλῃ   verb, ²aor. act. subjunc. 3 pers. sg. {5.B.1} . id.
    βάλητε   verb, ²aor. act. subjunc. 2 pers. pl.
    {5.B.1} . . . . id.
    βαλλάντια   noun, acc. pl. neut. {2.B} . . βαλλάντιον *G905*

G905 **βαλλάντιον**, -ου, τό   *a purse.*
    βαλλάντιον   noun, acc. sg. neut. {2.B} . βαλλάντιον *G905*
    βαλλαντίου   noun, gen. sg. neut. {2.B} . . . . id.
    βάλλει   verb, pres. act. indic. 3 pers. sg.
    {5.A.1.a} . . . . βάλλω *G906*
    βάλλειν   vbl., pres. act. inf. {6.B.1} . . . . id.
    βάλλεται   verb, pres. pass. indic. 3 pers. sg.
    {5.A.1.d} . . . . id.
    βάλλῃ   verb, pres. act. subjunc. 3 pers. sg. {5.B.1}id.

βάλλομεν   verb, pres. act. indic. 1 pers. pl.
{5.A.1.a} . . . . id.

βαλλόμενα   vbl., pres. pass. ptc. acc. pl. neut.
{6.A.1} . . . . id.

βαλλόμενον   vbl., pres. pass. ptc. acc. sg. masc.
{6.A.1} . . . . id.

βάλλοντας   vbl., pres. act. ptc. acc. pl. masc.
{6.A.1} . . . . id.

βάλλοντες   vbl., pres. act. ptc. nom. pl. masc.
{6.A.1} . . . . id.

βαλλόντων   vbl., pres. act. ptc. gen. pl. masc.
{6.A.1} . . . . id.

βάλλουσα   vbl., pres. act. ptc. nom. sg. fem. {6.A.1} id.

βάλλουσαν   vbl., pres. act. ptc. acc. sg. fem.
{6.A.1} . . . . id.

βάλλουσι   verb, pres. act. indic. 3 pers. pl. {5.A.1.a} id.

βάλλουσιν   verb, pres. act. indic. 3 pers. pl.
{5.A.1.a} . . . . id.

G906 **βάλλω**   (1) *I cast, throw;* (2) intrans., *I rush,* Acts
27:14; (3) often, in the weaker sense, *I place,
put, drop;* βεβλημένος, *lying in bed,* Matt 8:14.
βάλλω   verb, pres. act. indic. 1 pers. sg.
{5.A.1.a} . . . . βάλλω G906

βάλοντες   vbl., ²aor. act. ptc. nom. pl. masc.
{6.A.1} . . . . id.

βαλόντων   vbl., ²aor. act. ptc. gen. pl. masc.
{6.A.1.a} . . . . id.

βαλοῦσα   vbl., ²aor. act. ptc. nom. sg. fem.
{6.A.1.a} . . . . id.

βαλοῦσιν   verb, fut. act. indic. 3 pers. pl. {5.A.2} id.

βάλω   verb, fut. act. indic. 1 pers. sg. {5.A.1.a} . . id.

βάλω   verb, ²aor. act. subjunc. 1 pers. sg. {5.B.1}. id.

βάλωσιν   verb, ²aor. act. subjunc. 3 pers. pl. {5.B.1}. id.

βαπτίζει   verb, pres. act. indic. 3 pers. sg.
{5.A.1.a} . . . . βαπτίζω G907

βαπτίζειν   vbl., pres. act. inf. {6.B.1} . . . . id.

βαπτίζεις   verb, pres. act. indic. 2 pers. sg.
{5.A.1.a} . . . . id.

βαπτίζομαι   verb, pres. pass. indic. 1 pers. sg.
{5.A.1.d} . . . . id.

βαπτιζόμενοι   vbl., pres. pass. ptc. nom. pl.
masc. {6.A.1} . . . . id.

βαπτίζονται   verb, pres. pass. indic. 3 pers. pl.
{5.A.1.d} . . . . id.

βαπτίζοντες   vbl., pres. act. ptc. nom. pl. masc.
{6.A.1} . . . . id.

βαπτίζοντος   vbl., pres. act. ptc. gen. sg. masc.
{6.A.1} . . . . id.

G907 **βαπτίζω**   lit. *I dip, submerge,* but specifically of
ceremonial dipping (whether immersion or
pouring), *I baptize;* when the prep. εἰς with a
noun in the acc. follows, it appears to indicate
that through this ceremony the baptized
person becomes the property of the person
indicated after εἰς; met. Mark 10:38.
βαπτίζω   verb, pres. act. indic. 1 pers. sg.
{5.A.1.a} . . . . βαπτίζω G907

βαπτίζων   vbl., pres. act. ptc. nom. sg. masc.
{6.A.1} . . . . id.

βάπτισαι   verb, aor. mid. impv. 2 pers. sg. {5.D.1} . id.

βαπτίσει   verb, fut. act. indic. 3 pers. sg.
{5.A.1.a} . . . . id.

βαπτισθείς   vbl., aor. pass. ptc. nom. sg. masc.
{6.A.1.a} . . . . id.

βαπτισθέντες   vbl., aor. pass. ptc. nom. pl.
masc. {6.A.1.a} . . . . id.

βαπτισθέντος   vbl., aor. pass. ptc. gen. sg.
masc. {6.A.1.a} . . . . id.

βαπτισθῆναι   vbl., aor. pass. inf. {6.B.1} . . . . . id.

βαπτισθήσεσθε   verb, fut. pass. indic. 2 pers.
pl. {5.A.1.d} . . . . id.

βαπτισθήτω   verb, aor. pass. impv. 3 pers. sg.
{5.D.1} . . . . id.

G908 **βάπτισμα**, -ατος, τό   *a dipping, a baptism;*
with gen. μετανοίας, belonging to a change
of mental attitude, sign of a change of mental
attitude.
βάπτισμα   noun, acc. sg. neut. {2.C} . . . βάπτισμα G908

βάπτισμα   noun, nom. sg. neut. {2.C} . . . . . . id.

βαπτίσματι   noun, dat. sg. neut. {2.C} . . . . . . id.

βαπτισματος   noun, gen. sg. neut. {2.C} . . . . . id.

βαπτισμοῖς   noun, dat. pl. masc. {2.B} . . βαπτισμός G909

G909 **βαπτισμός**, -οῦ, ὁ   *dipping, washing* (of a
ceremonial character).
βαπτισμούς   noun, acc. pl. masc. {2.B} . βαπτισμός G909

βαπτισμῷ   noun, dat. sg. masc. {2.B} . . . . id.

βαπτισμῶν   noun, gen. pl. masc. {2.B} . . . . . . id.

βαπτιστήν   noun, acc. sg. masc. {2.A} . . βαπτιστής G910

G910 **βαπτιστής**, -οῦ, ὁ   *the baptizer, the baptist,*
epithet used only of John, the son of Zechariah
and Elizabeth, forerunner of Jesus.
βαπτιστής   noun, nom. sg. masc. {2.A} . βαπτιστής G910

βαπτιστοῦ   noun, gen. sg. masc. {2.A} . . . . . . id.

βαπτίσωνται   verb, aor. mid. subjunc. 3 pers. pl.
{5.B.1} . . . . βαπτίζω G907

G911 **βάπτω**   (1) *I dip;* (2) *I dye;* Rev 19:13, cf.
δίβαφα, twice-dyed garments.

βάρ   Aram. Βαριωνᾶ G920

Βαραββᾶν   noun prop., acc. sg. masc. {2.A;
2.D} . . . . Βαραββᾶς G912

G912 **Βαραββᾶς**, -ᾶ, ὁ   *Barabbas* (really *Jesus Barabbas,* according to certain MSS of Matt 27:17), a
highway robber.
Βαραββᾶς   noun prop., nom. sg. masc. {2.A;
2.D} . . . . Βαραββᾶς G912

G913 **Βαράκ**, ὁ   *Barak,* one of the judges of Israel
(Heb.).
Βαράκ   noun prop. . . . . Βαράκ G913

G914 **Βαραχίας**, -ου, ὁ   *Barachias, Baruch* (Heb.).
His identity is uncertain, perhaps father of the
Zacharias killed by the Zealots in the last Jew-
ish War (Josephus, *B.J.* 4.5.4). See Ζαχαρίας.
Βαραχίου   noun prop., gen. sg. masc. {2.A;
2.D} . . . . Βαραχίας G914

βάρβαροι   adj., nom. pl. masc. {3.C} . . . βάρβαρος G915

βαρβάροις   adj., dat. pl. masc. {3.C} . . . . id.

G915 **βάρβαρος**, -ον   *a foreigner,* one who speaks
neither Gk. nor Lat.; as adj., *foreign.*
βάρβαρος   adj., nom. sg. masc. {3.C} . . . βάρβαρος G915

βαρέα   adj., acc. pl. neut. {3.D} . . . . βαρύς G926 βάρει   noun, dat. sg. neut. {2.C} . . . . .βάρος *G922*

βαρεῖαι   adj., nom. pl. fem. {3.D}. . . . . .βαρύς *G926*

βαρεῖς   adj., nom. pl. masc. {3.D}. . . . . id.

βαρείσθω   verb, pres. pass. impv. 3 pers. sg.
{5.D.2}. . . . . .βαρέω *G916*

G916 **βαρέω**   *I weight, load, burden,* lit. and met.

G917 **βαρέως**   adv., *heavily, with difficulty.*

βαρέως   adv. {3.F} . . . . .βαρέως *G917*

βάρη   noun, acc. pl. neut. {2.C} . . . . βάρος *G922*

βαρηθῶσιν   verb, aor. pass. subjunc. 3 pers. pl.
{5.B.1}. . . . . .βαρέω *G916*

Βαρθολομαῖον   noun prop., acc. sg. masc. {2.B;
2.D}. Βαρθολομαῖος *G918*

G918 **Βαρθολομαῖος**, -ου, ὁ   *Bartholomew,* son of
Tholmai (Aram. for Ptolomaeus), one of the
twelve disciples of Jesus

Βαρθολομαῖος   noun prop., nom. sg. masc. {2.B;
2.D}. Βαρθολομαῖος *G918*

Βαριησοῦ   noun prop., gen. sg. masc. {2.B;
2.D}. . . . . Βαριησοῦς *G919*

G919 **Βαριησοῦς**, -οῦ, ὁ   *Bar-Jesus* (i.e., son of
Jesus), the name of the magician and false
prophet at Paphos in Cyprus. He is also called
Elymas (Aram.).

Βαριησοῦς   noun prop., nom. sg. masc. {2.B;
2.D}. . . . . Βαριησοῦς *G919*

Βαρϊησοῦς   noun prop., nom. sg. masc. {2.B;
2.D}. . . . . id.

G920 **Βαριωνᾶ** (Βαριωνᾶς), -ᾶ, ὁ   *Bar-Jonas,* son of
Jonas, the surname of Simon Peter (Aram.).

Βαριωνᾶ   noun prop.. . . . . Βαριωνᾶ *G920*

Βαρνάβα   noun prop., gen. sg. masc. {2.A;
2.D}. . . . . Βαρναβᾶς *G921*

Βαρνάββα   noun prop., dat. sg. masc. {2.A; 2.D} . id.

Βαρναβᾶ   noun prop., gen. sg. masc. {2.A; 2.D}. id.

Βαρναβᾶ   noun prop., dat. sg. masc. {2.A; 2.D} . id.

Βαρνάβαν   noun prop., acc. sg. masc. {2.A; 2.D} id.

Βαρναβᾶν   noun prop., acc. sg. masc. {2.A; 2.D} id.

G921 **Βαρναβᾶς**, -ᾶ, ὁ   *Barnabas* (son of Nebo), a
Cypriote Jew, uncle of John Mark; his other
name was Joseph (Aram.).

Βαρνάβας   noun prop., nom. sg. masc. {2.A;
2.D}. . . . . Βαρναβᾶς *G921*

Βαρναβᾶς   noun prop., nom. sg. masc. {2.A;
2.D}. . . . . id.

G922 **βάρος**, -ους, τό   (1) *a weight, a burden,* lit. or
met.; (2) in 1 Thess 2:7 there may be a play on
the derived sense, *authority, dignity.*

βάρος   noun, acc. sg. neut. {2.C} . . . . .βάρος *G922*

βαρούμενοι   vbl., pres. pass. ptc. nom. pl. masc.
{6.A.2}. . . . . .βαρέω *G916*

Βαρσαβᾶν   noun prop., acc. sg. masc. {2.A;
2.D}. . . . . .Βαρσαββᾶς *G923*

Βαρσαββᾶν   noun prop., acc. sg. masc. {2.A;
2.D}. . . . . id.

G923 **Βαρσαββᾶς**, Βαρσαβᾶς ᾶ, ὁ   *Barsabbas,* son
of Sabbas, a surname of Joseph (Acts 1:23) and
Judas (Acts 15:22) (Aram.).

Βαρτίμαιος   noun prop., nom. sg. masc. {2.B;
2.D}. . . . . Βαρτιμαῖος *G924*

G924 **Βαρτιμαῖος**, -ου, ὁ   *Bartimaeus,* son of(?)
Timaeus (Aram.).

Βαρτιμαῖος   noun prop., nom. sg. masc. {2.B;
2.D}. . . . . Βαρτιμαῖος *G924*

βαρυνθῶσιν   verb, aor. pass. subjunc. 3 pers. pl.
{5.B.1} . . . . βαρύνω *G925*

G925 **βαρύνω**   *I weigh down, burden.*

G926 **βαρύς**, -εῖα, -ύ   *heavy, weighty, burdensome,* lit.
and met.

βαρύτερα   adj. comp., acc. pl. neut. {3.D;
3.G}. . . . . .βαρύς *G926*

G927 **βαρύτιμος**, -ον   *heavy in price, very expensive.*

βαρυτίμου   adj., gen. sg. neut. {3.C}. . . . βαρύτιμος *G927*

βασανιζομένη   vbl., pres. pass. ptc. nom. sg. fem.
{6.A.1}. . . . . βασανίζω *G928*

βασανιζόμενον   vbl., pres. pass. ptc. nom. sg.
neut. {6.A.1} . . . . id.

βασανιζόμενος   vbl., pres. pass. ptc. nom. sg.
masc. {6.A.1}. . . . . id.

βασανιζομένους   vbl., pres. pass. ptc. acc. pl.
masc. {6.A.1}. . . . . id.

G928 **βασανίζω**   *I torture.*

βασανίσαι   vbl., aor. act. inf. {6.B.1} . . . βασανίζω *G928*

βασανίσῃς   verb, aor. act. subjunc. 2 pers. sg.
{5.B.1}. . . . . id.

βασανισθήσεται   verb, fut. pass. indic. 3 pers.
sg. {5.A.1.d}. . . . . id.

βασανισθήσονται   verb, fut. pass. indic.
3 pers. pl. {5.A.1.d} . . . . id.

βασανισθῶσι   verb, aor. pass. subjunc. 3 pers.
pl. {5.B.1}. . . . . id.

βασανισθῶσιν   verb, aor. pass. subjunc. 3 pers.
pl. {5.B.1}. . . . . id.

βασανισμόν   noun, acc. sg. masc.
{2.B} .βασανισμός *G929*

G929 **βασανισμός**, -οῦ, ὁ   *torture.*

βασανισμός   noun, nom. sg. masc.
{2.B} .βασανισμός *G929*

βασανισμοῦ   noun, gen. sg. masc. {2.B} . . . . . . id.

βασανισταῖς   noun, dat. pl. masc.
{2.A} .βασανιστής *G930*

G930 **βασανιστής**, -οῦ, ὁ   *a torturer.*

βασάνοις   noun, dat. pl. fem. {2.B} . . . . . βάσανος *G931*

G931 **βάσανος**, -ου, ἡ   *torture.*

βασάνου   noun, gen. sg. fem. {2.B} . . . . . βάσανος *G931*

βάσεις   noun, nom. pl. fem. {2.C} . . . . . . .βάσις *G939*

βασιλέα   noun, acc. sg. masc. {2.C} . . . . βασιλεύς *G935*

βασιλεῖ   noun, dat. sg. masc. {2.C}. . . . . id.

G932 **βασιλεία**, -ας, ἡ   (1) *kingship, sovereignty,
authority, rule,* esp. of God, both in the
world, and in the hearts of men; (2) hence,
kingdom, in the concr. sense; ἡ βασιλεία τῶν
οὐρανῶν perhaps always signifies the *coming*
kingdom, but ἡ βασιλεία τοῦ θεοῦ is wider.

βασιλεία   noun, nom. sg. fem. {2.A} . . . . βασιλεία *G932*

βασιλείᾳ   noun, dat. sg. fem. {2.A} . . . . id.

βασιλεῖαι   noun, nom. pl. fem. {2.A}. . . . . id.

βασιλείαν   noun, acc. sg. fem. {2.A} . . . . id.

βασιλείας   noun, acc. pl. fem. {2.A}. . . . . id.

βασιλείας   noun, gen. sg. fem. {2.A} . . . . id.

βασιλείοις   adj., dat. pl. masc. {3.C}. . . . βασίλειος *G934*
βασιλείοις   adj., dat. pl. neut. {3.C} . . . . id.
βασίλειον   adj., nom. sg. neut. {3.C} . . . . id.
G933 **βασίλειον**   *a palace* (neut. subs. of βασίλειος).
G934 **βασίλειος**, -ον   (1) in Luke 7:25 either masc.
    courtiers, or neut. *palaces;* (2) the LXX
    intended βασίλειον as subs., *a body of kings,*
    in the passage quoted by 1 Pet 2:9, but Peter
    clearly takes βασίλειον as adj., *royal.*
βασιλεῖς   noun, acc. pl. masc. {2.C} . . . . βασιλεύς *G935*
βασιλεῖς   noun, nom. pl. masc. {2.C} . . . . id.
βασιλείων   adj., gen. pl. masc. {3.C} . . . βασίλειος *G934*
βασιλεῦ   noun, voc. sg. masc. {2.C} . . . . βασιλεύς *G935*
βασιλεύει   verb, pres. act. indic. 3 pers. sg.
    {5.A.1.a} . . . . βασιλεύω *G936*
βασιλεύειν   vbl., pres. act. inf. {6.B.1} . . . . id.
βασιλευέτω   verb, pres. act. impv. 3 pers. sg.
    {5.D.1} . . . . id.
βασιλευόντων   vbl., pres. act. ptc. gen. pl.
    masc. {6.A.1} . . . . id.
βασιλεύουσιν   verb, pres. act. indic. 3 pers. pl.
    {5.A.1.a} . . . . id.
G935 **βασιλεύς**, -έως, ὁ   *a king,* but in some pas-
    sages, as 1 Pet 2:17, clearly to be translated
    emperor; ὁ βασιλεὺς τῶν βασιλέων (βα-
    σιλευόντων), *the King of Kings,* an oriental
    type of phrase, used for the Persian king as
    overlord of other kings, and in scripture of
    God.
βασιλεύς   noun, nom. sg. masc. {2.C} . . . βασιλεύς *G935*
βασιλεῦσαι   vbl., aor. act. inf. {6.B.1} . . .βασιλεύω *G936*
βασιλεύσει   verb, fut. act. indic. 3 pers. sg.
    {5.A.1.a} . . . . id.
βασιλεύσῃ   verb, aor. act. subjunc. 3 pers. sg.
    {5.B.1} . . . . id.
βασιλεῦσι   noun, dat. pl. masc. {2.C} . . . βασιλεύς *G935*
βασιλεῦσιν   noun, dat. pl. masc. {2.C} . . . . id.
βασιλεύσομεν   verb, fut. act. indic. 1 pers. pl.
    {5.A.1.a} . . . . βασιλεύω *G936*
βασιλεύσουσι   verb, fut. act. indic. 3 pers. pl.
    {5.A.1.a} . . . . id.
βασιλεύσουσιν   verb, fut. act. indic. 3 pers. pl.
    {5.A.1.a} . . . . id.
G936 **βασιλεύω**   (1) *I rule, reign;* (2) *I reign over,*
    with gen.
βασιλέων   noun, gen. pl. masc. {2.C} . . . . βασιλεύς *G935*
βασιλέως   noun, gen. sg. masc. {2.C} . . . . id.
βασιλικήν   adj., acc. sg. fem. {3.A} . . . . βασιλικός *G937*
βασιλικῆς   adj., gen. sg. fem. {3.A} . . . . id.
βασιλικόν   adj., acc. sg. masc. {3.A} . . . . id.
G937 **βασιλικός**, -ή, -όν   (1) *connected with a king,*
    royal, regal in Jas 2:8 βασιλικὸς νόμος, a
    supreme law is referred to, the more important
    parts of the law; (2) substantivally, (a) *an of-*
    ficer in the service of the king (Herod Antipas),
    John 4:46, 49; (b) ἡ βασιλικὴ (understand
    χώρα), *the king's country,* Acts 12:20.
βασιλικός   adj., nom. sg. masc. {3.A} . . . βασιλικός *G937*
G938 **βασίλισσα**, -ης, ἡ   *a queen.*
βασίλισσα   noun, nom. sg. fem. {2.A} . . .βασίλισσα *G938*

βασιλίσσης   noun, gen. sg. fem. {2.A} . . . . id.
G939 **βάσις**, -εως, ἡ   *a foot* (properly, that on which
    something may rest).
G940 **βασκαίνω**   *I give the evil eye to, fascinate,*
    bewitch, over power.
βαστάζει   verb, pres. act. indic. 3 pers. sg.
    {5.A.1.a} . . . . βαστάζω *G941*
βαστάζειν   vbl., pres. act. inf. {6.B.1} . . . . id.
βαστάζεις   verb, pres. act. indic. 2 pers. sg.
    {5.A.1.a} . . . . id.
βαστάζεσθαι   vbl., pres. pass. inf. {6.B.1} . . . . id.
βαστάζετε   verb, pres. act. impv. 2 pers. pl.
    {5.D.1} . . . . id.
βαστάζοντες   vbl., pres. act. ptc. nom. pl.
    masc. {6.A.1} . . . . id.
βαστάζοντος   vbl., pres. act. ptc. gen. sg. neut.
    {6.A.1} . . . . id.
G941 **βαστάζω**   (1) *I carry, bear;* (2) *I carry (take)*
    away, Matt 3:11; John 20:15; (3) *I pilfer,* John
    12:6.
βαστάζω   verb, pres. act. indic. 1 pers. sg.
    {5.A.1.a} . . . . βαστάζω *G941*
βαστάζων   vbl., pres. act. ptc. nom. sg. masc.
    {6.A.1} . . . . id.
βαστάσαι   vbl., aor. act. inf. {6.B.1} . . . . id.
βαστάσασα   vbl., aor. act. ptc. nom. sg. fem.
    {6.A.1.a} . . . . id.
βαστάσασι   vbl., aor. act. ptc. dat. pl. masc.
    {6.A.1.a} . . . . id.
βαστάσασιν   vbl., aor. act. ptc. dat. pl. masc.
    {6.A.1.a} . . . . id.
βαστάσει   verb, fut. act. indic. 3 pers. sg.
    {5.A.1.a} . . . . id.
G942 **βάτος**[1], -ου, ὁ or ἡ   *a thorn bush;* ἐπὶ τοῦ
    (Luke τῆς) βάτου, in the passage about the
    thorn bush, Mark 12:26; Luke 20:37.
G943 **βάτος**[2], -ου, ὁ   *a "bath"* (a liquid measure
    among the Jews, containing between eight and
    nine gallons) (Heb.).
βάτου   noun, gen. sg. fem. {2.B} . . . . βάτος[1] *G942*
βάτου   noun, gen. sg. masc. {2.B} . . . . id.
βάτους   noun, acc. pl. masc. {2.B} . . . . βάτος[2] *G943*
βάτραχοι   noun, nom. pl. masc. {2.B} . . . βάτραχος *G944*
βατράχοις   noun, dat. pl. masc. {2.B} . . . . id.
G944 **βάτραχος**, -ου, ὁ   *a frog.*
G945 **βατταλογέω**   *I chatter, am long-winded, utter*
    empty words.
βατταλογήσητε   verb, aor. act. subjunc. 2 pers. pl.
    {5.B.1} . . . . βατταλογέω *G945*
βαττολογήσητε   verb, aor. act. subjunc. 2 pers.
    pl. {5.B.1} . . . . id.
βάτῳ   noun, dat. sg. fem. {2.B} . . . . βάτος[1] *G942*
βάψας   vbl., aor. act. ptc. nom. sg. masc.
    {6.A.1.a} . . . . βάπτω *G911*
βάψῃ   verb, aor. act. subjunc. 3 pers. sg. {5.B.1} . id.
βάψω   verb, fut. act. indic. 1 pers. sg. {5.A.1.a} . id.
G946 **βδέλυγμα**, -ατος, τό   *an abominable thing, an*
    accursed thing.
βδέλυγμα   noun, acc. sg. neut. {2.C} . . . . . βδέλυγμα *G946*
βδέλυγμα   noun, nom. sg. neut. {2.C} . . . . id.

βδελυγμάτων   noun, gen. pl. neut. {2.C} . . . . . id.
βδελυκτοί   adj., nom. pl. masc. {3.A} . . . βδελυκτός G947
G947 **βδελυκτός**, -ή, -όν   abominable, detestable.
G948 **βδελύσσομαι**   I abominate, detest.
βδελυσσόμενος   vbl., pres. mid./pass. ptc. nom.
    sg. masc. {6.A.1} . . . . βδελύσσομαι G948
βεβαία   adj., nom. sg. fem. {3.A} . . . . βέβαιος G949
βεβαίαν   adj., acc. sg. fem. {3.A} . . . . id.
G949 **βέβαιος**, -α, -ον   firm, steadfast, enduring.
βέβαιος   adj., nom. sg. masc. {3.A} . . . . . . βέβαιος G949
βεβαιότερον   adj. comp., acc. sg. masc. {3.A; 3.G}. id.
βεβαιούμενοι   vbl., pres. pass. ptc. nom. pl. masc.
    {6.A.2}. βεβαιόω G950
βεβαιοῦντος   vbl., pres. act. ptc. gen. sg. masc.
    {6.A.2}. id.
βεβαιοῦσθαι   vbl., pres. pass. inf. {6.B.2}. . . . . id.
G950 **βεβαιόω**   I confirm, ratify.
βεβαιῶν   vbl., pres. act. ptc. nom. sg. masc.
    {6.A.2}. βεβαιόω G950
βεβαιῶσαι   vbl., aor. act. inf. {6.B.1} . . . . id.
βεβαιώσει   noun, dat. sg. fem. {2.C} . . . βεβαίωσις G951
βεβαιώσει   verb, fut. act. indic. 3 pers. sg.
    {5.A.1}. βεβαιόω G950
βεβαίωσιν   noun, acc. sg. fem. {2.C} . . . βεβαίωσις G951
G951 **βεβαίωσις**, -εως, ἡ   confirmation, ratification,
    establishment.
βεβαμμένον   vbl., perf. pass. ptc. acc. sg. neut.
    {6.A.1.b} . . . . βάπτω G911
βεβαπτισμένοι   vbl., perf. pass. ptc. nom. pl. masc.
    {6.A.1.b} . . . . βαπτίζω G907
βεβαρημένοι   vbl., perf. pass. ptc. nom. pl. masc.
    {6.A.2}. βαρέω G916
βεβήλοις   adj., dat. pl. masc. {3.A} . . . . . . βέβηλος G952
G952 **βέβηλος**, -ον   (1) profane, secular; (2) unspiri-
    tual, godless, worldly, Heb 12:16.
βέβηλος   adj., nom. sg. masc. {3.A} . . . . . βέβηλος G952
βεβήλους   adj., acc. pl. fem. {3.A} . . . . id.
βεβήλους   adj., acc. pl. masc. {3.A} . . . . id.
βεβηλοῦσιν   verb, pres. act. indic. 3 pers. pl.
    {5.A.2}. βεβηλόω G953
βεβηλοῦσιν   verb, pres. act. indic. 3 pers. pl.
    {5.A.2}. id.
G953 **βεβηλόω**   I profane.
βεβηλῶσαι   vbl., aor. act. inf. {6.B.1} . . . . βεβηλόω G953
βέβληκε   verb, perf. act. indic. 3 pers. sg.
    {5.A.1.c} . . . . βάλλω G906
βέβληκεν   verb, perf. act. indic. 3 pers. sg.
    {5.A.1.c} . . . . id.
βεβληκότος   vbl., perf. act. ptc. gen. sg. masc.
    {6.A.1.a} . . . . id.
βεβλημένην   vbl., perf. pass. ptc. acc. sg. fem.
    {6.A.1.b} . . . . id.
βεβλημένον   vbl., perf. pass. ptc. acc. sg. masc.
    {6.A.1.b} . . . . id.
βεβλημένον   vbl., perf. pass. ptc. acc. sg. neut.
    {6.A.1.b} . . . . id.
βεβλημένος   vbl., perf. pass. ptc. nom. sg.
    masc. {6.A.1.b} . . . . id.
βέβληται   verb, perf. pass. indic. 3 pers. sg.
    {5.A.1.f}. . . . . id.

βεβρωκόσιν   vbl., perf. act. ptc. dat. pl. masc.
    {6.A.1.a} . . . . βιβρώσκω G977
Βεεζεβούλ   noun prop. . . . . Βεελζεβούλ G954
G954 **Βεελζεβούλ** (Βεεζεβούλ), Βεελζεβούβ),
    ὁ   Beelzebul, a name of uncertain derivation,
    the chief of evil spirits among the Jews. The
    form Beelzebub = god of Flies at Ekron (2 Kgs
    1:2, 3); the better attested form perhaps = the
    Phoenician sun god as lord of the heavenly
    dwelling.
Βεελζεβούλ   noun prop. . . . . Βεελζεβούλ G954
βέλη   noun, acc. pl. neut. {2.C} . . . . βέλος G956
G955 **Βελιάρ** (Βελιάλ), ὁ   Beliar (spelled sometimes
    Belial, Beliab), a demon, among the Jews, and
    in fact a name for Satan (orig. a Heb. word =
    uselessness, corruption).
Βελιάρ   noun prop. . . . . Βελιάρ G955
Βελίαρ   noun prop. . . . . id.
G4476†‡ **βελόνη**, -ης, ἡ   needle. Var. for ῥαφίς, Luke
    18:25.
βελόνης   noun, gen. sg. fem. {2.A} . . . . . βελόνη G4476†‡
G956 **βέλος**, -ους, τό   a missile, dart.
βέλτιον   adv. comp. {3.F; 3.G} . . . . βελτίων G957
G957 **βελτίων**   neut. sg. comp. βέλτιον as adv., best
    (comp. in form, superl. in meaning; very rare
    in this period).
Βενιαμείν   noun prop. . . . . Βενιαμίν G958
G958 **Βενιαμίν** (Βενιαμείν), ὁ   Benjamin, youngest
    son of Jacob, founder of one of the twelve
    tribes of Israel (Heb.).
Βενιαμίν   noun prop. . . . . Βενιαμίν G958
G959 **Βερνίκη**, -ης, ἡ   Bernice (born in 29 A.D.),
    daughter of Agrippa I and Kypros, and sister
    of M. Iulius Agrippa II, in whose company she
    appears, Acts 25, 26.
Βερνίκη   noun prop., nom. sg. fem. {2.A;
    2.D}. . . . . Βερνίκη G959
Βερνίκης   noun prop., gen. sg. fem. {2.A; 2.D}. . id.
G960 **Βέροια**, -ας, ἡ   Beroea, a town of the province
    Macedonia.
Βεροίᾳ   noun prop., dat. sg. fem. {2.A; 2.D}. Βέροια G960
G961 **Βεροιαῖος**, -α, -ον   belonging to Beroea,
    Beroean.
Βεροιαῖος   adj. prop., nom. sg. masc. {3.A} .Βεροιαῖος G961
Βέροιαν   noun prop., acc. sg. fem. {2.A; 2.D}. Βέροια G960
Βεώρ   noun prop. . . . . Βοσόρ G1007
G962 **Βηθαβαρά**, ἡ   Bethabara, one reading in John
    1:28. If the place existed, it was on east side of
    Jordan, see Βηθανία.
Βηθαβαρᾶ   noun prop., dat. sg. fem. {2.A;
    2.D}. . . . . .Βηθαβαρά G962
Βηθανιά   noun prop., acc. sg. fem. {2.A;
    2.D}. . . . . Βηθανία G963
G963 **Βηθανία**, -ας, ἡ   (1) Bethany, the home of
    Lazarus, Martha, and Mary, near Jerusalem;
    (2) Bethany, beyond Jordan, the reading with
    the strongest attestation in John 1:28, see
    Βηθαβαρά.
Βηθανία   noun prop., nom. sg. fem. {2.A;
    2.D}. . . . . Βηθανία G963

Βηθανίᾳ   noun prop., dat. sg. fem. {2.A; 2.D} .. id.
Βηθανίαν   noun prop., acc. sg. fem. {2.A; 2.D} . id.
Βηθανίας   noun prop., gen. sg. fem. {2.A; 2.D} . id.

G964 **Βηθεσδά** (Βηθζαθά), ἡ   *Bethesda* or *Bethzatha*
(= House of Olives), name of a pool in Jerusa-
lem. (There is great doubt as to the real form).
Βηθεσδά   noun prop.. . . . . Βηθεσδά G964
Βηθζαθά   noun prop.. . . . . id.
Βηθλεέμ   noun prop.. . . . . .Βηθλέεμ G965

G965 **Βηθλέεμ**, ἡ   *Bethlehem,* a town of Judaea.
Βηθλέεμ   noun prop.. . . . . .Βηθλέεμ G965
Βηθσαιδά   noun prop.. . . . . Βηθσαϊδά G966

G966 **Βηθσαϊδά** (Βηθσαϊδάν), ἡ   *Bethsaida,* a city
of Galilee.
Βηθσαϊδά   noun prop.. . . . . Βηθσαϊδά G966
Βηθσαιδάν   noun prop.. . . . . id.
Βηθσαϊδάν   noun prop.. . . . . id.
Βηθσφαγή   noun prop. . . . . Βηθφαγή G967

G967 **Βηθφαγή**, ἡ   *Bethphage,* a village in the neigh-
borhood of Jerusalem, on the Mount of Olives.
Βηθφαγή   noun prop.. . . . . Βηθφαγή G967

G968 **βῆμα**, -ατος, τό   (1) βῆμα ποδός, the space
covered by a step of the foot; (2) *tribunal;*
(from root of ἔβην, *I went).*
βῆμα   noun, acc. sg. neut. {2.C} . . . . .βῆμα G968
βήματι   noun, dat. sg. neut. {2.C}. . . . . id.
βήματος   noun, gen. sg. neut. {2.C} . . . . id.

G969 **βήρυλλος**, -ου, ὁ   *a beryl,* a precious stone
of various colors, the best known being sea
green.
βήρυλλος   noun, nom. sg. masc. {2.B}. . .βήρυλλος G969

G970 **βία**, -ας, ἡ   *force.*
βιάζεται   verb, pres. mid. indic. 3 pers. sg.
{5.A.1.d} . . . . .βιάζω G971
βιάζεται   verb, pres. pass. indic. 3 pers. sg.
{5.A.1.d} . . . . id.

G971 **βιάζω**   (1) mid. *I use force, I force my way, I*
come forward violently, cf. Matt 11:12 (where
perhaps pass.); (2) pass. *I am forcibly treated.*
βιαίᾳ   adj., gen. sg. fem. {3.A}. . . . . . . .βίαιος G972

G972 **βίαιος**, -α, -ον   *strong, violent.*
βίαν   noun, acc. sg. fem. {2.A} . . . . βία G970
βίας   noun, gen. sg. fem. {2.A} . . . . id.
βιασταί   noun, nom. pl. masc. {2.A} . . . . . βιαστής G973

G973 **βιαστής**, -οῦ, ὁ   *a forceful, violent man.*

G974 **βιβλαρίδιον**, -ου, τό   *a little papyrus roll.*
βιβλαρίδιον   noun, acc. sg. neut. {2.B} βιβλαρίδιον G974
βιβλία   noun, acc. pl. neut. {2.B} . . . . . . .βιβλίον G975
βιβλία   noun, nom. pl. neut. {2.B} . . . . id.
βιβλιδάριον   noun, acc. sg. neut. {2.B} βιβλαρίδιον G974
βιβλίοις   noun, dat. pl. neut. {2.B} . . . . . . .βιβλίον G975

G975 **βιβλίον**, -ου, τό   (1) *a papyrus roll;* (2) ἀποστασίου, document of divorce, handed by
the husband to the wife whom he divorces;
(3) ζωῆς, of life, preserved in heaven and
containing the names of those who share in
(eternal) life; (orig. a diminutive).
βιβλίον   noun, acc. sg. neut. {2.B} . . . . . . .βιβλίον G975
βιβλίον   noun, nom. sg. neut. {2.B} . . . . id.
βιβλίου   noun, gen. sg. neut. {2.B} . . . . id.

βιβλίῳ   noun, dat. sg. neut. {2.B} . . . . id.

G976 **βίβλος**, -ου, ἡ   *a papyrus roll,* with a sacred
connotation; ζωῆς, see βιβλίον, which had
almost ousted it.
βίβλος   noun, nom. sg. fem. {2.B}. . . . . βίβλος G976
βίβλου   noun, gen. sg. fem. {2.B} . . . . id.
βίβλους   noun, acc. pl. fem. {2.B}. . . . . id.
βίβλῳ   noun, dat. sg. fem. {2.B} . . . . id.

G977 **βιβρώσκω**   *I eat.*

G978 **Βιθυνία**, -ας, ἡ   *Bithynia,* a Roman province,
northwest of Asia Minor and southwest of the
Black Sea.
Βιθυνίαν   noun prop., acc. sg. fem. {2.A;
2.D}. . . . . Βιθυνία G978
Βιθυνίας   noun prop., gen. sg. fem. {2.A; 2.D}. . id.
βίον   noun, acc. sg. masc. {2.B}. . . . . βίος G979

G979 **βίος**, -ου, ὁ   (1) *life;* (2) *manner of life;* (3)
livelihood.
βίου   noun, gen. sg. masc. {2.B} . . . . βίος G979

G980 **βιόω**   *I live.*
βιῶσαι   vbl., aor. act. inf. {6.B.1}. . . . . . . βιόω G980
βίωσιν   noun, acc. sg. fem. {2.C} . . . . . . βίωσις G981

G981 **βίωσις**, -εως, ἡ   *manner of life.*
βιωτικά   adj., acc. pl. neut. {3.A} . . . . . .βιωτικός G982
βιωτικαῖς   adj., dat. pl. fem. {3.A} . . . . id.

G982 **βιωτικός**, -ή, -όν   *belonging to ordinary life,*
with somewhat contemptuous attitude.
βλαβεράς   adj., acc. pl. fem. {3.A} . . . . . .βλαβερός G983

G983 **βλαβερός**, -ά, -όν   *injurious.*

G984 **βλάπτω**   *I injure.*
βλαστᾷ   verb, pres. act. subjunc. 3 pers. sg.
{5.B.1} . . . . βλαστάνω G985
βλαστάνῃ   verb, pres. act. subjunc. 3 pers. sg.
{5.B.1} . . . . id.

G985 **βλαστάνω** (βλαστάω)   (1) intrans., *I sprout;*
(2) trans., *I cause to sprout, make to grow up,*
Jas 5:18.
βλαστήσασα   vbl., aor. act. ptc. nom. sg. fem.
{6.A.1.a} . . . . βλαστάνω G985
Βλάστον   noun prop., acc. sg. masc. {2.B;
2.D}. . . . . .Βλάστος G986

G986 **Βλάστος**, -ου, ὁ   *Blastus,* chamberlain of King
Herod Agrippa I.
βλάσφημα   adj., acc. pl. neut. {3.C} . . . . . βλάσφημος G989
βλασφημεῖ   verb, pres. act. indic. 3 pers. sg.
{5.A.2}. . . . . βλασφημέω G987
βλασφημεῖν   vbl., pres. act. inf. {6.B.2} . . . . id.
βλασφημεῖς   verb, pres. act. indic. 2 pers. sg.
{5.A.2}. . . . . id.
βλασφημείσθω   verb, pres. pass. impv. 3 pers.
sg. {5.D.2} . . . . id.
βλασφημεῖται   verb, pres. pass. indic. 3 pers.
sg. {5.A.2} . . . . id.

G987 **βλασφημέω**   *I speak evil against, I use abusive*
or *scurrilous language about* (God or men).
βλασφημηθήσεται   verb, fut. pass. indic. 3 pers.
sg. {5.A.1} . . . . .βλασφημέω G987
βλασφημῆσαι   vbl., aor. act. inf. {6.B.1} . . . . . . id.
βλασφημήσαντι   vbl., aor. act. ptc. dat. sg.
masc. {6.A.2}. . . . . id.

βλασφημήση   verb, aor. act. subjunc. 3 pers.
 sg. {5.B.1} . . . . id.
βλασφημήσωσιν   verb, aor. act. subjunc.
 3 pers. pl. {5.B.1} . . . . id.
βλασφημῆται   verb, pres. pass. subjunc.
 3 pers. sg. {5.B.2} . . . . id.
G988 **βλασφημία**, -ας, ἡ   abusive or scurrilous
 language.
βλασφημία   noun, nom. sg. fem. {2.A} βλασφημία G988
βλασφημίαι   noun, nom. pl. fem. {2.A} . . . . . . id.
βλασφημίαν   noun, acc. sg. fem. {2.A} . . . . . . id.
βλασφημίας   noun, acc. pl. fem. {2.A} . . . . . . id.
βλασφημίας   noun, gen. sg. fem. {2.A} . . . . . . id.
βλάσφημοι   adj., nom. pl. masc. {3.C} . βλάσφημος G989
βλάσφημον   adj., acc. sg. fem. {3.C} . . . . id.
βλάσφημον   adj., acc. sg. masc. {3.C} . . . . id.
G989 **βλάσφημος**, -ον   abusive, scurrilous.
βλασφημοῦμαι   verb, pres. pass. indic. 1 pers. sg.
 {5.A.2} . . . . βλασφημέω G987
βλασφημούμεθα   verb, pres. pass. indic.
 1 pers. pl. {5.A.2} . . . . id.
βλασφημούμενοι   vbl., pres. pass. ptc. nom.
 pl. masc. {6.A.2} . . . . id.
βλασφημοῦντας   vbl., pres. act. ptc. acc. pl.
 masc. {6.A.2} . . . . id.
βλασφημοῦντες   vbl., pres. act. ptc. nom. pl.
 masc. {6.A.2} . . . . id.
βλασφημούντων   vbl., pres. act. ptc. gen. pl.
 masc. {6.A.2} . . . . id.
βλασφημοῦσι   verb, pres. act. indic. 3 pers. pl.
 {5.A.2} . . . . id.
βλασφημοῦσιν   verb, pres. act. indic. 3 pers.
 pl. {5.A.2} . . . . id.
βλάψαν   vbl., aor. act. ptc. nom. sg. neut.
 {6.A.1.a} . . . . βλάπτω G984
βλάψει   verb, fut. act. indic. 3 pers. sg. {5.A.1.a} . id.
βλάψῃ   verb, aor. act. subjunc. 3 pers. sg. {5.B.1} id.
G990 **βλέμμα**, -ατος, τό   look, the faculty of looking.
βλέμματι   noun, dat. sg. neut. {2.C} . . . . . . βλέμμα G990
βλέπε   verb, pres. act. impv. 2 pers. sg. {5.D.1} βλέπω G991
βλέπει   verb, pres. act. indic. 3 pers. sg. {5.A.1.a} id.
βλέπειν   vbl., pres. act. inf. {6.B.1} . . . . id.
βλέπεις   verb, pres. act. indic. 2 pers. sg.
 {5.A.1.a} . . . . id.
βλέπετε   verb, pres. act. impv. 2 pers. pl. {5.D.1} . id.
βλέπετε   verb, pres. act. indic. 2 pers. pl.
 {5.A.1.a} . . . . id.
βλεπέτω   verb, pres. act. impv. 3 pers. sg. {5.D.1} id.
βλέπῃ   verb, pres. act. subjunc. 3 pers. sg. {5.B.1} id.
βλέπῃς   verb, pres. act. subjunc. 2 pers. sg. {5.B.1} . id.
βλέπομεν   verb, pres. act. indic. 1 pers. pl.
 {5.A.1.a} . . . . id.
βλεπόμενα   vbl., pres. pass. ptc. acc. pl. neut.
 {6.A.1} . . . . id.
βλεπόμενα   vbl., pres. pass. ptc. nom. pl. neut.
 {6.A.1} . . . . id.
βλεπομένη   vbl., pres. pass. ptc. nom. sg. fem.
 {6.A.1} . . . . id.
βλεπόμενον   vbl., pres. pass. ptc. acc. sg. neut.
 {6.A.1} . . . . id.

βλεπομένων   vbl., pres. pass. ptc. gen. pl. neut.
 {6.A.1} . . . . id.
βλέποντα   vbl., pres. act. ptc. acc. sg. masc.
 {6.A.1} . . . . id.
βλέποντας   vbl., pres. act. ptc. acc. pl. masc.
 {6.A.1} . . . . id.
βλέποντες   vbl., pres. act. ptc. nom. pl. masc.
 {6.A.1} . . . . id.
βλεπόντων   vbl., pres. act. ptc. gen. pl. masc.
 {6.A.1} . . . . id.
βλέπουσι   verb, pres. act. indic. 3 pers. pl.
 {5.A.1.a} . . . . id.
βλέπουσιν   verb, pres. act. indic. 3 pers. pl.
 {5.A.1.a} . . . . id.
G991 **βλέπω**   (1) I look, see (primarily physical);
 βλέποντες βλέψετε, Hebraistic; βλέπειν
 ἀπό, to look away from, to beware of; βλέπειν
 μή, to take care lest; βλέπειν πῶς, to take care
 how; (2) almost I find, Rom 7:23 (cf. 21).
βλέπω   verb, pres. act. indic. 1 pers. sg.
 {5.A.1.a} . . . . βλέπω G991
βλέπων   vbl., pres. act. ptc. nom. sg. masc.
 {6.A.1} . . . . id.
βλέπωσι   verb, pres. act. subjunc. 3 pers. pl.
 {5.B.1} . . . . id.
βλέπωσιν   verb, pres. act. subjunc. 3 pers. pl.
 {5.B.1} . . . . id.
βλέψετε   verb, fut. act. indic. 2 pers. pl. {5.A.1.a} id.
βλέψον   verb, aor. act. impv. 2 pers. sg. {5.D.1} . . id.
βλέψουσιν   verb, fut. act. indic. 3 pers. pl.
 {5.A.1.a} . . . . id.
βληθείς   vbl., aor. pass. ptc. nom. sg. masc.
 {6.A.1.a} . . . . βάλλω G906
βληθείσῃ   vbl., aor. pass. ptc. dat. sg. fem.
 {6.A.1.a} . . . . id.
βληθέν   vbl., aor. pass. ptc. nom. sg. neut.
 {6.A.1.a} . . . . id.
βληθῇ   verb, aor. pass. subjunc. 3 pers. sg.
 {5.B.1} . . . . id.
βληθῆναι   vbl., aor. pass. inf. {6.B.1} . . . . id.
βληθήσεται   verb, fut. pass. indic. 3 pers. sg.
 {5.A.1.d} . . . . id.
βληθήσῃ   verb, fut. pass. indic. 2 pers. sg.
 {5.A.1.d} . . . . id.
βλήθητι   verb, aor. pass. impv. 2 pers. sg. {5.D.1} id.
βλητέον   adj., nom. sg. neut. {3.A} . . . . . . βλητέος G992
G992 **βλητέος**, -α, -ον   one must put (verbal adj.
 from βάλλω, understand ἐστίν).
βοαί   noun, nom. pl. fem. {2.A} . . . . βοή G995
Βοανεργές   noun prop. . . . . Βοανηργές G993
G993 **Βοανηργές**   Boanerges, a name of doubtful
 origin and meaning.
Βοανηργές   noun prop. . . . . Βοανηργές G993
βόας   noun, acc. pl. masc. {2.C} . . . . βοῦς G1016
G994 **βοάω**   I shout, call aloud.
Βοές   noun prop. . . . . Βόος G1003
Βόες   noun prop. . . . . id.
G995 **βοή**, -ῆς, ἡ   a shout.
βοήθει   verb, pres. act. impv. 2 pers. sg.
 {5.D.2} . . . . βοηθέω G997

G996 **βοήθεια**, -ας, ἡ (1) abstr., *assistance;* (2) concr.
(a technical term of nautical language), *a help.*
βοηθείαις   noun, dat. pl. fem. {2.A} . . . . . βοήθεια *G996*
βοήθειαν   noun, acc. sg. fem. {2.A} . . . . id.
βοηθεῖτε   verb, pres. act. impv. 2 pers. pl.
   {5.D.2} . . . . .βοηθέω *G997*

G997 **βοηθέω**   *I come to the rescue of, come to help, help.*
βοηθῆσαι   vbl., aor. act. inf. {6.B.1} . . . . . .βοηθέω *G997*
βοήθησον   verb, aor. act. impv. 2 pers. sg. {5.D.1} . id.

G998 **βοηθός**, όν   *helping;* subs., *a helper.*
βοηθός   adj., nom. sg. masc. {2.B} . . . . .βοηθός *G998*
βόησον   verb, aor. act. impv. 2 pers. sg. {5.D.1}βοάω *G994*
βόθυνον   noun, acc. sg. masc. {2.B} . . . . . βόθυνος *G999*

G999 **βόθυνος**, -ου, ὁ   *a hole in the earth, ditch.*

G1000 **βολή**, -ῆς, ἡ   *a casting, throw;* in acc. as measure of distance.
βολήν   noun, acc. sg. fem. {2.A} . . . . βολή *G1000*
βολίδι   noun, dat. sg. fem. {2.C} . . . . βολίς *G1002*

G1001 **βολίζω**   *I cast the line* (for sounding), *I sound.*

G1002 **βολίς**, -ίδος, ἡ   *an arrow, a javelin*
βολίσαντες   vbl., aor. act. ptc. nom. pl. masc.
   {6.A.1.a} . . . . βολίζω *G1001*
Βοόζ   noun prop. . . . . Βοός *G1003*

G1003 **Βόος** (Βόες)   *Boaz, son of Salmon (Sala) and*
Rahab, husband of Ruth, father of Iobed (Heb.).
Βόος   noun prop. . . . . Βοός *G1003*
Βοός   noun prop. . . . . id.

G1004 **βόρβορος**, -ου, ὁ   *a miry dungeon, hole.*
βορβόρου   noun, gen. sg. masc. {2.B} . . .βόρβορος *G1004*
βορρᾶ   noun, gen. sg. masc. {2.A} . . . . . . βορρᾶς *G1005*

G1005 **βορρᾶς**, -ᾶ, ὁ   *the north wind,* hence, *the north.*
βόσκε   verb, pres. act. impv. 2 pers. sg.
   {5.D.1} . . . . .βόσκω *G1006*
βόσκειν   vbl., pres. act. inf. {6.B.1} . . . . id.
βοσκομένη   vbl., pres. pass. ptc. nom. sg. fem.
   {6.A.1} . . . . id.
βοσκομένων   vbl., pres. pass. ptc. gen. pl.
   masc. {6.A.1} . . . . id.
βόσκοντες   vbl., pres. act. ptc. nom. pl. masc.
   {6.A.1} . . . . id.

G1006 **βόσκω**   *I feed.*

G1007 **Βοσόρ** (Βεώρ), ὁ   *Bosor or Beor, father of Balaam.*
(The var. Βοσόρ has no authority in LXX, and is
probably due to textual corruption here).
Βοσόρ   noun prop. . . . . .Βοσόρ *G1007*

G1008 **βοτάνη**, -ης, ἡ   *fodder, food.*
βοτάνην   noun, acc. sg. fem. {2.A} . . . . . . βοτάνη *G1008*
βότρυας   noun, acc. pl. masc. {2.C} . . . . . βότρυς *G1009*

G1009 **βότρυς**, -υος, ὁ   *cluster (bunch) of grapes.*
βουλάς   noun, acc. pl. fem. {2.A} . . . . βουλή *G1012*
βούλει   verb, pres. mid./pass. indic. 2 pers. sg.
   {5.A.1.d} . . . . βούλομαι *G1014*
βούλεσθε   verb, pres. mid./pass. indic. 2 pers.
   pl. {5.A.1.d} . . . . id.
βούλεται   verb, pres. mid./pass. indic. 3 pers.
   sg. {5.A.1.d} . . . . id.
βουλεύεται   verb, pres. mid./pass. indic. 3 pers.
   {5.A.1.d} . . . . βουλεύω *G1011*
βουλεύομαι   verb, pres. mid./pass. indic.
   1 pers. sg. {5.A.1.d} . . . . id.

βουλευόμενος   vbl., pres. mid./pass. ptc. nom.
   sg. masc. {6.A.1} . . . . id.
βουλεύσεται   verb, fut. mid. indic. 3 pers. sg.
   {5.A.1.d} . . . . id.

G1010 **βουλευτής**, -οῦ, ὁ   *a member of a βουλή* (city
council), in NT of the συνέδριον, Sanhedrin
at Jerusalem.
βουλευτής   noun, nom. sg. masc. {2.A} βουλευτής *G1010*

G1011 **βουλεύω**   mid. *I deliberate, take counsel.*

G1012 **βουλή**, -ῆς, ἡ   *counsel, deliberate wisdom.*
βουλή   noun, nom. sg. fem. {2.A} . . . . βουλή *G1012*
βουλῇ   noun, dat. sg. fem. {2.A} . . . . id.
βουληθείς   vbl., aor. pass. ptc. nom. sg. masc.
   {6.A.1.a} . . . . βούλομαι *G1014*
βουληθῇ   verb, aor. pass. subjunc. 3 pers. sg.
   {5.B.1} . . . . id.

G1013 **βούλημα**, -ατος, τό   *will, desire.*
βούλημα   noun, acc. sg. neut. {2.C} . . . .βούλημα *G1013*
βουλήματι   noun, dat. sg. neut. {2.C} . . . . id.
βουλήματος   noun, gen. sg. neut. {2.C} . . . . . . id.
βουλήν   noun, acc. sg. fem. {2.A} . . . . βουλή *G1012*
βουλῆς   noun, gen. sg. fem. {2.A} . . . . id.
βούληται   verb, pres. mid./pass. subjunc. 3 pers.
   sg. {5.B.1} . . . . βούλομαι *G1014*
βούλοιτο   verb, pres. mid./pass. opt. 3 pers. sg.
   {5.C.1} . . . . id.

G1014 **βούλομαι**   *I will.*
βούλομαι   verb, pres. mid./pass. indic. 1 pers. sg.
   {5.A.1.d} . . . . βούλομαι *G1014*
βουλόμεθα   verb, pres. mid./pass. indic. 1 pers.
   pl. {5.A.1.d} . . . . id.
βουλόμενοι   vbl., pres. mid./pass. ptc. nom. pl.
   masc. {6.A.1} . . . . id.
βουλόμενος   vbl., pres. mid./pass. ptc. nom. sg.
   masc. {6.A.1} . . . . id.
βουλομένου   vbl., pres. mid./pass. ptc. gen. sg.
   masc. {6.A.1} . . . . id.
βουλομένους   vbl., pres. mid./pass. ptc. acc. sg.
   masc. {6.A.1} . . . . id.
βοῦν   noun, acc. sg. masc. {2.C} . . . . βοῦς *G1016*
βουνοῖς   noun, dat. pl. masc. {2.B} . . . . . . βουνός *G1015*

G1015 **βουνός**, -οῦ, ὁ   *a hillock, hill.*
βουνός   noun, nom. sg. masc. {2.B} . . . . . . βουνός *G1015*

G1016 **βοῦς**, βοός, ὁ   *an ox, cow, head of cattle.*
βοῦς   noun, nom. sg. masc. {2.C} . . . . βοῦς *G1016*
βοῶν   noun, gen. pl. masc. {2.C} . . . . id.
βοῶντα   vbl., pres. act. ptc. acc. pl. neut. {6.A.2}. βοάω *G994*
βοῶντα   vbl., pres. act. ptc. nom. pl. neut. {6.A.2} id.
βοῶντες   vbl., pres. act. ptc. nom. pl. masc. {6.A.2} id.
βοῶντος   vbl., pres. act. ptc. gen. sg. masc. {6.A.2}. id.
βοώντων   vbl., pres. act. ptc. gen. pl. masc.
   {6.A.2} . . . . id.

G1017 **βραβεῖον**, -ου, τό   *a prize.*
βραβεῖον   noun, acc. sg. neut. {2.B} . . . . βραβεῖον *G1017*
βραβευέτω   verb, pres. act. impv. 3 pers. sg.
   {5.D.1} . . . . .βραβεύω *G1018*

G1018 **βραβεύω**   (1) *I decide* (in a conflict between
contending forces); (2) hence, *I rule, I*
administer.
βραδεῖς   adj., nom. pl. masc. {3.D} . . . . . . βραδύς *G1021*

βραδύνει   verb, pres. act. indic. 3 pers. sg.
   {5.A.1.a} . . . . .βραδύνω G1019
G1019 **βραδύνω**   *I am slow, I delay;* followed by gen.,
   2 Pet 3:9.
βραδύνω   verb, pres. act. subjunc. 1 pers. sg.
   {5.B.1} . . . . .βραδύνω G1019
G1020 **βραδυπλοέω**   *I sail slowly.*
βραδυπλοοῦντες   vbl., pres. act. ptc. nom. pl.
   masc. {6.A.2} . . . . .βραδυπλοέω G1020
G1021 **βραδύς**, -εῖα, -ύ   *slow.*
βραδύς   adj., nom. sg. masc. {3.D} . . . . . . βραδύς G1021
G1022 **βραδύτης**, -ητος, ἡ   *tardiness, dilatoriness.*
βραδύτητα   noun, acc. sg. fem. {2.C} . . βραδύτης G1022
βραχέων   adj., gen. pl. masc. {3.D} . . . . . . βραχύς G1024
βραχέων   adj., gen. pl. neut. {3.D} . . . . id.
βραχίονι   noun, dat. sg. masc. {2.C} . . . . βραχίων G1023
βραχίονος   noun, gen. sg. masc. {2.C} . . . . id.
G1023 **βραχίων**, -ονος, ὁ   *arm.*
βραχίων   noun, nom. sg. masc. {2.C} . . . βραχίων G1023
βραχύ   adj., acc. sg. neut. {3.D} . . . . βραχύς G1024
G1024 **βραχύς**, -εῖα, -ύ   *little;* mostly in various adv.
   phrases, indicating degree or time. βραχὺ τί,
   a little, for a short time.
βρέξαι   vbl., aor. act. inf. {6.B.1} . . . . βρέχω G1026
βρέφη   noun, acc. pl. neut. {2.C} . . . . βρέφος G1025
βρέφη   noun, nom. pl. neut. {2.C} . . . . id.
G1025 **βρέφος**, -ους, τό   *infant, baby, child in arms;*
   ἀπὸ βρέφους, *from babyhood.*
βρέφος   noun, acc. sg. neut. {2.C} . . . . βρέφος G1025
βρέφος   noun, nom. sg. neut. {2.C} . . . . id.
βρέφους   noun, gen. sg. neut. {2.C} . . . . id.
βρέχει   verb, pres. act. indic. 3 pers. sg.
   {5.A.1.a} . . . . βρέχω G1026
βρέχειν   vbl., pres. act. inf. {6.B.1} . . . . id.
βρέχῃ   verb, pres. act. subjunc. 3 pers. sg. {5.B.1} id.
G1026 **βρέχω**   (1) *I wet;* (2) *I rain,* having orig. the rain
   god (Ζεύς, Jupiter) as subj. (cf. Matt 5:45); (3)
   hence, of a shower from the sky other than
   rain, Luke 17:29.
βρονταί   noun, nom. pl. fem. {2.A} . . . . . βροντή G1027
G1027 **βροντή**, -ῆς, ἡ   *thunder.*
βροντήν   noun, acc. sg. fem. {2.A} . . . . . . βροντή G1027
βροντῆς   noun, gen. sg. fem. {2.A} . . . . id.
βροντῶν   noun, gen. pl. fem. {2.A} . . . . id.
G1028 **βροχή**, -ῆς, ἡ   *a wetting, rain.*
βροχή   noun, nom. sg. fem. {2.A} . . . . βροχή G1028
βρόχον   noun, acc. sg. masc. {2.B} . . . . . . βρόχος G1029

G1029 **βρόχος**, -ου, ὁ   *a noose.*
G1030 **βρυγμός**, -οῦ, ὁ   *gnashing, crunching.*
βρυγμός   noun, nom. sg. masc. {2.B} . . . . βρυγμός G1030
βρύει   verb, pres. act. indic. 3 pers. sg.
   {5.A.1.a} . . . . βρύω G1032
G1031 **βρύχω**   *I gnash, crunch.*
G1032 **βρύω**   *I cause to gush forth, send forth.*
G1033 **βρῶμα**, -ατος, τό   *food.*
βρῶμα   noun, acc. sg. neut. {2.C} . . . . .βρῶμα G1033
βρῶμα   noun, nom. sg. neut. {2.C} . . . . id.
βρώμασι   noun, dat. pl. neut. {2.C} . . . . id.
βρώμασιν   noun, dat. pl. neut. {2.C} . . . . id.
βρώματα   noun, acc. pl. neut. {2.C} . . . . id.
βρώματα   noun, nom. pl. neut. {2.C} . . . . id.
βρώματι   noun, dat. sg. neut. {2.C} . . . . id.
βρώματος   noun, gen. sg. neut. {2.C} . . . . id.
βρωμάτων   noun, gen. pl. neut. {2.C} . . . . id.
βρώσει   noun, dat. sg. fem. {2.C} . . . . βρῶσις G1035
βρώσεως   noun, gen. sg. fem. {2.C} . . . . id.
βρώσιμον   adj., acc. sg. neut. {3.A} . . . . βρώσιμος G1034
G1034 **βρώσιμος**, -ον   *eatable, suitable for food.*
βρῶσιν   noun, acc. sg. fem. {2.C} . . . . βρῶσις G1035
G1035 **βρῶσις**, -εως, ἡ   (1) (abstr.) *eating;* (2) *food, a
   meal,* Heb 12:16; (3) *rust.*
βρῶσις   noun, nom. sg. fem. {2.C} . . . . . . βρῶσις G1035
βυθίζεσθαι   vbl., pres. pass. inf. {6.B.1} . . . βυθίζω G1036
βυθίζουσι   verb, pres. act. indic. 3 pers. pl.
   {5.A.1.a} . . . . id.
βυθίζουσιν   verb, pres. act. indic. 3 pers. pl.
   {5.A.1.a} . . . . id.
G1036 **βυθίζω**   *I cause to sink.*
G1037 **βυθός**, -οῦ, ὁ   *the deep sea.*
βυθῷ   noun, dat. sg. masc. {2.B} . . . . βυθός G1037
βυρσεῖ   noun, dat. sg. masc. {2.C} . . . . . βυρσεύς G1038
G1038 **βυρσεύς**, -έως, ὁ   *a tanner.*
βυρσέως   noun, gen. sg. masc. {2.C} . . . . βυρσεύς G1038
βύσσινον   adj., acc. sg. neut. {3.A} . . . . βύσσινος G1039
βύσσινον   adj., nom. sg. neut. {3.A} . . . . id.
G1039 **βύσσινος**, -η, -ον   *of fine linen, of lawn.*
βυσσίνου   adj., gen. sg. neut. {3.A} . . . . βύσσινος G1039
βύσσον   noun, acc. sg. fem. {2.B} . . . . βύσσος G1040
G1040 **βύσσος**, -ου, ἡ   *fine linen* (Semitic origin, some
   authorities consider *cotton* to be meant; others
   silk).
βύσσου   noun, gen. sg. fem. {2.B} . . . . βύσσος G1040
βωμόν   noun, acc. sg. masc. {2.B} . . . . βωμός G1041
G1041 **βωμός**, -οῦ, ὁ   *an altar.*

Γ γ

G1042 **Γαββαθᾶ**   *Gabbatha,* i.e., *Gab Baitha,* "the
   ridge (back) of the House," i.e., the Aram.
   name for what the Greeks called Λιθόστρωτον, a sort of paved square, on which the
   procurator had his judgment seat.
Γαββαθα   noun prop. . . . . .Γαββαθᾶ G1042
Γαββαθᾶ   noun prop. . . . . id.

Γαββαθᾶ   noun prop. . . . . id.
G1043 **Γαβριήλ**, ὁ   *Gabriel,* a messenger of God (Heb.).
Γαβριήλ   noun prop. . . . . Γαβριήλ G1043
G1044 **γάγγραινα**, -ης, ἡ   *a cancerous sore, a cancer.*
γάγγραινα   noun, nom. sg. fem. {2.A} . .γάγγραινα G1044
G1045 **Γάδ**, ὁ   *Gad,* one of the twelve tribes of Israel (Heb.).
Γάδ   noun prop. Γάδ G1045

G1046 **Γαδαρηνός**, -ή, -όν *Gadarene, belonging to
Gadara* (an important Hellenized town, one
of the Decapolis, and southeast of the Sea of
Galilee). Var. Γερασηνός, Γεργεσηνός.
Γαδαρηνῶν adj. prop., gen. pl. masc.
 {3.A} . . . . .Γαδαρηνός G1046

G1047 **Γάζα**, -ης, ἡ *Gaza*, an old town in the south of
Palestine, on the sea coast.

G1048 **γάζα**, -ης, ἡ *treasure* (a Persian loanword).
Γάζαν noun prop., acc. sg. fem. {2.A; 2.D} . . Γάζα G1047
γάζης noun, gen. sg. fem. {2.A} . . . . γάζα G1048

G1049 **γαζοφυλάκιον**, -ου, τό *treasury*.
γαζοφυλάκιον noun, acc. sg. neut.
 {2.B} . . . . γαζοφυλάκιον G1049
γαζοφυλακίου noun, gen. sg. neut. {2.B} . . . . . id.
γαζοφυλακίῳ noun, dat. sg. neut. {2.B} . . . . . . id.
Γάιον noun prop., acc. sg. masc. {2.B; 2.D} . Γάϊος G1050
Γάϊον noun prop., acc. sg. masc. {2.B; 2.D} . . . . id.
Γαϊος noun prop., nom. sg. masc. {2.B; 2.D} . . . id.

G1050 **Γάϊος**, -ου, ὁ *Gaius*, (1) a Corinthian, Rom
16:23; 1 Cor 1:14; (2) a Macedonian(?), Acts
19:29; (3) a citizen of Derbe, Acts 20:4; (4) an
Ephesian(?), 3 John 1. (2), (3), and possibly (4)
may refer to the same person.
Γάϊος noun prop., nom. sg. masc. {2.B; 2.D} Γάϊος G1050
Γαΐῳ noun prop., dat. sg. masc. {2.B; 2.D} . . . . id.
Γαΐῳ noun prop., dat. sg. masc. {2.B; 2.D} . . . . id.

G1051 **γάλα**, γάλακτος, τό *milk*.
γάλα noun, acc. sg. neut. {2.C} . . . . γάλα G1051
γάλακτος noun, gen. sg. neut. {2.C} . . . . id.
Γαλάται noun prop., voc. pl. masc. {2.A;
 2.D}. . . . . Γαλάτης G1052
Γαλάτας noun prop., acc. sg. masc. {2.A; 2.D} . id.

G1052 **Γαλάτης**, -ου, ὁ *a Galatian* (meaning any
inhabitant of the Roman *province* Galatia).

G1053 **Γαλατία**, -ας, ἡ *Galatia*, a large Roman province in central Asia Minor, comprising the
districts of Paphlagonia, Pontus Galaticus, Galatia (in the narrower sense, which some still
think is intended in the NT), Phrygia Galatica,
Lycaonia Galatica, Pisidia and Isaurica. In
2 Tim 4:10 the reference may be to *Gaul*, even
if we read Γαλατίαν.
Γαλατίαν noun prop., acc. sg. fem. {2.A;
 2.D}. . . . . Γαλατία G1053
Γαλατίας noun prop., gen. sg. fem. {2.A; 2.D}. . id.
Γαλατικήν adj. prop., acc. sg. fem.
 {3.A} . . . . Γαλατικός G1054

G1054 **Γαλατικός**, -ή, -όν *Galatic*, belonging to the
province Galatia; τὴν Φρυγίαν καὶ Γαλα-
τικὴν χώραν, Acts 16:6, "the region which
is both Phrygian (racially) and Galatic (by
administration)."

G1055 **γαλήνη**, -ης, ἡ *a calm*.
γαλήνη noun, nom. sg. fem. {2.A}. . . . . . γαλήνη G1055

G1056 **Γαλιλαία**, -ας, ἡ *Galilee*, a district towards
the southern end of the Roman province Syria.
Γαλιλαία noun prop., nom. sg. fem. {2.A;
 2.D}. Γαλιλαία G1056
Γαλιλαία noun prop., voc. sg. fem. {2.A; 2.D}. . id.

Γαλιλαίᾳ noun prop., dat. sg. fem. {2.A; 2.D}. . id.
Γαλιλαίαν noun prop., acc. sg. fem. {2.A; 2.D} . id.
Γαλιλαίας noun prop., gen. sg. fem. {2.A; 2.D}. id.
Γαλιλαῖοι adj. prop., nom. pl. masc.
 {3.A} .Γαλιλαῖος G1057
Γαλιλαῖοι adj. prop., voc. pl. masc. {3.A} . . . . id.

G1057 **Γαλιλαῖος**, -α, -ον *Galilaean*, subs., an inhab-
itant of Galilee.
Γαλιλαῖος adj. prop., nom. sg. masc.
 {3.A} .Γαλιλαῖος G1057
Γαλιλαίου adj. prop., gen. sg. masc. {3.A} . . . id.
Γαλιλαίους adj. prop., acc. pl. masc. {3.A}. . . id.
Γαλιλαίων adj. prop., gen. pl. masc. {3.A} . . . id.

G1058 **Γαλλίων**, -ωνος, ὁ *Gallio*, Lucius Iunius
Gallio, who received this name by adoption
into another family, but was born brother of
the philosopher Seneca and orig. named L.
Annaeus Nouatus; proconsul of the Roman
province Achaia from spring 52 to spring
53 A.D.
Γαλλίων noun prop., nom. sg. masc. {2.C;
 2.D}. . . . . Γαλλίων G1058
Γαλλίωνι noun prop., dat. sg. masc. {2.C; 2.D} . id.
Γαλλίωνος noun prop., gen. sg. masc. {2.C;
 2.D}. . . . . id.

G1059 **Γαμαλιήλ**, ὁ *Gamaliel*, a noted Pharisee,
teacher of Saul (Heb.).
Γαμαλιήλ noun prop. . . . . Γαμαλιήλ G1059
γαμεῖν vbl., pres. act. inf. {6.B.2} . . . . γαμέω G1060
γαμείτωσαν verb, pres. act. impv. 3 pers. pl.
 {5.D.2}. . . . . id.

G1060 **γαμέω** *I marry*, used of either sex.
γαμηθῇ verb, aor. pass. subjunc. 3 pers. sg.
 {5.B.1} . . . . γαμέω G1060
γαμηθῆναι vbl., aor. pass. inf. {6.B.1} . . . . . . id.
γαμῆσαι vbl., aor. act. inf. {6.B.1} . . . . id.
γαμήσας vbl., aor. act. ptc. nom. sg. masc.
 {6.A.2} . . . . id.
γαμήσασα vbl., aor. act. ptc. nom. sg. fem.
 {6.A.2} . . . . id.
γαμησάτωσαν verb, aor. act. impv. 3 pers. pl.
 {5.D.1} . . . . id.
γαμήσῃ verb, aor. act. subjunc. 3 pers. sg.
 {5.B.1} . . . . id.
γαμήσῃς verb, aor. act. subjunc. 2 pers. sg.
 {5.B.1} . . . . id.
γαμίζονται verb, pres. pass. indic. 3 pers. pl.
 {5.A.1.d} . . . . γαμίζω G1061
γαμίζοντες vbl., pres. act. ptc. nom. pl. masc.
 {6.A.1}. . . . . id.

G1061 **γαμίζω** *I give in marriage; pass. I am given in
marriage*.
γαμίζων vbl., pres. act. ptc. nom. sg. masc.
 {6.A.1}. . . . . γαμίζω G1061
γαμίσκονται verb, pres. pass. indic. 3 pers. pl.
 {5.A.1.d} . . . . γαμίσκω G1061†

G1061† **γαμίσκω** *I give in marriage; pass. I am given in
marriage*. Var. for γαμίζω.
γάμον noun, acc. sg. masc. {2.B} . . . . γάμος G1062

G1062 **γάμος**, -ου, ὁ   (1) *a marriage, wedding, wedding ceremony;* (2) γάμοι (pl.), *a wedding feast.*
γάμος   noun, nom. sg. masc. {2.B} . . . . γάμος G1062
γάμου   noun, gen. sg. masc. {2.B} . . . . id.
γαμοῦντες   vbl., pres. act. ptc. nom. pl. masc.
     {6.A.2} . . . . γαμέω G1060
γάμους   noun, acc. pl. masc. {2.B} . . . . γάμος G1062
γαμοῦσι   verb, pres. act. indic. 3 pers. pl.
     {5.A.2} . . . . γαμέω G1060
γαμοῦσιν   verb, pres. act. indic. 3 pers. pl.
     {5.A.2} . . . . id.
γάμων   noun, gen. pl. masc. {2.B} . . . . γάμος G1062
γαμῶν   vbl., pres. act. ptc. nom. sg. masc.
     {6.A.2} . . . . γαμέω G1060
G1063 **γάρ**   conj., *for.*
γάρ   conj. . . . . γάρ G1063
γαστέρες   noun, nom. pl. fem. {2.C} . . . . . γαστήρ G1064
G1064 **γαστήρ**, τρός, ἡ   *belly;* often ἐν γαστρὶ ἔχειν, of a woman, *to be pregnant* (lit., *to have* a child *in the belly*).
γαστρί   noun, dat. sg. fem. {2.C} . . . . γαστήρ G1064
G1065 **γέ**   *at least, indeed, really,* an enclitic, emphasizing particle generally too subtle to be represented in Eng.; εἰ δὲ μήγε (Aramaism?), *otherwise.*
γε   part. . . . . γέ G1065
γεγαμηκόσι   vbl., perf. act. ptc. dat. pl. masc.
     {6.A.2} . . . . γαμέω G1060
γεγαμηκόσιν   vbl., perf. act. ptc. dat. pl. masc.
     {6.A.2} . . . . id.
γεγενημένα   vbl., perf. pass. ptc. nom. pl. neut.
     {6.A.1.b} . . . . γίνομαι G1096
γεγενημένον   vbl., perf. pass. ptc. acc. sg. neut.
     {6.A.1.b} . . . . id.
γεγενῆσθαι   vbl., perf. pass. inf. {6.B.1} . . . . id.
γεγένησθε   verb, perf. pass. indic. 2 pers. pl.
     {5.A.1.f} . . . . id.
γεγέννηκα   verb, perf. act. indic. 1 pers. sg.
     {5.A.1} . . . . γεννάω G1080
γεγέννημαι   verb, perf. pass. indic. 1 pers. sg.
     {5.A.1} . . . . id.
γεγεννήμεθα   verb, perf. pass. indic. 1 pers. pl.
     {5.A.1} . . . . id.
γεγεννημένα   vbl., perf. pass. ptc. nom. pl.
     neut. {6.A.2} . . . . id.
γεγεννημένον   vbl., perf. pass. ptc. acc. sg.
     masc. {6.A.2} . . . . id.
γεγεννημένον   vbl., perf. pass. ptc. nom. sg.
     neut. {6.A.2} . . . . id.
γεγεννημένος   vbl., perf. pass. ptc. nom. sg.
     masc. {6.A.2} . . . . id.
γεγεννημένου   vbl., perf. pass. ptc. gen. sg.
     masc. {6.A.2} . . . . id.
γεγέννηται   verb, perf. pass. indic. 3 pers. sg.
     {5.A.1} . . . . id.
γέγονα   verb, ²perf. act. indic. 1 pers. sg.
     {5.A.1.c} . . . . γίνομαι G1096
γεγόναμεν   verb, ²perf. act. indic. 1 pers. pl.
     {5.A.1.c} . . . . id.
γέγοναν   verb, ²perf. act. indic. 3 pers. pl.
     {5.A.1.c} . . . . id.

γέγονας   verb, ²perf. act. indic. 2 pers. sg.
     {5.A.1.c} . . . . id.
γεγόνασι   verb, ²perf. act. indic. 3 pers. pl.
     {5.A.1.c} . . . . id.
γεγόνασιν   verb, ²perf. act. indic. 3 pers. pl.
     {5.A.1.c} . . . . id.
γεγόνατε   verb, ²perf. act. indic. 2 pers. pl.
     {5.A.1.c} . . . . id.
γέγονε   verb, ²perf. act. indic. 3 pers. sg. {5.A.1.c} id.
γεγόνει   verb, plu. act. indic. 3 pers. sg. {5.A.1.b} id.
γέγονεν   verb, ²perf. act. indic. 3 pers. sg.
     {5.A.1.c} . . . . id.
γεγονέναι   vbl., ²perf. act. inf. {6.B.1} . . . . id.
γεγονός   vbl., ²perf. act. ptc. acc. sg. neut. {6.A.1} id.
γεγονός   vbl., ²perf. act. ptc. nom. sg. neut.
     {6.A.1} . . . . id.
γεγονότας   vbl., ²perf. act. ptc. acc. pl. masc.
     {6.A.1} . . . . id.
γεγονότες   vbl., ²perf. act. ptc. nom. pl. masc.
     {6.A.1} . . . . id.
γεγονότι   vbl., ²perf. act. ptc. dat. sg. neut.
     {6.A.1} . . . . id.
γεγονυῖα   vbl., ²perf. act. ptc. nom. sg. fem.
     {6.A.1} . . . . id.
γεγονώς   vbl., ²perf. act. ptc. nom. sg. masc.
     {6.A.1} . . . . id.
γεγραμμένα   vbl., perf. pass. ptc. acc. pl. neut.
     {6.A.1.b} . . . . γράφω G1125
γεγραμμένα   vbl., perf. pass. ptc. nom. pl. neut.
     {6.A.1.b} . . . . id.
γεγραμμένας   vbl., perf. pass. ptc. acc. pl. fem.
     {6.A.1.b} . . . . id.
γεγραμμένη   vbl., perf. pass. ptc. nom. sg. fem.
     {6.A.1.b} . . . . id.
γεγραμμένην   vbl., perf. pass. ptc. acc. sg. fem.
     {6.A.1.b} . . . . id.
γεγραμμένοι   vbl., perf. pass. ptc. nom. pl.
     masc. {6.A.1.b} . . . . id.
γεγραμμένοις   vbl., perf. pass. ptc. dat. pl. neut.
     {6.A.1.b} . . . . id.
γεγραμμένον   vbl., perf. pass. ptc. acc. sg. neut.
     {6.A.1.b} . . . . id.
γεγραμμένον   vbl., perf. pass. ptc. nom. sg.
     neut. {6.A.1.b} . . . . id.
γεγραμμένος   vbl., perf. pass. ptc. nom. sg.
     masc. {6.A.1.b} . . . . id.
γεγραμμένων   vbl., perf. pass. ptc. gen. pl. neut.
     {6.A.1.b} . . . . id.
γέγραπται   verb, perf. pass. indic. 3 pers. sg.
     {5.A.1.f} . . . . id.
γέγραφα   verb, ²perf. act. indic. 1 pers. sg.
     {5.A.1.c} . . . . id.
γεγυμνασμένα   vbl., perf. pass. ptc. acc. pl. neut.
     {6.A.1.b} . . . . γυμνάζω G1128
γεγυμνασμένην   vbl., perf. pass. ptc. acc. sg.
     fem. {6.A.1.b} . . . . id.
γεγυμνασμένοις   vbl., perf. pass. ptc. dat. pl.
     masc. {6.A.1.b} . . . . id.
G1066 **Γεδεών**, ὁ   *Gideon,* one of the Judges of Israel (Heb.).

Γεδεών   noun prop. . . . . Γεδεών G1066

G1067 **γέεννα**, -ης, ἡ   *gehenna,* and orig. *gē ben hinnôm,* name of a valley or cavity near Jerusalem, Jer 7:31; 2 Kgs 23:10, a place underneath the earth, a place of punishment (retributive or purificatory) for evil (Aram.).

Γέενναν   noun prop., acc. sg. fem. {2.A; 2.D} . . . . γέεννα G1067

Γεέννη   noun prop., dat. sg. fem. {2.A; 2.D} . . . . id.

Γεέννης   noun prop., gen. sg. fem. {2.A; 2.D} . . . id.

Γεθσημανεί   noun prop. . . . . Γεθσημανί G1068

Γεθσημανή   noun prop.

G1068 **Γεθσημανί**   *Gethsemani,* a small place between the brook Kidron and the Mount of Olives near Jerusalem.

Γεθσημανί   noun prop. . . . . Γεθσημανί G1068

γείτονας   noun, acc. pl. fem. {2.C} . . . . γείτων G1069

γείτονας   noun, acc. pl. masc. {2.C} . . . . id.

γείτονες   noun, nom. pl. masc. {2.C} . . . . id.

G1069 **γείτων**, -ονος, ὁ or ἡ   *a neighbor.*

γελάσετε   verb, fut. act. indic. 2 pers. pl. {5.A.1} . . . . γελάω G1070

G1070 **γελάω**   *I laugh.*

γελῶντες   vbl., pres. act. ptc. nom. pl. masc. {6.A.2} . . . . γελάω G1070

G1071 **γέλως**, -ωτος, ὁ   *laughter.*

γέλως   noun, nom. sg. masc. {2.C} . . . . γέλως G1071

γέμει   verb, pres. act. indic. 3 pers. sg. {5.A.1.a} γέμω G1073

γεμίζεσθαι   vbl., pres. pass. inf. {6.B.1} . . . . γεμίζω G1072

G1072 **γεμίζω**   *I fill, load.*

γεμίσαι   vbl., aor. act. inf. {6.B.1} . . . . γεμίζω G1072

γεμίσας   vbl., aor. act. ptc. nom. sg. masc. {6.A.1.a} . . . . id.

γεμίσατε   verb, aor. act. impv. 2 pers. pl. {5.D.1} . id.

γεμισθῇ   verb, aor. pass. subjunc. 3 pers. sg. {5.B.1} . . . . id.

γέμον   vbl., pres. act. ptc. acc. sg. neut. {6.A.1} γέμω G1073

γέμοντα   vbl., pres. act. ptc. acc. pl. neut. {6.A.1} id.

γέμοντα   vbl., pres. act. ptc. nom. pl. neut. {6.A.1} . . . . id.

γεμόντων   vbl., pres. act. ptc. gen. pl. fem. {6.A.1} . . . . id.

γεμόντων   vbl., pres. act. ptc. gen. pl. neut. {6.A.1} . . . . id.

γεμούσας   vbl., pres. act. ptc. acc. pl. fem. {6.A.1} . . . . id.

γέμουσιν   verb, pres. act. indic. 3 pers. pl. {5.A.1.a} . . . . id.

G1073 **γέμω**   *I am full of.*

G1074 **γενεά**, -ᾶς, ἡ   *a generation;* in combination with another γενεά, or with αἰών, practically indicates infinity of time.

γενεά   noun, nom. sg. fem. {2.A} . . . . .γενεά G1074

γενεά   noun, voc. sg. fem. {2.A} . . . . id.

γενεᾷ   noun, dat. sg. fem. {2.A} . . . . id.

γενεαί   noun, nom. pl. fem. {2.A} . . . . id.

γενεαῖς   noun, dat. pl. fem. {2.A} . . . . id.

G1075 **γενεαλογέω**   pass. *I am put into a genealogy; I am descended from.*

G1076 **γενεαλογία**, -ας, ἡ   *genealogy.*

γενεαλογίαις   noun, dat. pl. fem. {2.A} γενεαλογία G1076

γενεαλογίας   noun, acc. pl. fem. {2.A} . . . . id.

γενεαλογούμενος   vbl., pres. pass. ptc. nom. sg. masc. {6.A.2} . . . . .γενεαλογέω G1075

γενεάν   noun, acc. sg. fem. {2.A} . . . . .γενεά G1074

γενεάς   noun, acc. pl. fem. {2.A} . . . . id.

γενεᾶς   noun, gen. sg. fem. {2.A} . . . . id.

γένει   noun, dat. sg. neut. {2.C} . . . . . . .γένος G1085

γενέσει   noun, dat. sg. fem. {2.C} . . . . . . γένεσις G1078

γενέσεως   noun, gen. sg. fem. {2.C} . . . . id.

γενέσθαι   vbl., ²aor. mid. inf. {6.B.1} . . . . . . γίνομαι G1096

γένεσθε   verb, ²aor. mid. impv. 2 pers. pl. {5.D.1} id.

γενέσθω   verb, ²aor. mid. impv. 3 pers. sg. {5.D.1}id.

G1077 **γενέσια**, -ων, τά   *birthday or anniversary feast.*

γενεσίοις   noun, dat. pl. neut. {2.B} . . . . . γενέσια G1077

G1078 **γένεσις**, -εως, ἡ   *birth, creation, beginning.*

γένεσις   noun, nom. sg. fem. {2.C} . . . . . . γένεσις G1078

γενεσίων   noun, gen. pl. neut. {2.B} . . . . . γενέσια G1077

G1079 **γενετή**, -ῆς, ἡ   *birth.*

γενετῆς   noun, gen. sg. fem. {2.A} . . . . . . .γενετή G1079

γενεῶν   noun, gen. pl. fem. {2.A} . . . . .γενεά G1074

γένη   noun, acc. pl. neut. {2.C} . . . . γένος G1085

γένη   noun, nom. pl. neut. {2.C} . . . . id.

γενηθέντας   vbl., aor. pass. ptc. acc. pl. masc. {6.A.1.a} . . . . .γίνομαι G1096

γενηθέντες   vbl., aor. pass. ptc. nom. pl. masc. {6.A.1.a} . . . . id.

γενηθέντων   vbl., aor. pass. ptc. gen. pl. neut. {6.A.1.a} . . . . id.

γενηθῆναι   vbl., aor. pass. inf. {6.B.1} . . . . id.

γενηθῆτε   verb, aor. pass. impv. 2 pers. pl. {5.D.1} . . . . id.

γενηθήτω   verb, aor. pass. impv. 3 pers. sg. {5.D.1} . . . . id.

γενηθῶμεν   verb, aor. pass. subjunc. 1 pers. pl. {5.B.1} . . . . id.

G1081†‡ **γένημα**, -ατος, τό   *fruit, crop, produce of the earth* (of vegetable, never of animal, products, from γίνομαι). Var. for γέννημα.

γενήματα   noun, acc. pl. neut. {2.C} . . . . . γένημα G1081†‡

γενήματος   noun, gen. sg. neut. {2.C} . . . . id.

Γεννησαρέτ   noun prop. . . . . Γεννησαρέτ G1082

γενήσεσθε   verb, fut. mid. indic. 2 pers. pl. {5.A.1.d} . . . . γίνομαι G1096

γενήσεται   verb, fut. mid. indic. 3 pers. sg. {5.A.1.d} . . . . id.

γένησθε   verb, ²aor. mid. subjunc. 2 pers. pl. {5.B.1} . . . . id.

γενησόμενον   vbl., fut. mid. ptc. acc. sg. neut. {6.A.1.b} . . . . id.

γενήσονται   verb, fut. mid. indic. 3 pers. pl. {5.A.1.d} . . . . id.

γένηται   verb, ²aor. mid. subjunc. 3 pers. sg. {5.B.1} . . . . id.

γεννᾶται   verb, pres. pass. indic. 3 pers. sg. {5.A.2} . . . . γεννάω G1080

γεννᾶται   verb, pres. pass. subjunc. 3 pers. sg. {5.B.2} . . . . id.

G1080 **γεννάω**   *I beget* (of the male); more rarely (of the female) *I bring forth* (e.g., Luke 1:13).

γεννηθείς   vbl., aor. pass. ptc. nom. sg. masc.
  {6.A.1.a} . . . . γεννάω G1080
γεννηθέν   vbl., aor. pass. ptc. nom. sg. neut.
  {6.A.1.a} . . . . id.
γεννηθέντος   vbl., aor. pass. ptc. gen. sg. masc.
  {6.A.1.a} . . . . id.
γεννηθέντων   vbl., aor. pass. ptc. gen. pl. masc.
  {6.A.1.a} . . . . id.
γεννηθῇ   verb, aor. pass. subjunc. 3 pers. sg.
  {5.B.1} . . . . id.
γεννηθῆναι   vbl., aor. pass. inf. {6.B.1} . . . . . . id.
G1081 **γέννημα**, -ατος, τό   *offspring, child* (of animal,
  never of vegetable, products; from γεννάω).
γεννήματα   noun, acc. pl. neut. {2.C} . . . . γέννημα G1081
γεννήματα   noun, voc. pl. neut. {2.C} . . . . id.
γεννήματος   noun, gen. sg. neut. {2.C} . . . . . . id.
γεννήσαντα   vbl., aor. act. ptc. acc. sg. masc.
  {6.A.2} . . . . γεννάω G1080
G1082 **Γεννησαρέτ**, ἡ   *Gennesaret,* a fertile district by
  the lake of Tiberias, which was in consequence
  sometimes called the Lake of Gennesaret.
Γεννησαρέτ   noun prop. . . . . Γεννησαρέτ G1082
γεννήσει   noun, dat. sg. fem. {2.C} . . . . . γέννησις G1083
γεννήσει   verb, fut. act. indic. 3 pers. sg.
  {5.A.1} . . . . γεννάω G1080
γεννήσῃ   verb, aor. act. subjunc. 3 pers. sg.
  {5.B.1} . . . . id.
G1083 **γέννησις**, -εως, ἡ   *birth.*
γέννησις   noun, nom. sg. fem. {2.C} . . . . γέννησις G1083
γεννητοῖς   adj., dat. pl. masc. {3.A} . . . . . γεννητός G1084
G1084 **γεννητός**, -ή, -όν   *begotten,* used as subs.
γεννώμενον   vbl., pres. pass. ptc. nom. sg. neut.
  {6.A.2} . . . . γεννάω G1080
γεννῶσα   vbl., pres. act. ptc. nom. sg. fem.
  {6.A.2} . . . . id.
γεννῶσι   verb, pres. act. indic. 3 pers. pl. {5.A.2} id.
γεννῶσιν   verb, pres. act. indic. 3 pers. pl.
  {5.A.2} . . . . id.
γένοιτο   verb, ²aor. mid. opt. 3 pers. sg.
  {5.C.1} . . . . γίνομαι G1096
γενόμενα   vbl., ²aor. mid. ptc. acc. pl. neut.
  {6.A.1.b} . . . . id.
γενόμεναι   vbl., ²aor. mid. ptc. nom. pl. fem.
  {6.A.1.b} . . . . id.
γενομένην   vbl., ²aor. mid. ptc. acc. sg. fem.
  {6.A.1.b} . . . . id.
γενομένης   vbl., ²aor. mid. ptc. gen. sg. fem.
  {6.A.1.b} . . . . id.
γενόμενοι   vbl., ²aor. mid. ptc. nom. pl. masc.
  {6.A.1.b} . . . . id.
γενομένοις   vbl., ²aor. mid. ptc. dat. pl. masc.
  {6.A.1.b} . . . . id.
γενομένοις   vbl., ²aor. mid. ptc. dat. pl. neut.
  {6.A.1.b} . . . . id.
γενόμενον   vbl., ²aor. mid. ptc. acc. sg. masc.
  {6.A.1.b} . . . . id.
γενόμενον   vbl., ²aor. mid. ptc. acc. sg. neut.
  {6.A.1.b} . . . . id.
γενόμενος   vbl., ²aor. mid. ptc. nom. sg. masc.
  {6.A.1.b} . . . . id.

γενομένου   vbl., ²aor. mid. ptc. gen. sg. masc.
  {6.A.1.b} . . . . id.
γενομένου   vbl., ²aor. mid. ptc. gen. sg. neut.
  {6.A.1.b} . . . . id.
γενομένων   vbl., ²aor. mid. ptc. gen. pl. fem.
  {6.A.1.b} . . . . id.
γενομένων   vbl., ²aor. mid. ptc. gen. pl. masc.
  {6.A.1.b} . . . . id.
γενομένων   vbl., ²aor. mid. ptc. gen. pl. neut.
  {6.A.1.b} . . . . id.
γένος   noun, acc. sg. neut. {2.C} . . . . γένος G1085
G1085 **γένος**, -ους, τό   (1) *race;* (2) *kind.*
γένος   noun, nom. sg. neut. {2.C} . . . . γένος G1085
γένους   noun, gen. sg. neut. {2.C} . . . . id.
γένωμαι   verb, ²aor. mid. subjunc. 1 pers. sg.
  {5.B.1} . . . . γίνομαι G1096
γενώμεθα   verb, ²aor. mid. subjunc. 1 pers. pl.
  {5.B.1} . . . . id.
γένωνται   verb, ²aor. mid. subjunc. 3 pers. pl.
  {5.B.1} . . . . id.
G1086† **Γερασηνός**   *Gerasene, of Gerasa* (an important
  Hellenized town, one of the Decapolis, and
  southeast of the Sea of Galilee). Var. for Γαδαρηνός, Matt 8:28; Mark 5:1; Luke 8:26, 37.
Γερασηνῶν   noun prop., gen. pl. masc. {2.B;
  2.D} . . . . Γερασηνός G1086†
G1086 **Γεργεσηνός** (Γερασηνός), -ή, -όν   *Gergesene*
  or *Gerasene; of Gergesa* (mod. Kursi), a place
  on a hill on the Lake of Tiberias; or of Gerasa,
  a town on the east of the Lake of Tiberias.
  Wherever the one is mentioned, variants for
  the other occur.
Γεργεσηνῶν   noun prop., gen. pl. masc. {2.B;
  2.D} . . . . Γερασηνός G1086†
G1087 **γερουσία**, -ας, ἡ   *the assembly* or *body of
  elders,* probably as synonymous with or
  explicative of συνέδριον and πρεσβύτεροι.
  (The term γερουσία was often used in such a
  collective sense in the cities of Asia Minor.)
γερουσίαν   noun, acc. sg. fem. {2.A} . . . γερουσία G1087
G1088 **γέρων**, -οντος, ὁ   *an old man.*
γέρων   noun, nom. sg. masc. {2.C} . . . . γέρων G1088
G1089 **γεύομαι**   (1) *I taste;* (2) *I experience.*
γευσάμενος   vbl., aor. mid. ptc. nom. sg. masc.
  {6.A.1.b} . . . . γεύομαι G1089
γευσαμένους   vbl., aor. mid. ptc. acc. pl. masc.
  {6.A.1.b} . . . . id.
γεύσασθαι   vbl., aor. mid. inf. {6.B.1} . . . . id.
γεύσεται   verb, fut. mid. indic. 3 pers. sg.
  {5.A.1.d} . . . . id.
γεύσῃ   verb, aor. mid. subjunc. 2 pers. sg. {5.B.1} id.
γεύσηται   verb, aor. mid. subjunc. 3 pers. sg.
  {5.B.1} . . . . id.
γεύσονται   verb, fut. mid. indic. 3 pers. pl.
  {5.A.1.d} . . . . id.
γεύσωνται   verb, aor. mid. subjunc. 3 pers. pl.
  {5.B.1} . . . . id.
γεωργεῖται   verb, pres. pass. indic. 3 pers. sg.
  {5.A.2} . . . . γεωργέω G1090
G1090 **γεωργέω**   *I work the soil, I cultivate the soil.*

G1091 **γεώργιον**, -ου, τό   *a cultivated field.*
γεώργιον   noun, nom. sg. neut. {2.B} . . . . γεώργιον G1091
γεωργοί   noun, nom. pl. masc. {2.B} . . . . . .γεωργός G1092
γεωργοῖς   noun, dat. pl. masc. {2.B} . . . . id.
γεωργόν   noun, acc. sg. masc. {2.B} . . . . id.

G1092 **γεωργός**, -οῦ, ὁ   *a worker of the soil, husband-*
man, farmer, farm laborer.
γεωργός   noun, nom. sg. masc. {2.B}. . . . . .γεωργός G1092
γεωργούς   noun, acc. pl. masc. {2.B}. . . . . id.
γεωργῶν   noun, gen. pl. masc. {2.B} . . . . id.

G1093 **γῆ**, γῆς, ἡ   *the earth, soil, land.*
γῆ   noun, nom. sg. fem. {2.A} . . . . γῆ G1093
γῆ   noun, voc. sg. fem. {2.A} . . . . id.
γῆ   noun, dat. sg. fem. {2.A} . . . . id.
γήμας   vbl., aor. act. ptc. nom. sg. masc. {6.A.2}. . γαμέω G1060
γήμῃ   verb, aor. act. subjunc. 3 pers. sg. {5.B.1}. . id.
γήμῃς   verb, aor. act. subjunc. 2 pers. sg. {5.B.1}. id.
γῆν   noun, acc. sg. fem. {2.A} . . . . γῆ G1093
γήρᾳ   noun, dat. sg. neut. {2.C}. . . . . γῆρας G1094

G1094 **γῆρας**, -ως or ους, dat. γήρᾳ or γήρει, τό   *old*
age.
γηράσῃς   verb, aor. act. subjunc. 2 pers. sg.
{5.B.1} . . . . .γηράσκω G1095
γηράσκον   vbl., pres. act. ptc. nom. sg. neut.
{6.A.1} . . . . id.

G1095 **γηράσκω**   *I become old, grow old.*
γήρει   noun, dat. sg. neut. {2.C} . . . . γῆρας G1094
γῆς   noun, gen. sg. fem. {2.A} . . . . γῆ G1093
γίνεσθαι   vbl., pres. mid./pass. inf. {6.B.1} . γίνομαι G1096
γίνεσθε   verb, pres. mid./pass. impv. 2 pers. pl.
{5.D.1}. . . . . id.
γινέσθω   verb, pres. mid./pass. impv. 3 pers. sg.
{5.D.1} . . . . id.
γίνεται   verb, pres. mid./pass. indic. 3 pers. sg.
{5.A.1.d} . . . . id.

G1096 **γίνομαι**   (1) *I come into being, am born,* John
8:58; Gal 4:4, etc.; (2) *I become, come about,*
happen. (Aor. ἐγένετο is used by Luke to give
Hebraistic coloring in various constructions:
ἐγένετο ἦλθεν, ἐγένετο καὶ ἦλθεν, ἐγένετο
ἐλθεῖν, the latter of which is latest and
non-Hebraistic.)
γινόμενα   vbl., pres. mid./pass. ptc. acc. pl. neut.
{6.A.1}. . . . . .γίνομαι G1096
γινόμεναι   vbl., pres. mid./pass. ptc. nom. pl.
fem. {6.A.1}. . . . . id.
γινομένας   vbl., pres. mid./pass. ptc. acc. pl.
fem. {6.A.1}. . . . . id.
γινομένη   vbl., pres. mid./pass. ptc. dat. sg. fem.
{6.A.1}. . . . . id.
γινομένη   vbl., pres. mid./pass. ptc. nom. sg.
fem. {6.A.1}. . . . . id.
γινομένης   vbl., pres. mid./pass. ptc. gen. sg.
fem. {6.A.1}. . . . . id.
γινόμενοι   vbl., pres. mid./pass. ptc. nom. pl.
masc. {6.A.1}. . . . . id.
γινομένοις   vbl., pres. mid./pass. ptc. dat. pl.
neut. {6.A.1} . . . . id.
γινόμενον   vbl., pres. mid./pass. ptc. acc. sg.
masc. {6.A.1}. . . . . id.

γινόμενον   vbl., pres. mid./pass. ptc. acc. sg.
neut. {6.A.1} . . . . id.
γινόμενον   vbl., pres. mid./pass. ptc. nom. sg.
neut. {6.A.1} . . . . id.
γινομένου   vbl., pres. mid./pass. ptc. gen. sg.
neut. {6.A.1} . . . . id.
γινομένων   vbl., pres. mid./pass. ptc. gen. pl.
neut. {6.A.1} . . . . id.
γίνονται   verb, pres. mid./pass. indic. 3 pers. pl.
{5.A.1.d} . . . . id.
γίνου   verb, pres. mid./pass. impv. 2 pers. sg.
{5.D.1} . . . . id.
γινώμεθα   verb, pres. mid./pass. subjunc.
1 pers. pl. {5.B.1} . . . . id.
γίνωνται   verb, pres. mid./pass. subjunc. 3 pers.
pl. {5.B.1}. . . . . id.
γίνωσκε   verb, pres. act. impv. 2 pers. sg.
{5.D.1} . . . . γινώσκω G1097
γινώσκει   verb, pres. act. indic. 3 pers. sg.
{5.A.1.a} . . . . id.
γινώσκειν   vbl., pres. act. inf. {6.B.1} . . . . id.
γινώσκεις   verb, pres. act. indic. 2 pers. sg.
{5.A.1.a} . . . . id.
γινώσκεται   verb, pres. pass. indic. 3 pers. sg.
{5.A.1.d} . . . . id.
γινώσκετε   verb, pres. act. impv. 2 pers. pl.
{5.D.1}. . . . . id.
γινώσκετε   verb, pres. act. indic. 2 pers. pl.
{5.A.1.a} . . . . id.
γινωσκέτω   verb, pres. act. impv. 3 pers. sg.
{5.D.1} . . . . id.
γινώσκῃ   verb, pres. act. subjunc. 3 pers. sg.
{5.B.1} . . . . id.
γινώσκητε   verb, pres. act. subjunc. 2 pers. pl.
{5.B.1} . . . . id.
γινώσκομαι   verb, pres. pass. indic. 1 pers. sg.
{5.A.1.d} . . . . id.
γινώσκομεν   verb, pres. act. indic. 1 pers. pl.
{5.A.1.a} . . . . id.
γινωσκομένη   vbl., pres. pass. ptc. nom. sg.
fem. {6.A.1} . . . . id.
γινώσκοντες   vbl., pres. act. ptc. nom. pl. masc.
{6.A.1} . . . . id.
γινώσκουσι   verb, pres. act. indic. 3 pers. pl.
{5.A.1.a} . . . . id.
γινώσκουσι   vbl., pres. act. ptc. dat. pl. masc.
{6.A.1}. . . . . id.
γινώσκουσιν   vbl., pres. act. ptc. dat. pl. masc.
{6.A.1}. . . . . id.

G1097 **γινώσκω**   (1) *I am taking in knowledge, come to*
know, learn; (2) aor. *I ascertained, realized,* but
not in John 17:25; 2 Tim 2:19.
γινώσκω   verb, pres. act. indic. 1 pers. sg.
{5.A.1.a} . . . . γινώσκω G1097
γινώσκωμεν   verb, pres. act. subjunc. 1 pers. pl.
{5.B.1} . . . . id.
γινώσκων   vbl., pres. act. ptc. nom. sg. masc.
{6.A.1}. . . . . id.
γινώσκωσι   verb, pres. act. subjunc. 3 pers. pl.
{5.B.1} . . . . id.

γινώσκωσιν   verb, pres. act. subjunc. 3 pers. pl.
{5.B.1} . . . . id.

G1098 **γλεῦκος**, -ους, τό   *sweet wine,* made perhaps from a small specially sweet grape.
γλεύκους   noun, gen. sg. neut. {2.C} . . . . . γλεῦκος G1098
γλυκύ   adj., acc. sg. neut. {3.D} . . . . γλυκύς G1099
γλυκύ   adj., nom. sg. neut. {3.D} . . . . id.

G1099 **γλυκύς**, -εῖα, -ύ   *sweet.*

G1100 **γλῶσσα**, -ης, ἡ   (1) *tongue,* esp. as an organ of speech; (2) *tongue, language;* (3) also, usually in the pl., for the unintelligible sounds uttered in spiritual ecstasy.
γλῶσσα   noun, nom. sg. fem. {2.A} . . . . . γλῶσσα G1100
γλῶσσαι   noun, nom. pl. fem. {2.A} . . . . id.
γλώσσαις   noun, dat. pl. fem. {2.A} . . . . id.
γλῶσσαν   noun, acc. sg. fem. {2.A} . . . . id.
γλώσσας   noun, acc. pl. fem. {2.A} . . . . id.
γλώσση   noun, dat. sg. fem. {2.A} . . . . id.
γλώσσης   noun, gen. sg. fem. {2.A} . . . . id.

G1101 **γλωσσόκομον**, -ου, τό   *bag, purse;* some prefer to take as *box, chest* (a vernacular word).
γλωσσόκομον   noun, acc. sg. neut.
{2.B} . . . . γλωσσόκομον G1101
γλωσσῶν   noun, gen. pl. fem. {2.A} . . . . . γλῶσσα G1100

G1102 **γναφεύς**, -έως, ὁ   *fuller.*
γναφεύς   noun, nom. sg. masc. {2.C} . . . . γναφεύς G1102
γνήσιε   adj., voc. sg. masc. {3.A} . . . . γνήσιος G1103
γνήσιον   adj., acc. sg. neut. {3.A} . . . . id.

G1103 **γνήσιος**, -α, -ον   (lit. *born*), hence, *real, true, genuine;* τὸ γνήσιον, *the true, genuine element.*
γνησίῳ   adj., dat. sg. neut. {3.A} . . . . γνήσιος G1103

G1104 **γνησίως**   adv., (1) *truly, genuinely;* (2) *honorably.*
γνησίως   adv. {3.F} . . . . γνησίως G1104
γνοῖ   verb, ²aor. act. subjunc. 3 pers. sg.
{5.B.1} . . . . γινώσκω G1097
γνόντα   vbl., ²aor. act. ptc. acc. sg. masc.
{6.A.1.a} . . . . id.
γνόντες   vbl., ²aor. act. ptc. nom. pl. masc.
{6.A.1.a} . . . . id.
γνούς   vbl., ²aor. act. ptc. nom. sg. masc.
{6.A.1.a} . . . . id.

G1105 **γνόφος**, -ου, ὁ   *darkness.*
γνόφῳ   noun, dat. sg. masc. {2.B} . . . . γνόφος G1105
γνῶ   verb, ²aor. act. subjunc. 1 pers. sg.
{5.B.1} . . . . γινώσκω G1097
γνῷ   verb, ²aor. act. subjunc. 3 pers. sg. {5.B.1} . . id.
γνῶθι   verb, ²aor. act. impv. 2 pers. sg. {5.D.1} . . . id.

G1106 **γνώμη**, -ης, ἡ   *opinion, counsel.*
γνώμῃ   noun, dat. sg. fem. {2.A} . . . . γνώμη G1106
γνώμη   noun, nom. sg. fem. {2.A} . . . . id.
γνώμῃ   noun, dat. sg. fem. {2.A} . . . . id.
γνώμην   noun, acc. sg. fem. {2.A} . . . . id.
γνώμης   noun, gen. sg. fem. {2.A} . . . . id.
γνῶναι   vbl., ²aor. act. inf. {6.B.1} . . . . . . γινώσκω G1097
γνωριζέσθω   verb, pres. pass. impv. 3 pers. sg.
{5.D.1} . . . . γνωρίζω G1107
γνωρίζομεν   verb, pres. act. indic. 1 pers. pl.
{5.A.1.a} . . . . id.

G1107 **γνωρίζω**   *I make known.*

γνωρίζω   verb, pres. act. indic. 1 pers. sg.
{5.A.1.a} . . . . γνωρίζω G1107
γνωριοῦσι   verb, fut. act. indic. 3 pers. pl.
{5.A.2} . . . . id.
γνωριοῦσιν   verb, fut. act. indic. 3 pers. pl.
{5.A.2} . . . . id.
γνωρίσαι   vbl., aor. act. inf. {6.B.1} . . . . id.
γνωρίσας   vbl., aor. act. ptc. nom. sg. masc.
{6.A.1.a} . . . . id.
γνωρίσει   verb, fut. act. indic. 3 pers. sg.
{5.A.1.a} . . . . id.
γνωρίσῃ   verb, aor. act. subjunc. 3 pers. sg.
{5.B.1} . . . . id.
γνωρισθέντος   vbl., aor. pass. ptc. gen. sg. neut.
{6.A.1.a} . . . . id.
γνωρισθῇ   verb, aor. pass. subjunc. 3 pers. sg.
{5.B.1} . . . . id.
γνωρίσουσιν   verb, fut. act. indic. 3 pers. pl.
{5.A.1.a} . . . . id.
γνωρίσω   verb, fut. act. indic. 1 pers. sg.
{5.A.1.a} . . . . id.
γνῶς   verb, ²aor. act. subjunc. 2 pers. sg.
{5.B.1} . . . . γινώσκω G1097
γνώσει   noun, dat. sg. fem. {2.C} . . . . γνῶσις G1108
γνώσεσθε   verb, fut. mid. indic. 2 pers. pl.
{5.A.1.d} . . . . γινώσκω G1097
γνώσεται   verb, fut. mid. indic. 3 pers. sg.
{5.A.1.d} . . . . id.
γνώσεως   noun, gen. sg. fem. {2.C} . . . . γνῶσις G1108
γνώσῃ   verb, fut. mid. indic. 2 pers. sg.
{5.A.1.d} . . . . γινώσκω G1097
γνωσθέντες   vbl., aor. pass. ptc. nom. pl. masc.
{6.A.1.a} . . . . id.
γνωσθῇ   verb, aor. pass. subjunc. 3 pers. sg.
{5.B.1} . . . . id.
γνωσθήσεται   verb, fut. pass. indic. 3 pers. sg.
{5.A.1.d} . . . . id.
γνωσθήτω   verb, aor. pass. impv. 3 pers. sg.
{5.D.1} . . . . id.
γνῶσι   verb, ²aor. act. subjunc. 3 pers. pl. {5.B.1} . id.
γνῶσιν   noun, acc. sg. fem. {2.C} . . . . γνῶσις G1108
γνῶσιν   verb, ²aor. act. subjunc. 3 pers. pl.
{5.B.1} . . . . γινώσκω G1097

G1108 **γνῶσις**, -εως, ἡ   *knowledge.*
γνῶσις   noun, nom. sg. fem. {2.C} . . . . γνῶσις G1108
γνώσομαι   verb, fut. mid. indic. 1 pers. sg.
{5.A.1.d} . . . . γινώσκω G1097
γνωσόμεθα   verb, fut. mid. indic. 1 pers. pl.
{5.A.1.d} . . . . id.
γνώσονται   verb, fut. mid. indic. 3 pers. pl.
{5.A.1.d} . . . . id.
γνωστά   adj., acc. pl. neut. {3.A} . . . . γνωστός G1110
γνωστά   adj., nom. pl. neut. {3.A} . . . . id.
γνώστην   noun, acc. sg. masc. {2.A} . . . . . γνώστης G1109

G1109 **γνώστης**, -ου, ὁ   *a knower, expert.*
γνωστοί   adj., nom. pl. masc. {3.A} . . . . . . γνωστός G1110
γνωστοῖς   adj., dat. pl. masc. {3.A} . . . . id.
γνωστόν   adj., nom. sg. neut. {3.A} . . . . id.

G1110 **γνωστός**, -ή, -όν   (1) *known;* (2) subs. *an acquaintance.*

γνωστός adj., nom. sg. masc. {3.A} . . . . . γνωστός *G1110*

γνῶτε verb, ²aor. act. impv. 2 pers. pl. {5.D.1} . . γινώσκω *G1097*

γνῶτε verb, ²aor. act. subjunc. 2 pers. pl. {5.B.1} . id.

γνώτω verb, ²aor. act. impv. 3 pers. sg. {5.D.1} . . id.

γογγύζετε verb, pres. act. impv. 2 pers. pl.
{5.D.1} . . . . .γογγύζω *G1111*

γογγύζοντος vbl., pres. act. ptc. gen. sg. masc.
{6.A.1} . . . . id.

γογγύζουσι verb, pres. act. indic. 3 pers. pl.
{5.A.1.a} . . . . id.

γογγύζουσιν verb, pres. act. indic. 3 pers. pl.
{5.A.1.a} . . . . id.

G1111 **γογγύζω** *I whisper, murmur, grumble* (generally
of smoldering discontent).

G1112 **γογγυσμός**, -οῦ, ὁ *murmuring, grumbling.*

γογγυσμός noun, nom. sg. masc. {2.B} .γογγυσμός *G1112*

γογγυσμοῦ noun, gen. sg. masc. {2.B} . . . . id.

γογγυσμῶν noun, gen. pl. masc. {2.B} . . . . id.

γογγυσταί noun, nom. pl. masc. {2.A} .γογγυστής *G1113*

G1113 **γογγυστής**, -οῦ, ὁ *murmurer, grumbler.*

G1114 **γόης**, -ητος, ὁ (1) *a conjuror, juggler, sorcerer;*
(2) *a tricky (crafty) deceiver, impostor.*

γόητες noun, nom. pl. masc. {2.A} . . . . .γόης *G1114*

Γολγοθα noun prop. . . . . Γολγοθᾶ *G1115*

Γολγοθά noun prop. . . . . id.

G1115 **Γολγοθᾶ**, ἡ *Golgotha, a knoll outside the wall
of Jerusalem.*

Γολγοθᾶ noun prop., nom. sg. fem. {2.A;
2.D} . . . . Γολγοθᾶ *G1115*

Γολγοθᾶν noun prop., acc. sg. fem. {2.A; 2.D} . . id.

Γολγοθᾶν noun prop., acc. sg. fem. {2.A; 2.D} . . id.

γόμον noun, acc. sg. masc. {2.B} . . . . .γόμος *G1117*

G1116 **Γόμορρα**, -ας or ων, ἡ or τά *Gomorrha, one
of the destroyed cities on the Dead Sea.*

Γόμορρα noun prop., nom. sg. fem. {2.A;
2.D} . . . . .Γόμορρα *G1116*

Γομόρρας noun prop., gen. sg. fem. {2.A; 2.D} . id.

Γομόρροις noun prop., dat. pl. neut. {2.B; 2.D} . id.

Γομόρρων noun prop., gen. pl. neut. {2.B; 2.D} . id.

G1117 **γόμος**, -ου, ὁ *a cargo, freight.*

γόνασι noun, dat. pl. neut. {2.C} . . . . .γόνυ *G1119*

γόνασιν noun, dat. pl. neut. {2.C} . . . . id.

γόνατα noun, acc. pl. neut. {2.C} . . . . id.

γονεῖς noun, acc. pl. masc. {2.C} . . . . . . .γονεύς *G1118*

γονεῖς noun, nom. pl. masc. {2.C} . . . . id.

G1118 **γονεύς**, -έως, pl. γονεῖς, -έων, ὁ *parents.*

γονεῦσι noun, dat. pl. masc. {2.C} . . . . . . .γονεύς *G1118*

γονεῦσιν noun, dat. pl. masc. {2.C} . . . . id.

γονέων noun, gen. pl. masc. {2.C} . . . . id.

G1119 **γόνυ**, γόνατος, τό *a knee.*

γόνυ noun, acc. sg. neut. {2.C} . . . . .γόνυ *G1119*

γόνυ noun, nom. sg. neut. {2.C} . . . . id.

G1120 **γονυπετέω** *I fall on my knees before* (in supplication), *supplicate, entreat.*

γονυπετήσαντες vbl., aor. act. ptc. nom. pl. masc.
{6.A.2} . . . . γονυπετέω *G1120*

γονυπετήσας vbl., aor. act. ptc. nom. sg. masc.
{6.A.2} . . . . id.

γονυπετῶν vbl., pres. act. ptc. nom. sg. masc.
{6.A.2} . . . . id.

G1121 **γράμμα**, -ατος, τό *a letter of the alphabet;*
collectively, *written* (revelation), Rom 2:27:
γράμματα, *writings;* (1) *a written document,*
Luke 16:6, 7; *a letter an epistle,* Acts 28:21; (2)
writings, literature, John 5:47; 7:15; Acts 26:24;
2 Tim 3:15.

γράμμα noun, acc. sg. neut. {2.C} . . . . . . γράμμα *G1121*

γράμμα noun, nom. sg. neut. {2.C} . . . . id.

γράμμασιν noun, dat. pl. neut. {2.C} . . . . id.

γράμματα noun, acc. pl. neut. {2.C} . . . . id.

γράμματα noun, nom. pl. neut. {2.C} . . . . id.

γραμματεῖς noun, acc. pl. masc. {2.C}γραμματεύς *G1122*

γραμματεῖς noun, nom. pl. masc. {2.C} . . . . . . id.

γραμματεῖς noun, voc. pl. masc. {2.C} . . . . id.

G1122 **γραμματεύς**, -έως, ὁ (1) in Jerusalem, *a
scribe,* one learned in the Jewish Law, a religious teacher; (2) at Ephesus, *the town clerk,
the secretary of the city,* Acts 19:35.

γραμματεύς noun, nom. sg. masc.
{2.C} . . . . γραμματεύς *G1122*

γραμματεῦσι noun, dat. pl. masc. {2.C} . . . . . . id.

γραμματεῦσιν noun, dat. pl. masc. {2.C} . . . . . id.

γραμματέων noun, gen. pl. masc. {2.C} . . . . . . id.

γράμματι noun, dat. sg. neut. {2.C} . . . . . γράμμα *G1121*

γράμματος noun, gen. sg. neut. {2.C} . . . . id.

γραπτόν adj., acc. sg. neut. {3.A} . . . . γραπτός *G1123*

G1123 **γραπτός**, -ή, -όν *written.*

γραφαί noun, nom. pl. fem. {2.A} . . . . γραφή *G1124*

γραφαῖς noun, dat. pl. fem. {2.A} . . . . id.

γραφάς noun, acc. pl. fem. {2.A} . . . . id.

γράφε verb, pres. act. impv. 2 pers. sg.
{5.D.1} . . . . γράφω *G1125*

γράφει verb, pres. act. indic. 3 pers. sg. {5.A.1.a} id.

γράφειν vbl., pres. act. inf. {6.B.1} . . . . id.

γράφεσθαι vbl., pres. pass. inf. {6.B.1} . . . . id.

G1124 **γραφή**, -ῆς, ἡ (1) *a writing;* (2) *a passage of
scripture;* pl. αἱ γραφαί, *the scriptures* (of the
OT, and in 2 Pet 3:16 also of the New).

γραφή noun, nom. sg. fem. {2.A} . . . . γραφή *G1124*

γραφῇ noun, dat. sg. fem. {2.A} . . . . id.

γραφήν noun, acc. sg. fem. {2.A} . . . . id.

γραφῆς noun, gen. sg. fem. {2.A} . . . . id.

γράφηται verb, pres. pass. subjunc. 3 pers. sg.
{5.B.1} . . . . γράφω *G1125*

γράφομεν verb, pres. act. indic. 1 pers. pl.
{5.A.1.a} . . . . id.

γραφόμενα vbl., pres. pass. ptc. acc. pl. neut.
{6.A.1} . . . . id.

G1125 **γράφω** (1) *I write;* (2) γέγραπται, *it is written, it
stands written* (in the scriptures of the OT; so in
ordinary life, a formula introducing an unalter-
able agreement); (3) = προγράφω, Rom 15:4.

γράφω verb, pres. act. indic. 1 pers. sg.
{5.A.1.a} . . . . γράφω *G1125*

γράφων noun, gen. pl. fem. {2.A} . . . . γραφή *G1124*

γράφων vbl., pres. act. ptc. nom. sg. masc.
{6.A.1} . . . . γράφω *G1125*

γράψαι vbl., aor. act. inf. {6.B.1} . . . . id.

γράψαντες vbl., aor. act. ptc. nom. pl. masc.
{6.A.1.a} . . . . id.

γράψας   vbl., aor. act. ptc. nom. sg. masc.
{6.A.1.a} . . . . id.
γράψῃς   verb, aor. act. subjunc. 2 pers. sg. {5.B.1}id.
γράψον   verb, aor. act. impv. 2 pers. sg. {5.D.1}. . id.
γράψω   verb, aor. act. subjunc. 1 pers. sg. {5.B.1} id.
γράψω   verb, fut. act. indic. 1 pers. sg. {5.A.1.a} . id.
γραώδεις   adj., acc. pl. masc. {3.E} . . . . . . γραώδης G1126
G1126   **γραώδης**, -ες   *belonging to old women, such as old women tell.*
γρηγορεῖτε   verb, pres. act. impv. 2 pers. pl.
{5.D.2}. . . . . γρηγορέω G1127
G1127   **γρηγορέω**   (1) *I am awake* (in the night), *watch;* (2) *I am watchful, on the alert.*
γρηγορῇ   verb, pres. act. subjunc. 3 pers. sg.
{5.B.2}. . . . . γρηγορέω G1127
γρηγορῆσαι   vbl., aor. act. inf. {6.B.1} . . . . id.
γρηγορήσατε   verb, aor. act. impv. 2 pers. pl.
{5.D.1}. . . . . id.
γρηγορήσῃς   verb, aor. act. subjunc. 2 pers. sg.
{5.B.1} . . . . id.
γρηγοροῦντας   vbl., pres. act. ptc. acc. pl.
masc. {6.A.2} . . . . id.
γρηγοροῦντες   vbl., pres. act. ptc. nom. pl.
masc. {6.A.2} . . . . id.
γρηγορῶμεν   verb, pres. act. subjunc. 1 pers. pl.
{5.B.2} . . . . id.
γρηγορῶν   vbl., pres. act. ptc. nom. sg. masc.
{6.A.2} . . . . id.
γυμνά   adj., nom. pl. neut. {3.A} . . . . γυμνός G1131
γύμναζε   verb, pres. act. impv. 2 pers. sg.
{5.D.1} . . . . γυμνάζω G1128
G1128   **γυμνάζω**   (1) *I train by physical exercise;* (2) hence, *train* in widest sense; with gen. of sphere, 2 Pet 2:14.
G1129   **γυμνασία**, -ας, ἡ   (physical) *exercise,* in a wide sense.
γυμνασία   noun, nom. sg. fem. {2.A} . . . γυμνασία G1129
γυμνήν   adj., acc. sg. fem. {3.A} . . . . γυμνός G1131
γυμνητεύομεν   verb, pres. act. indic. 1 pers. pl.
{5.A.1.a} . . . . γυμνιτεύω G1130
γυμνιτεύομεν   verb, pres. act. indic. 1 pers. pl.
{5.A.1.a} . . . . id.
G1130   **γυμνιτεύω**   *I am habitually* γυμνός, i.e., *I wear the undergarment* (χιτών) *only,* it being the regular practice to wear two garments.

γυμνοί   adj., nom. pl. masc. {3.A} . . . . γυμνός G1131
γυμνόν   adj., acc. sg. masc. {3.A} . . . . id.
G1131   **γυμνός**, -ή, -όν   (1) rarely *stark naked,* generally *wearing only the undergarment* (χιτών), see γυμνιτεύω; (2) γυμνὸς κόκκος *a simple seed,* a seed per se.
γυμνός   adj., nom. sg. masc. {3.A} . . . . . . γυμνός G1131
G1132   **γυμνότης**, -ητος, ἡ   *nakedness,* cf. γυμνός, γυμνιτεύω.
γυμνότης   noun, nom. sg. fem. {2.C} . . . γυμνότης G1132
γυμνότητι   noun, dat. sg. fem. {2.C}. . . . . id.
γυμνότητος   noun, gen. sg. fem. {2.C} . . . . id.
γυμνοῦ   adj., gen. sg. neut. {3.A}. . . . . γυμνός G1131
γυμνούς   adj., acc. pl. masc. {3.A}. . . . . id.
γύναι   noun, voc. sg. fem. {2.A} . . . . γυνή G1135
γυναῖκα   noun, acc. sg. fem. {2.A} . . . . γυνή G1135
γυναικάρια   noun, acc. pl. neut. {2.B}γυναικάριον G1133
G1133   **γυναικάριον**, -ου, τό   *a poor weak woman* (physically or morally).
γυναῖκας   noun, acc. pl. fem. {2.A} . . . . γυνή G1135
G1134   **γυναικεῖος**, -α, -ον   *belonging to woman, of woman.*
γυναικείῳ   adj., dat. sg. neut. {3.A} . . . γυναικεῖος G1134
γυναῖκες   noun, nom. pl. fem. {2.A}. . . . . . . γυνή G1135
γυναῖκες   noun, voc. pl. fem. {2.A}. . . . . . . γυνή G1135
γυναικί   noun, dat. sg. fem. {2.A}. . . . . id.
γυναικός   noun, gen. sg. fem. {2.A} . . . . id.
γυναικῶν   noun, gen. pl. fem. {2.A} . . . . id.
γυναιξί   noun, dat. pl. fem. {2.A} . . . . id.
γυναιξίν   noun, dat. pl. fem. {2.A} . . . . id.
G1135   **γυνή**, -αικός, ἡ   (1) *a* (married) *woman, a wife;* so even in Matt 5:28 (2) voc., γύναι, *my lady,* Luke 22:57; John 2:4.
γυνή   noun, nom. sg. fem. {2.A} . . . . γυνή G1135
G1136   **Γώγ**, ὁ   *Gog,* a name borrowed from Ezekiel (38:2 ff., where = prince over Mesech and Thubal), to indicate a race or races to be led astray by Satan at the end of the thousand years.
Γώγ   noun prop. . . . . Γώγ G1136
G1137   **γωνία**, -ας, ἡ   *a corner.*
γωνίᾳ   noun, dat. sg. fem. {2.A} . . . . γωνία G1137
γωνίαις   noun, dat. pl. fem. {2.A} . . . . id.
γωνίας   noun, acc. pl. fem. {2.A}. . . . . id.
γωνίας   noun, gen. sg. fem. {2.A} . . . . id.

Δ δ

δ'   conj. . . . . δέ G1161
Δαβίδ   noun prop. . . . . .Δαυίδ G1138‡
δαίμονες   noun, nom. pl. masc. {2.C}. . . . δαίμων G1142
δαιμόνια   noun, acc. pl. neut. {2.B} . . . .δαιμόνιον G1140
δαιμόνια   noun, nom. pl. neut. {2.B} . . . . id.
δαιμονίζεται   verb, pres. mid./pass. indic. 3 pers.
sg. {5.A.1.d}. . . . . .δαιμονίζομαι G1139
G1139   **δαιμονίζομαι**   *I am under the power of an evil spirit* or *demon.*

δαιμονιζόμενοι   vbl., pres. mid./pass. ptc. nom. pl.
masc. {6.A.1}. . . . . .δαιμονίζομαι G1139
δαιμονιζόμενον   vbl., pres. mid./pass. ptc. acc.
sg. masc. {6.A.1} . . . . id.
δαιμονιζόμενος   vbl., pres. mid./pass. ptc.
nom. sg. masc. {6.A.1}. . . . . id.
δαιμονιζομένου   vbl., pres. mid./pass. ptc.
gen. sg. masc. {6.A.1}. . . . . id.
δαιμονιζομένους   vbl., pres. mid./pass. ptc.
acc. pl. masc. {6.A.1} . . . . id.

δαιμονιζομένῳ   vbl., pres. mid./pass. ptc. dat. sg. masc. {6.A.1} . . . . id.

δαιμονιζομένων   vbl., pres. mid./pass. ptc. gen. pl. masc. {6.A.1} . . . . id.

δαιμονίοις   noun, dat. pl. neut. {2.B} . . δαιμόνιον *G1140*

G1140 **δαιμόνιον**, -ου, τό   *an evil spirit, demon.*

δαιμόνιον   noun, acc. sg. neut. {2.B} . . δαιμόνιον *G1140*

δαιμόνιον   noun, nom. sg. neut. {2.B} . . . . id.

δαιμονίου   noun, gen. sg. neut. {2.B} . . . . id.

δαιμονισθείς   vbl., aor. pass. ptc. nom. sg. masc. {6.A.1.a} . . . . δαιμονίζομαι *G1139*

G1141 **δαιμονιώδης**, -ες   *demon-like, such as dem. have.*

δαιμονιώδης   adj., nom. sg. fem. {3.E} . . . . δαιμονιώδης *G1141*

δαιμονίων   noun, gen. pl. neut. {2.B} . . δαιμόνιον *G1140*

δαίμονος   noun, gen. sg. masc. {2.C} . . . . δαίμων *G1142*

δαιμόνων   noun, gen. pl. masc. {2.C} . . . . id.

G1142 **δαίμων**, -ονος, ὁ   *an evil spirit, a demon,* much less common than the diminutive δαιμόνιον.

δάκνετε   verb, pres. act. indic. 2 pers. pl. {5.A.1.a} . . . . δάκνω *G1143*

G1143 **δάκνω**   (1) *I bite;* (2) hence, *I backbite,* or *harm seriously.*

G1144 **δάκρυον** (δάκρυ), -ου, τό   *a tear.*

δάκρυον   noun, acc. sg. neut. {2.B} . . . . . δάκρυον *G1144*

δάκρυσι   noun, dat. pl. neut. {2.B} . . . . id.

δάκρυσιν   noun, dat. pl. neut. {2.B} . . . . id.

G1145 **δακρύω**   *I shed tears, weep.*

δακρύων   noun, gen. pl. neut. {2.B} . . . . δάκρυον *G1144*

δακτύλιον   noun, acc. sg. masc. {2.B} . . δακτύλιος *G1146*

G1146 **δακτύλιος**, -ου, ὁ   *a finger ring.*

δάκτυλον   noun, acc. sg. masc. {2.B} . . . δάκτυλος *G1147*

G1147 **δάκτυλος**, -ου, ὁ   *a finger;* the picturesque δακτύλῳ of Luke 11:20 is represented by πνεύματι in Matt 12:28.

δακτύλου   noun, gen. sg. masc. {2.B} . . . δάκτυλος *G1147*

δακτύλους   noun, acc. pl. masc. {2.B} . . . . id.

δακτύλῳ   noun, dat. sg. masc. {2.B} . . . . id.

δακτύλων   noun, gen. pl. masc. {2.B} . . . . id.

G1148 **Δαλμανουθά**, ἡ   *Dalmanutha;* nothing is known of name or place, and text is probably corrupt.

Δαλμανουθά   noun prop. . . . . Δαλμανουθά *G1148*

G1149 **Δαλματία**, -ας, ἡ   *Dalmatia,* a province of the Roman Empire, east of the Adriatic, a later name for part of what was earlier called *Illyricum* (Rom 15:19).

Δαλματίαν   noun prop., acc. sg. fem. {2.A; 2.D} . . . . Δαλματία *G1149*

δαμάζεται   verb, pres. pass. indic. 3 pers. sg. {5.A.1.d} . . . . δαμάζω *G1150*

G1150 **δαμάζω**   *I tame, subdue,* involving obedience and restraint.

δαμάλεως   noun, gen. sg. fem. {2.C} . . . . δάμαλις *G1151*

G1151 **δάμαλις**, -εως, ἡ   *a heifer.*

G1152 **Δάμαρις**, -ιδος, ἡ   *Damaris,* an Athenian woman.

Δάμαρις   noun prop., nom. sg. fem. {2.C; 2.D} . . . . Δάμαρις *G1152*

δαμάσαι   vbl., aor. act. inf. {6.B.1} . . . . . . δαμάζω *G1150*

G1153 **Δαμασκηνός**, -ή, -όν   *a Damascene, an inhabitant of Damascus.*

Δαμασκηνῶν   adj. prop., gen. pl. masc. {3.A} . . . . Δαμασκηνός *G1153*

Δαμασκόν   noun prop., acc. sg. fem. {2.B; 2.D} . . . . Δαμασκός *G1154*

G1154 **Δαμασκός**, -οῦ, ἡ   *Damascus,* an ancient city of Syria.

Δαμασκῷ   noun prop., dat. sg. fem. {2.B; 2.D} . . . . Δαμασκός *G1154*

δανείζετε   verb, pres. act. impv. 2 pers. pl. {5.D.1} . . . . δανείζω *G1155*

δανείζητε   verb, pres. act. subjunc. 2 pers. pl. {5.B.1} . . . . id.

δανείζουσιν   verb, pres. act. indic. 3 pers. pl. {5.A.1.a} . . . . id.

G1155 **δανείζω** (δανίζω)   (1) *I lend;* (2) mid. δαν(ε) ίζομαι, *I borrow.*

G1156 **δάνειον** (δάνιον), -ου, τό   *a loan.*

δάνειον   noun, acc. sg. neut. {2.B} . . . . . . δάνειον *G1156*

δανείσασθαι   vbl., aor. mid. inf. {6.B.1} . . δανείζω *G1155*

δανειστῇ   noun, dat. sg. masc. {2.A} . . . δανιστής *G1157‡*

δανίζετε   verb, pres. act. impv. 2 pers. pl. {5.D.1} . . . . δανείζω *G1155*

δανίζουσιν   verb, pres. act. indic. 3 pers. pl. {5.A.1.a} . . . . id.

G1158 **Δανιήλ**, ὁ   *Daniel,* loosely called a "prophet" (Heb.).

Δανιήλ   noun prop. . . . . Δανιήλ *G1158*

δάνιον   noun, acc. sg. neut. {2.B} . . . . δάνειον *G1156*

δανίσασθαι   vbl., aor. mid. inf. {6.B.1} . . δανείζω *G1155*

δανίσητε   verb, aor. act. subjunc. 2 pers. pl. {5.B.1} . . . . id.

δανιστῇ   noun, dat. sg. masc. {2.A} . . . . δανιστής *G1157‡*

G1157‡ **δανιστής** (δανειστής), -οῦ, ὁ   *a lender, creditor.*

G1159 **δαπανάω**   *I spend.*

G1160 **δαπάνη**, -ης, ἡ   *cost, expense.*

δαπάνην   noun, acc. sg. fem. {2.A} . . . . . . δαπάνη *G1160*

δαπανήσαντος   vbl., aor. act. ptc. gen. sg. masc. {6.A.2} . . . . δαπανάω *G1159*

δαπανήσασα   vbl., aor. act. ptc. nom. sg. fem. {6.A.2} . . . . id.

δαπανήσητε   verb, aor. act. subjunc. 2 pers. pl. {5.B.1} . . . . id.

δαπάνησον   verb, aor. act. impv. 2 pers. sg. {5.D.1} . . . . id.

δαπανήσω   verb, fut. act. indic. 1 pers. sg. {5.A.1} . . . . id.

δαρήσεσθε   verb, ²fut. pass. indic. 2 pers. pl. {5.A.1.d} . . . . δέρω *G1194*

δαρήσεται   verb, ²fut. pass. indic. 3 pers. sg. {5.A.1.d} . . . . id.

Δαυείδ   noun prop. Δαυίδ *G1138‡*

G1138‡ **Δαυίδ** (Δαυείδ), ὁ   *David,* King of Israel, to whose name the OT collection of Psalms was attached (Heb.).

Δαυίδ   noun prop. Δαυίδ *G1138‡*

G1161 **δέ**   a weak adversative conjunction, generally placed second in its clause, (1) *but, on the other hand;* (2) *and.* See μέν.

δέ   conj.............................δέ G1161

δεδάμασται   verb, perf. pass. indic. 3 pers. sg.
{5.A.1.f}..........................δαμάζω G1150

δεδεκάτωκε   verb, perf. act. indic. 3 pers. sg.
{5.A.1}..........................δεκατόω G1183

δεδεκάτωκεν   verb, perf. act. indic. 3 pers. sg.
{5.A.1}.................................. id.

δεδεκάτωται   verb, perf. pass. indic. 3 pers. sg.
{5.A.1}.................................. id.

δέδεκται   verb, perf. mid./pass. indic. 3 pers. sg.
{5.A.1.f}..........................δέχομαι G1209

δεδεκώς   vbl., perf. act. ptc. nom. sg. masc.
{6.A.2}............................. δέω G1210

δέδεμαι   verb, perf. pass. indic. 1 pers. sg. {5.A.1}id.

δεδεμένα   vbl., perf. pass. ptc. nom. pl. neut.
{6.A.2}.................................. id.

δεδεμένην   vbl., perf. pass. ptc. acc. sg. fem.
{6.A.2}.................................. id.

δεδεμένον   vbl., perf. pass. ptc. acc. sg. masc.
{6.A.2}.................................. id.

δεδεμένον   vbl., perf. pass. ptc. acc. sg. neut.
{6.A.2}.................................. id.

δεδεμένον   vbl., perf. pass. ptc. nom. sg. neut.
{6.A.2}.................................. id.

δεδεμένος   vbl., perf. pass. ptc. nom. sg. masc.
{6.A.2}.................................. id.

δεδεμένους   vbl., perf. pass. ptc. acc. pl. masc.
{6.A.2}.................................. id.

δέδεσαι   verb, perf. pass. indic. 2 pers. sg.
{5.A.1}.................................. id.

δεδέσθαι   vbl., perf. pass. inf. {6.B.1} . . . . id.

δέδεται   verb, perf. pass. indic. 3 pers. sg. {5.A.1}id.

δεδικαίωμαι   verb, perf. pass. indic. 1 pers. sg.
{5.A.1}..........................δικαιόω G1344

δεδικαιωμένος   vbl., perf. pass. ptc. nom. sg.
masc. {6.A.2}.............................. id.

δεδικαίωται   verb, perf. pass. indic. 3 pers. sg.
{5.A.1}.................................. id.

δεδιωγμένοι   vbl., perf. pass. ptc. nom. pl. masc.
{6.A.1.b}..........................διώκω G1377

δεδοκιμάσμεθα   verb, perf. pass. indic. 1 pers. pl.
{5.A.1.f}..........................δοκιμάζω G1381

δεδομένην   vbl., perf. pass. ptc. acc. sg. fem.
{6.A.3}..........................δίδωμι G1325

δεδομένον   vbl., perf. pass. ptc. nom. sg. neut.
{6.A.3}.................................. id.

δεδόξασμαι   verb, perf. pass. indic. 1 pers. sg.
{5.A.1.f}..........................δοξάζω G1392

δεδοξασμένη   vbl., perf. pass. ptc. dat. sg. fem.
{6.A.1.b}.................................. id.

δεδοξασμένον   vbl., perf. pass. ptc. nom. sg.
neut. {6.A.1.b}.............................. id.

δεδόξασται   verb, perf. pass. indic. 3 pers. sg.
{5.A.1.f}.................................. id.

δέδοται   verb, perf. pass. indic. 3 pers. sg.
{5.A.1}..........................δίδωμι G1325

δεδουλεύκαμεν   verb, perf. act. indic. 1 pers. pl.
{5.A.1.c}..........................δουλεύω G1398

δεδουλωμένας   vbl., perf. pass. ptc. acc. pl. fem.
{6.A.2}..........................δουλόω G1402

δεδουλωμένοι   vbl., perf. pass. ptc. nom. pl.
masc. {6.A.2}.............................. id.

δεδούλωται   verb, perf. pass. indic. 3 pers. sg.
{5.A.1}.................................. id.

δέδωκα   verb, perf. act. indic. 1 pers. sg.
{5.A.1}..........................δίδωμι G1325

δέδωκας   verb, perf. act. indic. 2 pers. sg. {5.A.1} id.

δέδωκε   verb, perf. act. indic. 3 pers. sg. {5.A.1} . id.

δεδώκει   verb, plu. act. indic. 3 pers. sg. {5.A.1} . id.

δεδώκεισαν   verb, plu. act. indic. 3 pers. pl.
{5.A.1}.................................. id.

δέδωκεν   verb, perf. act. indic. 3 pers. sg. {5.A.1} id.

δεδωκότι   vbl., perf. act. ptc. dat. sg. masc.
{6.A.3}.................................. id.

δεδωρημένης   vbl., perf. pass. ptc. gen. sg. fem.
{6.A.2}..........................δωρέομαι G1433

δεδώρηται   verb, perf. pass. indic. 3 pers. sg.
{5.A.1}.................................. id.

δέη   verb, pres. act. subjunc. 3 pers. sg. {5.B.1} . . δεῖ G1163

δεηθέντων   vbl., aor. pass. ptc. gen. pl. masc.
{6.A.1.a}..........................δέομαι G1189

δεήθητε   verb, aor. pass. impv. 2 pers. pl. {5.D.1} id.

δεήθητι   verb, aor. pass. impv. 2 pers. sg. {5.D.1} id.

δεήσει   noun, dat. sg. fem. {2.C}..........δέησις G1162

δεήσεις   noun, acc. pl. fem. {2.C}.............. id.

δεήσεσι   noun, dat. pl. fem. {2.C}.............. id.

δεήσεσιν   noun, dat. pl. fem. {2.C}.............. id.

δεήσεως   noun, gen. sg. fem. {2.C}.............. id.

δέησιν   noun, acc. sg. fem. {2.C} .... id.

G1162   **δέησις**, -εως, ἡ   *a requesting, a begging, request.*

δέησις   noun, nom. sg. fem. {2.C} ....δέησις G1162

δεθῆναι   vbl., aor. pass. inf. {6.B.1}..........δέω G1210

G1163   **δεῖ**   (1) *it is necessary, inevitable;* (2) *less
frequently, it is a duty,* τὰ μὴ δέοντα, *what
is improper, wrong;* δέον (ἐστίν) = δεῖ, *Acts
19:36; 1 Pet 1:6.*

δεῖ   verb, pres. act. indic. 3 pers. sg. {5.A.2}..... δεῖ G1163

G1164   **δεῖγμα**, -ατος, τό   *an example, type.*

δεῖγμα   noun, acc. sg. neut. {2.C} ....δεῖγμα G1164

G1165   **δειγματίζω**   *I hold up as an example.*

δειγματίσαι   vbl., aor. act. inf. {6.B.1} . δειγματίζω G1165

δεικνύειν   vbl., pres. act. inf. {6.B.1}..... δείκνυμι G1166

δεικνύεις   verb, pres. act. indic. 2 pers. sg.
{5.A.1.a} .... id.

G1166   **δείκνυμι** (δεικνύω)   *I point out, show.*

δείκνυμι   verb, pres. act. indic. 1 pers. sg.
{5.A.1.a}..........................δείκνυμι G1166

δεικνύοντος   vbl., pres. act. ptc. gen. sg. masc.
{6.A.1}.................................. id.

δείκνυσιν   verb, pres. act. indic. 3 pers. sg.
{5.A.1.a} .... id.

G1167   **δειλία**, -ας, ἡ   *cowardice.*

δειλίας   noun, gen. sg. fem. {2.A}........ δειλία G1167

δειλιάτω   verb, pres. act. impv. 3 pers. sg.
{5.D.2}..........................δειλιάω G1168

G1168   **δειλιάω**   *I shrink, am fearful.*

δειλοί   adj., nom. pl. masc. {3.A} .... δειλός G1169

δειλοῖς   adj., dat. pl. masc. {3.A}.............. id.

G1169   **δειλός**, -ή, -όν   *cowardly, timid.*

δεῖν   vbl., pres. act. inf. {6.B.1} .... δεῖ G1163

G1170 **δεῖνα**, ὁ, ἡ or τό   ὁ δεῖνα, *so and so, a certain one,* where the name of the person is known but not used.

δεῖνα   adj., acc. sg. masc. {3.A} . . . . .δεῖνα G1170

G1171 **δεινῶς**   adv., *terribly.*

δεινῶς   adv. {3.F} . . . . .δεινῶς G1171

δεῖξαι   vbl., aor. act. inf. {6.B.1} . . . . δείκνυμι G1166

δείξατε   verb, aor. act. impv. 2 pers. pl. {5.D.1} . . id.

δειξάτω   verb, aor. act. impv. 3 pers. sg. {5.D.1} . id.

δείξει   verb, fut. act. indic. 3 pers. sg. {5.A.1.a} . . id.

δείξον   verb, aor. act. impv. 2 pers. sg. {5.D.1} . . . id.

δείξω   verb, fut. act. indic. 1 pers. sg. {5.A.1.a} . . id.

δείξω   verb, fut. act. subjunc. 1 pers. sg. {5.A.1.a} id.

G1172 **δειπνέω**   *I dine.*

δειπνῆσαι   vbl., aor. act. inf. {6.B.1} . . . . .δειπνέω G1172

δειπνήσω   verb, aor. act. subjunc. 1 pers. sg. {5.B.1} . . . . id.

δειπνήσω   verb, fut. act. indic. 1 pers. sg. {5.A.1} id.

δείπνοις   noun, dat. pl. neut. {2.B} . . . . . .δεῖπνον G1173

G1173 **δεῖπνον**, -ου, τό   *a dinner, an afternoon* or *evening meal.*

δεῖπνον   noun, acc. sg. neut. {2.B} . . . . .δεῖπνον G1173

δείπνου   noun, gen. sg. neut. {2.B} . . . . id.

δείπνῳ   noun, dat. sg. neut. {2.B} . . . . id.

δείραντες   vbl., aor. act. ptc. nom. pl. masc. {6.A.1.a} . . . . δέρω G1194

δεισιδαιμονεστέρους   adj. comp., acc. pl. masc. {3.E; 3.G}. . . . . δεισιδαίμων G1174‡

G1175 **δεισιδαιμονία**, -ας, ἡ   *superstition, religion.*

δεισιδαιμονίας   noun, gen. sg. fem. {2.A} . . . . δεισιδαιμονία G1175

G1174‡ **δεισιδαίμων**, -ον gen. ονος   *respectful of what is divine, religious* perhaps, rather than *superstitious* (the usual meaning). Comp. δεισιδαιμονέστερος used as superl., *very devout* (Acts 17:22).

δειχθέντα   vbl., aor. pass. ptc. acc. sg. masc. {6.A.1.a} . . . . δείκνυμι G1166

G1176 **δέκα**   *ten.*

δέκα   adj. num. . . . . δέκα G1176

G1177 **δεκαδύο**   *twelve.*

δεκαδύο   adj. num.. . . . . δεκαδύο G1177

G1176†‡ **δεκαοκτώ**   *eighteen.* Var. for δέκα, Luke 13:4.

δεκαοκτώ   adj. num. . . . . .δεκαοκτώ G1176†‡

G1178 **δεκαπέντε**   *fifteen.*

δεκαπέντε   adj. num. . . . . .δεκαπέντε G1178

Δεκαπόλει   noun prop., dat. sg. fem. {2.C; 2.D}. Δεκάπολις G1179

Δεκαπόλεως   noun prop., gen. sg. fem. {2.C; 2.D}. . . . . id.

G1179 **Δεκάπολις**, -εως, ἡ   *Decapolis,* meaning a group or district of ten cities (of the Greek type) in Palestine, mostly southeast of the Lake of Tiberias. The names and number vary in ancient authorities.

δεκάτας   adj., acc. pl. fem. {3.A} . . . . δέκατος G1182

G1180 **δεκατέσσαρες**   *fourteen.*

δεκατέσσαρες   adj., nom. pl. fem. {3.E} . . . . δεκατέσσαρες G1180

δεκατεσσάρων   adj., gen. pl. neut. {3.E} . . . . . . id.

G1181 **δεκάτη**   *a tithe* (fem. subs. of δέκατος).

δεκάτη   adj., nom. sg. fem. {3.A} . . . . δέκατος G1182

δεκάτην   adj., acc. sg. fem. {3.A}. . . . . id.

δέκατον   adj., nom. sg. neut. {3.A}. . . . . id.

G1182 **δέκατος**, -η, -ον   *a tenth;* fem. or neut. subs., *a tithe.*

δέκατος   adj., nom. sg. masc. {3.A}. . . . . δέκατος G1182

G1183 **δεκατόω**   *I tithe, I collect tithe from.*

δεκτήν   adj., acc. sg. fem. {3.A}. . . . . δεκτός G1184

δεκτόν   adj., acc. sg. neut. {3.A}. . . . . id.

G1184 **δεκτός**, -ή, -όν   *acceptable.*

δεκτός   adj., nom. sg. masc. {3.A} . . . . . . δεκτός G1184

δεκτῷ   adj., dat. sg. masc. {3.A}. . . . . id.

δελεαζόμενος   vbl., pres. pass. ptc. nom. sg. masc. {6.A.1}. . . . . δελεάζω G1185

δελεάζοντες   vbl., pres. act. ptc. nom. pl. masc. {6.A.1}. . . . . id.

δελεάζουσιν   verb, pres. act. indic. 3 pers. pl. {5.A.1.a}. . . . . id.

G1185 **δελεάζω**   *I allure* (by a bait).

δένδρα   noun, acc. pl. neut. {2.B} . . . . δένδρον G1186

δένδρα   noun, nom. pl. neut. {2.B} . . . . id.

G1186 **δένδρον**, -ου, τό   *a tree.*

δένδρον   noun, acc. sg. neut. {2.B} . . . . . δένδρον G1186

δένδρον   noun, nom. sg. neut. {2.B} . . . . id.

δένδρων   noun, gen. pl. neut. {2.B} . . . . id.

δέξαι   verb, aor. mid. impv. 2 pers. sg. {5.D.1}. . . . . .δέχομαι G1209

δεξαμένη   vbl., aor. mid. ptc. nom. sg. fem. {6.A.1.b}. . . . . id.

δεξάμενοι   vbl., aor. mid. ptc. nom. pl. masc. {6.A.1.b}. . . . . id.

δεξάμενος   vbl., aor. mid. ptc. nom. sg. masc. {6.A.1.b}. . . . . id.

δέξασθαι   vbl., aor. mid. inf. {6.B.1}. . . . . id.

δέξασθε   verb, aor. mid. impv. 2 pers. pl. {5.D.1} id.

δέξηται   verb, aor. mid. subjunc. 3 pers. sg. {5.B.1}. . . . . id.

δεξιά   adj., acc. pl. neut. {3.A}. . . . . δεξιός G1188

δεξιά   adj., nom. sg. fem. {3.A}. . . . . id.

δεξιᾷ   adj., dat. sg. fem. {3.A}. . . . . id.

δεξιάν   adj., acc. sg. fem. {3.A}. . . . . id.

δεξιάς   adj., acc. pl. fem. {3.A}. . . . . id.

δεξιᾶς   adj., acc. pl. fem. {3.A}. . . . . id.

δεξιᾶς   adj., gen. sg. fem. {3.A}. . . . . id.

δεξιοῖς   adj., dat. pl. neut. {3.A} . . . . id.

G1187 **δεξιολάβος**, -ου, ὁ   a word of uncertain meaning, indicating some class of *soldier.*

δεξιολάβους   noun, acc. pl. masc. {2.B} . . . . .δεξιολάβος G1187

δεξιόν   adj., acc. sg. masc. {3.A} . . . . δεξιός G1188

δεξιόν   adj., acc. sg. neut. {3.A}. . . . . id.

G1188 **δεξιός**, -ά, -όν   *on the right hand, right hand, right.*

δεξιός   adj., nom. sg. masc. {3.A} . . . . . . δεξιός G1188

δεξιῶν   adj., gen. pl. fem. {3.A}. . . . . id.

δεξιῶν   adj., gen. pl. masc. {3.A}. . . . . id.

δεξιῶν   adj., gen. pl. neut. {3.A} . . . . id.

δέξωνται   verb, aor. mid. subjunc. 3 pers. pl. {5.B.1} . . . . .δέχομαι G1209

G1189 **δέομαι**   *I request, beg.*
δέομαι   verb, pres. mid./pass. indic. 1 pers. sg.
    {5.A.2} . . . . δέομαι G1189
δεόμεθα   verb, pres. mid./pass. indic. 1 pers. pl.
    {5.A.2} . . . . id.
δεόμενοι   vbl., pres. mid./pass. ptc. nom. pl.
    masc. {6.A.2} . . . . id.
δεόμενος   vbl., pres. mid./pass. ptc. nom. sg.
    masc. {6.A.2} . . . . id.
δέον   vbl., pres. act. ptc. nom. sg. neut. {6.A.1} . . δεῖ G1163
δέοντα   vbl., pres. act. ptc. acc. pl. neut. {6.A.1} . id.
G127†‡ **δέος**, -ους, τό   *fear.* Var. for αἰδώς, Heb 12:28.
δέους   noun, gen. sg. neut. {2.C} . . . . δέος G127†‡
G1190 **Δερβαῖος**, -α, -ον   *Derbean, belonging to*
    Derbe.
Δερβαῖος   adj. prop., nom. sg. masc.
    {3.A} . . . . Δερβαῖος G1190
G1191 **Δέρβη**, -ης, ἡ   *Derbe,* a town in Lycaonia and
    in the southern part of the Roman province
    Galatia.
Δέρβην   noun prop., acc. sg. fem. {2.A; 2.D}. Δέρβη G1191
δέρει   verb, pres. act. indic. 3 pers. sg. {5.A.1.a}δέρω G1194
δέρεις   verb, pres. act. indic. 2 pers. sg. {5.A.1.a}. id.
G1192 **δέρμα**, -ατος, τό   *a hide, skin.*
δέρμασιν   noun, dat. pl. neut. {2.C} . . . . . . δέρμα G1192
δερματίνην   adj., acc. sg. fem. {3.A}. . δερμάτινος G1193
G1193 **δερμάτινος**, -η, -ον   *made of hide or leather.*
δέροντες   vbl., pres. act. ptc. nom. pl. masc.
    {6.A.1} . . . . δέρω G1194
G1194 **δέρω**   *I flay, flog, beat.*
δέρων   vbl., pres. act. ptc. nom. sg. masc.
    {6.A.1} . . . . δέρω G1194
δεσμά   noun, acc. pl. neut. {2.B} . . . . δεσμός G1199
δεσμά   noun, nom. pl. neut. {2.B} . . . . id.
δεσμας   noun, acc. pl. fem. {2.A} . . . . δέσμη G1197
δεσμεύουσι   verb, pres. act. indic. 3 pers. pl.
    {5.A.1.a} . . . . δεσμεύω G1195
δεσμεύουσιν   verb, pres. act. indic. 3 pers. pl.
    {5.A.1.a} . . . . id.
G1195 **δεσμεύω**   *I bind, tie up.*
δεσμεύων   vbl., pres. act. ptc. nom. sg. masc.
    {6.A.1} . . . . δεσμεύω G1195
G1196 **δεσμέω**   *I bind, tie up.*
G1197 **δέσμη**, -ης, ἡ   *a bond.*
δέσμιοι   noun, nom. pl. masc. {2.B} . . . . . δέσμιος G1198
δεσμίοις   noun, dat. pl. masc. {2.B} . . . . id.
δέσμιον   noun, acc. sg. masc. {2.B} . . . . id.
G1198 **δέσμιος**, -α, -ον   (1) *bound, captive, in chains;*
    (2) sometimes substantively *prisoner, captive.*
δέσμιος   noun, nom. sg. masc. {2.B} . . . δέσμιος G1198
δεσμίους   noun, acc. pl. masc. {2.B} . . . . id.
δεσμίων   noun, gen. pl. masc. {2.B} . . . . id.
δεσμοῖς   noun, dat. pl. masc. {2.B} . . . . . . δεσμός G1199
G1199 **δεσμός**, -οῦ, ὁ   *a bond, chain;* in Acts 23:29;
    26:31, the reference is to the form of "capital"
    punishment involving loss of freedom and
    work in chains in the quarries; pl. sometimes
    δεσμά.
δεσμός   noun, nom. sg. masc. {2.B} . . . . . δεσμός G1199
δεσμοῦ   noun, gen. sg. masc. {2.B} . . . . id.

δεσμούς   noun, acc. pl. masc. {2.B} . . . . id.
δεσμοφύλακι   noun, dat. sg. masc.
    {2.C} . . . . δεσμοφύλαξ G1200
G1200 **δεσμοφύλαξ**, -ακος, ὁ   *a prison governor,*
    jailer.
δεσμοφύλαξ   noun, nom. sg. masc.
    {2.C} . . . . δεσμοφύλαξ G1200
δεσμῶν   noun, gen. pl. masc. {2.B} . . . . . . δεσμός G1199
δεσμῶν   noun, gen. pl. neut. {2.B} . . . . id.
δεσμώτας   noun, acc. pl. masc. {2.A} . . . δεσμώτης G1202
G1201 **δεσμωτήριον**, -ου, τό   *a prison, jail.*
δεσμωτήριον   noun, acc. sg. neut.
    {2.B} . . . . δεσμωτήριον G1201
δεσμωτηρίου   noun, gen. sg. neut. {2.B} . . . . id.
δεσμωτηρίῳ   noun, dat. sg. neut. {2.B} . . . . . . id.
G1202 **δεσμώτης**, -ου, ὁ   *a prisoner, captive.*
δέσποτα   noun, voc. sg. masc. {2.A}. . . . δεσπότης G1203
δεσπόταις   noun, dat. pl. masc. {2.A}. . . . . . . id.
δεσπότας   noun, acc. pl. masc. {2.A} . . . . id.
δεσπότῃ   noun, dat. sg. masc. {2.A} . . . . id.
δεσπότην   noun, acc. sg. masc. {2.A} . . . . id.
G1203 **δεσπότης**, -ου, ὁ   *a master.* particularly a mas-
    ter and owner of slaves, *lord.*
δεσπότης   noun, nom. sg. masc. {2.A} . . δεσπότης G1203
G1204 **δεῦρο**   adv. (1) excl., *come;* (2) temp., *now, the*
    present, Rom 1:13 (orig. *hither*); cf. δεῦτε.
δεῦρο   adv. . . . . δεῦρο G1204
δεῦρο   verb, pres. act. impv. 2 pers. sg. {5.D.1} . . id.
G1205 **δεῦτε**   adv., excl., *come hither, come, hither* (pl.
    of δεῦρο).
δεῦτε   adv. . . . . δεῦτε G1205
δευτέρα   adj., nom. sg. fem. {3.A}. . . . . δεύτερος G1208
δευτέρᾳ   adj., dat. sg. fem. {3.A}. . . . . id.
δευτεραῖοι   adj., nom. pl. masc. {3.A} . δευτεραῖος G1206
G1206 **δευτεραῖος**, -α, -ον   *on the second day, on the*
    next day (adj. where Eng. requires adv.).
δευτέραν   adj., acc. sg. fem. {3.A}. . . . . δεύτερος G1208
δευτέρας   adj., gen. sg. fem. {3.A} . . . . id.
δεύτερον   adj., acc. sg. neut. {3.A} . . . . id.
δεύτερον   adj., nom. sg. neut. {3.A} . . . . id.
δεύτερον   adv. . . . . id.
G1207 **δευτερόπρωτος**, -ον   a word of doubtful mean-
    ing (a doubtful var. in Luke 6:1).
δευτεροπρώτῳ   adj., dat. sg. neut.
    {3.C} . . . . δευτερόπρωτος G1207
G1208 **δεύτερος**, -α, -ον   (1) *second;* (2) (τὸ) δεύτε-
    ρον is used adverbially, *in the second place, for*
    the second time.
δεύτερος   adj., nom. sg. masc. {3.A} . . . . δεύτερος G1208
δευτέρου   adj., gen. sg. masc. {3.A} . . . . id.
δευτέρου   adj., gen. sg. neut. {3.A} . . . . id.
δευτέρῳ   adj., dat. sg. masc. {3.A}. . . . . id.
δευτέρῳ   adj., dat. sg. neut. {3.A} . . . . id.
δέχεται   verb, pres. mid./pass. indic. 3 pers. sg.
    {5.A.1.d} . . . . δέχομαι G1209
δέχηται   verb, pres. mid./pass. subjunc. 3 pers.
    sg. {5.B.1} . . . . id.
G1209 **δέχομαι**   *I receive, welcome.*
δεχόμενος   vbl., pres. mid./pass. ptc. nom. sg.
    masc. {6.A.1} . . . . δέχομαι G1209

δέχονται   verb, pres. mid./pass. indic. 3 pers. pl. {5.A.1.d} . . . . id.

δέχωνται   verb, pres. mid./pass. subjunc. 3 pers. pl. {5.B.1} . . . . id.

G1210 **δέω**   *I bind.*

G1211 **δή**   (1) in a clause expressing demand, *so, then,* 1 Cor 6:20; (2) *indeed,* Luke 2:15, etc.; (3) *truly,* Matt 13:23.

δή   part. . . . . δή *G1211*

G5081†‡ **δηλαυγῶς**   *with perfect clearness* (from δῆλος and αὐγή). Var. for τηλαυγῶς, Mark 8:25.

δηλαυγῶς   adv. {3.F} . . . . δηλαυγῶς *G5081†‡*

δηλοῖ   verb, pres. act. indic. 3 pers. sg. {5.A.2} . . . . δηλόω *G1213*

δῆλον   adj., acc. sg. masc. {3.A} . . . . δῆλος *G1212*

δῆλον   adj., nom. sg. neut. {3.A} . . . . id.

G1212 **δῆλος, -η, -ον**   *clear, manifest.*

δηλοῦντος   vbl., pres. act. ptc. gen. sg. neut. {6.A.2} . . . . δηλόω *G1213*

G1213 **δηλόω**   *I show, make clear, reveal.*

δηλώσας   vbl., aor. act. ptc. nom. sg. masc. {6.A.2} . . . . δηλόω *G1213*

δηλώσει   verb, fut. act. indic. 3 pers. sg. {5.A.1} . id.

G1214 **Δημᾶς, -ᾶ, ὁ**   *Demas,* a helper of Paul in Rome (a pet form, probably of Δημήτριος).

Δημᾶς   noun prop., nom. sg. masc. {2.A; 2.D} . . . . Δημᾶς *G1214*

G1215 **δημηγορέω**   *I make a public speech, I address a multitude.*

G1216 **Δημήτριος, -ου, ὁ**   *Demetrius;* a silversmith of Ephesus.

Δημήτριος   noun prop., nom. sg. masc. {2.B; 2.D} . . . . Δημήτριος *G1216*

Δημητρίῳ   noun prop., dat. sg. masc. {2.B; 2.D}. id.

G1217 **δημιουργός, -οῦ, ὁ**   *a constructor, builder.*

δημιουργός   noun, nom. sg. masc. {2.B} . . . . δημιουργός *G1217*

δῆμον   noun, acc. sg. masc. {2.B} . . . . δῆμος *G1218*

G1218 **δῆμος, -ου, ὁ**   properly *the people,* esp. the citizens of a Greek city in popular assembly (ἐκκλησία), but in NT = *multitude, rabble.*

δῆμος   noun, nom. sg. masc. {2.B} . . . . δῆμος *G1218*

δημοσίᾳ   adj., dat. sg. fem. {3.A} . . . . . . δημόσιος *G1219*

G1219 **δημόσιος, -α, -ον**   (1) *public;* (2) dat. as adv., δημοσίᾳ, *publicly.*

δήμῳ   noun, dat. sg. masc. {2.B} . . . . δῆμος *G1218*

δηνάρια   noun, acc. pl. neut. {2.B} . . . . . δηνάριον *G1220*

G1220 **δηνάριον, -ου, ὁ**   *a denarius,* a small Roman silver coin, weighing in Nero's time 53 grams. Its value and purchasing power varied from time to time.

δηνάριον   noun, acc. sg. neut. {2.B} . . . . δηνάριον *G1220*

δηναρίου   noun, gen. sg. neut. {2.B} . . . . id.

δηναρίων   noun, gen. pl. neut. {2.B} . . . . id.

G1221 **δήποτε**   adv., *even at that time, at any time* (var. in John 5:4).

δήποτε   adv. . . . . δήποτε *G1221*

G1222 **δήπου**   adv., *of course, surely,* qualifying and yet strengthening the assertion.

δήπου   adv. {3.F} . . . . δήπου *G1222*

δῆσαι   vbl., aor. act. inf. {6.B.1} . . . . δέω *G1210*

δήσαντες   vbl., aor. act. ptc. nom. pl. masc. {6.A.2} . . . . id.

δήσας   vbl., aor. act. ptc. nom. sg. masc. {6.A.2}. id.

δήσατε   verb, aor. act. impv. 2 pers. pl. {5.D.1} . . id.

δήσῃ   verb, aor. act. subjunc. 3 pers. sg. {5.B.1}. . id.

δήσῃς   verb, aor. act. subjunc. 2 pers. sg. {5.B.1}. id.

δήσητε   verb, aor. act. subjunc. 2 pers. pl. {5.B.1} id.

δήσουσιν   verb, fut. act. indic. 3 pers. pl. {5.A.1} id.

δι᾽   prep. . . . . διά *G1223*

Δία   noun prop., acc. sg. masc. {2.C; 2.D} . . . Ζεύς *G2203*

G1223 **διά**   (1) with gen. *through; throughout* (διὰ παντός, *always*); *by the instrumentality of;* denoting mediate and not original authorship, e.g., Matt 1:22; John 1:3; 1 Cor 8:6; (2) with acc. *on account of, by reason of, for the sake of, because of; through,* Luke 17:11(?). διὰ τί; *why?*

διά   prep. . . . . διά *G1223*

G1224 **διαβαίνω**   *I cross.*

G1225 **διαβάλλω**   (1) *I slander;* (2) merely *I complain of* (without idea of malice), Luke 16:1.

διαβάς   vbl., ²aor. act. ptc. nom. sg. masc. {6.A.1.a} . . . . διαβαίνω *G1224*

G1226 **διαβεβαιόομαι**   *I assert emphatically.*

διαβεβαιοῦνται   verb, pres. mid./pass. indic. 3 pers. pl. {5.A.2} . . . . διαβεβαιόομαι *G1226*

διαβεβαιοῦσθαι   vbl., pres. mid./pass. inf. {6.B.2} . . . . id.

διαβῆναι   vbl., ²aor. act. inf. {6.B.1} . . . . διαβαίνω *G1224*

G1227 **διαβλέπω**   *I see thoroughly.*

διαβλέψεις   verb, fut. act. indic. 2 pers. sg. {5.A.1.a} . . . . διαβλέπω *G1227*

διάβολοι   adj., nom. pl. masc. {3.C} . . . . διάβολος *G1228*

διάβολον   adj., acc. sg. masc. {3.C} . . . . id.

G1228 **διάβολος, -η, -ον**   (1) *slanderous* (1 Tim 3:11; 2 Tim 3:3; Titus 2:3); (2) adj. used oftener as noun, almost always ὁ Διάβολος, *the Slanderer* (par excellence), *the Devil.*

διάβολος   adj., nom. sg. masc. {3.C} . . . . διάβολος *G1228*

Διάβολος   adj., nom. sg. masc. {3.C} . . . . διάβολος *G1228*

διαβόλου   adj., gen. sg. masc. {3.C} . . . . id.

διαβόλοις   adj., acc. pl. fem. {3.C} . . . . id.

διαβόλῳ   adj., dat. sg. masc. {3.C} . . . . id.

διαγγελῇ   verb, ²aor. pass. subjunc. 3 pers. sg. {5.B.1} . . . . διαγγέλλω *G1229*

διάγγελλε   verb, pres. act. impv. 2 pers. sg. {5.D.1} . . . . id.

G1229 **διαγγέλλω**   *I announce throughout* the world, *I spread the news of.*

διαγγέλλων   vbl., pres. act. ptc. nom. sg. masc. {6.A.1} . . . . διαγγέλλω *G1229*

διαγενομένου   vbl., ²aor. mid. ptc. gen. sg. masc. {6.A.1.b} . . . . διαγίνομαι *G1230*

διαγενομένου   vbl., ²aor. mid. ptc. gen. sg. neut. {6.A.1.b} . . . . id.

διαγενομένων   vbl., ²aor. mid. ptc. gen. pl. fem. {6.A.1.b} . . . . id.

G1230 **διαγίνομαι**   *I pass* (of time).

διαγινώσκειν   vbl., pres. act. inf. {6.B.1} . . . . διαγινώσκω *G1231*

G1231 **διαγινώσκω**   *I learn thoroughly, I determine* (Acts 24:22).

G1232 **διαγνωρίζω**   *I give an exact report.*
διάγνωσιν   noun, acc. sg. fem. {2.C} . . .διάγνωσις G1233

G1233 **διάγνωσις,** -εως, ἡ   *decision resulting from an investigation.*
διαγνώσομαι   verb, fut. mid. indic. 1 pers. sg.
{5.A.1.d} . . . . διαγινώσκω G1231

G1234 **διαγογγύζω**   *I murmur greatly, I continue murmuring.*
διάγοντες   vbl., pres. act. ptc. nom. pl. masc.
{6.A.1} . . . . διάγω G1236

G1235 **διαγρηγορέω**   *I awake out of sleep, I am thoroughly awake.*
διαγρηγορήσαντες   vbl., aor. act. ptc. nom. pl.
masc. {6.A.2} . . . . διαγρηγορέω G1235

G1236 **διάγω**   *I spend time, pass time, live* (either trans. or intrans.).
διάγωμεν   verb, pres. act. subjunc. 1 pers. pl.
{5.B.1} . . . . διάγω G1236
διαδεξάμενοι   vbl., aor. mid. ptc. nom. pl. masc.
{6.A.1.b} .διαδέχομαι G1237

G1237 **διαδέχομαι**   *I receive in my turn.*

G1238 **διάδημα,** -ατος, τό   *a chaplet, crown.*
διαδήματα   noun, acc. pl. neut. {2.C} . . . διάδημα G1238
διαδήματα   noun, nom. pl. neut. {2.C} . . . . id.

G1239 **διαδίδωμι**   *I offer here and there, distribute.*
διαδίδωσιν   verb, pres. act. indic. 3 pers. sg.
{5.A.3.a} . . . . .διαδίδωμι G1239
διαδιδώσουσιν   verb, pres. act. indic. 3 pers.
pl. {5.A.3.a} . . . . id.
διάδος   verb, ²aor. act. impv. 2 pers. sg. {5.D.3} . . id.
διάδοχον   noun, acc. sg. masc. {2.B} . . . . διάδοχος G1240

G1240 **διάδοχος,** -ου, ὁ   *a successor.*

G1241 **διαζώννυμι**   *I gird myself,* by pulling up the tunic and allowing a fold to fall over the belt (ζώνη).
διαθέμενος   vbl., ²aor. mid. ptc. nom. sg. masc.
{6.A.3} . . . . διατίθημι G1303
διαθεμένου   vbl., ²aor. mid. ptc. gen. sg. masc.
{6.A.3} . . . . id.
διαθῆκαι   noun, nom. pl. fem. {2.A} . . . . διαθήκη G1242

G1242 **διαθήκη,** -ης, ἡ   (1) *a covenant* between two parties (= συνθήκη); (2) *a will, testament* (the ordinary, everyday sense, found a countless number of times in papyri), Gal 3:15, 17; Heb 9:16.
διαθήκη   noun, nom. sg. fem. {2.A} . . . . διαθήκη G1242
διαθήκη   noun, dat. sg. fem. {2.A} . . . . id.
διαθήκην   noun, acc. sg. fem. {2.A} . . . . id.
διαθήκης   noun, gen. sg. fem. {2.A} . . . . id.
διαθηκῶν   noun, gen. pl. fem. {2.A} . . . . id.
διαθήσομαι   verb, fut. mid. indic. 1 pers. sg.
{5.A.1} . . . . διατίθημι G1303
διαιρέσεις   noun, nom. pl. fem. {2.C} . . διαίρεσις G1243

G1243 **διαίρεσις,** -εως, ἡ   *division, distribution.*

G1244 **διαιρέω**   *I divide, distribute.*
διαιροῦν   vbl., pres. act. ptc. nom. sg. neut.
{6.A.2} . . . . .διαιρέω G1244

G1245† **διακαθαίρω,** *I clean out.* Var. for διακαθαρίζω.

διακαθᾶραι   vbl., aor. act. inf. {6.B.1}διακαθαίρω G1245†
διακαθαριεῖ   verb, fut. act. indic. 3 pers. sg.
{5.A.2} . . . . id.

G1245 **διακαθαρίζω**   *I clean thoroughly.*

G1246 **διακατελέγχομαι**   *I effectively (utterly) refute (confute).*
διακατηλέγχετο   verb, impf. mid./pass. indic.
3 pers. sg. {5.A.1.e} . . . . διακατελέγχομαι G1246
διακόνει   verb, pres. act. impv. 2 pers. sg.
{5.D.2} . . . . διακονέω G1247
διακονεῖ   verb, pres. act. indic. 3 pers. sg. {5.A.2}id.
διακονεῖν   vbl., pres. act. inf. {6.B.2} . . . . id.
διακονείτωσαν   verb, pres. act. impv. 3 pers.
pl. {5.D.2} . . . . id.

G1247 **διακονέω**   (1) *I wait at table* (particularly of a slave who pours out wine to the guests); (2) *I serve* (generally).
διακονῇ   verb, pres. act. subjunc. 3 pers. sg.
{5.B.2} . . . . διακονέω G1247
διακονηθεῖσα   vbl., aor. pass. ptc. nom. sg.
fem. {6.A.1.a} . . . . id.
διακονηθῆναι   vbl., aor. pass. inf. {6.B.1} . . . . . id.
διακονῆσαι   vbl., aor. act. inf. {6.B.1} . . . . id.
διακονήσαντες   vbl., aor. act. ptc. nom. pl.
masc. {6.A.2} . . . . id.
διακονήσει   verb, fut. act. indic. 3 pers. sg.
{5.A.1} . . . . id.

G1248 **διακονία,** -ας, ἡ   (1) *waiting at table;* (2) in a wider sense, *service, ministration.*
διακονία   noun, nom. sg. fem. {2.A} . . . .διακονία G1248
διακονίᾳ   noun, dat. sg. fem. {2.A} . . . . id.
διακονίαν   noun, acc. sg. fem. {2.A} . . . . id.
διακονίας   noun, gen. sg. fem. {2.A} . . . . id.
διακονιῶν   noun, gen. pl. fem. {2.A} . . . . id.
διάκονοι   noun, nom. pl. masc. {2.B} . . .διάκονος G1249
διακόνοις   noun, dat. pl. masc. {2.B} . . . . id.
διάκονον   noun, acc. sg. fem. {2.B} . . . . id.
διάκονον   noun, acc. sg. masc. {2.B} . . . . id.

G1249 **διάκονος,** -ου, ὁ or ἡ   (1) *a waiter, servant;* (2) then of anyone who performs any service, *an administrator,* etc.
διάκονος   noun, nom. sg. masc. {2.B} . . διάκονος G1249
διακόνου   noun, gen. sg. fem. {2.B} . . . . id.
διακονουμένη   vbl., pres. pass. ptc. dat. sg. fem.
{6.A.2} . . . . διακονέω G1247
διακονοῦντες   vbl., pres. act. ptc. nom. pl.
masc. {6.A.2} . . . . id.
διακονούντων   vbl., pres. act. ptc. gen. pl.
masc. {6.A.2} . . . . id.
διακόνους   noun, acc. pl. masc. {2.B} . . .διάκονος G1249
διακονοῦσαι   vbl., pres. act. ptc. nom. pl. fem.
{6.A.2} . . . . διακονέω G1247
διακονῶν   vbl., pres. act. ptc. nom. sg. masc.
{6.A.2} . . . . id.
διακόσιαι   adj., nom. pl. fem. {3.A} . . . .διακόσιοι G1250
διακοσίας   adj., acc. pl. fem. {3.A} . . . . id.

G1250 **διακόσιοι,** -αι, -α   *two hundred.*
διακοσίους   adj., acc. pl. masc. {3.A} . . .διακόσιοι G1250
διακοσίων   adj., gen. pl. masc. {3.A} . . . . id.
διακοσίων   adj., gen. pl. neut. {3.A} . . . . id.

διακούσομαι   verb, fut. mid. indic. 1 pers. sg.
{5.A.1.d} . . . . .διακούω G1251
G1251 **διακούω**   *I hear throughout,* of a judicial
hearing.
διακριθῇ   verb, aor. pass. subjunc. 3 pers. sg.
{5.B.1} . . . . .διακρίνω G1252
διακριθῆτε   verb, aor. pass. subjunc. 2 pers. pl.
{5.B.1} . . . . id.
διακρῖναι   vbl., aor. act. inf. {6.B.1} . . . . id.
διακρίναντα   vbl., aor. act. ptc. acc. sg. masc.
{6.A.1.a} . . . . id.
διακρίνει   verb, pres. act. indic. 3 pers. sg.
{5.A.1.a} . . . . id.
διακρίνειν   vbl., pres. act. inf. {6.B.1} . . . . id.
διακρινέτωσαν   verb, pres. act. impv. 3 pers.
pl. {5.D.1} . . . . id.
διακρινόμενοι   vbl., pres. mid. ptc. nom. pl.
masc. {6.A.1} . . . . id.
διακρινόμενον   vbl., pres. mid. ptc. acc. sg.
masc. {6.A.1} . . . . id.
διακρινόμενος   vbl., pres. mid. ptc. nom. sg.
masc. {6.A.1} . . . . id.
διακρινομένους   vbl., pres. mid. ptc. acc. pl.
masc. {6.A.1} . . . . id.
G1252 **διακρίνω**   (1) *I separate, distinguish, discern*
one thing *from* another; (2) mid., *I doubt,*
hesitate, waver.
διακρίνων   vbl., pres. act. ptc. nom. sg. masc.
{6.A.1} . . . . .διακρίνω G1252
διακρίσεις   noun, acc. pl. fem. {2.C} . . . διάκρισις G1253
διακρίσεις   noun, nom. pl. fem. {2.C} . . . . id.
διάκρισιν   noun, acc. sg. fem. {2.C} . . . . id.
G1253 **διάκρισις**, -εως, ἡ   (1) *distinguishing;* (2) hence,
deciding, passing sentence on (Rom 14:1).
G1254 **διακωλύω**   *I obstinately prevent.*
G1255 **διαλαλέω**   *I interchange talk,* of conversation
passing from mouth to mouth.
διαλέγεται   verb, pres. mid./pass. indic. 3 pers. sg.
{5.A.1.d} .διαλέγομαι G1256
G1256 **διαλέγομαι**   (1) *I converse,* Mark 9:34; (2)
elsewhere, *I address, preach, lecture.*
διαλεγόμενον   vbl., pres. mid./pass. ptc. acc. sg.
masc. {6.A.1} . . . . .διαλέγομαι G1256
διαλεγόμενος   vbl., pres. mid./pass. ptc. nom.
sg. masc. {6.A.1} . . . . id.
διαλεγομένου   vbl., pres. mid./pass. ptc. gen.
sg. masc. {6.A.1} . . . . id.
G1257 **διαλείπω**   *I cease, give over, give up.*
G1258 **διάλεκτος**, -ου, ἡ   *language, speech.*
διαλέκτῳ   noun, dat. sg. fem. {2.B} . . . . . διάλεκτος G1258
διαλλάγηθι   verb, ²aor. pass. impv. 2 pers. sg.
{5.D.1} . . . . .διαλλάσσομαι G1259
G1259 **διαλλάσσομαι**   *I become reconciled to, I recon-*
cile myself with.
διαλογίζεσθαι   vbl., pres. mid./pass. inf.
{6.B.1} . . . . .διαλογίζομαι G1260
διαλογίζεσθε   verb, pres. mid./pass. indic.
2 pers. pl. {5.A.1.d} . . . . id.
G1260 **διαλογίζομαι**   *I reason (with), debate (with),*
consider.

διαλογιζόμενοι   vbl., pres. mid./pass. ptc. nom. pl.
masc. {6.A.1} . . . . .διαλογίζομαι G1260
διαλογιζομένων   vbl., pres. mid./pass. ptc. gen.
pl. masc. {6.A.1} . . . . id.
διαλογίζονται   verb, pres. mid./pass. indic.
3 pers. pl. {5.A.1.d} . . . . id.
διαλογισμοί   noun, nom. pl. masc.
{2.B} . . . . .διαλογισμός G1261
διαλογισμοῖς   noun, dat. pl. masc. {2.B} . . . . . . id.
διαλογισμόν   noun, acc. sg. masc. {2.B} . . . . id.
G1261 **διαλογισμός**, -οῦ, ὁ   *a calculation, reasoning,*
thought, movement of thought, deliberation,
plotting.
διαλογισμός   noun, nom. sg. masc.
{2.B} . . . . .διαλογισμός G1261
διαλογισμοῦ   noun, gen. sg. masc. {2.B} . . . . . . id.
διαλογισμούς   noun, acc. pl. masc. {2.B} . . . . . . id.
διαλογισμῶν   noun, gen. pl. masc. {2.B} . . . . . . id.
G1262 **διαλύω**   *I break up, disperse.*
διαμαρτυράμενοι   vbl., aor. mid. ptc. nom. pl.
masc. {6.A.1.b} . . . . .διαμαρτύρομαι G1263
διαμαρτύρασθαι   vbl., aor. mid. inf. {6.B.1} . . . id.
διαμαρτύρεται   verb, pres. mid./pass. indic.
3 pers. sg. {5.A.1.d} . . . . id.
διαμαρτύρηται   verb, pres. mid./pass. sub-
junc. 3 pers. sg. {5.B.1} . . . . id.
G1263 **διαμαρτύρομαι**   *I give solemn evidence, I*
testify (declare) solemnly.
διαμαρτύρομαι   verb, pres. mid./pass. indic.
1 pers. sg. {5.A.1.d} . . . . .διαμαρτύρομαι G1263
διαμαρτυρόμενος   vbl., pres. mid./pass. ptc.
nom. sg. masc. {6.A.1} . . . . id.
G1264 **διαμάχομαι**   *I strive greatly.*
διαμείνῃ   verb, aor. act. subjunc. 3 pers. sg.
{5.B.1} . . . . .διαμένω G1265
διαμεμενηκότες   vbl., perf. act. ptc. nom. pl.
masc. {6.A.1.a} . . . . id.
διαμεμερισμένοι   vbl., perf. pass. ptc. nom. pl.
masc. {6.A.1.b} . . . . .διαμερίζω G1266
διαμένει   verb, pres. act. indic. 3 pers. sg.
{5.A.1.a} . . . . .διαμένω G1265
διαμένεις   verb, pres. act. indic. 2 pers. sg.
{5.A.1.a} . . . . id.
G1265 **διαμένω**   *I remain throughout.*
διαμεριζόμεναι   vbl., pres. mid./pass. ptc. nom. pl.
fem. {6.A.1} . . . . .διαμερίζω G1266
διαμεριζόμενοι   vbl., pres. mid. ptc. nom. pl.
masc. {6.A.1} . . . . id.
διαμερίζονται   verb, pres. mid. indic. 3 pers.
pl. {5.A.1.d} . . . . id.
G1266 **διαμερίζω**   (1) *I divide up into parts, break up;*
(2) *I distribute.*
διαμερίσατε   verb, aor. act. impv. 2 pers. pl.
{5.D.1} . . . . .διαμερίζω G1266
διαμερισθεῖσα   vbl., aor. pass. ptc. nom. sg.
fem. {6.A.1.a} . . . . id.
διαμερισθήσεται   verb, fut. pass. indic. 3 pers.
sg. {5.A.1.d} . . . . id.
διαμερισθήσονται   verb, fut. pass. indic.
3 pers. pl. {5.A.1.d} . . . . id.

διαμερισμόν   noun, acc. sg. masc.
  {2.B} . . . . .διαμερισμός G1267
G1267 **διαμερισμός**, -οῦ, ὁ   (1) *breaking up;* (2)
  discord, hostility.
διανεμηθῇ   verb, aor. pass. subjunc. 3 pers. sg.
  {5.B.1} . . . . διανέμω G1268
G1268 **διανέμω**   (1) *I divide into portions, distribute;*
  (2) *I spread abroad.*
G1269 **διανεύω**   *I nod continually.*
διανεύων   vbl., pres. act. ptc. nom. sg. masc.
  {6.A.1} . . . . διανεύω G1269
G1270 **διανόημα**, -ατος, τό   *a reasoning, thought,*
  cogitation.
διανοήματα   noun, acc. pl. neut. {2.C} . διανόημα G1270
G1271 **διάνοια**, -ας, ἡ   *understanding, intellect, mind*
  (*process of reasoning* in Plato).
διανοίᾳ   noun, dat. sg. fem. {2.A} . . . . . .διάνοια G1271
διάνοιαν   noun, acc. sg. fem. {2.A} . . . . id.
διανοίας   noun, gen. sg. fem. {2.A} . . . . id.
διανοῖγον   vbl., pres. act. ptc. nom. sg. neut.
  {6.A.1} . . . . .διανοίγω G1272
G1272 **διανοίγω**   *I open up.*
διανοίγων   vbl., pres. act. ptc. nom. sg. masc.
  {6.A.1} . . . . .διανοίγω G1272
διανοίχθητι   verb, aor. pass. impv. 2 pers. sg.
  {5.D.1} . . . . id.
διανοιῶν   noun, gen. pl. fem. {2.A} . . . . .διάνοια G1271
G1273 **διανυκτερεύω**   *I spend the whole night.*
διανυκτερεύων   vbl., pres. act. ptc. nom. sg. masc.
  {6.A.1} . . . . διανυκτερεύω G1273
διανύσαντες   vbl., aor. act. ptc. nom. pl. masc.
  {6.A.1.a} . . . . διανύω G1274
G1274 **διανύω**   *I finish, complete.*
G1275 **διαπαντός**   = διὰ παντός; see διά.
διαπαντός   adv. . . . . διαπαντός G1275
διαπαρατριβαί   noun, nom. pl. fem.
  {2.A} .διαπαρατριβή G3859†‡
G3859†‡ **διαπαρατριβή**, ῆς, ἡ   *perpetual wrangling.* Var.
  for παραδιατριβή, 1 Tim 6:5.
διαπεράσαντες   vbl., aor. act. ptc. nom. pl. masc.
  {6.A.2} . . . . .διαπεράω G1276
διαπεράσαντος   vbl., aor. act. ptc. gen. sg.
  masc. {6.A.2} . . . . id.
G1276 **διαπεράω**   *I cross over.*
διαπερῶν   vbl., pres. act. ptc. acc. sg. neut.
  {6.A.2} . . . . .διαπεράω G1276
διαπερῶσιν   verb, pres. act. subjunc. 3 pers. pl.
  {5.B.2} . . . . id.
διαπλεύσαντες   vbl., aor. act. ptc. nom. pl. masc.
  {6.A.2} . . . . διαπλέω G1277
G1277 **διαπλέω**   *I sail over (across).*
G1278 **διαπονέομαι**   *I am greatly troubled.*
διαπονηθείς   vbl., aor. pass. ptc. nom. sg. masc.
  {6.A.1.a} . . . . διαπονέομαι G1278
διαπονούμενοι   vbl., pres. mid./pass. ptc. nom.
  pl. masc. {6.A.2} . . . . id.
διαπορεῖσθαι   vbl., pres. pass. inf.
  {6.B.2} . . . . διαπορέω G1280
διαπορεύεσθαι   vbl., pres. mid./pass. inf.
  {6.B.1} . . . . διαπορεύομαι G1279

G1279 **διαπορεύομαι**   *I journey through (past).*
διαπορευόμενος   vbl., pres. mid./pass. ptc. nom.
  sg. masc. {6.A.1} . . . . διαπορεύομαι G1279
διαπορευομένου   vbl., pres. mid./pass. ptc.
  gen. sg. masc. {6.A.1} . . . . id.
G1280 **διαπορέω**   *I am in trouble, doubt, difficulty.*
G1281 **διαπραγματεύομαι**   *I gain by business*
  (*trading*).
G1282 **διαπρίω**   *I cut to the quick* (with indignation
  and envy), lit. *I saw through.*
διαρήξας   vbl., aor. act. ptc. nom. sg. masc.
  {6.A.3} .διαρρήγνυμι G1284
διαρήσσων   vbl., pres. act. ptc. nom. sg. masc.
  {6.A.3} . . . . id.
G1283 **διαρπάζω**   *I plunder, rob thoroughly.*
διαρπάσαι   vbl., aor. act. inf. {6.B.1} . . .διαρπάζω G1283
διαρπάσει   verb, fut. act. indic. 3 pers. sg.
  {5.A.1.a} . . . . id.
διαρπάσῃ   verb, aor. act. subjunc. 3 pers. sg.
  {5.B.1} . . . . id.
G1284 **διαρρήγνυμι** (διαρήγνυμι, διαρρήσσω,
  διαρήσσω)   *I tear asunder.*
διαρρήξαντες   vbl., aor. act. ptc. nom. pl. masc.
  {6.A.3} .διαρρήγνυμι G1284
διαρρήξας   vbl., aor. act. ptc. nom. sg. masc.
  {6.A.3} . . . . id.
διαρρήσσων   vbl., pres. act. ptc. nom. sg.
  masc. {6.A.3} . . . . id.
G1285 **διασαφέω**   *I make clear, explain.*
διασάφησον   verb, aor. act. impv. 2 pers. sg.
  {5.D.1} . . . . .διασαφέω G1285
διασείσητε   verb, aor. act. subjunc. 2 pers. pl.
  {5.B.1} . . . . διασείω G1286
G1286 **διασείω**   *I blackmail, extort from.*
G1287 **διασκορπίζω**   *I scatter.*
διασκορπίζων   vbl., pres. act. ptc. nom. sg. masc.
  {6.A.1} . . . . διασκορπίζω G1287
διασκορπισθήσεται   verb, fut. pass. indic.
  3 pers. sg. {5.A.1.d} . . . . id.
διασκορπισθήσονται   verb, fut. pass. indic.
  3 pers. pl. {5.A.1.d} . . . . id.
διασπαρέντες   vbl., ²aor. pass. ptc. nom. pl. masc.
  {6.A.1.a} .διασπείρω G1289
διασπασθῇ   verb, aor. pass. subjunc. 3 pers. sg.
  {5.B.1} . . . . .διασπάω G1288
G1288 **διασπάω**   *I tear apart, burst.*
G1289 **διασπείρω**   *I scatter (like seed).*
G1290 **διασπορά**, -ᾶς, ἡ   (1) lit. *scattering abroad of*
  seed by the sower; (2) hence, *dispersion,* used
  esp. of the Jews who had migrated and were
  scattered over the ancient world. In Jas 1:1
  and 1 Pet 1:1 the reference may be to the New
  Israel, the Christians.
διασπορᾷ   noun, dat. sg. fem. {2.A} . . . .διασπορά G1290
διασποράν   noun, acc. sg. fem. {2.A} . . . . id.
διασποράς   noun, gen. sg. fem. {2.A} . . . . id.
διαστάσης   vbl., ²aor. act. ptc. gen. sg. fem.
  {6.A.3} . . . . διΐστημι G1339
διαστελλόμενον   vbl., pres. pass. ptc. acc. sg. neut.
  {6.A.1} .διαστέλλω G1291

G1291 **διαστέλλω**   mid., *I give a commission (instructions), I order.*

G1292 **διάστημα**, -ατος, τό   *an interval.*
διάστημα   noun, nom. sg. neut. {2.C} . . διάστημα G1292
διαστήσαντες   vbl., aor. act. ptc. nom. pl. masc.
{6.A.3} . . . . διΐστημι G1339

G1293 **διαστολή**, -ῆς, ἡ   *distinction, separation.*
διαστολή   noun, nom. sg. fem. {2.A} . . . διαστολή G1293
διαστολήν   noun, acc. sg. fem. {2.A} . . . . id.
διαστρέφοντα   vbl., pres. act. ptc. acc. sg. masc.
{6.A.1} . . . . διαστρέφω G1294

G1294 **διαστρέφω**   *I pervert.*
διαστρέφων   vbl., pres. act. ptc. nom. sg. masc.
{6.A.1} . . . . διαστρέφω G1294
διαστρέψαι   vbl., aor. act. inf. {6.B.1} . . . . id.

G1295 **διασῴζω**   (1) *I save (rescue) through* (some danger); (2) διασώζω πρός (Acts 23:34), *I bring safely to,* so διεσώθησαν εἰς (1 Pet 3:20), *escaped into.*
διασωθέντα   vbl., aor. pass. ptc. acc. sg. masc.
{6.A.1.a} . . . . .διασῴζω G1295
διασωθέντες   vbl., aor. pass. ptc. nom. pl.
masc. {6.A.1.a} . . . . id.
διασωθῆναι   vbl., aor. pass. inf. {6.B.1} . . . . id.
διασῶσαι   vbl., aor. act. inf. {6.B.1} . . . . id.
διασώσῃ   verb, aor. act. subjunc. 3 pers. sg.
{5.B.1} . . . . id.
διασώσωσι   verb, aor. act. subjunc. 3 pers. pl.
{5.B.1} . . . . id.
διασώσωσιν   verb, aor. act. subjunc. 3 pers. pl.
{5.B.1} . . . . id.
διαταγάς   noun, acc. pl. fem. {2.A} . . . . . .διαταγή G1296
διαταγείς   vbl., ²aor. pass. ptc. nom. sg. masc.
{6.A.1.a} . . . . διατάσσω G1299

G1296 **διαταγή**, -ῆς, ἡ   *ordaining, ordinance, disposition.*
διαταγῇ   noun, dat. sg. fem. {2.A} . . . . . . διαταγή G1296

G1297 **διάταγμα**, -ατος, τό   *a commandment.*
διάταγμα   noun, acc. sg. neut. {2.C} . . . . διάταγμα G1297
διαταξάμενος   vbl., aor. mid. ptc. nom. sg. masc.
{6.A.1.b} .διατάσσω G1299
διατάξομαι   verb, fut. mid. indic. 1 pers. sg.
{5.A.1.d} . . . . id.

G1298 **διαταράσσω**   *I disturb greatly.*
διαταράσσομαι   verb, pres. mid. indic. 1 pers. sg.
{5.A.1.d} .διατάσσω G1299

G1299 **διατάσσω**   *I command.*
διατάσσων   vbl., pres. act. ptc. nom. sg. masc.
{6.A.1} . . . . .διατάσσω G1299
διαταχθέντα   vbl., aor. pass. ptc. acc. pl. neut.
{6.A.1.a} . . . . id.
διατελεῖτε   verb, pres. act. indic. 2 pers. pl.
{5.A.2} . . . . .διατελέω G1300

G1300 **διατελέω**   act. and mid., *I continue.*
διατεταγμένον   vbl., perf. pass. ptc. acc. sg. neut.
{6.A.1.b} .διατάσσω G1299
διατεταγμένος   vbl., perf. pass. ptc. nom. sg.
masc. {6.A.1.b} . . . . id.
διατεταχέναι   vbl., perf. act. inf. {6.B.1} . . . . . . id.

G1301 **διατηρέω**   *I keep safe, hold fast.*

διατηροῦντες   vbl., pres. act. ptc. nom. pl. masc.
{6.A.2} . . . . διατηρέω G1301

G1302 **διατί**   *why?* (= διὰ τί).
διατίθεμαι   verb, pres. mid. indic. 1 pers. sg.
{5.A.3.a} . . . . διατίθημι G1303

G1303 **διατίθημι**   mid., (1) *I appoint, make* (of a covenant); (2) *I make* (a will), Heb 9:16, 17, regular in papyri.
διατρίβοντες   vbl., pres. act. ptc. nom. pl. masc.
{6.A.1} . . . . .διατρίβω G1304

G1304 **διατρίβω**   *I tarry, continue, stay* in a place.
διατρίψας   vbl., aor. act. ptc. nom. sg. masc.
{6.A.1.a} . . . . .διατρίβω G1304
διατροφάς   noun, acc. pl. fem. {2.A} . . . διατροφή G1305

G1305 **διατροφή**, -ῆς, ἡ   *nourishment, food.*

G1306 **διαυγάζω**   *I dawn* (of the light coming *through* the shadows).
διαυγάσῃ   verb, aor. act. subjunc. 3 pers. sg.
{5.B.1} . . . . διαυγάζω G1306

G1307† **διαυγής**, -ες   *through which light passes, transparent.* Var. for διαφανής.
διαυγής   adj., nom. sg. masc. {3.E} . . . . . διαυγής G1307†

G1307 **διαφανής**   *transparent.*
διαφανής   adj., nom. sg. masc. {3.E} . . . διαφανής G1307
διαφέρει   verb, pres. act. indic. 3 pers. sg.
{5.A.1.a} . . . . διαφέρω G1308
διαφέρετε   verb, pres. act. indic. 2 pers. pl. {5.A.1.a} id.
διαφερομένων   vbl., pres. pass. ptc. gen. pl.
masc. {6.A.1} . . . . id.
διαφέροντα   vbl., pres. act. ptc. acc. pl. neut.
{6.A.1} . . . . id.

G1308 **διαφέρω**   (1) trans., *I carry through, hither and thither;* (2) intrans., *I am different, I differ,* sometimes with gen.; (3) hence with gen., *I surpass, I excel.*

G1309 **διαφεύγω**   *I flee through, I escape.*
διαφημίζειν   vbl., pres. act. inf. {6.B.1} διαφημίζω G1310

G1310 **διαφημίζω**   *I spread about* (by *word* of mouth).
διαφθεῖραι   vbl., aor. act. inf. {6.B.1} . .διαφθείρω G1311
διαφθείραντας   vbl., aor. act. ptc. acc. pl. masc.
{6.A.1} . . . . id.
διαφθείρει   verb, pres. act. indic. 3 pers. sg.
{5.A.1.a} . . . . id.
διαφθείρεται   verb, pres. pass. indic. 3 pers. sg.
{5.A.1.d} . . . . id.
διαφθείροντας   vbl., pres. act. ptc. acc. pl.
masc. {6.A.1} . . . . id.

G1311 **διαφθείρω**   (1) *I destroy, waste;* (2) hence met., *I corrupt.*

G1312 **διαφθορά**, -ᾶς, ἡ   (1) *destruction, dissolution;* (2) *corruption.*
διαφθοράν   noun, acc. sg. fem. {2.A} . . . διαφθορά G1312
διάφορα   adj., acc. pl. neut. {3.C} . . . . . διάφορος G1313
διαφόροις   adj., dat. pl. masc. {3.C} . . . . id.

G1313 **διάφορος**, -ον   (1) *differing, different;* (2) hence, *excellent.* Comp. διαφορώτερος, *more excellent.*
διαφορωτέρας   adj. comp., gen. sg. fem. {3.A; 3.G} . . . . διάφορος G1313
διαφορώτερον   adj. comp., acc. sg. neut. {3.A; 3.G} . . . . id.

διαφύγη   verb, ²aor. act. subjunc. 3 pers. sg.
  {5.B.1} . . . . διαφεύγω *G1309*
διαφύγοι   verb, ²aor. act. opt. 3 pers. sg. {5.C.1} . id.
διαφυλάξαι   vbl., aor. act. inf. {6.B.1}διαφυλάσσω *G1314*
G1314 **διαφυλάσσω**   *I guard securely, I preserve,* or *guard through* (a danger), *save.*
G1315 **διαχειρίζω**   mid., *I lay my hands upon,* and so, *I slay, kill.*
διαχειρίσασθαι   vbl., aor. mid. inf.
  {6.B.1} . . . . διαχειρίζω *G1315*
διαχλευάζοντες   vbl., pres. act. ptc. nom. pl. masc.
  {6.A.1} .διαχλευάζω *G5512†‡*
G5512†‡ **διαχλευάζω**   *I mock (scorn) greatly, with words and gesture.* Var. for χλευάζω, Acts 2:13.
διαχωρίζεσθαι   vbl., pres. mid./pass. inf.
  {6.B.1} . . . . διαχωρίζω *G1316*
G1316 **διαχωρίζω**   pass. *I am separated from, I depart from.*
διδακτικόν   adj., acc. sg. masc. {3.A} . . διδακτικός *G1317*
G1317 **διδακτικός**, -ή, -όν   *able to teach, apt to teach.*
διδακτοί   adj., nom. pl. masc. {3.A} . . . . . διδακτός *G1318*
διδακτοῖς   adj., dat. pl. masc. {3.A} . . . . id.
G1318 **διδακτός**, -ή, -όν   *taught.*
διδάξαι   vbl., aor. act. inf. {6.B.1} . . . . . . διδάσκω *G1321*
διδάξει   verb, fut. act. indic. 3 pers. sg. {5.A.1.a}. id.
διδάξῃ   verb, aor. act. subjunc. 3 pers. sg. {5.B.1} id.
διδάξον   verb, aor. act. impv. 2 pers. sg. {5.D.1} . id.
διδάξωσιν   verb, aor. act. subjunc. 3 pers. pl.
  {5.B.1} . . . . id.
διδάσκαλε   noun, voc. sg. masc. {2.B} διδάσκαλος *G1320*
G1319 **διδασκαλία**, -ας, ἡ   *teaching.*
διδασκαλία   noun, nom. sg. fem.
  {2.A} . . . . διδασκαλία *G1319*
διδασκαλίᾳ   noun, dat. sg. fem. {2.A} . . . . id.
διδασκαλίαις   noun, dat. pl. fem. {2.A} . . . . . id.
διδασκαλίαν   noun, acc. sg. fem. {2.A} . . . . . . id.
διδασκαλίας   noun, acc. pl. fem. {2.A} . . . . . . id.
διδασκαλίας   noun, gen. sg. fem. {2.A} . . . . . . id.
διδάσκαλοι   noun, nom. pl. masc.
  {2.B} . . . . διδάσκαλος *G1320*
διδάσκαλον   noun, acc. sg. masc. {2.B} . . . . . . id.
G1320 **διδάσκαλος**, -ου, ὁ   *teacher.*
διδάσκαλος   noun, nom. sg. masc.
  {2.B} . . . . διδάσκαλος *G1320*
διδασκάλους   noun, acc. pl. masc. {2.B} . . . . . . id.
διδασκάλων   noun, gen. pl. masc. {2.B} . . . . . . id.
δίδασκε   verb, pres. act. impv. 2 pers. sg.
  {5.D.1} . . . . διδάσκω *G1321*
διδάσκει   verb, pres. act. indic. 3 pers. sg.
  {5.A.1.a} . . . . id.
διδάσκειν   vbl., pres. act. inf. {6.B.1} . . . . id.
διδάσκεις   verb, pres. act. indic. 2 pers. sg.
  {5.A.1.a} . . . . id.
διδάσκῃ   verb, pres. act. subjunc. 3 pers. sg.
  {5.B.1} . . . . id.
διδάσκοντες   vbl., pres. act. ptc. nom. pl. masc.
  {6.A.1} . . . . id.
διδάσκοντι   vbl., pres. act. ptc. dat. sg. masc.
  {6.A.1} . . . . id.

διδάσκοντος   vbl., pres. act. ptc. gen. sg. masc.
  {6.A.1} . . . . id.
G1321 **διδάσκω**   *I teach.*
διδάσκω   verb, pres. act. indic. 1 pers. sg.
  {5.A.1.a} . . . . διδάσκω *G1321*
διδάσκων   vbl., pres. act. ptc. nom. sg. masc.
  {6.A.1} . . . . id.
διδαχαῖς   noun, dat. pl. fem. {2.A} . . . . . . διδαχή *G1322*
διδαχῇ   noun, dat. sg. fem. {2.A} . . . . id.
G1322 **διδαχή**, -ῆς, ἡ   *teaching.*
διδαχή   noun, nom. sg. fem. {2.A} . . . . . . διδαχή *G1322*
διδαχήν   noun, acc. sg. fem. {2.A} . . . . id.
διδαχῆς   noun, gen. sg. fem. {2.A} . . . . id.
διδόασιν   verb, pres. act. indic. 3 pers. pl.
  {5.A.3.a} . . . . δίδωμι *G1325*
διδόμενον   vbl., pres. pass. ptc. nom. sg. neut.
  {6.A.3} . . . . id.
διδόναι   vbl., pres. act. inf. {6.B.3} . . . . id.
διδόντα   vbl., pres. act. ptc. acc. sg. masc. {6.A.3}id.
διδόντα   vbl., pres. act. ptc. nom. pl. neut.
  {6.A.3} . . . . id.
διδόντες   vbl., pres. act. ptc. nom. pl. masc.
  {6.A.3} . . . . id.
διδόντι   vbl., pres. act. ptc. dat. sg. masc. {6.A.3} id.
διδόντος   vbl., pres. act. ptc. gen. sg. masc.
  {6.A.3} . . . . id.
δίδοται   verb, pres. pass. indic. 3 pers. sg.
  {5.A.3.a} . . . . id.
δίδοτε   verb, pres. act. impv. 2 pers. pl. {5.D.3} . id.
δίδου   verb, pres. act. impv. 2 pers. sg. {5.D.3}. . id.
διδούς   vbl., pres. act. ptc. nom. sg. masc. {6.A.3} id.
δίδραχμα   noun, acc. pl. neut. {2.B} . . . δίδραχμον *G1323*
G1323 **δίδραχμον**, -ου, τό   (1) *a double-drachma, two drachmae,* a Greek silver coin. In the time of Christ 1 drachma roughly = 1 denarius = ¼ shekel; (2) δίδραχμον, the yearly temple tax thus = ½ shekel.
G1324 **Δίδυμος**, -ου, ὁ   *the Twin.*
Δίδυμος   noun prop., nom. sg. masc. {2.B; 2.D} . . . . Δίδυμος *G1324*
διδῶ   verb, pres. act. subjunc. 1 pers. sg.
  {5.B.3} . . . . δίδωμι *G1325*
G1325 **δίδωμι**   (1) *I offer, give;* used elliptically in Rev 2:23; (2) Hebraistic (= τίθημι), *I put, place,* Rev 3:8.
δίδωμι   verb, pres. act. indic. 1 pers. sg.
  {5.A.3.a} . . . . δίδωμι *G1325*
δίδωσι   verb, pres. act. indic. 3 pers. sg. {5.A.3.a} id.
δίδωσιν   verb, pres. act. indic. 3 pers. sg.
  {5.A.3.a} . . . . id.
διέβησαν   verb, ²aor. act. indic. 3 pers. pl.
  {5.A.1.b} . . . . διαβαίνω *G1224*
διέβλεψεν   verb, aor. act. indic. 3 pers. sg.
  {5.A.1.b} . . . . διαβλέπω *G1227*
διεβλήθη   verb, aor. pass. indic. 3 pers. sg.
  {5.A.1.b} . . . . διαβάλλω *G1225*
διεγείρειν   vbl., pres. act. inf. {6.B.1} . . . . διεγείρω *G1326*
διεγείρετο   verb, impf. pass. indic. 3 pers. sg.
  {5.A.1.e} . . . . id.

διεγείρουσιν   verb, pres. act. indic. 3 pers. pl.
{5.A.1.a} . . . . id.

G1326 **διεγείρω**   (1) *I wake out of sleep;* (2) *I arouse,* in general.

διεγείρω   verb, pres. act. indic. 1 pers. sg.
{5.A.1.a} . . . . διεγείρω G1326

διεγερθείς   vbl., aor. pass. ptc. nom. sg. masc.
{6.A.1.a} . . . . id.

διεγνώρισαν   verb, aor. act. indic. 3 pers. pl.
{5.A.1.b} . . . . διαγνωρίζω G1232

διεγόγγυζον   verb, impf. act. indic. 3 pers. pl.
{5.A.1.b} . . . . .διαγογγύζω G1234

διεδίδετο   verb, impf. pass. indic. 3 pers. sg.
{5.A.3.a} . . . . .διαδίδωμι G1239

διεδίδοτο   verb, impf. pass. indic. 3 pers. sg.
{5.A.3.a} . . . . id.

διέδωκε   verb, aor. act. indic. 3 pers. sg. {5.A.3.b} id.

διέδωκεν   verb, aor. act. indic. 3 pers. sg.
{5.A.3.b} . . . . id.

διεζώσατο   verb, aor. mid. indic. 3 pers. sg.
{5.A.1} . . . . διαζώννυμι G1241

διέζωσεν   verb, aor. act. indic. 3 pers. sg.
{5.A.3.b} . . . . id.

διεζωσμένος   vbl., perf. mid./pass. ptc. nom. sg. masc. {6.A.3} . . . . id.

διέθετο   verb, ²aor. mid. indic. 3 pers. sg.
{5.A.3.b} . . . . διατίθημι G1303

διεῖλεν   verb, ²aor. act. indic. 3 pers. sg.
{5.A.1.b} .διαιρέω G1244

διεκρίθη   verb, aor. pass. indic. 3 pers. sg.
{5.A.1.b} .διακρίνω G1252

διεκρίθητε   verb, aor. pass. indic. 2 pers. pl.
{5.A.1.b} . . . . id.

διέκρινε   verb, aor. act. indic. 3 pers. sg.
{5.A.1.b} . . . . id.

διέκρινεν   verb, aor. act. indic. 3 pers. sg.
{5.A.1.b} . . . . id.

διεκρίνομεν   verb, impf. act. indic. 1 pers. pl.
{5.A.1.b} . . . . id.

διεκρίνοντο   verb, impf. mid. indic. 3 pers. pl.
{5.A.1.e} . . . . id.

διεκώλυεν   verb, impf. act. indic. 3 pers. sg.
{5.A.1.b} .διακωλύω G1254

διελαλεῖτο   verb, impf. pass. indic. 3 pers. sg.
{5.A.2} . . . . .διαλαλέω G1255

διελάλουν   verb, impf. act. indic. 3 pers. pl.
{5.A.2} . . . . id.

διελέγετο   verb, impf. mid./pass. indic. 3 pers. sg.
{5.A.1.e} . . . . .διαλέγομαι G1256

διελέξατο   verb, aor. mid. indic. 3 pers. sg.
{5.A.1.e} . . . . id.

διελεύσεται   verb, fut. mid. indic. 3 pers. sg.
{5.A.1.d} . . . . .διέρχομαι G1330

διελέχθη   verb, aor. pass. indic. 3 pers. sg.
{5.A.1.b} . . . . .διαλέγομαι G1256

διελέχθησαν   verb, aor. pass. indic. 3 pers. pl.
{5.A.1.b} . . . . id.

διεληλυθότα   vbl., ²perf. act. ptc. acc. sg. masc.
{6.A.1} . . . . .διέρχομαι G1330

διελθεῖν   vbl., ²aor. act. inf. {6.B.1} . . . . id.

διελθόντα   vbl., ²aor. act. ptc. acc. sg. masc.
{6.A.1.a} . . . . id.

διελθόντες   vbl., ²aor. act. ptc. nom. pl. masc.
{6.A.1.a} . . . . id.

διέλθω   verb, ²aor. act. subjunc. 1 pers. sg. {5.B.1}id.

διέλθωμεν   verb, ²aor. act. subjunc. 1 pers. pl.
{5.B.1} . . . . id.

διελθών   vbl., ²aor. act. ptc. nom. sg. masc.
{6.A.1.a} . . . . id.

διέλιπε   verb, ²aor. act. indic. 3 pers. sg.
{5.A.1.b} . . . . .διαλείπω G1257

διέλιπεν   verb, ²aor. act. indic. 3 pers. sg.
{5.A.1.b} . . . . id.

διελογίζεσθε   verb, impf. mid./pass. indic. 2 pers.
pl. {5.A.1.e} . . . . διαλογίζομαι G1260

διελογίζετο   verb, impf. mid./pass. indic.
3 pers. sg. {5.A.1.e} . . . . id.

διελογίζοντο   verb, impf. mid./pass. indic.
3 pers. pl. {5.A.1.e} . . . . id.

διελύθησαν   verb, aor. pass. indic. 3 pers. pl.
{5.A.1.b} . . . . διαλύω G1262

διεμαρτυράμεθα   verb, aor. mid. indic. 1 pers. pl.
{5.A.1.e} . . . . διαμαρτύρομαι G1263

διεμαρτύρατο   verb, aor. mid. indic. 3 pers. sg.
{5.A.1.e} . . . . id.

διεμαρτύρετο   verb, impf. mid./pass. indic.
3 pers. sg. {5.A.1.e} . . . . id.

διεμαρτύρω   verb, aor. mid. indic. 2 pers. sg.
{5.A.1.e} . . . . id.

διεμάχοντο   verb, impf. mid./pass. indic. 3 pers. pl.
{5.A.1.e} . . . . διαμάχομαι G1264

διέμενε   verb, impf. act. indic. 3 pers. sg.
{5.A.1.b} . . . . διαμένω G1265

διέμενεν   verb, impf. act. indic. 3 pers. sg.
{5.A.1.b} . . . . id.

διεμέριζον   verb, impf. act. indic. 3 pers. pl.
{5.A.1.b} . . . . .διαμερίζω G1266

διεμερίσαντο   verb, aor. mid. indic. 3 pers. pl.
{5.A.1.e} . . . . id.

διεμερίσθη   verb, aor. pass. indic. 3 pers. sg.
{5.A.1.b} . . . . id.

διενέγκη   verb, ²aor. act. subjunc. 3 pers. sg.
{5.B.1} . . . . .διαφέρω G1308

G1760†‡ **διενθυμέομαι**   *I weigh in my mind, ponder.*
Var. for ἐνθυμέομαι, Acts 10:19.

διενθυμουμένου   vbl., pres. mid./pass. ptc. gen. sg.
masc. {6.A.2} . . . . διενθυμέομαι G1760†‡

διεξελθοῦσα   vbl., ²aor. act. ptc. nom. sg. fem.
{6.A.1.a} . . . . .ἐξέρχομαι G1831

G1327 **διέξοδος**, -ου, ἡ   (1) *a going out in various directions, a parting;* (2) hence, *the issue* of a street, where it leads out of the city into the country.

διεξόδους   noun, acc. pl. fem. {2.B} . . . . . διέξοδος G1327

διεπέρασε   verb, aor. act. indic. 3 pers. sg.
{5.A.1} . . . . .διαπεράω G1276

διεπέρασεν   verb, aor. act. indic. 3 pers. sg.
{5.A.1} . . . . id.

διεπορεύετο   verb, impf. mid./pass. indic. 3 pers.
sg. {5.A.1.e} . . . . διαπορεύομαι G1279

διεπορεύοντο   verb, impf. mid./pass. indic.
     3 pers. pl. {5.A.1.e}. . . . . id.
διεπραγματεύσαντο   verb, aor. mid. indic. 3 pers.
     pl. {5.A.1.e}. . . . . διαπραγματεύομαι G1281
διεπραγματεύσατο   verb, aor. mid. indic.
     3 pers. sg. {5.A.1.e} . . . . id.
διεπρίοντο   verb, impf. pass. indic. 3 pers. pl.
     {5.A.1.e} . . . . διαπρίω G1282
διέρηξεν   verb, aor. act. indic. 3 pers. sg. {5.A.1.b;
     5.A.3.b}. . . . . .διαρρήγνυμι G1284
διερήσσετο   verb, impf. pass. indic. 3 pers. sg.
     {5.A.1.e; 5.A.3.a} . . . . id.
διερμηνεύει   verb, pres. act. indic. 3 pers. sg.
     {5.A.1.a} . . . . διερμηνεύω G1329
διερμηνευέτω   verb, pres. act. impv. 3 pers. sg.
     {5.D.1}. . . . . id.
διερμηνεύῃ   verb, pres. act. subjunc. 3 pers. sg.
     {5.B.1} . . . . id.
διερμηνευομένη   vbl., pres. pass. ptc. nom. sg.
     fem. {6.A.1} . . . . id.
διερμηνεύουσι   verb, pres. act. indic. 3 pers.
     pl. {5.A.1.a} . . . . id.
διερμηνεύουσιν   verb, pres. act. indic. 3 pers.
     pl. {5.A.1.a} . . . . id.
διερμήνευσεν   verb, aor. act. indic. 3 pers. sg.
     {5.A.1.b} . . . . id.
G1328 **διερμηνευτής**, -οῦ, ὁ   *an interpreter.*
διερμηνευτής   noun, nom. sg. masc.
     {2.A} .διερμηνευτής G1328
G1329 **διερμηνεύω**   *I translate, interpret, explain.*
διερρήγνυτο   verb, impf. pass. indic. 3 pers. sg.
     {5.A.1.e; 5.A.3.a} . . . . .διαρρήγνυμι G1284
διέρρηξε   verb, aor. act. indic. 3 pers. sg.
     {5.A.1.b; 5.A.3.b}. . . . . id.
διέρρηξεν   verb, aor. act. indic. 3 pers. sg.
     {5.A.1.b; 5.A.3.b}. . . . . id.
διερρήσσετο   verb, impf. pass. indic. 3 pers. sg.
     {5.A.1.e; 5.A.3.a} . . . . id.
διέρχεσθαι   vbl., pres. mid./pass. inf.
     {6.B.1} . . . . διέρχομαι G1330
διέρχεται   verb, pres. mid./pass. indic. 3 pers.
     sg. {5.A.1.d}. . . . . id.
G1330 **διέρχομαι**   (1) *I go (come, journey) all the way*
     through; (2) in Acts seems frequently to imply,
     I itinerate, evangelize as I go.
διέρχομαι   verb, pres. mid./pass. indic. 1 pers. sg.
     {5.A.1.d} . . . . διέρχομαι G1330
διερχόμενον   vbl., pres. mid./pass. ptc. acc. sg.
     masc. {6.A.1}. . . . . id.
διερχόμενος   vbl., pres. mid./pass. ptc. nom.
     sg. masc. {6.A.1} . . . . id.
διέρχωμαι   verb, pres. mid./pass. subjunc.
     1 pers. sg. {5.B.1} . . . . id.
G1331 **διερωτάω**   *I inquire for.*
διερωτήσαντες   vbl., aor. act. ptc. nom. pl. masc.
     {6.A.2}. . . . . διερωτάω G1331
διεσάφησαν   verb, aor. act. indic. 3 pers. pl.
     {5.A.1}. . . . . διασαφέω G1285
διεσκόρπισα   verb, aor. act. indic. 1 pers. sg.
     {5.A.1.b} . . . . διασκορπίζω G1287

διεσκόρπισας   verb, aor. act. indic. 2 pers. sg.
     {5.A.1.b} . . . . id.
διεσκόρπισε   verb, aor. act. indic. 3 pers. sg.
     {5.A.1.b} . . . . id.
διεσκόρπισεν   verb, aor. act. indic. 3 pers. sg.
     {5.A.1.b} . . . . id.
διεσκορπίσθησαν   verb, aor. pass. indic.
     3 pers. pl. {5.A.1.b} . . . . id.
διεσκορπισμένα   vbl., perf. pass. ptc. acc. pl.
     neut. {6.A.1.b}. . . . . id.
διεσπάρησαν   verb, ²aor. pass. indic. 3 pers. pl.
     {5.A.1.b} . . . . διασπείρω G1289
διεσπάσθαι   vbl., perf. pass. inf. {6.B.1}. .διασπάω G1288
διεσπᾶσθαι   vbl., perf. pass. inf. {6.B.1}. . . . . . . id.
διεστειλάμεθα   verb, aor. mid. indic. 1 pers. pl.
     {5.A.1.e} . . . . διαστέλλω G1291
διεστείλατο   verb, aor. mid. indic. 3 pers. sg.
     {5.A.1.e} . . . . id.
διεστέλλετο   verb, impf. mid. indic. 3 pers. sg.
     {5.A.1.e} . . . . id.
διέστη   verb, ²aor. act. indic. 3 pers. sg.
     {5.A.3.b} . . . . διΐστημι G1339
διεστραμμένα   vbl., perf. pass. ptc. acc. pl. neut.
     {6.A.1.b} . . . . διαστρέφω G1294
διεστραμμένη   vbl., perf. pass. ptc. nom. sg.
     fem. {6.A.1.b} . . . . id.
διεστραμμένης   vbl., perf. pass. ptc. gen. sg.
     fem. {6.A.1.b} . . . . id.
διεσώθησαν   verb, aor. pass. indic. 3 pers. pl.
     {5.A.1.b} . . . . διασῴζω G1295
διέταξα   verb, aor. act. indic. 1 pers. sg.
     {5.A.1.b} . . . . διατάσσω G1299
διεταξάμην   verb, aor. mid. indic. 1 pers. sg.
     {5.A.1.e} . . . . id.
διετάξατο   verb, aor. mid. indic. 3 pers. sg.
     {5.A.1.e} . . . . id.
διέταξε   verb, aor. act. indic. 3 pers. sg. {5.A.1.b} id.
διέταξεν   verb, aor. act. indic. 3 pers. sg.
     {5.A.1.b} . . . . id.
διεταράχθη   verb, aor. pass. indic. 3 pers. sg.
     {5.A.1.b} . . . . διαταράσσω G1298
διετήρει   verb, impf. act. indic. 3 pers. sg.
     {5.A.2}. . . . . διατηρέω G1301
G1332 **διετής**, -ές   *two years old.*
G1333 **διετία**, -ας, ἡ   *a period of two years, two years.*
     (According to ancient practice this means any
     period between one and two years.).
διετίαν   noun, acc. sg. fem. {2.A} . . . . διετία G1333
διετίας   noun, gen. sg. fem. {2.A} . . . . id.
διετοῦς   adj., gen. sg. masc. {3.E} . . . . διετής G1332
διέτριβε   verb, impf. act. indic. 3 pers. sg.
     {5.A.1.b} . . . . .διατρίβω G1304
διέτριβεν   verb, impf. act. indic. 3 pers. sg.
     {5.A.1.b} . . . . id.
διέτριβον   verb, impf. act. indic. 3 pers. pl.
     {5.A.1.b} . . . . id.
διετρίψαμεν   verb, aor. act. indic. 1 pers. pl.
     {5.A.1.b} . . . . id.
διέτριψαν   verb, aor. act. indic. 3 pers. pl.
     {5.A.1.b} . . . . id.

διεφέρετο   verb, impf. pass. indic. 3 pers. sg.
{5.A.1.e} . . . . διαφέρω *G1308*
διεφήμισαν   verb, aor. act. indic. 3 pers. pl.
{5.A.1.b} . . . . διαφημίζω *G1310*
διεφημίσθη   verb, aor. pass. indic. 3 pers. sg.
{5.A.1.b} . . . . id.
διεφθάρη   verb, ²aor. pass. indic. 3 pers. sg.
{5.A.1.e} . . . . διαφθείρω *G1311*
διεφθάρησαν   verb, ²aor. pass. indic. 3 pers. pl.
{5.A.1.e} . . . . id.
διεφθαρμένων   vbl., perf. pass. ptc. gen. pl.
masc. {6.A.1.b} . . . . id.
διέφθειρεν   verb, impf. act. indic. 3 pers. sg.
{5.A.1.b} . . . . id.
διεχειρίσασθε   verb, aor. mid. indic. 2 pers. pl.
{5.A.1.e} . . . . διαχειρίζω *G1315*
διήγειραν   verb, aor. act. indic. 3 pers. pl.
{5.A.1.b} . . . . διεγείρω *G1326*
διηγείρετο   verb, impf. pass. indic. 3 pers. sg.
{5.A.1.e} . . . . id.
G1334 **διηγέομαι**   *I relate, narrate.*
διηγήσαντο   verb, aor. mid. indic. 3 pers. pl.
{5.A.1} . . . . διηγέομαι *G1334*
διηγήσατο   verb, aor. mid. indic. 3 pers. sg.
{5.A.1} . . . . id.
διηγήσεται   verb, fut. mid. indic. 3 pers. sg.
{5.A.1} . . . . id.
διήγησιν   noun, acc. sg. fem. {2.C} . . . . . διήγησις *G1335*
G1335 **διήγησις**, -εως, ἡ   *a narrative.*
διηγήσωνται   verb, aor. mid. subjunc. 3 pers. pl.
{5.B.1} . . . . διηγέομαι *G1334*
διηγοῦ   verb, pres. mid./pass. impv. 2 pers. sg.
{5.D.2} . . . . id.
διηγούμενον   vbl., pres. mid./pass. ptc. acc. sg.
masc. {6.A.2} . . . . id.
διηκόνει   verb, impf. act. indic. 3 pers. sg.
{5.A.2} . . . . διακονέω *G1247*
διηκονήσαμεν   verb, aor. act. indic. 1 pers. pl.
{5.A.1} . . . . id.
διηκόνησε   verb, aor. act. indic. 3 pers. sg.
{5.A.1} . . . . id.
διηκόνησεν   verb, aor. act. indic. 3 pers. sg.
{5.A.1} . . . . id.
διηκόνουν   verb, impf. act. indic. 3 pers. pl.
{5.A.2} . . . . id.
διῆλθεν   verb, ²aor. act. indic. 3 pers. sg.
{5.A.1.b} . . . . διέρχομαι *G1330*
διῆλθον   verb, ²aor. act. indic. 1 pers. sg.
{5.A.1.b} . . . . id.
διῆλθον   verb, ²aor. act. indic. 3 pers. pl.
{5.A.1.b} . . . . id.
διηνεκές   adj., acc. sg. neut. {3.E} . . . . . . διηνεκής *G1336*
G1336 **διηνεκής**, -ές   (1) *continuous;* (2) εἰς τὸ διηνεκές, *perpetually.*
διήνοιγεν   verb, impf. act. indic. 3 pers. sg.
{5.A.1.b} . . . . διανοίγω *G1272*
διηνοιγμένους   vbl., perf. pass. ptc. acc. pl.
masc. {6.A.1.b} . . . . id.
διήνοιξε   verb, aor. act. indic. 3 pers. sg.
{5.A.1.b} . . . . id.

διήνοιξεν   verb, aor. act. indic. 3 pers. sg.
{5.A.1.b} . . . . id.
διηνοίχθησαν   verb, aor. pass. indic. 3 pers. pl.
{5.A.1.b} . . . . id.
διηπόρει   verb, impf. act. indic. 3 pers. sg.
{5.A.2} . . . . διαπορέω *G1280*
διηπόρουν   verb, impf. act. indic. 3 pers. pl.
{5.A.2} . . . . id.
διηπορούντο   verb, impf. mid. indic. 3 pers. pl.
{5.A.2} . . . . id.
διηρμήνευεν   verb, impf. act. indic. 3 pers. sg.
{5.A.1.b} . . . . διερμηνεύω *G1329*
διήρχετο   verb, impf. mid./pass. indic. 3 pers. sg.
{5.A.1.e} . . . . διέρχομαι *G1330*
διήρχοντο   verb, impf. mid./pass. indic. 3 pers.
pl. {5.A.1.e} . . . . id.
διθάλασσον   adj., acc. sg. masc. {3.C} διθάλασσος *G1337*
G1337 **διθάλασσος**, -ον   *between two seas, which has
sea on both sides.*
G1338 **διϊκνέομαι**   *I pass through (to), come through
(to).*
διϊκνούμενος   vbl., pres. mid./pass. ptc. nom. sg.
masc. {6.A.2} . . . . διϊκνέομαι *G1338*
G1339 **διΐστημι**   (1) διαστήσαντες (Acts 27:28)
trans. with τὸ πλοῖον understood, *having
moved (the ship) some distance;* (2) δι-
αστῆναι, intrans., *to be distant from, to be
separated from;* (3) *to pass away.*
διϊσχυρίζετο   verb, impf. mid./pass. indic. 3 pers.
sg. {5.A.1.e} . . . . διϊσχυρίζομαι *G1340*
διϊσχυρίζετο   verb, impf. mid./pass. indic.
3 pers. sg. {5.A.1.e} . . . . id.
G1340 **διϊσχυρίζομαι**   *I assert emphatically.*
δίκαια   adj., nom. pl. neut. {3.A} . . . . δίκαιος *G1342*
δικαία   adj., nom. pl. neut. {3.A} . . . . id.
δικαία   adj., nom. sg. fem. {3.A} . . . . id.
δίκαιαι   adj., nom. pl. fem. {3.A} . . . . id.
δικαίαν   adj., acc. sg. fem. {3.A} . . . . id.
δικαίας   adj., gen. sg. fem. {3.A} . . . . id.
δίκαιε   adj., voc. sg. masc. {3.A} . . . . id.
δίκαιοι   adj., nom. pl. masc. {3.A} . . . . . . δίκαιος *G1342*
δικαιοῖ   verb, pres. act. indic. 3 pers. sg.
{5.A.2} . . . . δικαιόω *G1344*
δικαίοις   adj., dat. pl. masc. {3.A} . . . . . . δίκαιος *G1342*
G1341 **δικαιοκρισία**, -ας, ἡ   *just judging, just
judgment.*
δικαιοκρισίας   noun, gen. sg. fem.
{2.A} . . . . δικαιοκρισία *G1341*
δίκαιον   adj., acc. sg. masc. {3.A} . . . . δίκαιος *G1342*
δίκαιον   adj., acc. sg. neut. {3.A} . . . . id.
δίκαιον   adj., nom. sg. neut. {3.A} . . . . id.
G1342 **δίκαιος**, -α, -ον   (1) *just;* (2) esp., *just in the
eyes of God, righteous;* (3) οἱ δίκαιοι in
Matt *the elect* (a Jewish idea); (4) κρίνω τὸ
δίκαιον, *I give just judgment,* Luke 12:57.
δίκαιος   adj., nom. sg. masc. {3.A} . . . . . . δίκαιος *G1342*
G1343 **δικαιοσύνη**, -ης, ἡ   (1) *justice, justness;* (2)
righteousness (cf. δίκαιος); (3) δικαιοσύνη
θεοῦ strictly, *righteousness of which God is
the source* or *author,* but practically, *a divine*

righteousness and equivalent to βασιλεία τοῦ θεοῦ (usually if not always in Jewish atmosphere).

δικαιοσύνη noun, nom. sg. fem. {2.A} . . . . δικαιοσύνη G1343
δικαιοσύνη noun, dat. sg. fem. {2.A} . . . . id.
δικαιοσύνην noun, acc. sg. fem. {2.A} . . . . . . id.
δικαιοσύνης noun, gen. sg. fem. {2.A} . . . . . . id.
δικαίου adj., gen. sg. masc. {3.A} . . . . . . δίκαιος G1342
δικαιούμενοι vbl., pres. pass. ptc. nom. pl. masc. {6.A.2} . . . . δικαιόω G1344
δικαιοῦν vbl., pres. act. inf. {6.B.2} . . . . id.
δικαιοῦντα vbl., pres. act. ptc. acc. sg. masc. {6.A.2} . . . . id.
δικαιοῦντες vbl., pres. act. ptc. nom. pl. masc. {6.A.2} . . . . id.
δικαίους adj., acc. pl. masc. {3.A} . . . . . . δίκαιος G1342
δικαιοῦσθαι vbl., pres. pass. inf. {6.B.2} . δικαιόω G1344
δικαιοῦσθε verb, pres. pass. indic. 2 pers. pl. {5.A.2} . . . . id.
δικαιοῦται verb, pres. pass. indic. 3 pers. sg. {5.A.2} . . . . id.

G1344 **δικαιόω** (1) *I make* δίκαιος *(righteous), I defend the cause of, plead for the righteousness (innocence) of, I acquit, justify;* (2) hence, *I regard as* δίκαιος *(righteous).*
δικαίῳ adj., dat. sg. masc. {3.A} . . . . δίκαιος G1342
δικαιωθέντες vbl., aor. pass. ptc. nom. pl. masc. {6.A.1.a} . . . . δικαιόω G1344
δικαιωθῆναι vbl., aor. pass. inf. {6.B.1} . . . . . . id.
δικαιωθῇς verb, aor. pass. subjunc. 2 pers. sg. {5.B.1} . . . . id.
δικαιωθήσεται verb, fut. pass. indic. 3 pers. sg. {5.A.1} . . . . id.
δικαιωθήσῃ verb, fut. pass. indic. 2 pers. sg. {5.A.1} . . . . id.
δικαιωθήσονται verb, fut. pass. indic. 3 pers. pl. {5.A.1} . . . . id.
δικαιωθήτω verb, aor. pass. impv. 3 pers. sg. {5.D.1} . . . . id.
δικαιωθῶμεν verb, aor. pass. subjunc. 1 pers. pl. {5.B.1} . . . . id.

G1345 **δικαίωμα**, -ατος, τό (1) *(an argument, a justificative piece),* hence, *a thing pronounced (by God) to be* δίκαιος *(just, the right);* (2) or the *restoration* of a criminal, a fresh chance given him; (3) *a righteous deed* (e.g., Rom 5:18).
δικαίωμα noun, acc. sg. neut. {2.C} . . . . δικαίωμα G1345
δικαίωμα noun, nom. sg. neut. {2.C} . . . . id.
δικαιώμασι noun, dat. pl. neut. {2.C} . . . . id.
δικαιώμασιν noun, dat. pl. neut. {2.C} . . . . id.
δικαιώματα noun, acc. pl. neut. {2.C} . . . . id.
δικαιώματα noun, nom. pl. neut. {2.C} . . . . id.
δικαιώματος noun, gen. sg. neut. {2.C} . . . . id.
δικαίων adj., gen. pl. masc. {3.A} . . . . δίκαιος G1342
δικαιῶν vbl., pres. act. ptc. nom. sg. masc. {6.A.2} . . . . δικαιόω G1344

G1346 **δικαίως** adv., *justly, righteously.*
δικαίως adv. {3.F} . . . . δικαίως G1346
δικαιῶσαι vbl., aor. act. inf. {6.B.1} . . . . δικαιόω G1344

δικαιώσει verb, fut. act. indic. 3 pers. sg. {5.A.1}id.
δικαίωσιν noun, acc. sg. fem. {2.C} . . . . δικαίωσις G1347
G1347 **δικαίωσις**, -εως, ἡ *justifying, justification, a process of absolution.*
δικαστήν noun, acc. sg. masc. {2.A} . . . δικαστής G1348
G1348 **δικαστής**, -οῦ, ὁ *a judge.*
G1349 **δίκη**, -ης, ἡ (1) (orig. *custom, usage);* hence, *right, justice,* Acts 28:4, where rather *Justice* (the goddess); (2) *process of law, judicial hearing;* (3) *execution of sentence, punishment, penalty,* 2 Thess 1:9; Jude 7.
δίκη noun, nom. sg. fem. {2.A} . . . . δίκη G1349
δίκην noun, acc. sg. fem. {2.A} . . . . id.
δίκτυα noun, acc. pl. neut. {2.B} . . . . δίκτυον G1350
δίκτυα noun, nom. pl. neut. {2.B} . . . . id.
G1350 **δίκτυον**, -ου, τό *a net.*
δίκτυον noun, acc. sg. neut. {2.B} . . . . . . δίκτυον G1350
δίκτυον noun, nom. sg. neut. {2.B} . . . . id.
G1351 **δίλογος**, -ον *double-tongued.*
διλόγους adj., acc. pl. masc. {3.C} . . . . . . δίλογος G1351
G1352 **διό** *wherefore* (= δι᾽ ὅ, *on account of which thing).*
διό conj. . . . . διό G1352
διοδεύσαντες vbl., aor. act. ptc. nom. pl. masc. {6.A.1.a} . . . . διοδεύω G1353
G1353 **διοδεύω** *I travel through.*
G1354 **Διονύσιος**, -ου, ὁ *Dionysius,* an Athenian.
Διονύσιος noun prop., nom. sg. masc. {2.B; 2.D} . . . . Διονύσιος G1354
G1355 **διόπερ** *therefore, for this very reason* (= δι᾽ ὅπερ, an emphatic διό).
διόπερ conj. . . . . διόπερ G1355
G1356 **διοπετής**, -ές *fallen from the sky.*
διοπετοῦς adj., gen. sg. masc. {3.E} . . . . . διοπετής G1356
διοπετοῦς adj., gen. sg. neut. {3.E} . . . . id.
G2735†‡ **διόρθωμα**, -ατος, τό *a correction, reform.* Var. for κατόρθωμα, Acts 24:2.
διορθωμάτων noun, gen. pl. neut. {2.C} . . . . διόρθωμα G2735†‡
διορθώσεως noun, gen. sg. fem. {2.C} . . διόρθωσις G1357
G1357 **διόρθωσις**, -εως, ἡ *amendment, improvement* (orig. *right ordering;* then *bettering).*
διορυγῆναι vbl., ²aor. pass. inf. {6.B.1} . διορύσσω G1358
διορύσσουσι verb, pres. act. indic. 3 pers. pl. {5.A.1.a} . . . . id.
διορύσσουσιν verb, pres. act. indic. 3 pers. pl. {5.A.1.a} . . . . id.
G1358 **διορύσσω** *I dig through, break through.*
διορυχθῆναι vbl., aor. pass. inf. {6.B.1} . διορύσσω G1358
Διός noun prop., gen. sg. masc. {2.C; 2.D} . . . Ζεύς G2203
G1359 **Διόσκουροι**, -ων, οἱ *the Dioscuri,* Castor and Pollux, sons of Zeus and Leda, and patrons of sailors (= Διὸς κοῦροι, *boys of Zeus).*
Διοσκούροις noun prop., dat. pl. masc. {2.B; 2.D} . . . . Διόσκουροι G1359
G1360 **διότι** (1) = διὰ ὅ τι, *wherefore;* (2) = ὅτι Rom 8:21 (var.).
διότι conj. . . . . διότι G1360
Διοτρεφής noun prop., nom. sg. masc. {2.A; 2.D} . . . . Διοτρέφης G1361

Διοτρέφης   noun prop., nom. sg. masc. {2.A;
2.D}. . . . . id.
G1361 **Διοτρέφης**, -ους, ὁ   *Diotrephes.*
διπλᾶ   adj., acc. pl. neut. {3.A} . . . . .διπλοῦς *G1362*
διπλῆς   adj., gen. sg. fem. {3.A}. . . . . id.
διπλότερον   adj. comp., acc. sg. masc. {3.A; 3.G} id.
διπλοῦν   adj., acc. sg. neut. {3.A} . . . . id.
G1362 **διπλοῦς**, -ῆ, -οῦν   *double* (contracted from
διπλόος).
G1363 **διπλόω**   *I double.*
διπλώσατε   verb, aor. act. impv. 2 pers. pl.
{5.D.1}. . . . . διπλόω *G1363*
G1364 **δίς**   adv., *twice.*
δίς   adv.. . . . . .δίς *G1364*
δισμυριάδες   noun, nom. pl. fem.
{2.C} . . . . δισμυριάς *G3461†‡*
G3461†‡ **δισμυριάς**, -άδος, ἡ   *a double myriad, i.e.,
20,000.* Var. for μυριάς, Rev 9:16.
G1365 **διστάζω**   *I doubt.*
δίστομον   adj., acc. sg. fem. {3.C}. . . . . . .δίστομος *G1366*
G1366 **δίστομος**, -ον   *two-edged* (lit. *two-mouthed;*
hence of a sword, as a drinker of blood).
δίστομος   adj., nom. sg. fem. {3.C}. . . . . .δίστομος *G1366*
δισχίλιοι   adj., nom. pl. masc. {3.A}. . . . . .δισχίλιοι *G1367*
G1367 **δισχίλιοι**, -αι, -α   *two-thousand.*
διυλίζοντες   vbl., pres. act. ptc. nom. pl. masc.
{6.A.1}. . . . . .διϋλίζω *G1368*
διϋλίζοντες   vbl., pres. act. ptc. nom. pl. masc.
{6.A.1}. . . . . id.
G1368 **διϋλίζω**   *I strain, put through a sieve.*
G1369 **διχάζω**   *I make to differ from, I make to be
hostile.*
διχάσαι   vbl., aor. act. inf. {6.B.1}. . . . . . . διχάζω *G1369*
G1370 **διχοστασία**, -ας, ἡ   *division* (between
persons).
διχοστασίαι   noun, nom. pl. fem.
{2.A} . . . . διχοστασία *G1370*
διχοστασίας   noun, acc. pl. fem. {2.A}. . . . . id.
G1371 **διχοτομέω**   *I cut in two.*
διχοτομήσει   verb, fut. act. indic. 3 pers. sg.
{5.A.1}. .διχοτομέω *G1371*
διψᾷ   verb, pres. act. subjunc. 3 pers. sg.
{5.B.2} . . . . διψάω *G1372*
G1372 **διψάω**   *I thirst.*
δίψει   noun, dat. sg. neut. {2.C} . . . . .δίψος *G1373*
διψήσει   verb, fut. act. indic. 3 pers. sg.
{5.A.1}. . . . . διψάω *G1372*
διψήσῃ   verb, aor. act. subjunc. 3 pers. sg. {5.B.1}id.
διψήσουσιν   verb, fut. act. indic. 3 pers. pl.
{5.A.1}. . . . . id.
G1373 **δίψος**, -ους, τό   *thirst.*
δίψυχοι   adj., voc. pl. masc. {3.C} . . . . . . .δίψυχος *G1374*
G1374 **δίψυχος**, -ον   *double-minded, wavering* (lit. *of
two souls, of two selves*).
δίψυχος   adj., nom. sg. masc. {3.C} . . . . . .δίψυχος *G1374*
διψῶ   verb, pres. act. indic. 1 pers. sg. {5.A.2}διψάω *G1372*
διψῶ   verb, pres. act. subjunc. 1 pers. sg. {5.B.2} . id.
διψῶμεν   verb, pres. act. indic. 1 pers. pl. {5.A.2} id.
διψῶν   vbl., pres. act. ptc. nom. sg. masc. {6.A.2} id.
διψῶντα   vbl., pres. act. ptc. acc. sg. masc. {6.A.2} id.

διψῶντες   vbl., pres. act. ptc. nom. pl. masc.
{6.A.2}. . . . . id.
διψῶντι   vbl., pres. act. ptc. dat. sg. masc. {6.A.2}id.
διωγμοῖς   noun, dat. pl. masc. {2.B} . . . . .διωγμός *G1375*
διωγμόν   noun, acc. sg. masc. {2.B} . . . . id.
G1375 **διωγμός**, -οῦ, ὁ   *persecution.*
διωγμός   noun, nom. sg. masc. {2.B}. . . . .διωγμός *G1375*
διωγμοῦ   noun, gen. sg. masc. {2.B} . . . . id.
διωγμούς   noun, acc. pl. masc. {2.B}. . . . . id.
διωγμῶν   noun, gen. pl. masc. {2.B}. . . . . id.
διώδευε   verb, impf. act. indic. 3 pers. sg.
{5.A.1.b} . . . . διοδεύω *G1353*
διώδευεν   verb, impf. act. indic. 3 pers. sg.
{5.A.1.b} . . . . id.
δίωκε   verb, pres. act. impv. 2 pers. sg.
{5.D.1}. . . . . διώκω *G1377*
διώκεις   verb, pres. act. indic. 2 pers. sg. {5.A.1.a}id.
διώκετε   verb, pres. act. impv. 2 pers. pl. {5.D.1} . id.
διώκομαι   verb, pres. pass. indic. 1 pers. sg.
{5.A.1.d} . . . . id.
διωκόμενοι   vbl., pres. pass. ptc. nom. pl. masc.
{6.A.1}. . . . . id.
διώκοντα   vbl., pres. act. ptc. nom. pl. neut.
{6.A.1}. . . . . id.
διώκοντας   vbl., pres. act. ptc. acc. pl. masc.
{6.A.1}. . . . . id.
διώκοντες   vbl., pres. act. ptc. nom. pl. masc.
{6.A.1}. . . . . id.
διωκόντων   vbl., pres. act. ptc. gen. pl. masc.
{6.A.1}. . . . . id.
διώκτην   noun, acc. sg. masc. {2.A} . . . . . .διώκτης *G1376*
G1376 **διώκτης**, -ου, ὁ   *a persecutor.*
G1377 **διώκω**   (1) *I pursue;* (2) hence, *I persecute.*
διώκω   verb, pres. act. indic. 1 pers. sg.
{5.A.1.a} . . . . διώκω *G1377*
διώκωμεν   verb, pres. act. subjunc. 1 pers. pl.
{5.B.1} . . . . id.
διώκων   vbl., pres. act. ptc. nom. sg. masc.
{6.A.1}. . . . . id.
διώκωνται   verb, pres. pass. subjunc. 3 pers. pl.
{5.B.1} . . . . id.
διώκωσιν   verb, pres. act. subjunc. 3 pers. pl.
{5.B.1} . . . . id.
διωξάτω   verb, aor. act. impv. 3 pers. sg. {5.D.1}. id.
διώξετε   verb, fut. act. indic. 2 pers. pl. {5.A.1.a}. id.
διώξητε   verb, aor. act. subjunc. 2 pers. pl.
{5.B.1} . . . . id.
διώξουσι   verb, fut. act. indic. 3 pers. pl.
{5.A.1.a} . . . . id.
διώξουσιν   verb, fut. act. indic. 3 pers. pl.
{5.A.1.a} . . . . id.
διώξωσι   verb, aor. act. subjunc. 3 pers. pl.
{5.B.1} . . . . id.
διώξωσιν   verb, aor. act. subjunc. 3 pers. pl.
{5.B.1} . . . . id.
διωχθήσονται   verb, fut. pass. indic. 3 pers. pl.
{5.A.1.d} . . . . id.
G1378 **δόγμα**, -ατος, τό   *a decree.*
δόγμα   noun, nom. sg. neut. {2.C} . . . . .δόγμα *G1378*
δόγμασι   noun, dat. pl. neut. {2.C} . . . . id.

δόγμασιν noun, dat. pl. neut. {2.C} . . . . id.

δόγματα noun, acc. pl. neut. {2.C} . . . . id.

δογματίζεσθε verb, pres. pass. indic. 2 pers. pl.
{5.A.1.d} . . . . δογματίζω G1379

G1379 **δογματίζω** pass. *I am subjected to regulations,*
or I am decree-ridden.

δογμάτων noun, gen. pl. neut. {2.C} . . . . . δόγμα G1378

δοθείη verb, aor. pass. opt. 3 pers. sg.
{5.C.3} . . . . δίδωμι G1325

δοθεῖσα vbl., aor. pass. ptc. nom. sg. fem.
{6.A.1.a} . . . . id.

δοθεῖσαν vbl., aor. pass. ptc. acc. sg. fem.
{6.A.1.a} . . . . id.

δοθείσῃ vbl., aor. pass. ptc. dat. sg. fem.
{6.A.1.a} . . . . id.

δοθείσης vbl., aor. pass. ptc. gen. sg. fem.
{6.A.1.a} . . . . id.

δοθέντος vbl., aor. pass. ptc. gen. sg. neut.
{6.A.1.a} . . . . id.

δοθῇ verb, aor. pass. subjunc. 3 pers. sg. {5.B.3}. id.

δοθῆναι vbl., aor. pass. inf. {6.B.1} . . . . id.

δοθήσεται verb, fut. pass. indic. 3 pers. sg.
{5.A.1} . . . . id.

δοῖ verb, ²aor. act. subjunc. 3 pers. sg. {5.B.3} . . . id.

δοκεῖ verb, pres. act. indic. 3 pers. sg. {5.A.2} δοκέω G1380

δοκεῖν vbl., pres. act. inf. {6.B.2} . . . . id.

δοκεῖς verb, pres. act. indic. 2 pers. sg. {5.A.2} . . id.

δοκεῖτε verb, pres. act. impv. 2 pers. pl. {5.D.2} . id.

δοκεῖτε verb, pres. act. indic. 2 pers. pl. {5.A.2} . id.

G1380 **δοκέω** (1) *I seem, am thought;* (2) δοκεῖ impers. with dat., *it seems good, it is resolved by.*

δοκῇ verb, pres. act. subjunc. 3 pers. sg.
{5.B.2} . . . . δοκέω G1380

δοκιμάζει verb, pres. act. indic. 3 pers. sg.
{5.A.1.a} . . . . δοκιμάζω G1381

δοκιμάζειν vbl., pres. act. inf. {6.B.1} . . . . id.

δοκιμάζεις verb, pres. act. indic. 2 pers. sg.
{5.A.1.a} . . . . id.

δοκιμαζέσθωσαν verb, pres. pass. impv.
3 pers. pl. {5.D.1} . . . . id.

δοκιμάζετε verb, pres. act. impv. 2 pers. pl.
{5.D.1} . . . . id.

δοκιμάζετε verb, pres. act. indic. 2 pers. pl.
{5.A.1.a} . . . . id.

δοκιμαζέτω verb, pres. act. impv. 3 pers. sg.
{5.D.1} . . . . id.

δοκιμαζομένου vbl., pres. pass. ptc. gen. sg.
neut. {6.A.1} . . . . id.

δοκιμάζοντες vbl., pres. act. ptc. nom. pl.
masc. {6.A.1} . . . . id.

δοκιμάζοντι vbl., pres. act. ptc. dat. sg. masc.
{6.A.1} . . . . id.

G1381 **δοκιμάζω** (1) *I put to the test, I prove, examine;*
(2) in Rom 2:18; Phil 1:10 either *I distinguish*
by testing, or, more probably, *I approve after*
testing; (3) *I think fit,* Rom 1:28. Var., δοκιμασία, -ας, ἡ, *testing, proving,* Heb 3:9.

δοκιμάζων vbl., pres. act. ptc. nom. sg. masc.
{6.A.1} . . . . δοκιμάζω G1381

δοκιμάσαι vbl., aor. act. inf. {6.B.1} . . . . id.

δοκιμάσει verb, fut. act. indic. 3 pers. sg.
{5.A.1.a} . . . . id.

δοκιμάσητε verb, aor. act. subjunc. 2 pers. pl.
{5.B.1} . . . . id.

G1381† **δοκιμασία**, -ας, ἡ *testing, proving.* Var. for
δοκιμάζω, Heb 3:9.

δοκιμασίᾳ noun, dat. sg. fem. {2.A} . . δοκιμασία G1381†

G1382 **δοκιμή**, -ῆς, ἡ (1) *approved status;* (2) hence,
character.

δοκιμή noun, nom. sg. fem. {2.A} . . . . δοκιμή G1382

δοκιμῇ noun, dat. sg. fem. {2.A} . . . . id.

δοκιμήν noun, acc. sg. fem. {2.A} . . . . id.

δοκιμῆς noun, gen. sg. fem. {2.A} . . . . id.

G1383 **δοκίμιον**, -ου, τό *what is genuine, the ap-*
proved part, the pure part (neut. of δοκίμιος
genuine, as opposed to *alloyed, counterfeit*).

δοκίμιον noun, nom. sg. neut. {2.B} . . . . δοκίμιον G1383

δόκιμοι adj., nom. pl. masc. {3.A} . . . . . . δόκιμος G1384

δόκιμον adj., acc. sg. masc. {3.A} . . . . id.

G1384 **δόκιμος**, -ον *approved.*

δόκιμος adj., nom. sg. masc. {3.A} . . . . . . δόκιμος G1384

δοκόν noun, acc. sg. fem. {2.B} . . . . δοκός G1385

G1385 **δοκός**, -οῦ, ἡ *a beam.*

δοκός noun, nom. sg. fem. {2.B} . . . . δοκός G1385

δοκοῦμεν verb, pres. act. indic. 1 pers. pl.
{5.A.2} . . . . δοκέω G1380

δοκοῦν vbl., pres. act. ptc. acc. sg. neut. {6.A.2}. id.

δοκοῦντα vbl., pres. act. ptc. nom. pl. neut.
{6.A.2} . . . . id.

δοκοῦντες vbl., pres. act. ptc. nom. pl. masc.
{6.A.2} . . . . id.

δοκούντων vbl., pres. act. ptc. gen. pl. masc.
{6.A.2} . . . . id.

δοκοῦσα vbl., pres. act. ptc. nom. sg. fem.
{6.A.2} . . . . id.

δοκοῦσι verb, pres. act. indic. 3 pers. pl. {5.A.2} id.

δοκοῦσι vbl., pres. act. ptc. dat. pl. masc. {6.A.2}id.

δοκοῦσιν verb, pres. act. indic. 3 pers. pl.
{5.A.2} . . . . id.

δοκοῦσιν vbl., pres. act. ptc. dat. pl. masc.
{6.A.2} . . . . id.

δοκῶ verb, pres. act. indic. 1 pers. sg. {5.A.2} . . . id.

δοκῶν vbl., pres. act. ptc. nom. sg. masc. {6.A.2} id.

δόλιοι adj., nom. pl. masc. {3.A} . . . . δόλιος G1386

G1386 **δόλιος**, -α, -ον *treacherous, deceitful.*

G1387 **δολιόω** *I act deceitfully, treacherously.*

δόλον noun, acc. sg. masc. {2.B} . . . . δόλος G1388

G1388 **δόλος**, -ου, ὁ *deceit, guile, treachery.*

δόλος noun, nom. sg. masc. {2.B} . . . . δόλος G1388

δόλου noun, gen. sg. masc. {2.B} . . . . id.

δολοῦντες vbl., pres. act. ptc. nom. pl. masc.
{6.A.2} . . . . δολόω G1389

G1389 **δολόω** *I adulterate* (cf. ἄδολος).

δόλῳ noun, dat. sg. masc. {2.B} . . . . δόλος G1388

G1390 **δόμα**, -ατος, τό *a gift.*

δόμα noun, acc. sg. neut. {2.C} . . . . δόμα G1390

δόματα noun, acc. pl. neut. {2.C} . . . . id.

δόντα vbl., ²aor. act. ptc. acc. sg. masc.
{6.A.3} . . . . δίδωμι G1325

δόντι vbl., ²aor. act. ptc. dat. sg. masc. {6.A.3} . . id.

δόντος   vbl., ²aor. act. ptc. gen. sg. masc. {6.A.3}. id.

G1391 **δόξα**, -ης, ἡ   (1) *glory,* an esp. divine quality, the unspoken manifestation of God; (2) in Jas 2:1 it is in apposition to Ἰησοῦ Χριστοῦ, and is personified (cf. 1 Cor 2:8; Acts 7:2, and the Shekinah of Targums and post-canonical Jewish writings).

δόξα   noun, nom. sg. fem. {2.A} . . . . δόξα G1391

δοξάζειν   vbl., pres. act. inf. {6.B.1} . . . . . δοξάζω G1392

δοξάζεται   verb, pres. pass. indic. 3 pers. sg. {5.A.1.d} . . . . id.

δοξαζέτω   verb, pres. act. impv. 3 pers. sg. {5.D.1} . . . . id.

δοξάζηται   verb, pres. pass. subjunc. 3 pers. sg. {5.B.1} . . . . id.

δοξάζητε   verb, pres. act. subjunc. 2 pers. pl. {5.B.1} . . . . id.

δοξαζόμενος   vbl., pres. pass. ptc. nom. sg. masc. {6.A.1} . . . . id.

δοξάζοντες   vbl., pres. act. ptc. nom. pl. masc. {6.A.1} . . . . id.

G1392 **δοξάζω**   (1) *I glorify, bestow glory on;* (2) τὸν θεόν, *I acknowledge the glory of God.*

δοξάζω   verb, pres. act. indic. 1 pers. sg. {5.A.1.a} . . . . δοξάζω G1392

δοξάζων   vbl., pres. act. ptc. nom. sg. masc. {6.A.1} . . . . id.

δόξαν   noun, acc. sg. fem. {2.A} . . . . δόξα G1391

δόξαντες   vbl., aor. act. ptc. nom. pl. masc. {6.A.2} . . . . δοκέω G1380

δόξας   noun, acc. pl. fem. {2.A} . . . . δόξα G1391

δοξάσαι   vbl., aor. act. inf. {6.B.1} . . . . . δοξάζω G1392

δοξάσατε   verb, aor. act. impv. 2 pers. pl. {5.D.1} id.

δοξάσει   verb, fut. act. indic. 3 pers. sg. {5.A.1.a} id.

δοξάσῃ   verb, aor. act. subjunc. 3 pers. sg. {5.B.1} . . . . id.

δοξασθῇ   verb, aor. pass. subjunc. 3 pers. sg. {5.B.1} . . . . id.

δοξασθῶσιν   verb, aor. pass. subjunc. 3 pers. pl. {5.B.1} . . . . id.

δόξασον   verb, aor. act. impv. 2 pers. sg. {5.D.1}. id.

δοξάσω   verb, aor. act. subjunc. 1 pers. sg. {5.B.1} . . . . id.

δοξάσω   verb, fut. act. indic. 1 pers. sg. {5.A.1.a} id.

δοξάσωσι   verb, aor. act. subjunc. 3 pers. pl. {5.B.1} . . . . id.

δοξάσωσιν   verb, aor. act. subjunc. 3 pers. pl. {5.B.1} . . . . id.

δόξῃ   noun, dat. sg. fem. {2.A} . . . . δόξα G1391

δόξῃ   verb, aor. act. subjunc. 3 pers. sg. {5.B.1} . . . . δοκέω G1380

δόξης   noun, gen. sg. fem. {2.A} . . . . δόξα G1391

δόξητε   verb, aor. act. subjunc. 2 pers. pl. {5.B.1} . . . . δοκέω G1380

δόξω   verb, aor. act. subjunc. 1 pers. sg. {5.B.1} . . id.

G1393 **Δορκάς**, -άδος, ἡ   the Gk. name of Tabitha, *Dorcas* (lit. *gazelle*).

Δορκάς   noun prop., nom. sg. fem. {2.C; 2.D} . . . . Δορκάς G1393

δός   verb, ²aor. act. impv. 2 pers. sg. {5.D.3}. . δίδωμι G1325

δόσεως   noun, gen. sg. fem. {2.C} . . . . δόσις G1394

δόσις   noun, nom. sg. fem. {2.C} . . . . id.

G1394 **δόσις**, -εως, ἡ   *giving* (from God).

δότε   verb, ²aor. act. impv. 2 pers. pl. {5.D.3} . δίδωμι G1325

δότην   noun, acc. sg. masc. {2.A} . . . . δότης G1395

G1395 **δότης**, -ου, ὁ   *giver.*

δότω   verb, ²aor. act. impv. 3 pers. sg. {5.D.3} δίδωμι G1325

δοῦλα   adj., acc. pl. neut. {3.A} . . . . δοῦλος G1400

G1396 **δουλαγωγέω**   *I enslave.*

δουλαγωγῶ   verb, pres. act. indic. 1 pers. sg. {5.A.2} . . . . δουλαγωγέω G1396

δούλας   noun, acc. pl. fem. {2.A} . . . . δούλη G1399

δοῦλε   noun, voc. sg. masc. {2.B} . . . . δοῦλος G1401

G1397 **δουλεία**, -ας, ἡ   *slavery.*

δουλείαν   noun, acc. sg. fem. {2.A} . . . . . δουλεία G1397

δουλείας   noun, gen. sg. fem. {2.A} . . . . id.

δουλεύει   verb, pres. act. indic. 3 pers. sg. {5.A.1.a} . . . . δουλεύω G1398

δουλεύειν   vbl., pres. act. inf. {6.B.1} . . . . id.

δουλεύετε   verb, pres. act. impv. 2 pers. pl. {5.D.1} . . . . id.

δουλεύετε   verb, pres. act. indic. 2 pers. pl. {5.A.1.a} . . . . id.

δουλευέτωσαν   verb, pres. act. impv. 3 pers. pl. {5.D.1} . . . . id.

δουλεύοντες   vbl., pres. act. ptc. nom. pl. masc. {6.A.1} . . . . id.

δουλεύουσιν   verb, pres. act. indic. 3 pers. pl. {5.A.1.a} . . . . id.

δουλεῦσαι   vbl., aor. act. inf. {6.B.1} . . . . id.

δουλεύσει   verb, fut. act. indic. 3 pers. sg. {5.A.1.a} . . . . id.

δουλεύσουσιν   verb, fut. act. indic. 3 pers. pl. {5.A.1.a} . . . . id.

δουλεύσωσι   verb, aor. act. subjunc. 3 pers. pl. {5.B.1} . . . . id.

δουλεύσωσιν   verb, aor. act. subjunc. 3 pers. pl. {5.B.1} . . . . id.

G1398 **δουλεύω**   *I serve as a slave, I am a slave.*

δουλεύω   verb, pres. act. indic. 1 pers. sg. {5.A.1.a} . . . . δουλεύω G1398

δουλεύων   vbl., pres. act. ptc. nom. sg. masc. {6.A.1} . . . . id.

G1399 **δούλη**, -ης, ἡ   *a female slave.*

δούλη   noun, nom. sg. fem. {2.A} . . . . δούλη G1399

δούλης   noun, gen. sg. fem. {2.A} . . . . id.

δοῦλοι   noun, nom. pl. masc. {2.B} . . . . . δοῦλος G1401

δοῦλοι   noun, voc. pl. masc. {2.B} . . . . id.

δούλοις   noun, dat. pl. masc. {2.B} . . . . id.

G1400 **δοῦλος**, -ή, -όν   *subservient, servile, subject.*

G1401 **δοῦλος**, -ου, ὁ   *a (male) slave.*

δοῦλος   noun, nom. sg. masc. {2.B} . . . . . δοῦλος G1401

δούλου   noun, gen. sg. masc. {2.B}. . . . . id.

δούλους   noun, acc. pl. masc. {2.B} . . . . id.

G1402 **δουλόω**   *I enslave.*

δούλῳ   noun, dat. sg. masc. {2.B} . . . . δοῦλος G1401

δουλωθέντες   vbl., aor. pass. ptc. nom. pl. masc. {6.A.1.a} . . . . δουλόω G1402

δούλων   noun, gen. pl. masc. {2.B} . . . . . . δοῦλος G1401

δουλώσουσιν   verb, fut. act. indic. 3 pers. pl.
   {5.A.1} . . . . δουλόω G1402
δοῦναι   vbl., ²aor. act. inf. {6.B.3} . . . . δίδωμι G1325
δούς   vbl., ²aor. act. ptc. nom. sg. masc. {6.A.3} . . id.
G1403 **δοχή**, -ῆς, ἡ   a reception, party.
   δοχήν   noun, acc. sg. fem. {2.A} . . . . δοχή G1403
   δράκοντα   noun, acc. sg. masc. {2.C} . . . . δράκων G1404
   δράκοντι   noun, dat. sg. masc. {2.C} . . . . id.
   δράκοντος   noun, gen. sg. masc. {2.C} . . . . id.
G1404 **δράκων**, -οντος, ὁ   a serpent.
   δράκων   noun, nom. sg. masc. {2.C} . . . . δράκων G1404
   δραμών   vbl., ²aor. act. ptc. nom. sg. masc.
   {6.A.1.a} . . . . τρέχω G5143
G1405 **δράσσομαι**   I take hold of, grasp.
   δρασσόμενος   vbl., pres. mid./pass. ptc. nom. sg.
   masc. {6.A.1} . . . . δράσσομαι G1405
   δραχμάς   noun, acc. pl. fem. {2.A} . . . . . . δραχμή G1406
G1406 **δραχμή**, -ῆς, ἡ   a drachma, a Gk. silver coin.
   δραχμήν   noun, acc. sg. fem. {2.A} . . . . . . δραχμή G1406
G1407 **δρέπανον**, -ου, τό   a sickle.
   δρέπανον   noun, acc. sg. neut. {2.B} . . . . δρέπανον G1407
   δρόμον   noun, acc. sg. masc. {2.B} . . . . . . δρόμος G1408
G1408 **δρόμος**, -ου, ὁ   a run, a course (in running).
G1409 **Δρούσιλλα**, -ης, ἡ   Drusilla (born in 39 A.D.),
   daughter of Herod Agrippa I and his cousin
   Kypros, wife, first of Azizos, King of Emesa, and
   then of Antonius Felix, procurator of Judaea.
   Δρουσίλλῃ   noun prop., dat. sg. fem. {2.A;
   2.D} . . . . Δρούσιλλα G1409
   δυναίμην   verb, pres. mid./pass. opt. 1 pers. sg.
   {5.C.3} . . . . δύναμαι G1410
   δύναιντο   verb, pres. mid./pass. opt. 3 pers. pl.
   {5.C.3} . . . . id.
G1410 **δύναμαι**   (1) I am powerful, I have (the) power;
   (2) I am able, I can.
   δύναμαι   verb, pres. mid./pass. indic. 1 pers. sg.
   {5.A.3.a} . . . . δύναμαι G1410
   δυνάμεθα   verb, pres. mid./pass. indic. 1 pers.
   pl. {5.A.3.a} . . . . id.
   δυνάμει   noun, dat. sg. fem. {2.C} . . . . . δύναμις G1411
   δυνάμεις   noun, acc. pl. fem. {2.C} . . . . id.
   δυνάμεις   noun, nom. pl. fem. {2.C} . . . . id.
   δυνάμενα   vbl., pres. mid./pass. ptc. acc. pl. neut.
   {6.A.3} . . . . δύναμαι G1410
   δυνάμεναι   vbl., pres. mid./pass. ptc. nom. pl.
   fem. {6.A.3} . . . . id.
   δυναμένη   vbl., pres. mid./pass. ptc. nom. sg.
   fem. {6.A.3} . . . . id.
   δυνάμενοι   vbl., pres. mid./pass. ptc. nom. pl.
   masc. {6.A.3} . . . . id.
   δυνάμενον   vbl., pres. mid./pass. ptc. acc. sg.
   masc. {6.A.3} . . . . id.
   δυνάμενος   vbl., pres. mid./pass. ptc. nom. sg.
   masc. {6.A.3} . . . . id.
   δυναμένου   vbl., pres. mid./pass. ptc. gen. sg.
   masc. {6.A.3} . . . . id.
   δυναμένου   vbl., pres. mid./pass. ptc. gen. sg.
   neut. {6.A.3} . . . . id.
   δυναμένους   vbl., pres. mid./pass. ptc. acc. pl.
   masc. {6.A.3} . . . . id.

δυναμένῳ   vbl., pres. mid./pass. ptc. dat. sg.
   masc. {6.A.3} . . . . id.
δυναμένων   vbl., pres. mid./pass. ptc. gen. pl.
   masc. {6.A.3} . . . . id.
δυνάμεσι   noun, dat. pl. fem. {2.C} . . . . δύναμις G1411
δυνάμεσιν   noun, dat. pl. fem. {2.C} . . . . id.
δυνάμεων   noun, gen. pl. fem. {2.C} . . . . id.
δυνάμεως   noun, gen. sg. fem. {2.C} . . . . id.
δύναμιν   noun, acc. sg. fem. {2.C} . . . . id.
G1411 **δύναμις**, -εως, ἡ   (1) physical power, force,
   might; (2) in pl., powerful deeds, deeds showing
   (physical) power, marvelous works.
   δύναμις   noun, nom. sg. fem. {2.C} . . . . δύναμις G1411
   δυναμούμενοι   vbl., pres. pass. ptc. nom. pl. masc.
   {6.A.2} . . . . δυναμόω G1412
G1412 **δυναμόω**   I empower, fill with power.
   δύνανται   verb, pres. mid./pass. indic. 3 pers. pl.
   {5.A.3.a} . . . . δύναμαι G1410
   δύνασαι   verb, pres. mid./pass. indic. 2 pers.
   sg. {5.A.3.a} . . . . id.
   δύνασθαι   vbl., pres. mid./pass. inf. {6.B.3} . . . . id.
   δύνασθε   verb, pres. mid./pass. indic. 2 pers. pl.
   {5.A.3.a} . . . . id.
   δυνάστας   noun, acc. pl. masc. {2.A} . . . δυνάστης G1413
G1413 **δυνάστης**, -ου, ὁ   (1) a ruler, potentate; (2)
   Acts 8:27 in apposition, seems = courtier,
   member of the court (lit. a man who rules by
   force).
   δυνάστης   noun, nom. sg. masc. {2.A} . . δυνάστης G1413
   δυνατά   adj., nom. pl. neut. {3.A} . . . . . . δυνατός G1415
   δύναται   verb, pres. mid./pass. indic. 3 pers. sg.
   {5.A.3.a} . . . . δύναμαι G1410
   δυνατεῖ   verb, pres. act. indic. 3 pers. sg.
   {5.A.2} . . . . δυνατέω G1414
G1414 **δυνατέω**   I am powerful, I have power, I am
   able.
   δυνατοί   adj., nom. pl. masc. {3.A} . . . . . δυνατός G1415
   δυνατόν   adj., acc. sg. neut. {3.A} . . . . id.
   δυνατόν   adj., nom. sg. neut. {3.A} . . . . id.
G1415 **δυνατός**, -ή, -όν   (1) of persons, powerful, able;
   (2) of things, possible.
   δυνατός   noun, nom. sg. masc. {3.A} . . . δυνατός G1415
   δύνῃ   verb, pres. mid./pass. indic. 2 pers. sg.
   {5.A.3} . . . . δύναμαι G1410
   δυνηθῆτε   verb, aor. pass. subjunc. 2 pers. pl.
   {5.B.3} . . . . id.
   δυνήσεσθε   verb, fut. mid. indic. 2 pers. pl.
   {5.A.1} . . . . id.
   δυνήσεται   verb, fut. mid. indic. 3 pers. sg.
   {5.A.1} . . . . id.
   δυνήσῃ   verb, fut. mid. indic. 2 pers. sg. {5.A.1} . . id.
   δυνησόμεθα   verb, fut. mid. indic. 1 pers. pl.
   {5.A.1} . . . . id.
   δυνήσονται   verb, fut. mid. indic. 3 pers. pl.
   {5.A.1} . . . . id.
   δύνηται   verb, pres. mid./pass. subjunc. 3 pers.
   sg. {5.B.2} . . . . id.
   δύνοντος   vbl., pres. act. ptc. gen. sg. masc.
   {6.A.1} . . . . δύνω G1416
G1416 **δύνω**   intrans., I sink.

δύνωνται   verb, pres. mid./pass. subjunc. 3 pers. pl.
    {5.B.2} . . . . δύναμαι G1410

G1417   **δύο**   (1) *two;* (2) δύο δύο and ἀνὰ (κατὰ) δύο,
    two by two; ἀνὰ δύο δύο in some MSS of Luke
    10:1 is a mistaken fusion of the two phrases.
    δύο   adj. num. . . . . δύο G1417

G1418   **δυσ-**   prefix, *hard, with difficulty.*
    δυσβάστακτα   adj., acc. pl. neut.
    {3.C} . . . . δυσβάστακτος G1419

G1419   **δυσβάστακτος**, -ον   *difficult to carry.*
    δυσεντερία   noun, dat. sg. fem. {2.B} δυσεντέριον G1420

G1420   **δυσεντέριον**, -ου, τό   *dysentery.*
    δυσεντερίῳ   noun, dat. sg. neut. {2.B} δυσεντέριον G1420

G1421   **δυσερμήνευτος**, -ον   *difficult to interpret.*
    δυσερμήνευτος   adj., nom. sg. masc.
    {3.C} . . . . δυσερμήνευτος G1421
    δύσεως   noun, gen. sg. fem. {2.C} . . . . δύσις G1424†‡
    δυσί   adj., num. dat. pl. fem. {3.E} . . . . δύο G1417
    δυσί   adj., num. dat. pl. masc. {3.E} . . . . id.
    δυσίν   adj., num. dat. pl. fem. {3.E} . . . . id.
    δυσίν   adj., num. dat. pl. masc. {3.E} . . . . id.

G1424†‡   **δύσις**, -εως, ἡ   *the west.*
    δύσκολον   adj., nom. sg. neut. {3.C} . . . δύσκολος G1422

G1422   **δύσκολος**, -ον   *difficult.*

G1423   **δυσκόλως**   adv., *with difficulty.*
    δυσκόλως   adv. {3.F} . . . . δυσκόλως G1423

G1424   **δυσμή**, -ῆς, ἡ   (1) *a setting* (of the sun); (2)
    hence, *the West;* always pl.
    δυσμῶν   noun, gen. pl. fem. {2.A} . . . . δυσμή G1424
    δυσνόητα   adj., nom. pl. neut. {3.C} . . δυσνόητος G1425

G1425   **δυσνόητος**, -ον   *hard to understand.*

G987†‡   **δυσφημέω**   pass., *I am badly spoken of, I have
    a bad reputation.* Var. for βλασφημέω, 1 Cor
    4:13.

G1426   **δυσφημία**, -ας, ἡ   *evil repute.*
    δυσφημίας   noun, gen. sg. fem. {2.A} . . δυσφημία G1426
    δυσφημούμενοι   vbl., pres. pass. ptc. nom. pl.
    masc. {6.A.2} . . . . δυσφημέω G987†‡
    δῷ   verb, ²aor. act. subjunc. 3 pers. sg. {5.B.3} δίδωμι G1325

G1427   **δώδεκα**   (1) *twelve;* (2) οἱ δώδεκα, the usual
    way in which *the Twelve* disciples of Jesus are
    referred to.
    δώδεκα   adj. num. . . . . δώδεκα G1427

G1428   **δωδέκατος**, -η, -ον   *twelfth.*
    δωδέκατος   adj., num. nom. sg. masc.
    {3.A} . . . . δωδέκατος G1428

G1429   **δωδεκάφυλον**, -ον, τό   *the twelve tribes* (of
    Israel).

δωδεκάφυλον   noun, nom. sg. neut.
    {2.B} . . . . δωδεκάφυλον G1429
δώῃ   verb, ²aor. act. opt. 3 pers. sg. {5.C.3} . . δίδωμι G1325
δώῃ   verb, ²aor. act. subjunc. 3 pers. sg. {5.B.3} . . id.

G1430   **δῶμα**, -ατος, τό   *the roof* (of a house), *the top
    of the house.*
    δῶμα   noun, acc. sg. neut. {2.C} . . . . δῶμα G1430
    δώματος   noun, gen. sg. neut. {2.C} . . . . id.
    δωμάτων   noun, gen. pl. neut. {2.C} . . . . id.
    δῶμεν   verb, ²aor. act. subjunc. 1 pers. pl.
    {5.B.3} . . . . δίδωμι G1325
    δῶρα   noun, acc. pl. neut. {2.B} . . . . δῶρον G1435
    δῶρα   noun, nom. pl. neut. {2.B} . . . . id.

G1431   **δωρεά**, -ᾶς, ἡ   *a (free) gift, a gift (without
    repayment).*
    δωρεά   noun, nom. sg. fem. {2.A} . . . . δωρεά G1431
    δωρεᾷ   noun, dat. sg. fem. {2.A} . . . . id.

G1432   **δωρεάν**   (= acc. of δωρεά used as adv.), *as a
    free gift, without payment, freely, gratis.*
    δωρεάν   adv. . . . . δωρεάν G1432
    δωρεάν   noun, acc. sg. fem. {2.A} . . . . δωρεά G1431
    δωρεᾶς   noun, gen. sg. fem. {2.A} . . . . id.

G1433   **δωρέομαι**   *I give, grant, donate.*

G1434   **δώρημα**, -ατος, τό   *a gift;* in Jas 1:17 *(of God).*
    δώρημα   noun, nom. sg. neut. {2.C} . . . . . . δώρημα G1434
    δώροις   noun, dat. pl. neut. {2.B} . . . . δῶρον G1435

G1435   **δῶρον**, -ου, τό   *a gift.*
    δῶρον   noun, acc. sg. neut. {2.B} . . . . δῶρον G1435
    δῶρον   noun, nom. sg. neut. {2.B} . . . . id.

G1248†‡   **δωροφορία**, -ας, ἡ   *bringing of a gift or offering.*
    Var. for διακονία, Rom 15:31.
    δωροφορία   noun, nom. sg. fem.
    {2.A} . . . . δωροφορία G1248†‡
    δώρῳ   noun, dat. sg. neut. {2.B} . . . . δῶρον G1435
    δῷς   verb, ²aor. act. subjunc. 2 pers. sg.
    {5.B.3} . . . . δίδωμι G1325
    δώσει   verb, fut. act. indic. 3 pers. sg. {5.A.1} . . . id.
    δώσεις   verb, fut. act. indic. 2 pers. sg. {5.A.1} . . id.
    δώσῃ   verb, aor. act. subjunc. 3 pers. sg. {5.B.3} . . id.
    δῶσιν   verb, ²aor. act. subjunc. 3 pers. pl. {5.B.3} id.
    δώσομεν   verb, fut. act. indic. 1 pers. pl. {5.A.1} . id.
    δώσουσι   verb, fut. act. indic. 3 pers. sg. {5.A.1} . id.
    δώσουσιν   verb, fut. act. indic. 3 pers. pl. {5.A.1} id.
    δώσω   verb, fut. act. indic. 1 pers. sg. {5.A.1} . . . id.
    δώσωμεν   verb, aor. act. subjunc. 1 pers. pl.
    {5.B.3} . . . . id.
    δώσωσιν   verb, aor. act. subjunc. 3 pers. pl. {5.B.3} id.
    δῶτε   verb, ²aor. act. subjunc. 2 pers. pl. {5.B.3} . . id.

E ε

G1436   **ἔα**   *ho!* Interj. implying surprise, fear and
    indignation.
    ἔα   interj. . . . . ἔα G1436

G3362‡   **ἐὰν μή**   *if not, unless,* combin. of ἐάν and μή.

G1437   **ἐάν**   (1) introducing a clause, *if,* with subjunc.,
    but 1 Thess 3:8; 1 John 5:15 have the indic.;

(2) within a clause, modifying, generalizing,
ὅς, ὅστις, ὅσος, ὁσάκις, ὅπου, οὗ (a usage
beginning about 133 B.C., exactly as ἄν does
in Attic Gk.), thus ὅς = *who,* ὅς ἐάν, *whosoever,* etc.
ἐάν   cond. part. . . . . ἐάν G1437

G1437† **ἐάνπερ**   *if indeed.* Var. for ἐάν, Heb 3:6.
ἐάνπερ   cond. part.....................ἐάνπερ G1437†
ἐᾷς   verb, pres. act. indic. 2 pers. sg. {5.A.2} . . . ἐάω G1439
ἐάσαντες   vbl., aor. act. ptc. nom. pl. masc.
   {6.A.2}................................. id.
ἐάσατε   verb, aor. act. impv. 2 pers. pl. {5.D.1} . . id.
ἐάσει   verb, fut. act. indic. 3 pers. sg. {5.A.1} . . . id.
ἐᾶτε   verb, pres. act. impv. 2 pers. pl. {5.D.2}.... id.
ἑαυτά   pron. refl., acc. pl. neut. {4.F} . . . . . ἑαυτοῦ G1438
ἑαυταῖς   pron. refl., dat. pl. fem. {4.F} . . . . id.
ἑαυτάς   pron. refl., acc. pl. fem. {4.F} . . . . id.
ἑαυτῇ   pron. refl., 3 pers. dat. sg. fem. {4.F} . . . id.
ἑαυτήν   pron. refl., 3 pers. acc. sg. fem. {4.F} . . . id.
ἑαυτῆς   pron. refl., 3 pers. gen. sg. fem. {4.F} . . . id.
ἑαυτό   pron. refl., 3 pers. acc. sg. neut. {4.F} . . . . id.
ἑαυτοῖς   pron. refl., dat. pl. masc. {4.F}. . . . . . . id.
ἑαυτόν   pron. refl., 3 pers. acc. sg. masc. {4.F} . . id.
G1438 **ἑαυτοῦ**, -ῆς, -οῦ   *self, selves; not used in*
   nom., used for all three persons, according to
   context, ourselves; yourself, yourselves; himself,
   herself, itself, themselves.
ἑαυτοῦ   pron. refl., 3 pers. gen. sg. masc.
   {4.F} . . . . ἑαυτοῦ G1438
ἑαυτοῦ   pron. refl., 3 pers. gen. sg. neut. {4.F} . . id.
ἑαυτούς   pron. refl., acc. pl. masc. {4.F} . . . . id.
ἑαυτῷ   pron. refl., 3 pers. dat. sg. masc. {4.F} . . . id.
ἑαυτῶν   pron. refl., gen. pl. fem. {4.F} . . . . id.
ἑαυτῶν   pron. refl., gen. pl. masc. {4.F} . . . . id.
ἑαυτῶν   pron. refl., gen. pl. neut. {4.F} . . . . id.
G1439 **ἐάω**   *I allow, permit, leave.*
ἐβάθυνε   verb, aor. act. indic. 3 pers. sg.
   {5.A.1.b} . . . . βαθύνω G900
ἐβάθυνεν   verb, aor. act. indic. 3 pers. sg.
   {5.A.1.b} . . . . id.
ἔβαλαν   verb, ²aor. act. indic. 3 pers. pl.
   {5.A.1.b} . . . . βάλλω G906
ἔβαλε   verb, ²aor. act. indic. 3 pers. sg. {5.A.1.b} . id.
ἔβαλεν   verb, ²aor. act. indic. 3 pers. sg. {5.A.1.b} id.
ἔβαλλον   verb, impf. act. indic. 3 pers. pl.
   {5.A.1.b} . . . . id.
ἔβαλον   verb, ²aor. act. indic. 3 pers. pl. {5.A.1.b} id.
ἐβάπτιζεν   verb, impf. act. indic. 3 pers. sg.
   {5.A.1.b} . . . . βαπτίζω G907
ἐβαπτίζοντο   verb, impf. pass. indic. 3 pers. pl.
   {5.A.1.e} . . . . id.
ἐβάπτισα   verb, aor. act. indic. 1 pers. sg.
   {5.A.1.b} . . . . id.
ἐβαπτίσαντο   verb, aor. mid. indic. 3 pers. pl.
   {5.A.1.e} . . . . id.
ἐβάπτισε   verb, aor. act. indic. 3 pers. sg.
   {5.A.1.b} . . . . id.
ἐβάπτισεν   verb, aor. act. indic. 3 pers. sg.
   {5.A.1.b} . . . . id.
ἐβαπτίσθη   verb, aor. pass. indic. 3 pers. sg.
   {5.A.1.b} . . . . id.
ἐβαπτίσθημεν   verb, aor. pass. indic. 1 pers. pl.
   {5.A.1.b} . . . . id.
ἐβαπτίσθησαν   verb, aor. pass. indic. 3 pers.
   pl. {5.A.1.b} . . . . id.

ἐβαπτίσθητε   verb, aor. pass. indic. 2 pers. pl.
   {5.A.1.b} . . . . id.
ἐβαρήθημεν   verb, aor. pass. indic. 1 pers. pl.
   {5.A.1} . . . . .βαρέω G916
ἐβασάνιζεν   verb, impf. act. indic. 3 pers. sg.
   {5.A.1.b} . . . . βασανίζω G928
ἐβασάνισαν   verb, aor. act. indic. 3 pers. pl.
   {5.A.1.b} . . . . id.
ἐβασίλευσαν   verb, aor. act. indic. 3 pers. pl.
   {5.A.1.b} . . . . .βασιλεύω G936
ἐβασίλευσας   verb, aor. act. indic. 2 pers. sg.
   {5.A.1.b} . . . . id.
ἐβασιλεύσατε   verb, aor. act. indic. 2 pers. pl.
   {5.A.1.b} . . . . id.
ἐβασίλευσε   verb, aor. act. indic. 3 pers. sg.
   {5.A.1.b} . . . . id.
ἐβασίλευσεν   verb, aor. act. indic. 3 pers. sg.
   {5.A.1.b} . . . . id.
ἐβάσκανε   verb, aor. act. indic. 3 pers. sg.
   {5.A.1.b} . . . . βασκαίνω G940
ἐβάσκανεν   verb, aor. act. indic. 3 pers. sg.
   {5.A.1.b} . . . . id.
ἐβάσταζεν   verb, impf. act. indic. 3 pers. sg.
   {5.A.1.b} . . . . βαστάζω G941
ἐβαστάζετο   verb, impf. pass. indic. 3 pers. sg.
   {5.A.1.e} . . . . id.
ἐβάστασαν   verb, aor. act. indic. 3 pers. pl.
   {5.A.1.b} . . . . id.
ἐβάστασας   verb, aor. act. indic. 2 pers. sg.
   {5.A.1.b} . . . . id.
ἐβάστασεν   verb, aor. act. indic. 3 pers. sg.
   {5.A.1.b} . . . . id.
ἐβδελυγμένοις   vbl., perf. pass. ptc. dat. pl. masc.
   {6.A.1.b} . . . . .βδελύσσομαι G948
ἑβδόμη   adj., dat. sg. fem. {3.A} . . . . ἕβδομος G1442
G1440 **ἑβδομήκοντα**   *seventy.*
ἑβδομήκοντα   adj. num. . . . . .ἑβδομήκοντα G1440
G1441 **ἑβδομηκοντάκις**   *seventy times.*
ἑβδομηκοντάκις   adv. . . . . ἑβδομηκοντάκις G1441
ἑβδόμην   adj., acc. sg. fem. {3.A} . . . . . . ἕβδομος G1442
ἑβδόμης   adj., gen. sg. fem. {3.A} . . . . id.
G1442 **ἕβδομος**, -η, -ον   *seventh.*
ἕβδομος   adj., nom. sg. masc. {3.A} . . . . . ἕβδομος G1442
ἑβδόμου   adj., gen. sg. masc. {3.A} . . . . id.
ἐβεβαιώθη   verb, aor. pass. indic. 3 pers. sg.
   {5.A.1} . . . . .βεβαιόω G950
ἐβέβλητο   verb, plu. pass. indic. 3 pers. sg.
   {5.A.1.e} . . . . βάλλω G906
G1443 **Ἔβερ**, ὁ   *Eber, father of Phalek and son of Sala*
   (Heb.).
Ἔβερ   noun prop. . . . . .Ἔβερ G1443
Ἑβέρ   noun prop. . . . . id.
ἐβλάστησε   verb, aor. act. indic. 3 pers. sg.
   {5.A.1.b} . . . . βλαστάνω G985
ἐβλάστησεν   verb, aor. act. indic. 3 pers. sg.
   {5.A.1.b} . . . . id.
ἐβλασφήμει   verb, impf. act. indic. 3 pers. sg.
   {5.A.2} . . . . .βλασφημέω G987
ἐβλασφήμησαν   verb, aor. act. indic. 3 pers. pl.
   {5.A.1} . . . . id.

ἐβλασφήμησεν   verb, aor. act. indic. 3 pers. sg.
{5.A.1}. . . . . id.
ἐβλασφήμουν   verb, impf. act. indic. 3 pers. pl.
{5.A.2}. . . . . id.
ἔβλεπε   verb, impf. act. indic. 3 pers. sg.
{5.A.1.b} . . . . .βλέπω G991
ἔβλεπεν   verb, impf. act. indic. 3 pers. sg.
{5.A.1.b} . . . . id.
ἔβλεπον   verb, impf. act. indic. 3 pers. pl.
{5.A.1.b} . . . . id.
ἔβλεψα   verb, aor. act. indic. 1 pers. sg. {5.A.1.b} id.
ἐβλήθη   verb, aor. pass. indic. 3 pers. sg.
{5.A.1.b} . . . . βάλλω G906
ἐβλήθησαν   verb, aor. pass. indic. 3 pers. pl.
{5.A.1.b} . . . . id.
ἐβοήθησα   verb, aor. act. indic. 1 pers. sg.
{5.A.1}. . . . . .βοηθέω G997
ἐβοήθησεν   verb, aor. act. indic. 3 pers. sg.
{5.A.1}. . . . . id.
ἐβόησε   verb, aor. act. indic. 3 pers. sg. {5.A.1} βοάω G994
ἐβόησεν   verb, aor. act. indic. 3 pers. sg. {5.A.1}. id.
ἐβούλετο   verb, impf. mid./pass. indic. 3 pers. sg.
{5.A.1.e} . . . . βούλομαι G1014
ἐβουλεύοντο   verb, impf. mid./pass. indic. 3 pers.
pl. {5.A.1.e} . . . . .βουλεύω G1011
ἐβουλεύσαντο   verb, aor. mid. indic. 3 pers. pl.
{5.A.1.e} . . . . id.
ἐβουλεύσατο   verb, aor. mid. indic. 3 pers. sg.
{5.A.1.e} . . . . id.
ἐβουλήθη   verb, aor. pass. indic. 3 pers. sg.
{5.A.1.b} . . . . βούλομαι G1014
ἐβουλήθην   verb, aor. pass. indic. 1 pers. sg.
{5.A.1.b} . . . . id.
ἐβουλόμην   verb, impf. mid./pass. indic.
1 pers. sg. {5.A.1.e} . . . . id.
ἐβούλοντο   verb, impf. mid./pass. indic. 3 pers.
pl. {5.A.1.e} . . . . id.
ἐβόων   verb, impf. act. indic. 3 pers. pl. {5.A.2} βοάω G994
Ἑβραΐδι   noun prop., dat. sg. fem. {2.C;
2.D}. . . . . Ἑβραΐς G1446
Ἑβραΐδι   noun prop., dat. sg. fem. {2.C; 2.D} . . . id.
Ἑβραϊκοῖς   adj. prop., dat. pl. neut.
{3.A} . . . . Ἑβραϊκός G1444
G1444 Ἑβραϊκός, -ή, -όν   Hebrew.
Ἑβραῖοι   noun prop., nom. pl. masc.
{3.A} . . . . Ἑβραῖος G1445
Ἑβραῖος   noun prop., nom. sg. masc. {3.A} . . . . id.
G1445 Ἑβραῖος, -ου, ὁ   a Hebrew, particularly one
who speaks Hebrew (Aramaic), cf. Acts 6:1;
Ἑβραῖος ἐξ Ἑβραίων, a Hebrew descended
from Hebrews (Phil 3:5).
Ἑβραῖος   noun prop., nom. sg. masc.
{3.A} . . . . Ἑβραῖος G1445
Ἑβραίους   noun prop., acc. pl. masc. {3.A} . . . . id.
Ἑβραίους   noun prop., acc. pl. masc. {3.A} . . . . id.
G1446 Ἑβραΐς, ίδος, ἡ   Hebrew, or rather Aramaic.
Ἑβραϊστί   adv. prop. . . . . Ἑβραϊστί G1447
G1447 Ἑβραϊστί   adv., in the Hebrew, or rather, in the
Aramaic dialect.
Ἑβραϊστί   adv. prop. . . . . Ἑβραϊστί G1447

Ἑβραίων   noun prop., gen. pl. masc.
{3.A} . . . . Ἑβραῖος G1445
Ἑβραίων   noun prop., gen. pl. masc. {3.A} . . . . id.
ἔβρεξε   verb, aor. act. indic. 3 pers. sg.
{5.A.1.b} . . . . βρέχω G1026
ἔβρεξεν   verb, aor. act. indic. 3 pers. sg. {5.A.1.b} id.
ἔβρυχον   verb, impf. act. indic. 3 pers. pl.
{5.A.1.b} . . . . βρύχω G1031
ἐγάμησεν   verb, aor. act. indic. 3 pers. sg.
{5.A.1}. . . . . γαμέω G1060
ἐγαμίζοντο   verb, impf. pass. indic. 3 pers. pl.
{5.A.1.e} . . . . γαμίζω G1061
ἐγάμουν   verb, impf. act. indic. 3 pers. pl.
{5.A.2}. . . . . γαμέω G1060
ἐγγεγραμμένη   vbl., perf. pass. ptc. nom. sg. fem.
{6.A.1.b} . . . . ἐγγράφω G1449
ἐγγέγραπται   verb, perf. pass. indic. 3 pers. sg.
{5.A.1.f}. . . . . id.
ἐγγιεῖ   verb, fut. act. indic. 3 pers. sg. {5.A.2}. ἐγγίζω G1448
ἐγγίζει   verb, pres. act. indic. 3 pers. sg. {5.A.1.a} id.
ἐγγίζειν   vbl., pres. act. inf. {6.B.1} . . . . id.
ἐγγίζομεν   verb, pres. act. indic. 1 pers. pl.
{5.A.1.a} . . . . id.
ἐγγίζοντες   vbl., pres. act. ptc. nom. pl. masc.
{6.A.1} . . . . id.
ἐγγίζοντι   vbl., pres. act. ptc. dat. sg. masc.
{6.A.1} . . . . id.
ἐγγίζοντος   vbl., pres. act. ptc. gen. sg. masc.
{6.A.1} . . . . id.
ἐγγιζόντων   vbl., pres. act. ptc. gen. pl. masc.
{6.A.1} . . . . id.
ἐγγίζουσαν   vbl., pres. act. ptc. acc. sg. fem.
{6.A.1} . . . . id.
ἐγγίζουσιν   verb, pres. act. indic. 3 pers. pl.
{5.A.1.a} . . . . id.
G1448 ἐγγίζω   I come near, approach.
ἐγγίσαι   vbl., aor. act. inf. {6.B.1} . . . . ἐγγίζω G1448
ἐγγίσαντος   vbl., aor. act. ptc. gen. sg. masc.
{6.A.1.a} . . . . id.
ἐγγίσας   vbl., aor. act. ptc. nom. sg. masc.
{6.A.1.a} . . . . id.
ἐγγίσατε   verb, aor. act. impv. 2 pers. pl. {5.D.1} . id.
ἐγγίσει   verb, fut. act. indic. 3 pers. sg. {5.A.1.a} . id.
G1449 ἐγγράφω   I write (in), inscribe.
G1450 ἔγγυος, -ου, ὁ   a surety, security.
ἔγγυος   adj., nom. sg. masc. {3.A} . . . . ἔγγυος G1450
G1451 ἐγγύς   adv., near; comp. ἐγγύτερον, nearer;
superl. ἔγγιστα, nearest.
ἐγγύς   adv.. . . . . ἐγγύς G1451
G1452 ἐγγύτερον   adv., nearer (comp. of ἐγγύς).
ἐγγύτερον   adv. comp. {3.F; 3.G}. . . . . . ἐγγύτερον G1452
ἐγεγόνει   verb, plu. act. indic. 3 pers. sg.
{5.A.1.b} . . . . γίνομαι G1096
ἔγειραι   verb, aor. mid. impv. 2 pers. sg.
{5.D.1}. . . . . ἐγείρω G1453
ἐγεῖραι   vbl., aor. act. inf. {6.B.1}. . . . . id.
ἐγείραντα   vbl., aor. act. ptc. acc. sg. masc.
{6.A.1.a} . . . . id.
ἐγείραντος   vbl., aor. act. ptc. gen. sg. masc.
{6.A.1.a} . . . . id.

ἐγείρας   vbl., aor. act. ptc. nom. sg. masc.
{6.A.1.a} . . . . id.
ἔγειρε   verb, pres. act. impv. 2 pers. sg. {5.D.1} . . id.
ἐγείρει   verb, pres. act. indic. 3 pers. sg. {5.A.1.a} id.
ἐγείρειν   vbl., pres. act. inf. {6.B.1} . . . . id.
ἐγείρεσθε   verb, pres. mid./pass. impv. 2 pers.
pl. {5.D.1} . . . . id.
ἐγείρεται   verb, pres. pass. indic. 3 pers. sg.
{5.A.1.d} . . . . id.
ἐγείρετε   verb, pres. act. impv. 2 pers. pl. {5.D.1} . id.
ἐγείρηται   verb, pres. pass. subjunc. 3 pers. sg.
{5.B.1} . . . . id.
ἐγείρομαι   verb, pres. pass. indic. 1 pers. sg.
{5.A.1.d} . . . . id.
ἐγείρονται   verb, pres. pass. indic. 3 pers. pl.
{5.A.1.d} . . . . id.
ἐγείροντι   vbl., pres. act. ptc. dat. sg. masc.
{6.A.1} . . . . id.
ἐγείρου   verb, pres. mid./pass. impv. 2 pers. sg.
{5.D.1} . . . . id.
ἐγείρουσιν   verb, pres. act. indic. 3 pers. pl.
{5.A.1.a} . . . . id.
G1453 **ἐγείρω**   (1) *I wake, arouse;* intrans. in impv.,
ἔγειρε, ἐγείρεσθε, *wake up!;* (2) *I raise up;*
pass. some times = *I rise,* e.g., Mark 16:6.
ἐγέμισαν   verb, aor. act. indic. 3 pers. pl.
{5.A.1.b} . . . . γεμίζω G1072
ἐγέμισεν   verb, aor. act. indic. 3 pers. sg.
{5.A.1.b} . . . . id.
ἐγεμίσθη   verb, aor. pass. indic. 3 pers. sg.
{5.A.1.b} . . . . id.
ἐγένεσθε   verb, ²aor. mid. indic. 2 pers. pl.
{5.A.1.e} . . . . γίνομαι G1096
ἐγένετο   verb, ²aor. mid. indic. 3 pers. sg.
{5.A.1.e} . . . . id.
ἐγενήθη   verb, aor. pass. indic. 3 pers. sg.
{5.A.1.b} . . . . id.
ἐγενήθημεν   verb, aor. pass. indic. 1 pers. pl.
{5.A.1.b} . . . . id.
ἐγενήθην   verb, aor. pass. indic. 1 pers. sg.
{5.A.1.b} . . . . id.
ἐγενήθησαν   verb, aor. pass. indic. 3 pers. pl.
{5.A.1.b} . . . . id.
ἐγενήθητε   verb, aor. pass. indic. 2 pers. pl.
{5.A.1.b} . . . . id.
ἐγεννήθη   verb, aor. pass. indic. 3 pers. sg.
{5.A.1} . . . . γεννάω G1080
ἐγεννήθημεν   verb, aor. pass. indic. 1 pers. pl.
{5.A.1} . . . . id.
ἐγεννήθης   verb, aor. pass. indic. 2 pers. sg.
{5.A.1} . . . . id.
ἐγεννήθησαν   verb, aor. pass. indic. 3 pers. pl.
{5.A.1} . . . . id.
ἐγέννησα   verb, aor. act. indic. 1 pers. sg. {5.A.1} id.
ἐγέννησαν   verb, aor. act. indic. 3 pers. pl.
{5.A.1} . . . . id.
ἐγέννησε   verb, aor. act. indic. 3 pers. sg. {5.A.1} id.
ἐγέννησεν   verb, aor. act. indic. 3 pers. sg. {5.A.1} id.
ἐγενόμην   verb, ²aor. mid. indic. 1 pers. sg.
{5.A.1.e} . . . . γίνομαι G1096

ἐγένοντο   verb, ²aor. mid. indic. 3 pers. pl.
{5.A.1.e} . . . . id.
ἐγένου   verb, ²aor. mid. indic. 2 pers. sg. {5.A.1.e} id.
ἐγερεῖ   verb, fut. act. indic. 3 pers. sg. {5.A.2} ἐγείρω G1453
ἐγερεῖς   verb, fut. act. indic. 2 pers. sg. {5.A.2} . . id.
ἐγερθείς   vbl., aor. pass. ptc. nom. sg. masc.
{6.A.1.a} . . . . id.
ἐγερθέντι   vbl., aor. pass. ptc. dat. sg. masc.
{6.A.1.a} . . . . id.
ἐγερθῇ   verb, aor. pass. subjunc. 3 pers. sg. {5.B.1} . id.
ἐγερθῆναι   vbl., aor. pass. inf. {6.B.1} . . . . id.
ἐγερθήσεται   verb, fut. pass. indic. 3 pers. sg.
{5.A.1.d} . . . . id.
ἐγερθήσονται   verb, fut. pass. indic. 3 pers. pl.
{5.A.1.d} . . . . id.
ἐγέρθητε   verb, aor. pass. impv. 2 pers. pl. {5.D.1} id.
ἐγέρθητι   verb, aor. pass. impv. 2 pers. sg. {5.D.1} id.
ἔγερσιν   noun, acc. sg. fem. {2.C} . . . . ἔγερσις G1454
G1454 **ἔγερσις**, -εως, ἡ   *a waking up.*
ἐγερῶ   verb, fut. act. indic. 1 pers. sg. {5.A.2} ἐγείρω G1453
ἐγεύσασθε   verb, aor. mid. indic. 2 pers. pl.
{5.A.1.e} . . . . γεύομαι G1089
ἐγεύσατο   verb, aor. mid. indic. 3 pers. sg.
{5.A.1.e} . . . . id.
ἐγηγερμένον   vbl., perf. pass. ptc. acc. sg. masc.
{6.A.1.b} . . . . ἐγείρω G1453
ἐγήγερται   verb, perf. pass. indic. 3 pers. sg.
{5.A.1.f} . . . . id.
ἔγημα   verb, aor. act. indic. 1 pers. sg. {5.A.1} γαμέω G1060
ἐγίνετο   verb, impf. mid./pass. indic. 3 pers. sg.
{5.A.1.e} . . . . γίνομαι G1096
ἐγίνωσκε   verb, impf. act. indic. 3 pers. sg.
{5.A.1.b} . . . . γινώσκω G1097
ἐγίνωσκεν   verb, impf. act. indic. 3 pers. sg.
{5.A.1.b} . . . . id.
ἐγίνωσκον   verb, impf. act. indic. 3 pers. pl.
{5.A.1.b} . . . . id.
G1455 **ἐγκάθετος**, -ου, ὁ   *a snare setter, spy.*
ἐγκαθέτους   adj., acc. pl. masc. {3.C} . . . ἐγκάθετος G1455
G1456 **ἐγκαίνια**, -ίων, τά   *festival of dedication* of the
Temple, to celebrate the rededication of the
Temple by Judas Maccabeus in 164 B.C., held
at Jerusalem about the middle of December.
ἐγκαίνια   noun, nom. pl. neut. {2.B} . . . . ἐγκαίνια G1456
G1457 **ἐγκαινίζω**   (*I restore or carry out anew,* then) *I
dedicate.*
ἐγκακεῖν   vbl., pres. act. inf. {6.B.2} . . . . . ἐκκακέω G1573
ἐγκακήσητε   verb, aor. act. subjunc. 2 pers. pl.
{5.B.1} . . . . id.
ἐγκακοῦμεν   verb, pres. act. indic. 1 pers. pl.
{5.A.2} . . . . id.
ἐγκακῶμεν   verb, pres. act. subjunc. 1 pers. pl.
{5.B.2} . . . . id.
ἐγκαλεῖσθαι   vbl., pres. pass. inf. {6.B.2} . ἐγκαλέω G1458
ἐγκαλείτωσαν   verb, pres. act. impv. 3 pers. pl.
{5.D.2} . . . . id.
ἐγκαλέσει   verb, fut. act. indic. 3 pers. sg. {5.A.1} id.
G1458 **ἐγκαλέω**   *I bring a charge against.*
ἐγκαλοῦμαι   verb, pres. pass. indic. 1 pers. sg.
{5.A.2} . . . . ἐγκαλέω G1458

ἐγκαλούμενον   vbl., pres. pass. ptc. acc. sg.
    masc. {6.A.2} . . . . id.

ἐγκαταλειπόμενοι   vbl., pres. pass. ptc. nom. pl.
    masc. {6.A.1} . . . . ἐγκαταλείπω G1459

ἐγκαταλείποντες   vbl., pres. act. ptc. nom. pl.
    masc. {6.A.1} . . . . id.

G1459   **ἐγκαταλείπω**   *I leave in the lurch, I abandon*
    (one who is in straits), *I desert.*

ἐγκαταλείπω   verb, pres. act. subjunc. 1 pers. sg.
    {5.B.1} . . . . ἐγκαταλείπω G1459

ἐγκαταλείψεις   verb, fut. act. indic. 2 pers. sg.
    {5.A.1.a} . . . . id.

ἐγκαταλίπω   verb, ²aor. act. subjunc. 1 pers. sg.
    {5.B.1} . . . . id.

ἐγκατέλειπεν   verb, impf. act. indic. 3 pers. sg.
    {5.A.1.b} . . . . id.

ἐγκατέλειπον   verb, impf. act. indic. 3 pers. pl.
    {5.A.1.b} . . . . id.

ἐγκατελείφθη   verb, aor. pass. indic. 3 pers. sg.
    {5.A.1.b} . . . . id.

ἐγκατέλιπεν   verb, ²aor. act. indic. 3 pers. sg.
    {5.A.1.b} . . . . id.

ἐγκατέλιπες   verb, ²aor. act. indic. 2 pers. sg.
    {5.A.1.b} . . . . id.

ἐγκατέλιπον   verb, ²aor. act. indic. 3 pers. pl.
    {5.A.1.b} . . . . id.

G1460   **ἐγκατοικέω**   *I am settled among, dwell among.*

ἐγκατοικῶν   vbl., pres. act. ptc. nom. sg. masc.
    {6.A.2} . . . . ἐγκατοικέω G1460

G2744†‡ **ἐγκαυχάομαι**   *I boast in (because of) some-*
    thing. Var. for καυχάομαι, 2 Thess. 1:4.

ἐγκαυχᾶσθαι   vbl., pres. mid./pass. inf.
    {6.B.2} . . . . ἐγκαυχάομαι G2744†‡

ἐγκεκαίνισται   verb, perf. pass. indic. 3 pers. sg.
    {5.A.1.f} . . . . ἐγκαινίζω G1457

G1461   **ἐγκεντρίζω**   *I graft.*

ἐγκεντρίσαι   vbl., aor. act. inf. {6.B.1} . . ἐγκεντρίζω G1461

ἐγκεντρισθήσονται   verb, fut. pass. indic.
    3 pers. pl. {5.A.1.d} . . . . id.

ἐγκεντρισθῶ   verb, aor. pass. subjunc. 1 pers.
    sg. {5.B.1} . . . . id.

G1462   **ἔγκλημα**, -ατος, τό   *an accusation, charge.*

ἔγκλημα   noun, acc. sg. neut. {2.C} . . . . . ἔγκλημα G1462

ἐγκλήματος   noun, gen. sg. neut. {2.C} . . . . . . id.

G1463   **ἐγκομβόομαι**   *I clothe myself* (orig., *I tie round*
    in a knot).

ἐγκομβώσασθε   verb, aor. mid. impv. 2 pers. pl.
    {5.D.1} . . . . ἐγκομβόομαι G1463

G1464   **ἐγκοπή** (ἐκκοπή), -ῆς, ἡ   *a block, check,*
    obstacle, hindrance.

ἐγκοπήν   noun, acc. sg. fem. {2.A} . . . . . . ἐγκοπή G1464

ἐγκόπτεσθαι   vbl., pres. pass. inf. {6.B.1} . ἐγκόπτω G1465

G1465   **ἐγκόπτω**   *I block, check, hinder* (by introduc-
    ing an obstacle sharply in the way of a moving
    object).

ἐγκόπτω   verb, pres. act. subjunc. 1 pers. sg.
    {5.B.1} . . . . ἐγκόπτω G1465

G1466   **ἐγκράτεια**, -ας, ἡ   *self-mastery, self-restraint,*
    self-control, continence.

ἐγκράτεια   noun, nom. sg. fem. {2.A} . . . ἐγκράτεια G1466

ἐγκρατεία   noun, dat. sg. fem. {2.A} . . . . id.

ἐγκράτειαν   noun, acc. sg. fem. {2.A} . . . . id.

ἐγκρατείας   noun, gen. sg. fem. {2.A} . . . . id.

ἐγκρατεύεται   verb, pres. mid./pass. indic. 3 pers.
    sg. {5.A.1.d} . . . . ἐγκρατεύομαι G1467

G1467   **ἐγκρατεύομαι**   *I exercise self-control, I am*
    continent.

ἐγκρατεύονται   verb, pres. mid./pass. indic. 3 pers.
    pl. {5.A.1.d} . . . . ἐγκρατεύομαι G1467

ἐγκρατή   adj., acc. sg. masc. {3.E} . . . . . . ἐγκρατής G1468

G1468   **ἐγκρατής**, -ές   *self-controlled.*

ἐγκρῖναι   vbl., aor. act. inf. {6.B.1} . . . . . . ἐγκρίνω G1469

G1469   **ἐγκρίνω**   *I judge (reckon) to belong to, I class with.*

G1470   **ἐγκρύπτω**   *I hide (within).*

G1471   **ἔγκυος**, -ον   *pregnant.*

ἐγκύῳ   adj., dat. sg. fem. {2.B} . . . . ἔγκυος G1471

ἔγνω   verb, ²aor. act. indic. 3 pers. sg.
    {5.A.1.b} . . . . γινώσκω G1097

ἔγνωκα   verb, perf. act. indic. 1 pers. sg. {5.A.1.c}id.

ἐγνώκαμεν   verb, perf. act. indic. 1 pers. pl.
    {5.A.1.c} . . . . id.

ἔγνωκαν   verb, perf. act. indic. 3 pers. pl.
    {5.A.1.c} . . . . id.

ἔγνωκας   verb, perf. act. indic. 2 pers. sg.
    {5.A.1.c} . . . . id.

ἐγνώκατε   verb, perf. act. indic. 2 pers. pl.
    {5.A.1.c} . . . . id.

ἔγνωκε   verb, perf. act. indic. 3 pers. sg. {5.A.1.c} id.

ἐγνώκειτε   verb, plu. act. indic. 2 pers. pl.
    {5.A.1.b} . . . . id.

ἔγνωκεν   verb, perf. act. indic. 3 pers. sg.
    {5.A.1.c} . . . . id.

ἐγνωκέναι   vbl., perf. act. inf. {6.B.1} . . . . id.

ἐγνωκότες   vbl., perf. act. ptc. nom. pl. masc.
    {6.A.1.a} . . . . id.

ἔγνων   verb, ²aor. act. indic. 1 pers. sg. {5.A.1.b} . id.

ἐγνώρισα   verb, aor. act. indic. 1 pers. sg.
    {5.A.1.b} . . . . γνωρίζω G1107

ἐγνωρίσαμεν   verb, aor. act. indic. 1 pers. pl.
    {5.A.1.b} . . . . id.

ἐγνώρισαν   verb, aor. act. indic. 3 pers. pl.
    {5.A.1.b} . . . . id.

ἐγνώρισας   verb, aor. act. indic. 2 pers. sg.
    {5.A.1.b} . . . . id.

ἐγνώρισε   verb, aor. act. indic. 3 pers. sg.
    {5.A.1.b} . . . . id.

ἐγνώρισεν   verb, aor. act. indic. 3 pers. sg.
    {5.A.1.b} . . . . id.

ἐγνωρίσθη   verb, aor. pass. indic. 3 pers. sg.
    {5.A.1.b} . . . . id.

ἔγνως   verb, ²aor. act. indic. 2 pers. sg.
    {5.A.1.b} . . . . γινώσκω G1097

ἔγνωσαν   verb, ²aor. act. indic. 3 pers. pl.
    {5.A.1.b} . . . . id.

ἐγνώσθη   verb, ²aor. pass. indic. 3 pers. sg.
    {5.A.1.e} . . . . id.

ἔγνωσται   verb, perf. pass. indic. 3 pers. sg.
    {5.A.1.f} . . . . id.

ἐγόγγυζον   verb, impf. act. indic. 3 pers. pl.
    {5.A.1.b} . . . . γογγύζω G1111

ἐγόγγυσαν   verb, aor. act. indic. 3 pers. pl.
    {5.A.1.b} . . . . id.
ἔγραφεν   verb, impf. act. indic. 3 pers. sg.
    {5.A.1.b} . . . . γράφω G1125
ἐγράφη   verb, ²aor. pass. indic. 3 pers. sg.
    {5.A.1.e} . . . . id.
ἔγραψα   verb, aor. act. indic. 1 pers. sg. {5.A.1.b} id.
ἔγραψαν   verb, aor. act. indic. 3 pers. pl.
    {5.A.1.b} . . . . id.
ἐγράψατε   verb, aor. act. indic. 2 pers. pl.
    {5.A.1.b} . . . . id.
ἔγραψε   verb, aor. act. indic. 3 pers. sg. {5.A.1.b} id.
ἔγραψεν   verb, aor. act. indic. 3 pers. sg.
    {5.A.1.b} . . . . id.
ἐγρηγόρησεν   verb, aor. act. indic. 3 pers. sg.
    {5.A.1} . . . . γρηγορέω G1127
ἐγχρῖσαι   vbl., aor. act. inf. {6.B.1} . . . . ἐγχρίω G1472
ἐγχρίσῃ   verb, aor. act. subjunc. 3 pers. sg.
    {5.B.1} . . . . id.
ἔγχρισον   verb, aor. act. impv. 2 pers. sg. {5.D.1} id.
G1472 **ἐγχρίω**   I besmear, anoint.
G1473 **ἐγώ**   First pers. pron., I, me; pl. ἡμεῖς; τί ἐμοὶ
    (ἡμῖν) καὶ σοί; What have I (we) to do with
    thee?, but in John 2:4 ἐμοὶ καὶ σοί may be
    simply equal to ἡμῖν; τὸ (τὰ) κατ᾽ ἐμέ, so
    far as I am concerned; in letters ἡμεῖς often
    alternates with ἐγώ without real difference of
    meaning.
ἐγώ   pron. pers., 1 pers. nom. sg. {4.A} . . . . . . ἐγώ G1473
ἐδάκρυσεν   verb, aor. act. indic. 3 pers. sg.
    {5.A.1.b} . . . . δακρύω G1145
G1474 **ἐδαφίζω**   I dash to the ground.
ἐδαφιοῦσί   verb, fut. act. indic. 3 pers. pl.
    {5.A.2} . . . . ἐδαφίζω G1474
ἐδαφιοῦσίν   verb, fut. act. indic. 3 pers. pl.
    {5.A.2} . . . . id.
G1475 **ἔδαφος, -ους, τό**   ground.
ἔδαφος   noun, acc. sg. neut. {2.C} . . . . ἔδαφος G1475
ἐδέετο   verb, impf. mid./pass. indic. 3 pers. sg.
    {5.A.2} . . . . δέομαι G1189
ἐδεήθη   verb, aor. pass. indic. 3 pers. sg. {5.A.1} . id.
ἐδεήθην   verb, aor. pass. indic. 1 pers. sg. {5.A.1} id.
ἔδει   verb, impf. act. indic. 3 pers. sg. {5.A.1.b} . . δεῖ G1163
ἐδειγμάτισεν   verb, aor. act. indic. 3 pers. sg.
    {5.A.1.b} . . . . δειγματίζω G1165
ἔδειξα   verb, aor. act. indic. 1 pers. sg.
    {5.A.1.b} . . . . δείκνυμι G1166
ἔδειξε   verb, aor. act. indic. 3 pers. sg. {5.A.1.b} . id.
ἔδειξεν   verb, aor. act. indic. 3 pers. sg. {5.A.1.b} id.
ἔδειραν   verb, aor. act. indic. 3 pers. pl.
    {5.A.1.b} . . . . δέρω G1194
ἐδεῖτο   verb, impf. mid./pass. indic. 3 pers. sg.
    {5.A.2} . . . . δέομαι G1189
ἐδεξάμεθα   verb, aor. mid. indic. 1 pers. pl.
    {5.A.1.e} . . . . δέχομαι G1209
ἐδέξαντο   verb, aor. mid. indic. 3 pers. pl.
    {5.A.1.e} . . . . id.
ἐδέξασθε   verb, aor. mid. indic. 2 pers. pl.
    {5.A.1.e} . . . . id.

ἐδέξατο   verb, aor. mid. indic. 3 pers. sg.
    {5.A.1.e} . . . . id.
ἐδεσμεῖτο   verb, impf. pass. indic. 3 pers. sg.
    {5.A.2} . . . . δεσμέω G1196
ἐδεσμεύετο   verb, impf. pass. indic. 3 pers. sg.
    {5.A.1.e} . . . . δεσμεύω G1195
ἐδήλου   verb, impf. act. indic. 3 pers. sg.
    {5.A.2} . . . . δηλόω G1213
ἐδηλώθη   verb, aor. pass. indic. 3 pers. sg.
    {5.A.1} . . . . id.
ἐδήλωσε   verb, aor. act. indic. 3 pers. sg. {5.A.1} id.
ἐδήλωσεν   verb, aor. act. indic. 3 pers. sg.
    {5.A.1} . . . . id.
ἐδημηγόρει   verb, impf. act. indic. 3 pers. sg.
    {5.A.2} . . . . δημηγορέω G1215
ἔδησαν   verb, aor. act. indic. 3 pers. pl. {5.A.1}. δέω G1210
ἔδησεν   verb, aor. act. indic. 3 pers. sg. {5.A.1} . . id.
ἐδίδαξα   verb, aor. act. indic. 1 pers. sg.
    {5.A.1.b} . . . . διδάσκω G1321
ἐδίδαξαν   verb, aor. act. indic. 3 pers. pl.
    {5.A.1.b} . . . . id.
ἐδίδαξας   verb, aor. act. indic. 2 pers. sg.
    {5.A.1.b} . . . . id.
ἐδίδαξε   verb, aor. act. indic. 3 pers. sg. {5.A.1.b} id.
ἐδίδαξεν   verb, aor. act. indic. 3 pers. sg.
    {5.A.1.b} . . . . id.
ἐδίδασκε   verb, impf. act. indic. 3 pers. sg.
    {5.A.1.b} . . . . id.
ἐδίδασκεν   verb, impf. act. indic. 3 pers. sg.
    {5.A.1.b} . . . . id.
ἐδίδασκον   verb, impf. act. indic. 3 pers. pl.
    {5.A.1.b} . . . . id.
ἐδιδάχθην   verb, aor. pass. indic. 1 pers. sg.
    {5.A.1.b} . . . . id.
ἐδιδάχθησαν   verb, aor. pass. indic. 3 pers. pl.
    {5.A.1.b} . . . . id.
ἐδιδάχθητε   verb, aor. pass. indic. 2 pers. pl.
    {5.A.1.b} . . . . id.
ἐδίδοσαν   verb, impf. act. indic. 3 pers. pl.
    {5.A.3.a} . . . . δίδωμι G1325
ἐδίδου   verb, impf. act. indic. 3 pers. sg. {5.A.3.a} id.
ἐδίδουν   verb, impf. act. indic. 3 pers. pl.
    {5.A.3.a} . . . . id.
ἐδικαιώθη   verb, aor. pass. indic. 3 pers. sg.
    {5.A.1} . . . . δικαιόω G1344
ἐδικαιώθητε   verb, aor. pass. indic. 2 pers. pl.
    {5.A.1} . . . . id.
ἐδικαίωσαν   verb, aor. act. indic. 3 pers. pl.
    {5.A.1} . . . . id.
ἐδικαίωσε   verb, aor. act. indic. 3 pers. sg.
    {5.A.1} . . . . id.
ἐδικαίωσεν   verb, aor. act. indic. 3 pers. sg.
    {5.A.1} . . . . id.
ἐδίστασαν   verb, aor. act. indic. 3 pers. pl.
    {5.A.1.b} . . . . διστάζω G1365
ἐδίστασας   verb, aor. act. indic. 2 pers. sg.
    {5.A.1.b} . . . . id.
ἐδίψησα   verb, aor. act. indic. 1 pers. sg.
    {5.A.1} . . . . διψάω G1372

ἐδίωκε   verb, impf. act. indic. 3 pers. sg.
  {5.A.1.b} . . . . διώκω G1377
ἐδίωκεν   verb, impf. act. indic. 3 pers. sg.
  {5.A.1.b} . . . . id.
ἐδίωκον   verb, impf. act. indic. 1 pers. sg.
  {5.A.1.b} . . . . id.
ἐδίωκον   verb, impf. act. indic. 3 pers. pl.
  {5.A.1.b} . . . . id.
ἐδίωξα   verb, aor. act. indic. 1 pers. sg. {5.A.1.b}. id.
ἐδίωξαν   verb, aor. act. indic. 3 pers. pl. {5.A.1.b}id.
ἐδίωξε   verb, aor. act. indic. 3 pers. sg. {5.A.1}. id.
ἐδίωξεν   verb, aor. act. indic. 3 pers. sg. {5.A.1.b}id.
ἐδόθη   verb, aor. pass. indic. 3 pers. sg.
  {5.A.1} . . . . .δίδωμι G1325
ἐδόθησαν   verb, aor. pass. indic. 3 pers. pl.
  {5.A.1} . . . . id.
ἐδόκει   verb, impf. act. indic. 3 pers. sg.
  {5.A.2} . . . . δοκέω G1380
ἐδοκιμάσαμεν   verb, aor. act. indic. 1 pers. pl.
  {5.A.1.b} . . . . δοκιμάζω G1381
ἐδοκίμασαν   verb, aor. act. indic. 3 pers. pl.
  {5.A.1.b} . . . . id.
ἐδόκουν   verb, impf. act. indic. 3 pers. pl.
  {5.A.2} . . . . δοκέω G1380
ἐδολιοῦσαν   verb, impf. act. indic. 3 pers. pl.
  {5.A.2} . . . . δολιόω G1387
ἔδοξα   verb, aor. act. indic. 1 pers. sg. {5.A.1} δοκέω G1380
ἐδόξαζε   verb, impf. act. indic. 3 pers. sg.
  {5.A.1.b} . . . . δοξάζω G1392
ἐδόξαζεν   verb, impf. act. indic. 3 pers. sg.
  {5.A.1.b} . . . . id.
ἐδόξαζον   verb, impf. act. indic. 3 pers. pl.
  {5.A.1.b} . . . . id.
ἔδοξαν   verb, aor. act. indic. 3 pers. pl.
  {5.A.1} . . . . δοκέω G1380
ἐδόξασα   verb, aor. act. indic. 1 pers. sg.
  {5.A.1.b} . . . . δοξάζω G1392
ἐδόξασαν   verb, aor. act. indic. 3 pers. pl.
  {5.A.1.b} . . . . id.
ἐδόξασε   verb, aor. act. indic. 3 pers. sg.
  {5.A.1.b} . . . . id.
ἐδόξασεν   verb, aor. act. indic. 3 pers. sg.
  {5.A.1.b} . . . . id.
ἐδοξάσθη   verb, aor. pass. indic. 3 pers. sg.
  {5.A.1.b} . . . . id.
ἔδοξε   verb, aor. act. indic. 3 pers. sg. {5.A.1} δοκέω G1380
ἔδοξεν   verb, aor. act. indic. 3 pers. sg. {5.A.1} . . id.
ἐδουλεύσατε   verb, aor. act. indic. 2 pers. pl.
  {5.A.1.b} . . . . δουλεύω G1398
ἐδούλευσεν   verb, aor. act. indic. 3 pers. sg.
  {5.A.1.b} . . . . id.
ἐδουλώθητε   verb, aor. pass. indic. 2 pers. pl.
  {5.A.1} . . . . δουλόω G1402
ἐδούλωσα   verb, aor. act. indic. 1 pers. sg.
  {5.A.1} . . . . id.
ἑδραῖοι   adj., nom. pl. masc. {3.A} . . . . . . ἑδραῖος G1476
G1476 ἑδραῖος, -α, -ον   firm, steadfast (lit. seated).
ἑδραῖος   adj., nom. sg. masc. {3.A} . . . . . . ἑδραῖος G1476
G1477 ἑδραίωμα, -ατος, τό   a foundation.
ἑδραίωμα   noun, nom. sg. neut. {2.C} . . ἑδραίωμα G1477

ἔδραμε   verb, ²aor. act. indic. 3 pers. sg.
  {5.A.1.b} . . . . τρέχω G5143
ἔδραμεν   verb, ²aor. act. indic. 3 pers. sg.
  {5.A.1.b} . . . . id.
ἔδραμον   verb, ²aor. act. indic. 1 pers. sg.
  {5.A.1.b} . . . . id.
ἔδραμον   verb, ²aor. act. indic. 3 pers. pl.
  {5.A.1.b} . . . . id.
ἔδυ   verb, ²aor. act. indic. 3 pers. sg. {5.A.1.b} . δύνω G1416
ἐδυναμώθησαν   verb, aor. pass. indic. 3 pers. pl.
  {5.A.1} .δυναμόω G1412
ἐδύναντο   verb, impf. mid./pass. indic. 3 pers. pl.
  {5.A.3.a} . . . . δύναμαι G1410
ἐδύνασθε   verb, impf. mid./pass. indic. 2 pers.
  pl. {5.A.3.a} . . . . id.
ἐδύνατο   verb, impf. mid./pass. indic. 3 pers.
  sg. {5.A.3.a} . . . . id.
ἔδυσεν   verb, aor. act. indic. 3 pers. sg.
  {5.A.1.b} . . . . δύνω G1416
ἔδωκα   verb, aor. act. indic. 1 pers. sg.
  {5.A.3.b} .δίδωμι G1325
ἐδώκαμεν   verb, aor. act. indic. 1 pers. pl.
  {5.A.3.b} . . . . id.
ἔδωκαν   verb, aor. act. indic. 3 pers. pl. {5.A.3.b} id.
ἔδωκας   verb, aor. act. indic. 2 pers. sg. {5.A.3.b} id.
ἐδώκατε   verb, aor. act. indic. 2 pers. pl.
  {5.A.3.b} . . . . id.
ἔδωκε   verb, aor. act. indic. 3 pers. sg. {5.A.3.b}. . id.
ἔδωκεν   verb, aor. act. indic. 3 pers. sg. {5.A.3.b} id.
ἐδωρήσατο   verb, aor. mid. indic. 3 pers. sg.
  {5.A.1} . . . . δωρέομαι G1433
Ἑζεκίαν   noun prop., acc. sg. masc. {2.A;
  2.D} . . . . Ἑζεκίας G1478
Ἑζεκίαν   noun prop., acc. sg. masc. {2.A; 2.D} . . id.
Ἑζεκίας   noun prop., nom. sg. masc. {2.A; 2.D}. id.
G1478 Ἑζεκίας, -ου, ὁ   Hezekiah, son of Achas
  (Ahaz), father of Manasseh, and king of Judah
  (727–686? B.C.) (Heb.).
Ἑζεκίας   noun prop., nom. sg. masc. {2.A;
  2.D} . . . . Ἑζεκίας G1478
ἐζημιώθην   verb, aor. pass. indic. 1 pers. sg.
  {5.A.1} . . . . ζημιόω G2210
ἔζησα   verb, aor. act. indic. 1 pers. sg. {5.A.1}. ζάω G2198
ἔζησαν   verb, aor. act. indic. 3 pers. pl. {5.A.1}. . id.
ἔζησε   verb, aor. act. indic. 3 pers. sg. {5.A.1} . . . id.
ἔζησεν   verb, aor. act. indic. 3 pers. sg. {5.A.1} . . id.
ἐζῆτε   verb, impf. act. indic. 2 pers. pl. {5.A.2} . . id.
ἐζήτει   verb, impf. act. indic. 3 pers. sg.
  {5.A.2} . . . . ζητέω G2212
ἐζητεῖτε   verb, impf. act. indic. 2 pers. pl. {5.A.2} id.
ἐζητεῖτο   verb, impf. pass. indic. 3 pers. sg.
  {5.A.2} . . . . id.
ἐζητήσαμεν   verb, aor. act. indic. 1 pers. pl.
  {5.A.1} . . . . id.
ἐζήτησαν   verb, aor. act. indic. 3 pers. pl. {5.A.1}id.
ἐζήτησε   verb, aor. act. indic. 3 pers. sg. {5.A.1}. id.
ἐζήτησεν   verb, aor. act. indic. 3 pers. sg. {5.A.1} id.
ἐζητοῦμεν   verb, impf. act. indic. 1 pers. pl.
  {5.A.2} . . . . id.
ἐζήτουν   verb, impf. act. indic. 3 pers. pl. {5.A.2}id.

ἐζυμώθη   verb, aor. pass. indic. 3 pers. sg.
  {5.A.1}..............................ζυμόω G2220
ἐζωγρημένοι   vbl., perf. pass. ptc. nom. pl. masc.
  {6.A.2}..............................ζωγρέω G2221
ἔζων   verb, impf. act. indic. 1 pers. sg. {5.A.2}..ζάω G2198
ἐζώννυες   verb, impf. act. indic. 2 pers. sg.
  {5.A.3.a}...........................ζώννυμι G2224
ἐθαμβήθησαν   verb, aor. pass. indic. 3 pers. pl.
  {5.A.1}..............................θαμβέω G2284
ἐθαμβοῦντο   verb, impf. pass. indic. 3 pers. pl.
  {5.A.2}..............................id.
ἐθανατώθητε   verb, aor. pass. indic. 2 pers. pl.
  {5.A.1}..............................θανατόω G2289
ἐθαύμαζε   verb, impf. act. indic. 3 pers. sg.
  {5.A.1.b}...........................θαυμάζω G2296
ἐθαύμαζεν   verb, impf. act. indic. 3 pers. sg.
  {5.A.1.b}...........................id.
ἐθαύμαζον   verb, impf. act. indic. 3 pers. pl.
  {5.A.1.b}...........................id.
ἐθαύμασα   verb, aor. act. indic. 1 pers. sg.
  {5.A.1.b}...........................id.
ἐθαύμασαν   verb, aor. act. indic. 3 pers. pl.
  {5.A.1.b}...........................id.
ἐθαύμασας   verb, aor. act. indic. 2 pers. sg.
  {5.A.1.b}...........................id.
ἐθαύμασε   verb, aor. act. indic. 3 pers. sg.
  {5.A.1.b}...........................id.
ἐθαύμασεν   verb, aor. act. indic. 3 pers. sg.
  {5.A.1.b}...........................id.
ἐθαυμάσθη   verb, aor. pass. indic. 3 pers. sg.
  {5.A.1.b}...........................id.
ἔθαψαν   verb, aor. act. indic. 3 pers. pl.
  {5.A.1.b}...........................θάπτω G2290
ἐθεάθη   verb, aor. pass. indic. 3 pers. sg.
  {5.A.1}..............................θεάομαι G2300
ἐθεασάμεθα   verb, aor. mid. indic. 1 pers. pl.
  {5.A.1}..............................id.
ἐθεάσαντο   verb, aor. mid. indic. 3 pers. pl.
  {5.A.1}..............................id.
ἐθεάσασθε   verb, aor. mid. indic. 2 pers. pl.
  {5.A.1}..............................id.
ἐθεάσατο   verb, aor. mid. indic. 3 pers. sg. {5.A.1}. id.
ἔθει   noun, dat. sg. neut. {2.C}...........ἔθος G1485
ἐθελοθρησκεία   noun, dat. sg. fem.
  {2.A}.......................ἐθελοθρησκία G1479
G1479   **ἐθελοθρησκία**, -ας, ἡ   service (worship) of the
  will, worship of self, self-made religion; practically, worship of the angels (cf. ἐθελοδουλεία).
ἐθελοθρησκία   noun, dat. sg. fem.
  {2.A}.......................ἐθελοθρησκία G1479
ἐθεμελίωσας   verb, aor. act. indic. 2 pers. sg.
  {5.A.1}..............................θεμελιόω G2311
ἔθεντο   verb, ²aor. mid. indic. 3 pers. pl.
  {5.A.3.b}...........................τίθημι G5087
ἐθεράπευεν   verb, impf. act. indic. 3 pers. sg.
  {5.A.1.b}...........................θεραπεύω G2323
ἐθεραπεύθη   verb, aor. pass. indic. 3 pers. sg.
  {5.A.1.b}...........................id.
ἐθεραπεύθησαν   verb, aor. pass. indic. 3 pers.
  pl. {5.A.1.b}.......................id.

ἐθεράπευον   verb, impf. act. indic. 3 pers. pl.
  {5.A.1.b}...........................id.
ἐθεραπεύοντο   verb, impf. pass. indic. 3 pers.
  pl. {5.A.1.e}.......................id.
ἐθεράπευσε   verb, aor. act. indic. 3 pers. sg.
  {5.A.1.b}...........................id.
ἐθεράπευσεν   verb, aor. act. indic. 3 pers. sg.
  {5.A.1.b}...........................id.
ἐθερίσθη   verb, aor. pass. indic. 3 pers. sg.
  {5.A.1.b}...........................θερίζω G2325
ἐθερμαίνοντο   verb, impf. mid./pass. indic. 3 pers.
  pl. {5.A.1.e}.......................θερμαίνω G2328
ἔθεσθε   verb, ²aor. mid. indic. 2 pers. pl.
  {5.A.3.b}...........................τίθημι G5087
ἔθεσι   noun, dat. pl. neut. {2.C}..........ἔθος G1485
ἔθεσιν   noun, dat. pl. neut. {2.C}..........id.
ἔθετο   verb, ²aor. mid. indic. 3 pers. sg.
  {5.A.3.b}...........................τίθημι G5087
ἐθεώρει   verb, impf. act. indic. 3 pers. sg.
  {5.A.2}..............................θεωρέω G2334
ἐθεώρησαν   verb, aor. act. indic. 3 pers. pl.
  {5.A.1}..............................id.
ἐθεώρουν   verb, impf. act. indic. 1 pers. sg.
  {5.A.2}..............................id.
ἐθεώρουν   verb, impf. act. indic. 3 pers. pl.
  {5.A.2}..............................id.
ἔθη   noun, acc. pl. neut. {2.C}............ἔθος G1485
ἔθηκα   verb, aor. act. indic. 1 pers. sg.
  {5.A.3.b}...........................τίθημι G5087
ἔθηκαν   verb, aor. act. indic. 3 pers. pl. {5.A.3.b} id.
ἔθηκας   verb, aor. act. indic. 2 pers. sg. {5.A.3.b} id.
ἔθηκε   verb, aor. act. indic. 3 pers. sg. {5.A.3.b}.. id.
ἔθηκεν   verb, aor. act. indic. 3 pers. sg. {5.A.3.b}. id.
ἐθήλασαν   verb, aor. act. indic. 3 pers. pl.
  {5.A.1.b}...........................θηλάζω G2337
ἐθήλασας   verb, aor. act. indic. 2 pers. sg.
  {5.A.1.b}...........................id.
ἐθηριομάχησα   verb, aor. act. indic. 1 pers. sg.
  {5.A.1}..............................θηριομαχέω G2341
ἐθησαυρίσατε   verb, aor. act. indic. 2 pers. pl.
  {5.A.1.b}...........................θησαυρίζω G2343
G1480   **ἐθίζω**   (1) I accustom; (2) τὸ εἰθισμένον, the
  custom.
G1481   **ἐθνάρχης**, -ου, ὁ   ethnarch, tribal lord, a subordinate ruler.
ἐθνάρχης   noun, nom. sg. masc. {2.A}.. ἐθνάρχης G1481
ἔθνει   noun, dat. sg. neut. {2.C}..........ἔθνος G1484
ἔθνεσι   noun, dat. pl. neut. {2.C}..........id.
ἔθνεσιν   noun, dat. pl. neut. {2.C}..........id.
ἔθνη   noun, acc. pl. neut. {2.C}............id.
ἔθνη   noun, nom. pl. neut. {2.C}............id.
ἔθνη   noun, voc. pl. neut. {2.C}............id.
ἐθνικοί   adj., nom. pl. masc. {3.A}.......ἐθνικός G1482
G1482   **ἐθνικός**, -ή, -όν   a Gentile, a non-Jew (in biblical Hebrew = nation, but in rabbinic Heb. =
  non-Jew).
ἐθνικός   adj., nom. sg. masc. {3.A}.......ἐθνικός G1482
ἐθνικῶν   adj., gen. pl. masc. {3.A}...........id.
G1483   **ἐθνικῶς**   adv., in the manner of Gentiles.

ἐθνικῶς   adv. {3.F} . . . . .ἐθνικῶς *G1483*

G1484 **ἔθνος**, -ους, τό   (1) *a race, people* (orig., a rustic or village people as opposed to those dwelling in organized cities or πόλεις; usually outside the privileged Jewish people, but also sometimes in the singular for it; sometimes = the inhabitants of a Roman province); (2) τὰ ἔθνη, *the nations* outside Judaism, *the Gentiles.*

ἔθνος   noun, acc. sg. neut. {2.C} . . . . .ἔθνος *G1484*
ἔθνος   noun, nom. sg. neut. {2.C}. . . . . id.
ἔθνους   noun, gen. sg. neut. {2.C}. . . . . id.
ἐθνῶν   noun, gen. pl. neut. {2.C} . . . . id.
ἐθορύβουν   verb, impf. act. indic. 3 pers. pl. {5.A.2}. . . . . .θορυβέω *G2350*

G1485 **ἔθος**, -ους, τό   *a custom.*

ἔθος   noun, acc. sg. neut. {2.C} . . . . .ἔθος *G1485*
ἔθος   noun, nom. sg. neut. {2.C} . . . . id.
ἔθου   verb, ²aor. mid. indic. 2 pers. sg. {5.A.3.b} . . . . .τίθημι *G5087*
ἐθρέψαμεν   verb, aor. act. indic. 1 pers. pl. {5.A.1.b} . . . . .τρέφω *G5142*
ἔθρεψαν   verb, aor. act. indic. 3 pers. pl. {5.A.1.b} . . . . id.
ἐθρέψατε   verb, aor. act. indic. 2 pers. pl. {5.A.1.b} . . . . id.
ἐθρηνήσαμεν   verb, aor. act. indic. 1 pers. pl. {5.A.1}. . . . . θρηνέω *G2354*
ἐθρήνουν   verb, impf. act. indic. 3 pers. pl. {5.A.2}. . . . . id.
ἐθυμώθη   verb, aor. pass. indic. 3 pers. sg. {5.A.1}. . . . . θυμόω *G2373*
ἔθυον   verb, impf. act. indic. 3 pers. pl. {5.A.1.b} . . . . θύω *G2380*
ἔθυσας   verb, aor. act. indic. 2 pers. sg. {5.A.1.b} id.
ἔθυσεν   verb, aor. act. indic. 3 pers. sg. {5.A.1.b} . id.

G1486 **ἔθω**   Plu. εἴωθα, (1) *I am accustomed;* (2) τὸ εἰωθός (verbal adj. as subs.), *custom, what was customary.*

ἐθῶν   noun, gen. pl. neut. {2.C} . . . . .ἔθος *G1485*

G1487 **εἰ**   (1) *if;* (2) *verily, indeed, assuredly* (Semitic, sometimes negative, *assuredly not,* Mark 8:12; Heb 3:11); (a) in strong statements, approaching oaths in character, and as the first word in an interrog. clause, probably a mere graphic equivalent, first appearing second c. B.C., of ἤ; (b) merely a particle asking a question, εἰ μή; (3) *but only,* e.g., Luke 4:26–27; John 15:4; Acts 27:22; Rev 21:27; (4) *and not,* in Mark 6:8, probably due to a misreading of an Aram. word; (5) εἰ δὲ μή, εἰ δὲ μήγε (Aramaism?), *otherwise;* (6) εἴπερ (= εἴ περ) a more emphatic εἰ, *if indeed.*

εἰ   cond. part. . . . . εἰ *G1487*
εἴ   cond. part. . . . . id.
εἶ   verb, pres. indic. 2 pers. sg. {7.A} . . . . . εἰμί *G1510*

G1490 **εἰ δὲ μήγε**   see εἰ.
G1499‡ **εἰ καί**   *if also, if even* (from εἰ and καί).
G1508‡ **εἰ μή**   *except, unless* (from εἰ and μή).

G1509‡ **εἰ μήτι**   *unless indeed, unless perhaps* (from εἰ and μήτι).
G1512‡ **εἴ περ** (εἴπερ)   *if perhaps, since* (from εἰ and περ).
G1513‡ **εἴ πως** (εἴπως)   *if somehow; if perhaps* (from εἰ and πως).
G1536‡ **εἴ τις**   *if any* (from εἰ and τις).

εἴα   verb, impf. act. indic. 3 pers. sg. {5.A.2} . . . ἐάω *G1439*
εἴασαν   verb, aor. act. indic. 3 pers. pl. {5.A.1} . . id.
εἴασε   verb, aor. act. indic. 3 pers. sg. {5.A.1} . . . id.
εἴασεν   verb, aor. act. indic. 3 pers. sg. {5.A.1} . . id.

G1489 **εἴγε**   *if indeed, seeing that, unless.*

εἴγε   cond. part.. . . . . εἴγε *G1489*
εἴδαμεν   verb, ²aor. act. indic. 1 pers. pl. {5.A.1.b} . . . . .ὁράω *G3708*
εἴδαν   verb, ²aor. act. indic. 3 pers. pl. {5.A.1.b} . id.
εἴδε   verb, ²aor. act. indic. 3 pers. sg. {5.A.1.b}. . . id.
εἰδέα   noun, nom. sg. fem. {2.A}. . . . . .ἰδέα *G2397*
εἴδει   noun, dat. sg. neut. {2.C} . . . . .εἶδος *G1491*
εἴδεν   verb, ²aor. act. indic. 3 pers. sg. {5.A.1.b} . . . . .ὁράω *G3708*
εἰδέναι   vbl., ²perf. act. inf. {6.B.1} . . . . .εἰδῶ *G1492*
εἶδες   verb, ²aor. act. indic. 2 pers. sg. {5.A.1.b} . . . . .ὁράω *G3708*
εἴδετε   verb, ²aor. act. indic. 2 pers. pl. {5.A.1.b} . id.
εἰδῆς   verb, ²perf. act. subjunc. 2 pers. sg. {5.B.1} . . . . .εἰδῶ *G1492*
εἰδήσουσι   verb, fut. act. indic. 3 pers. pl. {5.A.1.a} . . . . id.
εἰδήσουσιν   verb, fut. act. indic. 3 pers. pl. {5.A.1.a} . . . . id.
εἰδῆτε   verb, ²perf. act. subjunc. 2 pers. pl. {5.B.1}id.
εἴδομεν   verb, ²aor. act. indic. 1 pers. pl. {5.A.1.b} . . . . .ὁράω *G3708*
εἶδον   verb, ²aor. act. indic. 1 pers. sg. {5.A.1.b} . id.
εἶδον   verb, ²aor. act. indic. 3 pers. pl. {5.A.1.b}. . id.

G1491 **εἶδος**, -ους, τό   (1) *visible form, shape, appearance, outward show;* (2) in 1 Thess 5:22 = *kind, species, class.*

εἶδος   noun, acc. sg. neut. {2.C} . . . . .εἶδος *G1491*
εἶδος   noun, nom. sg. neut. {2.C} . . . . id.
εἰδόσι   vbl., ²perf. act. ptc. dat. pl. masc. {6.A.1}. . . . . .εἰδῶ *G1492*
εἰδόσιν   vbl., ²perf. act. ptc. dat. pl. masc. {6.A.1}id.
εἰδότα   vbl., ²perf. act. ptc. nom. pl. neut. {6.A.1}id.
εἰδότας   vbl., ²perf. act. ptc. acc. pl. masc. {6.A.1}id.
εἰδότες   vbl., ²perf. act. ptc. nom. pl. masc. {6.A.1}. . . . . id.
εἰδότι   vbl., ²perf. act. ptc. dat. sg. masc. {6.A.1} . id.
εἴδους   noun, gen. sg. neut. {2.C} . . . . .εἶδος *G1491*
εἰδυῖα   vbl., ²perf. act. ptc. nom. sg. fem. {6.A.1}. . . . . .εἰδῶ *G1492*

G1492 **εἰδῶ** (οἶδα)   *I know a fact;* perhaps, *I remember,* 1 Cor 1:16; 2 Cor 12:3; with inf. *I know how to;* (2) *I know* (am acquainted with) a person (obsolete pres. tense associated with the ²perf. form οἶδα used as present tense in the NT. Plu. ᾔδειν used as impf. or aor.).

εἰδῶ   verb, ²perf. act. subjunc. 1 pers. sg. {5.B.1} . . . . .εἰδῶ *G1492* εἴδωλα   noun, acc. pl. neut. {2.B} . . . . . . .εἴδωλον G1497

G1493 **εἰδωλεῖον**, -ου, τό   *a temple for (containing) an image* (of a god).
εἰδωλείῳ   noun, dat. sg. neut. {2.B} . . . . εἰδωλεῖον G1493
εἰδωλίῳ   noun, dat. sg. neut. {2.B} . . . . id.
εἰδωλόθυτα   adj., acc. pl. neut. {3.C} .εἰδωλόθυτος G1494
εἰδωλόθυτον   adj., acc. sg. neut. {3.C} . . . . id.
εἰδωλόθυτον   adj., nom. sg. neut. {3.C} . . . . . . id.

G1494 **εἰδωλόθυτος**, -ου, τό   (meat) *sacrificed to an image* (of a god).
εἰδωλοθύτων   adj., gen. pl. neut.
   {3.C} . . . . .εἰδωλόθυτος G1494
εἰδωλολάτραι   noun, nom. pl. masc.
   {2.A} . . . . .εἰδωλολάτρης G1496‡
εἰδωλολάτραις   noun, dat. pl. masc. {2.A}. . . . . id.
εἰδωλολατρεία   noun, nom. sg. fem.
   {2.A} . . . . εἰδωλολατρία G1495
εἰδωλολατρείαις   noun, dat. pl. fem. {2.A} . . . . id.
εἰδωλολατρείας   noun, gen. sg. fem. {2.A} . . . . id.

G1496‡ **εἰδωλολάτρης**, -ου, ὁ   *a server (worshipper) of an image* (of a god).
εἰδωλολάτρης   noun, nom. sg. masc.
   {2.A} . . . . .εἰδωλολάτρης G1496‡

G1495 **εἰδωλολατρία**, -ας, ἡ   *service (worship) of an image* (of a god).
εἰδωλολατρία   noun, nom. sg. fem.
   {2.A} . . . . εἰδωλολατρία G1495
εἰδωλολατρίαις   noun, dat. pl. fem. {2.A} . . . . id.
εἰδωλολατρίας   noun, gen. sg. fem. {2.A} . . . . id.

G1497 **εἴδωλον**, -ου, τό   *an image of a god.*
εἴδωλον   noun, nom. sg. neut. {2.B} . . . . .εἴδωλον G1497
εἰδώλου   noun, gen. sg. neut. {2.B}. . . . . id.
εἰδώλῳ   noun, dat. sg. neut. {2.B}. . . . . id.
εἰδώλων   noun, gen. pl. neut. {2.B}. . . . . id.
εἴδωμεν   verb, ²perf. act. subjunc. 1 pers. pl.
   {5.B.1} . . . . .εἴδω G1492
εἰδώς   vbl., ²perf. act. ptc. nom. sg. masc. {6.A.1} id.
εἴη   verb, pres. opt. 3 pers. sg. {7.B}. . . . . εἰμί G1510

G1498 **εἴην**   opt. form of εἰμί.
εἴης   verb, pres. opt. 2 pers. sg. {7.B}. . . . . εἰμί G1510
εἰθισμένον   vbl., perf. pass. ptc. acc. sg. neut.
   {6.A.1.b} . . . . .ἐθίζω G1480

G1500 **εἰκῆ**   adv. (1) *without a cause or purpose, haphazardly*; (2) *purposelessly, in vain, for nothing,* used both with reference to antecedent causes and purposes for the future.
εἰκῆ   adv. . . . . .εἰκῆ G1500
εἰκῇ   adv. . . . . id.
εἰκόνα   noun, acc. sg. fem. {2.C} . . . . .εἰκών G1504
εἰκόνι   noun, dat. sg. fem. {2.C} . . . . id.
εἰκόνος   noun, gen. sg. fem. {2.C}. . . . . id.

G1501 **εἴκοσι**   *twenty.*
εἴκοσι   adj. num. . . . . .εἴκοσι G1501
εἴκοσιν   adj. num. . . . . id.

G1502 **εἴκω**   *I yield.*

G1504 **εἰκών**, -όνος, ἡ   *image, likeness, bust.*
εἰκών   noun, nom. sg. fem. {2.C} . . . . .εἰκών G1504
εἵλατο   verb, aor. mid. indic. 3 pers. sg.
   {5.A.1}. . . . . .αἱρέω G138‡
εἵλετο   verb, ²aor. mid. indic. 3 pers. sg. {5.A.1.e} id.

εἴληφα   verb, ²perf. act. indic. 1 pers. sg.
   {5.A.1.c} . . . . λαμβάνω G2983
εἴληφας   verb, ²perf. act. indic. 2 pers. sg.
   {5.A.1.c} . . . . id.
εἴληφε   verb, ²perf. act. indic. 3 pers. sg. {5.A.1.c}id.
εἴληφεν   verb, ²perf. act. indic. 3 pers. sg.
   {5.A.1.c} . . . . id.
εἴληφες   verb, ²perf. act. indic. 2 pers. sg.
   {5.A.1.c} . . . . id.
εἰληφώς   vbl., ²perf. act. ptc. nom. sg. masc.
   {6.A.1.a} . . . . id.

G1505 **εἰλικρίνεια**, -ας, ἡ   *purity.*
εἰλικρινείᾳ   noun, dat. sg. fem. {2.A}. .εἰλικρίνεια G1505
εἰλικρινείας   noun, gen. sg. fem. {2.A} . . . . . . id.
εἰλικρινεῖς   adj., nom. pl. masc. {3.E}. . εἰλικρινής G1506
εἰλικρινῆ   adj., acc. sg. fem. {3.E}. . . . . id.

G1506 **εἰλικρινής**, -ές   (orig. *unmixed*), *pure, uncontaminated.*
εἰλικρινίᾳ   noun, dat. sg. fem. {2.A} . .εἰλικρίνεια G1505
εἰλικρινίας   noun, gen. sg. fem. {2.A} . . . . id.
εἱλισσόμενον   vbl., pres. pass. ptc. nom. sg. neut.
   {6.A.1} . . . . .ἑλίσσω G1667

G1507 **εἱλίσσω**   alt. spelling of ἑλίσσω.
εἷλκον   verb, impf. act. indic. 3 pers. pl.
   {5.A.1.b} . . . . .ἑλκύω G1670
εἵλκυσαν   verb, aor. act. indic. 3 pers. pl.
   {5.A.1.b} . . . . id.
εἵλκυσε   verb, aor. act. indic. 3 pers. sg. {5.A.1.b} id.
εἵλκυσεν   verb, aor. act. indic. 3 pers. sg.
   {5.A.1.b} . . . . id.
εἱλκωμένος   vbl., perf. pass. ptc. nom. sg. masc.
   {6.A.2}. . . . . .ἑλκόω G1669

G1510 **εἰμί**   *I am, exist, happen.* Used with participles in periphrastic constructions, the special frequency of which in the impf. is due to the Aramaic basis of the language. ὁ ἦν ungrammatically, in Rev, where an aor. ptc. would be expected.
εἰμί   verb, pres. indic. 1 pers. sg. {7.A} . . . . . . εἰμί G1510
εἶναι   vbl., pres. inf. {7.C.2} . . . . εἰμί G1510
εἵνεκεν   prep. . . . . ἕνεκα G1752
εἴξαμεν   verb, aor. act. indic. 1 pers. pl.
   {5.A.1.b} . . . . .εἴκω G1502
εἶπα   verb, ²aor. act. indic. 1 pers. sg. {5.A.1.b} λέγω G3004
εἶπαν   verb, ²aor. act. indic. 3 pers. pl. {5.A.1.b} . id.
εἴπας   vbl., ²aor. act. ptc. nom. sg. masc. {6.A.1.a}id.
εἶπας   verb, ²aor. act. indic. 2 pers. sg. {5.A.1.b} . id.
εἴπασα   vbl., ²aor. act. ptc. nom. sg. fem.
   {6.A.1.a} . . . . id.
εἴπατε   verb, ²aor. act. impv. 2 pers. pl. {5.D.1} . . id.
εἴπατε   verb, ²aor. act. indic. 2 pers. pl. {5.A.1.b}. id.
εἰπάτω   verb, ²aor. act. impv. 3 pers. sg. {5.D.1} . id.
εἰπάτωσαν   verb, ²aor. act. impv. 3 pers. pl.
   {5.D.1} . . . . id.
εἰπέ   verb, ²aor. act. impv. 2 pers. sg. {5.D.1} . . . . id.
εἶπε   verb, ²aor. act. indic. 3 pers. sg. {5.A.1.b}. . . id.
εἰπεῖν   vbl., ²aor. act. inf. {6.B.1} . . . . id.
εἶπεν   verb, ²aor. act. indic. 3 pers. sg. {5.A.1.b}. . id.
εἴπερ   cond. part. . . . . .εἴ περ G1512‡

εἶπες   verb, ²aor. act. indic. 2 pers. sg. {5.A.1.b} λέγω G3004
εἴπῃ   verb, ²aor. act. subjunc. 3 pers. sg. {5.B.1} . id.
εἴπῃς   verb, ²aor. act. subjunc. 2 pers. sg. {5.B.1} . id.
εἴπητε   verb, ²aor. act. subjunc. 2 pers. pl. {5.B.1} id.
εἰπόν   verb, ²aor. act. impv. 2 pers. sg. {5.D.1} . λέγω G3004
εἶπον   verb, ²aor. act. indic. 1 pers. sg. {5.A.1.b} . id.
εἶπον   verb, ²aor. act. indic. 3 pers. pl. {5.A.1.b} . id.
εἰπόντα   vbl., ²aor. act. ptc. acc. sg. masc.
   {6.A.1.a} . . . . id.
εἰπόντες   vbl., ²aor. act. ptc. nom. pl. masc.
   {6.A.1.a} . . . . id.
εἰπόντι   vbl., ²aor. act. ptc. dat. sg. masc.
   {6.A.1.a} . . . . id.
εἰπόντος   vbl., ²aor. act. ptc. gen. sg. masc.
   {6.A.1.a} . . . . id.
εἰποῦσα   vbl., ²aor. act. ptc. nom. sg. fem.
   {6.A.1.a} . . . . id.
εἴπω   verb, ²aor. act. subjunc. 1 pers. sg. {5.B.1} . . id.
εἴπωμεν   verb, ²aor. act. subjunc. 1 pers. pl.
   {5.B.1} . . . . id.
εἰπών   vbl., ²aor. act. ptc. nom. sg. masc.
   {6.A.1.a} . . . . id.
εἴπωσι   verb, ²aor. act. subjunc. 3 pers. pl. {5.B.1} id.
εἴπωσιν   verb, ²aor. act. subjunc. 3 pers. pl.
   {5.B.1} . . . . id.
εἰργάζετο   verb, impf. mid./pass. indic. 3 pers. sg.
   {5.A.1.e} . . . . ἐργάζομαι G2038
εἰργασάμεθα   verb, aor. mid. indic. 1 pers. pl.
   {5.A.1.e} . . . . id.
εἰργάσαντο   verb, aor. mid. indic. 3 pers. pl.
   {5.A.1.e} . . . . id.
εἰργάσατο   verb, aor. mid. indic. 3 pers. sg.
   {5.A.1.e} . . . . id.
εἰργασμένα   vbl., perf. pass. ptc. nom. pl. neut.
   {6.A.1.b} . . . . id.
εἴρηκα   verb, perf. act. indic. 1 pers. sg.
   {5.A.1} . . . . ἐρέω G2046
εἴρηκαν   verb, perf. act. indic. 3 pers. pl. {5.A.1} id.
εἴρηκας   verb, perf. act. indic. 2 pers. sg. {5.A.1} id.
εἰρήκασι   verb, perf. act. indic. 3 pers. pl.
   {5.A.1} . . . . id.
εἰρήκασιν   verb, perf. act. indic. 3 pers. pl.
   {5.A.1} . . . . id.
εἰρήκατε   verb, perf. act. indic. 2 pers. pl. {5.A.1}id.
εἴρηκε   verb, perf. act. indic. 3 pers. sg. {5.A.1} . id.
εἰρήκει   verb, plu. indic. 3 pers. sg. {5.A.1} . . id.
εἴρηκεν   verb, perf. act. indic. 3 pers. sg. {5.A.1} . id.
εἰρηκέναι   vbl., perf. act. inf. {6.B.2} . . . . id.
εἰρηκότος   vbl., perf. act. ptc. gen. sg. masc.
   {6.A.2} . . . . id.
εἰρημένον   vbl., perf. pass. ptc. acc. sg. neut.
   {6.A.2} . . . . id.
εἰρημένον   vbl., perf. pass. ptc. nom. sg. neut.
   {6.A.2} . . . . id.
εἰρηνεύετε   verb, pres. act. impv. 2 pers. pl.
   {5.D.1} . . . . εἰρηνεύω G1514
εἰρηνεύοντες   vbl., pres. act. ptc. nom. pl.
   masc. {6.A.1} . . . . id.
G1514 **εἰρηνεύω**   *I am peaceful, I keep the peace, I am*
   at peace.

G1515 **εἰρήνη**, -ης, ἡ   (1) *peace, undisturbed condi-*
   tion; (2) invocation of peace a common Jewish
   farewell (Mark 5:34, etc.), in the Hebraistic
   sense of *the health (welfare)* of an individual.
   εἰρήνη   noun, nom. sg. fem. {2.A} . . . . . . .εἰρήνη G1515
   εἰρήνη   noun, dat. sg. fem. {2.A} . . . . id.
   εἰρήνην   noun, acc. sg. fem. {2.A} . . . . id.
   εἰρήνης   noun, gen. sg. fem. {2.A} . . . . id.
   εἰρηνική   adj., nom. sg. fem. {3.A} . . . . . εἰρηνικός G1516
   εἰρηνικόν   adj., acc. sg. masc. {3.A} . . . . id.
G1516 **εἰρηνικός**, -ή, -όν   *making for peace, produc-*
   tive of peace.
G1517 **εἰρηνοποιέω**   *I make peace.*
   εἰρηνοποιήσας   vbl., aor. act. ptc. nom. sg. masc.
   {6.A.2} . . . . .εἰρηνοποιέω G1517
   εἰρηνοποιοί   adj., nom. pl. masc.
   {3.C} . . . . .εἰρηνοποιός G1518
G1518 **εἰρηνοποιός**, -οῦ, ὁ   *peacemaking, peacemaker.*
   εἴρηται   verb, perf. pass. indic. 3 pers. sg.
   {5.A.1} . . . . ἐρέω G2046
G1527‡ **εἷς καθ’ εἷς**   *one by one, severally.*
G1519 **εἰς**   prep. with acc. (1) *into, until, for;* (2) εἰς
   τό with inf., (a) generally final; (b) but also
   expressing tendency, result, e.g., Rom 12:3;
   2 Cor 8:6; Gal 3:17; (c) content of command
   or entreaty, e.g., 1 Thess 2:12; (d) simply =
   explanatory inf., 1 Thess 4:9; (3) encroaches
   on ἐν and = *in,* e.g., John 1:18; Acts 7:12;
   2 Cor 11:10; 1 John 5:8; (4) εἰς ἑκατόν, etc., *a*
   hundredfold.
   εἰς   prep. . . . . εἰς G1519
   εἷς   prep. . . . . id.
   εἷς   adj., nom. sg. masc. {3.D} . . . . εἷς G1520
G1520 **εἷς**, μία, ἕν, gen. ἑνός, μιᾶς, ἑνός   *one;* καθ’
   εἷς, *each single one, one by one;* sometimes no
   different from τις (Mark 14:10), and sometimes too = πρῶτος, *first.*
   εἰσάγαγε   verb, ²aor. act. impv. 2 pers. sg.
   {5.D.1} . . . . εἰσάγω G1521
   εἰσαγαγεῖν   vbl., ²aor. act. inf. {6.B.1} . . . . id.
   εἰσαγάγῃ   verb, ²aor. act. subjunc. 3 pers. sg.
   {5.B.1} . . . . id.
   εἰσάγεσθαι   vbl., pres. pass. inf. {6.B.1} . . . . id.
G1521 **εἰσάγω**   *I lead in, bring in.*
   εἰσακουσθείς   vbl., aor. pass. ptc. nom. sg. masc.
   {6.A.1.a} . . . . εἰσακούω G1522
   εἰσακουσθήσονται   verb, fut. pass. indic.
   3 pers. pl. {5.A.1.d} . . . . id.
   εἰσακούσονται   verb, fut. mid. indic. 3 pers.
   pl. {5.A.1.d} . . . . id.
G1522 **εἰσακούω**   *I hear.*
   εἰσδέξομαι   verb, fut. mid. indic. 1 pers. sg.
   {5.A.1.d} . . . . εἰσδέχομαι G1523
G1523 **εἰσδέχομαι**   *I welcome in.*
   εἰσδραμοῦσα   vbl., ²aor. act. ptc. nom. sg. fem.
   {6.A.1.a} . . . . .εἰστρέχω G1532
G1524 **εἴσειμι** (from εἶμι)   *I go in, enter* (orig., *I shall*
   go in).
   εἰσελεύσεσθαι   vbl., fut. mid. inf.
   {6.B.1} . . . . .εἰσέρχομαι G1525

εἰσελεύσεται   verb, fut. mid. indic. 3 pers. sg.
{5.A.1.d} . . . . id.
εἰσελεύσομαι   verb, fut. mid. indic. 1 pers. sg.
{5.A.1.d} . . . . id.
εἰσελεύσονται   verb, fut. mid. indic. 3 pers. pl.
{5.A.1.d} . . . . id.
εἰσελήλυθαν   verb, ²perf. act. indic. 3 pers. pl.
{5.A.1.c} . . . . id.
εἰσεληλύθασιν   verb, ²perf. act. indic. 3 pers.
pl. {5.A.1.c} . . . . id.
εἰσεληλύθατε   verb, ²perf. act. indic. 2 pers. pl.
{5.A.1.c} . . . . id.
εἰσέλθατε   verb, ²aor. act. impv. 2 pers. pl.
{5.D.1} . . . . id.
εἰσελθάτω   verb, ²aor. act. impv. 3 pers. sg.
{5.D.1} . . . . id.
εἴσελθε   verb, ²aor. act. impv. 2 pers. sg. {5.D.1} . id.
εἰσελθεῖν   vbl., ²aor. act. inf. {6.B.1} . . . . id.
εἰσέλθετε   verb, ²aor. act. impv. 2 pers. pl.
{5.D.1} . . . . id.
εἰσελθέτω   verb, ²aor. act. impv. 3 pers. sg.
{5.D.1} . . . . id.
εἰσέλθῃ   verb, ²aor. act. subjunc. 3 pers. sg.
{5.B.1} . . . . id.
εἰσέλθῃς   verb, ²aor. act. subjunc. 2 pers. sg.
{5.B.1} . . . . id.
εἰσέλθητε   verb, ²aor. act. subjunc. 2 pers. pl.
{5.B.1} . . . . id.
εἰσελθόντα   vbl., ²aor. act. ptc. acc. sg. masc.
{6.A.1.a} . . . . id.
εἰσελθόντα   vbl., ²aor. act. ptc. nom. pl. neut.
{6.A.1.a} . . . . id.
εἰσελθόντες   vbl., ²aor. act. ptc. nom. pl. masc.
{6.A.1.a} . . . . id.
εἰσελθόντι   vbl., ²aor. act. ptc. dat. sg. masc.
{6.A.1.a} . . . . id.
εἰσελθόντος   vbl., ²aor. act. ptc. gen. sg. masc.
{6.A.1.a} . . . . id.
εἰσελθόντων   vbl., ²aor. act. ptc. gen. pl. masc.
{6.A.1.a} . . . . id.
εἰσελθοῦσα   vbl., ²aor. act. ptc. nom. sg. fem.
{6.A.1.a} . . . . id.
εἰσελθοῦσαι   vbl., ²aor. act. ptc. nom. pl. fem.
{6.A.1.a} . . . . id.
εἰσελθούσης   vbl., ²aor. act. ptc. gen. sg. fem.
{6.A.1.a} . . . . id.
εἰσέλθωμεν   verb, ²aor. act. subjunc. 1 pers. pl.
{5.B.1} . . . . id.
εἰσελθών   vbl., ²aor. act. ptc. nom. sg. masc.
{6.A.1.a} . . . . id.
εἰσέλθωσι   verb, ²aor. act. subjunc. 3 pers. pl.
{5.B.1} . . . . id.
εἰσέλθωσιν   verb, ²aor. act. subjunc. 3 pers. pl.
{5.B.1} . . . . id.
εἰσενεγκεῖν   vbl., ²aor. act. inf. {6.B.1} . . . εἰσφέρω G1533
εἰσενέγκῃς   verb, aor. act. subjunc. 2 pers. sg.
{5.B.1} . . . . id.
εἰσενέγκωσιν   verb, ²aor. act. subjunc. 3 pers.
pl. {5.B.1} . . . . id.

εἰσεπήδησαν   verb, aor. act. indic. 3 pers. pl.
{5.A.1} . . . . εἰσπηδάω G1530
εἰσεπήδησε   verb, aor. act. indic. 3 pers. sg.
{5.A.1} . . . . id.
εἰσεπήδησεν   verb, aor. act. indic. 3 pers. sg.
{5.A.1} . . . . id.
εἰσεπορεύετο   verb, impf. mid./pass. indic. 3 pers.
sg. {5.A.1.e} . . . . εἰσπορεύομαι G1531
εἰσέρχεσθε   verb, pres. mid./pass. indic. 2 pers. pl.
{5.A.1.d} . . . . εἰσέρχομαι G1525
εἰσερχέσθωσαν   verb, pres. mid./pass. impv.
3 pers. pl. {5.D.1} . . . . id.
εἰσέρχεται   verb, pres. mid./pass. indic. 3 pers.
sg. {5.A.1.d} . . . . id.
εἰσέρχησθε   verb, pres. mid./pass. subjunc.
2 pers. pl. {5.B.1} . . . . id.
G1525   **εἰσέρχομαι**   *I go in.*
εἰσερχόμεθα   verb, pres. mid./pass. indic. 1 pers.
pl. {5.A.1.d} . . . . εἰσέρχομαι G1525
εἰσερχομένην   vbl., pres. mid./pass. ptc. acc.
sg. fem. {6.A.1} . . . . id.
εἰσερχόμενοι   vbl., pres. mid./pass. ptc. nom.
pl. masc. {6.A.1} . . . . id.
εἰσερχόμενον   vbl., pres. mid./pass. ptc. nom.
sg. neut. {6.A.1} . . . . id.
εἰσερχόμενος   vbl., pres. mid./pass. ptc. nom.
sg. masc. {6.A.1} . . . . id.
εἰσερχομένου   vbl., pres. mid./pass. ptc. gen.
sg. masc. {6.A.1} . . . . id.
εἰσερχομένους   vbl., pres. mid./pass. ptc. acc.
pl. masc. {6.A.1} . . . . id.
εἰσήγαγε   verb, ²aor. act. indic. 3 pers. sg.
{5.A.1.b} . . . . εἰσάγω G1521
εἰσήγαγεν   verb, ²aor. act. indic. 3 pers. sg.
{5.A.1.b} . . . . id.
εἰσήγαγον   verb, ²aor. act. indic. 3 pers. pl.
{5.A.1.b} . . . . id.
εἰσῄει   verb, impf. act. indic. 3 pers. sg.
{7.A} . . . . εἴσειμι G1524
εἰσηκούσθη   verb, aor. pass. indic. 3 pers. sg.
{5.A.1.b} . . . . εἰσακούω G1522
εἰσήλθαμεν   verb, ²aor. act. indic. 1 pers. pl.
{5.A.1.b} . . . . εἰσέρχομαι G1525
εἰσήλθατε   verb, ²aor. act. indic. 2 pers. pl.
{5.A.1.b} . . . . id.
εἰσῆλθε   verb, ²aor. act. indic. 3 pers. sg.
{5.A.1.b} . . . . id.
εἰσῆλθεν   verb, ²aor. act. indic. 3 pers. sg.
{5.A.1.b} . . . . id.
εἰσῆλθες   verb, ²aor. act. indic. 2 pers. sg.
{5.A.1.b} . . . . id.
εἰσήλθετε   verb, ²aor. act. indic. 2 pers. pl.
{5.A.1.b} . . . . id.
εἰσήλθομεν   verb, ²aor. act. indic. 1 pers. pl.
{5.A.1.b} . . . . id.
εἰσῆλθον   verb, ²aor. act. indic. 1 pers. sg.
{5.A.1.b} . . . . id.
εἰσῆλθον   verb, ²aor. act. indic. 3 pers. pl.
{5.A.1.b} . . . . id.

εἰσηνέγκαμεν verb, aor. act. indic. 1 pers. pl.
 {5.A.1.b} . . . . εἰσφέρω G1533
εἶσι verb, pres. indic. 3 pers. pl. {7.A} . . . . εἰμί G1510
εἰσί verb, pres. indic. 3 pers. pl. {7.A} . . . . id.
εἰσίασιν verb, pres. act. indic. 3 pers. pl. {7.A} .εἴσειμι G1524
εἰσιέναι vbl., pres. act. inf. {6.B.3} . . . . id.
εἰσιν verb, pres. indic. 3 pers. pl. {7.A} . . . . . . εἰμί G1510
εἰσίν verb, pres. indic. 3 pers. pl. {7.A} . . . . id.
G1528 **εἰσκαλέομαι** *I invite in.*
 εἰσκαλεσάμενος vbl., aor. mid. ptc. nom. sg.
  masc. {6.A.2} . . . . εἰσκαλέομαι G1528
 εἴσοδον noun, acc. sg. fem. {2.B} . . . . εἴσοδος G1529
G1529 **εἴσοδος**, -ου, ἡ (1) abstr., *(act of) entering,*
  entrance, entry; (2) concr., *the entrance* itself,
  Heb 10:19 (cf. 20); 2 Pet 1:11.
 εἴσοδος noun, nom. sg. fem. {2.B} . . . . . . εἴσοδος G1529
 εἰσόδου noun, gen. sg. fem. {2.B} . . . . id.
G1530 **εἰσπηδάω** *I leap into, rush into.*
G1531 **εἰσπορεύομαι** *I journey in(to), I go in(to).*
 εἰσπορεύεται verb, pres. mid./pass. indic. 3 pers.
  sg. {5.A.1.d} . . . . εἰσπορεύομαι G1531
 εἰσπορευόμεναι vbl., pres. mid./pass. ptc.
  nom. pl. fem. {6.A.1} . . . . id.
 εἰσπορευόμενοι vbl., pres. mid./pass. ptc.
  nom. pl. masc. {6.A.1} . . . . id.
 εἰσπορευόμενον vbl., pres. mid./pass. ptc.
  nom. sg. neut. {6.A.1} . . . . id.
 εἰσπορευόμενος vbl., pres. mid./pass. ptc.
  nom. sg. masc. {6.A.1} . . . . id.
 εἰσπορευομένους vbl., pres. mid./pass. ptc.
  acc. pl. masc. {6.A.1} . . . . id.
 εἰσπορευομένων vbl., pres. mid./pass. ptc.
  gen. pl. masc. {6.A.1} . . . . id.
 εἰσπορεύονται verb, pres. mid./pass. indic.
  3 pers. pl. {5.A.1.d} . . . . id.
 εἰστήκει verb, plu. act. indic. 3 pers. sg.
  {5.A.1} . . . . ἵστημι G2476
 εἰστήκεισαν verb, plu. act. indic. 3 pers. pl.
  {5.A.1} . . . . id.
G1532 **εἰστρέχω** *I run in(to).*
 εἰσφέρεις verb, pres. act. indic. 2 pers. sg.
  {5.A.1.a} . . . . εἰσφέρω G1533
 εἰσφέρεται verb, pres. pass. indic. 3 pers. sg.
  {5.A.1.d} . . . . id.
G1533 **εἰσφέρω** *I carry (bring) in.*
 εἰσφέρωσιν verb, pres. act. subjunc. 3 pers. pl.
  {5.B.1} . . . . εἰσφέρω G1533
G1534 **εἶτα** (εἶτεν) adv., *then, thereafter, next* (marking a fresh stage).
 εἶτα adv. . . . . εἶτα G1534
G1535 **εἴτε** lit. *and if;* εἴτε . . . εἴτε, *whether . . . or.*
 εἴτε conj. . . . . εἴτε G1535
 εἴτεν adv. . . . . εἶτα G1534
 εἴχαμεν verb, impf. act. indic. 1 pers. pl.
  {5.A.1.b} . . . . ἔχω G2192
 εἶχαν verb, impf. act. indic. 3 pers. pl. {5.A.1.b} . id.
 εἶχε verb, impf. act. indic. 3 pers. sg. {5.A.1.b} . . id.
 εἶχεν verb, impf. act. indic. 3 pers. sg. {5.A.1.b} . id.
 εἶχες verb, impf. act. indic. 2 pers. sg. {5.A.1.b} . id.
 εἴχετε verb, impf. act. indic. 2 pers. pl. {5.A.1.b} id.

εἴχομεν verb, impf. act. indic. 1 pers. pl.
 {5.A.1.b} . . . . id.
εἶχον verb, impf. act. indic. 1 pers. sg. {5.A.1.b} . id.
εἶχον verb, impf. act. indic. 3 pers. pl. {5.A.1.b} . id.
εἴχοσαν verb, impf. act. indic. 3 pers. pl.
 {5.A.1.b} . . . . id.
εἰώθει verb, plu. act. indic. 3 pers. sg. {5.A.1.b} ἔθω G1486
εἰωθός vbl., ²perf. act. ptc. acc. sg. neut. {6.A.1} . id.
εἴων verb, impf. act. indic. 3 pers. pl. {5.A.2} . . ἐάω G1439
G1537 **ἐκ**, ἐξ prep. with gen., *from out, out from*
  among, from, suggesting from the interior out-
  wards; ἐξ Ἑβραίων, *descended from Hebrews,*
  Phil 3:5; with gen. of price, Matt 20:2; Acts
  1:18; in partitive phrase, as subj. of sentence,
  John 16:17; cf. the periphrasis οἱ ἐξ ἐριθείας,
  Rom 2:8.
 ἐκ prep. . . . . ἐκ G1537
 ἐκαθάρισε verb, aor. act. indic. 3 pers. sg.
  {5.A.1.b} . . . . καθαρίζω G2511
 ἐκαθάρισεν verb, aor. act. indic. 3 pers. sg.
  {5.A.1.b} . . . . id.
 ἐκαθαρίσθη verb, aor. pass. indic. 3 pers. sg.
  {5.A.1.b} . . . . id.
 ἐκαθαρίσθησαν verb, aor. pass. indic. 3 pers.
  pl. {5.A.1.b} . . . . id.
 ἐκαθέζετο verb, impf. mid./pass. indic. 3 pers. sg.
  {5.A.1.e} . . . . καθέζομαι G2516
 ἐκαθεζόμην verb, impf. mid./pass. indic.
  1 pers. sg. {5.A.1.e} . . . . id.
 ἐκαθερίσθη verb, aor. pass. indic. 3 pers. sg.
  {5.A.1.b} . . . . καθαρίζω G2511
 ἐκάθευδε verb, impf. act. indic. 3 pers. sg.
  {5.A.1.b} . . . . καθεύδω G2518
 ἐκάθευδεν verb, impf. act. indic. 3 pers. sg.
  {5.A.1.b} . . . . id.
 ἐκάθευδον verb, impf. act. indic. 3 pers. pl.
  {5.A.1.b} . . . . id.
 ἐκάθητο verb, impf. mid./pass. indic. 3 pers. sg.
  {5.A.3.a} . . . . κάθημαι G2521
 ἐκάθισα verb, aor. act. indic. 1 pers. sg.
  {5.A.1.b} . . . . καθίζω G2523
 ἐκάθισαν verb, aor. act. indic. 3 pers. pl.
  {5.A.1.b} . . . . id.
 ἐκάθισε verb, aor. act. indic. 3 pers. sg. {5.A.1.b} id.
 ἐκάθισεν verb, aor. act. indic. 3 pers. sg.
  {5.A.1.b} . . . . id.
 ἐκάκωσαν verb, aor. act. indic. 3 pers. pl.
  {5.A.1} . . . . κακόω G2559
 ἐκάκωσε verb, aor. act. indic. 3 pers. sg. {5.A.1} id.
 ἐκάκωσεν verb, aor. act. indic. 3 pers. sg.
  {5.A.1} . . . . id.
 ἐκάλεσα verb, aor. act. indic. 1 pers. sg.
  {5.A.1} . . . . καλέω G2564
 ἐκάλεσαν verb, aor. act. indic. 3 pers. pl. {5.A.1} id.
 ἐκάλεσε verb, aor. act. indic. 3 pers. sg. {5.A.1} . id.
 ἐκάλεσεν verb, aor. act. indic. 3 pers. sg. {5.A.1} id.
 ἐκάλουν verb, impf. act. indic. 3 pers. pl.
  {5.A.2} . . . . id.
 ἐκάμμυσαν verb, aor. act. indic. 3 pers. pl.
  {5.A.1.b} . . . . καμμύω G2576

ἔκαμψαν   verb, aor. act. indic. 3 pers. pl.
{5.A.1.b} . . . . .κάμπτω G2578
ἐκαρτέρησε   verb, aor. act. indic. 3 pers. sg.
{5.A.1} . . . . καρτερέω G2594
ἐκαρτέρησεν   verb, aor. act. indic. 3 pers. sg.
{5.A.1} . . . . id.
ἑκάστη   adj., nom. sg. fem. {3.A} . . . . ἕκαστος G1538
ἑκάστην   adj., acc. sg. fem. {3.A} . . . . id.
ἕκαστοι   adj., nom. pl. masc. {3.A} . . . . id.
ἑκάστοις   adj., dat. pl. masc. {3.A} . . . . id.
ἕκαστον   adj., acc. sg. masc. {3.A} . . . . id.
ἕκαστον   adj., acc. sg. neut. {3.A} . . . . id.
ἕκαστον   adj., nom. sg. neut. {3.A} . . . . id.
G1538 **ἕκαστος**, -η, -ον   each (of more than two); εἷς
        ἕκαστος, each individual; pl. ἕκαστοι, etc.,
        each class, group.
ἕκαστος   adj., nom. sg. masc. {3.A} . . . . . ἕκαστος G1538
G1539 **ἑκάστοτε**   adv., on each occasion.
ἑκάστοτε   adv. . . . . ἑκάστοτε G1539
ἑκάστου   adj., gen. sg. masc. {3.A} . . . . . . ἕκαστος G1538
ἑκάστου   adj., gen. sg. neut. {3.A} . . . . id.
ἑκάστῳ   adj., dat. sg. masc. {3.A} . . . . id.
ἑκάστῳ   adj., dat. sg. neut. {3.A} . . . . id.
G1540 **ἑκατόν**   a hundred; εἰς ἑκατόν, see εἰς.
ἑκατόν   adj. num. ἑκατόν G1540
G1541 **ἑκατονταετής**, -ές   a hundred years old.
ἑκατονταετής   adj., nom. sg. masc.
        {3.E} . . . . ἑκατονταετής G1541
ἑκατονταπλασίονα   adj., acc. pl. neut.
        {3.E} . . . . .ἑκατονταπλασίων G1542
ἑκατονταπλασίονα   adj., acc. sg. masc. {3.E} . . id.
G1542 **ἑκατονταπλασίων**, -ον   a hundredfold.
ἑκατοντάρχας   noun, acc. pl. masc.
        {2.A} . . . . ἑκατοντάρχης G1543
ἑκατοντάρχη   noun, dat. sg. masc. {2.A} . . . . . . id.
G1543 **ἑκατοντάρχης** (-ος), -ου, ὁ   a centurion of the
        Roman army (see κεντυρίων).
ἑκατοντάρχης   noun, nom. sg. masc.
        {2.A} . . . . ἑκατοντάρχης G1543
ἑκατόνταρχον   noun, acc. sg. masc. {2.A} . . . . id.
ἑκατόνταρχος   noun, nom. sg. masc. {2.A} . . . . id.
ἑκατοντάρχου   noun, gen. sg. masc. {2.A} . . . . id.
ἑκατοντάρχους   noun, acc. pl. masc. {2.A} . . . . id.
ἑκατοντάρχῳ   noun, dat. sg. masc. {2.A} . . . . . id.
ἑκατονταρχῶν   noun, gen. pl. masc. {2.A} . . . . id.
ἑκατοντάρχων   noun, gen. pl. masc. {2.A} . . . . id.
ἐκαυματίσθη   verb, aor. pass. indic. 3 pers. sg.
        {5.A.1.b} . . . . καυματίζω G2739
ἐκαυματίσθησαν   verb, aor. pass. indic.
        3 pers. pl. {5.A.1.b} . . . . id.
G1831‡ ἐκβαίνω, I go out. Var. for ἐξέρχομαι, Heb
        11:15.
ἔκβαλε   verb, ²aor. act. impv. 2 pers. sg.
        {5.D.1} . . . . .ἐκβάλλω G1544
ἐκβαλεῖν   vbl., ²aor. act. inf. {6.B.1} . . . . id.
ἐκβάλετε   verb, ²aor. act. impv. 2 pers. pl. {5.D.1} id.
ἐκβάλῃ   verb, ²aor. act. subjunc. 3 pers. sg.
        {5.B.1} . . . . id.
ἐκβάλλει   verb, pres. act. indic. 3 pers. sg.
        {5.A.1.a} . . . . id.

ἐκβάλλειν   vbl., pres. act. inf. {6.B.1} . . . . id.
ἐκβάλλεις   verb, pres. act. indic. 2 pers. sg.
        {5.A.1.a} . . . . id.
ἐκβάλλεται   verb, pres. pass. indic. 3 pers. sg.
        {5.A.1.d} . . . . id.
ἐκβάλλετε   verb, pres. act. impv. 2 pers. pl.
        {5.D.1} . . . . id.
ἐκβάλλῃ   verb, pres. act. subjunc. 3 pers. sg.
        {5.B.1} . . . . id.
ἐκβαλλόμενοι   vbl., pres. mid. ptc. nom. pl.
        masc. {6.A.1} . . . . id.
ἐκβαλλομένους   vbl., pres. pass. ptc. acc. pl.
        masc. {6.A.1} . . . . id.
ἐκβάλλοντα   vbl., pres. act. ptc. acc. sg. masc.
        {6.A.1} . . . . id.
ἐκβάλλουσι   verb, pres. act. indic. 3 pers. pl.
        {5.A.1.a} . . . . id.
ἐκβάλλουσιν   verb, pres. act. indic. 3 pers. pl.
        {5.A.1.a} . . . . id.
G1544 **ἐκβάλλω** (1) I throw (cast, put) out; (2) I
        banish, Gal 4:30; 3 John 10; (3) I bring forth, I
        produce, Matt 12:35.
ἐκβάλλω   verb, pres. act. indic. 1 pers. sg.
        {5.A.1.a} . . . . .ἐκβάλλω G1544
ἐκβάλλων   vbl., pres. act. ptc. nom. sg. masc.
        {6.A.1} . . . . id.
ἐκβάλλωσιν   verb, pres. act. subjunc. 3 pers. pl.
        {5.B.1} . . . . id.
ἐκβαλόντες   vbl., ²aor. act. ptc. nom. pl. masc.
        {6.A.1.a} . . . . id.
ἐκβαλοῦσα   vbl., ²aor. act. ptc. nom. sg. fem.
        {6.A.1.a} . . . . id.
ἐκβαλοῦσι   verb, fut. act. indic. 3 pers. pl.
        {5.A.2} . . . . id.
ἐκβαλοῦσιν   verb, fut. act. indic. 3 pers. pl.
        {5.A.2} . . . . id.
ἐκβάλω   verb, ²aor. act. subjunc. 1 pers. sg.
        {5.B.1} . . . . id.
ἐκβαλών   vbl., ²aor. act. ptc. nom. sg. masc.
        {6.A.1.a} . . . . id.
ἐκβάλωσι   verb, ²aor. act. subjunc. 3 pers. pl.
        {5.B.1} . . . . id.
ἐκβάλωσιν   verb, ²aor. act. subjunc. 3 pers. pl.
        {5.B.1} . . . . id.
ἔκβασιν   noun, acc. sg. fem. {2.C} . . . . . ἔκβασις G1545
G1545 **ἔκβασις**, -εως, ἡ   (1) a way out, escape, 1 Cor
        10:13; (2) result, Heb 13:7.
ἐκβεβλήκει   verb, plu. act. indic. 3 pers. sg.
        {5.A.1.b} . . . . .ἐκβάλλω G1544
ἐκβληθέντος   vbl., aor. pass. ptc. gen. sg. neut.
        {6.A.1.a} . . . . id.
ἐκβληθήσεται   verb, fut. pass. indic. 3 pers. sg.
        {5.A.1.d} . . . . id.
ἐκβληθήσονται   verb, fut. pass. indic. 3 pers.
        pl. {5.A.1.d} . . . . id.
G1546 **ἐκβολή**, -ῆς, ἡ   a throwing out, a jettisoning of
        cargo, to lighten a ship.
ἐκβολήν   noun, acc. sg. fem. {2.A} . . . . . . ἐκβολή G1546
ἐκγαμίζονται   verb, pres. pass. indic. 3 pers. pl.
        {5.A.1.d} .ἐκγαμίζω G1547

ἐκγαμίζοντες vbl., pres. act. ptc. nom. pl.
  masc. {6.A.1} . . . . id.
G1547 **ἐκγαμίζω** *I give in marriage.*
  ἐκγαμίζων vbl., pres. act. ptc. nom. sg. masc.
  {6.A.1} . . . . .ἐκγαμίζω G1547
  ἐκγαμίσκονται verb, pres. pass. indic. 3 pers. pl.
  {5.A.1.d} .ἐκγαμίσκω G1548
G1548 **ἐκγαμίσκω** *I give in marriage.*
  ἔκγονα adj., acc. pl. neut. {3.C} . . . . .ἔκγονος G1549
G1549 **ἔκγονος**, -ον, τό *descended,* hence subs., *a*
  descendant.
G1550 **ἐκδαπανάω** *I spend (give out) completely.*
  ἐκδαπανηθήσομαι verb, fut. pass. indic. 1 pers.
  sg. {5.A.1} . . . . ἐκδαπανάω G1550
  ἐκδέχεσθε verb, pres. mid./pass. impv. 2 pers. pl.
  {5.D.1} . . . . .ἐκδέχομαι G1551
  ἐκδέχεται verb, pres. mid./pass. indic. 3 pers.
  sg. {5.A.1.d} . . . . id.
G1551 **ἐκδέχομαι** *I wait for, expect.*
  ἐκδέχομαι verb, pres. mid./pass. indic. 1 pers. sg.
  {5.A.1.d} . . . . .ἐκδέχομαι G1551
  ἐκδεχόμενος vbl., pres. mid./pass. ptc. nom.
  sg. masc. {6.A.1} . . . . id.
  ἐκδεχομένου vbl., pres. mid./pass. ptc. gen. sg.
  masc. {6.A.1} . . . . id.
  ἐκδεχομένων vbl., pres. mid./pass. ptc. gen. pl.
  masc. {6.A.1} . . . . id.
G1552 **ἔκδηλος**, -ον *perfectly evident, manifest.*
  ἔκδηλος adj., nom. sg. fem. {3.C} . . . . . . ἔκδηλος G1552
G1553 **ἐκδημέω** *I am away from the* δῆμος, *from my*
  parish, from home.
  ἐκδημῆσαι vbl., aor. act. inf. {6.B.1} . . . . ἐκδημέω G1553
  ἐκδημοῦμεν verb, pres. act. indic. 1 pers. pl.
  {5.A.2} . . . . id.
  ἐκδημοῦντες vbl., pres. act. ptc. nom. pl. masc.
  {6.A.2} . . . . id.
G1554 **ἐκδίδωμι** (1) *I give out, let;* (2) mid., *I let out*
  for my own advantage, Mark 12:1.
G1555 **ἐκδιηγέομαι** *I give a complete narrative of.*
  ἐκδιηγῆται verb, pres. mid./pass. subjunc. 3 pers.
  sg. {5.B.2} . . . . ἐκδιηγέομαι G1555
  ἐκδιηγούμενοι vbl., pres. mid./pass. ptc. nom.
  pl. masc. {6.A.2} . . . . id.
  ἐκδικεῖς verb, pres. act. indic. 2 pers. sg.
  {5.A.2} . . . . .ἐκδικέω G1556
G1556 **ἐκδικέω** *I give justice over, defend, avenge,*
  vindicate.
  ἐκδικῆσαι vbl., aor. act. inf. {6.B.1} . . . . .ἐκδικέω G1556
  ἐκδικήσεως noun, gen. sg. fem. {2.C} . . ἐκδίκησις G1557
  ἐκδίκησιν noun, acc. sg. fem. {2.C} . . . . id.
G1557 **ἐκδίκησις**, -εως, ἡ (1) *defense, avenging,*
  vindication, vengeance; (2) *full (complete)*
  punishment, 2 Thess 1:8; 1 Pet 2:14.
  ἐκδίκησις noun, nom. sg. fem. {2.C} . . . ἐκδίκησις G1557
  ἐκδίκησον verb, aor. act. impv. 2 pers. sg.
  {5.D.1} . . . . .ἐκδικέω G1556
  ἐκδικήσω verb, fut. act. indic. 1 pers. sg. {5.A.1} id.
G1558 **ἔκδικος**, -ου, ὁ *avenging, an avenger.* (The
  word occurs frequently in the sense of a special *advocate* or *champion* of a city.).

ἔκδικος adj., nom. sg. masc. {3.C} . . . . . . ἔκδικος G1558
ἐκδικοῦντες vbl., pres. act. ptc. nom. pl. masc.
  {6.A.2} . . . . .ἐκδικέω G1556
G1559 **ἐκδιώκω** *I drive out.*
  ἐκδιωξάντων vbl., aor. act. ptc. gen. pl. masc.
  {6.A.1.a} . . . . .ἐκδιώκω G1559
  ἐκδιώξουσιν verb, fut. act. indic. 3 pers. pl.
  {5.A.1.a} . . . . id.
  ἐκδόσεται verb, fut. mid. indic. 3 pers. sg.
  {5.A.1} . . . . .ἐκδίδωμι G1554
  ἔκδοτον adj., acc. sg. masc. {3.C} . . . . . . ἔκδοτος G1560
G1560 **ἔκδοτος**, -ον *given up, delivered up.*
G1561 **ἐκδοχή**, -ῆς, ἡ *waiting, expectation.*
  ἐκδοχή noun, nom. sg. fem. {2.A} . . . . . . .ἐκδοχή G1561
  ἐκδυσάμενοι vbl., aor. mid. ptc. nom. pl. masc.
  {6.A.1.b} . . . . ἐκδύω G1562
  ἐκδύσαντες vbl., aor. act. ptc. nom. pl. masc.
  {6.A.1.a} . . . . id.
  ἐκδύσασθαι vbl., aor. mid. inf. {6.B.1} . . . . . . id.
G1562 **ἐκδύω** *I put off, take off, strip off* with acc. of
  person or garment or both.
  ἐκδώσεται verb, fut. mid. indic. 3 pers. sg.
  {5.A.1} . . . . .ἐκδίδωμι G1554
G1563 **ἐκεῖ** adv. (1) *there, yonder;* (2) *thither, there.*
  ἐκεῖ adv. . . . . ἐκεῖ G1563
G1564 **ἐκεῖθεν** adv., *thence, from that place.*
  ἐκεῖθεν adv. ἐκεῖθεν G1564
  ἐκεῖνα pron. dem., acc. pl. neut. {4.B} . . . . ἐκεῖνος G1565
  ἐκεῖνα pron. dem., nom. pl. neut. {4.B} . . . . id.
  ἐκεῖναι pron. dem., nom. pl. fem. {4.B} . . . . id.
  ἐκείναις pron. dem., dat. pl. fem. {4.B} . . . . id.
  ἐκείνας pron. dem., acc. pl. fem. {4.B} . . . . id.
  ἐκείνη pron. dem., nom. sg. fem. {4.B} . . . . id.
  ἐκείνῃ pron. dem., dat. sg. fem. {4.B} . . . . id.
  ἐκείνην pron. dem., acc. sg. fem. {4.B} . . . . . . id.
G1565†‡ **ἐκείνης** adv., *there.* Var. for ἐκεῖνος, Luke
  19:4.
  ἐκείνης adv. . . . . .ἐκείνης G1565†‡
  ἐκείνης pron. dem., gen. sg. fem. {4.B} . . . . id.
  ἐκεῖνο pron. dem., acc. sg. neut. {4.B} . . . . id.
  ἐκεῖνο pron. dem., nom. sg. neut. {4.B} . . . . . . id.
  ἐκεῖνοι pron. dem., nom. pl. masc. {4.B} . . . . . . id.
  ἐκείνοις pron. dem., dat. pl. masc. {4.B} . . . . . . id.
  ἐκεῖνον pron. dem., acc. sg. masc. {4.B} . . . . . . id.
G1565 **ἐκεῖνος**, -η, -ο *that, yonder* (of what is distant,
  or great); in 1 John, "that one" = Christ. Var.
  adv. ἐκείνης, Luke 19:4.
  ἐκεῖνος pron. dem., nom. sg. masc. {4.B} . . ἐκεῖνος G1565
  ἐκείνου pron. dem., gen. sg. masc. {4.B} . . . . . . id.
  ἐκείνου pron. dem., gen. sg. neut. {4.B} . . . . id.
  ἐκείνους pron. dem., acc. pl. masc. {4.B} . . . . . . id.
  ἐκείνῳ pron. dem., dat. sg. masc. {4.B} . . . . id.
  ἐκείνων pron. dem., gen. pl. fem. {4.B} . . . . id.
  ἐκείνων pron. dem., gen. pl. masc. {4.B} . . . . . . id.
  ἐκείνων pron. dem., gen. pl. neut. {4.B} . . . . id.
G1566 **ἐκεῖσε** adv. (1) *thither,* Acts 21:3; (2) *there,*
  Acts 22:5.
  ἐκεῖσε adv. . . . . ἐκεῖσε G1566
  ἔκειτο verb, impf. mid./pass. indic. 3 pers. sg.
  {5.A.3.a} . . . . κεῖμαι G2749

ἐκέκραξα   verb, aor. act. indic. 1 pers. sg.
{5.A.1.b} . . . . κράζω G2896
ἐκέλευον   verb, impf. act. indic. 3 pers. pl.
{5.A.1.b} . . . . κελεύω G2753
ἐκέλευσα   verb, aor. act. indic. 1 pers. sg.
{5.A.1.b} . . . . id.
ἐκέλευσε   verb, aor. act. indic. 3 pers. sg.
{5.A.1.b} . . . . id.
ἐκέλευσεν   verb, aor. act. indic. 3 pers. sg.
{5.A.1.b} . . . . id.
ἐκένωσε   verb, aor. act. indic. 3 pers. sg. {5.A.1} .κενόω G2758
ἐκένωσεν   verb, aor. act. indic. 3 pers. sg. {5.A.1} id.
ἐκέρασε   verb, aor. act. indic. 3 pers. sg.
{5.A.3.b} . . . . κεράννυμι G2767
ἐκέρασεν   verb, aor. act. indic. 3 pers. sg.
{5.A.3.b} . . . . id.
ἐκέρδησα   verb, aor. act. indic. 1 pers. sg.
{5.A.1.b} . . . . κερδαίνω G2770
ἐκέρδησας   verb, aor. act. indic. 2 pers. sg.
{5.A.1.b} . . . . id.
ἐκέρδησε   verb, aor. act. indic. 3 pers. sg.
{5.A.1.b} . . . . id.
ἐκέρδησεν   verb, aor. act. indic. 3 pers. sg.
{5.A.1.b} . . . . id.
ἐκεφαλαίωσαν   verb, aor. act. indic. 3 pers. pl.
{5.A.1} . . . . κεφαλαιόω G2775
ἐκεφαλίωσαν   verb, aor. act. indic. 3 pers. pl.
{5.A.1} . . . . id.
G1567 **ἐκζητέω**   *I seek out.*
ἐκζητηθῇ   verb, aor. pass. subjunc. 3 pers. sg.
{5.B.1} . . . . ἐκζητέω G1567
ἐκζητηθήσεται   verb, fut. pass. indic. 3 pers.
sg. {5.A.1} . . . . id.
ἐκζητήσας   vbl., aor. act. ptc. nom. sg. masc.
{6.A.2} . . . . id.
ἐκζητήσεις   noun, acc. pl. fem. {2.C} . ἐκζήτησις G2214†‡
G2214†‡ **ἐκζήτησις**, -εως, ἡ   *a seeking out, searching
questioning.* Var. for ζήτησις, 1 Tim. 1:4.
ἐκζητήσωσιν   verb, aor. act. subjunc. 3 pers. pl.
{5.B.1} . . . . ἐκζητέω G1567
ἐκζητοῦσιν   vbl., pres. act. ptc. dat. pl. masc.
{6.A.2} . . . . id.
ἐκζητῶν   vbl., pres. act. ptc. nom. sg. masc.
{6.A.2} . . . . id.
ἐκηρύξαμεν   verb, aor. act. indic. 1 pers. pl.
{5.A.1.b} . . . . κηρύσσω G2784
ἐκήρυξαν   verb, aor. act. indic. 3 pers. pl.
{5.A.1.b} . . . . id.
ἐκήρυξεν   verb, aor. act. indic. 3 pers. sg.
{5.A.1.b} . . . . id.
ἐκήρυσσε   verb, impf. act. indic. 3 pers. sg.
{5.A.1.b} . . . . id.
ἐκήρυσσεν   verb, impf. act. indic. 3 pers. sg.
{5.A.1.b} . . . . id.
ἐκήρυσσον   verb, impf. act. indic. 3 pers. pl.
{5.A.1.b} . . . . id.
ἐκηρύχθη   verb, aor. pass. indic. 3 pers. sg.
{5.A.1.b} . . . . id.
ἐκθαμβεῖσθαι   vbl., pres. pass. inf.
{6.B.2} . . . . ἐκθαμβέω G1568

ἐκθαμβεῖσθε   verb, pres. pass. impv. 2 pers. pl.
{5.D.2} . . . . id.
G1568 **ἐκθαμβέω**   pass., *I am greatly astonished.*
ἔκθαμβοι   adj., nom. pl. masc. {3.C} . . . ἔκθαμβος G1569
G1569 **ἔκθαμβος**, -ον   *full of astonishment.*
G2296†‡ **ἐκθαυμάζω**   *I wonder greatly.* Var. for
θαυμάζω, 1 Tim 1:4.
ἔκθετα   adj., acc. pl. neut. {3.C} . . . . ἔκθετος G1570
G1570 **ἔκθετος**, -ον   *exposed* (to the elements).
ἐκινδύνευον   verb, impf. act. indic. 3 pers. pl.
{5.A.1.b} . . . . κινδυνεύω G2793
ἐκινήθη   verb, aor. pass. indic. 3 pers. sg.
{5.A.1} . . . . .κινέω G2795
ἐκινήθησαν   verb, aor. pass. indic. 3 pers. pl.
{5.A.1} . . . . id.
G1571 **ἐκκαθαίρω**   (1) *I clean (cleanse) out,* 1 Cor 5:7;
(2) *I clean thoroughly,* 2 Tim 2:21.
ἐκκαθάρατε   verb, aor. act. impv. 2 pers. pl.
{5.D.1} . . . . ἐκκαθαίρω G1571
ἐκκαθάρῃ   verb, aor. act. subjunc. 3 pers. sg.
{5.B.1} . . . . id.
G1572 **ἐκκαίω**   pass. *I am inflamed (with lust).*
ἐκκακεῖν   vbl., pres. act. inf. {6.B.2} . . . . . ἐκκακέω G1573
G1573 **ἐκκακέω** (ἐγκακέω)   (1) *I grow tired;* (2) *I lose
heart* (from κακός in the sense of *cowardly;*
very rare outside the Bible).
ἐκκακήσητε   verb, aor. act. subjunc. 2 pers. pl.
{5.B.1} . . . . ἐκκακέω G1573
ἐκκακοῦμεν   verb, pres. act. indic. 1 pers. pl.
{5.A.2} . . . . id.
ἐκκακῶμεν   verb, pres. act. subjunc. 1 pers. pl.
{5.B.2} . . . . id.
G1574 **ἐκκεντέω**   *I pierce through* (or *deeply*).
ἐκκεχυμένον   vbl., perf. pass. ptc. nom. sg. neut.
{6.A.2} . . . . ἐκχέω G1632
ἐκκέχυται   verb, perf. pass. indic. 3 pers. sg.
{5.A.1} . . . . id.
G1575 **ἐκκλάω**   *I break off.*
ἐκκλεῖσαι   vbl., aor. act. inf. {6.B.1} . . . . . .ἐκκλείω G1576
G1576 **ἐκκλείω**   *I shut out, exclude.*
G1577 **ἐκκλησία**, -ας, ἡ   *an assembly, meeting of
assembly* (lit., *a calling out*), Acts 19:39; (1) *a
community, congregation, church, society* (first
used in LXX for *the congregation* of Israel),
the assembly of Christians in *one* city or community; in Matt 16:18; 18:17 the body of Palestinian adherents of the Messiah is intended;
(2) much more rarely, in a developed sense,
esp. with ὅλη, *the Church* (the whole body of
Christians in the world).
ἐκκλησία   noun, nom. sg. fem. {2.A} . . . ἐκκλησία G1577
ἐκκλησίᾳ   noun, dat. sg. fem. {2.A} . . . . id.
ἐκκλησίαι   noun, nom. pl. fem. {2.A} . . . . id.
ἐκκλησίαις   noun, dat. pl. fem. {2.A} . . . . id.
ἐκκλησίαν   noun, acc. sg. fem. {2.A} . . . . id.
ἐκκλησίας   noun, acc. pl. fem. {2.A} . . . . id.
ἐκκλησίας   noun, gen. sg. fem. {2.A} . . . . id.
ἐκκλησιῶν   noun, gen. pl. fem. {2.A} . . . . id.
ἐκκλίνατε   verb, aor. act. impv. 2 pers. pl.
{5.D.1} . . . . ἐκκλίνω G1578

ἐκκλινάτω   verb, aor. act. impv. 3 pers. sg.
 {5.D.1} . . . . id.
ἐκκλίνετε   verb, pres. act. impv. 2 pers. pl.
 {5.D.1} . . . . id.
G1578 **ἐκκλίνω**   *I fall away from, I turn away* (from);
 (lit. *I bend away from*).
G1579 **ἐκκολυμβάω**   *I swim out* (of the water).
ἐκκολυμβήσας   vbl., aor. act. ptc. nom. sg. masc.
 {6.A.2} . . . . .ἐκκολυμβάω G1579
G1580 **ἐκκομίζω**   *I carry out* (of the city gate for
 burial).
ἐκκοπήσῃ   verb, ²fut. pass. indic. 2 pers. sg.
 {5.A.1.d} . . . . ἐκκόπτω G1581
ἐκκόπτεσθαι   vbl., pres. pass. inf. {6.B.1} . . . . . . id.
ἐκκόπτεται   verb, pres. pass. indic. 3 pers. sg.
 {5.A.1.d} . . . . id.
G1581 **ἐκκόπτω**   *I cut out (off, away).*
ἐκκόψεις   verb, fut. act. indic. 2 pers. sg.
 {5.A.1.a} . . . . ἐκκόπτω G1581
ἔκκοψον   verb, aor. act. impv. 2 pers. sg. {5.D.1}. id.
ἐκκόψω   verb, aor. act. subjunc. 1 pers. sg.
 {5.B.1} . . . . id.
G1582 **ἐκκρεμάννυμι** (ἐκκρέμαμαι)   mid. or pass., *I
 hang upon, pay attention to* with gen. (met.).
ἔκλαιε   verb, impf. act. indic. 3 pers. sg.
 {5.A.1.b} . . . . κλαίω G2799
ἔκλαιεν   verb, impf. act. indic. 3 pers. sg.
 {5.A.1.b} . . . . id.
ἔκλαιον   verb, impf. act. indic. 1 pers. sg.
 {5.A.1.b} . . . . id.
ἔκλαιον   verb, impf. act. indic. 3 pers. pl.
 {5.A.1.b} . . . . id.
G1583 **ἐκλαλέω**   *I speak out, tell out.*
ἐκλαλῆσαι   vbl., aor. act. inf. {6.B.1} . . . . ἐκλαλέω G1583
G1584 **ἐκλάμπω**   *I shine forth (out).*
ἐκλάμψουσιν   verb, fut. act. indic. 3 pers. pl.
 {5.A.1.a} . . . . ἐκλάμπω G1584
G1585 **ἐκλανθάνομαι**   *I quite forget.*
ἔκλασα   verb, aor. act. indic. 1 pers. sg. {5.A.1} κλάω G2806
ἔκλασε   verb, aor. act. indic. 3 pers. sg. {5.A.1} . . id.
ἔκλασεν   verb, aor. act. indic. 3 pers. sg. {5.A.1}. id.
ἐκλαύσατε   verb, aor. act. indic. 2 pers. pl.
 {5.A.1.b} . . . . κλαίω G2799
ἔκλαυσε   verb, aor. act. indic. 3 pers. sg.
 {5.A.1.b} . . . . id.
ἔκλαυσεν   verb, aor. act. indic. 3 pers. sg.
 {5.A.1.b} . . . . id.
G1586 **ἐκλέγομαι**   *I pick out for myself, I choose.*
ἐκλείπῃ   verb, pres. act. subjunc. 3 pers. sg.
 {5.B.1} .ἐκλείπω G1587
ἐκλείποντος   vbl., pres. act. ptc. gen. sg. masc.
 {6.A.1} . . . . id.
G1587 **ἐκλείπω**   intrans., (1) *I fail utterly;* (2) *I am in a
 state of eclipse* (of the sun) Luke 23:45.
ἔκλεισεν   verb, aor. act. indic. 3 pers. sg.
 {5.A.1.b} . . . . .κλείω G2808
ἐκλείσθη   verb, aor. pass. indic. 3 pers. sg.
 {5.A.1.b} . . . . id.
ἐκλείσθησαν   verb, aor. pass. indic. 3 pers. pl.
 {5.A.1.b} . . . . id.

ἐκλείψουσι   verb, fut. act. indic. 3 pers. pl.
 {5.A.1.a} . . . . ἐκλείπω G1587
ἐκλείψουσιν   verb, fut. act. indic. 3 pers. pl.
 {5.A.1.a} . . . . id.
ἐκλεκτῇ   adj., dat. sg. fem. {3.A} . . . . ἐκλεκτός G1588
ἐκλεκτῆς   adj., gen. sg. fem. {3.A} . . . . id.
ἐκλεκτοί   adj., nom. pl. masc. {3.A} . . . . id.
ἐκλεκτοῖς   adj., dat. pl. masc. {3.A} . . . . id.
ἐκλεκτόν   adj., acc. sg. masc. {3.A} . . . . id.
ἐκλεκτόν   adj., nom. sg. neut. {3.A} . . . . id.
G1588 **ἐκλεκτός**, -ή, -όν   *chosen out, selected,* sometimes as subs., of those chosen out by God for
 the rendering of special service to Him (of the
 Hebrew race, particular Hebrews, the Messiah,
 and the Christians); an adj. in 2 John 1, 13.
ἐκλεκτός   adj., nom. sg. masc. {3.A} . . . . ἐκλεκτός G1588
ἐκλεκτούς   adj., acc. pl. masc. {3.A} . . . . id.
ἐκλεκτῶν   adj., gen. pl. masc. {3.A} . . . . id.
ἐκλελεγμένος   vbl., perf. pass. ptc. nom. sg. masc.
 {6.A.1.b} . . . . .ἐκλέγομαι G1586
ἐκλέλησθε   verb, perf. pass. indic. 2 pers. pl.
 {5.A.1.f} . . . . .ἐκλανθάνομαι G1585
ἐκλελυμένοι   vbl., perf. pass. ptc. nom. pl. masc.
 {6.A.1.b} . . . . ἐκλύω G1590
ἐκλεξαμένοις   vbl., aor. mid. ptc. dat. pl. masc.
 {6.A.1.b} . . . . .ἐκλέγομαι G1586
ἐκλεξάμενος   vbl., aor. mid. ptc. nom. sg.
 masc. {6.A.1.b} . . . . id.
ἐκλεξαμένους   vbl., aor. mid. ptc. acc. pl. masc.
 {6.A.1.b} . . . . id.
ἔκλεψαν   verb, aor. act. indic. 3 pers. pl.
 {5.A.1.b} . . . . κλέπτω G2813
ἐκλήθη   verb, aor. pass. indic. 3 pers. sg.
 {5.A.1} .καλέω G2564
ἐκλήθης   verb, aor. pass. indic. 2 pers. sg. {5.A.1}id.
ἐκλήθητε   verb, aor. pass. indic. 2 pers. pl.
 {5.A.1} . . . . id.
ἐκληρώθημεν   verb, aor. pass. indic. 1 pers. pl.
 {5.A.1} .κληρόω G2820
ἔκλιναν   verb, aor. act. indic. 3 pers. pl.
 {5.A.1.b} . . . . κλίνω G2827
ἐκλίπῃ   verb, ²aor. act. subjunc. 3 pers. sg.
 {5.B.1} .ἐκλείπω G1587
ἐκλίπητε   verb, ²aor. act. subjunc. 2 pers. pl.
 {5.B.1} . . . . id.
ἐκλιπόντος   vbl., ²aor. act. ptc. gen. sg. masc.
 {6.A.1.a} . . . . id.
G1589 **ἐκλογή**, -ῆς, ἡ   *choosing out, selecting, choice*
 (by God); in Acts 9:15 a Hebraistic gen.,
 equivalent to ἐκλεκτόν.
ἐκλογή   noun, nom. sg. fem. {2.A} . . . . ἐκλογή G1589
ἐκλογήν   noun, acc. sg. fem. {2.A} . . . . id.
ἐκλογῆς   noun, gen. sg. fem. {2.A} . . . . id.
ἐκλυθήσονται   verb, fut. pass. indic. 3 pers. pl.
 {5.A.1.d} . . . . ἐκλύω G1590
ἐκλυθῶσιν   verb, aor. pass. subjunc. 3 pers. pl.
 {5.B.1} . . . . id.
ἐκλυόμενοι   vbl., pres. pass. ptc. nom. pl. masc.
 {6.A.1} . . . . id.
ἐκλύου   verb, pres. pass. impv. 2 pers. sg. {5.D.1} id.

G1590 **ἐκλύω**   pass., *I am unstrung, become weak, fail.*
ἐκμάξασα   vbl., aor. act. ptc. nom. sg. fem.
  {6.A.1.a} . . . . .ἐκμάσσω G1591
ἐκμάσσειν   vbl., pres. act. inf. {6.B.1} . . . . id.
G1591 **ἐκμάσσω**   *I wipe (off) thoroughly.*
G1592 **ἐκμυκτηρίζω**   *I mock greatly.*
G1593 **ἐκνεύω**   *I retire, withdraw* (lit. *I bend the head
    aside,* to avoid a blow).
G1594 **ἐκνήφω**   *I am thoroughly sober* (in mind).
ἐκνήψατε   verb, aor. act. impv. 2 pers. pl.
  {5.D.1} . . . . .ἐκνήφω G1594
ἐκοιμήθη   verb, aor. pass. indic. 3 pers. sg.
  {5.A.1} . . . . κοιμάω G2837
ἐκοιμήθησαν   verb, aor. pass. indic. 3 pers. pl.
  {5.A.1} . . . . id.
ἐκοινώνησαν   verb, aor. act. indic. 3 pers. pl.
  {5.A.1} . . . . κοινωνέω G2841
ἐκοινώνησεν   verb, aor. act. indic. 3 pers. sg.
  {5.A.1} . . . . id.
ἐκολάφισαν   verb, aor. act. indic. 3 pers. pl.
  {5.A.1.b} . . . . κολαφίζω G2852
ἐκολλήθη   verb, aor. pass. indic. 3 pers. sg.
  {5.A.1} . . . . .κολλάω G2853
ἐκολλήθησαν   verb, aor. pass. indic. 3 pers. pl.
  {5.A.1} . . . . id.
ἐκολοβώθησαν   verb, aor. pass. indic. 3 pers. pl.
  {5.A.1} . . . . .κολοβόω G2856
ἐκολόβωσε   verb, aor. act. indic. 3 pers. sg. {5.A.1} . id.
ἐκολόβωσεν   verb, aor. act. indic. 3 pers. sg.
  {5.A.1} . . . . id.
ἐκομισάμην   verb, aor. mid. indic. 1 pers. sg.
  {5.A.1.e} . . . . κομίζω G2865
ἐκομίσαντο   verb, aor. mid. indic. 3 pers. pl.
  {5.A.1.e} . . . . id.
ἐκομίσατο   verb, aor. mid. indic. 3 pers. sg.
  {5.A.1.e} . . . . id.
ἐκόπασεν   verb, aor. act. indic. 3 pers. sg.
  {5.A.1.b} . . . . .κοπάζω G2869
ἐκοπίασα   verb, aor. act. indic. 1 pers. sg.
  {5.A.1} . . . . .κοπιάω G2872
ἐκοπίασας   verb, aor. act. indic. 2 pers. sg.
  {5.A.1} . . . . id.
ἐκοπίασεν   verb, aor. act. indic. 3 pers. sg.
  {5.A.1} . . . . id.
ἔκοπτον   verb, impf. act. indic. 3 pers. pl.
  {5.A.1.b} . . . . κόπτω G2875
ἐκόπτοντο   verb, impf. mid. indic. 3 pers. pl.
  {5.A.1.e} . . . . id.
ἐκόσμησαν   verb, aor. act. indic. 3 pers. pl.
  {5.A.1} . . . . .κοσμέω G2885
ἐκόσμουν   verb, impf. act. indic. 3 pers. pl.
  {5.A.2} . . . . id.
ἐκοῦσα   adj., nom. sg. fem. {3.D} . . . . ἑκών G1635
ἑκούσιον   adj., acc. sg. neut. {3.A} . . . . .ἑκούσιος G1595
G1595 **ἑκούσιος**, -α, -ον   *willing;* κατὰ ἑκούσιον,
    with right good will.
G1596 **ἑκουσίως**   adv., *willingly, with the will.*
ἑκουσίως   adv. {3.F} . . . . ἑκουσίως G1596
ἐκούφιζον   verb, impf. act. indic. 3 pers. pl.
  {5.A.1.b} . . . . κουφίζω G2893

ἐκόψασθε   verb, aor. mid. indic. 2 pers. pl.
  {5.A.1.e} . . . . κόπτω G2875
G1597 **ἔκπαλαι**   adv., *from of old, long since.*
ἔκπαλαι   adv. . . . . ἔκπαλαι G1597
ἐκπειράζοντες   vbl., pres. act. ptc. nom. pl. masc.
  {6.A.1} . . . . ἐκπειράζω G1598
G1598 **ἐκπειράζω**   *I put to a thorough test.*
ἐκπειράζωμεν   verb, pres. act. subjunc. 1 pers. pl.
  {5.B.1} . . . . ἐκπειράζω G1598
ἐκπειράζων   vbl., pres. act. ptc. nom. sg. masc.
  {6.A.1} . . . . id.
ἐκπειράσεις   verb, fut. act. indic. 2 pers. sg.
  {5.A.1.a} . . . . id.
G1599 **ἐκπέμπω**   *I send out.*
ἐκπεμφθέντες   vbl., aor. pass. ptc. nom. pl. masc.
  {6.A.1.a} . . . . ἐκπέμπω G1599
ἐκπεπλήρωκε   verb, perf. act. indic. 3 pers. sg.
  {5.A.1} . . . . .ἐκπληρόω G1603
ἐκπεπλήρωκεν   verb, perf. act. indic. 3 pers. sg.
  {5.A.1} . . . . id.
ἐκπέπτωκας   verb, perf. act. indic. 2 pers. sg.
  {5.A.1.c} . . . . .ἐκπίπτω G1601
ἐκπέπτωκεν   verb, perf. act. indic. 3 pers. sg.
  {5.A.1.c} . . . . id.
G4053†‡ **ἐκπερισσοῦ** (ἐκπερισσῶς)   adv., *most
    exceedingly, with exceeding emphasis.* Var. for
    περισσός, Mark 14:31.
ἐκπερισσοῦ   adv. {3.F} . . . . ἐκπερισσοῦ G4053†‡
ἐκπερισσῶς   adv. {3.F} . . . . id.
ἐκπεσεῖν   vbl., ²aor. act. inf. {6.B.1} . . . . . .ἐκπίπτω G1601
ἐκπέσητε   verb, ²aor. act. subjunc. 2 pers. pl.
  {5.B.1} . . . . id.
ἐκπέσωμεν   verb, ²aor. act. subjunc. 1 pers. pl.
  {5.B.1} . . . . id.
ἐκπέσωσι   verb, ²aor. act. subjunc. 3 pers. pl.
  {5.B.1} . . . . id.
ἐκπέσωσιν   verb, ²aor. act. subjunc. 3 pers. pl.
  {5.B.1} . . . . id.
G1600 **ἐκπετάννυμι**   *I spread (stretch) out.*
ἐκπεφευγέναι   vbl., ²perf. act. inf. {6.B.1} . ἐκφεύγω G1628
G1530†‡ **ἐκπηδάω**   *I leap (rush) out.* Var. for εἰσπηδάω,
    Acts 14:14.
ἐκπίπτει   verb, pres. act. indic. 3 pers. sg.
  {5.A.1.a} . . . . .ἐκπίπτω G1601
ἐκπίπτοντες   vbl., pres. act. ptc. nom. pl. masc.
  {6.A.1} . . . . id.
G1601 **ἐκπίπτω**   (1) *I fall out, I fall off, I fall away;* (2)
    hence, in nautical language, *I fall off* from the
    straight course; (3) of flowers, *I fade away,
    wither away.*
ἐκπλεῦσαι   vbl., aor. act. inf. {6.B.1} . . . . . ἐκπλέω G1602
G1602 **ἐκπλέω**   *I sail out* (of harbor), *I sail away.*
G1603 **ἐκπληρόω**   *I fill completely, I fulfill in every
    particular (to the utmost), I make good.*
ἐκπλήρωσιν   noun, acc. sg. fem.
  {2.C} . . . . ἐκπλήρωσις G1604
G1604 **ἐκπλήρωσις**, -εως, ἡ   *completion, fulfillment.*
ἐκπλήσσεσθαι   vbl., pres. pass. inf.
  {6.B.1} . . . . .ἐκπλήσσω G1605

ἐκπλησσόμενος   vbl., pres. pass. ptc. nom. sg.
  masc. {6.A.1} . . . . id.
G1605 **ἐκπλήσσω**   pass., *I am thunderstruck,*
  astounded.
ἐκπλήττεσθαι   vbl., pres. pass. inf.
  {6.B.1} . . . . .ἐκπλήσσω G1605
ἐκπληττόμενος   vbl., pres. pass. ptc. nom. sg.
  masc. {6.A.1} . . . . id.
G1606 **ἐκπνέω**   *I breathe my last, I expire* (lit. *I breathe*
  out).
ἐκπορεύεσθαι   vbl., pres. mid./pass. inf.
  {6.B.1} . . . . ἐκπορεύομαι G1607
ἐκπορεύέσθω   verb, pres. mid./pass. impv.
  3 pers. sg. {5.D.1} . . . . id.
ἐκπορεύεται   verb, pres. mid./pass. indic.
  3 pers. sg. {5.A.1.d} . . . . id.
G1607 **ἐκπορεύομαι**   (1) *I journey out;* (2) *I come*
  forth.
ἐκπορευόμενα   vbl., pres. mid./pass. ptc. nom. pl.
  neut. {6.A.1} . . . . ἐκπορεύομαι G1607
ἐκπορευομένη   vbl., pres. mid./pass. ptc. dat.
  sg. fem. {6.A.1} . . . . id.
ἐκπορευομένη   vbl., pres. mid./pass. ptc. nom.
  sg. fem. {6.A.1} . . . . id.
ἐκπορευόμενοι   vbl., pres. mid./pass. ptc. nom.
  pl. masc. {6.A.1} . . . . id.
ἐκπορευομένοις   vbl., pres. mid./pass. ptc. dat.
  pl. masc. {6.A.1} . . . . id.
ἐκπορευόμενον   vbl., pres. mid./pass. ptc. acc.
  sg. masc. {6.A.1} . . . . id.
ἐκπορευόμενον   vbl., pres. mid./pass. ptc.
  nom. sg. neut. {6.A.1} . . . . id.
ἐκπορευόμενος   vbl., pres. mid./pass. ptc.
  nom. sg. masc. {6.A.1} . . . . id.
ἐκπορευομένου   vbl., pres. mid./pass. ptc. gen.
  sg. masc. {6.A.1} . . . . id.
ἐκπορευομένου   vbl., pres. mid./pass. ptc. gen.
  sg. neut. {6.A.1} . . . . id.
ἐκπορευομένῳ   vbl., pres. mid./pass. ptc. dat.
  sg. neut. {6.A.1} . . . . id.
ἐκπορευομένων   vbl., pres. mid./pass. ptc. gen.
  pl. masc. {6.A.1} . . . . id.
ἐκπορεύονται   verb, pres. mid./pass. indic.
  3 pers. pl. {5.A.1.d} . . . . id.
ἐκπορεύσονται   verb, fut. mid. indic. 3 pers.
  pl. {5.A.1.d} . . . . id.
ἐκπορνεύσασαι   vbl., aor. act. ptc. nom. pl. fem.
  {6.A.1.a} . . . . ἐκπορνεύω G1608
G1608 **ἐκπορνεύω**   *I am guilty of fornication* (the force
  of ἐκ is uncertain).
G1609 **ἐκπτύω**   *I spit upon, disdain.*
ἔκραζε   verb, impf. act. indic. 3 pers. sg.
  {5.A.1.b} . . . . κράζω G2896
ἔκραζεν   verb, impf. act. indic. 3 pers. sg.
  {5.A.1.b} . . . . id.
ἔκραζον   verb, impf. act. indic. 3 pers. pl.
  {5.A.1.b} . . . . id.
ἔκραξα   verb, aor. act. indic. 1 pers. sg. {5.A.1.b} id.
ἔκραξαν   verb, aor. act. indic. 3 pers. pl.
  {5.A.1.b} . . . . id.

ἔκραξε   verb, aor. act. indic. 3 pers. sg. {5.A.1.b}. id.
ἔκραξεν   verb, aor. act. indic. 3 pers. sg. {5.A.1.b}id.
ἐκραταιοῦτο   verb, impf. pass. indic. 3 pers. sg.
  {5.A.2} . . . . κραταιόω G2901
ἐκρατήσαμεν   verb, aor. act. indic. 1 pers. pl.
  {5.A.1} . . . . κρατέω G2902
ἐκράτησαν   verb, aor. act. indic. 3 pers. pl.
  {5.A.1} . . . . id.
ἐκρατήσατε   verb, aor. act. indic. 2 pers. pl.
  {5.A.1} . . . . id.
ἐκράτησε   verb, aor. act. indic. 3 pers. sg. {5.A.1}id.
ἐκράτησεν   verb, aor. act. indic. 3 pers. sg.
  {5.A.1} . . . . id.
ἐκρατοῦντο   verb, impf. pass. indic. 3 pers. pl.
  {5.A.2} . . . . id.
ἐκραύγαζον   verb, impf. act. indic. 3 pers. pl.
  {5.A.1.b} . . . . κραυγάζω G2905
ἐκραύγασαν   verb, aor. act. indic. 3 pers. pl.
  {5.A.1.b} . . . . id.
ἐκραύγασε   verb, aor. act. indic. 3 pers. sg.
  {5.A.1.b} . . . . id.
ἐκραύγασεν   verb, aor. act. indic. 3 pers. sg.
  {5.A.1.b} . . . . id.
G1610 **ἐκριζόω**   *I root out, root up.*
ἐκριζωθέντα   vbl., aor. pass. ptc. nom. pl. neut.
  {6.A.1.a.} . . . . .ἐκριζόω G1610
ἐκριζωθήσεται   verb, fut. pass. indic. 3 pers.
  sg. {5.A.1} . . . . id.
ἐκριζώθητι   verb, aor. pass. impv. 2 pers. sg.
  {5.D.1} . . . . id.
ἐκριζώσητε   verb, aor. act. subjunc. 2 pers. pl.
  {5.B.1} . . . . id.
ἐκρίθη   verb, aor. pass. indic. 3 pers. sg.
  {5.A.1.b} . . . . κρίνω G2919
ἐκρίθησαν   verb, aor. pass. indic. 3 pers. pl.
  {5.A.1.b} . . . . id.
ἔκρινα   verb, aor. act. indic. 1 pers. sg. {5.A.1.b}. id.
ἔκρινας   verb, aor. act. indic. 2 pers. sg. {5.A.1.b}id.
ἔκρινε   verb, aor. act. indic. 3 pers. sg. {5.A.1.b} . id.
ἔκρινεν   verb, aor. act. indic. 3 pers. sg. {5.A.1.b} id.
ἐκρινόμεθα   verb, impf. pass. indic. 1 pers. pl.
  {5.A.1.e} . . . . id.
ἐκρύβη   verb, ²aor. pass. indic. 3 pers. sg.
  {5.A.1.e} . . . . κρύπτω G2928
ἔκρυψα   verb, aor. act. indic. 1 pers. sg. {5.A.1.b} id.
ἔκρυψαν   verb, aor. act. indic. 3 pers. pl.
  {5.A.1.b} . . . . id.
ἔκρυψας   verb, aor. act. indic. 2 pers. sg.
  {5.A.1.b} . . . . id.
ἔκρυψεν   verb, aor. act. indic. 3 pers. sg.
  {5.A.1.b} . . . . id.
ἐκστάσει   noun, dat. sg. fem. {2.C} . . . . .ἔκστασις G1611
ἐκστάσεως   noun, gen. sg. fem. {2.C} . . . . . id.
G1611 **ἔκστασις**, -εως, ἡ   *bewilderment* (properly,
  distraction or *disturbance* of mind caused by a
  shock).
ἔκστασις   noun, nom. sg. fem. {2.C} . . . .ἔκστασις G1611
G1612 **ἐκστρέφω**   *I pervert.*
G1856†‡ **ἐκσῴζω**   *I save completely.* Var. for ἐξωθέω,
  Acts 27:39.

ἐκσῶσαι vbl., aor. act. inf. {6.B.1} . . . . ἐκσῴζω G1856†‡
ἐκταράσσουσιν verb, pres. act. indic. 3 pers. pl.
{5.A.1.a} . . . . ἐκταράσσω G1613
G1613 **ἐκταράσσω** *I disturb (trouble) greatly*
(exceedingly).
ἐκτεθέντα vbl., aor. pass. ptc. acc. sg. masc.
{6.A.3} . . . . ἐκτίθημι G1620
ἐκτεθέντος vbl., aor. pass. ptc. gen. sg. masc.
{6.A.3} . . . . id.
ἐκτείνας vbl., aor. act. ptc. nom. sg. masc.
{6.A.1.a} . . . . ἐκτείνω G1614
ἐκτείνειν vbl., pres. act. inf. {6.B.1} . . . . id.
ἔκτεινον verb, aor. act. impv. 2 pers. sg. {5.D.1}. id.
G1614 **ἐκτείνω** *I stretch out (forth).*
ἐκτελέσαι vbl., aor. act. inf. {6.B.1} . . . . . ἐκτελέω G1615
G1615 **ἐκτελέω** *I complete, bring to completion, carry*
out, perform.
G1616 **ἐκτένεια**, -ας, ἡ *earnestness, strenuousness.*
ἐκτενείᾳ noun, dat. sg. fem. {2.A} . . . . . ἐκτένεια G1616
ἐκτενεῖς verb, fut. act. indic. 2 pers. sg.
{5.A.2} . . . . ἐκτείνω G1614
G1617 **ἐκτενέστερον** *more intently, more earnestly*
(comp.).
ἐκτενέστερον adv. comp. {3.F; 3.G} ἐκτενέστερον G1617
ἐκτενῆ adj., acc. sg. fem. {3.E} . . . . ἐκτενής G1618
G1618 **ἐκτενής**, -ές (1) *intent, constant, strenuous;*
(2) comp. adv., ἐκτενέστερον, *more earnestly,*
very fervently.
ἐκτενής adj., nom. sg. fem. {3.E} . . . . ἐκτενής G1618
G1619 **ἐκτενῶς** adv., *earnestly, strenuously.*
ἐκτενῶς adv. {3.F} . . . . ἐκτενῶς G1619
ἕκτη adj., nom. sg. fem. {3.A} . . . . ἕκτος G1623
ἕκτην adj., acc. sg. fem. {3.A} . . . . id.
ἕκτης adj., gen. sg. fem. {3.A} . . . . id.
ἐκτησάμην verb, aor. mid. indic. 1 pers. sg.
{5.A.1} . . . . κτάομαι G2932
ἐκτήσατο verb, aor. mid. indic. 3 pers. sg. {5.A.1}. .id.
G1620 **ἐκτίθημι** (1) *I abandon* or *expose* a child; (2)
mid. *I set forth, expound, explain.*
ἐκτιναξάμενοι vbl., aor. mid. ptc. nom. pl. masc.
{6.A.1.b} . . . . ἐκτινάσσω G1621
ἐκτιναξάμενος vbl., aor. mid. ptc. nom. sg.
masc. {6.A.1.b} . . . . id.
ἐκτινάξατε verb, aor. act. impv. 2 pers. pl.
{5.D.1} . . . . id.
G1621 **ἐκτινάσσω** *I shake off;* mid. *I shake off from*
myself.
ἔκτισας verb, aor. act. indic. 2 pers. sg.
{5.A.1.b} . . . . .κτίζω G2936
ἔκτισε verb, aor. act. indic. 3 pers. sg. {5.A.1.b} . id.
ἔκτισεν verb, aor. act. indic. 3 pers. sg. {5.A.1.b} id.
ἐκτίσθη verb, aor. pass. indic. 3 pers. sg.
{5.A.1.b} . . . . id.
ἐκτίσθησαν verb, aor. pass. indic. 3 pers. pl.
{5.A.1.b} . . . . id.
ἔκτισται verb, perf. pass. indic. 3 pers. sg.
{5.A.1.f} . . . . id.
G1622 **ἐκτός** (1) adv., (a) *without, outside;* (b) *except;*
(c) τὸ ἐκτός, substantivally, *the outside;* (2)
prep. with gen., *outside, apart from.*

ἐκτός adv. . . . . ἐκτός G1622
G1623 **ἕκτος**, -η, -ον *sixth.*
ἕκτος adj., nom. sg. masc. {3.A} . . . . .ἕκτος G1623
ἐκτραπῇ verb, ²aor. pass. subjunc. 3 pers. sg.
{5.B.1} . . . . ἐκτρέπω G1624
ἐκτραπήσονται verb, ²fut. pass. indic. 3 pers.
pl. {5.A.1.d} . . . . id.
ἐκτρεπόμενος vbl., pres. mid. ptc. nom. sg.
masc. {6.A.1} . . . . id.
G1624 **ἐκτρέπω** mid. and pass. *I turn aside* (from
the right road), *I wander,* and with an obj. *I*
remove from myself, 1 Tim 6:20 (lit. *I turn out*
from).
ἐκτρέφει verb, pres. act. indic. 3 pers. sg.
{5.A.1.a} . . . . ἐκτρέφω G1625
ἐκτρέφετε verb, pres. act. impv. 2 pers. pl.
{5.D.1} . . . . id.
G1625 **ἐκτρέφω** *I nourish, nurture.*
ἐκτρέφωσιν verb, pres. act. subjunc. 3 pers. pl.
{5.B.1} . . . . ἐκτρέφω G1625
G1626 **ἔκτρωμα**, -ατος, τό *an untimely birth* (strictly
a lifeless abortion).
ἐκτρώματι noun, dat. sg. neut. {2.C} . . . . ἔκτρωμα G1626
ἕκτῳ adj., dat. sg. masc. {3.A} . . . . .ἕκτος G1623
ἐκύκλευσαν verb, aor. act. indic. 3 pers. pl.
{5.A.1.b} .κυκλεύω G2944†‡
ἐκύκλωσαν verb, aor. act. indic. 3 pers. pl. {5.A.1} id.
ἐκυλίετο verb, impf. mid./pass. indic. 3 pers. sg.
{5.A.1.e} . . . . κυλίω G2947
ἐκφέρειν vbl., pres. act. inf. {6.B.1} . . . . . . ἐκφέρω G1627
ἐκφέρουσα vbl., pres. act. ptc. nom. sg. fem.
{6.A.1} . . . . id.
G1627 **ἐκφέρω** (1) *I bring out, carry out,* sometimes
out of the city for burial; (2) *I bring forth, bear,*
Heb 6:8.
G1628 **ἐκφεύγω** *I flee out, away, I escape;* with an acc.
I escape something.
ἐκφεύξῃ verb, fut. mid. indic. 2 pers. sg.
{5.A.1.d} . . . . ἐκφεύγω G1628
ἐκφευξόμεθα verb, fut. mid. indic. 1 pers. pl.
{5.A.1.d} . . . . id.
ἐκφοβεῖν vbl., pres. act. inf. {6.B.2} . . . . . ἐκφοβέω G1629
G1629 **ἐκφοβέω** *I terrify exceedingly.*
ἔκφοβοι adj., nom. pl. masc. {3.C} . . . . . . ἔκφοβος G1630
G1630 **ἔκφοβος**, -ον *exceedingly afraid.*
ἔκφοβος adj., nom. sg. masc. {3.C} . . . . . ἔκφοβος G1630
ἐκφυγεῖν vbl., ²aor. act. inf. {6.B.1} . . . . . . ἐκφεύγω G1628
ἐκφύγωσιν verb, ²aor. act. subjunc. 3 pers. pl.
{5.B.1} . . . . id.
ἐκφύῃ verb, pres. act. subjunc. 3 pers. sg.
{5.B.1} . . . . .ἐκφύω G1631
G1631 **ἐκφύω** *I put forth, cause to sprout.*
ἐκχέαι vbl., aor. act. inf. {6.B.1} . . . . ἐκχέω G1632
ἐκχέατε verb, aor. act. impv. 2 pers. pl. {5.D.1}. . id.
ἐκχέετε verb, pres. act. impv. 2 pers. pl. {5.D.2} . id.
ἐκχεῖται verb, pres. pass. indic. 3 pers. sg.
{5.A.2} . . . . id.
G1632 **ἐκχέω** (ἐκχύννω) (1) *I pour out* (liquid or
solid), *I shed;* (2) pass. *I am swept on, rush* or *I*
surrender, Jude 11.

ἐκχεῶ   verb, fut. act. indic. 1 pers. sg. {5.A.1} ἐκχέω *G1632*

ἐκχυθήσεται   verb, fut. pass. indic. 3 pers. sg.
{5.A.1}. . . . . id.

ἐκχυννόμενον   vbl., pres. pass. ptc. nom. sg.
neut. {6.A.2} . . . . id.

ἐκχυνόμενον   vbl., pres. pass. ptc. nom. sg.
neut. {6.A.2} . . . . id.

ἐκχωρείτωσαν   verb, pres. act. impv. 3 pers. pl.
{5.D.2}. . . . . ἐκχωρέω *G1633*

G1633 **ἐκχωρέω**   *I go out.*

G1634 **ἐκψύχω**   *I breathe my last, I die.*

ἐκωλύθην   verb, aor. pass. indic. 1 pers. sg.
{5.A.1.b}. .κωλύω *G2967*

ἐκωλύομεν   verb, impf. act. indic. 1 pers. pl.
{5.A.1.b} . . . . id.

ἐκωλύσαμεν   verb, aor. act. indic. 1 pers. pl.
{5.A.1.b} . . . . id.

ἐκωλύσατε   verb, aor. act. indic. 2 pers. pl.
{5.A.1.b} . . . . id.

ἐκώλυσε   verb, aor. act. indic. 3 pers. sg.
{5.A.1.b} . . . . id.

ἐκώλυσεν   verb, aor. act. indic. 3 pers. sg.
{5.A.1.b} . . . . id.

G1635 **ἑκών**, -οῦσα, -όν   *willing, willingly.*

ἑκών   adj., nom. sg. masc. {3.D} . . . . ἑκών *G1635*

ἔλαβε   verb, ²aor. act. indic. 3 pers. sg.
{5.A.1.b} . . . . λαμβάνω *G2983*

ἔλαβεν   verb, ²aor. act. indic. 3 pers. sg. {5.A.1.b} id.

ἔλαβες   verb, ²aor. act. indic. 2 pers. sg. {5.A.1.b} id.

ἐλάβετε   verb, ²aor. act. indic. 2 pers. pl.
{5.A.1.b} . . . . id.

ἐλάβομεν   verb, ²aor. act. indic. 1 pers. pl.
{5.A.1.b} . . . . id.

ἔλαβον   verb, ²aor. act. indic. 1 pers. sg. {5.A.1.b}id.

ἔλαβον   verb, ²aor. act. indic. 3 pers. pl. {5.A.1.b} id.

ἔλαθε   verb, ²aor. act. indic. 3 pers. sg.
{5.A.1.b} . . . . λανθάνω *G2990*

ἔλαθεν   verb, ²aor. act. indic. 3 pers. sg. {5.A.1.b} id.

ἔλαθον   verb, ²aor. act. indic. 3 pers. pl. {5.A.1.b} id.

G1636 **ἐλαία**, -ας, ἡ   *an olive tree; see* ἐλαίων.

ἐλαία   noun, dat. sg. fem. {2.A} . . . . ἐλαία *G1636*

ἐλαίαι   noun, nom. pl. fem. {2.A}. . . . . id.

ἐλαίας   noun, acc. pl. fem. {2.A} . . . . id.

ἐλαίας   noun, gen. sg. fem. {2.A} . . . . id.

G1637 **ἔλαιον**, -ου, τό   *olive oil;* ἔλαιον ἀγαλλιάσεως, *oil of enjoyment,* the oil with which
the heads of guests at banquets are anointed,
Heb 1:9.

ἔλαιον   noun, acc. sg. neut. {2.B} . . . . ἔλαιον *G1637*

ἐλαίου   noun, gen. sg. neut. {2.B}. . . . . id.

ἐλαίῳ   noun, dat. sg. neut. {2.B} . . . . id.

G1638 **ἐλαιών** (Ἐλαιών), -ῶνος, ὁ   *olive orchard,
olive grove, olive yard;* as a proper noun, "the
mount called Olives" (**Ἐλαιών** probably the
right text in Luke 19:29; 21:37; Acts 1:12).

ἐλαιῶν   noun, gen. pl. fem. {2.A} . . . . ἐλαία *G1636*

Ἐλαιῶνος   noun prop., gen. sg. masc. {2.C;
2.D}. . . . . ἐλαιών *G1638*

ἐλάκησε   verb, aor. act. indic. 3 pers. sg.
{5.A.1.b} . . . . λακάω *G2997‡*

ἐλάκησεν   verb, aor. act. indic. 3 pers. sg.
{5.A.1.b} . . . . id.

ἐλάλει   verb, impf. act. indic. 3 pers. sg.
{5.A.2}. . . . . λαλέω *G2980*

ἐλαλήθη   verb, aor. pass. indic. 3 pers. sg.
{5.A.1}. . . . . id.

ἐλάλησα   verb, aor. act. indic. 1 pers. sg. {5.A.1} id.

ἐλαλήσαμεν   verb, aor. act. indic. 1 pers. pl.
{5.A.1}. . . . . id.

ἐλάλησαν   verb, aor. act. indic. 3 pers. pl.
{5.A.1}. . . . . id.

ἐλαλήσατε   verb, aor. act. indic. 2 pers. pl.
{5.A.1}. . . . . id.

ἐλάλησε   verb, aor. act. indic. 3 pers. sg. {5.A.1} id.

ἐλάλησεν   verb, aor. act. indic. 3 pers. sg.
{5.A.1}. . . . . id.

ἐλαλοῦμεν   verb, impf. act. indic. 1 pers. pl.
{5.A.2}. . . . . id.

ἐλάλουν   verb, impf. act. indic. 1 pers. sg.
{5.A.2}. . . . . id.

ἐλάλουν   verb, impf. act. indic. 3 pers. pl.
{5.A.2}. . . . . id.

ἐλάμβανον   verb, impf. act. indic. 3 pers. pl.
{5.A.1.b}. . . . . λαμβάνω *G2983*

Ἐλαμεῖται   noun prop., nom. pl. masc. {2.A;
2.D}. . . . . .Ἐλαμίτης *G1639*

Ἐλαμῖται   noun prop., nom. pl. masc. {2.A;
2.D}. . . . . id.

G1639 **Ἐλαμίτης**, -ου, ὁ   *an Elamite,* one of a people
living to the north of the Persian Gulf in the
southern part of Persia.

ἔλαμψε   verb, aor. act. indic. 3 pers. sg.
{5.A.1.b} .λάμπω *G2989*

ἔλαμψεν   verb, aor. act. indic. 3 pers. sg.
{5.A.1.b} . . . . id.

ἐλάσσονι   adj. comp., dat. sg. masc. {3.E;
3.G}. . . . . .ἐλάσσων *G1640*

ἐλάσσω   adj. comp., acc. sg. masc. {3.E; 3.G} . . . id.

G1640 **ἐλάσσων** (ἐλάττων), -ον   (1) *less, smaller;* (2)
poorer, inferior, John 2:10; (3) adv., ἔλαττον,
less.

ἐλατόμησεν   verb, aor. act. indic. 3 pers. sg.
{5.A.1}. . . . . .λατομέω *G2998*

ἐλάτρευσαν   verb, aor. act. indic. 3 pers. pl.
{5.A.1.b} . . . . .λατρεύω *G3000*

ἔλαττον   adj. comp., nom. sg. neut. {3.E;
3.G}. . . . . .ἐλάσσων *G1640*

ἔλαττον   adv. comp. {3.F; 3.G} . . . . id.

G1641 **ἐλαττονέω**   *I have less, I lack.*

ἐλαττοῦσθαι   vbl., pres. mid./pass. inf.
{6.B.2}. .ἐλαττόω *G1642*

G1642 **ἐλαττόω**   *I make less (inferior).*

ἐλαύνειν   vbl., pres. act. inf. {6.B.1} . . . . . ἐλαύνω *G1643*

ἐλαυνόμενα   vbl., pres. pass. ptc. nom. pl.
neut. {6.A.1} . . . . id.

ἐλαυνόμεναι   vbl., pres. pass. ptc. nom. pl.
fem. {6.A.1} . . . . id.

G1643 **ἐλαύνω**   (1) trans., *I drive (on), propel;* (2)
intrans., *I row,* Mark 6:48; John 6:19.

G1644 **ἐλαφρία**, -ας, ἡ   *levity, fickleness.*

ἐλαφρία   noun, dat. sg. fem. {2.A} . . . . . ἐλαφρία G1644
ἐλαφρόν   adj., nom. sg. neut. {3.A} . . . . ἐλαφρός G1645
G1645 **ἐλαφρός**, -ά, -όν   light.
ἔλαχε   verb, ²aor. act. indic. 3 pers. sg.
   {5.A.1.b} . . . . .λαγχάνω G2975
ἔλαχεν   verb, ²aor. act. indic. 3 pers. sg. {5.A.1.b} id.
ἐλαχίστη   adj. superl., nom. sg. fem.
   {3.A} . . . . .ἐλάχιστος G1646
ἐλάχιστον   adj. superl., acc. sg. neut. {3.A} . . . . id.
G1646 **ἐλάχιστος**, -η, -ον   (1) least, smallest (Matt;
   1 Cor 15:9), but perhaps oftener in the weaker
   sense, very little, very small (Luke; 1 Cor 4:3;
   6:2; James); ὁ ἐλαχιστότερος, the smallest,
   the least important; εἰς ἐλάχιστόν ἐστιν, it
   matters very little; (2) adv., ἐλάχιστον, a very
   little.
ἐλάχιστος   adj. superl., nom. sg. masc.
   {3.A} . . . . .ἐλάχιστος G1646
G1647 **ἐλαχιστότερος**   smallest, very small (comp.).
ἐλαχιστοτέρῳ   adj. superl., dat. sg. masc.
   {3.A} . . . . .ἐλαχιστότερος G1647
ἐλαχίστου   adj. superl., gen. sg. neut.
   {3.A} . . . . .ἐλάχιστος G1646
ἐλαχίστῳ   adj. superl., dat. sg. neut. {3.A} . . . . id.
ἐλαχίστων   adj. superl., gen. pl. fem. {3.A} . . . id.
ἐλαχίστων   adj. superl., gen. pl. masc. {3.A} . . . id.
ἐλαχίστων   adj. superl., gen. pl. neut. {3.A} . . . id.
G1648 **Ἐλεάζαρ**, ὁ   Eleazar, son of Eliud, and father
   of Matthan (Heb.).
Ἐλεάζαρ   noun prop. . . . . Ἐλεάζαρ G1648
ἐλεᾶτε   verb, pres. act. impv. 2 pers. pl.
   {5.D.2} . . . . ἐλεέω G1653
ἔλεγε   verb, impf. act. indic. 3 pers. sg.
   {5.A.1.b} . . . . λέγω G3004
ἔλεγεν   verb, impf. act. indic. 3 pers. sg. {5.A.1.b} id.
ἐλέγετε   verb, impf. act. indic. 2 pers. pl.
   {5.A.1.b} . . . . id.
ἐλεγμόν   noun, acc. sg. masc. {2.B} . . . . . ἐλεγμός G1650†‡
G1650†‡ **ἐλεγμός**, -οῦ, ὁ   reproof. Var. for ἔλεγχος,
   2 Tim 3:16.
ἐλέγξαι   vbl., aor. act. inf. {6.B.1} . . . . .ἐλέγχω G1651
ἐλέγξει   verb, fut. act. indic. 3 pers. sg. {5.A.1.a} . id.
ἔλεγξιν   noun, acc. sg. fem. {2.C} . . . . ἔλεγξις G1649
G1649 **ἔλεγξις**, -εως, ἡ   rebuke, reproof.
ἔλεγξον   verb, aor. act. impv. 2 pers. sg.
   {5.D.1} . . . . .ἐλέγχω G1651
ἔλεγον   verb, impf. act. indic. 1 pers. sg.
   {5.A.1.b} . . . . λέγω G3004
ἔλεγον   verb, impf. act. indic. 3 pers. pl. {5.A.1.b} id.
ἔλεγχε   verb, pres. act. impv. 2 pers. sg.
   {5.D.1} . . . . .ἐλέγχω G1651
ἐλέγχει   verb, pres. act. indic. 3 pers. sg. {5.A.1.a}id.
ἐλέγχειν   vbl., pres. act. inf. {6.B.1} . . . . id.
ἐλέγχεται   verb, pres. pass. indic. 3 pers. sg.
   {5.A.1.d} . . . . id.
ἐλέγχετε   verb, pres. act. impv. 2 pers. pl. {5.D.1} id.
ἐλεγχθῇ   verb, aor. pass. subjunc. 3 pers. sg.
   {5.B.1} . . . . id.
ἐλεγχόμενα   vbl., pres. pass. ptc. nom. pl. neut.
   {6.A.1} . . . . id.

ἐλεγχόμενοι   vbl., pres. pass. ptc. nom. pl.
   masc. {6.A.1} . . . . id.
ἐλεγχόμενος   vbl., pres. pass. ptc. nom. sg.
   masc. {6.A.1} . . . . id.
ἔλεγχον   noun, acc. sg. masc. {2.B} . . . . . . ἔλεγχος G1650
G1650 **ἔλεγχος**, -ου, ὁ   (1) a proof; (2) possibly a
   persuasion.
ἔλεγχος   noun, nom. sg. masc. {2.B} . . . . . ἔλεγχος G1650
G1651 **ἐλέγχω**   (1) I reprove, rebuke; (2) I expose, show
   to be guilty, John 3:20; 1 Cor 14:24; Eph 5:11,
   13; Jas 2:9.
ἐλέγχω   verb, pres. act. indic. 1 pers. sg.
   {5.A.1.a} . . . . .ἐλέγχω G1651
ἐλέει   noun, dat. sg. neut. {2.C} . . . . .ἔλεος G1656
ἐλεεῖ   verb, pres. act. indic. 3 pers. sg. {5.A.2} ἐλεέω G1653
G1652 **ἐλεεινός**, -ή, -όν   merciful, pitiful.
ἐλεεινός   adj., nom. sg. masc. {3.A} . . . . ἐλεεινός G1652
ἐλεεινότεροι   adj. comp., nom. pl. masc. {3.A;
   3.G} . . . . id.
ἐλεεῖτε   verb, pres. act. impv. 2 pers. pl.
   {5.D.2} . . . . ἐλεέω G1653
G1653 **ἐλεέω** (ἐλεάω)   I pity; I have mercy on, show
   mercy (to).
ἐλεηθέντες   vbl., aor. pass. ptc. nom. pl. masc.
   {6.A.1.a.} . . . . ἐλεέω G1653
ἐλεηθήσονται   verb, fut. pass. indic. 3 pers. pl.
   {5.A.1} . . . . id.
ἐλεηθῶσι   verb, aor. pass. subjunc. 3 pers. pl.
   {5.B.1} . . . . id.
ἐλεηθῶσιν   verb, aor. pass. subjunc. 3 pers. pl.
   {5.B.1} . . . . id.
ἐλεήμονες   adj., nom. pl. masc. {3.E} . . . . ἐλεήμων G1655
ἐλεημοσύναι   noun, nom. pl. fem.
   {2.A} . . . . .ἐλεημοσύνη G1654
ἐλεημοσύνας   noun, acc. pl. fem. {2.A} . . . . . . id.
G1654 **ἐλεημοσύνη**, -ης, ἡ   (1) abstr. almsgiving,
   charity; (2) concr. alms, charity.
ἐλεημοσύνη   noun, nom. sg. fem.
   {2.A} . . . . .ἐλεημοσύνη G1654
ἐλεημοσύνην   noun, acc. sg. fem. {2.A} . . . . . . id.
ἐλεημοσυνῶν   noun, gen. pl. fem. {2.A} . . . . . . id.
G1655 **ἐλεήμων**, -ον gen. ονος   pitiful, merciful.
ἐλεήμων   adj., nom. sg. masc. {3.E} . . . . . ἐλεήμων G1655
ἐλεῆσαι   vbl., aor. act. inf. {6.B.1} . . . . ἐλεέω G1653
ἐλεήσῃ   verb, aor. act. subjunc. 3 pers. sg. {5.B.1} id.
ἐλέησον   verb, aor. act. impv. 2 pers. sg. {5.D.1} . id.
ἐλεήσω   verb, fut. act. indic. 1 pers. sg. {5.A.1} . . id.
ἐλεινός   adj., nom. sg. masc. {3.A} . . . . . . ἐλεεινός G1652
Ἐλεισάβετ   noun prop. . . . . Ἐλισάβετ G1665
ἔλεον   noun, acc. sg. masc. {2.B} . . . . .ἔλεος G1656
ἔλεος   noun, acc. sg. neut. {2.C} . . . . id.
G1656 **ἔλεος**, -ους, τό   pity, mercy.
ἔλεος   noun, nom. sg. neut. {2.C} . . . . .ἔλεος G1656
ἐλεοῦντος   vbl., pres. act. ptc. gen. sg. masc.
   {6.A.2} . . . . ἐλεέω G1653
ἐλέους   noun, gen. sg. neut. {2.C} . . . . .ἔλεος G1656
ἐλευθέρα   adj., nom. sg. fem. {3.A} . . . .ἐλεύθερος G1658
ἐλευθέρας   adj., gen. sg. fem. {3.A} . . . . id.
G1657 **ἐλευθερία**, -ας, ἡ   freedom, liberty, esp. a state
   of freedom from slavery.

ἐλευθερία	noun, nom. sg. fem. {2.A} . .ἐλευθερία G1657
ἐλευθερίᾳ	noun, dat. sg. fem. {2.A} . . . . id.
ἐλευθερίαν	noun, acc. sg. fem. {2.A} . . . . id.
ἐλευθερίας	noun, gen. sg. fem. {2.A} . . . . id.
ἐλεύθεροι	adj., nom. pl. masc. {3.A} . . .ἐλεύθερος G1658
G1658 ἐλεύθερος, -α, -ον	free (opp. enslaved, cf.
	1 Cor 12:13).
ἐλεύθερος	adj., nom. sg. masc. {3.A}. . .ἐλεύθερος G1658
ἐλευθέρους	adj., acc. pl. masc. {3.A} . . . . id.
G1659 ἐλευθερόω	I free, set free, liberate.
ἐλευθερωθέντες	vbl., aor. pass. ptc. nom. pl. masc.
	{6.A.1.a} . . . . .ἐλευθερόω G1659
ἐλευθερωθήσεται	verb, fut. pass. indic.
	3 pers. sg. {5.A.1} . . . . id.
ἐλευθέρων	adj., gen. pl. masc. {3.A} . . .ἐλεύθερος G1658
ἐλευθερώσει	verb, fut. act. indic. 3 pers. sg.
	{5.A.1} .ἐλευθερόω G1659
ἐλευθερώσῃ	verb, aor. act. subjunc. 3 pers. sg.
	{5.B.1} . . . . id.
ἐλεύκαναν	verb, aor. act. indic. 3 pers. pl.
	{5.A.1.b} . . . . .λευκαίνω G3021
ἐλεύσεται	verb, fut. mid. indic. 3 pers. sg.
	{5.A.1.d} . . . . .ἔρχομαι G2064
ἐλεύσεως	noun, gen. sg. fem. {2.C} . . . . .ἔλευσις G1660
G1660 ἔλευσις, -εως, ἡ	coming, arrival.
ἐλεύσομαι	verb, fut. mid. indic. 1 pers. sg.
	{5.A.1.d} . . . . .ἔρχομαι G2064
ἐλευσόμεθα	verb, fut. mid. indic. 1 pers. pl.
	{5.A.1.d} . . . . id.
ἐλεύσονται	verb, fut. mid. indic. 3 pers. pl.
	{5.A.1.d} . . . . id.
ἐλεφάντινον	adj., acc. sg. neut. {3.A} ἐλεφάντινος G1661
G1661 ἐλεφάντινος, -η, -ον	made of ivory.
ἐλεῶ	verb, pres. act. subjunc. 1 pers. sg.
	{5.B.2} . . . . .ἐλεέω G1653
ἐλεῶν	vbl., pres. act. ptc. nom. sg. masc. {6.A.2} id.
ἐλεῶντος	vbl., pres. act. ptc. gen. sg. masc.
	{6.A.2} . . . . id.
ἐληλακότες	vbl., perf. act. ptc. nom. pl. masc.
	{6.A.1.a} . . . . .ἐλαύνω G1643
ἐλήλυθα	verb, ²perf. act. indic. 1 pers. sg.
	{5.A.1.c} . . . . .ἔρχομαι G2064
ἐλήλυθας	verb, ²perf. act. indic. 2 pers. sg.
	{5.A.1.c} . . . . id.
ἐλήλυθε	verb, ²perf. act. indic. 3 pers. sg.
	{5.A.1.c} . . . . id.
ἐληλύθει	verb, plu. act. indic. 3 pers. sg.
	{5.A.1.b} . . . . id.
ἐληλύθεισαν	verb, plu. act. indic. 3 pers. pl.
	{5.A.1.b} . . . . id.
ἐλήλυθεν	verb, ²perf. act. indic. 3 pers. sg.
	{5.A.1.c} . . . . id.
ἐληλυθότα	vbl., ²perf. act. ptc. acc. sg. masc.
	{6.A.1} . . . . id.
ἐληλυθότες	vbl., ²perf. act. ptc. nom. pl. masc.
	{6.A.1} . . . . id.
ἐληλυθυῖαν	vbl., ²perf. act. ptc. acc. sg. fem.
	{6.A.1} . . . . id.
ἐλθάτω	verb, ²aor. act. impv. 3 pers. sg. {5.D.1} . id.
ἐλθέ	verb, ²aor. act. impv. 2 pers. sg. {5.D.1} . . . . id.

ἐλθεῖν	vbl., ²aor. act. inf. {6.B.1} . . . . id.
ἐλθέτω	verb, ²aor. act. impv. 3 pers. sg. {5.D.1} . id.
ἔλθῃ	verb, ²aor. act. subjunc. 3 pers. sg. {5.B.1} . id.
ἔλθῃς	verb, ²aor. act. subjunc. 2 pers. sg. {5.B.1}. id.
ἔλθητε	verb, ²aor. act. subjunc. 2 pers. pl. {5.B.1} id.
ἐλθόν	vbl., ²aor. act. ptc. nom. sg. neut. {6.A.1.a} id.
ἐλθόντα	vbl., ²aor. act. ptc. acc. sg. masc.
	{6.A.1.a} . . . . id.
ἐλθόντα	vbl., ²aor. act. ptc. nom. pl. neut.
	{6.A.1.a} . . . . id.
ἐλθόντας	vbl., ²aor. act. ptc. acc. pl. masc.
	{6.A.1.a} . . . . id.
ἐλθόντες	vbl., ²aor. act. ptc. nom. pl. masc.
	{6.A.1.a} . . . . id.
ἐλθόντι	vbl., ²aor. act. ptc. dat. sg. masc.
	{6.A.1.a} . . . . id.
ἐλθόντος	vbl., ²aor. act. ptc. gen. sg. masc.
	{6.A.1.a} . . . . id.
ἐλθόντων	vbl., ²aor. act. ptc. gen. pl. masc.
	{6.A.1.a} . . . . id.
ἐλθοῦσα	vbl., ²aor. act. ptc. nom. sg. fem.
	{6.A.1.a} . . . . id.
ἐλθοῦσαι	vbl., ²aor. act. ptc. nom. pl. fem.
	{6.A.1.a} . . . . id.
ἐλθούσης	vbl., ²aor. act. ptc. gen. sg. fem.
	{6.A.1.a} . . . . id.
ἔλθω	verb, ²aor. act. subjunc. 1 pers. sg. {5.B.1} . id.
ἐλθών	vbl., ²aor. act. ptc. nom. sg. masc.
	{6.A.1.a} . . . . id.
ἔλθωσι	verb, ²aor. act. subjunc. 3 pers. pl.
	{5.B.1} . . . . id.
ἔλθωσιν	verb, ²aor. act. subjunc. 3 pers. pl.
	{5.B.1} . . . . id.
Ἐλιακείμ	noun prop. . . . . .Ἐλιακίμ G1662
G1662 Ἐλιακίμ, ὁ	Eliakim, son of Abiud and father
	of Azor (Matt 1:13), son of Melea and father of
	Jonam (Luke 3:30) (Heb.).
Ἐλιακίμ	noun prop. . . . . .Ἐλιακίμ G1662
G3395†‡ ἔλιγμα, -ατος, τό	a roll. Var. for μίγμα, John
	19:39.
ἔλιγμα	noun, acc. sg. neut. {2.C} . . . . . .ἔλιγμα G3395†‡
G1663 Ἐλιέζερ, ὁ	Eliezer, son of Joreim and father of
	Joshua (Heb.).
Ἐλιέζερ	noun prop. . . . . .Ἐλιέζερ G1663
ἐλιθάσθην	verb, aor. pass. indic. 1 pers. sg.
	{5.A.1.b} . . . . .λιθάζω G3034
ἐλιθάσθησαν	verb, aor. pass. indic. 3 pers. pl.
	{5.A.1.b} . . . . id.
ἐλιθοβόλησαν	verb, aor. act. indic. 3 pers. pl.
	{5.A.1} . . . . .λιθοβολέω G3036
ἐλιθοβόλουν	verb, impf. act. indic. 3 pers. pl.
	{5.A.2} . . . . id.
ἑλίξεις	verb, fut. act. indic. 2 pers. sg.
	{5.A.1.a} . . . . .ἑλίσσω G1667
G1664 Ἐλιούδ, ὁ	Eliud, son of Acheim, and father of
	Eleazar (Heb.).
Ἐλιούδ	noun prop. . . . . .Ἐλιούδ G1664
G1665 Ἐλισάβετ, ἡ	Elisabeth, mother of John the
	Baptizer (Heb.).
Ἐλισάβετ	noun prop. . . . . .Ἐλισάβετ G1665

G1666 **Ἐλισαῖος,** -ου, ὁ   *Helisaeus, Graecized form of Elisha.*
Ἐλισαίου   noun prop., gen. sg. masc. {2.B;
2.D} . . . . Ἐλισαῖος G1666
Ἐλισσαίου   noun prop., gen. sg. masc. {2.B;
2.D} . . . . id.
ἐλισσόμενον   vbl., pres. pass. ptc. nom. sg. neut.
{6.A.1} . . . . ἑλίσσω G1667
G1667 **ἑλίσσω** (εἱλίσσω)   *I roll, roll up.*
ἕλκη   noun, acc. pl. neut. {2.C} . . . . .ἕλκος G1668
G1668 **ἕλκος,** -ους, τό   *a (festering) sore.*
ἕλκος   noun, nom. sg. neut. {2.C} . . . . .ἕλκος G1668
ἕλκουσιν   verb, pres. act. indic. 3 pers. pl.
{5.A.1.a} . . . . ἑλκύω G1670
G1669 **ἑλκόω**   pass., *I am covered with sores.*
ἑλκύσαι   vbl., aor. act. inf. {6.B.1} . . . . ἑλκύω G1670
ἑλκύσῃ   verb, aor. act. subjunc. 3 pers. sg. {5.B.1}id.
ἑλκύσω   verb, fut. act. indic. 1 pers. sg. {5.A.1.a} id.
G1670 **ἑλκύω,** ἕλκω   *I drag, draw, pull.*
ἑλκῶν   noun, gen. pl. neut. {2.C} . . . . .ἕλκος G1668
Ἑλλάδα   noun prop., acc. sg. fem. {2.C;
2.D} . . . . .Ἑλλάς G1671
G1671 **Ἑλλάς,** -άδος, ἡ   *Hellas, the native name for Greece.*
G1672 **Ἕλλην,** -ηνος, ὁ   *a Hellene, the native word for a Greek;* it is, however, a term wide enough for to include all Greek-speaking (i.e., educated) non-Jews.
Ἕλλην   noun prop., nom. sg. masc. {2.C;
2.D} . . . . Ἕλλην G1672
Ἕλληνας   noun prop., acc. pl. masc. {2.C; 2.D} . id.
Ἕλληνες   noun prop., nom. pl. masc. {2.C; 2.D} id.
Ἕλληνι   noun prop., dat. sg. masc. {2.C; 2.D} . . id.
Ἑλληνίδων   noun prop., gen. pl. fem. {2.C;
2.D} . . . . Ἑλληνίς G1674
Ἑλληνικῇ   adj. prop., dat. sg. fem. {3.A} Ἑλληνικός G1673
Ἑλληνικοῖς   adj. prop., dat. pl. neut. {3.A} . . . . id.
G1673 **Ἑλληνικός,** -ή, -όν   *Greek;* ἡ Ἑλληνικὴ (γλῶσσα), *the Greek language.*
G1674 **Ἑλληνίς,** -ίδος, ἡ   *Greek; see* Ἕλλην.
Ἑλληνίς   noun prop., nom. sg. fem. {2.C;
2.D} . . . . Ἑλληνίς G1674
G1675 **Ἑλληνιστής,** -οῦ, ὁ   *a Hellenist, Grecian Jew,* a Greek-speaking Jew, i.e., one who can speak Greek only and not Hebrew (or Aramaic).
Ἑλληνιστάς   noun prop., acc. pl. masc. {2.A;
2.D} . . . . Ἑλληνιστής G1675
G1676 **Ἑλληνιστί**   *in the Greek language.*
Ἑλληνιστί   adv. prop. . . . . Ἑλληνιστί G1676
Ἑλληνιστῶν   noun prop., gen. pl. masc. {2.A;
2.D} . . . . Ἑλληνιστής G1675
Ἕλληνος   noun prop., gen. sg. masc. {2.C;
2.D} . . . . Ἕλλην G1672
Ἑλλήνων   noun prop., gen. pl. masc. {2.C; 2.D}. id.
Ἕλλησι   noun prop., dat. pl. masc. {2.C; 2.D} . . id.
Ἕλλησιν   noun prop., dat. pl. masc. {2.C; 2.D} . id.
ἐλλόγα   verb, pres. act. impv. 2 pers. sg.
{5.D.2} . . . . ἐλλογέω G1677
ἐλλογᾶται   verb, pres. pass. indic. 3 pers. sg.
{5.A.2} . . . . id.

ἐλλόγει   verb, pres. act. impv. 2 pers. sg. {5.D.2} . id.
ἐλλογεῖται   verb, pres. pass. indic. 3 pers. sg.
{5.A.2} . . . . id.
G1677 **ἐλλογέω** (ἐλλογάω)   *I put down (set) to some one's account, reckon, impute.*
G1678 **Ἐλμαδάμ,** ὁ   *Elmadam, father of Kosam, son of Er* (Heb.).
Ἐλμαδάμ   noun prop. . . . . Ἐλμαδάμ G1678
Ἐλμωδάμ   noun prop. . . . . id.
ἐλογιζόμην   verb, impf. mid./pass. indic. 1 pers. sg.
{5.A.1.e} . . . . λογίζομαι G3049
ἐλογίζοντο   verb, impf. mid./pass. indic. 3 pers.
pl. {5.A.1.e} . . . . id.
ἐλογίσθη   verb, aor. pass. indic. 3 pers. sg.
{5.A.1.b} . . . . id.
ἐλογίσθημεν   verb, aor. pass. indic. 1 pers. pl.
{5.A.1.b} . . . . id.
ἐλοιδόρησαν   verb, aor. act. indic. 3 pers. pl.
{5.A.1} . . . . λοιδορέω G3058
ἑλόμενος   vbl., ²aor. mid. ptc. nom. sg. masc.
{6.A.2} . . . . αἱρέω G138‡
ἔλουσεν   verb, aor. act. indic. 3 pers. sg.
{5.A.1.b} . . . . λούω G3068
ἐλπίδα   noun, acc. sg. fem. {2.C} . . . . ἐλπίς G1680
ἐλπίδι   noun, dat. sg. fem. {2.C} . . . . id.
ἐλπίδι   noun, dat. sg. fem. {2.C} . . . . id.
ἐλπίδος   noun, gen. sg. fem. {2.C} . . . . id.
ἐλπίζει   verb, pres. act. indic. 3 pers. sg.
{5.A.1.a} . . . . .ἐλπίζω G1679
ἐλπίζετε   verb, pres. act. indic. 2 pers. pl.
{5.A.1.a} . . . . id.
ἐλπίζομεν   verb, pres. act. indic. 1 pers. pl.
{5.A.1.a} . . . . id.
ἐλπιζομένων   vbl., pres. pass. ptc. gen. pl. neut.
{6.A.1} . . . . id.
ἐλπίζουσαι   vbl., pres. act. ptc. nom. pl. fem.
{6.A.1} . . . . id.
G1679 **ἐλπίζω**   *I hope, hope for;* the subs. following ἐν, εἰς, ἐπί with dat. or acc., is the ground of the hope, that which makes hope possible.
ἐλπίζω   verb, pres. act. indic. 1 pers. sg.
{5.A.1.a} . . . . .ἐλπίζω G1679
ἐλπίζων   vbl., pres. act. ptc. nom. sg. masc.
{6.A.1} . . . . id.
ἐλπιοῦσιν   verb, fut. act. indic. 3 pers. pl. {5.A.2}id.
G1680 **ἐλπίς,** -ίδος, ἡ   *hope.*
ἐλπίς   noun, nom. sg. fem. {2.C} . . . . ἐλπίς G1680
ἐλπίσατε   verb, aor. act. impv. 2 pers. pl.
{5.D.1} . . . . ἐλπίζω G1679
ἔλυε   verb, impf. act. indic. 3 pers. sg. {5.A.1.b} λύω G3089
ἔλυεν   verb, impf. act. indic. 3 pers. sg. {5.A.1.b} id.
ἐλύετο   verb, impf. pass. indic. 3 pers. sg.
{5.A.1.e} . . . . id.
ἐλύθη   verb, aor. pass. indic. 3 pers. sg. {5.A.1.b} id.
ἐλύθησαν   verb, aor. pass. indic. 3 pers. pl.
{5.A.1.b} . . . . id.
ἐλυμαίνετο   verb, impf. mid./pass. indic. 3 pers.
sg. {5.A.1.e} . . . . λυμαίνω G3075
G1681 **Ἐλύμας,** -α, ὁ   *Elymas,* the name of the sorcerer at Paphos (the form of the name is

doubtful; some MSS read Ἑτοιμᾶς, *Son of the Ready*).

Ἐλύμας   noun prop., nom. sg. masc. {2.A; 2.D}. . . . . Ἐλύμας *G1681*

ἐλυπήθη   verb, aor. pass. indic. 3 pers. sg. {5.A.1}. . . . . λυπέω *G3076*

ἐλυπήθησαν   verb, aor. pass. indic. 3 pers. pl. {5.A.1}. . . . . id.

ἐλυπήθητε   verb, aor. pass. indic. 2 pers. pl. {5.A.1}. . . . . id.

ἐλύπησα   verb, aor. act. indic. 1 pers. sg. {5.A.1} id.

ἐλύπησεν   verb, aor. act. indic. 3 pers. sg. {5.A.1}id.

ἔλυσεν   verb, aor. act. indic. 3 pers. sg. {5.A.1.b}. . . . . λύω *G3089*

ἐλυτρώθητε   verb, aor. pass. indic. 2 pers. pl. {5.A.1}. . . . . λυτρόω *G3084*

G1682   **ἐλωΐ** (ἐλωΐ)   *my God* (Aram. form of word is doubtful; cf. ἠλί).

ἐλωΐ   Aram. . . . . .ἐλωΐ *G1682*

ελωΐ   Aram. . . . . id.

ἐλωΐ   Aram. . . . . id.

ἐμά   pron. posses, 1 pers. sg. acc. pl. neut. {4.H}. . . . . .ἐμός *G1699*

ἐμά   pron. posses, 1 pers. sg. nom. pl. neut. {4.H} id.

ἔμαθεν   verb, 2aor. act. indic. 3 pers. sg. {5.A.1.b} . . . . μανθάνω *G3129*

ἔμαθες   verb, 2aor. act. indic. 2 pers. sg. {5.A.1.b} id.

ἐμάθετε   verb, 2aor. act. indic. 2 pers. pl. {5.A.1.b} . id.

ἐμαθητεύθη   verb, aor. pass. indic. 3 pers. sg. {5.A.1.b} .μαθητεύω *G3100*

ἐμαθήτευσε   verb, aor. act. indic. 3 pers. sg. {5.A.1.b} . . . . id.

ἐμαθήτευσεν   verb, aor. act. indic. 3 pers. sg. {5.A.1.b} . . . . id.

ἔμαθον   verb, 2aor. act. indic. 1 pers. sg. {5.A.1.b} . . . . μανθάνω *G3129*

ἐμαρτύρει   verb, impf. act. indic. 3 pers. sg. {5.A.2}. . . . . μαρτυρέω *G3140*

ἐμαρτυρεῖτο   verb, impf. pass. indic. 3 pers. sg. {5.A.2}. . . . . id.

ἐμαρτυρήθη   verb, aor. pass. indic. 3 pers. sg. {5.A.1}. . . . . id.

ἐμαρτυρήθησαν   verb, aor. pass. indic. 3 pers. pl. {5.A.1}. . . . . id.

ἐμαρτυρήσαμεν   verb, aor. act. indic. 1 pers. pl. {5.A.1}. . . . . id.

ἐμαρτύρησαν   verb, aor. act. indic. 3 pers. pl. {5.A.1}. . . . . id.

ἐμαρτύρησε   verb, aor. act. indic. 3 pers. sg. {5.A.1}. . . . . id.

ἐμαρτύρησεν   verb, aor. act. indic. 3 pers. sg. {5.A.1}. . . . . id.

ἐμαρτύρουν   verb, impf. act. indic. 3 pers. pl. {5.A.2}. . . . . id.

ἐμάς   pron. posses, 1 pers. sg. acc. pl. fem. {4.H}. . . . . ἐμός *G1699*

ἐμασσῶντο   verb, impf. mid./pass. indic. 3 pers. pl. {5.A.2}. . . . . μασάομαι *G3145*

ἐμαστίγωσε   verb, aor. act. indic. 3 pers. sg. {5.A.1}. . . . . μαστιγόω *G3146*

ἐμαστίγωσεν   verb, aor. act. indic. 3 pers. sg. {5.A.1}. . . . . id.

ἐμασῶντο   verb, impf. mid./pass. indic. 3 pers. pl. {5.A.2}. . . . . μασάομαι *G3145*

ἐματαιώθησαν   verb, aor. pass. indic. 3 pers. pl. {5.A.1}. . . . . ματαιόω *G3154*

ἐμαυτόν   pron. refl., 1 pers. acc. sg. masc. {4.F}. . . . . ἐμαυτοῦ *G1683*

G1683   **ἐμαυτοῦ**, -ῆς   *of myself.*

ἐμαυτοῦ   pron. refl., 1 pers. gen. sg. masc. {4.F}. . . . . ἐμαυτοῦ *G1683*

ἐμαυτῷ   pron. refl., 1 pers. dat. sg. masc. {4.F} . . id.

ἐμάχοντο   verb, impf. mid./pass. indic. 3 pers. pl. {5.A.1.e} . . . . μάχομαι *G3164*

ἐμβαίνοντος   vbl., pres. act. ptc. gen. sg. masc. {6.A.1}. . . . . ἐμβαίνω *G1684*

G1684   **ἐμβαίνω**   *I embark.*

ἐμβαλεῖν   vbl., 2aor. act. inf. {6.B.1} . . . . .ἐμβάλλω *G1685*

G1685   **ἐμβάλλω**   *I cast in, throw in.*

ἐμβάντα   vbl., 2aor. act. ptc. acc. sg. masc. {6.A.1.a}. . . . . ἐμβαίνω *G1684*

ἐμβάντες   vbl., 2aor. act. ptc. nom. pl. masc. {6.A.1.a}. . . . . id.

ἐμβάντι   vbl., 2aor. act. ptc. dat. sg. masc. {6.A.1.a}. id.

ἐμβάντος   vbl., 2aor. act. ptc. gen. sg. masc. {6.A.1.a}. . . . . id.

ἐμβάντων   vbl., 2aor. act. ptc. gen. pl. masc. {6.A.1.a}. . . . . id.

ἐμβαπτόμενος   vbl., pres. mid. ptc. nom. sg. masc. {6.A.1}. . . . . ἐμβάπτω *G1686*

G1686   **ἐμβάπτω**   act. and mid. *I dip in.*

ἐμβάς   vbl., 2aor. act. ptc. nom. sg. masc. {6.A.1.a}. . . . . ἐμβαίνω *G1684*

G1687   **ἐμβατεύω**   (*I enter on, take possession of*), hence a technical expression connected with the pagan Mysteries, *I enter, set foot on* (the inner shrine, after the first initiation). It indicates the final act in mystic ceremonial, the entrance on a new life in presence of the god.

ἐμβατεύων   vbl., pres. act. ptc. nom. sg. masc. {6.A.1}. . . . . ἐμβατεύω *G1687*

ἐμβάψας   vbl., aor. act. ptc. nom. sg. masc. {6.A.1.a}. . . . . ἐμβάπτω *G1686*

ἐμβῆναι   vbl., 2aor. act. inf. {6.B.1} . . . . . ἐμβαίνω *G1684*

G1688   **ἐμβιβάζω**   trans., *I embark, put on board.*

ἐμβλέποντες   vbl., pres. act. ptc. nom. pl. masc. {6.A.1}. . . . . ἐμβλέπω *G1689*

G1689   **ἐμβλέπω**   *I look into (upon).*

ἐμβλέψας   vbl., aor. act. ptc. nom. sg. masc. {6.A.1.a}. . . . . ἐμβλέπω *G1689*

ἐμβλέψασα   vbl., aor. act. ptc. nom. sg. fem. {6.A.1.a}. . . . . id.

ἐμβλέψατε   verb, aor. act. impv. 2 pers. pl. {5.D.1}. . . . . id.

G1690   **ἐμβριμάομαι**   *I groan* (with the notion of coercion springing out of displeasure, anger, indignation, antagonism), *I express indignant displeasure,* with dat. of person with whom it is felt, Matt 9:30; Mark 1:43; 14:5; absol. John 11:33, 38.

ἐμβριμησάμενος   vbl., aor. mid. ptc. nom. sg.
   masc. {6.A.2} . . . . ἐμβριμάομαι G1690
ἐμβριμώμενος   vbl., pres. mid./pass. ptc. nom.
   sg. masc. {6.A.2} . . . . id.
ἐμέ   pron. pers., 1 pers. acc. sg. {4.A} . . . . ἐγώ G1473
ἐμεγάλυνε   verb, impf. act. indic. 3 pers. sg.
   {5.A.1.b} . . . . μεγαλύνω G3170
ἐμεγάλυνεν   verb, impf. act. indic. 3 pers. sg.
   {5.A.1.b} . . . . id.
ἐμεγαλύνετο   verb, impf. pass. indic. 3 pers. sg.
   {5.A.1.e} . . . . id.
ἐμεθύσθησαν   verb, aor. pass. indic. 3 pers. pl.
   {5.A.1.b} . . . . μεθύσκω G3182
ἐμείναμεν   verb, aor. act. indic. 1 pers. pl.
   {5.A.1.b} . . . . μένω G3306
ἔμειναν   verb, aor. act. indic. 3 pers. pl. {5.A.1.b} id.
ἔμεινε   verb, aor. act. indic. 3 pers. sg. {5.A.1.b} . id.
ἔμεινεν   verb, aor. act. indic. 3 pers. sg. {5.A.1.b} id.
ἔμελεν   verb, impf. act. indic. 3 pers. sg.
   {5.A.1.b} . . . . μέλει G3199‡
ἐμελέτησαν   verb, aor. act. indic. 3 pers. pl.
   {5.A.1} . . . . μελετάω G3191
ἔμελλε   verb, impf. act. indic. 3 pers. sg.
   {5.A.1.b} . . . . μέλλω G3195
ἔμελλεν   verb, impf. act. indic. 3 pers. sg.
   {5.A.1.b} . . . . id.
ἔμελλες   verb, impf. act. indic. 2 pers. sg.
   {5.A.1.b} . . . . id.
ἔμελλον   verb, impf. act. indic. 1 pers. sg.
   {5.A.1.b} . . . . id.
ἔμελλον   verb, impf. act. indic. 3 pers. pl.
   {5.A.1.b} . . . . id.
ἐμέμψαντο   verb, aor. mid. indic. 3 pers. pl.
   {5.A.1.e} . . . . μέμφομαι G3201
ἔμενε   verb, impf. act. indic. 3 pers. sg.
   {5.A.1.b} . . . . μένω G3306
ἔμενεν   verb, impf. act. indic. 3 pers. sg. {5.A.1.b} id.
ἔμενον   verb, impf. act. indic. 3 pers. pl.
   {5.A.1.b} . . . . id.
ἐμέρισε   verb, aor. act. indic. 3 pers. sg.
   {5.A.1.b} . . . . μερίζω G3307
ἐμέρισεν   verb, aor. act. indic. 3 pers. sg.
   {5.A.1.b} . . . . id.
ἐμερίσθη   verb, aor. pass. indic. 3 pers. sg.
   {5.A.1.b} . . . . id.
ἐμέσαι   vbl., aor. act. inf. {6.B.1} . . . . ἐμέω G1692
ἐμεσίτευσεν   verb, aor. act. indic. 3 pers. sg.
   {5.A.1.b} . . . . μεσιτεύω G3315
ἐμέτρησε   verb, aor. act. indic. 3 pers. sg.
   {5.A.1} . . . . μετρέω G3354
ἐμέτρησεν   verb, aor. act. indic. 3 pers. sg.
   {5.A.1} . . . . id.
G1692 ἐμέω   I vomit.
ἐμῇ   pron. posses, 1 pers. sg. dat. sg. fem. {4.H} ἐμός G1699
ἐμή   pron. posses, 1 pers. sg. nom. sg. fem. {4.H} id.
ἐμήν   pron. posses, 1 pers. sg. acc. sg. fem. {4.H} id.
ἐμήνυσεν   verb, aor. act. indic. 3 pers. sg.
   {5.A.1.b} . . . . μηνύω G3377

ἐμῆς   pron. posses, 1 pers. sg. gen. sg. fem.
   {4.H} . . . . ἐμός G1699
ἔμιξε   verb, aor. act. indic. 3 pers. sg.
   {5.A.3.b} . . . . μίγνυμι G3396
ἔμιξεν   verb, aor. act. indic. 3 pers. sg. {5.A.3.b} . id.
ἐμίσησα   verb, aor. act. indic. 1 pers. sg.
   {5.A.1} . . . . μισέω G3404
ἐμίσησαν   verb, aor. act. indic. 3 pers. pl. {5.A.1} id.
ἐμίσησας   verb, aor. act. indic. 2 pers. sg. {5.A.1} id.
ἐμίσησεν   verb, aor. act. indic. 3 pers. sg. {5.A.1} id.
ἐμισθώσατο   verb, aor. mid. indic. 3 pers. sg.
   {5.A.1} . . . . μισθόω G3409
ἐμίσουν   verb, impf. act. indic. 3 pers. pl.
   {5.A.2} . . . . μισέω G3404
G1693 ἐμμαίνομαι   I am madly enraged with.
ἐμμαινόμενος   vbl., pres. mid./pass. ptc. nom. sg.
   masc. {6.A.1} . . . . ἐμμαίνομαι G1693
G1694 Ἐμμανουήλ, ὁ   Emmanuel, a Messianic title
   derived from Isa 7:14 = God with us (Heb.).
Ἐμμανουήλ   noun prop. . . . . Ἐμμανουήλ G1694
Ἐμμαούς   noun prop. . . . . Ἐμμαοῦς G1695
G1695 Ἐμμαοῦς, ἡ   Emmaus (Ammaus), a village not
   far from Jerusalem.
Ἐμμαοῦς   noun prop. . . . . Ἐμμαοῦς G1695
ἐμμένει   verb, pres. act. indic. 3 pers. sg.
   {5.A.1.a} . . . . ἐμμένω G1696
ἐμμένειν   vbl., pres. act. inf. {6.B.1} . . . . id.
G1696 ἐμμένω   (1) I remain (abide) in, Acts 28:30; (2)
   hence met., Heb 8:9; (3) with dat., I abide by,
   maintain, Acts 14:22; Gal 3:10.
Ἐμμόρ   noun prop. . . . . Ἐμμώρ G1697
G1697 Ἐμμώρ, ὁ   Hamor, a man whose sons sold a
   field at Shechem to Jacob (Heb.).
Ἐμμώρ   noun prop. . . . . Ἐμμώρ G1697
ἐμνημόνευον   verb, impf. act. indic. 3 pers. pl.
   {5.A.1.b} . . . . μνημονεύω G3421
ἐμνημόνευσε   verb, aor. act. indic. 3 pers. sg.
   {5.A.1.b} . . . . id.
ἐμνημόνευσεν   verb, aor. act. indic. 3 pers. sg.
   {5.A.1.b} . . . . id.
ἐμνήσθη   verb, aor. pass. indic. 3 pers. sg.
   {5.A.1.b} . . . . μιμνήσκομαι G3403
ἐμνήσθημεν   verb, aor. pass. indic. 1 pers. pl.
   {5.A.1.b} . . . . id.
ἐμνήσθην   verb, aor. pass. indic. 1 pers. sg.
   {5.A.1.b} . . . . id.
ἐμνήσθησαν   verb, aor. pass. indic. 3 pers. pl.
   {5.A.1.b} . . . . id.
ἐμνηστευμένη   vbl., perf. pass. ptc. dat. sg. fem.
   {6.A.1.b} . . . . μνηστεύω G3423
ἐμνηστευμένην   vbl., perf. pass. ptc. acc. sg.
   fem. {6.A.1.b} . . . . id.
ἐμοί   pron. pers., 1 pers. dat. sg. {4.A} . . . . ἐγώ G1473
ἐμοί   pron. posses, 1 pers. sg. nom. pl. masc.
   {4.H} . . . . ἐμός G1699
ἐμοῖς   pron. posses, 1 pers. sg. dat. pl. neut. {4.H} id.
ἐμοίχευσεν   verb, aor. act. indic. 3 pers. sg.
   {5.A.1.b} . . . . μοιχεύω G3431

ἐμόλυναν   verb, aor. act. indic. 3 pers. pl.
     {5.A.1.b} . . . . .μολύνω G3435
ἐμολύνθησαν   verb, aor. pass. indic. 3 pers. pl.
     {5.A.1.b} . . . . id.
ἐμόν   pron. posses, 1 pers. sg. acc. sg. masc.
     {4.H} . . . . .ἐμός G1699
ἐμόν   pron. posses, 1 pers. sg. acc. sg. neut. {4.H} id.
ἐμόν   pron. posses, 1 pers. sg. nom. sg. neut.
     {4.H} . . . . id.
ἐμός   pron. posses, 1 pers. sg. nom. sg. masc.
     {4.H} . . . . id.
G1699 **ἐμός**, -ή, -όν   *my, mine* (predominates in John).
ἐμοσχοποίησαν   verb, aor. act. indic. 3 pers. pl.
     {5.A.1} . . . . μοσχοποιέω G3447
ἐμοῦ   pron. pers., 1 pers. gen. sg. {4.A} . . . . ἐγώ G1473
ἐμοῦ   pron. posses, 1 pers. sg. gen. sg. neut.
     {4.H} . . . . .ἐμός G1699
ἐμούς   pron. posses, 1 pers. sg. acc. pl. masc.
     {4.H} . . . . id.
G1701†‡ **ἐμπαιγμονή**, -ῆς, ἡ   *mockery, public ridicule.*
ἐμπαιγμονῆ   noun, dat. sg. fem.
     {2.A} . . . . ἐμπαιγμονή G1701†‡
G1701 **ἐμπαιγμός**, -οῦ, ὁ   *mockery.*
ἐμπαιγμῶν   noun, gen. pl. masc. {2.B} . .ἐμπαιγμός G1701
ἐμπαίζειν   vbl., pres. act. inf. {6.B.1} . . . . ἐμπαίζω G1702
ἐμπαίζοντες   vbl., pres. act. ptc. nom. pl. masc.
     {6.A.1} . . . . id.
G1702 **ἐμπαίζω**   *I mock.*
ἐμπαῖκται   noun, nom. pl. masc. {2.A} .ἐμπαίκτης G1703
G1703 **ἐμπαίκτης**, -ου, ὁ   *a mocker.*
ἐμπαῖξαι   vbl., aor. act. inf. {6.B.1} . . . . . . ἐμπαίζω G1702
ἐμπαίξας   vbl., aor. act. ptc. nom. sg. masc.
     {6.A.1.a} . . . . id.
ἐμπαίξουσιν   verb, fut. act. indic. 3 pers. pl.
     {5.A.1.a} . . . . id.
ἐμπαιχθήσεται   verb, fut. pass. indic. 3 pers.
     sg. {5.A.1.d} . . . . id.
ἐμπεπλησμένοι   vbl., perf. pass. ptc. nom. pl.
     masc. {6.A.3} . . . . .ἐμπίπλημι G1705
G1704 **ἐμπεριπατέω**   *I walk among.*
ἐμπεριπατήσω   verb, fut. act. indic. 1 pers. sg.
     {5.A.1} . . . . ἐμπεριπατέω G1704
ἐμπεσεῖν   vbl., ²aor. act. inf. {6.B.1} . . . . . ἐμπίπτω G1706
ἐμπεσεῖται   verb, fut. mid. indic. 3 pers. sg.
     {5.A.2} . . . . id.
ἐμπέσῃ   verb, ²aor. act. subjunc. 3 pers. sg.
     {5.B.1} . . . . id.
ἐμπεσόντος   vbl., ²aor. act. ptc. gen. sg. masc.
     {6.A.1.a} . . . . id.
ἐμπεσοῦνται   verb, fut. mid. indic. 3 pers. pl.
     {5.A.2} . . . . id.
G1705 **ἐμπίπλημι** (ἐμπιπλάω, ἐμπιμπλάω,
     ἐμπίμπλημι)   *I fill up, fill; pass., be satisfied.*
ἐμπιπλῶν   vbl., pres. act. ptc. nom. sg. masc.
     {6.A.3} .ἐμπίπλημι G1705
G1714‡ **ἐμπίπρημι** (ἐμπίμπρημι)   (1) *I burn, set on
     fire;* (2) pass. *I suffer inflammation* (from
     ἐμπρήθω = *I cause to swell*), Acts 28:6 (var.).

ἐμπίπτουσιν   verb, pres. act. indic. 3 pers. pl.
     {5.A.1.a} . . . . ἐμπίπτω G1706
G1706 **ἐμπίπτω**   *I fall in, am cast in.*
ἐμπλακέντες   vbl., ²aor. pass. ptc. nom. pl. masc.
     {6.A.1.a} . . . . ἐμπλέκω G1707
ἐμπλέκεται   verb, pres. pass. indic. 3 pers. sg.
     {5.A.1.d} . . . . id.
G1707 **ἐμπλέκω**   *I enfold, entangle.*
ἐμπλησθῶ   verb, aor. pass. subjunc. 1 pers. sg.
     {5.B.3} .ἐμπίπλημι G1705
G1708 **ἐμπλοκή**, -ῆς, ἡ   *braiding.*
ἐμπλοκῆς   noun, gen. sg. fem. {2.A} . . . . . ἐμπλοκή G1708
G1709 **ἐμπνέω**   *I breathe of, breathe* (lit. *I breathe in*).
ἐμπνέων   vbl., pres. act. ptc. nom. sg. masc.
     {6.A.2} . . . . ἐμπνέω G1709
G1710 **ἐμπορεύομαι**   (1) *I travel as a merchant, engage
     in trade;* (2) with acc. *I traffic in, make gain* or
     business of.
ἐμπορευσόμεθα   verb, fut. mid. indic. 1 pers. pl.
     {5.A.1.d} . . . . ἐμπορεύομαι G1710
ἐμπορεύσονται   verb, fut. mid. indic. 3 pers.
     pl. {5.A.1.d} . . . . id.
ἐμπορευσώμεθα   verb, aor. mid. subjunc.
     1 pers. pl. {5.B.1} . . . . id.
G1711 **ἐμπορία**, -ας, ἡ   *trading, trade, trafficking,
     business.*
ἐμπορίαν   noun, acc. sg. fem. {2.A} . . . . . ἐμπορία G1711
G1712 **ἐμπόριον**, -ου, τό   *a place of traffic, mart.,
     market, market house.*
ἐμπορίου   noun, gen. sg. neut. {2.B} . . . .ἐμπόριον G1712
ἔμποροι   noun, nom. pl. masc. {2.B} . . . ἔμπορος G1713
G1713 **ἔμπορος**, -ου, ὁ   *a merchant, trader.*
ἐμπόρῳ   noun, dat. sg. masc. {2.B} . . . . . . ἔμπορος G1713
G1715 **ἔμπροσθεν**   (1) prep., usually with gen., *in
     front of, before the face of;* (2) adv., *in front,
     before the face;* sometimes made a subs. by the
     addition of the article.
ἔμπροσθεν   adv. . . . . ἔμπροσθεν G1715
ἔμπροσθεν   prep. . . . . id.
ἐμπτύειν   vbl., pres. act. inf. {6.B.1} . . . . . . ἐμπτύω G1716
ἐμπτύσαντες   vbl., aor. act. ptc. nom. pl. masc.
     {6.A.1.a} . . . . id.
ἐμπτυσθήσεται   verb, fut. pass. indic. 3 pers.
     sg. {5.A.1.d} . . . . id.
ἐμπτύσουσιν   verb, fut. act. indic. 3 pers. pl.
     {5.A.1.a} . . . . id.
G1716 **ἐμπτύω**   *I spit upon.*
ἐμφανῆ   adj., acc. sg. masc. {3.E} . . . . . . ἐμφανής G1717
ἐμφανής   adj., nom. sg. masc. {3.E} . . . . id.
G1717 **ἐμφανής**, -ές   *manifest, visible.*
ἐμφανίζειν   vbl., pres. act. inf. {6.B.1} . . ἐμφανίζω G1718
ἐμφανίζουσιν   verb, pres. act. indic. 3 pers. pl.
     {5.A.1.a} . . . . id.
G1718 **ἐμφανίζω**   (1) *I make visible (manifest);* (2)
     hence, act. *I report (inform) against,* Acts 24:1;
     25:2, 15; (3) pass. (quasi-technical) *I appear
     before.*
ἐμφανίσατε   verb, aor. act. impv. 2 pers. pl.
     {5.D.1} . . . . ἐμφανίζω G1718

ἐμφανισθῆναι   vbl., aor. pass. inf. {6.B.1} . . . . . id.
ἐμφανίσω   verb, fut. act. indic. 1 pers. sg.
   {5.A.1.a} . . . . id.
ἔμφοβοι   adj., nom. pl. masc. {3.C} . . . . . ἔμφοβος *G1719*
G1719 **ἔμφοβος**, -ον   *full of fear, terrified.*
ἔμφοβος   adj., nom. sg. masc. {3.C} . . . . ἔμφοβος *G1719*
ἐμφόβων   adj., gen. pl. fem. {3.C} . . . . id.
G1720 **ἐμφυσάω**   *I breathe into, breathe upon.*
ἔμφυτον   adj., acc. sg. masc. {3.C} . . . . . ἔμφυτος *G1721*
G1721 **ἔμφυτος**, -ον   *inborn, ingrown, congenital,*
   natural.
ἐμῷ   pron. posses, 1 pers. sg. dat. sg. masc.
   {4.H} . . . . .ἐμός *G1699*
ἐμῷ   pron. posses, 1 pers. sg. dat. sg. neut. {4.H}. id.
ἐμῶν   pron. posses, 1 pers. sg. gen. pl. neut.
   {4.H} . . . . id.
ἐμώρανεν   verb, aor. act. indic. 3 pers. sg.
   {5.A.1.b} . . . . .μωραίνω *G3471*
ἐμωράνθησαν   verb, aor. pass. indic. 3 pers. pl.
   {5.A.1.b} . . . . id.
G1722 **ἐν**   prep. with dat., (1) of place, *in; ἐν τοῖς*, see
   ὅ; *ἐν Χριστῷ*, of mystic indwelling; (2) = εἰς,
   into, e.g., Matt 10:16; (3) of time, *in, during, at;*
   (4) of instrument, *(armed) with,* Luke 22:49;
   1 Cor 4:21, etc.; (5) *amounting to,* Acts 7:14
   (cf. Mark 4:8 twice); (6) *consisting in,* Eph 2:15;
   (7) *in the department of,* cf. 1 Cor 6:2; (8) *in*
   the judgment of; cf. 1 Cor 14:11; (9) Hebraistic
   use, Matt 10:32; Luke 12:8. For *ἐν ᾧ*, see ὅς.
ἐν   prep. . . . . .ἐν *G1722*
ἔν   prep. . . . . id.
ἕν   adj., acc. sg. neut. {3.D} . . . . .εἷς *G1520*
ἕν   adj., nom. sg. neut. {3.D} . . . . id.
ἕνα   adj., acc. sg. masc. {3.D} . . . . id.
G1723 **ἐναγκαλίζομαι**   *I take (fold) in my arms.*
ἐναγκαλισάμενος   vbl., aor. mid. ptc. nom. sg.
   masc. {6.A.1.b} . . . . .ἐναγκαλίζομαι *G1723*
G1724 **ἐνάλιος**, -ον   of creatures, *living in the sea*
   (poetic).
ἐναλίων   adj., gen. pl. neut. {3.C} . . . . . . .ἐνάλιος *G1724*
G1725 **ἔναντι**   prep. with gen., *before, in the presence*
   of.
ἔναντι   adv. . . . . .ἔναντι *G1725*
ἐναντία   adj., acc. pl. neut. {3.A} . . . . . . ἐναντίος *G1727*
ἐναντίας   adj., gen. sg. fem. {3.A}. . . . . id.
G1726 **ἐναντίον**   prep. with gen., (1) *before, in the*
   presence of; (2) *in the eyes of;* adv. *τοὐναντίον,*
   on the contrary (from τὸ ἐναντίον, neut. subs.
   of ἐναντίος, *the opposite*).
ἐναντίον   adj., acc. sg. neut. {3.A} . . . . . . ἐναντίος *G1727*
ἐναντίον   adv. and prep. {3.F} . . . . .ἐναντίον *G1726*
ἐναντίος   adj., nom. sg. masc. {3.A} . . . . id.
G1727 **ἐναντίος**, -α, -ον   *opposite, opposed, contrary;*
   ἐξ ἐναντίας (adv.), *opposite; ὁ ἐξ ἐναντίας,*
   the adversary.
ἐναντίους   adj., acc. pl. masc. {3.A} . . . . ἐναντίος *G1727*
ἐναντίων   adj., gen. pl. masc. {3.A} . . . . id.
ἐναρξάμενοι   vbl., aor. mid. ptc. nom. pl. masc.
   {6.A.1.b} . . . . ἐνάρχομαι *G1728*

ἐναρξάμενος   vbl., aor. mid. ptc. nom. sg.
   masc. {6.A.1.b} . . . . id.
G1728 **ἐνάρχομαι**   *I begin (in).*
ἐνάτη   adj., dat. sg. fem. {3.A}. . . . . .ἔνατος *G1766‡*
ἐνάτην   adj., acc. sg. fem. {3.A} . . . . id.
ἐνάτης   adj., gen. sg. fem. {3.A} . . . . id.
G1766‡ **ἔνατος**, -η, -ον   *ninth.*
ἔνατος   adj., nom. sg. masc. {3.A}. . . . . . .ἔνατος *G1766‡*
ἐναυάγησα   verb, aor. act. indic. 1 pers. sg.
   {5.A.1}. . . . . .ναυαγέω *G3489*
ἐναυάγησαν   verb, aor. act. indic. 3 pers. pl.
   {5.A.1}. . . . . id.
ἐνγεγραμμένη   vbl., perf. pass. ptc. nom. sg. fem.
   {6.A.1.b} . . . . ἐγγράφω *G1449*
ἐνγέγραπται   verb, perf. pass. indic. 3 pers. sg.
   {5.A.1.f}. . . . . id.
ἐνδεδυμένοι   vbl., perf. mid. ptc. nom. pl. masc.
   {6.A.1.b} . . . . .ἐνδύω *G1746*
ἐνδεδυμένον   vbl., perf. mid. ptc. acc. sg. masc.
   {6.A.1.b} . . . . id.
ἐνδεδυμένος   vbl., perf. mid. ptc. nom. sg.
   masc. {6.A.1.b} . . . . id.
ἐνδέδυσθαι   verb, perf. mid./pass. inf. {6.B.1} . . id.
G1729 **ἐνδεής**, -ές   *in need, needy.*
ἐνδεής   adj., nom. sg. masc. {3.E} . . . . .ἐνδεής *G1729*
G1730 **ἔνδειγμα**, -ατος, τό   *(a thing proved),* hence, *a*
   plain token (sign, proof).
ἔνδειγμα   noun, nom. sg. neut. {2.C} . . . .ἔνδειγμα *G1730*
ἐνδεικνύμενοι   vbl., pres. mid. ptc. nom. pl. masc.
   {6.A.3} . . . . .ἐνδείκνυμι *G1731*
ἐνδεικνυμένους   vbl., pres. mid. ptc. acc. pl.
   masc. {6.A.3} . . . . id.
G1731 **ἐνδείκνυμι**   (in the mid. voice ἐνδείκνυμαι
   only), *I show forth.*
ἐνδείκνυνται   verb, pres. mid. indic. 3 pers. pl.
   {5.A.3.a} . . . . ἐνδείκνυμι *G1731*
ἐνδείκνυσθαι   vbl., pres. mid. inf. {6.B.3} . . . . . id.
ἐνδείξασθαι   vbl., aor. mid. inf. {6.B.3} . . . . id.
ἐνδείξασθε   verb, aor. mid. impv. 2 pers. pl.
   {5.D.3}. . . . . id.
ἐνδείξηται   verb, aor. mid. subjunc. 3 pers. sg.
   {5.B.1} . . . . id.
ἔνδειξιν   noun, acc. sg. fem. {2.C} . . . . . . ἔνδειξις *G1732*
G1732 **ἔνδειξις**, -εως, ἡ   *a showing, proof,*
   demonstration.
ἔνδειξις   noun, nom. sg. fem. {2.C} . . . . . .ἔνδειξις *G1732*
ἐνδείξωμαι   verb, aor. mid. subjunc. 1 pers. sg.
   {5.B.1} . . . . ἐνδείκνυμι *G1731*
G1733 **ἔνδεκα**   *eleven.*
ἔνδεκα   adj. num. . . . . ἔνδεκα *G1733*
ἐνδεκάτην   adj., num. acc. sg. fem. {3.A}ἐνδέκατος *G1734*
G1734 **ἐνδέκατος**, -η, -ον   *eleventh.*
ἐνδέκατος   adj., num. nom. sg. masc.
   {3.A} . . . . .ἐνδέκατος *G1734*
ἐνδέχεται   verb, pres. mid./pass. indic. 3 pers. sg.
   {5.A.1.d} . . . . .ἐνδέχομαι *G1735*
G1735 **ἐνδέχομαι**   ἐνδέχεται, impers., *it is possible.*
G1736 **ἐνδημέω**   *I am in my δῆμος (parish), I am at*
   home.
ἐνδημῆσαι   vbl., aor. act. inf. {6.B.1} . . . . ἐνδημέω *G1736*

ἐνδημοῦντες   vbl., pres. act. ptc. nom. pl. masc.
   {6.A.2} . . . . id.
ἐνδιδύσκουσιν   verb, pres. act. indic. 3 pers. pl.
   {5.A.1.a} . . . . ἐνδιδύσκω G1737
G1737 **ἐνδιδύσκω**   (of clothing, *I put on* another);
   mid. *I put on* (myself); somewhat rare.
G1738 **ἔνδικος**, -ον   *just.*
   ἔνδικον   adj., acc. sg. fem. {3.C} . . . . ἔνδικος G1738
   ἔνδικον   adj., nom. sg. neut. {3.C} . . . . id.
G1739 **ἐνδόμησις** (ἐνδώμησις), -εως, ἡ   *roofing,
   coping* (probably from δῶμα = *roof,* but most
   interpret *building*).
   ἐνδόμησις   noun, nom. sg. fem. {2.C} . ἐνδόμησις G1739
G1740 **ἐνδοξάζομαι**   pass., *I am glorified, recognized
   as* ἔνδοξος.
   ἐνδοξασθῇ   verb, aor. pass. subjunc. 3 pers. sg.
   {5.B.1} . . . . ἐνδοξάζομαι G1740
   ἐνδοξασθῆναι   vbl., aor. pass. inf. {6.B.1} . . . . . id.
   ἔνδοξοι   adj., nom. pl. masc. {3.C} . . . . . . ἔνδοξος G1741
   ἐνδόξοις   adj., dat. pl. neut. {3.C} . . . . id.
G1741 **ἔνδοξος**, -ον   *glorious.*
   ἔνδοξον   adj., acc. sg. fem. {3.C} . . . . .ἔνδοξος G1741
   ἐνδόξῳ   adj., dat. sg. masc. {3.C} . . . . id.
   ἔνδυμα   noun, acc. sg. neut. {2.C} . . . . ἔνδυμα G1742
G1742 **ἔνδυμα**, -ατος, τό   *a garment, dress.*
   ἔνδυμα   noun, nom. sg. neut. {2.C} . . . . . ἔνδυμα G1742
   ἐνδύμασι   noun, dat. pl. neut. {2.C} . . . . id.
   ἐνδύμασιν   noun, dat. pl. neut. {2.C} . . . . id.
   ἐνδύματος   noun, gen. sg. neut. {2.C} . . . . id.
   ἐνδυναμοῦ   verb, pres. pass. impv. 2 pers. sg.
   {5.D.2} . . . . .ἐνδυναμόω G1743
   ἐνδυναμοῦντι   vbl., pres. act. ptc. dat. sg.
   masc. {6.A.2} . . . . id.
   ἐνδυναμοῦσθε   verb, pres. pass. impv. 2 pers.
   pl. {5.D.2} . . . . id.
G1743 **ἐνδυναμόω**   *I fill with* δύναμις *(power);* almost
   = δυναμόω.
   ἐνδυναμώσαντι   vbl., aor. act. ptc. dat. sg. masc.
   {6.A.2} . . . . .ἐνδυναμόω G1743
   ἐνδύνοντες   vbl., pres. act. ptc. nom. pl. masc.
   {6.A.1} . . . . ἐνδύνω G1744
G1744 **ἐνδύνω**   *I slip in* (deviously).
   ἐνδύουσιν   verb, pres. act. indic. 3 pers. pl.
   {5.A.1.a} . . . . ἐνδύω G1746
   ἐνδυσάμενοι   vbl., aor. mid. ptc. nom. pl.
   masc. {6.A.1.b} . . . . id.
   ἐνδυσάμενος   vbl., aor. mid. ptc. nom. sg.
   masc. {6.A.1.b} . . . . id.
   ἐνδύσασθαι   vbl., aor. mid. inf. {6.B.1} . . . . . . id.
   ἐνδύσασθε   verb, aor. mid. impv. 2 pers. pl.
   {5.D.1} . . . . id.
   ἐνδύσατε   verb, aor. act. impv. 2 pers. pl. {5.D.1} id.
   ἐνδύσεως   noun, gen. sg. fem. {2.C} . . . . . .ἔνδυσις G1745
   ἐνδύσησθε   verb, aor. mid. subjunc. 2 pers. pl.
   {5.B.1} . . . . ἐνδύω G1746
   ἐνδύσηται   verb, aor. mid. subjunc. 3 pers. sg.
   {5.B.1} . . . . id.
G1745 **ἔνδυσις**, -εως, ἡ   *putting on* (of a garment).
   ἐνδυσώμεθα   verb, aor. mid. subjunc. 1 pers. pl.
   {5.B.1} . . . . ἐνδύω G1746

G1746 **ἐνδύω**   (1) *I put on, clothe* (another); mid.
   I clothe (myself), *dress;* (2) hence, met., of
   acquiring qualities; = ἐπενδύομαι, 2 Cor 5:3.
   ἐνδώμησις   noun, nom. sg. fem. {2.C} . ἐνδόμησις G1739
   ἐνέβη   verb, ²aor. act. indic. 3 pers. sg.
   {5.A.1.b} . . . . ἐμβαίνω G1684
   ἐνέβημεν   verb, ²aor. act. indic. 1 pers. pl.
   {5.A.1.b} . . . . id.
   ἐνέβησαν   verb, ²aor. act. indic. 3 pers. pl.
   {5.A.1.b} . . . . id.
   ἐνεβίβασεν   verb, aor. act. indic. 3 pers. sg.
   {5.A.1.b} . . . . ἐμβιβάζω G1688
   ἐνέβλεπεν   verb, impf. act. indic. 3 pers. sg.
   {5.A.1.b} . . . . ἐμβλέπω G1689
   ἐνέβλεπον   verb, impf. act. indic. 1 pers. sg.
   {5.A.1.b} . . . . id.
   ἐνέβλεψε   verb, aor. act. indic. 3 pers. sg.
   {5.A.1.b} . . . . id.
   ἐνέβλεψεν   verb, aor. act. indic. 3 pers. sg.
   {5.A.1.b} . . . . id.
   ἐνεβριμήθη   verb, aor. pass. indic. 3 pers. sg.
   {5.A.1} . . . . ἐμβριμάομαι G1690
   ἐνεβριμήσατο   verb, aor. mid. indic. 3 pers. sg.
   {5.A.1} . . . . id.
   ἐνεβριμῶντο   verb, impf. mid./pass. indic.
   3 pers. pl. {5.A.2} . . . . id.
   ἐνέγκαι   vbl., ²aor. act. inf. {6.B.1} . . . . φέρω G5342
   ἐνέγκαντες   vbl., aor. act. ptc. nom. pl. masc.
   {6.A.1.a} . . . . id.
   ἐνέγκας   vbl., aor. act. ptc. nom. sg. masc.
   {6.A.1.a} . . . . id.
   ἐνέγκατε   verb, aor. act. impv. 2 pers. pl. {5.D.1}. id.
   ἐνεγκεῖν   vbl., ²aor. act. inf. {6.B.1} . . . . id.
   ἐνεδείξασθε   verb, aor. mid. indic. 2 pers. pl.
   {5.A.3.b} . . . . ἐνδείκνυμι G1731
   ἐνεδείξατο   verb, aor. mid. indic. 3 pers. sg.
   {5.A.3.b} . . . . id.
   ἐνεδιδύσκετο   verb, impf. mid. indic. 3 pers. sg.
   {5.A.1.e} . . . . ἐνδιδύσκω G1737
G1747 **ἐνέδρα**, -ας, ἡ   (1) *ambush;* (2) hence, *plot,
   treachery, fraud.*
   ἐνέδραν   noun, acc. sg. fem. {2.A} . . . . ἐνέδρα G1747
   ἐνεδρεύοντες   vbl., pres. act. ptc. nom. pl. masc.
   {6.A.1} . . . . ἐνεδρεύω G1748
   ἐνεδρεύουσι   verb, pres. act. indic. 3 pers. pl.
   {5.A.1.a} . . . . id.
   ἐνεδρεύουσιν   verb, pres. act. indic. 3 pers. pl.
   {5.A.1.a} . . . . id.
G1748 **ἐνεδρεύω**   *I lie in wait* (ambush) *for, seek to
   entrap* (hence, *I defraud, deceive*).
G1749 **ἔνεδρον**   (1) *ambush;* (2) hence, *plot, treachery,
   fraud.*
   ἔνεδρον   noun, acc. sg. neut. {2.B} . . . . . . ἔνεδρον G1749
   ἐνεδυναμοῦτο   verb, impf. pass. indic. 3 pers. sg.
   {5.A.2} . . . . .ἐνδυναμόω G1743
   ἐνεδυναμώθη   verb, aor. pass. indic. 3 pers. sg.
   {5.A.1} . . . . id.
   ἐνεδυναμώθησαν   verb, aor. pass. indic.
   3 pers. pl. {5.A.1} . . . . id.

ἐνεδυνάμωσε verb, aor. act. indic. 3 pers. sg.
{5.A.1}. . . . . id.
ἐνεδυνάμωσεν verb, aor. act. indic. 3 pers. sg.
{5.A.1}. . . . . id.
ἐνέδυσαν verb, aor. act. indic. 3 pers. pl.
{5.A.1.b}. . . . . ἐνδύω G1746
ἐνεδύσασθε verb, aor. mid. indic. 2 pers. pl.
{5.A.1.e}. . . . . id.
ἐνεδύσατο verb, aor. mid. indic. 3 pers. sg.
{5.A.1.e}. . . . . id.
G1750 **ἐνειλέω** *I wrap up, roll up in* (something).
ἐνείλησε verb, aor. act. indic. 3 pers. sg.
{5.A.1}. . . . . ἐνειλέω G1750
ἐνείλησεν verb, aor. act. indic. 3 pers. sg.
{5.A.1}. . . . . id.
G1751 **ἔνειμι** (from εἰμί) *I am in (within);* τὰ
ἐνόντα, probably *the contents* (of the dish),
or perhaps *what you can* (but the words are
obscure and may be a mistranslation of an
Aram. original).
ἐνεῖχεν verb, impf. act. indic. 3 pers. sg.
{5.A.1.b}. . . . . ἐνέχω G1758
G1752 **ἔνεκα** (ἕνεκεν, εἵνεκεν) prep. with gen., *for
the sake of, on account of;* οὗ (neut.) εἵνεκεν,
on account of which, wherefore, Luke 4:18;
τίνος ἕνεκα, *on account of what, wherefore,
why,* Acts 19:32.
ἕνεκα prep. . . . . ἕνεκα G1752
ἐνεκαίνισεν verb, aor. act. indic. 3 pers. sg.
{5.A.1.b}. . . . . ἐγκαινίζω G1457
ἐνεκάλουν verb, impf. act. indic. 3 pers. pl.
{5.A.2}. . . . . ἐγκαλέω G1458
ἕνεκεν prep. . . . . ἕνεκα G1752
ἐνεκεντρίσθης verb, aor. pass. indic. 2 pers. sg.
{5.A.1.b}. . . . . ἐγκεντρίζω G1461
ἐνεκοπτόμην verb, impf. pass. indic. 1 pers. sg.
{5.A.1.e}. . . . . ἐγκόπτω G1465
ἐνέκοψεν verb, aor. act. indic. 3 pers. sg.
{5.A.1.b}. . . . . id.
ἐνέκρυψεν verb, aor. act. indic. 3 pers. sg.
{5.A.1.b}. . . . . ἐγκρύπτω G1470
ἐνέμειναν verb, aor. act. indic. 3 pers. pl.
{5.A.1.b}. . . . . ἐμμένω G1696
ἐνέμεινεν verb, aor. act. indic. 3 pers. sg.
{5.A.1.b}. . . . . id.
ἐνένευον verb, impf. act. indic. 3 pers. pl.
{5.A.1.b}. . . . . ἐννεύω G1770
G1768†‡ **ἐνενήκοντα** (ἐννενήκοντα) *ninety.*
ἐνενήκοντα adj. num. . . . . ἐνενήκοντα G1768†‡
ἐνεοί adj., nom. pl. masc. {3.A} . . . . . ἐνεός G1769†‡
G1769†‡ **ἐνεός** (ἐννεός), -ά, -όν *speechless, dumb, un-
able to speak* (= ἄνεως).
ἐνέπαιζον verb, impf. act. indic. 3 pers. pl.
{5.A.1.b}. . . . . ἐμπαίζω G1702
ἐνέπαιξαν verb, aor. act. indic. 3 pers. pl.
{5.A.1.b}. . . . . id.
ἐνεπαίχθη verb, aor. pass. indic. 3 pers. sg.
{5.A.1.b}. . . . . id.
ἐνέπλησεν verb, aor. act. indic. 3 pers. sg.
{5.A.3.b}. . . . . ἐμπίπλημι G1705

ἐνεπλήσθησαν verb, aor. pass. indic. 3 pers.
pl. {5.A.1}. . . . . id.
ἐνέπρησε verb, aor. act. indic. 3 pers. sg.
{5.A.3.b}. . . . . ἐμπίπρημι G1714‡
ἐνέπρησεν verb, aor. act. indic. 3 pers. sg.
{5.A.3.b}. . . . . id.
ἐνέπτυον verb, impf. act. indic. 3 pers. pl.
{5.A.1.b}. . . . . ἐμπτύω G1716
ἐνέπτυσαν verb, aor. act. indic. 3 pers. pl.
{5.A.1.b}. . . . . id.
ἐνεργεῖ verb, pres. act. indic. 3 pers. sg.
{5.A.2}. . . . . ἐνεργέω G1754
G1753 **ἐνέργεια**, -ας, ἡ *working, action productive
of* ἔργον (concr. *work*), *activity;* in the NT
confined to superhuman activity.
ἐνέργειαν noun, acc. sg. fem. {2.A} . . . . ἐνέργεια G1753
ἐνεργείας noun, gen. sg. fem. {2.A}. . . . . id.
ἐνεργεῖν vbl., pres. act. inf. {6.B.2}. . . . . ἐνεργέω G1754
ἐνεργεῖται verb, pres. mid. indic. 3 pers. sg.
{5.A.2}. . . . . id.
G1754 **ἐνεργέω** (1) intrans., *I am at work, work;* (2)
trans., *I work,* the acc. expressing "that which
is worked," *effect.* In the NT the word is generally connected with miraculous interventions;
(3) pass. always with non-personal subj., as
ἐνεργεῖν always with personal, *I am made
operative (effective), I am made to produce my
appropriate result, I am set in operation, I am
made to work.* Mid. absent from NT.
G1755 **ἐνέργημα**, -ατος, τό *a working.*
ἐνεργήματα noun, nom. pl. neut. {2.C}. ἐνέργημα G1755
ἐνεργημάτων noun, gen. pl. neut. {2.C} . . . . id.
ἐνεργής adj., nom. sg. fem. {3.E}. . . . . . ἐνεργής G1756
G1756 **ἐνεργής**, -ές *effective, productive of due result.*
ἐνεργής adj., nom. sg. masc. {3.E} . . . . . ἐνεργής G1756
ἐνεργήσας vbl., aor. act. ptc. nom. sg. masc.
{6.A.2}. . . . . ἐνεργέω G1754
ἐνεργουμένη vbl., pres. mid. ptc. nom. sg. fem.
{6.A.2}. . . . . id.
ἐνεργουμένην vbl., pres. mid. ptc. acc. sg. fem.
{6.A.2}. . . . . id.
ἐνεργουμένης vbl., pres. mid. ptc. gen. sg.
fem. {6.A.2}. . . . . id.
ἐνεργοῦντος vbl., pres. act. ptc. gen. sg. masc.
{6.A.2}. . . . . id.
ἐνεργοῦντος vbl., pres. act. ptc. gen. sg. neut.
{6.A.2}. . . . . id.
ἐνεργοῦσιν verb, pres. act. indic. 3 pers. pl.
{5.A.2}. . . . . id.
ἐνεργῶν vbl., pres. act. ptc. nom. sg. masc. {6.A.2} id.
ἐνέστηκεν verb, perf. act. indic. 3 pers. sg.
{5.A.1}. . . . . ἐνίστημι G1764
ἐνεστηκότα vbl., perf. act. ptc. acc. sg. masc.
{6.A.3}. . . . . id.
ἐνεστῶσαν vbl., ²perf. act. ptc. acc. sg. fem.
{6.A.3}. . . . . id.
ἐνεστῶτα vbl., ²perf. act. ptc. nom. pl. neut.
{6.A.3}. . . . . id.
ἐνεστῶτος vbl., ²perf. act. ptc. gen. sg. masc.
{6.A.3}. . . . . id.

ἐνετειλάμην   verb, aor. mid. indic. 1 pers. sg.
　{5.A.1.e} . . . . ἐντέλλω G1781
ἐνετείλατο   verb, aor. mid. indic. 3 pers. sg.
　{5.A.1.e} . . . . id.
ἐνετρεπόμεθα   verb, impf. pass. indic. 1 pers. pl.
　{5.A.1.e} . . . . ἐντρέπω G1788
ἐνετύλιξεν   verb, aor. act. indic. 3 pers. sg.
　{5.A.1.b} . . . . ἐντυλίσσω G1794
ἐνέτυχεν   verb, ²aor. act. indic. 3 pers. sg.
　{5.A.1.b} . . . . ἐντυγχάνω G1793
ἐνέτυχον   verb, ²aor. act. indic. 3 pers. pl.
　{5.A.1.b} . . . . id.
G1757 **ἐνευλογέω**   I bless (of God); ἐν is considered to
　have instrumental force.
ἐνευλογηθήσονται   verb, fut. pass. indic. 3 pers.
　pl. {5.A.1} . . . . ἐνευλογέω G1757
ἐνεφάνισαν   verb, aor. act. indic. 3 pers. pl.
　{5.A.1.b} . . . . ἐμφανίζω G1718
ἐνεφάνισας   verb, aor. act. indic. 2 pers. sg.
　{5.A.1.b} . . . . id.
ἐνεφανίσθησαν   verb, aor. pass. indic. 3 pers.
　pl. {5.A.1.b} . . . . id.
ἐνεφύσησε   verb, aor. act. indic. 3 pers. sg.
　{5.A.1} . . . . ἐμφυσάω G1720
ἐνεφύσησεν   verb, aor. act. indic. 3 pers. sg.
　{5.A.1} . . . . id.
ἐνέχειν   vbl., pres. act. inf. {6.B.1} . . . . . . ἐνέχω G1758
ἐνέχεσθε   verb, pres. pass. impv. 2 pers. pl. {5.D.1}. id.
ἐνεχθεῖσαν   vbl., aor. pass. ptc. acc. sg. fem.
　{6.A.1.a} . . . . φέρω G5342
ἐνεχθείσης   vbl., aor. pass. ptc. gen. sg. fem.
　{6.A.1.a} . . . . id.
ἐνεχθῆναι   vbl., aor. pass. inf. {6.B.1} . . . . id.
G1758 **ἐνέχω**   (1) I have a grudge against, I am angry
　(with); (2) pass. or mid. I am entangled, en-
　tangle myself (var. in 2 Thess 1:4).
ἐνηργεῖτο   verb, impf. mid. indic. 3 pers. sg.
　{5.A.2} . . . . .ἐνεργέω G1754
ἐνήργηκεν   verb, perf. act. indic. 3 pers. sg.
　{5.A.1} . . . . id.
ἐνήργησε   verb, aor. act. indic. 3 pers. sg. {5.A.1} id.
ἐνήργησεν   verb, aor. act. indic. 3 pers. sg.
　{5.A.1} . . . . id.
G1759 **ἐνθάδε**   adv., here, in this place.
ἐνθάδε   adv. . . . . .ἐνθάδε G1759
G1782†‡ **ἔνθεν**   from here. Var. for ἐντεῦθεν, Matt
　17:20; Luke 16:26.
ἔνθεν   adv. ἔνθεν G1782†‡
ἐνθυμεῖσθε   verb, pres. mid./pass. indic. 2 pers. pl.
　{5.A.2} . . . . ἐνθυμέομαι G1760
G1760 **ἐνθυμέομαι**   I meditate upon, reflect upon.
ἐνθυμηθέντος   vbl., aor. pass. ptc. gen. sg. masc.
　{6.A.1.a.} . . . . ἐνθυμέομαι G1760
ἐνθυμήσεις   noun, acc. pl. fem. {2.C} . ἐνθύμησις G1761
ἐνθυμήσεων   noun, gen. pl. fem. {2.C} . . . . . . id.
ἐνθυμήσεως   noun, gen. sg. fem. {2.C} . . . . . . id.
G1761 **ἐνθύμησις**, -εως, ἡ   inward thought, medita-
　tion; pl. thoughts.
ἐνθυμουμένου   vbl., pres. mid./pass. ptc. gen. sg.
　masc. {6.A.2} . . . . ἐνθυμέομαι G1760

G1762 **ἔνι**   there is; οὐκ ἔνι, there is (or can be) no
　room for.
ἔνι   verb, pres. act. indic. 3 pers. sg.. . . . . ἔνι G1762
ἐνί   adj., dat. sg. masc. {3.D} . . . . εἷς G1520
ἐνί   adj., dat. sg. neut. {3.D}. . . . . id.
ἐνιαυτόν   noun, acc. sg. masc. {2.B}. . . . . ἐνιαυτός G1763
G1763 **ἐνιαυτός**, -οῦ, ὁ   a year.
ἐνιαυτοῦ   noun, gen. sg. masc. {2.B} . . . . ἐνιαυτός G1763
ἐνιαυτούς   noun, acc. pl. masc. {2.B}. . . . . id.
ἐνίκησα   verb, aor. act. indic. 1 pers. sg.
　{5.A.1}. . . . . νικάω G3528
ἐνίκησαν   verb, aor. act. indic. 3 pers. pl. {5.A.1} id.
ἐνίκησεν   verb, aor. act. indic. 3 pers. sg. {5.A.1} id.
G1764 **ἐνίστημι**   only intrans., I impend, am at hand,
　am present; perf. ptc. ἐνεστηκώς (ἐνεστώς)
　as adj., present.
ἐνισχύθη   verb, aor. pass. indic. 3 pers. sg.
　{5.A.1.b} . . . . ἐνισχύω G1765
ἐνίσχυσεν   verb, aor. act. indic. 3 pers. sg.
　{5.A.1.b} . . . . id.
G1765 **ἐνισχύω**   I strengthen within, I fill with strength.
ἐνισχύων   vbl., pres. act. ptc. nom. sg. masc.
　{6.A.1}. . . . . ἐνισχύω G1765
ἔνιψα   verb, aor. act. indic. 1 pers. sg.
　{5.A.1.b} . . . . νίπτω G3538
ἐνιψάμην   verb, aor. mid. indic. 1 pers. sg.
　{5.A.1.e} . . . . id.
ἐνίψατο   verb, aor. mid. indic. 3 pers. sg.
　{5.A.1.e} . . . . id.
ἔνιψε   verb, aor. act. indic. 3 pers. sg. {5.A.1.b} . . id.
ἔνιψεν   verb, aor. act. indic. 3 pers. sg. {5.A.1.b} . id.
ἐνκαθέτους   adj., acc. pl. masc. {3.C} . . ἐγκάθετος G1455
ἐνκαίνια   noun, nom. pl. neut. {2.B} . . . ἐγκαίνια G1456
ἐνκακεῖν   vbl., pres. act. inf. {6.B.2} . . . . . ἐκκακέω G1573
ἐνκακήσητε   verb, aor. act. subjunc. 2 pers. pl.
　{5.B.1} . . . . id.
ἐνκακῶμεν   verb, pres. act. subjunc. 1 pers. pl.
　{5.B.2} . . . . id.
ἐνκαταλείψεις   verb, fut. act. indic. 2 pers. sg.
　{5.A.1.a} . . . . ἐγκαταλείπω G1459
ἐνκατελείφθη   verb, aor. pass. indic. 3 pers. sg.
　{5.A.1.b} . . . . id.
ἐνκατοικῶν   vbl., pres. act. ptc. nom. sg. masc.
　{6.A.2}. ἐγκατοικέω G1460
ἐνκαυχᾶσθαι   vbl., pres. mid./pass. inf.
　{6.B.2} . . . . .ἐγκαυχάομαι G2744†‡
ἐνκεκαίνισται   verb, perf. pass. indic. 3 pers. sg.
　{5.A.1.f}. ἐγκαινίζω G1457
ἐνκεντρίσαι   vbl., aor. act. inf. {6.B.1} . ἐγκεντρίζω G1461
ἐνκεντρισθήσονται   verb, fut. pass. indic.
　3 pers. pl. {5.A.1.d} . . . . id.
ἐνκεντρισθῶ   verb, aor. pass. subjunc. 1 pers.
　sg. {5.B.1} . . . . id.
ἐνκοπήν   noun, acc. sg. fem. {2.A} . . . . . . ἐγκοπή G1464
ἐνκόπτω   verb, pres. act. subjunc. 1 pers. sg.
　{5.B.1} . . . . ἐγκόπτω G1465
ἐνκρῖναι   vbl., aor. act. inf. {6.B.1} . . . . ἐγκρίνω G1469
ἐνκύῳ   noun, dat. sg. fem. {2.B} . . . . ἔγκυος G1471
ἐννάτη   adj., dat. sg. fem. {3.A} . . . . ἔνατος G1766‡
ἐννάτην   adj., acc. sg. fem. {3.A} . . . . id.

ἐννάτης   adj., gen. sg. fem. {3.A} . . . . id.
G1767 **ἐννέα**   nine.
ἐννέα   adj. num. . . . . ἐννέα G1767
ἐννενήκοντα   adj. num. . . . . ἐνενήκοντα G1768†‡
G1768 ἐννενηκονταεννέα, *ninety nine.* Var. for
      ἐνενήκοντα εννέα (G1768 and G1782), Matt
      18:12; Luke 15:4, 7.
ἐννενηκονταεννέα   adj.
      num. . . . . ἐννενηκονταεννέα G1768
ἐννεοί   adj., nom. pl. masc. {3.A} . . . . ἐνεός G1769†‡
G1770 **ἐννεύω**   *I make a sign to by nodding.*
G1771 **ἔννοια**, -ας, ἡ   *(intelligence, thought), intention,*
      purpose.
ἔννοιαν   noun, acc. sg. fem. {2.A} . . . . ἔννοια G1771
ἐννοιῶν   noun, gen. pl. fem. {2.A} . . . . id.
G1772 **ἔννομος**, -ον   (1) *legal, statutory, duly consti-*
      tuted, Acts 19:39; (2) *under the law, obedient to*
      the law, 1 Cor 9:21.
ἔννομος   adj., nom. sg. masc. {3.C} . . . . . ἔννομος G1772
ἐννόμῳ   adj., dat. sg. fem. {3.C} . . . . id.
ἔννυχα   adv. . . . . .ἔννυχος G1773
ἔννυχον   adv. . . . . id.
G1773 **ἔννυχος**, -ον   *in the night;* neut. pl. ἔννυχα as
      adv., *at night.*
ἐνοικείτω   verb, pres. act. impv. 3 pers. sg.
      {5.D.2} . . . . .ἐνοικέω G1774
G1774 **ἐνοικέω**   *I dwell in, am settled (stationary) in.*
ἐνοικήσω   verb, fut. act. indic. 1 pers. sg.
      {5.A.1} . . . . .ἐνοικέω G1774
ἐνοικοῦν   vbl., pres. act. ptc. acc. sg. neut.
      {6.A.2} . . . . id.
ἐνοικοῦντος   vbl., pres. act. ptc. gen. neut.
      {6.A.2} . . . . id.
ἐνοικοῦσα   vbl., pres. act. ptc. nom. sg. fem.
      {6.A.2} . . . . id.
ἐνόμιζε   verb, impf. act. indic. 3 pers. sg.
      {5.A.1.b} . . . . νομίζω G3543
ἐνόμιζεν   verb, impf. act. indic. 3 pers. sg.
      {5.A.1.b} . . . . id.
ἐνομίζετο   verb, impf. pass. indic. 3 pers. sg.
      {5.A.1.e} . . . . id.
ἐνομίζομεν   verb, impf. act. indic. 1 pers. pl.
      {5.A.1.b} . . . . id.
ἐνόμιζον   verb, impf. act. indic. 3 pers. pl.
      {5.A.1.b} . . . . id.
ἐνόμισαν   verb, aor. act. indic. 3 pers. pl.
      {5.A.1.b} . . . . id.
ἐνόμισας   verb, aor. act. indic. 2 pers. sg.
      {5.A.1.b} . . . . id.
ἐνόντα   vbl., pres. act. ptc. acc. pl. neut.
      {7.C.1} . . . . ἔνειμι G1751
G3726†‡ **ἐνορκίζω**   *I adjure someone by, I solemnly ap-*
      peal to someone by (a strengthened ὁρκίζω).
      Var. for ὁρκίζω, 1 Thess 5:27.
ἐνορκίζω   verb, pres. act. indic. 1 pers. sg.
      {5.A.1.a} . . . . ἐνορκίζω G3726†‡
ἑνός   adj., gen. sg. masc. {3.D} . . . . εἷς G1520
ἑνός   adj., gen. sg. neut. {3.D} . . . . id.
ἐνοσφίσατο   verb, aor. mid. indic. 3 pers. sg.
      {5.A.1.e} . . . . νοσφίζω G3557

G1775 **ἑνότης**, -ητος, ἡ   *oneness, unity.*
ἑνότητα   noun, acc. sg. fem. {2.C} . . . . . . .ἑνότης G1775
G1776 **ἐνοχλέω**   *I disturb, torment* (Heb 12:15 is from
      the LXX, where ἐνοχλῇ appears to be a cor-
      ruption for ἐν χολῇ, *in gall*).
ἐνοχλῇ   verb, pres. act. subjunc. 3 pers. sg.
      {5.B.2} . . . . ἐνοχλέω G1776
ἐνοχλούμενοι   vbl., pres. pass. ptc. nom. pl.
      masc. {6.A.2} . . . . id.
ἔνοχοι   adj., nom. pl. masc. {3.C} . . . . .ἔνοχος G1777
ἔνοχον   adj., acc. sg. masc. {3.C} . . . . id.
G1777 **ἔνοχος**, -ον   *involved in,* hence, *liable,* generally
      with dat. (or gen.) of the punishment.
ἔνοχος   adj., nom. sg. masc. {3.C} . . . . .ἔνοχος G1777
ἐνπεριπατήσω   verb, fut. act. indic. 1 pers. sg.
      {5.A.1} . . . . ἐμπεριπατέω G1704
ἐνπνέων   vbl., pres. act. ptc. nom. sg. masc.
      {6.A.2} . . . . ἐμπνέω G1709
ἐνστήσονται   verb, fut. mid. indic. 3 pers. pl.
      {5.A.1} . . . . ἐνίστημι G1764
G1778 **ἔνταλμα**, -ατος, τό   *an injunction, ordinance.*
ἐντάλματα   noun, acc. pl. neut. {2.C} . . . . .ἔνταλμα G1778
ἐνταφιάζειν   vbl., pres. act. inf. {6.B.1} ἐνταφιάζω G1779
G1779 **ἐνταφιάζω**   *I embalm, prepare for burial.*
ἐνταφιάσαι   vbl., aor. act. inf. {6.B.1} . . ἐνταφιάζω G1779
ἐνταφιασμόν   noun, acc. sg. masc.
      {2.B} . . . . ἐνταφιασμός G1780
G1780 **ἐνταφιασμός**, -οῦ, ὁ   *embalming, preparation*
      of corpse *for burial.*
ἐνταφιασμοῦ   noun, gen. sg. masc.
      {2.B} . . . . ἐνταφιασμός G1780
ἐντειλάμενος   vbl., aor. mid. ptc. nom. sg. masc.
      {6.A.1.b} . . . . ἐντέλλω G1781
ἐντελεῖται   verb, fut. mid. indic. 3 pers. sg.
      {5.A.2} . . . . id.
ἐντέλλομαι   verb, pres. mid./pass. indic. 1 pers.
      sg. {5.A.1.d} . . . . id.
G1781 **ἐντέλλω**   mid., *I give orders (injunctions,*
      instructions, commands).
ἐντέταλται   verb, perf. mid./pass. indic. 3 pers. sg.
      {5.A.1.f} . . . . ἐντέλλω G1781
ἐντετυλιγμένον   vbl., perf. pass. ptc. acc. sg. neut.
      {6.A.1.b} . . . . ἐντυλίσσω G1794
ἐντετυπωμένη   vbl., perf. pass. ptc. nom. sg. fem.
      {6.A.2} . . . . ἐντυπόω G1795
G1782 **ἐντεῦθεν**   adv., (1) *hence, from this place;* (2)
      ἐντεῦθεν καὶ ἐντεῦθεν, *on this side and on*
      that, cf. Rev 22:2.
ἐντεῦθεν   adv. .ἐντεῦθεν G1782
ἐντεύξεις   noun, acc. pl. fem. {2.C} . . . . . ἔντευξις G1783
ἐντεύξεως   noun, gen. sg. fem. {2.C} . . . . id.
G1783 **ἔντευξις**, -εως, ἡ   (lit. *approaching* the king,
      hence a technical term), *a petition.*
ἔντιμον   adj., acc. sg. masc. {3.C} . . . . ἔντιμος G1784
G1784 **ἔντιμος**, -ον   *(held precious),* hence, (1) *pre-*
      cious; (2) *honored, honorable* in rank, etc.,
      Luke 14:8.
ἔντιμος   adj., nom. sg. masc. {3.C} . . . . . . .ἔντιμος G1784
ἐντιμότερος   adj. comp., nom. sg. masc. {3.C;
      3.G} . . . . id.

ἐντίμους   adj., acc. pl. masc. {3.C} . . . . id.

ἐντολαί   noun, nom. pl. fem. {2.A} . . . . . . ἐντολή G1785

ἐντολαῖς   noun, dat. pl. fem. {2.A} . . . . id.

ἐντολάς   noun, acc. pl. fem. {2.A} . . . . id.

G1785   **ἐντολή**, -ῆς, ἡ   *an ordinance, injunction, command.*

ἐντολή   noun, nom. sg. fem. {2.A} . . . . . . ἐντολή G1785

ἐντολήν   noun, acc. sg. fem. {2.A} . . . . id.

ἐντολῆς   noun, gen. sg. fem. {2.A} . . . . id.

ἐντολῶν   noun, gen. pl. fem. {2.A} . . . . id.

ἐντόπιοι   adj., nom. pl. masc. {3.C} . . . . ἐντόπιος G1786

G1786   **ἐντόπιος**, -α, -ον   *belonging to the place, native, resident.*

G1787   **ἐντός**   prep. with gen., *within, inside* (so also Luke 17:21); τὸ ἐντός, *the inside.*

ἐντός   adv. ἐντός G1787

ἐντραπῇ   verb, ²aor. pass. subjunc. 3 pers. sg. {5.B.1} . . . . ἐντρέπω G1788

ἐντραπήσονται   verb, ²fut. pass. indic. 3 pers. pl. {5.A.1.d} . . . . id.

ἐντρέπομαι   verb, pres. pass. indic. 1 pers. sg. {5.A.1.d} . . . . id.

ἐντρεπόμενος   vbl., pres. pass. ptc. nom. sg. masc. {6.A.1} . . . . id.

G1788   **ἐντρέπω**   (1) *I turn to confusion, put to shame,* e.g., 1 Cor 4:14; 2 Thess 3:14; Titus 2:8; (2) mid. with acc., meaning *I reverence,* e.g., Mark 12:6; Heb 12:9.

ἐντρέπων   vbl., pres. act. ptc. nom. sg. masc. {6.A.1} . . . . ἐντρέπω G1788

ἐντρεφόμενος   vbl., pres. pass. ptc. nom. sg. masc. {6.A.1} . . . . ἐντρέφω G1789

G1789   **ἐντρέφω**   *I nourish (sustain) on.*

ἔντρομος   adj., nom. sg. masc. {3.C} . . . . ἔντρομος G1790

G1790   **ἔντρομος**, -ον   *trembling.*

G1791   **ἐντροπή**, -ῆς, ἡ   *shame* (from ἐντρέπω).

ἐντροπήν   noun, acc. sg. fem. {2.A} . . . . ἐντροπή G1791

G1792   **ἐντρυφάω**   *I revel (in).*

ἐντρυφῶντες   vbl., pres. act. ptc. nom. pl. masc. {6.A.2} . . . . ἐντρυφάω G1792

ἐντυγχάνει   verb, pres. act. indic. 3 pers. sg. {5.A.1.a} . . . . ἐντυγχάνω G1793

ἐντυγχάνειν   vbl., pres. act. inf. {6.B.1} . . . . id.

G1793   **ἐντυγχάνω**   (1) *I meet, encounter;* hence, (2) *I call (upon), I make a petition, I make suit, supplication,* cf. ἔντευξις.

G1794   **ἐντυλίσσω**   *I wrap up, roll round, envelop.*

G1795   **ἐντυπόω**   *I engrave.*

G1796   **ἐνυβρίζω**   *I insult, outrage.*

ἐνυβρίσας   vbl., aor. act. ptc. nom. sg. masc. {6.A.1.a} . . . . ἐνυβρίζω G1796

ἔνυξε   verb, aor. act. indic. 3 pers. sg. {5.A.1.b} . . . . νύσσω G3572

ἔνυξεν   verb, aor. act. indic. 3 pers. sg. {5.A.1.b}. id.

ἐνύπνια   noun, acc. pl. neut. {2.B} . . . . ἐνύπνιον G1798

G1797   **ἐνυπνιάζομαι**   *I dream (see visions)* in my sleep.

ἐνυπνιαζόμενοι   vbl., pres. mid./pass. ptc. nom. pl. masc. {6.A.1} . . . . ἐνυπνιάζομαι G1797

ἐνυπνιασθήσονται   verb, fut. pass. indic. 3 pers. pl. {5.A.1.d} . . . . id.

ἐνυπνίοις   noun, dat. pl. neut. {2.B} . . . . ἐνύπνιον G1798

G1798   **ἐνύπνιον**, -ου, τό   *a dream, vision.*

ἐνύσταξαν   verb, aor. act. indic. 3 pers. pl. {5.A.1.b} . . . . νυστάζω G3573

ἐνῴκησε   verb, aor. act. indic. 3 pers. sg. {5.A.1} . . . . ἐνοικέω G1774

ἐνῴκησεν   verb, aor. act. indic. 3 pers. sg. {5.A.1} . . . . id.

G1799   **ἐνώπιον**   prep. with gen., (1) *before the face of, in the presence of;* (2) *in the eyes of* (vernacular).

ἐνώπιον   prep. . . . . ἐνώπιον G1799

Ἐνώς   noun prop.. . . . . Ἐνώς G1800

G1800   **Ἐνώς**, ὁ   *Enos,* son of Seth, and father of Cainam (Heb.).

G1801   **ἐνωτίζομαι**   *I take into my ear, give ear to* (from ἐν and οὖς).

ἐνωτίσασθε   verb, aor. mid. impv. 2 pers. pl. {5.D.1} . . . . ἐνωτίζομαι G1801

Ἐνώχ   noun prop. . . . . Ἐνώχ G1802

G1802   **Ἐνώχ**, ὁ   *Enoch,* son of Jaret and father of Mathusala (Heb.); Jude 14 refers to the apocryphal *Book of Enoch.*

Ἐνώχ   noun prop. . . . . Ἐνώχ G1802

G1803   **ἕξ**   *six.*

ἕξ   adj. num. ἕξ G1803

ἐξ   prep. . . . . ἐκ G1537

ἐξαγαγεῖν   vbl., ²aor. act. inf. {6.B.1} . . . . ἐξάγω G1806

ἐξαγαγέτωσαν   verb, ²aor. act. impv. 3 pers. pl. {5.D.1} . . . . id.

ἐξαγαγόντες   vbl., ²aor. act. ptc. nom. pl. masc. {6.A.1.a} . . . . id.

ἐξαγαγών   vbl., ²aor. act. ptc. nom. sg. masc. {6.A.1.a} . . . . id.

ἐξαγγείλητε   verb, aor. act. subjunc. 2 pers. pl. {5.B.1} . . . . ἐξαγγέλλω G1804

G1804   **ἐξαγγέλλω**   *I announce publicly, proclaim.*

ἐξάγει   verb, pres. act. indic. 3 pers. sg. {5.A.1.a} . . . . ἐξάγω G1806

ἐξαγοραζόμενοι   vbl., pres. mid. ptc. nom. pl. masc. {6.A.1} . . . . ἐξαγοράζω G1805

G1805   **ἐξαγοράζω**   (1) *I buy out, buy away from, ransom;* (2) mid., *I purchase out, buy, redeem.*

ἐξαγοράσῃ   verb, aor. act. subjunc. 3 pers. sg. {5.B.1} . . . . ἐξαγοράζω G1805

ἐξάγουσιν   verb, pres. act. indic. 3 pers. pl. {5.A.1.a} . . . . ἐξάγω G1806

G1806   **ἐξάγω**   *I lead out,* sometimes to death, execution.

G1807   **ἐξαιρέω**   (1) *I take out, remove;* (2) sometimes (mid.) *I choose,* sometimes *I rescue.*

ἐξαιρούμενος   vbl., pres. mid. ptc. nom. sg. masc. {6.A.2} . . . . ἐξαιρέω G1807

G1808   **ἐξαίρω**   *I remove.*

G1809   **ἐξαιτέω**   mid. (1) *I beg earnestly for;* (2) aor. = *I have procured to be given up to me.*

G1810   **ἐξαίφνης** (ἐξέφνης)   adv., *suddenly.*

ἐξαίφνης   adv. . . . . ἐξαίφνης G1810

G1811 **ἐξακολουθέω**   *I follow closely, adhere to.*
ἐξακολουθήσαντες   vbl., aor. act. ptc. nom. pl.
   masc. {6.A.2}................ἐξακολουθέω G1811
ἐξακολουθήσουσιν   verb, fut. act. indic.
   3 pers. pl. {5.A.1}................... id.
ἐξακόσια   adj., num. nom. pl. neut.
   {3.A}.....................ἐξακόσιοι G1812

G1812 **ἐξακόσιοι, -αι, -α**   *six hundred.*
ἐξακόσιοι   adj., num. nom. pl. masc.
   {3.A}.....................ἐξακόσιοι G1812
ἐξακοσίων   adj., num. gen. pl. masc. {3.A} .... id.
ἐξαλειφθῆναι   vbl., aor. pass. inf. {6.B.1} ἐξαλείφω G1813

G1813 **ἐξαλείφω**   *I wipe away, obliterate.*
ἐξαλείψας   vbl., aor. act. ptc. nom. sg. masc.
   {6.A.1.a}.................. ἐξαλείφω G1813
ἐξαλείψει   verb, fut. act. indic. 3 pers. sg.
   {5.A.1.a}........................ id.
ἐξαλείψω   verb, fut. act. indic. 1 pers. sg.
   {5.A.1.a}........................ id.
ἐξαλιφθῆναι   vbl., aor. pass. inf. {6.B.1}...... id.

G1814 **ἐξάλλομαι**   *I leap up* (for joy).
ἐξαλλόμενος   vbl., pres. mid./pass. ptc. nom. sg.
   masc. {6.A.1}............. ἐξάλλομαι G1814
ἐξανάστασιν   noun, acc. sg. fem.
   {2.C}.................. ἐξανάστασις G1815

G1815 **ἐξανάστασις, -εως, ἡ**   *rising up and out,*
   resurrection.
ἐξαναστήσῃ   verb, aor. act. subjunc. 3 pers. sg.
   {5.B.3}.................ἐξανίστημι G1817

G1816 **ἐξανατέλλω**   *I rise (spring) up out* (of the
   ground).
ἐξανέστησαν   verb, ²aor. act. indic. 3 pers. pl.
   {5.A.3.b}.................ἐξανίστημι G1817
ἐξανέτειλε   verb, aor. act. indic. 3 pers. sg.
   {5.A.1.b}................ἐξανατέλλω G1816
ἐξανέτειλεν   verb, aor. act. indic. 3 pers. sg.
   {5.A.1.b}........................ id.

G1817 **ἐξανίστημι**   (1) trans., *I raise up, cause to
   grow;* (2) intrans., *I rise up.*
ἐξαπατάτω   verb, pres. act. impv. 3 pers. sg.
   {5.D.2}.................ἐξαπατάω G1818

G1818 **ἐξαπατάω**   *I deceive.*
ἐξαπατηθεῖσα   vbl., aor. pass. ptc. nom. sg. fem.
   {6.A.1.a.}................ἐξαπατάω G1818
ἐξαπατήσῃ   verb, aor. act. subjunc. 3 pers. sg.
   {5.B.1}......................... id.
ἐξαπατῶσι   verb, pres. act. indic. 3 pers. pl.
   {5.A.2}......................... id.
ἐξαπατῶσιν   verb, pres. act. indic. 3 pers. pl.
   {5.A.2}......................... id.
ἐξαπεστάλη   verb, ²aor. pass. indic. 3 pers. sg.
   {5.A.1.e}................ἐξαποστέλλω G1821
ἐξαπέστειλαν   verb, aor. act. indic. 3 pers. pl.
   {5.A.1.b}....................... id.
ἐξαπέστειλε   verb, aor. act. indic. 3 pers. sg.
   {5.A.1.b}....................... id.
ἐξαπέστειλεν   verb, aor. act. indic. 3 pers. sg.
   {5.A.1.b}....................... id.

G1819 **ἐξάπινα**   adv., *suddenly.*
ἐξάπινα   adv.................. ἐξάπινα G1819

G1820 **ἐξαπορέω**   pass., *I am at my wits' end, I despair*
   (w. gen. = *about*), 2 Cor 1:8.
ἐξαπορηθῆναι   vbl., aor. pass. inf.
   {6.B.1}..................ἐξαπορέω G1820
ἐξαπορούμενοι   vbl., pres. mid./pass. ptc.
   nom. pl. masc. {6.A.2}................ id.

G1821 **ἐξαποστέλλω**   *I send away out, I send forth* (a
   person qualified for a task).
ἐξαποστέλλω   verb, pres. act. indic. 1 pers. sg.
   {5.A.1.a}................ἐξαποστέλλω G1821
ἐξαποστελῶ   verb, fut. act. indic. 1 pers. sg.
   {5.A.2}......................... id.
ἐξάρατε   verb, aor. act. impv. 2 pers. pl.
   {5.D.1}..................ἐξαίρω G1808
ἐξαρεῖτε   verb, fut. act. indic. 2 pers. pl. {5.A.2} . id.
ἐξαρθῇ   verb, aor. pass. subjunc. 3 pers. sg.
   {5.B.1}......................... id.

G1822 **ἐξαρτίζω**   (1) *I fit up, equip, furnish, supply,*
   2 Tim 3:17; (2) *I accomplish, finish,* Acts 21:5.
ἐξαρτίσαι   vbl., aor. act. inf. {6.B.1} .... ἐξαρτίζω G1822

G1823 **ἐξαστράπτω**   *I flash forth like lightning.*
ἐξαστράπτων   vbl., pres. act. ptc. nom. sg. masc.
   {6.A.1}.................ἐξαστράπτω G1823

G1824 **ἐξαυτῆς**   adv., *immediately* (= ἐξ αὐτῆς τῆς
   ὥρας).
ἐξαυτῆς   adv................... ἐξαυτῆς G1824
ἐξέβαλε   verb, ²aor. act. indic. 3 pers. sg.
   {5.A.1.b}.................ἐκβάλλω G1544
ἐξέβαλεν   verb, ²aor. act. indic. 3 pers. sg.
   {5.A.1.b}....................... id.
ἐξέβαλλον   verb, impf. act. indic. 3 pers. pl.
   {5.A.1.b}....................... id.
ἐξεβάλομεν   verb, ²aor. act. indic. 1 pers. pl.
   {5.A.1.b}....................... id.
ἐξέβαλον   verb, ²aor. act. indic. 3 pers. pl.
   {5.A.1.b}....................... id.
ἐξέβησαν   verb, ²aor. act. indic. 3 pers. pl.
   {5.A.1.b}.................ἐκβαίνω G1831†‡
ἐξεβλήθη   verb, aor. pass. indic. 3 pers. sg.
   {5.A.1.b}.................ἐκβάλλω G1544
ἐξεγαμίζοντο   verb, impf. pass. indic. 3 pers. pl.
   {5.A.1.e}.................ἐκγαμίζω G1547

G1825 **ἐξεγείρω**   *I raise up, arouse.*
ἐξεγερεῖ   verb, fut. act. indic. 3 pers. sg.
   {5.A.2}..................ἐξεγείρω G1825
ἐξέδετο   verb, ²aor. mid. indic. 3 pers. sg.
   {5.A.3.b}.................ἐκδίδωμι G1554
ἐξεδέχετο   verb, impf. mid./pass. indic. 3 pers. sg.
   {5.A.1.e}.................ἐκδέχομαι G1551
ἐξεδίκησε   verb, aor. act. indic. 3 pers. sg.
   {5.A.1}..................ἐκδικέω G1556
ἐξεδίκησεν   verb, aor. act. indic. 3 pers. sg. {5.A.1}. id.
ἐξέδοτο   verb, ²aor. mid. indic. 3 pers. sg.
   {5.A.3.b}.................ἐκδίδωμι G1554
ἐξέδυσαν   verb, aor. act. indic. 3 pers. pl.
   {5.A.1.b}.................ἐκδύω G1562
ἐξεζήτησαν   verb, aor. act. indic. 3 pers. pl.
   {5.A.1}..................ἐκζητέω G1567
ἐξεθαμβήθη   verb, aor. pass. indic. 3 pers. sg.
   {5.A.1}..................ἐκθαμβέω G1568

ἐξεθαμβήθησαν   verb, aor. pass. indic. 3 pers.
    pl. {5.A.1} . . . . id.
ἐξεθαύμαζον   verb, impf. act. indic. 3 pers. pl.
    {5.A.1.b} . . . . ἐκθαυμάζω *G2296†‡*
ἐξέθεντο   verb, ²aor. mid. indic. 3 pers. pl.
    {5.A.3.b} . . . . ἐκτίθημι *G1620*
ἔξει   verb, fut. act. indic. 3 pers. sg. {5.A.1.a} . . . ἔχω *G2192*
ἐξειλάμην   verb, ²aor. mid. indic. 1 pers. sg.
    {5.A.1.e} . . . . ἐξαιρέω *G1807*
ἐξείλατο   verb, aor. mid. indic. 3 pers. sg. {5.A.1}   id.
ἐξείλετο   verb, ²aor. mid. indic. 3 pers. sg.
    {5.A.1.e} . . . . id.
ἐξειλόμην   verb, ²aor. mid. indic. 1 pers. sg.
    {5.A.1.e} . . . . id.
G1826 **ἔξειμι** (from εἶμι)   *I go out (away), depart*
    (orig., *I shall go out*).
ἔξεις   verb, fut. act. indic. 2 pers. sg. {5.A.1.a} . . ἔχω *G2192*
ἐξεκαύθησαν   verb, aor. pass. indic. 3 pers. pl.
    {5.A.1.b} . . . . ἐκκαίω *G1572*
ἐξεκέντησαν   verb, aor. act. indic. 3 pers. pl.
    {5.A.1} . . . . ἐκκεντέω *G1574*
ἐξεκλάσθησαν   verb, aor. pass. indic. 3 pers. pl.
    {5.A.1} . . . . ἐκκλάω *G1575*
ἐξεκλείσθη   verb, aor. pass. indic. 3 pers. sg.
    {5.A.1.b} . . . . ἐκκλείω *G1576*
ἐξέκλιναν   verb, aor. act. indic. 3 pers. pl.
    {5.A.1.b} . . . . ἐκκλίνω *G1578*
ἐξεκομίζετο   verb, impf. pass. indic. 3 pers. sg.
    {5.A.1.e} . . . . ἐκκομίζω *G1580*
ἐξεκόπης   verb, ²aor. pass. indic. 2 pers. sg.
    {5.A.1.e} . . . . ἐκκόπτω *G1581*
ἐξεκρέματο   verb, impf. mid. indic. 3 pers. sg.
    {5.A.3.a} . . . . ἐκκρεμάννυμι *G1582*
ἐξεκρέμετο   verb, impf. mid. indic. 3 pers. sg.
    {5.A.3.a} . . . . id.
ἔξελε   verb, ²aor. act. impv. 2 pers. sg.
    {5.D.1} . . . . ἐξαιρέω *G1807*
ἐξελέγξαι   vbl., aor. act. inf. {6.B.1} . . . . . ἐξελέγχω *G1827*
ἐξελέγοντο   verb, impf. mid. indic. 3 pers. pl.
    {5.A.1.e} . . . . ἐκλέγομαι *G1586*
G1827 **ἐξελέγχω**   *I convict.*
ἐξελεξάμην   verb, aor. mid. indic. 1 pers. sg.
    {5.A.1.e} . . . . ἐκλέγομαι *G1586*
ἐξελέξαντο   verb, aor. mid. indic. 3 pers. pl.
    {5.A.1.e} . . . . id.
ἐξελέξασθε   verb, aor. mid. indic. 2 pers. pl.
    {5.A.1.e} . . . . id.
ἐξελέξατο   verb, aor. mid. indic. 3 pers. sg.
    {5.A.1.e} . . . . id.
ἐξελέξω   verb, aor. mid. indic. 2 pers. sg.
    {5.A.1.e} . . . . id.
ἐξελέσθαι   vbl., ²aor. mid. inf. {6.B.1} . . . ἐξαιρέω *G1807*
ἐξελεύσεται   verb, fut. mid. indic. 3 pers. sg.
    {5.A.1.d} . . . . ἐξέρχομαι *G1831*
ἐξελεύσονται   verb, fut. mid. indic. 3 pers. pl.
    {5.A.1.d} . . . . id.
ἐξελήλυθα   verb, ²perf. act. indic. 1 pers. sg.
    {5.A.1.c} . . . . id.
ἐξεληλύθασιν   verb, ²perf. act. indic. 3 pers. pl.
    {5.A.1.c} . . . . id.

ἐξεληλύθατε   verb, ²perf. act. indic. 2 pers. pl.
    {5.A.1.c} . . . . id.
ἐξελήλυθε   verb, ²perf. act. indic. 3 pers. sg.
    {5.A.1.c} . . . . id.
ἐξεληλύθει   verb, plu. act. indic. 3 pers. sg.
    {5.A.1.b} . . . . id.
ἐξελήλυθεν   verb, ²perf. act. indic. 3 pers. sg.
    {5.A.1.c} . . . . id.
ἐξεληλυθός   vbl., ²perf. act. ptc. acc. sg. neut.
    {6.A.1.a} . . . . id.
ἐξεληλυθότας   vbl., ²perf. act. ptc. acc. pl.
    masc. {6.A.1.a} . . . . id.
ἐξεληλυθυῖαν   vbl., ²perf. act. ptc. acc. sg. fem.
    {6.A.1.a} . . . . id.
ἐξέληται   verb, ²aor. mid. subjunc. 3 pers. sg.
    {5.B.1} . . . . ἐξαιρέω *G1807*
ἐξέλθατε   verb, ²aor. act. impv. 2 pers. pl.
    {5.D.1} . . . . ἐξέρχομαι *G1831*
ἔξελθε   verb, ²aor. act. impv. 2 pers. sg. {5.D.1} . . id.
ἐξελθεῖν   vbl., ²aor. act. inf. {6.B.1} . . . . id.
ἐξέλθετε   verb, ²aor. act. impv. 2 pers. pl. {5.D.1} id.
ἐξέλθη   verb, ²aor. act. subjunc. 3 pers. sg. {5.B.1}id.
ἐξέλθης   verb, ²aor. act. subjunc. 2 pers. sg.
    {5.B.1} . . . . id.
ἐξέλθητε   verb, ²aor. act. subjunc. 2 pers. pl.
    {5.B.1} . . . . id.
ἐξελθόντα   vbl., ²aor. act. ptc. acc. sg. masc.
    {6.A.1.a} . . . . id.
ἐξελθόντα   vbl., ²aor. act. ptc. nom. pl. neut.
    {6.A.1.a} . . . . id.
ἐξελθόντες   vbl., ²aor. act. ptc. nom. pl. masc.
    {6.A.1.a} . . . . id.
ἐξελθόντι   vbl., ²aor. act. ptc. dat. sg. masc.
    {6.A.1.a} . . . . id.
ἐξελθόντος   vbl., ²aor. act. ptc. gen. sg. masc.
    {6.A.1.a} . . . . id.
ἐξελθόντος   vbl., ²aor. act. ptc. gen. sg. neut.
    {6.A.1.a} . . . . id.
ἐξελθόντων   vbl., ²aor. act. ptc. gen. pl. masc.
    {6.A.1.a} . . . . id.
ἐξελθοῦσα   vbl., ²aor. act. ptc. nom. sg. fem.
    {6.A.1.a} . . . . id.
ἐξελθοῦσαι   vbl., ²aor. act. ptc. nom. pl. fem.
    {6.A.1.a} . . . . id.
ἐξελθοῦσαν   vbl., ²aor. act. ptc. acc. sg. fem.
    {6.A.1.a} . . . . id.
ἐξελθούση   vbl., ²aor. act. ptc. dat. sg. fem.
    {6.A.1.a} . . . . id.
ἐξελθών   vbl., ²aor. act. ptc. nom. sg. masc.
    {6.A.1.a} . . . . id.
ἐξελκόμενος   vbl., pres. pass. ptc. nom. sg. masc.
    {6.A.1} . . . . ἐξέλκω *G1828*
G1828 **ἐξέλκω**   *I entice* (lit. *I draw out* of the right
    place, or *I draw aside* out of the right way).
ἐξέμαξε   verb, aor. act. indic. 3 pers. sg.
    {5.A.1.b} . . . . ἐκμάσσω *G1591*
ἐξέμαξεν   verb, aor. act. indic. 3 pers. sg.
    {5.A.1.b} . . . . id.
ἐξέμασσε   verb, impf. act. indic. 3 pers. sg.
    {5.A.1.b} . . . . id.

ἐξέμασσεν   verb, impf. act. indic. 3 pers. sg.
{5.A.1.b} . . . . id.
ἐξεμυκτήριζον   verb, impf. act. indic. 3 pers. pl.
{5.A.1.b} . . . . ἐκμυκτηρίζω G1592
ἐξενέγκαντες   vbl., aor. act. ptc. nom. pl. masc.
{6.A.1.a} . . . . ἐκφέρω G1627
ἐξενέγκατε   verb, aor. act. impv. 2 pers. pl. {5.D.1} . id.
ἐξενεγκεῖν   vbl., ²aor. act. inf. {6.B.1} . . . . id.
ἐξένευσεν   verb, aor. act. indic. 3 pers. sg.
{5.A.1.b} . . . . ἐκνεύω G1593
ἐξένισε   verb, aor. act. indic. 3 pers. sg.
{5.A.1.b} . . . . ξενίζω G3579
ἐξένισεν   verb, aor. act. indic. 3 pers. sg.
{5.A.1.b} . . . . id.
ἐξενοδόχησεν   verb, aor. act. indic. 3 pers. sg.
{5.A.1} . . . . ξενοδοχέω G3580
ἐξέπεμψαν   verb, aor. act. indic. 3 pers. pl.
{5.A.1.b} . . . . ἐκπέμπω G1599
ἐξέπεσαν   verb, ²aor. act. indic. 3 pers. pl.
{5.A.1.b} . . . . ἐκπίπτω G1601
ἐξεπέσατε   verb, ²aor. act. indic. 2 pers. pl.
{5.A.1.b} . . . . id.
ἐξέπεσε   verb, ²aor. act. indic. 3 pers. sg.
{5.A.1.b} . . . . id.
ἐξέπεσεν   verb, ²aor. act. indic. 3 pers. sg.
{5.A.1.b} . . . . id.
ἐξέπεσον   verb, ²aor. act. indic. 3 pers. pl.
{5.A.1.b} . . . . id.
ἐξεπέτασα   verb, aor. act. indic. 1 pers. sg.
{5.A.3.b} . . . . ἐκπετάννυμι G1600
ἐξεπήδησαν   verb, aor. act. indic. 3 pers. pl.
{5.A.1} . . . . ἐκπηδάω G1530†‡
ἐξεπλάγησαν   verb, ²aor. pass. indic. 3 pers. pl.
{5.A.1.e} . . . . ἐκπλήσσω G1605
ἐξέπλει   verb, impf. act. indic. 3 pers. sg.
{5.A.2} . . . . ἐκπλέω G1602
ἐξεπλεύσαμεν   verb, aor. act. indic. 1 pers. pl.
{5.A.1} . . . . id.
ἐξεπλήσσετο   verb, impf. pass. indic. 3 pers. sg.
{5.A.1.e} . . . . ἐκπλήσσω G1605
ἐξεπλήσσοντο   verb, impf. pass. indic. 3 pers.
pl. {5.A.1.e} . . . . id.
ἐξέπνευσε   verb, aor. act. indic. 3 pers. sg.
{5.A.1} . . . . ἐκπνέω G1606
ἐξέπνευσεν   verb, aor. act. indic. 3 pers. sg.
{5.A.1} . . . . id.
ἐξεπορεύετο   verb, impf. mid./pass. indic. 3 pers.
sg. {5.A.1.e} . . . . ἐκπορεύομαι G1607
ἐξεπορεύοντο   verb, impf. mid./pass. indic.
3 pers. pl. {5.A.1.e} . . . . id.
ἐξεπτύσατε   verb, aor. act. indic. 2 pers. pl.
{5.A.1.b} . . . . ἐκπτύω G1609
G1829 **ἐξέραμα**, -ατος, τό   *vomit, purge.*
ἐξέραμα   noun, acc. sg. neut. {2.C} . . . . . ἐξέραμα G1829
G1830 **ἐξεραυνάω** (ἐξερευνάω)   *I search diligently, I examine carefully (minutely).*
ἐξέρχεσθαι   vbl., pres. mid./pass. inf.
{6.B.1} . . . . ἐξέρχομαι G1831
ἐξέρχεσθε   verb, pres. mid./pass. impv. 2 pers.
pl. {5.D.1} . . . . id.

ἐξέρχεται   verb, pres. mid./pass. indic. 3 pers.
sg. {5.A.1.d} . . . . id.
G1831 **ἐξέρχομαι**   *I go out.*
ἐξερχόμενοι   vbl., pres. mid./pass. ptc. nom. pl.
masc. {6.A.1} . . . . ἐξέρχομαι G1831
ἐξερχόμενος   vbl., pres. mid./pass. ptc. nom.
sg. masc. {6.A.1} . . . . id.
ἐξερχομένων   vbl., pres. mid./pass. ptc. gen. pl.
masc. {6.A.1} . . . . id.
ἐξέρχονται   verb, pres. mid./pass. indic. 3 pers.
pl. {5.A.1.d} . . . . id.
ἐξερχώμεθα   verb, pres. mid./pass. subjunc.
1 pers. pl. {5.B.1} . . . . id.
ἐξεστακέναι   vbl., perf. act. inf. {6.B.3} . . ἐξίστημι G1839
ἐξέστη   verb, ²aor. act. indic. 3 pers. sg. {5.A.3.b} id.
ἐξέστημεν   verb, ²aor. act. indic. 1 pers. pl.
{5.A.3.b} . . . . id.
ἐξέστησαν   verb, ²aor. act. indic. 3 pers. pl.
{5.A.3.b} . . . . id.
G1832 **ἔξεστι** (ν)   impers. *it is permitted (allowed),*
sometimes followed by acc. + inf.; ἐξόν
(ἐστιν) = ἔξεστιν, the ἐστιν being understood in Acts 2:29; 2 Cor 12:4.
ἔξεστι   verb, pres. act. indic. 3 pers. sg.
{5.A.1.a} . . . . ἔξεστι G1832
ἔξεστιν   verb, pres. act. indic. 3 pers. sg.
{5.A.1.a} . . . . id.
ἐξέστραπται   verb, perf. pass. indic. 3 pers. sg.
{5.A.1.f} . . . . ἐκστρέφω G1612
G1833 **ἐξετάζω**   (indicates precise and careful inquiry), *I examine, question, inquire at.*
ἐξετάσαι   vbl., aor. act. inf. {6.B.1} . . . . . ἐξετάζω G1833
ἐξετάσατε   verb, aor. act. impv. 2 pers. pl.
{5.D.1} . . . . id.
ἔξετε   verb, fut. act. indic. 2 pers. pl. {5.A.1.a} . . ἔχω G2192
ἐξετείνατε   verb, aor. act. indic. 2 pers. pl.
{5.A.1.b} . . . . ἐκτείνω G1614
ἐξέτεινε   verb, aor. act. indic. 3 pers. sg. {5.A.1.b}id.
ἐξέτεινεν   verb, aor. act. indic. 3 pers. sg.
{5.A.1.b} . . . . id.
ἐξετίθετο   verb, impf. mid. indic. 3 pers. sg.
{5.A.3.a} . . . . ἐκτίθημι G1620
ἐξετράπησαν   verb, ²aor. pass. indic. 3 pers. pl.
{5.A.1.e} . . . . ἐκτρέπω G1624
ἐξέφνης   adv. . . . . ἐξαίφνης G1810
ἐξέφυγον   verb, ²aor. act. indic. 1 pers. sg.
{5.A.1.b} . . . . ἐκφεύγω G1628
ἐξέφυγον   verb, ²aor. act. indic. 3 pers. pl.
{5.A.1.b} . . . . id.
ἐξέχεαν   verb, aor. act. indic. 3 pers. pl.
{5.A.1} . . . . ἐκχέω G1632
ἐξέχεε   verb, aor. act. indic. 3 pers. sg. {5.A.1} . . id.
ἐξέχεεν   verb, aor. act. indic. 3 pers. sg. {5.A.1} . id.
ἐξεχεῖτο   verb, impf. pass. indic. 3 pers. sg.
{5.A.2} . . . . id.
ἐξεχύθη   verb, aor. pass. indic. 3 pers. sg. {5.A.1} id.
ἐξεχύθησαν   verb, aor. pass. indic. 3 pers. pl.
{5.A.1} . . . . id.
ἐξεχύννετο   verb, impf. pass. indic. 3 pers. sg.
{5.A.2} . . . . id.

ἐξέψυξε   verb, aor. act. indic. 3 pers. sg.
{5.A.1.b} . . . . ἐκψύχω G1634
ἐξέψυξεν   verb, aor. act. indic. 3 pers. sg.
{5.A.1.b} . . . . id.
ἐξήγαγε   verb, ²aor. act. indic. 3 pers. sg.
{5.A.1.b} . . . . ἐξάγω G1806
ἐξήγαγεν   verb, ²aor. act. indic. 3 pers. sg.
{5.A.1.b} . . . . id.
ἐξήγγειλαν   verb, aor. act. indic. 3 pers. pl.
{5.A.1.b} . . . . ἐξαγγέλλω G1804
ἐξήγειρα   verb, aor. act. indic. 1 pers. sg.
{5.A.1.b} . . . . ἐξεγείρω G1825
ἐξηγεῖτο   verb, impf. mid./pass. indic. 3 pers. sg.
{5.A.2} . . . . .ἐξηγέομαι G1834
G1834 **ἐξηγέομαι**   (1) *(I interpret) I relate, expound,*
explain; (2) *make declaration (John 1:18).*
ἐξηγησάμενος   vbl., aor. mid. ptc. nom. sg. masc.
{6.A.2} . . . . .ἐξηγέομαι G1834
ἐξηγήσατο   verb, aor. mid. indic. 3 pers. sg.
{5.A.1} . . . . id.
ἐξηγόρασεν   verb, aor. act. indic. 3 pers. sg.
{5.A.1.b} . . . . ἐξαγοράζω G1805
ἐξηγουμένων   vbl., pres. mid./pass. ptc. gen. pl.
masc. {6.A.2} . . . . .ἐξηγέομαι G1834
ἐξηγοῦντο   verb, impf. mid./pass. indic. 3 pers.
pl. {5.A.2} . . . . id.
ἐξήεσαν   verb, impf. act. indic. 3 pers. pl.
{7.A} . . . . ἔξειμι G1826
G1835 **ἑξήκοντα**   *sixty.*
ἑξήκοντα   adj. num. . . . . ἑξήκοντα G1835
ἐξῆλθαν   verb, ²aor. act. indic. 3 pers. pl.
{5.A.1.b} . . . . .ἐξέρχομαι G1831
ἐξήλθατε   verb, ²aor. act. indic. 2 pers. pl.
{5.A.1.b} . . . . id.
ἐξῆλθε   verb, ²aor. act. indic. 3 pers. sg. {5.A.1.b} id.
ἐξῆλθεν   verb, ²aor. act. indic. 3 pers. sg.
{5.A.1.b} . . . . id.
ἐξῆλθες   verb, ²aor. act. indic. 2 pers. sg.
{5.A.1.b} . . . . id.
ἐξήλθετε   verb, ²aor. act. indic. 2 pers. pl.
{5.A.1.b} . . . . id.
ἐξήλθομεν   verb, ²aor. act. indic. 1 pers. pl.
{5.A.1.b} . . . . id.
ἐξῆλθον   verb, ²aor. act. indic. 1 pers. sg.
{5.A.1.b} . . . . id.
ἐξῆλθον   verb, ²aor. act. indic. 3 pers. pl.
{5.A.1.b} . . . . id.
ἐξήνεγκεν   verb, aor. act. indic. 3 pers. sg.
{5.A.1.b} . . . . ἐκφέρω G1627
ἐξηπάτησε   verb, aor. act. indic. 3 pers. sg.
{5.A.1} . . . . ἐξαπατάω G1818
ἐξηπάτησεν   verb, aor. act. indic. 3 pers. sg.
{5.A.1} . . . . id.
ἐξηραμμένην   vbl., perf. pass. ptc. acc. sg. fem.
{6.A.1.b} . . . . ξηραίνω G3583
ἐξήρανε   verb, aor. act. indic. 3 pers. sg. {5.A.1.b} id.
ἐξήρανεν   verb, aor. act. indic. 3 pers. sg.
{5.A.1.b} . . . . id.
ἐξηράνθη   verb, aor. pass. indic. 3 pers. sg.
{5.A.1.b} . . . . id.

ἐξήρανται   verb, perf. pass. indic. 3 pers. sg.
{5.A.1.f} . . . . id.
ἐξηραύνησαν   verb, aor. act. indic. 3 pers. pl.
{5.A.1} . . . . ἐξεραυνάω G1830
ἐξηρεύνησαν   verb, aor. act. indic. 3 pers. pl.
{5.A.1} . . . . id.
ἐξηρτισμένος   vbl., perf. pass. ptc. nom. sg. masc.
{6.A.1.b} . . . . ἐξαρτίζω G1822
ἐξήρχετο   verb, impf. mid./pass. indic. 3 pers. sg.
{5.A.1.e} . . . . .ἐξέρχομαι G1831
ἐξήρχοντο   verb, impf. mid./pass. indic. 3 pers.
pl. {5.A.1.e} . . . . id.
G1836 **ἑξῆς**   adv., *next in order;* ἡ ἑξῆς (understand
ἡμέρᾳ), *the next day, the following day;* τῷ
ἑξῆς (Luke 7:11, var.), perhaps = τῷ ἑξῆς
χρόνῳ, *at the period immediately following.*
ἑξῆς   adv. . . . . .ἑξῆς G1836
ἐξητήσατο   verb, aor. mid. indic. 3 pers. sg.
{5.A.1} . . . . ἐξαιτέω G1809
G1837 **ἐξηχέω**   *I sound out (forth),* referring either to
the clearness or to the loudness of the sound.
ἐξήχηται   verb, perf. pass. indic. 3 pers. sg.
{5.A.1} . . . . ἐξηχέω G1837
ἐξιέναι   vbl., pres. act. inf. {7.C.2} . . . . . ἔξειμι G1826
ἔξιν   noun, acc. sg. fem. {2.C} . . . . ἕξις G1838
ἐξιόντων   vbl., pres. act. ptc. gen. pl. masc.
{7.C.1} . . . . ἔξειμι G1826
G1838 **ἕξις**, -εως, ἡ   *condition, state,* esp. *good condi-*
tion of body or soul.
ἐξίσταντο   verb, impf. mid. indic. 3 pers. pl.
{5.A.3.a} . . . . ἐξίστημι G1839
ἐξιστάνων   vbl., pres. act. ptc. nom. sg. masc.
{6.A.3} . . . . id.
ἐξίστασθαι   vbl., pres. mid. inf. {6.B.3} . . . . id.
ἐξίστατο   verb, impf. mid. indic. 3 pers. sg.
{5.A.3.a} . . . . id.
G1839 **ἐξίστημι**   (ἐξιστάνω), ἐξιστάω   (1) trans.
(including ἐξέστακα), *I astonish, amaze;* (2)
intrans., *I am astonished, amazed;* (3) *I am out
of my mind, I am mad,* Mark 3:21; 2 Cor 5:13;
(lit. *I remove from a standing position*).
ἐξιστῶν   vbl., pres. act. ptc. nom. sg. masc.
{6.A.3} . . . . ἐξίστημι G1839
ἐξισχύσητε   verb, aor. act. subjunc. 2 pers. pl.
{5.B.1} . . . . ἐξισχύω G1840
G1840 **ἐξισχύω**   *I have strength for* (a difficult task).
ἔξοδον   noun, acc. sg. fem. {2.B} . . . . .ἔξοδος G1841
G1841 **ἔξοδος**, -ου, ἡ   (1) *going out, departure* from a
place; (2) *death,* Luke 9:31; 2 Pet 1:15.
ἐξόδου   noun, gen. sg. fem. {2.B} . . . . .ἔξοδος G1841
ἐξοίσουσι   verb, fut. act. indic. 3 pers. pl.
{5.A.1.a} . . . . ἐκφέρω G1627
ἐξοίσουσιν   verb, fut. act. indic. 3 pers. pl.
{5.A.1.a} . . . . id.
ἐξολεθρευθήσεται   verb, fut. pass. indic. 3 pers.
sg. {5.A.1.d} . . . . ἐξολεθρεύω G1842
G1842 **ἐξολεθρεύω**   *I destroy utterly, annihilate,
exterminate.*
ἐξολοθρευθήσεται   verb, fut. pass. indic. 3 pers.
sg. {5.A.1.d} . . . . ἐξολεθρεύω G1842

ἐξομολογεῖσθε   verb, pres. mid. impv. 2 pers. pl.
{5.A.2}. . . . . ἐξομολογέω *G1843*

G1843 **ἐξομολογέω**   (1) *I consent fully, agree out and out,* Luke 22:6; (2) *I confess, admit, acknowledge* (cf. the early Hellenistic sense of the mid., *I acknowledge* a debt); (3) in certain passages there is a difficulty as to the sense: in Matt 11:25 (Luke 10:21) the Vulgate (w. the Sahidic) renders by *confiteor,* but modern scholars prefer either *I give thanks* or *I praise.*

ἐξομολογήσεται   verb, fut. mid. indic. 3 pers. sg.
{5.A.1}. . . . . ἐξομολογέω *G1843*
ἐξομολογήσηται   verb, aor. mid. subjunc.
3 pers. sg. {5.B.1}. . . . . id.
ἐξομολογήσομαι   verb, fut. mid. indic. 1 pers.
sg. {5.A.1} . . . . id.
ἐξομολογοῦμαι   verb, pres. mid. indic. 1 pers.
sg. {5.A.2} . . . . id.
ἐξομολογούμενοι   vbl., pres. mid. ptc. nom. pl.
masc. {6.A.2}. . . . . id.
ἐξόν   vbl., pres. act. ptc. nom. sg. neut.
{6.A.1}. . . . . ἔξεστι *G1832*

G1844 **ἐξορκίζω**   *I exorcise, cast out by appeal to a god.*
ἐξορκίζω   verb, pres. act. indic. 1 pers. sg.
{5.A.1.a} .ἐξορκίζω *G1844*

G1845 **ἐξορκιστής,** -οῦ, ὁ   *an exorcist, a caster out of evil spirits* by the use of names or spells.
ἐξορκιστῶν   noun, gen. pl. masc. {2.A}ἐξορκιστής *G1845*
ἐξορύξαντες   vbl., aor. act. ptc. nom. pl. masc.
{6.A.1.a} .ἐξορύσσω *G1846*

G1846 **ἐξορύσσω**   (1) *I dig out;* (2) hence, *I open up;* (3) *I gouge,* Gal 4:15.

G1847 **ἐξουδενέω** (-όω)   *I despise, disdain.* see ἐξουθενέω.
ἐξουδενηθῇ   verb, aor. pass. subjunc. 3 pers. sg.
{5.B.1}. . . . . ἐξουδενέω *G1847*
ἐξουδενωθῇ   verb, aor. pass. subjunc. 3 pers.
sg. {5.B.1} . . . . id.
ἐξουθενεῖς   verb, pres. act. indic. 2 pers. sg.
{5.A.2}. . . . . ἐξουθενέω *G1848*
ἐξουθενεῖτε   verb, pres. act. impv. 2 pers. pl.
{5.D.2}. . . . . id.
ἐξουθενείτω   verb, pres. act. impv. 3 pers. sg.
{5.D.2}. . . . . id.

G1848 **ἐξουθενέω** (-όω)   (1) *I set at naught, ignore;* (2) *I despise, disdain.*
ἐξουθενηθείς   vbl., aor. pass. ptc. nom. sg. masc.
{6.A.1.a.}. . . . . ἐξουθενέω *G1848*
ἐξουθενημένα   vbl., perf. pass. ptc. acc. pl.
neut. {6.A.2} . . . . id.
ἐξουθενημένος   vbl., perf. pass. ptc. nom. sg.
masc. {6.A.2}. . . . . id.
ἐξουθενημένους   vbl., perf. pass. ptc. acc. pl.
masc. {6.A.2}. . . . . id.
ἐξουθενήσας   vbl., aor. act. ptc. nom. sg. masc.
{6.A.2}. . . . . id.
ἐξουθενήσατε   verb, aor. act. indic. 2 pers. pl.
{5.A.1} . . . . id.

ἐξουθενήσῃ   verb, aor. act. subjunc. 3 pers. sg.
{5.B.1} . . . . id.
ἐξουθενοῦντας   vbl., pres. act. ptc. acc. pl.
masc. {6.A.2}. . . . . id.
ἔξουσι   verb, fut. act. indic. 3 pers. pl. {5.A.1.a} ἔχω *G2192*

G1849 **ἐξουσία,** -ας, ἡ   (1) *power, authority, weight,* esp. *moral authority, influence;* in 1 Cor 11:10 the *authority* which the wearing of the veil gives the woman, making her sacrosanct; with gen. indicates *over* any one; (2) in a quasi-personal sense, derived from later Judaism, of a *spiritual power,* 1 Pet 3:22, and hence of *an earthly power* (e.g., Luke 12:11 and often, in combination with ἀρχή).
ἐξουσία   noun, nom. sg. fem. {2.A} . . . . . ἐξουσία *G1849*
ἐξουσίᾳ   noun, dat. sg. fem. {2.A} . . . . id.
ἐξουσιάζει   verb, pres. act. indic. 3 pers. sg.
{5.A.1.a} .ἐξουσιάζω *G1850*
ἐξουσιάζοντες   vbl., pres. act. ptc. nom. pl.
masc. {6.A.1} . . . . id.

G1850 **ἐξουσιάζω**   *I exercise (wield) power (authority),* with gen., *over;* pass. 1 Cor 6:12, *I am ruled.*
ἐξουσίαι   noun, nom. pl. fem. {2.A}. . . . . ἐξουσία *G1849*
ἐξουσίαις   noun, dat. pl. fem. {2.A} . . . . id.
ἐξουσίαν   noun, acc. sg. fem. {2.A} . . . . id.
ἐξουσίας   noun, acc. pl. fem. {2.A} . . . . id.
ἐξουσίας   noun, gen. sg. fem. {2.A} . . . . id.
ἐξουσιασθήσομαι   verb, fut. pass. indic. 1 pers.
sg. {5.A.1.d}. . . . . ἐξουσιάζω *G1850*
ἕξουσιν   verb, fut. act. indic. 3 pers. pl.
{5.A.1.a} . . . . ἔχω *G2192*
ἐξουσιῶν   noun, gen. pl. fem. {2.A} . . . . . ἐξουσία *G1849*

G1851 **ἐξοχή,** -ῆς, ἡ   *projection, prominence;* οἱ κατ᾽ ἐξοχήν, *the prominent persons, the chief men.*
ἐξοχήν   noun, acc. sg. fem. {2.A} . . . . ἐξοχή *G1851*

G1852 **ἐξυπνίζω**   *I wake* out of sleep.
ἐξυπνίσω   verb, aor. act. subjunc. 1 pers. sg.
{5.B.1} . . . . ἐξυπνίζω *G1852*

G1853 **ἔξυπνος,** -ον   *awake* out of sleep.
ἔξυπνος   adj., nom. sg. masc. {3.C} . . . . . ἔξυπνος *G1853*
ἐξυρημένη   vbl., perf. pass. ptc. dat. sg. fem.
{6.A.2}. . . . . ξυράω *G3587*

G1854 **ἔξω**   (1) prep. with gen., *outside;* (2) adv., *without, outside;* ἐν ὁ ἔξω, etc., the adv. is equivalent to an adj., τὰς ἔξω πόλεις, *foreign cities,* Acts 26:11; ὁ ἔξω ἄνθρωπος, *the outer (physical) nature,* 2 Cor 4:16; esp. οἱ ἔξω, *the outsiders, the non-Christians.*
ἔξω   adv. . . . . ἔξω *G1854*

G1855 **ἔξωθεν**   (1) prep. with gen., *outside* (Mark 7:15; Rev 11:2; 14:20, etc.); (2) adv., *from outside, from without;* τὸ ἔξωθεν, *the outside,* etc., οἱ ἔξωθεν = οἱ ἔξω; equivalent to ἔξω, both as adv. and as prep.
ἔξωθεν   adv. . . . . ἔξωθεν *G1855*

G1856 **ἐξωθέω**   *I push out, thrust out;* εἰς αἰγιαλὸν ἐξῶσαι, *to drive the ship upon the beach,* Acts 27:39.
ἐξωμολόγησε   verb, aor. act. indic. 3 pers. sg.
{5.A.1}. . . . . ἐξομολογέω *G1843*

ἐξωμολόγησεν   verb, aor. act. indic. 3 pers. sg.
   {5.A.1} . . . . id.
ἐξῶσαι   vbl., aor. act. inf. {6.B.1} . . . . ἐξωθέω *G1856*
ἐξῶσεν   verb, aor. act. indic. 3 pers. sg. {5.A.1} . . id.
ἔξωσεν   verb, aor. act. indic. 3 pers. sg. {5.A.1} . . id.
ἐξώτερον   adj. comp., acc. sg. neut. {3.C;
   3.G} . . . . ἐξώτερος *G1857*
G1857 **ἐξώτερος**, -α, -ον   outermost, farthest.
G1503‡ **ἔοικα**   perf., I resemble, I am like.
ἔοικε   verb, perf. act. indic. 3 pers. sg.
   {5.A.1.c} . . . . ἔοικα *G1503‡*
ἔοικεν   verb, perf. act. indic. 3 pers. sg. {5.A.1.c} id.
ἑόρακα   verb, perf. act. indic. 1 pers. sg.
   {5.A.1} . . . . ὁράω *G3708*
ἑόρακαν   verb, perf. act. indic. 3 pers. pl. {5.A.1} id.
ἑόρακεν   verb, perf. act. indic. 3 pers. sg. {5.A.1} id.
G1858 **ἑορτάζω**   I take part in a festival, keep a feast
   (allegorically).
ἑορτάζωμεν   verb, pres. act. subjunc. 1 pers. pl.
   {5.B.1} . . . . ἑορτάζω *G1858*
G1859 **ἑορτή**, -ῆς, ἡ   a festival, feast, periodically
   recurring; ποιεῖν ἑορτήν, Acts 18:21 =
   ἑορτάζειν.
ἑορτή   noun, nom. sg. fem. {2.A} . . . . ἑορτή *G1859*
ἑορτῇ   noun, dat. sg. fem. {2.A} . . . . id.
ἑορτήν   noun, acc. sg. fem. {2.A} . . . . id.
ἑορτῆς   noun, gen. sg. fem. {2.A} . . . . id.
ἐπ'   prep. . . . . ἐπί *G1909*
ἐπαγαγεῖν   vbl., 2aor. act. inf. {6.B.1} . . . . . . ἐπάγω *G1863*
ἐπαγγειλάμενον   vbl., aor. mid. ptc. acc. sg. masc.
   {6.A.1.b} . . . . ἐπαγγέλλομαι *G1861*
ἐπαγγειλάμενος   vbl., aor. mid. ptc. nom. sg.
   masc. {6.A.1.b} . . . . id.
G1860 **ἐπαγγελία**, -ας, ἡ   a promise; cf. τέκνον (2).
ἐπαγγελία   noun, nom. sg. fem. {2.A} . . ἐπαγγελία *G1860*
ἐπαγγελίᾳ   noun, dat. sg. fem. {2.A} . . . . id.
ἐπαγγελίαι   noun, nom. pl. fem. {2.A} . . . . id.
ἐπαγγελίαις   noun, dat. pl. fem. {2.A} . . . . id.
ἐπαγγελίαν   noun, acc. sg. fem. {2.A} . . . . id.
ἐπαγγελίας   noun, acc. pl. fem. {2.A} . . . . id.
ἐπαγγελίας   noun, gen. sg. fem. {2.A} . . . . id.
ἐπαγγελιῶν   noun, gen. pl. fem. {2.A} . . . . id.
G1861 **ἐπαγγέλλομαι**   (1) I promise; (2) I profess,
   1 Tim 2:10; 6:21.
ἐπαγγελλομέναις   vbl., pres. mid./pass. ptc. dat. pl.
   fem. {6.A.1} . . . . ἐπαγγέλλομαι *G1861*
ἐπαγγελλόμενοι   vbl., pres. mid./pass. ptc.
   nom. pl. masc. {6.A.1} . . . . id.
G1862 **ἐπάγγελμα**, -ατος, τό   a promise.
ἐπάγγελμα   noun, acc. sg. neut. {2.C} . . ἐπάγγελμα *G1862*
ἐπαγγέλματα   noun, acc. pl. neut. {2.C} . . . . . . id.
ἐπαγγέλματα   noun, nom. pl. neut. {2.C} . . . . . id.
ἐπάγοντες   vbl., pres. act. ptc. nom. pl. masc.
   {6.A.1} . . . . ἐπάγω *G1863*
G1863 **ἐπάγω**   I bring upon.
ἐπαγωνίζεσθαι   vbl., pres. mid./pass. inf.
   {6.B.1} . . . . ἐπαγωνίζομαι *G1864*
G1864 **ἐπαγωνίζομαι**   I contend for.
ἔπαθε   verb, 2aor. act. indic. 3 pers. sg.
   {5.A.1.b} . . . . πάσχω *G3958*

ἔπαθεν   verb, 2aor. act. indic. 3 pers. sg. {5.A.1.b} id.
ἐπάθετε   verb, 2aor. act. indic. 2 pers. pl.
   {5.A.1.b} . . . . id.
ἔπαθον   verb, 2aor. act. indic. 1 pers. sg. {5.A.1.b} id.
ἐπαθροιζομένων   vbl., pres. pass. ptc. gen. pl.
   masc. {6.A.1} . . . . ἐπαθροίζω *G1865*
G1865 **ἐπαθροίζω**   I gather together in addition, I
   increase.
ἐπαιδεύθη   verb, aor. pass. indic. 3 pers. sg.
   {5.A.1.b} . . . . παιδεύω *G3811*
ἐπαίδευον   verb, impf. act. indic. 3 pers. pl.
   {5.A.1.b} . . . . id.
ἐπαινέσατε   verb, aor. act. impv. 2 pers. pl.
   {5.D.1} . . . . ἐπαινέω *G1867*
ἐπαινεσάτωσαν   verb, aor. act. impv. 3 pers.
   pl. {5.D.1} . . . . id.
ἐπαινέσω   verb, aor. act. subjunc. 1 pers. sg.
   {5.B.1} . . . . id.
Ἐπαίνετον   noun prop., acc. sg. masc. {2.B;
   2.D} . . . . Ἐπαίνετος *G1866*
G1866 **Ἐπαίνετος**, -ου, ὁ   Epaenetus, a Christian in
   Rome.
G1867 **ἐπαινέω**   I praise, commend.
ἔπαινον   noun, acc. sg. masc. {2.B} . . . . . ἔπαινος *G1868*
G1868 **ἔπαινος**, -ου, ὁ   praise.
ἔπαινος   noun, nom. sg. masc. {2.B} . . . . . ἔπαινος *G1868*
ἐπαινῶ   verb, pres. act. indic. 1 pers. sg.
   {5.A.2} . . . . ἐπαινέω *G1867*
ἐπαίρεται   verb, pres. mid. indic. 3 pers. sg.
   {5.A.1.d} . . . . ἐπαίρω *G1869*
ἐπαιρόμενον   vbl., pres. mid. ptc. acc. sg. neut.
   {6.A.1} . . . . id.
ἐπαίροντας   vbl., pres. act. ptc. acc. pl. masc.
   {6.A.1} . . . . id.
G1869 **ἐπαίρω**   I raise, lift up.
ἔπαισε   verb, aor. act. indic. 3 pers. sg.
   {5.A.1.b} . . . . παίω *G3817*
ἔπαισεν   verb, aor. act. indic. 3 pers. sg. {5.A.1.b} id.
ἐπαισχύνεσθε   verb, pres. mid./pass. indic. 2 pers.
   pl. {5.A.1.d} . . . . ἐπαισχύνομαι *G1870*
ἐπαισχύνεται   verb, pres. mid./pass. indic.
   3 pers. sg. {5.A.1.d} . . . . id.
ἐπαισχύνθη   verb, aor. pass. indic. 3 pers. sg.
   {5.A.1.b} . . . . id.
ἐπαισχυνθῇ   verb, aor. pass. subjunc. 3 pers.
   sg. {5.B.1} . . . . id.
ἐπαισχυνθῇς   verb, aor. pass. subjunc. 2 pers.
   sg. {5.B.1} . . . . id.
ἐπαισχυνθήσεται   verb, fut. pass. indic.
   3 pers. sg. {5.A.1.d} . . . . id.
G1870 **ἐπαισχύνομαι**   I am ashamed of.
ἐπαισχύνομαι   verb, pres. mid./pass. indic. 1 pers.
   sg. {5.A.1.d} . . . . ἐπαισχύνομαι *G1870*
ἐπαιτεῖν   vbl., pres. act. inf. {6.B.2} . . . . . . ἐπαιτέω *G1871*
G1871 **ἐπαιτέω**   I beg, am a beggar.
ἐπαιτῶν   vbl., pres. act. ptc. nom. sg. masc.
   {6.A.2} . . . . ἐπαιτέω *G1871*
G1872 **ἐπακολουθέω**   I follow close after, I accompany,
   dog; I promote, 1 Tim 5:10; hence, I endorse
   Mark 16:20.

ἐπακολουθήσητε   verb, aor. act. subjunc. 2 pers.
 pl. {5.B.1}. . . . . .ἐπακολουθέω G1872
ἐπακολουθούντων   vbl., pres. act. ptc. gen. pl.
 neut. {6.A.2} . . . . id.
ἐπακολουθοῦσιν   verb, pres. act. indic. 3 pers.
 pl. {5.A.2} . . . . id.
G1873 **ἐπακούω**   I listen to, hear.
G1874 **ἐπακροάομαι**   I listen to, hearken to.
G1875 **ἐπάν**   whenever.
ἐπάν   conj. ἐπάν G1875
ἐπανάγαγε   verb, ²aor. act. impv. 2 pers. sg.
 {5.D.1} . . . . ἐπανάγω G1877
ἐπαναγαγεῖν   vbl., ²aor. act. inf. {6.B.1} . . . . id.
ἐπαναγαγών   vbl., ²aor. act. ptc. nom. sg. masc.
 {6.A.1.a} . . . . id.
G1876 **ἐπάναγκες**   adv. used as adj., necessary, inevitable, obligatory.
ἐπάναγκες   adv. . . . . .ἐπάναγκες G1876
G1877 **ἐπανάγω**   (1) nautical, I put out (from the
 shore; lit. I take up a ship on to the high seas);
 (2) I go up, possibly I go up again, return.
ἐπανάγω   vbl., pres. act. ptc. nom. sg. masc.
 {6.A.1} . . . . .ἐπανάγω G1877
G344†‡ **ἐπανακάμπτω**   I return. Var. for ἀνακάμπτω
 in Luke 10:6.
ἐπανακάμψει   verb, fut. act. indic. 3 pers. sg.
 {5.A.1.a} . . . . .ἐπανακάμπτω G344†‡
G1878 **ἐπαναμιμνήσκω**   I remind, possibly I remind
 again.
ἐπαναμιμνήσκων   vbl., pres. act. ptc. nom. sg.
 masc. {6.A.1} . . . . ἐπαναμιμνήσκω G1878
ἐπαναμιμνήσκων   vbl., pres. act. ptc. nom. sg.
 masc. {6.A.1} . . . . id.
ἐπαναπαήσεται   verb, ²fut. pass. indic. 3 pers.
 {5.A.1.d} . . . . ἐπαναπαύομαι G1879
ἐπαναπαύη   verb, pres. mid./pass. indic.
 2 pers. sg. {5.A.1.d} . . . . id.
G1879 **ἐπαναπαύομαι**   I rest upon.
ἐπαναπαύσεται   verb, fut. mid. indic. 3 pers. sg.
 {5.A.1.d} . . . . ἐπαναπαύομαι G1879
ἐπαναστήσονται   verb, fut. mid. indic. 3 pers. pl.
 {5.A.1.e} . . . . ἐπανίστημι G1881
ἐπανελθεῖν   vbl., ²aor. act. inf. {6.B.1}ἐπανέρχομαι G1880
ἐπανέρχεσθαι   vbl., pres. mid./pass. inf. {6.B.1} id.
G1880 **ἐπανέρχομαι**   I return.
G1881 **ἐπανίστημι**   intrans., I rise against.
ἐπανόρθωσιν   noun, acc. sg. fem.
 {2.C} . . . . ἐπανόρθωσις G1882
G1882 **ἐπανόρθωσις**, -εως, ἡ   setting straight (right)
 again.
G1883 **ἐπάνω**   (1) adv., on the top, above; (2) prep. with
 gen., on the top of, above, over, on; met. of rule,
 over, Luke 19:17, etc.; above, more than, Mark
 14:5; 1 Cor 15:6.
ἐπάνω   adv., prep. . . . . ἐπάνω G1883
ἐπάξας   vbl., aor. act. ptc. nom. sg. masc.
 {6.A.1.a} . . . . ἐπάγω G1863
ἐπάραι   vbl., aor. act. inf. {6.B.1}. . . . . . . ἐπαίρω G1869
ἐπάραντες   vbl., aor. act. ptc. nom. pl. masc.
 {6.A.1.a} . . . . id.

ἐπάρας   vbl., aor. act. ptc. nom. sg. masc. {6.A.1.a}. id.
ἐπάρασα   vbl., aor. act. ptc. nom. sg. fem. {6.A.1.a} .id.
ἐπάρατε   verb, aor. act. impv. 2 pers. pl. {5.D.1} . id.
G1944†‡ **ἐπάρατος**, -ον   accursed, cursed. Var. for ἐπικατάρατος, John 7:49.
ἐπάρατοι   adj., nom. pl. masc. {3.C}. . .ἐπάρατος G1944†‡
ἐπαρκείτω   verb, pres. act. impv. 3 pers. sg.
 {5.D.2}. .ἐπαρκέω G1884
ἐπαρκέση   verb, aor. act. subjunc. 3 pers. sg. {5.B.1}.id.
G1884 **ἐπαρκέω**   I do service, render help.
ἐπαρρησιάζετο   verb, impf. mid./pass. indic.
 3 pers. sg. {5.A.1.e} . . . . .παρρησιάζομαι G3955
ἐπαρρησιασάμεθα   verb, aor. mid. indic.
 1 pers. pl. {5.A.1.e}. . . . . id.
ἐπαρρησιάσατο   verb, aor. mid. indic. 3 pers.
 sg. {5.A.1.e} . . . . id.
G1885 **ἐπαρχεία** (ἐπαρχία), -ας, ἡ   sphere of duty,
 province.
ἐπαρχεία   noun, dat. sg. fem. {2.A} . . . . ἐπαρχεία G1885
ἐπαρχείας   noun, gen. sg. fem. {2.A} . . . . id.
G1885† **ἐπάρχειος**, -ον, belonging to the province; τῇ
 ἐπαρχείᾳ (understand ἐξουσίᾳ), the power
 over the province, the province. Var. for ἐπαρχεία, Acts 25:1.
ἐπαρχία   noun, dat. sg. fem. {2.A} . . . . . ἐπαρχεία G1885
ἐπαρχίας   noun, gen. sg. fem. {2.A}. . . . . id.
ἐπάταξεν   verb, aor. act. indic. 3 pers. sg.
 {5.A.1.b} . . . . πατάσσω G3960
ἐπατήθη   verb, aor. pass. indic. 3 pers. sg.
 {5.A.1} . . . . πατέω G3961
G1886 **ἔπαυλις**, -εως, ἡ   a farm, estate.
ἔπαυλις   noun, nom. sg. fem. {2.C} . . .ἔπαυλις G1886
ἐπαύοντο   verb, impf. mid. indic. 3 pers. pl.
 {5.A.1.e} . . . . .παύω G3973
G1887 **ἐπαύριον**   adv., tomorrow.
ἐπαύριον   adv. . . . . ἐπαύριον G1887
ἐπαυσάμην   verb, aor. mid. indic. 1 pers. sg.
 {5.A.1.e} . . . . .παύω G3973
ἐπαύσαντο   verb, aor. mid. indic. 3 pers. pl.
 {5.A.1.e} . . . . id.
ἐπαύσατο   verb, aor. mid. indic. 3 pers. sg.
 {5.A.1.e} . . . . id.
G1888 **ἐπαυτοφώρῳ**   = ἐπ' αὐτοφώρῳ, from
 αὐτόφωρος (αὐτοφόρῳ), ον, (caught) in the
 act (from αὐτός and φώρ, a thief).
ἐπαυτοφώρῳ   adv. . . . . ἐπαυτοφώρῳ G1888
Ἐπαφρᾶ   noun prop., gen. sg. masc. {2.A;
 2.D}. . . . . Ἐπαφρᾶς G1889
G1889 **Ἐπαφρᾶς**, -ᾶ, ὁ   Epaphras, Epaphroditus, a
 Colossian Christian, in captivity with Paul in
 Rome (the pet form of Ἐπαφρόδιτος).
Ἐπαφρᾶς   noun prop., nom. sg. masc. {2.A;
 2.D}. . . . . Ἐπαφρᾶς G1889
ἐπαφρίζοντα   vbl., pres. act. ptc. nom. pl. neut.
 {6.A.1} . . . . .ἐπαφρίζω G1890
G1890 **ἐπαφρίζω**   I foam out (a metaphor from the
 seaweed and refuse borne on the crest of waves).
Ἐπαφρόδιτον   noun prop., acc. sg. masc. {2.B;
 2.D}. . . . . Ἐπαφρόδιτος G1891
G1891 **Ἐπαφρόδιτος**, -ου, ὁ   see Ἐπαφρᾶς.

Ἐπαφροδίτου   noun prop., gen. sg. masc. {2.B;
2.D}. Ἐπαφρόδιτος *G1891*
ἐπαχύνθη   verb, aor. pass. indic. 3 pers. sg.
  {5.A.1.b} .παχύνω *G3975*
ἐπέβαλαν   verb, ²aor. act. indic. 3 pers. pl.
  {5.A.1.b} . . . . ἐπιβάλλω *G1911*
ἐπέβαλεν   verb, ²aor. act. indic. 3 pers. sg.
  {5.A.1.b} . . . . id.
ἐπέβαλλεν   verb, impf. act. indic. 3 pers. sg.
  {5.A.1.b} . . . . id.
ἐπέβαλον   verb, ²aor. act. indic. 3 pers. pl.
  {5.A.1.b} . . . . id.
ἐπέβημεν   verb, ²aor. act. indic. 1 pers. pl.
  {5.A.1.b} . . . . ἐπιβαίνω *G1910*
ἐπέβην   verb, ²aor. act. indic. 1 pers. sg. {5.A.1.b} id.
ἐπεβίβασαν   verb, aor. act. indic. 3 pers. pl.
  {5.A.1.b} . . . . .ἐπιβιβάζω *G1913*
ἐπέβλεψεν   verb, aor. act. indic. 3 pers. sg.
  {5.A.1.b} . . . . ἐπιβλέπω *G1914*
ἐπεγέγραπτο   verb, plu. pass. indic. 3 pers. sg.
  {5.A.1.e} . . . . ἐπιγράφω *G1924*
G1892 **ἐπεγείρω**   *I arouse, stimulate.*
ἐπεγίνωσκον   verb, impf. act. indic. 3 pers. pl.
  {5.A.1.b} . . . . ἐπιγινώσκω *G1921*
ἐπεγνωκέναι   vbl., perf. act. inf. {6.B.1} . . . . id.
ἐπεγνωκόσι   vbl., perf. act. ptc. dat. pl. masc.
  {6.A.1.a} . . . . id.
ἐπεγνωκόσιν   vbl., perf. act. ptc. dat. pl. masc.
  {6.A.1.a} . . . . id.
ἐπέγνωμεν   verb, ²aor. act. indic. 1 pers. pl.
  {5.A.1.b} . . . . id.
ἐπέγνωσαν   verb, ²aor. act. indic. 3 pers. pl.
  {5.A.1.b} . . . . id.
ἐπεγνώσθην   verb, aor. pass. indic. 1 pers. sg.
  {5.A.1.b} . . . . id.
ἐπέγνωτε   verb, ²aor. act. indic. 2 pers. pl.
  {5.A.1.b} . . . . id.
ἐπέδειξεν   verb, aor. act. indic. 3 pers. sg.
  {5.A.3.b} . . . . ἐπιδείκνυμι *G1925*
ἐπεδίδου   verb, impf. act. indic. 3 pers. sg.
  {5.A.3.a} . . . . ἐπιδίδωμι *G1929*
ἐπεδόθη   verb, aor. pass. indic. 3 pers. sg. {5.A.1} id.
ἐπέδωκαν   verb, aor. act. indic. 3 pers. pl.
  {5.A.3.b} . . . . id.
ἐπεζήτησεν   verb, aor. act. indic. 3 pers. sg.
  {5.A.1} . . . . .ἐπιζητέω *G1934*
ἐπεζήτουν   verb, impf. act. indic. 3 pers. pl.
  {5.A.2} . . . . id.
ἐπέθεντο   verb, ²aor. mid. indic. 3 pers. pl.
  {5.A.3.b} . . . . ἐπιτίθημι *G2007*
ἐπέθηκαν   verb, aor. act. indic. 3 pers. pl.
  {5.A.3.b} . . . . id.
ἐπέθηκε   verb, aor. act. indic. 3 pers. sg. {5.A.3.b} id.
ἐπέθηκεν   verb, aor. act. indic. 3 pers. sg.
  {5.A.3.b} . . . . id.
ἐπεθύμει   verb, impf. act. indic. 3 pers. sg.
  {5.A.2} . . . . ἐπιθυμέω *G1937*
ἐπεθύμησα   verb, aor. act. indic. 1 pers. sg. {5.A.1} id.
ἐπεθύμησαν   verb, aor. act. indic. 3 pers. pl.
  {5.A.1} . . . . id.

G1893 **ἐπεί**   (1) *after,* Luke 7:1 (var.); Acts 13:46 (var.);
  (2) *for, since;* (3) *otherwise,* Rom 11:6, 22;
  1 Cor 5:10, etc.
ἐπεί   conj. . . . . ἐπεί *G1893*
ἐπεῖδεν   verb, ²aor. act. indic. 3 pers. sg.
  {5.A.1.b} . . . . ἐπεῖδον *G1896*
G1894 **ἐπειδή**   (1) *when,* Luke 7:1; (2) *since.*
ἐπειδή   conj. . . . . .ἐπειδή *G1894*
G1895 **ἐπειδήπερ**   *since.*
ἐπειδήπερ   conj. . . . . .ἐπειδήπερ *G1895*
G1896 **ἐπεῖδον**   *I regard, look upon;* ²aor. of ἐφοράω.
ἔπειθε   verb, impf. act. indic. 3 pers. sg.
  {5.A.1.b} .πείθω *G3982*
ἔπειθεν   verb, impf. act. indic. 3 pers. sg.
  {5.A.1.b} . . . . id.
ἐπείθετο   verb, impf. pass. indic. 3 pers. sg.
  {5.A.1.e} . . . . id.
ἔπειθον   verb, impf. act. indic. 3 pers. pl.
  {5.A.1.b} . . . . id.
ἐπείθοντο   verb, impf. pass. indic. 3 pers. pl.
  {5.A.1.e} . . . . id.
G1966‡ **ἔπειμι**   (from εἶμι)   in the ptc. ἐπιοῦσα, *coming
on, next;* τῇ ἐπιούσῃ (understand ἡμέρᾳ),
next day.
ἐπείνασα   verb, aor. act. indic. 1 pers. sg.
  {5.A.1} . . . . πεινάω *G3983*
ἐπείνασαν   verb, aor. act. indic. 3 pers. pl.
  {5.A.1} . . . . id.
ἐπείνασε   verb, aor. act. indic. 3 pers. sg. {5.A.1} id.
ἐπείνασεν   verb, aor. act. indic. 3 pers. sg.
  {5.A.1} . . . . id.
G1897 **ἐπείπερ**   *since indeed* (var. in Rom 3:30).
ἐπείπερ   conj. . . . . ἐπείπερ *G1897*
ἐπείραζεν   verb, impf. act. indic. 3 pers. sg.
  {5.A.1.b} . . . . πειράζω *G3985*
ἐπείραζον   verb, impf. act. indic. 3 pers. pl.
  {5.A.1.b} . . . . id.
ἐπείρασαν   verb, aor. act. indic. 3 pers. pl.
  {5.A.1.b} . . . . id.
ἐπείρασας   verb, aor. act. indic. 2 pers. sg.
  {5.A.1.b} . . . . id.
ἐπείρασε   verb, aor. act. indic. 3 pers. sg.
  {5.A.1.b} . . . . id.
ἐπείρασεν   verb, aor. act. indic. 3 pers. sg.
  {5.A.1.b} . . . . id.
ἐπειράσθησαν   verb, aor. pass. indic. 3 pers.
  pl. {5.A.1.b} . . . . id.
ἐπειράσω   verb, aor. mid. indic. 2 pers. sg.
  {5.A.1.e} . . . . id.
ἐπειρᾶτο   verb, impf. mid./pass. indic. 3 pers. sg.
  {5.A.2} . . . . πειράω *G3987*
ἐπειρῶντο   verb, impf. mid./pass. indic. 3 pers.
  pl. {5.A.2} . . . . id.
G1898 **ἐπεισαγωγή**, -ῆς, ἡ   *bringing in, introduction,
importation.*
ἐπεισαγωγή   noun, nom. sg. fem. {2.A} ἐπεισαγωγή *G1898*
ἔπεισαν   verb, aor. act. indic. 3 pers. pl.
  {5.A.1.b} .πείθω *G3982*
ἐπεισελεύσεται   verb, fut. mid. indic. 3 pers. sg.
  {5.A.1.d} . . . . .ἐπεισέρχομαι *G1904†‡*

G1904†‡ **ἐπεισέρχομαι**   *I come (in) upon suddenly* or
     forcibly. Var. for ἐπέρχομαι, Luke 21:35.
ἐπείσθησαν   verb, aor. pass. indic. 3 pers. pl.
     {5.A.1.b} . . . . .πείθω G3982
G1899 **ἔπειτα**   adv., *then, thereafter, afterwards.*
ἔπειτα   adv.. . . . . ἔπειτα G1899
ἐπεῖχεν   verb, impf. act. indic. 3 pers. sg.
     {5.A.1.b} . . . . ἐπέχω G1907
ἐπεκάθισαν   verb, aor. act. indic. 3 pers. pl.
     {5.A.1.b} . . . . .ἐπικαθίζω G1940
ἐπεκάθισεν   verb, aor. act. indic. 3 pers. sg.
     {5.A.1.b} . . . . id.
ἐπεκάλεσαν   verb, aor. act. indic. 3 pers. pl.
     {5.A.1}. ἐπικαλέω G1941
ἐπεκαλύφθησαν   verb, aor. pass. indic. 3 pers. pl.
     {5.A.1.b} . . . . .ἐπικαλύπτω G1943
ἐπέκειλαν   verb, aor. act. indic. 3 pers. pl.
     {5.A.1.b} . . . . ἐπικέλλω G2027†‡
G1900 **ἐπέκεινα**   adv., prep. with gen., *beyond.*
ἐπέκεινα   adv., prep. . . . . ἐπέκεινα G1900
ἐπέκειντο   verb, impf. mid./pass. indic. 3 pers. pl.
     {5.A.3.a} . . . . ἐπίκειμαι G1945
ἐπέκειτο   verb, impf. mid./pass. indic. 3 pers.
     sg. {5.A.3.a} . . . . id.
ἐπεκέκλητο   verb, plu. mid. indic. 3 pers. sg.
     {5.A.1}. ἐπικαλέω G1941
ἐπεκλήθη   verb, aor. pass. indic. 3 pers. sg.
     {5.A.1}. . . . . id.
ἐπέκρινε   verb, aor. act. indic. 3 pers. sg.
     {5.A.1.b} . . . . .ἐπικρίνω G1948
ἐπέκρινεν   verb, aor. act. indic. 3 pers. sg.
     {5.A.1.b} . . . . id.
G1901 **ἐπεκτείνομαι**   *I strain after.*
ἐπεκτεινόμενος   vbl., pres. mid./pass. ptc. nom. sg.
     masc. {6.A.1}. . . . . ἐπεκτείνομαι G1901
ἐπελάβετο   verb, ²aor. mid. indic. 3 pers. sg.
     {5.A.1.e} . . . . ἐπιλαμβάνομαι G1949
ἐπελάθετο   verb, ²aor. mid. indic. 3 pers. sg.
     {5.A.1.e} . . . . ἐπιλανθάνομαι G1950
ἐπελάθοντο   verb, ²aor. mid. indic. 3 pers. pl.
     {5.A.1.e} . . . . id.
ἐπέλειχον   verb, impf. act. indic. 3 pers. pl.
     {5.A.1.b} . . . . ἐπιλείχω G621†‡
ἐπελεύσεται   verb, fut. mid. indic. 3 pers. sg.
     {5.A.1.d} . . . . .ἐπέρχομαι G1904
ἐπέλθῃ   verb, ²aor. act. subjunc. 3 pers. sg. {5.B.1} id.
ἐπελθόντος   vbl., ²aor. act. ptc. gen. sg. neut.
     {6.A.1.a} . . . . id.
ἐπελθών   vbl., ²aor. act. ptc. nom. sg. masc.
     {6.A.1.a} . . . . id.
ἐπέλυε   verb, impf. act. indic. 3 pers. sg.
     {5.A.1.b} . . . . ἐπιλύω G1956
ἐπέλυεν   verb, impf. act. indic. 3 pers. sg.
     {5.A.1.b} . . . . id.
ἐπέμεινα   verb, aor. act. indic. 1 pers. sg.
     {5.A.1.b} . . . . .ἐπιμένω G1961
ἐπεμείναμεν   verb, aor. act. indic. 1 pers. pl.
     {5.A.1.b} . . . . id.
ἐπεμελήθη   verb, aor. pass. indic. 3 pers. sg.
     {5.A.1}. . . . . .ἐπιμελέομαι G1959

ἐπέμενε   verb, impf. act. indic. 3 pers. sg.
     {5.A.1.b} . . . . .ἐπιμένω G1961
ἐπέμενεν   verb, impf. act. indic. 3 pers. sg.
     {5.A.1.b} . . . . id.
ἐπέμενον   verb, impf. act. indic. 3 pers. pl.
     {5.A.1.b} . . . . id.
ἐπέμφθη   verb, aor. pass. indic. 3 pers. sg.
     {5.A.1.b} . . . . πέμπω G3992
ἔπεμψα   verb, aor. act. indic. 1 pers. sg. {5.A.1.b} id.
ἐπέμψαμεν   verb, aor. act. indic. 1 pers. pl.
     {5.A.1.b} . . . . id.
ἐπέμψατε   verb, aor. act. indic. 2 pers. pl.
     {5.A.1.b} . . . . id.
ἔπεμψε   verb, aor. act. indic. 3 pers. sg. {5.A.1.b} id.
ἔπεμψεν   verb, aor. act. indic. 3 pers. sg.
     {5.A.1.b} . . . . id.
G1902 **ἐπενδύομαι**   *I put on* (as a garment).
ἐπενδύσασθαι   vbl., aor. mid. inf.
     {6.B.1} . . . . ἐπενδύομαι G1902
ἐπενδύτην   noun, acc. sg. masc. {2.A} ..ἐπενδύτης G1903
G1903 **ἐπενδύτης**, -ου, ὁ   *a coat, outer wrap.*
ἐπενεγκεῖν   vbl., ²aor. act. inf. {6.B.1} . . . . ἐπιφέρω G2018
ἐπένευσεν   verb, aor. act. indic. 3 pers. sg.
     {5.A.1.b} . . . . .ἐπινεύω G1962
ἐπενθήσατε   verb, aor. act. indic. 2 pers. pl.
     {5.A.1}. . . . . πενθέω G3996
ἐπέπεσαν   verb, aor. act. indic. 3 pers. pl.
     {5.A.1.b} . . . . .ἐπιπίπτω G1968
ἐπέπεσε   verb, ²aor. act. indic. 3 pers. sg.
     {5.A.1.b} . . . . id.
ἐπέπεσεν   verb, ²aor. act. indic. 3 pers. sg.
     {5.A.1.b} . . . . id.
ἐπέπεσον   verb, ²aor. act. indic. 3 pers. sg.
     {5.A.1.b} . . . . id.
ἐπέπνιξαν   verb, aor. act. indic. 3 pers. pl.
     {5.A.1.b} . . . . .ἐπιπνίγω G1970
ἐπεποίθει   verb, plu. act. indic. 3 pers. sg.
     {5.A.1.b} . . . . πείθω G3982
ἐπερίσσευον   verb, impf. act. indic. 3 pers. pl.
     {5.A.1.b} . . . . περισσεύω G4052
ἐπερίσσευσαν   verb, aor. act. indic. 3 pers. pl.
     {5.A.1.b} . . . . id.
ἐπερίσσευσε   verb, aor. act. indic. 3 pers. sg.
     {5.A.1.b} . . . . id.
ἐπερίσσευσεν   verb, aor. act. indic. 3 pers. sg.
     {5.A.1.b} . . . . id.
G1904 **ἐπέρχομαι**   *I come upon,* sometimes with
     hostility.
ἐπερχομέναις   vbl., pres. mid./pass. ptc. dat. pl.
     fem. {6.A.1}. . . . . .ἐπέρχομαι G1904
ἐπερχομένοις   vbl., pres. mid./pass. ptc. dat. pl.
     masc. {6.A.1} . . . . id.
ἐπερχομένων   vbl., pres. mid./pass. ptc. gen. pl.
     neut. {6.A.1} . . . . id.
ἐπερχομένων   vbl., pres. mid./pass. ptc. gen. pl.
     masc. {6.A.1} . . . . id.
ἐπερωτᾶν   vbl., pres. act. inf. {6.B.2} ...ἐπερωτάω G1905
ἐπερωτᾶν   vbl., pres. act. inf. {6.B.2} . . . . id.
ἐπερωτᾷς   verb, pres. act. indic. 2 pers. sg.
     {5.A.2}. . . . . id.

ἐπερωτάτωσαν   verb, pres. act. impv. 3 pers.
  pl. {5.D.2} . . . . id.
G1905 **ἐπερωτάω**   *I ask, question.*
ἐπερωτηθείς   vbl., aor. pass. ptc. nom. sg. masc.
  {6.A.1.a.} . . . . .ἐπερωτάω G1905
G1906 **ἐπερώτημα**, -ατος, τό   *a request.*
ἐπερώτημα   noun, nom. sg. neut. {2.C}ἐπερώτημα G1906
ἐπερωτῆσαι   vbl., aor. act. inf. {6.B.1} . .ἐπερωτάω G1905
ἐπερωτήσας   vbl., aor. act. ptc. nom. sg. masc.
  {6.A.2} . . . . id.
ἐπερωτήσατε   verb, aor. act. impv. 2 pers. pl.
  {5.D.1} . . . . id.
ἐπερώτησον   verb, aor. act. impv. 2 pers. sg.
  {5.D.1} . . . . id.
ἐπερωτήσω   verb, fut. act. indic. 1 pers. sg. {5.A.1} id.
ἐπερωτῶ   verb, pres. act. indic. 1 pers. sg. {5.A.2}id.
ἐπερωτῶντα   vbl., pres. act. ptc. acc. sg. masc.
  {6.A.2} . . . . id.
ἐπερωτῶσι   vbl., pres. act. ptc. dat. pl. masc.
  {6.A.2} . . . . id.
ἐπερωτῶσιν   verb, pres. act. indic. 3 pers. pl.
  {5.A.2} . . . . id.
ἐπερωτῶσιν   vbl., pres. act. ptc. dat. pl. masc.
  {6.A.2} . . . . id.
ἔπεσα   verb, ²aor. act. indic. 1 pers. sg.
  {5.A.1.b} . . . . πίπτω G4098
ἔπεσαν   verb, ²aor. act. indic. 3 pers. pl. {5.A.1.b} id.
ἔπεσε   verb, ²aor. act. indic. 3 pers. sg. {5.A.1.b} . id.
ἔπεσεν   verb, ²aor. act. indic. 3 pers. sg. {5.A.1.b} id.
ἐπεσκέψασθε   verb, aor. mid. indic. 2 pers. pl.
  {5.A.1.e} . . . . .ἐπισκέπτομαι G1980
ἐπεσκέψατο   verb, aor. mid. indic. 3 pers. sg.
  {5.A.1.e} . . . . id.
ἐπεσκίαζεν   verb, impf. act. indic. 3 pers. sg.
  {5.A.1.b} . . . . .ἐπισκιάζω G1982
ἐπεσκίασεν   verb, aor. act. indic. 3 pers. sg.
  {5.A.1.b} . . . . id.
ἔπεσον   verb, ²aor. act. indic. 1 pers. sg.
  {5.A.1.b} . . . . πίπτω G4098
ἔπεσον   verb, ²aor. act. indic. 3 pers. pl. {5.A.1.b} id.
ἐπέσπειρεν   verb, aor. act. indic. 3 pers. sg.
  {5.A.1.b} . . . . .ἐπισπείρω G4687†‡
ἐπέστειλα   verb, aor. act. indic. 1 pers. sg.
  {5.A.1.b} . . . . .ἐπιστέλλω G1989
ἐπεστείλαμεν   verb, aor. act. indic. 1 pers. pl.
  {5.A.1.b} . . . . id.
ἐπέστη   verb, ²aor. act. indic. 3 pers. sg.
  {5.A.3.b} . . . . .ἐφίστημι G2186
ἐπεστήριξαν   verb, aor. act. indic. 3 pers. pl.
  {5.A.1.b} . . . . .ἐπιστηρίζω G1991
ἐπέστησαν   verb, ²aor. act. indic. 3 pers. pl.
  {5.A.3.b} . . . . .ἐφίστημι G2186
ἐπεστράφητε   verb, ²aor. pass. indic. 2 pers. pl.
  {5.A.1.e} . . . . .ἐπιστρέφω G1994
ἐπέστρεψα   verb, aor. act. indic. 1 pers. sg.
  {5.A.1.b} . . . . id.
ἐπέστρεψαν   verb, aor. act. indic. 3 pers. pl.
  {5.A.1.b} . . . . id.
ἐπεστρέψατε   verb, aor. act. indic. 2 pers. pl.
  {5.A.1.b} . . . . id.

ἐπέστρεψε   verb, aor. act. indic. 3 pers. sg.
  {5.A.1.b} . . . . id.
ἐπέστρεψεν   verb, aor. act. indic. 3 pers. sg.
  {5.A.1.b} . . . . id.
ἐπέσχε   verb, ²aor. act. indic. 3 pers. sg.
  {5.A.1.b} . . . . ἐπέχω G1907
ἐπέσχεν   verb, ²aor. act. indic. 3 pers. sg.
  {5.A.1.b} . . . . id.
ἐπέταξας   verb, aor. act. indic. 2 pers. sg.
  {5.A.1.b} . . . . .ἐπιτάσσω G2004
ἐπέταξε   verb, aor. act. indic. 3 pers. sg. {5.A.1.b} id.
ἐπέταξεν   verb, aor. act. indic. 3 pers. sg.
  {5.A.1.b} . . . . id.
ἐπετίθεσαν   verb, impf. act. indic. 3 pers. pl.
  {5.A.3.a} . . . . .ἐπιτίθημι G2007
ἐπετίθουν   verb, impf. act. indic. 3 pers. pl.
  {5.A.3.a} . . . . id.
ἐπετίμα   verb, impf. act. indic. 3 pers. sg.
  {5.A.2} . . . . .ἐπιτιμάω G2008
ἐπετίμησαν   verb, aor. act. indic. 3 pers. pl.
  {5.A.1} . . . . id.
ἐπετίμησε   verb, aor. act. indic. 3 pers. sg.
  {5.A.1} . . . . id.
ἐπετίμησεν   verb, aor. act. indic. 3 pers. sg.
  {5.A.1} . . . . id.
ἐπετίμων   verb, impf. act. indic. 3 pers. pl.
  {5.A.2} . . . . id.
ἐπετράπη   verb, aor. pass. indic. 3 pers. sg.
  {5.A.1.b} . . . . .ἐπιτρέπω G2010
ἐπέτρεψε   verb, aor. act. indic. 3 pers. sg.
  {5.A.1.b} . . . . id.
ἐπέτρεψεν   verb, aor. act. indic. 3 pers. sg.
  {5.A.1.b} . . . . id.
ἐπέτυχε   verb, ²aor. act. indic. 3 pers. sg.
  {5.A.1.b} . . . . .ἐπιτυγχάνω G2013
ἐπέτυχεν   verb, ²aor. act. indic. 3 pers. sg.
  {5.A.1.b} . . . . id.
ἐπέτυχον   verb, ²aor. act. indic. 3 pers. pl.
  {5.A.1.b} . . . . id.
ἐπεφάνη   verb, ²aor. pass. indic. 3 pers. sg.
  {5.A.1.e} . . . . .ἐπιφαίνω G2014
ἐπέφερον   verb, impf. act. indic. 3 pers. pl.
  {5.A.1.b} . . . . .ἐπιφέρω G2018
ἐπεφώνει   verb, impf. act. indic. 3 pers. sg.
  {5.A.2} . . . . .ἐπιφωνέω G2019
ἐπεφώνουν   verb, impf. act. indic. 3 pers. pl.
  {5.A.2} . . . . id.
ἐπέφωσκε   verb, impf. act. indic. 3 pers. sg.
  {5.A.1.b} . . . . .ἐπιφώσκω G2020
ἐπέφωσκεν   verb, impf. act. indic. 3 pers. sg.
  {5.A.1.b} . . . . id.
ἔπεχε   verb, pres. act. impv. 2 pers. sg. {5.D.1}ἐπέχω G1907
ἐπεχείρησαν   verb, aor. act. indic. 3 pers. pl.
  {5.A.1} . . . . .ἐπιχειρέω G2021
ἐπεχείρουν   verb, impf. act. indic. 3 pers. pl.
  {5.A.2} . . . . id.
ἐπέχοντες   vbl., pres. act. ptc. nom. pl. masc.
  {6.A.1} . . . . ἐπέχω G1907
ἐπέχρισε   verb, aor. act. indic. 3 pers. sg.
  {5.A.1.b} . . . . .ἐπιχρίω G2025

ἐπέχρισεν   verb, aor. act. indic. 3 pers. sg.
{5.A.1.b} . . . . id.

G1907 **ἐπέχω**   (1) trans., *I hold forth;* (2) intrans. (νοῦν being understood), *I mark, pay attention (heed), note,* Acts 3:5; 1 Tim 4:16; (3) *I delay,* Acts 19:22.

ἐπέχων   vbl., pres. act. ptc. nom. sg. masc.
{6.A.1} . . . . ἐπέχω G1907

ἐπηγγείλαντο   verb, aor. mid. indic. 3 pers. pl.
{5.A.1.e} . . . . ἐπαγγέλλομαι G1861

ἐπηγγείλατο   verb, aor. mid. indic. 3 pers. sg.
{5.A.1.e} . . . . id.

ἐπήγγελται   verb, perf. mid./pass. indic. 3 pers. sg. {5.A.1.f} . . . . id.

ἐπήγγελται   verb, perf. pass. indic. 3 pers. sg.
{5.A.1.f} . . . . id.

ἐπήγειραν   verb, aor. act. indic. 3 pers. pl.
{5.A.1.b} . . . . ἐπεγείρω G1892

ἐπηκολούθησε   verb, aor. act. indic. 3 pers. sg.
{5.A.1} . . . . ἐπακολουθέω G1872

ἐπηκολούθησεν   verb, aor. act. indic. 3 pers. sg. {5.A.1} . . . . id.

ἐπήκουσα   verb, aor. act. indic. 1 pers. sg.
{5.A.1.b} . . . . ἐπακούω G1873

ἐπηκροῶντο   verb, impf. mid./pass. indic. 3 pers. pl. {5.A.2} . . . . ἐπακροάομαι G1874

ἐπῆλθαν   verb, ²aor. act. indic. 3 pers. pl.
{5.A.1.b} . . . . ἐπέρχομαι G1904

ἐπῆλθον   verb, ²aor. act. indic. 3 pers. pl.
{5.A.1.b} . . . . id.

ἐπήνεσεν   verb, aor. act. indic. 3 pers. sg.
{5.A.1} . . . . ἐπαινέω G1867

ἔπηξεν   verb, aor. act. indic. 3 pers. sg.
{5.A.3.b} . . . . πήγνυμι G4078

ἐπῆραν   verb, aor. act. indic. 3 pers. pl.
{5.A.1.b} . . . . ἐπαίρω G1869

ἐπῆρε   verb, aor. act. indic. 3 pers. sg. {5.A.1.b} . id.

ἐπηρεάζοντες   vbl., pres. act. ptc. nom. pl. masc.
{6.A.1} . . . . ἐπηρεάζω G1908

ἐπηρεαζόντων   vbl., pres. act. ptc. gen. pl. masc. {6.A.1} . . . . id.

G1908 **ἐπηρεάζω**   *I insult, treat wrongfully, molest.*

ἐπῆρεν   verb, aor. act. indic. 3 pers. sg.
{5.A.1.b} . . . . ἐπαίρω G1869

ἐπήρθη   verb, aor. pass. indic. 3 pers. sg.
{5.A.1.b} . . . . id.

ἐπήρκεσεν   verb, aor. act. indic. 3 pers. sg.
{5.A.1} . . . . ἐπαρκέω G1884

ἐπηρώτα   verb, impf. act. indic. 3 pers. sg.
{5.A.2} . . . . ἐπερωτάω G1905

ἐπηρώτησαν   verb, aor. act. indic. 3 pers. pl.
{5.A.1} . . . . id.

ἐπηρώτησε   verb, aor. act. indic. 3 pers. sg.
{5.A.1} . . . . id.

ἐπηρώτησεν   verb, aor. act. indic. 3 pers. sg.
{5.A.1} . . . . id.

ἐπηρώτων   verb, impf. act. indic. 3 pers. pl.
{5.A.2} . . . . id.

ἐπῃσχύνθη   verb, aor. pass. indic. 3 pers. sg.
{5.A.1.b} . . . . ἐπαισχύνομαι G1870

G1909 **ἐπί**   prep., (1) with gen. locally, *on, upon;* and so met. of that *on* which anything rests, e.g., ἐπ᾽ ἀληθείας, *in truth;* of authority *over,* e.g., Matt 24:45; *concerning,* Gal 3:16; *in presence of,* e.g., Matt 28:14; *at, in,* Mark 12:26; *in (at) the time (period) of,* e.g., Mark 2:26; (2) with dat. *on, upon; near,* e.g., Matt 24:33; *on the basis (ground) of,* e.g., Matt 4:4; *on account of,* e.g., Luke 5:5, ἐφ᾽ ᾧ = (ἐπὶ τούτῳ, ὅ, τι), *in view of the fact that; over* (cf. under #1), Luke 12:44; *against,* Luke 12:52; *in addition to,* e.g., 2 Cor 7:13; *in, at,* ἐπὶ τούτῳ, *meantime,* John 4:27; *for, with a view to,* cf. Acts 5:35; (3) with acc. locally, *on, upon,* generally after verbs indicating motion, but afterwards more widely used, both lit. and met., ἐπὶ τὸ αὐτό, *in the same place, together, in all,* cf. Acts 1:15; 2:47; *near, to, towards* (after word expressing motion, and then more widely), both lit. and met.; *against; in addition to* (cf. under #2), Phil 2:27; of number or degree attained, *as far as,* e.g., ἐπὶ πλεῖον, ἐφ᾽ ὅσον; of charge, rule, or power *over; concerning,* e.g., Luke 23:28; *on account of, with a view to,* Mark 15:24; John 19:24; of time, *for, during,* e.g., Luke 4:25; of time, *about,* e.g., Luke 10:35.

ἐπί   prep. . . . . ἐπί G1909

ἐπίασαν   verb, aor. act. indic. 3 pers. pl.
{5.A.1.b} . . . . πιάζω G4084

ἐπιάσατε   verb, aor. act. indic. 2 pers. pl.
{5.A.1.b} . . . . id.

ἐπίασεν   verb, aor. act. indic. 3 pers. sg. {5.A.1.b} id.

ἐπιάσθη   verb, aor. pass. indic. 3 pers. sg.
{5.A.1.b} . . . . id.

ἐπιβαίνειν   vbl., pres. act. inf. {6.B.1} . . . ἐπιβαίνω G1910

G1910 **ἐπιβαίνω**   (1) *I set foot on, I step on;* (2) *I mount* (a horse), *board* (a vessel).

ἐπιβαλεῖν   vbl., ²aor. act. inf. {6.B.1} . . . . ἐπιβάλλω G1911

ἐπιβάλλει   verb, pres. act. indic. 3 pers. sg.
{5.A.1.a} . . . . id.

ἐπιβάλλον   vbl., pres. act. ptc. acc. sg. neut.
{6.A.1} . . . . id.

ἐπιβάλλουσιν   verb, pres. act. indic. 3 pers. pl.
{5.A.1.a} . . . . id.

G1911 **ἐπιβάλλω**   (1) *I throw upon, cast over,* 1 Cor 7:35; Rev 18:19 (var.); (2) *I place upon;* (3) *I lay,* with τήν χεῖρα (τὰς χεῖρας), either with innocent, or with hostile, intent; (4) intrans., *I strike upon,* Mark 4:37; (5) intrans., τὸ ἐπιβάλλον μέρος, *the share that falls to (belongs to) one,* Luke 15:12; (6) intrans., ἐπιβαλὼν ἔκλαιεν, *he set to and wept,* Mark 14:72.

ἐπιβαλοῦσιν   verb, fut. act. indic. 3 pers. pl.
{5.A.2} . . . . ἐπιβάλλω G1911

ἐπιβάλω   verb, ²aor. act. subjunc. 1 pers. sg.
{5.B.1} . . . . id.

ἐπιβαλών   vbl., ²aor. act. ptc. nom. sg. masc.
{6.A.1.a} . . . . id.

ἐπιβάντες   vbl., ²aor. act. ptc. nom. pl. masc.
{6.A.1.a} . . . . ἐπιβαίνω G1910

G1912 **ἐπιβαρέω**   *I put a burden on, burden.*
ἐπιβαρῆσαι   vbl., aor. act. inf. {6.B.1} . . ἐπιβαρέω G1912
ἐπιβαρῶ   verb, pres. act. subjunc. 1 pers. sg.
   {5.B.2} . . . . id.
ἐπιβάς   vbl., ²aor. act. ptc. nom. sg. masc.
   {6.A.1.a} . . . . ἐπιβαίνω G1910
ἐπιβεβηκώς   vbl., perf. act. ptc. nom. sg. masc.
   {6.A.1.a} . . . . id.
G1913 **ἐπιβιβάζω**   *I place upon* (a horse, mule).
ἐπιβιβάσαντες   vbl., aor. act. ptc. nom. pl. masc.
   {6.A.1.a} .ἐπιβιβάζω G1913
ἐπιβιβάσας   vbl., aor. act. ptc. nom. sg. masc.
   {6.A.1.a} . . . . id.
G1914 **ἐπιβλέπω**   *I look with favor on.*
ἐπιβλέψαι   vbl., aor. act. inf. {6.B.1} . . . . ἐπιβλέπω G1914
ἐπιβλέψαι   verb, aor. mid. impv. 2 pers. sg. (5.D.1) . . id
ἐπιβλέψητε   verb, aor. act. subjunc. 2 pers. pl.
   {5.B.1} . . . . id.
ἐπίβλεψον   verb, aor. act. impv. 2 pers. sg. {5.D.1} . id.
G1915 **ἐπίβλημα**, -ατος, τό   *something put on, a
   patch.*
ἐπίβλημα   noun, acc. sg. neut. {2.C} . . . ἐπίβλημα G1915
ἐπίβλημα   noun, nom. sg. neut. {2.C} . . . . id.
G1916 **ἐπιβοάω**   *I cry out.*
ἐπιβουλαῖς   noun, dat. pl. fem. {2.A} . . . ἐπιβουλή G1917
G1917 **ἐπιβουλή**, -ῆς, ἡ   *a plot.*
ἐπιβουλή   noun, nom. sg. fem. {2.A} . . . ἐπιβουλή G1917
ἐπιβουλῆς   noun, gen. sg. fem. {2.A} . . . . id.
ἐπιβοῶντες   vbl., pres. act. ptc. nom. pl. masc.
   {6.A.2} . . . . ἐπιβοάω G1916
ἐπιγαμβρεύσει   verb, fut. act. indic. 3 pers. sg.
   {5.A.1.a} . . . . ἐπιγαμβρεύω G1918
G1918 **ἐπιγαμβρεύω**   *I take to wife after.*
ἐπιγεγραμμένα   vbl., perf. pass. ptc. acc. pl. neut.
   {6.A.1.b} . . . . ἐπιγράφω G1924
ἐπιγεγραμμένη   vbl., perf. pass. ptc. nom. sg.
   fem. {6.A.1.b} . . . . id.
ἐπίγεια   adj., acc. pl. neut. {3.C} . . . . . . .ἐπίγειος G1919
ἐπίγεια   adj., nom. pl. neut. {3.C} . . . . id.
G1919 **ἐπίγειος**, -ον   (1) *on the earth, belonging to the
   earth* (as opposed to the sky); (2) in a spiritual
   sense, *belonging to the earthly sphere, earthly*
   (as opposed to heavenly); opp. to ἐπουράνιος
   in both senses.
ἐπίγειος   adj., nom. sg. fem. {3.C} . . . . . . ἐπίγειος G1919
ἐπιγείων   adj., gen. pl. masc. {3.C} . . . . id.
ἐπιγείων   adj., gen. pl. neut. {3.C} . . . . id.
ἐπιγενομένου   vbl., ²aor. mid. ptc. gen. sg. masc.
   {6.A.1.b} . . . . ἐπιγίνομαι G1920
G1920 **ἐπιγίνομαι**   *I come on, supervene.*
ἐπιγινώσκει   verb, pres. act. indic. 3 pers. sg.
   {5.A.1.a} . . . . ἐπιγινώσκω G1921
ἐπιγινώσκεις   verb, pres. act. indic. 2 pers. sg.
   {5.A.1.a} . . . . id.
ἐπιγινώσκετε   verb, pres. act. impv. 2 pers. pl.
   {5.D.1} . . . . id.
ἐπιγινώσκετε   verb, pres. act. indic. 2 pers. pl.
   {5.A.1.a} . . . . id.
ἐπιγινωσκέτω   verb, pres. act. impv. 3 pers. sg.
   {5.D.1} . . . . id.

ἐπιγινωσκόμενοι   vbl., pres. pass. ptc. nom. pl.
   masc. {6.A.1} . . . . id.
G1921 **ἐπιγινώσκω**   *I come to know* by directing my
   attention to (ἐπί) him or it, *I perceive, discern,
   recognize;* aor. *I found out.*
ἐπιγνόντες   vbl., ²aor. act. ptc. nom. pl. masc.
   {6.A.1.a} . . . . ἐπιγινώσκω G1921
ἐπιγνόντων   vbl., ²aor. act. ptc. gen. pl. masc.
   {6.A.1.a} . . . . id.
ἐπιγνούς   vbl., ²aor. act. ptc. nom. sg. masc.
   {6.A.1.a} . . . . id.
ἐπιγνοῦσα   vbl., ²aor. act. ptc. nom. sg. fem.
   {6.A.1.a} . . . . id.
ἐπιγνοῦσιν   vbl., ²aor. act. ptc. dat. pl. masc.
   {6.A.1.a} . . . . id.
ἐπιγνῷ   verb, ²aor. act. subjunc. 3 pers. sg. {5.B.1} id.
ἐπιγνῶναι   vbl., ²aor. act. inf. {6.B.1} . . . . id.
ἐπιγνῷς   verb, ²aor. act. subjunc. 2 pers. sg.
   {5.B.1} . . . . id.
ἐπιγνώσει   noun, dat. sg. fem. {2.C} . . . . ἐπίγνωσις G1922
ἐπιγνώσεσθε   verb, fut. mid. indic. 2 pers. pl.
   {5.A.1.d} . . . . ἐπιγινώσκω G1921
ἐπιγνώσεως   noun, gen. sg. fem. {2.C} . . ἐπίγνωσις G1922
ἐπίγνωσιν   noun, acc. sg. fem. {2.C} . . . . id.
G1922 **ἐπίγνωσις**, -εως, ἡ   *knowledge* of a particular
   point (directed towards a particular object);
   perception, discernment, recognition; intuition.
ἐπίγνωσις   noun, nom. sg. fem. {2.C} . . ἐπίγνωσις G1922
ἐπιγνώσομαι   verb, fut. mid. indic. 1 pers. sg.
   {5.A.1.d} . . . . ἐπιγινώσκω G1921
G1923 **ἐπιγραφή**, -ῆς, ἡ   *an inscription.*
ἐπιγραφή   noun, nom. sg. fem. {2.A} . . . ἐπιγραφή G1923
ἐπιγραφήν   noun, acc. sg. fem. {2.A} . . . . id.
G1924 **ἐπιγράφω**   *I write upon, inscribe.*
ἐπιγράψω   verb, fut. act. indic. 1 pers. sg.
   {5.A.1.a} . . . . ἐπιγράφω G1924
ἔπιδε   verb, ²aor. act. impv. 2 pers. sg.
   {5.D.1}. . . . . ἐπεῖδον G1896
ἐπιδεικνύμεναι   vbl., pres. mid. ptc. nom. pl. fem.
   {6.A.3} .ἐπιδείκνυμι G1925
G1925 **ἐπιδείκνυμι**   *I show, display, point out, indicate;
   I prove, demonstrate,* Acts 18:28; Heb 6:17.
ἐπιδεικνύς   vbl., pres. act. ptc. nom. sg. masc.
   {6.A.3} .ἐπιδείκνυμι G1925
ἐπιδεῖξαι   vbl., aor. act. inf. {6.B.3} . . . . id.
ἐπιδείξατε   verb, aor. act. impv. 2 pers. pl.
   {5.D.3} . . . . id.
ἐπιδέχεται   verb, pres. mid./pass. indic. 3 pers. sg.
   {5.A.1.d} . . . . ἐπιδέχομαι G1926
G1926 **ἐπιδέχομαι**   *I welcome.*
G1927 **ἐπιδημέω**   *I am resident* (temporarily, in a
   foreign city).
ἐπιδημοῦντες   vbl., pres. act. ptc. nom. pl. masc.
   {6.A.2} . . . . ἐπιδημέω G1927
ἐπιδιατάσσεται   verb, pres. mid./pass. indic.
   3 pers. sg. {5.A.1.d} . . . . ἐπιδιατάσσομαι G1928
G1928 **ἐπιδιατάσσομαι**   *I make an additional testa-
   mentary disposition, I furnish with additions.*
G1929 **ἐπιδίδωμι**   (1) trans., *I hand in;* (2) intrans., *I
   give way* (to the wind), Acts 27:15.

G1930 **ἐπιδιορθόω** *I put besides into a state of order, I put in order.*
ἐπιδιορθώσῃ verb, aor. mid. subjunc. 2 pers. sg.
{5.B.1}. . . . . .ἐπιδιορθόω G1930
ἐπιδόντες vbl., ²aor. act. ptc. nom. pl. masc.
{6.A.3}. . . . . ἐπιδίδωμι G1929
ἐπιδυέτω verb, pres. act. impv. 3 pers. sg.
{5.D.1}. . . . . ἐπιδύω G1931
G1931 **ἐπιδύω** *I sink, set.*
ἐπιδώσει verb, fut. act. indic. 3 pers. sg.
{5.A.1}. . . . . .ἐπιδίδωμι G1929
ἐπιδώσω verb, fut. act. indic. 1 pers. sg. {5.A.1}. id.
ἔπιε verb, ²aor. act. indic. 3 pers. sg. {5.A.1.b}. πίνω G4095
G1932 **ἐπιείκεια**, -ας, ἡ *considerateness, forbearance, fairness.*
ἐπιεικείᾳ noun, dat. sg. fem. {2.A}. . . . .ἐπιείκεια G1932
ἐπιεικείας noun, gen. sg. fem. {2.A} . . . . id.
ἐπιεικεῖς adj., acc. pl. masc. {3.E}. . . . . . ἐπιεικής G1933
ἐπιεικές adj., nom. sg. neut. {3.E} . . . . id.
ἐπιεικέσιν adj., dat. pl. masc. {3.E} . . . . id.
ἐπιεικῆ adj., acc. sg. masc. {3.E}. . . . . id.
G1933 **ἐπιεικής**, -ές *forbearing, fair, reasonable.*
ἐπιεικής adj., nom. sg. fem. {3.E}. . . . . . ἐπιεικής G1933
ἐπιεικίᾳ noun, dat. sg. fem. {2.A} . . . . .ἐπιείκεια G1932
ἐπιεικίας noun, gen. sg. fem. {2.A} . . . . id.
ἔπιεν verb, ²aor. act. indic. 3 pers. sg. {5.A.1.b} πίνω G4095
ἐπιζητεῖ verb, pres. act. indic. 3 pers. sg.
{5.A.2}. . . . . .ἐπιζητέω G1934
ἐπιζητεῖτε verb, pres. act. indic. 2 pers. pl.
{5.A.2}. . . . . id.
G1934 **ἐπιζητέω** *I seek after, search for, make inquiries about.*
ἐπιζητήσας vbl., aor. act. ptc. nom. sg. masc.
{6.A.2}. . . . . .ἐπιζητέω G1934
ἐπιζητοῦμεν verb, pres. act. indic. 1 pers. pl.
{5.A.2}. . . . . id.
ἐπιζητοῦσι verb, pres. act. indic. 3 pers. pl.
{5.A.2}. . . . . id.
ἐπιζητοῦσιν verb, pres. act. indic. 3 pers. pl.
{5.A.2}. . . . . id.
ἐπιζητῶ verb, pres. act. indic. 1 pers. sg. {5.A.2} id.
G1935 **ἐπιθανάτιος**, -ον *at the point of death, doomed to death.*
ἐπιθανατίους adj., acc. pl. masc.
{3.C} . . . . .ἐπιθανάτιος G1935
ἐπιθεῖναι vbl., ²aor. act. inf. {6.B.3} . . . . ἐπιτίθημι G2007
ἐπιθείς vbl., ²aor. act. ptc. nom. sg. masc. {6.A.3} id.
ἐπιθέντα vbl., ²aor. act. ptc. acc. sg. masc.
{6.A.3}. . . . . id.
ἐπιθέντες vbl., ²aor. act. ptc. nom. pl. masc.
{6.A.3}. . . . . id.
ἐπιθέντος vbl., ²aor. act. ptc. gen. sg. masc.
{6.A.3}. . . . . id.
ἐπίθες verb, ²aor. act. impv. 2 pers. sg. {5.D.3} . . id.
ἐπιθέσεως noun, gen. sg. fem. {2.C} . . . . ἐπίθεσις G1936
G1936 **ἐπίθεσις**, -εως, ἡ *laying on.*
ἐπιθῇ verb, ²aor. act. subjunc. 3 pers. sg.
{5.B.3}. . . . . .ἐπιτίθημι G2007
ἐπιθῇς verb, ²aor. act. subjunc. 2 pers. sg. {5.B.3} id.
ἐπιθήσαι verb, aor. act. opt. 3 pers. sg. {5.C.3}. . id.

ἐπιθήσει verb, fut. act. indic. 3 pers. sg. {5.A.1}. id.
ἐπιθήσεται verb, fut. mid. indic. 3 pers. sg.
{5.A.1}. id.
ἐπιθήσουσι verb, fut. act. indic. 3 pers. pl.
{5.A.1}. id.
ἐπιθήσουσιν verb, fut. act. indic. 3 pers. pl.
{5.A.1}. id.
ἐπιθυμεῖ verb, pres. act. indic. 3 pers. sg.
{5.A.2}. . . . . ἐπιθυμέω G1937
ἐπιθυμεῖτε verb, pres. act. indic. 2 pers. pl.
{5.A.2}. id.
G1937 **ἐπιθυμέω** *I desire, long; ἐπιθυμίᾳ ἐπιθυμεῖν,* Hebraistic, *to long eagerly,* Luke 22:15.
ἐπιθυμῆσαι vbl., aor. act. inf. {6.B.1}. . . ἐπιθυμέω G1937
ἐπιθυμήσεις verb, fut. act. indic. 2 pers. sg.
{5.A.1}. id.
ἐπιθυμήσετε verb, fut. act. indic. 2 pers. pl.
{5.A.1}. id.
ἐπιθυμήσουσιν verb, fut. act. indic. 3 pers. pl.
{5.A.1}. id.
ἐπιθυμητάς noun, acc. pl. masc. {2.A}ἐπιθυμητής G1938
G1938 **ἐπιθυμητής**, -οῦ, ὁ *a longer after, luster after.*
G1939 **ἐπιθυμία**, -ας, ἡ *eager (passionate) desire, passion; see ἐπιθυμέω.*
ἐπιθυμία noun, nom. sg. fem. {2.A} . . . .ἐπιθυμία G1939
ἐπιθυμίᾳ noun, dat. sg. fem. {2.A}. . . . . id.
ἐπιθυμίαι noun, nom. pl. fem. {2.A} . . . . id.
ἐπιθυμίαις noun, dat. pl. fem. {2.A} . . . . id.
ἐπιθυμίαν noun, acc. sg. fem. {2.A}. . . . . id.
ἐπιθυμίας noun, acc. pl. fem. {2.A} . . . . id.
ἐπιθυμίας noun, gen. sg. fem. {2.A} . . . . id.
ἐπιθυμιῶν noun, gen. pl. fem. {2.A} . . . . id.
ἐπιθυμοῦμεν verb, pres. act. indic. 1 pers. pl.
{5.A.2}. . . . . ἐπιθυμέω G1937
ἐπιθυμοῦσιν verb, pres. act. indic. 3 pers. pl.
{5.A.2}. id.
ἐπιθυμῶν vbl., pres. act. ptc. nom. sg. masc.
{6.A.2}. id.
ἐπιθῶ verb, ²aor. act. subjunc. 1 pers. sg.
{5.B.3} . . . . ἐπιτίθημι G2007
G1940 **ἐπικαθίζω** *I sit.*
ἐπικαλεῖσθαι vbl., pres. pass. inf. {6.B.2}ἐπικαλέω G1941
ἐπικαλεῖσθε verb, pres. mid. indic. 2 pers. pl.
{5.A.2}. id.
ἐπικαλεῖται verb, pres. pass. indic. 3 pers. sg.
{5.A.2}. id.
ἐπικαλεσάμενος vbl., aor. mid. ptc. nom. sg.
masc. {6.A.2}. . . . . id.
ἐπικαλεσαμένου vbl., aor. mid. ptc. gen. sg.
masc. {6.A.2}. . . . . id.
ἐπικαλέσασθαι vbl., aor. mid. inf. {6.B.1}. . . . . id.
ἐπικαλέσηται verb, aor. mid. subjunc. 3 pers.
sg. {5.B.1}. . . . . id.
ἐπικαλέσονται verb, fut. mid. indic. 3 pers. pl.
{5.A.1}. id.
ἐπικαλέσωνται verb, aor. mid. subjunc.
3 pers. pl. {5.B.1}. . . . . id.
G1941 **ἐπικαλέω** (1) *I call (name) by a supplementary (additional, alternative) name;* (2) mid. *I call upon, appeal to, address.*

ἐπικαλοῦμαι verb, pres. mid. indic. 1 pers. sg.
{5.A.2} . . . . ἐπικαλέω G1941
ἐπικαλουμένοις vbl., pres. mid. ptc. dat. pl.
masc. {6.A.2} . . . . id.
ἐπικαλούμενον vbl., pres. mid. ptc. acc. sg.
masc. {6.A.2} . . . . id.
ἐπικαλούμενον vbl., pres. pass. ptc. acc. sg.
masc. {6.A.2} . . . . id.
ἐπικαλούμενος vbl., pres. pass. ptc. nom. sg.
masc. {6.A.2} . . . . id.
ἐπικαλουμένου vbl., pres. pass. ptc. gen. sg.
masc. {6.A.2} . . . . id.
ἐπικαλουμένους vbl., pres. mid. ptc. acc. pl.
masc. {6.A.2} . . . . id.
ἐπικαλουμένων vbl., pres. mid. ptc. gen. pl.
masc. {6.A.2} . . . . id.
G1942 **ἐπικάλυμμα**, -ατος, τό a covering, pretext.
ἐπικάλυμμα noun, acc. sg. neut.
{2.C} . . . . ἐπικάλυμμα G1942
G1943 **ἐπικαλύπτω** I put a cover on, cover up.
ἐπικατάρατοι adj., nom. pl. masc.
{3.C} . . . . ἐπικατάρατος G1944
G1944 **ἐπικατάρατος**, -ον on whom a curse has been
invoked, accursed.
ἐπικατάρατος adj., nom. sg. masc.
{3.C} . . . . ἐπικατάρατος G1944
G1945 **ἐπίκειμαι** (1) with dat. or with ἐπί + dat. I
am placed upon, am laid upon, lie upon, am
imposed; I press upon, Luke 5:1; (2) absol. I
press hard, Acts 27:20; I am insistent, insist,
Luke 23:23.
ἐπικείμενα vbl., pres. mid./pass. ptc. nom. pl.
neut. {6.A.3} . . . . ἐπίκειμαι G1945
ἐπικείμενον vbl., pres. mid./pass. ptc. acc. sg.
neut. {6.A.3} . . . . id.
ἐπικειμένου vbl., pres. mid./pass. ptc. gen. sg.
masc. {6.A.3} . . . . id.
ἐπικεῖσθαι vbl., pres. mid./pass. inf. {6.B.3} . . . id.
ἐπίκειται verb, pres. mid./pass. indic. 3 pers.
sg. {5.A.3.a} . . . . id.
ἐπικέκλησαι verb, perf. mid. indic. 2 pers. sg.
{5.A.1} . . . . ἐπικαλέω G1941
ἐπικέκληται verb, perf. pass. indic. 3 pers. sg.
{5.A.1} . . . . id.
G2027†‡ **ἐπικέλλω** I beach, run aground, drive a ship on
to. Var. for ἐποκέλλω, Acts 27:41.
ἐπικληθείς vbl., aor. pass. ptc. nom. sg. masc.
{6.A.1.a.} . . . . ἐπικαλέω G1941
ἐπικληθέν vbl., aor. pass. ptc. acc. sg. neut.
{6.A.1.a.} . . . . id.
ἐπικληθέντα vbl., aor. pass. ptc. acc. sg. masc.
{6.A.1.a.} . . . . id.
G1946 **Ἐπικούρειος**, -ου, ὁ an Epicurean, one who
holds the tenets of Epicurus (341–270 B.C.).
Ἐπικουρείων noun prop., gen. pl. masc. {2.B;
2.D} . . . . Ἐπικούρειος G1946
G1947 **ἐπικουρία**, -ας, ἡ succor (against foes), help.
ἐπικουρίας noun, gen. sg. fem. {2.A} . . ἐπικουρία G1947
Ἐπικουρίων noun prop., gen. pl. masc. {2.B;
2.D} . . . . Ἐπικούρειος G1946

ἐπικράνθη verb, aor. pass. indic. 3 pers. sg.
{5.A.1.b} . . . . πικραίνω G4087
ἐπικράνθησαν verb, aor. pass. indic. 3 pers.
pl. {5.A.1.b} . . . . id.
G1948 **ἐπικρίνω** I give decision, decide.
ἐπιλαβέσθαι vbl., ²aor. mid. inf.
{6.B.1} . . . . ἐπιλαμβάνομαι G1949
ἐπιλαβόμενοι vbl., ²aor. mid. ptc. nom. pl.
masc. {6.A.1.b} . . . . id.
ἐπιλαβόμενος vbl., ²aor. mid. ptc. nom. sg.
masc. {6.A.1.b} . . . . id.
ἐπιλαβομένου vbl., ²aor. mid. ptc. gen. sg.
masc. {6.A.1.b} . . . . id.
ἐπιλαβοῦ verb, ²aor. mid. impv. 2 pers. sg.
{5.D.1} . . . . id.
ἐπιλάβωνται verb, ²aor. mid. subjunc. 3 pers.
pl. {5.B.1} . . . . id.
ἐπιλαθέσθαι vbl., ²aor. mid. inf.
{6.B.1} . . . . ἐπιλανθάνομαι G1950
ἐπιλαμβάνεται verb, pres. mid./pass. indic.
3 pers. sg. {5.A.1.d} . . . . ἐπιλαμβάνομαι G1949
G1949 **ἐπιλαμβάνομαι** I lay hold of, take hold of,
seize (some times with beneficent, sometimes
with hostile, intent).
ἐπιλανθάνεσθε verb, pres. mid./pass. impv.
2 pers. pl. {5.D.1} . . . . ἐπιλανθάνομαι G1950
G1950 **ἐπιλανθάνομαι** I forget.
ἐπιλανθανόμενος vbl., pres. mid./pass. ptc. nom.
sg. masc. {6.A.1} . . . . ἐπιλανθάνομαι G1950
ἐπιλεγομένη vbl., pres. pass. ptc. nom. sg. fem.
{6.A.1} . . . . ἐπιλέγω G1951
G1951 **ἐπιλέγω** (1) mid. I choose for myself, Acts
15:40; (2) pass. I am named.
G1952 **ἐπιλείπω** I fail, leave behind.
G621‡ **ἐπιλείχω**, I lick. Var. for ἀπολείχω, Luke 16:21.
ἐπιλείψει verb, fut. act. indic. 3 pers. sg.
{5.A.1.a} . . . . ἐπιλείπω G1952
ἐπιλελησμένον vbl., perf. pass. ptc. nom. sg. neut.
{6.A.1.b} . . . . ἐπιλανθάνομαι G1950
ἐπιλεξάμενος vbl., aor. mid. ptc. nom. sg. masc.
{6.A.1.b} . . . . ἐπιλέγω G1951
G1953 **ἐπιλησμονή**, -ῆς, ἡ forgetting, in Jas 1:25 a
Hebraistic gen. = that forgets.
ἐπιλησμονῆς noun, gen. sg. fem.
{2.A} . . . . ἐπιλησμονή G1953
ἐπίλοιπον adj., acc. sg. masc. {3.C} . . . . ἐπίλοιπος G1954
G1954 **ἐπίλοιπος**, -ον remaining, i.e., left over.
ἐπιλυθήσεται verb, fut. pass. indic. 3 pers. sg.
{5.A.1.d} . . . . ἐπιλύω G1956
ἐπιλύσεως noun, gen. sg. fem. {2.C} . . . ἐπίλυσις G1955
G1955 **ἐπίλυσις**, -εως, ἡ solution, explanation,
interpretation.
G1956 **ἐπιλύω** I explain.
G1957 **ἐπιμαρτυρέω** I call to witness.
ἐπιμαρτυρῶν vbl., pres. act. ptc. nom. sg. masc.
{6.A.2} . . . . ἐπιμαρτυρέω G1957
ἐπιμεῖναι vbl., aor. act. inf. {6.B.1} . . . . . ἐπιμένω G1961
ἐπιμείνης verb, aor. act. subjunc. 3 pers. sg.
{5.B.1} . . . . id.

ἐπιμείνωσι   verb, aor. act. subjunc. 3 pers. pl.
{5.B.1} . . . . id.
ἐπιμείνωσιν   verb, aor. act. subjunc. 3 pers. pl.
{5.B.1} . . . . id.
G1958 **ἐπιμέλεια**, -ας, ἡ   care, attention.
ἐπιμελείας   noun, gen. sg. fem. {2.A} . . . ἐπιμέλεια G1958
G1959 **ἐπιμελέομαι**   I care for, attend to.
ἐπιμελήθητι   verb, aor. pass. impv. 2 pers. sg.
{5.D.1} . . . . ἐπιμελέομαι G1959
ἐπιμελήσεται   verb, fut. mid. indic. 3 pers. sg.
{5.A.1} . . . . id.
G1960 **ἐπιμελῶς**   adv., carefully, attentively.
ἐπιμελῶς   adv. {3.F} . . . . ἐπιμελῶς G1960
ἐπίμενε   verb, pres. act. impv. 2 pers. sg.
{5.D.1} . . . . ἐπιμένω G1961
ἐπιμένειν   vbl., pres. act. inf. {6.B.1} . . . . id.
ἐπιμένετε   verb, pres. act. indic. 2 pers. pl.
{5.A.1.a} . . . . id.
ἐπιμένῃς   verb, pres. act. subjunc. 2 pers. sg.
{5.B.1} . . . . id.
ἐπιμένομεν   verb, pres. act. indic. 1 pers. pl.
{5.A.1.a} . . . . id.
ἐπιμενόντων   vbl., pres. act. ptc. gen. pl. masc.
{6.A.1} . . . . id.
ἐπιμενοῦμεν   verb, fut. act. indic. 1 pers. pl.
{5.A.2} . . . . id.
G1961 **ἐπιμένω**   (1) I remain, tarry; (2) with dat. I
remain in, persist in.
ἐπιμένω   verb, fut. act. indic. 1 pers. sg.
{5.A.1.a} . . . . ἐπιμένω G1961
ἐπιμενῶ   verb, fut. act. indic. 1 pers. sg. {5.A.2} . id.
ἐπιμένωμεν   verb, pres. act. subjunc. 1 pers. pl.
{5.B.1} . . . . id.
ἐπιμένωσι   verb, pres. act. subjunc. 3 pers. pl.
{5.B.1} . . . . id.
ἐπιμένωσιν   verb, pres. act. subjunc. 3 pers. pl.
{5.B.1} . . . . id.
G1962 **ἐπινεύω**   I consent.
G1963 **ἐπίνοια**, -ας, ἡ   thought.
ἐπίνοια   noun, nom. sg. fem. {2.A} . . . . . . ἐπίνοια G1963
ἔπινον   verb, impf. act. indic. 3 pers. pl.
{5.A.1.b} . . . . πίνω G4095
ἐπίομεν   verb, ²aor. act. indic. 1 pers. pl. {5.A.1.b} id.
ἔπιον   verb, ²aor. act. indic. 3 pers. pl. {5.A.1.b} . id.
G1964 **ἐπιορκέω** (ἐφιορκέω)   I take an oath, swear.
ἐπιορκήσεις   verb, fut. act. indic. 2 pers. sg.
{5.A.1} . . . . ἐπιορκέω G1964
ἐπιόρκοις   adj., dat. pl. masc. {3.C} . . . . . ἐπίορκος G1965
G1965 **ἐπίορκος**, -ου, ὁ   perjuring, a perjurer.
ἐπιούσῃ   vbl., pres. act. ptc. dat. sg. fem.
{7.C.1} . . . . ἔπειμι G1966‡
ἐπιούσιον   adj., acc. sg. masc. {3.C} . . . ἐπιούσιος G1967
G1967 **ἐπιούσιος**, -ον   belonging to the morrow, from
ἡ ἐπιοῦσα (ἡμέρα).
ἐπιπεπτωκός   vbl., perf. act. ptc. nom. sg. neut.
{6.A.1.a} . . . . ἐπιπίπτω G1968
ἐπιπεσόντες   vbl., ²aor. act. ptc. nom. pl. masc.
{6.A.1.a} . . . . id.
ἐπιπεσών   vbl., ²aor. act. ptc. nom. sg. masc.
{6.A.1.a} . . . . id.

ἐπιπίπτειν   vbl., pres. act. inf. {6.B.1} . . . . id.
G1968 **ἐπιπίπτω**   I fall upon; I press upon, Mark 3:10.
ἐπιπλήξῃς   verb, aor. act. subjunc. 2 pers. sg.
{5.B.1} . . . . ἐπιπλήσσω G1969
G1969 **ἐπιπλήσσω**   I reprove.
G1970 **ἐπιπνίγω**   I choke, i.e., (fig.) overgrow. Var. for
ἀποπνίγω, Luke 8:7.
ἐπιποθεῖ   verb, pres. act. indic. 3 pers. sg.
{5.A.2} . . . . ἐπιποθέω G1971
ἐπιπόθειαν   noun, acc. sg. fem. {2.A} . . . ἐπιποθία G1974
G1971 **ἐπιποθέω**   I long for, strain after, desire greatly.
ἐπιποθήσατε   verb, aor. act. impv. 2 pers. pl.
{5.D.1} . . . . ἐπιποθέω G1971
ἐπιπόθησιν   noun, acc. sg. fem. {2.C} . . ἐπιπόθησις G1972
G1972 **ἐπιπόθησις**, -εως, ἡ   eager longing (desire).
ἐπιπόθητοι   adj., voc. pl. masc. {3.C} . . ἐπιπόθητος G1973
G1973 **ἐπιπόθητος**, -ον   longed for, missed.
G1974 **ἐπιποθία**, -ας, ἡ   longing, eager desire.
ἐπιποθίαν   noun, acc. sg. fem. {2.A} . . . . ἐπιποθία G1974
ἐπιποθοῦντες   vbl., pres. act. ptc. nom. pl. masc.
{6.A.2} . . . . ἐπιποθέω G1971
ἐπιποθούντων   vbl., pres. act. ptc. gen. pl.
masc. {6.A.2} . . . . id.
ἐπιποθῶ   verb, pres. act. indic. 1 pers. sg. {5.A.2} id.
ἐπιποθῶν   vbl., pres. act. ptc. nom. sg. masc.
{6.A.2} . . . . id.
G1975 **ἐπιπορεύομαι**   I journey (to).
ἐπιπορευομένων   vbl., pres. mid./pass. ptc. gen. pl.
masc. {6.A.1} . . . . ἐπιπορεύομαι G1975
ἐπίπρασκον   verb, impf. act. indic. 3 pers. pl.
{5.A.1.b} . . . . πιπράσκω G4097
ἔπιπτεν   verb, impf. act. indic. 3 pers. sg.
{5.A.1.b} . . . . πίπτω G4098
ἐπιράπτει   verb, pres. act. indic. 3 pers. sg.
{5.A.1.a} . . . . ἐπιράπτω G1976
G1976 **ἐπιράπτω** (ἐπιρράπτω)   I sew (on).
G1977 **ἐπιρίπτω** (ἐπιρρίπτω)   I throw, I cast upon.
ἐπιρίψαντες   vbl., aor. act. ptc. nom. pl. masc.
{6.A.1.a} . . . . ἐπιρίπτω G1977
ἐπιρράπτει   verb, pres. act. indic. 3 pers. sg.
{5.A.1.a} . . . . ἐπιράπτω G1976
ἐπιρρίψαντες   vbl., aor. act. ptc. nom. pl. masc.
{6.A.1.a} . . . . ἐπιρίπτω G1977
ἐπίσημοι   adj., nom. pl. masc. {3.C} . . . . ἐπίσημος G1978
ἐπίσημον   adj., acc. sg. masc. {3.C} . . . . id.
G1978 **ἐπίσημος**, -ον   notable, conspicuous.
ἐπισιτισμόν   noun, acc. sg. masc.
{2.B} . . . . ἐπισιτισμός G1979
G1979 **ἐπισιτισμός**, -οῦ, ὁ   provision, nourishment,
food.
ἐπισκέπτεσθαι   vbl., pres. mid./pass. inf.
{6.B.1} . . . . ἐπισκέπτομαι G1980
ἐπισκέπτῃ   verb, pres. mid./pass. indic. 2 pers.
sg. {5.A.1.d} . . . . id.
G1980 **ἐπισκέπτομαι**   (1) I look out, Acts 6:3; (2) I
visit.
G643‡ **ἐπισκευάζω**   I equip (horses); I make preparations. Var. for ἀποσκευάζω, Acts 21:15.
ἐπισκευασάμενοι   vbl., aor. mid. ptc. nom. pl.
masc. {6.A.1.b} . . . . ἐπισκευάζω G643‡

ἐπισκέψασθαι   vbl., aor. mid. inf.
   {6.B.1} .ἐπισκέπτομαι G1980

ἐπισκέψασθε   verb, aor. mid. impv. 2 pers. pl.
   {5.D.1} . . . . id.

ἐπισκέψεται   verb, fut. mid. indic. 3 pers. sg.
   {5.A.1.d} . . . . id.

ἐπισκεψώμεθα   verb, aor. mid. subjunc. 1 pers.
   pl. {5.B.1} . . . . id.

G1981 **ἐπισκηνόω**   *I raise a tent (over).*

ἐπισκηνώση   verb, aor. act. subjunc. 3 pers. sg.
   {5.B.1} . . . . ἐπισκηνόω G1981

ἐπισκιάζουσα   vbl., pres. act. ptc. nom. sg. fem.
   {6.A.1} . . . . .ἐπισκιάζω G1982

G1982 **ἐπισκιάζω**   *I overshadow, envelop.*

ἐπισκιάσει   verb, fut. act. indic. 3 pers. sg.
   {5.A.1.a} . . . . .ἐπισκιάζω G1982

ἐπισκιάση   verb, aor. act. subjunc. 3 pers. sg.
   {5.B.1} . . . . id.

G1983 **ἐπισκοπέω**   *I exercise oversight (care).*

G1984 **ἐπισκοπή**, -ῆς, ἡ   (1) *visitation* (of judgment), Luke 19:44; 1 Pet 2:12; (2) *oversight,*
   supervision.

ἐπισκοπήν   noun, acc. sg. fem. {2.A} . . . ἐπισκοπή G1984

ἐπισκοπῆς   noun, gen. sg. fem. {2.A} . . . . id.

ἐπισκόποις   noun, dat. pl. masc. {2.B} . ἐπίσκοπος G1985

ἐπίσκοπον   noun, acc. sg. masc. {2.B} . . . . id.

G1985 **ἐπίσκοπος**, -ου, ὁ   *overseer, supervisor, ruler*
   (used as an official title in civil life), esp. used
   with reference to the supervising function
   exercised by an elder or presbyter of a church
   or congregation, and therefore (at first) practically synonymous with πρεσβύτερος.

ἐπισκοποῦντες   vbl., pres. act. ptc. nom. pl. masc.
   {6.A.2} . . . . ἐπισκοπέω G1983

ἐπισκόπους   noun, acc. pl. masc. {2.B}. ἐπίσκοπος G1985

G1986 **ἐπισπάομαι**   mid. *I undo the effects of circumci-
   sion on myself* (lit. *I draw over*).

ἐπισπάσθω   verb, pres. mid./pass. impv. 3 pers. sg.
   {5.D.2} . . . . ἐπισπάομαι G1986

G4687†‡ **ἐπισπείρω**   *I sow above (over), I replant.* Var.
   for σπείρω, Matt 13:25.

G1987 **ἐπίσταμαι**   *I know, understand.*

ἐπίσταμαι   verb, pres. mid./pass. indic. 1 pers. sg.
   {5.A.3.a} . . . . .ἐπίσταμαι G1987

ἐπιστάμενος   vbl., pres. mid./pass. ptc. nom.
   sg. masc. {6.A.3} . . . . id.

ἐπίστανται   verb, pres. mid./pass. indic. 3 pers.
   pl. {5.A.3.a} . . . . id.

ἐπιστάντες   vbl., ²aor. act. ptc. nom. pl. masc.
   {6.A.3} . . . . .ἐφίστημι G2186

ἐπιστάς   vbl., ²aor. act. ptc. nom. sg. masc.
   {6.A.3} . . . . id.

ἐπιστᾶσα   vbl., ²aor. act. ptc. nom. sg. fem.
   {6.A.3} . . . . id.

ἐπίστασθε   verb, pres. mid./pass. indic. 2 pers. pl.
   {5.A.3.a} . . . . .ἐπίσταμαι G1987

ἐπίστασιν   noun, acc. sg. fem. {2.C}. .ἐπίστασις G1999†‡

G1999†‡ **ἐπίστασις**, -εως, ἡ   *plotting (conspiring)*
   against. Var. for ἐπισύστασις, Acts 24:12;
   2 Cor 11:28.

ἐπίστασις   noun, nom. sg. fem. {2.C}. .ἐπίστασις G1999†‡

ἐπιστάτα   noun, voc. sg. masc. {2.A} . . .ἐπιστάτης G1988

ἐπίσταται   verb, pres. mid./pass. indic. 3 pers. sg.
   {5.A.3.a} . . . . .ἐπίσταμαι G1987

G1988 **ἐπιστάτης**, -ου, ὁ   *master, teacher.*

ἐπιστεῖλαι   vbl., aor. act. inf. {6.B.1} . . . ἐπιστέλλω G1989

G1989 **ἐπιστέλλω**   *I enjoin,* generally *in writing, I*
   write.

ἐπίστευεν   verb, impf. act. indic. 3 pers. sg.
   {5.A.1.b} . . . . πιστεύω G4100

ἐπιστεύετε   verb, impf. act. indic. 2 pers. pl.
   {5.A.1.b} . . . . id.

ἐπιστεύθη   verb, aor. pass. indic. 3 pers. sg.
   {5.A.1.b} . . . . id.

ἐπιστεύθην   verb, aor. pass. indic. 1 pers. sg.
   {5.A.1.b} . . . . id.

ἐπιστεύθησαν   verb, aor. pass. indic. 3 pers. pl.
   {5.A.1.b} . . . . id.

ἐπίστευον   verb, impf. act. indic. 3 pers. pl.
   {5.A.1.b} . . . . id.

ἐπίστευσα   verb, aor. act. indic. 1 pers. sg.
   {5.A.1.b} . . . . id.

ἐπιστεύσαμεν   verb, aor. act. indic. 1 pers. pl.
   {5.A.1.b} . . . . id.

ἐπίστευσαν   verb, aor. act. indic. 3 pers. pl.
   {5.A.1.b} . . . . id.

ἐπίστευσας   verb, aor. act. indic. 2 pers. sg.
   {5.A.1.b} . . . . id.

ἐπιστεύσατε   verb, aor. act. indic. 2 pers. pl.
   {5.A.1.b} . . . . id.

ἐπίστευσε   verb, aor. act. indic. 3 pers. sg.
   {5.A.1.b} . . . . id.

ἐπίστευσεν   verb, aor. act. indic. 3 pers. sg.
   {5.A.1.b} . . . . id.

ἐπιστῇ   verb, ²aor. act. subjunc. 3 pers. sg.
   {5.B.3} . . . . .ἐφίστημι G2186

ἐπίστηθι   verb, ²aor. act. impv. 2 pers. sg. {5.D.3} id.

G1990 **ἐπιστήμων**, -ον gen. ονος   *knowing* by experience (personal acquaintance).

ἐπιστήμων   adj., nom. sg. masc. {3.E} . ἐπιστήμων G1990

ἐπιστηρίζοντες   vbl., pres. act. ptc. nom. pl. masc.
   {6.A.1} . . . . ἐπιστηρίζω G1991

G1991 **ἐπιστηρίζω**   *I prop. up, uphold, support, confirm.*

ἐπιστηρίζων   vbl., pres. act. ptc. nom. sg. masc.
   {6.A.1} . . . . .ἐπιστηρίζω G1991

ἐπιστολαί   noun, nom. pl. fem. {2.A}. . . .ἐπιστολή G1992

ἐπιστολαῖς   noun, dat. pl. fem. {2.A} . . . . id.

ἐπιστολάς   noun, acc. pl. fem. {2.A}. . . . . id.

G1992 **ἐπιστολή**, -ῆς, ἡ   *a letter, dispatch.*

ἐπιστολή   noun, nom. sg. fem. {2.A} . . . ἐπιστολή G1992

ἐπιστολῇ   noun, dat. sg. fem. {2.A} . . . . id.

ἐπιστολήν   noun, acc. sg. fem. {2.A} . . . . id.

ἐπιστολῆς   noun, gen. sg. fem. {2.A} . . . . id.

ἐπιστολῶν   noun, gen. pl. fem. {2.A} . . . . id.

ἐπιστομίζειν   vbl., pres. act. inf. {6.B.1}ἐπιστομίζω G1993

G1993 **ἐπιστομίζω**   *I muzzle, silence.*

ἐπιστραφείς   vbl., ²aor. pass. ptc. nom. sg. masc.
   {6.A.1.a} . . . . ἐπιστρέφω G1994

ἐπιστραφήτω   verb, ²aor. pass. impv. 3 pers. sg.
   {5.D.1} . . . . id.

ἐπιστραφῶσι   verb, ²aor. pass. subjunc. 3 pers.
pl. {5.B.1} . . . . id.

ἐπιστραφῶσιν   verb, ²aor. pass. subjunc.
3 pers. pl. {5.B.1} . . . . id.

ἐπιστρέφειν   vbl., pres. act. inf. {6.B.1}. . . . . . . id.

ἐπιστρέφετε   verb, pres. act. indic. 2 pers. pl.
{5.A.1.a} . . . . id.

ἐπιστρέφουσιν   vbl., pres. act. ptc. dat. pl.
masc. {6.A.1} . . . . id.

G1994 **ἐπιστρέφω**   (1) trans., *I turn (back) to (to-wards); (2) intrans., I turn (back to, towards); I come to myself,* Luke 22:32.

ἐπιστρέψαι   vbl., aor. act. inf. {6.B.1} . . ἐπιστρέφω G1994

ἐπιστρέψαντες   vbl., aor. act. ptc. nom. pl.
masc. {6.A.1.a}. . . . . id.

ἐπιστρέψας   vbl., aor. act. ptc. nom. sg. masc.
{6.A.1.a} . . . . id.

ἐπιστρέψατε   verb, aor. act. impv. 2 pers. pl.
{5.D.1} . . . . id.

ἐπιστρεψάτω   verb, aor. act. impv. 3 pers. sg.
{5.D.1}. . . . . id.

ἐπιστρέψει   verb, fut. act. indic. 3 pers. sg.
{5.A.1.a} . . . . id.

ἐπιστρέψῃ   verb, aor. act. subjunc. 3 pers. sg.
{5.B.1} . . . . id.

ἐπιστρέψω   verb, fut. act. indic. 1 pers. sg.
{5.A.1.a} . . . . id.

ἐπιστρέψωσι   verb, aor. act. subjunc. 3 pers. pl.
{5.B.1} . . . . id.

ἐπιστρέψωσιν   verb, aor. act. subjunc. 3 pers.
pl. {5.B.1} . . . . id.

G1995 **ἐπιστροφή**, -ῆς, ἡ   *a turning (to God).*

ἐπιστροφήν   noun, acc. sg. fem. {2.A} . ἐπιστροφή G1995

ἐπιστώθης   verb, aor. pass. indic. 2 pers. sg.
{5.A.1}. . . . . πιστόω G4104

ἐπισυναγαγεῖν   vbl., ²aor. act. inf.
{6.B.1} . . . . ἐπισυνάγω G1996

ἐπισυνάγει   verb, pres. act. indic. 3 pers. sg.
{5.A.1.a} . . . . id.

G1996 **ἐπισυνάγω**   *I collect, gather together.*

G1997 **ἐπισυναγωγή**, -ῆς, ἡ   *gathering (collecting) together, assembling.*

ἐπισυναγωγήν   noun, acc. sg. fem.
{2.A} . . . . ἐπισυναγωγή G1997

ἐπισυναγωγῆς   noun, gen. sg. fem. {2.A} . . . . . . id.

ἐπισυνάξαι   vbl., aor. act. inf. {6.B.1} . . ἐπισυνάγω G1996

ἐπισυνάξει   verb, fut. act. indic. 3 pers. sg.
{5.A.1.a} . . . . id.

ἐπισυνάξουσι   verb, fut. act. indic. 3 pers. pl.
{5.A.1.a} . . . . id.

ἐπισυνάξουσιν   verb, fut. act. indic. 3 pers. pl.
{5.A.1.a} . . . . id.

ἐπισυναχθεισῶν   vbl., aor. pass. ptc. gen. pl.
fem. {6.A.1.a}. . . . . id.

ἐπισυναχθήσονται   verb, fut. pass. indic.
3 pers. pl. {5.A.1.d} . . . . id.

ἐπισυνηγμένη   vbl., perf. pass. ptc. nom. sg.
fem. {6.A.1.b} . . . . id.

ἐπισυντρέχει   verb, pres. act. indic. 3 pers. sg.
{5.A.1.a} . . . . ἐπισυντρέχω G1998

G1998 **ἐπισυντρέχω**   *I run together to (towards).*

ἐπισύστασιν   noun, acc. sg. fem. {2.C} .ἐπισύστασις G1999

G1999 **ἐπισύστασις**   *a disturbance, an insurrection.*

ἐπισύστασις   noun, nom. sg. fem.
{2.C} . . . . .ἐπισύστασις G1999

G2000 **ἐπισφαλής**, -ές   *dangerous.*

ἐπισφαλοῦς   adj., gen. sg. masc. {3.E} . ἐπισφαλής G2000

ἐπίσχυον   verb, impf. act. indic. 3 pers. pl.
{5.A.1.b} . . . . ἐπισχύω G2001

G2001 **ἐπισχύω**   *I persist, insist.*

ἐπισωρεύσουσι   verb, fut. act. indic. 3 pers. pl.
{5.A.1.a} . . . . ἐπισωρεύω G2002

ἐπισωρεύσουσιν   verb, fut. act. indic. 3 pers.
pl. {5.A.1.a} . . . . id.

G2002 **ἐπισωρεύω**   *I heap up.*

G2003 **ἐπιταγή**, -ῆς, ἡ   *instruction, command, order, authority* (often of a god).

ἐπιταγήν   noun, acc. sg. fem. {2.A}. . . . . .ἐπιταγή G2003

ἐπιταγῆς   noun, gen. sg. fem. {2.A} . . . . id.

ἐπιτάξῃ   verb, aor. act. subjunc. 3 pers. sg.
{5.B.1} . . . . ἐπιτάσσω G2004

ἐπιτάσσει   verb, pres. act. indic. 3 pers. sg.
{5.A.1.a} . . . . id.

ἐπιτάσσειν   vbl., pres. act. inf. {6.B.1} . . . . id.

G2004 **ἐπιτάσσω**   *I give order, command.*

ἐπιτάσσω   verb, pres. act. indic. 1 pers. sg.
{5.A.1.a} . . . . ἐπιτάσσω G2004

ἐπιτεθῇ   verb, aor. pass. subjunc. 3 pers. sg.
{5.B.3} . . . . ἐπιτίθημι G2007

ἐπιτελεῖν   vbl., pres. act. inf. {6.B.2} . . .ἐπιτελέω G2005

ἐπιτελεῖσθαι   vbl., pres. pass. inf. {6.B.2} . . . . . id.

ἐπιτελεῖσθε   verb, pres. mid./pass. indic.
2 pers. pl. {5.A.2} . . . . id.

ἐπιτελέσαι   vbl., aor. act. inf. {6.B.1} . . . . id.

ἐπιτελέσας   vbl., aor. act. ptc. nom. sg. masc.
{6.A.2}. . . . . id.

ἐπιτελέσατε   verb, aor. act. impv. 2 pers. pl.
{5.D.1} . . . . id.

ἐπιτελέσει   verb, fut. act. indic. 3 pers. sg.
{5.A.1} . . . . id.

ἐπιτελέσῃ   verb, aor. act. subjunc. 3 pers. sg.
{5.B.1} . . . . id.

G2005 **ἐπιτελέω**   *I complete, accomplish, perfect.*

ἐπιτελοῦντες   vbl., pres. act. ptc. nom. pl. masc.
{6.A.2}. . . . . ἐπιτελέω G2005

ἐπιτελῶ   verb, pres. act. indic. 1 pers. sg. {5.A.2} id.

ἐπιτέτραπται   verb, perf. pass. indic. 3 pers.
{5.A.1.f}. . . . . .ἐπιτρέπω G2010

ἐπιτήδεια   adj., acc. pl. neut. {3.C} . . . . ἐπιτήδειος G2006

G2006 **ἐπιτήδειος**, -α, -ον   *necessary.*

ἐπιτιθέασιν   verb, pres. act. indic. 3 pers. pl.
{5.A.3.a} . . . . ἐπιτίθημι G2007

ἐπιτίθει   verb, pres. act. impv. 2 pers. sg. {5.D.3}. id.

ἐπιτιθείς   vbl., pres. act. ptc. nom. sg. masc.
{6.A.3}. . . . . id.

ἐπιτίθεσθαι   vbl., pres. mid./pass. inf. {6.B.3}. . . id.

ἐπιτιθῇ   verb, pres. act. subjunc. 3 pers. sg.
{5.B.3} . . . . id.

G2007 **ἐπιτίθημι**   *I place upon, lay on; with* ὄνομα, *I add, give in addition.*

ἐπιτίθησιν   verb, pres. act. indic. 3 pers. sg.
   {5.A.3.a} . . . . ἐπιτίθημι G2007
ἐπιτιμᾶν   vbl., pres. act. inf. {6.B.2} . . . . ἐπιτιμάω G2008
ἐπιτιμᾶν   vbl., pres. act. inf. {6.B.2} . . . . id.
G2008 **ἐπιτιμάω**   (1) *I rebuke, chide, censure;* (2) with
   ἵνα, *I warn.*
ἐπιτιμῆσαι   verb, aor. act. opt. 3 pers. sg.
   {5.C.1} . . . . ἐπιτιμάω G2008
ἐπιτιμήσας   vbl., aor. act. ptc. nom. sg. masc.
   {6.A.2} . . . . id.
ἐπιτίμησον   verb, aor. act. impv. 2 pers. sg. {5.D.1} id.
G2009 **ἐπιτιμία**, -ας, ἡ   *punishment.*
ἐπιτιμία   noun, nom. sg. fem. {2.A} . . . . . ἐπιτιμία G2009
ἐπιτιμῶν   vbl., pres. act. ptc. nom. sg. masc.
   {6.A.2} . . . . ἐπιτιμάω G2008
ἐπιτρέπεται   verb, pres. pass. indic. 3 pers. sg.
   {5.A.1.d} . . . . ἐπιτρέπω G2010
ἐπιτρέπῃ   verb, pres. act. subjunc. 3 pers. sg.
   {5.B.1} . . . . id.
G2010 **ἐπιτρέπω**   *I allow, permit.*
ἐπιτρέπω   verb, pres. act. indic. 1 pers. sg.
   {5.A.1.a} . . . . ἐπιτρέπω G2010
ἐπιτρέψαντος   vbl., aor. act. ptc. gen. sg. masc.
   {6.A.1.a} . . . . id.
ἐπιτρέψῃ   verb, aor. act. subjunc. 3 pers. sg.
   {5.B.1} . . . . id.
ἐπίτρεψον   verb, aor. act. impv. 2 pers. sg.
   {5.D.1} . . . . id.
G2011 **ἐπιτροπή**, -ῆς, ἡ   *commission.*
ἐπιτροπῆς   noun, gen. sg. fem. {2.A} . . . ἐπιτροπή G2011
G2012 **ἐπίτροπος**, -ου, ὁ   (1) (procurator) *a steward;*
   (2) (tutor) *a guardian* (appointed for an
   "infant," under 14 perhaps, by the father or by
   a magistrate), Gal 4:2.
ἐπιτρόπου   noun, gen. sg. masc. {2.B} . . ἐπίτροπος G2012
ἐπιτρόπους   noun, acc. pl. masc. {2.B} . . . . id.
ἐπιτρόπῳ   noun, dat. sg. masc. {2.B} . . . . id.
G2013 **ἐπιτυγχάνω**   *I attain, obtain.*
ἐπιτυχεῖν   vbl., ²aor. act. inf. {6.B.1} . . ἐπιτυγχάνω G2013
ἐπιφαινόντων   vbl., pres. act. ptc. gen. pl. neut.
   {6.A.1} . . . . ἐπιφαίνω G2014
G2014 **ἐπιφαίνω**   *I appear* (as of a light in the heavens
   or from the heavens); cf. Acts 27:20.
ἐπιφᾶναι   vbl., aor. act. inf. {6.B.1} . . . . . ἐπιφαίνω G2014
G2015 **ἐπιφάνεια**, -ας, ἡ   *appearing, manifestation* (of
   a conspicuous intervention from the sky on
   behalf of a worshipper).
ἐπιφανείᾳ   noun, dat. sg. fem. {2.A} . . . ἐπιφάνεια G2015
ἐπιφάνειαν   noun, acc. sg. fem. {2.A} . . . . id.
ἐπιφανείας   noun, gen. sg. fem. {2.A} . . . . id.
ἐπιφανῆ   adj., acc. sg. fem. {3.E} . . . . . . ἐπιφανής G2016
G2016 **ἐπιφανής**, -ές   *manifest.*
ἐπιφαύσει   verb, fut. act. indic. 3 pers. sg.
   {5.A.1.a} . . . . ἐπιφαύσκω G2017
G2017 **ἐπιφαύσκω**   *I shine upon.*
ἐπιφέρειν   vbl., pres. act. inf. {6.B.1} . . . . . ἐπιφέρω G2018
ἐπιφέρεσθαι   vbl., pres. pass. inf. {6.B.1} . . . . . . id.
G2018 **ἐπιφέρω**   *I bring forward (against).*
ἐπιφέρων   vbl., pres. act. ptc. nom. sg. masc.
   {6.A.1} . . . . ἐπιφέρω G2018

G2019 **ἐπιφωνέω**   *I call out, shout;* with dat. *against,*
   Acts 22:24.
ἐπιφωσκούσῃ   vbl., pres. act. ptc. dat. sg. fem.
   {6.A.1} . . . . ἐπιφώσκω G2020
G2020 **ἐπιφώσκω**   *I draw near, dawn,* of the next day.
G2021 **ἐπιχειρέω**   *I take in hand, I attempt.*
G2022 **ἐπιχέω**   *I pour on.*
ἐπιχέων   vbl., pres. act. ptc. nom. sg. masc.
   {6.A.2} . . . . ἐπιχέω G2022
G2023 **ἐπιχορηγέω**   *I supply, provide* (perhaps
   lavishly).
ἐπιχορηγηθήσεται   verb, fut. pass. indic. 3 pers.
   sg. {5.A.1} . . . . ἐπιχορηγέω G2023
ἐπιχορηγήσατε   verb, aor. act. impv. 2 pers. pl.
   {5.D.1} . . . . id.
G2024 **ἐπιχορηγία**, -ας, ἡ   *supply, provision,*
   equipment.
ἐπιχορηγίας   noun, gen. sg. fem. {2.A}. ἐπιχορηγία G2024
ἐπιχορηγούμενον   vbl., pres. pass. ptc. nom.
   neut. {6.A.2} . . . . ἐπιχορηγέω G2023
ἐπιχορηγῶν   vbl., pres. act. ptc. nom. sg. masc.
   {6.A.2} . . . . id.
G2025 **ἐπιχρίω**   *I besmear, anoint.*
ἐπλανήθησαν   verb, aor. pass. indic. 3 pers. pl.
   {5.A.1} . . . . πλανάω G4105
ἐπλάνησε   verb, aor. act. indic. 3 pers. sg. {5.A.1} id.
ἐπλάνησεν   verb, aor. act. indic. 3 pers. sg.
   {5.A.1} . . . . id.
ἐπλάσθη   verb, aor. pass. indic. 3 pers. sg.
   {5.A.1.b} . . . . πλάσσω G4111
ἐπλέομεν   verb, impf. act. indic. 1 pers. pl.
   {5.A.2} . . . . πλέω G4126
ἐπλεόνασε   verb, aor. act. indic. 3 pers. sg.
   {5.A.1.b} . . . . πλεονάζω G4121
ἐπλεόνασεν   verb, aor. act. indic. 3 pers. sg.
   {5.A.1.b} . . . . id.
ἐπλεονέκτησα   verb, aor. act. indic. 1 pers. sg.
   {5.A.1} . . . . πλεονεκτέω G4122
ἐπλεονεκτήσαμεν   verb, aor. act. indic. 1 pers.
   pl. {5.A.1} . . . . id.
ἐπλεονέκτησεν   verb, aor. act. indic. 3 pers. sg.
   {5.A.1} . . . . id.
ἐπλήγη   verb, ²aor. pass. indic. 3 pers. sg.
   {5.A.1.e} . . . . πλήσσω G4141
ἐπληθύνετο   verb, impf. pass. indic. 3 pers. sg.
   {5.A.1.e} . . . . πληθύνω G4129
ἐπληθύνθη   verb, aor. pass. indic. 3 pers. sg.
   {5.A.1.b} . . . . id.
ἐπληθύνοντο   verb, impf. pass. indic. 3 pers.
   pl. {5.A.1.e} . . . . id.
ἐπλήρου   verb, impf. act. indic. 3 pers. sg.
   {5.A.2} . . . . πληρόω G4137
ἐπληροῦντο   verb, impf. pass. indic. 3 pers. pl.
   {5.A.2} . . . . id.
ἐπληροῦτο   verb, impf. pass. indic. 3 pers. sg.
   {5.A.2} . . . . id.
ἐπληρώθη   verb, aor. pass. indic. 3 pers. sg.
   {5.A.1} . . . . id.
ἐπλήρωσαν   verb, aor. act. indic. 3 pers. pl.
   {5.A.1} . . . . id.

ἐπλήρωσε   verb, aor. act. indic. 3 pers. sg.
{5.A.1}. . . . . id.
ἐπλήρωσεν   verb, aor. act. indic. 3 pers. sg.
{5.A.1}. . . . . id.
ἔπλησαν   verb, aor. act. indic. 3 pers. pl.
{5.A.1.b} . . . . πίμπλημι G4130‡
ἐπλήσθη   verb, aor. pass. indic. 3 pers. sg.
{5.A.1.b} . . . . id.
ἐπλήσθησαν   verb, aor. pass. indic. 3 pers. pl.
{5.A.1.b} . . . . id.
ἐπλούτησαν   verb, aor. act. indic. 3 pers. pl.
{5.A.1}. . . . . πλουτέω G4147
ἐπλουτήσατε   verb, aor. act. indic. 2 pers. pl.
{5.A.1}. . . . . id.
ἐπλουτίσθητε   verb, aor. pass. indic. 2 pers. pl.
{5.A.1.b} . . . . πλουτίζω G4148
ἔπλυναν   verb, aor. act. indic. 3 pers. pl.
{5.A.1.b} . . . . πλύνω G4150
ἔπλυνον   verb, impf. act. indic. 3 pers. pl.
{5.A.1.b} . . . . id.
ἔπνευσαν   verb, aor. act. indic. 3 pers. pl.
{5.A.1}. . . . . πνέω G4154
ἔπνιγε   verb, impf. act. indic. 3 pers. sg.
{5.A.1.b} . . . . πνίγω G4155
ἔπνιγεν   verb, impf. act. indic. 3 pers. sg.
{5.A.1.b} . . . . id.
ἐπνίγοντο   verb, impf. pass. indic. 3 pers. pl.
{5.A.1.e} . . . . id.
ἔπνιξαν   verb, aor. act. indic. 3 pers. pl. {5.A.1.b} id.
ἐποίει   verb, impf. act. indic. 3 pers. sg.
{5.A.2}. . . . . ποιέω G4160
ἐποιεῖτε   verb, impf. act. indic. 2 pers. pl. {5.A.2} id.
ἐποίησα   verb, aor. act. indic. 1 pers. sg. {5.A.1}. id.
ἐποιήσαμεν   verb, aor. act. indic. 1 pers. pl.
{5.A.1}. . . . . id.
ἐποιησάμην   verb, aor. mid. indic. 1 pers. sg.
{5.A.1}. . . . . id.
ἐποίησαν   verb, aor. act. indic. 3 pers. pl. {5.A.1} id.
ἐποιήσαντο   verb, aor. mid. indic. 3 pers. pl.
{5.A.1}. . . . . id.
ἐποίησας   verb, aor. act. indic. 2 pers. sg. {5.A.1} id.
ἐποιήσατε   verb, aor. act. indic. 2 pers. pl.
{5.A.1}. . . . . id.
ἐποιήσατο   verb, aor. mid. indic. 3 pers. sg.
{5.A.1.e} . . . . id.
ἐποίησε   verb, aor. act. indic. 3 pers. sg. {5.A.1}. id.
ἐποίησεν   verb, aor. act. indic. 3 pers. sg. {5.A.1} id.
ἐποικοδομεῖ   verb, pres. act. indic. 3 pers. sg.
{5.A.2}. ἐποικοδομέω G2026
G2026 ἐποικοδομέω   I build upon (above) a
foundation.
ἐποικοδομηθέντες   vbl., aor. pass. ptc. nom. pl.
masc. {6.A.1.a.} . . . . ἐποικοδομέω G2026
ἐποικοδομῆσαι   vbl., aor. act. inf. {6.B.1} . . . . . id.
ἐποικοδόμησεν   verb, aor. act. indic. 3 pers. sg.
{5.A.1}. . . . . id.
ἐποικοδομούμενοι   vbl., pres. pass. ptc. nom.
pl. masc. {6.A.2} . . . . id.
ἐποικοδομοῦντες   vbl., pres. act. ptc. nom. pl.
masc. {6.A.2}. . . . . id.

ἐποίουν   verb, impf. act. indic. 3 pers. pl.
{5.A.2}. . . . . ποιέω G4160
ἐποιοῦντο   verb, impf. mid. indic. 3 pers. pl.
{5.A.2}. . . . . id.
G2027 ἐποκέλλω   I run aground.
ἐπολέμησαν   verb, aor. act. indic. 3 pers. pl.
{5.A.1}. . . . . πολεμέω G4170
ἐπολέμησε   verb, aor. act. indic. 3 pers. sg. {5.A.1}. id.
ἐπολέμησεν   verb, aor. act. indic. 3 pers. sg.
{5.A.1}. . . . . id.
ἐπονομάζῃ   verb, pres. mid./pass. indic. 2 pers. sg.
{5.A.1.d} . . . . ἐπονομάζω G2028
G2028 ἐπονομάζω   I name, impose a name on.
ἐπόπται   noun, nom. pl. masc. {2.A} . . . . ἐπόπτης G2030
ἐποπτεύοντες   vbl., pres. act. ptc. nom. pl. masc.
{6.A.1}. . . . . ἐποπτεύω G2029
ἐποπτεύσαντες   vbl., aor. act. ptc. nom. pl.
masc. {6.A.1.a}. . . . . id.
G2029 ἐποπτεύω   I am an eyewitness of, behold.
G2030 ἐπόπτης, -ου, ὁ   an eye witness (orig. of one
initiated into the mysteries, but also found of a
surveyor, supervisor).
ἐπορεύετο   verb, impf. mid./pass. indic. 3 pers. sg.
{5.A.1.e} . . . . πορεύομαι G4198
ἐπορεύθη   verb, aor. pass. indic. 3 pers. sg.
{5.A.1.b} . . . . id.
ἐπορεύθησαν   verb, aor. pass. indic. 3 pers. pl.
{5.A.1.b} . . . . id.
ἐπορευόμεθα   verb, impf. mid./pass. indic.
1 pers. pl. {5.A.1.e}. id.
ἐπορευόμην   verb, impf. mid./pass. indic.
1 pers. sg. {5.A.1.e} . . . . id.
ἐπορεύοντο   verb, impf. mid./pass. indic.
3 pers. pl. {5.A.1.e}. id.
ἐπόρθει   verb, impf. act. indic. 3 pers. sg.
{5.A.2}. . . . . πορθέω G4199
ἐπόρθουν   verb, impf. act. indic. 1 pers. sg.
{5.A.2}. . . . . id.
ἐπόρνευσαν   verb, aor. act. indic. 3 pers. pl.
{5.A.1.b} . . . . πορνεύω G4203
G2031 ἔπος, -ους, τό   a word; ὡς ἔπος εἰπεῖν (a literary phrase), one might almost say, modifying a
statement, Heb 7:9.
ἔπος   noun, acc. sg. neut. {2.C} . . . . ἔπος G2031
ἐπότιζεν   verb, impf. act. indic. 3 pers. sg.
{5.A.1.b} . . . . ποτίζω G4222
ἐπότισα   verb, aor. act. indic. 1 pers. sg. {5.A.1.b} id.
ἐποτίσαμεν   verb, aor. act. indic. 1 pers. pl.
{5.A.1.b} . . . . id.
ἐποτίσατε   verb, aor. act. indic. 2 pers. pl.
{5.A.1.b} . . . . id.
ἐπότισεν   verb, aor. act. indic. 3 pers. sg.
{5.A.1.b} . . . . id.
ἐποτίσθημεν   verb, aor. pass. indic. 1 pers. pl.
{5.A.1.b} . . . . id.
ἐπουράνια   adj., acc. pl. neut. {3.C} . . ἐπουράνιος G2032
ἐπουράνια   adj., nom. pl. neut. {3.C}. . . . . id.
ἐπουράνιοι   adj., nom. pl. masc. {3.C}. . . . . id.
ἐπουρανίοις   adj., dat. pl. neut. {3.C}. . . . . id.
ἐπουράνιον   adj., acc. sg. fem. {3.C} . . . . id.

G2032 **ἐπουράνιος**, -ον   *heavenly, in heaven;* ἐν τοῖς
ἐπουρανίοις, *in the heavenly sphere,* the
sphere of spiritual activities (opp. ἐπίγειος).
ἐπουράνιος   adj., nom. sg. masc. {3.C}ἐπουράνιος G2032
ἐπουρανίου   adj., gen. sg. fem. {3.C} . . . . id.
ἐπουρανίου   adj., gen. sg. masc. {3.C} . . . . id.
ἐπουρανίῳ   adj., dat. sg. fem. {3.C} . . . . id.
ἐπουρανίων   adj., gen. pl. masc. {3.C} . . . . id.
ἐπουρανίων   adj., gen. pl. neut. {3.C} . . . . id.
ἐπράθη   verb, aor. pass. indic. 3 pers. sg.
{5.A.1.b} . . . . πιπράσκω G4097
ἔπραξα   verb, aor. act. indic. 1 pers. sg.
{5.A.1.b} . . . . πράσσω G4238
ἐπράξαμεν   verb, aor. act. indic. 1 pers. pl.
{5.A.1.b} . . . . id.
ἔπραξαν   verb, aor. act. indic. 3 pers. pl.
{5.A.1.b} . . . . id.
ἐπράξατε   verb, aor. act. indic. 2 pers. pl.
{5.A.1.b} . . . . id.
ἔπραξε   verb, aor. act. indic. 3 pers. sg. {5.A.1.b} id.
ἔπραξεν   verb, aor. act. indic. 3 pers. sg.
{5.A.1.b} . . . . id.
ἔπρεπε   verb, impf. act. indic. 3 pers. sg.
{5.A.1.b} . . . . πρέπω G4241
ἔπρεπεν   verb, impf. act. indic. 3 pers. sg.
{5.A.1.b} . . . . id.
ἐπρίσθησαν   verb, aor. pass. indic. 3 pers. pl.
{5.A.1.b} . . . . πρίζω G4249
ἐπροφήτευον   verb, impf. act. indic. 3 pers. pl.
{5.A.1.b} . . . . προφητεύω G4395
ἐπροφητεύσαμεν   verb, aor. act. indic. 1 pers.
pl. {5.A.1.b} . . . . id.
ἐπροφήτευσαν   verb, aor. act. indic. 3 pers. pl.
{5.A.1.b} . . . . id.
ἐπροφήτευσεν   verb, aor. act. indic. 3 pers. sg.
{5.A.1.b} . . . . id.
G2033 **ἑπτά**   *seven;* οἱ ἑπτά, *the seven* ("deacons" of
Acts 6:3–6).
ἑπτά   adj. num. . . . . ἑπτά G2033
ἔπταισαν   verb, aor. act. indic. 3 pers. pl.
{5.A.1.b} . . . . πταίω G4417
G2034 **ἑπτάκις**   adv., *seven times;* ἑπτάκις τῆς
ἡμέρας, *seven times in the day.*
ἑπτάκις   adv. . . . . ἑπτάκις G2034
G2035 **ἑπτακισχίλιοι**, -αι, -α   *seven thousand.*
ἑπτακισχιλίους   adj., num. acc. pl. masc.
{3.A} . . . . ἑπτακισχίλιοι G2035
ἔπτυσε   verb, aor. act. indic. 3 pers. sg.
{5.A.1.b} . . . . πτύω G4429
ἔπτυσεν   verb, aor. act. indic. 3 pers. sg. {5.A.1.b}id.
ἐπτώχευσε   verb, aor. act. indic. 3 pers. sg.
{5.A.1.b} . . . . πτωχεύω G4433
ἐπτώχευσεν   verb, aor. act. indic. 3 pers. sg.
{5.A.1.b} . . . . id.
ἐπύθετο   verb, ²aor. mid. indic. 3 pers. sg.
{5.A.1.e} . . . . πυνθάνομαι G4441
ἐπύθοντο   verb, ²aor. mid. indic. 3 pers. pl.
{5.A.1.e} . . . . id.
ἐπυνθάνετο   verb, impf. mid./pass. indic.
3 pers. sg. {5.A.1.e} . . . . id.

ἐπυνθάνοντο   verb, impf. mid./pass. indic.
3 pers. pl. {5.A.1.e} . . . . id.
ἐπώκειλαν   verb, aor. act. indic. 3 pers. pl.
{5.A.1.b} . . . . ἐποκέλλω G2027
ἐπῳκοδόμησε   verb, aor. act. indic. 3 pers. sg.
{5.A.1} . . . . ἐποικοδομέω G2026
ἐπώλησε   verb, aor. act. indic. 3 pers. sg.
{5.A.1} . . . . πωλέω G4453
ἐπώλησεν   verb, aor. act. indic. 3 pers. sg.
{5.A.1} . . . . id.
ἐπώλουν   verb, impf. act. indic. 3 pers. pl.
{5.A.2} . . . . id.
ἐπωρώθη   verb, aor. pass. indic. 3 pers. sg.
{5.A.1} . . . . πωρόω G4456
ἐπωρώθησαν   verb, aor. pass. indic. 3 pers. pl.
{5.A.1} . . . . id.
ἐπώρωσεν   verb, aor. pass. indic. 3 pers. sg.
{5.A.1} . . . . id.
ἐραβδίσθην   verb, aor. pass. indic. 1 pers. sg.
{5.A.1.b} . . . . ῥαβδίζω G4463
ἐράντισεν   verb, aor. act. indic. 3 pers. sg.
{5.A.1.b} . . . . ῥαντίζω G4472
ἐράπισαν   verb, aor. act. indic. 3 pers. pl.
{5.A.1.b} . . . . ῥαπίζω G4474
Ἔραστον   noun prop., acc. sg. masc. {2.B;
2.D} . . . . Ἔραστος G2037
G2037 **Ἔραστος**, -ου, ὁ   *Erastus,* steward of Corinth,
a Christian.
Ἔραστος   noun prop., nom. sg. masc. {2.B;
2.D} . . . . Ἔραστος G2037
ἐραυνᾷ   verb, pres. act. indic. 3 pers. sg.
{5.A.2} . . . . ἐραυνάω G2045‡
ἐραυνᾶτε   verb, pres. act. impv. 2 pers. pl.
{5.D.2} . . . . id.
ἐραυνᾶτε   verb, pres. act. indic. 2 pers. pl.
{5.A.2} . . . . id.
G2045‡ **ἐραυνάω**   *I search;* = ἐξεραυνάω, 1 Pet 1:11;
(a form of ἐρευνάω not known before first c.
A.D.).
ἐραύνησον   verb, aor. act. impv. 2 pers. sg.
{5.D.1} . . . . ἐραυνάω G2045‡
ἐραυνῶν   vbl., pres. act. ptc. nom. sg. masc.
{6.A.2} . . . . id.
ἐραυνῶντες   vbl., pres. act. ptc. nom. pl. masc.
{6.A.2} . . . . id.
ἔργα   noun, acc. pl. neut. {2.B} . . . . ἔργον G2041
ἔργα   noun, nom. pl. neut. {2.B}
ἐργάζεσθαι   vbl., pres. mid./pass. inf.
{6.B.1} . . . . ἐργάζομαι G2038
ἐργάζεσθε   verb, pres. mid./pass. impv. 2 pers.
pl. {5.D.1} . . . . id.
ἐργάζεσθε   verb, pres. mid./pass. indic. 2 pers.
pl. {5.A.1.d} . . . . id.
ἐργάζεται   verb, pres. mid./pass. indic. 3 pers.
sg. {5.A.1.d} . . . . id.
ἐργάζῃ   verb, pres. mid./pass. indic. 2 pers.
{5.A.1.d} . . . . id.
G2038 **ἐργάζομαι**   (1) *I am at work, I work;* (2) trans.,
*I produce by work, put in force, give operation
to, realize,* e.g., Matt 7:23; with cog. acc. ἔργον,

ἔργα, Matt 26:10, etc.; with acc. βρῶσιν, *I work for,* John 6:27.

ἐργάζομαι   verb, pres. mid./pass. indic. 1 pers. sg.
{5.A.1.d} . . . . ἐργάζομαι *G2038*

ἐργαζόμενοι   vbl., pres. mid./pass. ptc. nom.
pl. masc. {6.A.1} . . . . id.

ἐργαζόμενος   vbl., pres. mid./pass. ptc. nom.
sg. masc. {6.A.1} . . . . id.

ἐργαζομένους   vbl., pres. mid./pass. ptc. acc.
pl. masc. {6.A.1} . . . . id.

ἐργαζομένῳ   vbl., pres. mid./pass. ptc. dat. sg.
masc. {6.A.1} . . . . id.

ἐργάζονται   verb, pres. mid./pass. indic. 3 pers.
pl. {5.A.1.d} . . . . id.

ἐργάζου   verb, pres. mid./pass. impv. 2 pers. sg.
{5.D.1} . . . . id.

ἐργαζώμεθα   verb, pres. mid./pass. subjunc.
1 pers. pl. {5.B.1} . . . . id.

ἐργάσῃ   verb, aor. mid. subjunc. 2 pers. sg.
{5.B.1} . . . . id.

G2039 **ἐργασία**, -ας, ἡ   *working, activity, work, service, trade, business, gains of business;* δὸς ἐργασίαν, *take pains to, see to it that you,* Luke 12:58; *performance, practice,* Eph 4:19.

ἐργασίαν   noun, acc. sg. fem. {2.A} . . . . . ἐργασία *G2039*

ἐργασίας   noun, gen. sg. fem. {2.A} . . . . id.

ἐργάται   noun, nom. pl. masc. {2.A} . . . . . ἐργάτης *G2040*

ἐργάται   noun, nom. pl. voc. {2.A} . . . . id.

ἐργάτας   noun, acc. pl. masc. {2.A} . . . . id.

ἐργάτην   noun, acc. sg. masc. {2.A} . . . . id.

G2040 **ἐργάτης**, -ου, ὁ   *a field laborer;* then, *a laborer, workman* in general.

ἐργάτης   noun, nom. sg. masc. {2.A} . . . . ἐργάτης *G2040*

ἐργατῶν   noun, gen. pl. masc. {2.A} . . . . id.

ἔργοις   noun, dat. pl. neut. {2.B} . . . . ἔργον *G2041*

G2041 **ἔργον**, -ου, τό   (1) *work, labor* (in the physical, orig. in the agricultural, sphere); (2) moral *action, deed,* hence with adjs. or gens. defining its character.

ἔργον   noun, acc. sg. neut. {2.B} . . . . ἔργον *G2041*

ἔργον   noun, nom. sg. neut. {2.B} . . . . id.

ἔργου   noun, gen. sg. neut. {2.B} . . . . id.

ἔργῳ   noun, dat. sg. neut. {2.B} . . . . id.

ἔργων   noun, gen. pl. neut. {2.B} . . . . id.

ἐρεθίζετε   verb, pres. act. impv. 2 pers. pl.
{5.D.1} . . . . ἐρεθίζω *G2042*

G2042 **ἐρεθίζω**   *I stir up,* 2 Cor 9:2: *I arouse to anger, provoke,* Col 3:21.

ἐρεῖ   verb, fut. act. indic. 3 pers. sg. {5.A.1} . . . ἐρέω *G2046*

G2043 **ἐρείδω**   *I strike; I run aground* (of a ship).

ἔρεις   noun, acc. pl. fem. {2.C} . . . . ἔρις *G2054*

ἔρεις   noun, nom. pl. fem. {2.C} . . . . id.

ἐρεῖς   verb, fut. act. indic. 2 pers. sg. {5.A.1} . . ἐρέω *G2046*

ἐρείσασα   vbl., aor. act. ptc. nom. sg. fem.
{6.A.1.a} . . . . ἐρείδω *G2043*

ἐρεῖτε   verb, fut. act. indic. 2 pers. pl. {5.A.2} . ἐρέω *G2046*

G2044 **ἐρεύγομαι**   *I utter, declare.* (lit. *I belch forth*).

ἐρευνᾷ   verb, pres. act. indic. 3 pers. sg.
{5.A.2} . . . . ἐραυνάω *G2045‡*

ἐρευνᾶτε   verb, pres. act. impv. 2 pers. pl.
{5.D.2} . . . . id.

ἐρευνᾶτε   verb, pres. act. indic. 2 pers. pl.
{5.A.2} . . . . id.

ἐρεύνησον   verb, aor. act. impv. 2 pers. sg.
{5.D.1} . . . . id.

ἐρευνῶν   vbl., pres. act. ptc. nom. sg. masc.
{6.A.2} . . . . id.

ἐρευνῶντες   vbl., pres. act. ptc. nom. pl. masc.
{6.A.2} . . . . id.

ἐρεύξομαι   verb, fut. mid. indic. 1 pers. sg.
{5.A.1.d} . . . . ἐρεύγομαι *G2044*

G2046 **ἐρέω** (ἐρῶ)   fut. act. of λέγω, *I shall say;* with acc. pers. ὑμᾶς εἴρηκα φίλους, *I have called you friends,* John 15:15; ἄρχοντα οὐκ ἐρεῖς κακῶς, *you shall not speak evilly of a leader,* Acts 23:5, cf. Rom 4:1 (var.); cf. εἶπον.

G2047 **ἐρημία**, -ας, ἡ   *a desert place, a desert.*

ἐρημία   noun, dat. sg. fem. {2.A} . . . . ἐρημία *G2047*

ἐρημίαις   noun, dat. pl. fem. {2.A} . . . . id.

ἐρημίας   noun, gen. sg. fem. {2.A} . . . . id.

ἐρήμοις   adj., dat. pl. fem. {3.C} . . . . ἔρημος *G2048*

ἐρήμοις   adj., dat. pl. masc. {3.C} . . . . id.

ἔρημον   adj., acc. sg. fem. {3.C} . . . . id.

ἔρημον   adj., acc. sg. masc. {3.C} . . . . id.

G2048 **ἔρημος**, -ου, ἡ   adj., *desert;* hence, ἡ ἔρημος (understand χώρα), *the desert,* to the east and south of Palestine; of a person, *deserted, abandoned, desolate,* Gal 4:27.

ἔρημος   adj., nom. sg. fem. {3.C} . . . . ἔρημος *G2048*

ἔρημος   adj., nom. sg. masc. {3.C} . . . . id.

ἐρήμου   adj., gen. sg. fem. {3.C} . . . . id.

ἐρήμους   adj., acc. pl. fem. {3.C} . . . . id.

ἐρημοῦται   verb, pres. pass. indic. 3 pers. sg.
{5.A.2} . . . . ἐρημόω *G2049*

G2049 **ἐρημόω**   (1) *I make desolate, bring to desolation, destroy, waste;* (2) of a person, *I strip, rob.*

ἐρήμῳ   adj., dat. sg. fem. {3.C} . . . . ἔρημος *G2048*

ἐρήμῳ   adj., dat. sg. masc. {3.C} . . . . id.

ἐρημώσεως   noun, gen. sg. fem. {2.C} . . ἐρήμωσις *G2050*

G2050 **ἐρήμωσις**, -εως, ἡ   *making into a desert, wasting, desolating, desolation.*

ἐρήμωσις   noun, nom. sg. fem. {2.C} . . . ἐρήμωσις *G2050*

ἔριδες   noun, nom. pl. fem. {2.C} . . . . ἔρις *G2054*

ἔριδι   noun, dat. sg. fem. {2.C} . . . . id.

ἔριδος   noun, gen. sg. fem. {2.C} . . . . id.

G2051 **ἐρίζω**   *I strive.*

G2052 **ἐριθεία**, -ας, ἡ   *ambition, rivalry* (lit. the *seeking of followers and adherents by means of gifts, the seeking of followers*).

ἐριθεία   noun, nom. sg. fem. {2.A} . . . . . . ἐριθεία *G2052*

ἐριθείαι   noun, nom. pl. fem. {2.A} . . . . id.

ἐριθεῖαι   noun, nom. pl. fem. {2.A} . . . . id.

ἐριθείαν   noun, acc. sg. fem. {2.A} . . . . id.

ἐριθείας   noun, gen. sg. fem. {2.A} . . . . id.

ἐριθία   noun, nom. sg. fem. {2.A} . . . . id.

ἐριθίαι   noun, nom. pl. fem. {2.A} . . . . id.

ἐριθίαν   noun, acc. sg. fem. {2.A} . . . . id.

ἐριθίας   noun, gen. sg. fem. {2.A} . . . . id.

ἐριμμένοι   vbl., perf. pass. ptc. nom. pl. masc.
{6.A.1.b} . . . . ῥίπτω *G4496*
ἔριν   noun, acc. sg. fem. {2.C}. . . . . ἔρις *G2054*
G2053 **ἔριον**, -ου, τό   *wool.*
ἔριον   noun, nom. sg. neut. {2.B} . . . . .ἔριον *G2053*
ἐρίου   noun, gen. sg. neut. {2.B} . . . . id.
G2054 **ἔρις**, -ιδος, ἡ   *strife.*
ἔρις   noun, nom. sg. fem. {2.C}. . . . . ἔρις *G2054*
ἐρίσει   verb, fut. act. indic. 3 pers. sg.
{5.A.1.a} . . . . .ἐρίζω *G2051*
ἐρίφια   noun, acc. pl. neut. {2.B} . . . . ἐρίφιον *G2055*
G2055 **ἐρίφιον**, -ου, τό   *a goat,* or *kid.*
ἔριφον   noun, acc. sg. masc. {2.B}. . . . . . . .ἔριφος *G2056*
G2056 **ἔριφος**, -ου, ὁ   *a goat.*
ἐρίφων   noun, gen. pl. masc. {2.B} . . . . .ἔριφος *G2056*
ἔριψαν   verb, aor. act. indic. 3 pers. pl.
{5.A.1.b} . . . . .ῥίπτω *G4496*
Ἑρμᾶν   noun prop., acc. sg. masc. {2.A;
2.D} . . . . Ἑρμᾶς *G2057*
G2057 **Ἑρμᾶς**, -ᾶ, ὁ   *Hermas,* a Roman Christian.
Ἑρμῆν   noun prop., acc. sg. masc. {2.A;
2.D} . . . . Ἑρμῆς *G2060*
G2058 **ἑρμηνεία**, -ας, ἡ   *translation, interpretation.*
ἑρμηνεία   noun, nom. sg. fem. {2.A} . . . ἑρμηνεία *G2058*
ἑρμηνείαν   noun, acc. sg. fem. {2.A} . . . . id.
ἑρμηνεύεται   verb, pres. pass. indic. 3 pers. sg.
{5.A.1.d} . . . . .ἑρμηνεύω *G2059*
ἑρμηνευόμενον   vbl., pres. pass. ptc. nom. sg.
neut. {6.A.1} . . . . id.
ἑρμηνευόμενος   vbl., pres. pass. ptc. nom. sg.
masc. {6.A.1} . . . . id.
G1328†‡ **ἑρμηνευτής**   *translator, interpreter.* Var. for
διερμηνευτής, 1 Cor 14:28.
G2059 **ἑρμηνεύω**   (1) *I translate;* (2) *I interpret* the
meaning of, Luke 24:27 (var.).
ἑρμηνία   noun, nom. sg. fem. {2.A} . . . . ἑρμηνεία *G2058*
ἑρμηνίαν   noun, acc. sg. fem. {2.A} . . . . id.
G2060 **Ἑρμῆς**, -οῦ, ὁ   (1) *Hermes,* the messenger
and herald of the Greek gods, or rather the
corresponding Lycaonian deity; to him also
corresponded the Lat. *Mercurius,* Acts 14:12;
(2) *Hermes,* a Roman Christian.
G2061 **Ἑρμογένης**, -ους, ὁ   *Hermogenes,* a faithless
Christian at Rome.
Ἑρμογένης   noun prop., nom. sg. masc. {2.A;
2.D}. Ἑρμογένης *G2061*
ἐροῦμεν   verb, fut. act. indic. 1 pers. pl.
{5.A.2} . . . . .ἐρέω *G2046*
ἐροῦσι   verb, fut. act. indic. 3 pers. pl. {5.A.2} . . id.
ἐροῦσιν   verb, fut. act. indic. 3 pers. pl. {5.A.2} . id.
ἑρπετά   noun, acc. pl. neut. {2.B} . . . . . . .ἑρπετόν *G2062*
ἑρπετά   noun, nom. pl. neut. {2.B} . . . . id.
G2062 **ἑρπετόν**, -οῦ, τό   *a creeping creature, reptile,*
esp. *a serpent.*
ἑρπετῶν   noun, gen. pl. neut. {2.B} . . . . . .ἑρπετόν *G2062*
ἐρραβδίσθην   verb, aor. pass. indic. 1 pers. sg.
{5.A.1.b} .ῥαβδίζω *G4463*
ἐρράντισε   verb, aor. act. indic. 3 pers. sg.
{5.A.1.b} .ῥαντίζω *G4472*

ἐρράντισεν   verb, aor. act. indic. 3 pers. sg.
{5.A.1.b} . . . . id.
ἐρραντισμένοι   vbl., perf. pass. ptc. nom. pl.
masc. {6.A.1.b} . . . . id.
ἐρράπισαν   verb, aor. act. indic. 3 pers. pl.
{5.A.1.b} . . . . .ῥαπίζω *G4474*
ἐρρέθη   verb, aor. pass. indic. 3 pers. sg. {5.A.1} . .ἐρέω *G2046*
ἐρρέθησαν   verb, aor. pass. indic. 3 pers. pl.
{5.A.1}. . . . . id.
ἐρρήθη   verb, aor. pass. indic. 3 pers. sg. {5.A.1}. id.
ἐρρήθησαν   verb, aor. pass. indic. 3 pers. pl.
{5.A.1}. . . . . id.
ἔρρηξεν   verb, aor. act. indic. 3 pers. sg.
{5.A.3.b} . . . . .ῥήγνυμι *G4486*
ἐρριζωμένοι   vbl., perf. pass. ptc. nom. pl. masc.
{6.A.2} . . . . .ῥιζόω *G4492*
ἐρριμμένοι   vbl., perf. pass. ptc. nom. pl. masc.
{6.A.1.b} . . . . .ῥίπτω *G4496*
ἔρριπται   verb, perf. pass. indic. 3 pers. sg.
{5.A.1.f}. . . . . id.
ἐρρίψαμεν   verb, aor. act. indic. 1 pers. pl.
{5.A.1.b} . . . . id.
ἔρριψαν   verb, aor. act. indic. 3 pers. pl.
{5.A.1.b} . . . . id.
ἐρρύσατο   verb, aor. mid. indic. 3 pers. sg.
{5.A.1.e} . . . . .ῥύομαι *G4506*
ἐρρύσθην   verb, aor. pass. indic. 1 pers. sg.
{5.A.1.b} . . . . id.
ἔρρωσθε   verb, perf. pass. impv. 2 pers. pl.
{5.D.3}. . . . . .ῥώννυμι *G4517*
ἔρρωσο   verb, perf. pass. impv. 2 pers. sg. {5.D.3}id.
ἐρυθρᾷ   adj., dat. sg. fem. {3.A} . . . . .ἐρυθρός *G2063*
ἐρυθράν   adj., acc. sg. fem. {3.A} . . . . id.
G2063 **ἐρυθρός**, -ά, -όν   *red.*
ἐρύσατο   verb, aor. mid. indic. 3 pers. sg.
{5.A.1.e} . . . . .ῥύομαι *G4506*
ἐρύσθην   verb, aor. pass. indic. 1 pers. sg.
{5.A.1.b} . . . . id.
ἔρχεσθαι   vbl., pres. mid./pass. inf. {6.B.1}.ἔρχομαι *G2064*
ἔρχεσθε   verb, pres. mid./pass. impv. 2 pers. pl.
{5.D.1}. . . . . id.
ἐρχέσθω   verb, pres. mid./pass. impv. 3 pers. sg.
{5.D.1}. . . . . id.
ἔρχεται   verb, pres. mid./pass. indic. 3 pers. sg.
{5.A.1.d} . . . . id.
ἔρχῃ   verb, pres. mid./pass. indic. 2 pers. sg.
{5.A.1.d} . . . . id.
ἔρχηται   verb, pres. mid./pass. subjunc. 3 pers.
sg. {5.B.1} . . . . id.
G2064 **ἔρχομαι**   (1) *I go;* with acc. of extent, ὁδόν; (2)
I come; εἰς ἑαυτὸν ἐλθών, *having come to
himself, having come to his right mind, "having
reasoned with him self"* (Sahidic), Luke 15:17.
ἔρχομαι   verb, pres. mid./pass. indic. 1 pers. sg.
{5.A.1.d} . . . . .ἔρχομαι *G2064*
ἐρχόμεθα   verb, pres. mid./pass. indic. 1 pers.
pl. {5.A.1.d} . . . . id.
ἐρχόμενα   vbl., pres. mid./pass. ptc. acc. pl.
neut. {6.A.1} . . . . id.

ἐρχομένη   vbl., pres. mid./pass. ptc. nom. sg.
  fem. {6.A.1} . . . . id.
ἐρχομένην   vbl., pres. mid./pass. ptc. acc. sg.
  fem. {6.A.1} . . . . id.
ἐρχομένης   vbl., pres. mid./pass. ptc. gen. sg.
  fem. {6.A.1} . . . . id.
ἐρχόμενοι   vbl., pres. mid./pass. ptc. nom. pl.
  masc. {6.A.1} . . . . id.
ἐρχόμενον   vbl., pres. mid./pass. ptc. acc. sg.
  masc. {6.A.1} . . . . id.
ἐρχόμενον   vbl., pres. mid./pass. ptc. acc. sg.
  neut. {6.A.1} . . . . id.
ἐρχόμενον   vbl., pres. mid./pass. ptc. nom. sg.
  neut. {6.A.1} . . . . id.
ἐρχόμενος   vbl., pres. mid./pass. ptc. nom. sg.
  masc. {6.A.1} . . . . id.
ἐρχομένου   vbl., pres. mid./pass. ptc. gen. sg.
  masc. {6.A.1} . . . . id.
ἐρχόμενου   vbl., pres. mid./pass. ptc. gen. sg.
  masc. {6.A.1} . . . . id.
ἐρχομένους   vbl., pres. mid./pass. ptc. acc. pl.
  masc. {6.A.1} . . . . id.
ἐρχομένῳ   vbl., pres. mid./pass. ptc. dat. sg.
  masc. {6.A.1} . . . . id.
ἐρχομένῳ   vbl., pres. mid./pass. ptc. dat. sg.
  neut. {6.A.1} . . . . id.
ἐρχομένων   vbl., pres. mid./pass. ptc. gen. pl.
  masc. {6.A.1} . . . . id.
ἔρχονται   verb, pres. mid./pass. indic. 3 pers.
  pl. {5.A.1.d} . . . . id.
ἔρχου   verb, pres. mid./pass. impv. 2 pers. sg.
  {5.D.1} . . . . id.
ἔρχωμαι   verb, pres. mid./pass. subjunc. 1 pers.
  sg. {5.B.1} . . . . id.
ἐρῶ   verb, fut. act. indic. 1 pers. sg. {5.A.1} . . . ἐρέω G2046
ἐρωτᾷ   verb, pres. act. indic. 3 pers. sg.
  {5.A.2} . . . . ἐρωτάω G2065
ἐρωτᾷ   verb, pres. act. subjunc. 3 pers. sg. {5.B.2} id.
ἐρωτᾶν   vbl., pres. act. inf. {6.B.2} . . . . id.
ἐρωτᾷν   vbl., pres. act. inf. {6.B.2} . . . . id.
ἐρωτᾷς   verb, pres. act. indic. 2 pers. sg. {5.A.2} . id.
G2065 ἐρωτάω   (1) *I ask* (a question), *I question;* (2) *I*
  request, make a request to, I pray (= αἰτέω).
ἐρωτῆσαι   vbl., aor. act. inf. {6.B.1} . . . . . . ἐρωτάω G2065
ἐρωτήσατε   verb, aor. act. impv. 2 pers. pl.
  {5.D.1} . . . . id.
ἐρωτήσετε   verb, fut. act. indic. 2 pers. pl.
  {5.A.1} . . . . id.
ἐρωτήσῃ   verb, aor. act. subjunc. 3 pers. sg.
  {5.B.1} . . . . id.
ἐρώτησον   verb, aor. act. impv. 2 pers. sg.
  {5.D.1} . . . . id.
ἐρωτήσω   verb, aor. act. subjunc. 1 pers. sg.
  {5.B.1} . . . . id.
ἐρωτήσω   verb, fut. act. indic. 1 pers. sg. {5.A.1} id.
ἐρωτήσωσιν   verb, aor. act. subjunc. 3 pers. pl.
  {5.B.1} . . . . id.
ἐρωτῶ   verb, pres. act. indic. 1 pers. sg. {5.A.2} . . id.
ἐρωτῶμεν   verb, pres. act. indic. 1 pers. pl.
  {5.A.2} . . . . id.

ἐρωτῶν   vbl., pres. act. ptc. nom. sg. masc.
  {6.A.2} . . . . id.
ἐρωτῶντες   vbl., pres. act. ptc. nom. pl. masc.
  {6.A.2} . . . . id.
ἐρωτώντων   vbl., pres. act. ptc. gen. pl. masc.
  {6.A.2} . . . . id.
ἐσαλεύθη   verb, aor. pass. indic. 3 pers. sg.
  {5.A.1.b} . . . . σαλεύω G4531
ἐσάλευσε   verb, aor. act. indic. 3 pers. sg.
  {5.A.1.b} . . . . id.
ἐσάλευσεν   verb, aor. act. indic. 3 pers. sg.
  {5.A.1.b} . . . . id.
ἐσάλπισε   verb, aor. act. indic. 3 pers. sg.
  {5.A.1.b} . . . . σαλπίζω G4537
ἐσάλπισεν   verb, aor. act. indic. 3 pers. sg.
  {5.A.1.b} . . . . id.
ἔσβεσαν   verb, aor. act. indic. 3 pers. pl.
  {5.A.3.b} . . . . σβέννυμι G4570
ἐσεβάσθησαν   verb, aor. pass. indic. 3 pers. pl.
  {5.A.1.e} . . . . σεβάζομαι G4573
ἐσείσθη   verb, aor. pass. indic. 3 pers. sg.
  {5.A.1.b} . . . . σείω G4579
ἐσείσθησαν   verb, aor. pass. indic. 3 pers. pl.
  {5.A.1.b} . . . . id.
ἔσεσθαι   vbl., fut. inf. {7.C.2} . . . . εἰμί G1510
ἔσεσθε   verb, fut. indic. 2 pers. pl. {7.A} . . . . id.
ἔσῃ   verb, fut. indic. 2 pers. sg. {7.A} . . . . id.
ἐσήμαινεν   verb, impf. act. indic. 3 pers. sg.
  {5.A.1.b} . . . . σημαίνω G4591
ἐσήμανε   verb, aor. act. indic. 3 pers. sg.
  {5.A.1.b} . . . . id.
ἐσήμανεν   verb, aor. act. indic. 3 pers. sg.
  {5.A.1.b} . . . . id.
G2066 ἐσθής, -ῆτος, ἡ   *clothing;* ἐσθήσεσι = ἔσθεσι,
  dat. pl. of ἐσθής.
ἐσθήσεσι   noun, dat. pl. fem. {2.C} . . . . ἐσθής G2066
ἐσθήσεσιν   noun, dat. pl. fem. {2.C} . . . . id.
G2067 ἔσθησις   *clothing;* cf. ἐσθής.
ἐσθῆτα   noun, acc. sg. fem. {2.C} . . . . ἐσθής G2066
ἔσθητε   verb, pres. act. subjunc. 2 pers. pl.
  {5.B.1} . . . . ἐσθίω G2068
ἐσθῆτι   noun, dat. sg. fem. {2.C} . . . . ἐσθής G2066
ἐσθίει   verb, pres. act. indic. 3 pers. sg.
  {5.A.1.a} . . . . ἐσθίω G2068
ἐσθίειν   vbl., pres. act. inf. {6.B.1} . . . . id.
ἐσθίετε   verb, pres. act. impv. 2 pers. pl. {5.D.1} . . id.
ἐσθίετε   verb, pres. act. indic. 2 pers. pl. {5.A.1.a} id.
ἐσθιέτω   verb, pres. act. impv. 3 pers. sg. {5.D.1} id.
ἐσθίῃ   verb, pres. act. subjunc. 3 pers. sg. {5.B.1} id.
ἐσθίητε   verb, pres. act. subjunc. 2 pers. pl.
  {5.B.1} . . . . id.
ἐσθίοντα   vbl., pres. act. ptc. acc. sg. masc.
  {6.A.1} . . . . id.
ἐσθίοντας   vbl., pres. act. ptc. acc. pl. masc.
  {6.A.1} . . . . id.
ἐσθίοντες   vbl., pres. act. ptc. nom. pl. masc.
  {6.A.1} . . . . id.
ἐσθίοντι   vbl., pres. act. ptc. dat. sg. masc. {6.A.1} id.
ἐσθιόντων   vbl., pres. act. ptc. gen. pl. masc.
  {6.A.1} . . . . id.

ἐσθίουσι   verb, pres. act. indic. 3 pers. pl.
{5.A.1.a} . . . . id.
ἐσθίουσιν   verb, pres. act. indic. 3 pers. pl.
{5.A.1.a} . . . . id.
G2068   **ἐσθίω** (ἔσθω)   trans. and intrans., *I eat, I am eating; I take a meal;* aor. φαγεῖν, *to eat,* but in Rev 10:10 = καταφαγεῖν.
ἐσθίων   vbl., pres. act. ptc. nom. sg. masc.
{6.A.1} . . . . ἐσθίω G2068
ἐσθίωσιν   verb, pres. act. subjunc. 3 pers. pl.
{5.B.1} . . . . id.
ἔσθοντες   vbl., pres. act. ptc. nom. pl. masc.
{6.A.1} . . . . id.
ἔσθων   vbl., pres. act. ptc. nom. sg. masc. {6.A.1} id.
ἐσίγησαν   verb, aor. act. indic. 3 pers. pl.
{5.A.1} . . . . σιγάω G4601
ἐσίγησε   verb, aor. act. indic. 3 pers. sg. {5.A.1} . id.
ἐσίγησεν   verb, aor. act. indic. 3 pers. sg. {5.A.1} id.
ἐσιώπα   verb, impf. act. indic. 3 pers. sg.
{5.A.2} . . . . .σιωπάω G4623
ἐσιώπων   verb, impf. act. indic. 3 pers. pl.
{5.A.2} . . . . id.
ἐσκανδαλίζοντο   verb, impf. pass. indic. 3 pers. pl. {5.A.1.e} . . . . σκανδαλίζω G4624
ἐσκανδαλίσθησαν   verb, aor. pass. indic. 3 pers. pl. {5.A.1.b} . . . . id.
ἔσκαψε   verb, aor. act. indic. 3 pers. sg.
{5.A.1.b} . . . . .σκάπτω G4626
ἔσκαψεν   verb, aor. act. indic. 3 pers. sg.
{5.A.1.b} . . . . id.
ἐσκήνωσεν   verb, aor. act. indic. 3 pers. sg.
{5.A.1} . . . . .σκηνόω G4637
ἐσκίρτησε   verb, aor. act. indic. 3 pers. sg.
{5.A.1} . . . . .σκιρτάω G4640
ἐσκίρτησεν   verb, aor. act. indic. 3 pers. sg.
{5.A.1} . . . . id.
ἐσκληρύνοντο   verb, impf. pass. indic. 3 pers. pl.
{5.A.1.e} . . . . σκληρύνω G4645
ἐσκόρπισεν   verb, aor. act. indic. 3 pers. sg.
{5.A.1.b} . . . . σκορπίζω G4650
ἐσκοτίσθη   verb, aor. pass. indic. 3 pers. sg.
{5.A.1.b} . . . . σκοτίζω G4654
ἐσκοτισμένοι   vbl., perf. pass. ptc. nom. pl.
masc. {6.A.1.b} . . . . id.
ἐσκοτώθη   verb, aor. pass. indic. 3 pers. sg.
{5.A.1} . . . . .σκοτόω G4656
ἐσκοτωμένη   vbl., perf. pass. ptc. nom. sg. fem.
{6.A.2} . . . . id.
ἐσκοτωμένοι   vbl., perf. pass. ptc. nom. pl.
masc. {6.A.2} . . . . id.
ἐσκυλμένοι   vbl., perf. pass. ptc. nom. pl. masc.
{6.A.1.b} . . . . .σκύλλω G4660
Ἐσλεί   noun prop. . . . . Ἐσλί G2069
Ἐσλί   noun prop. . . . . id.
G2069   **Ἐσλί**, ὁ   *Esli,* son of Naggai and father of Nahum (Heb.).
Ἐσλί   noun prop. . . . . Ἐσλί G2069
Ἐσλίμ   noun prop. . . . . id.
ἐσμεν   verb, pres. indic. 1 pers. pl. {7.A} . . . . . . εἰμί G1510

ἐσμέν   verb, pres. indic. 1 pers. pl. {7.A} . . . . . . id.
ἐσμυρνισμένον   vbl., perf. pass. ptc. acc. sg. masc.
{6.A.1.b} . . . . σμυρνίζω G4669
ἔσομαι   verb, fut. indic. 1 pers. sg. {7.A} . . . . . εἰμί G1510
ἐσόμεθα   verb, fut. indic. 1 pers. pl. {7.A} . . . . . id.
ἐσόμενον   vbl., fut. ptc. acc. sg. neut. {7.C.1} . . . id.
ἔσονται   verb, fut. indic. 3 pers. pl. {7.A} . . . . . id.
G2072   **ἔσοπτρον**, -ου, τό   *a mirror, looking glass* (made of highly polished metal).
ἐσόπτρου   noun, gen. sg. neut. {2.B} . . . ἔσοπτρον G2072
ἐσόπτρῳ   noun, dat. sg. neut. {2.B}. . . . . id.
ἐσπάραξεν   verb, aor. act. indic. 3 pers. sg.
{5.A.1.b} . . . . σπαράσσω G4682
ἐσπαργανωμένον   vbl., perf. pass. ptc. acc. sg.
neut. {6.A.2} . . . . σπαργανόω G4683
ἐσπαργάνωσεν   verb, aor. act. indic. 3 pers. sg.
{5.A.1} . . . . id.
ἐσπαρμένον   vbl., perf. pass. ptc. acc. sg. masc.
{6.A.1.b} . . . . σπείρω G4687
ἐσπαρμένον   vbl., perf. pass. ptc. acc. sg. neut.
{6.A.1.b} . . . . id.
ἐσπαταλήσατε   verb, aor. act. indic. 2 pers. pl.
{5.A.1} . . . . σπαταλάω G4684
ἔσπειρα   verb, aor. act. indic. 1 pers. sg.
{5.A.1.b} . . . . σπείρω G4687
ἐσπείραμεν   verb, aor. act. indic. 1 pers. pl.
{5.A.1.b} . . . . id.
ἔσπειρας   verb, aor. act. indic. 2 pers. sg.
{5.A.1.b} . . . . id.
ἔσπειρε   verb, aor. act. indic. 3 pers. sg. {5.A.1.b} id.
ἔσπειρεν   verb, aor. act. indic. 3 pers. sg.
{5.A.1.b} . . . . id.
G2073   **ἑσπέρα**, -ας, ἡ   *evening.*
ἑσπέρα   noun, nom. sg. fem. {2.A} . . . . ἑσπέρα G2073
ἑσπέραν   noun, acc. sg. fem. {2.A} . . . . id.
ἑσπέρας   noun, gen. sg. fem. {2.A} . . . . id.
ἔσπευδε   verb, impf. act. indic. 3 pers. sg.
{5.A.1.b} . . . . σπεύδω G4692
ἔσπευδεν   verb, impf. act. indic. 3 pers. sg.
{5.A.1.b} . . . . id.
ἐσπιλωμένον   vbl., perf. pass. ptc. acc. sg. masc.
{6.A.2} . . . . σπιλόω G4695‡
ἐσπλαγχνίσθη   verb, aor. pass. indic. 3 pers. sg.
{5.A.1.b} . . . . σπλαγχνίζομαι G4697
ἐσπούδασα   verb, aor. act. indic. 1 pers. sg.
{5.A.1.b} . . . . σπουδάζω G4704
ἐσπουδάσαμεν   verb, aor. act. indic. 1 pers. pl.
{5.A.1.b} . . . . id.
Ἐσρώμ   noun prop. . . . . Ἐσρώμ G2074
G2074   **Ἐσρώμ**, ὁ   *Hezron,* son of Phares, father of Aram. (Heb.).
Ἐσρώμ   noun prop. . . . . Ἐσρώμ G2074
Ἐσρώμ   noun prop. id.
G2274†‡   **ἐσσόομαι**   *be worse off than, be inferior to.* Var. for ἡττάομαι, 2 Cor 12:13.
ἐστάθη   verb, aor. pass. indic. 3 pers. sg.
{5.A.1} . . . . ἵστημι G2476
ἐστάθην   verb, aor. pass. indic. 1 pers. sg. {5.A.1}id.
ἐστάθησαν   verb, aor. pass. indic. 3 pers. pl.
{5.A.1} . . . . id.

ἔσται   verb, fut. indic. 3 pers. sg. {7.A} . . . . . . εἰμί G1510
ἑστάναι   vbl., ²perf. act. inf. {6.B.3} . . . . . . ἵστημι G2476
ἐσταυρώθη   verb, aor. pass. indic. 3 pers. sg.
    {5.A.1} . . . . .σταυρόω G4717
ἐσταυρωμένον   vbl., perf. pass. ptc. acc. sg.
    masc. {6.A.2} . . . . id.
ἐσταυρωμένος   vbl., perf. pass. ptc. nom. sg.
    masc. {6.A.2} . . . . id.
ἐσταύρωσαν   verb, aor. act. indic. 3 pers. pl.
    {5.A.1} . . . . id.
ἐσταυρώσατε   verb, aor. act. indic. 2 pers. pl.
    {5.A.1} . . . . id.
ἐσταύρωται   verb, perf. pass. indic. 3 pers. sg.
    {5.A.1} . . . . id.
ἐστε   verb, pres. indic. 2 pers. pl. {7.A} . . . . . . εἰμί G1510
ἐστέ   verb, pres. indic. 2 pers. pl. {7.A} . . . . id.
ἐστέναξε   verb, aor. act. indic. 3 pers. sg.
    {5.A.1.b} . . . . στενάζω G4727
ἐστέναξεν   verb, aor. act. indic. 3 pers. sg.
    {5.A.1.b} . . . . id.
ἐστερεοῦντο   verb, impf. pass. indic. 3 pers. pl.
    {5.A.2} . . . . στερεόω G4732
ἐστερεώθησαν   verb, aor. pass. indic. 3 pers.
    pl. {5.A.1} . . . . id.
ἐστερέωσε   verb, aor. act. indic. 3 pers. sg.
    {5.A.1} . . . . id.
ἐστερέωσεν   verb, aor. act. indic. 3 pers. sg.
    {5.A.1} . . . . id.
ἐστεφανωμένον   vbl., perf. pass. ptc. acc. sg. masc.
    {6.A.2} . . . . .στεφανόω G4737
ἐστεφάνωσας   verb, aor. act. indic. 2 pers. sg.
    {5.A.1} . . . . id.
ἔστη   verb, ²aor. act. indic. 3 pers. sg.
    {5.A.3.b} . . . . ἵστημι G2476
ἔστηκα   verb, perf. act. indic. 1 pers. sg. {5.A.1} . id.
ἑστήκαμεν   verb, perf. act. indic. 1 pers. pl.
    {5.A.1} . . . . id.
ἔστηκας   verb, perf. act. indic. 2 pers. sg. {5.A.1} id.
ἑστήκασι   verb, perf. act. indic. 3 pers. pl.
    {5.A.1} . . . . id.
ἑστήκασιν   verb, perf. act. indic. 3 pers. pl.
    {5.A.1} . . . . id.
ἑστήκατε   verb, perf. act. indic. 2 pers. pl.
    {5.A.1} . . . . id.
ἔστηκε   verb, perf. act. indic. 3 pers. sg. {5.A.1} . id.
ἔστηκεν   verb, impf. act. indic. 3 pers. sg.
    {5.A.1.b} . . . . στήκω G4739
ἕστηκεν   verb, perf. act. indic. 3 pers. sg.
    {5.A.1} . . . . ἵστημι G2476
ἑστήκεσαν   verb, plu. act. indic. 3 pers. pl.
    {5.A.1} . . . . id.
ἑστηκός   vbl., perf. act. ptc. acc. sg. neut. {6.A.3} id.
ἑστηκός   vbl., perf. act. ptc. nom. sg. neut.
    {6.A.3} . . . . id.
ἑστηκότα   vbl., perf. act. ptc. acc. sg. masc.
    {6.A.3} . . . . id.
ἑστηκότες   vbl., perf. act. ptc. nom. pl. masc.
    {6.A.3} . . . . id.
ἑστηκότων   vbl., perf. act. ptc. gen. pl. masc.
    {6.A.3} . . . . id.

ἑστηκώς   vbl., perf. act. ptc. nom. sg. masc.
    {6.A.3} . . . . id.
ἐστηριγμένους   vbl., perf. pass. ptc. acc. pl. masc.
    {6.A.1.b} . . . . στηρίζω G4741
ἐστήρικται   verb, perf. pass. indic. 3 pers. sg.
    {5.A.1.f} . . . . id.
ἐστήριξε   verb, aor. act. indic. 3 pers. sg.
    {5.A.1.b} . . . . id.
ἐστήριξεν   verb, aor. act. indic. 3 pers. sg.
    {5.A.1.b} . . . . id.
ἐστήρισεν   verb, aor. act. indic. 3 pers. sg.
    {5.A.1.b} . . . . id.
ἔστησαν   verb, aor. act. indic. 3 pers. pl.
    {5.A.3.b} . . . . ἵστημι G2476
ἔστησεν   verb, aor. act. indic. 3 pers. sg.
    {5.A.3.b} . . . . id.
ἐστι   verb, pres. indic. 3 pers. sg. {7.A} . . . . . . εἰμί G1510
ἐστί   verb, pres. indic. 3 pers. sg. {7.A} . . . . id.
ἔστι   verb, pres. indic. 3 pers. sg. {7.A} . . . . id.
ἐστιν   verb, pres. indic. 3 pers. sg. {7.A} . . . . . εἰμί G1510
ἐστίν   verb, pres. indic. 3 pers. sg. {7.A} . . . . id.
ἔστιν   verb, pres. indic. 3 pers. sg. {7.A} . . . . id.
ἑστός   vbl., ²perf. act. ptc. acc. sg. neut.
    {6.A.3} . . . . ἵστημι G2476
ἑστός   vbl., ²perf. act. ptc. nom. sg. neut. {6.A.3}. id.
ἐστράφη   verb, ²aor. pass. indic. 3 pers. sg.
    {5.A.1.e} . . . . στρέφω G4762
ἐστράφησαν   verb, ²aor. pass. indic. 3 pers. pl.
    {5.A.1.e} . . . . id.
ἔστρεψε   verb, aor. act. indic. 3 pers. sg.
    {5.A.1.b} . . . . id.
ἔστρεψεν   verb, aor. act. indic. 3 pers. sg.
    {5.A.1.b} . . . . id.
ἐστρηνίασε   verb, aor. act. indic. 3 pers. sg.
    {5.A.1} . . . . .στρηνιάω G4763
ἐστρηνίασεν   verb, aor. act. indic. 3 pers. sg.
    {5.A.1} . . . . id.
ἐστρωμένον   vbl., perf. pass. ptc. acc. sg. neut.
    {6.A.3} . . . . στρώννυμι G4766
ἐστρώννυον   verb, impf. act. indic. 3 pers. pl.
    {5.A.3.a} . . . . id.
ἔστρωσαν   verb, aor. act. indic. 3 pers. pl.
    {5.A.3.b} . . . . id.
ἔστω   verb, pres. impv. 3 pers. sg. {7.B} . . . . . . εἰμί G1510
ἑστώς   vbl., ²perf. act. ptc. nom. sg. masc.
    {6.A.3} . . . . ἵστημι G2476
ἑστῶσα   vbl., ²perf. act. ptc. nom. sg. fem.
    {6.A.3} . . . . id.
ἑστῶσαι   vbl., ²perf. act. ptc. nom. pl. fem.
    {6.A.3} . . . . id.
ἔστωσαν   verb, pres. impv. 3 pers. pl. {7.B} . . . εἰμί G1510
ἑστῶτα   vbl., ²perf. act. ptc. acc. pl. neut.
    {6.A.3} . . . . ἵστημι G2476
ἑστῶτα   vbl., ²perf. act. ptc. acc. sg. masc. {6.A.3}id.
ἑστῶτας   vbl., ²perf. act. ptc. acc. pl. masc.
    {6.A.3} . . . . id.
ἑστῶτες   vbl., ²perf. act. ptc. nom. pl. masc.
    {6.A.3} . . . . id.
ἑστῶτος   vbl., ²perf. act. ptc. gen. sg. masc.
    {6.A.3} . . . . id.

ἑστώτων   vbl., ²perf. act. ptc. gen. pl. masc.
{6.A.3} . . . . id.
ἐσυκοφάντησα   verb, aor. act. indic. 1 pers. sg.
{5.A.1} . . . . .συκοφαντέω *G4811*
ἐσύλησα   verb, aor. act. indic. 1 pers. sg.
{5.A.1} . . . . .συλάω *G4813*
ἔσυραν   verb, aor. act. indic. 3 pers. pl.
{5.A.1.b} . . . . .σύρω *G4951*
ἔσυρον   verb, impf. act. indic. 3 pers. pl. {5.A.1.b} . id.
ἐσφάγης   verb, ²aor. pass. indic. 2 pers. sg.
{5.A.1.e} . . . . .σφάζω *G4969*
ἐσφαγμένην   vbl., perf. pass. ptc. acc. sg. fem.
{6.A.1.b} . . . . id.
ἐσφαγμένον   vbl., perf. pass. ptc. acc. sg. neut.
{6.A.1.b} . . . . id.
ἐσφαγμένον   vbl., perf. pass. ptc. nom. sg. neut.
{6.A.1.b} . . . . id.
ἐσφαγμένου   vbl., perf. pass. ptc. gen. sg. neut.
{6.A.1.b} . . . . id.
ἐσφαγμένων   vbl., perf. pass. ptc. gen. pl. masc.
{6.A.1.b} . . . . id.
ἔσφαξε   verb, aor. act. indic. 3 pers. sg. {5.A.1.b} id.
ἔσφαξεν   verb, aor. act. indic. 3 pers. sg.
{5.A.1.b} . . . . id.
ἐσφράγισεν   verb, aor. act. indic. 3 pers. sg.
{5.A.1.b} . . . . σφραγίζω *G4972*
ἐσφραγίσθητε   verb, aor. pass. indic. 2 pers. pl.
{5.A.1.b} . . . . id.
ἐσφραγισμέναι   vbl., perf. pass. ptc. nom. pl.
fem. {6.A.1.b} . . . . id.
ἐσφραγισμένοι   vbl., perf. pass. ptc. nom. pl.
masc. {6.A.1.b} . . . . id.
ἐσφραγισμένων   vbl., perf. pass. ptc. gen. pl.
masc. {6.A.1.b} . . . . id.
ἔσχατα   adj., acc. pl. neut. {3.A} . . . . ἔσχατος *G2078*
ἔσχατα   adj., nom. pl. neut. {3.A} . . . . id.
ἐσχάταις   adj., dat. pl. fem. {3.A} . . . . id.
ἐσχάτας   adj., acc. pl. fem. {3.A} . . . . id.
ἐσχάτη   adj., nom. sg. fem. {3.A} . . . . id.
ἐσχάτη   adj., dat. sg. fem. {3.A} . . . . id.
ἔσχατοι   adj., nom. pl. masc. {3.A} . . . . id.
ἔσχατον   adj., acc. sg. masc. {3.A} . . . . id.
ἔσχατον   adj., acc. sg. neut. {3.A} . . . . id.
G2078 **ἔσχατος**, -η, -ον   *last;* ἔσχατον, neut. acc. as
adv., *at the last, finally;* ἐπ᾽ ἐσχάτου, *at the
end;* ἕως ἐσχάτου, *till the end.*
ἔσχατος   adj., nom. sg. masc. {3.A} . . . . . ἔσχατος *G2078*
ἐσχάτου   adj., gen. sg. masc. {3.A} . . . . id.
ἐσχάτου   adj., gen. sg. neut. {3.A} . . . . id.
ἐσχάτους   adj., acc. pl. masc. {3.A} . . . . id.
ἐσχάτῳ   adj., dat. sg. masc. {3.A} . . . . id.
ἐσχάτων   adj., gen. pl. fem. {3.A} . . . . id.
ἐσχάτων   adj., gen. pl. masc. {3.A} . . . . id.
G2079 **ἐσχάτως**   adv., ἐσχάτως ἔχειν, *to be at the
extremity, to be "in extremis," to be at the last
gasp.*
ἐσχάτως   adv. {3.F} . . . . ἐσχάτως *G2079*
ἔσχε   verb, ²aor. act. indic. 3 pers. sg. {5.A.1.b} . ἔχω *G2192*
ἔσχεν   verb, ²aor. act. indic. 3 pers. sg. {5.A.1.b} . id.
ἔσχες   verb, ²aor. act. indic. 2 pers. sg. {5.A.1.b} . id.

ἔσχηκα   verb, perf. act. indic. 1 pers. sg.
{5.A.1.c} . . . . id.
ἐσχήκαμεν   verb, perf. act. indic. 1 pers. pl.
{5.A.1.c} . . . . id.
ἔσχηκεν   verb, perf. act. indic. 3 pers. sg.
{5.A.1.c} . . . . id.
ἐσχηκότα   vbl., perf. act. ptc. acc. sg. masc.
{6.A.1.a} . . . . id.
ἐσχίσθη   verb, aor. pass. indic. 3 pers. sg.
{5.A.1.b} . . . . .σχίζω *G4977*
ἐσχίσθησαν   verb, aor. pass. indic. 3 pers. pl.
{5.A.1.b} . . . . id.
ἔσχομεν   verb, ²aor. act. indic. 1 pers. pl.
{5.A.1.b} . . . . .ἔχω *G2192*
ἔσχον   verb, ²aor. act. indic. 1 pers. sg. {5.A.1.b} . id.
ἔσχον   verb, ²aor. act. indic. 3 pers. pl. {5.A.1.b} . id.
G2080 **ἔσω**   adv., *within, inside,* with verbs either of
rest or of motion; ὁ ἔσω ἄνθρωπος, *that part
of man which is spiritual;* οἱ ἔσω, *those within*
(the church), *members of the church,* 1 Cor
5:12; prep. with gen., *within, to within, inside,*
Mark 15:16.
ἔσω   adv. . . . . ἔσω *G2080*
ἐσώζοντο   verb, impf. pass. indic. 3 pers. pl.
{5.A.1.e} . . . . .σῴζω *G4982*
ἐσῴζοντο   verb, impf. pass. indic. 3 pers. pl.
{5.A.1.e} . . . . id.
G2081 **ἔσωθεν**   adv. (1) *from within, from inside;* (2)
within, inside; τὸ ἔσωθεν, *the inner part, the
inner element.*
ἔσωθεν   adv. . . . . ἔσωθεν *G2081*
ἐσώθη   verb, aor. pass. indic. 3 pers. sg.
{5.A.1.b} . . . . .σῴζω *G4982*
ἐσώθημεν   verb, aor. pass. indic. 1 pers. pl.
{5.A.1.b} . . . . id.
ἔσωσε   verb, aor. act. indic. 3 pers. sg. {5.A.1.b} . id.
ἔσωσεν   verb, aor. act. indic. 3 pers. sg. {5.A.1.b} id.
ἐσωτέραν   adj. comp., acc. sg. fem. {3.A;
3.G} . . . . ἐσώτερος *G2082*
ἐσώτερον   adj. comp., acc. sg. neut. {3.A; 3.G} . . id.
G2082 **ἐσώτερος**, -α, -ον   *inner;* τὸ ἐσώτερον, *the
part that is within,* with gen.
ἑταῖρε   noun, voc. sg. masc. {2.B} . . . . . . ἑταῖρος *G2083*
ἑταίροις   noun, dat. pl. masc. {2.B} . . . . id.
G2083 **ἑταῖρος**, -ου, ὁ   *companion, comrade.*
ἔταξαν   verb, aor. act. indic. 3 pers. pl.
{5.A.1.b} . . . . .τάσσω *G5021*
ἐτάξατο   verb, aor. mid. indic. 3 pers. sg.
{5.A.1.e} . . . . id.
ἐταπείνωσεν   verb, aor. act. indic. 3 pers. sg.
{5.A.1} . . . . ταπεινόω *G5013*
ἐτάραξαν   verb, aor. act. indic. 3 pers. pl.
{5.A.1.b} . . . . ταράσσω *G5015*
ἐτάραξεν   verb, aor. act. indic. 3 pers. sg. {5.A.1.b} id.
ἐτάρασσε   verb, impf. act. indic. 3 pers. sg.
{5.A.1.b} . . . . id.
ἐτάρασσεν   verb, impf. act. indic. 3 pers. sg.
{5.A.1.b} . . . . id.
ἐταράσσετο   verb, impf. mid./pass. indic.
3 pers. sg. {5.A.1.e} . . . . id.

ἐταράχθη   verb, aor. pass. indic. 3 pers. sg.
{5.A.1.b} . . . . id.
ἐταράχθησαν   verb, aor. pass. indic. 3 pers. pl.
{5.A.1.b} . . . . id.
ἐτάφη   verb, ²aor. pass. indic. 3 pers. sg.
{5.A.1.e} . . . . θάπτω G2290
ἐτέθη   verb, aor. pass. indic. 3 pers. sg.
{5.A.1} . . . . τίθημι G5087
ἐτέθην   verb, aor. pass. indic. 1 pers. sg. {5.A.1} . id.
ἐτέθησαν   verb, aor. pass. indic. 3 pers. pl.
{5.A.1} . . . . id.
ἐτεθνήκει   verb, plu. act. indic. 3 pers. sg.
{5.A.1.b} . . . . .θνῄσκω G2348
ἔτει   noun, dat. sg. neut. {2.C} . . . . .ἔτος G2094
ἔτεκε   verb, ²aor. act. indic. 3 pers. sg.
{5.A.1.b} . . . . .τίκτω G5088
ἔτεκεν   verb, ²aor. act. indic. 3 pers. sg. {5.A.1.b}. id.
ἐτεκνοτρόφησεν   verb, aor. act. indic. 3 pers. sg.
{5.A.1} . . . . τεκνοτροφέω G5044
ἐτελειώθη   verb, aor. pass. indic. 3 pers. sg.
{5.A.1} . . . . .τελειόω G5048
ἐτελείωσα   verb, aor. act. indic. 1 pers. sg.
{5.A.1} . . . . id.
ἐτελείωσεν   verb, aor. act. indic. 3 pers. sg.
{5.A.1} . . . . id.
ἐτέλεσαν   verb, aor. act. indic. 3 pers. pl.
{5.A.1} . . . . τελέω G5055
ἐτέλεσεν   verb, aor. act. indic. 3 pers. sg. {5.A.1} id.
ἐτελέσθη   verb, aor. pass. indic. 3 pers. sg.
{5.A.1} . . . . id.
ἐτελεύτησε   verb, aor. act. indic. 3 pers. sg.
{5.A.1} . . . . τελευτάω G5053
ἐτελεύτησεν   verb, aor. act. indic. 3 pers. sg.
{5.A.1} . . . . id.
ἕτερα   adj., acc. pl. neut. {3.A} . . . . .ἕτερος G2087
ἑτέρα   adj., nom. sg. fem. {3.A} . . . . id.
ἑτέρᾳ   adj., dat. sg. fem. {3.A} . . . . id.
ἕτεραι   adj., nom. pl. fem. {3.A} . . . . id.
ἑτέραις   adj., dat. pl. fem. {3.A} . . . . id.
ἑτέραν   adj., acc. sg. fem. {3.A} . . . . id.
ἑτέρας   adj., gen. sg. fem. {3.A} . . . . id.
ἑτερογλώσσοις   adj., dat. pl. masc.
{3.C} . . . . ἑτερόγλωσσος G2084
G2084   ἑτερόγλωσσος, -ον   speaking another language.
ἑτεροδιδασκαλεῖ   verb, pres. act. indic. 3 pers. sg.
{5.A.2} . . . . ἑτεροδιδασκαλέω G2085
ἑτεροδιδασκαλεῖν   vbl., pres. act. inf. {6.B.2} . . id.
G2085   ἑτεροδιδασκαλέω   I teach different things, i.e.,
different from the true or necessary teaching.
G2086   ἑτεροζυγέω   I am yoked with one different from
myself, unequally yoked.
ἑτεροζυγοῦντες   vbl., pres. act. ptc. nom. pl. masc.
{6.A.2} .ἑτεροζυγέω G2086
ἕτεροι   adj., nom. pl. masc. {3.A} . . . . ἕτερος G2087
ἑτέροις   adj., dat. pl. masc. {3.A} . . . . id.
ἑτέροις   adj., dat. pl. neut. {3.A} . . . . id.
ἕτερον   adj., acc. sg. masc. {3.A} . . . . id.
ἕτερον   adj., acc. sg. neut. {3.A} . . . . id.
ἕτερον   adj., nom. sg. neut. {3.A} . . . . id.

G2087   ἕτερος, -α, -ον   (1) of two, another, a second:
ἐν ἑτέρῳ (understand ψαλμῷ), Heb 5:6;
ὁ ἕτερος, the other, the second, τῇ ἑτέρᾳ
(understand ἡμέρᾳ), on the second day, Acts
20:15; 27:3; ἕτεροι, others, another group; (2)
sometimes it does not differ from ἄλλος, being
used of more than two, other, different, cf. Luke
8:6–8; 2 Cor 11:4; in Gal 1:6, 7 ἕτερος appears
to mean another of the same kind, as contrasted
with ἄλλος, another of a different kind.
ἕτερος   adj., nom. sg. masc. {3.A} . . . . .ἕτερος G2087
ἑτέρου   adj., gen. sg. masc. {3.A} . . . . id.
ἑτέρους   adj., acc. pl. masc. {3.A} . . . . id.
ἑτέρῳ   adj., dat. sg. masc. {3.A} . . . . id.
ἑτέρῳ   adj., dat. sg. neut. {3.A} . . . . id.
ἑτέρων   adj., gen. pl. masc. {3.A} . . . . id.
ἑτέρων   adj., gen. pl. neut. {3.A} . . . . id.
G2088   ἑτέρως   adv., differently.
ἑτέρως   adv. {3.F} . . . . .ἑτέρως G2088
ἔτεσι   noun, dat. pl. neut. {2.C} . . . . .ἔτος G2094
ἔτεσιν   noun, dat. pl. neut. {2.C} . . . . id.
ἐτέχθη   verb, aor. pass. indic. 3 pers. sg.
{5.A.1.b} . . . . .τίκτω G5088
ἔτη   noun, acc. pl. neut. {2.C} . . . . .ἔτος G2094
ἔτη   noun, nom. pl. neut. {2.C} . . . . id.
ἐτηρεῖτο   verb, impf. pass. indic. 3 pers. sg.
{5.A.2} . . . . τηρέω G5083
ἐτήρησα   verb, aor. act. indic. 1 pers. sg. {5.A.1} id.
ἐτήρησαν   verb, aor. act. indic. 3 pers. pl.
{5.A.1} . . . . id.
ἐτήρησας   verb, aor. act. indic. 2 pers. sg. {5.A.1}id.
ἐτήρουν   verb, impf. act. indic. 1 pers. sg. {5.A.2}id.
ἐτήρουν   verb, impf. act. indic. 3 pers. pl. {5.A.2}id.
G2089   ἔτι   adv. (1) of time, still, yet; even now; οὐκ ἔτι,
no longer, and similarly with other negatives;
(2) of degree, even; further, more, in addition.
ἔτι   adv. . . . . ἔτι G2089
ἐτίθει   verb, impf. act. indic. 3 pers. sg.
{5.A.3.a} . . . . τίθημι G5087
ἐτίθεσαν   verb, impf. act. indic. 3 pers. pl.
{5.A.3.a} . . . . id.
ἐτίθουν   verb, impf. act. indic. 3 pers. pl.
{5.A.3.a} . . . . id.
ἔτιλλον   verb, impf. act. indic. 3 pers. pl.
{5.A.1.b} . . . . .τίλλω G5089
ἐτίμησαν   verb, aor. act. indic. 3 pers. pl.
{5.A.1} . . . . τιμάω G5091
ἐτιμήσαντο   verb, aor. mid. indic. 3 pers. pl.
{5.A.1} . . . . id.
ἕτοιμα   adj., acc. pl. neut. {3.A} . . . . .ἕτοιμος G2092
ἕτοιμα   adj., nom. pl. neut. {3.A} . . . . id.
ἑτοίμαζε   verb, pres. act. impv. 2 pers. sg.
{5.D.1} . . . . ἑτοιμάζω G2090
G2090   ἑτοιμάζω   I make ready, prepare.
ἑτοιμάσαι   vbl., aor. act. inf. {6.B.1} . . . . ἑτοιμάζω G2090
ἑτοιμάσας   vbl., aor. act. ptc. nom. sg. masc.
{6.A.1.a} . . . . id.
ἑτοιμάσατε   verb, aor. act. impv. 2 pers. pl.
{5.D.1} . . . . id.

ἑτοιμασθῇ   verb, aor. pass. subjunc. 3 pers. sg.
  {5.B.1} . . . . id.
G2091 **ἑτοιμασία**, -ας, ἡ   *readiness* (of bearer of good
   tidings; in LXX, *a stand, base*).
ἑτοιμασία   noun, dat. sg. fem. {2.A} . . . ἑτοιμασία G2091
ἑτοιμάσομεν   verb, fut. act. indic. 1 pers. pl.
  {5.A.1.a} . . . . ἑτοιμάζω G2090
ἑτοίμασον   verb, aor. act. impv. 2 pers. sg.
  {5.D.1} . . . . id.
ἑτοιμάσω   verb, aor. act. subjunc. 1 pers. sg.
  {5.B.1} . . . . id.
ἑτοιμάσω   verb, fut. act. indic. 1 pers. sg.
  {5.A.1.a} . . . . id.
ἑτοιμάσωμεν   verb, aor. act. subjunc. 1 pers. pl.
  {5.B.1} . . . . id.
ἑτοίμην   adj., acc. sg. fem. {3.A} . . . . ἕτοιμος G2092
ἕτοιμοι   adj., nom. pl. fem. {3.A} . . . . id.
ἕτοιμοι   adj., nom. pl. masc. {3.A} . . . . id.
ἕτοιμον   adj., acc. sg. neut. {3.A} . . . . id.
G2092 **ἕτοιμος**, -η, -ον   *ready, prepared;* ἐν ἑτοίμῳ
   ἔχοντες, *being ready,* 2 Cor 10:6, cf. ἑτοίμως.
ἕτοιμος   adj., nom. sg. masc. {3.A} . . . . . . ἕτοιμος G2092
ἑτοίμους   adj., acc. pl. masc. {3.A} . . . . id.
ἑτοίμῳ   adj., dat. sg. neut. {3.A} . . . . id.
G2093 **ἑτοίμως**   adv., *readily;* ἑτοίμως ἔχειν, *to be
   ready.*
ἑτοίμως   adv. {3.F} . . . . ἑτοίμως G2093
ἐτόλμα   verb, impf. act. indic. 3 pers. sg.
  {5.A.2} . . . . τολμάω G5111
ἐτόλμησε   verb, aor. act. indic. 3 pers. sg. {5.A.1} id.
ἐτόλμησεν   verb, aor. act. indic. 3 pers. sg.
  {5.A.1} . . . . id.
ἐτόλμων   verb, impf. act. indic. 3 pers. pl. {5.A.2} id.
G2094 **ἔτος**, -ους, τό   *a year;* κατ᾿ ἔτος (καθ᾿ ἔτος),
   annually; ἀπ᾿ or ἐξ ἐτῶν followed by a number *(for),* lit. *from . . . years.*
ἔτος   noun, acc. sg. neut. {2.C} . . . . ἔτος G2094
ἐτρέχετε   verb, impf. act. indic. 2 pers. pl.
  {5.A.1.b} . . . . τρέχω G5143
ἔτρεχον   verb, impf. act. indic. 3 pers. pl.
  {5.A.1.b} . . . . id.
ἐτροποφόρησεν   verb, aor. act. indic. 3 pers. sg.
  {5.A.1} . . . . τροποφορέω G5159
ἐτρύγησε   verb, aor. act. indic. 3 pers. sg.
  {5.A.1} . . . . τρυγάω G5166
ἐτρύγησεν   verb, aor. act. indic. 3 pers. sg.
  {5.A.1} . . . . id.
ἐτρυφήσατε   verb, aor. act. indic. 2 pers. pl.
  {5.A.1} . . . . τρυφάω G5171
ἐτύθη   verb, aor. pass. indic. 3 pers. sg.
  {5.A.1.b} . . . . θύω G2380
ἐτυμπανίσθησαν   verb, aor. pass. indic. 3 pers. pl.
  {5.A.1.b} . . . . τυμπανίζω G5178
ἔτυπτε   verb, impf. act. indic. 3 pers. sg.
  {5.A.1.b} . . . . τύπτω G5180
ἔτυπτεν   verb, impf. act. indic. 3 pers. sg.
  {5.A.1.b} . . . . id.
ἔτυπτον   verb, impf. act. indic. 3 pers. pl.
  {5.A.1.b} . . . . id.

ἐτύφλωσε   verb, aor. act. indic. 3 pers. sg.
  {5.A.1} . . . . τυφλόω G5186
ἐτύφλωσεν   verb, aor. act. indic. 3 pers. sg.
  {5.A.1} . . . . id.
ἐτῶν   noun, gen. pl. neut. {2.C} . . . . ἔτος G2094
G2095 **εὖ**   adv., *well;* as interj., *well done! bravo!*
εὖ   adv., interj. . . . . εὖ G2095
Εὔα   noun prop., nom. sg. fem. {2.A; 2.D} . . . . Εὔα G2096
G2096 **Εὔα**, -ας, ἡ   *Eve,* wife of Adam, the first man
   (Heb.).
Εὔα   noun prop., nom. sg. fem. {2.A; 2.D} . . . . Εὔα G2096
εὐαγγελίζεσθαι   vbl., pres. mid. inf.
  {6.B.1} . . . . εὐαγγελίζω G2097
εὐαγγελίζεται   verb, pres. mid. indic. 3 pers.
  sg. {5.A.1.d} . . . . id.
εὐαγγελίζεται   verb, pres. pass. indic. 3 pers.
  sg. {5.A.1.d} . . . . id.
εὐαγγελίζηται   verb, pres. mid. subjunc.
  3 pers. sg. {5.B.1} . . . . id.
εὐαγγελίζομαι   verb, pres. mid. indic. 1 pers.
  sg. {5.A.1.d} . . . . id.
εὐαγγελιζόμεθα   verb, pres. mid. indic. 1 pers.
  pl. {5.A.1.d} . . . . id.
εὐαγγελιζόμενοι   vbl., pres. mid. ptc. nom. pl.
  masc. {6.A.1} . . . . id.
εὐαγγελιζόμενος   vbl., pres. mid. ptc. nom. pl.
  masc. {6.A.1} . . . . id.
εὐαγγελιζομένου   vbl., pres. mid. ptc. gen. sg.
  masc. {6.A.1} . . . . id.
εὐαγγελιζομένῳ   vbl., pres. mid. ptc. dat. sg.
  masc. {6.A.1} . . . . id.
εὐαγγελιζομένων   vbl., pres. mid. ptc. gen. pl.
  masc. {6.A.1} . . . . id.
εὐαγγελίζονται   verb, pres. pass. indic. 3 pers.
  pl. {5.A.1.d} . . . . id.
G2097 εὐαγγελίζω   *I bring good news, I preach good
   tidings,* normally mid., with or without an obj.,
   expressing either the persons who receive the
   good news or the good news itself (the good
   news being sometimes expressed as a person,
   e.g., Acts 5:42).
εὐαγγελίζωμαι   verb, pres. mid. subjunc. 1 pers.
  sg. {5.B.1} . . . . εὐαγγελίζω G2097
G2098 **εὐαγγέλιον**, -ου, τό   *the good news* of the coming of the Messiah, *the gospel;* the gen. after it
   expresses some times the giver (God), sometimes the subj. (the Messiah, etc.), sometimes
   the human transmitter (an apostle).
εὐαγγέλιον   noun, acc. sg. neut. {2.B} . εὐαγγέλιον G2098
εὐαγγέλιον   noun, nom. sg. neut. {2.B} . . . . id.
εὐαγγελίου   noun, gen. sg. neut. {2.B} . . . . id.
εὐαγγελίσαι   vbl., aor. act. inf. {6.B.1} . εὐαγγελίζω G2097
εὐαγγελισάμενοι   vbl., aor. mid. ptc. nom. pl.
  masc. {6.A.1.b} . . . . id.
εὐαγγελισαμένου   vbl., aor. mid. ptc. gen. sg.
  masc. {6.A.1.b} . . . . id.
εὐαγγελισαμένων   vbl., aor. mid. ptc. gen. pl.
  masc. {6.A.1.b} . . . . id.
εὐαγγελίσασθαι   vbl., aor. mid. inf. {6.B.1} . . . . id.

εὐαγγελίσηται   verb, aor. mid. subjunc. 3 pers.
  sg. {5.B.1} . . . . id.
εὐαγγελισθέν   vbl., aor. pass. ptc. acc. sg. neut.
  {6.A.1.a} . . . . id.
εὐαγγελισθέν   vbl., aor. pass. ptc. nom. sg.
  neut. {6.A.1.a} . . . . id.
εὐαγγελισθέντες   vbl., aor. pass. ptc. nom. pl.
  masc. {6.A.1.a} . . . . id.
εὐαγγελιστάς   noun, acc. pl. masc.
  {2.A} . . . . εὐαγγελιστής G2099
G2099 **εὐαγγελιστής**, -οῦ, ὁ   *a missionary* (an occurrence on a pagan inscription = priest of
  Εὐάγγελος, i.e., of Ἑρμῆς, is found).
εὐαγγελιστοῦ   noun, gen. sg. masc.
  {2.A} . . . . εὐαγγελιστής G2099
εὐαγγελίσωμαι   verb, aor. mid. subjunc. 1 pers. sg.
  {5.B.1} . . . . εὐαγγελίζω G2097
εὐαγγελίῳ   noun, dat. sg. neut. {2.B} . . εὐαγγέλιον G2098
Εὖαν   noun prop., acc. sg. fem. {2.A; 2.D} . . . . Εὖα G2096
Εὖαν   noun prop., acc. sg. fem. {2.A; 2.D} . . . . . id.
εὐαρεστεῖται   verb, pres. pass. indic. 3 pers. sg.
  {5.A.2} . . . . εὐαρεστέω G2100
G2100 **εὐαρεστέω**   *I give pleasure to, I please* (perhaps
  with the added idea of *rendering good service
  to*, cf. ἀρέσκω).
εὐαρεστηκέναι   vbl., perf. act. inf. {6.B.1} εὐαρεστέω G2100
εὐαρεστῆσαι   vbl., aor. act. inf. {6.B.1} . . . . id.
εὐάρεστοι   adj., nom. pl. masc. {3.C} . . εὐάρεστος G2101
εὐάρεστον   adj., acc. sg. fem. {3.C} . . . . id.
εὐάρεστον   adj., acc. sg. neut. {3.C} . . . . id.
εὐάρεστον   adj., nom. sg. neut. {3.C} . . . . id.
G2101 **εὐάρεστος**, -ον   *well-pleasing* (esp. to God).
εὐάρεστος   adj., nom. sg. masc. {3.C} . εὐάρεστος G2101
εὐαρέστους   adj., acc. pl. masc. {3.C} . . . . id.
G2102 **εὐαρέστως**   adv., *in a well-pleasing way.*
εὐαρέστως   adv. {3.F} . . . . εὐαρέστως G2102
G2103 **Εὔβουλος**, -ου, ὁ   *Eubulus,* a Christian with
  Paul in Rome.
Εὔβουλος   noun prop., nom. sg. masc. {2.B;
  2.D} . . . . Εὔβουλος G2103
G2095†‡ **εὖγε**   interj., *well done! excellent!* Var. for εὖ,
  Luke 19:17.
εὖγε   adv. . . . . εὖγε G2095†‡
εὐγενεῖς   adj., nom. pl. masc. {3.E} . . . . . . εὐγενής G2104
εὐγενέστεροι   adj. comp., nom. pl. masc. {3.E;
  3.G} . . . . id.
G2104 **εὐγενής**, -ές   (1) *of noble birth, of high birth;* (2)
  noble in nature, Acts 17:11.
εὐγενής   adj., nom. sg. masc. {3.E} . . . . . . εὐγενής G2104
G2105 **εὐδία**, -ας, ἡ   *fair weather, good weather.*
εὐδία   noun, nom. sg. fem. {2.A} . . . . εὐδία G2105
εὐδοκεῖ   verb, pres. act. indic. 3 pers. sg.
  {5.A.2} . . . . εὐδοκέω G2106
G2106 **εὐδοκέω**   *I am well pleased,* with acc. expressing *with,* Matt 12:18, etc.; *I think it good, am
  resolved* (a characteristic word of Jewish Gk.).
εὐδόκησα   verb, aor. act. indic. 1 pers. sg.
  {5.A.1} . . . . εὐδοκέω G2106
εὐδοκήσαμεν   verb, aor. act. indic. 1 pers. pl.
  {5.A.1} . . . . id.

εὐδόκησαν   verb, aor. act. indic. 3 pers. pl.
  {5.A.1} . . . . id.
εὐδοκήσαντες   vbl., aor. act. ptc. nom. pl.
  masc. {6.A.2} . . . . id.
εὐδόκησας   verb, aor. act. indic. 2 pers. sg.
  {5.A.1} . . . . id.
εὐδόκησε   verb, aor. act. indic. 3 pers. sg. {5.A.1} id.
εὐδόκησεν   verb, aor. act. indic. 3 pers. sg.
  {5.A.1} . . . . id.
G2107 **εὐδοκία**, -ας, ἡ   (1) *goodwill* (*good pleasure*),
  favor, feeling of complacency of God to man;
  ἄνθρωποι εὐδοκίας (Hebraistic), *men with
  whom God is well pleased,* Luke 2:14; (2) *good
  pleasure, satisfaction, happiness, delight* of
  men, e.g., 2 Thess 1:11, though even in such
  passages there may be a latent reference to
  (divine) approval.
εὐδοκία   noun, nom. sg. fem. {2.A} . . . . . . εὐδοκία G2107
εὐδοκίαν   noun, acc. sg. fem. {2.A} . . . . id.
εὐδοκίας   noun, gen. sg. fem. {2.A} . . . . id.
εὐδοκοῦμεν   verb, impf. act. indic. 1 pers. pl.
  {5.A.2} . . . . εὐδοκέω G2106
εὐδοκοῦμεν   verb, pres. act. indic. 1 pers. pl.
  {5.A.2} . . . . id.
εὐδοκῶ   verb, pres. act. indic. 1 pers. sg. {5.A.2} . id.
G2108 **εὐεργεσία**, -ας, ἡ   *good action, well doing,
  benefiting, kind service.*
εὐεργεσίᾳ   noun, dat. sg. fem. {2.A} . . . . εὐεργεσία G2108
εὐεργεσίας   noun, gen. sg. fem. {2.A} . . . . id.
εὐεργέται   noun, nom. pl. masc. {2.A} . . εὐεργέτης G2110
G2109 **εὐεργετέω**   *I do good deeds, perform kind
  service, benefit.*
G2110 **εὐεργέτης**, -ου, ὁ   *Benefactor,* an honorary title
  of kings and governors.
εὐεργετῶν   vbl., pres. act. ptc. nom. sg. masc.
  {6.A.2} . . . . εὐεργετέω G2109
εὐηγγελίζετο   verb, impf. mid. indic. 3 pers. sg.
  {5.A.1.e} . . . . εὐαγγελίζω G2097
εὐηγγελίζοντο   verb, impf. mid. indic. 3 pers.
  pl. {5.A.1.e} . . . . id.
εὐηγγελισάμεθα   verb, aor. mid. indic. 1 pers.
  pl. {5.A.1.e} . . . . id.
εὐηγγελισάμην   verb, aor. mid. indic. 1 pers.
  sg. {5.A.1.e} . . . . id.
εὐηγγελίσαντο   verb, aor. mid. indic. 3 pers.
  pl. {5.A.1.e} . . . . id.
εὐηγγελίσατο   verb, aor. mid. indic. 3 pers. sg.
  {5.A.1.e} . . . . id.
εὐηγγέλισε   verb, aor. act. indic. 3 pers. sg.
  {5.A.1.b} . . . . id.
εὐηγγέλισεν   verb, aor. act. indic. 3 pers. sg.
  {5.A.1.b} . . . . id.
εὐηγγελίσθη   verb, aor. pass. indic. 3 pers. sg.
  {5.A.1.b} . . . . id.
εὐηγγελισμένοι   vbl., perf. pass. ptc. nom. pl.
  masc. {6.A.1.b} . . . . id.
εὐηρεστηκέναι   vbl., perf. act. inf.
  {6.B.1} . . . . εὐαρεστέω G2100
εὐθεῖα   adj., nom. sg. fem. {3.D} . . . . εὐθύς G2117
εὐθεῖαν   adj., acc. sg. fem. {3.D} . . . . id.

εὐθεῖαν   adj., acc. sg. fem. {3.D} . . . . id.
εὐθείας   adj., acc. pl. fem. {3.D} . . . . id.
εὔθετον   adj., acc. sg. fem. {3.C} . . . . εὔθετος G2111
εὔθετον   adj., nom. sg. neut. {3.C} . . . . id.
G2111 **εὔθετος**, -ον   *fitted, suitable;* absol. Heb 6:7.
εὔθετος   adj., nom. sg. masc. {3.C} . . . . . . εὔθετος G2111
G2112 **εὐθέως**   adv., *immediately.* Var. adv. εὐθύς.
εὐθέως   adv. εὐθέως G2112
G2113 **εὐθυδρομέω**   *I run a straight course.*
εὐθυδρομήσαμεν   verb, aor. act. indic. 1 pers. pl.
    {5.A.1} . . . . εὐθυδρομέω G2113
εὐθυδρομήσαντες   vbl., aor. act. ptc. nom. pl.
    masc. {6.A.2} . . . . id.
εὐθυμεῖ   verb, pres. act. indic. 3 pers. sg.
    {5.A.2} . . . . εὐθυμέω G2114
εὐθυμεῖν   vbl., pres. act. inf. {6.B.2} . . . . id.
εὐθυμεῖτε   verb, pres. act. impv. 2 pers. pl.
    {5.D.2} . . . . id.
G2114 **εὐθυμέω**   *I keep up spirit, am of good courage.*
εὔθυμοι   adj., nom. pl. masc. {3.C} . . . . . εὔθυμος G2115
G2115 **εὔθυμος**, -ον   *in good spirits.* Comp. adv.
    εὐθυμότερον, *most cheerfully.*
G2115† **εὐθύμως**   adv., *with good courage.* Var. for
    εὔθυμος, Acts 24:10.
εὐθυμότερον   adv. comp. {3.G; 3.F} . . . . εὔθυμος G2115
εὐθύμως   adv. {3.F} . . . . εὐθύμως G2115†
εὐθύνατε   verb, aor. act. impv. 2 pers. pl.
    {5.D.1} . . . . εὐθύνω G2116
εὐθύνοντος   vbl., pres. act. ptc. gen. sg. masc.
    {6.A.1} . . . . id.
G2116 **εὐθύνω**   (1) *I make straight* (of the direction,
    not the surface, of a road); (2) *I steer,* Jas 3:4.
G2117 **εὐθύς**, -εῖα, -ύ gen. -έως   (1) *straight,* of direc-
    tion, as opposed to crooked (σκολιός); (2)
    met. *upright.*
G2112†‡ **εὐθύς**   adv., *immediately.* Var. for εὐθέως.
εὐθύς   adj., nom. sg. masc. {3.D} . . . . εὐθύς G2117
εὐθύς   adv. εὐθύς G2112†‡
G2118 **εὐθύτης**, -ητος, ἡ   *straightness, uprightness.*
εὐθύτητος   noun, gen. sg. fem. {2.C} . . . . εὐθύτης G2118
G2119 **εὐκαιρέω**   *I have a good (favorable) opportu-
    nity, I have leisure.*
εὐκαιρήσῃ   verb, aor. act. subjunc. 3 pers. sg.
    {5.B.1} . . . . εὐκαιρέω G2119
G2120 **εὐκαιρία**, -ας, ἡ   *a good opportunity, an
    opportunity.*
εὐκαιρίαν   noun, acc. sg. fem. {2.A} . . . . εὐκαιρία G2120
εὔκαιρον   adj., acc. sg. fem. {3.C} . . . . εὔκαιρος G2121
G2121 **εὔκαιρος**, -ον   *opportune, timely, suitable;* in
    Mark 6:21 per haps = *empty, holiday, festal.*
εὐκαίρου   adj., gen. sg. fem. {3.C} . . . . εὔκαιρος G2121
εὐκαίρουν   verb, impf. act. indic. 3 pers. pl.
    {5.A.2} . . . . εὐκαιρέω G2119
G2122 **εὐκαίρως**   adv., *opportunely, in season,
    conveniently.*
εὐκαίρως   adv. {3.F} . . . . εὐκαίρως G2122
G2123 **εὔκοπος**, -η, -ον   *easy;* εὐκοπώτερόν ἐστιν, *it
    is easier.*
εὐκοπώτερον   adj. comp., nom. sg. neut. {3.C;
    3.G} . . . . εὔκοπος G2123

G2124 **εὐλάβεια**, -ας, ἡ   *caution, care;* then *anxiety,
    fear* (in a good sense); then almost *piety.*
εὐλαβείας   noun, gen. sg. fem. {2.A} . . . εὐλάβεια G2124
εὐλαβεῖς   adj., nom. pl. masc. {3.E} . . . . . εὐλαβής G2126
G2125 **εὐλαβέομαι**   *I am anxious,* περί, *about,* cf.
    εὐλάβεια).
εὐλαβηθείς   vbl., aor. pass. ptc. nom. sg. masc.
    {6.A.1.a.} . . . . εὐλαβέομαι G2125
G2126 **εὐλαβής**, -ές   (lit. *handling well*), hence, *cau-
    tious, circumspect;* hence, *God-fearing, pious.*
εὐλαβής   adj., nom. sg. masc. {3.E} . . . . . εὐλαβής G2126
εὐλόγει   verb, impf. act. indic. 3 pers. sg.
    {5.A.2} . . . . εὐλογέω G2127
εὐλογεῖν   vbl., pres. act. inf. {6.B.2} . . . . id.
εὐλογεῖται   verb, pres. pass. indic. 3 pers. sg.
    {5.A.2} . . . . id.
εὐλογεῖτε   verb, pres. act. impv. 2 pers. pl.
    {5.D.2} . . . . id.
G2127 **εὐλογέω**   *I bless* (lit. *I speak well of,* opp. *I abuse,
    curse*); εὐλογημένος, of a man, *blessed* (by
    God; contrast εὐλογητός); εὐλογῶν (or
    ἐν εὐλογίᾳ) εὐλογῶ (Hebraistic), *I bless
    abundantly.*
εὐλογηθήσονται   verb, fut. pass. indic. 3 pers. pl.
    {5.A.1} . . . . εὐλογέω G2127
εὐλόγηκε   verb, perf. act. indic. 3 pers. sg.
    {5.A.1} . . . . id.
εὐλόγηκεν   verb, perf. act. indic. 3 pers. sg.
    {5.A.1} . . . . id.
εὐλογημένη   vbl., perf. pass. ptc. nom. sg. fem.
    {6.A.2} . . . . id.
εὐλογημένοι   vbl., perf. pass. ptc. nom. pl.
    masc. {6.A.2} . . . . id.
εὐλογημένος   vbl., perf. pass. ptc. nom. sg.
    masc. {6.A.2} . . . . id.
εὐλογῇς   verb, pres. act. subjunc. 2 pers. sg.
    {5.B.2} . . . . id.
εὐλογήσας   vbl., aor. act. ptc. nom. sg. masc.
    {6.A.2} . . . . id.
εὐλόγησε   verb, aor. act. indic. 3 pers. sg. {5.A.1} id.
εὐλόγησεν   verb, aor. act. indic. 3 pers. sg.
    {5.A.1} . . . . id.
εὐλογήσῃς   verb, aor. act. subjunc. 2 pers. sg.
    {5.B.1} . . . . id.
εὐλογήσω   verb, fut. act. indic. 1 pers. sg. {5.A.1} id.
G2128 **εὐλογητός**, -ή, -όν   *blessed* (used only of God,
    as entitled to receive blessing from man).
εὐλογητός   adj., nom. sg. masc. {3.C} . . . εὐλογητός G2128
εὐλογητοῦ   adj., gen. sg. masc. {3.C} . . . . id.
G2129 **εὐλογία**, -ας, ἡ   *blessing.*
εὐλογία   noun, dat. sg. fem. {2.A} . . . . . . εὐλογία G2129
εὐλογία   noun, nom. sg. fem. {2.A} . . . . id.
εὐλογίᾳ   noun, dat. sg. fem. {2.A} . . . . id.
εὐλογίαις   noun, dat. pl. fem. {2.A} . . . . id.
εὐλογίαν   noun, acc. sg. fem. {2.A} . . . . id.
εὐλογίας   noun, gen. sg. fem. {2.A} . . . . id.
εὐλογοῦμεν   verb, pres. act. indic. 1 pers. pl.
    {5.A.2} . . . . εὐλογέω G2127
εὐλογοῦντα   vbl., pres. act. ptc. acc. sg. masc.
    {6.A.2} . . . . id.

εὐλογοῦνται   verb, pres. pass. indic. 3 pers. pl.
{5.A.2}. . . . . id.
εὐλογοῦντες   vbl., pres. act. ptc. nom. pl. masc.
{6.A.2}. . . . . id.
εὐλογῶν   vbl., pres. act. ptc. nom. sg. masc. {6.A.2} id.
G2130 **εὐμετάδοτος**, -ον   willingly sharing, ready to
impart.
εὐμεταδότους   adj., acc. pl. masc.
{3.C}. .εὐμετάδοτος G2130
G2131 **Εὐνίκη**, -ης, ἡ   Eunice, mother of Timothy.
Εὐνίκη   noun prop., dat. sg. fem. {2.A; 2.D} Εὐνίκη G2131
G2132 **εὐνοέω**   I have goodwill.
G2133 **εὔνοια**, -ας, ἡ   goodwill.
εὔνοιαν   noun, acc. sg. fem. {2.A}. . . . . . .εὔνοια G2133
εὐνοίας   noun, gen. sg. fem. {2.A}. . . . . id.
G2134 **εὐνουχίζω**   I make into a eunuch, emasculate,
castrate.
εὐνούχισαν   verb, aor. act. indic. 3 pers. pl.
{5.A.1.b}. εὐνουχίζω G2134
εὐνουχίσθησαν   verb, aor. pass. indic. 3 pers.
pl. {5.A.1.b}. . . . . id.
εὐνοῦχοι   noun, nom. pl. masc. {2.B}. . . εὐνοῦχος G2135
G2135 **εὐνοῦχος**, -ου, ὁ   (1) a chamberlain, keeper of
the bedchamber of an Eastern potentate, eunuch, Acts 8; (2) hence, as such were castrated,
a eunuch, a castrated person.
εὐνοῦχος   noun, nom. sg. masc. {2.B}. . εὐνοῦχος G2135
εὐνοῶν   vbl., pres. act. ptc. nom. sg. masc.
{6.A.2}. . . . . εὐνοέω G2132
εὐξαίμην   verb, aor. mid. opt. 1 pers. sg.
{5.C.1}. . . . . εὔχομαι G2172
G2136 **Εὐοδία**, -ας, ἡ   Euodia, Evodia, or rather Euho-
dia, a Christian woman of Philippi.
Εὐοδίαν   noun prop., acc. sg. fem. {2.A;
2.D}. . . . . Εὐοδία G2136
εὐοδοῦσθαι   vbl., pres. pass. inf. {6.B.2}. . . εὐοδόω G2137
εὐοδοῦται   verb, pres. pass. indic. 3 pers. sg.
{5.A.2}. . . . . id.
G2137 **εὐοδόω**   pass. I have a happy (successful)
journey; hence, I prosper, succeed, with the acc.
in 1 Cor 16:2 expressing the concrete sign of
prosperity.
εὐοδωθήσομαι   verb, fut. pass. indic. 1 pers. sg.
{5.A.1}. . . . . εὐοδόω G2137
εὐοδῶται   verb, pres. pass. subjunc. 3 pers. sg.
{5.B.2}. . . . . id.
εὐπάρεδρον   adj., acc. sg. neut. {3.C}εὐπάρεδρος G2145†‡
G2145†‡ **εὐπάρεδρος**, -ον   constant in service. Var. for
εὐπρόσεδρος, 1 Cor 7:35.
G2138 **εὐπειθής**, -ές, gen. οὖς   compliant.
εὐπειθής   adj., nom. sg. fem. {3.E}. . . . . .εὐπειθής G2138
εὐπερίστατον   adj., acc. sg. fem.
{3.C}. . . . . .εὐπερίστατος G2139
G2139 **εὐπερίστατος**, -ον   easily surrounding, easily
encircling.
G2140 **εὐποιΐα**, -ας, ἡ   good doing, doing of good.
εὐποιΐας   noun, gen. sg. fem. {2.A}. . . . . .εὐποιΐα G2140
εὐποιῖας   noun, gen. sg. fem. {2.A}. . . . . id.
εὐπορεῖτο   verb, impf. mid. indic. 3 pers. sg.
{5.A.2}. . . . . εὐπορέω G2141

G2141 **εὐπορέω**   mid. I am prosperous.
G2142 **εὐπορία**, -ας, ἡ   wealth, gain.
εὐπορία   noun, nom. sg. fem. {2.A}. . . . . εὐπορία G2142
G2143 **εὐπρέπεια**, -ας, ἡ   glory (with a notion of state-
liness or majesty).
εὐπρέπεια   noun, nom. sg. fem. {2.A}. .εὐπρέπεια G2143
G2144 **εὐπρόσδεκτος**, -ον   well-received, acceptable,
welcome.
εὐπρόσδεκτος   adj., nom. sg. fem.
{3.C}. . . . . εὐπρόσδεκτος G2144
εὐπρόσδεκτος   adj., nom. sg. masc. {3.C}. . . . . id.
εὐπροσδέκτους   adj., acc. pl. fem. {3.C}. . . . . . id.
εὐπρόσεδρον   adj., acc. sg. neut.
{3.C}. . . . . εὐπρόσεδρος G2145
G2145 **εὐπρόσεδρος**   constant in service.
G2146 **εὐπροσωπέω**   I look well, I make a fair show
(a good outward appearance, and so win good
opinion).
εὐπροσωπῆσαι   vbl., aor. act. inf.
{6.B.1}. εὐπροσωπέω G2146
G2148†‡ **Εὐρακύλων**, -ονος, ὁ   Euraquilo, an east-
northeast wind. Var. for Εὐροκλύδων, Acts
27:14.
Εὐρακύλων   noun prop., nom. sg. masc. {2.C;
2.D}. . . . . Εὐρακύλων G2148†‡
εὕραμεν   verb, ²aor. act. indic. 1 pers. pl.
{5.A.1.b}. . . . . εὑρίσκω G2147
εὑράμενος   vbl., ²aor. mid. ptc. nom. sg. masc.
{6.A.1.b}. . . . . id.
εὗραν   verb, ²aor. act. indic. 3 pers. pl {5.A.1.b}. . id.
εὗρε   verb, ²aor. act. indic. 3 pers. sg. {5.A.1.b}. . id.
εὑρεθείς   vbl., aor. pass. ptc. nom. sg. masc.
{6.A.1.a}. . . . . id.
εὑρέθη   verb, aor. pass. indic. 3 pers. sg.
{5.A.1.b}. . . . . id.
εὑρεθῇ   verb, aor. pass. subjunc. 3 pers. sg.
{5.B.1}. . . . . id.
εὑρέθημεν   verb, aor. pass. indic. 1 pers. pl.
{5.A.1.b}. . . . . id.
εὑρέθην   verb, aor. pass. indic. 1 pers. sg.
{5.A.1.b}. . . . . id.
εὑρεθῆναι   vbl., aor. pass. inf. {6.B.1}. . . . . id.
εὑρέθησαν   verb, aor. pass. indic. 3 pers. pl.
{5.A.1.b}. . . . . id.
εὑρεθήσεται   verb, fut. pass. indic. 3 pers. sg.
{5.A.1.d}. . . . . id.
εὑρεθησόμεθα   verb, fut. pass. indic. 1 pers. pl.
{5.A.1.d}. . . . . id.
εὑρεθῆτε   verb, aor. pass. subjunc. 2 pers. pl.
{5.B.1}. . . . . id.
εὑρεθῶ   verb, aor. pass. subjunc. 1 pers. sg.
{5.B.1}. . . . . id.
εὑρεθῶσι   verb, aor. pass. subjunc. 3 pers. pl.
{5.B.1}. . . . . id.
εὑρεθῶσιν   verb, aor. pass. subjunc. 3 pers. pl.
{5.B.1}. . . . . id.
εὑρεῖν   vbl., ²aor. act. inf. {6.B.1}. . . . . id.
εὗρεν   verb, ²aor. act. indic. 3 pers. sg. {5.A.1.b}. . id.
εὗρες   verb, ²aor. act. indic. 2 pers. sg. {5.A.1.b}. . id.
εὕρη   verb, ²aor. act. subjunc. 3 pers. sg. {5.B.1}. . id.

εὕρηκα   verb, perf. act. indic. 1 pers. sg.
{5.A.1.c} . . . . id.
εὑρήκαμεν   verb, perf. act. indic. 1 pers. pl.
{5.A.1.c} . . . . id.
εὑρηκέναι   vbl., perf. act. inf. {6.B.1} . . . . id.
εὕρῃς   verb, ²aor. act. subjunc. 2 pers. sg. {5.B.1} id.
εὑρήσει   verb, fut. act. indic. 3 pers. sg. {5.A.1.a} id.
εὑρήσεις   verb, fut. act. indic. 2 pers. sg.
{5.A.1.a} . . . . id.
εὑρήσετε   verb, fut. act. indic. 2 pers. pl.
{5.A.1.a} . . . . id.
εὑρήσῃς   verb, aor. act. subjunc. 2 pers. sg. {5.B.1}. id.
εὑρήσομεν   verb, fut. act. indic. 1 pers. pl.
{5.A.1.a} . . . . id.
εὑρήσουσιν   verb, fut. act. indic. 3 pers. pl.
{5.A.1.a} . . . . id.
εὕρητε   verb, ²aor. act. subjunc. 2 pers. pl. {5.B.1}id.
εὑρίσκει   verb, pres. act. indic. 3 pers. sg.
{5.A.1.a} . . . . id.
εὑρίσκετο   verb, impf. pass. indic. 3 pers. sg.
{5.A.1.e} . . . . id.
εὑρισκόμεθα   verb, pres. pass. indic. 1 pers. pl.
{5.A.1.d} . . . . id.
εὑρίσκομεν   verb, pres. act. indic. 1 pers. pl.
{5.A.1.a} . . . . id.
εὑρίσκον   vbl., pres. act. ptc. nom. sg. neut.
{6.A.1} . . . . id.
εὕρισκον   verb, impf. act. indic. 3 pers. pl.
{5.A.1.b} . . . . id.
εὑρίσκον   vbl., pres. act. ptc. nom. sg. neut.
{6.A.1} . . . . id.
εὑρίσκοντες   vbl., pres. act. ptc. nom. pl. masc.
{6.A.1} . . . . id.
G2147 **εὑρίσκω**   *I find,* esp. after searching; but in Phil
3:9 possibly *I surprise.*
εὑρίσκω   verb, pres. act. indic. 1 pers. sg.
{5.A.1.a} . . . . εὑρίσκω G2147
εὕροιεν   verb, ²aor. act. opt. 3 pers. pl. {5.C.1} . . id.
G2148 **Εὐροκλύδων,** -ωνος, ὁ   *Euroclydon,* a southeast wind.
Εὐροκλύδων   noun prop., nom. sg. masc. {2.C;
2.D} . . . . Εὐροκλύδων G2148
εὕρομεν   verb, ²aor. act. indic. 1 pers. pl.
{5.A.1.b} . . . . εὑρίσκω G2147
εὗρον   verb, ²aor. act. indic. 1 pers. sg. {5.A.1.b}. id.
εὗρον   verb, ²aor. act. indic. 3 pers. pl. {5.A.1.b}. id.
εὑρόντες   vbl., ²aor. act. ptc. nom. pl. masc.
{6.A.1.a} . . . . id.
εὑροῦσα   vbl., ²aor. act. ptc. nom. sg. fem.
{6.A.1.a} . . . . id.
εὑροῦσαι   vbl., ²aor. act. ptc. nom. pl. fem.
{6.A.1.a} . . . . id.
G2149 **εὐρύχωρος,** -ον   *broad.*
εὐρύχωρος   adj., nom. sg. fem. {3.C} . . εὐρύχωρος G2149
εὕρω   verb, ²aor. act. subjunc. 1 pers. sg.
{5.B.1} . . . . εὑρίσκω G2147
εὕρωμεν   verb, ²aor. act. subjunc. 1 pers. pl.
{5.B.1} . . . . id.
εὑρών   vbl., ²aor. act. ptc. nom. sg. masc.
{6.A.1.a} . . . . id.

εὕρωσι   verb, ²aor. act. subjunc. 3 pers. pl.
{5.B.1} . . . . id.
εὕρωσιν   verb, ²aor. act. subjunc. 3 pers. pl.
{5.B.1} . . . . id.
G2150 **εὐσέβεια,** -ας, ἡ   *piety* (towards God),
godliness.
εὐσεβείᾳ   noun, dat. sg. fem. {2.A} . . . . .εὐσέβεια G2150
εὐσέβεια   noun, nom. sg. fem. {2.A} . . . . id.
εὐσεβείαις   noun, dat. pl. fem. {2.A} . . . . id.
εὐσέβειαν   noun, acc. sg. fem. {2.A} . . . . id.
εὐσεβείας   noun, gen. sg. fem. {2.A} . . . . id.
εὐσεβεῖν   vbl., pres. act. inf. {6.B.2} . . . . εὐσεβέω G2151
εὐσεβεῖς   adj., acc. pl. masc. {3.E} . . . . . εὐσεβής G2152
εὐσεβεῖτε   verb, pres. act. indic. 2 pers. pl.
{5.A.2} . . . . εὐσεβέω G2151
G2151 **εὐσεβέω**   *I am dutiful, pious;* with acc. pers. *to-*
wards one who has the right to it, man or God.
εὐσεβῆ   adj., acc. sg. masc. {3.E} . . . . εὐσεβής G2152
G2152 **εὐσεβής,** -ές   *pious, God fearing.*
εὐσεβής   adj., nom. sg. masc. {3.E} . . . . . . εὐσεβής G2152
G2153 **εὐσεβῶς**   adv., *piously.*
εὐσεβῶς   adv. {3.F} . . . . εὐσεβῶς G2153
εὔσημον   adj., acc. sg. masc. {3.C} . . . εὔσημος G2154
G2154 **εὔσημος,** -ον   *with clear meaning.*
εὔσπλαγχνοι   adj., nom. pl. masc.
{3.C} . . . . εὔσπλαγχνος G2155
G2155 **εὔσπλαγχνος,** -ον   *tender-hearted, merciful.*
εὐσχῆμον   adj., acc. sg. neut. {3.E} . . . .εὐσχήμων G2158
εὐσχήμονα   adj., nom. pl. neut. {3.E} . . . . id.
εὐσχήμονας   adj., acc. pl. fem. {3.E} . . . . id.
εὐσχήμονα   adj., acc. pl. masc. {3.E} . . . . id.
εὐσχημόνων   adj., gen. pl. fem. {3.E} . . . . id.
εὐσχημόνων   adj., gen. pl. masc. {3.E} . . . . id.
G2156 **εὐσχημόνως**   adv., *becomingly, decorously.*
εὐσχημόνως   adv. {3.F} . . . . .εὐσχημόνως G2156
G2157 **εὐσχημοσύνη,** -ης, ἡ   *comeliness.*
εὐσχημοσύνην   noun, acc. sg. fem.
{2.A} . . . . εὐσχημοσύνη G2157
G2158 **εὐσχήμων,** -ον gen. ονος   (1) *comely, seemly,*
decorous; (2) *of honorable position* (in society).
εὐσχήμων   adj., nom. sg. masc. {3.E} . . .εὐσχήμων G2158
G2159 **εὐτόνως**   adv., *vehemently, powerfully.*
εὐτόνως   adv. {3.F} . . . . εὐτόνως G2159
G2160 **εὐτραπελία,** -ας, ἡ   *versatility* (esp. of speech);
facetiousness, raillery.
εὐτραπελία   noun, nom. sg. fem.
{2.A} . . . . εὐτραπελία G2160
G2161 **Εὔτυχος,** -ου, ὁ   *Eutychus,* a young hearer of
Paul at Troas.
Εὔτυχος   noun prop., nom. sg. masc. {2.B;
2.D} . . . . Εὔτυχος G2161
εὔφημα   adj., nom. pl. neut. {3.C} . . . . . εὔφημος G2163
G2162 **εὐφημία,** -ας, ἡ   *good reputation.*
εὐφημίας   noun, gen. sg. fem. {2.A} . . . . εὐφημία G2162
G2163 **εὔφημος,** -ον   *well reported of.*
G2164 **εὐφορέω**   *I bear well, I bring a good harvest.*
εὐφόρησεν   verb, aor. act. indic. 3 pers. sg.
{5.A.1} . . . . εὐφορέω G2164
εὐφραίνεσθαι   vbl., pres. pass. inf.
{6.B.1} . . . . εὐφραίνω G2165

εὐφραίνεσθε   verb, pres. pass. impv. 2 pers. pl.
{5.D.1} . . . . id.
εὐφραινόμενος   vbl., pres. pass. ptc. nom. sg.
masc. {6.A.1} . . . . id.
εὐφραίνονται   verb, pres. pass. indic. 3 pers.
pl. {5.A.1.d} . . . . id.
εὐφραίνοντο   verb, impf. pass. indic. 3 pers. pl.
{5.A.1.e} . . . . id.
εὐφραίνου   verb, pres. pass. impv. 2 pers. sg.
{5.D.1} . . . . id.
G2165 **εὐφραίνω**   I cheer, make glad; generally mid.
or pass. I am glad; I make merry, revel, feast.
εὐφραίνων   vbl., pres. act. ptc. nom. sg. masc.
{6.A.1} . . . . εὐφραίνω G2165
εὐφράνθη   verb, aor. pass. indic. 3 pers. sg.
{5.A.1.b} . . . . id.
εὐφρανθῆναι   vbl., aor. pass. inf. {6.B.1} . . . . . . id.
εὐφρανθήσονται   verb, fut. pass. indic. 3 pers.
pl. {5.A.1.d} . . . . id.
εὐφράνθητε   verb, aor. pass. impv. 2 pers. pl.
{5.D.1} . . . . id.
εὐφράνθητι   verb, aor. pass. impv. 2 pers. sg.
{5.D.1} . . . . id.
εὐφρανθῶ   verb, aor. pass. subjunc. 1 pers. sg.
{5.B.1} . . . . id.
εὐφρανθῶμεν   verb, aor. pass. subjunc. 1 pers.
pl. {5.B.1} . . . . id.
Εὐφράτη   noun prop., dat. sg. masc. {2.A;
2.D} . . . . Εὐφράτης G2166
Εὐφράτην   noun prop., acc. sg. masc. {2.A; 2.D} id.
G2166 **Εὐφράτης**, -ου, ὁ   the Euphrates, boundary
river of the province Syria.
G2167 **εὐφροσύνη**, -ης, ἡ   gladness.
εὐφροσύνης   noun, gen. sg. fem. {2.A} εὐφροσύνη G2167
εὐχαριστεῖ   verb, pres. act. indic. 3 pers. sg.
{5.A.2} . . . . εὐχαριστέω G2168
εὐχαριστεῖν   vbl., pres. act. inf. {6.B.2} . . . . . . id.
εὐχαριστεῖς   verb, pres. act. indic. 2 pers. sg.
{5.A.2} . . . . id.
εὐχαριστεῖτε   verb, pres. act. impv. 2 pers. pl.
{5.D.2} . . . . id.
G2168 **εὐχαριστέω**   I give thanks; pass. 3 sg. is received
with thanks, 2 Cor 1:11.
εὐχαριστηθῇ   verb, aor. pass. subjunc. 3 pers.
{5.B.1} . . . . εὐχαριστέω G2168
εὐχαρίστησαν   verb, aor. act. indic. 3 pers. pl.
{5.A.1} . . . . id.
εὐχαριστήσαντος   vbl., aor. act. ptc. gen. sg.
masc. {6.A.2} . . . . id.
εὐχαριστήσας   vbl., aor. act. ptc. nom. sg.
masc. {6.A.2} . . . . id.
εὐχαρίστησε   verb, aor. act. indic. 3 pers. sg.
{5.A.1} . . . . id.
εὐχαρίστησεν   verb, aor. act. indic. 3 pers. sg.
{5.A.1} . . . . id.
G2169 **εὐχαριστία**, -ας, ἡ   thankfulness, gratitude.
εὐχαριστία   noun, nom. sg. fem. {2.A} εὐχαριστία G2169
εὐχαριστίᾳ   noun, dat. sg. fem. {2.A} . . . . id.
εὐχαριστίαν   noun, acc. sg. fem. {2.A} . . . . id.
εὐχαριστίας   noun, acc. pl. fem. {2.A} . . . . id.

εὐχαριστίας   noun, gen. sg. fem. {2.A} . . . . . . id.
εὐχαριστιῶν   noun, gen. pl. fem. {2.A} . . . . . . id.
εὐχάριστοι   adj., nom. pl. masc. {3.C} εὐχάριστος G2170
G2170 **εὐχάριστος**, -ον   thankful.
εὐχαριστοῦμεν   verb, pres. act. indic. 1 pers. pl.
{5.A.2} . . . . εὐχαριστέω G2168
εὐχαριστοῦντες   vbl., pres. act. ptc. nom. pl.
masc. {6.A.2} . . . . id.
εὐχαριστῶ   verb, pres. act. indic. 1 pers. sg.
{5.A.2} . . . . id.
εὐχαριστῶν   vbl., pres. act. ptc. nom. sg. masc.
{6.A.2} . . . . id.
εὔχεσθε   verb, pres. mid./pass. impv. 2 pers. pl.
{5.D.1} . . . . εὔχομαι G2172
G2171 **εὐχή**, -ῆς, ἡ   a prayer comprising a vow, as was
usual; a prayer; a vow.
εὐχή   noun, nom. sg. fem. {2.A} . . . . εὐχή G2171
εὐχήν   noun, acc. sg. fem. {2.A} . . . . id.
G2172 **εὔχομαι**   I pray.
εὔχομαι   verb, pres. mid./pass. indic. 1 pers. sg.
{5.A.1.d} . . . . εὔχομαι G2172
εὐχόμεθα   verb, pres. mid./pass. indic. 1 pers.
pl. {5.A.1.d} . . . . id.
εὐχόμην   verb, impf. mid./pass. indic. 1 pers.
sg. {5.A.1.e} . . . . id.
εὔχρηστον   adj., acc. sg. masc. {3.C} . . εὔχρηστος G2173
εὔχρηστον   adj., nom. sg. neut. {3.C} . . . . id.
G2173 **εὔχρηστος**, -ον   useful, serviceable.
εὔχρηστος   adj., nom. sg. masc. {3.C} . εὔχρηστος G2173
G2174 **εὐψυχέω**   I am of good cheer.
εὐψυχῶ   verb, pres. act. subjunc. 1 pers. sg.
{5.B.2} . . . . εὐψυχέω G2174
G2175 **εὐωδία**, -ας, ἡ   a sweet smell.
εὐωδία   noun, nom. sg. fem. {2.A} . . . . εὐωδία G2175
εὐωδίας   noun, gen. sg. fem. {2.A} . . . . id.
εὐώνυμον   adj., acc. sg. fem. {3.C} . . . . . εὐώνυμος G2176
εὐώνυμον   adj., acc. sg. masc. {3.C} . . . . id.
εὐώνυμον   adj., acc. sg. neut. {3.C} . . . . id.
G2176 **εὐώνυμος**, -ον   on the left-hand side, left; ἐξ
εὐωνύμων, on the left (lit. well-named, to
avoid the evil omen attaching to the left).
εὐωνύμων   adj., gen. pl. neut. {3.C} . . . . εὐώνυμος G2176
ἐφ᾽   prep. . . . . ἐπί G1909
ἔφαγε   verb, ²aor. act. indic. 3 pers. sg.
{5.A.1.b} . . . . ἐσθίω G2068
ἔφαγεν   verb, ²aor. act. indic. 3 pers. sg. {5.A.1.b} id.
ἐφάγετε   verb, ²aor. act. indic. 2 pers. pl. {5.A.1.b} id.
ἐφάγομεν   verb, ²aor. act. indic. 1 pers. pl.
{5.A.1.b} . . . . id.
ἔφαγον   verb, ²aor. act. indic. 1 pers. sg. {5.A.1.b} id.
ἔφαγον   verb, ²aor. act. indic. 3 pers. pl. {5.A.1.b} id.
G2177 **ἐφάλλομαι**   I leap upon.
ἐφαλλόμενος   vbl., pres. mid./pass. ptc. nom. sg.
masc. {6.A.1} . . . . ἐφάλλομαι G2177
ἐφαλόμενος   vbl., aor. mid. ptc. nom. sg. masc.
{6.A.1.b} . . . . id.
ἐφανερώθη   verb, aor. pass. indic. 3 pers. sg.
{5.A.1} . . . . φανερόω G5319
ἐφανερώθησαν   verb, aor. pass. indic. 3 pers.
pl. {5.A.1} . . . . id.

ἐφανέρωσα   verb, aor. act. indic. 1 pers. sg.
　{5.A.1} . . . . id.
ἐφανέρωσε   verb, aor. act. indic. 3 pers. sg.
　{5.A.1} . . . . id.
ἐφανέρωσεν   verb, aor. act. indic. 3 pers. sg.
　{5.A.1} . . . . id.
ἐφάνη   verb, ²aor. pass. indic. 3 pers. sg.
　{5.A.1.e} . . . . φαίνω G5316
ἐφάνησαν   verb, ²aor. pass. indic. 3 pers. pl.
　{5.A.1.e} . . . . id.
G2178 ἐφάπαξ (ἐφ᾽ ἅπαξ)   adv., once, once for all.
ἐφάπαξ   adv.. . . . . .ἐφάπαξ G2178
ἔφασκεν   verb, impf. act. indic. 3 pers. sg.
　{5.A.1.b} . . . . φάσκω G5335
ἐφείσατο   verb, aor. mid. indic. 3 pers. sg.
　{5.A.1.e} . . . . φείδομαι G5339
ἔφερεν   verb, impf. act. indic. 3 pers. sg.
　{5.A.1.b} . . . . φέρω G5342
ἐφερόμεθα   verb, impf. pass. indic. 1 pers. pl.
　{5.A.1.e} . . . . id.
ἔφερον   verb, impf. act. indic. 3 pers. pl.
　{5.A.1.b} . . . . id.
ἐφέροντο   verb, impf. pass. indic. 3 pers. pl.
　{5.A.1.e} . . . . id.
Ἐφεσίνης   noun prop., gen. sg. fem. {2.B;
　2.D}. . . . . Ἐφεσῖνος G2179
G2179 Ἐφεσῖνος, -η, -ον   Ephesian, of Ephesus.
Ἐφέσιοι   adj. prop., nom. pl. masc. {3.A}. Ἐφέσιος G2180
Ἐφέσιοι   adj. prop., voc. pl. masc. {3.A} . . . . . . id.
Ἐφέσιον   adj. prop., acc. sg. masc. {3.A} . . . . . id.
G2180 Ἐφέσιος, -α, -ον   Ephesian, of Ephesus.
Ἐφεσίους   adj. prop., acc. pl. masc. {3.A}. Ἐφέσιος G2180
Ἐφεσίων   adj. prop., gen. pl. masc. {3.A} . . . . . . id.
Ἔφεσον   noun prop., acc. sg. fem. {2.B;
　2.D}. . . . . Ἔφεσος G2181
G2181 Ἔφεσος, -ου, ἡ   Ephesus, a coast city, capital of
　the Roman province Asia.
Ἐφέσου   noun prop., gen. sg. fem. {2.B;
　2.D}. . . . . Ἔφεσος G2181
ἐφέστηκε   verb, perf. act. indic. 3 pers. sg.
　{5.A.1} . . . . .ἐφίστημι G2186
ἐφέστηκεν   verb, perf. act. indic. 3 pers. sg.
　{5.A.1} . . . . id.
ἐφεστώς   vbl., ²perf. act. ptc. nom. sg. masc.
　{6.A.3} . . . . id.
ἐφεστῶτα   vbl., ²perf. act. ptc. acc. sg. masc.
　{6.A.3} . . . . id.
Ἐφέσῳ   noun prop., dat. sg. fem. {2.B;
　2.D}. . . . . Ἔφεσος G2181
ἐφευρετάς   noun, acc. pl. masc. {2.A} . .ἐφευρετής G2182
G2182 ἐφευρετής, -οῦ, ὁ   a finder out, discoverer.
ἔφη   verb, impf. act. indic. 3 pers. sg. {5.A.3.a} φημί G5346
G2183 ἐφημερία, -ας, ἡ   a class of priests who served
　for a stated number of days.
ἐφημερίας   noun, gen. sg. fem. {2.A} . . . ἐφημερία G2183
G2184 ἐφήμερος, -ον   for the day, for a day.
ἐφημέρου   adj., gen. sg. fem. {3.C} . . . . . ἐφήμερος G2184
ἐφθάσαμεν   verb, aor. act. indic. 1 pers. pl.
　{5.A.1.b} . . . . φθάνω G5348
ἔφθασε   verb, aor. act. indic. 3 pers. sg. {5.A.1.b} id.

ἔφθασεν   verb, aor. act. indic. 3 pers. sg.
　{5.A.1.b} . . . . id.
ἐφθείραμεν   verb, aor. act. indic. 1 pers. pl.
　{5.A.1.b} . . . . φθείρω G5351
ἔφθειρε   verb, impf. act. indic. 3 pers. sg.
　{5.A.1.b} . . . . id.
ἔφθειρεν   verb, impf. act. indic. 3 pers. sg.
　{5.A.1.b} . . . . id.
ἐφικέσθαι   vbl., ²aor. mid. inf. {6.B.1} . . ἐφικνέομαι G2185
G2185 ἐφικνέομαι   I reach as far as.
ἐφικνούμενοι   vbl., pres. mid./pass. ptc. nom. pl.
　masc. {6.A.2} . . . . ἐφικνέομαι G2185
ἐφίλει   verb, impf. act. indic. 3 pers. sg.
　{5.A.2} . . . . φιλέω G5368
ἐφιμώθη   verb, aor. pass. indic. 3 pers. sg.
　{5.A.1} . . . . φιμόω G5392
ἐφίμωσε   verb, aor. act. indic. 3 pers. sg. {5.A.1}. id.
ἐφίμωσεν   verb, aor. act. indic. 3 pers. sg. {5.A.1}id.
ἐφίσταται   verb, pres. mid. indic. 3 pers. sg.
　{5.A.3.a} . . . . ἐφίστημι G2186
G2186 ἐφίστημι   intrans. and pass., I come upon
　(suddenly or unexpectedly) and stand by; met. I
　press forward, 2 Tim 4:2.
ἐφνίδιος   adj., nom. sg. fem. {3.A} . . . . . αἰφνίδιος G160
ἐφοβεῖτο   verb, impf. mid./pass. indic. 3 pers. sg.
　{5.A.2} . . . . φοβέω G5399
ἐφοβήθη   verb, aor. pass. indic. 3 pers. sg.
　{5.A.1} . . . . id.
ἐφοβήθησαν   verb, aor. pass. indic. 3 pers. pl.
　{5.A.1} . . . . id.
ἐφοβούμην   verb, impf. mid./pass. indic.
　1 pers. sg. {5.A.2} . . . . id.
ἐφοβοῦντο   verb, impf. mid./pass. indic. 3 pers.
　pl. {5.A.2} . . . . id.
ἐφονεύσατε   verb, aor. act. indic. 2 pers. pl.
　{5.A.1.b} . . . . φονεύω G5407
ἐφορέσαμεν   verb, aor. act. indic. 1 pers. pl.
　{5.A.1} . . . . φορέω G5409
G2187 Ἐφραίμ, ὁ   Ephraim, a city of uncertain
　location.
Ἐφραίμ   noun prop.. . . . . Ἐφραίμ G2187
Ἐφραΐμ   noun prop.. . . . . id.
ἔφραξαν   verb, aor. act. indic. 3 pers. pl.
　{5.A.1.b} . . . . φράσσω G5420
ἐφρονεῖτε   verb, impf. act. indic. 2 pers. pl.
　{5.A.2} . . . . φρονέω G5426
ἐφρόνουν   verb, impf. act. indic. 1 pers. sg.
　{5.A.2} . . . . id.
ἐφρούρει   verb, impf. act. indic. 3 pers. sg.
　{5.A.2} . . . . .φρουρέω G5432
ἐφρουρούμεθα   verb, impf. pass. indic. 1 pers.
　pl. {5.A.2} . . . . id.
ἐφρύαξαν   verb, aor. act. indic. 3 pers. pl.
　{5.A.1.b} . . . . φρυάσσω G5433
ἔφυγε   verb, ²aor. act. indic. 3 pers. sg.
　{5.A.1.b} . . . . φεύγω G5343
ἔφυγεν   verb, ²aor. act. indic. 3 pers. sg. {5.A.1.b} id.
ἔφυγον   verb, ²aor. act. indic. 3 pers. pl. {5.A.1.b} id.
ἐφύλαξα   verb, aor. act. indic. 1 pers. sg.
　{5.A.1.b} . . . . φυλάσσω G5442

ἐφυλαξάμην   verb, aor. mid. indic. 1 pers. sg.
{5.A.1.e} . . . . id.
ἐφυλάξατε   verb, aor. act. indic. 2 pers. pl.
{5.A.1.b} . . . . id.
ἐφύλαξε   verb, aor. act. indic. 3 pers. sg.
{5.A.1.b} . . . . id.
ἐφύλαξεν   verb, aor. act. indic. 3 pers. sg.
{5.A.1.b} . . . . id.
ἐφυσιώθησαν   verb, aor. pass. indic. 3 pers. pl.
{5.A.1} . . . . φυσιόω G5448
ἐφύτευον   verb, impf. act. indic. 3 pers. pl.
{5.A.1.b} . . . . φυτεύω G5452
ἐφύτευσα   verb, aor. act. indic. 1 pers. sg.
{5.A.1.b} . . . . id.
ἐφύτευσεν   verb, aor. act. indic. 3 pers. sg.
{5.A.1.b} . . . . id.
εφφαθα   Aram. ἐφφαθά G2188
G2188   **ἐφφαθά**   *be opened up* (Aram.).
ἐφφαθά   Aram. ἐφφαθά G2188
ἐφώνει   verb, impf. act. indic. 3 pers. sg.
{5.A.2} . . . . φωνέω G5455
ἐφώνησαν   verb, aor. act. indic. 3 pers. pl.
{5.A.1} . . . . id.
ἐφώνησε   verb, aor. act. indic. 3 pers. sg. {5.A.1} id.
ἐφώνησεν   verb, aor. act. indic. 3 pers. sg.
{5.A.1} . . . . id.
ἐφώτισεν   verb, aor. act. indic. 3 pers. sg.
{5.A.1.b} . . . . φωτίζω G5461
ἐφωτίσθη   verb, aor. pass. indic. 3 pers. sg.
{5.A.1.b} . . . . id.
ἔχαιρεν   verb, impf. act. indic. 3 pers. sg.
{5.A.1.b} . . . . χαίρω G5463
ἔχαιρον   verb, impf. act. indic. 3 pers. pl.
{5.A.1.b} . . . . id.
ἐχαλάσθην   verb, aor. pass. indic. 1 pers. sg.
{5.A.1} . . . . χαλάω G5465
ἐχάρη   verb, ²aor. pass. indic. 3 pers. sg.
{5.A.1.e} . . . . χαίρω G5463
ἐχάρημεν   verb, ²aor. pass. indic. 1 pers. pl.
{5.A.1.e} . . . . id.
ἐχάρην   verb, ²aor. pass. indic. 1 pers. sg.
{5.A.1.e} . . . . id.
ἐχάρησαν   verb, ²aor. pass. indic. 3 pers. pl.
{5.A.1.e} . . . . id.
ἐχάρητε   verb, ²aor. pass. indic. 2 pers. pl.
{5.A.1.e} . . . . id.
ἐχαρίσατο   verb, aor. mid. indic. 3 pers. sg.
{5.A.1.e} . . . . χαρίζομαι G5483
ἐχαρίσθη   verb, aor. pass. indic. 3 pers. sg.
{5.A.1.b} . . . . id.
ἐχαρίτωσεν   verb, aor. act. indic. 3 pers. sg.
{5.A.1} . . . . χαριτόω G5487
ἔχε   verb, pres. act. impv. 2 pers. sg. {5.D.1} . . . ἔχω G2192
ἔχει   verb, pres. act. indic. 3 pers. sg. {5.A.1.a} . . id.
ἔχειν   vbl., pres. act. inf. {6.B.1} . . . . id.
ἔχεις   verb, pres. act. indic. 2 pers. sg. {5.A.1.a} . . id.
ἔχετε   verb, pres. act. impv. 2 pers. pl. {5.D.1} . . . id.
ἔχετε   verb, pres. act. indic. 2 pers. pl. {5.A.1.a} . id.
ἐχέτω   verb, pres. act. impv. 3 pers. sg. {5.D.1} . . id.
ἔχη   verb, pres. act. subjunc. 3 pers. sg. {5.B.1} . . id.

ἔχητε   verb, pres. act. subjunc. 2 pers. pl. {5.B.1}. id.
G5504†‡   **ἐχθές**   adv., *yesterday.* Var. for χθές.
ἐχθές   adv. ἐχθές G5504†‡
G2189   **ἔχθρα**, -ας, ἡ   *enmity, hostility.*
ἔχθρα   noun, nom. sg. fem. {2.A} . . . . ἔχθρα G2189
ἔχθρᾳ   noun, dat. sg. fem. {2.A} . . . . id.
ἔχθραι   noun, nom. pl. fem. {2.A} . . . . id.
ἔχθραν   noun, acc. sg. fem. {2.A} . . . . id.
ἐχθρέ   adj., voc. sg. masc. {3.A} . . . . ἐχθρός G2190
ἐχθροί   adj., nom. pl. masc. {3.A} . . . . id.
ἐχθρόν   adj., acc. sg. masc. {3.A} . . . . id.
G2190   **ἐχθρός**, -ή, -όν   *an enemy.*
ἐχθρός   adj., nom. sg. masc. {3.A}. . . . . ἐχθρός G2190
ἐχθροῦ   adj., gen. sg. masc. {3.A} . . . . id.
ἐχθρούς   adj., acc. pl. masc. {3.A} . . . . id.
ἐχθρῶν   adj., gen. pl. masc. {3.A} . . . . id.
G2191   **ἔχιδνα**, -ης, ἡ   *a serpent, snake;* in Acts 28:3
    probably *Coronella leopardinus,* a constric-
    tor snake like a viper without poison fangs,
    which fixes its small teeth into the skin, but is
    harmless.
ἔχιδνα   noun, nom. sg. fem. {2.A} . . . . ἔχιδνα G2191
ἐχιδνῶν   noun, gen. pl. fem. {2.A} . . . . id.
ἐχλεύαζον   verb, impf. act. indic. 3 pers. pl.
{5.A.1.b} . . . . χλευάζω G5512
ἔχοι   verb, pres. act. opt. 3 pers. sg. {5.C.1} . . . ἔχω G2192
ἔχοιεν   verb, pres. act. opt. 3 pers. pl. {5.C.1} . . . id.
ἔχομεν   verb, pres. act. indic. 1 pers. pl. {5.A.1.a} id.
ἐχόμενα   vbl., pres. mid./pass. ptc. acc. pl. neut.
{6.A.1} . . . . id.
ἐχομένας   vbl., pres. mid./pass. ptc. acc. pl.
fem. {6.A.1} . . . . id.
ἐχομένη   vbl., pres. mid./pass. ptc. dat. sg. fem.
{6.A.1} . . . . id.
ἔχον   vbl., pres. act. ptc. acc. sg. neut. {6.A.1} . . . id.
ἔχον   vbl., pres. act. ptc. nom. sg. neut. {6.A.1} . . id.
ἔχοντα   vbl., pres. act. ptc. acc. sg. masc. {6.A.1} id.
ἔχοντα   vbl., pres. act. ptc. nom. pl. neut. {6.A.1} id.
ἔχοντας   vbl., pres. act. ptc. acc. pl. masc. {6.A.1} id.
ἔχοντες   vbl., pres. act. ptc. nom. pl. masc.
{6.A.1} . . . . id.
ἔχοντι   vbl., pres. act. ptc. dat. sg. masc. {6.A.1} . id.
ἔχοντος   vbl., pres. act. ptc. gen. sg. masc.
{6.A.1} . . . . id.
ἔχοντος   vbl., pres. act. ptc. gen. sg. neut. {6.A.1} id.
ἐχόντων   vbl., pres. act. ptc. gen. pl. masc.
{6.A.1} . . . . id.
ἐχορτάσθησαν   verb, aor. pass. indic. 3 pers. pl.
{5.A.1.b} . . . . χορτάζω G5526
ἐχορτάσθητε   verb, aor. pass. indic. 2 pers. pl.
{5.A.1.b} . . . . id.
ἔχουσα   vbl., pres. act. ptc. nom. sg. fem.
{6.A.1} . . . . ἔχω G2192
ἔχουσαι   vbl., pres. act. ptc. nom. pl. fem.
{6.A.1} . . . . id.
ἐχούσαις   vbl., pres. act. ptc. dat. pl. fem. {6.A.1} id.
ἔχουσαν   vbl., pres. act. ptc. acc. sg. fem. {6.A.1} id.
ἐχούσῃ   vbl., pres. act. ptc. dat. sg. fem. {6.A.1} . id.
ἐχούσης   vbl., pres. act. ptc. gen. sg. fem. {6.A.1} id.
ἔχουσι   verb, pres. act. indic. 3 pers. pl. {5.A.1.a} id.

ἔχουσιν   verb, pres. act. indic. 3 pers. pl.
{5.A.1.a} . . . . id.
ἐχρηματίσθη   verb, aor. pass. indic. 3 pers. sg.
{5.A.1.b} . . . . χρηματίζω G5537
ἐχρησάμεθα   verb, aor. mid. indic. 1 pers. pl.
{5.A.1} . . . . χράομαι G5530
ἐχρησάμην   verb, aor. mid. indic. 1 pers. sg.
{5.A.1} . . . . id.
ἔχρισας   verb, aor. act. indic. 2 pers. sg.
{5.A.1.b} . . . . χρίω G5548
ἔχρισε   verb, aor. act. indic. 3 pers. sg. {5.A.1.b} . id.
ἔχρισεν   verb, aor. act. indic. 3 pers. sg. {5.A.1.b} id.
ἐχρῶντο   verb, impf. mid./pass. indic. 3 pers. pl.
{5.A.2} . . . . χράομαι G5530
G2192   ἔχω   (1) trans., *I hold, have, possess*; ἔσχον, generally, *I got, received, acquired*, ἔσχηκα, *I possessed*; ἔχω τι κατά (εἰς), *I have a ground of complaint against*; ἐν γαστρὶ ἔχειν, *to have* (a child) *in the womb*; with double acc., the second being in the pred. (with or without εἰς), *to have so and so as . . . , to regard so and so as* (cf. Mark 11:32); with obj. indicating time to be so and so days etc. old; (2) with inf. *I am able*; (3) with adv. equal to εἰμί with corresponding adj.; intrans., κατὰ κεφαλῆς ἔχων, *having a covering over the head, with head covered*, 1 Cor 11:4; (5) Mid. *I am neighboring, I am next to*, e.g., Mark 1:38; τῇ ἐχομένῃ (understand ἡμέρᾳ), *next day*, Luke 13:33; cf. Acts 13:44 (var.); etc.
ἔχω   verb, pres. act. indic. 1 pers. sg. {5.A.1.a} . . ἔχω G2192
ἔχω   verb, pres. act. subjunc. 1 pers. sg. {5.B.1} . . id.
ἔχωμεν   verb, pres. act. subjunc. 1 pers. pl.
{5.B.1} . . . . id.
ἔχων   vbl., pres. act. ptc. nom. sg. masc. {6.A.1} . id.
ἐχωρίσθη   verb, aor. pass. indic. 3 pers. sg.
{5.A.1.b} . . . . χωρίζω G5563
ἔχωσι   verb, pres. act. subjunc. 3 pers. pl. {5.B.1} ἔχω G2192
ἔχωσιν   verb, pres. act. subjunc. 3 pers. pl. {5.B.1} id.

ἐψευδομαρτύρουν   verb, impf. act. indic. 3 pers. pl. {5.A.2} . . . . ψευδομαρτυρέω G5576
ἐψεύσω   verb, aor. mid. indic. 2 pers. sg.
{5.A.1.e} . . . . ψεύδομαι G5574
ἐψηλάφησαν   verb, aor. act. indic. 3 pers. pl.
{5.A.1} . . . . ψηλαφάω G5584
ἑώρακα   verb, perf. act. indic. 1 pers. sg.
{5.A.1} . . . . ὁράω G3708
ἑωράκαμεν   verb, perf. act. indic. 1 pers. pl.
{5.A.1} . . . . id.
ἑώρακαν   verb, perf. act. indic. 3 pers. pl.
{5.A.1} . . . . id.
ἑώρακας   verb, perf. act. indic. 2 pers. sg. {5.A.1} id.
ἑωράκασι   verb, perf. act. indic. 3 pers. pl.
{5.A.1} . . . . id.
ἑωράκασιν   verb, perf. act. indic. 3 pers. pl.
{5.A.1} . . . . id.
ἑωράκατε   verb, perf. act. indic. 2 pers. pl.
{5.A.1} . . . . id.
ἑώρακε   verb, perf. act. indic. 3 pers. sg. {5.A.1} . id.
ἑωράκει   verb, plu. act. indic. 3 pers. sg. {5.A.1} . id.
ἑώρακεν   verb, perf. act. indic. 3 pers. sg. {5.A.1} id.
ἑωρακέναι   vbl., perf. act. inf. {6.B.1} . . . . id.
ἑωρακότες   vbl., perf. act. ptc. nom. pl. masc.
{6.A.2} . . . . id.
ἑωρακώς   vbl., perf. act. ptc. nom. sg. masc.
{6.A.2} . . . . id.
ἑώρων   verb, impf. act. indic. 3 pers. pl. {5.A.2} . id.
G2193   ἕως   (1) conj., *until*; followed by the indic. where a def. time in the past is indicated; with or with out οὗ or ὅτου, and followed by the subjunc. aor. with or without ἄν or ἐάν, indicating an indef. time, *until . . . shall have*, e.g., ἕως ἂν πάντα γένηται, *until all shall have happened*, Matt 5:18; (2) prep. with gen., *as far as, up to, as much as, until*, both in local and temp. connections, both with nouns in gen. and with advs. (or preps.).
ἕως   conj., prep. . . . . ἕως G2193

Z ζ

G2194   **Ζαβουλών**, ὁ   *Zebulon*, one of the sons of Jacob, and founder of one of the twelve tribes (Heb.).
Ζαβουλών   noun prop. . . . . Ζαβουλών G2194
Ζακχαῖε   noun prop., voc. sg. masc. {2.B; 2.D} . . . . Ζακχαῖος G2195
G2195   **Ζακχαῖος**, -ου, ὁ   *Zacchaeus*, a Jewish tax gatherer.
Ζακχαῖος   noun prop., nom. sg. masc. {2.B; 2.D} . . . . Ζακχαῖος G2195
Ζαρά   noun prop. . . . . Ζαρά G2196
G2196   **Ζαρά**, Ζαρά, ὁ   *Zara*, son of Judah and Thamar (Heb.).
Ζαρά   noun prop. . . . . Ζαρά G2196
Ζαχαρία   noun prop., voc. sg. masc. {2.A; 2.D} . . . . Ζαχαρίας G2197

Ζαχαρίαν   noun prop., acc. sg. masc. {2.A; 2.D} id.
G2197   **Ζαχαρίας**, -ου, ὁ   *Zechariah*: (1) a priest referred to in 2 Chr 24:20 as a son of Jehoiada, in most copies of Matt 23:35, and some of Luke 11:51, perhaps confused with Zechariah the prophet, who was son of Berechiah (Zech 1:1), but see also Βαραχίας; (2) another priest, father of John the Baptist (Heb.).
Ζαχαρίας   noun prop., nom. sg. masc. {2.A; 2.D} . . . . Ζαχαρίας G2197
Ζαχαρίου   noun prop., gen. sg. masc. {2.A; 2.D} id.
G2198   **ζάω**   *I live*; ἑαυτῷ ζῆν, *to be one's own master*.
Ζεβεδαῖον   noun prop., acc. sg. masc. {2.B; 2.D} . . . . Ζεβεδαῖος G2199
G2199   **Ζεβεδαῖος**, -ου, ὁ   *Zebedee*, father of the disciples James and John.

Ζεβεδαίου   noun prop., gen. sg. masc. {2.B;
2.D}. . . . . .Ζεβεδαῖος G2199
ζέοντες   vbl., pres. act. ptc. nom. pl. masc.
    {6.A.2}. . . . . ζέω G2204
G2200 **ζεστός**, -ή, -όν   boiling hot.
ζεστός   adj., nom. sg. masc. {3.A}. . . . . . . .ζεστός G2200
ζεύγη   noun, acc. pl. neut. {2.C}. . . . . .ζεῦγος G2201
G2201 **ζεῦγος**, -ους, τό   (1) a yoke, team; (2) hence, a
    pair.
ζεῦγος   noun, acc. sg. neut. {2.C}. . . . . . . .ζεῦγος G2201
G2202 **ζευκτηρία**, -ας, ἡ   a band, a fastening.
ζευκτηρίας   noun, acc. pl. fem. {2.A}. . .ζευκτηρία G2202
G2203 **Ζεύς**, gen. Διός, acc. Δία, ὁ   Zeus, the Greek
    god of the sky in all its manifestations, cor-
    responding to the Roman Jupiter and to the
    leading god of the native Lycaonians, etc.
G2204 **ζέω**   I burn (in spirit); (lit. I boil, I am boiling).
ζέων   vbl., pres. act. ptc. nom. sg. masc. {6.A.2} ζέω G2204
ζῇ   verb, pres. act. indic. 3 pers. sg. {5.A.2} . . . .ζάω G2198
ζήλευε   verb, pres. act. impv. 2 pers. sg.
    {5.D.1}. . . . . .ζηλεύω G2206†‡
G2206†‡ **ζηλεύω**   I am eager, earnest. Var. for ζηλόω,
    Rev. 3:19.
ζῆλοι   noun, nom. pl. masc. {2.B}. . . . . ζῆλος G2205
ζηλοῖ   verb, pres. act. indic. 3 pers. sg.
    {5.A.2}. . . . . .ζηλόω G2206
ζῆλον   noun, acc. sg. masc. {2.B}. . . . . id.
G2205 **ζῆλος**, -ου, ὁ   (1) eagerness, zeal, enthusiasm;
    (2) jealousy, rivalry.
ζῆλος   noun, nom. sg. masc. {2.B}. . . . . ζῆλος G2205
ζῆλος   noun, acc. sg. neut. {2.C}. . . . . id.
ζῆλος   noun, nom. sg. neut. {2.C}. . . . . id.
ζήλου   noun, gen. sg. masc. {2.B}. . . . . id.
ζηλοῦσθαι   vbl., pres. pass. inf. {6.B.2} . . . .ζηλόω G2206
ζηλοῦσιν   verb, pres. act. indic. 3 pers. pl.
    {5.A.2}. . . . . id.
ζηλοῦτε   verb, pres. act. impv. 2 pers. pl. {5.D.2} id.
ζηλοῦτε   verb, pres. act. indic. 2 pers. pl. {5.A.2} id.
ζηλοῦτε   verb, pres. act. subjunc. 2 pers. pl.
    {5.B.2}. . . . . id.
G2206 **ζηλόω**   (1) intrans., I am jealous; (2) trans., I
    am jealous of, with acc. of a person; I am eager
    for, I am eager to possess, with acc. of a thing.
ζηλῶ   verb, pres. act. indic. 1 pers. sg.
    {5.A.2}. . . . . .ζηλόω G2206
ζήλῳ   noun, dat. sg. masc. {2.B} . . . . ζῆλος G2205
ζηλώσαντες   vbl., aor. act. ptc. nom. pl. masc.
    {6.A.2}. . . . . .ζηλόω G2206
ζήλωσον   verb, aor. act. impv. 2 pers. sg. {5.D.1} id.
ζηλωταί   noun, nom. pl. masc. {2.A} . . . .ζηλωτής G2207
ζηλωτήν   noun, acc. sg. masc. {2.A} . . . . id.
G2207 **ζηλωτής**, -οῦ, ὁ   one who is eagerly devoted to a
    person or thing, a zealot.
ζηλωτής   noun, nom. sg. masc. {2.A} . . . .ζηλωτής G2207
G2208 **Ζηλωτής**   a Zealot, i.e., (spec.) a member of a
    Jewish sect dedicated to political independence;
    cf. ζηλωτής.
G2209 **ζημία**, -ας, ἡ   loss.
ζημίαν   noun, acc. sg. fem. {2.A} . . . . ζημία G2209
ζημίας   noun, gen. sg. fem. {2.A} . . . . id.

G2210 **ζημιόω**   I inflict loss (damage) upon, I fine, I
    punish, sometimes with the acc. of the penalty,
    even when verb is pass.
ζημιωθείς   vbl., aor. pass. ptc. nom. sg. masc.
    {6.A.1.a.}. . . . . .ζημιόω G2210
ζημιωθῇ   verb, aor. pass. subjunc. 3 pers. sg.
    {5.B.1}. . . . . id.
ζημιωθῆναι   vbl., aor. pass. inf. {6.B.1} . . . . id.
ζημιωθήσεται   verb, fut. pass. indic. 3 pers. sg.
    {5.A.1}. . . . . id.
ζημιωθῆτε   verb, aor. pass. subjunc. 2 pers. pl.
    {5.B.1}. . . . . id.
ζῆν   vbl., pres. act. inf. {6.B.2}. . . . . .ζάω G2198
ζῆν   vbl., pres. act. inf. {6.B.2}. . . . . id.
Ζηνᾶν   noun prop., acc. sg. masc. {2.A; 2.D} Ζηνᾶς G2211
G2211 **Ζηνᾶς**, acc. ᾶν, ὁ   Zenas, a lawyer in Rome
    (pet form of Ζηνόδοτος or Ζηνόδωρος).
ζῇς   verb, pres. act. indic. 2 pers. sg. {5.A.2} . . ζάω G2198
ζήσασα   vbl., aor. act. ptc. nom. sg. fem. {6.A.2} id.
ζήσει   verb, fut. act. indic. 3 pers. sg. {5.A.1} . . . id.
ζήσεσθε   verb, fut. mid. indic. 2 pers. pl. {5.A.1} id.
ζήσεται   verb, fut. mid. indic. 3 pers. sg. {5.A.1} id.
ζήσετε   verb, fut. act. indic. 2 pers. pl. {5.A.1} . . id.
ζήσῃ   verb, aor. act. subjunc. 3 pers. sg. {5.B.1}. . id.
ζήσῃ   verb, fut. mid. indic. 2 pers. sg. {5.A.1}. . . id.
ζησόμεθα   verb, fut. mid. indic. 1 pers. pl.
    {5.A.1}. . . . . id.
ζήσομεν   verb, fut. act. indic. 1 pers. pl. {5.A.1} . id.
ζήσονται   verb, fut. mid. indic. 3 pers. pl. {5.A.1} id.
ζήσουσιν   verb, fut. act. indic. 3 pers. pl. {5.A.1} id.
ζήσω   verb, aor. act. subjunc. 1 pers. sg. {5.B.1} id.
ζήσωμεν   verb, aor. act. subjunc. 1 pers. pl.
    {5.B.1}. . . . . id.
ζῆτε   verb, pres. act. indic. 2 pers. pl. {5.A.2} . . . id.
ζήτει   verb, pres. act. impv. 2 pers. sg. {5.D.2} ζητέω G2212
ζητεῖ   verb, pres. act. impv. 2 pers. sg. {5.D.2} . . id.
ζητεῖ   verb, pres. act. indic. 3 pers. sg. {5.A.2}. . . id.
ζητεῖν   vbl., pres. act. inf. {6.B.2} . . . . id.
ζητεῖς   verb, pres. act. indic. 2 pers. sg. {5.A.2}. . id.
ζητεῖται   verb, pres. pass. indic. 3 pers. sg.
    {5.A.2}. . . . . id.
ζητεῖτε   verb, pres. act. impv. 2 pers. pl. {5.D.2} . id.
ζητεῖτε   verb, pres. act. indic. 2 pers. pl. {5.A.2} . id.
ζητείτω   verb, pres. act. impv. 3 pers. sg. {5.D.2}. id.
G2212 **ζητέω**   I seek, search for.
ζητηθήσεται   verb, fut. pass. indic. 3 pers. sg.
    {5.A.1}. . . . . .ζητέω G2212
G2213 **ζήτημα**, -ατος, τό   a question, subject of
    inquiry.
ζήτημα   noun, nom. sg. neut. {2.C} . . . . . .ζήτημα G2213
ζήτημα   noun, acc. pl. neut. {2.C} . . . . id.
ζητήματα   noun, nom. pl. neut. {2.C} . . . . id.
ζητήματος   noun, gen. sg. neut. {2.C} . . . . id.
ζητημάτων   noun, gen. pl. neut. {2.C} . . . . id.
ζητῆσαι   vbl., aor. act. inf. {6.B.1} . . . . . . .ζητέω G2212
ζητησάτω   verb, aor. act. impv. 3 pers. sg.
    {5.D.1}. . . . . id.
ζητήσεις   noun, acc. pl. fem. {2.C} . . . . .ζήτησις G2214
ζητήσετε   verb, fut. act. indic. 2 pers. pl.
    {5.A.1}. . . . . .ζητέω G2212

ζητήσεως   noun, gen. sg. fem. {2.C} . . . . . ζήτησις G2214
ζητήσῃ   verb, aor. act. subjunc. 3 pers. sg.
  {5.B.1} . . . . ζητέω G2212
ζήτησιν   noun, acc. sg. fem. {2.C} . . . . . . ζήτησις G2214
G2214 **ζήτησις**, -εως, ἡ   questioning.
ζήτησις   noun, nom. sg. fem. {2.C} . . . . . ζήτησις G2214
ζήτησον   verb, aor. act. impv. 2 pers. sg.
  {5.D.1} . . . . ζητέω G2212
ζητήσουσιν   verb, fut. act. indic. 3 pers. pl.
  {5.A.1} . . . . id.
ζητοῦμεν   verb, pres. act. indic. 1 pers. pl.
  {5.A.2} . . . . id.
ζητοῦν   vbl., pres. act. ptc. nom. sg. neut. {6.A.2} id.
ζητοῦντες   vbl., pres. act. ptc. nom. pl. masc.
  {6.A.2} . . . . id.
ζητοῦντι   vbl., pres. act. ptc. dat. sg. masc.
  {6.A.2} . . . . id.
ζητούντων   vbl., pres. act. ptc. gen. pl. masc.
  {6.A.2} . . . . id.
ζητοῦσι   verb, pres. act. indic. 3 pers. pl. {5.A.2} id.
ζητοῦσι   vbl., pres. act. ptc. dat. pl. masc. {6.A.2} id.
ζητοῦσιν   verb, pres. act. indic. 3 pers. pl.
  {5.A.2} . . . . id.
ζητοῦσιν   vbl., pres. act. ptc. dat. pl. masc.
  {6.A.2} . . . . id.
ζητῶ   verb, pres. act. indic. 1 pers. sg. {5.A.2} . . . id.
ζητῶν   vbl., pres. act. ptc. nom. sg. masc. {6.A.2} id.
ζιζάνια   noun, acc. pl. neut. {2.B} . . . . . . ζιζάνιον G2215
ζιζάνια   noun, nom. pl. neut. {2.B} . . . . id.
G2215 **ζιζάνιον**, -ου, τό   pl. darnel.
ζιζανίων   noun, gen. pl. neut. {2.B} . . . . . ζιζάνιον G2215
G2216 **Ζοροβαβέλ**, ὁ   Zerubbabel (flourished sixth
  c. B.C.), son of Salathiel, according to one of
  three traditions, all of which agree on Davidic
  descent, and father Abiud and Resa (Heb.).
Ζοροβαβέλ   noun prop. . . . . Ζοροβαβέλ G2216
Ζοροβάβελ   noun prop. . . . . id.
ζόφον   noun, acc. sg. masc. {2.B} . . . . ζόφος G2217
G2217 **ζόφος**, -ου, ὁ   darkness, murkiness.
ζόφος   noun, nom. sg. masc. {2.B} . . . . ζόφος G2217
ζόφου   noun, gen. sg. masc. {2.B} . . . . id.
ζόφῳ   noun, dat. sg. masc. {2.B} . . . . id.
ζυγόν   noun, acc. sg. masc. {2.B} . . . . ζυγός G2218
G2218 **ζυγός**, -οῦ, ὁ   a yoke; hence met. (a Jewish
  idea) of a heavy burden, comparable to the
  heavy yokes resting on the bullocks' necks.
ζυγός   noun, nom. sg. masc. {2.B} . . . . ζυγός G2218
ζυγῷ   noun, dat. sg. masc. {2.B} . . . . id.
G2219 **ζύμη**, -ης, ἡ   leaven, ferment, both lit. and met.
ζύμη   noun, nom. sg. fem. {2.A} . . . . ζύμη G2219
ζύμῃ   noun, dat. sg. fem. {2.A} . . . . id.
ζύμην   noun, acc. sg. fem. {2.A} . . . . id.
ζύμης   noun, gen. sg. fem. {2.A} . . . . id.
ζυμοῖ   verb, pres. act. indic. 3 pers. sg.
  {5.A.2} . . . . ζυμόω G2220
G2220 **ζυμόω**   I leaven.
ζῶ   verb, pres. act. indic. 1 pers. sg. {5.A.2} . . . . ζάω G2198
ζῷα   noun, nom. pl. neut. {2.B} . . . . ζῷον G2226
ζῷα   noun, nom. pl. neut. {2.B} . . . . id.
G2221 **ζωγρέω**   I capture alive or I capture for life.

ζωγρῶν   vbl., pres. act. ptc. nom. sg. masc.
  {6.A.2} . . . . ζωγρέω G2221
G2222 **ζωή**, -ῆς, ἡ   life, both of physical (present) and
  of spiritual (particularly future) existence;
  sometimes, e.g., Mark 10:17, = Heb. hayyim (a
  pl. form) = all the days you are alive (nearer to
  βίος than ζωή), of a place in the New Age.
ζωή   noun, nom. sg. fem. {2.A} . . . . ζωή G2222
ζωῇ   noun, dat. sg. fem. {2.A} . . . . id.
ζωήν   noun, acc. sg. fem. {2.A} . . . . id.
ζωῆς   noun, gen. sg. fem. {2.A} . . . . id.
ζῶμεν   verb, pres. act. indic. 1 pers. pl. {5.A.2} . ζάω G2198
ζῶμεν   verb, pres. act. subjunc. 1 pers. pl. {5.B.2} id.
ζῶν   vbl., pres. act. ptc. acc. sg. neut. {6.A.2} . . . id.
ζῶν   vbl., pres. act. ptc. nom. sg. masc. {6.A.2} . . id.
ζώνας   noun, acc. pl. fem. {2.A} . . . . ζώνη G2223
G2223 **ζώνη**, -ης, ἡ   a girdle, belt, waistband; because
  the purse was kept there, also a purse.
ζώνη   noun, nom. sg. fem. {2.A} . . . . ζώνη G2223
ζώνην   noun, acc. sg. fem. {2.A} . . . . id.
G2224 **ζώννυμι** (ζωννύω)   I gird, I put on the girdle,
  esp. as preparatory to active work; in John
  21:18 there a double entendre, the second occurrence referring to binding by another.
ζῶντα   vbl., pres. act. ptc. acc. pl. neut. {6.A.2} . ζάω G2198
ζῶντα   vbl., pres. act. ptc. acc. sg. masc. {6.A.2} . id.
ζῶντας   vbl., pres. act. ptc. acc. pl. masc. {6.A.2} id.
ζῶντες   vbl., pres. act. ptc. nom. pl. masc. {6.A.2} id.
ζῶντι   vbl., pres. act. ptc. dat. sg. masc. {6.A.2} . . id.
ζῶντος   vbl., pres. act. ptc. gen. sg. masc. {6.A.2} id.
ζῶντος   vbl., pres. act. ptc. gen. sg. neut. {6.A.2} . id.
ζώντων   vbl., pres. act. ptc. gen. pl. masc. {6.A.2} id.
ζῳογονεῖσθαι   vbl., pres. pass. inf.
  {6.B.2} . . . . ζῳογονέω G2225
ζῳογονεῖσθαι   vbl., pres. pass. inf. {6.B.2} . . . . . id.
G2225 **ζῳογονέω**   I preserve alive (lit. bring to birth).
ζῳογονήσει   verb, fut. act. indic. 3 pers. sg.
  {5.A.1} . . . . ζῳογονέω G2225
ζῳογονήσει   verb, fut. act. indic. 3 pers. sg.
  {5.A.1} . . . . id.
ζῳογονοῦντος   vbl., pres. act. ptc. gen. sg.
  masc. {6.A.2} . . . . id.
ζῳογονοῦντος   vbl., pres. act. ptc. gen. sg.
  masc. {6.A.2} . . . . id.
G2226 **ζῷον**, -ου, τό   an animal.
ζῷον   noun, nom. sg. neut. {2.B} . . . . ζῷον G2226
ζῷον   noun, nom. sg. neut. {2.B} . . . . id.
ζῳοποιεῖ   verb, pres. act. indic. 3 pers. sg.
  {5.A.2} . . . . ζῳοποιέω G2227
ζῳοποιεῖ   verb, pres. act. indic. 3 pers. sg.
  {5.A.2} . . . . id.
ζῳοποιεῖται   verb, pres. pass. indic. 3 pers. sg.
  {5.A.2} . . . . id.
ζῳοποιεῖται   verb, pres. pass. indic. 3 pers. sg.
  {5.A.2} . . . . id.
G2227 **ζῳοποιέω**   I make that which was dead to live.
ζῳοποιηθείς   vbl., aor. pass. ptc. nom. sg. masc.
  {6.A.1.a.} . . . . ζῳοποιέω G2227
ζῳοποιηθείς   vbl., aor. pass. ptc. nom. sg.
  masc. {6.A.1.a.} . . . . id.

ζωοποιηθήσονται verb, fut. pass. indic.
3 pers. pl. {5.A.1} . . . . id.
ζωοποιηθήσονται verb, fut. pass. indic.
3 pers. pl. {5.A.1} . . . . id.
ζωοποιῆσαι vbl., aor. act. inf. {6.B.1} . . . . id.
ζωοποιῆσαι vbl., aor. act. inf. {6.B.1} . . . . id.
ζωοποιήσει verb, fut. act. indic. 3 pers. sg.
{5.A.1} . . . . id.
ζωοποιήσει verb, fut. act. indic. 3 pers. sg.
{5.A.1} . . . . id.
ζωοποιοῦν vbl., pres. act. ptc. acc. sg. neut.
{6.A.2} . . . . id.
ζωοποιοῦν vbl., pres. act. ptc. nom. sg. neut.
{6.A.2} . . . . id.
ζωοποιοῦν vbl., pres. act. ptc. acc. sg. neut.
{6.A.2} . . . . id.
ζωοποιοῦν vbl., pres. act. ptc. nom. sg. neut.
{6.A.2} . . . . id.

ζωοποιοῦντος vbl., pres. act. ptc. gen. sg.
masc. {6.A.2} . . . . id.
ζωοποιοῦντος vbl., pres. act. ptc. gen. sg.
masc. {6.A.2} . . . . id.
ζῴου noun, gen. sg. neut. {2.B} . . . . ζῷον G2226
ζῴου noun, gen. sg. neut. {2.B} . . . . id.
ζῶσα vbl., pres. act. ptc. nom. sg. fem. {6.A.2} . ζάω G2198
ζῶσαι verb, aor. mid. impv. 2 pers. sg.
{5.D.3} . . . . ζώννυμι G2224
ζῶσαν vbl., pres. act. ptc. acc. sg. fem. {6.A.2} . ζάω G2198
ζώσας vbl., pres. act. ptc. acc. pl. fem. {6.A.2} . . id.
ζώσει verb, fut. act. indic. 3 pers. sg.
{5.A.1} . . . . ζώννυμι G2224
ζῶσι verb, pres. act. subjunc. 3 pers. pl. {5.B.2} ζάω G2198
ζῶσιν verb, pres. act. indic. 3 pers. pl. {5.A.2} . . id.
ζῶσιν verb, pres. act. subjunc. 3 pers. pl. {5.B.2} id.
ζῴων noun, gen. pl. neut. {2.B} . . . . ζῷον G2226
ζῴων noun, gen. pl. neut. {2.B} . . . . id.

Η η

ἡ art., nom. sg. fem. {1} . . . . ὁ G3588
G2228 ἤ conj., (1) *or*, both in rel. and interrog. clauses;
in interrog. sentences we ought perhaps sometimes to accent ἤ (cf. εἰ) and regard simply
as an interrog. particle, not to be translated;
(2) *than*, sometimes almost otiose after πρίν;
ἀλλ᾽ ἤ (i.e., ἄλλο ἤ; Luke 12:51; 2 Cor 1:13),
nothing but; ἤ γάρ in Luke 18:14 (var.) is
corrupt.
ἤ conj. . . . . ἤ G2228
G2229 ἦ adv. *truly, indeed.*
ἦ adv. . . . . ἦ G2229
ᾖ verb, pres. subjunc. 3 pers. sg. {7.B} . . . . εἰμί G1510
ᾗ art., nom. sg. fem. {1} . . . . ὁ G3588
ἥ pron. rel., nom. sg. fem. {4.C} . . . . ὅς G3739
ᾗ pron. rel., dat. sg. fem. {4.C} . . . . id.
ἠβουλήθην verb, aor. pass. indic. 1 pers. sg.
{5.A.1.b} . . . . βούλομαι G1014
ἤγαγε verb, ²aor. act. indic. 3 pers. sg. {5.A.1.b} . ἄγω G71
ἤγαγεν verb, ²aor. act. indic. 3 pers. sg. {5.A.1.b} id.
ἠγάγετε verb, ²aor. act. indic. 2 pers. pl. {5.A.1.b} id.
ἤγαγον verb, ²aor. act. indic. 3 pers. pl. {5.A.1.b} id.
ἠγαλλιάσατο verb, aor. mid. indic. 3 pers. sg.
{5.A.1} . . . . ἀγαλλιάω G21
ἠγαλλίασε verb, aor. act. indic. 3 pers. sg.
{5.A.1} . . . . id.
ἠγαλλίασεν verb, aor. act. indic. 3 pers. sg.
{5.A.1} . . . . id.
ἠγαλλιᾶτο verb, impf. mid./pass. indic. 3 pers.
sg. {5.A.2} . . . . id.
ἠγανάκτησαν verb, aor. act. indic. 3 pers. pl.
{5.A.1} . . . . ἀγανακτέω G23
ἠγανάκτησε verb, aor. act. indic. 3 pers. sg.
{5.A.1} . . . . id.
ἠγανάκτησεν verb, aor. act. indic. 3 pers. sg.
{5.A.1} . . . . id.

ἠγάπα verb, impf. act. indic. 3 pers. sg.
{5.A.2} . . . . ἀγαπάω G25
ἠγαπᾶτε verb, impf. act. indic. 2 pers. pl. {5.A.2} id.
ἠγαπήκαμεν verb, perf. act. indic. 1 pers. pl.
{5.A.1} . . . . id.
ἠγαπηκόσι vbl., perf. act. ptc. dat. pl. masc.
{6.A.2} . . . . id.
ἠγαπηκόσιν vbl., perf. act. ptc. dat. pl. masc.
{6.A.2} . . . . id.
ἠγαπημένην vbl., perf. pass. ptc. acc. sg. fem.
{6.A.2} . . . . id.
ἠγαπημένοι vbl., perf. pass. ptc. nom. pl.
masc. {6.A.2} . . . . id.
ἠγαπημένοις vbl., perf. pass. ptc. dat. pl. masc.
{6.A.2} . . . . id.
ἠγαπημένῳ vbl., perf. pass. ptc. dat. sg. masc.
{6.A.2} . . . . id.
ἠγάπησα verb, aor. act. indic. 1 pers. sg. {5.A.1} id.
ἠγαπήσαμεν verb, aor. act. indic. 1 pers. pl.
{5.A.1} . . . . id.
ἠγάπησαν verb, aor. act. indic. 3 pers. pl.
{5.A.1} . . . . id.
ἠγάπησας verb, aor. act. indic. 2 pers. sg.
{5.A.1} . . . . id.
ἠγάπησε verb, aor. act. indic. 3 pers. sg. {5.A.1} id.
ἠγάπησεν verb, aor. act. indic. 3 pers. sg.
{5.A.1} . . . . id.
ἠγγάρευσαν verb, aor. act. indic. 3 pers. pl.
{5.A.1.b} . . . . ἀγγαρεύω G29
ἤγγιζε verb, impf. act. indic. 3 pers. sg.
{5.A.1.b} . . . . ἐγγίζω G1448
ἤγγιζεν verb, impf. act. indic. 3 pers. sg.
{5.A.1.b} . . . . id.
ἤγγικε verb, perf. act. indic. 3 pers. sg. {5.A.1.c}. id.
ἤγγικεν verb, perf. act. indic. 3 pers. sg. {5.A.1.c} id.
ἤγγισαν verb, aor. act. indic. 3 pers. pl. {5.A.1.b} id.

ἤγγισε   verb, aor. act. indic. 3 pers. sg. {5.A.1.b} . id.

ἤγγισεν   verb, aor. act. indic. 3 pers. sg. {5.A.1.b} id.

ἤγειραν   verb, aor. act. indic. 3 pers. pl.
{5.A.1.b} . . . . .ἐγείρω *G1453*

ἤγειρε   verb, aor. act. indic. 3 pers. sg. {5.A.1.b} . id.

ἤγειρεν   verb, aor. act. indic. 3 pers. sg. {5.A.1.b} id.

ἡγεῖσθαι   vbl., pres. mid./pass. inf. {6.B.2} .ἡγέομαι *G2233*

ἡγεῖσθε   verb, pres. mid./pass. impv. 2 pers. pl.
{5.D.2} . . . . id.

ἡγείσθωσαν   verb, pres. mid./pass. impv.
3 pers. pl. {5.D.2} . . . . id.

ἡγεμόνα   noun, acc. sg. masc. {2.C} . . . . . ἡγεμών *G2232*

ἡγεμόνας   noun, acc. pl. masc. {2.C} . . . . id.

ἡγεμονεύοντος   vbl., pres. act. ptc. gen. sg. masc.
{6.A.1} . . . . ἡγεμονεύω *G2230*

G2230 **ἡγεμονεύω**   *I govern.*

ἡγεμόνι   noun, dat. sg. masc. {2.C} . . . . . . ἡγεμών *G2232*

G2231 **ἡγεμονία**, -ας, ἡ   *rule, authority.*

ἡγεμονίας   noun, gen. sg. fem. {2.A} . . . ἡγεμονία *G2231*

ἡγεμόνος   noun, gen. sg. masc. {2.C} . . . . . ἡγεμών *G2232*

ἡγεμόνων   noun, gen. pl. masc. {2.C} . . . . id.

ἡγεμόσιν   noun, dat. pl. masc. {2.C} . . . . id.

G2232 **ἡγεμών**, -όνος, ὁ   *a* (Roman) *governor.*

ἡγεμών   noun, nom. sg. masc. {2.C} . . . . . ἡγεμών *G2232*

ἦγεν   verb, impf. act. indic. 3 pers. sg. {5.A.1.b} . ἄγω *G71*

G2233 **ἡγέομαι**   (1) *I lead;* ὁ ἡγούμενος (as subs.), *the
leader;* (2) *I think, I am of opinion.*

ἠγέρθη   verb, aor. pass. indic. 3 pers. sg.
{5.A.1.b} . . . . .ἐγείρω *G1453*

ἠγέρθησαν   verb, aor. pass. indic. 3 pers. pl.
{5.A.1.b} . . . . id.

ἤγεσθε   verb, impf. pass. indic. 2 pers. pl.
{5.A.1.e} . . . . ἄγω *G71*

ἤγετο   verb, impf. pass. indic. 3 pers. sg. {5.A.1.e}id.

ἤγημαι   verb, perf. mid./pass. indic. 1 pers. sg.
{5.A.1} . . . . .ἡγέομαι *G2233*

ἡγησάμενος   vbl., aor. mid. ptc. nom. sg. masc.
{6.A.2} . . . . id.

ἡγησάμην   verb, aor. mid. indic. 1 pers. sg.
{5.A.1} . . . . id.

ἡγήσασθε   verb, aor. mid. impv. 2 pers. pl.
{5.D.1} . . . . id.

ἡγήσατο   verb, aor. mid. indic. 3 pers. sg. {5.A.1}id.

ἡγίασε   verb, aor. act. indic. 3 pers. sg.
{5.A.1.b} . . . . .ἁγιάζω *G37*

ἡγίασεν   verb, aor. act. indic. 3 pers. sg. {5.A.1.b}id.

ἡγιάσθη   verb, aor. pass. indic. 3 pers. sg.
{5.A.1.b} . . . . id.

ἡγιάσθητε   verb, aor. pass. indic. 2 pers. pl.
{5.A.1.b} . . . . id.

ἡγιασμένη   vbl., perf. pass. ptc. nom. sg. fem.
{6.A.1.b} . . . . id.

ἡγιασμένοι   vbl., perf. pass. ptc. nom. pl. masc.
{6.A.1.b} . . . . id.

ἡγιασμένοις   vbl., perf. pass. ptc. dat. pl. masc.
{6.A.1.b} . . . . id.

ἡγιασμένον   vbl., perf. pass. ptc. nom. sg. neut.
{6.A.1.b} . . . . id.

ἡγίασται   verb, perf. pass. indic. 3 pers. sg.
{5.A.1.f}. . . . . id.

ἡγνικότες   vbl., perf. act. ptc. nom. pl. masc.
{6.A.1.a} . . . . .ἁγνίζω *G48*

ἡγνισμένον   vbl., perf. pass. ptc. acc. sg. masc.
{6.A.1.b} . . . . id.

ἠγνόουν   verb, impf. act. indic. 3 pers. pl.
{5.A.2} . . . . .ἀγνοέω *G50*

ἤγοντο   verb, impf. pass. indic. 3 pers. pl.
{5.A.1.e} . . . . ἄγω *G71*

ἠγόραζον   verb, impf. act. indic. 3 pers. pl.
{5.A.1.b} .ἀγοράζω *G59*

ἠγόρασα   verb, aor. act. indic. 1 pers. sg.
{5.A.1.b} . . . . id.

ἠγόρασαν   verb, aor. act. indic. 3 pers. pl.
{5.A.1.b} . . . . id.

ἠγόρασας   verb, aor. act. indic. 2 pers. sg.
{5.A.1.b} . . . . id.

ἠγόρασεν   verb, aor. act. indic. 3 pers. sg.
{5.A.1.b} . . . . id.

ἠγοράσθησαν   verb, aor. pass. indic. 3 pers. pl.
{5.A.1.b} . . . . id.

ἠγοράσθητε   verb, aor. pass. indic. 2 pers. pl.
{5.A.1.b} . . . . id.

ἠγορασμένοι   vbl., perf. pass. ptc. nom. pl.
masc. {6.A.1.b} . . . . id.

ἡγοῦμαι   verb, pres. mid./pass. indic. 1 pers. sg.
{5.A.2} . . . . .ἡγέομαι *G2233*

ἡγούμενοι   vbl., pres. mid./pass. ptc. nom. pl.
masc. {6.A.2} . . . . id.

ἡγουμένοις   vbl., pres. mid./pass. ptc. dat. pl.
masc. {6.A.2} . . . . id.

ἡγούμενον   vbl., pres. mid./pass. ptc. acc. sg.
masc. {6.A.2} . . . . id.

ἡγούμενος   vbl., pres. mid./pass. ptc. nom. sg.
masc. {6.A.2} . . . . id.

ἡγουμένους   vbl., pres. mid./pass. ptc. acc. pl.
masc. {6.A.2} . . . . id.

ἡγουμένων   vbl., pres. mid./pass. ptc. gen. pl.
masc. {6.A.2} . . . . id.

ἡγοῦνται   verb, pres. mid./pass. indic. 3 pers.
pl. {5.A.2} . . . . id.

ἠγωνίζοντο   verb, impf. mid./pass. indic. 3 pers. pl.
{5.A.1.e} .ἀγωνίζομαι *G75*

ἠγώνισμαι   verb, perf. mid./pass. indic. 1 pers.
sg. {5.A.1.f} . . . . id.

ᾔδει   verb, plu. act. indic. 3 pers. sg. {5.A.1.c} . .εἴδω *G1492*

ᾔδειν   verb, plu. act. indic. 1 pers. sg. {5.A.1.c} . . id.

ᾔδεις   verb, plu. act. indic. 2 pers. sg. {5.A.1.c} . . id.

ᾔδεισαν   verb, plu. act. indic. 3 pers. pl. {5.A.1.c}id.

ᾔδειτε   verb, plu. act. indic. 2 pers. pl. {5.A.1.c} . id.

G2234 **ἡδέως**   adv., *gladly, pleasantly;* superl ἥδιστα as
elative, *all the more gladly.*

ἡδέως   adv. {3.F; 3.G} . . . . ἡδέως *G2234*

G2235 **ἤδη**   adv., *already; now at length, now after all
this waiting* Rom 1:10.

ἤδη   adv. . . . . ἤδη *G2235*

ἠδίκηκα   verb, perf. act. indic. 1 pers. sg.
{5.A.1} . . . . .ἀδικέω *G91*

ἠδίκησα   verb, aor. act. indic. 1 pers. sg. {5.A.1}. id.

ἠδικήσαμεν   verb, aor. act. indic. 1 pers. pl.
{5.A.1} . . . . id.

ἠδικήσατε   verb, aor. act. indic. 2 pers. pl.
   {5.A.1}. . . . . id.
ἠδίκησε   verb, aor. act. indic. 3 pers. sg. {5.A.1} . id.
ἠδίκησεν   verb, aor. act. indic. 3 pers. sg. {5.A.1} id.
G2236 **ἥδιστα**   adv., elative, *with great pleasure, most
   gladly;* superl. neut. pl. of ἡδέως.
ἥδιστα   adv. super {3.F; 3.G} . . . . ἥδιστα G2236
ἡδοναῖς   noun, dat. pl. fem. {2.A} . . . . ἡδονή G2237
G2237 **ἡδονή**, -ῆς, ἡ   *pleasure, a pleasure,* esp. sensuous pleasure.
ἡδονήν   noun, acc. sg. fem. {2.A}. . . . . ἡδονή G2237
ἡδονῶν   noun, gen. pl. fem. {2.A}. . . . . id.
ἠδύναντο   verb, impf. mid./pass. indic. 3 pers. pl.
   {5.A.3.a} . . . . δύναμαι G1410
ἠδύνασθε   verb, impf. mid./pass. indic. 2 pers.
   pl. {5.A.3.a} . . . . id.
ἠδυνάσθη   verb, aor. pass. indic. 3 pers. sg.
   {5.A.1}. . . . . id.
ἠδύνατο   verb, impf. mid./pass. indic. 3 pers.
   sg. {5.A.3.a} . . . . id.
ἠδυνήθη   verb, aor. pass. indic. 3 pers. sg.
   {5.A.1}. . . . . id.
ἠδυνήθημεν   verb, aor. pass. indic. 1 pers. pl.
   {5.A.1}. . . . . id.
ἠδυνήθην   verb, aor. pass. indic. 1 pers. sg.
   {5.A.1}. . . . . id.
ἠδυνήθησαν   verb, aor. pass. indic. 3 pers. pl.
   {5.A.1}. . . . . id.
ἠδυνήθητε   verb, aor. pass. indic. 2 pers. pl.
   {5.A.1}. . . . . id.
G2238 **ἡδύοσμον**, -ου, τό   *mint, peppermint.*
ἡδύοσμον   noun, acc. sg. neut. {2.B} . . . ἡδύοσμον G2238
ἤθελε   verb, impf. act. indic. 3 pers. sg.
   {5.A.1.b} . . . . θέλω G2309
ἤθελεν   verb, impf. act. indic. 3 pers. sg.
   {5.A.1.b} . . . . id.
ἤθελες   verb, impf. act. indic. 2 pers. sg.
   {5.A.1.b} . . . . id.
ἠθέλησα   verb, aor. act. indic. 1 pers. sg.
   {5.A.1.b} . . . . id.
ἠθελήσαμεν   verb, aor. act. indic. 1 pers. pl.
   {5.A.1.b} . . . . id.
ἠθέλησαν   verb, aor. act. indic. 3 pers. pl.
   {5.A.1.b} . . . . id.
ἠθέλησας   verb, aor. act. indic. 2 pers. sg.
   {5.A.1.b} . . . . id.
ἠθελήσατε   verb, aor. act. indic. 2 pers. pl.
   {5.A.1.b} . . . . id.
ἠθέλησε   verb, aor. act. indic. 3 pers. sg.
   {5.A.1.b} . . . . id.
ἠθέλησεν   verb, aor. act. indic. 3 pers. sg.
   {5.A.1.b} . . . . id.
ἤθελον   verb, impf. act. indic. 1 pers. sg.
   {5.A.1.b} . . . . id.
ἤθελον   verb, impf. act. indic. 3 pers. pl.
   {5.A.1.b} . . . . id.
ἠθέτησαν   verb, aor. act. indic. 3 pers. pl.
   {5.A.1}. . . . . ἀθετέω G114
ἤθη   noun, acc. pl. neut. {2.C}. . . . . ἦθος G2239
G2239 **ἦθος**, -ους, τό   *a habit.*

ἠθροισμένους   vbl., perf. pass. ptc. acc. pl. masc.
   {6.A.1.b} . . . . ἀθροίζω G4867†‡
ἠθῶν   noun, gen. pl. neut. {2.C} . . . . ἦθος G2239
ᾔδει   verb, plu. act. indic. 3 pers. sg. {5.A.1.c} . εἴδω G1492
ἠκαιρεῖσθε   verb, impf. mid./pass. indic. 2 pers. pl.
   {5.A.2}. . . . . ἀκαιρέομαι G170
ἥκασι   verb, perf. act. indic. 3 pers. pl. {5.A.1.c}ἥκω G2240
ἥκασιν   verb, perf. act. indic. 3 pers. pl. {5.A.1.c}id.
ἥκει   verb, pres. act. indic. 3 pers. sg. {5.A.1.a} . . id.
ἤκμασαν   verb, aor. act. indic. 3 pers. pl.
   {5.A.1.b} . . . . ἀκμάζω G187
ἤκμασεν   verb, aor. act. indic. 3 pers. sg. {5.A.1.b}. id.
ἠκολούθει   verb, impf. act. indic. 3 pers. sg.
   {5.A.2}. ἀκολουθέω G190
ἠκολουθήκαμεν   verb, perf. act. indic. 1 pers.
   pl. {5.A.1} . . . . id.
ἠκολουθήσαμεν   verb, aor. act. indic. 1 pers.
   pl. {5.A.1} . . . . id.
ἠκολούθησαν   verb, aor. act. indic. 3 pers. pl.
   {5.A.1}. . . . . id.
ἠκολούθησε   verb, aor. act. indic. 3 pers. sg.
   {5.A.1}. . . . . id.
ἠκολούθησεν   verb, aor. act. indic. 3 pers. sg.
   {5.A.1}. . . . . id.
ἠκολούθουν   verb, impf. act. indic. 3 pers. pl.
   {5.A.2}. . . . . id.
ἧκον   verb, impf. act. indic. 3 pers. pl. {5.A.1.b} ἥκω G2240
ἤκουε   verb, impf. act. indic. 3 pers. sg.
   {5.A.1.b} . . . . ἀκούω G191
ἤκουεν   verb, impf. act. indic. 3 pers. sg.
   {5.A.1.b} . . . . id.
ἤκουον   verb, impf. act. indic. 3 pers. pl.
   {5.A.1.b} . . . . id.
ἤκουσα   verb, aor. act. indic. 1 pers. sg. {5.A.1.b}id.
ἠκούσαμεν   verb, aor. act. indic. 1 pers. pl.
   {5.A.1.b} . . . . id.
ἤκουσαν   verb, aor. act. indic. 3 pers. pl.
   {5.A.1.b} . . . . id.
ἤκουσας   verb, aor. act. indic. 2 pers. sg.
   {5.A.1.b} . . . . id.
ἠκούσατε   verb, aor. act. indic. 2 pers. pl.
   {5.A.1.b} . . . . id.
ἤκουσε   verb, aor. act. indic. 3 pers. sg. {5.A.1.b} id.
ἤκουσεν   verb, aor. act. indic. 3 pers. sg.
   {5.A.1.b} . . . . id.
ἠκούσθη   verb, aor. pass. indic. 3 pers. sg.
   {5.A.1.b} . . . . id.
ἥκουσιν   verb, pres. act. indic. 3 pers. pl.
   {5.A.1.a} . . . . ἥκω G2240
ἠκρίβωσε   verb, aor. act. indic. 3 pers. sg.
   {5.A.1}. . . . . ἀκριβόω G198
ἠκρίβωσεν   verb, aor. act. indic. 3 pers. sg.
   {5.A.1}. . . . . id.
ἠκυρώσατε   verb, aor. act. indic. 2 pers. sg.
   {5.A.1}. . . . . ἀκυρόω G208
G2240 **ἥκω**   *I have come,* but other tenses are translated as if the pres. meant *I come.*
ἥκω   verb, pres. act. indic. 1 pers. sg. {5.A.1.a} . ἥκω G2240
ἥλατο   verb, aor. mid. indic. 3 pers. sg.
   {5.A.1.e} . . . . ἅλλομαι G242

ἠλαττόνησε   verb, aor. act. indic. 3 pers. sg.
{5.A.1} . . . . ἐλαττονέω G1641
ἠλαττόνησεν   verb, aor. act. indic. 3 pers. sg.
{5.A.1} . . . . id.
ἠλαττωμένον   vbl., perf. pass. ptc. acc. sg. masc.
{6.A.2} . . . . ἐλαττόω G1642
ἠλάττωσας   verb, aor. act. indic. 2 pers. sg.
{5.A.1} . . . . id.
ἠλαύνετο   verb, impf. pass. indic. 3 pers. sg.
{5.A.1.e} . . . . ἐλαύνω G1643
ἠλεήθημεν   verb, aor. pass. indic. 1 pers. pl.
{5.A.1} . . . . ἐλεέω G1653
ἠλεήθην   verb, aor. pass. indic. 1 pers. sg.
{5.A.1} . . . . id.
ἠλεήθητε   verb, aor. pass. indic. 2 pers. pl.
{5.A.1} . . . . id.
ἠλεημένοι   vbl., perf. pass. ptc. nom. pl. masc.
{6.A.2} . . . . id.
ἠλεημένος   vbl., perf. pass. ptc. nom. sg. masc.
{6.A.2} . . . . id.
ἠλέησα   verb, aor. act. indic. 1 pers. sg. {5.A.1} . id.
ἠλέησε   verb, aor. act. indic. 3 pers. sg. {5.A.1} . id.
ἠλέησεν   verb, aor. act. indic. 3 pers. sg. {5.A.1} . id.
Ἠλεί   noun prop. . . . . Ἠλί G2242
Ἠλεία   noun prop., gen. sg. masc. {2.A; 2.D} Ἠλίας G2243
Ἠλείᾳ   noun prop., dat. sg. masc. {2.A; 2.D} . . . id.
Ἠλείαν   noun prop., acc. sg. masc. {2.A; 2.D} . . id.
Ἠλείας   noun prop., nom. sg. masc. {2.A; 2.D} . id.
Ἠλείου   noun prop., gen. sg. masc. {2.A; 2.D} . . id.
ἤλειφε   verb, impf. act. indic. 3 pers. sg.
{5.A.1.b} . . . . ἀλείφω G218
ἤλειφεν   verb, impf. act. indic. 3 pers. sg.
{5.A.1.b} . . . . id.
ἤλειφον   verb, impf. act. indic. 3 pers. pl.
{5.A.1.b} . . . . id.
ἤλειψας   verb, aor. act. indic. 2 pers. sg.
{5.A.1.b} . . . . id.
ἤλειψε   verb, aor. act. indic. 3 pers. sg. {5.A.1.b}. id.
ἤλειψεν   verb, aor. act. indic. 3 pers. sg. {5.A.1.b}id.
ἠλευθέρωσε   verb, aor. act. indic. 3 pers. sg.
{5.A.1} . . . . ἐλευθερόω G1659
ἠλευθέρωσεν   verb, aor. act. indic. 3 pers. sg.
{5.A.1} . . . . id.
ἤλθαμεν   verb, ²aor. act. indic. 1 pers. pl.
{5.A.1.b} . . . . ἔρχομαι G2064
ἦλθαν   verb, ²aor. act. indic. 3 pers. pl. {5.A.1.b}. id.
ἤλθατε   verb, ²aor. act. indic. 2 pers. pl. {5.A.1.b} id.
ἦλθε   verb, ²aor. act. indic. 3 pers. sg. {5.A.1.b} . . id.
ἦλθεν   verb, ²aor. act. indic. 3 pers. sg. {5.A.1.b} . id.
ἦλθες   verb, ²aor. act. indic. 2 pers. sg. {5.A.1.b} . id.
ἤλθετε   verb, ²aor. act. indic. 2 pers. pl. {5.A.1.b} id.
ἤλθομεν   verb, ²aor. act. indic. 1 pers. pl.
{5.A.1.b} . . . . id.
ἦλθον   verb, ²aor. act. indic. 1 pers. sg. {5.A.1.b}. id.
ἦλθον   verb, ²aor. act. indic. 3 pers. pl. {5.A.1.b}. id.
ηλι   Heb. . . . . .ἠλί G2241
G2241 ἠλί (ἠλεί), ἠλεί)   my God (from Heb., as
contrasted with the var. ἐλωΐ, from Aram.).
G2242 Ἠλί, ὁ   Eli, the father of Joseph, husband of
Mary, Luke 3:23 (Heb.).

ἠλί   Heb. . . . . .ἠλί G2241
Ἠλί   noun prop. . . . . Ἠλί G2242
Ἠλί   noun prop. . . . . Ἠλί G2242
Ἠλίᾳ   noun prop., dat. sg. masc. {2.A; 2.D} Ἠλίας G2243
Ἠλίᾳ   noun prop., dat. sg. masc. {2.A; 2.D} . . . id.
Ἠλίαν   noun prop., acc. sg. masc. {2.A; 2.D} . . . id.
Ἠλίαν   noun prop., acc. sg. masc. {2.A; 2.D} . . . id.
G2243 Ἠλίας, -ου, ὁ   Elias, Elijah, the prophet (Heb.).
Ἠλίας   noun prop., nom. sg. masc. {2.A;
2.D} . . . . Ἠλίας G2243
Ἠλίας   noun prop., nom. sg. masc. {2.A; 2.D} . . id.
ἠλίκην   pron. correl., acc. sg. fem. {4.D} . . . .ἡλίκος G2245
G2244 ἡλικία, -ας, ἡ   age, term of life; full age,
ἡλικίαν ἔχει, he has come to maturity, John
9:21, 23, cf. Eph 4:13; stature, only in Luke
19:3.
ἡλικίᾳ   noun, dat. sg. fem. {2.A} . . . . ἡλικία G2244
ἡλικίαν   noun, acc. sg. fem. {2.A} . . . . id.
ἡλικίας   noun, gen. sg. fem. {2.A} . . . . id.
ἡλίκον   pron. correl., acc. sg. masc. {4.D} . . .ἡλίκος G2245
ἡλίκον   pron. correl., nom. sg. neut. {4.D} . . . . id.
G2245 ἡλίκος, -η, -ον   rel. and interrog. of which size,
of what size, e.g., in Jas 3:5 ἡλίκον means how
small, ἡλίκην, how much. Context determines
the sense in each case.
ἥλιον   noun, acc. sg. masc. {2.B} . . . . ἥλιος G2246
G2246 ἥλιος, -ου, ὁ   the sun; μὴ βλέπων τὸν ἥλιον,
equivalent to stone-blind, Acts 13:11.
ἥλιος   noun, nom. sg. masc. {2.B} . . . . .ἥλιος G2246
Ἠλίου   noun prop., gen. sg. masc. {2.A; 2.D}Ἠλίας G2243
ἡλίου   noun, gen. sg. masc. {2.B} . . . . id.
Ἠλίου   noun prop., gen. sg. masc. {2.A; 2.D}Ἠλίας G2243
ἡλίῳ   noun, dat. sg. masc. {2.B} . . . . .ἥλιος G2246
ἡλκωμένος   vbl., perf. pass. ptc. nom. sg. masc.
{6.A.2} . . . . ἑλκόω G1669
ἤλλαξαν   verb, aor. act. indic. 3 pers. pl.
{5.A.1.b} . . . . ἀλλάσσω G236
ἤλλετο   verb, impf. mid./pass. indic. 3 pers. sg.
{5.A.1.e} . . . . .ἅλλομαι G242
G2247 ἧλος, -ου, ὁ   a nail.
ἤλπιζε   verb, impf. act. indic. 3 pers. sg.
{5.A.1.b} . . . . ἐλπίζω G1679
ἤλπιζεν   verb, impf. act. indic. 3 pers. sg.
{5.A.1.b} . . . . id.
ἠλπίζομεν   verb, impf. act. indic. 1 pers. pl.
{5.A.1.b} . . . . id.
ἠλπίκαμεν   verb, perf. act. indic. 1 pers. pl.
{5.A.1.c} . . . . id.
ἠλπίκατε   verb, perf. act. indic. 2 pers. pl.
{5.A.1.c} . . . . id.
ἤλπικεν   verb, perf. act. indic. 3 pers. sg.
{5.A.1.c} . . . . id.
ἠλπικέναι   vbl., perf. act. inf. {6.B.1} . . . . . . id.
ἠλπικότες   vbl., perf. act. ptc. nom. pl. masc.
{6.A.1.a} . . . . id.
ἠλπίσαμεν   verb, aor. act. indic. 1 pers. pl.
{5.A.1.b} . . . . id.
ἥλων   noun, gen. pl. masc. {2.B} . . . . ἧλος G2247
ἥμαρτε   verb, ²aor. act. indic. 3 pers. sg.
{5.A.1.b} . . . . ἁμαρτάνω G264

ἥμαρτεν   verb, ²aor. act. indic. 3 pers. sg.
{5.A.1.b} . . . . id.
ἥμαρτες   verb, ²aor. act. indic. 2 pers. sg.
{5.A.1.b} . . . . id.
ἡμαρτήκαμεν   verb, perf. act. indic. 1 pers. pl.
{5.A.1.c} . . . . id.
ἥμαρτον   verb, ²aor. act. indic. 1 pers. sg.
{5.A.1.b} . . . . id.
ἥμαρτον   verb, ²aor. act. indic. 3 pers. pl.
{5.A.1.b} . . . . id.
ἡμᾶς   pron. pers., 1 pers. acc. pl. {4.A} . . . . . . ἐγώ G1473
ἥμεθα   verb, impf. indic. 1 pers. pl. {7.A} . . . . εἰμί G1510
ἡμεῖς   pron. pers., 1 pers. nom. pl. {4.A} . . . . . ἐγώ G1473
ἠμέλησα   verb, aor. act. indic. 1 pers. sg.
{5.A.1} . . . . .ἀμελέω G272
ἤμελλε   verb, impf. act. indic. 3 pers. sg.
{5.A.1.b} . . . . μέλλω G3195
ἤμελλεν   verb, impf. act. indic. 3 pers. sg.
{5.A.1.b} . . . . id.
ἤμελλον   verb, impf. act. indic. 1 pers. sg.
{5.A.1.b} . . . . id.
ἤμεν   verb, impf. indic. 1 pers. pl. {7.A} . . . . . . εἰμί G1510
G2250   ἡμέρα, -ας, ἡ   *a day*, the period from sunrise
to sunset; (ἡ) ἡμέρα κρίσεως, ἡ ἡμέρα
ἐκείνη, ἡ ἡμέρα τοῦ κυρίου, *the judgment
day*, coinciding with the end of the world,
according to late Jewish belief; τῇ τρίτῃ
ἡμέρᾳ, etc., *on the third day, after two days*, so
διὰ τριῶν ἡμερῶν, Matt 26:61, etc.; νύκτα
καὶ ἡμέραν, *through night as well as day*;
νυκτὸς καὶ ἡμέρας, *by night as well as day*,
imply merely *before dawn* as well as *during
the day*; (τὸ) καθ᾽ ἡμέραν, *day by day, each
day*; πάσας τὰς ἡμέρας (vernacular phrase),
perpetually, Matt 28:20.
ἡμέρα   noun, nom. sg. fem. {2.A} . . . . ἡμέρα G2250
ἡμέρᾳ   noun, dat. sg. fem. {2.A} . . . . id.
ἡμέραι   noun, nom. pl. fem. {2.A} . . . . id.
ἡμέραις   noun, dat. pl. fem. {2.A} . . . . id.
ἡμέραν   noun, acc. sg. fem. {2.A} . . . . id.
ἡμέρας   noun, acc. pl. fem. {2.A} . . . . id.
ἡμέρας   noun, gen. sg. fem. {2.A} . . . . id.
ἡμερῶν   noun, gen. pl. fem. {2.A} . . . . id.
ἡμετέρα   pron. posses, 1 pers. pl. nom. sg. fem.
{4.H} .ἡμέτερος G2251
ἡμετέραις   pron. posses, 1 pers. pl. dat. pl. fem.
{4.H} . . . . id.
ἡμετέραν   pron. posses, 1 pers. pl. acc. sg. fem.
{4.H} . . . . id.
ἡμετέρας   pron. posses, 1 pers. pl. gen. sg. fem.
{4.H} . . . . id.
ἡμέτεροι   pron. posses, 1 pers. pl. nom. pl.
masc. {4.H} . . . . id.
ἡμετέροις   pron. posses, 1 pers. pl. dat. pl.
masc. {4.H} . . . . id.
ἡμέτερον   pron. posses, 1 pers. pl. acc. sg.
masc. {4.H} . . . . id.

ἡμέτερον   pron. posses, 1 pers. pl. acc. sg. neut.
{4.H} . . . . id.
G2251   ἡμέτερος, -α, -ον   *our.*
ἡμετέρων   pron. posses, 1 pers. pl. gen. pl. fem.
{4.H} . . . . .ἡμέτερος G2251
ἤμην   verb, impf. mid. indic. 1 pers. sg. {7.A} . . εἰμί G1510
ἡμιθανῆ   adj., acc. sg. masc. {3.E} . . . . . ἡμιθανής G2253
G2253   ἡμιθανής, -ές   *half-dead.*
ἡμῖν   pron. pers., 1 pers. dat. pl. {4.A} . . . . ἐγώ G1473
ἡμίση   adj., acc. pl. neut. {3.D} . . . . ἥμισυς G2255
ἡμίσια   adj., acc. pl. neut. {3.D} . . . . id.
ἡμίσους   adj., gen. sg. neut. {3.D} . . . . id.
ἥμισυ   adj., acc. sg. neut. {3.D} . . . . id.
G2255   ἥμισυς, -εια, -υ, gen. ἡμίσους   *half*; (τὸ)
ἥμισυν, τὰ ἡμίσια (ἡμίσεια, elsewhere
unparalleled; usual form ἡμίση), *the half.*
ἡμιώριον   noun, acc. sg. neut. {2.B} . . . . . ἡμίωρον G2256
G2256   ἡμίωρον (ἡμιώριον), -ου, τό   *half an hour*,
but see ὥρα.
ἡμίωρον   noun, acc. sg. neut. {2.B} . . . . . ἡμίωρον G2256
ἠμύνατο   verb, aor. mid. indic. 3 pers. sg.
{5.A.1.e} . . . . .ἀμύνομαι G292
ἠμφιεσμένον   vbl., perf. pass. ptc. acc. sg. masc.
{6.A.3} . . . . ἀμφιέννυμι G294
ἡμῶν   pron. pers., 1 pers. gen. pl. {4.A} . . . . . . ἐγώ G1473
ἥν   pron. rel., acc. sg. fem. {4.C} . . . . .ὅς G3739
ἦν   verb, impf. indic. 3 pers. sg. {7.A} . . . . εἰμί G1510
ἠνάγκαζον   verb, impf. act. indic. 1 pers. sg.
{5.A.1.b} . . . . ἀναγκάζω G315
ἠναγκάσατε   verb, aor. act. indic. 2 pers. pl.
{5.A.1.b} . . . . id.
ἠνάγκασε   verb, aor. act. indic. 3 pers. sg.
{5.A.1.b} . . . . id.
ἠνάγκασεν   verb, aor. act. indic. 3 pers. sg.
{5.A.1.b} . . . . id.
ἠναγκάσθη   verb, aor. pass. indic. 3 pers. sg.
{5.A.1.b} . . . . id.
ἠναγκάσθην   verb, aor. pass. indic. 1 pers. sg.
{5.A.1.b} . . . . id.
ἤνεγκα   verb, aor. act. indic. 1 pers. sg.
{5.A.1.b} . . . . φέρω G5342
ἤνεγκαν   verb, aor. act. indic. 3 pers. pl.
{5.A.1.b} . . . . id.
ἤνεγκε   verb, aor. act. indic. 3 pers. sg. {5.A.1.b} . id.
ἤνεγκεν   verb, aor. act. indic. 3 pers. sg. {5.A.1.b} id.
ἠνείχεσθε   verb, impf. mid./pass. indic. 2 pers. pl.
{5.A.1.e} . . . . .ἀνέχω G430
ἠνεσχόμην   verb, ²aor. mid. indic. 1 pers. sg.
{5.A.1.e} . . . . id.
ἠνέχθη   verb, aor. pass. indic. 3 pers. sg.
{5.A.1.b} . . . . φέρω G5342
ἠνεῳγμένη   vbl., perf. pass. ptc. nom. sg. fem.
{6.A.1.b} . . . . .ἀνοίγω G455
ἠνεῳγμένην   vbl., perf. pass. ptc. acc. sg. fem.
{6.A.1.b} . . . . id.
ἠνεῳγμένον   vbl., perf. pass. ptc. acc. sg. masc.
{6.A.1.b} . . . . id.

ἠνεῳγμένον vbl., perf. pass. ptc. acc. sg. neut.
{6.A.1.b} . . . . id.
ἠνέῳξεν verb, aor. act. indic. 3 pers. sg.
{5.A.1.b} . . . . id.
ἠνεῴχθη verb, aor. pass. indic. 3 pers. sg.
{5.A.1.b} . . . . id.
ἠνεῴχθησαν verb, aor. pass. indic. 3 pers. pl.
{5.A.1.b} . . . . id.
G2259 ἡνίκα part., *when; ἡνίκα ἄν, whenever.*
ἡνίκα part. . . . . ἡνίκα G2259
ἠνοίγη verb, ²aor. pass. indic. 3 pers. sg.
{5.A.1.e} . . . . ἀνοίγω G455
ἠνοίγησαν verb, ²aor. pass. indic. 3 pers. pl.
{5.A.1.e} . . . . id.
ἤνοιξε verb, aor. act. indic. 3 pers. sg. {5.A.1.b} . id.
ἤνοιξεν verb, aor. act. indic. 3 pers. sg. {5.A.1.b} id.
ἠνοίχθη verb, aor. pass. indic. 3 pers. sg.
{5.A.1.b} . . . . id.
ἠνοίχθησαν verb, aor. pass. indic. 3 pers. pl.
{5.A.1.b} . . . . id.
ἠντληκότες vbl., perf. act. ptc. nom. pl. masc.
{6.A.2} . . . . ἀντλέω G501
ἤξει verb, fut. act. indic. 3 pers. sg. {5.A.1.a} . ἥκω G2240
ἤξῃ verb, aor. act. subjunc. 3 pers. sg. {5.B.1} . . . id.
ἠξίου verb, impf. act. indic. 3 pers. sg. {5.A.2} ἀξιόω G515
ἠξίωσα verb, aor. act. indic. 1 pers. sg. {5.A.1} . id.
ἠξίωται verb, perf. pass. indic. 3 pers. sg.
{5.A.1} . . . . id.
ἥξουσι verb, fut. act. indic. 3 pers. pl. {5.A.1.a} ἥκω G2240
ἥξουσιν verb, fut. act. indic. 3 pers. pl. {5.A.1.a} id.
ἥξω verb, fut. act. indic. 1 pers. sg. {5.A.1.a} . id.
ἥξω verb, aor. act. subjunc. 1 pers. sg. {5.B.1} . . . id.
ἥξωσι verb, aor. act. subjunc. 3 pers. pl. {5.B.1} . id.
ἥξωσιν verb, aor. act. subjunc. 3 pers. pl. {5.B.1} id.
ἠπατήθη verb, aor. pass. indic. 3 pers. sg.
{5.A.1} . . . . ἀπατάω G538
ἠπείθησαν verb, aor. act. indic. 3 pers. pl.
{5.A.1} . . . . ἀπειθέω G544
ἠπειθήσατε verb, aor. act. indic. 2 pers. pl.
{5.A.1} . . . . id.
ἠπείθουν verb, impf. act. indic. 3 pers. pl.
{5.A.2} . . . . id.
ἠπείλει verb, impf. act. indic. 3 pers. sg.
{5.A.2} . . . . ἀπειλέω G546
G2260 ἤπερ conj., an intensified form of ἤ, *than.*
ἤπερ conj. . . . . ἤπερ G2260
ἤπιοι adj., nom. pl. masc. {3.A} . . . . ἤπιος G2261
ἤπιον adj., acc. sg. masc. {3.A} . . . . id.
G2261 ἤπιος, -α, -ον *gentle.*
ἠπίστησαν verb, aor. act. indic. 3 pers. pl.
{5.A.1} . . . . ἀπιστέω G569
ἠπίστουν verb, impf. act. indic. 3 pers. pl.
{5.A.2} . . . . id.
ἠπόρει verb, impf. act. indic. 3 pers. sg.
{5.A.2} . . . . ἀπορέω G639
ἥπτοντο verb, impf. mid./pass. indic. 3 pers. pl.
{5.A.1.e} . . . . ἅπτομαι G680
G2262 Ἤρ, ὁ *Er, son of Joshua and father of Elmadam
(Heb.).*

Ἤρ noun prop. . . . . Ἤρ G2262
ἦραν verb, aor. act. indic. 3 pers. pl. {5.A.1.b} . αἴρω G142
ἤρατε verb, aor. act. indic. 2 pers. pl. {5.A.1.b} . id.
ἠργάζετο verb, impf. mid./pass. indic. 3 pers. sg.
{5.A.1.e} . . . . ἐργάζομαι G2038
ἠργάζοντο verb, impf. mid./pass. indic. 3 pers.
pl. {5.A.1.e} . . . . id.
ἠργασάμεθα verb, aor. mid. indic. 1 pers. pl.
{5.A.1.e} . . . . id.
ἠργάσαντο verb, aor. mid. indic. 3 pers. pl.
{5.A.1.e} . . . . id.
ἠργάσατο verb, aor. mid. indic. 3 pers. sg.
{5.A.1.e} . . . . id.
ἦρε verb, aor. act. indic. 3 pers. sg. {5.A.1.b} . . αἴρω G142
ἠρέθισε verb, aor. act. indic. 3 pers. sg.
{5.A.1.b} . . . . ἐρεθίζω G2042
ἠρέθισεν verb, aor. act. indic. 3 pers. sg.
{5.A.1.b} . . . . id.
ἤρεμον adj., acc. sg. masc. {3.A} . . . . ἤρεμος G2263
G2263 ἤρεμος, -ον *undisturbed.*
ἦρεν verb, aor. act. indic. 3 pers. sg. {5.A.1.b} . αἴρω G142
ἤρεσε verb, aor. act. indic. 3 pers. sg.
{5.A.1.b} . . . . ἀρέσκω G700
ἤρεσεν verb, aor. act. indic. 3 pers. sg. {5.A.1.b} id.
ἤρεσκον verb, impf. act. indic. 1 pers. sg.
{5.A.1.b} . . . . id.
ἠρέτισα verb, aor. act. indic. 1 pers. sg.
{5.A.1.b} . . . . αἱρετίζω G140
ἠρημώθη verb, aor. pass. indic. 3 pers. sg.
{5.A.1} . . . . ἐρημόω G2049
ἠρημωμένην vbl., perf. pass. ptc. acc. sg. fem.
{6.A.2} . . . . id.
ἤρθη verb, aor. pass. indic. 3 pers. sg. {5.A.1.b} αἴρω G142
ἠριθμημέναι vbl., perf. pass. ptc. nom. pl. fem.
{6.A.2} . . . . ἀριθμέω G705
ἠρίθμηνται verb, perf. pass. indic. 3 pers. pl.
{5.A.1} . . . . id.
ἠρίστησαν verb, aor. act. indic. 3 pers. pl.
{5.A.1} . . . . ἀριστάω G709
ἦρκεν verb, perf. act. indic. 3 pers. sg.
{5.A.1.c.E11235} . . . . αἴρω G142
ἠρμένον vbl., perf. pass. ptc. acc. sg. masc.
{6.A.1.b} . . . . id.
ἡρμοσάμην verb, aor. mid. indic. 1 pers. sg.
{5.A.1.e} . . . . ἁρμόζω G718
ἠρνεῖτο verb, impf. mid./pass. indic. 3 pers. sg.
{5.A.2} . . . . ἀρνέομαι G720
ἠρνημένοι vbl., perf. mid./pass. ptc. nom. pl.
masc. {6.A.2} . . . . id.
ἠρνήσαντο verb, aor. mid. indic. 3 pers. pl.
{5.A.1} . . . . id.
ἠρνήσασθε verb, aor. mid. indic. 2 pers. pl.
{5.A.1} . . . . id.
ἠρνήσατο verb, aor. mid. indic. 3 pers. sg.
{5.A.1} . . . . id.
ἠρνήσω verb, aor. mid. indic. 2 pers. sg. {5.A.1} id.
ἤρνηται verb, perf. mid. indic. 3 pers. sg.
{5.A.1} . . . . id.

ἤρξαντο   verb, aor. mid. indic. 3 pers. pl.
{5.A.1.e} . . . . .ἄρχομαι G756

ἤρξατο   verb, aor. mid. indic. 3 pers. sg.
{5.A.1.e} . . . . id.

Ἡροδίωνα   noun prop., acc. sg. masc. {2.C;
2.D}. .Ἡρῳδίων G2267

ἡρπάγη   verb, ²aor. pass. indic. 3 pers. sg.
{5.A.1.e} . . . . ἁρπάζω G726

ἥρπασε   verb, aor. act. indic. 3 pers. sg. {5.A.1.b} id.

ἥρπασεν   verb, aor. act. indic. 3 pers. sg.
{5.A.1.b} . . . . id.

ἡρπάσθη   verb, aor. pass. indic. 3 pers. sg.
{5.A.1.b} . . . . id.

ἠρτυμένος   vbl., perf. pass. ptc. nom. sg. masc.
{6.A.1.b} . . . . ἀρτύω G741

ἤρχετο   verb, impf. mid./pass. indic. 3 pers. sg.
{5.A.1.e} .ἔρχομαι G2064

ἤρχοντο   verb, impf. mid./pass. indic. 3 pers.
pl. {5.A.1.e} . . . . id.

ἤρχου   verb, impf. mid./pass. indic. 2 pers. sg.
{5.A.1.e} . . . . id.

Ἡρώδη   noun prop., dat. sg. masc. {2.A;
2.D}. .Ἡρῴδης G2264

Ἡρῴδη   noun prop., dat. sg. masc. {2.A; 2.D}. . . id.

Ἡρώδην   noun prop., acc. sg. masc. {2.A; 2.D}. . id.

Ἡρῴδην   noun prop., acc. sg. masc. {2.A; 2.D}. . id.

Ἡρώδης   noun prop., nom. sg. masc. {2.A; 2.D}. id.

G2264   **Ἡρῴδης**, -ου, ὁ   *Herod:* (1) *"Herod the King,"*
"Herod the Great," Herod I (73–4 B.C.), Matt
2 *passim;* Luke 1:5; Acts 23:35; (2) *"Herod, the*
Tetrarch," son of (1), Herod Antipas, ruled 4
B.C.–39 A.D.; (3) *"Herod the King,"* Agrippa
I, grandson of (1), brother of Herodias (10
B.C.–44 A.D.), ruled 37–44 A.D., Acts 12
passim.

Ἡρῴδης   noun prop., nom. sg. masc. {2.A;
2.D}. .Ἡρῴδης G2264

Ἡρωδιάδα   noun prop., acc. sg. fem. {2.C;
2.D}. .Ἡρῳδιάς G2266

Ἡρωδιάδα   noun prop., acc. sg. fem. {2.C; 2.D}. id.

Ἡρωδιάδος   noun prop., gen. sg. fem. {2.C; 2.D} id.

Ἡρωδιάδος   noun prop., gen. sg. fem. {2.C; 2.D} id.

G2265   **Ἡρῳδιανοί**, -ῶν, -οἱ   *the Herodians, the parti-*
sans of Herod (Antipas).

Ἡρῳδιανῶν   noun prop., gen. pl. masc. {2.B;
2.D}. .Ἡρῳδιανοί G2265

Ἡρῳδιανῶν   noun prop., gen. pl. masc. {2.B; 2.D} id.

Ἡρῳδιάς   noun prop., nom. sg. fem. {2.C;
2.D}. .Ἡρῳδιάς G2266

G2266   **Ἡρῳδιάς**, -άδος, ἡ   *Herodias* (died after 40
A.D.), daughter of Aristobulus and grand-
daughter of Herod I, wife, first, of her uncle
Herod, second, of his half brother, her uncle
Herod Antipas.

Ἡρῳδιάς   noun prop., nom. sg. fem. {2.C;
2.D}. .Ἡρῳδιάς G2266

G2267   **Ἡρῳδίων**, -ωνος, ὁ   *Herodion,* a Christian in
Rome, a "relative" of Paul.

Ἡρῳδίωνα   noun prop., acc. sg. masc. {2.C;
2.D}. .Ἡρῳδίων G2267

Ἡρῴδου   noun prop., gen. sg. masc. {2.A;
2.D}. .Ἡρῴδης G2264

Ἡρῴδου   noun prop., gen. sg. masc. {2.A; 2.D} . id.

ἠρώτα   verb, impf. act. indic. 3 pers. sg.
{5.A.2}. .ἐρωτάω G2065

ἠρώτησαν   verb, aor. act. indic. 3 pers. pl.
{5.A.1}. . . . . id.

ἠρώτησε   verb, aor. act. indic. 3 pers. sg. {5.A.1} id.

ἠρώτησεν   verb, aor. act. indic. 3 pers. sg.
{5.A.1}. . . . . id.

ἠρώτουν   verb, impf. act. indic. 3 pers. pl.
{5.A.2}. . . . . id.

ἠρώτων   verb, impf. act. indic. 3 pers. pl. {5.A.2} id.

ἦς   verb, impf. indic. 2 pers. sg. {7.A} . . . . . . .εἰμί G1510

ἦς   pron. rel., gen. sg. fem. {4.C} . . . . .ὅς G3739

ἦς   verb, pres. subjunc. 2 pers. sg. {7.B} . . . . . .εἰμί G1510

Ἡσαΐᾳ   noun prop., dat. sg. masc. {2.A;
2.D}. .Ἡσαΐας G2268

Ἡσαΐᾳ   noun prop., dat. sg. masc. {2.A; 2.D}. . . id.

Ἡσαΐαν   noun prop., acc. sg. masc. {2.A; 2.D}. . id.

Ἡσαΐαν   noun prop., acc. sg. masc. {2.A; 2.D}. . id.

Ἡσαΐαν   noun prop., acc. sg. masc. {2.A; 2.D}. . id.

Ἡσαΐας   noun prop., nom. sg. masc. {2.A; 2.D} . id.

G2268   **Ἡσαΐας** (Ἡσαΐας), -ου, ὁ   *Isaiah,* the prophet
(Heb.).

Ἡσαΐας   noun prop., nom. sg. masc. {2.A;
2.D}. .Ἡσαΐας G2268

Ἡσαΐας   noun prop., nom. sg. masc. {2.A; 2.D}. id.

Ἡσαΐου   noun prop., gen. sg. masc. {2.A; 2.D}. . id.

Ἡσαΐου   noun prop., gen. sg. masc. {2.A; 2.D}. . id.

Ἡσαΐου   noun prop., gen. sg. masc. {2.A; 2.D}. . id.

ἦσαν   verb, impf. indic. 3 pers. pl. {7.A} . . . . . .εἰμί G1510

G2269   **Ἡσαῦ**, ὁ   *Esau,* elder son of Isaac the patriarch,
brother of Jacob (Heb.).

Ἡσαῦ   noun prop. . . . . .Ἡσαῦ G2269

ἠσέβησαν   verb, aor. act. indic. 3 pers. pl.
{5.A.1}. .ἀσεβέω G764

ἦσθα   verb, impf. indic. 2 pers. sg. {7.A} . . . . . .εἰμί G1510

ἠσθένει   verb, impf. act. indic. 3 pers. sg.
{5.A.2}. .ἀσθενέω G770

ἠσθενήκαμεν   verb, perf. act. indic. 1 pers. pl.
{5.A.1}. . . . . id.

ἠσθένησα   verb, aor. act. indic. 1 pers. sg.
{5.A.1}. . . . . id.

ἠσθενήσαμεν   verb, aor. act. indic. 1 pers. pl.
{5.A.1}. . . . . id.

ἠσθένησε   verb, aor. act. indic. 3 pers. sg.
{5.A.1}. . . . . id.

ἠσθένησεν   verb, aor. act. indic. 3 pers. sg.
{5.A.1}. . . . . id.

ἤσθιον   verb, impf. act. indic. 3 pers. pl.
{5.A.1.b} . . . . .ἐσθίω G2068

ἠσπάζοντο   verb, impf. mid./pass. indic. 3 pers. pl.
{5.A.1.e} .ἀσπάζομαι G782

ἠσπάσατο   verb, aor. mid. indic. 3 pers. sg.
{5.A.1.e} . . . . id.

ἧσσον   adj. comp., acc. sg. neut. {3.E; 3.G} .ἥσσων G2276‡

ἧσσον   adv. comp. {3.F; 3.G} . . . . id.

ἡσσώθητε   verb, aor. pass. indic. 2 pers. pl.
{5.A.1}. .ἑσσόομαι G2274†‡

G2276‡ **ἥσσων** (ἥττων), -ον, gen. ονος   *less; worse.*

ἠστόχησαν   verb, aor. act. indic. 3 pers. pl.
{5.A.1}. . . . . ἀστοχέω *G795*

ἠσυχάζειν   vbl., pres. act. inf. {6.B.1}. . . ἡσυχάζω *G2270*

G2270 **ἡσυχάζω**   *I am quiet, I keep quiet, I rest; I am silent.*

ἡσυχάσαμεν   verb, aor. act. indic. 1 pers. pl.
{5.A.1.b} . . . . ἡσυχάζω *G2270*

ἡσύχασαν   verb, aor. act. indic. 3 pers. pl.
{5.A.1.b} . . . . id.

G2271 **ἡσυχία**, -ας, ἡ   *quietness; silence.*

ἡσυχίᾳ   noun, dat. sg. fem. {2.A} . . . . ἡσυχία *G2271*

ἡσυχίαν   noun, acc. sg. fem. {2.A}. . . . . id.

ἡσυχίας   noun, gen. sg. fem. {2.A}. . . . . id.

ἡσύχιον   adj., acc. sg. masc. {3.A} . . . . . ἡσύχιος *G2272*

G2272 **ἡσύχιος**, -ον   *quiet.*

ἡσυχίου   adj., gen. sg. neut. {3.A} . . . . . . ἡσύχιος *G2272*

ἠσφαλίσαντο   verb, aor. mid. indic. 3 pers. pl.
{5.A.1.e} . . . . ἀσφαλίζω *G805*

ἠσφαλίσατο   verb, aor. mid. indic. 3 pers. sg.
{5.A.1.e} . . . . id.

ἠτακτήσαμεν   verb, aor. act. indic. 1 pers. pl.
{5.A.1} . . . . ἀτακτέω *G812*

ἦτε   verb, impf. indic. 2 pers. pl. {7.A}. . . . . . . εἰμί *G1510*

ἦτε   verb, pres. subjunc. 2 pers. pl. {7.B} . . . . id.

ἠτήκαμεν   verb, perf. act. indic. 1 pers. pl.
{5.A.1} . . . . αἰτέω *G154*

ἠτήσαντο   verb, aor. mid. indic. 3 pers. pl.
{5.A.1} . . . . id.

ἤτησας   verb, aor. act. indic. 2 pers. sg. {5.A.1} . id.

ἠτήσασθε   verb, aor. mid. indic. 2 pers. pl.
{5.A.1} . . . . id.

ἠτήσατε   verb, aor. act. indic. 2 pers. pl. {5.A.1}. id.

ἠτήσατο   verb, aor. mid. indic. 3 pers. sg.
{5.A.1} . . . . id.

ἠτίμασαν   verb, aor. act. indic. 3 pers. pl.
{5.A.1.b} . . . . ἀτιμάζω *G818*

ἠτιμάσατε   verb, aor. act. indic. 2 pers. pl.
{5.A.1.b} . . . . id.

ἠτιμωμένον   vbl., perf. pass. ptc. acc. sg. masc.
{6.A.2} . . . . ἀτιμόω *G821*

ἥτις   pron. indef. rel., nom. sg. fem. {4.C} . . . . ὅστις *G3748*

G2273 **ἤτοι**   *or of course.*

ἤτοι   conj. . . . . .ἤτοι *G2273*

ἡτοίμακα   verb, perf. act. indic. 1 pers. sg.
{5.A.1.c} . . . . ἑτοιμάζω *G2090*

ἡτοίμασα   verb, aor. act. indic. 1 pers. sg.
{5.A.1.b} . . . . id.

ἡτοίμασαν   verb, aor. act. indic. 3 pers. pl.
{5.A.1.b} . . . . id.

ἡτοίμασας   verb, aor. act. indic. 2 pers. sg.
{5.A.1.b} . . . . id.

ἡτοίμασε   verb, aor. act. indic. 3 pers. sg.
{5.A.1.b} . . . . id.

ἡτοίμασεν   verb, aor. act. indic. 3 pers. sg.
{5.A.1.b} . . . . id.

ἡτοιμασμένην   vbl., perf. pass. ptc. acc. sg.
fem. {6.A.1.b} . . . . id.

ἡτοιμασμένοι   vbl., perf. pass. ptc. nom. pl.
masc. {6.A.1.b} . . . . id.

ἡτοιμασμένοις   vbl., perf. pass. ptc. dat. pl.
masc. {6.A.1.b} . . . . id.

ἡτοιμασμένον   vbl., perf. pass. ptc. acc. sg.
masc. {6.A.1.b} . . . . id.

ἡτοιμασμένον   vbl., perf. pass. ptc. acc. sg.
neut. {6.A.1.b} . . . . id.

ἡτοιμασμένον   vbl., perf. pass. ptc. nom. sg.
neut. {6.A.1.b} . . . . id.

ἡτοίμασται   verb, perf. pass. indic. 3 pers. sg.
{5.A.1.f}. . . . . id.

ἠτοῦντο   verb, impf. mid. indic. 3 pers. pl.
{5.A.2}. . . . . αἰτέω *G154*

G2274 **ἡττάομαι**   pass. *I am defeated, I am worsted, I am made inferior.*

ἡττήθητε   verb, aor. pass. indic. 2 pers. pl.
{5.A.1} . . . . ἡττάομαι *G2274*

G2275 **ἥττημα**, -ατος, τό   *a defeat (failure).*

ἥττημα   noun, nom. sg. neut. {2.C} . . . . . ἥττημα *G2275*

ἥττηται   verb, perf. mid./pass. indic. 3 pers. sg.
{5.A.1} . . . . ἡττάομαι *G2274*

ἧττον   adj. comp., acc. sg. neut. {3.E; 3.G} . ἥσσων *G2276‡*

ἧττον   adv. comp. {3.F; 3.G} . . . . id.

ἡττῶνται   verb, pres. mid./pass. indic. 3 pers. pl.
{5.A.2}. . . . . ἡττάομαι *G2274*

ἤτω   verb, pres. impv. 3 pers. sg. {7.B}. . . . . . . εἰμί *G1510*

ηὐδόκησα   verb, aor. act. indic. 1 pers. sg.
{5.A.1} . . . . εὐδοκέω *G2106*

ηὐδοκήσαμεν   verb, aor. act. indic. 1 pers. pl.
{5.A.1} . . . . id.

ηὐδόκησαν   verb, aor. act. indic. 3 pers. pl.
{5.A.1} . . . . id.

ηὐδόκησεν   verb, aor. act. indic. 3 pers. sg.
{5.A.1} . . . . id.

ηὐδοκοῦμεν   verb, impf. act. indic. 1 pers. pl.
{5.A.2} . . . . id.

ηὐκαίρουν   verb, impf. act. indic. 3 pers. pl.
{5.A.2} . . . . εὐκαιρέω *G2119*

ηὐλήσαμεν   verb, aor. act. indic. 1 pers. pl.
{5.A.1} . . . . αὐλέω *G832*

ηὐλίζετο   verb, impf. mid./pass. indic. 3 pers. sg.
{5.A.1.e} . . . . αὐλίζομαι *G835*

ηὐλίσθη   verb, aor. pass. indic. 3 pers. sg.
{5.A.1.b} . . . . id.

ηὐλόγει   verb, impf. act. indic. 3 pers. sg.
{5.A.2} . . . . εὐλογέω *G2127*

ηὔξανε   verb, impf. act. indic. 3 pers. sg.
{5.A.1.b} . . . . αὐξάνω *G837*

ηὔξανεν   verb, impf. act. indic. 3 pers. sg.
{5.A.1.b} . . . . id.

ηὔξησε   verb, aor. act. indic. 3 pers. sg. {5.A.1.b} id.

ηὔξησεν   verb, aor. act. indic. 3 pers. sg.
{5.A.1.b} . . . . id.

ηὐπορεῖτο   verb, impf. mid. indic. 3 pers. sg.
{5.A.2}. . . . . εὐπορέω *G2141*

ηὑρίσκετο   verb, impf. pass. indic. 3 pers. sg.
{5.A.1.e} . . . . εὑρίσκω *G2147*

ηὕρισκον   verb, impf. act. indic. 3 pers. pl.
{5.A.1.b} . . . . id.

ηὐφράνθη   verb, aor. pass. indic. 3 pers. sg.
{5.A.1.b} . . . . εὐφραίνω *G2165*

ηὐχαρίστησαν   verb, aor. act. indic. 3 pers. pl.
{5.A.1}. . . . . εὐχαριστέω *G2168*
ηὐχόμην   verb, impf. mid./pass. indic. 1 pers. sg.
{5.A.1.e} . . . . εὔχομαι *G2172*
ηὔχοντο   verb, impf. mid./pass. indic. 3 pers.
pl. {5.A.1.e} . . . . id.
ἤφιε   verb, impf. act. indic. 3 pers. sg.
{5.A.3.a} . . . . ἀφίημι *G863*
ἤφιεν   verb, impf. act. indic. 3 pers. sg. {5.A.3.a}. id.
G2278 **ἠχέω**   *I make a sound, give forth a sound, sound*
(when struck).
ἤχθη   verb, aor. pass. indic. 3 pers. sg. {5.A.1.b} . ἄγω *G71*
ἤχθημεν   verb, aor. pass. indic. 1 pers. pl.
{5.A.1.b} . . . . id.
ἠχμαλώτευσεν   verb, aor. act. indic. 3 pers. sg.
{5.A.1.b} . . . . αἰχμαλωτεύω *G162*

G2279 **ἦχος**, -ους, τό   (1) *a sound;* (2) *a rumor,* Luke
4:37.
ἦχος   noun, nom. sg. masc. {2.B} . . . . ἦχος *G2279*
ἠχοῦς   noun, gen. sg. fem. {2.B} . . . . id.
ἤχους   noun, gen. sg. neut. {2.C} . . . . id.
ἠχούσης   vbl., pres. act. ptc. gen. sg. fem.
{6.A.2} . . . . ἠχέω *G2278*
ἠχρειώθησαν   verb, aor. pass. indic. 3 pers. pl.
{5.A.1} . . . . ἀχρειόω *G889*
ἠχρεώθησαν   verb, aor. pass. indic. 3 pers. pl.
{5.A.1} . . . . id.
ἤχῳ   noun, dat. sg. masc. {2.B} . . . . ἦχος *G2279*
ἠχῶν   vbl., pres. act. ptc. nom. sg. masc. {6.A.2}. ἠχέω *G2278*
ἥψαντο   verb, aor. mid. indic. 3 pers. pl.
{5.A.1.e} . . . . ἅπτομαι *G680*
ἥψατο   verb, aor. mid. indic. 3 pers. sg. {5.A.1.e} id.

Θ θ

θά   Aram. . . . . μαρὰν ἀθά *G3134*
Θαδδαῖον   noun prop., acc. sg. masc. {2.B;
2.D} . . . . Θαδδαῖος *G2280*
G2280 **Θαδδαῖος**, -ου, ὁ   *Thaddaeus,* one of the twelve
disciples (var. Λεββαῖος, Aram. = *Theodotus*
or some similar name).
Θαδδαῖος   noun prop., nom. sg. masc. {2.B;
2.D} . . . . Θαδδαῖος *G2280*
G2281 **θάλασσα**, -ης, ἡ   (1) *the sea,* in contrast to the
land (γῆ); τὸ πέλαγος τῆς θαλάσσης, *the depth
of the sea,* Matt 18:6; (2) *a particular sea* or *lake,*
e.g., *the sea of Galilee (Tiberias), the Red Sea.*
θάλασσα   noun, nom. sg. fem. {2.A} . . . θάλασσα *G2281*
θάλασσαν   noun, acc. sg. fem. {2.A} . . . . id.
θαλάσσῃ   noun, dat. sg. fem. {2.A} . . . . id.
θαλάσσης   noun, gen. sg. fem. {2.A} . . . . id.
θάλπει   verb, pres. act. indic. 3 pers. sg.
{5.A.1.a} . . . . θάλπω *G2282*
θάλπῃ   verb, pres. act. subjunc. 3 pers. sg. {5.B.1} id.
G2282 **θάλπω**   (properly *I warm,* then) *I cherish.*
G2283 **Θαμάρ**, ἡ   *Tamar,* mother of Phares and Zara
by Judah, son of Jacob (Heb.).
Θαμάρ   noun prop. . . . . Θαμάρ *G2283*
Θάμαρ   noun prop. . . . . id.
G2284 **θαμβέω**   pass. *I am amazed* (almost *terrified*).
G2285 **θάμβος**, -ους, τό   *astonishment, amazement*
(allied to terror or awe).
θάμβος   noun, nom. sg. neut. {2.C} . . . . . θάμβος *G2285*
θάμβους   noun, gen. sg. neut. {2.C} . . . . id.
θαμβῶν   vbl., pres. act. ptc. nom. sg. masc.
{6.A.2} . . . . θαμβέω *G2284*
θανάσιμον   adj., acc. sg. neut. {3.A} . . θανάσιμος *G2286*
G2286 **θανάσιμος**, -ον   *deadly.*
θάνατε   noun, voc. sg. masc. {2.B} . . . . . . θάνατος *G2288*
G2287 **θανατηφόρος**, -ον   *death-bringing, deadly.*
θανατηφόρου   adj., gen. sg. masc.
{3.C} . . . . θανατηφόρος *G2287*
θανάτοις   noun, dat. pl. masc. {2.B} . . . . θάνατος *G2288*

θάνατον   noun, acc. sg. masc. {2.B} . . . . id.
G2288 **θάνατος**, -ου, ὁ   *death,* physical or spiritual;
θάνατοι appears to mean *risks to life,* 2 Cor
11:23; ὁ δεύτερος θάνατος (ὁ θάνατος ὁ
δεύτερος), spiritual death.
θάνατος   noun, nom. sg. masc. {2.B} . . . . θάνατος *G2288*
θανάτου   noun, gen. sg. masc. {2.B} . . . . id.
θανατούμεθα   verb, pres. pass. indic. 1 pers. pl.
{5.A.2} . . . . θανατόω *G2289*
θανατούμενοι   vbl., pres. pass. ptc. nom. pl.
masc. {6.A.2} . . . . id.
θανατοῦτε   verb, pres. act. indic. 2 pers. pl.
{5.A.2} . . . . id.
G2289 **θανατόω**   *I put to death.*
θανάτῳ   noun, dat. sg. masc. {2.B} . . . . . . θάνατος *G2288*
θανατωθείς   vbl., aor. pass. ptc. nom. sg. masc.
{6.A.1.a} . . . . θανατόω *G2289*
θανατῶσαι   vbl., aor. act. inf. {6.B.1} . . . . id.
θανατώσουσιν   verb, fut. act. indic. 3 pers. pl.
{5.A.1} . . . . id.
θανατώσωσι   verb, aor. act. subjunc. 3 pers. pl.
{5.B.1} . . . . id.
θανατώσωσιν   verb, aor. act. subjunc. 3 pers.
pl. {5.B.1} . . . . id.
G2290 **θάπτω**   *I bury.*
Θαρά   noun prop. . . . . Θάρα *G2291*
G2291 **Θάρα**, ὁ   *Terah,* the father of Abraham (Heb.).
Θάρα   noun prop. . . . . Θάρα *G2291*
G2292 **θαρρέω**   *I am courageous, I am of good cheer,* a
by-form of θαρσέω.
θαρρῆσαι   vbl., aor. act. inf. {6.B.1} . . . . . . θαρρέω *G2292*
θαρροῦμεν   verb, pres. act. indic. 1 pers. pl.
{5.A.2} . . . . id.
θαρροῦντας   vbl., pres. act. ptc. acc. pl. masc.
{6.A.2} . . . . id.
θαρροῦντες   vbl., pres. act. ptc. nom. pl. masc.
{6.A.2} . . . . id.
θαρρῶ   verb, pres. act. indic. 1 pers. sg. {5.A.2} . id.

θάρσει verb, pres. act. impv. 2 pers. sg.
{5.D.2}. . . . . .θαρσέω G2293
θαρσεῖτε verb, pres. act. impv. 2 pers. pl. {5.D.2}id.
G2293 **θαρσέω** *be of good cheer,* a by-form of
θαρρέω, only in the impv.
G2294 **θάρσος,** -ους, τό *courage.*
θάρσος noun, acc. sg. neut. {2.C} . . . . . . θάρσος G2294
G2295 **θαῦμα,** -ατος, τό (1) concr., *a marvel, a wonder;* (2) abstr., *wonder.*
θαῦμα noun, acc. sg. neut. {2.C} . . . . .θαῦμα G2295
θαῦμα noun, nom. sg. neut. {2.C} . . . . id.
θαυμάζειν vbl., pres. act. inf. {6.B.1}. . . θαυμάζω G2296
θαυμάζετε verb, pres. act. impv. 2 pers. pl.
{5.D.1}. id.
θαυμάζετε verb, pres. act. indic. 2 pers. pl.
{5.A.1.a}. . . . . id.
θαυμάζητε verb, pres. act. subjunc. 2 pers. pl.
{5.B.1}. id.
θαυμάζοντες vbl., pres. act. ptc. nom. pl.
masc. {6.A.1}. . . . . id.
θαυμαζόντων vbl., pres. act. ptc. gen. pl.
masc. {6.A.1}. . . . . id.
G2296 **θαυμάζω** (1) intrans., *I wonder;* cog. acc.
θαυμάζειν θαῦμα μέγα, Rev 17:6, *to wonder
greatly;* (2) trans., *I wonder at, admire.*
θαυμάζω verb, pres. act. indic. 1 pers. sg.
{5.A.1.a} . . . . θαυμάζω G2296
θαυμάζων vbl., pres. act. ptc. nom. sg. masc.
{6.A.1}. id.
θαυμάσαι vbl., aor. act. inf. {6.B.1} . . . . id.
θαυμάσαντες vbl., aor. act. ptc. nom. pl. masc.
{6.A.1.a} . . . . id.
θαυμάσατε verb, aor. act. impv. 2 pers. pl.
{5.D.1}. id.
θαυμάσῃς verb, aor. act. subjunc. 2 pers. sg.
{5.B.1} . . . . id.
θαυμασθῆναι vbl., aor. pass. inf. {6.B.1}. . . . id.
θαυμασθήσονται verb, fut. pass. indic. 3 pers.
pl. {5.A.1.d} . . . . id.
θαυμάσια adj., acc. pl. neut. {3.A} . . . θαυμάσιος G2297
G2297 **θαυμάσιος,** -α, -ον *wonderful.*
θαυμάσονται verb, fut. mid. indic. 3 pers. pl.
{5.A.1.d} . . . . θαυμάζω G2296
θαυμαστά adj., nom. pl. neut. {3.A} . .θαυμαστός G2298
θαυμαστή adj., nom. sg. fem. {3.A}. . . . . id.
θαυμαστόν adj., acc. sg. neut. {3.A} . . . . id.
θαυμαστόν adj., nom. sg. neut. {3.A} . . . . . . id.
G2298 **θαυμαστός,** -ή, -όν *to be wondered at,
wonderful.*
θάψαι vbl., aor. act. inf. {6.B.1} . . . . .θάπτω G2290
θαψάντων vbl., aor. act. ptc. gen. pl. masc.
{6.A.1.a} . . . . id.
G2299 **θεά,** -ᾶς, ἡ *a goddess.*
θεαθῆναι vbl., aor. pass. inf. {6.B.1} . . . . θεάομαι G2300
θεάν noun, acc. sg. fem. {2.A} . . . . θεά G2299
G2300 **θεάομαι** *I behold.*
θεᾶς noun, gen. sg. fem. {2.A} . . . . θεά G2299
θεασάμενοι vbl., aor. mid. ptc. nom. pl. masc.
{6.A.2}. . . . . θεάομαι G2300

θεασαμένοις vbl., aor. mid. ptc. dat. pl. masc.
{6.A.2}. id.
θεασάμενος vbl., aor. mid. ptc. nom. sg. masc.
{6.A.2}. id.
θεάσασθαι vbl., aor. mid. inf. {6.B.1} . . . . id.
θεάσασθε verb, aor. mid. impv. 2 pers. pl.
{5.D.1}. id.
θεατριζόμενοι vbl., pres. pass. ptc. nom. pl. masc.
{6.A.1}. . . . . θεατρίζω G2301
G2301 **θεατρίζω** *I make a public show of, I expose to
public shame.*
G2302 **θέατρον,** -ου, τό (1) *a theatre,* a semicircular
stone building, generally open to the sky; (2) *a
spectacle,* 1 Cor 4:9.
θέατρον noun, acc. sg. neut. {2.B}. . . . . . θέατρον G2302
θέατρον noun, nom. sg. neut. {2.B}. . . . . id.
θεέ noun, voc. sg. masc. {2.B} . . . . .θεός G2316
θείας adj., gen. sg. fem. {3.A} . . . . θεῖος G2304
θεῖναι vbl., ²aor. act. inf. {6.B.3}. . . . . . . τίθημι G5087
G2303 **θεῖον,** -ου, τό *brimstone, sulfur.*
θεῖον adj., acc. sg. neut. {3.A} . . . . θεῖος G2304
θεῖον noun, acc. sg. neut. {2.B} . . . . θεῖον G2303
θεῖον noun, nom. sg. neut. {2.B} . . . . id.
G2304 **θεῖος,** -α, -ον *divine;* τὸ θεῖον, *the divine, the
divine nature,* Acts 17:29.
G2305 **θειότης,** -ητος, ἡ *divinity.*
θειότης noun, nom. sg. fem. {2.C}. . . . . . θειότης G2305
θείου noun, gen. sg. neut. {2.B} . . . . θεῖον G2303
θείς vbl., ²aor. act. ptc. nom. sg. masc.
{6.A.3}. . . . . τίθημι G5087
θείῳ noun, dat. sg. neut. {2.B} . . . . θεῖον G2303
θειώδεις adj., acc. pl. masc. {3.E}. . . . . .θειώδης G2306
G2306 **θειώδης,** -ες *of brimstone, sulfurous.*
θέλει verb, pres. act. indic. 3 pers. sg.
{5.A.1.a} . . . . θέλω G2309
θέλειν vbl., pres. act. inf. {6.B.1} . . . . id.
θέλεις verb, pres. act. indic. 2 pers. sg. {5.A.1.a}. id.
θέλετε verb, pres. act. indic. 2 pers. pl. {5.A.1.a} id.
θέλῃ verb, pres. act. subjunc. 3 pers. sg. {5.B.1} . id.
G2307 **θέλημα,** -ατος, τό *an act of will, will;* pl.
wishes, desires; τὸ θέλημα τοῦ Θεοῦ, *the will
of God,* sometimes as a will to be recognized,
sometimes as a will to be obeyed.
θέλημα noun, acc. sg. neut. {2.C} . . . . . . .θέλημα G2307
θέλημα noun, nom. sg. neut. {2.C} . . . . id.
θελήματα noun, acc. pl. neut. {2.C} . . . . id.
θελήματι noun, dat. sg. neut. {2.C} . . . . id.
θελήματος noun, gen. sg. neut. {2.C} . . . . id.
θέλῃς verb, pres. act. subjunc. 2 pers. sg.
{5.B.1}. . . . . θέλω G2309
θελήσαντας vbl., aor. act. ptc. acc. pl. masc.
{6.A.1.a} . . . . id.
θελήσῃ verb, aor. act. subjunc. 3 pers. sg. {5.B.1}id.
θέλησιν noun, acc. sg. fem. {2.C} . . . . . . .θέλησις G2308
G2308 **θέλησις,** -εως, ἡ *willing, will.*
θελήσω verb, aor. act. subjunc. 1 pers. sg.
{5.B.1} . . . . θέλω G2309
θελήσωσι verb, aor. act. subjunc. 3 pers. pl.
{5.B.1} . . . . id.

θελήσωσιν   verb, aor. act. subjunc. 3 pers. pl.
{5.B.1} . . . . id.

θέλητε   verb, pres. act. subjunc. 2 pers. pl.
{5.B.1} . . . . id.

θέλοι   verb, pres. act. opt. 3 pers. sg. {5.C.1} . . . . id.

θέλομεν   verb, pres. act. indic. 1 pers. pl.
{5.A.1.a} . . . . id.

θέλοντα   vbl., pres. act. ptc. acc. sg. masc.
{6.A.1} . . . . id.

θέλοντας   vbl., pres. act. ptc. acc. pl. masc.
{6.A.1} . . . . id.

θέλοντες   vbl., pres. act. ptc. nom. pl. masc.
{6.A.1} . . . . id.

θέλοντι   vbl., pres. act. ptc. dat. sg. masc. {6.A.1} id.

θέλοντος   vbl., pres. act. ptc. gen. sg. masc.
{6.A.1} . . . . id.

θελόντων   vbl., pres. act. ptc. gen. pl. masc.
{6.A.1} . . . . id.

θέλουσι   verb, pres. act. indic. 3 pers. pl.
{5.A.1.a} . . . . id.

θέλουσιν   verb, pres. act. indic. 3 pers. pl.
{5.A.1.a} . . . . id.

G2309   **θέλω**   (1) intrans., *I will*; οὐ θέλω, *I refuse*;
θέλειν ἐν, *to fix one's will on, to stick reso-
lutely to*, Col 2:18; followed by subjunc. with
or without ἵνα, *I will that*; (2) trans., *I wish,
desire*.

θέλω   verb, pres. act. indic. 1 pers. sg. {5.A.1.a}θέλω G2309

θέλω   verb, pres. act. subjunc. 1 pers. sg. {5.B.1} . id.

θέλων   vbl., pres. act. ptc. nom. sg. masc. {6.A.1} id.

θέλωσι   verb, pres. act. subjunc. 3 pers. pl.
{5.B.1} . . . . id.

θέλωσιν   verb, pres. act. subjunc. 3 pers. pl.
{5.B.1} . . . . id.

θεμέλια   noun, acc. pl. neut. {2.B} . . . . θεμέλιον G2310†‡

θεμέλιοι   noun, nom. pl. masc. {2.B} . . . . θεμέλιος G2310

G2310†‡ **θεμέλιον**, τό   *a foundation, a basis*. Var. for
θεμέλιος.

θεμέλιον   noun, acc. sg. masc. {2.B} . . . θεμέλιον G2310†‡

θεμέλιον   noun, acc. sg. masc. {2.B} . . . . . θεμέλιος G2310

G2310   **θεμέλιος**, -ου, ὁ   *a foundation*. Var. θεμέλιον.

θεμέλιος   noun, nom. sg. masc. {2.B} . . . . θεμέλιος G2310

θεμελίου   noun, gen. sg. masc. {2.B} . . θεμέλιον G2310†‡

θεμελίους   noun, acc. pl. masc. {2.B} . . . θεμέλιος G2310

G2311   **θεμελιόω**   *I found (lay a foundation)*, lit., and
met.

θεμελίῳ   noun, dat. sg. masc. {2.B} . . . . . . θεμέλιος G2310

θεμελιῶσαι   verb, aor. act. opt. 3 pers. sg.
{5.C.1} . . . . θεμελιόω G2311

θεμελιώσει   verb, fut. act. indic. 3 pers. sg.
{5.A.1} . . . . id.

θέμενος   vbl., ²aor. mid. ptc. nom. sg. masc.
{6.A.3} . . . . τίθημι G5087

θέντες   vbl., ²aor. act. ptc. nom. pl. masc. {6.A.3} id.

θέντος   vbl., ²aor. act. ptc. gen. sg. masc. {6.A.3} . id.

θεοδίδακτοι   adj., nom. pl. masc.
{3.C} . . . . θεοδίδακτος G2312

G2312   **θεοδίδακτος**, -ον   *taught by the god*.

θεοί   noun, nom. pl. masc. {2.B} . . . . θεός G2316

θεοῖς   noun, dat. pl. masc. {2.B} . . . . id.

G2313   **θεομαχέω**   *I oppose God, I fight against God*.

θεομάχοι   adj., nom. pl. masc. {3.C} . . . . θεομάχος G2314

G2314   **θεομάχος**, -ον   *fighting against the god*.

θεομαχῶμεν   verb, pres. act. subjunc. 1 pers. pl.
{5.B.2} . . . . θεομαχέω G2313

θεόν   noun, acc. sg. fem. {2.B} . . . . θεός G2316

θεόν   noun, acc. sg. masc. {2.B} . . . . id.

G2315   **θεόπνευστος**, -ον   *inspired by the god, due to
the inspiration of the god*.

θεόπνευστος   adj., nom. sg. fem.
{3.C} . . . . θεόπνευστος G2315

G2316   **θεός**, -οῦ, ὁ   (1) *a god* or *goddess*, John 10:34,
35; Acts 7:40; 14:11; 19:26, 37; 1 Cor 8:5; Gal
4:8; (2) *the god*. The word is an appellative.
The Christian, like the Jew and many pagans,
avoided *naming* his God, and referred to him
as *the god*.

θεός   noun, nom. sg. masc. {2.B} . . . . θεός G2316

G2317   **θεοσέβεια**, -ας, ἡ   *reverence for the god*.

θεοσέβειαν   noun, acc. sg. fem. {2.A} . . θεοσέβεια G2317

G2318   **θεοσεβής**, -ές   *devout, religious*.

θεοσεβής   adj., nom. sg. masc. {3.E} . . . . θεοσεβής G2318

θεοστυγεῖς   adj., acc. pl. masc. {3.E} . . . θεοστυγής G2319

G2319   **θεοστυγής**, -ές   *hating the god*.

G2320   **θεότης**, -ητος, ἡ   *deity, godhead*.

θεότητος   noun, gen. sg. fem. {2.C} . . . . . . θεότης G2320

θεοῦ   noun, gen. sg. masc. {2.B} . . . . θεός G2316

θεούς   noun, acc. pl. masc. {2.B} . . . . id.

Θεόφιλε   noun prop., voc. sg. masc. {2.B;
2.D} . . . . Θεόφιλος G2321

G2321   **Θεόφιλος**, -ου, ὁ   *Theophilus*, a friend of Luke
of equestrian rank, to whom the Gospel and
Acts are dedicated.

G2322   **θεραπεία**, -ας, ἡ   *care, attention* (Luke 12:42),
esp. *medical attention (treatment)*, Luke 9:11;
hence almost *healing* (Rev 22:2). In Luke 12:42
may, however, be taken as abstr. for concr., *the
slaves*.

θεραπείαν   noun, acc. sg. fem. {2.A} . . . θεραπεία G2322

θεραπείας   noun, gen. sg. fem. {2.A} . . . . id.

θεραπεύει   verb, pres. act. indic. 3 pers. sg.
{5.A.1.a} . . . . θεραπεύω G2323

θεραπεύειν   vbl., pres. act. inf. {6.B.1} . . . . . . id.

θεραπεύεσθαι   vbl., pres. pass. inf. {6.B.1} . . . . id.

θεραπεύεσθε   verb, pres. pass. impv. 2 pers. pl.
{5.D.1} . . . . id.

θεραπεύεται   verb, pres. pass. indic. 3 pers. sg.
{5.A.1.d} . . . . id.

θεραπεύετε   verb, pres. act. impv. 2 pers. pl.
{5.D.1} . . . . id.

θεραπευθῆναι   vbl., aor. pass. inf. {6.B.1} . . . . id.

θεραπεύοντες   vbl., pres. act. ptc. nom. pl.
masc. {6.A.1} . . . . id.

θεραπεῦσαι   vbl., aor. act. inf. {6.B.1} . . . . . . id.

θεραπεύσει   verb, fut. act. indic. 3 pers. sg.
{5.A.1.a} . . . . id.

θεράπευσον   verb, aor. act. impv. 2 pers. sg.
{5.D.1} . . . . id.

θεραπεύσω   verb, fut. act. indic. 1 pers. sg.
{5.A.1.a} . . . . id.

G2323 **θεραπεύω** *I care for, attend, serve, treat,* esp. of a
physician; hence, *I heal,* sometimes with ἀπό, *of.*
θεραπεύων vbl., pres. act. ptc. nom. sg. masc.
{6.A.1} . . . . θεραπεύω G2323

G2324 **θεράπων**, -οντος, ὁ *a servant, slave.*
θεράπων noun, nom. sg. masc. {2.C} . . . θεράπων G2324
θερίζειν vbl., pres. act. inf. {6.B.1} . . . . θερίζω G2325
θερίζεις verb, pres. act. indic. 2 pers. sg.
{5.A.1.a} . . . . id.
θερίζουσιν verb, pres. act. indic. 3 pers. pl.
{5.A.1.a} . . . . id.

G2325 **θερίζω** *I reap.*
θερίζω verb, pres. act. indic. 1 pers. sg.
{5.A.1.a} . . . . θερίζω G2325
θερίζων vbl., pres. act. ptc. nom. sg. masc.
{6.A.1} . . . . id.
θερίσαι vbl., aor. act. inf. {6.B.1} . . . . id.
θερισάντων vbl., aor. act. ptc. gen. pl. masc.
{6.A.1} . . . . id.
θερίσει verb, fut. act. indic. 3 pers. sg. {5.A.1.a}. id.
θερισμόν noun, acc. sg. masc. {2.B} . . . . θερισμός G2326

G2326 **θερισμός**, -οῦ, ὁ *reaping, harvest.*
θερισμός noun, nom. sg. masc. {2.B} . . θερισμός G2326
θερισμοῦ noun, gen. sg. masc. {2.B} . . . . id.
θερίσομεν verb, fut. act. indic. 1 pers. pl.
{5.A.1.a} . . . . θερίζω G2325
θέρισον verb, aor. act. impv. 2 pers. sg. {5.D.1} . id.
θερισταί noun, nom. pl. masc. {2.A} . . . θεριστής G2327
θερισταῖς noun, dat. pl. masc. {2.A} . . . . id.

G2327 **θεριστής**, -οῦ, ὁ *a reaper, harvester.*
θερμαίνεσθε verb, pres. mid./pass. impv. 2 pers.
pl. {5.D.1} . . . . θερμαίνω G2328
θερμαινόμενον vbl., pres. mid. ptc. acc. sg.
masc. {6.A.1} . . . . id.
θερμαινόμενος vbl., pres. mid. ptc. nom. sg.
masc. {6.A.1} . . . . id.

G2328 θερμαίνω mid., I warm myself.

G2329 **θέρμη**, -ης, ἡ *heat.*
θέρμης noun, gen. sg. fem. {2.A} . . . . θέρμη G2329

G2330 **θέρος**, -ους, τό *summer.*
θέρος noun, nom. sg. neut. {2.C} . . . . θέρος G2330
θέσθε verb, ²aor. mid. impv. 2 pers. pl.
{5.D.3} . . . . τίθημι G5087
Θεσσαλονικεῖς noun prop., acc. pl. masc. {2.C;
2.D} . . . . Θεσσαλονικεύς G2331

G2331 **Θεσσαλονικεύς**, -έως, ὁ *a man of
Thessalonica.*
Θεσσαλονικέων noun prop., gen. pl. masc. {2.C;
2.D} . . . . Θεσσαλονικεύς G2331
Θεσσαλονικέως noun prop., gen. sg. masc.
{2.C; 2.D} . . . . id.

G2332 **Θεσσαλονίκη**, -ης, ἡ *Thessalonica* (mod.
Salonika), an important city of the Roman
province Macedonia.
Θεσσαλονίκη noun prop., dat. sg. fem. {2.A;
2.D} . . . . Θεσσαλονίκη G2332
Θεσσαλονίκην noun prop., acc. sg. fem. {2.A;
2.D} . . . . id.
Θεσσαλονίκης noun prop., gen. sg. fem. {2.A;
2.D} . . . . id.

θέτε verb, ²aor. act. impv. 2 pers. pl. {5.D.3} . τίθημι G5087

G2333 **Θευδᾶς**, -ᾶ, ὁ *Theudas,* a Jewish pretender of
date about 4 B.C., otherwise unknown.
Θευδᾶς noun prop., nom. sg. masc. {2.A;
2.D} . . . . Θευδᾶς G2333
θεω noun, dat. sg. masc. {2.B} . . . . θεός G2316
θεῷ noun, dat. sg. masc. {2.B} . . . . id.
θεωρεῖ verb, pres. act. indic. 3 pers. sg.
{5.A.2} . . . . θεωρέω G2334
θεωρεῖν vbl., pres. act. inf. {6.B.2} . . . . id.
θεωρεῖς verb, pres. act. indic. 2 pers. sg. {5.A.2} id.
θεωρεῖτε verb, pres. act. impv. 2 pers. pl. {5.D.2} id.
θεωρεῖτε verb, pres. act. indic. 2 pers. pl. {5.A.2} id.

G2334 **θεωρέω** *I behold, look at.*
θεωρῇ verb, pres. act. subjunc. 3 pers. sg.
{5.B.2} . . . . θεωρέω G2334
θεωρῆσαι vbl., aor. act. inf. {6.B.1} . . . . id.
θεωρήσαντες vbl., aor. act. ptc. nom. pl. masc.
{6.A.2} . . . . id.
θεωρήσῃ verb, aor. act. subjunc. 3 pers. sg.
{5.B.1} . . . . id.
θεωρήσουσιν verb, fut. act. indic. 3 pers. pl.
{5.A.1} . . . . id.
θεωρήσωσι verb, aor. act. subjunc. 3 pers. pl.
{5.B.1} . . . . id.
θεωρήσωσιν verb, aor. act. subjunc. 3 pers. pl.
{5.B.1} . . . . id.
θεωρῆτε verb, pres. act. subjunc. 2 pers. pl. {5.B.2} id.

G2335 **θεωρία**, -ας, ἡ *a sight.*
θεωρίαν noun, acc. sg. fem. {2.A} . . . . θεωρία G2335
θεωροῦντας vbl., pres. act. ptc. acc. pl. masc.
{6.A.2} . . . . θεωρέω G2334
θεωροῦντες vbl., pres. act. ptc. nom. pl. masc.
{6.A.2} . . . . id.
θεωροῦντι vbl., pres. act. ptc. dat. sg. masc.
{6.A.2} . . . . id.
θεωροῦντος vbl., pres. act. ptc. gen. sg. masc.
{6.A.2} . . . . id.
θεωρούντων vbl., pres. act. ptc. gen. pl. masc.
{6.A.2} . . . . id.
θεωροῦσαι vbl., pres. act. ptc. nom. pl. fem.
{6.A.2} . . . . id.
θεωροῦσι verb, pres. act. indic. 3 pers. pl.
{5.A.2} . . . . id.
θεωροῦσιν verb, pres. act. indic. 3 pers. pl.
{5.A.2} . . . . id.
θεωρῶ verb, pres. act. indic. 1 pers. sg. {5.A.2} . id.
θεωρῶν vbl., pres. act. ptc. nom. sg. masc.
{6.A.2} . . . . id.
θεωρῶσι verb, pres. act. subjunc. 3 pers. pl.
{5.B.2} . . . . id.
θεωρῶσιν verb, pres. act. subjunc. 3 pers. pl.
{5.B.2} . . . . id.
θῇ verb, ²aor. act. subjunc. 3 pers. sg. {5.B.3} τίθημι G5087

G2336 **θήκη**, -ης, ἡ *a scabbard, a sheath.*
θήκην noun, acc. sg. fem. {2.A} . . . . θήκη G2336
θηλαζόντων vbl., pres. act. ptc. gen. pl. masc.
{6.A.1} . . . . .θηλάζω G2337
θηλαζούσαις vbl., pres. act. ptc. dat. pl. fem.
{6.A.1} . . . . id.

G2337 **θηλάζω** (1) *I give suck;* (2) *I suck.*
θήλειαι adj., nom. pl. fem. {3.A} . . . . θῆλυς G2338
θηλείας adj., gen. sg. fem. {3.A} . . . . id.
θῆλυ adj., acc. sg. neut. {3.A} . . . . id.
θῆλυ adj., nom. sg. neut. {3.A} . . . . id.
G2338 **θῆλυς, -εια, -υ** *female.*
G2339 **θήρα, -ας, ἡ** *hunting, entrapping.*
θήραν noun, acc. sg. fem. {2.A} . . . . θήρα G2339
θηρεῦσαι vbl., aor. act. inf. {6.B.1} . . . . . θηρεύω G2340
G2340 **θηρεύω** *I hunt, I seek to catch* or *entrap.*
θηρία noun, acc. pl. neut. {2.B} . . . . θηρίον G2342
θηρία noun, nom. pl. neut. {2.B} . . . . id.
G2341 **θηριομαχέω** *I fight with wild beasts* (i.e., wild
beasts in human form).
G2342 **θηρίον, -ου, τό** properly *a wild beast,* hence,
any *animal.*
θηρίον noun, acc. sg. neut. {2.B} . . . . θηρίον G2342
θηρίον noun, nom. sg. neut. {2.B} . . . . id.
θηρίου noun, gen. sg. neut. {2.B} . . . . id.
θηρίῳ noun, dat. sg. neut. {2.B} . . . . id.
θηρίων noun, gen. pl. neut. {2.B} . . . . id.
θησαυρίζειν vbl., pres. act. inf. {6.B.1}θησαυρίζω G2343
θησαυρίζεις verb, pres. act. indic. 2 pers. sg.
{5.A.1.a} . . . . id.
θησαυρίζετε verb, pres. act. impv. 2 pers. pl.
{5.D.1} . . . . id.
G2343 **θησαυρίζω** *I store up, I treasure up, I save.*
θησαυρίζων vbl., pres. act. ptc. nom. sg. masc.
{6.A.1} . . . . θησαυρίζω G2343
θησαυροί noun, nom. pl. masc. {2.B} . . θησαυρός G2344
θησαυρόν noun, acc. sg. masc. {2.B} . . . . id.
G2344 **θησαυρός, -οῦ, ὁ** *a storehouse* for precious
things; hence, *a treasure, a store.*
θησαυρός noun, nom. sg. masc. {2.B} . . θησαυρός G2344
θησαυροῦ noun, gen. sg. masc. {2.B} . . . . id.
θησαυρούς noun, acc. pl. masc. {2.B} . . . . id.
θησαυρῷ noun, dat. sg. masc. {2.B} . . . . id.
θησαυρῶν noun, gen. pl. masc. {2.B} . . . . id.
θήσει verb, fut. act. indic. 3 pers. sg. {5.A.1} τίθημι G5087
θήσεις verb, fut. act. indic. 2 pers. sg. {5.A.1} . . id.
θήσω verb, aor. act. subjunc. 1 pers. sg. {5.B.3} . id.
θήσω verb, fut. act. indic. 1 pers. sg. {5.A.1} . . . id.
G2345 **θιγγάνω** *I touch.*
θίγῃ verb, ²aor. act. subjunc. 3 pers. sg.
{5.B.1} . . . . θιγγάνω G2345
θίγῃς verb, ²aor. act. subjunc. 2 pers. sg. {5.B.1} . id.
θλίβεσθαι vbl., pres. pass. inf. {6.B.1} . . . . θλίβω G2346
θλιβόμεθα verb, pres. pass. indic. 1 pers. pl.
{5.A.1.d} . . . . id.
θλιβόμενοι vbl., pres. pass. ptc. nom. pl. masc.
{6.A.1} . . . . id.
θλιβομένοις vbl., pres. pass. ptc. dat. pl. masc.
{6.A.1} . . . . id.
θλίβουσιν vbl., pres. act. ptc. dat. pl. masc.
{6.A.1} . . . . id.
G2346 **θλίβω** (1) *I make narrow* (strictly *by pressure*),
Matt 7:14; *I press upon,* Mark 3:9; (2) *I persecute, press hard.*
θλίβωσιν verb, pres. act. subjunc. 3 pers. pl.
{5.B.1} . . . . θλίβω G2346

θλίψει noun, dat. sg. fem. {2.C} . . . . θλῖψις G2347
θλίψεις noun, nom. pl. fem. {2.C} . . . . id.
θλίψεσι noun, dat. pl. fem. {2.C} . . . . id.
θλίψεσιν noun, dat. pl. fem. {2.C} . . . . id.
θλίψεων noun, gen. pl. fem. {2.C} . . . . id.
θλίψεως noun, gen. sg. fem. {2.C} . . . . id.
θλίψιν noun, acc. sg. fem. {2.C} . . . . id.
θλῖψιν noun, acc. sg. fem. {2.C} . . . . id.
θλῖψις noun, nom. sg. fem. {2.C} . . . . id.
G2347 **θλῖψις, -εως, ἡ** *persecution, affliction, distress.*
θλῖψις noun, nom. sg. fem. {2.C} . . . . θλῖψις G2347
G2348 **θνήσκω** *I am dying;* perf. τέθνηκα, *I am dead;*
τεθνηκώς, *dead.*
θνητά adj., acc. pl. neut. {3.A} . . . . θνητός G2349
θνητῇ adj., dat. sg. fem. {3.A} . . . . id.
θνητόν adj., acc. sg. neut. {3.A} . . . . id.
θνητόν adj., nom. sg. neut. {3.A} . . . . id.
G2349 **θνητός, -ή, -όν** *mortal.*
θνητῷ adj., dat. sg. neut. {3.A} . . . . θνητός G2349
θορυβάζῃ verb, pres. pass. indic. 2 pers. sg.
{5.A.1.d} . . . . θορυβάζω G5182†‡
G5182†‡ **θορυβάζω** *I disturb greatly.* Var. for τυρβάζω,
Luke 10:41.
θορυβεῖσθε verb, pres. pass. impv. 2 pers. pl.
{5.D.2} . . . . θορυβέω G2350
θορυβεῖσθε verb, pres. pass. indic. 2 pers. pl.
{5.A.2} . . . . id.
G2350 **θορυβέω** *I disturb greatly, I terrify, I strike with
panic.*
θόρυβον noun, acc. sg. masc. {2.B} . . . . . θόρυβος G2351
G2351 **θόρυβος, -ου, ὁ** (1) *din, hubbub, confused
noise,* Acts 21:34, cf. Mark 5:38; (2) *riot,
disturbance.*
θόρυβος noun, nom. sg. masc. {2.B} . . . . θόρυβος G2351
θορύβου noun, gen. sg. masc. {2.B} . . . . id.
θορυβούμενον vbl., pres. pass. ptc. acc. sg. masc.
{6.A.2} . . . . θορυβέω G2350
G2352 **θραύω** *I crush.*
G2353 **θρέμμα, -ατος, τό** (lit. *a nursling*), hence pl.,
probably *cattle* (rather than *household, slaves*).
θρέμματα noun, nom. pl. neut. {2.C} . . . . θρέμμα G2353
G2354 **θρηνέω** *I lament.*
θρηνήσετε verb, fut. act. indic. 2 pers. pl.
{5.A.1} . . . . θρηνέω G2354
G2355 **θρῆνος, -ου, ὁ** *a dirge, lamentation* (Matt 2:18,
var.).
θρῆνος noun, nom. sg. masc. {2.B} . . . . . . θρῆνος G2355
G2356 **θρησκεία, -ας, ἡ** *worship* as expressed in
ritual acts, *religion* (underlying sense = *reverence* or *worship* of the gods).
θρησκεία noun, nom. sg. fem. {2.A} . . . θρησκεία G2356
θρησκεία noun, dat. sg. fem. {2.A} . . . . id.
θρησκείας noun, gen. sg. fem. {2.A} . . . . id.
G2357 **θρησκός, -όν** *religious* (probably in a limited
sense, referring to a careful observance of
religious restrictions), Jas 1:26.
θρησκός adj., nom. sg. masc. {3.A} . . . . . θρησκός G2357
θρῆσκος adj., nom. sg. masc. {3.A} . . . . id.
θριαμβεύοντι vbl., pres. act. ptc. dat. sg. masc.
{6.A.1} . . . . θριαμβεύω G2358

θριαμβεύσας   vbl., aor. act. ptc. nom. sg. masc.
{6.A.1.a} . . . . id.

G2358 **θριαμβεύω**   (properly, *I lead* one as my prisoner *in a triumphal procession,* hence) *I lead
around, I make a show (spectacle) of.*

G2359 **θρίξ**, τριχός, ἡ   *a hair;* pl. *hair.*
θρίξ   noun, nom. sg. fem. {2.C} . . . . .θρίξ G2359
θριξί   noun, dat. pl. fem. {2.C} . . . . id.
θριξίν   noun, dat. pl. fem. {2.C} . . . . id.
θροεῖσθαι   vbl., pres. pass. inf. {6.B.2} . . . . . θροέω G2360
θροεῖσθε   verb, pres. pass. impv. 2 pers. pl.
{5.D.2} . . . . id.

G2360 **θροέω**   *I disturb, agitate.*
θρόμβοι   noun, nom. pl. masc. {2.B} . . . . θρόμβος G2361

G2361 **θρόμβος**, -ου, ὁ   *a clot.*
θρόνοι   noun, nom. pl. masc. {2.B}. . . . . . θρόνος G2362
θρόνον   noun, acc. sg. masc. {2.B} . . . . id.

G2362 **θρόνος**, -ου, ὁ   *a (king's) throne, seat.*
θρόνος   noun, nom. sg. masc. {2.B} . . . . . . θρόνος G2362
θρόνου   noun, gen. sg. masc. {2.B}. . . . . id.
θρόνους   noun, acc. pl. masc. {2.B} . . . . id.
θρόνῳ   noun, dat. sg. masc. {2.B} . . . . id.
θρόνων   noun, gen. pl. masc. {2.B}. . . . . id.
Θυάτειρα   noun prop., acc. pl. neut. {2.B;
2.D} . . . . .Θυάτιρα G2363
Θυατείροις   noun prop., dat. pl. neut. {2.B; 2.D} id.
Θυατείρων   noun prop., gen. pl. neut. {2.B; 2.D} id.

G2363 **Θυάτιρα**, -ων, τό   *Thyatira,* a city of the old
district Lydia, in the Roman province Asia.
θύγατερ   noun, voc. sg. fem. {2.C} . . . . . . θυγάτηρ G2364
θυγατέρα   noun, acc. sg. fem. {2.C} . . . . id.
θυγατέρας   noun, acc. pl. fem. {2.C} . . . . id.
θυγατέρες   noun, nom. pl. fem. {2.C}. . . . . id.
θυγατέρες   noun, voc. pl. fem. {2.C}. . . . . id.
θυγατέρων   noun, gen. pl. fem. {2.C} . . . . id.

G2364 **θυγάτηρ**, τρός, ἡ   *a daughter;* hence (Hebraistic?), of any female *descendant,* however far removed, Luke 1:5; 13:16; even of one unrelated,
my young lady, Mark 5:34, etc.
θυγάτηρ   noun, nom. sg. fem. {2.C} . . . . θυγάτηρ G2364
θυγάτηρ   noun, voc. sg. fem. {2.C}. . . . . id.
θυγατρί   noun, dat. sg. fem. {2.C}. . . . . id.

G2365 **θυγάτριον**, -ου, τό   *a little (young) daughter.*
θυγάτριον   noun, nom. sg. neut. {2.B} . .θυγάτριον G2365
θυγατρός   noun, gen. sg. fem. {2.C} . . . . θυγάτηρ G2364
θύει   verb, pres. act. indic. 3 pers. sg. {5.A.1.a} . θύω G2380
θύειν   vbl., pres. act. inf. {6.B.1} . . . . id.

G2366 **θύελλα**, -ης, ἡ   *a storm, tempest.*
θυέλλῃ   noun, dat. sg. fem. {2.A} . . . . θύελλα G2366
θύεσθαι   vbl., pres. pass. inf. {6.B.1} . . . . θύω G2380
θύϊνον   adj., acc. sg. neut. {3.A} . . . . .θύϊνος G2367
θύϊνον   adj., acc. sg. neut. {3.A} . . . . id.

G2367 **θύϊνος**, -η, -ον   *of the sandarac* (so-called
citron) tree.

G2368 **θυμίαμα**, -ατος, τό   *incense.*
θυμίαμα   noun, acc. pl. neut. {2.C} . . . θυμίαμα G2368
θυμιάματα   noun, nom. pl. neut. {2.C} . . . . id.
θυμιάματος   noun, gen. sg. neut. {2.C} . . . . id.
θυμιαμάτων   noun, gen. pl. neut. {2.C} . . . . . . id.
θυμιᾶσαι   vbl., aor. act. inf. {6.B.1} . . . . . . θυμιάω G2370

G2369 **θυμιατήριον**, -ου, τό   (ordinarily *censer,* but)
either the *altar of incense* (Exod 30:1–10), or
the *shovel,* on which the high priest poured
the coals, when he entered the Holy of Holies
on the Day of Atonement (Lev 16:12).
θυμιατήριον   noun, acc. sg. neut.
{2.B} . . . . θυμιατήριον G2369

G2370 **θυμιάω**   *I burn incense.*
θυμοί   noun, nom. pl. masc. {2.B} . . . . θυμός G2372

G2371 **θυμομαχέω**   (lit. *I fight desperately*), hence, *I
am furiously angry with.*
θυμομαχῶν   vbl., pres. act. ptc. nom. sg. masc.
{6.A.2} . . . . θυμομαχέω G2371
θυμόν   noun, acc. sg. masc. {2.B} . . . . θυμός G2372

G2372 **θυμός**, -οῦ, ὁ   *an outburst of passion, wrath.*
θυμός   noun, nom. sg. masc. {2.B} . . . . θυμός G2372
θυμοῦ   noun, gen. sg. masc. {2.B}. . . . . id.

G2373 **θυμόω**   pass. *I am full of angry passion.*
θύουσιν   verb, pres. act. indic. 3 pers. pl.
{5.A.1.a} . . . . θύω G2380

G2374 **θύρα**, -ας, ἡ   (1) *a door;* (2) met. *an opportunity,* Acts 14:27; 1 Cor 16:9, etc.
θύρα   noun, nom. sg. fem. {2.A}. . . . . θύρα G2374
θύρᾳ   noun, dat. sg. fem. {2.A} . . . . id.
θύραι   noun, nom. pl. fem. {2.A} . . . . id.
θύραις   noun, dat. pl. fem. {2.A}. . . . . id.
θύραν   noun, acc. sg. fem. {2.A} . . . . id.
θύρας   noun, acc. pl. fem. {2.A} . . . . id.
θύρας   noun, gen. sg. fem. {2.A} . . . . id.
θυρεόν   noun, acc. sg. masc. {2.B} . . . . . . θυρεός G2375

G2375 **θυρεός**, -οῦ, ὁ   the heavy oblong Roman *shield.*
θυρίδος   noun, gen. sg. fem. {2.C} . . . . .θυρίς G2376

G2376 **θυρίς**, -ίδος, ἡ   *a window sill.*
θυρῶν   noun, gen. pl. fem. {2.A}. . . . . θύρα G2374

G2377 **θυρωρός**, -οῦ, ὁ or ἡ   *doorkeeper, porter.*
θυρωρός   noun, nom. sg. fem. {2.B} . . . . θυρωρός G2377
θυρωρός   noun, nom. sg. masc. {2.B}. . . . . id.
θυρωρῷ   noun, dat. sg. fem. {2.B}. . . . . id.
θυρωρῷ   noun, dat. sg. masc. {2.B}. . . . . id.
θύσατε   verb, aor. act. impv. 2 pers. pl. {5.D.1} . θύω G2380
θύσῃ   verb, aor. act. subjunc. 3 pers. sg. {5.B.1}. . id.

G2378 **θυσία**, -ας, ἡ   abstr. and concr., *sacrifice; a
sacrifice.*
θυσία   noun, nom. sg. fem. {2.A} . . . . θυσία G2378
θυσίᾳ   noun, dat. sg. fem. {2.A} . . . . id.
θυσίαι   noun, nom. pl. fem. {2.A} . . . . id.
θυσίαις   noun, dat. pl. fem. {2.A} . . . . id.
θυσίαν   noun, acc. sg. fem. {2.A} . . . . id.
θυσίας   noun, acc. pl. fem. {2.A} . . . . id.
θυσίας   noun, gen. sg. fem. {2.A} . . . . id.
θυσιαστήρια   noun, acc. pl. neut.
{2.B} . . . . θυσιαστήριον G2379

G2379 **θυσιαστήριον**, -ου, τό   *an altar* (for sacrifice).
θυσιαστήριον   noun, acc. sg. neut.
{2.B} . . . . θυσιαστήριον G2379
θυσιαστήριον   noun, nom. sg. neut. {2.B}. . . . . id.
θυσιαστηρίου   noun, gen. sg. neut. {2.B} . . . . . id.
θυσιαστηρίῳ   noun, dat. sg. neut. {2.B}. . . . . . id.
θυσιῶν   noun, gen. pl. fem. {2.A}. . . . . θυσία G2378
θῦσον   verb, aor. act. impv. 2 pers. sg. {5.D.1}. . θύω G2380

G2380 **θύω** *I sacrifice*, generally an animal; hence, *I kill*.

θῶ verb, ²aor. act. subjunc. 1 pers. sg. {5.B.3} τίθημι G5087

Θωμᾶ noun prop., voc. sg. masc. {2.A; 2.D} Θωμᾶς G2381

Θωμᾷ noun prop., dat. sg. masc. {2.A; 2.D} . . . . id.

Θωμᾶν noun prop., acc. sg. masc. {2.A; 2.D} . . . id.

G2381 **Θωμᾶς**, -ᾶ, ὁ *Thomas*, also called Didymus, one of the Twelve.

Θωμᾶς noun prop., nom. sg. masc. {2.A; 2.D} . . . . Θωμᾶς G2381

θῶμεν verb, ²aor. act. subjunc. 1 pers. pl. {5.B.3} . . . . τίθημι G5087

θώρακα noun, acc. sg. masc. {2.C} . . . . . . θώραξ G2382

θώρακας noun, acc. pl. masc. {2.C} . . . . id.

G2382 **θώραξ**, -ακος, ὁ *a breastplate, corselet, cuirass*.

I ι

Ἰάειρος noun prop., nom. sg. masc. {2.B; 2.D} . . . . Ἰάϊρος G2383

ἰαθείς vbl., aor. pass. ptc. nom. sg. masc. {6.A.1.a.} . . . . ἰάομαι G2390

ἰαθέντος vbl., aor. pass. ptc. gen. sg. masc. {6.A.1.a.} . . . . id.

ἰάθη verb, aor. pass. indic. 3 pers. sg. {5.A.1} . . . id.

ἰαθῇ verb, aor. pass. subjunc. 3 pers. sg. {5.B.1} . id.

ἰαθῆναι vbl., aor. pass. inf. {6.B.1} . . . . id.

ἰαθήσεται verb, fut. pass. indic. 3 pers. sg. {5.A.1} . . . . id.

ἰάθητε verb, aor. pass. indic. 2 pers. pl. {5.A.1} . id.

ἰαθῆτε verb, aor. pass. subjunc. 2 pers. pl. {5.B.1} . . . . id.

ἰαθήτω verb, aor. pass. impv. 3 pers. sg. {5.D.1} . id.

G2383 **Ἰάϊρος**, -ου, ὁ *Jairus*, a Jewish ruler of the synagogue.

Ἰάϊρος noun prop., nom. sg. masc. {2.B; 2.D} . . . . Ἰάϊρος G2383

G2384 **Ἰακώβ**, ὁ *Jacob*, (1) the patriarch, son of Isaac; (2) father of Joseph, the husband of Mary, according to Matt 1:15, 16 (Heb.).

Ἰακώβ noun prop. . . . . Ἰακώβ G2384

Ἰάκωβον noun prop., acc. sg. masc. {2.B; 2.D} . . . . Ἰάκωβος G2385

G2385 **Ἰάκωβος**, -ου, ὁ *James*, (1) the Small, son of Alphaeus, and one of the Twelve, Matt 10:3; 27:56; Mark 2:13 (var.); 3:18; 15:40; 16:1; Luke 6:15; 24:10; Acts 1:13; (2) brother of Jesus, Matt 13:55; Mark 6:3; Acts 12:17; 15:13; 21:18; 1 Cor 15:7; Gal 1:19; 2:9, 12; Jas 1:1(?); Jude 1; (3) father(?) of Jude, Luke 6:16; Acts 1:13; (4) son of Zebedee, and brother of John, one of the Twelve, killed 44 A.D.; (5) a late Egyptian(?) author, if not to be identified with (2), Jas 1:1.

Ἰάκωβος noun prop., nom. sg. masc. {2.B; 2.D} . . . . Ἰάκωβος G2385

Ἰακώβου noun prop., gen. sg. masc. {2.B; 2.D} . id.

Ἰακώβῳ noun prop., dat. sg. masc. {2.B; 2.D} . . id.

G2386 **ἴαμα**, -ατος, τό *a healing, a curing*.

ἰαμάτων noun, gen. pl. neut. {2.C} . . . . ἴαμα G2386

G2387 **Ἰαμβρῆς**, ὁ *Jambres*, a sorcerer at the court of the Pharaoh (var. Μαμβρῆς).

Ἰαμβρῆς noun prop., nom. sg. masc. {2.A; 2.D} . . . . Ἰαμβρῆς G2387

Ἰαννά noun prop. . . . . Ἰανναί G2388

G2388 **Ἰανναί**, ὁ *Jannai*, an ancestor of Jesus, son of Joseph, and father of Melchi (Heb.).

Ἰανναί noun prop. . . . . Ἰανναί G2388

Ἰαννῆς noun prop., nom. sg. masc. {2.A; 2.D} . . . . Ἰαννῆς G2389

G2389 **Ἰαννῆς**, ὁ *Jannes*, a sorcerer at the court of the Pharaoh (var. Ἰαμνῆς).

Ἰαννῆς noun prop., nom. sg. masc. {2.A; 2.D} . . . . Ἰαννῆς G2389

G2390 **ἰάομαι** *I heal*, generally of physical, sometimes of spiritual, disease.

Ἰαρέδ noun prop. . . . . Ἰάρετ G2391

G2391 **Ἰάρετ**, ὁ *Jareth*, son of Maleleel and father of Enoch. (Heb.).

Ἰάρετ noun prop. . . . . Ἰάρετ G2391

ἰάσασθαι vbl., aor. mid. inf. {6.B.1} . . . . . ἰάομαι G2390

ἰάσατο verb, aor. mid. indic. 3 pers. sg. {5.A.1}. id.

ἰάσεις noun, acc. pl. fem. {2.C} . . . . ἴασις G2392

ἰάσεως noun, gen. sg. fem. {2.C} . . . . id.

ἰάσηται verb, aor. mid. subjunc. 3 pers. sg. {5.B.1} . . . . ἰάομαι G2390

ἰᾶσθαι vbl., pres. mid./pass. inf. {6.B.2} . . . . . id.

ἴασιν noun, acc. sg. fem. {2.C} . . . . ἴασις G2392

G2392 **ἴασις**, -εως, ἡ *healing*.

ἰάσομαι verb, fut. mid. indic. 1 pers. sg. {5.A.1} . . . . ἰάομαι G2390

Ἰάσονα noun prop., acc. sg. masc. {2.C; 2.D} . . . . Ἰάσων G2394

Ἰάσονος noun prop., gen. sg. masc. {2.C; 2.D} . id.

ἰάσπιδι noun, dat. sg. fem. {2.C} . . . . ἴασπις G2393

G2393 **ἴασπις**, -ιδος, ἡ *jasper*.

ἴασπις noun, nom. sg. fem. {2.C} . . . . ἴασπις G2393

ἰάσωμαι verb, aor. mid. subjunc. 1 pers. sg. {5.B.1} . . . . ἰάομαι G2390

G2394 **Ἰάσων**, -ονος, ὁ *Jason*, a Christian of Thessalonica, perhaps the same as the "relative" of Paul in Rom 16:21.

Ἰάσων noun prop., nom. sg. masc. {2.C; 2.D} . . . . Ἰάσων G2394

ἰᾶται verb, pres. mid./pass. indic. 3 pers. sg. {5.A.2} . . . . ἰάομαι G2390

ἴαται verb, perf. pass. indic. 3 pers. sg. {5.A.1} . . id.

ἰᾶτο verb, impf. mid./pass. indic. 3 pers. sg. {5.A.2} . . . . id.

ἰατρέ noun, voc. sg. masc. {2.B} . . . . ἰατρός G2395

ἰατροῖς noun, dat. pl. masc. {2.B} . . . . id.

G2395 **ἰατρός**, -οῦ, ὁ *a physician*.

ἰατρός   noun, nom. sg. masc. {2.B} . . . . . . .ἰατρός *G2395*
ἰατροῦ   noun, gen. sg. masc. {2.B} . . . . id.
ἰατρούς   noun, acc. pl. masc. {2.B} . . . . id.
ἰατρῶν   noun, gen. pl. masc. {2.B} . . . . id.
G2396 **ἴδε**   *behold!* dem. part., from ²aor. act. impv. of
            ὁράω.
ἴδε   dem. part. . . . . ἴδε *G2396*
ἴδε   verb, ²aor. act. impv. 2 pers. sg. {5.D.1} . . .ὁράω *G3708*
G2397 **ἰδέα**, -ας, ἡ   *appearance.* Var. spelling εἰδέα,
            Matt 28:3.
ἰδέα   noun, nom. sg. fem. {2.A} . . . . .ἰδέα *G2397*
ἰδεῖν   vbl., ²aor. act. inf. {6.B.1} . . . . .ὁράω *G3708*
ἴδετε   verb, ²aor. act. impv. 2 pers. pl. {5.D.1}. . . . id.
ἴδῃ   verb, ²aor. act. subjunc. 3 pers. sg. {5.B.1}. . . id.
ἴδῃς   verb, ²aor. act. subjunc. 2 pers. sg. {5.B.1}. . id.
ἴδητε   verb, ²aor. act. subjunc. 2 pers. pl. {5.B.1} . id.
ἴδια   adj., acc. pl. neut. {3.A}. . . . . ἴδιος *G2398*
ἴδια   adj., nom. pl. neut. {3.A}. . . . . id.
ἰδίᾳ   adj., dat. sg. fem. {3.A} . . . . id.
ἰδίαις   adj., dat. pl. fem. {3.A}. . . . . id.
ἰδίαν   adj., acc. sg. fem. {3.A} . . . . id.
ἰδίας   adj., acc. pl. fem. {3.A} . . . . id.
ἰδίας   adj., gen. sg. fem. {3.A} . . . . id.
ἴδιοι   adj., nom. pl. masc. {3.A}. . . . . id.
ἰδίοις   adj., dat. pl. masc. {3.A} . . . . id.
ἰδίοις   adj., dat. pl. neut. {3.A} . . . . id.
ἴδιον   adj., acc. sg. masc. {3.A} . . . . id.
ἴδιον   adj., acc. sg. neut. {3.A} . . . . id.
G2398 **ἴδιος**, -α, -ον   *one's own, belonging to one,*
            private, personal; οἱ ἴδιοι, *one's own people,*
            one's own family, John 1:11; ὁ ἴδιος, possibly
            his own (son), Acts 20:28; τὰ ἴδια, *one's own*
            home, one's own property, John 1:11, etc.; ἰδίᾳ,
            κατ᾽ ἰδίαν (καθ᾽ ἰδίαν) *privately, apart,*
            in private, by oneself, individually (possibly
            understand ὁδόν).
ἴδιος   adj., nom. sg. masc. {3.A} . . . . ἴδιος *G2398*
ἰδίου   adj., gen. sg. masc. {3.A}. . . . . id.
ἰδίου   adj., gen. sg. neut. {3.A}. . . . . id.
ἰδίους   adj., acc. pl. masc. {3.A} . . . . id.
ἰδίῳ   adj., dat. sg. masc. {3.A} . . . . id.
ἰδίῳ   adj., dat. sg. neut. {3.A}. . . . . id.
ἰδίων   adj., gen. pl. fem. {3.A} . . . . id.
ἰδίων   adj., gen. pl. masc. {3.A} . . . . id.
ἰδίων   adj., gen. pl. neut. {3.A} . . . . id.
ἰδιῶται   noun, nom. pl. masc. {2.A} . . . . . . .ἰδιώτης *G2399*
G2399 **ἰδιώτης**, -ου, ὁ   (*unofficial*), hence, *an amateur,*
            an unprofessional man, a layman.
ἰδιώτης   noun, nom. sg. masc. {2.A} . . . . .ἰδιώτης *G2399*
ἰδιώτου   noun, gen. sg. masc. {2.A} . . . . id.
ἰδόντες   vbl., ²aor. act. ptc. nom. pl. masc.
            {6.A.2} . . . . .ὁράω *G3708*
ἰδού   interj. . . . . .ἰδού *G2400*
ἰδού   verb, ²aor. act. impv. 2 pers. sg. {5.D.1} . .ὁράω *G3708*
G2400 **ἰδού**   interj., *behold!,* from ²aor. act. impv. of
            ὁράω.
G2401 **Ἰδουμαία**, -ας, ἡ   *Idumaea, Edom,* a district of
            Arabia, immediately south of Judaea.
Ἰδουμαίας noun prop., gen. sg. fem. {2.A;
            2.D} . . . . .Ἰδουμαία *G2401*

ἰδοῦσα   vbl., ²aor. act. ptc. nom. sg. fem.
            {6.A.2} . . . . .ὁράω *G3708*
G2402 **ἱδρώς**, -ῶτος, ὁ   *sweat, perspiration.*
ἱδρώς   noun, nom. sg. masc. {2.C} . . . . .ἱδρώς *G2402*
ἴδω   verb, ²aor. act. subjunc. 1 pers. sg. {5.B.1}.ὁράω *G3708*
ἴδωμεν   verb, ²aor. act. subjunc. 1 pers. pl. {5.B.1}id.
ἰδών   vbl., ²aor. act. ptc. nom. sg. masc. {6.A.2}. . id.
ἴδωσι   verb, ²aor. act. subjunc. 3 pers. pl. {5.B.1} . id.
ἴδωσιν   verb, ²aor. act. subjunc. 3 pers. pl. {5.B.1}id.
G2403 **Ἰεζάβελ**, ἡ   *Jezebel* (Old Lat. and Armenian
            Zezabel), name given to a false prophetess of
            Thyatira, possibly borrowed from the name of
            Ahab's wife, queen of Israel (I Kgs 16:31, etc.).
Ἰεζάβελ   noun prop. . . . . Ἰεζάβελ *G2403*
Ἰεζαβήλ   noun prop. . . . . id.
ἱερά   adj., acc. pl. neut. {3.A} . . . . ἱερός *G2413*
ἱερᾷ   adj., dat. sg. fem. {3.A} . . . . id.
Ἱεραπόλει noun prop., dat. sg. fem. {2.C;
            2.D} . . . . Ἱεράπολις *G2404*
G2404 **Ἱεράπολις**, -εως, ἡ   *Hierapolis,* a city of the
            Lycus valley in Phrygia, near Laodicea and
            Colossae.
G2405 **ἱερατεία**, -ας, ἡ   *the duty (office) of a priest.*
ἱερατείαν noun, acc. sg. fem. {2.A} . . . . . ἱερατεία *G2405*
ἱερατείας noun, gen. sg. fem. {2.A}. . . . . id.
ἱερατεύειν vbl., pres. act. inf. {6.B.1} . . . ἱερατεύω *G2407*
G2406 **ἱεράτευμα**, -ατος, τό   *act* or *office of*
            priesthood.
ἱεράτευμα noun, acc. sg. neut. {2.C} . . ἱεράτευμα *G2406*
ἱεράτευμα noun, nom. sg. neut. {2.C}. . . . . id.
G2407 **ἱερατεύω**   *I serve as priest.*
ἱερατίαν   noun, acc. sg. fem. {2.A}. . . . . . ἱερατεία *G2405*
ἱερατίας   noun, gen. sg. fem. {2.A}. . . . . id.
ἱερέα   noun, acc. sg. masc. {2.C}. . . . . . ἱερεύς *G2409*
ἱερεῖ   noun, dat. sg. masc. {2.C} . . . . id.
ἱερεῖς   noun, acc. pl. masc. {2.C}. . . . . id.
ἱερεῖς   noun, nom. pl. masc. {2.C} . . . . id.
Ἱεριχώ   noun prop. . . . . Ἱεριχώ *G2410*
Ἰερεμίαν   noun prop., acc. sg. masc. {2.A;
            2.D} . . . . .Ἰερεμίας *G2408*
Ἰερεμίαν   noun prop., acc. sg. masc. {2.A; 2.D} . id.
G2408 **Ἰερεμίας**, -ου, ὁ   *Jeremiah,* OT prophet (wrote
            about 603–586 B.C.) (Heb.).
Ἰερεμίου   noun prop., gen. sg. masc. {2.A;
            2.D} . . . . .Ἰερεμίας *G2408*
Ἰερεμίου   noun prop., gen. sg. masc. {2.A; 2.D} . id.
G2409 **ἱερεύς**, -έως, ὁ   *a priest,* one who offers sacri-
            fice to a god (in Jewish and pagan religions; of
            Christians only met.).
ἱερεύς   noun, nom. sg. masc. {2.C} . . . . .ἱερεύς *G2409*
ἱερεῦσι   noun, dat. pl. masc. {2.C} . . . . id.
ἱερεῦσιν   noun, dat. pl. masc. {2.C} . . . . id.
ἱερέων   noun, gen. pl. masc. {2.C} . . . . id.
G2410 **Ἱεριχώ**, ἡ   *Jericho,* a city a little north of the
            Dead Sea.
Ἱεριχώ   noun prop. . . . . Ἱεριχώ *G2410*
Ἱεριχώ   noun prop. . . . . id.
ἱερόθυτον adj., nom. sg. neut. {3.C} . . ἱερόθυτος *G1494†‡*
G1494†‡ **ἱερόθυτος**, -ον   *slain as sacred, slain in sacrifice.*
            Var. for εἰδωλόθυτος, 1 Cor. 10:28.

G2411 **ἱερόν**, -οῦ, τό   *a temple,* either the whole building, or specifically the outer courts, open to worshippers (subs. from ἱερός); contrast ναός.

ἱερόν   adj., acc. sg. neut. {3.A} . . . . ἱερός G2413
ἱερόν   noun, acc. sg. neut. {2.B} . . . . .ἱερόν G2411
ἱεροπρεπεῖς   adj., acc. pl. fem. {3.E} . . .ἱεροπρεπής G2412

G2412 **ἱεροπρεπής**, -ές   *like those employed in sacred service.*

G2413 **ἱερός**, -ά, -όν   *holy, sacred;* neut. sg. subs. ἱερόν, *temple;* pl. subs. ἱερά, *holy things.*

Ἱεροσόλυμα   noun prop., acc. sg. fem. {2.A; 2.D} . . . . .Ἱεροσόλυμα G2414
Ἱεροσόλυμα   noun prop., nom. sg. fem. {2.A; 2.D} id.

G2414 **Ἱεροσόλυμα**, ἡ or τά   Gk. form of the Heb. name *Jerusalem* (cf. Heb. form Ἱερουσαλήμ).

Ἱεροσόλυμα   noun prop., acc. sg. fem. {2.A; 2.D} . . . . .Ἱεροσόλυμα G2414
Ἱεροσόλυμα   noun prop., nom. sg. fem. {2.A; 2.D} . . . . id.
Ἱεροσολυμεῖται   noun prop., nom. pl. masc. {2.A; 2.D} . . . . Ἱεροσολυμίτης G2415
Ἱεροσολυμειτῶν   noun prop., gen. pl. masc. {2.A; 2.D} . . . . id.
Ἱεροσολυμῖται   noun prop., nom. pl. masc. {2.A; 2.D} . . . . id.

G2415 **Ἱεροσολυμίτης**, -ου, ὁ   *an inhabitant of Jerusalem,* see Ἱερουσαλήμ.

Ἱεροσολυμιτῶν   noun prop., gen. pl. masc. {2.A; 2.D} . . . . Ἱεροσολυμίτης G2415
Ἱεροσολύμοις   noun prop., dat. pl. neut. {2.B; 2.D} . . . . .Ἱεροσόλυμα G2414
Ἱεροσολύμοις   noun prop., dat. pl. neut. {2.B; 2.D} . . . . id.
Ἱεροσολύμων   noun prop., gen. pl. neut. {2.B; 2.D} . . . . id.
Ἱεροσολύμων   noun prop., gen. pl. neut. {2.B; 2.D} . . . . id.
ἱεροσυλεῖς   verb, pres. act. indic. 2 pers. sg. {5.A.2} . . . . ἱεροσυλέω G2416

G2416 **ἱεροσυλέω**   *I rob temples.*

G2417 **ἱερόσυλος**, -ου, ὁ   *a robber of temples,* but possibly simply *sacrilegious.*

ἱεροσύλους   adj., acc. pl. masc. {3.C} . . ἱερόσυλος G2417
ἱεροῦ   adj, gen. sg. neut. {2.B} . . . . ἱερός G2413
ἱεροῦ   noun, gen. sg. neut. {2.B} . . . . . . .ἱερόν G2411

G2418 **ἱερουργέω**   *I sacrifice.*

ἱερουργοῦντα   vbl., pres. act. ptc. acc. sg. masc. {6.A.2} . . . . .ἱερουργέω G2418

G2419 **Ἱερουσαλήμ**, ἡ   *Jerusalem,* the capital of Palestine; hence, *Judaism,* Gal 4:25, and allegorically, *Christendom, the Christian Church,* Gal 4:26, etc. (Aram. form). (cf. Gk. form Ἱεροσόλυμα).

Ἱερουσαλήμ   noun prop. . . . . Ἱερουσαλήμ G2419
Ἱερουσαλήμ   noun prop. . . . . id.
ἱερῷ   adj., dat. sg. neut. {2.B} . . . . ἱερός G2413
ἱερῷ   noun, dat. sg. neut. {2.B} . . . . .ἱερόν G2411

G2420 **ἱερωσύνη**, -ης, ἡ   the abstr. notion of the *priestly office* (earlier ἱερεωσύνη from ἱερεύς).

ἱερωσύνην   noun, acc. sg. fem. {2.A} . . . ἱερωσύνη G2420
ἱερωσύνης   noun, gen. sg. fem. {2.A} . . . . id.

G2421 **Ἰεσσαί**, ὁ   *Jesse,* son of Obed (Iobed), and father of King David (Heb.).

Ἰεσσαί   noun prop. . . . . Ἰεσσαί G2421

G2422 **Ἰεφθάε**, ὁ   *Jephthah,* one of the Judges of Israel (Heb.).

Ἰεφθάε   noun prop. . . . . Ἰεφθάε G2422
Ἰεχονίαν   noun prop., acc. sg. masc. {2.A; 2.D} . . . . .Ἰεχονίας G2423

G2423 **Ἰεχονίας**, -ου, ὁ   *Jechoniah,* son of Josiah and father of Salathiel (Heb.).

Ἰεχονίας   noun prop., nom. sg. masc. {2.A; 2.D} . . . . .Ἰεχονίας G2423
Ἰησοῦ   noun prop., dat. sg. masc. {2.B; 2.D} . . . . Ἰησοῦς G2424
Ἰησοῦ   noun prop., gen. sg. masc. {2.B; 2.D} . . . id.
Ἰησοῦ   noun prop., voc. sg. masc. {2.B; 2.D} . . . id.
Ἰησοῦν   noun prop., acc. sg. masc. {2.B; 2.D} . . . id.
Ἰησους   noun prop., nom. sg. masc. {2.B; 2.D} . . id.

G2424 **Ἰησοῦς**, gen., dat. οῦ, acc. οῦν   (1) *Jesus,* the Gk. form of Joshua, and the human name of our Savior (see Χριστός). The name is generally contracted thus, IC, IHC, in MSS., as a sign of sanctity; (2) according to certain manuscripts, one of the names of Barabbas, the robber, Matt 27:16, 17; (3) *Joshua,* Moses' successor as leader of the children of Israel, Acts 7:45; Heb 4:8; (4) an ancestor of our Lord, Luke 3:29; (5) *Jesus,* who was also called Justus, an early Christian, with Paul, Col 4:11. In these cases the name is not contracted.

Ἰησοῦς   noun prop., nom. sg. masc. {2.B; 2.D} . . . . Ἰησοῦς G2424
ἱκανά   adj., acc. pl. neut. {3.A} . . . . ἱκανός G2425
ἱκαναί   adj., nom. pl. fem. {3.A} . . . . id.
ἱκαναῖς   adj., dat. pl. fem. {3.A} . . . . id.
ἱκανάς   adj., acc. pl. fem. {3.A} . . . . id.
ἱκανοί   adj., nom. pl. masc. {3.A} . . . . id.
ἱκανοῖς   adj., dat. pl. masc. {3.A} . . . . id.
ἱκανόν   adj., acc. sg. masc. {3.A} . . . . id.
ἱκανόν   adj., acc. sg. neut. {3.A} . . . . id.
ἱκανόν   adj., nom. sg. neut. {3.A} . . . . id.

G2425 **ἱκανός**, -ή, -όν   (1) *considerable, sufficient,* of number, quantity, time: ἐξ ἱκανῶν χρόνων (var. ἱκανοῦ), *already for a long time,* Luke 23:8 (cf. 8:27); ἐφ᾽ ἱκανόν, *for a sufficiently long time,* Acts 20:11; ἱκανόν ἐστιν, *enough of this subject,* Luke 22:38 (cf. 2 Cor 2:6); τὸ ἱκανὸν ποιεῖν τινι, *to satisfy one, to give him no ground of complaint,* Mark 15:15, τὸ ἱκανὸν λαμβάνω, *I get surety (security),* Acts 17:9; (2) of persons, *sufficiently strong (good, etc.), worthy, suitable,* with various constructions.

ἱκανός   adj., nom. sg. masc. {3.A} . . . . .ἱκανός G2425

G2426 **ἱκανότης**, -ητος, ἡ   *sufficiency, ability, power.*

ἱκανότης   noun, nom. sg. fem. {2.C} . . .ἱκανότης G2426
ἱκανοῦ   adj., gen. sg. masc. {3.A} . . . . . . .ἱκανός G2425
ἱκανούς   adj., acc. pl. masc. {3.A} . . . . id.

G2427 **ἱκανόω**   *I make sufficient, I make fit.*
ἱκανῷ   adj., dat. sg. masc. {3.A} . . . . .ἱκανός G2425
ἱκανῶν   adj., gen. pl. masc. {3.A} . . . . id.
ἱκανώσαντι   vbl., aor. act. ptc. dat. sg. masc.
     {6.A.2}. . . . . ἱκανόω G2427
ἱκάνωσεν   verb, aor. act. indic. 3 pers. sg. {5.A.1}id.
G2428 **ἱκετηρία**, -ας, ἡ   *supplication, entreaty;* (orig.
     ἱκετηρίας ῥάβδος, the olive branch held in
     the hand of the suppliant).
ἱκετηρίας   noun, acc. pl. fem. {2.A} . . . . . ἱκετηρία G2428
ἰκμάδα   noun, acc. sg. fem. {2.C} . . . . .ἰκμάς G2429
G2429 **ἰκμάς**, -άδος, ἡ   *moisture.*
G2430 **Ἰκόνιον**, -ου, τό   *Iconium,* a Phrygian city of
     the Roman province Galatia (mod. Konya).
Ἰκόνιον   noun prop., acc. sg. neut. {2.B;
     2.D}. . . . . Ἰκόνιον G2430
Ἰκονίου   noun prop., gen. sg. neut. {2.B; 2.D} . . id.
Ἰκονίῳ   noun prop., dat. sg. neut. {2.B; 2.D} . . . id.
ἱλαρόν   adj., acc. sg. masc. {3.A} . . . . ἱλαρός G2431
G2431 **ἱλαρός**, -ά, -όν   *cheerful.*
G2432 **ἱλαρότης**, -ητος, ἡ   *cheerfulness.*
ἱλαρότητι   noun, dat. sg. fem. {2.C}. . . . ἱλαρότης G2432
ἱλάσθητι   verb, aor. pass. impv. 2 pers. sg.
     {5.D.1}. . . . . ἱλάσκομαι G2433
ἱλάσκεσθαι   vbl., pres. pass. inf. {6.B.1}. . . . . . id.
G2433 **ἱλάσκομαι**   (1) with dat. *I have mercy on, I
     show favor to;* (2) trans. with obj. of sins, *I
     forgive.*
ἱλασμόν   noun, acc. sg. masc. {2.B} . . . . . ἱλασμός G2434
G2434 **ἱλασμός**, -οῦ, ὁ   *a propitiation* (of an angry
     god).
ἱλασμός   noun, nom. sg. masc. {2.B} . . . . ἱλασμός G2434
G2435 **ἱλαστήριον**, -ου, τό   (1) *a sin offering,* by
     which the wrath of the deity shall be appeased,
     a means of propitiation, Rom 3:25; (2) *the cov-
     ering* of the ark, which was sprinkled with the
     atoning blood on the Day of Atonement (Heb.
     kappōret), Heb 9:5 (original idea, *propitiation*
     of an angry god).
ἱλαστήριον   noun, acc. sg. neut. {2.B} ἱλαστήριον G2435
G2436 **ἵλεως**, -ων   *propitious, forgiving,* Heb 8:12:
     ἵλεως σοι = ἵλεως εἴη σοι ὁ Θεός, *may the
     god be favorable to you, God be merciful to you,
     may God help you, God forbid!* Matt 16:22.
ἵλεως   adj., nom. sg. masc. {3.E} . . . . .ἵλεως G2436
G2437 **Ἰλλυρικόν**, -οῦ, τό   *Illyricum,* a Roman prov-
     ince, afterwards called Dalmatia, bounded
     by Pannonia on the north, Macedonia on the
     south, Moesia on the east, and the Adriatic Sea
     on the west.
Ἰλλυρικοῦ   noun prop., gen. sg. neut. {2.B;
     2.D}. . . . . Ἰλλυρικόν G2437
ἱμάντα   noun, acc. sg. masc. {2.C} . . . . .ἱμάς G2438
G2438 **ἱμάς**, -άντος, ὁ   *a thong, strap,* (1) for binding
     a man who is to be flogged, Acts 22:25; (2) for
     fastening a sandal or shoe.
ἱμᾶσιν   noun, dat. pl. masc. {2.C}. . . . . .ἱμάς G2438
ἱμάτια   noun, acc. pl. neut. {2.B} . . . . ἱμάτιον G2440
ἱμάτια   noun, nom. pl. neut. {2.B} . . . . id.
G2439 **ἱματίζω**   *I clothe, I provide clothing for.*

ἱματίοις   noun, dat. pl. neut. {2.B} . . . . . . ἱμάτιον G2440
G2440 **ἱμάτιον**, -ου, τό   a long flowing *outer garment.*
ἱμάτιον   noun, acc. sg. neut. {2.B} . . . . . . ἱμάτιον G2440
ἱμάτιον   noun, nom. sg. neut. {2.B} . . . . id.
ἱματίου   noun, gen. sg. neut. {2.B} . . . . id.
ἱματισμένον   vbl., perf. pass. ptc. acc. sg. masc.
     {6.A.1.b} . . . . .ἱματίζω G2439
ἱματισμόν   noun, acc. sg. masc. {2.B}. . .ἱματισμός G2441
G2441 **ἱματισμός**, -οῦ, ὁ   *raiment, clothing,* a collec-
     tive word.
ἱματισμός   noun, nom. sg. masc. {2.B}. . ἱματισμός G2441
ἱματισμοῦ   noun, gen. sg. masc. {2.B} . . . . id.
ἱματισμῷ   noun, dat. sg. masc. {2.B} . . . . id.
ἱματίῳ   noun, dat. sg. neut. {2.B} . . . . . . ἱμάτιον G2440
ἱματίων   noun, gen. pl. neut. {2.B} . . . . id.
G2442 **ἱμείρομαι**   *I long for,* with gen. (perhaps a
     nursery word, derived from a word indicating
     "remembrance").
ἱμειρόμενοι   vbl., pres. mid. ptc. nom. pl. masc.
     {6.A.1}. . . . . ἱμείρομαι G2442
G2443 **ἵνα**   (1) in statements: (a) indicating purpose,
     in order that; (b) indicating a command or
     wish, *that,* Mark 5:23; 6:25; 10:35, 51; John
     17:24; 1 Cor 7:29; 2 Cor 8:7; Gal 2:10; Eph
     5:33; (c) indicating consequence, *so that,* e.g.,
     Rom 11:11; (d) a mere introduction to a noun
     clause, *that,* e.g., John 17:3; (2) in interroga-
     tions ἵνα τί, *why? wherefore?*
ἵνα   conj. . . . . .ἵνα G2443
G3363‡ **ἵνα μή**   *lest, in order that not.*
G2444 **ἱνατί**   = ἵνα τί; see ἵνα (2).
ἱνατί   adv. . . . . .ἱνατί G2444
G2445 **Ἰόππη**, -ης, ἡ   *Joppa,* a coast town of Judaea,
     west northwest of Jerusalem.
Ἰόππη   noun prop., dat. sg. fem. {2.A; 2.D}. . Ἰόππη G2445
Ἰόππην   noun prop., acc. sg. fem. {2.A; 2.D} . . . id.
Ἰόππης   noun prop., gen. sg. fem. {2.A; 2.D} . . . id.
Ἰορδάνη   noun prop., dat. sg. masc. {2.A;
     2.D}. . . . . .Ἰορδάνης G2446
Ἰορδάνην   noun prop., acc. sg. masc. {2.A; 2.D} id.
G2446 **Ἰορδάνης**, -ου, ὁ   *Jordan,* a great river flowing
     due south and bounding Galilee, Samaria, and
     Judaea on the east.
Ἰορδάνου   noun prop., gen. sg. masc. {2.A;
     2.D}. . . . . .Ἰορδάνης G2446
G2447 **ἰός**, -οῦ, ὁ   *poison;* hence, *rust,* Jas 5:3.
ἰός   noun, nom. sg. masc. {2.B}. . . . . .ἰός G2447
ἰοῦ   noun, gen. sg. masc. {2.B} . . . . id.
G2448 **Ἰούδα**   see Ἰούδας.
Ἰούδα   noun prop., gen. sg. masc. {2.A;
     2.D}. . . . . .Ἰούδας G2455
Ἰούδα   noun prop., voc. sg. masc. {2.A; 2.D} . . . id.
Ἰούδᾳ   noun prop., dat. sg. masc. {2.A; 2.D}. . . . id.
G2449 **Ἰουδαία**, -ας, ἡ   *Judaea,* a Roman province,
     capital Jerusalem.
Ἰουδαία   noun prop., nom. sg. fem. {2.A;
     2.D}. . . . . .Ἰουδαία G2449
Ἰουδαίᾳ   noun prop., dat. sg. fem. {2.A; 2.D}. . . id.
Ἰουδαίᾳ   adj. prop., dat. sg. fem. {3.A}. . Ἰουδαῖος G2453
Ἰουδαίαν   adj. prop., acc. sg. fem. {3.A}. . . . . . id.

Ἰουδαίαν noun prop., acc. sg. fem. {2.A;
2.D} . . . . Ἰουδαία G2449
Ἰουδαίας adj. prop., gen. sg. fem. {3.A}. Ἰουδαῖος G2453
Ἰουδαίας noun prop., gen. sg. fem. {2.A;
2.D} . . . . Ἰουδαία G2449
ἰουδαΐζειν vbl., pres. act. inf. {6.B.1} . . . ἰουδαΐζω G2450
G2450 ἰουδαΐζω I live as a Jew (in religion,
ceremonially).
Ἰουδαϊκοῖς adj. prop., dat. pl. masc.
{3.A} . . . . Ἰουδαϊκός G2451
G2451 Ἰουδαϊκός, -ή, -όν Jewish, Judaic.
G2452 Ἰουδαϊκῶς adv., in the manner of Jews (reli-
giously, ceremonially).
Ἰουδαϊκῶς adv. prop. {3.F} . . . . Ἰουδαϊκῶς G2452
Ἰουδαῖοι adj. prop., nom. pl. masc.
{3.A} . . . . Ἰουδαῖος G2453
Ἰουδαῖοι adj. prop., voc. pl. masc. {3.A} . . . . . id.
Ἰουδαίοις adj. prop., dat. pl. masc. {3.A} . . . . . id.
Ἰουδαῖον adj. prop., acc. sg. masc. {3.A} . . . . . id.
G2453 Ἰουδαῖος, -α, -ον Jewish.
Ἰουδαῖος adj. prop., nom. sg. masc.
{3.A} . . . . Ἰουδαῖος G2453
Ἰουδαίου adj. prop., gen. sg. masc. {3.A} . . . . id.
Ἰουδαίους adj. prop., acc. pl. masc. {3.A} . . . . id.
G2454 Ἰουδαϊσμός, -οῦ, ὁ the Jewish religion,
Judaism.
Ἰουδαϊσμῷ noun prop., dat. sg. masc. {2.B;
2.D} . . . . Ἰουδαϊσμός G2454
Ἰουδαίῳ adj. prop., dat. sg. masc. {3.A}. Ἰουδαῖος G2453
Ἰουδαίων adj. prop., gen. pl. masc. {3.A} . . . . . id.
Ἰουδαίων noun prop., gen. pl. masc. {3.A} . . . . id.
Ἰούδαν noun prop., acc. sg. masc. {2.A;
2.D} . . . . Ἰούδας G2455
G2455 Ἰούδας (Ἰούδα, Ἰωδά), -α, ὁ (1) Judah, son
of Jacob, the tribe founded by him, and the
country occupied by it, Matt 1:2, 3; 2:6; Luke
1:39 (but some think Ἰούδα the name of
a city); 3:33; Heb 7:14; 8:8; Rev 5:5; 7:5; (2)
Judas, Iscariot (son of Simon), the disciple
who betrayed Jesus; (3) Jude, the brother of
Jesus, Matt 13:55; Mark 6:3; Jude 1(?); (4) Jude,
an ancestor of Jesus, Luke 3:30; (5) Jude (son
of James), the apostle, Luke 6:16; John 14:22;
Acts 1:13; (6) Judas, a Galilean rebel about 4
B.C., Acts 5:37; (7) Judas, a resident of Damascus, Acts 9:11; (8) Judas, surnamed Barsabbas,
a leading Christian and "prophet" sent by the
Jerusalem church to Antioch, Acts 15:22–34,
perhaps identical with (7); (Heb.).
Ἰούδας noun prop., nom. sg. masc. {2.A;
2.D} . . . . Ἰούδας G2455
G2456 Ἰουλία, -ας, ἡ Julia, a Roman Christian, probably a slave or freedwoman of the Imperial
household (Rom 16:15).
Ἰουλίαν noun prop., acc. sg. fem. {2.A;
2.D} . . . . Ἰουλία G2456
G2457 Ἰούλιος, -ου, ὁ Julius, a Roman centurion on
special service.
Ἰούλιος noun prop., nom. sg. masc. {2.B;
2.D} . . . . Ἰούλιος G2457

Ἰουλίῳ noun prop., dat. sg. masc. {2.B; 2.D} . . . id.
Ἰουνιᾶν noun prop., acc. sg. masc. {2.A;
2.D} . . . . Ἰουνιᾶς G2458
Ἰουνίαν noun prop., acc. sg. fem. {2.A; 2.D} . . . id.
G2458 Ἰουνιᾶς, -ᾶ, ὁ Junias a Roman Christian
(Rom 16:7).
G2459 Ἰοῦστος, -ου, ὁ Justus, (1) a surname of Jo-
seph Barsabbas, one of the two nominated to
fill Judas' place as apostle, Acts 1:23; (2) Titius
Justus, a Corinthian Christian, Acts 18:7; (3)
surname of Jesus, a Christian with Paul in
Rome.
Ἰοῦστος noun prop., nom. sg. masc. {2.B;
2.D} . . . . Ἰοῦστος G2459
Ἰούστου noun prop., gen. sg. masc. {2.B; 2.D} . id.
ἱππεῖς noun, acc. pl. masc. {2.C} . . . . ἱππεύς G2460
G2460 ἱππεύς, -έως, ὁ a horse soldier, a mounted
soldier, a cavalryman.
G2461 ἱππικός, -ή, -όν pertaining to horses; adj. used
as collective subs., cavalry.
ἱππικοῦ adj., gen. sg. neut. {3.A} . . . . ἱππικός G2461
ἵπποις noun, dat. pl. masc. {2.B} . . . . ἵππος G2462
G2462 ἵππος, -ου, ὁ a horse.
ἵππος noun, nom. sg. masc. {2.B} . . . . ἵππος G2462
ἵππου noun, gen. sg. masc. {2.B} . . . . id.
ἵππους noun, acc. pl. masc. {2.B} . . . . id.
ἵππων noun, gen. pl. masc. {2.B} . . . . id.
G2463 ἶρις, -ιδος, ἡ a rainbow.
ἶρις noun, nom. sg. fem. {2.C} . . . . ἶρις G2463
ἴσα adj., acc. pl. neut. {3.A} . . . . ἴσος G2470
ἴσα adj., nom. pl. neut. {3.A} . . . . id.
G2464 Ἰσαάκ, Ἰσάκ, ὁ Isaac, the patriarch (Heb.).
Ἰσαάκ noun prop . . . . Ἰσαάκ G2464
ἰσάγγελοι adj., nom. pl. masc. {3.C} . . . ἰσάγγελος G2465
G2465 ἰσάγγελος, -ον like the angels.
ἴσαι adj., nom. pl. fem. {3.A} . . . . ἴσος G2470
ἴσασι verb, ²perf. act. indic. 3 pers. pl.
{5.A.1.c} . . . . εἴδω G1492
ἴσασιν verb, ²perf. act. indic. 3 pers. pl. {5.A.1.c} id.
G2466 Ἰσαχάρ (Ἰσσαχάρ) Issachar, one of the sons
of Jacob and founder of a tribe of Israel (Heb.).
Ἰσαχάρ noun prop . . . . Ἰσαχάρ G2466
ἴση adj., nom. sg. fem. {3.A} . . . . ἴσος G2470
ἴσην adj., acc. sg. fem. {3.A} . . . . id.
ἴσθι verb, pres. act. impv. 2 pers. sg. {7.B} . . . εἰμί G1510
Ἰσκαριώθ noun prop . . . . Ἰσκαριώτης G2469
Ἰσκαριώτῃ noun prop., dat. sg. masc. {2.A;
2.D} . . . . id.
Ἰσκαριώτην noun prop., acc. sg. masc. {2.A;
2.D} . . . . id.
G2469 Ἰσκαριώτης (Ἰσκαριώθ) Iscariot, the sur-
name of Judas the Betrayer, which would seem
to indicate the place from which he came (var.
Σκαριώθ). Ἰσκαριώτης is the Graecized
form of Ἰσκαριώθ (var. ἀπὸ Καρυώτου,
from Kerioth, in John 6:71; 12:4; 14:22).
Ἰσκαριώτης noun prop., nom. sg. masc. {2.A;
2.D} . . . . Ἰσκαριώτης G2469
Ἰσκαριώτου noun prop., gen. sg. masc. {2.A;
2.D} . . . . id.

ἴσον adj., acc. sg. masc. {3.A}. . . . . .ἴσος G2470

G2470 ἴσος, -η, -ον *equal, equivalent, identical;* τὰ
ἴσα, *the equivalent,* Luke 6:34; ἴσα, adverbially, *on an equality,* Phil 2:6 (if text be sound).

G2471 ἰσότης, -ητος, ἡ *equality; equality of treatment, fairness.*
ἰσότης noun, nom. sg. fem. {2.C}. . . . . . .ἰσότης G2471
ἰσότητα noun, acc. sg. fem. {2.C}. . . . . id.
ἰσότητος noun, gen. sg. fem. {2.C}. . . . . id.
ἰσότιμος adj., acc. sg. fem. {3.C}. . . . . .ἰσότιμος G2472

G2472 ἰσότιμος, -ον *equally privileged, equal.*
ἴσους adj., acc. pl. masc. {3.A}. . . . . .ἴσος G2470
ἰσόψυχον adj., acc. sg. masc. {3.C}. . . ἰσόψυχος G2473

G2473 ἰσόψυχος, -ον *likeminded.*

G2474 Ἰσραήλ, ὁ *Israel,* surname of Jacob, then the
Jewish people, the people of God (Heb.).
Ἰσραήλ noun prop.. . . . . .Ἰσραήλ G2474
Ἰσραηλεῖται noun prop., nom. pl. masc. {2.A;
2.D}. . . . . .Ἰσραηλίτης G2475
Ἰσραηλεῖται noun prop., voc. pl. masc. {2.A;
2.D}. . . . . id.
Ἰσραηλείτης noun prop., nom. sg. masc. {2.A;
2.D}. . . . . id.
Ἰσραηλῖται noun prop., nom. pl. masc. {2.A;
2.D}. . . . . id.
Ἰσραηλῖται noun prop., voc. pl. masc. {2.A;
2.D}. . . . . id.

G2475 Ἰσραηλίτης, -ου, ὁ *an Israelite,* one of the
chosen people Israel, a Jew.
Ἰσραηλίτης noun prop., nom. sg. masc. {2.A;
2.D}. . . . . .Ἰσραηλίτης G2475
Ἰσσαχάρ noun prop.. . . . . .Ἰσαχάρ G2466
ἱστάνομεν verb, pres. act. indic. 1 pers. pl.
{5.A.3.a}. .ἵστημι G2476
ἴστε verb, ²perf. act. impv. 2 pers. pl. {5.D.1}. .εἴδω G1492
ἴστε verb, ²perf. act. indic. 2 pers. pl. {5.A.1.c}. . id.
ἱστήκει verb, plu. act. indic. 3 pers. sg.
{5.A.1}. . . . . .ἵστημι G2476
ἱστήκεισαν verb, plu. act. indic. 3 pers. pl.
{5.A.1}. . . . . id.

G2476 ἵστημι (ἱστάνω) (1) trans. (with act. of pres.,
fut., impf., 1aor, and perf. tenses), *I make to
stand, I set up; I weigh* (pay), Matt 26:15; (2)
intrans. (with act. of ²aor., perf., and plup.
tenses, and with fut. mid., fut. pass., and
aor. pass.), *I am set up, I am made to stand, I
stand, I take an erect position, I stand firm* (=
ἀντιστῆναι, Eph 6:13). The form ἱστάνω
first appeared in third c. B.C.
ἵστησιν verb, pres. act. indic. 3 pers. sg.
{5.A.3.a} . . . . .ἵστημι G2476

G2477 ἱστορέω *I visit, see* (some person or object of
importance).
ἱστορῆσαι vbl., aor. act. inf. {6.B.1}. . . . .ἱστορέω G2477
ἱστῶμεν verb, pres. act. indic. 1 pers. pl.
{5.A.3.a} . . . . .ἵστημι G2476
ἴσχυε verb, impf. act. indic. 3 pers. sg.
{5.A.1.b} . . . . .ἰσχύω G2480
ἰσχύει verb, pres. act. indic. 3 pers. sg. {5.A.1.a} id.
ἰσχύειν vbl., pres. act. inf. {6.B.1} . . . . id.

ἴσχυεν verb, impf. act. indic. 3 pers. sg. {5.A.1.b} id.
ἰσχύι noun, dat. sg. fem. {2.C}. . . . . .ἰσχύς G2479
ἰσχύϊ noun, dat. sg. fem. {2.C}. . . . . id.
ἰσχύν noun, acc. sg. fem. {2.C} . . . . id.
ἴσχυον verb, impf. act. indic. 3 pers. pl.
{5.A.1.b} . . . . .ἰσχύω G2480
ἰσχύοντες vbl., pres. act. ptc. nom. pl. masc.
{6.A.1}. . . . . id.
ἰσχύοντος vbl., pres. act. ptc. gen. sg. masc.
{6.A.1}. . . . . id.
ἰσχύος noun, gen. sg. fem. {2.C}. . . . . .ἰσχύς G2479
ἰσχυρά adj., acc. pl. neut. {3.A}. . . . . . ἰσχυρός G2478
ἰσχυρά adj., nom. sg. fem. {3.A}. . . . . id.
ἰσχυρά adj., voc. sg. fem. {3.A}. . . . . id.
ἰσχυρᾷ adj., dat. sg. fem. {3.A}. . . . . id.
ἰσχυραί adj., nom. pl. fem. {3.A}. . . . . id.
ἰσχυράν adj., acc. sg. fem. {3.A}. . . . . id.
ἰσχυράς adj., gen. sg. fem. {3.A}. . . . . id.
ἰσχυροί adj., nom. pl. masc. {3.A}. . . . . id.
ἰσχυρόν adj., acc. sg. masc. {3.A}. . . . . id.

G2478 ἰσχυρός, -ά, -όν *strong* (originally and generally of physical strength); *powerful.*
ἰσχυρός adj., nom. sg. masc. {3.A} . . . .ἰσχυρός G2478
ἰσχυρότεροι adj. comp., nom. pl. masc. {3.A;
3.G}. . . . . id.
ἰσχυρότερον adj. comp., nom. sg. neut. {3.A;
3.G}. . . . . id.
ἰσχυρότερος adj. comp., nom. sg. masc. {3.A;
3.G}. . . . . id.
ἰσχυροῦ adj., gen. sg. masc. {3.A}. . . . . id.
ἰσχυρῶν adj., gen. pl. fem. {3.A}. . . . . id.
ἰσχυρῶν adj., gen. pl. masc. {3.A}. . . . . id.

G2479 ἰσχύς, -ύος, ἡ *strength* (absol.).
ἰσχύς noun, nom. sg. fem. {2.C} . . . . .ἰσχύς G2479
ἰσχύσαμεν verb, aor. act. indic. 1 pers. pl.
{5.A.1.b} . . . . .ἰσχύω G2480
ἴσχυσαν verb, aor. act. indic. 3 pers. pl.
{5.A.1.b} . . . . id.
ἰσχύσαντος vbl., aor. act. ptc. gen. sg. masc.
{6.A.1.a} . . . . id.
ἴσχυσας verb, aor. act. indic. 2 pers. sg.
{5.A.1.b} . . . . id.
ἰσχύσατε verb, aor. act. indic. 2 pers. pl.
{5.A.1.b} . . . . id.
ἴσχυσε verb, aor. act. indic. 3 pers. sg. {5.A.1.b} id.
ἴσχυσεν verb, aor. act. indic. 3 pers. sg. {5.A.1.b} id.
ἰσχύσουσιν verb, fut. act. indic. 3 pers. pl.
{5.A.1.a} . . . . id.

G2480 ἰσχύω *I have strength, I am strong, I am in full
health and vigor* (opp. κακῶς ἔχω), Matt 9:12;
and so *I am able,* sometimes followed by the
inf. or εἰς with acc. to indicate the purpose for
which the strength is used, e.g., Matt 26:40;
5:13; with acc. adverbially, qualifying the
strength, τι ἰσχύει, *has any validity* (value),
Gal 5:6; cf. Heb 9:17; πάντα ἰσχύω, *I have all
strength* (power), Phil 4:13, πολὺ ἰσχύει, *has
great power,* Jas 5:16.
ἰσχύω verb, pres. act. indic. 1 pers. sg.
{5.A.1.a} . . . . .ἰσχύω G2480

G2481 **ἴσως** adv., *perhaps* (cf. Eng. *likely*).
ἴσως adv. {3.F} . . . . ἴσως G2481
G2482 **Ἰταλία, -ας, ἡ** *Italy.*
Ἰταλίαν noun prop., acc. sg. fem. {2.A;
  2.D} . . . . Ἰταλία G2482
Ἰταλίας noun prop., gen. sg. fem. {2.A; 2.D} . . . id.
Ἰταλικῆς adj. prop., gen. sg. fem. {3.A} . . Ἰταλικός G2483
G2483 **Ἰταλικός, -ή, -όν** *Italic,* the name of a cohort
  forming part of the Syrian army.
Ἰτουραίας adj. prop., gen. sg. fem. {3.A} Ἰτουραῖος G2484
G2484 **Ἰτουραῖος, -α, -ον** *Iturean,* an adj. applied
  to the district (χώρα) of Iturea (also called
  Trachonitis), about sixty miles east of the Sea
  of Galilee, and partly inhabited by the nomad
  tribe called Itureans (Ἰτουραῖοι).
ἰχθύας noun, acc. pl. masc. {2.C} . . . . ἰχθύς G2486
ἰχθύδια noun, acc. pl. neut. {2.B} . . . . . ἰχθύδιον G2485
G2485 **ἰχθύδιον, -ου, τό** *a little fish.*
ἰχθύες noun, nom. pl. masc. {2.C} . . . . ἰχθύς G2486
ἰχθύν noun, acc. sg. masc. {2.C} . . . . id.
ἰχθύος noun, gen. sg. masc. {2.C} . . . . id.
G2486 **ἰχθύς, -ύος, ὁ** *a fish.*
ἰχθύων noun, gen. pl. masc. {2.C} . . . . ἰχθύς G2486
ἴχνεσι noun, dat. pl. neut. {2.C} . . . . ἴχνος G2487
ἴχνεσιν noun, dat. pl. neut. {2.C} . . . . id.
G2487 **ἴχνος, -ους, τό** *a track, footstep.*
G2488 **Ἰωαθάμ, ὁ** *Jotham,* son of Ozias and father of
  Achaz (Heb.).
Ἰωαθάμ noun prop. . . . . Ἰωαθάμ G2488
Ἰωάθαμ noun prop. id.
Ἰωάνα noun prop., nom. sg. fem. {2.A;
  2.D} . . . . Ἰωάννα G2489
Ἰωανάν noun prop. . . . . Ἰωαννᾶς G2490
Ἰωάνει noun prop., dat. sg. masc. {2.A;
  2.D} . . . . Ἰωάννης G2491
Ἰωάνη noun prop., dat. sg. masc. {2.A; 2.D} . . . id.
Ἰωάνην noun prop., acc. sg. masc. {2.A; 2.D} . . id.
Ἰωάνης noun prop., nom. sg. masc. {2.A; 2.D} . id.
Ἰωαννᾶ noun prop. . . . . Ἰωαννᾶς G2490
G2489 **Ἰωάννα (Ἰωάνα), -ας, ἡ** *Joanna,* wife of
  Chuza, Herod's steward (Heb.).
Ἰωάννα noun prop., nom. sg. fem. {2.A;
  2.D} . . . . Ἰωάννα G2489
Ἰωαννάν noun prop. . . . . Ἰωαννᾶς G2490
G2490 **Ἰωαννᾶς (Ἰωανάν)** *Joannas* or *Joanan,* an
  ancestor of Jesus. (Luke 3:27). (Heb.)
Ἰωάννη noun prop., dat. sg. masc. {2.A;
  2.D} . . . . Ἰωάννης G2491
Ἰωάννην noun prop., acc. sg. masc. {2.A; 2.D} . id.
G2491 **Ἰωάννης (Ἰωάνης), Ἰωαννᾶς), -ου, ὁ** *John:*
  (1) the Baptizer, son of Zacharias and Elizabeth; (2) son of Zebedee and brother of James;
  (3) the writer of the Apocalypse, by very
  many identified with (2); (4) also called Mark,
  cousin of Barnabas, generally regarded as author of the second Gospel, Acts 12, 13, 15; (5)
  the father of Simon Peter and Andrew, John
  1, 21; (6) var. Ἰωνάθας i.e., *Jonathan,* son of
  Annas, who succeeded Caiaphas, otherwise
  unknown, unless to be identified with Johanan

ben Zacchai, president of the Great Synagogue
  after 70 A.D. (Heb.).
Ἰωάννης noun prop., nom. sg. masc. {2.A;
  2.D} . . . . Ἰωάννης G2491
Ἰωάννου noun prop., gen. sg. masc. {2.A; 2.D} . id.
Ἰωάνου noun prop., gen. sg. masc. {2.A; 2.D} . . id.
G2492 **Ἰώβ, ὁ** *Job,* the hero of the OT book of that
  name (Heb.).
Ἰώβ noun prop. Ἰώβ G2492
Ἰωβήδ noun prop. . . . . Ὠβήδ G5601
Ἰωβήλ noun prop. . . . . id.
Ἰωδά noun prop. . . . . Ἰούδας G2455
G2493 **Ἰωήλ, ὁ** *Joel,* the OT prophet (Heb.).
Ἰωήλ noun prop. . . . . Ἰωήλ G2493
ἰώμενος vbl., pres. mid./pass. ptc. nom. sg. masc.
  {6.A.2} . . . . ἰάομαι G2390
Ἰωνᾶ noun prop., gen. sg. masc. {2.A; 2.D} . Ἰωνᾶς G2495
G2494 **Ἰωνάμ, ὁ** *Jonam,* an ancestor of Jesus (Heb.).
Ἰωνάμ noun prop. . . . . Ἰωνάμ G2494
Ἰωνάν noun prop. . . . . id.
G2495 **Ἰωνᾶς (Ἰωνᾶ), -ᾶ, ὁ** *Jonah,* the OT prophet (Heb.).
Ἰωνᾶς noun prop., nom. sg. masc. {2.A;
  2.D} . . . . Ἰωνᾶς G2495
G2496 **Ἰωράμ, ὁ** *Joram,* son of Jehoshaphat and father
  of Ozias (Heb.).
Ἰωράμ noun prop. . . . . Ἰωράμ G2496
Ἰωρείμ noun prop. . . . . Ἰωρίμ G2497
G2497 **Ἰωρίμ, ὁ** *Jorim,* an ancestor of Jesus (Heb.).
Ἰωρίμ noun prop. . . . . Ἰωρίμ G2497
G2498 **Ἰωσαφάτ, ὁ** *Jehoshaphat,* king of Judah, son
  of Asaph, father of Joram, an ancestor of Jesus
  (Heb.).
Ἰωσαφάτ noun prop. . . . . Ἰωσαφάτ G2498
Ἰωσείαν noun prop., acc. sg. masc. {2.A;
  2.D} . . . . Ἰωσίας G2502
Ἰωσείας noun prop., nom. sg. masc. {2.A; 2.D} . id.
G2499 **Ἰωσή** a form of Ἰωσῆς.
Ἰωσή noun prop., gen. sg. masc. {2.A; 2.D} . Ἰωσῆς G2500
Ἰωσῆ noun prop., gen. sg. masc. {2.A; 2.D} . . . . id.
G2500 **Ἰωσῆς, -ῆ or ῆτος, ὁ** *Joses,* son of Mary, sister
  of Mary, the mother of Jesus; see Ἰωσήφ (4)
  (Heb.).
Ἰωσῆς noun prop., nom. sg. masc. {2.A; 2.D} . Ἰωσῆς G2500
Ἰωσῆτος noun prop., gen. sg. masc. {2.A; 2.D} . id.
G2501 **Ἰωσήφ, ὁ** *Joseph:* (1) son of Jacob the patriarch, John 4:5; Acts 7:9, 13, 14, 18; Heb 11:21,
  22; Rev 7:8; (2) husband of Mary; (3) of Ari-
  mathea, rich member of the Sanhedrin, Matt
  27:57, 59; Mark 15:43, 45; Luke 23:50; John
  19:38; (4) Ἰωσῆς, a by-form of Ἰωσήφ, and
  add Matt 13:55; 27:56; (5) an ancestor of Jesus,
  Luke 3:24; (6) another ancestor of Jesus, Luke
  3:30; (7) also called Barsabbas and Justus,
  one of the two nominated to fill the place of
  the Betrayer Judas among the apostles, Acts
  1:23; (8) another name of Barnabas of Cyprus,
  cousin of Mark, colleague of Paul.
Ἰωσήφ noun prop. . . . . Ἰωσήφ G2501
G2501† **Ἰωσήχ, ὁ** *Josech,* an ancestor of Jesus (Heb.).
  Var. for Ἰωσήφ, Luke 3:26.

Ἰωσήχ   noun prop.. . . . . Ἰωσήχ *G2501†*

Ἰωσίαν   noun prop., acc. sg. masc. {2.A; 2.D}. . . . . Ἰωσίας *G2502*

G2502 **Ἰωσίας**   *Josiah,* king of Judah, son of Amos and father of Jechoniah (Heb.).

Ἰωσίας   noun prop., nom. sg. masc. {2.A; 2.D}. . . . . Ἰωσίας *G2502*

G2503 **ἰῶτα,** τό   *yod,* the Heb. or rather Aram. letter which was smallest of all.

ἰῶτα   noun, letter . . . . ἰῶτα *G2503*

Κ κ

G2504 **κἀγώ**   conj. or adv. contracted from καὶ ἐγώ, *I also, I too.*

κἀγώ   conj. + pron. pers., 1 pers. nom. sg. {4.A} . . . . κἀγώ *G2504*

καθ᾽   prep.. . . . . κατά *G2596*

G2505 **καθά**   *just as* (from καθ᾽ ἅ, *according to which things*).

καθά   adv., conj.. . . . . καθά *G2505*

καθαίρει   verb, pres. act. indic. 3 pers. sg. {5.A.1.a} . . . . .καθαίρω *G2508*

καθαιρεῖσθαι   vbl., pres. pass. inf. {6.B.2} . . . . καθαιρέω *G2507*

καθαίρεσιν   noun, acc. sg. fem. {2.C} .καθαίρεσις *G2506*

G2506 **καθαίρεσις,** -εως, ἡ   *taking down, razing, destroying.*

G2507 **καθαιρέω**   (1) *I take down, pull down;* (2) *I depose,* Luke 1:52, cf. 2 Cor 10:4, with gen. *I diminish* something *from,* Acts 19:27; (3) *I destroy,* Acts 13:19.

καθαιροῦντες   vbl., pres. act. ptc. nom. pl. masc. {6.A.2} . . . . καθαιρέω *G2507*

G2508 **καθαίρω**   *I cleanse, purify.*

G2509 **καθάπερ**   adv. or conj. (i.e., καθ᾽ ἅπερ, *according to which things*), *even as.*

καθάπερ   adv., conj.. . . . . καθάπερ *G2509*

G2510 **καθάπτω**   *I lay hold of, I fasten on to,* of a snake with short teeth harmless to the skin.

καθαρά   adj., nom. pl. neut. {3.A} . . . . . καθαρός *G2513*

καθαρά   adj., nom. sg. fem. {3.A}. . . . . id.

καθαρᾷ   adj., dat. sg. fem. {3.A} . . . . id.

καθαρᾶς   adj., gen. sg. fem. {3.A}. . . . . id.

καθαριεῖ   verb, fut. act. indic. 3 pers. sg. {5.A.2} . . . . .καθαρίζω *G2511*

καθαρίζει   verb, pres. act. indic. 3 pers. sg. {5.A.1.a} . . . . id.

καθαρίζεσθαι   vbl., pres. pass. inf. {6.B.1} . . . . id.

καθαρίζεται   verb, pres. pass. indic. 3 pers. sg. {5.A.1.d} . . . . id.

καθαρίζετε   verb, pres. act. impv. 2 pers. pl. {5.D.1} . . . . id.

καθαρίζετε   verb, pres. act. indic. 2 pers. pl. {5.A.1.a} . . . . id.

καθαρίζον   vbl., pres. act. ptc. nom. sg. neut. {6.A.1} . . . . id.

καθαρίζονται   verb, pres. pass. indic. 3 pers. pl. {5.A.1.d} . . . . id.

G2511 **καθαρίζω**   *I make clean,* literally, ceremonially, or spiritually, according to context, ἀπό with gen. being sometimes added, of the dirt removed. (Alternative spelling καθερίζω, perhaps = καθαιρίζω, but it occurs only in augmented and reduplicated forms and has been otherwise explained).

καθαρίζων   vbl., pres. act. ptc. nom. sg. masc. {6.A.1} . . . . .καθαρίζω *G2511*

καθαρίσαι   vbl., aor. act. inf. {6.B.1} . . . . id.

καθαρίσας   vbl., aor. act. ptc. nom. sg. masc. {6.A.1.a} . . . . id.

καθαρίσατε   verb, aor. act. impv. 2 pers. pl. {5.D.1} . . . . id.

καθαρίσῃ   verb, aor. act. subjunc. 3 pers. sg. {5.B.1} . . . . id.

καθαρισθητι   verb, aor. pass. impv. 2 pers. sg. {5.D.1} . . . . id.

καθαρισμόν   noun, acc. sg. masc. {2.B}. καθαρισμός *G2512*

G2512 **καθαρισμός,** -οῦ, ὁ   *cleansing, purifying, purification,* literal, ceremonial, or moral.

καθαρισμοῦ   noun, gen. sg. masc. {2.B} . . . . καθαρισμός *G2512*

καθάρισον   verb, aor. act. impv. 2 pers. sg. {5.D.1} . . . . .καθαρίζω *G2511*

καθαρίσωμεν   verb, aor. act. subjunc. 1 pers. pl. {5.B.1} . . . . id.

καθαροί   adj., nom. pl. masc. {3.A} . . . . καθαρός *G2513*

καθαροῖς   adj., dat. pl. masc. {3.A}. . . . . id.

καθαρόν   adj., acc. sg. masc. {3.A} . . . . id.

καθαρόν   adj., acc. sg. neut. {3.A} . . . . id.

καθαρόν   adj., nom. sg. neut. {3.A} . . . . id.

G2513 **καθαρός,** -ά, -όν   *clean, pure, unstained,* either literally or ceremonially or spiritually; καθαρὸς ἀπό, *unstained by.*

καθαρός   adj., nom. sg. masc. {3.A} . . . . .καθαρός *G2513*

G2514 **καθαρότης,** -ητος, ἡ   *cleanness.*

καθαρότητα   noun, acc. sg. fem. {2.C} καθαρότης *G2514*

καθαρῷ   adj., dat. sg. masc. {3.A}. . . . . . .καθαρός *G2513*

καθαρῷ   adj., dat. sg. neut. {3.A} . . . . id.

G2515 **καθέδρα,** -ας, ἡ   *a seat, chair.*

καθέδρας   noun, acc. pl. fem. {2.A} . . . . . καθέδρα *G2515*

καθέδρας   noun, gen. sg. fem. {2.A}. . . . . id.

G2516 **καθέζομαι**   *I am sitting, I sit, I am seated.*

καθεζόμενοι   vbl., pres. mid./pass. ptc. nom. pl. masc. {6.A.1}. . . . . καθέζομαι *G2516*

καθεζόμενον   vbl., pres. mid./pass. ptc. acc. sg. masc. {6.A.1} . . . . id.

καθεζόμενος   vbl., pres. mid./pass. ptc. nom. sg. masc. {6.A.1} . . . . id.

καθεζομένους   vbl., pres. mid./pass. ptc. acc. pl. masc. {6.A.1} . . . . id.

καθεῖλε   verb, ²aor. act. indic. 3 pers. sg.
{5.A.1.b} . . . . καθαιρέω *G2507*

καθεῖλεν   verb, ²aor. act. indic. 3 pers. sg.
{5.A.1.b} . . . . id.

καθελεῖν   vbl., ²aor. act. inf. {6.B.1} . . . . id.

καθελόντες   vbl., ²aor. act. ptc. nom. pl. masc.
{6.A.2} . . . . id.

καθελῶ   verb, ²fut. act. indic. 1 pers. sg. {5.A.1} . id.

καθελών   vbl., ²aor. act. ptc. nom. sg. masc.
{6.A.2} . . . . id.

G2517 **καθεξῆς**   adv., *in order, in succession; ἐν τῷ*
καθεξῆς (understand χρόνῳ), *in the time
immediately after, just after,* Luke 8:1; οἱ καθεξῆς, *those who followed,* Acts 3:24.

καθεξῆς   adv. . . . . καθεξῆς *G2517*

καθεύδει   verb, pres. act. indic. 3 pers. sg.
{5.A.1.a} . . . . καθεύδω *G2518*

καθεύδειν   vbl., pres. act. inf. {6.B.1} . . . . id.

καθεύδεις   verb, pres. act. indic. 2 pers. sg.
{5.A.1.a} . . . . id.

καθεύδετε   verb, pres. act. impv. 2 pers. pl.
{5.D.1} . . . . id.

καθεύδετε   verb, pres. act. indic. 2 pers. pl.
{5.A.1.a} . . . . id.

καθεύδῃ   verb, pres. act. subjunc. 3 pers. sg.
{5.B.1} . . . . id.

καθεύδοντας   vbl., pres. act. ptc. acc. pl. masc.
{6.A.1} . . . . id.

καθεύδοντες   vbl., pres. act. ptc. nom. pl. masc.
{6.A.1} . . . . id.

καθεύδουσι   verb, pres. act. indic. 3 pers. pl.
{5.A.1.a} . . . . id.

καθεύδουσιν   verb, pres. act. indic. 3 pers. pl.
{5.A.1.a} . . . . id.

G2518 **καθεύδω**   *I am sleeping (asleep), I sleep.*

καθεύδωμεν   verb, pres. act. subjunc. 1 pers. pl.
{5.B.1} . . . . καθεύδω *G2518*

καθεύδων   vbl., pres. act. ptc. nom. sg. masc.
{6.A.1} . . . . id.

κάθη   verb, pres. mid./pass. indic. 2 pers. sg.
{5.A.3} . . . . κάθημαι *G2521*

καθηγηταί   noun, nom. pl. masc. {2.A} καθηγητής *G2519*

G2519 **καθηγητής**, -οῦ, ὁ   *a leader, a teacher.*

καθηγητής   noun, nom. sg. masc. {2.A}καθηγητής *G2519*

καθῆκαν   verb, aor. act. indic. 3 pers. pl.
{5.A.3.b} . . . . καθίημι *G2524*

καθῆκεν   verb, impf. act. indic. 3 pers. sg.
{5.A.1.b} . . . . καθήκω *G2520*

καθῆκον   vbl., pres. act. ptc. nom. sg. neut. {6.A.1} id.

καθήκοντα   vbl., pres. act. ptc. acc. pl. neut.
{6.A.1} . . . . id.

G2520 **καθήκω**   impers. καθήκει, *it is fitting;* τὰ μὴ
καθήκοντα (a technical phrase of the Stoic
philosophy), *what is unfitting.*

G2521 **κάθημαι**   *I am seated, I sit;* καθήμενος, *seated,
sitting.*

κάθημαι   verb, pres. mid./pass. indic. 1 pers. sg.
{5.A.3.a} . . . . κάθημαι *G2521*

καθήμεναι   vbl., pres. mid./pass. ptc. nom. pl.
fem. {6.A.3} . . . . id.

καθημένην   vbl., pres. mid./pass. ptc. acc. sg.
fem. {6.A.3} . . . . id.

καθημένης   vbl., pres. mid./pass. ptc. gen. sg.
fem. {6.A.3} . . . . id.

καθήμενοι   vbl., pres. mid./pass. ptc. nom. pl.
masc. {6.A.3} . . . . id.

καθημένοις   vbl., pres. mid./pass. ptc. dat. pl.
masc. {6.A.3} . . . . id.

καθημένοις   vbl., pres. mid./pass. ptc. dat. pl.
neut. {6.A.3} . . . . id.

καθήμενον   vbl., pres. mid./pass. ptc. acc. sg.
masc. {6.A.3} . . . . id.

καθήμενος   vbl., pres. mid./pass. ptc. nom. sg.
masc. {6.A.3} . . . . id.

καθημένου   vbl., pres. mid./pass. ptc. gen. sg.
masc. {6.A.3} . . . . id.

καθημένους   vbl., pres. mid./pass. ptc. acc. pl.
masc. {6.A.3} . . . . id.

καθημένῳ   vbl., pres. mid./pass. ptc. dat. sg.
masc. {6.A.3} . . . . id.

καθημένων   vbl., pres. mid./pass. ptc. gen. pl.
masc. {6.A.3} . . . . id.

καθημερινῇ   adj., dat. sg. fem. {3.A} καθημερινός *G2522*

G2522 **καθημερινός**, -ή, -όν   *daily.*

κάθηνται   verb, pres. mid./pass. indic. 3 pers. pl.
{5.A.3.a} . . . . κάθημαι *G2521*

καθήσεσθε   verb, fut. mid. indic. 2 pers. pl.
{5.A.1} . . . . id.

καθῆσθαι   vbl., pres. mid./pass. inf. {6.B.3} . . . . id.

καθῆσθε   verb, pres. mid./pass. indic. 2 pers.
pl. {5.A.3.a} . . . . id.

κάθηται   verb, pres. mid./pass. indic. 3 pers. sg.
{5.A.3.a} . . . . id.

καθῆψε   verb, aor. act. indic. 3 pers. sg.
{5.A.1.b} . . . . .καθάπτω *G2510*

καθῆψεν   verb, aor. act. indic. 3 pers. sg.
{5.A.1.b} . . . . id.

καθιεμένην   vbl., pres. pass. ptc. acc. sg. fem.
{6.A.3} . . . . .καθίημι *G2524*

καθιέμενον   vbl., pres. pass. ptc. acc. sg. neut.
{6.A.3} . . . . id.

καθίζετε   verb, pres. act. indic. 2 pers. pl.
{5.A.1.a} . . . . καθίζω *G2523*

G2523 **καθίζω**   (1) trans., *I make to sit, I set;* (2)
intrans. aor., *I sat down.*

G2524 **καθίημι**   *I let down.*

καθίσαι   vbl., aor. act. inf. {6.B.1} . . . . καθίζω *G2523*

καθίσαντες   vbl., aor. act. ptc. nom. pl. masc.
{6.A.1.a} . . . . id.

καθίσαντος   vbl., aor. act. ptc. gen. sg. masc.
{6.A.1.a} . . . . id.

καθίσας   vbl., aor. act. ptc. nom. sg. masc.
{6.A.1.a} . . . . id.

καθίσατε   verb, aor. act. impv. 2 pers. pl. {5.D.1} id.

καθίσει   verb, fut. act. indic. 3 pers. sg. {5.A.1.a} id.

καθίσεσθε   verb, fut. mid. indic. 2 pers. pl.
{5.A.1.d} . . . . id.

καθίσῃ   verb, aor. act. subjunc. 3 pers. sg. {5.B.1}id.

καθίσησθε   verb, aor. mid. subjunc. 2 pers. pl.
{5.B.1} . . . . id.

καθιστάνοντες vbl., pres. act. ptc. nom. pl. masc.
{6.A.3} . . . . καθίστημι G2525
καθίσταται verb, pres. pass. indic. 3 pers. sg.
{5.A.3.a} . . . . id.

G2525 **καθίστημι** (καθιστάνω) trans. (see ἵστημι),
I set, establish, appoint, constitute, make; I
conduct, Acts 17:15; καθίσταται, shows itself,
acts its part, Jas 3:6.
καθίστησιν verb, pres. act. indic. 3 pers. sg.
{5.A.3.a} . . . . καθίστημι G2525
καθιστῶντες vbl., pres. act. ptc. nom. pl. masc.
{6.A.3} . . . . id.
καθίσωμεν verb, aor. act. subjunc. 1 pers. pl.
{5.B.1} . . . . καθίζω G2523
καθίσωσιν verb, aor. act. subjunc. 3 pers. pl.
{5.B.1} . . . . id.

G2526 **καθό** adv., as, according as (i.e., καθ᾽ ὅ, according to which thing).
καθό adv. . . . . καθό G2526

G2527 **καθόλου** adv., at all (i.e., καθ᾽ ὅλου).
καθόλου adv. . . . . καθόλου G2527

G2528 **καθοπλίζω** trans., I arm completely, I arm
head-to-toe.
καθορᾶται verb, pres. pass. indic. 3 pers. sg.
{5.A.2} . . . . καθοράω G2529

G2529 **καθοράω** I see clearly.

G2530 **καθότι** (1) in proportion as, according as, Acts
2:45; 4:35; (2) because, Luke 1:7; 19:9; Acts
2:24; 17:31 (from, καθ᾽ ὅ, τι, neut. of ὅστις,
cf. καθό, καθά).
καθότι adv., conj. . . . . καθότι G2530
κάθου verb, pres. mid./pass. impv. 2 pers. sg.
{5.D.3} . . . . κάθημαι G2521
καθωπλισμένος vbl., perf. mid./pass. ptc. nom.
sg. masc. {6.A.1.b} . . . . καθοπλίζω G2528

G2531 **καθώς** adv., according to the manner in which,
in the degree that, as.
καθώς adv. . . . . καθώς G2531

G2509†‡ **καθώσπερ** adv., according to the very manner
in which, even as. Var. for καθάπερ, 2 Cor
3:18.
καθώσπερ adv. . . . . καθώσπερ G2509†‡
και conj. . . . . καί G2532

G2532 **καί** and; sometimes modifying a following
word, even.
καί conj. . . . . καί G2532
Καιάφα noun prop., gen. sg. masc. {2.A;
2.D} . . . . Καϊάφας G2533
Καϊάφα noun prop., gen. sg. masc. {2.A; 2.D} . . id.
Καιάφαν noun prop., acc. sg. masc. {2.A; 2.D} . id.
Καϊάφαν noun prop., acc. sg. masc. {2.A; 2.D} . id.
Καϊάφας noun prop., nom. sg. masc. {2.A; 2.D} id.

G2533 **Καϊάφας**, -α, ὁ Caiaphas, Jewish high priest
(Old Lat. and Sahidic = Καίφας).
Καϊάφας noun prop., nom. sg. masc. {2.A;
2.D} . . . . Καϊάφας G2533

G2534 **καίγε** at least, even, indeed; from καί γε.
καίεται verb, pres. pass. indic. 3 pers. sg.
{5.A.1.d} . . . . καίω G2545

Καίν noun prop. . . . . Κάϊν G2535

G2535 **Κάϊν**, ὁ Cain, son of Adam and Eve and
brother of Abel (Heb.).
Κάϊν noun prop. . . . . Κάϊν G2535
καινά adj., acc. pl. neut. {3.A} . . . . .καινός G2537
καινά adj., nom. pl. neut. {3.A} . . . . id.
καιναῖς adj., dat. pl. fem. {3.A} . . . . id.
Καινάμ noun prop. . . . . .Καϊνάμ G2536

G2536 **Καϊνάμ** (Καϊνάν), ὁ Cainan, one of the
ancestors of Jesus (Heb.).
Καϊνάμ noun prop. . . . . .Καϊνάμ G2536
Καϊνάν noun prop. . . . . id.
καινή adj., nom. sg. fem. {3.A} . . . . .καινός G2537
καινήν adj., acc. sg. fem. {3.A} . . . . id.
καινῆς adj., gen. sg. fem. {3.A} . . . . id.
καινόν adj., acc. sg. masc. {3.A}. . . . . id.
καινόν adj., acc. sg. neut. {3.A} . . . . id.
καινόν adj., nom. sg. neut. {3.A} . . . . id.

G2537 **καινός**, -ή, -όν fresh, new.
καινότερον adj. comp., acc. sg. neut. {3.A;
3.G} . . . . .καινός G2537

G2538 **καινότης**, -ητος, ἡ freshness, newness.
καινότητι noun, dat. sg. fem. {2.C} . . . .καινότης G2538
καινοῦ adj., gen. sg. neut. {3.A} . . . . .καινός G2537
καινούς adj., acc. pl. masc. {3.A} . . . . id.
καινῷ adj., dat. sg. neut. {3.A} . . . . id.
καιόμεναι vbl., pres. pass. ptc. nom. pl. fem.
{6.A.1} . . . . καίω G2545
καιομένη vbl., pres. pass. ptc. nom. sg. fem.
{6.A.1} . . . . id.
καιομένῃ vbl., pres. pass. ptc. dat. sg. fem.
{6.A.1} . . . . id.
καιομένην vbl., pres. pass. ptc. acc. sg. fem.
{6.A.1} . . . . id.
καιομένης vbl., pres. pass. ptc. gen. sg. fem.
{6.A.1} . . . . id.
καιόμενοι vbl., pres. pass. ptc. nom. pl. masc.
{6.A.1} . . . . id.
καιόμενον vbl., pres. pass. ptc. nom. sg. neut.
{6.A.1} . . . . id.
καιόμενος vbl., pres. pass. ptc. nom. sg. masc.
{6.A.1} . . . . id.
καίουσι verb, pres. act. indic. 3 pers. sg.
{5.A.1.a} . . . . id.
καίουσιν verb, pres. act. indic. 3 pers. pl.
{5.A.1.a} . . . . id.

G2539 **καίπερ** although.
καίπερ conj. . . . . καίπερ G2539
καιροί noun, nom. pl. masc. {2.B} . . . . καιρός G2540
καιροῖς noun, dat. pl. masc. {2.B} . . . . id.
καιρόν noun, acc. sg. masc. {2.B} . . . . id.

G2540 **καιρός**, -οῦ, ὁ fitting season, season, opportunity, occasion, time; πρὸς καιρόν, for a time.
καιρός noun, nom. sg. masc. {2.B} . . . . καιρός G2540
καιροῦ noun, gen. sg. masc. {2.B} . . . . id.
καιρούς noun, acc. pl. masc. {2.B} . . . . id.
καιρῷ noun, dat. sg. masc. {2.B} . . . . id.
καιρῶν noun, gen. pl. masc. {2.B} . . . . id.

G2541 **Καῖσαρ**, -ος, ὁ Caesar, a surname of the gens
Iulia, which became practically synonymous

with *the Emperor* for the time being; in
the Gospels it refers always to Tiberius
(14–37 A.D.) except in Luke 2:1 to Augustus
(23 B.C.–14 A.D.), in Acts 17:7 to Claudius
(41–54 A.D.), in Acts 25–28 and Phil 4:22 to
Nero (54–68 A.D.).
Καίσαρα   noun prop., acc. sg. masc. {2.C;
2.D}. . . . . Καῖσαρ G2541
G2542 **Καισάρεια**, -ας, ἡ   *Caesarea*, (1) *Caesarea
of Philip* (Luke 3:1), Matt 16:13; Mark 8:27,
otherwise called *Caesarea Panias*, a city in
Phoenice at the foot of Mount Hermon, by the
source of the Jordan; (2) *Caesarea of Strato* (a
king of Sidon) or *of Palestine*, on the coast of
Palestine, about sixty miles north northwest of
Jerusalem.
Καισαρείᾳ   noun prop., dat. sg. fem. {2.A;
2.D}. . . . . Καισάρεια G2542
Καισάρειαν   noun prop., acc. sg. fem. {2.A;
2.D}. . . . . id.
Καισαρείας   noun prop., gen. sg. fem. {2.A;
2.D}. . . . . id.
Καίσαρι   noun prop., dat. sg. masc. {2.C;
2.D}. . . . . Καῖσαρ G2541
Καισαρίᾳ   noun prop., dat. sg. fem. {2.A;
2.D}. Καισάρεια G2542
Καισαρίαν   noun prop., acc. sg. fem. {2.A; 2.D} id.
Καισαρίας   noun prop., gen. sg. fem. {2.A; 2.D} id.
Καίσαρος   noun prop., gen. sg. masc. {2.C;
2.D}. . . . . Καῖσαρ G2541
G2543 **καίτοι**   *and yet.*
καίτοι   conj. καίτοι G2543
G2544 **καίτοιγε**   *and yet.*
καίτοιγε   conj. . . . . καίτοιγε G2544
G2545 **καίω**   trans., *I ignite, I light, I burn*, lit. and met.
κακά   adj., acc. pl. neut. {3.A}. . . . . κακός G2556
κακά   adj., nom. pl. neut. {3.A}. . . . . id.
κακαί   adj., nom. pl. fem. {3.A} . . . . id.
G2546 **κἀκεῖ**   adv., *and there, and yonder* (contraction
of καὶ ἐκεῖ).
κἀκεῖ   conj. + adv. . . . . κἀκεῖ G2546
G2547 **κἀκεῖθεν**   adv., *and thence, and from there*
(contraction of καὶ ἐκεῖθεν).
κἀκεῖθεν   conj. + adv. . . . . κἀκεῖθεν G2547
κἀκεῖνα   conj. + pron. dem., acc. pl. neut.
{4.B} . . . . κἀκεῖνος G2548
κἀκεῖνα   conj. + pron. dem., nom. pl. neut. {4.B} id.
κἀκεῖνοι   conj. + pron. dem., nom. pl. masc.
{4.B} . . . . id.
κἀκείνοις   conj. + pron. dem., dat. pl. masc.
{4.B} . . . . id.
κἀκεῖνον   conj. + pron. dem., acc. sg. masc.
{4.B} . . . . id.
G2548 **κἀκεῖνος**, -η, -ο   *and he, and that* (contraction
of καὶ ἐκεῖνος).
κἀκεῖνος   conj. + pron. dem., nom. sg. masc.
{4.B} . . . . κἀκεῖνος G2548
κἀκείνους   conj. + pron. dem., acc. pl. masc.
{4.B} . . . . id.
κακήν   adj., acc. sg. fem. {3.A} . . . . κακός G2556

G2549 **κακία**, -ας, ἡ   (1) *evil* (i.e., trouble, labor, misfortune), Matt 6:34; (2) *wickedness*, Acts 8:22;
(3) *vicious disposition, malice, spite.*
κακία   noun, nom. sg. fem. {2.A} . . . . κακία G2549
κακίᾳ   noun, dat. sg. fem. {2.A} . . . . id.
κακίαν   noun, acc. sg. fem. {2.A} . . . . id.
κακίας   noun, gen. sg. fem. {2.A} . . . . id.
G2550 **κακοήθεια**, -ας, ἡ   *evil-mindedness*, the
tendency to put the worst construction on
everything.
κακοηθείας   noun, gen. sg. fem. {2.A}. κακοήθεια G2550
κακοηθίας   noun, gen. sg. fem. {2.A}. . . . . id.
κακοί   adj., nom. pl. masc. {3.A} . . . . κακός G2556
G2551 **κακολογέω**   *I speak evil of* (not so strong a
word as βλασφημέω).
κακολογῆσαι   vbl., aor. act. inf. {6.B.1} κακολογέω G2551
κακολογοῦντες   vbl., pres. act. ptc. nom. pl.
masc. {6.A.2}. id.
κακολογῶν   vbl., pres. act. ptc. nom. sg. masc.
{6.A.2}. . . . . id.
κακόν   adj., acc. sg. neut. {3.A}. . . . . κακός G2556
κακόν   adj., nom. sg. neut. {3.A}. . . . . id.
κακοπαθεῖ   verb, pres. act. indic. 3 pers. sg.
{5.A.2} . . . . κακοπαθέω G2553
G2552 **κακοπάθεια**, -ας, ἡ   *experience of evil,
suffering.*
κακοπαθείας   noun, gen. sg. fem.
{2.A} . . . . κακοπάθεια G2552
G2553 **κακοπαθέω**   *I am ill-treated.*
κακοπάθησον   verb, aor. act. impv. 2 pers. sg.
{5.D.1}. . . . . κακοπαθέω G2553
κακοπαθίας   noun, gen. sg. fem.
{2.A} . . . . κακοπάθεια G2552
κακοπαθῶ   verb, pres. act. indic. 1 pers. sg.
{5.A.2}. . . . . κακοπαθέω G2553
G2554 **κακοποιέω**   *I do evil.*
κακοποιῆσαι   vbl., aor. act. inf. {6.B.1} κακοποιέω G2554
G2555 **κακοποιός**, -οῦ, ὁ   *an evildoer*; in 1 Pet 4:15
probably *a sorcerer, magician*, or *poisoner.*
κακοποιός   adj., nom. sg. masc. {3.C} . κακοποιός G2555
κακοποιοῦντας   vbl., pres. act. ptc. acc. pl. masc.
{6.A.2}. . . . . κακοποιέω G2554
κακοποιῶν   adj., gen. pl. masc. {3.C}. . κακοποιός G2555
κακοποιῶν   vbl., pres. act. ptc. nom. sg. masc.
{6.A.2}. . . . . κακοποιέω G2554
G2556 **κακός**, -ή, -όν   *bad, evil*, in the widest sense.
κακός   adj., nom. sg. masc. {3.A} . . . . κακός G2556
κακοῦ   adj., gen. sg. neut. {3.A} . . . . id.
κακοῦργοι   adj., nom. pl. masc. {3.C} . κακοῦργος G2557
G2557 **κακοῦργος**, -ου, ὁ   *a criminal* (lit. *an
evil-worker*).
κακοῦργος   adj., nom. sg. masc. {3.C} . κακοῦργος G2557
κακούργους   adj., acc. pl. masc. {3.C} . . . . . id.
κακούργων   adj., gen. pl. masc. {3.C}. . . . . . id.
κακούς   adj., acc. pl. masc. {3.A} . . . . κακός G2556
G2558 **κακουχέω**   *I treat evilly.*
κακουχούμενοι   vbl., pres. pass. ptc. nom. pl.
masc. {6.A.2}. . . . . κακουχέω G2558
κακουχουμένων   vbl., pres. pass. ptc. gen. pl.
masc. {6.A.2}. . . . . id.

G2559 **κακόω**   *I treat badly.*
κακῷ   adj., dat. sg. neut. {3.A}. . . . . κακός G2556
κακῶν   adj., gen. pl. neut. {3.A} . . . . id.
G2560 **κακῶς**   adv., *badly, evilly;* κακῶς ἔχω, see ἔχω.
κακῶς   adv. {3.F} . . . . κακῶς G2560
κακῶσαι   vbl., aor. act. inf. {6.B.1} . . . . κακόω G2559
κάκωσιν   noun, acc. sg. fem. {2.C} . . . . . . κάκωσις G2561
G2561 **κάκωσις**, -εως, ἡ   *ill-treating, ill treatment.*
κακώσουσιν   verb, fut. act. indic. 3 pers. pl.
   {5.A.1}. . . . . κακόω G2559
κακώσων   vbl., fut. act. ptc. nom. sg. masc.
   {6.A.2}. . . . . id.
καλά   adj., acc. pl. neut. {3.A}. . . . . καλός G2570
καλά   adj., nom. pl. neut. {3.A} . . . . id.
G2562 **καλάμη**, -ης, ἡ   *stubble.*
καλάμην   noun, acc. sg. fem. {2.A} . . . . . καλάμη G2562
κάλαμον   noun, acc. sg. masc. {2.B} . . . . κάλαμος G2563
G2563 **κάλαμος**, -ου, ὁ   *a reed; a reed pen,* 3 John 13.
κάλαμος   noun, nom. sg. masc. {2.B} . . . . κάλαμος G2563
καλάμου   noun, gen. sg. masc. {2.B} . . . . id.
καλάμῳ   noun, dat. sg. masc. {2.B} . . . . id.
καλεῖ   verb, pres. act. indic. 3 pers. sg.
   {5.A.2}. . . . . καλέω G2564
κάλει   verb, pres. act. impv. 2 pers. sg. {5.D.2} . . id.
καλεῖν   vbl., pres. act. inf. {6.B.2} . . . . id.
καλεῖσθαι   vbl., pres. pass. inf. {6.B.2} . . . . id.
καλεῖται   verb, pres. pass. indic. 3 pers. sg.
   {5.A.2}. . . . . id.
καλεῖτε   verb, pres. act. indic. 2 pers. pl. {5.A.2}. id.
καλέσαι   vbl., aor. act. inf. {6.B.1} . . . . id.
καλέσαντα   vbl., aor. act. ptc. acc. sg. masc.
   {6.A.2}. . . . . id.
καλέσαντες   vbl., aor. act. ptc. nom. pl. masc.
   {6.A.2}. . . . . id.
καλέσαντος   vbl., aor. act. ptc. gen. sg. masc.
   {6.A.2}. . . . . id.
καλέσας   vbl., aor. act. ptc. nom. sg. masc.
   {6.A.2}. . . . . id.
καλέσατε   verb, aor. act. impv. 2 pers. pl. {5.D.1} id.
καλέσεις   verb, fut. act. indic. 2 pers. sg. {5.A.1} id.
καλέσητε   verb, aor. act. subjunc. 2 pers. pl.
   {5.B.1} . . . . id.
κάλεσον   verb, aor. act. impv. 2 pers. sg. {5.D.1}. id.
καλέσουσι   verb, fut. act. indic. 3 pers. pl.
   {5.A.1}. . . . . id.
καλέσουσιν   verb, fut. act. indic. 3 pers. pl.
   {5.A.1}. . . . . id.
καλέσω   verb, fut. act. indic. 1 pers. sg. {5.A.1} . id.
G2564 **καλέω**   (1) *I call, summon, invite;* (2) *I call,*
   name; ἐπί, *after,* Luke 1:59.
καλῇ   adj., dat. sg. fem. {3.A} . . . . καλός G2570
καλήν   adj., acc. sg. fem. {3.A} . . . . id.
καλῆς   adj., gen. sg. fem. {3.A} . . . . id.
καλλιέλαιον   noun, acc. sg. fem.
   {2.B} . . . . καλλιέλαιος G2565
G2565 **καλλιέλαιος**, -ου, ἡ   *a cultivated olive tree.*
G2566 **κάλλιον**   adv. comp. of καλῶς, *very well.*
κάλλιον   adv. comp. {3.F; 3.G} . . . . κάλλιον G2566
G2567 **καλοδιδάσκαλος**, -ον   *a teacher of that which*
   is noble (honorable).

καλοδιδασκάλους   adj., acc. pl. fem.
   {3.C} . . . . καλοδιδάσκαλος G2567
καλοί   adj., nom. pl. masc. {3.A} . . . . καλός G2570
G2568 **Καλοὶ Λιμένες**, -οί   *Fair Havens.*
Καλοὶ Λιμένες   noun prop. . . . . . . Καλοὶ Λιμένες G2568
καλοῖς   adj., dat. pl. masc. {3.A} . . . . καλός G2570
καλοῖς   adj., dat. pl. neut. {3.A} . . . . id.
καλόν   adj., acc. sg. masc. {3.A} . . . . id.
καλόν   adj., acc. sg. neut. {3.A}. . . . . id.
καλόν   adj., nom. sg. neut. {3.A} . . . . id.
G2569 **καλοποιέω**   *I do the noble (honorable) thing.*
καλοποιοῦντες   vbl., pres. act. ptc. nom. pl. masc.
   {6.A.2}. . . . . καλοποιέω G2569
G2570 **καλός**, -ή, -όν   *beautiful,* as an outward sign of
   the inward *good, noble, honorable character;*
   good, worthy, honorable, noble, and seen to be so.
καλός   adj., nom. sg. masc. {3.A} . . . . καλός G2570
καλοῦ   adj., gen. sg. neut. {3.A} . . . . id.
καλουμένη   vbl., pres. pass. ptc. nom. sg. fem.
   {6.A.2}. . . . . καλέω G2564
καλουμένη   vbl., pres. pass. ptc. dat. sg. fem.
   {6.A.2}. . . . . id.
καλουμένην   vbl., pres. pass. ptc. acc. sg. fem.
   {6.A.2}. . . . . id.
καλουμένης   vbl., pres. pass. ptc. gen. sg. fem.
   {6.A.2}. . . . . id.
καλούμενον   vbl., pres. pass. ptc. acc. sg. masc.
   {6.A.2}. . . . . id.
καλούμενον   vbl., pres. pass. ptc. acc. sg. neut.
   {6.A.2}. . . . . id.
καλούμενος   vbl., pres. pass. ptc. nom. sg.
   masc. {6.A.2} . . . . id.
καλουμένου   vbl., pres. pass. ptc. gen. sg.
   masc. {6.A.2} . . . . id.
καλουμένου   vbl., pres. pass. ptc. gen. sg. neut.
   {6.A.2}. . . . . id.
καλοῦνται   verb, pres. pass. indic. 3 pers. pl.
   {5.A.2}. . . . . id.
καλοῦντες   vbl., pres. act. ptc. nom. pl. masc.
   {6.A.2}. . . . . id.
καλοῦντος   vbl., pres. act. ptc. gen. sg. masc.
   {6.A.2}. . . . . id.
καλούς   adj., acc. pl. masc. {3.A} . . . . καλός G2570
καλοῦσα   vbl., pres. act. ptc. nom. sg. fem.
   {6.A.2}. . . . . καλέω G2564
G2571 **κάλυμμα**, -ατος, τό   *a covering,* esp. a covering of head and face, *a veil.*
κάλυμμα   noun, acc. sg. neut. {2.C} . . . . . κάλυμμα G2571
κάλυμμα   noun, nom. sg. neut. {2.C} . . . . id.
καλύπτει   verb, pres. act. indic. 3 pers. sg.
   {5.A.1.a} . . . . καλύπτω G2572
καλύπτεσθαι   vbl., pres. pass. inf. {6.B.1} . . . . id.
G2572 **καλύπτω**   *I veil, hide, conceal, envelop.*
καλύψατε   verb, aor. act. impv. 2 pers. pl.
   {5.D.1} . . . . καλύπτω G2572
καλύψει   verb, fut. act. indic. 3 pers. sg. {5.A.1.a} id.
καλῷ   adj., dat. sg. neut. {3.A} . . . . καλός G2570
καλῶν   adj., gen. pl. neut. {3.A} . . . . καλός G2570
καλῶν   vbl., pres. act. ptc. nom. sg. masc.
   {6.A.2}. . . . . καλέω G2564

G2573 **καλῶς**   adv., *well, nobly, honorably; in a good place,* Jas 2:3: comp. adv. κάλλιον, *very well;* καλῶς ποιήσεις, esp. with aor. ptc., is idiomatic for *please,* 3 John 6, cf. Acts 10:33; Phil 4:14; 2 Pet 1:19.

καλῶς   adv. {3.F} . . . . καλῶς G2573

κἀμέ   conj. + pron. pers., 1 pers. acc. sg. {4.A} κἀγώ G2504

κάμηλον   noun, acc. sg. masc. {2.B} . . . . . κάμηλος G2574

κάμηλον   noun, acc. sg. fem. {2.B} . . . . . κάμηλος G2574

G2574 **κάμηλος**, -ου, ὁ or ἡ   *camel; dromedary.*

καμήλου   noun, gen. sg. masc. {2.B} . . . . κάμηλος G2574

καμήλου   noun, gen. sg. fem. {2.B} . . . . κάμηλος G2574

κάμητε   verb, ²aor. act. subjunc. 2 pers. pl.
{5.B.1} . . . . κάμνω G2577

κάμινον   noun, acc. sg. fem. {2.B} . . . . . . κάμινος G2575

G2575 **κάμινος**, -ου, ἡ   *a furnace.*

καμίνου   noun, gen. sg. fem. {2.B} . . . . . . κάμινος G2575

καμίνῳ   noun, dat. sg. fem. {2.B} . . . . id.

G2576 **καμμύω**   *I close.*

κάμνοντα   vbl., pres. act. ptc. acc. sg. masc.
{6.A.1} . . . . κάμνω G2577

G2577 **κάμνω**   (1) *I am weary,* Heb 12:3; (2) *I am ill,* Jas 5:15.

κἀμοί   conj. + pron. pers., 1 pers. dat. sg. {4.A} κἀγώ G2504

G2578 **κάμπτω**   *I bend.*

κάμπτω   verb, pres. act. indic. 1 pers. sg.
{5.A.1.a} . . . . κάμπτω G2578

κάμψει   verb, fut. act. indic. 3 pers. sg. {5.A.1.a}. id.

κάμψῃ   verb, aor. act. subjunc. 3 pers. sg. {5.B.1} id.

G2579 **κἂν**   *and if; even if* (= καὶ ἐάν).

κἄν   conj. + cond. part. . . . . κἄν G2579

G2580 **Κανά**, ἡ   *Cana,* a town in Galilee.

Κανά   noun prop.. . . . . Κανά G2580

Κανᾷ   noun prop.. . . . . id.

Καναναῖον   noun prop., acc. sg. masc. {2.B;
2.D} . . . . Καναναῖος G2581

G2581 **Καναναῖος**, -ου, ὁ   *a Cananaean,* a (former) adherent of the party of Zealots (= ζηλωτής).

Καναναῖος   noun prop., nom. sg. masc. {2.B;
2.D} . . . . Καναναῖος G2581

Κανανίτην   noun prop., acc. sg. masc. {2.B;
2.D} . . . . Κανανίτης G2581†

G2581† **Κανανίτης**, -ου, ὁ   *A Cananite, a man from Cana.* Var. for Καναναῖος, Matt 10:4; Mark 3:18.

Κανανίτης   noun prop., nom. sg. masc. {2.B;
2.D} . . . . Κανανίτης G2581†

G2582 **Κανδάκη**, -ης, ἡ   *the Candace,* a dynastic name for queens of the Ethiopians in Abyssinia.

Κανδάκης   noun prop., gen. sg. fem. {2.A;
2.D} . . . . Κανδάκη G2582

κανόνα   noun, acc. sg. masc. {2.C} . . . . κανών G2583

κανόνι   noun, dat. sg. masc. {2.C} . . . . id.

κανόνος   noun, gen. sg. masc. {2.C} . . . . id.

G2583 **κανών**, -όνος, ὁ   (1) *rule, regulation,* Gal 6:16; (2) *a measured (defined) area, province* (lit. *a level, ruler*).

G2584 **Καπερναούμ** (Καφαρναούμ), ἡ   *Capernaum* (the form appears to be a conscious alteration

made in Syria not earlier than the fourth c.), perhaps = mod. *Tell Hum.*

Καπερναούμ   noun prop. . . . . Καπερναούμ G2584

καπηλεύοντες   vbl., pres. act. ptc. nom. pl. masc.
{6.A.1} . . . . καπηλεύω G2585

G2585 **καπηλεύω**   *I hawk, trade in, deal in for purposes of gain.*

καπνόν   noun, acc. sg. masc. {2.B}

G2586 **καπνός**, -οῦ, ὁ   *smoke.*

καπνός   noun, nom. sg. masc. {2.B} . . . . . καπνός G2586

καπνοῦ   noun, gen. sg. masc. {2.B} . . . . id.

G2587 **Καππαδοκία**, -ας, ἡ   *Cappadocia,* a large Roman province in the central eastern part of Asia Minor.

Καππαδοκίαν   noun prop., acc. sg. fem. {2.A;
2.D} . . . . Καππαδοκία G2587

Καππαδοκίας   noun prop., gen. sg. fem. {2.A; 2.D} id.

G2588 **καρδία**, -ας, ἡ   (1) lit. *the heart.,* as an organ of the body; (2) *mind* covers the nonphysical sense best: (a) *personality, character, inner life,* e.g., 1 Cor 14:25; 1 Pet 1:22; (b) *emotional state,* e.g., Rom 9:2; (c) *mind, intellect,* e.g., Rom 1:21; (d) *will, volition, intention,* e.g., Rom 2:5 (Heb. *lēb, lēbāb*).

καρδία   noun, nom. sg. fem. {2.A} . . . . . . καρδία G2588

καρδίᾳ   noun, dat. sg. fem. {2.A} . . . . id.

καρδίαι   noun, nom. pl. fem. {2.A} . . . . id.

καρδίαις   noun, dat. pl. fem. {2.A} . . . . id.

καρδίαν   noun, acc. sg. fem. {2.A} . . . . id.

καρδίας   noun, acc. pl. fem. {2.A} . . . . id.

καρδίας   noun, gen. sg. fem. {2.A} . . . . id.

καρδιογνῶστα   noun, voc. sg. masc.
{2.A} . . . . καρδιογνώστης G2589

G2589 **καρδιογνώστης**, -ου, ὁ   *one who knows the inner life (character).*

καρδιογνώστης   noun, nom. sg. masc.
{2.A} . . . . καρδιογνώστης G2589

καρδιῶν   noun, gen. pl. fem. {2.A} . . . . . . καρδία G2588

καρπόν   noun, acc. sg. masc. {2.B} . . . . . . καρπός G2590

G2590 **καρπός**, -οῦ, ὁ   (1) *fruit,* generally vegetable, sometimes animal (e.g., Luke 1:42; Acts 2:30); (2) met. *fruit, deed, action, result,* Matt 3:8; Luke 3:8; Jas 3:17–18, etc.; (3) *profit, gain,* Rom 1:13, etc.

καρπός   noun, nom. sg. masc. {2.B} . . . . . καρπός G2590

G2591 **Κάρπος**, -ου, ὁ   *Carpus,* a Christian of Troas.

καρποῦ   noun, gen. sg. masc. {2.B} . . . . . καρπός G2590

καρπούς   noun, acc. pl. masc. {2.B} . . . . id.

καρποφορεῖ   verb, pres. act. indic. 3 pers. sg.
{5.A.2} . . . . καρποφορέω G2592

G2592 **καρποφορέω**   act. and mid. *I bear fruit.*

καρποφορῆσαι   vbl., aor. act. inf.
{6.B.1} . . . . καρποφορέω G2592

καρποφορήσωμεν   verb, aor. act. subjunc.
1 pers. pl. {5.B.1} . . . . id.

G2593 **καρποφόρος**, -ον   *fruit-bearing.*

καρποφορούμενον   vbl., pres. mid. ptc. nom. sg.
neut. {6.A.2} . . . . καρποφορέω G2592

καρποφοροῦντες   vbl., pres. act. ptc. nom. pl.
masc. {6.A.2} . . . . id.

καρποφόρους   adj., acc. pl. masc.
{3.C} . . . . .καρποφόρος G2593

καρποφοροῦσιν   verb, pres. act. indic. 3 pers. pl.
{5.A.2} . . . . καρποφορέω G2592

Κάρπῳ   noun prop., dat. sg. masc. {2.B;
2.D} . . . . Κάρπος G2591

καρπῶν   noun, gen. pl. masc. {2.B} . . . . . καρπός G2590

G2594   **καρτερέω**   *I persevere, endure.*

G2595   **κάρφος**, -ους, τό   *a dry stalk; a chip of wood.*

κάρφος   noun, acc. sg. neut. {2.C} . . . . κάρφος G2595

κατ᾽   prep. . . . . κατά G2596

G2596   **κατά**   prep. (1) with gen., (a) *against,* Matt
12:30; (b) *down from,* Matt 8:32, κατὰ κε-
φαλῆς, *down over the head, on the head,* 1 Cor
11:4; (c) *throughout,* Luke 4:14; 23:5; Acts 9:31;
10:37, always with ὅλος; ἡ κατὰ βάθους
πτωχεία, *deep (abject) poverty,* 2 Cor 8:2; (d)
in oaths, *by,* Matt 26:63; Heb 6:13, 16; (2) with
acc. (lit. *down along*), (a) *over against,* Acts
2:10; 16:7; (b) *among,* νόμος ὁ καθ᾽ ὑμᾶς, *the
law among you, your law,* Acts 18:15; cf. 17:28;
26:3; Eph 1:15; Col 4:7; etc.; (c) with distribu-
tive force, (τὸ) καθ᾽ ἡμέραν, *daily, day by
day, each day,* κατὰ ἑορτήν *at each feast,* Matt
27:15; Mark 15:6; κατὰ ἑκατόν, *by hundreds,*
Mark 6:40; ungrammatically εἷς κατὰ (καθ᾽)
εἷς, Mark 14:19; (John 8:9; contrast Eph 5:33);
τὸ δὲ καθ᾽ εἷς (καθεῖς), *singly, with reference
to each individual,* Rom 12:5, etc.; (d) *according to, by way of,* Matt 2:16, καθ᾽ ὅσον, etc.;
in titles of Gospels, κατά practically indicates
the author; (e) various adv. phrases: τὸ κατ᾽
ἐμέ, *as far as in me lies,* with πρόθυμος,
Rom 1:15; cf. τὸ κατὰ σάρκα, Rom 9:5, etc.;
κατ᾽ ἰδίαν (καθ᾽ ἰδίαν), *privately, by oneself,
individually* (opp. δημοσίᾳ), Matt 14:13, etc.;
κατὰ μόνας, *alone,* Mark 4:10; Luke 9:18;
κατὰ πρόσωπον, in a Hebraistic periphrasis,
in the presence of, Luke 2:31; Acts 3:13, cf.
25:16.

κατά   prep. κατά G2596

κατάβα   verb, ²aor. act. impv. 2 pers. sg.
{5.D.1} .καταβαίνω G2597

καταβαίνει   verb, pres. act. indic. 3 pers. sg.
{5.A.1.a} . . . . id.

καταβαίνειν   vbl., pres. act. inf. {6.B.1} . . . . id.

καταβαινέτω   verb, pres. act. impv. 3 pers. sg.
{5.D.1} . . . . id.

καταβαίνῃ   verb, pres. act. subjunc. 3 pers. sg.
{5.B.1} . . . . id.

καταβαῖνον   vbl., pres. act. ptc. acc. sg. neut.
{6.A.1} . . . . id.

καταβαῖνον   vbl., pres. act. ptc. nom. sg. neut.
{6.A.1} . . . . id.

καταβαίνοντα   vbl., pres. act. ptc. acc. sg.
masc. {6.A.1} . . . . id.

καταβαίνοντας   vbl., pres. act. ptc. acc. pl.
masc. {6.A.1} . . . . id.

καταβαίνοντες   vbl., pres. act. ptc. nom. pl.
masc. {6.A.1} . . . . id.

καταβαίνοντος   vbl., pres. act. ptc. gen. sg.
masc. {6.A.1} . . . . id.

καταβαινόντων   vbl., pres. act. ptc. gen. pl.
masc. {6.A.1} . . . . id.

καταβαίνουσα   vbl., pres. act. ptc. nom. sg.
fem. {6.A.1} . . . . id.

καταβαίνουσαν   vbl., pres. act. ptc. acc. sg.
fem. {6.A.1} . . . . id.

G2597   **καταβαίνω**   *I go down, I come down,* either
from the sky or from higher land.

καταβαίνων   vbl., pres. act. ptc. nom. sg. masc.
{6.A.1} . . . . καταβαίνω G2597

καταβαλλόμενοι   vbl., pres. mid. ptc. nom. pl.
masc. {6.A.1} . . . . καταβάλλω G2598

καταβαλλόμενοι   vbl., pres. pass. ptc. nom. pl.
masc. {6.A.1} . . . . id.

G2598   **καταβάλλω**   (1) mid. I lay, of a foundation,
Heb 6:1 (cf. καταβολή); (2) met. I cast down,
2 Cor 4:9.

καταβάν   vbl., ²aor. act. ptc. acc. sg. neut.
{6.A.1.a} .καταβαίνω G2597

καταβάντες   vbl., ²aor. act. ptc. nom. pl. masc.
{6.A.1.a} . . . . id.

καταβάντι   vbl., ²aor. act. ptc. dat. sg. masc.
{6.A.1.a} . . . . id.

καταβάντος   vbl., ²aor. act. ptc. gen. sg. masc.
{6.A.1.a} . . . . id.

G2599   **καταβαρέω**   *I burden, oppress.*

G2599†   **καταβαρύνω**   *I weigh down, make heavy.* Var.
for καταβαρέω, Mark 14:40.

καταβαρυνόμενοι   vbl., pres. pass. ptc. nom. pl.
masc. {6.A.1} . . . . καταβαρύνω G2599†

καταβάς   vbl., ²aor. act. ptc. nom. sg. masc.
{6.A.1.a} .καταβαίνω G2597

καταβάσει   noun, dat. sg. fem. {2.C} . . κατάβασις G2600

G2600   **κατάβασις**, -εως, ἡ   *descent.*

καταβάτω   verb, ²aor. act. impv. 3 pers. sg.
{5.D.1} .καταβαίνω G2597

καταβέβηκα   verb, perf. act. indic. 1 pers. sg.
{5.A.1.c} . . . . id.

καταβεβηκότες   vbl., perf. act. ptc. nom. pl.
masc. {6.A.1.a} . . . . id.

καταβῇ   verb, ²aor. act. subjunc. 3 pers. sg.
{5.B.1} . . . . id.

κατάβηθι   verb, ²aor. act. impv. 2 pers. sg.
{5.D.1} . . . . id.

καταβῆναι   vbl., ²aor. act. inf. {6.B.1} . . . . . . id.

καταβήσεται   verb, fut. mid. indic. 3 pers. sg.
{5.A.1.d} . . . . id.

καταβήσῃ   verb, fut. mid. indic. 2 pers. sg.
{5.A.1.d} . . . . id.

G2601   **καταβιβάζω**   *I bring down, I cause to go down.*

καταβιβασθήσῃ   verb, fut. pass. indic. 2 pers. sg.
{5.A.1.d} .καταβιβάζω G2601

G2602   **καταβολή**, -ῆς, ἡ   (1) *foundation,* only in Matt
13:35 (var.) without κόσμου; (2) *depositing,
sowing, deposit,* σπέρματος, technically used
of the act of conception, Heb 11:11.

καταβολήν   noun, acc. sg. fem. {2.A} . .καταβολή G2602

καταβολῆς   noun, gen. sg. fem. {2.A} . . . . id.

καταβραβευέτω   verb, pres. act. impv. 3 pers. sg.
{5.D.1}. . . . . καταβραβεύω *G2603*

G2603 **καταβραβεύω**   of the umpire in a contest,
I decide against, take part against, condemn
(perhaps with the idea of *unjust assumption,
officialism*).

καταγαγεῖν   vbl., ²aor. act. inf. {6.B.1} . . . . κατάγω *G2609*
καταγάγῃ   verb, ²aor. act. subjunc. 3 pers. sg.
{5.B.1}. . . . . id.
καταγάγῃς   verb, ²aor. act. subjunc. 2 pers. sg.
{5.B.1}. . . . . id.
καταγαγόντες   vbl., ²aor. act. ptc. nom. pl.
masc. {6.A.1.a}. . . . . id.
καταγαγών   vbl., ²aor. act. ptc. nom. sg. masc.
{6.A.1.a} . . . . id.

G2604 **καταγγελεύς**, -έως, ὁ   *a reporter, announcer,
proclaimer, herald, setter forth.*
καταγγελεύς   noun, nom. sg. masc.
{2.C}. .καταγγελεύς *G2604*
καταγγέλλειν   vbl., pres. act. inf.
{6.B.1} . . . . καταγγέλλω *G2605*
καταγγέλλεται   verb, pres. pass. indic. 3 pers.
sg. {5.A.1.d} . . . . id.
καταγγέλλετε   verb, pres. act. indic. 2 pers. pl.
{5.A.1.a} . . . . id.
καταγγέλλομεν   verb, pres. act. indic. 1 pers.
pl. {5.A.1.a} . . . . id.
καταγγέλλουσιν   verb, pres. act. indic. 3 pers.
pl. {5.A.1.a} . . . . id.
καταγγέλλουσιν   vbl., pres. act. ptc. dat. pl.
masc. {6.A.1} . . . . id.

G2605 **καταγγέλλω**   *I announce.*
καταγγέλλω   verb, pres. act. indic. 1 pers. sg.
{5.A.1.a} . . . . καταγγέλλω *G2605*
καταγγέλλων   vbl., pres. act. ptc. nom. sg.
masc. {6.A.1}. id.

G2606 **καταγελάω**   *I laugh at, ridicule.*
καταγινώσκῃ   verb, pres. act. subjunc. 3 pers. sg.
{5.B.1} . . . . .καταγινώσκω *G2607*

G2607 **καταγινώσκω**   *I condemn;* κατεγνωσμένος,
reprehensible, Gal 2:11.

G2608 **κατάγνυμι**   *I break.*

G2609 **κατάγω**   *I lead down, I bring down,* either from
a high place on land to a lower (or actually to
the seacoast), or from the high seas to land.

G2610 **καταγωνίζομαι**   *I subdue* (in warfare).

G2611 **καταδέω**   *I bind up.*
κατάδηλον   adj., nom. sg. neut. {3.C} . κατάδηλος *G2612*

G2612 **κατάδηλος**, -ον   *quite clear.*
καταδικάζετε   verb, pres. act. impv. 2 pers. pl.
{5.D.1}. . . . . .καταδικάζω *G2613*

G2613 **καταδικάζω**   *I condemn.*
καταδικασθήσῃ   verb, fut. pass. indic. 2 pers. sg.
{5.A.1.d} . . . . .καταδικάζω *G2613*
καταδικασθῆτε   verb, aor. pass. subjunc.
2 pers. pl. {5.B.1} . . . . id.

G1349†‡ **καταδίκη**, -ης, ἡ   *sentence of condemnation,
condemnation.* Var. for δίκη, Acts 25:15.
καταδίκην   noun, acc. sg. fem. {2.A} . . καταδίκη *G1349†‡*

G2614 **καταδιώκω**   *I hunt down.*
καταδουλοῖ   verb, pres. act. indic. 3 pers. sg.
{5.A.2}. . . . . .καταδουλόω *G2615*

G2615 **καταδουλόω**   *I enslave.*
καταδουλώσουσιν   verb, fut. act. indic. 3 pers. pl.
{5.A.1}. . . . . .καταδουλόω *G2615*
καταδουλώσωνται   verb, aor. mid. subjunc.
3 pers. pl. {5.B.1} . . . . id.
καταδυναστευομένους   vbl., pres. pass. ptc. acc.
pl. masc. {6.A.1} . . . . καταδυναστεύω *G2616*
καταδυναστεύουσιν   verb, pres. act. indic.
3 pers. pl. {5.A.1.a} . . . . id.

G2616 **καταδυναστεύω**   *I overpower, quell; I treat
harshly.*

G2652†‡ **κατάθεμα**, -ατος, τό   *an accursed thing.* Var.
for κατανάθεμα, Rev 22:3.
κατάθεμα   noun, nom. sg. neut. {2.C} κατάθεμα *G2652†‡*
καταθεματίζειν   vbl., pres. act. inf.
{6.B.1} . . . . .καταθεματίζω *G2653†‡*

G2653†‡ **καταθεματίζω**   *I curse.* Var. for κατανάθε-
ματίζω, Matt 26:74.
καταθέσθαι   vbl., ²aor. mid. inf.
{6.B.3} . . . . .κατατίθημι *G2698*
καταισχύνει   verb, pres. act. indic. 3 pers. sg.
{5.A.1.a} . . . . .καταισχύνω *G2617*
καταισχύνετε   verb, pres. act. indic. 2 pers. pl.
{5.A.1.a} . . . . id.
καταισχύνῃ   verb, pres. act. subjunc. 3 pers.
sg. {5.B.1} . . . . id.
καταισχυνθῇ   verb, aor. pass. subjunc. 3 pers.
sg. {5.B.1} . . . . id.
καταισχυνθήσεται   verb, fut. pass. indic.
3 pers. sg. {5.A.1.d} . . . . id.
καταισχυνθῶμεν   verb, aor. pass. subjunc.
1 pers. pl. {5.B.1} . . . . id.
καταισχυνθῶσιν   verb, aor. pass. subjunc.
3 pers. pl. {5.B.1} . . . . id.

G2617 **καταισχύνω**   *I shame, disgrace, bring to shame,
put to utter confusion.*
κατακαήσεται   verb, ²fut. pass. indic. 3 pers. sg.
{5.A.1.d} . . . . .κατακαίω *G2618*
κατακαίεται   verb, pres. pass. indic. 3 pers. sg.
{5.A.1.d} . . . . id.

G2618 **κατακαίω**   *I burn down.*
κατακαλύπτεσθαι   vbl., pres. mid. inf.
{6.B.1} . . . . κατακαλύπτω *G2619*
κατακαλυπτέσθω   verb, pres. mid. impv.
3 pers. sg. {5.D.1}. . . . . id.
κατακαλύπτεται   verb, pres. mid. indic.
3 pers. sg. {5.A.1.d} . . . . id.

G2619 **κατακαλύπτω**   mid. *I veil myself, I cover my
head.*
κατακαυθήσεται   verb, fut. pass. indic. 3 pers. sg.
{5.A.1.d} . . . . .κατακαίω *G2618*
κατακαῦσαι   vbl., aor. act. inf. {6.B.1}. . . . . . . id.
κατακαύσει   verb, fut. act. indic. 3 pers. sg.
{5.A.1.a} . . . . id.
κατακαύσουσιν   verb, fut. act. indic. 3 pers.
pl. {5.A.1.a} . . . . id.

G2620 **κατακαυχάομαι** *I boast against.*
κατακαυχᾶσαι verb, pres. mid./pass. indic.
  2 pers. sg. {5.A.2} . . . . κατακαυχάομαι *G2620*
κατακαυχᾶσθε verb, pres. mid./pass. impv.
  2 pers. pl. {5.D.2} . . . . id.
κατακαυχᾶται verb, pres. mid./pass. indic.
  3 pers. sg. {5.A.2} . . . . id.
κατακαυχῶ verb, pres. mid./pass. impv.
  2 pers. sg. {5.D.2} . . . . id.
G2621 **κατάκειμαι** *I recline* (at table); more often, *I keep my bed, I am lying ill* (in bed).
κατακείμενοι vbl., pres. mid./pass. ptc. nom. pl.
  masc. {6.A.3} . . . . κατάκειμαι *G2621*
κατακείμενον vbl., pres. mid./pass. ptc. acc.
  sg. masc. {6.A.3} . . . . id.
κατακειμένου vbl., pres. mid./pass. ptc. gen.
  sg. masc. {6.A.3} . . . . id.
κατακεῖσθαι vbl., pres. mid./pass. inf. {6.B.3} . . id.
κατάκειται verb, pres. mid./pass. indic. 3 pers.
  sg. {5.A.3.a} . . . . id.
κατακέκριται verb, perf. pass. indic. 3 pers. sg.
  {5.A.1.f} . . . . κατακρίνω *G2632*
G2622 **κατακλάω** *I break up.*
G2623 **κατακλείω** *I shut up.*
G2624 **κατακληροδοτέω** *I distribute by lot, give as an inheritance.* Var. for κατακληρονομέω, Acts 13:9.
G2624† **κατακληρονομέω** *I give as a rightful inheritance.* Var. κατακληροδοτέω, Acts 13:9.
κατακλιθῆναι vbl., aor. pass. inf.
  {6.B.1} . . . . κατακλίνω *G2625*
κατακλιθῇς verb, aor. pass. subjunc. 2 pers. sg.
  {5.B.1} . . . . id.
κατακλίνατε verb, aor. act. impv. 2 pers. pl.
  {5.D.1} . . . . id.
G2625 **κατακλίνω** *I cause to recline at table;* mid. (and pass.) *I recline at table.*
G2626 **κατακλύζω** *I flood over, overwhelm.*
κατακλυσθείς vbl., aor. pass. ptc. nom. sg. masc.
  {6.A.1.a} . . . . κατακλύζω *G2626*
κατακλυσμόν noun, acc. sg. masc.
  {2.B} . . . . κατακλυσμός *G2627*
G2627 **κατακλυσμός**, -οῦ, ὁ *a flood.*
κατακλυσμός noun, nom. sg. masc.
  {2.B} . . . . κατακλυσμός *G2627*
κατακλυσμοῦ noun, gen. sg. masc. {2.B} . . . . . id.
G2628 **κατακολουθέω** *I follow after.*
κατακολουθήσασα vbl., aor. act. ptc. nom. sg.
  fem. {6.A.2} . . . . κατακολουθέω *G2628*
κατακολουθήσασαι vbl., aor. act. ptc. nom.
  pl. fem. {6.A.2} . . . . id.
κατακολουθοῦσα vbl., pres. act. ptc. nom. sg.
  fem. {6.A.2} . . . . id.
G2629 **κατακόπτω** *I beat.*
κατακόπτων vbl., pres. act. ptc. nom. sg. masc.
  {6.A.1} . . . . κατακόπτω *G2629*
G2630 **κατακρημνίζω** *I throw down a precipice.*
κατακρημνίσαι vbl., aor. act. inf.
  {6.B.1} . . . . κατακρημνίζω *G2630*

κατακριθήσεται verb, fut. pass. indic. 3 pers. sg.
  {5.A.1.d} . . . . κατακρίνω *G2632*
κατακριθῆτε verb, aor. pass. subjunc. 2 pers.
  pl. {5.B.1} . . . . id.
κατακριθῶμεν verb, aor. pass. subjunc. 1 pers.
  pl. {5.B.1} . . . . id.
G2631 **κατάκριμα**, -ατος, τό *punishment following condemnation, penal servitude.*
κατάκριμα noun, acc. sg. neut. {2.C} . κατάκριμα *G2631*
κατάκριμα noun, nom. sg. neut. {2.C} . . . . id.
κατακρινεῖ verb, fut. act. indic. 3 pers. sg.
  {5.A.2} . . . . κατακρίνω *G2632*
κατακρίνεις verb, pres. act. indic. 2 pers. sg.
  {5.A.1.a} . . . . id.
κατακρινοῦσιν verb, fut. act. indic. 3 pers. pl.
  {5.A.2} . . . . id.
G2632 **κατακρίνω** *I condemn.*
κατακρίνω verb, pres. act. indic. 1 pers. sg.
  {5.A.1.a} . . . . κατακρίνω *G2632*
κατακρίνων vbl., pres. act. ptc. nom. sg. masc.
  {6.A.1} . . . . id.
κατακρινῶν vbl., pres. act. ptc. nom. sg. masc.
  {6.A.1} . . . . id.
κατακρινῶν vbl., fut. act. ptc. nom. sg. masc.
  {6.A.1.a} . . . . id.
κατακρίσεως noun, gen. sg. fem.
  {2.C} . . . . κατάκρισις *G2633*
κατάκρισιν noun, acc. sg. fem. {2.C} . . . . id.
G2633 **κατάκρισις**, -εως, ἡ *condemnation.*
G2955†‡ **κατακύπτω** *I stoop down, I look down.* Var. for κύπτω, John 8:8.
κατακυριεύοντες vbl., pres. act. ptc. nom. pl.
  masc. {6.A.1} . . . . κατακυριεύω *G2634*
κατακυριεύουσιν verb, pres. act. indic.
  3 pers. pl. {5.A.1.a} . . . . id.
κατακυριεύσαν vbl., aor. act. ptc. nom. sg.
  neut. {6.A.1.a} . . . . id.
κατακυριεύσας vbl., aor. act. ptc. nom. sg.
  masc. {6.A.1.a} . . . . id.
G2634 **κατακυριεύω** *I exercise lordship over, I overpower.*
κατακύψας vbl., aor. act. ptc. nom. sg. masc.
  {6.A.1.a} . . . . κατακύπτω *G2955†‡*
καταλαβέσθαι vbl., ²aor. mid. inf.
  {6.B.1} . . . . καταλαμβάνω *G2638*
καταλάβῃ verb, ²aor. act. subjunc. 3 pers. sg.
  {5.B.1} . . . . id.
καταλάβητε verb, ²aor. act. subjunc. 2 pers. pl.
  {5.B.1} . . . . id.
καταλαβόμενοι vbl., ²aor. mid. ptc. nom. pl.
  masc. {6.A.1.b} . . . . id.
καταλαβόμενος vbl., ²aor. mid. ptc. nom. sg.
  masc. {6.A.1.b} . . . . id.
καταλάβω verb, ²aor. act. subjunc. 1 pers. sg.
  {5.B.1} . . . . id.
καταλαλεῖ verb, pres. act. indic. 3 pers. sg.
  {5.A.2} . . . . καταλαλέω *G2635*
καταλαλεῖσθε verb, pres. pass. indic. 2 pers.
  pl. {5.A.2} . . . . id.

καταλαλεῖτε   verb, pres. act. impv. 2 pers. pl.
{5.D.2}. . . . . id.

G2635 **καταλαλέω**   *I speak evil of.*

G2636 **καταλαλιά**, -ᾶς, ἡ   *evil-speaking, backbiting, detraction.*
καταλαλιαί   noun, nom. pl. fem. {2.A}καταλαλιά G2636
καταλαλιάς   noun, acc. pl. fem. {2.A}. . . . . . . id.

G2637 **κατάλαλος**, -ου, ὁ   *speaking against; a backbiter.*
καταλάλους   adj., acc. pl. masc. {3.C} κατάλαλος G2637
καταλαλοῦσιν   verb, pres. act. indic. 3 pers. pl.
{5.A.2}. . . . . καταλαλέω G2635
καταλαλῶν   vbl., pres. act. ptc. nom. sg. masc.
{6.A.2}. . . . . id.
καταλαλῶσιν   verb, pres. act. subjunc. 3 pers.
pl. {5.B.2}. . . . . id.
καταλαμβάνομαι   verb, pres. mid. indic. 1 pers.
sg. {5.A.1.d}. . . . . καταλαμβάνω G2638

G2638 **καταλαμβάνω**   (1) act., (a) I seize tight hold of, arrest, catch, capture, appropriate, Mark 9:18; (John 8:3, 4); Rom 9:30; 1 Cor 9:24; Phil 3:12, 13; (b) I overtake, John 1:5; 6:17 (var.); 12:35; 1 Thess 5:4; (2) mid. aor. I perceived, comprehended.
καταλεγέσθω   verb, pres. pass. impv. 3 pers. sg.
{5.D.1}. . . . . καταλέγω G2639

G2639 **καταλέγω**   *I enter in a list, register.*

G2640 **κατάλειμμα**, -ατος, τό   *a remnant.*
κατάλειμμα   noun, nom. sg. neut. {2.C} κατάλειμμα G2640
καταλείπει   verb, pres. act. indic. 3 pers. sg.
{5.A.1.a}. . . . . καταλείπω G2641
καταλειπομένης   vbl., pres. pass. ptc. gen. sg.
fem. {6.A.1}. . . . . id.
καταλείποντες   vbl., pres. act. ptc. nom. pl.
masc. {6.A.1}. . . . . id.

G2641 **καταλείπω**   *I leave behind; I desert, abandon.*
καταλειφθῆναι   vbl., aor. pass. inf.
{6.B.1}. . . . . καταλείπω G2641
καταλείψαντας   vbl., aor. act. ptc. acc. pl.
masc. {6.A.1.a}. . . . . id.
καταλείψει   verb, fut. act. indic. 3 pers. sg.
{5.A.1.a}. . . . . id.
καταλελειμμένος   vbl., perf. pass. ptc. nom.
sg. masc. {6.A.1.b}. id.
καταλελιμμένος   vbl., perf. pass. ptc. nom. sg.
masc. {6.A.1.b} . . . . id.
καταληφθεῖσαν   vbl., aor. pass. ptc. acc. sg. fem.
{6.A.1.a} . . . . καταλαμβάνω G2638

G2642 **καταλιθάζω**   *I stone down, stone to death, overwhelm with stones.*
καταλιθάσει   verb, fut. act. indic. 3 pers. sg.
{5.A.1.a} . . . . καταλιθάζω G2642
καταλίπῃ   verb, ²aor. act. subjunc. 3 pers. sg.
{5.B.1} . . . . καταλείπω G2641
καταλιπόντες   vbl., ²aor. act. ptc. nom. pl.
masc. {6.A.1.a}. . . . . id.
καταλιπών   vbl., ²aor. act. ptc. nom. sg. masc.
{6.A.1.a} . . . . id.
καταλλαγέντες   vbl., ²aor. pass. ptc. nom. pl. masc.
{6.A.1.a} . . . . καταλλάσσω G2644

G2643 **καταλλαγή**, -ῆς, ἡ   *reconciliation.*
καταλλαγή   noun, nom. sg. fem. {2.A} καταλλαγή G2643
καταλλαγήν   noun, acc. sg. fem. {2.A} . . . . . . id.
καταλλαγῆς   noun, gen. sg. fem. {2.A} . . . . . . id.
καταλλαγῆτε   verb, ²aor. pass. impv. 2 pers. pl.
{5.D.1}. . . . . καταλλάσσω G2644
καταλλαγήτω   verb, ²aor. pass. impv. 3 pers.
sg. {5.D.1} . . . . id.
καταλλάξαντος   vbl., aor. act. ptc. gen. sg.
masc. {6.A.1.a}. . . . . id.

G2644 **καταλλάσσω**   *I reconcile.*
καταλλάσσων   vbl., pres. act. ptc. nom. sg. masc.
{6.A.1}. . . . . καταλλάσσω G2644
κατάλοιποι   adj., nom. pl. masc. {3.C}κατάλοιπος G2645

G2645 **κατάλοιπος**, -ον   *left behind;* οἱ κατάλοιποι, *the rest, the remainder.*
κατάλυε   verb, pres. act. impv. 2 pers. sg.
{5.D.1}. . . . . καταλύω G2647
καταλυθῇ   verb, aor. pass. subjunc. 3 pers. sg.
{5.B.1} . . . . id.
καταλυθήσεται   verb, fut. pass. indic. 3 pers.
sg. {5.A.1.d} . . . . id.

G2646 **κατάλυμα**, -ατος, τό   *an inn, lodging.*
κατάλυμα   noun, nom. sg. neut. {2.C} κατάλυμα G2646
καταλύματι   noun, dat. sg. neut. {2.C} . . . . . . id.
καταλῦσαι   vbl., aor. act. inf. {6.B.1} . . . καταλύω G2647
καταλύσει   verb, fut. act. indic. 3 pers. sg.
{5.A.1.a} . . . . id.
καταλύσω   verb, fut. act. indic. 1 pers. sg.
{5.A.1.a} . . . . id.
καταλύσωσι   verb, aor. act. subjunc. 3 pers. pl.
{5.B.1} . . . . id.
καταλύσωσιν   verb, aor. act. subjunc. 3 pers.
pl. {5.B.1}. . . . . id.

G2647 **καταλύω**   (1) trans., I break up, overthrow, destroy, both lit. and met., ὁ καταλύων, you would-be destroyer (of), Matt 27:40; (2) I unyoke, unharness a carriage horse or pack animal; hence, I put up, I lodge, I find a lodging, Luke 9:12; 19:7; (lit. I loosen thoroughly).
καταλύων   vbl., pres. act. ptc. nom. sg. masc.
{6.A.1}. . . . . καταλύω G2647
καταμάθετε   verb, ²aor. act. impv. 2 pers. pl.
{5.D.1}. καταμανθάνω G2648

G2648 **καταμανθάνω**   *I understand, take in a fact about.*

G2649 **καταμαρτυρέω**   *I give evidence against.*
καταμαρτυροῦσι   verb, pres. act. indic. 3 pers. pl.
{5.A.2}. καταμαρτυρέω G2649
καταμαρτυροῦσιν   verb, pres. act. indic.
3 pers. pl. {5.A.2}. . . . . id.
καταμένοντες   vbl., pres. act. ptc. nom. pl. masc.
{6.A.1}. . . . . καταμένω G2650
καταμενῶ   verb, fut. act. indic. 1 pers. sg.
{5.A.2}. . . . . id.

G2650 **καταμένω**   *I wait, Acts 1:13; I stay,* πρός, *with,* 1 Cor 16:6.

G2651 **καταμόνας**   *alone* (= κατὰ μόνας, see μόνος).
καταμόνας   adv. . . . . καταμόνας G2651

G2652 **κατανάθεμα**   *an accursed thing.*

κατανάθεμα   noun, nom. sg. neut.
{2.C} . . . . .κατανάθεμα *G2652*
καταναθεματίζειν   vbl., pres. act. inf.
{6.B.1} . . . . .καταναθεματίζω *G2653*
G2653 **καταναθεματίζω**   *I curse.*
καταναλίσκον   vbl., pres. act. ptc. nom. sg. neut.
{6.A.1} . . . . καταναλίσκω *G2654*
G2654 **καταναλίσκω**   *I consume utterly.*
G2655 **καταναρκάω**   (properly a medical term, *I stupefy*), hence, *I burden, encumber.*
καταναρκήσω   verb, fut. act. indic. 1 pers. sg.
{5.A.1} . . . . καταναρκάω *G2655*
G2656 **κατανεύω**   *I nod, make a sign.*
κατανοεῖς   verb, pres. act. indic. 2 pers. sg.
{5.A.2} . . . . .κατανοέω *G2657*
G2657 **κατανοέω**   *I understand, take in a fact about, take knowledge of, take notice of, perceive; I detect,* Luke 20:23; *I master,* Acts 7:31.
κατανοῆσαι   vbl., aor. act. inf. {6.B.1} . .κατανοέω *G2657*
κατανοήσας   vbl., aor. act. ptc. nom. sg. masc.
{6.A.2} . . . . id.
κατανοήσατε   verb, aor. act. impv. 2 pers. pl.
{5.D.1} . . . . id.
κατανοοῦντι   vbl., pres. act. ptc. dat. sg. masc.
{6.A.2} . . . . id.
κατανοῶμεν   verb, pres. act. subjunc. 1 pers.
pl. {5.B.2} . . . . id.
G2658 **καταντάω**   (1) *I come down,* either from high land to lower (or actually to the sea coast), or from the high seas to the coast; hence met., *I reach* (my destination), Acts 26:7; Eph 4:13; Phil 3:11; (2) of property, *I come down (descend)* by inheritance to an heir, 1 Cor 10:11; 14:36.
καταντῆσαι   vbl., aor. act. inf. {6.B.1} . .καταντάω *G2658*
καταντήσαντες   vbl., aor. act. ptc. nom. pl.
masc. {6.A.2} . . . . id.
καταντήσω   verb, aor. act. subjunc. 1 pers. sg.
{5.B.1} . . . . id.
καταντήσωμεν   verb, aor. act. subjunc. 1 pers.
pl. {5.B.1} . . . . id.
κατανύξεως   noun, gen. sg. fem. {2.C} κατάνυξις *G2659*
G2659 **κατάνυξις**, -εως, ἡ   *deep sleep, torpor, insensibility.*
G2660 **κατανύσσομαι**   met. *I am pierced, stung.*
G2661 **καταξιόω**   *I deem (count) worthy.*
καταξιωθέντες   vbl., aor. pass. ptc. nom. pl. masc.
{6.A.1.a} . . . . καταξιόω *G2661*
καταξιωθῆναι   vbl., aor. pass. inf. {6.B.1} . . . . id.
καταξιωθῆτε   verb, aor. pass. subjunc. 2 pers.
pl. {5.B.1} . . . . id.
καταπατεῖν   vbl., pres. act. inf. {6.B.2}.καταπατέω *G2662*
καταπατεῖσθαι   vbl., pres. pass. inf. {6.B.2} . . . id.
G2662 **καταπατέω**   lit. and met. *I trample down.*
καταπατήσας   vbl., aor. act. ptc. nom. sg. masc.
{6.A.2} . . . . .καταπατέω *G2662*
καταπατήσουσιν   verb, fut. act. indic. 3 pers.
pl. {5.A.1} . . . . id.
καταπατήσωσιν   verb, aor. act. subjunc.
3 pers. pl. {5.B.1} . . . . id.

καταπαύσεως   noun, gen. sg. fem.
{2.C} . . . . .κατάπαυσις *G2663*
κατάπαυσιν   noun, acc. sg. fem. {2.C}. . . . . . . id.
G2663 **κατάπαυσις**, -εως, ἡ   *resting, rest* (in OT of *the rest* attained by the settlement in Canaan).
G2664 **καταπαύω**   (1) trans., *I cause to rest, bring to rest;* with gen. *I cause to refrain,* Acts 14:18; (2) intrans., *I rest,* Heb 4:4, 10.
καταπεσόντων   vbl., ²aor. act. ptc. gen. pl. masc.
{6.A.1.a} . . . . καταπίπτω *G2667*
G2665 **καταπέτασμα**, -ατος, τό   *curtain* (lit. *that which is spread out downwards, that which hangs down*), of that which separated the Holy of Holies from the outer parts of the temple at Jerusalem, also of an outer curtain at the entrance to the Holy Place in the same temple; the latter is strictly denoted by κάλυμμα; yet Heb 9:3 speaks of the former as τὸ δεύτερον καταπέτασμα.
καταπέτασμα   noun, acc. sg. neut.
{2.C} . . . . καταπέτασμα *G2665*
καταπέτασμα   noun, nom. sg. neut. {2.C}. . . . . id.
καταπετάσματος   noun, gen. sg. neut. {2.C}. . . id.
καταπιεῖν   vbl., ²aor. act. inf. {6.B.1}   . . . καταπίνω *G2666*
καταπίῃ   verb, ²aor. act. subjunc. 3 pers. sg.
{5.B.1} . . . . id.
καταπίνοντες   vbl., pres. act. ptc. nom. pl.
masc. {6.A.1} . . . . id.
G2666 **καταπίνω**   (1) *I drink up, swallow, gulp down; I gobble* (orig. of liquids, extended to solids); (2) pass. lit. and met. *I drown, am drowning.*
καταπίπτειν   vbl., pres. act. inf. {6.B.1} καταπίπτω *G2667*
G2667 **καταπίπτω**   *I fall down.*
G2668 **καταπλέω**   *I sail down* (from the high seas to the shore).
καταποθῇ   verb, aor. pass. subjunc. 3 pers. sg.
{5.B.1} . . . . καταπίνω *G2666*
G2669 **καταπονέω**   *I ill treat; pass. I am getting the worse.*
καταπονούμενον   vbl., pres. pass. ptc. acc. sg.
masc. {6.A.2} . . . . .καταπονέω *G2669*
καταπονουμένῳ   vbl., pres. pass. ptc. dat. sg.
masc. {6.A.2} . . . . id.
καταποντίζεσθαι   vbl., pres. pass. inf.
{6.B.1} . . . . καταποντίζω *G2670*
G2670 **καταποντίζω**   mid. I am submerged, I drown.
καταποντισθῇ   verb, aor. pass. subjunc. 3 pers. sg.
{5.B.1} . . . . καταποντίζω *G2670*
G2671 **κατάρα**, -ας, ἡ   *cursing; a curse.*
κατάρα   noun, nom. sg. fem. {2.A} . . . . . κατάρα *G2671*
κατάραν   noun, acc. sg. fem. {2.A}. . . . . id.
G2672 **καταράομαι**   *I curse;* κατηραμένοι, *having become the subjects of a curse,* Matt 25:41.
κατάρας   noun, gen. sg. fem. {2.A} . . . .κατάρα *G2671*
καταρᾶσθε   verb, pres. mid./pass. impv. 2 pers. pl.
{5.D.2} .καταράομαι *G2672*
καταργεῖ   verb, pres. act. indic. 3 pers. sg.
{5.A.2} . . . . .καταργέω *G2673*
καταργεῖται   verb, pres. pass. indic. 3 pers. sg.
{5.A.2} . . . . id.

G2673 **καταργέω**   (1) *I make idle (inactive), I make of no effect, I annul, abolish, bring to naught;* (2) with ἀπό, *I discharge, sever, separate from.*
καταργηθῇ   verb, aor. pass. subjunc. 3 pers. sg.
{5.B.1} . . . . καταργέω G2673
καταργηθήσεται   verb, fut. pass. indic. 3 pers.
sg. {5.A.1} . . . . id.
καταργηθήσονται   verb, fut. pass. indic.
3 pers. pl. {5.A.1} . . . . id.
καταργῆσαι   vbl., aor. act. inf. {6.B.1} . . . . id.
καταργήσαντος   vbl., aor. act. ptc. gen. sg.
masc. {6.A.2} . . . . id.
καταργήσας   vbl., aor. act. ptc. nom. sg. masc.
{6.A.2} . . . . id.
καταργήσει   verb, fut. act. indic. 3 pers. sg.
{5.A.1} . . . . id.
καταργήσῃ   verb, aor. act. subjunc. 3 pers. sg.
{5.B.1} . . . . id.
καταργοῦμεν   verb, pres. act. indic. 1 pers. pl.
{5.A.2} . . . . id.
καταργουμένην   vbl., pres. pass. ptc. acc. sg.
fem. {6.A.2} . . . . id.
καταργούμενον   vbl., pres. pass. ptc. nom. sg.
neut. {6.A.2} . . . . id.
καταργουμένου   vbl., pres. pass. ptc. gen. sg.
neut. {6.A.2} . . . . id.
καταργουμένων   vbl., pres. pass. ptc. gen. pl.
masc. {6.A.2} . . . . id.
G2674 **καταριθμέω**   *I number.*
καταρτίζεσθε   verb, pres. pass. impv. 2 pers. pl.
{5.D.1} . . . . καταρτίζω G2675
καταρτίζετε   verb, pres. act. impv. 2 pers. pl.
{5.D.1} . . . . id.
καταρτίζοντας   vbl., pres. act. ptc. acc. pl.
masc. {6.A.1} . . . . id.
G2675 **καταρτίζω**   (1) I fit (join) together, Mark 1:19; Matt 4:21; met. I compact together, 1 Cor 1:10; (2) act. and mid. I prepare, I perfect, for his (its) full destination or use, I bring into its proper condition (whether for the first time, or after a lapse).
καταρτίσαι   vbl., aor. act. inf. {6.B.1} . . καταρτίζω G2675
καταρτίσαι   verb, aor. act. opt. 3 pers. sg.
{5.C.1} . . . . id.
καταρτίσει   verb, fut. act. indic. 3 pers. sg.
{5.A.1.a} . . . . id.
κατάρτισιν   noun, acc. sg. fem. {2.C} . κατάρτισις G2676
G2676 **κατάρτισις,** -εως, ἡ   *restoration.*
καταρτισμόν   noun, acc. sg. masc.
{2.B} . . . . καταρτισμός G2677
G2677 **καταρτισμός,** -οῦ, ὁ   *bringing to a condition of fitness, perfecting.*
καταρώμεθα   verb, pres. mid./pass. indic. 1 pers.
pl. {5.A.2} . . . . καταράομαι G2672
καταρωμένους   vbl., pres. mid./pass. ptc. acc.
pl. masc. {6.A.2} . . . . id.
κατασείσας   vbl., aor. act. ptc. nom. sg. masc.
{6.A.1.a} . . . . κατασείω G2678
G2678 **κατασείω**   *I shake (the hand) up and* down, *I wave;* intrans., *I beckon for silence.*

G2679 **κατασκάπτω**   *I dig down.*
κατασκευάζεται   verb, pres. pass. indic. 3 pers. sg.
{5.A.1.d} . . . . κατασκευάζω G2680
κατασκευαζομένης   vbl., pres. pass. ptc. gen.
sg. fem. {6.A.1} . . . . id.
G2680 **κατασκευάζω**   *I build, construct, prepare, make.*
κατασκευάσας   vbl., aor. act. ptc. nom. sg. masc.
{6.A.1.a} . . . . κατασκευάζω G2680
κατασκευάσει   verb, fut. act. indic. 3 pers. sg.
{5.A.1.a} . . . . id.
κατασκηνοῖν   vbl., pres. act. inf.
{6.B.2} . . . . κατασκηνόω G2681
κατασκηνοῦν   vbl., pres. act. inf. {6.B.2} . . . . . . id.
G2681 **κατασκηνόω**   *I encamp, take up my quarters, tabernacle, dwell.*
κατασκηνώσει   verb, fut. act. indic. 3 pers. sg.
{5.A.1} . . . . κατασκηνόω G2681
κατασκηνώσεις   noun, acc. pl. fem.
{2.C} . . . . κατασκήνωσις G2682
G2682 **κατασκήνωσις,** -εως, ἡ   *a dwelling.*
κατασκιάζοντα   vbl., pres. act. ptc. nom. pl. neut.
{6.A.1} . . . . κατασκιάζω G2683
G2683 **κατασκιάζω**   *I overshadow.*
G2684 **κατασκοπέω**   *I spy out.*
κατασκοπῆσαι   vbl., aor. act. inf.
{6.B.1} . . . . κατασκοπέω G2684
G2685 **κατάσκοπος,** -ου, ὁ   *a spy.*
κατασκόπους   noun, acc. pl. masc.
{2.B} . . . . κατάσκοπος G2685
G2686 **κατασοφίζομαι**   *I circumvent by trickery.*
κατασοφισάμενος   vbl., aor. mid. ptc. nom. sg.
masc. {6.A.1.b} . . . . κατασοφίζομαι G2686
κατασταθήσονται   verb, fut. pass. indic. 3 pers.
pl. {5.A.1} . . . . καθίστημι G2525
καταστείλας   vbl., aor. act. ptc. nom. sg. masc.
{6.A.1.a} . . . . καταστέλλω G2687
G2687 **καταστέλλω**   *I restrain, quiet.*
G2688 **κατάστημα,** -ατος, τό   *demeanor, deportment* (a man's outward bearing, including *gait, posture, expression of countenance, dress,* etc., involving the idea of *calmness* and *composure*).
καταστήματι   noun, dat. sg. neut.
{2.C} . . . . κατάστημα G2688
καταστήσει   verb, fut. act. indic. 3 pers. sg.
{5.A.1} . . . . καθίστημι G2525
καταστήσῃς   verb, aor. act. subjunc. 2 pers. sg.
{5.B.3} . . . . id.
καταστήσομεν   verb, fut. act. indic. 1 pers. pl.
{5.A.1} . . . . id.
καταστήσω   verb, fut. act. indic. 1 pers. sg.
{5.A.1} . . . . id.
καταστήσωμεν   verb, aor. act. subjunc. 1 pers.
pl. {5.B.3} . . . . id.
G2689 **καταστολή,** -ῆς, ἡ   *garb, clothing.*
καταστολῇ   noun, dat. sg. fem. {2.A} . καταστολή G2689
G2690 **καταστρέφω**   *I overturn.*
καταστρηνιάσωσι   verb, aor. act. subjunc. 3 pers.
pl. {5.B.1} . . . . καταστρηνιάω G2691
καταστρηνιάσωσιν   verb, aor. act. subjunc.
3 pers. pl. {5.B.1} . . . . id.

G2691 **καταστρηνιάω**   *I exercise my youthful vigor against.*

G2692 **καταστροφή**, -ῆς, ἡ   *destruction,* material or spiritual.
καταστροφῇ   noun, dat. sg. fem.
{2.A} . . . . καταστροφή *G2692*

G2693 **καταστρώννυμι**   *I scatter on the ground.*
κατασύρῃ   verb, aor. act. subjunc. 3 pers. sg.
{5.B.1} . . . . κατασύρω *G2694*
κατασύρῃ   verb, pres. act. subjunc. 3 pers. sg.
{5.B.1} . . . . id.

G2694 **κατασύρω**   *I drag (down).*

G2695 **κατασφάζω**   *I slaughter.*
κατασφάξατε   verb, aor. act. impv. 2 pers. pl.
{5.D.1} . . . . κατασφάζω *G2695*

G2696 **κατασφραγίζω**   *I seal* and thus close.
κατασχέσει   noun, dat. sg. fem. {2.C} κατάσχεσις *G2697*
κατάσχεσιν   noun, acc. sg. fem. {2.C} . . . . id.

G2697 **κατάσχεσις**, -εως, ἡ   abstr., (permanent) *possession.*
κατάσχωμεν   verb, ²aor. act. subjunc. 1 pers. pl.
{5.B.1} . . . . κατέχω *G2722*

G2698 **κατατίθημι**   (1) I lay down, deposit; (2) mid. χάριν, χάριτα, I lay down or deposit a favor, with the view of receiving one in return, I seek favor.

G2699 **κατατομή**, -ῆς, ἡ   *a cutting up, spoiling* (a wordplay with περιτομή).
κατατομήν   noun, acc. sg. fem. {2.A} . . . κατατομή *G2699*
κατατοξευθήσεται   verb, fut. pass. indic. 3 pers. sg. {5.A.1.d} . . . . κατατοξεύω *G2700*

G2700 **κατατοξεύω**   *I shoot down* (with arrows).

G2701 **κατατρέχω**   *I run down.*
κατάφαγε   verb, ²aor. act. impv. 2 pers. sg.
{5.D.1} . . . . κατεσθίω *G2719*
καταφάγεται   verb, fut. mid. indic. 3 pers. sg.
{5.A.1.d} . . . . id.
καταφάγῃ   verb, ²aor. act. subjunc. 3 pers. sg.
{5.B.1} . . . . id.
καταφαγών   vbl., ²aor. act. ptc. nom. sg. masc.
{6.A.1.a} . . . . id.
καταφερόμενος   vbl., pres. pass. ptc. nom. sg.
masc. {6.A.1} . . . . καταφέρω *G2702*
καταφέροντες   vbl., pres. act. ptc. nom. pl.
masc. {6.A.1} . . . . id.

G2702 **καταφέρω**   (1) *I bring down,* ψῆφον, *the pebble* into the urn, i.e., *I give my vote;* αἴτίωμα, *I bring a charge against;* (2) *I oppress;* καταφερόμενος, *being gradually oppressed, becoming oppressed,* Acts 20:9, κατενεχθείς, *being borne down, overcome,* Acts 20:9.

G2703 **καταφεύγω**   *I flee for refuge* (implying that the refuge is reached); aor. indicates moment of arrival.
καταφθαρήσονται   verb, ²fut. pass. indic. 3 pers. pl. {5.A.1.d} . . . . καταφθείρω *G2704*

G2704 **καταφθείρω**   *I destroy, I corrupt.*

G2705 **καταφιλέω**   *I kiss affectionately.*
καταφιλοῦσα   vbl., pres. act. ptc. nom. sg. fem.
{6.A.2} . . . . καταφιλέω *G2705*

καταφρονεῖς   verb, pres. act. indic. 2 pers. sg.
{5.A.2} . . . . καταφρονέω *G2706*
καταφρονεῖτε   verb, pres. act. indic. 2 pers. pl.
{5.A.2} . . . . id.
καταφρονείτω   verb, pres. act. impv. 3 pers. sg.
{5.D.2} . . . . id.
καταφρονείτωσαν   verb, pres. act. impv.
3 pers. pl. {5.D.2} . . . . id.

G2706 **καταφρονέω**   *I despise, scorn,* and show it by active insult.
καταφρονήσας   vbl., aor. act. ptc. nom. sg. masc.
{6.A.2} . . . . καταφρονέω *G2706*
καταφρονήσει   verb, fut. act. indic. 3 pers. sg.
{5.A.1} . . . . id.
καταφρονήσητε   verb, aor. act. subjunc.
2 pers. pl. {5.B.1} . . . . id.
καταφρονηταί   noun, nom. pl. masc.
{2.A} . . . . καταφρονητής *G2707*
καταφρονηταί   noun, voc. pl. masc. {2.A} . . . . id.

G2707 **καταφρονητής**, -οῦ, ὁ   *a despiser.*
καταφρονοῦντας   vbl., pres. act. ptc. acc. pl. masc.
{6.A.2} . . . . καταφρονέω *G2706*
καταφυγόντες   vbl., ²aor. act. ptc. nom. pl. masc.
{6.A.1.a} . . . . καταφεύγω *G2703*

G2708 **καταχέω**   *I pour (down) over.*
καταχθέντες   vbl., aor. pass. ptc. nom. pl. masc.
{6.A.1.a} . . . . κατάγω *G2609*

G2709 **καταχθόνιος**, -ον   *under the earth, subterranean.*
καταχθονίων   adj., gen. pl. masc.
{3.C} . . . . καταχθόνιος *G2709*

G2710 **καταχράομαι**   *I use to the full, I use up.*
καταχρήσασθαι   vbl., aor. mid. inf.
{6.B.1} . . . . καταχράομαι *G2710*
καταχρώμενοι   vbl., pres. mid./pass. ptc. nom.
pl. masc. {6.A.2} . . . . id.
καταψύξῃ   verb, aor. act. subjunc. 3 pers. sg.
{5.B.1} . . . . καταψύχω *G2711*

G2711 **καταψύχω**   *I cool, I refresh.*
κατεαγῶσιν   verb, ²aor. pass. subjunc. 3 pers. pl.
{5.B.3} . . . . κατάγνυμι *G2608*
κατέαξαν   verb, aor. act. indic. 3 pers. pl.
{5.A.3.b} . . . . id.
κατεάξει   verb, fut. act. indic. 3 pers. sg. {5.A.1} id.
κατέβαινεν   verb, impf. act. indic. 3 pers. sg.
{5.A.1.b} . . . . καταβαίνω *G2597*
κατεβάρησα   verb, aor. act. indic. 1 pers. sg.
{5.A.1} . . . . καταβαρέω *G2599*
κατέβη   verb, ²aor. act. indic. 3 pers. sg.
{5.A.1.b} . . . . καταβαίνω *G2597*
κατέβην   verb, ²aor. act. indic. 1 pers. sg.
{5.A.1.b} . . . . id.
κατέβησαν   verb, ²aor. act. indic. 3 pers. pl.
{5.A.1.b} . . . . id.
κατεβλήθη   verb, aor. pass. indic. 3 pers. sg.
{5.A.1.b} . . . . καταβάλλω *G2598*
κατεγέλων   verb, impf. act. indic. 3 pers. pl.
{5.A.2} . . . . καταγελάω *G2606*
κατεγνωσμένος   vbl., perf. pass. ptc. nom. sg.
masc. {6.A.1.b} . . . . καταγινώσκω *G2607*

κατέγραφεν   verb, impf. act. indic. 3 pers. sg.
{5.A.1.b} . . . . γράφω G1125
κατέδησε   verb, aor. act. indic. 3 pers. sg.
{5.A.1} . . . . καταδέω G2611
κατέδησεν   verb, aor. act. indic. 3 pers. sg.
{5.A.1} . . . . id.
κατεδικάσατε   verb, aor. act. indic. 2 pers. pl.
{5.A.1.b} . . . . καταδικάζω G2613
κατεδίωξαν   verb, aor. act. indic. 3 pers. pl.
{5.A.1.b} . . . . καταδιώκω G2614
κατεδίωξεν   verb, aor. act. indic. 3 pers. sg.
{5.A.1.b} . . . . id.
κατέδραμεν   verb, ²aor. act. indic. 3 pers. sg.
{5.A.1.b} . . . . κατατρέχω G2701
κατέθηκεν   verb, aor. act. indic. 3 pers. sg.
{5.A.3.b} . . . . κατατίθημι G2698
κατείδωλον   adj., acc. sg. fem. {3.C} . . κατείδωλος G2712
G2712 **κατείδωλος**, -ον   *full of images* of gods.
κατειλημμένην   vbl., perf. pass. ptc. acc. sg. fem.
{6.A.1.b} . . . . καταλαμβάνω G2638
κατείληπται   verb, perf. pass. indic. 3 pers. sg.
{5.A.1.f} . . . . id.
κατειληφέναι   vbl., ²perf. act. inf. {6.B.1} . . . . . . id.
κατειλήφθη   verb, aor. pass. indic. 3 pers. sg.
{5.A.1.b} . . . . id.
κατειργάσατο   verb, aor. mid. indic. 3 pers. sg.
{5.A.1.e} . . . . κατεργάζομαι G2716
κατειργάσθαι   vbl., perf. mid./pass. inf. {6.B.1} . id.
κατειργάσθη   verb, aor. pass. indic. 3 pers. sg.
{5.A.1.b} . . . . id.
κατείχετο   verb, impf. pass. indic. 3 pers. sg.
{5.A.1.e} . . . . κατέχω G2722
κατειχόμεθα   verb, impf. pass. indic. 1 pers. pl.
{5.A.1.e} . . . . id.
κατεῖχον   verb, impf. act. indic. 3 pers. pl.
{5.A.1.b} . . . . id.
κατεκάη   verb, ²aor. pass. indic. 3 pers. sg.
{5.A.1.e} . . . . κατακαίω G2618
κατέκαιον   verb, impf. act. indic. 3 pers. pl.
{5.A.1.b} . . . . id.
κατέκειτο   verb, impf. mid./pass. indic. 3 pers. sg.
{5.A.3.a} . . . . κατάκειμαι G2621
κατέκλασε   verb, aor. act. indic. 3 pers. sg.
{5.A.1} . . . . κατακλάω G2622
κατέκλασεν   verb, aor. act. indic. 3 pers. sg.
{5.A.1} . . . . id.
κατέκλεισα   verb, aor. act. indic. 1 pers. sg.
{5.A.1.b} . . . . κατακλείω G2623
κατέκλεισε   verb, aor. act. indic. 3 pers. sg.
{5.A.1.b} . . . . id.
κατέκλεισεν   verb, aor. act. indic. 3 pers. sg.
{5.A.1.b} . . . . id.
κατεκληροδότησεν   verb, aor. act. indic. 3 pers.
sg. {5.A.1} . . . . κατακληροδοτέω G2624
κατεκληρονόμησεν   verb, aor. act. indic. 3 pers.
sg. {5.A.1} . . . . κατακληρονομέω G2624†
κατεκλίθη   verb, aor. pass. indic. 3 pers. sg.
{5.A.1.b} . . . . κατακλίνω G2625
κατέκλιναν   verb, aor. act. indic. 3 pers. pl.
{5.A.1.b} . . . . id.

κατεκρίθη   verb, aor. pass. indic. 3 pers. sg.
{5.A.1.b} . . . . κατακρίνω G2632
κατέκριναν   verb, aor. act. indic. 3 pers. pl.
{5.A.1.b} . . . . id.
κατέκρινε   verb, aor. act. indic. 3 pers. sg.
{5.A.1.b} . . . . id.
κατέκρινεν   verb, aor. act. indic. 3 pers. sg.
{5.A.1.b} . . . . id.
κατέλαβε   verb, ²aor. act. indic. 3 pers. sg.
{5.A.1.b} . . . . καταλαμβάνω G2638
κατέλαβεν   verb, ²aor. act. indic. 3 pers. sg.
{5.A.1.b} . . . . id.
κατελαβόμην   verb, ²aor. mid. indic. 1 pers. sg.
{5.A.1.e} . . . . id.
κατέλειπεν   verb, impf. act. indic. 3 pers. sg.
{5.A.1.b} . . . . καταλείπω G2641
κατελείφθη   verb, aor. pass. indic. 3 pers. sg.
{5.A.1.b} . . . . id.
κατελήμφθην   verb, aor. pass. indic. 1 pers. sg.
{5.A.1.b} . . . . καταλαμβάνω G2638
κατελήφθη   verb, aor. pass. indic. 3 pers. sg.
{5.A.1.b} . . . . id.
κατελήφθην   verb, aor. pass. indic. 1 pers. sg.
{5.A.1.b} . . . . id.
κατελθεῖν   vbl., ²aor. act. inf. {6.B.1} . κατέρχομαι G2718
κατελθόντες   vbl., ²aor. act. ptc. nom. pl. masc.
{6.A.1.a} . . . . id.
κατελθόντων   vbl., ²aor. act. ptc. gen. pl. masc.
{6.A.1.a} . . . . id.
κατελθών   vbl., ²aor. act. ptc. nom. sg. masc.
{6.A.1.a} . . . . id.
κατέλιπε   verb, ²aor. act. indic. 3 pers. sg.
{5.A.1.b} . . . . καταλείπω G2641
κατέλιπεν   verb, ²aor. act. indic. 3 pers. sg.
{5.A.1.b} . . . . id.
κατέλιπον   verb, ²aor. act. indic. 1 pers. sg.
{5.A.1.b} . . . . id.
κατέλιπον   verb, ²aor. act. indic. 3 pers. pl.
{5.A.1.b} . . . . id.
κατέλυσα   verb, aor. act. indic. 1 pers. sg.
{5.A.1.b} . . . . καταλύω G2647
G2713 **κατέναντι**   adv. and prep. with gen., *opposite,
in front (of)*.
κατέναντι   adv. . . . . κατέναντι G2713
κατενάρκησα   verb, aor. act. indic. 1 pers. sg.
{5.A.1} . . . . καταναρκάω G2655
κατένευσαν   verb, aor. act. indic. 3 pers. pl.
{5.A.1.b} . . . . κατανεύω G2656
κατενεχθείς   vbl., aor. pass. ptc. nom. sg. masc.
{6.A.1.a} . . . . καταφέρω G2702
κατενόησε   verb, aor. act. indic. 3 pers. sg.
{5.A.1} . . . . κατανοέω G2657
κατενόησεν   verb, aor. act. indic. 3 pers. sg.
{5.A.1} . . . . id.
κατενόουν   verb, impf. act. indic. 1 pers. sg.
{5.A.2} . . . . id.
κατενόουν   verb, impf. act. indic. 3 pers. pl.
{5.A.2} . . . . id.
κατενύγησαν   verb, ²aor. pass. indic. 3 pers. pl.
{5.A.1.e} . . . . κατανύσσομαι G2660

G2714 κατενώπιον prep. with gen., *before the face of.*
κατενώπιον adv. . . . . κατενώπιον *G2714*
κατεξουσιάζουσιν verb, pres. act. indic. 3 pers.
   pl. {5.A.1.a} . . . . κατεξουσιάζω *G2715*
G2715 κατεξουσιάζω *I have (exercise) power (authority) over.*
κατεπατήθη verb, aor. pass. indic. 3 pers. sg.
   {5.A.1} . . . . καταπατέω *G2662*
κατέπαυσαν verb, aor. act. indic. 3 pers. pl.
   {5.A.1.b} . . . . καταπαύω *G2664*
κατέπαυσεν verb, aor. act. indic. 3 pers. sg.
   {5.A.1.b} . . . . id.
κατέπεσεν verb, ²aor. act. indic. 3 pers. sg.
   {5.A.1.b} . . . . καταπίπτω *G2667*
κατεπέστησαν verb, ²aor. act. indic. 3 pers. pl.
   {5.A.3.b} . . . . κατεφίσταμαι *G2721*
κατέπιε verb, ²aor. act. indic. 3 pers. sg.
   {5.A.1.b} . . . . καταπίνω *G2666*
κατέπιεν verb, ²aor. act. indic. 3 pers. sg. {5.A.1.b} id.
κατέπλευσαν verb, aor. act. indic. 3 pers. pl.
   {5.A.1} . . . . καταπλέω *G2668*
κατέπλευσεν verb, aor. act. indic. 3 pers. sg.
   {5.A.1} . . . . id.
κατεπόθη verb, aor. pass. indic. 3 pers. sg.
   {5.A.1.b} . . . . καταπίνω *G2666*
κατεπόθησαν verb, aor. pass. indic. 3 pers. pl.
   {5.A.1.b} . . . . id.
κατεργάζεσθαι vbl., pres. mid./pass. inf.
   {6.B.1} . . . . κατεργάζομαι *G2716*
κατεργάζεσθε verb, pres. mid./pass. impv.
   2 pers. pl. {5.D.1} . . . . id.
κατεργάζεται verb, pres. mid./pass. indic.
   3 pers. sg. {5.A.1.d} . . . . id.
G2716 κατεργάζομαι *I work out; I produce, accomplish.*
κατεργάζομαι verb, pres. mid./pass. indic. 1 pers.
   sg. {5.A.1.d} . . . . κατεργάζομαι *G2716*
κατεργαζομένη vbl., pres. mid./pass. ptc.
   nom. sg. fem. {6.A.1} . . . . id.
κατεργαζόμενοι vbl., pres. mid./pass. ptc.
   nom. pl. masc. {6.A.1} . . . . id.
κατεργαζομένου vbl., pres. mid./pass. ptc.
   gen. sg. masc. {6.A.1} . . . . id.
κατεργασάμενοι vbl., aor. mid. ptc. nom. pl.
   masc. {6.A.1.b} . . . . id.
κατεργασάμενον vbl., aor. mid. ptc. acc.
   masc. {6.A.1.b} . . . . id.
κατεργασάμενος vbl., aor. mid. ptc. nom. sg.
   masc. {6.A.1.b} . . . . id.
κατεργάσασθαι vbl., aor. mid. inf. {6.B.1} . . . . id.
G2718 κατέρχομαι *I come down from sky to earth, or from high land to lower land (or to the coast), or from the high seas to the shore; ptc. qualitative in Jas 3:15.*
κατερχομένη vbl., pres. mid./pass. ptc. nom. sg.
   fem. {6.A.1} . . . . κατέρχομαι *G2718*
κατέσεισε verb, aor. act. indic. 3 pers. sg.
   {5.A.1.b} . . . . κατασείω *G2678*
κατέσεισεν verb, aor. act. indic. 3 pers. sg.
   {5.A.1.b} . . . . id.

κατεσθίει verb, pres. act. indic. 3 pers. sg.
   {5.A.1.a} . . . . κατεσθίω *G2719*
κατεσθίετε verb, pres. act. indic. 2 pers. pl.
   {5.A.1.a} . . . . id.
κατεσθίοντες vbl., pres. act. ptc. nom. pl.
   masc. {6.A.1} . . . . id.
κατεσθίουσι verb, pres. act. indic. 3 pers. pl.
   {5.A.1.a} . . . . id.
κατεσθίουσιν verb, pres. act. indic. 3 pers. pl.
   {5.A.1.a} . . . . id.
G2719 κατεσθίω (κατέσθω) *I eat up, I eat till it is finished* (cf. καταπίνω); aor. inf. καταφαγεῖν.
κατέσθοντες vbl., pres. act. ptc. nom. pl. masc.
   {6.A.1} . . . . κατεσθίω *G2719*
κατεσκαμμένα vbl., perf. pass. ptc. acc. pl. neut.
   {6.A.1.b} . . . . κατασκάπτω *G2679*
κατέσκαψαν verb, aor. act. indic. 3 pers. pl.
   {5.A.1.b} . . . . id.
κατεσκεύασε verb, aor. act. indic. 3 pers. sg.
   {5.A.1.b} . . . . κατασκευάζω *G2680*
κατεσκεύασεν verb, aor. act. indic. 3 pers. sg.
   {5.A.1.b} . . . . id.
κατεσκευάσθη verb, aor. pass. indic. 3 pers.
   sg. {5.A.1.b} . . . . id.
κατεσκευασμένον vbl., perf. pass. ptc. acc. sg.
   masc. {6.A.1.b} . . . . id.
κατεσκευασμένων vbl., perf. pass. ptc. gen.
   pl. masc. {6.A.1.b} . . . . id.
κατεσκήνωσεν verb, aor. act. indic. 3 pers. sg.
   {5.A.1} . . . . κατασκηνόω *G2681*
κατεστάθησαν verb, aor. pass. indic. 3 pers. pl.
   {5.A.1} . . . . καθίστημι *G2525*
κατεσταλμένους vbl., perf. pass. ptc. acc. pl.
   masc. {6.A.1.b} . . . . καταστέλλω *G2687*
κατέστησας verb, aor. act. indic. 2 pers. sg.
   {5.A.3.b} . . . . καθίστημι *G2525*
κατέστησε verb, aor. act. indic. 3 pers. sg. {5.A.3.b} id.
κατέστησεν verb, aor. act. indic. 3 pers. sg.
   {5.A.3.b} . . . . id.
κατεστραμμένα vbl., perf. pass. ptc. acc. pl. neut.
   {6.A.1.b} . . . . καταστρέφω *G2690*
κατέστρεψε verb, aor. act. indic. 3 pers. sg.
   {5.A.1.b} . . . . id.
κατέστρεψεν verb, aor. act. indic. 3 pers. sg.
   {5.A.1.b} . . . . id.
κατεστρώθησαν verb, aor. pass. indic. 3 pers. pl.
   {5.A.1} . . . . καταστρώννυμι *G2693*
κατεσφραγισμένον vbl., perf. pass. ptc. acc. sg.
   neut. {6.A.1.b} . . . . κατασφραγίζω *G2696*
κατευθύναι verb, aor. act. opt. 3 pers. sg.
   {5.C.1} . . . . κατευθύνω *G2720*
κατευθύναι vbl., aor. act. inf. {6.B.1} . . . . id.
G2720 κατευθύνω (1) *I make straight,* 1 Thess 3:11; (2) met. *I put in the right way, I direct.*
κατευλόγει verb, impf. act. indic. 3 pers. sg.
   {5.A.2} . . . . κατευλογέω *G2127†‡*
G2127†‡ κατευλογέω *I bless.* Var. for εὐλογέω, Mark 10:16.
κατέφαγε verb, ²aor. act. indic. 3 pers. sg.
   {5.A.1.b} . . . . κατεσθίω *G2719*

κατέφαγεν verb, ²aor. act. indic. 3 pers. sg.
{5.A.1.b} . . . . id.
κατέφαγον verb, ²aor. act. indic. 1 pers. sg.
{5.A.1.b} . . . . id.
κατεφθαρμένοι vbl., perf. pass. ptc. nom. pl.
masc. {6.A.1.b} . . . . κατεφθείρω G2704
κατεφίλει verb, impf. act. indic. 3 pers. sg.
{5.A.2} . . . . κατεφιλέω G2705
κατεφίλησεν verb, aor. act. indic. 3 pers. sg.
{5.A.1} . . . . id.
κατεφίλουν verb, impf. act. indic. 3 pers. pl.
{5.A.2} . . . . id.
G2721 **κατεφίσταμαι** aor. intrans., *I set upon, I rise up against.*
κατέφυγον verb, ²aor. act. indic. 3 pers. pl.
{5.A.1.b} . . . . κατεφεύγω G2703
κατέχεεν verb, aor. act. indic. 3 pers. sg.
{5.A.1} . . . . κατεχέω G2708
κατέχειν vbl., pres. act. inf. {6.B.1} . . . . . . κατέχω G2722
κατέχετε verb, pres. act. impv. 2 pers. pl. {5.D.1} id.
κατέχετε verb, pres. act. indic. 2 pers. pl.
{5.A.1.a} . . . . id.
κατέχον vbl., pres. act. ptc. acc. sg. neut. {6.A.1} id.
κατέχοντες vbl., pres. act. ptc. nom. pl. masc.
{6.A.1} . . . . id.
κατεχόντων vbl., pres. act. ptc. gen. pl. masc.
{6.A.1} . . . . id.
κατέχουσι verb, pres. act. indic. 3 pers. pl.
{5.A.1.a} . . . . id.
κατέχουσιν verb, pres. act. indic. 3 pers. pl.
{5.A.1.a} . . . . id.
G2722 **κατέχω** (1) *I hold fast, bind, arrest;* (2) *I take possession of, lay hold of,* Luke 14:9; (3) *I hold back, detain, restrain,* Luke 4:42; Rom 1:18; 2 Thess 2:6, 7; Phlm 13; (4) *I hold a ship* (supply τὴν ναῦν), *keep its heading,* Acts 27:40.
κατέχομεν verb, pres. act. subjunc. 1 pers. pl.
{5.B.1} . . . . κατέχω G2722
κατέχων vbl., pres. act. ptc. nom. sg. masc.
{6.A.1} . . . . id.
κατήγαγον verb, ²aor. act. indic. 1 pers. sg.
{5.A.1.b} . . . . κατάγω G2609
κατήγαγον verb, ²aor. act. indic. 3 pers. pl.
{5.A.1.b} . . . . id.
κατηγγείλαμεν verb, aor. act. indic. 1 pers. pl.
{5.A.1.b} . . . . καταγγέλλω G2605
κατήγγειλαν verb, aor. act. indic. 3 pers. pl.
{5.A.1.b} . . . . id.
κατηγγέλη verb, ²aor. pass. indic. 3 pers. sg.
{5.A.1.e} . . . . id.
κατήγγελλον verb, impf. act. indic. 3 pers. pl.
{5.A.1.b} . . . . id.
κατηγορεῖν vbl., pres. act. inf. {6.B.2} . κατηγορέω G2723
κατηγορεῖσθαι vbl., pres. pass. inf. {6.B.2} . . . . id.
κατηγορεῖται verb, pres. pass. indic. 3 pers.
sg. {5.A.2} . . . . id.
κατηγορεῖτε verb, pres. act. indic. 2 pers. pl.
{5.A.2} . . . . id.
κατηγορείτωσαν verb, pres. act. impv. 3 pers.
pl. {5.D.2} . . . . id.

G2723 **κατηγορέω** *I accuse, charge; I prosecute.*
κατηγορῆσαι vbl., aor. act. inf. {6.B.1} κατηγορέω G2723
κατηγορήσω verb, fut. act. indic. 1 pers. sg.
{5.A.1} . . . . id.
κατηγορήσωσιν verb, aor. act. subjunc.
3 pers. pl. {5.B.1} . . . . id.
G2724 **κατηγορία**, -ας, ἡ *a charge, an accusation.*
κατηγορίᾳ noun, dat. sg. fem. {2.A} . . κατηγορία G2724
κατηγορίαν noun, acc. sg. fem. {2.A} . . . . id.
κατήγοροι noun, nom. pl. masc. {2.B} κατήγορος G2725
κατηγόροις noun, dat. pl. masc. {2.B} . . . . id.
G2725 **κατήγορος**, -ου, ὁ *a prosecutor, an accuser.*
κατηγόρος noun, nom. sg. masc. {2.B} κατήγορος G2725
κατηγορούμεν verb, pres. act. indic. 1 pers. pl.
{5.A.2} . . . . κατηγορέω G2723
κατηγορούμενος vbl., pres. pass. ptc. nom. sg.
masc. {6.A.2} . . . . id.
κατηγόρουν verb, impf. act. indic. 3 pers. pl.
{5.A.2} . . . . id.
κατηγοροῦντες vbl., pres. act. ptc. nom. pl.
masc. {6.A.2} . . . . id.
κατηγορούντων vbl., pres. act. ptc. gen. pl.
masc. {6.A.2} . . . . id.
κατηγόρους noun, acc. pl. masc. {2.B} κατήγορος G2725
κατηγοροῦσι verb, pres. act. indic. 3 pers. pl.
{5.A.2} . . . . κατηγορέω G2723
κατηγοροῦσιν verb, pres. act. indic. 3 pers. pl.
{5.A.2} . . . . id.
κατηγορῶν vbl., pres. act. ptc. nom. sg. masc.
{6.A.2} . . . . id.
κατηγωνίσαντο verb, aor. mid. indic. 3 pers. pl.
{5.A.1.e} . . . . καταγωνίζομαι G2610
G2725† **κατήγωρ**, -ορος, ὁ *an accuser* (an abbreviated vulgar form of κατήγορος). Var. for κατήγορος, Rev 12:10.
κατήγωρ noun, nom. sg. masc. {2.B} . . . κατήγωρ G2725†
κατήλθαμεν verb, ²aor. act. indic. 1 pers. pl.
{5.A.1.b} . . . . κατέρχομαι G2718
κατῆλθε verb, ²aor. act. indic. 3 pers. sg. {5.A.1.b} . id.
κατῆλθεν verb, ²aor. act. indic. 3 pers. sg.
{5.A.1.b} . . . . id.
κατήλθομεν verb, ²aor. act. indic. 1 pers. pl.
{5.A.1.b} . . . . id.
κατῆλθον verb, ²aor. act. indic. 3 pers. pl.
{5.A.1.b} . . . . id.
κατηλλάγημεν verb, ²aor. pass. indic. 1 pers. pl.
{5.A.1.e} . . . . καταλλάσσω G2644
κατήνεγκα verb, aor. act. indic. 1 pers. sg.
{5.A.1.b} . . . . καταφέρω G2702
κατήντηκεν verb, perf. act. indic. 3 pers. sg.
{5.A.1} . . . . καταντάω G2658
κατηντήσαμεν verb, aor. act. indic. 1 pers. pl.
{5.A.1} . . . . id.
κατήντησαν verb, aor. act. indic. 3 pers. pl.
{5.A.1} . . . . id.
κατήντησε verb, aor. act. indic. 3 pers. sg. {5.A.1} id.
κατήντησεν verb, aor. act. indic. 3 pers. sg.
{5.A.1} . . . . id.
κατηξιώθησαν verb, aor. pass. indic. 3 pers. pl.
{5.A.1} . . . . καταξιόω G2661

κατηραμένοι   vbl., perf. pass. ptc. nom. pl. masc.
{6.A.2}. . . . . .καταράομαι *G2672*
κατηράσω   verb, aor. mid. indic. 2 pers. sg. {5.A.1} id.
κατηργήθημεν   verb, aor. pass. indic. 1 pers. pl.
{5.A.1}. καταργέω *G2673*
κατηργήθητε   verb, aor. pass. indic. 2 pers. pl.
{5.A.1}. . . . . id.
κατήργηκα   verb, perf. act. indic. 1 pers. sg. {5.A.1} id.
κατήργηται   verb, perf. pass. indic. 3 pers. sg.
{5.A.1}. . . . . id.
κατηριθμημένος   vbl., perf. pass. ptc. nom. sg.
masc. {6.A.2}. . . . . καταριθμέω *G2674*
κατηρτίσθαι   vbl., perf. pass. inf.
{6.B.1}. καταρτίζω *G2675*
κατηρτισμένα   vbl., perf. pass. ptc. acc. pl.
neut. {6.A.1.b}. id.
κατηρτισμένοι   vbl., perf. pass. ptc. nom. pl.
masc. {6.A.1.b} . . . . id.
κατηρτισμένος   vbl., perf. pass. ptc. nom. sg.
masc. {6.A.1.b} . . . . id.
κατηρτίσω   verb, aor. mid. indic. 2 pers. sg.
{5.A.1.e} . . . . id.
κατησχύνθην   verb, aor. pass. indic. 1 pers. sg.
{5.A.1.b} . . . . .καταισχύνω *G2617*
κατησχύνοντο   verb, impf. pass. indic. 3 pers.
pl. {5.A.1.e} . . . . id.
κατηυλόγει   verb, impf. act. indic. 3 pers. sg.
{5.A.2}. . . . . .κατευλογέω *G2127†‡*
G2726 **κατήφεια**, -ας, ἡ   *a downcast countenance* as a
sign of sorrow, *gloominess, gloom, dejection.*
κατήφειαν   noun, acc. sg. fem. {2.A} . . . κατήφεια *G2726*
G2727 **κατηχέω**   *I instruct orally.*
κατηχήθης   verb, aor. pass. indic. 2 pers. sg.
{5.A.1}. . . . . .κατηχέω *G2727*
κατηχήθησαν   verb, aor. pass. indic. 3 pers. pl.
{5.A.1}. . . . . id.
κατηχημένος   vbl., perf. pass. ptc. nom. sg.
masc. {6.A.2}. . . . . id.
κατήχηνται   verb, perf. pass. indic. 3 pers. pl.
{5.A.1}. . . . . id.
κατηχήσω   verb, aor. act. subjunc. 1 pers. sg.
{5.B.1}. . . . . id.
κατήχθημεν   verb, ²aor. pass. indic. 1 pers. pl.
{5.A.1.e} . . . . κατάγω *G2609*
κατηχούμενος   vbl., pres. pass. ptc. nom. sg. masc.
{6.A.2}. . . . . .κατηχέω *G2727*
κατηχοῦντι   vbl., pres. act. ptc. dat. sg. masc.
{6.A.2}. . . . . id.
G2728 **κατιόω**   *I rust; pass. I am rusted.*
κατίσχυον   verb, impf. act. indic. 3 pers. pl.
{5.A.1.b} . . . . κατισχύω *G2729*
κατισχύσητε   verb, aor. act. subjunc. 2 pers. pl.
{5.B.1}. . . . . id.
κατισχύσουσιν   verb, fut. act. indic. 3 pers. pl.
{5.A.1.a} . . . . id.
G2729 **κατισχύω**   (1) *I have strength against, I prevail
against,* Matt 16:18; (2) *I prevail,* Luke 23:23; (3)
I have strength, I am able, with inf., Luke 21:36.
κατίωται   verb, perf. pass. indic. 3 pers. sg.
{5.A.1}. κατιόω *G2728*

κατοικεῖ   verb, pres. act. indic. 3 pers. sg.
{5.A.2}. κατοικέω *G2730*
κατοικεῖν   vbl., pres. act. inf. {6.B.2} . . . . id.
κατοικεῖς   verb, pres. act. indic. 2 pers. sg. {5.A.2} . id.
κατοικεῖτε   verb, pres. act. indic. 2 pers. pl.
{5.A.2}. . . . . id.
G2730 **κατοικέω**   *I dwell in* (implying a more permanent settlement than παροικέω), *I settle in, I
am established in* (permanently).
κατοικῆσαι   vbl., aor. act. inf. {6.B.1}. . . κατοικέω *G2730*
κατοικήσαντι   vbl., aor. act. ptc. dat. sg. masc.
{6.A.2}. . . . . id.
κατοικήσας   vbl., aor. act. ptc. nom. sg. masc.
{6.A.2}. . . . . id.
κατοίκησιν   noun, acc. sg. fem. {2.C} .κατοίκησις *G2731*
G2731 **κατοίκησις**, -εως, ἡ   *dwelling, abode.*
G2732 **κατοικητήριον**, -ου, τό   *a habitation, dwelling
place.*
κατοικητήριον   noun, acc. sg. neut.
{2.B} .κατοικητήριον *G2732*
κατοικητήριον   noun, nom. sg. neut. {2.B}. . . . id.
G2733 **κατοικία**, -ας, ἡ   *dwelling, habitation.*
κατοικίας   noun, gen. sg. fem. {2.A} . . . .κατοικία *G2733*
G2730†‡ **κατοικίζω**   *I take up a dwelling.* Var. for
κατοικέω (κατῴκισεν is probably an iota-
cism for κατῴκησεν, from κατοικέω, as
κατοικίζω is properly trans.), James 4:5.
κατοικοῦντας   vbl., pres. act. ptc. acc. pl. masc.
{6.A.2}. κατοικέω *G2730*
κατοικοῦντες   vbl., pres. act. ptc. nom. pl.
masc. {6.A.2}. . . . . id.
κατοικοῦντι   vbl., pres. act. ptc. dat. sg. masc.
{6.A.2}. . . . . id.
κατοικούντων   vbl., pres. act. ptc. gen. pl.
masc. {6.A.2}. . . . . id.
κατοικοῦσι   vbl., pres. act. ptc. dat. pl. masc.
{6.A.2}. . . . . id.
κατοικοῦσιν   vbl., pres. act. ptc. dat. pl. masc.
{6.A.2}. . . . . id.
κατοικῶν   vbl., pres. act. ptc. nom. sg. masc.
{6.A.2}. . . . . id.
κατοπτριζόμενοι   vbl., pres. mid. ptc. nom. pl.
masc. {6.A.1}. . . . . κατοπτρίζω *G2734*
G2734 **κατοπτρίζω**   mid. for act., *I mirror, reflect;*
elsewhere mid., *I gaze upon myself in a mirror.*
G2735 **κατόρθωμα**, -ατος, τό   *success, prosperity.*
κατορθωμάτων   noun, gen. pl. neut.
{2.C} . . . . κατόρθωμα *G2735*
G2736 **κάτω**   adv., (1) *down, below,* also *downwards;*
(2) comp. κατωτέρω, *lower, under, less,* of a
length of a time, Matt 2:16.
κάτω   adv.. .κάτω *G2736*
κατῴκησεν   verb, aor. act. indic. 3 pers. sg.
{5.A.1}. κατοικέω *G2730*
κατῴκισεν   verb, aor. act. indic. 3 pers. sg.
{5.A.1.b} . . . . κατοικίζω *G2730†‡*
κατώτερα   adj. comp., acc. pl. neut. {3.C;
3.G} . . . . κατώτερος *G2737*
G2737 **κατώτερος**, -α, -ον   comp. adj., *lower,* Hebraistic, with ref. to Sheol.

G2736†‡ **κατωτέρω**   adv. *lower, below.* Var. for κάτω,
     Matt 2:16.
     κατωτέρω   adv. comp. {3.F; 3.G} . . . . κατωτέρω G2736†‡
     Καῦδα   noun prop.. . . . . Κλαῦδα G2802
     καυθήσομαι   verb, fut. pass. indic. 1 pers. sg.
         {5.A.1.d} . . . . καίω G2545
     καυθήσωμαι   verb, fut. pass. subjunc. 1 pers.
         sg. {5.A.1.d} . . . . id.
G2738 **καῦμα**, -ατος, τό   *burning heat, heat.*
     καῦμα   noun, acc. sg. neut. {2.C} . . . . καῦμα G2738
     καῦμα   noun, nom. sg. neut. {2.C} . . . . id.
G2739 **καυματίζω**   trans., *I burn, I scorch.*
     καυματίσαι   vbl., aor. act. inf. {6.B.1} . καυματίζω G2739
     καῦσιν   noun, acc. sg. fem. {2.C} . . . . καῦσις G2740
G2740 **καῦσις**, -εως, ἡ   *burning.*
     καυσούμενα   vbl., pres. pass. ptc. nom. pl. neut.
         {6.A.2} . . . . καυσόω G2741
G2741 **καυσόω**   trans., *I burn* (perhaps by internal
     heat).
G2742 **καύσων**, -ωνος, ὁ   *the East wind* of Palestine,
     the Simoom, which blows from February to
     June.
     καύσων   noun, nom. sg. masc. {2.C} . . . καύσων G2742
     καύσωνα   noun, acc. sg. masc. {2.C} . . . . id.
     καύσωνι   noun, dat. sg. masc. {2.C} . . . . id.
G2743 **καυτηριάζω** (καυστηριάζω)   *I cauterize, I*
     burn with a hot iron; hence met., *I sear.*
G2744 **καυχάομαι**   *I boast; I glory (exult) proudly.*
     καυχᾶσαι   verb, pres. mid./pass. indic. 2 pers. sg.
         {5.A.2} . . . . καυχάομαι G2744
     καυχᾶσθαι   vbl., pres. mid./pass. inf. {6.B.2} . . . id.
     καυχᾶσθε   verb, pres. mid./pass. indic. 2 pers.
         pl. {5.A.2} . . . . id.
     καυχάσθω   verb, pres. mid./pass. impv. 3 pers.
         sg. {5.D.2} . . . . id.
G2745 **καύχημα**, -ατος, τό   *a boasting, a ground of*
     boasting (glorying, exultation).
     καύχημα   noun, acc. sg. neut. {2.C} . . . καύχημα G2745
     καύχημα   noun, nom. sg. neut. {2.C} . . . . id.
     καυχήματος   noun, gen. sg. neut. {2.C} . . . . id.
     καυχήσασθαι   vbl., aor. mid. inf.
         {6.B.1} . . . . καυχάομαι G2744
     καυχήσεως   noun, gen. sg. fem. {2.C} . . καύχησις G2746
     καυχήσηται   verb, aor. mid. subjunc. 3 pers. sg.
         {5.B.1} . . . . καυχάομαι G2744
     καύχησιν   noun, acc. sg. fem. {2.C} . . . . καύχησις G2746
G2746 **καύχησις**, -εως, ἡ   *boasting; glorying,*
     exultation.
     καύχησις   noun, nom. sg. fem. {2.C} . . . καύχησις G2746
     καυχήσομαι   verb, fut. mid. indic. 1 pers. sg.
         {5.A.1} . . . . καυχάομαι G2744
     καυχησόμεθα   verb, fut. mid. indic. 1 pers. pl.
         {5.A.1} . . . . id.
     καυχήσωμαι   verb, aor. mid. subjunc. 1 pers.
         sg. {5.B.1} . . . . id.
     καυχήσωνται   verb, aor. mid. subjunc. 3 pers.
         pl. {5.B.1} . . . . id.
     καυχῶμαι   verb, pres. mid./pass. indic. 1 pers.
         sg. {5.A.2} . . . . id.

     καυχώμεθα   verb, pres. mid./pass. indic.
         1 pers. pl. {5.A.2} . . . . id.
     καυχώμενοι   vbl., pres. mid./pass. ptc. nom. pl.
         masc. {6.A.2} . . . . id.
     καυχώμενος   vbl., pres. mid./pass. ptc. nom.
         sg. masc. {6.A.2} . . . . id.
     καυχωμένους   vbl., pres. mid./pass. ptc. acc.
         pl. masc. {6.A.2} . . . . id.
     καυχῶνται   verb, pres. mid./pass. indic. 3 pers.
         pl. {5.A.2} . . . . id.
     Καφαρναούμ   noun prop. . . . . Καπερναούμ G2584
G2747 **Κεγχρεαί** (Κενχρεαί), -ῶν, -αί   *Cenchrea,* the
     harbor town of Corinth on the Saronic Gulf.
     Κεγχρεαῖς   noun prop., dat. pl. fem. {2.A;
         2.D} . . . . Κεγχρεαί G2747
G2748 **Κεδρών**, ὁ   *Kidron;* The var. τῶν κέδρων, *the*
     cedars (from κέδρος, ὁ, a *cedar*) in John 18:1
     is probably due to a popular misunderstand-
     ing of the orig. name τοῦ Κεδρών (cf. 1 Kgs
     2:37, etc.), esp. as cedars grew in the vicinity.
     Κεδρών   noun prop. . . . . Κεδρών G2748
     Κέδρων   noun prop. id.
G2749 **κεῖμαι**   *I have been placed (put, laid),* hence,
     I lie; a perf. used instead of the perf. pass. of
     τίθημι, the former sense explains the constr.
     with εἰς and acc.
     κεῖμαι   verb, pres. mid./pass. indic. 1 pers. sg.
         {5.A.3.a} . . . . κεῖμαι G2749
     κείμεθα   verb, pres. mid./pass. indic. 1 pers. pl.
         {5.A.3.a} . . . . id.
     κείμενα   vbl., pres. mid./pass. ptc. acc. pl. neut.
         {6.A.3} . . . . id.
     κείμεναι   vbl., pres. mid./pass. ptc. nom. pl.
         fem. {6.A.3} . . . . id.
     κειμένη   vbl., pres. mid./pass. ptc. nom. sg.
         fem. {6.A.3} . . . . id.
     κειμένην   vbl., pres. mid./pass. ptc. acc. sg. fem.
         {6.A.3} . . . . id.
     κείμενον   vbl., pres. mid./pass. ptc. acc. sg.
         masc. {6.A.3} . . . . id.
     κείμενον   vbl., pres. mid./pass. ptc. acc. sg.
         neut. {6.A.3} . . . . id.
     κείμενος   vbl., pres. mid./pass. ptc. nom. sg.
         masc. {6.A.3} . . . . id.
     κειράμενος   vbl., aor. mid. ptc. nom. sg. masc.
         {6.A.1.b} . . . . κείρω G2751
     κείραντος   vbl., aor. act. ptc. gen. sg. masc.
         {6.A.1.a} . . . . id.
     κείρασθαι   vbl., aor. mid. inf. {6.B.1} . . . . id.
     κειράσθω   verb, aor. mid. impv. 3 pers. sg.
         {5.D.1} . . . . id.
G2750 **κειρία**, -ας, ἡ   a kind of *girdle* made of cords; *a*
     bandage.
     κειρίαις   noun, dat. pl. fem. {2.A} . . . . κειρία G2750
     κείροντος   vbl., pres. act. ptc. gen. sg. masc.
         {6.A.1} . . . . κείρω G2751
G2751 **κείρω**   *I shear, I cut the hair of;* mid. *I cut my*
     own hair, I have my hair cut.
     Κείς   noun prop. . . . . Κίς G2797

κεῖται   verb, pres. mid./pass. indic. 3 pers. sg.
{5.A.3} . . . . κεῖμαι G2749
κεκαθαρισμένους   vbl., perf. pass. ptc. acc. pl.
masc. {6.A.1.b} . . . . καθαρίζω G2511
κεκαθαρμένους   vbl., perf. pass. ptc. acc. pl. masc.
{6.A.1.b} . . . . καθαίρω G2508
κεκάθικε   verb, perf. act. indic. 3 pers. sg.
{5.A.1.c} . . . . καθίζω G2523
κεκάθικεν   verb, perf. act. indic. 3 pers. sg.
{5.A.1.c} . . . . id.
κεκαλυμμένον   vbl., perf. pass. ptc. nom. sg. neut.
{6.A.1.b} . . . . καλύπτω G2572
κεκαυμένῳ   vbl., perf. pass. ptc. dat. sg. neut.
{6.A.1.b} . . . . καίω G2545
κεκαυστηριασμένων   vbl., perf. pass. ptc. gen. pl.
masc. {6.A.1.b} . . . . καυτηριάζω G2743
κεκαυτηριασμένων   vbl., perf. pass. ptc. gen.
pl. masc. {6.A.1.b} . . . . id.
κεκαύχημαι   verb, perf. mid./pass. indic. 1 pers.
sg. {5.A.1} . . . . καυχάομαι G2744
κεκένωται   verb, perf. pass. indic. 3 pers. sg.
{5.A.1} . . . . κενόω G2758
κεκερασμένου   vbl., perf. pass. ptc. gen. sg. masc.
{6.A.3} . . . . κεράννυμι G2767
κεκλεισμένον   vbl., perf. pass. ptc. acc. sg. neut.
{6.A.1.b} . . . . κλείω G2808
κεκλεισμένων   vbl., perf. pass. ptc. gen. pl.
fem. {6.A.1.b} . . . . id.
κέκλεισται   verb, perf. pass. indic. 3 pers. sg.
{5.A.1.f} . . . . id.
κέκληκεν   verb, perf. act. indic. 3 pers. sg.
{5.A.1} . . . . καλέω G2564
κεκληκότι   vbl., perf. act. ptc. dat. sg. masc. {6.A.2} .id.
κεκληκώς   vbl., perf. act. ptc. nom. sg. masc.
{6.A.2} . . . . id.
κεκλημένοι   vbl., perf. pass. ptc. nom. pl. masc.
{6.A.2} . . . . id.
κεκλημένοις   vbl., perf. pass. ptc. dat. pl. masc.
{6.A.2} . . . . id.
κεκλημένος   vbl., perf. pass. ptc. nom. sg.
masc. {6.A.2} . . . . id.
κεκλημένους   vbl., perf. pass. ptc. acc. pl. masc.
{6.A.2} . . . . id.
κεκλημένων   vbl., perf. pass. ptc. gen. pl. masc.
{6.A.2} . . . . id.
κεκληρονόμηκεν   verb, perf. act. indic. 3 pers. sg.
{5.A.1} . . . . κληρονομέω G2816
κέκληται   verb, perf. pass. indic. 3 pers. sg.
{5.A.1} . . . . καλέω G2564
κέκλικεν   verb, perf. act. indic. 3 pers. sg.
{5.A.1.c} . . . . κλίνω G2827
κέκμηκας   verb, perf. act. indic. 2 pers. sg.
{5.A.1.c} . . . . κάμνω G2577
κεκοιμημένων   vbl., perf. pass. ptc. gen. pl. masc.
{6.A.2} . . . . κοιμάω G2837
κεκοίμηται   verb, perf. pass. indic. 3 pers. sg.
{5.A.1} . . . . id.
κεκοίνωκε   verb, perf. act. indic. 3 pers. sg.
{5.A.1} . . . . κοινόω G2840

κεκοίνωκεν   verb, perf. act. indic. 3 pers. sg.
{5.A.1} . . . . id.
κεκοινωμένους   vbl., perf. pass. ptc. acc. pl.
masc. {6.A.2} . . . . id.
κεκοινώνηκε   verb, perf. act. indic. 3 pers. sg.
{5.A.1} . . . . κοινωνέω G2841
κεκοινώνηκεν   verb, perf. act. indic. 3 pers. sg.
{5.A.1} . . . . id.
κεκονιαμένε   vbl., perf. pass. ptc. voc. sg. masc.
{6.A.2} . . . . κονιάω G2867
κεκονιαμένοις   vbl., perf. pass. ptc. dat. pl.
masc. {6.A.2} . . . . id.
κεκοπίακα   verb, perf. act. indic. 1 pers. sg.
{5.A.1} . . . . κοπιάω G2872
κεκοπίακας   verb, perf. act. indic. 2 pers. sg.
{5.A.1} . . . . id.
κεκοπιάκασι   verb, perf. act. indic. 3 pers. pl.
{5.A.1} . . . . id.
κεκοπιάκασιν   verb, perf. act. indic. 3 pers. pl.
{5.A.1} . . . . id.
κεκοπιάκατε   verb, perf. act. indic. 2 pers. pl.
{5.A.1} . . . . id.
κεκοπίακες   verb, perf. act. indic. 2 pers. sg.
{5.A.1} . . . . id.
κεκοπιακώς   vbl., perf. act. ptc. nom. sg. masc.
{6.A.2} . . . . id.
κεκορεσμένοι   vbl., perf. pass. ptc. nom. pl. masc.
{6.A.3} . . . . κορέννυμι G2880
κεκοσμημένην   vbl., perf. pass. ptc. acc. sg. fem.
{6.A.2} . . . . κοσμέω G2885
κεκοσμημένοι   vbl., perf. pass. ptc. nom. pl.
masc. {6.A.2} . . . . id.
κεκοσμημένον   vbl., perf. pass. ptc. acc. sg.
masc. {6.A.2} . . . . id.
κεκόσμηται   verb, perf. pass. indic. 3 pers. sg.
{5.A.1} . . . . id.
κέκραγε   verb, ²perf. act. indic. 3 pers. sg.
{5.A.1.c} . . . . κράζω G2896
κέκραγεν   verb, ²perf. act. indic. 3 pers. sg.
{5.A.1.c} . . . . id.
κεκράξονται   verb, fut. mid. indic. 3 pers. pl.
{5.A.1.d} . . . . id.
κεκρατηκέναι   vbl., perf. act. inf. {6.B.1} . . κρατέω G2902
κεκράτηνται   verb, perf. pass. indic. 3 pers. pl.
{5.A.1} . . . . id.
κέκρικα   verb, perf. act. indic. 1 pers. sg.
{5.A.1.c} . . . . κρίνω G2919
κεκρίκατε   verb, perf. act. indic. 2 pers. pl.
{5.A.1.c} . . . . id.
κέκρικει   verb, plu. act. indic. 3 pers. sg.
{5.A.1.b} . . . . id.
κέκρικεν   verb, perf. act. indic. 3 pers. sg.
{5.A.1.c} . . . . id.
κεκριμένα   vbl., perf. pass. ptc. acc. pl. neut.
{6.A.1.b} . . . . id.
κέκριται   verb, perf. pass. indic. 3 pers. sg.
{5.A.1.f} . . . . id.
κεκρυμμένα   vbl., perf. pass. ptc. acc. pl. neut.
{6.A.1.b} . . . . κρύπτω G2928

κεκρυμμένον   vbl., perf. pass. ptc. nom. sg.
neut. {6.A.1.b} . . . . id.
κεκρυμμένος   vbl., perf. pass. ptc. nom. sg.
masc. {6.A.1.b} . . . . id.
κεκρυμμένου   vbl., perf. pass. ptc. gen. sg.
neut. {6.A.1.b} . . . . id.
κεκρυμμένῳ   vbl., perf. pass. ptc. dat. sg. masc.
{6.A.1.b} . . . . id.
κέκρυπται   verb, perf. pass. indic. 3 pers. sg.
{5.A.1.f} . . . . id.
κεκυρωμένην   vbl., perf. pass. ptc. acc. sg. fem.
{6.A.2} . . . . κυρόω *G2964*
κελεύεις   verb, pres. act. indic. 2 pers. sg.
{5.A.1.a} . . . . κελεύω *G2753*
κελεύσαντες   vbl., aor. act. ptc. nom. pl. masc.
{6.A.1.a} . . . . id.
κελεύσαντος   vbl., aor. act. ptc. gen. sg. masc.
{6.A.1.a} . . . . id.
κελεύσας   vbl., aor. act. ptc. nom. sg. masc.
{6.A.1.a} . . . . id.
G2752 **κέλευσμα**, -ατος, τό   *a word of command, a
call.*
κελεύσματι   noun, dat. sg. neut. {2.C} . . κέλευσμα *G2752*
κέλευσον   verb, aor. act. impv. 2 pers. sg.
{5.D.1} . . . . κελεύω *G2753*
G2753 **κελεύω**   *I command, I order.*
κενά   adj., acc. pl. neut. {3.A} . . . . .κενός *G2756*
κενέ   adj., voc. sg. masc. {3.A} . . . . id.
κενή   adj., nom. sg. fem. {3.A} . . . . id.
κενῆς   adj., gen. sg. fem. {3.A} . . . . id.
G2754 **κενοδοξία**, -ας, ἡ   *vainglory.*
κενοδοξίαν   noun, acc. sg. fem. {2.A} . .κενοδοξία *G2754*
κενόδοξοι   adj., nom. pl. masc. {3.C} . . .κενόδοξος *G2755*
G2755 **κενόδοξος**, -ον   *vainglorious.*
κενοῖς   adj., dat. pl. masc. {3.A} . . . . .κενός *G2756*
κενόν   adj., acc. sg. masc. {3.A} . . . . id.
κενόν   adj., acc. sg. neut. {3.A} . . . . id.
κενόν   adj., nom. sg. neut. {3.A} . . . . id.
G2756 **κενός**, -ή, -όν   (1) *empty;* (2) met. *empty* (in
moral content), *vain, ineffective, foolish, worthless;* εἰς κενόν, *in vain, to no purpose;* (3) *false,
unreal, pretentious, hollow,* Eph 5:6; Col 2:8; Jas
2:20.
κενός   adj., nom. sg. masc. {3.A} . . . . .κενός *G2756*
κενούς   adj., acc. pl. masc. {3.A} . . . . id.
G2757 **κενοφωνία**, -ας, ἡ   *a worthless utterance.*
κενοφωνίας   noun, acc. pl. fem. {2.A} . . κενοφωνία *G2757*
G2758 **κενόω**   (1) *I empty,* Phil 2:7; (2) *I deprive of
content; make unreal.*
κέντρα   noun, acc. pl. neut. {2.B} . . . . .κέντρον *G2759*
G2759 **κέντρον**, -ου, τό   *a goad.*
κέντρον   noun, nom. sg. neut. {2.B} . . . . . .κέντρον *G2759*
G2760 **κεντυρίων**, -ωνος, ὁ   *a centurion,* an officer
commanding about a hundred infantry in the
Roman army (Lat., = Gk. ἑκατοντάρχης).
κεντυρίων   noun, nom. sg. masc. {2.C} .κεντυρίων *G2760*
κεντυρίωνα   noun, acc. sg. masc. {2.C} . . . . . . id.
κεντυρίωνος   noun, gen. sg. masc. {2.C} . . . . . . id.
Κεγχρεαῖς   noun prop., dat. pl. fem. {2.A;
2.D} . . . . .Κεγχρεαί *G2747*

κενωθῇ   verb, aor. pass. subjunc. 3 pers. sg.
{5.B.1} . . . . κενόω *G2758*
G2761 **κενῶς**   adv., *falsely.*
κενῶς   adv. {3.F} . . . . κενῶς *G2761*
κενώσει   verb, fut. act. indic. 3 pers. sg.
{5.A.1} . . . . κενόω *G2758*
κενώσῃ   verb, aor. act. subjunc. 3 pers. sg.
{5.B.1} . . . . id.
G2762 **κεραία** (κεραία), -ας, ἡ   *a little hook, an
apostrophe* on letters of the alphabet, distinguishing them from other like letters, or *a
separation stroke* between letters.
κεραία   noun, nom. sg. fem. {2.A} . . . . . . κεραία *G2762*
κεραίαν   noun, acc. sg. fem. {2.A} . . . . id.
G2763 **κεραμεύς**, -έως, ὁ   *a potter.*
κεραμεύς   noun, nom. sg. masc. {2.C} . . κεραμεύς *G2763*
κεραμέως   noun, gen. sg. masc. {2.C} . . . . id.
κεραμικά   adj., nom. pl. neut. {3.A} . . . .κεραμικός *G2764*
G2764 **κεραμικός**, -ή, -όν   *of clay, made by a potter.*
G2765 **κεράμιον**, -ου, τό   *an earthenware pitcher.*
κεράμιον   noun, acc. sg. neut. {2.B} . . . . κεράμιον *G2765*
G2766 **κέραμος**, -ου, ὁ   *a tile;* οἱ κέραμοι, practically
the roof.
κεράμων   noun, gen. pl. masc. {2.B} . . . . κέραμος *G2766*
G2767 **κεράννυμι**   *I mix.*
G2768 **κέρας**, -ατος, τό   (1) *a horn;* (2) as a symbol
of strength, κέρας σωτηρίας, *a powerful
support of salvation,* Luke 1:69; (3) a dwarfed
column set upon or at the corner of an altar,
with ritual significance, Rev 9:13.
κέρας   noun, acc. sg. neut. {2.C} . . . . κέρας *G2768*
κεράσατε   verb, aor. act. impv. 2 pers. pl.
{5.D.3} . . . . κεράννυμι *G2767*
κέρατα   noun, acc. pl. neut. {2.C} . . . . κέρας *G2768*
κέρατα   noun, nom. pl. neut. {2.C} . . . . id.
G2769 **κεράτιον**, -ου, τό   *a husk (pod) of the carob*
(siliqua graeca).
κερατίων   noun, gen. pl. neut. {2.B} . . . . .κεράτιον *G2769*
κεράτων   noun, gen. pl. neut. {2.C} . . . . κέρας *G2768*
G2770 **κερδαίνω**   *I gain;* ὕβριν καὶ ζημίαν, *I gain
injury and loss,* i.e., I gain by shunning injury
and loss, I do not suffer (I am spared) injury
and loss, Acts 27:21.
κερδανῶ   verb, aor. act. subjunc. 1 pers. sg.
{5.B.1} . . . . κερδαίνω *G2770*
κερδάνω   verb, aor. act. subjunc. 1 pers. sg.
{5.B.1} . . . . id.
κέρδη   noun, nom. pl. neut. {2.C} . . . . .κέρδος *G2771*
κερδηθήσονται   verb, fut. pass. indic. 3 pers. pl.
{5.A.1.d} . . . . κερδαίνω *G2770*
κερδηθήσωνται   verb, aor. pass. subjunc.
3 pers. pl. {5.B.1} . . . . id.
κερδῆσαι   vbl., aor. act. inf. {6.B.1} . . . . id.
κερδήσας   vbl., aor. act. ptc. nom. sg. masc.
{6.A.1.a} . . . . id.
κερδήσῃ   verb, aor. act. subjunc. 3 pers. sg. {5.B.1} id.
κερδήσομεν   verb, fut. act. indic. 1 pers. pl.
{5.A.1.a} . . . . id.
κερδήσω   verb, aor. act. subjunc. 1 pers. sg.
{5.B.1} . . . . id.

κερδήσωμεν   verb, aor. act. subjunc. 1 pers. pl.
     {5.B.1} . . . . id.

G2771   **κέρδος**, -ους, τό   *gain.*
     κέρδος   noun, nom. sg. neut. {2.C} . . . . κέρδος *G2771*
     κέρδους   noun, gen. sg. neut. {2.C}. . . . . id.
     κερέα   noun, nom. sg. fem. {2.A} . . . . κεραία *G2762*
     κερέαν   noun, acc. sg. fem. {2.A} . . . . id.

G2772   **κέρμα**, -ατος, τό   *a small coin; pl. small change.*
     κέρμα   noun, acc. sg. neut. {2.C} . . . . κέρμα *G2772*
     κέρματα   noun, acc. pl. neut. {2.C}. . . . . id.
     κερματιστάς   noun, acc. pl. masc.
        {2.A} . . . . κερματιστής *G2773*

G2773   **κερματιστής**, -ου, ὁ   *a moneychanger,* prop-
     erly *a changer of* large into smaller *coins.*
     κεφαλαί   noun, nom. pl. fem. {2.A} . . . . . κεφαλή *G2776*

G2774   **κεφάλαιον**, -ου, τό   (1) *the chief matter, the*
     main point, Heb 8:1; (2) *a sum* of money, Acts
     22:28.
     κεφάλαιον   noun, nom. sg. neut. {2.B} κεφάλαιον *G2774*
     κεφαλαίου   noun, gen. sg. neut. {2.B} . . . . id.

G2775   **κεφαλαιόω** (κεφαλιόω)   *a roll* (lit. *little head,*
     then the *knob* at the end of the wooden core of
     a roll of papyrus).
     κεφαλάς   noun, acc. pl. fem. {2.A} . . . . . . κεφαλή *G2776*

G2776   **κεφαλή**, -ῆς, ἡ   (1) *head,* κατὰ κεφαλῆς
     ἔχων, see κατά; (2) met. κεφαλὴ γωνίας, *a*
     corner stone, uniting two walls, Mark 12:10
     and parallels; *head, ruler, lord,* 1 Cor 11:3, etc.
     κεφαλή   noun, nom. sg. fem. {2.A} . . . . . . κεφαλή *G2776*
     κεφαλῇ   noun, dat. sg. fem. {2.A} . . . . id.
     κεφαλήν   noun, acc. sg. fem. {2.A} . . . . id.
     κεφαλῆς   noun, gen. sg. fem. {2.A} . . . . id.
     κεφαλίδι   noun, dat. sg. fem. {2.C} . . . . κεφαλίς *G2777*

G2777   **κεφαλίς**, -ίδος, ἡ   *a roll* (lit. *little head,* then
     the *knob* at the end of the wooden core of a
     roll of papyrus).
     κεφαλῶν   noun, gen. pl. fem. {2.A} . . . . . κεφαλή *G2776*
     κεχάρισμαι   verb, perf. mid./pass. indic. 1 pers. sg.
        {5.A.1.f}. . . . . χαρίζομαι *G5483*
     κεχάρισται   verb, perf. mid./pass. indic. 3 pers.
        sg. {5.A.1.f} . . . . id.
     κεχαριτωμένη   vbl., perf. pass. ptc. nom. sg. fem.
        {6.A.2} . . . . χαριτόω *G5487*
     κέχρημαι   verb, perf. mid./pass. indic. 1 pers. sg.
        {5.A.1} . . . . χράομαι *G5530*
     κεχρηματισμένον   vbl., perf. pass. ptc. nom. sg.
        neut. {6.A.1.b} . . . . χρηματίζω *G5537*
     κεχρημάτισται   verb, perf. pass. indic. 3 pers.
        sg. {5.A.1.f} . . . . id.
     κεχρυσωμένη   vbl., perf. pass. ptc. nom. sg. fem.
        {6.A.2} . . . . χρυσόω *G5558*
     κεχωρισμένος   vbl., perf. pass. ptc. nom. sg. masc.
        {6.A.1.b} . . . . χωρίζω *G5563*

G5392†‡   **κημόω**   *I muzzle* (from κημός, *a muzzle*). Var.
     for φιμόω, 1 Cor 9:9.
     κημώσεις   verb, fut. act. indic. 2 pers. sg.
        {5.A.1} . . . . κημόω *G5392†‡*
     κῆνσον   noun, acc. sg. masc. {2.B} . . . . . κῆνσος *G2778*

G2778   **κῆνσος**, -ου, ὁ   *poll tax* (Lat. *census*).
     κήνσου   noun, gen. sg. masc. {2.B} . . . . . . κῆνσος *G2778*

     κῆπον   noun, acc. sg. masc. {2.B} . . . . κῆπος *G2779*

G2779   **κῆπος**, -ου, ὁ   *a garden.*
     κῆπος   noun, nom. sg. masc. {2.B} . . . . κῆπος *G2779*

G2780   **κηπουρός**, -οῦ, ὁ   *keeper of a garden.*
     κηπουρός   noun, nom. sg. masc. {2.B} . . κηπουρός *G2780*
     κήπῳ   noun, dat. sg. masc. {2.B} . . . . κῆπος *G2779*

G2781   **κηρίον**, -ου, τό   *a honeycomb.*
     κηρίου   noun, gen. sg. neut. {2.B}. . . . . . . κηρίον *G2781*

G2782   **κήρυγμα**, -ατος, τό   *a proclamation.*
     κήρυγμα   noun, acc. sg. neut. {2.C} . . . . κήρυγμα *G2782*
     κήρυγμα   noun, nom. sg. neut. {2.C} . . . . id.
     κηρύγματι   noun, dat. sg. neut. {2.C} . . . . id.
     κηρύγματος   noun, gen. sg. neut. {2.C} . . . . . . id.
     κήρυκα   noun, acc. sg. masc. {2.C} . . . . κῆρυξ *G2783*

G2783   **κῆρυξ**, -υκος, ὁ   *a herald, proclaimer.*
     κῆρυξ   noun, nom. sg. masc. {2.C} . . . . κῆρυξ *G2783*
     κηρύξαι   vbl., aor. act. inf. {6.B.1} . . . . . κηρύσσω *G2784*
     κηρύξας   vbl., aor. act. ptc. nom. sg. masc.
        {6.A.1.a} . . . . id.
     κηρύξατε   verb, aor. act. impv. 2 pers. pl. {5.D.1} id.
     κήρυξον   verb, aor. act. impv. 2 pers. sg. {5.D.1}. id.
     κηρύξουσιν   verb, fut. act. indic. 3 pers. pl.
        {5.A.1.a} . . . . id.
     κηρύξω   verb, aor. act. subjunc. 1 pers. sg.
        {5.B.1} . . . . id.
     κηρύξωσιν   verb, aor. act. subjunc. 3 pers. pl.
        {5.B.1} . . . . id.
     κηρύσσει   verb, pres. act. indic. 3 pers. sg.
        {5.A.1.a} . . . . id.
     κηρύσσειν   vbl., pres. act. inf. {6.B.1} . . . . id.
     κηρύσσεται   verb, pres. pass. indic. 3 pers. sg.
        {5.A.1.d} . . . . id.
     κηρύσσετε   verb, pres. act. impv. 2 pers. pl.
        {5.D.1} . . . . id.
     κηρύσσομεν   verb, pres. act. indic. 1 pers. pl.
        {5.A.1.a} . . . . id.
     κηρύσσοντα   vbl., pres. act. ptc. acc. sg. masc.
        {6.A.1} . . . . id.
     κηρύσσοντας   vbl., pres. act. ptc. acc. pl. masc.
        {6.A.1} . . . . id.
     κηρύσσοντος   vbl., pres. act. ptc. gen. sg. masc.
        {6.A.1} . . . . id.
     κηρύσσουσιν   verb, pres. act. indic. 3 pers. pl.
        {5.A.1.a} . . . . id.

G2784   **κηρύσσω**   *I proclaim, herald, preach.*
     κηρύσσω   verb, pres. act. indic. 1 pers. sg.
        {5.A.1.a} . . . . κηρύσσω *G2784*
     κηρύσσων   vbl., pres. act. ptc. nom. sg. masc.
        {6.A.1} . . . . id.
     κηρυχθείς   vbl., aor. pass. ptc. nom. sg. masc.
        {6.A.1.a} . . . . id.
     κηρυχθέντος   vbl., aor. pass. ptc. gen. sg. neut.
        {6.A.1.a} . . . . id.
     κηρυχθῇ   verb, aor. pass. subjunc. 3 pers. sg.
        {5.B.1} . . . . id.
     κηρυχθῆναι   vbl., aor. pass. inf. {6.B.1} . . . . . . id.
     κηρυχθήσεται   verb, fut. pass. indic. 3 pers. sg.
        {5.A.1.d} . . . . id.

G2785   **κῆτος**, -ους, τό   *a sea monster, a huge sea fish.*
     κήτους   noun, gen. sg. neut. {2.C} . . . . κῆτος *G2785*

Κηφᾶ   noun prop., gen. sg. masc. {2.A; 2.D}.Κηφᾶς *G2786*
Κηφᾶ   noun prop., dat. sg. masc. {2.A; 2.D} . . . . id.
Κηφᾶν   noun prop., acc. sg. masc. {2.A; 2.D} . . . id.
G2786 **Κηφᾶς,** -ᾶ, ὁ   *Cephas* (Aram. for *rock*), the new
    name given to Simon, the disciple.
Κηφᾶς   noun prop., nom. sg. masc. {2.A;
    2.D}. . . . . .Κηφᾶς *G2786*
κιβωτόν   noun, acc. sg. fem. {2.B} . . . . .κιβωτός *G2787*
G2787 **κιβωτός,** -οῦ, ἡ   (properly *a wooden box*),
    hence, *the Ark*, in which Noah sailed.
κιβωτός   noun, nom. sg. fem. {2.B} . . . .κιβωτός *G2787*
κιβωτοῦ   noun, gen. sg. fem. {2.B} . . . . id.
G2788 **κιθάρα,** -ας, ἡ   *a harp*.
κιθάρα   noun, nom. sg. fem. {2.A} . . . . . . κιθάρα *G2788*
κιθάραις   noun, dat. pl. fem. {2.A}. . . . . id.
κιθάραν   noun, acc. sg. fem. {2.A} . . . . id.
κιθάρας   noun, acc. pl. fem. {2.A} . . . . id.
κιθαριζόμενον   vbl., pres. pass. ptc. nom. sg. neut.
    {6.A.1}. . . . . .κιθαρίζω *G2789*
κιθαριζόντων   vbl., pres. act. ptc. gen. pl.
    masc. {6.A.1}. id.
G2789 **κιθαρίζω**   intrans. and trans., *I play on the*
    harp, I harp, with acc. of the tune.
G2790 **κιθαρῳδός,** -οῦ, ὁ   *a harpist*.
κιθαρῳδῶν   noun, gen. pl. masc. {2.B}. κιθαρῳδός *G2790*
G2791 **Κιλικία,** -ας, ἡ   *Cilicia*, a Roman province be-
    tween the Taurus range of mountains and the
    coast in the southeast corner of Asia Minor,
    linked up with the province of Syria.
Κιλικίαν   noun prop., acc. sg. fem. {2.A;
    2.D}. . . . . .Κιλικία *G2791*
Κιλικίας   noun prop., gen. sg. fem. {2.A; 2.D} . . id.
G2792 **κινάμωμον** (κιννάμωμον), -ου, τό   *cinna-*
    mon (a Semitic word).
κινάμωμον   noun, acc. sg. neut. {2.B} . κινάμωμον *G2792*
κινδυνεύει   verb, pres. act. indic. 3 pers. sg.
    {5.A.1.a} . . . . κινδυνεύω *G2793*
κινδυνεύομεν   verb, pres. act. indic. 1 pers. pl.
    {5.A.1.a} . . . . id.
G2793 **κινδυνεύω**   *I am in danger,* sometimes with
    inf. *of . . .*
κινδύνοις   noun, dat. pl. masc. {2.B} . . . .κίνδυνος *G2794*
G2794 **κίνδυνος,** -ου, ὁ   *danger, peril, risk.*
κίνδυνος   noun, nom. sg. masc. {2.B}. . . .κίνδυνος *G2794*
G2795 **κινέω**   trans., *I move; I stir, excite.*
κινῆσαι   vbl., aor. act. inf. {6.B.1}. . . . . . . .κινέω *G2795*
κίνησιν   noun, acc. sg. fem. {2.C}. . . . . . .κίνησις *G2796*
G2796 **κίνησις,** -εως, ἡ   *moving, stirring.*
κινήσω   verb, fut. act. indic. 1 pers. sg.
    {5.A.1} . . . . .κινέω *G2795*
κινάμωμον   noun, acc. sg. neut.
    {2.B} . . . . κινάμωμον *G2792*
κινούμεθα   verb, pres. pass. indic. 1 pers. pl.
    {5.A.2}. . . . . .κινέω *G2795*
κινοῦντα   vbl., pres. act. ptc. acc. sg. masc.
    {6.A.2}. . . . . id.
κινοῦντες   vbl., pres. act. ptc. nom. pl. masc.
    {6.A.2}. . . . . id.
G2797 **Κίς,** Κείς, ὁ   *Kish,* father of Saul, king of Israel
    (Heb.).

Κίς   noun prop.. . . . . .Κίς *G2797*
G5531†‡ **κίχρημι**   *I lend.* Var. for χράω, Luke 11:5.
κλάδοι   noun, nom. pl. masc. {2.B} . . . . . . κλάδος *G2798*
κλάδοις   noun, dat. pl. masc. {2.B}. . . . . id.
G2798 **κλάδος,** -ου, ὁ   *a branch* of a tree.
κλάδος   noun, nom. sg. masc. {2.B} . . . . . κλάδος *G2798*
κλάδους   noun, acc. pl. masc. {2.B} . . . . id.
κλάδων   noun, gen. pl. masc. {2.B}. . . . . id.
κλαῖε   verb, pres. act. impv. 2 pers. sg. {5.D.1}κλαίω *G2799*
κλαίειν   vbl., pres. act. inf. {6.B.1}. . . . . id.
κλαίεις   verb, pres. act. indic. 2 pers. sg. {5.A.1.a}id.
κλαίετε   verb, pres. act. impv. 2 pers. pl. {5.D.1} . id.
κλαίετε   verb, pres. act. indic. 2 pers. pl.
    {5.A.1.a} . . . . id.
κλαίοντας   vbl., pres. act. ptc. acc. pl. masc.
    {6.A.1}. . . . . id.
κλαίοντες   vbl., pres. act. ptc. nom. pl. masc.
    {6.A.1}. . . . . id.
κλαιόντων   vbl., pres. act. ptc. gen. pl. masc.
    {6.A.1}. . . . . id.
κλαίουσα   vbl., pres. act. ptc. nom. sg. fem.
    {6.A.1}. . . . . id.
κλαίουσαι   vbl., pres. act. ptc. nom. pl. fem.
    {6.A.1}. . . . . id.
κλαίουσαν   vbl., pres. act. ptc. acc. sg. fem.
    {6.A.1}. . . . . id.
κλαίουσι   verb, pres. act. indic. 3 pers. pl.
    {5.A.1.a} . . . . id.
κλαίουσι   vbl., pres. act. ptc. dat. pl. masc.
    {6.A.1}. . . . . id.
κλαίουσιν   verb, pres. act. indic. 3 pers. pl.
    {5.A.1.a} . . . . id.
κλαίουσιν   vbl., pres. act. ptc. dat. pl. masc.
    {6.A.1}. . . . . id.
G2799 **κλαίω**   *I weep;* with acc. or ἐπί with acc. *I weep*
    for, mourn.
κλαίων   vbl., pres. act. ptc. nom. sg. masc.
    {6.A.1}. . . . . .κλαίω *G2799*
κλάσαι   vbl., aor. act. inf. {6.B.1} . . . . .κλάω *G2806*
κλάσας   vbl., aor. act. ptc. nom. sg. masc. {6.A.2}id.
κλάσει   noun, dat. sg. fem. {2.C} . . . . κλάσις *G2800*
G2800 **κλάσις,** -εως, ἡ   *breaking.*
G2801 **κλάσμα,** -ατος, τό   *a fragment.*
κλάσματα   noun, acc. pl. neut. {2.C}. . . . .κλάσμα *G2801*
κλασμάτων   noun, gen. pl. neut. {2.C}. . . . . . . id.
G2802 **Κλαῦδα** (Καῦδα)   *Clauda* or *Cauda* (mod.
    Gaudho), an island twenty-three miles south
    of the western end of Crete (var. Γαύδη).
Κλαύδην   noun prop., acc. sg. fem. {2.A;
    2.D}. . . . . .Κλαῦδα *G2802*
G2803 **Κλαυδία,** -ας, ἡ   *Claudia,* a Christian woman
    in Rome; if historical, probably a freedwoman
    of the imperial household.
Κλαυδία   noun prop., nom. sg. fem. {2.A;
    2.D}. . . . . .Κλαυδία *G2803*
Κλαύδιον   noun prop., acc. sg. masc. {2.B;
    2.D}. . . . . .Κλαύδιος *G2804*
G2804 **Κλαύδιος,** -ου, ὁ   (1) *Claudius,* the fourth
    of the Roman Emperors, Tiberius Claudius
    Caesar Augustus Germanicus, who ruled from

41–54 A.D.; (2) *Claudius* Lysias, a tribune at Jerusalem.

Κλαύδιος   noun prop., nom. sg. masc. {2.B; 2.D}. . . . . Κλαύδιος *G2804*

Κλαυδίου   noun prop., gen. sg. masc. {2.B; 2.D} id.

G2805 **κλαυθμός**, -οῦ, ὁ   *weeping.*

κλαυθμός   noun, nom. sg. masc. {2.B}. . κλαυθμός *G2805*

κλαύσατε   verb, aor. act. impv. 2 pers. pl. {5.D.1}. . . . . κλαίω *G2799*

κλαύσετε   verb, fut. act. indic. 2 pers. pl. {5.A.1.a} . . . . id.

κλαύσῃ   verb, aor. act. subjunc. 3 pers. sg. {5.B.1} . id.

κλαύσονται   verb, fut. mid. indic. 3 pers. pl. {5.A.1.d} . . . . id.

κλαύσουσιν   verb, fut. act. indic. 3 pers. pl. {5.A.1.a} . . . . id.

G2806 **κλάω**   *I break.*

κλεῖδα   noun, acc. sg. fem. {2.C}. . . . . κλείς *G2807*

κλεῖδας   noun, acc. pl. fem. {2.C}. . . . . id.

κλείει   verb, pres. act. indic. 3 pers. sg. {5.A.1.a} . . . . κλείω *G2808*

κλείετε   verb, pres. act. indic. 2 pers. pl. {5.A.1.a} id.

κλεῖν   noun, acc. sg. fem. {2.C}. . . . . κλείς *G2807*

G2807 **κλείς**, κλειδός, ἡ   *a key.*

κλείς   noun, acc. pl. fem. {2.C} . . . . κλείς *G2807*

κλείς   noun, nom. sg. fem. {2.C} . . . . id.

κλεῖς   noun, acc. pl. fem. {2.C} . . . . id.

κλεῖσαι   vbl., aor. act. inf. {6.B.1} . . . . .κλείω *G2808*

κλείσας   vbl., aor. act. ptc. nom. sg. masc. {6.A.1.a} . . . . id.

κλείσει   verb, fut. act. indic. 3 pers. sg. {5.A.1.a}. id.

κλείσῃ   verb, aor. act. subjunc. 3 pers. sg. {5.B.1} id.

κλεισθῶσιν   verb, aor. pass. subjunc. 3 pers. pl. {5.B.1} . . . . id.

G2808 **κλείω**   *I shut.*

κλείων   vbl., pres. act. ptc. nom. sg. masc. {6.A.1} . . . . .κλείω *G2808*

G2809 **κλέμμα**, -ατος, τό   *a theft.*

κλεμμάτων   noun, gen. pl. neut. {2.C} . . . . κλέμμα *G2809*

G2810 **Κλεοπᾶς**, -ᾶ, ὁ   *Cleopas,* one of the two companions of the risen Jesus from Jerusalem to Emmaus.

Κλεοπᾶς   noun prop., nom. sg. masc. {2.A; 2.D}. . . . . Κλεοπᾶς *G2810*

Κλεόπας   noun prop., nom. sg. masc. {2.A; 2.D} id.

G2811 **κλέος**, -ους, τό   *glory, fame.*

κλέος   noun, nom. sg. neut. {2.C}. . . . . .κλέος *G2811*

κλέπται   noun, nom. pl. masc. {2.A}. . . . . .κλέπτης *G2812*

κλέπτας   noun, acc. pl. masc. {2.A} . . . . id.

κλέπτειν   vbl., pres. act. inf. {6.B.1} . . . κλέπτω *G2813*

κλέπτεις   verb, pres. act. indic. 2 pers. sg. {5.A.1.a} . . . . id.

κλεπτέτω   verb, pres. act. impv. 3 pers. sg. {5.D.1}. . . . . id.

G2812 **κλέπτης**, -ου, ὁ   *a thief.*

κλέπτης   noun, nom. sg. masc. {2.A} . . . . .κλέπτης *G2812*

κλέπτουσι   verb, pres. act. indic. 3 pers. pl. {5.A.1.a} . . . . κλέπτω *G2813*

κλέπτουσιν   verb, pres. act. indic. 3 pers. pl. {5.A.1.a} . . . . id.

G2813 **κλέπτω**   *I steal;* ὁ κλέπτων, *the stealer,* Eph 4:28.

κλέπτων   vbl., pres. act. ptc. nom. sg. masc. {6.A.1}. . . . . κλέπτω *G2813*

κλέψεις   verb, fut. act. indic. 2 pers. sg. {5.A.1.a} id.

κλέψῃ   verb, aor. act. subjunc. 3 pers. sg. {5.B.1}. id.

κλέψῃς   verb, aor. act. subjunc. 2 pers. sg. {5.B.1}id.

κλέψωσιν   verb, aor. act. subjunc. 3 pers. pl. {5.B.1} . . . . id.

κληθείς   vbl., aor. pass. ptc. nom. sg. masc. {6.A.1.a.} . . . . .καλέω *G2564*

κληθέν   vbl., aor. pass. ptc. nom. sg. neut. {6.A.1.a.} . . . . id.

κληθέντος   vbl., aor. pass. ptc. gen. sg. masc. {6.A.1.a.} . . . . id.

κληθῆναι   vbl., aor. pass. inf. {6.B.1} . . . . id.

κληθῇς   verb, aor. pass. subjunc. 2 pers. sg. {5.B.1} . . . . id.

κληθήσεται   verb, fut. pass. indic. 3 pers. sg. {5.A.1} . . . . id.

κληθήσῃ   verb, fut. pass. indic. 2 pers. sg. {5.A.1} . . . . id.

κληθήσονται   verb, fut. pass. indic. 3 pers. pl. {5.A.1} . . . . id.

κληθῆτε   verb, aor. pass. subjunc. 2 pers. pl. {5.B.1} . . . . id.

κληθῶμεν   verb, aor. pass. subjunc. 1 pers. pl. {5.B.1} . . . . id.

G2814 **κλῆμα**, -ατος, τό   *a branch.*

κλῆμα   noun, acc. sg. neut. {2.C} . . . . .κλῆμα *G2814*

κλῆμα   noun, nom. sg. neut. {2.C} . . . . id.

κλήματα   noun, nom. pl. neut. {2.C} . . . . id.

Κλήμεντος   noun prop., gen. sg. masc. {2.A; 2.D}. . . . . .Κλήμης *G2815*

G2815 **Κλήμης**, -εντος, ὁ   *Clement,* a fellow worker of Paul in Rome (Lat. = *Clemens*).

κλῆρον   noun, acc. sg. masc. {2.B} . . . . κλῆρος *G2819*

κληρονομεῖ   verb, pres. act. indic. 3 pers. sg. {5.A.2}. . . . . .κληρονομέω *G2816*

κληρονομεῖν   vbl., pres. act. inf. {6.B.2}. . . . . . . id.

G2816 **κληρονομέω**   *I inherit, I obtain (possess) by inheritance.*

κληρονομῆσαι   vbl., aor. act. inf. {6.B.1}. . . . . .κληρονομέω *G2816*

κληρονομήσατε   verb, aor. act. impv. 2 pers. pl. {5.D.1} . . . . id.

κληρονομήσει   verb, fut. act. indic. 3 pers. sg. {5.A.1} . . . . id.

κληρονομήσῃ   verb, aor. act. subjunc. 3 pers. sg. {5.B.1} . . . . id.

κληρονομήσητε   verb, aor. act. subjunc. 2 pers. pl. {5.B.1} . . . . id.

κληρονομήσουσι   verb, fut. act. indic. 3 pers. pl. {5.A.1} . . . . id.

κληρονομήσουσιν   verb, fut. act. indic. 3 pers. pl. {5.A.1} . . . . id.

κληρονομήσω   verb, aor. act. subjunc. 1 pers. sg. {5.B.1} . . . . id.

κληρονομήσω   verb, fut. act. indic. 1 pers. sg. {5.A.1}. . . . . id.

G2817 **κληρονομία**, -ας, ἡ   *an inheritance, an heritage,* regularly the gift of God to His chosen people, in OT the Promised Land, in NT a possession viewed in one sense as present, in another as future.
κληρονομία   noun, nom. sg. fem.
{2.A} . . . . κληρονομία G2817
κληρονομίαν   noun, acc. sg. fem. {2.A} . . . . . . id.
κληρονομίας   noun, gen. sg. fem. {2.A} . . . . . . id.
κληρονόμοι   noun, nom. pl. masc.
{2.B} . . . . κληρονόμος G2818
κληρονόμοις   noun, dat. pl. masc. {2.B} . . . . . . id.
κληρονόμον   noun, acc. sg. masc. {2.B} . . . . . . id.
G2818 **κληρονόμος**, -ου, ὁ   *an heir, an inheritor;* cf. κληρονομία.
κληρονόμος   noun, nom. sg. masc.
{2.B} . . . . κληρονόμος G2818
κληρονομούντων   vbl., pres. act. ptc. gen. pl.
masc. {6.A.2} . . . . κληρονομέω G2816
κληρονόμους   noun, acc. pl. masc.
{2.B} . . . . κληρονόμος G2818
G2819 **κλῆρος**, -ου, ὁ   (1) *a lot;* (2) *a portion* assigned, Acts 1:17; 8:21; 26:18; Col 1:12; hence, a portion of the people of God assigned to one's care, *a congregation,* 1 Pet 5:3.
κλῆρος   noun, nom. sg. masc. {2.B} . . . . . . κλῆρος G2819
κλήρου   noun, gen. sg. masc. {2.B} . . . . id.
κλήρους   noun, acc. pl. masc. {2.B} . . . . id.
G2820 **κληρόω**   lit. I choose by lot, I appoint by lot; hence, I assign; mid. I assign to myself, choose; pass. I am assigned, I am chosen as God's portion (κλῆρος), Eph 1:11.
κλήρων   noun, gen. pl. masc. {2.B} . . . . . . κλῆρος G2819
κλήσει   noun, dat. sg. fem. {2.C} . . . . κλῆσις G2821
κλήσεως   noun, gen. sg. fem. {2.C} . . . . id.
κλῆσιν   noun, acc. sg. fem. {2.C} . . . . id.
G2821 **κλῆσις**, -εως, ἡ   *a calling, invitation, summons* of God to the religious life; sometimes, e.g., Phil 3:14; 2 Thess 1:11; Heb 3:1, it may include a reference to the final issue of this invitation.
κλῆσις   noun, nom. sg. fem. {2.C} . . . . κλῆσις G2821
κλητοί   adj., nom. pl. masc. {3.A} . . . . . . κλητός G2822
κλητοῖς   adj., dat. pl. masc. {3.A} . . . . id.
G2822 **κλητός**, -ή, -όν   *called, invited, summoned* by God to the religious life.
κλητός   adj., nom. sg. masc. {3.A} . . . . . . κλητός G2822
κλίβανον   noun, acc. sg. masc. {2.B} . . . κλίβανος G2823
G2823 **κλίβανος**, -ου, ὁ   *an oven, a furnace.*
G2824 **κλίμα**, -ατος, τό   a small geographical division, district, or *territory,* a portion of a χώρα (q.v.).
κλίμασι   noun, dat. pl. neut. {2.C} . . . . κλίμα G2824
κλίμασιν   noun, dat. pl. neut. {2.C} . . . . id.
κλίματα   noun, acc. pl. neut. {2.C} . . . . id.
G2825†‡ **κλινάριον**, -ου, τό   *a couch or litter* of a sick person. Var. for κλίνη, Acts 5:15.
κλιναρίων   noun, gen. pl. neut. {2.B} . . κλινάριον G2825†‡
κλίνας   vbl., aor. act. ptc. nom. sg. masc.
{6.A.1.a} . . . . κλίνω G2827
κλίνειν   vbl., pres. act. inf. {6.B.1} . . . . id.

G2825 **κλίνη**, -ης, ἡ   *a couch, a bed,* alike a mere mat (e.g., Matt 9:2, 6), and a more elaborate structure (e.g., Mark 4:21); possibly *a bier* in Rev 2:22.
κλίνη   verb, pres. act. subjunc. 3 pers. sg.
{5.B.1} . . . . κλίνω G2827
κλίνην   noun, acc. sg. fem. {2.A} . . . . κλίνη G2825
κλίνης   noun, gen. sg. fem. {2.A} . . . . id.
G2826 **κλινίδιον**, -ου, τό   *a couch* or *litter* of a sick person.
κλινίδιον   noun, acc. sg. neut. {2.B} . . . . κλινίδιον G2826
κλινιδίῳ   noun, dat. sg. neut. {2.B} . . . . id.
κλινουσῶν   vbl., pres. act. ptc. gen. pl. fem.
{6.A.1} . . . . κλίνω G2827
G2827 **κλίνω**   (1) trans., (a) *I rest, recline* (even in John 19:30); (b) *I bend, incline;* (c) *I cause to give ground, I make to yield,* Heb 11:34; (2) intrans. of the day, *declines, approaches its end,* Luke 9:12; 24:29.
κλινῶν   noun, gen. pl. fem. {2.A} . . . . κλίνη G2825
G2828 **κλισία**, -ας, ἡ   properly *a dining couch;* hence, *a group of diners.*
κλισίας   noun, acc. pl. fem. {2.A} . . . . κλισία G2828
κλοπαί   noun, nom. pl. fem. {2.A} . . . . κλοπή G2829
G2829 **κλοπή**, -ῆς, ἡ   *thieving, theft.*
G2830 **κλύδων**, -ωνος, ὁ   *rough water, roughness of water;* κλύδωνι θαλάσσης *a rough sea,* Jas 1:6.
κλύδωνι   noun, dat. sg. masc. {2.C} . . . . . . κλύδων G2830
G2831 **κλυδωνίζομαι**   pass. *I am tossed as in a storm at sea.*
κλυδωνιζόμενοι   vbl., pres. mid./pass. ptc. nom.
pl. masc. {6.A.1} . . . . κλυδωνίζομαι G2831
κλῶμεν   verb, pres. act. indic. 1 pers. pl.
{5.A.2} . . . . κλάω G2806
κλώμενον   vbl., pres. pass. ptc. nom. sg. neut.
{6.A.2} . . . . id.
κλῶντες   vbl., pres. act. ptc. nom. pl. masc.
{6.A.2} . . . . id.
Κλωπᾶ   noun prop., gen. sg. masc. {2.A;
2.D} . . . . Κλωπᾶς G2832
G2832 **Κλωπᾶς**, -ᾶ, ὁ   *Clopas,* husband of one Mary, who stood by the cross.
κνηθόμενοι   vbl., pres. pass. ptc. nom. pl. masc.
{6.A.1} . . . . κνήθω G2833
G2833 **κνήθω**   *I rub, tickle;* κνηθόμενοι τὴν ἀκοήν, *with ears itching* with eagerness to hear pleasant things, 2 Tim 4:3.
Κνίδον   noun prop., acc. sg. fem. {2.B; 2.D} Κνίδος G2834
G2834 **Κνίδος**, -ου, ἡ   *Cnidus,* a town on the coast of Caria (southwest Asia Minor) near the island of Cos.
κοδράντην   noun, acc. sg. masc. {2.A} . κοδράντης G2835
G2835 **κοδράντης**, -ου, ὁ   *a quadrans,* the smallest Roman copper coin, a quarter of an *assarion,* the sixteenth part of a *sestertius.*
κοδράντης   noun, nom. sg. masc. {2.A} κοδράντης G2835
G2836 **κοιλία**, -ας, ἡ   *belly, abdomen,* a general term covering any organ in the abdomen, e.g., stomach, womb; ἐκ κοιλίας μητρός, *from birth.*

κοιλία   noun, nom. sg. fem. {2.A} . . . . . . .κοιλία *G2836*
κοιλίᾳ   noun, dat. sg. fem. {2.A}. . . . . id.
κοιλίαι   noun, nom. pl. fem. {2.A} . . . . id.
κοιλίαν   noun, acc. sg. fem. {2.A} . . . . id.
κοιλίας   noun, gen. sg. fem. {2.A} . . . . id.

G2837 **κοιμάω**   pass. *I am asleep, I fall asleep,* some-
    times of the sleep of death (e.g., Matt 27:52).
κοιμηθέντας   vbl., aor. pass. ptc. acc. pl. masc.
    {6.A.1.a.}. . . . . .κοιμάω *G2837*
κοιμηθέντες   vbl., aor. pass. ptc. nom. pl. masc.
    {6.A.1.a.}. . . . . id.
κοιμηθῇ   verb, aor. pass. subjunc. 3 pers. sg.
    {5.B.1}. . . . . id.
κοιμηθησόμεθα   verb, fut. pass. indic. 1 pers.
    pl. {5.A.1}. . . . . id.
κοιμήσεως   noun, gen. sg. fem. {2.C}. . . .κοίμησις *G2838*

G2838 **κοίμησις**, -εως, ἡ   *sleeping,* followed by con-
    stituent gen. τοῦ ὕπνου, *which is slumber.*
κοιμώμενος   vbl., pres. mid./pass. ptc. nom. sg.
    masc. {6.A.2}. . . . . .κοιμάω *G2837*
κοιμωμένους   vbl., pres. mid./pass. ptc. acc. pl.
    masc. {6.A.2}. . . . . id.
κοιμωμένων   vbl., pres. mid./pass. ptc. gen. pl.
    masc. {6.A.2}. . . . . id.
κοιμῶνται   verb, pres. mid./pass. indic. 3 pers.
    pl. {5.A.2}. . . . . id.
κοινά   adj., acc. pl. neut. {3.A} . . . . . . .κοινός *G2839*
κοινά   adj., nom. pl. neut. {3.A} . . . . id.
κοιναῖς   adj., dat. pl. fem. {3.A} . . . . id.
κοινήν   adj., acc. sg. fem. {3.A}. . . . . id.
κοινῆς   adj., gen. sg. fem. {3.A} . . . . id.
κοινοῖ   verb, pres. act. indic. 3 pers. sg.
    {5.A.2}. . . . . κοινόω *G2840*
κοινόν   adj., acc. sg. masc. {3.A}. . . . . .κοινός *G2839*
κοινόν   adj., acc. sg. neut. {3.A} . . . . id.
κοινόν   adj., nom. sg. neut. {3.A} . . . . id.

G2839 **κοινός**, -ή, -όν   (1) *common, shared;* (2) Heb.
    use (in contrast to ἅγιος), *profane; dirty,*
    unclean, unwashed, Mark 7:2; Acts 10:14, 28;
    11:8; Rom 14:14; Heb 10:29; Rev 21:27.
κοίνου   verb, pres. act. impv. 2 pers. sg.
    {5.D.2}. . . . . κοινόω *G2840*
κοινοῦν   vbl., pres. act. ptc. nom. sg. neut.
    {6.A.2}. . . . . id.
κοινοῦντα   vbl., pres. act. ptc. nom. pl. neut.
    {6.A.2}. . . . . id.

G2840 **κοινόω**   (1) I make unclean, I pollute; (2) mid.
    I regard (treat) as unclean, Acts 10:15; 11:9.
    (Cf. κοινός.)
κοινωνεῖ   verb, pres. act. indic. 3 pers. sg.
    {5.A.2}. . . . . .κοινωνέω *G2841*
κοινώνει   verb, pres. act. impv. 2 pers. sg. {5.D.2}id.
κοινωνεῖτε   verb, pres. act. indic. 2 pers. pl.
    {5.A.2}. . . . . id.
κοινωνείτω   verb, pres. act. impv. 3 pers. sg.
    {5.D.2}. . . . . id.

G2841 **κοινωνέω**   (1) *I share, communicate, contrib-*
    ute, impart, Rom 12:13; Gal 6:6; (2) *I share in,*
    I have a share of, I have fellowship with, with
    gen. or dat.

G2842 **κοινωνία**, -ας, ἡ   (1) *contributory help,* Acts
    2:42; Rom 15:26; 2 Cor 8:4; 9:13; Heb 13:16;
    (2) *sharing in,* Phil 1:5; 3:10; Phlm 6, cf. (3);
    (3) spiritual *fellowship,* a *fellowship* in the
    spirit, 1 Cor 1:9; 10:16; 2 Cor 6:14; 13:13; Gal
    2:9; Phil 2:1; 1 John 1:3, 6, 7 (lit. *partner-*
    ship, frequently outside NT, of the marriage
    relationship).
κοινωνία   noun, nom. sg. fem. {2.A} . . . κοινωνία *G2842*
κοινωνίᾳ   noun, dat. sg. fem. {2.A} . . . . id.
κοινωνίαν   noun, acc. sg. fem. {2.A} . . . . id.
κοινωνίας   noun, gen. sg. fem. {2.A} . . . . id.

G2843 **κοινωνικός**, -ή, -όν   *willing to share.*
κοινωνικούς   adj., acc. pl. masc. {3.A}.κοινωνικός *G2843*
κοινωνοί   noun, nom. pl. masc. {2.B}. . . κοινωνός *G2844*
κοινωνόν   noun, acc. sg. masc. {2.B} . . . . id.

G2844 **κοινωνός**, -οῦ, ὁ and ἡ   *a sharer; a partner.*
κοινωνός   noun, nom. sg. masc. {2.B} . . κοινωνός *G2844*
κοινωνοῦντες   vbl., pres. act. ptc. nom. pl. masc.
    {6.A.2}. . . . . .κοινωνέω *G2841*
κοινωνούς   noun, acc. pl. masc. {2.B} . . κοινωνός *G2844*
κοινῶσαι   vbl., aor. act. inf. {6.B.1} . . . . . κοινόω *G2840*
κοίταις   noun, dat. pl. fem. {2.A} . . . . .κοίτη *G2845*

G2845 **κοίτη**, -ης, ἡ   (1) *a bed,* Luke 11:7; (2) *a*
    marriage bed, Heb 13:4; κοίτην ἔχειν ἐκ, *to*
    conceive seed from, Rom 9:10; pl. *repeated* (im-
    moral) sexual intercourse, Rom 13:13.
κοίτη   noun, nom. sg. fem. {2.A} . . . . .κοίτη *G2845*
κοίτην   noun, acc. sg. fem. {2.A} . . . . id.

G2846 **κοιτών**, -ῶνος, ὁ   *bedchamber;* ὁ ἐπὶ τοῦ
    κοιτῶνος, *chamberlain.*
κοιτῶνος   noun, gen. sg. masc. {2.C} . . . . . κοιτών *G2846*
κοκκίνην   adj., acc. sg. fem. {3.A}. . . . . .κόκκινος *G2847*
κόκκινον   adj., acc. sg. neut. {3.A} . . . . id.

G2847 **κόκκινος**, -η, -ον   *crimson,* dyed with Kermes,
    the female coccus of the Kermes oak.
κοκκίνου   adj., gen. sg. neut. {3.A}. . . . .κόκκινος *G2847*
κοκκίνῳ   adj., dat. sg. neut. {3.A} . . . . id.
κόκκον   noun, acc. sg. masc. {2.B} . . . . . κόκκος *G2848*

G2848 **κόκκος**, -ου, ὁ   *a grain.*
κόκκος   noun, nom. sg. masc. {2.B} . . . κόκκος *G2848*
κόκκῳ   noun, dat. sg. masc. {2.B} . . . . id.
κολαζομένους   vbl., pres. pass. ptc. acc. pl. masc.
    {6.A.1}. . . . . .κολάζω *G2849*

G2849 **κολάζω**   I punish; mid. I cause to be punished.

G2850 **κολακεία**, -ας, ἡ   *flattery,* with a view to
    advantage or gain.
κολακείας   noun, gen. sg. fem. {2.A} . . . κολακεία *G2850*
κολακίας   noun, gen. sg. fem. {2.A}. . . . . id.
κόλασιν   noun, acc. sg. fem. {2.C} . . . . . . κόλασις *G2851*

G2851 **κόλασις**, -εως, ἡ   *punishing, punishment,* per-
    haps with the idea of *deprivation,* 1 John 4:18.
κολάσονται   verb, fut. mid. indic. 3 pers. pl.
    {5.A.1.d}. . . . . .κολάζω *G2849*
Κολασσαεῖς   noun prop., acc. pl. masc. {2.C;
    2.D}. . . . . Κολοσσαεύς *G2858*
Κολασσαῖς   noun prop., dat. pl. fem. {2.A;
    2.D}. . . . . .Κολοσσαί *G2857‡*
κολάσωνται   verb, aor. mid. subjunc. 3 pers. pl.
    {5.B.1}. . . . . .κολάζω *G2849*

κολαφίζειν   vbl., pres. act. inf. {6.B.1} . . κολαφίζω *G2852*
κολαφίζῃ   verb, pres. act. subjunc. 3 pers. sg.
{5.B.1} . . . . id.
κολαφιζόμεθα   verb, pres. pass. indic. 1 pers.
pl. {5.A.1.d} . . . . id.
κολαφιζόμενοι   vbl., pres. pass. ptc. nom. pl.
masc. {6.A.1} . . . . id.
G2852 **κολαφίζω**   *I strike with the fist; hence, I mal-
treat violently.*
κολλᾶσθαι   vbl., pres. pass. inf. {6.B.2} . . .κολλάω *G2853*
G2853 **κολλάω**   (lit. I glue); hence, mid. and pass. I
join myself closely, I cleave, I adhere (to), I
keep company (with), of friendly intercourse;
of inanimate objects, Luke 10:11.
κολληθέντα   vbl., aor. pass. ptc. acc. sg. masc.
{6.A.1.a.} . . . . .κολλάω *G2853*
κολληθέντες   vbl., aor. pass. ptc. nom. pl.
masc. {6.A.1.a.} . . . . id.
κολληθήσεται   verb, fut. pass. indic. 3 pers. sg.
{5.A.1} . . . . id.
κολλήθητι   verb, aor. pass. impv. 2 pers. sg. {5.D.1} id.
G2854 **κολλούριον** (κολλύριον), -ου, τό   *eye salve.*
κολλούριον   noun, acc. sg. neut. {2.B}κολλούριον *G2854*
G2855 **κολλυβιστής**, -οῦ, ὁ   *a moneychanger,* who
changed heathen into Jewish money, for
payment into the Temple treasury (from
κόλλυβος, *a commission paid on exchange*).
κολλυβιστῶν   noun, gen. pl. masc.
{2.A} . . . . κολλυβιστής *G2855*
κολλύριον   noun, acc. sg. neut. {2.B}. κολλούριον *G2854*
κολλώμενοι   vbl., pres. pass. ptc. nom. pl. masc.
{6.A.2} . . . . .κολλάω *G2853*
κολλώμενος   vbl., pres. pass. ptc. nom. sg.
masc. {6.A.2} . . . . id.
G2856 **κολοβόω**   (lit. *I maim, mutilate*), *I cut short,
shorten, abbreviate.*
κολοβωθήσονται   verb, fut. pass. indic. 3 pers. pl.
{5.A.1} . . . . .κολοβόω *G2856*
G2858 **Κολοσσαεύς**   *a Colossian,* an inhabitant of
Colossae.
G2857‡ **Κολοσσαί**, -ῶν, -αί   *Colossae,* a town of the
Roman province Asia, in the Lycus valley, near
Laodicea and Hierapolis.
Κολοσσαῖς   noun prop., dat. pl. fem. {2.A;
2.D} . . . . Κολοσσαί *G2857‡*
κόλποις   noun, dat. pl. masc. {2.B} . . . . . . κόλπος *G2859*
κόλπον   noun, acc. sg. masc. {2.B} . . . . id.
G2859 **κόλπος**, -ου, ὁ   (1) sg. and pl. *bosom, breast,
chest;* (2) the overhanging fold of the garment
used as a pocket, Luke 6:38; (3) *a bay, gulf,*
Acts 27:39.
κόλπῳ   noun, dat. sg. masc. {2.B} . . . . κόλπος *G2859*
κολυμβᾶν   vbl., pres. act. inf. {6.B.2} . . κολυμβάω *G2860*
κολυμβᾶν   vbl., pres. act. inf. {6.B.2} . . . . id.
G2860 **κολυμβάω**   (properly *I dive*); hence, *I swim.*
G2861 **κολυμβήθρα**, -ας, ἡ   (lit. a *diving* or *swimming
place*), *a pool.*
κολυμβήθρα   noun, nom. sg. fem.
{2.A} . . . . κολυμβήθρα *G2861*
κολυμβήθρᾳ   noun, dat. sg. fem. {2.A} . . . . id.

κολυμβήθραν   noun, acc. sg. fem. {2.A} . . . . . id.
κολωνεία   noun, nom. sg. fem. {2.A} . . . . κολωνία *G2862*
G2862 **κολωνία**, -ας, ἡ   *a colony,* a city settlement of
Roman (soldier) citizens; *a garrison city.*
κολωνία   noun, nom. sg. fem. {2.A} . . . . . κολωνία *G2862*
κομᾷ   verb, pres. act. subjunc. 3 pers. sg.
{5.B.2} . . . . .κομάω *G2863*
G2863 **κομάω**   *I wear the hair long, I allow the hair to
grow long.*
G2864 **κόμη**, -ης, ἡ   *hair, long hair.*
κόμη   noun, nom. sg. fem. {2.A} . . . . κόμη *G2864*
κομεῖσθε   verb, fut. mid. indic. 2 pers. pl.
{5.A.2} . . . . κομίζω *G2865*
κομεῖται   verb, fut. mid. indic. 3 pers. sg.
{5.A.2} . . . . id.
κομιζόμενοι   vbl., pres. mid. ptc. nom. pl.
masc. {6.A.1} . . . . id.
G2865 **κομίζω**   (1) act. I convey, bring, Luke 7:37;
(2) mid. I receive back, I receive what has
belonged to myself but has been lost, or else
promised but kept back, or I get what has
come to be my own by earning, I recover.
κομιούμενοι   vbl., fut. mid. ptc. nom. pl. masc.
{6.A.1.b} . . . . κομίζω *G2865*
κομισάμενοι   vbl., aor. mid. ptc. nom. pl.
masc. {6.A.1.b} . . . . id.
κομίσασα   vbl., aor. act. ptc. nom. sg. fem.
{6.A.1.a} . . . . id.
κομίσεται   verb, fut. mid. indic. 3 pers. sg.
{5.A.1.d} . . . . id.
κομίσησθε   verb, aor. mid. subjunc. 2 pers. pl.
{5.B.1} . . . . id.
κομίσηται   verb, aor. mid. subjunc. 3 pers. sg.
{5.B.1} . . . . id.
G2866 **κομψότερον**   comp. adv. *better* (of sick
persons).
κομψότερον   adv. comp. {3.F; 3.G} . . κομψότερον *G2866*
G2867 **κονιάω**   *I whitewash.*
κονιορτόν   noun, acc. sg. masc. {2.B} . .κονιορτός *G2868*
G2868 **κονιορτός**, -οῦ, ὁ   *dust.*
G2869 **κοπάζω**   *I cease, drop.*
κοπετόν   noun, acc. sg. masc. {2.B} . . . . .κοπετός *G2870*
G2870 **κοπετός**, -οῦ, ὁ   *beating of the breast* or *head* in
lamentation, *lamentation.*
G2871 **κοπή**, -ῆς, ἡ   *slaughter.*
κοπῆς   noun, gen. sg. fem. {2.A} . . . . .κοπή *G2871*
κοπιᾷ   verb, pres. act. indic. 3 pers. sg.
{5.A.2} . . . . κοπιάω *G2872*
κοπιάσαντες   vbl., aor. act. ptc. nom. pl. masc.
{6.A.2} . . . . id.
κοπιάτω   verb, pres. act. impv. 3 pers. sg. {5.D.2} id.
G2872 **κοπιάω**   (1) *I grow weary,* Matt 11:28; John 4:6;
Rev 2:3; (2) *I toil, work with effort* (of bodily
and mental labor alike).
κοπιῶ   verb, pres. act. indic. 1 pers. sg.
{5.A.2} . . . . κοπιάω *G2872*
κοπιῶμεν   verb, pres. act. indic. 1 pers. pl.
{5.A.2} . . . . id.
κοπιῶντα   vbl., pres. act. ptc. acc. sg. masc.
{6.A.2} . . . . id.

κοπιῶντας   vbl., pres. act. ptc. acc. pl. masc.
{6.A.2}. . . . . id.

κοπιῶντες   vbl., pres. act. ptc. nom. pl. masc.
{6.A.2}. . . . . id.

κοπιῶντι   vbl., pres. act. ptc. dat. sg. masc.
{6.A.2}. . . . . id.

κοπιώσας   vbl., pres. act. ptc. acc. pl. fem.
{6.A.2}. . . . . id.

κοπιῶσιν   verb, pres. act. indic. 3 pers. pl.
{5.A.2}. . . . . id.

κόποις   noun, dat. pl. masc. {2.B}. . . . . κόπος G2873

κόπον   noun, acc. sg. masc. {2.B} . . . . id.

G2873   **κόπος**, -ου, ὁ   (1) *trouble;* κόπους (κόπον)
τινι παρέχειν, *to give trouble to one, to annoy
one;* (2) *toil, labor, laborious toil,* involving
weariness and fatigue.

κόπος   noun, nom. sg. masc. {2.B} . . . . κόπος G2873

κόπου   noun, gen. sg. masc. {2.B}. . . . . id.

κόπους   noun, acc. pl. masc. {2.B} . . . . id.

G2874   **κοπρία**, -ας, ἡ   *manure.*

κόπρια   noun, acc. pl. neut. {2.B} . . . . . κόπριον G2874†

κοπρίαν   noun, acc. sg. fem. {2.A} . . . . id.

G2874†   **κόπριον**, -ου, τό   *manure.* Var. for κοπρία,
Luke 13:8.

G2875   **κόπτω**   (1) I cut, I cut of, Matt 21:8; Mark 11:8;
(2) mid. I beat my breast or head in lam-
entation, I lament, mourn, sometimes with
acc. (ἐπί with acc.) of person whose loss is
mourned.

κόπῳ   noun, dat. sg. masc. {2.B} . . . . κόπος G2873

κόπων   noun, gen. pl. masc. {2.B}. . . . . id.

κόρακας   noun, acc. pl. masc. {2.C} . . . . . . κόραξ G2876

G2876   **κόραξ**, -ακος, ὁ   *a raven.*

G2877   **κοράσιον**, -ου, τό   *a little girl, a young girl; a
girl* (colloquial).

κοράσιον   noun, nom. sg. neut. {2.B} . . κοράσιον G2877

κορασίῳ   noun, dat. sg. neut. {2.B} . . . . id.

κορβάν   Heb. κορβᾶν G2878

G2878   **κορβᾶν**   *a gift consecrated to God* (Aram.).

κορβάν   Heb. κορβᾶν G2878

κορβανᾶν   noun, acc. sg. masc. {2.A} . κορβανᾶς G2878†

G2878†   **κορβανᾶς**, -ᾶ, ὁ   *the temple treasure.* Var. for
κορβᾶν, Matt 27:6.

Κορέ   noun prop. . . . . Κόρε G2879

G2879   **Κόρε**, ὁ   *Korah* (Num 16:1ff.) (Heb.).

Κόρε   noun prop. . . . . Κόρε G2879

G2880   **κορέννυμι**   *I fill, sate, glut, feed full.*

κορεσθέντες   vbl., aor. pass. ptc. nom. pl. masc.
{6.A.3}. . . . . κορέννυμι G2880

Κορίνθιοι   adj. prop., voc. pl. masc.
{3.A} . . . . Κορίνθιος G2881

G2881   **Κορίνθιος**, -ου, ὁ   *Corinthian, of Corinth.*

Κορινθίους   adj. prop., acc. pl. masc.
{3.A} . . . . Κορίνθιος G2881

Κορινθίων   adj. prop., gen. pl. masc. {3.A}. . . . . id.

Κόρινθον   noun prop., acc. sg. fem. {2.B;
2.D}. . . . . Κόρινθος G2882

G2882   **Κόρινθος**, -ου, ἡ   *Corinth,* in northeast Pelo-
ponnese, the capital of the Roman province
Achaia.

Κορίνθου   noun prop., gen. sg. fem. {2.B;
2.D}. . . . . Κόρινθος G2882

Κορίνθῳ   noun prop., dat. sg. fem. {2.B; 2.D}. . . id.

Κορνήλιε   noun prop., voc. sg. masc. {2.B;
2.D}. . . . . Κορνήλιος G2883

G2883   **Κορνήλιος**, -ου, ὁ   *Cornelius,* a centurion of
the Roman army, stationed at Caesarea (2).

Κορνήλιος   noun prop., nom. sg. masc. {2.B;
2.D}. . . . . Κορνήλιος G2883

Κορνηλίου   noun prop., gen. sg. masc. {2.B;
2.D}. . . . . id.

Κορνηλίῳ   noun prop., dat. sg. masc. {2.B; 2.D} id.

G2884   **κόρος**, -ου, ὁ   *a (dry) measure,* equivalent to
ten Attic μέδιμνοι or 120 gallons (Heb.).

κόρους   noun, acc. pl. masc. {2.B} . . . . κόρος G2884

κοσμεῖν   vbl., pres. act. inf. {6.B.2} . . . . . . κοσμέω G2885

κοσμεῖτε   verb, pres. act. indic. 2 pers. pl. {5.A.2}id.

G2885   **κοσμέω**   *I put into order; I decorate, deck,
adorn.*

κοσμικάς   adj., acc. pl. fem. {3.A}. . . . . κοσμικός G2886

κοσμικόν   adj., acc. sg. neut. {3.A} . . . . id.

G2886   **κοσμικός**, -ή, -όν   *earthly, worldly* (belonging
to the present, earthly world as opposed to the
heavenly and future).

κόσμιον   adj., acc. sg. masc. {3.A} . . . . . . κόσμιος G2887

G2887   **κόσμιος**, -ον   *orderly, virtuous.*

κοσμίῳ   adj., dat. sg. fem. {3.A} . . . . κόσμιος G2887

κοσμοκράτορας   noun, acc. pl. masc.
{2.C} . . . . κοσμοκράτωρ G2888

G2888   **κοσμοκράτωρ**, -ορος, ὁ   *ruler of this world,*
i.e., of the world as asserting its independence
of God; used of the angelic or demonic powers
controlling the sublunary world, cf. ἀρχή,
ἐξουσία, στοιχεῖον.

κόσμον   noun, acc. sg. masc. {2.B} . . . . . . κόσμος G2889

G2889   **κόσμος**, -ου, ὁ   (1) *the universe, the world,*
the sum total of created things; (2) a Jewish
conception; the word has acquired a bad sense
in Isaiah (e.g., 13:11), the sum of the fierce
surrounding heathen nations, the powers of
the heathen world, at once destructive and
corruptive. Hence, *the world* as apart from
God its Creator, the world as self-sufficient,
consequently running counter to its Creator,
and thus evil in its tendency, cf. John, 1 John
(e.g., 2:15), Jas (e.g., 4:4), 2 Pet 2:20; (3) sometimes seems not different from, *the inhabited
world;* (4) *adornment,* 1 Pet 3:3.

κόσμος   noun, nom. sg. masc. {2.B} . . . . . . κόσμος G2889

κόσμου   noun, gen. sg. masc. {2.B}. . . . . id.

κόσμῳ   noun, dat. sg. masc. {2.B}. . . . . id.

κοσμῶσιν   verb, pres. act. subjunc. 3 pers. pl.
{5.B.2} . . . . κοσμέω G2885

G2890   **Κούαρτος**, -ου, ὁ   *Quartus,* a Christian,
brother of Erastus the Corinthian. Cf.
ἀδελφός.

Κούαρτος   noun prop., nom. sg. masc. {2.B;
2.D}. . . . . Κούαρτος G2890

κουμ   Aram. . . . . κούμ G2891

κούμ   Aram. . . . . id.

G2891 **κοῦμ** (κουμι)   *arise* (Aram.).
κοῦμι   Aram. . . . . κοῦμ G2891
G2892 **κουστωδία**, -ας, ἡ   concr., *a guard* (Lat. custodia).
κουστωδίαν   noun, acc. sg. fem. {2.A}. κουστωδία G2892
κουστωδίας   noun, gen. sg. fem. {2.A}. . . . . . . id.
G2893 **κουφίζω**   *I lighten.*
κόφινοι   noun, nom. pl. masc. {2.B} . . . . . κόφινος G2894
G2894 **κόφινος**, -ου, ὁ   a stiff wicker *basket.*
κοφίνους   noun, acc. pl. masc. {2.B}. . . . . .κόφινος G2894
κοφίνων   noun, gen. pl. masc. {2.B} . . . . id.
κόψαντες   vbl., aor. act. ptc. nom. pl. masc.
   {6.A.1.a} . . . . κόπτω G2875
κόψονται   verb, fut. mid. indic. 3 pers. pl.
   {5.A.1.d} . . . . id.
κραβάττοις   noun, dat. pl. masc. {2.B}. κράβαττος G2895
κράβαττον   noun, acc. sg. masc. {2.B} . . . . id.
G2895 **κράβαττος**, -ου, ὁ   a bed, mattress, mat of a poor man (spelled κράβακτος in Egyptian documents).
κραβάττου   noun, gen. sg. masc. {2.B}. κράβαττος G2895
κραβάττῳ   noun, dat. sg. masc. {2.B}. . . . . id.
κραβάττων   noun, gen. pl. masc. {2.B}. . . . . . . id.
κραββάτοις   noun, dat. pl. masc. {2.B}. . . . . . . id.
κράββατον   noun, acc. sg. masc. {2.B} . . . . id.
κραββάτῳ   noun, dat. sg. masc. {2.B}. . . . . id.
κραββάτων   noun, gen. pl. masc. {2.B} . . . . . . id.
κράζει   verb, pres. act. indic. 3 pers. sg.
   {5.A.1.a} . . . . .κράζω G2896
κράζειν   vbl., pres. act. inf. {6.B.1} . . . . id.
κράζομεν   verb, pres. act. indic. 1 pers. pl.
   {5.A.1.a} . . . . id.
κράζον   vbl., pres. act. ptc. acc. sg. neut. {6.A.1}. id.
κράζοντα   vbl., pres. act. ptc. nom. pl. neut.
   {6.A.1} . . . . id.
κράζοντας   vbl., pres. act. ptc. acc. pl. masc.
   {6.A.1} . . . . id.
κράζοντες   vbl., pres. act. ptc. nom. pl. masc.
   {6.A.1} . . . . id.
κραζόντων   vbl., pres. act. ptc. gen. pl. masc.
   {6.A.1} . . . . id.
κράζουσι   verb, pres. act. indic. 3 pers. pl.
   {5.A.1.a} . . . . id.
κράζουσιν   verb, pres. act. indic. 3 pers. pl.
   {5.A.1.a} . . . . id.
G2896 **κράζω**   *I cry aloud, shriek.*
κράζων   vbl., pres. act. ptc. nom. sg. masc.
   {6.A.1} . . . . .κράζω G2896
G2897 **κραιπάλη** (κρεπάλη), -ης, ἡ   *excessive drunkenness, carousing, surfeiting.*
κραιπάλη   noun, dat. sg. fem. {2.A} . . . . κραιπάλη G2897
G2898 **κρανίον**, -ου, τό   *the skull.*
κρανίον   noun, acc. sg. neut. {2.B; 2.D} . . κρανίον G2898
Κρανίον   noun, acc. sg. neut. {2.B; 2.D} . . . . . id.
κρανίου   noun, gen. sg. neut. {2.B; 2.D} . . . . . . id.
Κρανίου   noun, gen. sg. neut. {2.B; 2.D} . . . . . . id.
κράξαν   vbl., aor. act. ptc. nom. sg. neut.
   {6.A.1.a} . . . . .κράζω G2896
κράξαντες   vbl., aor. act. ptc. nom. pl. masc.
   {6.A.1.a} . . . . id.

κράξας   vbl., aor. act. ptc. nom. sg. masc.
   {6.A.1.a} . . . . id.
κράξουσιν   verb, fut. act. indic. 3 pers. pl.
   {5.A.1.a} . . . . id.
κράσπεδα   noun, acc. pl. neut. {2.B} . . κράσπεδον G2899
G2899 **κράσπεδον**, -ου, τό   *the fringe, the edge.*
κρασπέδου   noun, gen. sg. neut. {2.B} . κράσπεδον G2899
κραταιάν   adj., acc. sg. fem. {3.A} . . . . κραταιός G2900
G2900 **κραταιός**, -ά, -όν   *strong, powerful.*
κραταιοῦσθε   verb, pres. pass. impv. 2 pers. pl.
   {5.D.2} . . . . κραταιόω G2901
G2901 **κραταιόω**   *I strengthen, pass. I become strong.*
κραταιωθῆναι   vbl., aor. pass. inf.
   {6.B.1} . . . . κραταιόω G2901
κράτει   noun, dat. sg. neut. {2.C} . . . . κράτος G2904
κράτει   verb, pres. act. impv. 2 pers. sg.
   {5.D.2} . . . . κρατέω G2902
κρατεῖν   vbl., pres. act. inf. {6.B.2} . . . . id.
κρατεῖς   verb, pres. act. indic. 2 pers. sg. {5.A.2}. id.
κρατεῖσθαι   vbl., pres. pass. inf. {6.B.2} . . . . . . id.
κρατεῖτε   verb, pres. act. impv. 2 pers. pl. {5.D.2} id.
κρατεῖτε   verb, pres. act. indic. 2 pers. pl. {5.A.2} id.
G2902 **κρατέω**   *I lay hold of, take possession of, obtain,* with gen. and (much oftener) with acc.
κρατῆσαι   vbl., aor. act. inf. {6.B.1} . . . . . . κρατέω G2902
κρατήσαντες   vbl., aor. act. ptc. nom. pl. masc.
   {6.A.2} . . . . id.
κρατήσας   vbl., aor. act. ptc. nom. sg. masc. {6.A.2} id.
κρατήσατε   verb, aor. act. impv. 2 pers. pl.
   {5.D.1} . . . . id.
κρατήσει   verb, fut. act. indic. 3 pers. sg. {5.A.1} id.
κρατήσωσι   verb, aor. act. subjunc. 3 pers. pl.
   {5.B.1} . . . . id.
κρατήσωσιν   verb, aor. act. subjunc. 3 pers. pl.
   {5.B.1} . . . . id.
κρατῆτε   verb, pres. act. subjunc. 2 pers. pl.
   {5.B.1} . . . . id.
κράτιστε   adj. superl., voc. sg. masc.
   {3.A} . . . . .κράτιστος G2903
G2903 **κράτιστος**, -η, -ον   *most excellent,* an official epithet, used in addressing a Roman of high rank, and in the second c. one of equestrian (as distinguished from senatorial) rank.
κρατίστῳ   adj. superl., dat. sg. masc.
   {3.A} . . . . .κράτιστος G2903
G2904 **κράτος**, -ους, τό   *might, rule, power,* divine except in Heb 2:14.
κράτος   noun, acc. sg. neut. {2.C} . . . . κράτος G2904
κράτος   noun, nom. sg. neut. {2.C}. . . . . id.
κρατοῦντας   vbl., pres. act. ptc. acc. pl. masc.
   {6.A.2} . . . . κρατέω G2902
κρατοῦντες   vbl., pres. act. ptc. nom. pl. masc.
   {6.A.2} . . . . id.
κρατοῦντος   vbl., pres. act. ptc. gen. sg. masc.
   {6.A.2} . . . . id.
κράτους   noun, gen. sg. neut. {2.C} . . . . . . κράτος G2904
κρατοῦσιν   verb, pres. act. indic. 3 pers. pl.
   {5.A.2} . . . . κρατέω G2902
κρατῶμεν   verb, pres. act. subjunc. 1 pers. pl.
   {5.B.2} . . . . id.

κρατῶν   vbl., pres. act. ptc. nom. sg. masc.
    {6.A.2} . . . . id.

κραυγάζοντα   vbl., pres. act. ptc. nom. pl. neut.
    {6.A.1} . . . . κραυγάζω G2905

κραυγαζόντων   vbl., pres. act. ptc. gen. pl.
    masc. {6.A.1} . . . . id.

G2905 **κραυγάζω**   *I cry aloud, shout.*

κραυγάσει   verb, fut. act. indic. 3 pers. sg.
    {5.A.1.a} . . . . κραυγάζω G2905

G2906 **κραυγή**, -ῆς, ἡ   (1) *a shout, cry, clamor;* (2)
    outcry, clamoring against another, Eph 4:31.

κραυγή   noun, nom. sg. fem. {2.A} . . . . . . κραυγή G2906

κραυγῇ   noun, dat. sg. fem. {2.A} . . . . id.

κραυγῆς   noun, gen. sg. fem. {2.A} . . . . id.

κρέα   noun, acc. pl. neut. {2.C} . . . . κρέας G2907

G2907 **κρέας**, κρέως and κρέατος, acc. pl. κρέα,
    τό   *flesh; pieces of flesh, kinds of flesh.*

κρεῖσσον   adj. comp., acc. sg. neut. {3.E;
    3.G} . . . . κρείσσων G2908

κρεῖσσον   adj. comp., nom. sg. neut. {3.E; 3.G} . id.

κρεῖσσον   adv. comp. {3.F; 3.G} . . . . id.

κρείσσονα   adj. comp., acc. pl. neut. {3.E; 3.G} . . id.

κρείσσονα   adj. comp., acc. sg. fem. {3.E; 3.G} . . id.

G2908 **κρείσσων**   Alt. spelling of κρείσσων.

κρεῖττον   adj. comp., acc. sg. neut. {3.E;
    3.G} . . . . κρείττων G2909

κρεῖττον   adj. comp., nom. sg. neut. {3.E; 3.G} . id.

κρεῖττον   adv. comp. {3.F; 3.G} . . . . id.

κρείττονα   adj. comp., acc. pl. neut. {3.E; 3.G} . . id.

κρείττονα   adj. comp., acc. sg. fem. {3.E; 3.G} . . id.

κρείττονος   adj. comp., gen. sg. fem. {3.E; 3.G} . id.

κρείττονος   adj. comp., gen. sg. masc. {3.E; 3.G} id.

κρείττοσι   adj. comp., dat. pl. fem. {3.E; 3.G} . . id.

κρείττοσιν   adj. comp., dat. pl. fem. {3.E; 3.G} . . id.

G2909 **κρείττων** (κρείσσων), -ον gen. ονος   *better.*

κρείττων   adj. comp., nom. sg. masc. {3.E;
    3.G} . . . . κρείττων G2909

κρεμάμενον   vbl., pres. mid. ptc. acc. sg. neut.
    {6.A.3} . . . . κρεμάννυμι G2910

κρεμάμενος   vbl., pres. mid. ptc. nom. sg.
    masc. {6.A.3} . . . . id.

G2910 **κρεμάννυμι**   I hang, I suspend; mid. I am
    hanging, I hang.

κρέμανται   verb, pres. pass. indic. 3 pers. pl.
    {5.A.3.a} . . . . κρεμάννυμι G2910

κρεμάσαντες   vbl., aor. act. ptc. nom. pl. masc.
    {6.A.3} . . . . id.

κρεμασθέντων   vbl., aor. pass. ptc. gen. pl.
    masc. {6.A.3} . . . . id.

κρεμασθῇ   verb, aor. pass. subjunc. 3 pers. sg.
    {5.B.3} . . . . id.

κρέμαται   verb, pres. pass. indic. 3 pers. sg.
    {5.A.3.a} . . . . id.

κρεπάλη   noun, dat. sg. fem. {2.A} . . . . . κραιπάλη G2897

G2911 **κρημνός**, -οῦ, ὁ   *a crag, precipice.*

κρημνοῦ   noun, gen. sg. masc. {2.B} . . . . . κρημνός G2911

G2912 **Κρής**, -ητός, ὁ   *a Cretan, an inhabitant of*
    Crete.

G2913 **Κρήσκης**, -εντος, ὁ   *Crescens*, a Christian,
    coadjutor of Paul.

Κρήσκης   noun prop., nom. sg. masc. {2.A;
    2.D} . . . . Κρήσκης G2913

Κρῆτες   noun prop., nom. pl. masc. {2.C; 2.D}Κρής G2912

G2914 **Κρήτη**, -ης, ἡ   *Crete;* see Κυρήνη.

Κρήτῃ   noun prop., dat. sg. fem. {2.A; 2.D} . Κρήτη G2914

Κρήτην   noun prop., acc. sg. fem. {2.A; 2.D} . . . id.

Κρήτης   noun prop., gen. sg. fem. {2.A; 2.D} . . . id.

Κρητῶν   noun prop., gen. pl. masc. {2.C; 2.D}Κρής G2912

G2915 **κριθή**, -ῆς, ἡ   *barley.*

κριθῆναι   vbl., aor. pass. inf. {6.B.1} . . . . κρίνω G2919

κριθῆς   noun, gen. sg. fem. {2.A} . . . . κριθή G2915

κριθήσεσθε   verb, fut. pass. indic. 2 pers. pl.
    {5.A.1.d} . . . . κρίνω G2919

κριθήσονται   verb, fut. pass. indic. 3 pers. pl.
    {5.A.1.d} . . . . id.

κριθῆτε   verb, aor. pass. subjunc. 2 pers. pl.
    {5.B.1} . . . . id.

G2916 **κρίθινος**, -η, -ον   *made of barley.*

κριθίνους   adj., acc. pl. masc. {3.A} . . . . κρίθινος G2916

κριθίνων   adj., gen. pl. masc. {3.A} . . . . id.

κριθῶν   noun, gen. pl. fem. {2.A} . . . . κριθή G2915

κριθῶσι   verb, aor. pass. subjunc. 3 pers. pl.
    {5.B.1} . . . . κρίνω G2919

κριθῶσιν   verb, aor. pass. subjunc. 3 pers. pl.
    {5.B.1} . . . . id.

G2917 **κρίμα**, -ατος, τό   (1) *a judgment, a verdict;*
    sometimes implying *an adverse verdict, a con-*
    demnation; (2) *a case at law, a lawsuit,* 1 Cor
    6:7.

κρίμα   noun, acc. sg. neut. {2.C} . . . . κρίμα G2917

κρίμα   noun, nom. sg. neut. {2.C} . . . . id.

κρίματα   noun, acc. pl. neut. {2.C} . . . . id.

κρίματα   noun, nom. pl. neut. {2.C} . . . . id.

κρίματι   noun, dat. sg. neut. {2.C} . . . . id.

κρίματος   noun, gen. sg. neut. {2.C} . . . . id.

κρίνα   noun, acc. pl. neut. {2.B} . . . . κρίνον G2918

κρῖναι   vbl., aor. act. inf. {6.B.1} . . . . κρίνω G2919

κρίναντας   vbl., aor. act. ptc. acc. pl. masc.
    {6.A.1.a} . . . . id.

κρίναντες   vbl., aor. act. ptc. nom. pl. masc.
    {6.A.1.a} . . . . id.

κρίναντος   vbl., aor. act. ptc. gen. sg. masc.
    {6.A.1.a} . . . . id.

κρίνας   vbl., aor. act. ptc. nom. sg. masc.
    {6.A.1.a} . . . . id.

κρίνατε   verb, aor. act. impv. 2 pers. pl. {5.D.1}. . id.

κρινεῖ   verb, fut. act. indic. 3 pers. sg. {5.A.2} . . . id.

κρίνει   verb, pres. act. indic. 3 pers. sg. {5.A.1.a}. id.

κρίνειν   vbl., pres. act. inf. {6.B.1} . . . . id.

κρίνεις   verb, pres. act. indic. 2 pers. sg. {5.A.1.a}id.

κρίνεσθαι   vbl., pres. pass. inf. {6.B.1} . . . . id.

κρίνεται   verb, pres. pass. indic. 3 pers. sg.
    {5.A.1.d} . . . . id.

κρίνετε   verb, pres. act. impv. 2 pers. pl. {5.D.1} . id.

κρίνετε   verb, pres. act. indic. 2 pers. pl. {5.A.1.a}id.

κρινέτω   verb, pres. act. impv. 3 pers. sg. {5.D.1} id.

κρίνη   verb, aor. act. subjunc. 3 pers. sg. {5.B.1} . id.

κρίνη   verb, pres. act. subjunc. 3 pers. sg. {5.B.1} id.

κρίνομαι   verb, pres. pass. indic. 1 pers. sg.
    {5.A.1.d} . . . . id.

κρινόμενοι   vbl., pres. pass. ptc. nom. pl. masc.
{6.A.1}. . . . . id.

κρινόμενος   vbl., pres. pass. ptc. nom. sg. masc.
{6.A.1}. . . . . id.

G2918 **κρίνον**, -ου, τό   *a lily* growing wild, variously
identified with the red anemone, the white lily,
the sword lily.

κρίνοντα   vbl., pres. act. ptc. acc. sg. masc.
{6.A.1}. . . . . κρίνω G2919

κρίνοντες   vbl., pres. act. ptc. nom. pl. masc.
{6.A.1}. . . . . id.

κρίνοντι   vbl., pres. act. ptc. dat. sg. masc.
{6.A.1}. . . . . id.

κρινοῦμεν   verb, fut. act. indic. 1 pers. pl.
{5.A.2}. . . . . id.

κρινοῦσι   verb, fut. act. indic. 3 pers. pl. {5.A.2}. id.
κρινοῦσιν   verb, fut. act. indic. 3 pers. pl. {5.A.2}id.
κρινῶ   verb, fut. act. indic. 1 pers. sg. {5.A.2} . . . id.

G2919 **κρίνω**   (1) *I judge,* whether in a law court or
privately; sometimes with cog. nouns κρίμα,
κρίματι, κρίσιν, emphasizing the notion of
the verb; (2) *I decide, I think (it) good,* with inf.
Acts 3:13; 15:19, etc. (cf. Acts 27:1).

κρίνω   verb, fut. act. indic. 1 pers. sg.
{5.A.1.a} . . . . κρίνω G2919

κρίνω   verb, pres. act. indic. 1 pers. sg. {5.A.1.a}. id.
κρίνω   verb, pres. act. subjunc. 1 pers. sg. {5.B.1} id.
κρίνωμεν   verb, pres. act. subjunc. 1 pers. pl.
{5.B.1} . . . . id.

κρίνων   vbl., pres. act. ptc. nom. sg. masc.
{6.A.1}. . . . . id.

κρίσει   noun, dat. sg. fem. {2.C} . . . . κρίσις G2920
κρίσεις   noun, nom. pl. fem. {2.C} . . . . id.
κρίσεως   noun, gen. sg. fem. {2.C} . . . . id.
κρίσιν   noun, acc. sg. fem. {2.C}. . . . . id.

G2920 **κρίσις**, -εως, ἡ   *judging, judgment;* generally
divine judgment; accusation, Jude 9.

κρίσις   noun, nom. sg. fem. {2.C} . . . . . . κρίσις G2920
Κρίσπον   noun prop., acc. sg. masc. {2.B;
2.D}. . . . . Κρίσπος G2921

G2921 **Κρίσπος**, -ου, ὁ   *Crispus,* ruler of the synagogue at Corinth, converted and baptized by
Paul.

Κρίσπος   noun prop., nom. sg. masc. {2.B;
2.D}. . . . . Κρίσπος G2921

κριταί   noun, nom. pl. masc. {2.A}. . . . . . . κριτής G2923
κριτάς   noun, acc. pl. masc. {2.A}. . . . . id.
κριτῇ   noun, dat. sg. masc. {2.A}. . . . . id.
κριτήν   noun, acc. sg. masc. {2.A} . . . . id.
κριτήρια   noun, acc. pl. neut. {2.B} . . . . κριτήριον G2922

G2922 **κριτήριον**, -ου, τό   (1) *a law court,* Jas 2:6; (2)
a law case before an arbiter.

κριτηρίων   noun, gen. pl. neut. {2.B} . . . κριτήριον G2922

G2923 **κριτής**, -ου, ὁ   *a judge.*

κριτής   noun, nom. sg. masc. {2.A}. . . . . . . κριτής G2923

G2924 **κριτικός**, -ή, -όν   *able to judge.*

κριτικός   adj., nom. sg. masc. {3.A} . . . . κριτικός G2924
κρούειν   vbl., pres. act. inf. {6.B.1} . . . . κρούω G2925
κρούετε   verb, pres. act. impv. 2 pers. pl. {5.D.1}. id.

κρούοντι   vbl., pres. act. ptc. dat. sg. masc.
{6.A.1}. . . . . id.

κρούσαντος   vbl., aor. act. ptc. gen. sg. masc.
{6.A.1.a}. . . . . id.

G2925 **κρούω**   *I beat* a door with a stick, to gain
admittance.

κρούω   verb, pres. act. indic. 1 pers. sg.
{5.A.1.a} . . . . κρούω G2925

κρούων   vbl., pres. act. ptc. nom. sg. masc.
{6.A.1}. . . . . id.

κρυβῆναι   vbl., ²aor. pass. inf. {6.B.1}. . . . κρύπτω G2928
κρυπτά   adj., acc. pl. neut. {3.A}. . . . . . . κρυπτός G2927
κρυπτά   adj., nom. pl. neut. {3.A}. . . . . id.

G2926 **κρύπτη**, -ης, ἡ   *a hidden place,* cf. κρυπτός.

κρύπτην   noun, acc. sg. fem. {2.A} . . . . . . κρύπτη G2926
κρυπτόν   adj., acc. sg. neut. {3.A} . . . . . . κρυπτός G2927
κρυπτόν   adj., nom. sg. neut. {3.A}. . . . . id.

G2927 **κρυπτός**, -ή, -όν   *hidden, secret;* τὰ κρυπτά,
as subs. *the hidden (secret) things (parts), the
inward nature (character);* ἐν (τῷ) κρυπτῷ, *in
the secret place, in the hidden sphere, inwardly.*

κρυπτός   adj., nom. sg. masc. {3.A} . . . . κρυπτός G2927
κρυπτῷ   adj., dat. sg. neut. {3.A}. . . . . id.

G2928 **κρύπτω**   *I hide, conceal.*

κρυσταλλίζοντι   vbl., pres. act. ptc. dat. sg. masc.
{6.A.1}. . . . . κρυσταλλίζω G2929

G2929 **κρυσταλλίζω**   *I am clear as crystal.*

κρύσταλλον   noun, acc. sg. masc.
{2.B} . . . . κρύσταλλος G2930

G2930 **κρύσταλλος**, -ου, ὁ   *crystal.*

κρυστάλλῳ   noun, dat. sg. masc.
{2.B} . . . . κρύσταλλος G2930

G2927†‡ **κρυφαῖος**, -α, -ον   *hidden, secret.* Var. for
κρυπτός, Matt 6:18.

κρυφαίῳ   adj., dat. sg. neut. {3.A}. . . . . κρυφαῖος G2927†‡

G2931 **κρυφῇ**   adv., *in secret, secretly.*

κρυφῇ   adv.. . . . . κρυφῇ G2931
κρυφῆ   adv.. . . . . id.
κρύψατε   verb, aor. act. impv. 2 pers. pl.
{5.D.1}. . . . . κρύπτω G2928

G2932 **κτάομαι**   (1) *I acquire, win, get, purchase, buy;*
(2) *I possess,* 1 Thess 4:4.

κτᾶσθαι   vbl., pres. mid./pass. inf. {6.B.2} κτάομαι G2932

G2933 **κτῆμα**, -ατος, τό   *a piece of landed property,
a field,* Acts 5:1; pl. *possessions, property,* possibly *landed property, property in land* in Mark
10:22; Matt 19:22, as it is in Acts 2:45.

κτῆμα   noun, acc. sg. neut. {2.C} . . . . κτῆμα G2933
κτήματα   noun, acc. pl. neut. {2.C} . . . . id.
κτήνη   noun, nom. pl. neut. {2.C}. . . . . κτῆνος G2934

G2934 **κτῆνος**, -ους, τό   *a beast of burden* (generally,
a horse or mule), either for riding or for carry-
ing loads on its back, or for yoking to a cart or
carriage.

κτῆνος   noun, acc. sg. neut. {2.C}. . . . . κτῆνος G2934
κτηνῶν   noun, gen. pl. neut. {2.C} . . . . id.
κτήσασθε   verb, aor. mid. impv. 2 pers. pl.
{5.D.1}. . . . . κτάομαι G2932

κτήσεσθε   verb, fut. mid. indic. 2 pers. pl. {5.A.1} id.

κτήσησθε   verb, aor. mid. subjunc. 2 pers. pl. {5.B.1} . . . . id.

κτήτορες   noun, nom. pl. masc. {2.C}. . . . . κτήτωρ *G2935*

G2935 **κτήτωρ**, -ορος, ὁ   *a possessor, owner.*

G2936 **κτίζω**   *I create, found, make,* always of God.

κτίσαντα   vbl., aor. act. ptc. acc. sg. masc. {6.A.1.a} . . . . .κτίζω *G2936*

κτίσαντι   vbl., aor. act. ptc. dat. sg. masc. {6.A.1.a} . . . . id.

κτίσαντος   vbl., aor. act. ptc. gen. sg. masc. {6.A.1.a} . . . . id.

κτίσας   vbl., aor. act. ptc. nom. sg. masc. {6.A.1.a} . . . . id.

κτίσει   noun, dat. sg. fem. {2.C} . . . . κτίσις *G2937*

κτίσεως   noun, gen. sg. fem. {2.C} . . . . id.

κτίση   verb, aor. act. subjunc. 3 pers. sg. {5.B.1} . . . . .κτίζω *G2936*

κτισθέντα   vbl., aor. pass. ptc. acc. sg. masc. {6.A.1.a} . . . . id.

κτισθέντες   vbl., aor. pass. ptc. nom. pl. masc. {6.A.1.a} . . . . id.

G2937 **κτίσις**, -εως, ἡ   (1) abstr., *creation;* (2) concr., *creation, creature, institution* (often of the *founding* of a city). Always of Divine work.

κτίσις   noun, nom. sg. fem. {2.C} . . . . κτίσις *G2937*

G2938 **κτίσμα**, -ατος, τό   *a created thing, a creature,* of God.

κτίσμα   noun, acc. sg. neut. {2.C} . . . . κτίσμα *G2938*

κτίσμα   noun, nom. sg. neut. {2.C}. . . . . id.

κτισμάτων   noun, gen. pl. neut. {2.C} . . . . id.

κτίστη   noun, dat. sg. masc. {2.A}. . . . . . . κτίστης *G2939*

G2939 **κτίστης**, -ου, ὁ   *creator, the creator* (of God).

κτῶμαι   verb, pres. mid./pass. indic. 1 pers. sg. {5.A.2} . . . . κτάομαι *G2932*

G2940 **κυβεία**, -ας, ἡ   (lit. *playing with dice, gaming,* hence) *trickery, sleight.*

κυβεία   noun, dat. sg. fem. {2.A} . . . . .κυβεία *G2940*

κυβερνήσεις   noun, acc. pl. fem. {2.C} κυβέρνησις *G2941*

G2941 **κυβέρνησις**, -εως, ἡ   (lit. *steering, piloting*), *governing, government,* supposed to refer to such duty as was, later at least, performed by any presbyter or by that presbyter who was ἐπίσκοπος.

κυβερνήτη   noun, dat. sg. masc. {2.A} κυβερνήτης *G2942*

G2942 **κυβερνήτης**, -ου, ὁ   *a steersman, a pilot.*

κυβερνήτης   noun, nom. sg. masc. {2.A} . . . . κυβερνήτης *G2942*

κυβία   noun, dat. sg. fem. {2.A} . . . . .κυβεία *G2940*

G2944†‡ **κυκλεύω**   *I encircle, invest, surround.* Var. for κυκλόω, John 10:24; Rev 20:9.

G2943 **κυκλόθεν**   adv. and prep. with gen., *in a circle round, round about.*

κυκλόθεν   adv., prep. . . . . κυκλόθεν *G2943*

κυκλουμένην   vbl., pres. pass. ptc. acc. sg. fem. {6.A.2} . . . . .κυκλόω *G2944*

G2944 **κυκλόω**   *I encircle, invest, surround.*

G2945 **κύκλῳ**   adv., *in a circle;* prep. w. gen., *around, round about* (dat. of κύκλος, *a circle*).

κύκλῳ   adv. and prep. . . . . .κύκλῳ *G2945*

κυκλωθέντα   vbl., aor. pass. ptc. nom. pl. neut. {6.A.1.a.} . . . . κυκλόω *G2944*

κυκλωσάντων   vbl., aor. act. ptc. gen. pl. masc. {6.A.2} . . . . id.

κύλισμα   noun, acc. sg. neut. {2.B}. . . . κυλισμός *G2946*

κυλισμόν   noun, acc. sg. masc. {2.B} . . . . id.

G2946 **κυλισμός**, -οῦ, ὁ   *rolling, wallowing.*

G2947 **κυλίω**   trans., *I roll;* mid. intrans., *I roll (myself).*

κυλλόν   adj., acc. sg. masc. {3.A} . . . . κυλλός *G2948*

G2948 **κυλλός**, -ή, -όν   *maimed.*

κυλλούς   adj., acc. pl. masc. {3.A} . . . . . . κυλλός *G2948*

G2949 **κῦμα**, -ατος, τό   *a wave.*

κύματα   noun, nom. pl. neut. {2.C} . . . . . . κῦμα *G2949*

κυμάτων   noun, gen. pl. neut. {2.C} . . . . id.

G2950 **κύμβαλον**, -ου, τό   *a cymbal.*

κύμβαλον   noun, nom. sg. neut. {2.B} . .κύμβαλον *G2950*

G2951 **κύμινον**, -ου, τό   *cumin,* a plant used as a spice (a Semitic word).

κύμινον   noun, acc. sg. neut. {2.B} . . . . . κύμινον *G2951*

κυνάρια   noun, nom. pl. neut. {2.B}. . . . κυνάριον *G2952*

κυναρίοις   noun, dat. pl. neut. {2.B} . . . . id.

G2952 **κυνάριον**, -ου, τό   *a house dog,* possibly with a touch of contempt.

κύνας   noun, acc. pl. masc. {2.C} . . . . .κύων *G2965*

κύνες   noun, nom. pl. masc. {2.C} . . . . id.

Κύπριοι   noun prop., nom. pl. masc. {2.B; 2.D} . . . . Κύπριος *G2953*

G2953 **Κύπριος**, -ου, ὁ   *Cypriote, belonging to Cyprus.*

Κύπριος   noun prop., nom. sg. masc. {2.B; 2.D} . . . . Κύπριος *G2953*

Κυπρίῳ   noun prop., dat. sg. masc. {2.B; 2.D}. . . id.

Κύπρον   noun prop., acc. sg. fem. {2.B; 2.D} . . . . Κύπρος *G2954*

G2954 **Κύπρος**, -ου, ἡ   *Cyprus.*

Κύπρου   noun prop., gen. sg. fem. {2.B; 2.D} . . . . Κύπρος *G2954*

G2955 **κύπτω**   *I stoop.*

Κυρηναῖοι   noun prop., nom. pl. masc. {2.B; 2.D} . . . . .Κυρηναῖος *G2956*

Κυρηναῖον   noun prop., acc. sg. masc. {2.B; 2.D} . . . . id.

G2956 **Κυρηναῖος**, -ου, ὁ   *belonging to Cyrene.*

Κυρηναῖος   noun prop., nom. sg. masc. {2.B; 2.D} . . . . .Κυρηναῖος *G2956*

Κυρηναίου   noun prop., gen. sg. masc. {2.B; 2.D} . . . . id.

Κυρηναίων   noun prop., gen. pl. masc. {2.B; 2.D} . . . . id.

G2957 **Κυρήνη**, -ης, ἡ   *Cyrene,* a district west of Egypt on the Mediterranean coast, forming with Crete a Roman province.

Κυρήνην   noun prop., acc. sg. fem. {2.A; 2.D} . . . . Κυρήνη *G2957*

G2958 **Κυρήνιος**, -ου, ὁ   Publius Sulpicius *Quirinius* (died in 21 A.D.), who conducted two censuses of the province Syria, one in 8, 7, or 6 B.C., Luke 2:2, as plenipotentiary of the Emperor, and another as *legatus pro praetore* in 7 A.D., Acts 5:37.

Κυρηνίου   noun prop., gen. sg. masc. {2.B;
     2.D}. . . . . Κυρήνιος *G2958*

G2959 **κυρία**, -ας, ἡ   *a lady;* voc. *my lady,* an address
     of courtesy.
κυρία   noun, voc. sg. fem. {2.A}. . . . . κυρία *G2959*
κυρίᾳ   noun, dat. sg. fem. {2.A} . . . . id.
κυριακῇ   adj., dat. sg. fem. {3.A} . . . . . κυριακός *G2960*
κυριακόν   adj., acc. sg. neut. {3.A} . . . . id.

G2960 **κυριακός**, -ή, -όν   *of the Lord* (κύριος), *special
     to the Lord* (in constitutional law, *imperial*);
     δεῖπνον, supper (dinner) for church mem-
     bers, combined with the Eucharist; ἡμέρα,
     Sunday.
κύριε   noun, voc. sg. masc. {2.B}. . . . . .κύριος *G2962*
κυριεύει   verb, pres. act. indic. 3 pers. sg.
     {5.A.1.a} . . . . κυριεύω *G2961*
κυριεύομεν   verb, pres. act. indic. 1 pers. pl.
     {5.A.1.a} . . . . id.
κυριευόντων   vbl., pres. act. ptc. gen. pl. masc.
     {6.A.1}. . . . . id.
κυριεύουσιν   verb, pres. act. indic. 3 pers. pl.
     {5.A.1.a} . . . . id.
κυριεύσει   verb, fut. act. indic. 3 pers. sg.
     {5.A.1.a} . . . . id.
κυριεύσῃ   verb, aor. act. subjunc. 3 pers. sg.
     {5.B.1} . . . . id.

G2961 **κυριεύω**   *I rule;* with gen. *I rule over, lord it
     over, master.*
κύριοι   noun, nom. pl. masc. {2.B}. . . . . . .κύριος *G2962*
κύριοι   noun, voc. pl. masc. {2.B}. . . . . id.
κυρίοις   noun, dat. pl. masc. {2.B}. . . . . id.
κύριον   noun, acc. sg. masc. {2.B; 2.D}. . . . . . . id.

G2962 **κύριος**, -ου, ὁ   (1) *an owner* of property, par-
     ticularly of slaves (δοῦλοι), *a lord, master* (cf.
     1 Pet 3:6); pl. οἱ κύριοι, *master and mistress,*
     Matt 15:27(?), Luke 19:33; Acts 16:16, 19, and
     perhaps elsewhere; (2) weaker sense, in the
     voc., as a polite address, κύριε, *sir!,* κύριοι,
     gentlemen, sirs, Acts 16:30, cf. κυρία; (3) of
     divine beings, κύριος, *Lord,* without article,
     generally refers to God, whereas ὁ κύριος, *the
     Lord,* generally refers to Jesus, the Messiah (cf.
     Acts 2:34). In this sense the word connotes
     that these Divine Beings are absolute rulers
     (kings) of the whole world, and that we are
     their slaves (subjects). As the term was also ap-
     plied to oriental sovereigns and to the Roman
     Emperors (particularly frequently in Nero's
     case) in the same sense, it focused the deadly
     rivalry between the two powers (cf. Acts 25:26).
κύριος   noun, nom. sg. masc. {2.B}. . . . . . . .κύριος *G2962*

G2963 **κυριότης**, -ητος, ἡ   (1) abstr., *lordship,* 2 Pet
     2:10; (2) concr., *divine* or *angelic lordship,
     domination, dignity,* Eph 1:21; Col 1:16; Jude 8,
     usually with reference to a celestial hierarchy.
κυριότητα   noun, acc. sg. fem. {2.C} . . . .κυριότης *G2963*
κυριότητες   noun, nom. pl. fem. {2.C}. . . . . id.
κυριότητος   noun, gen. sg. fem. {2.C} . . . . id.
κυρίου   noun, gen. sg. masc. {2.B} . . . . . . .κύριος *G2962*
κυρίῳ   noun, dat. sg. masc. {2.B} . . . . id.

κυριων   noun, gen. pl. masc. {2.B} . . . . id.
κυρίων   noun, gen. pl. masc. {2.B} . . . . id.

G2964 **κυρόω**   *I ratify, confirm.*
κυρῶσαι   vbl., aor. act. inf. {6.B.1} . . . . . . .κυρόω *G2964*
κυσί   noun, dat. pl. masc. {2.C}. . . . . .κύων *G2965*
κυσίν   noun, dat. pl. masc. {2.C}. . . . . id.
κύψας   vbl., aor. act. ptc. nom. sg. masc.
     {6.A.1.a} .κύπτω *G2955*

G2965 **κύων**, κυνός, dat. pl. κυσί, ὁ   *a dog;* univer-
     sally despised in the east, and thus the name is
     applied contemptuously to persons, Phil 3:2;
     Rev 22:15 (cf. Matt 15:26).
κύων   noun, nom. sg. masc. {2.C}. . . . . .κύων *G2965*
Κῶ   noun prop., acc. sg. fem. {2.B; 2.D} . . . . .Κῶς *G2972*
κῶλα   noun, nom. pl. neut. {2.B} . . . . .κῶλον *G2966*

G2966 **κῶλον**, -ου, τό   *a limb;* pl. *bodies.*
κωλύει   verb, pres. act. indic. 3 pers. sg.
     {5.A.1.a} . . . . .κωλύω *G2967*
κωλύειν   vbl., pres. act. inf. {6.B.1} . . . . id.
κωλύεσθαι   vbl., pres. pass. inf. {6.B.1} . . . . . . id.
κωλύετε   verb, pres. act. impv. 2 pers. pl. {5.D.1} id.
κωλυθέντες   vbl., aor. pass. ptc. nom. pl. masc.
     {6.A.1.a} . . . . id.
κωλύοντα   vbl., pres. act. ptc. acc. sg. masc.
     {6.A.1}. . . . . id.
κωλυόντων   vbl., pres. act. ptc. gen. pl. masc.
     {6.A.1}. . . . . id.
κωλῦσαι   vbl., aor. act. inf. {6.B.1} . . . . id.
κωλύσῃς   verb, aor. act. subjunc. 2 pers. sg. {5.B.1} id.

G2967 **κωλύω**   *I prevent, debar, hinder;* with inf. *from*
     doing so and so.
κώμας   noun, acc. pl. fem. {2.A} . . . . .κώμη *G2968*
κωμῇ   noun, dat. sg. fem. {2.A}. . . . . id.

G2968 **κώμη**, -ης, ἡ   *a village.*
κώμη   noun, dat. sg. fem. {2.A}. . . . . .κώμη *G2968*
κώμην   noun, acc. sg. fem. {2.A}. . . . . id.
κώμης   noun, gen. sg. fem. {2.A} . . . . id.
κῶμοι   noun, nom. pl. masc. {2.B} . . . . . . .κῶμος *G2970*
κώμοις   noun, dat. pl. masc. {2.B}. . . . . id.
κωμοπόλεις   noun, acc. pl. fem. {2.C} . κωμόπολις *G2969*

G2969 **κωμόπολις**, -εως, ἡ   a city which in constitu-
     tion has only the status of a village.

G2970 **κῶμος**, -ου, ὁ   *a revel, a reveling,* such as took
     place at the gathering of the grapes.
Κῶν   noun prop., acc. sg. fem. {2.B; 2.D} . . . . .Κῶς *G2972*
κώνωπα   noun, acc. sg. masc. {2.C} . . . . . .κώνωψ *G2971*

G2971 **κώνωψ**, -ωπος, ὁ   *a gnat, mosquito,* referred to
     proverbially as something small.

G2972 **Κῶς**, Κῶ, ἡ   *Cos,* an island in the Aegean Sea,
     southwest of Asia Minor.

G2973 **Κωσάμ**, ὁ   *Cosam,* son of Elmadam and father
     of Addei (Heb.).
Κωσάμ   noun prop. . . . . Κωσάμ *G2973*
κωφοί   adj., nom. pl. masc. {3.A} . . . . . . .κωφός *G2974*
κωφόν   adj., acc. sg. masc. {3.A} . . . . id.
κωφόν   adj., acc. sg. neut. {3.A} . . . . id.
κωφόν   adj., nom. sg. neut. {3.A} . . . . id.

G2974 **κωφός**, -ή, -όν   *dumb.*
κωφός   adj., nom. sg. masc. {3.A}. . . . . . . .κωφός *G2974*
κωφούς   adj., acc. pl. masc. {3.A} . . . . id.

Λ λ

λάβε   verb, ²aor. act. impv. 2 pers. sg.
{5.D.1}. . . . . λαμβάνω G2983
λαβεῖν   vbl., ²aor. act. inf. {6.B.1} . . . . id.
λάβετε   verb, ²aor. act. impv. 2 pers. pl. {5.D.1} . . id.
λαβέτω   verb, ²aor. act. impv. 3 pers. sg. {5.D.1} . id.
λάβῃ   verb, ²aor. act. subjunc. 3 pers. sg. {5.B.1} . id.
λάβητε   verb, ²aor. act. subjunc. 2 pers. pl.
{5.B.1} . . . . id.
λάβοι   verb, ²aor. act. opt. 3 pers. sg. {5.C.1}. . . . id.
λαβόντα   vbl., ²aor. act. ptc. acc. sg. masc.
{6.A.1.a} . . . . id.
λαβόντας   vbl., ²aor. act. ptc. acc. pl. masc.
{6.A.1.a} . . . . id.
λαβόντες   vbl., ²aor. act. ptc. nom. pl. masc.
{6.A.1.a} . . . . id.
λαβοῦσα   vbl., ²aor. act. ptc. nom. sg. fem.
{6.A.1.a} . . . . id.
λαβοῦσαι   vbl., ²aor. act. ptc. nom. pl. fem.
{6.A.1.a} . . . . id.
λάβω   verb, ²aor. act. subjunc. 1 pers. sg. {5.B.1} . id.
λάβωμεν   verb, ²aor. act. subjunc. 1 pers. pl.
{5.B.1} . . . . id.
λαβών   vbl., ²aor. act. ptc. nom. sg. masc.
{6.A.1.a} . . . . id.
λάβωσι   verb, ²aor. act. subjunc. 3 pers. pl.
{5.B.1} . . . . id.
λάβωσιν   verb, ²aor. act. subjunc. 3 pers. pl.
{5.B.1} . . . . id.
G2975   **λαγχάνω**   (1) *I obtain (receive) by lot, my lot
(turn) is;* (2) *I cast lots,* John 19:24.
Λάζαρε   noun prop., voc. sg. masc. {2.B;
2.D}. . . . . .Λάζαρος G2976
Λάζαρον   noun prop., acc. sg. masc. {2.B; 2.D} . id.
G2976   **Λάζαρος**, -ου, ὁ   *Lazarus,* (1) the beggar, Luke
16:20ff.; (2) the brother of Martha and Mary,
of Bethany, John 11, 12 (Ἐλεάζαρος, *Eliezer,*
in old Western documents).
Λάζαρος   noun prop., nom. sg. masc. {2.B;
2.D}. . . . . .Λάζαρος G2976
λαθεῖν   vbl., ²aor. act. inf. {6.B.1} . . . . . . λανθάνω G2990
λάθρα   adv. . . . . .λάθρα G2977
G2977   **λάθρα**   adv., *secretly.*
λάθρα   adv. . . . . .λάθρα G2977
λαίλαπος   noun, gen. sg. fem. {2.C}. . . . . λαῖλαψ G2978
G2978   **λαῖλαψ**, -απος, ἡ   *a sudden storm, a squall.*
λαῖλαψ   noun, nom. sg. fem. {2.C}. . . . . . λαῖλαψ G2978
G2997‡   **λακάω** (λάσκω)   *I burst apart, burst open,
burst asunder with a loud noise.* Λακάω,
rather than λάσκω, is currently believed to be
the source of ἐλάκησεν, Acts 1:18.
λακτίζειν   vbl., pres. act. inf. {6.B.1}. . . . . λακτίζω G2979
G2979   **λακτίζω**   *I kick.*
λάλει   verb, pres. act. impv. 2 pers. sg.
{5.D.2}. . . . . .λαλέω G2980
λαλεῖ   verb, pres. act. impv. 2 pers. sg. {5.D.2} . . id.
λαλεῖ   verb, pres. act. indic. 3 pers. sg. {5.A.2} . . id.
λαλεῖν   vbl., pres. act. inf. {6.B.2} . . . . id.

λαλεῖς   verb, pres. act. indic. 2 pers. sg. {5.A.2} . id.
λαλεῖσθαι   vbl., pres. pass. inf. {6.B.2} . . . . id.
λαλεῖται   verb, pres. mid. indic. 3 pers. sg.
{5.A.2}. . . . . id.
λαλεῖτε   verb, pres. act. impv. 2 pers. pl. {5.D.2} . id.
λαλείτω   verb, pres. act. impv. 3 pers. sg. {5.D.2} id.
λαλείτωσαν   verb, pres. act. impv. 3 pers. pl.
{5.D.2}. . . . . id.
G2980   **λαλέω**   *I speak; I say* (*I talk, chatter* in classical
Gk., but in NT a more dignified word).
λαλῇ   verb, pres. act. subjunc. 3 pers. sg.
{5.B.2}. . . . . .λαλέω G2980
λαληθείς   vbl., aor. pass. ptc. nom. sg. masc.
{6.A.1.a.}. . . . . id.
λαληθείσης   vbl., aor. pass. ptc. gen. sg. fem.
{6.A.1.a.}. . . . . id.
λαληθέντος   vbl., aor. pass. ptc. gen. sg. neut.
{6.A.1.a.}. . . . . id.
λαληθέντων   vbl., aor. pass. ptc. gen. pl. neut.
{6.A.1.a.}. . . . . id.
λαληθῆναι   vbl., aor. pass. inf. {6.B.1} . . . . id.
λαληθήσεται   verb, fut. pass. indic. 3 pers. sg.
{5.A.1}. . . . . id.
λαληθησομένων   vbl., fut. pass. ptc. gen. pl.
neut. {6.A.1.b} . . . . id.
λαλῆσαι   vbl., aor. act. inf. {6.B.1} . . . . id.
λαλήσαντες   vbl., aor. act. ptc. nom. pl. masc.
{6.A.2} . . . . id.
λαλήσαντος   vbl., aor. act. ptc. gen. sg. masc.
{6.A.2} . . . . id.
λαλήσας   vbl., aor. act. ptc. nom. sg. masc.
{6.A.2} . . . . id.
λαλήσει   verb, fut. act. indic. 3 pers. sg. {5.A.1} . id.
λαλήσετε   verb, fut. act. indic. 2 pers. pl. {5.A.1} id.
λαλήσῃ   verb, aor. act. subjunc. 3 pers. sg.
{5.B.1} . . . . id.
λαλήσητε   verb, aor. act. subjunc. 2 pers. pl.
{5.B.1} . . . . id.
λαλήσομεν   verb, fut. act. indic. 1 pers. pl.
{5.A.1} . . . . id.
λαλήσουσι   verb, fut. act. indic. 3 pers. pl.
{5.A.1} . . . . id.
λαλήσουσιν   verb, fut. act. indic. 3 pers. pl.
{5.A.1} . . . . id.
λαλήσω   verb, aor. act. subjunc. 1 pers. sg.
{5.B.1} . . . . id.
λαλήσω   verb, fut. act. indic. 1 pers. sg. {5.A.1} . id.
λαλήσωσιν   verb, aor. act. subjunc. 3 pers. pl.
{5.B.1} . . . . id.
G2981   **λαλιά**, -ᾶς, ἡ   *speech, talk; manner of speech* (in
classical Gk. *babble, chattering*).
λαλιά   noun, nom. sg. fem. {2.A}. . . . . λαλιά G2981
λαλιάν   noun, acc. sg. fem. {2.A} . . . . id.
λαλοῦμεν   verb, pres. act. indic. 1 pers. pl.
{5.A.2}. . . . . .λαλέω G2980
λαλουμένη   vbl., pres. pass. ptc. nom. sg. fem.
{6.A.2} . . . . id.

λαλουμένοις vbl., pres. pass. ptc. dat. pl. neut.
{6.A.2}............................... id.
λαλούμενον vbl., pres. pass. ptc. acc. sg. masc.
{6.A.2}............................... id.
λαλούμενον vbl., pres. pass. ptc. nom. sg.
neut. {6.A.2} .... id.
λαλοῦν vbl., pres. act. ptc. nom. sg. neut.
{6.A.2}............................... id.
λαλοῦντα vbl., pres. act. ptc. acc. sg. masc.
{6.A.2}............................... id.
λαλοῦντας vbl., pres. act. ptc. acc. pl. masc.
{6.A.2}............................... id.
λαλοῦντες vbl., pres. act. ptc. nom. pl. masc.
{6.A.2}............................... id.
λαλοῦντι vbl., pres. act. ptc. dat. sg. masc.
{6.A.2}............................... id.
λαλοῦντος vbl., pres. act. ptc. gen. sg. masc.
{6.A.2}............................... id.
λαλούντων vbl., pres. act. ptc. gen. pl. masc.
{6.A.2}............................... id.
λαλοῦσα vbl., pres. act. ptc. nom. sg. fem.
{6.A.2}............................... id.
λαλοῦσαι vbl., pres. act. ptc. nom. pl. fem.
{6.A.2}............................... id.
λαλοῦσαν vbl., pres. act. ptc. acc. sg. fem.
{6.A.2}............................... id.
λαλούσης vbl., pres. act. ptc. gen. sg. fem.
{6.A.2}............................... id.
λαλοῦσι verb, pres. act. indic. 3 pers. pl. {5.A.2} id.
λαλοῦσιν verb, pres. act. indic. 3 pers. pl. {5.A.2} . id.
λαλῶ verb, pres. act. indic. 1 pers. sg. {5.A.2} . . id.
λαλῶ verb, pres. act. subjunc. 1 pers. sg. {5.B.2} id.
λαλῶν vbl., pres. act. ptc. nom. sg. masc. {6.A.2} id.
λαλῶσιν verb, pres. act. subjunc. 3 pers. pl.
{5.B.2}............................... id.
G2982 **λαμά** (λεμα) *why* (Heb.).
λαμά Aram........................ λαμά G2982
λαμβάνει verb, pres. act. indic. 3 pers. sg.
{5.A.1.a} .... λαμβάνω G2983
λαμβάνειν vbl., pres. act. inf. {6.B.1}......... id.
λαμβάνεις verb, pres. act. indic. 2 pers. sg.
{5.A.1.a} .... id.
λαμβάνετε verb, pres. act. impv. 2 pers. pl.
{5.D.1}............................... id.
λαμβάνετε verb, pres. act. indic. 2 pers. pl.
{5.A.1.a} .... id.
λαμβανέτω verb, pres. act. impv. 3 pers. sg.
{5.D.1}............................... id.
λαμβάνῃ verb, pres. act. subjunc. 3 pers. sg.
{5.B.1}............................... id.
λαμβάνομεν verb, pres. act. indic. 1 pers. pl.
{5.A.1.a} .... id.
λαμβανόμενον vbl., pres. pass. ptc. nom. sg.
neut. {6.A.1}........................ id.
λαμβανόμενος vbl., pres. pass. ptc. nom. sg.
masc. {6.A.1}........................ id.
λαμβάνοντες vbl., pres. act. ptc. nom. pl.
masc. {6.A.1}........................ id.
λαμβάνουσι verb, pres. act. indic. 3 pers. pl.
{5.A.1.a} .... id.

λαμβάνουσιν verb, pres. act. indic. 3 pers. pl.
{5.A.1.a} .... id.
G2983 **λαμβάνω** (1) *I receive, get;* πρόσωπον
λαμβάνειν τινός (Hebraistic), lit. *to receive
the face of, to accept the person of,* i.e., *to favor
specially;* (2) *I take;* συμβούλιον λαβεῖν, *to
deliberate,* Matt 12:14; (3) = παραλαμβάνω,
John 1:12.
λαμβάνω verb, pres. act. indic. 1 pers. sg.
{5.A.1.a} .... λαμβάνω G2983
λαμβάνων vbl., pres. act. ptc. nom. sg. masc.
{6.A.1}............................... id.
G2984 **Λάμεχ**, ὁ *Lamech,* son of Methuselah and
father of Noah (Heb.).
Λάμεχ noun prop.................. Λάμεχ G2984
λαμμᾶ Aram....................... λαμά G2982
λαμπάδας noun, acc. pl. fem. {2.C}..... λαμπάς G2985
λαμπάδες noun, nom. pl. fem. {2.C}........ id.
λαμπάδων noun, gen. pl. fem. {2.C}........ id.
G2985 **λαμπάς**, -άδος, ἡ *a lamp, a lantern.*
λαμπάς noun, nom. sg. fem. {2.C}..... λαμπάς G2985
λάμπει verb, pres. act. indic. 3 pers. sg.
{5.A.1.a} .... λάμπω G2989
λαμπρά adj., nom. pl. neut. {3.A} .. λαμπρός G2986
λαμπρᾷ adj., dat. sg. fem. {3.A}.......... id.
λαμπράν adj., acc. sg. fem. {3.A}......... id.
λαμπρόν adj., acc. sg. masc. {3.A}........ id.
λαμπρόν adj., acc. sg. neut. {3.A}......... id.
G2986 **λαμπρός**, -ά, -όν *shining, glossy, bright.*
λαμπρός adj., nom. sg. masc. {3.A}.... λαμπρός G2986
G2987 **λαμπρότης**, -ητος, ἡ *brightness.*
λαμπρότητα noun, acc. sg. fem. {2.C} λαμπρότης G2987
G2988 **λαμπρῶς** adv., *sumptuously.*
λαμπρῶς adv. {3.F} .... λαμπρῶς G2988
G2989 **λάμπω** *I shine.*
λάμψαι vbl., aor. act. inf. {6.B.1} .... λάμπω G2989
λαμψάτω verb, aor. act. impv. 3 pers. sg. {5.D.1} id.
λάμψει verb, fut. act. indic. 3 pers. sg. {5.A.1.a}. id.
λανθάνει verb, pres. act. indic. 3 pers. sg.
{5.A.1.a} .... λανθάνω G2990
λανθάνειν vbl., pres. act. inf. {6.B.1}......... id.
λανθανέτω verb, pres. act. impv. 3 pers. sg.
{5.D.1}............................... id.
G2990 **λανθάνω** *I am hidden (concealed), I lie hid, I
escape notice,* sometimes with acc. of person
from whom concealment takes place, Acts
26:26; 2 Pet 3:8; with parts. (classical constr.), I
do so and so *unconsciously, unknown to myself,
I shut my eyes to* so and so, Heb 13:2.
G2991 **λαξευτός**, -ή, -όν *hewn* out of the rock.
λαξευτῷ adj., dat. sg. neut. {3.A}. .... λαξευτός G2991
Λαοδικαίων noun prop., gen. pl. masc. {2.C;
2.D}...................... Λαοδικεύς G2994
G2993 **Λαοδίκεια**, -ας, ἡ *Laodicea,* a city in the
Lycos valley in the Roman province Asia, near
Colossae and Hierapolis.
Λαοδικείᾳ noun prop., dat. sg. fem. {2.A;
2.D}...................... Λαοδίκεια G2993
Λαοδίκειαν noun prop., acc. sg. fem. {2.A; 2.D} id.
Λαοδικείας noun prop., gen. sg. fem. {2.A; 2.D} id.

G2994 **Λαοδικεύς**, -έως, ὁ *a Laodicean, an inhabitant of Laodicea.*
Λαοδικέων noun prop., gen. pl. masc. {2.C; 2.D} . . . . Λαοδικεύς G2994
Λαοδικία noun prop., dat. sg. fem. {2.A; 2.D} . . . . Λαοδίκεια G2993
Λαοδικίαν noun prop., acc. sg. fem. {2.A; 2.D} . id.
Λαοδικίας noun prop., gen. sg. fem. {2.A; 2.D} . id.
λαοί noun, nom. pl. masc. {2.B} . . . . λαός G2992‡
λαοῖς noun, dat. pl. masc. {2.B} . . . . id.
λαόν noun, acc. sg. masc. {2.B} . . . . id.

G2992‡ **λαός**, -οῦ, ὁ (1) *a people,* characteristically of God's chosen people, first the Jews, then the Christians; (2) sometimes, but rarely, *the people, the crowd,* e.g., Luke 9:13; 20:6.
λαός noun, nom. sg. masc. {2.B} . . . . λαός G2992‡
λαός noun, voc. sg. masc. {2.B} . . . . id.
λαοῦ noun, gen. sg. masc. {2.B} . . . . id.

G2995 **λάρυγξ**, γγος, ὁ *the throat.*
λάρυγξ noun, nom. sg. masc. {2.C} . . . . . . λάρυγξ G2995

G2996 **Λασαία** (Λασέα), -ας, ἡ *Lasaea* (Lasea), a city in Crete, about the middle of the south coast.
Λασαία noun prop., nom. sg. fem. {2.A; 2.D} . . . . .Λασαία G2996
Λασέα noun prop., nom. sg. fem. {2.A; 2.D} . . . id.

G2998 **λατομέω** *I hew* (of stone).

G2999 **λατρεία**, -ας, ἡ *service* rendered to God, perhaps simply *worship.*
λατρεία noun, nom. sg. fem. {2.A} . . . . . λατρεία G2999
λατρείαν noun, acc. sg. fem. {2.A} . . . . id.
λατρείας noun, acc. pl. fem. {2.A}. . . . . id.
λατρείας noun, gen. sg. fem. {2.A} . . . . id.
λατρεύειν vbl., pres. act. inf. {6.B.1} . . . λατρεύω G3000
λατρεύομεν verb, pres. act. indic. 1 pers. pl. {5.A.1.a} . . . . id.
λατρεῦον vbl., pres. act. ptc. nom. sg. neut. {6.A.1} . . . . id.
λατρεύοντα vbl., pres. act. ptc. acc. sg. masc. {6.A.1} . . . . id.
λατρεύοντας vbl., pres. act. ptc. acc. pl. masc. {6.A.1} . . . . id.
λατρεύοντες vbl., pres. act. ptc. nom. pl. masc. {6.A.1} . . . . id.
λατρεύουσα vbl., pres. act. ptc. nom. sg. fem. {6.A.1} . . . . id.
λατρεύουσι verb, pres. act. indic. 3 pers. pl. {5.A.1.a} . . . . id.
λατρεύουσιν verb, pres. act. indic. 3 pers. pl. {5.A.1.a} . . . . id.
λατρεύσεις verb, fut. act. indic. 2 pers. sg. {5.A.1.a} . . . . id.
λατρεύσω verb, fut. act. indic. 3 pers. pl. {5.A.1.a} . . . . id.
λατρεύσουσιν verb, fut. act. indic. 3 pers. pl. {5.A.1.a} . . . . id.

G3000 **λατρεύω** *I serve,* esp. God, perhaps simply *I worship.*
λατρεύω verb, pres. act. indic. 1 pers. sg. {5.A.1.a} . . . . λατρεύω G3000

λατρεύωμεν verb, pres. act. subjunc. 1 pers. pl. {5.B.1} . . . . id.
λάχανα noun, acc. pl. neut. {2.B} . . . . . λάχανον G3001

G3001 **λάχανον**, -ου, τό *a vegetable.*
λάχανον noun, acc. sg. neut. {2.B} . . . . λάχανον G3001
λαχάνων noun, gen. pl. neut. {2.B} . . . . id.
λαχοῦσι vbl., ²aor. act. ptc. dat. pl. masc. {6.A.1.a} . . . . λαγχάνω G2975
λαχοῦσιν vbl., ²aor. act. ptc. dat. pl. masc. {6.A.1.a} . . . . id.
λάχωμεν verb, ²aor. act. subjunc. 1 pers. pl. {5.B.1} . . . . id.
λαῷ noun, dat. sg. masc. {2.B} . . . . λαός G2992‡
λαῶν noun, gen. pl. masc. {2.B} . . . . id.

G3002 **Λεββαῖος**, -ου, ὁ *Lebbaeus,* a pet name, a var. for Thaddaeus, one of the twelve disciples of Jesus. The full form of the name is not known.
Λεββαῖος noun prop., nom. sg. masc. {2.B; 2.D} . . . . Λεββαῖος G3002
λέγε verb, pres. act. impv. 2 pers. sg. {5.D.1} . . λέγω G3004
λέγει verb, pres. act. indic. 3 pers. sg. {5.A.1.a} . . id.
λέγειν vbl., pres. act. inf. {6.B.1} . . . . id.
λέγεις verb, pres. act. indic. 2 pers. sg. {5.A.1.a} . id.
λέγεσθαι vbl., pres. pass. inf. {6.B.1} . . . . id.
λέγεται verb, pres. pass. indic. 3 pers. sg. {5.A.1.d} . . . . id.
λέγετε verb, pres. act. impv. 2 pers. pl. {5.D.1} . . id.
λέγετε verb, pres. act. indic. 2 pers. pl. {5.A.1.a} . id.
λεγέτω verb, pres. act. impv. 3 pers. sg. {5.D.1} . . id.
λεγών noun, nom. sg. masc. {2.C} . . . . λεγιών G3003
λεγεώνα noun, acc. sg. masc. {2.C} . . . . id.
λεγεῶνας noun, acc. pl. fem. {2.C} . . . . id.
λέγῃ verb, pres. act. subjunc. 3 pers. sg. {5.B.1}λέγω G3004
λέγητε verb, pres. act. subjunc. 2 pers. pl. {5.B.1}id.

G3003 **λεγιών** (λεγεών), -ῶνος, ἡ properly a division of the Roman army, numbering about 6,000 infantry with additional cavalry (cf. Matt 26:53); hence, *a very large number* (Lat. *legio*).
λεγιών noun, nom. sg. fem. {2.C} . . . . λεγιών G3003
λεγιῶνα noun, acc. sg. fem. {2.C} . . . . id.
λεγιῶνας noun, acc. pl. fem. {2.C} . . . . id.
λέγομεν verb, pres. act. indic. 1 pers. pl. {5.A.1.a} . . . . λέγω G3004
λεγόμενα vbl., pres. pass. ptc. acc. pl. neut. {6.A.1} id.
λεγομένη vbl., pres. pass. ptc. nom. sg. fem. {6.A.1} . . . . id.
λεγομένην vbl., pres. pass. ptc. acc. sg. fem. {6.A.1} . . . . id.
λεγομένης vbl., pres. pass. ptc. gen. sg. fem. {6.A.1} . . . . id.
λεγόμενοι vbl., pres. pass. ptc. nom. pl. masc. {6.A.1} . . . . id.
λεγομένοις vbl., pres. pass. ptc. dat. pl. neut. {6.A.1} . . . . id.
λεγόμενον vbl., pres. pass. ptc. acc. sg. masc. {6.A.1} . . . . id.
λεγόμενον vbl., pres. pass. ptc. acc. sg. neut. {6.A.1} . . . . id.
λεγόμενος vbl., pres. pass. ptc. nom. sg. masc. {6.A.1} . . . . id.

λεγομένου vbl., pres. pass. ptc. gen. sg. masc.
{6.A.1}. . . . . id.
λέγον vbl., pres. act. ptc. nom. sg. neut. {6.A.1} . id.
λέγοντα vbl., pres. act. ptc. acc. sg. masc. {6.A.1}id.
λέγοντα vbl., pres. act. ptc. nom. pl. neut.
{6.A.1}. . . . . id.
λέγοντας vbl., pres. act. ptc. acc. pl. masc.
{6.A.1}. . . . . id.
λέγοντες vbl., pres. act. ptc. nom. pl. masc.
{6.A.1}. . . . . id.
λέγοντι vbl., pres. act. ptc. dat. sg. masc. {6.A.1} id.
λέγοντος vbl., pres. act. ptc. gen. sg. masc.
{6.A.1}. . . . . id.
λέγοντος vbl., pres. act. ptc. gen. sg. neut.
{6.A.1}. . . . . id.
λεγόντων vbl., pres. act. ptc. gen. pl. masc.
{6.A.1}. . . . . id.
λέγουσα vbl., pres. act. ptc. nom. sg. fem.
{6.A.1}. . . . . id.
λέγουσαι vbl., pres. act. ptc. nom. pl. fem.
{6.A.1}. . . . . id.
λέγουσαν vbl., pres. act. ptc. acc. sg. fem.
{6.A.1}. . . . . id.
λεγούσης vbl., pres. act. ptc. gen. sg. fem. {6.A.1} id.
λέγουσι verb, pres. act. indic. 3 pers. pl.
{5.A.1.a} . . . . id.
λέγουσιν verb, pres. act. indic. 3 pers. pl.
{5.A.1.a} . . . . id.
λέγουσιν vbl., pres. act. ptc. dat. pl. neut.
{6.A.1}. . . . . id.
G3004 **λέγω** (1) *I say, speak; I mean; I mention, tell;* (2)
I call, name, esp. in the pass., e.g., Matt 1:16;
John 1:38, but also act., e.g., Mark 10:18; (3) *I
tell, I command,* e.g., Matt 5:34, 39; Rom 2:22.
Fut. ἐρῶ. Aor. εἶπον or εἶπα, I spoke, said;
ὡς ἔπος εἰπεῖν, *one might almost say (almost,
about).*
λέγω verb, pres. act. indic. 1 pers. sg. {5.A.1.a} λέγω G3004
λέγω verb, pres. act. subjunc. 1 pers. sg. {5.B.1} . id.
λέγωμεν verb, pres. act. subjunc. 1 pers. pl.
{5.B.1} . . . . id.
λέγων vbl., pres. act. ptc. nom. sg. masc. {6.A.1} id.
λέγωσι verb, pres. act. subjunc. 3 pers. pl.
{5.B.1} . . . . id.
λέγωσιν verb, pres. act. subjunc. 3 pers. pl.
{5.B.1} . . . . id.
λείας adj., acc. pl. fem. {3.A} . . . . λεῖος G3006
G3005 **λεῖμμα** (λίμμα), -ατος, τό *a remnant, a
remainder.*
λεῖμμα noun, nom. sg. neut. {2.C}. . . . . . λεῖμμα G3005
G3006 **λεῖος**, -α, -ον *smooth.*
λείπει verb, pres. act. indic. 3 pers. sg.
{5.A.1.a} . . . . λείπω G3007
λείπεται verb, pres. mid./pass. indic. 3 pers. sg.
{5.A.1.d} . . . . id.
λείπῃ verb, pres. act. subjunc. 3 pers. sg. {5.B.1} id.
λειπόμενοι vbl., pres. mid./pass. ptc. nom. pl.
masc. {6.A.1}. . . . . id.
λείποντα vbl., pres. act. ptc. acc. pl. neut.
{6.A.1}. . . . . id.

G3007 **λείπω** (1) *I am wanting;* τὰ λείποντα, *what
is defective,* Titus 1:5; (2) mid. e.g., with gen. *I
come behind* (in a race), *I am left behind in, I
fall short of* (some standard), *I am wanting in.*
(Earlier meaning, *I leave behind, abandon*),
G3008 **λειτουργέω** *I act in the public service, I render
service, I minister,* in the widest sense, Rom
15:27, of some special public religious service,
Acts 13:2; but also of the service of priests and
Levites, Heb 10:11.
λειτουργῆσαι vbl., aor. act. inf. {6.B.1}λειτουργέω G3008
G3009 **λειτουργία**, -ας, ἡ *public service* in the widest
sense, 2 Cor 9:12; Phil 2:30; *service* as of priest
or Levite ritual, Luke 1:23; Phil 2:17; Heb 8:6;
9:21.
λειτουργίᾳ noun, dat. sg. fem. {2.A} . . λειτουργία G3009
λειτουργίας noun, gen. sg. fem. {2.A}. . . . . . . id.
λειτουργικά adj., nom. pl. neut.
{3.A} . . . . λειτουργικός G3010
G3010 **λειτουργικός**, -ή, -όν *given to serving (ministration), ministering.*
λειτουργοί noun, nom. pl. masc. {2.B} λειτουργός G3011
λειτουργόν noun, acc. sg. masc. {2.B}. . . . . id.
G3011 **λειτουργός**, -οῦ, ὁ *minister, servant,* of an
official character; of priests and Levites, Heb
8:2.
λειτουργός noun, nom. sg. masc. {2.B}λειτουργός G3011
λειτουργούντων vbl., pres. act. ptc. gen. pl. masc.
{6.A.2}. . . . . .λειτουργέω G3008
λειτουργούς noun, acc. pl. masc. {2.B}λειτουργός G3011
λειτουργῶν vbl., pres. act. ptc. nom. sg. masc.
{6.A.2}. . . . . .λειτουργέω G3008
λελάληκα verb, perf. act. indic. 1 pers. sg.
{5.A.1}. . . . . λαλέω G2980
λελάληκεν verb, perf. act. indic. 3 pers. sg.
{5.A.1}. . . . . id.
λελαλημένοις vbl., perf. pass. ptc. dat. pl.
neut. {6.A.2} . . . . id.
λελάληται verb, perf. pass. indic. 3 pers. sg.
{5.A.1}. . . . . id.
λελατομημένον vbl., perf. pass. ptc. nom. sg.
neut. {6.A.2} . . . . λατομέω G2998
λελουμένοι vbl., perf. mid./pass. ptc. nom. pl.
masc. {6.A.1.b} . . . . λούω G3068
λελουμένος vbl., perf. mid./pass. ptc. nom. sg.
masc. {6.A.1.b} . . . . id.
λελουσμένοι vbl., perf. mid./pass. ptc. nom.
pl. masc. {6.A.1.b} . . . . id.
λελυμένα vbl., perf. pass. ptc. nom. pl. neut.
{6.A.1.b} . . . . λύω G3089
λελυμένον vbl., perf. pass. ptc. nom. sg. neut.
{6.A.1.b} . . . . id.
λελύπηκεν verb, perf. act. indic. 3 pers. sg.
{5.A.1}. . . . . λυπέω G3076
λέλυσαι verb, perf. pass. indic. 2 pers. sg.
{5.A.1.f} . . . . λύω G3089
λεμα Aram. . . . . λαμά G2982
λεμά Aram. . . . . id.
G3012 **λέντιον**, -ου, τό *a towel* (loan word from Lat.
linteum).

λέντιον   noun, acc. sg. neut. {2.B} . . . . . . λέντιον G3012
λεντίῳ   noun, dat. sg. neut. {2.B} . . . . id.
λέοντι   noun, dat. sg. masc. {2.C} . . . . λέων G3023
λέοντος   noun, gen. sg. masc. {2.C} . . . . id.
λεόντων   noun, gen. pl. masc. {2.C} . . . . id.
λεπίδες   noun, nom. pl. fem. {2.C} . . . . λεπίς G3013
G3013 **λεπίς**, -ίδος, ἡ   *a scale, a scaly substance* thrown
     off from the body.
G3014 **λέπρα**, -ας, ἡ   *leprosy.*
λέπρα   noun, nom. sg. fem. {2.A} . . . . λέπρα G3014
λέπρας   noun, gen. sg. fem. {2.A} . . . . id.
λεπροί   adj., nom. pl. masc. {3.A} . . . . λεπρός G3015
G3015 **λεπρός**, -οῦ, ὁ   *a leprous person, a leper.*
λεπρός   adj., nom. sg. masc. {3.A} . . . . . . λεπρός G3015
λεπροῦ   adj., gen. sg. masc. {3.A} . . . . id.
λεπρούς   adj., acc. pl. masc. {3.A} . . . . id.
λεπτά   noun, acc. pl. neut. {2.B} . . . . λεπτός G3016
λεπτόν   noun, acc. sg. neut. {2.B} . . . . id.
G3016 **λεπτός**, -οῦ, τό   *small, light;* neut. subs. *a small*
     piece of money, probably *the smallest piece of*
     money = a half quadrans (see κοδράντης).
Λευί   noun prop.. . . . . Λευί G3017
Λευείν   noun prop., acc. sg. masc. {2.C; 2.D} . . Λευί G3018
Λευείς   noun prop., nom. sg. masc. {2.C; 2.D} . . id.
Λευείτας   noun prop., acc. pl. masc. {2.A;
     2.D}. . . . . Λευίτης G3019
Λευείτης   noun prop., nom. sg. masc. {2.A; 2.D} id.
Λευειτικῆς   adj. prop., gen. sg. fem.
     {3.A} . . . . Λευιτικός G3020
G3017 **Λευί** (Λευίς), ὁ   *Levi,* (1) an ancestor of Jesus,
     Luke 3:24; (2) another ancestor of Jesus, Luke
     3:29; (3) third son of Jacob, the patriarch, and
     founder of a tribe named after him, Heb 7:5,
     9; Rev 7:7; (4) son of Alphaeus, and called
     also Matthew, a revenue officer and one of the
     twelve disciples of Jesus (Heb.).
Λευί   noun prop. Λευί G3017
Λευῖ   noun prop. .Λευίς G3018
Λευῖ   noun prop. . . . . id.
Λευίν   noun prop., acc. sg. masc. {2.C; 2.D} . . . . id.
Λευίν   noun prop., acc. sg. masc. {2.C; 2.D} . . . . id.
G3018 **Λευίς**   Alt. spelling of Λευί.
Λευίς   noun prop., nom. sg. masc. {2.C; 2.D} .Λευίς G3018
Λευῖς   noun prop., nom. sg. masc. {2.C; 2.D} . . . id.
Λευίτας   noun prop., acc. pl. masc. {2.A;
     2.D}. . . . . .Λευίτης G3019
Λευίτας   noun prop., acc. pl. masc. {2.A; 2.D} . . id.
G3019 **Λευίτης**, -ου, ὁ   *a Levite,* properly a man of
     the tribe of Levi; hence, *a priest's assistant, an*
     under priest; as the members of that tribe were
     charged with this duty.
Λευίτης   noun prop., nom. sg. masc. {2.A;
     2.D}. . . . . .Λευίτης G3019
Λευῖτης   noun prop., nom. sg. masc. {2.A; 2.D} . id.
Λευιτικῆς   adj. prop., gen. sg. fem. {3.A} Λευιτικός G3020
Λευϊτικῆς   adj. prop., gen. sg. fem. {3.A} . . . . id.
G3020 **Λευιτικός**, -ή, -όν   *belonging to the tribe of*
     Levi, levitical.
λευκά   adj., acc. pl. neut. {3.A} . . . . λευκός G3022
λευκά   adj., nom. pl. neut. {3.A} . . . . id.

λευκαί   adj., nom. pl. fem. {3.A}. . . . . id.
G3021 **λευκαίνω**   *I whiten.*
λευκαῖς   adj., dat. pl. fem. {3.A} . . . . λευκός G3022
λευκᾶναι   vbl., aor. act. inf. {6.B.1} . . . . λευκαίνω G3021
λευκάς   adj., acc. pl. fem. {3.A}. . . . . λευκός G3022
λευκή   adj., nom. sg. fem. {3.A} . . . . id.
λευκῇ   adj., dat. sg. fem. {3.A} . . . . id.
λευκήν   adj., acc. sg. fem. {3.A} . . . . id.
λευκοῖς   adj., dat. pl. masc. {3.A} . . . . id.
λευκοῖς   adj., dat. pl. neut. {3.A}. . . . . id.
λευκόν   adj., acc. sg. masc. {3.A} . . . . id.
λευκόν   adj., acc. sg. neut. {3.A}. . . . . id.
λευκόν   adj., nom. sg. neut. {3.A}. . . . . id.
G3022 **λευκός**, -ή, -όν   *white.*
λευκός   adj., nom. sg. masc. {3.A} . . . . . . λευκός G3022
G3023 **λέων**, -οντος, ὁ   *a lion;* ἐκ τῆς φυλῆς Ἰούδα
     applied to Jesus, Rev 5:5 (after Gen. 49:9); in
     2 Tim 4:17 used proverbially for very great
     danger.
λέων   noun, nom. sg. masc. {2.C} . . . . λέων G3023
G3024 **λήθη**, -ης, ἡ   *forgetfulness.*
λήθην   noun, acc. sg. fem. {2.A} . . . . λήθη G3024
λήμψεσθε   verb, fut. mid. indic. 2 pers. pl.
     {5.A.1.d} . . . . λαμβάνω G2983
λήμψεται   verb, fut. mid. indic. 3 pers. sg. {5.A.1.d} id.
λήμψεως   noun, gen. sg. fem. {2.C} . . . . . λῆμψις G3028‡
G3028‡ **λῆμψις** (λῆψις), -εως, ἡ   *a receiving.*
λημψόμεθα   verb, fut. mid. indic. 1 pers. pl.
     {5.A.1.d} . . . . λαμβάνω G2983
λήμψονται   verb, fut. mid. indic. 3 pers. pl.
     {5.A.1.d} . . . . id.
ληνόν   noun, acc. sg. fem. {2.B} . . . . ληνός G3025
G3025 **ληνός**, -οῦ, ἡ   *a winepress;* hence met., Rev
     14:19; 19:15.
ληνός   noun, nom. sg. fem. {2.B} . . . . ληνός G3025
ληνοῦ   noun, gen. sg. fem. {2.B}. . . . . id.
G3026 **λῆρος**, -ου, ὁ   *folly, nonsense, idle talk.*
λῆρος   noun, nom. sg. masc. {2.B} . . . . λῆρος G3026
λησταί   noun, nom. pl. masc. {2.A} . . . . . . λῃστής G3027
λῃσταῖς   noun, dat. pl. masc. {2.A} . . . . id.
λῃστάς   noun, acc. pl. masc. {2.A} . . . . id.
λῃστήν   noun, acc. sg. masc. {2.A} . . . . id.
G3027 **λῃστής**, -οῦ, ὁ   *a robber, brigand, bandit.*
λῃστής   noun, nom. sg. masc. {2.A} . . . . . . λῃστής G3027
λῃστῶν   noun, gen. pl. masc. {2.A} . . . . id.
λήψεσθε   verb, fut. mid. indic. 2 pers. pl.
     {5.A.1.d} . . . . λαμβάνω G2983
λήψεται   verb, fut. mid. indic. 3 pers. sg.
     {5.A.1.d} . . . . id.
λήψεως   noun, gen. sg. fem. {2.C} . . . . . .λῆμψις G3028‡
ληψόμεθα   verb, fut. mid. indic. 1 pers. pl.
     {5.A.1.d} . . . . λαμβάνω G2983
λήψονται   verb, fut. mid. indic. 3 pers. pl.
     {5.A.1.d} . . . . id.
G3029 **λίαν**   adv., *very; very much, exceedingly.*
λίαν   adv. . . . . λίαν G3029
λίβα   noun, acc. sg. masc. {2.C} . . . . λίψ G3047
λίβανον   noun, acc. sg. masc. {2.B} . . . . . λίβανος G3030
G3030 **λίβανος**, -ου, ὁ   *frankincense, incense* (Semitic
     word).

λιβανωτόν   noun, acc. sg. masc. {2.B} . λιβανωτός G3031
G3031 **λιβανωτός**, -οῦ, ὁ   a censer.
G3032 **Λιβερτίνος**, -ου, ὁ   a freedman, one of the
    class of manumitted slaves (Lat. libertinus). A
    synagogue at Jerusalem appears to have been
    reserved for them.
  Λιβερτίνων   noun prop., gen. pl. masc. {2.B;
    2.D}. . . . . Λιβερτῖνος G3032
G3033 **Λιβύη**, -ης, ἡ   Libya, Africa (in the mod.
    sense).
  Λιβύης   noun prop., gen. sg. fem. {2.A; 2.D} Λιβύη G3033
  λιθάζειν   vbl., pres. act. inf. {6.B.1} . . . . . λιθάζω G3034
  λιθάζετε   verb, pres. act. indic. 2 pers. pl.
    {5.A.1.a} . . . . id.
  λιθάζομεν   verb, pres. act. indic. 1 pers. pl.
    {5.A.1.a} . . . . id.
G3034 **λιθάζω**   I stone.
  λιθάσαι   vbl., aor. act. inf. {6.B.1}. . . . . . . λιθάζω G3034
  λιθάσαντες   vbl., aor. act. ptc. nom. pl. masc.
    {6.A.1.a} . . . . id.
  λιθασθῶσιν   verb, aor. pass. subjunc. 3 pers. pl.
    {5.B.1} . . . . id.
  λιθάσωσιν   verb, aor. act. subjunc. 3 pers. pl.
    {5.B.1} . . . . id.
  λίθινα   adj., acc. pl. neut. {3.A}. . . . . λίθινος G3035
  λίθιναι   adj., nom. pl. fem. {3.A} . . . . id.
  λιθίναις   adj., dat. pl. fem. {3.A}. . . . . id.
G3035 **λίθινος**, -η, -ον   made of stone.
  λιθοβολεῖσθαι   vbl., pres. pass. inf.
    {6.B.2} . . . . λιθοβολέω G3036
G3036 **λιθοβολέω**   I stone, I cast stones (at).
  λιθοβοληθήσεται   verb, fut. pass. indic. 3 pers. sg.
    {5.A.1} . . . . λιθοβολέω G3036
  λιθοβολῆσαι   vbl., aor. act. inf. {6.B.1} . . . . . . id.
  λιθοβολήσαντες   vbl., aor. act. ptc. nom. pl.
    masc. {6.A.2}. . . . . id.
  λιθοβολοῦσα   vbl., pres. act. ptc. nom. sg. fem.
    {6.A.2}. . . . . id.
  λίθοι   noun, nom. pl. masc. {2.B} . . . . . . .λίθος G3037
  λίθοις   noun, dat. pl. masc. {2.B} . . . . id.
  λίθον   noun, acc. sg. masc. {2.B}. . . . . id.
G3037 **λίθος**, -ου, ὁ   a stone; met. of Jesus as the chief
    stone in a building, etc., Acts 4:11, etc.
  λίθος   noun, nom. sg. masc. {2.B}. . . . . . . .λίθος G3037
  λιθόστρωτον   adj., acc. sg. neut.
    {3.C} . . . . λιθόστρωτος G3038
  Λιθόστρωτον   adj. prop., acc. sg. neut.
    {3.C} . . . . λιθόστρωτος G3038
G3038 **λιθόστρωτος**, -ου, τό   paved with stone; neut.
    subs. stone pavement. Possibly a proper noun
    in John 19:13.
  λίθου   noun, gen. sg. masc. {2.B} . . . . .λίθος G3037
  λίθους   noun, acc. pl. masc. {2.B}. . . . . id.
  λίθῳ   noun, dat. sg. masc. {2.B} . . . . id.
  λίθων   noun, gen. pl. masc. {2.B} . . . . id.
G3039 **λικμάω**   I crush to powder.
  λικμήσει   verb, fut. act. indic. 3 pers. sg.
    {5.A.1}. . . . . λικμάω G3039
  λιμά   Aram. . . . . .λαμά G2982
  λιμένα   noun, acc. sg. masc. {2.C} . . . . λιμήν G3040

  Λιμένας   noun prop., acc. pl. masc. {2.C; 2.D} . . id.
  λιμένος   noun, gen. sg. masc. {2.C} . . . . id.
G3040 **λιμήν**, -ένος, ὁ   a harbor, port.
  λίμμα   noun, nom. sg. neut. {2.C} . . . . . . λεῖμμα G3005
G3041 **λίμνη**, -ης, ἡ   a lake.
  λίμνη   noun, nom. sg. fem. {2.A} . . . . λίμνη G3041
  λίμνῃ   noun, dat. sg. fem. {2.A} . . . . id.
  λίμνην   noun, acc. sg. fem. {2.A} . . . . id.
  λίμνης   noun, gen. sg. fem. {2.A} . . . . id.
  λιμοί   noun, nom. pl. masc. {2.B} . . . . .λιμός G3042
  λιμόν   noun, acc. sg. masc. {2.B}. . . . . id.
  λιμόν   noun, acc. sg. masc. {2.B}. . . . . id.
G3042 **λιμός**, -οῦ, ὁ and ἡ   a famine.
  λιμός   noun, nom. sg. fem. {2.B}. . . . . .λιμός G3042
  λιμός   noun, nom. sg. masc. {2.B}. . . . . id.
  λιμῷ   noun, dat. sg. fem. {2.B} . . . . id.
  λιμῷ   noun, dat. sg. masc. {2.B} . . . . id.
G3043 **λίνον**, -ου, τό   flax; linen.
  λίνον   noun, acc. sg. neut. {2.B} . . . . .λίνον G3043
G3044 **Λίνος**, -ου, ὁ   Linus, a Christian in Rome.
  Λίνος   noun prop., nom. sg. masc. {2.B; 2.D} Λίνος G3044
  Λῖνος   noun prop., nom. sg. masc. {2.B; 2.D} . . id.
  λιπαρά   adj., nom. pl. neut. {3.A}. . . . . . . λιπαρός G3045
G3045 **λιπαρός**, -ά, -όν   (lit. fat) rich, sumptuous.
G3046 **λίτρα**, -ας, ἡ   a Roman pound, of about twelve
    ounces, 327½ grams.
  λίτραν   noun, acc. sg. fem. {2.A} . . . . .λίτρα G3046
  λίτρας   noun, acc. pl. fem. {2.A}. . . . . id.
G3047 **λίψ**, λιβός, acc. λίβα, ὁ   the southwest wind,
    and thus the quarter from which it comes.
G3048 **λογεία** (λογία), -ας, ἡ   a collection, collecting
    (of money), particularly of an irregular local
    contribution for religious purposes (from
    λογεύω, "I collect").
  λογεῖαι   noun, nom. pl. fem. {2.A} . . . . . . λογεία G3048
  λογείας   noun, gen. sg. fem. {2.A} . . . . id.
  λόγια   noun, acc. pl. neut. {2.B} . . . . λόγιον G3051
  λογίαι   noun, nom. pl. fem. {2.A}. . . . . λογεία G3048
  λογίας   noun, gen. sg. fem. {2.A} . . . . id.
  λογίζεσθαι   vbl., pres. pass. inf. {6.B.1} . λογίζομαι G3049
  λογίζεσθε   verb, pres. mid./pass. impv. 2 pers.
    pl. {5.D.1} . . . . id.
  λογίζεσθε   verb, pres. mid./pass. indic. 2 pers.
    pl. {5.A.1.d} . . . . id.
  λογιζέσθω   verb, pres. mid./pass. impv. 3 pers.
    sg. {5.D.1} . . . . id.
  λογίζεται   verb, pres. mid./pass. indic. 3 pers.
    sg. {5.A.1.d}. . . . . id.
  λογίζῃ   verb, pres. mid./pass. indic. 2 pers. sg.
    {5.A.1.d} . . . . id.
G3049 **λογίζομαι**   (1) I reckon, count, put down to
    one's account, τι or τινί τι, Rom 4:6; 1 Cor
    13:5; 2 Cor 5:19; 2 Tim 4:16; also with εἴς τι
    = as some thing, as of some value, e.g., Acts
    19:27; Rom 4:3; Gal 3:6; (2) I number, class
    amongst, Mark 15:28; Luke 22:37; (3) I reckon
    up accounts, I weigh arguments, I deliberate,
    Mark 11:31 (var.); (4) hence, I consider, weigh,
    John 11:50; 2 Cor 10:11; Phil 4:8; Heb 11:19;
    (5) I think, I judge, often; (6) I decide, deter-

mine, 2 Cor 10:2. (Properly of an accountant, bookkeeper, *I count, reckon up.*)

λογίζομαι   verb, pres. mid./pass. indic. 1 pers. sg. {5.A.1.d} . . . . λογίζομαι *G3049*

λογιζόμεθα   verb, pres. mid./pass. indic. 1 pers. pl. {5.A.1.d} . . . . id.

λογιζόμενος   vbl., pres. mid./pass. ptc. nom. sg. masc. {6.A.1} . . . . id.

λογιζομένους   vbl., pres. mid./pass. ptc. acc. pl. masc. {6.A.1} . . . . id.

λογιζομένῳ   vbl., pres. mid./pass. ptc. dat. sg. masc. {6.A.1} . . . . id.

λογικήν   adj., acc. sg. fem. {3.A} . . . . . λογικός *G3050*

λογικόν   adj., acc. sg. neut. {3.A} . . . . id.

G3050 **λογικός,** -ή, -όν   (1) *reasonable, rational,* Rom 12:1; (2) *metaphorical,* as contrasted with lit., 1 Pet 2:2 (so perhaps also in Rom 12:1).

G3051 **λόγιον,** -ου, τό   pl. *oracles, divine responses* or *utterances* (it can include the entire OT scriptures); in Rom 3:2 mainly of the promises in the OT; in Heb 5:12 probably of Jesus' teaching.

G3052 **λόγιος,** -α, -ον   *eloquent.*

λόγιος   adj., nom. sg. masc. {3.A} . . . . λόγιος *G3052*

λογισάμενος   vbl., aor. mid. ptc. nom. sg. masc. {6.A.1.b} . . . . λογίζομαι *G3049*

λογίσασθαι   vbl., aor. mid. inf. {6.B.1} . . . . id.

λογίσηται   verb, aor. mid. subjunc. 3 pers. sg. {5.B.1} . . . . id.

λογισθείη   verb, aor. pass. opt. 3 pers. sg. {5.C.1} id.

λογισθῆναι   vbl., aor. pass. inf. {6.B.1} . . . . . . id.

λογισθήσεται   verb, fut. pass. indic. 3 pers. sg. {5.A.1.d} . . . . id.

G3053 **λογισμός,** -οῦ, ὁ   *reasoning, thinking.*

λογισμούς   noun, acc. pl. masc. {2.B} . . . λογισμός *G3053*

λογισμῶν   noun, gen. pl. masc. {2.B} . . . . id.

λογίων   noun, gen. pl. neut. {2.B} . . . . λόγιον *G3051*

λόγοι   noun, nom. pl. masc. {2.B} . . . . λόγος *G3056*

λόγοις   noun, dat. pl. masc. {2.B} . . . . id.

λογομαχεῖν   vbl., pres. act. inf. {6.B.2} . λογομαχέω *G3054*

G3054 **λογομαχέω**   *I battle with (for) words.*

G3055 **λογομαχία,** -ας, ἡ   *a battling with (for) words, a battle of words.*

λογομαχίας   noun, acc. pl. fem. {2.A} . λογομαχία *G3055*

λόγον   noun, acc. sg. masc. {2.B} . . . . λόγος *G3056*

G3056 **λόγος,** -ου, ὁ   (speech in progress); (1) *a word, an utterance, speech, discourse, saying,* frequently of God through his messengers; the gen. expresses either this origin or the subj. of the word; διὰ λόγου, *by spoken word, by word of mouth;* ὁ λόγος, the Gospel news, e.g., Luke 1:2; Acts 14:25; (2) *the personalized Word* or *Divine utterance,* a conception of Palestinian or Alexandrian theology, referred by the Fourth Evangelist to Jesus the Messiah, John 1:1, 14; (3) *an account,* Acts 20:24; 1 Pet 4:5; hence, (4) *reason, a reason,* 1 Pet 3:15; κατὰ λόγον, *rightly, deservedly,* Acts 18:14; (5) *analogy,* ἐπέχειν λόγον τινος, *to correspond*

to, be analogous to, be instead of something, Phil 2:16.

λόγος   noun, nom. sg. masc. {2.B} . . . . λόγος *G3056*

λόγου   noun, gen. sg. masc. {2.B} . . . . id.

λόγους   noun, acc. pl. masc. {2.B} . . . . id.

G3057 **λόγχη,** -ης, ἡ   *a long lance.*

λόγχη   noun, dat. sg. fem. {2.A} . . . . λόγχη *G3057*

λόγχην   noun, acc. sg. fem. {2.A} . . . . id.

λόγῳ   noun, dat. sg. masc. {2.B} . . . . λόγος *G3056*

λόγων   noun, gen. pl. masc. {2.B} . . . . id.

λοιδορεῖς   verb, pres. act. indic. 2 pers. sg. {5.A.2} . . . . λοιδορέω *G3058*

G3058 **λοιδορέω**   *I revile* a person *to his face, I abuse insultingly.*

G3059 **λοιδορία,** -ας, ἡ   *reviling, abuse.*

λοιδορίαν   noun, acc. sg. fem. {2.A} . . . . λοιδορία *G3059*

λοιδορίας   noun, gen. sg. fem. {2.A} . . . . id.

λοίδοροι   noun, nom. pl. masc. {3.A} . . . λοίδορος *G3060*

G3060 **λοίδορος,** -ου, ὁ   *a railer, reviler, abuser.*

λοίδορος   noun, nom. sg. masc. {3.A} . . λοίδορος *G3060*

λοιδορούμενοι   vbl., pres. pass. ptc. nom. pl. masc. {6.A.2} . . . . λοιδορέω *G3058*

λοιδορούμενος   vbl., pres. pass. ptc. nom. sg. masc. {6.A.2} . . . . id.

λοιμοί   noun, nom. pl. masc. {2.B} . . . . λοιμός *G3061*

λοιμόν   adj., acc. sg. masc. {2.B} . . . . id.

G3061 **λοιμός,** ή, όν and λοιμός, -οῦ, ὁ   adj., *diseased, pestilential; a pestilent fellow,* Acts 24:5; noun, *a pestilence, plague.*

λοιπά   adj., acc. pl. neut. {3.A} . . . . λοιπός *G3062†*

λοιπά   adj., nom. pl. neut. {3.A} . . . . id.

λοιπαί   adj., nom. pl. fem. {3.A} . . . . id.

λοιπάς   adj., acc. pl. fem. {3.A} . . . . id.

λοιποί   adj., nom. pl. masc. {3.A} . . . . id.

λοιποῖς   adj., dat. pl. masc. {3.A} . . . . id.

λοιποῖς   adj., dat. pl. neut. {3.A} . . . . id.

λοιπόν   adj., acc. sg. neut. {3.A} . . . . id.

λοιπόν   adv. . . . . id.

G3062† **λοιπός,** -ή, -όν   (1) *left, left behind,* οἱ λοιποί, *the remainder, the rest, the others;* (2) adv. phrases, acc. neut., λοιπόν, τὸ λοιπόν, *for the rest, now, already;* temp. gen., τοῦ λοιποῦ (supply χρόνου), *henceforth.*

λοιποῦ   adv. {3.F} . . . . λοιπός *G3062†*

λοιπούς   adj., acc. pl. masc. {3.A} . . . . id.

λοιπῶν   adj., gen. pl. masc. {3.A} . . . . id.

λοιπῶν   adj., gen. pl. neut. {3.A} . . . . id.

Λουκᾶ   noun prop., gen. sg. masc. {2.A; 2.D} . Λουκᾶς *G3065*

G3065 **Λουκᾶς,** -ᾶ, ὁ   *Lucas, Luke,* Christian physician and writer of the Third Gospel and Acts, an abbreviated pet form either of Λουκανός, as the Old Latin Bible gave in the title of the Third Gospel, or of Λουκίος, as some moderns have thought.

Λουκᾶς   noun prop., nom. sg. masc. {2.A; 2.D} . . . . Λουκᾶς *G3065*

G3066 **Λούκιος,** -ου, ὁ   *Lucius,* (1) of Cyrene, an early Christian, in the church of Antioch, Acts 13:1, by some identified with the evangelist Luke;

(2) a Christian with Paul at Corinth, by some
identified with (1), Rom 16:21.

Λούκιος   noun prop., nom. sg. masc. {2.B;
 2.D}. . . . . Λούκιος G3066

λουσαμένη   vbl., aor. mid. ptc. nom. sg. fem.
 {6.A.1.b} . . . . λούω G3068

λούσαντες   vbl., aor. act. ptc. nom. pl. masc.
 {6.A.1.a} . . . . id.

λούσαντι   vbl., aor. act. ptc. dat. sg. masc.
 {6.A.1.a} . . . . id.

G3067 **λουτρόν**, -οῦ, τό   *a bath* (of the water, not the
 vessel), *water for washing, washing.*

λουτροῦ   noun, gen. sg. neut. {2.B} . . . . . λουτρόν G3067

λουτρῷ   noun, dat. sg. neut. {2.B} . . . . id.

G3068 **λούω**   *I wash, bathe* (the body, literally or merely
 ceremonially); mid. of *washing, bathing oneself.*

G3069 **Λύδδα**, -ας, ἡ   *Lydda, Diospolis, Lod* (mod.
 Ludd), a city on the way to Joppa within a
 day's journey of Jerusalem.

Λύδδα   noun prop., acc. sg. fem. {2.A; 2.D} . Λύδδα G3069

Λύδδαν   noun prop., acc. sg. fem. {2.A; 2.D} . . . id.

Λύδδας   noun prop., gen. sg. fem. {2.A; 2.D} . . . id.

Λύδδης   noun prop., gen. sg. fem. {2.A; 2.D} . . . id.

G3070 **Λυδία**, -ας, ἡ   *Lydia,* a lady resident of Philippi,
 native of Thyatira in Lydia (Asia Minor), and
 engaged in the clothing trade.

Λυδία   noun prop., nom. sg. fem. {2.A; 2.D} Λυδία G3070

Λυδίαν   noun prop., acc. sg. fem. {2.A; 2.D} . . . . id.

λύει   verb, pres. act. indic. 3 pers. sg. {5.A.1.a} . λύω G3089

λύετε   verb, pres. act. indic. 2 pers. pl. {5.A.1.a} . id.

λυθείσης   vbl., aor. pass. ptc. gen. sg. fem.
 {6.A.1.a} . . . . id.

λυθῇ   verb, aor. pass. subjunc. 3 pers. sg. {5.B.1}. id.

λυθῆναι   vbl., aor. pass. inf. {6.B.1} . . . . id.

λυθήσεται   verb, fut. pass. indic. 3 pers. sg.
 {5.A.1.d} . . . . id.

λυθήσονται   verb, fut. pass. indic. 3 pers. pl.
 {5.A.1.d} . . . . id.

G3071 **Λυκαονία**, -ας, ἡ   *Lycaonia, the country of the
 Lykaones,* a district of Asia Minor, comprised
 within the Roman province Galatia and
 including the cities Derbe and Lystra.

Λυκαονίας   noun prop., gen. sg. fem. {2.A;
 2.D}. . . . . Λυκαονία G3071

G3072 **Λυκαονιστί**   *in the Lycaonian language.*

Λυκαονιστί   adv. prop. . . . . Λυκαονιστί G3072

G3073 **Λυκία**, -ας, ἡ   *Lycia,* a small Roman province
 on the south coast of Asia Minor.

Λυκίας   noun prop., gen. sg. fem. {2.A; 2.D} Λυκία G3073

λύκοι   noun, nom. pl. masc. {2.B} . . . . λύκος G3074

λύκον   noun, acc. sg. masc. {2.B} . . . . id.

G3074 **λύκος**, -ου, ὁ   *a wolf,* or perhaps *a jackal;* often
 applied to persons of wolfish proclivities.

λύκος   noun, nom. sg. masc. {2.B} . . . . λύκος G3074

λύκων   noun, gen. pl. masc. {2.B}. . . . . id.

G3075 **λυμαίνω**   mid. *I ravage, harry, devastate.*

λυομένων   vbl., pres. pass. ptc. gen. pl. neut.
 {6.A.1} . . . . λύω G3089

λύοντες   vbl., pres. act. ptc. nom. pl. masc.
 {6.A.1} . . . . id.

λυόντων   vbl., pres. act. ptc. gen. pl. masc.
 {6.A.1}. . . . . id.

λύουσιν   verb, pres. act. indic. 3 pers. pl.
 {5.A.1.a} . . . . id.

λύπας   noun, acc. pl. fem. {2.A} . . . . λύπη G3077

λυπεῖσθαι   vbl., pres. pass. inf. {6.B.2} . . . . λυπέω G3076

λυπεῖται   verb, pres. pass. indic. 3 pers. sg.
 {5.A.2}. . . . . id.

λυπεῖτε   verb, pres. act. impv. 2 pers. pl. {5.D.2} . id.

G3076 **λυπέω**   *I pain, grieve, vex.*

G3077 **λύπη**, -ης, ἡ   *pain, grief.*

λύπη   noun, nom. sg. fem. {2.A}. . . . . λύπη G3077

λύπῃ   noun, dat. sg. fem. {2.A}. . . . . id.

λυπηθείς   vbl., aor. pass. ptc. nom. sg. masc.
 {6.A.1.a.} . . . . λυπέω G3076

λυπηθέντες   vbl., aor. pass. ptc. nom. pl. masc.
 {6.A.1.a.} . . . . id.

λυπηθῆναι   vbl., aor. pass. inf. {6.B.1} . . . . id.

λυπηθήσεσθε   verb, fut. pass. indic. 2 pers. pl.
 {5.A.1} . . . . id.

λυπηθῆτε   verb, aor. pass. subjunc. 2 pers. pl.
 {5.B.1} . . . . id.

λύπην   noun, acc. sg. fem. {2.A} . . . . λύπη G3077

λύπης   noun, gen. sg. fem. {2.A} . . . . id.

λυπῆσθε   verb, pres. pass. subjunc. 2 pers. pl.
 {5.B.2}. . . . . λυπέω G3076

λυπούμενοι   vbl., pres. pass. ptc. nom. pl.
 masc. {6.A.2}. . . . . id.

λυπούμενος   vbl., pres. pass. ptc. nom. sg.
 masc. {6.A.2}. . . . . id.

λυπῶ   verb, pres. act. indic. 1 pers. sg. {5.A.2}. . . id.

λῦσαι   vbl., aor. act. inf. {6.B.1} . . . . λύω G3089

G3078 **Λυσανίας**, -ου, ὁ   *Lysanias,* tetrarch of
 Abilene.

Λυσανίου   noun prop., gen. sg. masc. {2.A;
 2.D}. . . . . Λυσανίας G3078

λύσαντες   vbl., aor. act. ptc. nom. pl. masc.
 {6.A.1.a} . . . . λύω G3089

λύσαντι   vbl., aor. act. ptc. dat. sg. masc.
 {6.A.1.a} . . . . id.

λύσας   vbl., aor. act. ptc. nom. sg. masc.
 {6.A.1.a} . . . . id.

λύσατε   verb, aor. act. impv. 2 pers. pl. {5.D.1} . . id.

λύσῃ   verb, aor. act. subjunc. 3 pers. sg. {5.B.1}. . id.

λύσῃς   verb, aor. act. subjunc. 2 pers. sg. {5.B.1}. id.

λύσητε   verb, aor. act. subjunc. 2 pers. pl. {5.B.1} id.

G3079 **Λυσίας**, -ου, ὁ   Claudius *Lysias,* a Roman
 tribune of the soldiers in Jerusalem.

Λυσίας   noun prop., nom. sg. masc. {2.A;
 2.D}. . . . . Λυσίας G3079

λύσιν   noun, acc. sg. fem. {2.C} . . . . λύσις G3080

G3080 **λύσις**, -εως, ἡ   *dissolution, release.*

λυσιτελεῖ   verb, impers., pres. act. indic. 3 pers. sg.
 {5.A.2}. . . . . λυσιτελέω G3081

G3081 **λυσιτελέω**   impers. 3 sg. *it is advantageous to,
 it profits.*

λῦσον   verb, aor. act. impv. 2 pers. sg. {5.D.1} . . λύω G3089

G3082 **Λύστρα**, dat. Λύστροις, acc. Λύστραν, ἡ and
 τό   *Lystra,* a Lycaonian city in the southern
 part of the Roman province Galatia.

Λύστραν   noun prop., acc. sg. fem. {2.A;
2.D} . . . . .Λύστρα G3082
Λύστροις   noun prop., dat. pl. neut. {2.B; 2.D} . . id.
λύσω   verb, aor. act. subjunc. 1 pers. sg. {5.B.1} λύω G3089
G3083 λύτρον, -ου, τό   the purchasing money for
manumitting slaves, a ransom, the price of
ransoming; esp. the sacrifice by which expiation
is effected, an offering of expiation.
λύτρον   noun, acc. sg. neut. {2.B} . . . . λύτρον G3083
λυτροῦσθαι   vbl., pres. mid. inf. {6.B.2} . . . λυτρόω G3084
G3084 λυτρόω   (orig., I deliver captives from robbers
or enemies in war by payment, I manumit or
liberate a slave from slavery), I ransom, liberate, deliver.
λυτρώσηται   verb, aor. mid. subjunc. 3 pers. sg.
{5.B.1} . . . . λυτρόω G3084
λύτρωσιν   noun, acc. sg. fem. {2.C} . . . . λύτρωσις G3085
G3085 λύτρωσις, -εως, ἡ   liberation, deliverance,
release (cf. λυτρόω). (In OT ransoming from
imprisonment for debt, or from slavery, release
from national misfortune, etc.).
λυτρωτήν   noun, acc. sg. masc. {2.A} . . λυτρωτής G3086
G3086 λυτρωτής, -οῦ, ὁ   a redeemer, one who pays a
ransom, a liberator.
G3087 λυχνία, -ας, ἡ   a lamp stand.

λυχνία   noun, nom. sg. fem. {2.A} . . . . . . λυχνία G3087
λυχνίαι   noun, nom. pl. fem. {2.A} . . . . id.
λυχνίαν   noun, acc. sg. fem. {2.A} . . . . id.
λυχνίας   noun, acc. pl. fem. {2.A} . . . . id.
λυχνίας   noun, gen. sg. fem. {2.A} . . . . id.
λυχνιῶν   noun, gen. pl. fem. {2.A} . . . . id.
λύχνοι   noun, nom. pl. masc. {2.B} . . . . . λύχνος G3088
λύχνον   noun, acc. sg. masc. {2.B} . . . . id.
G3088 λύχνος, -ου, ὁ   a lamp.
λύχνος   noun, nom. sg. masc. {2.B} . . . . . λύχνος G3088
λύχνου   noun, gen. sg. masc. {2.B} . . . . id.
λύχνῳ   noun, dat. sg. masc. {2.B} . . . . id.
G3089 λύω   (1) I unloose, loose, loosen, untie, release,
Mark 1:7, etc.; thus I break (in a phrase
where the time order of the two processes is
inverted), Rev 5:2; (2) met. I break, destroy,
set at naught, contravene; sometimes merely,
I declare a law to be not binding, John 5:18; I
break up a meeting, Acts 13:43; I annul, 1 John
4:3 (var.).
Λωΐδι   noun prop., dat. sg. fem. {2.C; 2.D} . . . Λωΐς G3090
Λωΐδι   noun prop., dat. sg. fem. {2.C; 2.D} . . . id.
G3090 Λωΐς, ΐδος, ἡ   Lois, grandmother of Timothy.
G3091 Λώτ, ὁ   Lot, nephew of Abraham (Heb.).
Λώτ   noun prop. .Λώτ G3091

M μ

Μαάθ   noun prop. . . . . Μαάθ G3092
G3092 Μαάθ, ὁ   Maath, Mahath, an ancestor of Jesus
(Heb.).
Μαάθ   noun prop. . . . . Μαάθ G3092
Μαγαδάν   noun prop. . . . . Μαγδαλά G3093
G3093 Μαγδαλά (Μαγαδάν), -ῆς, ἡ   Magada(n) or
Magdala(n). Μαγαδάν is a place of uncertain
location on Lake Gennesaret. Regarding Μα-
γδαλά, the reading and the site are uncertain.
Two views are held with regard to the latter:
(1) that it was in the Decapolis near Gerasa;
(2) that it was at Megdel on the western bank
of the Sea of Galilee.
Μαγδαλά   noun prop. . . . . Μαγδαλά G3093
G3094 Μαγδαληνή   a woman from Magdala, Mag-
dalene (of a place identical with mod. Megdel,
near Tiberias; see Μαγαδάν); surname of
Mary from Magdala; see Μαρία (2).
Μαγδαληνή   noun prop., nom. sg. fem. {2.A;
2.D} . . . . Μαγδαληνή G3094
Μαγδαληνῇ   noun prop., dat. sg. fem. {2.A; 2.D} id.
Μαγεδών   noun prop. . . . . Ἁρμαγεδών G717
G3095 μαγεία, -ας, ἡ   sorcery, magic.
μαγείαις   noun, dat. pl. fem. {2.A} . . . . . . .μαγεία G3095
G3096 μαγεύω   I practice sorcery or magic.
μαγεύων   vbl., pres. act. ptc. nom. sg. masc.
{6.A.1} . . . . .μαγεύω G3096
μαγίαις   noun, dat. pl. fem. {2.A} . . . . . . .μαγεία G3095
μάγοι   noun, nom. pl. masc. {2.B} . . . . μάγος G3097

μάγον   noun, acc. sg. masc. {2.B} . . . . id.
G3097 μάγος, -ου, ὁ   a sorcerer, a magician, a wizard.
μάγος   noun, nom. sg. masc. {2.B} . . . . μάγος G3097
μάγους   noun, acc. pl. masc. {2.B} . . . . id.
G3098 Μαγώγ, ὁ   Magog, sometimes as name of a
people, sometimes as name of a country in OT
(Gen. 10:2; Ezek 38:2; 39:6), probably the Scyth-
ians; hence, used in apocalyptic literature (Heb.).
Μαγώγ   noun prop. . . . . .Μαγώγ G3098
μάγων   noun, gen. pl. masc. {2.B} . . . . μάγος G3097
G3099 Μαδιάμ, ὁ   Madiam, Midian, generally taken to
mean or to include the peninsula of Sinai (Heb.).
Μαδιάμ   noun prop. . . . . .Μαδιάμ G3099
μαθεῖν   vbl., ²aor. act. inf. {6.B.1} . . . . . μανθάνω G3129
μάθετε   verb, ²aor. act. impv. 2 pers. pl. {5.D.1} . . id.
μαθηταί   noun, nom. pl. masc. {2.A} . . . μαθητής G3101
μαθηταῖς   noun, dat. pl. masc. {2.A} . . . . id.
μαθητάς   noun, acc. pl. masc. {2.A} . . . . id.
μάθητε   verb, ²aor. act. subjunc. 2 pers. pl.
{5.B.1} . . . . μανθάνω G3129
μαθητευθείς   vbl., aor. pass. ptc. nom. sg. masc.
{6.A.1.a} . . . . .μαθητεύω G3100
μαθητεύσαντες   vbl., aor. act. ptc. nom. pl.
masc. {6.A.1.a} . . . . id.
μαθητεύσατε   verb, aor. act. impv. 2 pers. pl.
{5.D.1} . . . . id.
G3100 μαθητεύω   I make disciples, I make into
disciples; followed by dat. of instrument, Matt
13:52.

μαθητῇ   noun, dat. sg. masc. {2.A}. . . . . μαθητής G3101
μαθητήν   noun, acc. sg. masc. {2.A}. . . . . id.
G3101 **μαθητής**, -οῦ, ὁ   a learner, disciple, pupil.
μαθητής   noun, nom. sg. masc. {2.A}. . . . μαθητής G3101
μαθητοῦ   noun, gen. sg. masc. {2.A} . . . . id.
G3102 **μαθήτρια**, -ας, ἡ   a woman disciple.
μαθήτρια   noun, nom. sg. fem. {2.A}. . . μαθήτρια G3102
μαθητῶν   noun, gen. pl. masc. {2.A} . . . . μαθητής G3101
Μαθθαῖον   noun prop., acc. sg. masc. {2.B;
   2.D}. . . . . Ματθαῖος G3156
Μαθθαῖος   noun prop., nom. sg. masc. {2.B;
   2.D}. . . . . id.
Μαθθάν   noun prop. . . . . Ματθάν G3157
Μαθθάτ   noun prop. . . . . Ματθάτ G3158
Μαθθίαν   noun prop., acc. sg. masc. {2.A;
   2.D}. . . . . Ματθίας G3159
G3103 **Μαθουσαλά**, ὁ   Methuselah, son of Enoch and
   father of Lamech (Heb.).
Μαθουσαλά   noun prop. . . . . .Μαθουσαλά G3103
Μαθουσάλα   noun prop. . . . . id.
μαθών   vbl., ²aor. act. ptc. nom. sg. masc.
   {6.A.1.a} . . . . μανθάνω G3129
G3104 **Μαϊνάν** (Μεννά)   Mainan or Menna, one of
   the ancestors of Jesus (Heb.).
Μαϊνάν   noun prop. . . . . .Μαϊνάν G3104
μαίνεσθε   verb, pres. mid./pass. indic. 2 pers. pl.
   {5.A.1.d} . . . . μαίνομαι G3105
μαίνεται   verb, pres. mid./pass. indic. 3 pers.
   sg. {5.A.1.d}. . . . . id.
μαίνῃ   verb, pres. mid./pass. indic. 2 pers. sg.
   {5.A.1.d} . . . . id.
G3105 **μαίνομαι**   I am raving mad, I speak as a
   madman.
μαίνομαι   verb, pres. mid./pass. indic. 1 pers. sg.
   {5.A.1.d} . . . . μαίνομαι G3105
μακαρία   adj., nom. sg. fem. {3.A} . . . . μακάριος G3107
μακάριαι   adj., nom. pl. fem. {3.A} . . . . id.
μακαρίαν   adj., acc. sg. fem. {3.A} . . . . id.
μακαρίζομεν   verb, pres. act. indic. 1 pers. pl.
   {5.A.1.a} . . . . μακαρίζω G3106
G3106 **μακαρίζω**   I deem (declare) happy.
μακάριοι   adj., nom. pl. masc. {3.A}. . . μακάριος G3107
μακάριον   adj., acc. sg. masc. {3.A} . . . . id.
μακάριον   adj., nom. sg. neut. {3.A}. . . . . id.
G3107 **μακάριος**, -α, -ον   happy, to be envied.
μακάριος   adj., nom. sg. masc. {3.A} . . . μακάριος G3107
μακαρίου   adj., gen. sg. masc. {3.A} . . . . id.
μακαριοῦσί   verb, fut. act. indic. 3 pers. pl.
   {5.A.2}. . . . . μακαρίζω G3106
μακαριοῦσίν   verb, fut. act. indic. 3 pers. pl.
   {5.A.2}. . . . . id.
μακαρισμόν   noun, acc. sg. masc.
   {2.B} . . . . .μακαρισμός G3108
G3108 **μακαρισμός**, -οῦ, ὁ   felicitation, regarding as
   happy or enviable.
μακαρισμός   noun, nom. sg. masc.
   {2.B} . . . . .μακαρισμός G3108
μακαριωτέρα   adj. comp., nom. sg. fem. {3.A;
   3.G}. . . . . μακάριος G3107

Μακεδόνας   noun prop., acc. pl. masc. {2.C;
   2.D}. . . . . Μακεδών G3110
Μακεδόνες   noun prop., nom. pl. masc. {2.C;
   2.D}. . . . . id.
G3109 **Μακεδονία**, -ας, ἡ   Macedonia, a Roman
   province north of Achaia (Greece) (Heb.).
Μακεδονία   noun prop., nom. sg. fem. {2.A;
   2.D}. . . . . .Μακεδονία G3109
Μακεδονίᾳ   noun prop., dat. sg. fem. {2.A; 2.D} id.
Μακεδονίαν   noun prop., acc. sg. fem. {2.A;
   2.D}. . . . . id.
Μακεδονίας   noun prop., gen. sg. fem. {2.A;
   2.D}. . . . . id.
Μακεδόνος   noun prop., gen. sg. masc. {2.C;
   2.D}. . . . . Μακεδών G3110
Μακεδόσιν   noun prop., dat. pl. masc. {2.C;
   2.D}. . . . . id.
G3110 **Μακεδών**, -όνος, ὁ   a Macedonian, an inhabitant of the Roman province Macedonia.
Μακεδών   noun prop., nom. sg. masc. {2.C;
   2.D}. . . . . Μακεδών G3110
G3111 **μάκελλον**, -ου, τό   meat market (Lat.
   macellum).
μακέλλῳ   noun, dat. sg. neut. {2.B} . . . . μάκελλον G3111
μακρά   adj., acc. pl. neut. {3.A}. . . . . μακρός G3117
G3112 **μακράν**   adv., sometimes used adjectivally, at a
   distance, far away.
μακράν   adj., acc. sg. fem. {3.A} . . . . μακρός G3117
μακράν   adv. μακράν G3112
G3113 **μακρόθεν**   adv., from a (long) distance, often in
   the tautological expression ἀπὸ μακρόθεν =
   μακρόθεν, ἀπὸ μακράν (cf. Luke 18:13).
μακρόθεν   adv.. . . . . μακρόθεν G3113
μακροθυμεῖ   verb, pres. act. indic. 3 pers. sg.
   {5.A.2}. . . . . μακροθυμέω G3114
μακροθυμεῖτε   verb, pres. act. impv. 2 pers. pl.
   {5.D.2}. . . . . id.
G3114 **μακροθυμέω**   I defer my anger, I am longsuffering, i.e., the opp. of short- or quick-tempered.
μακροθυμήσας   vbl., aor. act. ptc. nom. sg. masc.
   {6.A.2}. . . . . μακροθυμέω G3114
μακροθυμήσατε   verb, aor. act. impv. 2 pers.
   pl. {5.D.1}. . . . . id.
μακροθύμησον   verb, aor. act. impv. 2 pers. sg.
   {5.D.1}. . . . . id.
G3115 **μακροθυμία**, -ας, ἡ   longsuffering.
μακροθυμία   noun, nom. sg. fem.
   {2.A} . . . . .μακροθυμία G3115
μακροθυμίᾳ   noun, dat. sg. fem. {2.A}. . . . . . . id.
μακροθυμίαν   noun, acc. sg. fem. {2.A}. . . . . . id.
μακροθυμίας   noun, gen. sg. fem. {2.A}. . . . . . id.
μακροθυμῶν   vbl., pres. act. ptc. nom. sg. masc.
   {6.A.2}. . . . . μακροθυμέω G3114
G3116 **μακροθύμως**   adv., with longsuffering, patiently.
μακροθύμως   adv. {3.F}. . . . . μακροθύμως G3116
G3117 **μακρός**, -ά, -όν   (1) long; acc. neut. pl. as adv.
   long, Mark 12:40; Luke 20:47; (2) distant.
G3118 **μακροχρόνιος**, -ον   long-timed, long-lived.
μακροχρόνιος   adj., nom. sg. masc.
   {3.C} . . . . μακροχρόνιος G3118

μαλακά   adj., acc. pl. neut. {3.A} . . . . . . μαλακός *G3120*

G3119 **μαλακία**, -ας, ἡ   *weakness, illness.*

μαλακίαν   noun, acc. sg. fem. {2.A} . . . . μαλακία *G3119*

μαλακοί   adj., nom. pl. masc. {3.A} . . . . μαλακός *G3120*

μαλακοῖς   adj., dat. pl. neut. {3.A} . . . . id.

G3120 **μαλακός**, -ή, -όν   (1) *soft, (τὰ) μαλακά,* as subs., *soft material;* (2) of persons, *soft, voluptuous, effeminate.*

G3121 **Μαλελεήλ**, ὁ   *Maleleel,* one of the ancestors of Jesus (Heb.).

Μαλελεήλ   noun prop. . . . . Μαλελεήλ *G3121*

G3122 **μάλιστα**   adv., *most of all, especially* (superl., see μᾶλλον).

μάλιστα   adv. super {3.F; 3.G} . . . . μάλιστα *G3122*

G3123 **μᾶλλον**   adv., *more, rather* (comp., see μάλιστα).

μᾶλλον   adv. {3.F} . . . . μᾶλλον *G3123*

G3124 **Μάλχος**, -ου, ὁ   *Malchus,* a slave of the high priest at Jerusalem (Aram. *Malchu*).

Μάλχος   noun prop., nom. sg. masc. {2.B; 2.D} .Μάλχος *G3124*

G3125 **μάμμη**, -ης, ἡ   *a grandmother.*

μάμμη   noun, dat. sg. fem. {2.A} . . . . .μάμμη *G3125*

μαμμωνᾷ   noun, dat. sg. masc. {2.A} . . .μαμωνᾶς *G3126*

μαμωνᾷ   noun, dat. sg. masc. {2.A} . . . . id.

μαμωνᾶ   noun, gen. sg. masc. {2.A} . . . . id.

G3126 **μαμωνᾶς**, -ᾶ, ὁ   *riches, money, possessions, property* (Aram., with cog. words in Heb. and Punic).

G3127 **Μαναήν**, ὁ   *Manaen,* probably a member of Herod Antipas' court (Graecized form of Aram. *Menahem*).

Μαναήν   noun prop. . . . . Μαναήν *G3127*

Μανασσῆ   noun prop., acc. sg. masc. {2.A; 2.D} .Μανασσῆς *G3128*

Μανασσῆ   noun prop., gen. sg. masc. {2.A; 2.D} id.

G3128 **Μανασσῆς**, -ῆ, ὁ   *Manasseh,* (1) son of Joseph, founder of a tribe of Israel, Rev 7:6; (2) son of Hezekiah and father of Amon (Amos) (Lat.).

Μανασσῆς   noun prop., nom. sg. masc. {2.A; 2.D} . . . . .Μανασσῆς *G3128*

μανθάνειν   vbl., pres. act. inf. {6.B.1} . . . μανθάνω *G3129*

μανθανέτω   verb, pres. act. impv. 3 pers. sg. {5.D.1} . . . . id.

μανθανέτωσαν   verb, pres. act. impv. 3 pers. pl. {5.D.1} . . . . id.

μανθάνοντα   vbl., pres. act. ptc. acc. pl. neut. {6.A.1} . . . . id.

μανθάνουσι   verb, pres. act. indic. 3 pers. pl. {5.A.1.a} . . . . id.

μανθάνουσιν   verb, pres. act. indic. 3 pers. pl. {5.A.1.a} . . . . id.

G3129 **μανθάνω**   *I learn;* with adjs. or nouns, *I learn to be so and so,* 1 Tim 5:13; with acc. of person who is the object of knowledge, Eph 4:20; aor. sometimes to *ascertain,* Acts 23:27; Gal 3:2.

μανθάνωσι   verb, pres. act. subjunc. 3 pers. pl. {5.B.1} . . . . μανθάνω *G3129*

μανθάνωσιν   verb, pres. act. subjunc. 3 pers. pl. {5.B.1} . . . . id.

G3130 **μανία**, -ας, ἡ   *raving madness.*

μανίαν   noun, acc. sg. fem. {2.A} . . . . μανία *G3130*

G3131 **μάννα**, τό   *manna,* the supernatural food eaten by the Israelites in the desert; of spiritual food, Rev 2:17 (Lat.).

μάννα   Heb. . . . . .μάννα *G3131*

G3132 **μαντεύομαι**   *I practice soothsaying,* suggesting the fraud involved in the practice.

μαντευομένη   vbl., pres. mid./pass. ptc. nom. sg. fem. {6.A.1} . . . . μαντεύομαι *G3132*

G3133 **μαραίνω**   pass. *I die, I wither* (like the grass).

μαράν   Aram. .μαρὰν ἀθά *G3134*

G3134 **μαρὰν ἀθά** (μαρὰν ἀθᾶ)   Aram., early Christian (eucharistic?) formula meaning, *Lord, come!* or *Our Lord hath come* or *Our Lord cometh (will come, is at hand).*

μαράνα   Aram. . . . . .μαρὰν ἀθά *G3134*

μαρανθήσεται   verb, fut. pass. indic. 3 pers. sg. {5.A.1.d} . . . . μαραίνω *G3133*

μαργαρῖται   noun, nom. pl. masc. {2.A} . . . . μαργαρίτης *G3135*

μαργαρίταις   noun, dat. pl. masc. {2.A} . . . . . . id.

μαργαρίτας   noun, acc. pl. masc. {2.A} . . . . . . id.

μαργαρίτῃ   noun, dat. sg. masc. {2.A} . . . . . . id.

μαργαρίτην   noun, acc. sg. masc. {2.A} . . . . . . id.

G3135 **μαργαρίτης**, -ου, ὁ   *a pearl.*

μαργαρίτου   noun, gen. sg. masc. {2.A} . . . . μαργαρίτης *G3135*

μαργαριτῶν   noun, gen. pl. masc. {2.A} . . . . . . id.

G3136 **Μάρθα**, -ας, ἡ   *Martha,* sister of Mary and Lazarus of Bethany.

Μάρθα   noun prop., nom. sg. fem. {2.A; 2.D}   Μάρθα *G3136*

Μάρθα   noun prop., voc. sg. fem. {2.A; 2.D} . . . id.

Μάρθαν   noun prop., acc. sg. fem. {2.A; 2.D}. . . id.

Μάρθας   noun prop., gen. sg. fem. {2.A; 2.D}. . . id.

G3137 **Μαρία** (Μαριάμ), -ας, ἡ   *Mary, Miriam* (the former is the Graecized form), (1) the mother of Jesus; (2) of Magdala, which epithet is always attached (except John 20:11, 16 where it is unnecessary; (3) sister of Martha and Lazarus, Luke 10:39, 42; John 11; 12:3; (4) mother of James and Joseph (or Joses), Matt 27:56; Mark 15:40, and presumably in Mark 15:47; 16:1; Luke 24:10; wife of Clopas, John 19:25. Also referred to in Matt 27:61; 28:1; (5) mother of John Mark, Acts 12:12; (6) a Christian in Rome, Rom 16:6.

Μαρία   noun prop., nom. sg. fem. {2.A; 2.D} . . . . .Μαρία *G3137*

Μαρία   noun prop., voc. sg. fem. {2.A; 2.D} . . . . id.

Μαρίᾳ   noun prop., dat. sg. fem. {2.A; 2.D} . . . . id.

Μαριάμ   noun prop. . . . . id.

Μαρίαν   noun prop., acc. sg. fem. {2.A; 2.D} . . . id.

Μαρίας   noun prop., gen. sg. fem. {2.A; 2.D} . . . id.

Μάρκον   noun prop., acc. sg. masc. {2.B; 2.D} . . . . Μᾶρκος *G3138*

Μάρκον   noun prop., acc. sg. masc. {2.B; 2.D} . . id.

Μάρκος   noun prop., nom. sg. masc. {2.B; 2.D} . id.

G3138 **Μᾶρκος**, -ου, ὁ   *Marcus, Mark,* who also had the Heb. name John, son of Mary (#5 above), nephew of Barnabas, coadjutor of Barnabas, Saul (Paul), and Peter.

Μᾶρκος   noun prop., nom. sg. masc. {2.B; 2.D}. . . . . Μᾶρκος *G3138*

Μᾶρκου   noun prop., gen. sg. masc. {2.B; 2.D}. . id.

G3139 **μάρμαρος**, -ου, ὁ *marble.*

μαρμάρου   noun, gen. sg. masc. {2.B} . . μάρμαρος *G3139*

μάρτυρα   noun, acc. sg. masc. {2.C}. . . . . μάρτυς *G3144*

μάρτυρας   noun, acc. pl. masc. {2.C}. . . . . id.

μαρτυρεῖ   verb, pres. act. indic. 3 pers. sg. {5.A.2}. . . . . .μαρτυρέω *G3140*

μαρτυρεῖν   vbl., pres. act. inf. {6.B.2}. . . . . id.

μαρτυρεῖς   verb, pres. act. indic. 2 pers. sg. {5.A.2}. . . . . id.

μαρτυρεῖται   verb, pres. pass. indic. 3 pers. sg. {5.A.2}. . . . . id.

μαρτυρεῖτε   verb, pres. act. indic. 2 pers. pl. {5.A.2}. . . . . id.

μάρτυρες   noun, nom. pl. masc. {2.C} . . . . μάρτυς *G3144*

G3140 **μαρτυρέω**   *I witness, I bear witness, I give evidence, I testify,* with dat. pers. or quality, in one's favor, in favor of; with acc. cog., μαρτυρίαν, ὁμολογίαν, practically otiose; in the pass., *I am witnessed to, I am borne witness to,* sometimes with nom. and dependent inf. (impers., 3 John 12), corresponding to the act.; Rev 1:2; 22:16, 18, 20.

μαρτυρηθέντες   vbl., aor. pass. ptc. nom. pl. masc. {6.A.1.a.}. . . . . μαρτυρέω *G3140*

μαρτυρῆσαι   vbl., aor. act. inf. {6.B.1}. . . . . . . id.

μαρτυρήσαντος   vbl., aor. act. ptc. gen. sg. masc. {6.A.2}. . . . . id.

μαρτυρήσας   vbl., aor. act. ptc. nom. sg. masc. {6.A.2}. . . . . id.

μαρτυρήσει   verb, fut. act. indic. 3 pers. sg. {5.A.1}. . . . . id.

μαρτυρήσῃ   verb, aor. act. subjunc. 3 pers. sg. {5.B.1}. . . . . id.

μαρτύρησον   verb, aor. act. impv. 2 pers. sg. {5.D.1}. . . . . id.

μαρτυρήσω   verb, aor. act. subjunc. 1 pers. sg. {5.B.1}. . . . . id.

G3141 **μαρτυρία**, -ας, ἡ   *witness, evidence, testimony.*

μαρτυρία   noun, nom. sg. fem. {2.A}. . . μαρτυρία *G3141*

μαρτυρίαι   noun, nom. pl. fem. {2.A} . . . . . . id.

μαρτυρίαν   noun, acc. sg. fem. {2.A}. . . . . id.

μαρτυρίας   noun, gen. sg. fem. {2.A}. . . . . id.

G3142 **μαρτύριον**, -ου, τό   *witness, evidence* (of recovery, Matt 8:4; Mark 1:44; Luke 5:14; so of other occurrences or thoughts); ἡ σκηνὴ τοῦ μαρτυρίου, *the tent* of the congregation, *the tent* of meeting of God with His people, because it contained the ark and the tablets *of the testimony* to the covenant between God and his people, cf. Exod 25:9, 10.

μαρτύριον   noun, acc. sg. neut. {2.B}. . μαρτύριον *G3142*

μαρτύριον   noun, nom. sg. neut. {2.B}. . . . . . . id.

μαρτυρίου   noun, gen. sg. neut. {2.B} . . . . id.

G3143 **μαρτύρομαι**   (properly, *I call* or *summon to witness,* and then, absol.) *I testify, I protest, I*

asseverate; I conjure, solemnly charge, 1 Thess 2:12; Eph 4:17.

μαρτύρομαι   verb, pres. mid./pass. indic. 1 pers. sg. {5.A.1.d}. . . . . .μαρτύρομαι *G3143*

μαρτυρόμενοι   vbl., pres. mid./pass. ptc. nom. pl. masc. {6.A.1} . . . . id.

μαρτυρόμενος   vbl., pres. mid./pass. ptc. nom. sg. masc. {6.A.1} . . . . id.

μάρτυρος   noun, gen. sg. masc. {2.C}. . . . . μάρτυς *G3144*

μαρτυροῦμεν   verb, pres. act. indic. 1 pers. pl. {5.A.2}. . . . . .μαρτυρέω *G3140*

μαρτυρουμένη   vbl., pres. pass. ptc. nom. sg. fem. {6.A.2}. . . . . id.

μαρτυρούμενοι   vbl., pres. mid. ptc. nom. pl. masc. {6.A.2}. . . . . id.

μαρτυρούμενος   vbl., pres. pass. ptc. nom. sg. masc. {6.A.2}. . . . . id.

μαρτυρουμένους   vbl., pres. pass. ptc. acc. pl. masc. {6.A.2}. . . . . id.

μαρτυροῦν   vbl., pres. act. ptc. nom. sg. neut. {6.A.2}. . . . . id.

μαρτυροῦντες   vbl., pres. act. ptc. nom. pl. masc. {6.A.2}. . . . . id.

μαρτυροῦντι   vbl., pres. act. ptc. dat. sg. masc. {6.A.2}. . . . . id.

μαρτυροῦντος   vbl., pres. act. ptc. gen. sg. masc. {6.A.2}. . . . . id.

μαρτυρούντων   vbl., pres. act. ptc. gen. pl. masc. {6.A.2}. . . . . id.

μαρτυροῦσαι   vbl., pres. act. ptc. nom. pl. fem. {6.A.2}. . . . . id.

μαρτυρούσης   vbl., pres. act. ptc. gen. sg. fem. {6.A.2}. . . . . id.

μαρτυροῦσιν   verb, pres. act. indic. 3 pers. pl. {5.A.2}. . . . . id.

μαρτυρῶ   verb, pres. act. indic. 1 pers. sg. {5.A.2}. . . . . id.

μαρτυρῶ   verb, pres. act. subjunc. 1 pers. sg. {5.B.2}. . . . . id.

μαρτύρων   noun, gen. pl. masc. {2.C} . . . . μάρτυς *G3144*

μαρτυρῶν   vbl., pres. act. ptc. nom. sg. masc. {6.A.2}. . . . . .μαρτυρέω *G3140*

G3144 **μάρτυς**, μάρτυρος, dat. pl. μάρτυσιν, ὁ   *a witness, eyewitness* or *ear witness.* In Acts 22:20; Rev 2:13 it approaches the ecclesiastical sense of *martyr,* i.e., one who gives public testimony to his faith before a tribunal, and suffers the penalty.

μάρτυς   noun, nom. sg. masc. {2.C}. . . . . . μάρτυς *G3144*

μάρτυσι   noun, dat. pl. masc. {2.C} . . . . id.

μάρτυσιν   noun, dat. pl. masc. {2.C} . . . . id.

G3145 **μασάομαι**   *I gnaw.*

μάστιγας   noun, acc. pl. fem. {2.C}. . . . . . . μάστιξ *G3148*

μαστιγοῖ   verb, pres. act. indic. 3 pers. sg. {5.A.2}. . . . . .μαστιγόω *G3146*

μάστιγος   noun, gen. sg. fem. {2.C} . . . . . μάστιξ *G3148*

G3146 **μαστιγόω**   *I flog, scourge,* the victim being strapped to a pole or frame, see μάστιξ.

μαστίγων   noun, gen. pl. fem. {2.C} . . . . . . μάστιξ *G3148*

μαστιγῶσαι   vbl., aor. act. inf. {6.B.1} . . μαστιγόω *G3146*

μαστιγώσαντες vbl., aor. act. ptc. nom. pl.
  masc. {6.A.2} . . . . id.
μαστιγώσετε verb, fut. act. indic. 2 pers. pl.
  {5.A.1} . . . . id.
μαστιγώσουσιν verb, fut. act. indic. 3 pers. pl.
  {5.A.1} . . . . id.
μαστίζειν vbl., pres. act. inf. {6.B.1} . . . μαστίζω G3147
G3147 **μαστίζω** I flog, scourge, see μάστιξ.
G3148 **μάστιξ**, -ιγος, ἡ (1) a scourge, lash, of leathern
  thongs with pieces of metal sewn up in them,
  Acts 22:24; Heb 11:36; (2) met. severe pains
  (sufferings) sent by God.
μάστιξιν noun, dat. pl. fem. {2.C} . . . . . . μάστιξ G3148
μαστοί noun, nom. pl. masc. {2.B} . . . . . μαστός G3149
μαστοῖς noun, dat. pl. masc. {2.B} . . . . id.
G3149 **μαστός** (μασθός), -οῦ, ὁ a breast, esp. a nipple
  of a woman's breast.
ματαία adj., nom. sg. fem. {3.A} . . . . . . μάταιος G3152
ματαίας adj., gen. sg. fem. {3.A} . . . . id.
μάταιοι adj., nom. pl. fem. {3.A} . . . . id.
μάταιοι adj., nom. pl. masc. {3.A} . . . . id.
G3150 **ματαιολογία**, -ας, ἡ vain speaking, foolish
  talking.
ματαιολογίαν noun, acc. sg. fem.
  {2.A} . . . . ματαιολογία G3150
ματαιολόγοι adj., nom. pl. masc.
  {3.C} . . . . ματαιολόγος G3151
G3151 **ματαιολόγος**, -ου, ὁ speaking vain things.
G3152 **μάταιος**, -α, -ον vain, unreal, ineffectual,
  unproductive; practically godless.
μάταιος adj., nom. sg. fem. {3.A} . . . . . μάταιος G3152
G3153 **ματαιότης**, -ητος, ἡ vanity, emptiness, unreal-
  ity, purposelessness, ineffectiveness, instability.
ματαιότητι noun, dat. sg. fem. {2.C} . . ματαιότης G3153
ματαιότητος noun, gen. sg. fem. {2.C} . . . . . . id.
G3154 **ματαιόω** pass. I am made vain, ineffective,
  godless.
ματαίων adj., gen. pl. neut. {3.A} . . . . μάταιος G3152
G3155 **μάτην** adv., in vain, in an unreal way.
μάτην adv. . . . . μάτην G3155
Ματθαῖον noun prop., acc. sg. masc. {2.B;
  2.D} . . . . Ματθαῖος G3156
G3156 **Ματθαῖος** (Μαθθαῖος), -ου, ὁ Matthew, a
  revenue officer, then one of the twelve disciples of Jesus.
Ματθαῖος noun prop., nom. sg. masc. {2.B;
  2.D} . . . . Ματθαῖος G3156
G3157 **Ματθάν** (Μαθθάν), ὁ Matthan, son of Eleazar
  and father of Jacob, an ancestor of Jesus (Heb.).
Ματθάν noun prop. . . . . Ματθάν G3157
G3158 **Ματθάτ** (Μαθθάθ, Μαθθάτ, Ματθάτ) Mat-
  that, son of Levi and father of Jorem, an ances-
  tor of Jesus (Heb.).
Ματθάτ noun prop. . . . . Ματθάτ G3158
Ματθίαν noun prop., acc. sg. masc. {2.A;
  2.D} . . . . Ματθίας G3159
G3159 **Ματθίας** (Μαθθίας), -ου, ὁ Matthias, elected
  one of the Twelve in room of the deceased
  Judas.

G3160 **Ματταθά**, ὁ Mattathah, an ancestor of Jesus
  (Heb.).
Ματταθά noun prop. . . . . Ματταθά G3160
G3161 **Ματταθίας**, -ου, ὁ Mattathias, an ancestor of
  Jesus (Heb.).
Ματταθίου noun prop., gen. sg. masc. {2.A;
  2.D} . . . . Ματταθίας G3161
μάχαι noun, nom. pl. fem. {2.A} . . . . μάχη G3163
G3162 **μάχαιρα**, -ης, ἡ a sword; met. of the spirit,
  Eph 6:17.
μάχαιρα noun, nom. sg. fem. {2.A} . . . . . μάχαιρα G3162
μαχαίρᾳ noun, dat. sg. fem. {2.A} . . . . id.
μάχαιραι noun, nom. pl. fem. {2.A} . . . . id.
μάχαιραν noun, acc. sg. fem. {2.A} . . . . id.
μαχαίρας noun, gen. sg. fem. {2.A} . . . . id.
μαχαίρη noun, dat. sg. fem. {2.A} . . . . id.
μαχαίρης noun, gen. sg. fem. {2.A} . . . . id.
μαχαιρῶν noun, gen. pl. fem. {2.A} . . . . id.
μάχας noun, acc. pl. fem. {2.A} . . . . μάχη G3163
μάχεσθαι vbl., pres. mid./pass. inf.
  {6.B.1} . . . . μάχομαι G3164
μάχεσθε verb, pres. mid./pass. indic. 2 pers. pl.
  {5.A.1.d} . . . . id.
G3163 **μάχη**, -ης, ἡ (earlier, a battle, conflict, perhaps
  in Jas 4:1; hence, in the sphere of words, etc.)
  strife, contention, quarrel.
G3164 **μάχομαι** I engage in battle, I fight; hence, I
  strive, John 6:52.
μαχομένοις vbl., pres. mid./pass. ptc. dat. pl.
  masc. {6.A.1} . . . . μάχομαι G3164
με pron. pers., 1 pers. acc. sg. {4.A} . . . . ἐγώ G1473
μέ pron. pers., 1 pers. acc. sg. {4.A} . . . . id.
μέγα adj., acc. sg. neut. {3.B} . . . . μέγας G3173
μέγα adj., nom. sg. neut. {3.B} . . . . id.
μεγάλα adj., acc. pl. neut. {3.B} . . . . id.
μεγάλα adj., nom. pl. neut. {3.B} . . . . id.
μεγάλαι adj., nom. pl. fem. {3.B} . . . . id.
μεγάλαις adj., dat. pl. fem. {3.B} . . . . id.
μεγάλας adj., acc. pl. fem. {3.B} . . . . id.
μεγαλαυχεῖ verb, pres. act. indic. 3 pers. sg.
  {5.A.2} . . . . μεγαλαυχέω G3166
G3166 **μεγαλαυχέω** I boast, brag.
μεγαλεῖα adj., acc. pl. neut. {3.A} . . . . μεγαλεῖος G3167
G3167 **μεγαλεῖος**, -α, -ον neut. subs. greatness; pl. τὰ
  μεγαλεῖα, the mighty deeds.
G3168 **μεγαλειότης**, -ητος, ἡ (divine) majesty or
  magnificence.
μεγαλειότητα noun, acc. sg. fem.
  {2.C} . . . . μεγαλειότης G3168
μεγαλειότητι noun, dat. sg. fem. {2.C} . . . . . id.
μεγαλειότητος noun, gen. sg. fem. {2.C} . . . . id.
μεγάλη adj., nom. sg. fem. {3.B} . . . . . . μέγας G3173
μεγάλη adj., voc. sg. fem. {3.B} . . . . id.
μεγάλῃ adj., dat. sg. fem. {3.B} . . . . id.
μεγάλην adj., acc. sg. fem. {3.B} . . . . id.
μεγάλης adj., gen. sg. fem. {3.B} . . . . id.
μεγάλοι adj., nom. pl. masc. {3.B} . . . . id.
μεγάλοι adj., voc. pl. masc. {3.B} . . . . id.
μεγάλοις adj., dat. pl. masc. {3.B} . . . . id.

G3169 **μεγαλοπρεπής**, -ές *magnificent, superb, transcendent.*
μεγαλοπρεποῦς adj., gen. sg. fem.
{3.E} . . . . μεγαλοπρεπής G3169
μεγάλου adj., gen. sg. masc. {3.B} . . . . .μέγας G3173
μεγάλους adj., acc. pl. masc. {3.B} . . . . id.
μεγαλύνει verb, pres. act. indic. 3 pers. sg.
{5.A.1.a} . . . . μεγαλύνω G3170
μεγαλυνθῆναι vbl., aor. pass. inf. {6.B.1} . . . . id.
μεγαλυνθήσεται verb, fut. pass. indic. 3 pers.
sg. {5.A.1.d} . . . . id.
μεγαλυνόντων vbl., pres. act. ptc. gen. pl.
masc. {6.A.1} . . . . id.
μεγαλύνουσι verb, pres. act. indic. 3 pers. pl.
{5.A.1.a} . . . . id.
μεγαλύνουσιν verb, pres. act. indic. 3 pers. pl.
{5.A.1.a} . . . . id.
G3170 **μεγαλύνω** (1) *I enlarge, lengthen,* Matt 23:5;
(2) *I increase, magnify.*
μεγάλῳ adj., dat. sg. masc. {3.B} . . . . .μέγας G3173
μεγάλων adj., gen. pl. masc. {3.B} . . . . id.
G3171 **μεγάλως** adv., *greatly;* comp. μεῖζον.
μεγάλως adv. {3.F} . . . . μεγάλως G3171
G3172 **μεγαλωσύνη**, -ης, ἡ *(divine) majesty;* in Heb
1:3; 8:1, a sort of substitute for the divine
Name.
μεγαλωσύνη noun, nom. sg. fem.
{2.A} . . . . μεγαλωσύνη G3172
μεγαλωσύνης noun, gen. sg. fem. {2.A} . . . . . id.
μέγαν adj., acc. sg. masc. {3.B} . . . . .μέγας G3173
G3173 **μέγας**, μεγάλη, μέγα *large, great,* in the widest
sense. Comp. μέγιστος, elative, *very great*
(practically obsolete and only literary). See
comp. μείζων.
μέγας adj., nom. sg. masc. {3.B} . . . . .μέγας G3173
G3174 **μέγεθος**, -ους, τό *greatness.*
μέγεθος noun, nom. sg. neut. {2.C} . . . . . μέγεθος G3174
μέγιστα adj. superl., acc. pl. neut. {3.B} . . .μέγας G3173
μέγιστα adj. superl., nom. pl. neut. {3.B} . . . . . id.
G3175 **μεγιστάν**, -άνος, ὁ *a great one, a lord, a courtier, a satrap.* (The word has an oriental flavor
and belongs to late Gk.).
μεγιστᾶνες noun, nom. pl. masc. {2.C} . .μεγιστάν G3175
μεγιστᾶσιν noun, dat. pl. masc. {2.C} . . . . . . id.
G3176 **μέγιστος** *greatest, very great* (superl. of μέγας).
μεθ᾽ prep. . . . . μετά G3326
μέθαι noun, nom. pl. fem. {2.A} . . . . μέθη G3178
μέθαις noun, dat. pl. fem. {2.A} . . . . id.
μεθερμηνεύεται verb, pres. pass. indic. 3 pers. sg.
{5.A.1.d} . . . . .μεθερμηνεύω G3177
μεθερμηνευόμενον vbl., pres. pass. ptc. nom.
sg. neut. {6.A.1} . . . . id.
μεθερμηνευόμενος vbl., pres. pass. ptc. nom.
sg. masc. {6.A.1} . . . . id.
G3177 **μεθερμηνεύω** *I translate* (from one language
into another).
G3178 **μέθη**, -ης, ἡ *deep drinking, drunkenness.*
μέθη noun, dat. sg. fem. {2.A} . . . . μέθη G3178
μεθιστάναι vbl., pres. act. inf. {6.B.3} . .μεθίστημι G3179

μεθιστάνειν vbl., pres. act. inf. {6.B.3} . . . . . . id.
G3179 **μεθίστημι** (μεθιστάνω) *I cause to change its
place, I move out of its place, I translate, transfer, remove.*
G3180 **μεθοδεία**, -ας, ἡ *scheming, craftiness* (from
μέθοδος, *a way of search after something, an
inquiry; a method*).
μεθοδείαν noun, acc. sg. fem. {2.A} . . . .μεθοδεία G3180
μεθοδείας noun, acc. pl. fem. {2.A} . . . . id.
μεθοδίαν noun, acc. sg. fem. {2.A} . . . . id.
μεθοδίας noun, acc. pl. fem. {2.A} . . . . id.
μεθόρια noun, acc. pl. neut. {2.B} . . . . . .μεθόριον G3181
G3181 **μεθόριον**, -ου, τό *a boundary, a border.*
μεθύει verb, pres. act. indic. 3 pers. sg.
{5.A.1.a} . . . . μεθύω G3184
μεθυόντων vbl., pres. act. ptc. gen. pl. masc.
{6.A.1} . . . . id.
μεθύουσαν vbl., pres. act. ptc. acc. sg. fem.
{6.A.1} . . . . id.
μεθύουσιν verb, pres. act. indic. 3 pers. pl.
{5.A.1.a} . . . . id.
μεθυσθῶσι verb, aor. pass. subjunc. 3 pers. pl.
{5.B.1} . . . . id.
μεθυσθῶσιν verb, aor. pass. subjunc. 3 pers.
pl. {5.B.1} . . . . id.
μεθύσκεσθαι vbl., pres. pass. inf. {6.B.1}.μεθύσκω G3182
μεθύσκεσθε verb, pres. pass. impv. 2 pers. pl.
{5.D.1} . . . . id.
μεθυσκόμενοι vbl., pres. pass. ptc. nom. pl.
masc. {6.A.1} . . . . id.
G3182 **μεθύσκω** *I intoxicate; pass., I become intoxicated with wine, I become drunk.*
μέθυσοι noun, nom. pl. masc. {2.B} . . . . μέθυσος G3183
G3183 **μέθυσος**, -ου, ὁ *a drunkard* (orig., *tipsy*).
μέθυσος noun, nom. sg. masc. {2.B} . . . μέθυσος G3183
G3184 **μεθύω** *I am intoxicated with wine, I am drunk.*
μεῖζον adj. comp., acc. sg. neut. {3.E; 3.G} .μείζων G3187
μεῖζον adv. {3.F} . . . . id.
μεῖζον adj. comp., nom. sg. neut. {3.E; 3.G} . . . id.
μείζονα adj. comp., acc. sg. fem. {3.E; 3.G} . . . . id.
μείζονα adj. comp., acc. sg. masc. {3.E; 3.G} . . . id.
μείζονα adj. comp., acc. pl. neut. {3.E; 3.G} . . . . id.
μείζονας adj. comp., acc. pl. fem. {3.E; 3.G} . . . id.
μείζονες adj. comp., nom. pl. masc. {3.E; 3.G}. . . id.
μείζονος adj. comp., gen. sg. neut. {3.E; 3.G} . . . id.
μείζονος adj. comp., gen. sg. masc. {3.E; 3.G} . . id.
μειζοτέραν adj. comp., acc. sg. fem. {3.A; 3.G} . id.
μείζω adj. comp., acc. pl. neut. {3.E; 3.G}. . . . . id.
μείζω adj. comp., acc. sg. fem. {3.E; 3.G} . . . . . id.
G3187 **μείζων**, -ον, -ον *greater* (comp. of μέγας). Superl. μειζότερος, *greatest,* Matt 13:32; 23:11;
1 Cor 13:13, etc. Adv. μεῖζον, *all the more.*
μείζων adj. comp., nom. sg. fem. {3.E; 3.G} .μείζων G3187
μείζων adj. comp., nom. sg. masc. {3.E; 3.G} . . . id.
μεῖναι vbl., aor. act. inf. {6.B.1} . . . . .μένω G3306
μείναντες vbl., aor. act. ptc. nom. pl. masc.
{6.A.1.a} . . . . id.
μείνατε verb, aor. act. impv. 2 pers. pl. {5.D.1} . . id.
μείνῃ verb, aor. act. subjunc. 3 pers. sg. {5.B.1} . id.

μείνητε   verb, aor. act. subjunc. 2 pers. pl. {5.B.1}id.
μεῖνον   verb, aor. act. impv. 2 pers. sg. {5.D.1} .. id.
μείνωσιν   verb, aor. act. subjunc. 3 pers. pl.
   {5.B.1} . . . . id.
μέλαιναν   adj., acc. sg. fem. {3.D} . . . . μέλας G3189
G3188 **μέλαν**, -ανος, τό   ink (neut. sg. subs. of
   μέλας), 2 Cor 3:3; 2 John 12; 3 John 13.
μέλανι   adj., dat. sg. neut. {3.D} . . . . μέλας G3189
μέλανος   adj., gen. sg. neut. {3.D} . . . . id.
G3189 **μέλας**, -αινα, -αν, gen. ανος, -αίνης,
   -ανος   black. Cf. μέλαν.
μέλας   adj., nom. sg. masc. {3.D} . . . . μέλας G3189
G3190 **Μελεά**, ὁ   Melea, one of the ancestors of Jesus
   (Heb.).
Μελεά   noun prop. .Μελεά G3190
Μελεά   noun prop. . . . . id.
G3199‡ **μέλει**   impers., it is a care, it is an object of
   anxiety, with dat. of the person; pers., διὸ
   μελλήσω, wherefore I will take care, true text
   in 2 Pet 1:12.
μέλει   verb, pres. act. indic. 3 pers. sg.
   {5.A.1.a} . . . . μέλει G3199‡
μέλεσι   noun, dat. pl. neut. {2.C} . . . . μέλος G3196
μέλεσιν   noun, dat. pl. neut. {2.C} . . . . id.
μελέτα   verb, pres. act. impv. 2 pers. sg.
   {5.D.2} . . . . .μελετάω G3191
μελετᾶτε   verb, pres. act. impv. 2 pers. pl. {5.D.2}id.
G3191 **μελετάω**   I devise, plan; practice, exercise myself
   in.
μελέτω   verb, pres. act. impv. 3 pers. sg.
   {5.D.1} . . . . μέλει G3199‡
μέλη   noun, acc. pl. neut. {2.C} . . . . μέλος G3196
μέλη   noun, nom. pl. neut. {2.C} . . . . id.
G3192 **μέλι**, -ιτος, τό   honey.
μέλι   noun, acc. sg. neut. {2.C} . . . . μέλι G3192
μέλι   noun, nom. sg. neut. {2.C} . . . . id.
G3193 **μελίσσιος**, -ον   belonging to bees, coming from
   bees.
μελισσίου   adj., gen. sg. neut. {3.A} . . . .μελίσσιος G3193
G3194 **Μελίτη** (Μελιτήνη), -ης, ἡ   Malta.
Μελίτη   noun prop., nom. sg. fem. {2.A;
   2.D} . . . . Μελίτη G3194
Μελιτήνη   noun prop., nom. sg. fem. {2.A; 2.D} id.
μέλλει   verb, pres. act. indic. 3 pers. sg.
   {5.A.1.a} . . . . μέλλω G3195
μέλλειν   vbl., pres. act. inf. {6.B.1} . . . . id.
μέλλεις   verb, pres. act. indic. 2 pers. sg.
   {5.A.1.a} . . . . id.
μέλλετε   verb, pres. act. indic. 2 pers. pl.
   {5.A.1.a} . . . . id.
μέλλη   verb, pres. act. subjunc. 3 pers. sg. {5.B.1} id.
μελλήσετε   verb, fut. act. indic. 2 pers. pl.
   {5.A.1.a} . . . . id.
μελλήσω   verb, fut. act. indic. 1 pers. sg.
   {5.A.1.a} . . . . id.
μέλλομεν   verb, pres. act. indic. 1 pers. pl.
   {5.A.1.a} . . . . id.
μέλλον   vbl., pres. act. ptc. acc. sg. neut. {6.A.1}. id.

μέλλοντα   vbl., pres. act. ptc. acc. pl. neut.
   {6.A.1} . . . . id.
μέλλοντα   vbl., pres. act. ptc. acc. sg. masc.
   {6.A.1} . . . . id.
μέλλοντα   vbl., pres. act. ptc. nom. pl. neut.
   {6.A.1} . . . . id.
μέλλοντας   vbl., pres. act. ptc. acc. pl. masc.
   {6.A.1} . . . . id.
μέλλοντες   vbl., pres. act. ptc. nom. pl. masc.
   {6.A.1} . . . . id.
μέλλοντι   vbl., pres. act. ptc. dat. sg. masc.
   {6.A.1} . . . . id.
μέλλοντι   vbl., pres. act. ptc. dat. sg. neut. {6.A.1} id.
μέλλοντος   vbl., pres. act. ptc. gen. sg. masc.
   {6.A.1} . . . . id.
μέλλοντος   vbl., pres. act. ptc. gen. sg. neut.
   {6.A.1} . . . . id.
μελλόντων   vbl., pres. act. ptc. gen. pl. masc.
   {6.A.1} . . . . id.
μελλόντων   vbl., pres. act. ptc. gen. pl. neut.
   {6.A.1} . . . . id.
μέλλουσαν   vbl., pres. act. ptc. acc. sg. fem.
   {6.A.1} . . . . id.
μελλούσης   vbl., pres. act. ptc. gen. sg. fem.
   {6.A.1} . . . . id.
μέλλουσι   verb, pres. act. indic. 3 pers. pl.
   {5.A.1.a} . . . . id.
μέλλουσιν   verb, pres. act. indic. 3 pers. pl.
   {5.A.1.a} . . . . id.
G3195 **μέλλω**   (1) with inf. I am about to, I intend;
   (2) absol., in pres. ptc., coming, future; so τὸ
   μέλλον, the future, εἰς τὸ μέλλον (supply
   ἔτος), next year, Luke 13:9, τὰ μέλλοντα, the
   things that are to be (come to pass). See μέλει.
μέλλω   verb, pres. act. indic. 1 pers. sg.
   {5.A.1.a} . . . . μέλλω G3195
μέλλων   vbl., pres. act. ptc. nom. sg. masc.
   {6.A.1} . . . . id.
G3196 **μέλος**, -ους, τό   a bodily organ, limb, member
   (wider in sense than κῶλον).
μέλος   noun, nom. sg. neut. {2.C} . . . . μέλος G3196
Μελχεί   noun prop. Μελχί G3197
G3197 **Μελχί**, ὁ   Melchi, one of the ancestors of Jesus
   (Heb.).
Μελχί   noun prop. Μελχί G3197
Μελχισεδέκ   noun prop. . . . . Μελχισεδέκ G3198
G3198 **Μελχισεδέκ**, ὁ   Melchizedek, king and priest of
   Salem (Gen. 14:18–20) (Heb.).
Μελχισεδέκ   noun prop. . . . . Μελχισεδέκ G3198
μελῶν   noun, gen. pl. neut. {2.C} . . . . μέλος G3196
μεμαθηκώς   vbl., perf. act. ptc. nom. sg. masc.
   {6.A.1.a} . . . . μανθάνω G3129
μεμαρτύρηκα   verb, perf. act. indic. 1 pers. sg.
   {5.A.1} . . . . .μαρτυρέω G3140
μεμαρτύρηκας   verb, perf. act. indic. 2 pers.
   sg. {5.A.1} . . . . id.
μεμαρτύρηκε   verb, perf. act. indic. 3 pers. sg.
   {5.A.1} . . . . id.

μεμαρτύρηκεν   verb, perf. act. indic. 3 pers. sg.
{5.A.1} . . . . id.
μεμαρτύρηται   verb, perf. pass. indic. 3 pers.
   sg. {5.A.1} . . . . id.
G3200 **μεμβράνα**, -ης, ἡ   *a parchment leaf,* perhaps
   for notes (Lat. *membrana*).
μεμβράνας   noun, acc. pl. fem. {2.A} . . .μεμβράνα G3200
μεμενήκεισαν   verb, plu. act. indic. 3 pers. pl.
   {5.A.1.b} . . . . μένω G3306
μεμέρικεν   verb, perf. act. indic. 3 pers. sg.
   {5.A.1.c} . . . . μερίζω G3307
μεμέρισται   verb, perf. pass. indic. 3 pers. sg.
   {5.A.1.f} . . . . id.
μεμεστωμένοι   vbl., perf. pass. ptc. nom. pl. masc.
   {6.A.2} . . . . μεστόω G3325
μεμιαμμένοις   vbl., perf. pass. ptc. dat. pl. masc.
   {6.A.1.b} . . . . μιαίνω G3392
μεμίανται   verb, perf. pass. indic. 3 pers. sg.
   {5.A.1.f} . . . . id.
μεμιασμένοις   vbl., perf. pass. ptc. dat. pl.
   masc. {6.A.1.b} . . . . id.
μεμιγμένα   vbl., perf. pass. ptc. nom. pl. neut.
   {6.A.3} . . . . μίγνυμι G3396
μεμιγμένην   vbl., perf. pass. ptc. acc. sg. fem.
   {6.A.3} . . . . id.
μεμιγμένον   vbl., perf. pass. ptc. acc. sg. masc.
   {6.A.3} . . . . id.
μεμιγμένον   vbl., perf. pass. ptc. acc. sg. neut.
   {6.A.3} . . . . id.
μεμισήκασι   verb, perf. act. indic. 3 pers. pl.
   {5.A.1} . . . . μισέω G3404
μεμισήκασιν   verb, perf. act. indic. 3 pers. pl.
   {5.A.1} . . . . id.
μεμίσηκεν   verb, perf. act. indic. 3 pers. sg. {5.A.1} id.
μεμισημένου   vbl., perf. pass. ptc. gen. sg.
   neut. {6.A.2} . . . . id.
μεμνημένος   vbl., perf. mid./pass. ptc. nom. sg.
   masc. {6.A.1.b} . . . . μιμνήσκομαι G3403
μέμνησθε   verb, perf. mid./pass. indic. 2 pers.
   pl. {5.A.1.f} . . . . id.
μεμνηστευμένη   vbl., perf. pass. ptc. dat. sg. fem.
   {6.A.1.b} . . . . μνηστεύω G3423
μεμνηστευμένην   vbl., perf. pass. ptc. acc. sg.
   fem. {6.A.1.b} . . . . id.
μεμονωμένη   vbl., perf. pass. ptc. nom. sg. fem.
   {6.A.2} . . . . μονόω G3443
μεμύημαι   verb, perf. pass. indic. 1 pers. sg.
   {5.A.1} . . . . μυέω G3453
μέμφεται   verb, pres. mid./pass. indic. 3 pers. sg.
   {5.A.1.d} . . . . μέμφομαι G3201
G3201 **μέμφομαι**   *I blame.*
μεμφόμενος   vbl., pres. mid./pass. ptc. nom. sg.
   masc. {6.A.1} . . . . μέμφομαι G3201
μεμψίμοιροι   adj., nom. pl. masc.
   {3.C} . . . . μεμψίμοιρος G3202
G3202 **μεμψίμοιρος**, -ον   *blaming one's lot* or *destiny,*
   discontented.
G3303 **μέν**   an untranslatable particle, generally
   answered by δέ (sometimes by ἀλλά, πλήν),
   each of the two introducing a clause intended

to be contrasted with the other. (The μέν is
very often omitted as compared with classical
Gk.) Other uses are: (1) μέν followed by καί
(e.g., Luke 8:5), where an additional detail
is given, not explicitly contrasted with the
earlier; (2) μέν followed by no contrasting
particle in the following clause (e.g., πρῶτον
almost *at the very first,* Rom 1:8; 1 Cor 11:18);
and (3) μὲν οὖν, for the most part in narrative
passages, where the μέν brings the accompa-
nying noun or pron. into relief, without any
contrast being expressed by a following δέ
(e.g., Acts 1:6), (a) where what has preceded is
summed up on the way to the relation of some
new detail, or (b) where it acts as the introduction to a further occurrence; but see μενοῦν
for another use.
μέν   part. . . . . μέν G3303
Μεναμ   noun prop. . . . . .Μαϊνάν G3104
μένε   verb, pres. act. impv. 2 pers. sg. {5.D.1} . μένω G3306
μενεῖ   verb, fut. act. indic. 3 pers. sg. {5.A.2}. . . . id.
μένει   verb, pres. act. indic. 3 pers. sg. {5.A.1.a} . id.
μένειν   vbl., pres. act. inf. {6.B.1} . . . . id.
μένεις   verb, pres. act. indic. 2 pers. sg. {5.A.1.a} id.
μενεῖτε   verb, fut. act. indic. 2 pers. pl. {5.A.2} . . id.
μένετε   verb, pres. act. impv. 2 pers. pl. {5.D.1} . . id.
μένετε   verb, pres. act. indic. 2 pers. pl. {5.A.1.a} . id.
μενέτω   verb, pres. act. impv. 3 pers. sg. {5.D.1} . id.
μένῃ   verb, pres. act. subjunc. 3 pers. sg. {5.B.1} . id.
μένητε   verb, pres. act. subjunc. 2 pers. pl.
   {5.B.1} . . . . id.
Μεννά   noun prop. . . . . .Μαϊνάν G3104
μένομεν   verb, pres. act. indic. 1 pers. pl.
   {5.A.1.a} . . . . μένω G3306
μένον   vbl., pres. act. ptc. acc. sg. neut. {6.A.1} . . id.
μένον   vbl., pres. act. ptc. nom. sg. neut. {6.A.1}. . id.
μένοντα   vbl., pres. act. ptc. acc. sg. masc.
   {6.A.1} . . . . id.
μένοντος   vbl., pres. act. ptc. gen. sg. masc.
   {6.A.1} . . . . id.
G3304† **μενοῦν**   *rather, more than that, on the contrary.*
   Var. for μενοῦνγε.
μενοῦν   part. . . . . .μενοῦν G3304†
G3304 **μενοῦνγε**   *rather, more than that, on the*
   contrary, esp. in an answer (strengthening or
   correcting).
μενοῦνγε   part. . . . . .μενοῦν G3304†
μένουσαν   vbl., pres. act. ptc. acc. sg. fem.
   {6.A.1} . . . . μένω G3306
μένουσιν   verb, pres. act. indic. 3 pers. pl.
   {5.A.1.a} . . . . id.
G3305 **μέντοι**   (1) *indeed, really,* Jas 2:8; (2) *yet, how-*
   ever, nevertheless.
μέντοι   conj. . . . . .μέντοι G3305
μενῶ   verb, fut. act. indic. 1 pers. sg. {5.A.2} . . μένω G3306
G3306 **μένω**   *I remain, abide, wait;* with acc. *I wait for,*
   await.
μένω   verb, pres. act. indic. 1 pers. sg. {5.A.1.a}μένω G3306
μένων   vbl., pres. act. ptc. nom. sg. masc. {6.A.1} id.
μέρει   noun, dat. sg. neut. {2.C} . . . . μέρος G3313

μέρη   noun, acc. pl. neut. {2.C} . . . . id.

μερίδα   noun, acc. sg. fem. {2.C} . . . . μερίς G3310

μερίδος   noun, gen. sg. fem. {2.C} . . . . id.

G3307   **μερίζω**   *I divide into parts, I divide, I part, I share, I distribute;* mid. *I go shares, I share* (with others; in this case with Paul, Apollos, Cephas), *I take part in a partitioning,* 1 Cor 1:13; *I distract,* 1 Cor 7:34.

G3308   **μέριμνα**, -ης, ἡ   *care, worry, anxiety.*

μέριμνα   noun, nom. sg. fem. {2.A} . . . . . μέριμνα G3308

μεριμνᾷ   verb, pres. act. indic. 3 pers. sg. {5.A.2} . . . . μεριμνάω G3309

μέριμναι   noun, nom. pl. fem. {2.A} . . . . μέριμνα G3308

μερίμναις   noun, dat. pl. fem. {2.A} . . . . id.

μέριμναν   noun, acc. sg. fem. {2.A} . . . . id.

μεριμνᾶς   verb, pres. act. indic. 2 pers. sg. {5.A.2} . . . . μεριμνάω G3309

μεριμνᾶτε   verb, pres. act. impv. 2 pers. pl. {5.D.2}. id.

μεριμνᾶτε   verb, pres. act. indic. 2 pers. pl. {5.A.2} . . . . id.

G3309   **μεριμνάω**   *I am overanxious;* with acc. *I am anxious about, I care for.*

μεριμνήσει   verb, fut. act. indic. 3 pers. sg. {5.A.1} . . . . μεριμνάω G3309

μεριμνήσητε   verb, aor. act. subjunc. 2 pers. pl. {5.B.1} . . . . id.

μεριμνῶν   noun, gen. pl. fem. {2.A} . . . . . μέριμνα G3308

μεριμνῶν   vbl., pres. act. ptc. nom. sg. masc. {6.A.2} . . . . μεριμνάω G3309

μεριμνῶσι   verb, pres. act. subjunc. 3 pers. pl. {5.B.2} . . . . id.

μεριμνῶσιν   verb, pres. act. subjunc. 3 pers. pl. {5.B.2} . . . . id.

G3310   **μερίς**, -ίδος, ἡ   (1) *a part, division* of a country, Acts 16:12 (a sense amply attested outside); (2) *a share, portion.*

μερίς   noun, nom. sg. fem. {2.C} . . . . μερίς G3310

μερίσασθαι   vbl., aor. mid. inf. {6.B.1} . . . . μερίζω G3307

μερισθεῖσα   vbl., aor. pass. ptc. nom. sg. fem. {6.A.1.a} . . . . id.

μερισθῇ   verb, aor. pass. subjunc. 3 pers. sg. {5.B.1} . . . . id.

μερισμοῖς   noun, dat. pl. masc. {2.B} . . . μερισμός G3311

G3311   **μερισμός**, -οῦ, ὁ   (1) *a distributing, a distribution,* Heb 2:4; (2) *a parting, dividing, severance, separation.*

μερισμοῦ   noun, gen. sg. masc. {2.B} . . . . μερισμός G3311

μεριστήν   noun, acc. sg. masc. {2.A} . . . . μεριστής G3312

G3312   **μεριστής**, -οῦ, ὁ   *a divider, arbitrator, distributor.*

G3313   **μέρος**, -ους, τό   *a part, portion;* τὰ μέρη, territorially, *the region;* adv., phrases are ἀπὸ μέρους, ἐκ μέρους, *in part, partly,* ἀνὰ μέρος, κατὰ μέρος, *part by part, each part separately, in detail; a party,* Acts 23:9.

μέρος   noun, acc. sg. neut. {2.C} . . . . μέρος G3313

μέρος   noun, nom. sg. neut. {2.C} . . . . id.

μέρους   noun, gen. sg. neut. {2.C} . . . . id.

G3314   **μεσημβρία**, -ας, ἡ   *the south* (lit. *midday,* hence, the position of the sun at midday).

μεσημβρίαν   noun, acc. sg. fem. {2.A} . μεσημβρία G3314

μέσης   adj., gen. sg. fem. {3.A} . . . . μέσος G3319

Μεσίαν   noun prop., acc. sg. masc. {2.A; 2.D}. . . . . Μεσσίας G3323

Μεσίας   noun prop., nom. sg. masc. {2.A; 2.D} . id.

G3315   **μεσιτεύω**   *I mediate, interpose;* but probably in Heb 6:17 rather *I am surety, I give bail.*

μεσίτῃ   noun, dat. sg. masc. {2.A} . . . . . . μεσίτης G3316

G3316   **μεσίτης**, -ου, ὁ   (1) *a mediator, intermediary,* 1 Tim 2:5; (2) *a go-between, arbiter, agent* of something good, Gal 3:19, 20; Heb 8:6; 9:15; 12:24.

μεσίτης   noun, nom. sg. masc. {2.A} . . . . μεσίτης G3316

μεσίτου   noun, gen. sg. masc. {2.A} . . . . id.

μέσον   adj., acc. sg. neut. {3.A} . . . . μέσος G3319

G3317   **μεσονύκτιον**, -ου, τό   *midnight,* the middle of the period between sunset and sunrise.

μεσονύκτιον   noun, acc. sg. neut. {2.B} . . . . μεσονύκτιον G3317

μεσονυκτίου   noun, gen. sg. neut. {2.B} . . . . . . id.

G3318   **Μεσοποταμία**, -ας, ἡ   *Mesopotamia, the Country between the* (two) *Rivers,* i.e., the Euphrates and the Tigris.

Μεσοποταμίᾳ   noun prop., dat. sg. fem. {2.A; 2.D} . . . . Μεσοποταμία G3318

Μεσοποταμίαν   noun prop., acc. sg. fem. {2.A; 2.D} . . . . id.

G3319   **μέσος**, -η, -ον   *middle, in the middle,* sometimes followed by the gen. of the whole area referred to; adv. (with or without gen.) are μέσον (acc. neut.), ἀνὰ μέσον (elliptical in 1 Cor 6:5), κατὰ μέσον, ἐν (τῷ) μέσῳ, *in the middle, before them all,* ἐκ μέσου, *from the midst.*

μέσος   adj., nom. sg. masc. {3.A} . . . . μέσος G3319

G3320   **μεσότοιχον**, -ου, τό   *dividing wall.*

μεσότοιχον   noun, acc. sg. neut. {2.B} . μεσότοιχον G3320

μέσου   adj., gen. sg. neut. {3.A} . . . . μέσος G3319

G3321   **μεσουράνημα**, -ατος, τό   *mid-heaven, the zenith of heaven.*

μεσουρανήματι   noun, dat. sg. neut. {2.C} . . . . μεσουράνημα G3321

μεσούσης   vbl., pres. act. ptc. gen. sg. fem. {6.A.2} . . . . μεσόω G3322

G3322   **μεσόω**   *I am in the middle* of my course.

Μεσσίαν   noun prop., acc. sg. masc. {2.A; 2.D} . . . . Μεσσίας G3323

G3323   **Μεσσίας**, -ου, ὁ   *Messiah, the Anointed One* (Heb.), generally translated into Gk. as Χριστός.

Μεσσίας   noun prop., nom. sg. masc. {2.A; 2.D} . . . . Μεσσίας G3323

μεστή   adj., nom. sg. fem. {3.A} . . . . μεστός G3324

μεστοί   adj., nom. pl. masc. {3.A} . . . . id.

μεστόν   adj., acc. sg. masc. {3.A} . . . . id.

μεστόν   adj., acc. sg. neut. {3.A} . . . . id.

μεστόν   adj., nom. sg. neut. {3.A} . . . . id.

G3324   **μεστός**, -ή, -όν   *full;* met. (cf. πλήρης) almost *tainted, diseased with,* Matt 23:28; Rom 1:29.

μεστούς   adj., acc. pl. masc. {3.A} . . . . μεστός G3324

G3325   **μεστόω**   *I fill.*

μέσῳ   adj., dat. sg. neut. {3.A} . . . . μέσος *G3319*

μετ᾽   prep. . . . . μετά *G3326*

G3326 **μετά**   prep. (1) with gen. *with, in company with;* merely, *in connection with,* Luke 1:58; (2) with acc., (a) *behind, beyond, after,* of place; (b) *after,* of time, with nouns, neut. of adjs., or τό with inf.

μετά   prep. . . . . μετά *G3326*

μετάβα   verb, ²aor. act. impv. 2 pers. sg. {5.D.1} . . . . μεταβαίνω *G3327*

μεταβαίνετε   verb, pres. act. impv. 2 pers. pl. {5.D.1} . . . . id.

G3327 **μεταβαίνω**   *I change my place (abode), I leave, I depart, I remove.*

μεταβαλλόμενοι   vbl., pres. mid. ptc. nom. pl. masc. {6.A.1.b} . . . . μεταβάλλω *G3328*

G3328 **μεταβάλλω**   mid. *I change my mind.*

μεταβαλόμενοι   vbl., ²aor. mid. ptc. nom. pl. masc. {6.A.1.b} . . . . μεταβάλλω *G3328*

μεταβάς   vbl., ²aor. act. ptc. nom. sg. masc. {6.A.1.a} . . . . μεταβαίνω *G3327*

μεταβεβήκαμεν   verb, perf. act. indic. 1 pers. pl. {5.A.1.c} . . . . id.

μεταβέβηκεν   verb, perf. act. indic. 3 pers. sg. {5.A.1.c} . . . . id.

μεταβῇ   verb, ²aor. act. subjunc. 3 pers. sg. {5.B.1} . . . . id.

μετάβηθι   verb, ²aor. act. impv. 2 pers. sg. {5.D.1}id.

μεταβήσεται   verb, fut. mid. indic. 3 pers. sg. {5.A.1.d} . . . . id.

μετάγεται   verb, pres. pass. indic. 3 pers. sg. {5.A.1.d} . . . . μετάγω *G3329*

μετάγομεν   verb, pres. act. indic. 1 pers. pl. {5.A.1.a} . . . . id.

G3329 **μετάγω**   (usually *transfer, transport,* and met., to a better mind), *I turn about, I change the position of.*

μεταδιδόναι   vbl., pres. act. inf. {6.B.3}μεταδίδωμι *G3330*

μεταδιδούς   vbl., pres. act. ptc. nom. sg. masc. {6.A.3} . . . . id.

G3330 **μεταδίδωμι**   (lit. *I offer by way of change, I offer so that a change* of owner is produced), *I share;* sometimes merely, *I impart.*

μεταδότω   verb, ²aor. act. impv. 3 pers. sg. {5.D.3} . . . . μεταδίδωμι *G3330*

μεταδοῦναι   vbl., ²aor. act. inf. {6.B.3} . . . . id.

μεταδῶ   verb, ²aor. act. subjunc. 1 pers. sg. {5.B.3} . . . . id.

μεταθέσεως   noun, gen. sg. fem. {2.C} . . μετάθεσις *G3331*

μετάθεσιν   noun, acc. sg. fem. {2.C} . . . . id.

G3331 **μετάθεσις**, -εως, ἡ   (1) *change, transformation,* Heb 7:12; 12:27; (2) *removal,* Heb 11:5.

μετάθεσις   noun, nom. sg. fem. {2.C} . . μετάθεσις *G3331*

G3332 **μεταίρω**   *I change my position, remove.*

μετακάλεσαι   verb, aor. mid. impv. 2 pers. sg. {5.D.1} . . . . μετακαλέω *G3333*

μετακαλέσομαι   verb, fut. mid. indic. 1 pers. sg. {5.A.1.d} . . . . id.

G3333 **μετακαλέω**   mid. *I summon to myself, I send for.*

G3334 **μετακινέω**   trans., *I move away, I dislodge.*

μετακινούμενοι   vbl., pres. pass. ptc. nom. pl. masc. {6.A.2} . . . . μετακινέω *G3334*

μεταλαβεῖν   vbl., ²aor. act. inf. {6.B.1} . . . . μεταλαμβάνω *G3335*

μεταλαβών   vbl., ²aor. act. ptc. nom. sg. masc. {6.A.1.a} . . . . id.

μεταλαμβάνει   verb, pres. act. indic. 3 pers. sg. {5.A.1.a} . . . . id.

μεταλαμβάνειν   vbl., pres. act. inf. {6.B.1} . . . . id.

G3335 **μεταλαμβάνω**   (1) with gen. *I take a share (part) of, I share in, I partake of;* (2) with acc. *I take after (later)* or *I take instead,* Acts 24:25.

μετάλημψιν   noun, acc. sg. fem. {2.C} μετάλημψις *G3336*

G3336 **μετάλημψις**, -εως, ἡ   *partaking of, sharing in.*

μετάληψιν   noun, acc. sg. fem. {2.C} . μετάλημψις *G3336*

G3337 **μεταλλάσσω**   *I transform, alter.*

μεταμεληθείς   vbl., aor. pass. ptc. nom. sg. masc. {6.A.1.a} . . . . μεταμέλομαι *G3338*

μεταμεληθήσεται   verb, fut. pass. indic. 3 pers. sg. {5.A.1.d} . . . . id.

G3338 **μεταμέλομαι**   (lit. *I change one care* or *interest for another), I change my mind* (generally for a better).

μεταμέλομαι   verb, pres. mid./pass. indic. 1 pers. sg. {5.A.1.d} . . . . μεταμέλομαι *G3338*

μεταμορφούμεθα   verb, pres. pass. indic. 1 pers. pl. {5.A.2} . . . . μεταμορφόω *G3339*

μεταμορφοῦσθαι   vbl., pres. pass. inf. {6.B.2} . . id.

μεταμορφοῦσθε   verb, pres. pass. impv. 2 pers. pl. {5.D.2} . . . . id.

G3339 **μεταμορφόω**   *I change a form* (involving a change of inmost nature; contrast the creatures described in Ovid's *Metamorphoses*); mid. with acc. *I assume some thing through a change,* 2 Cor 3:18.

μετανοεῖν   vbl., pres. act. inf. {6.B.2} . . . μετανοέω *G3340*

μετανοεῖτε   verb, pres. act. impv. 2 pers. pl. {5.D.2} . . . . id.

G3340 **μετανοέω**   *I change my mind, I change the inner man* (particularly with reference to acceptance of the will of God by the νοῦς (mind) instead of rejection); with ἀπό or ἐκ, the giving up definitely of the courses denoted by the following words is indicated.

μετανοῆσαι   vbl., aor. act. inf. {6.B.1} . . μετανοέω *G3340*

μετανοησάντων   vbl., aor. act. ptc. gen. pl. masc. {6.A.2} . . . . id.

μετανοήσατε   verb, aor. act. impv. 2 pers. pl. {5.D.1} . . . . id.

μετανοήσῃ   verb, aor. act. subjunc. 3 pers. sg. {5.B.1} . . . . id.

μετανοήσῃς   verb, aor. act. subjunc. 2 pers. sg. {5.B.1} . . . . id.

μετανοήσητε   verb, aor. act. subjunc. 2 pers. pl. {5.B.1} . . . . id.

μετανοήσον   verb, aor. act. impv. 2 pers. sg. {5.D.1} . . . . id.

μετανοήσουσιν   verb, fut. act. indic. 3 pers. pl. {5.A.1} . . . . id.

μετανοήσωσι   verb, aor. act. subjunc. 3 pers.
   pl. {5.B.1}. . . . . id.
μετανοήσωσιν   verb, aor. act. subjunc. 3 pers.
   pl. {5.B.1}. . . . . id.
μετανοῆτε   verb, pres. act. subjunc. 2 pers. pl.
   {5.B.2} . . . . id.
G3341 **μετάνοια**, -ας, ἡ   *a change of mind, a change in*
   the inner man; ἀπό indicates what is given up
   in this change, Heb 6:1.
μετάνοιαν   noun, acc. sg. fem. {2.A} . . . μετάνοια G3341
μετανοίας   noun, gen. sg. fem. {2.A} . . . . id.
μετανοοῦντι   vbl., pres. act. ptc. dat. sg. masc.
   {6.A.2}. . . . . μετανοέω G3340
μετανοῶ   verb, pres. act. indic. 1 pers. sg. {5.A.2}id.
μετανοῶσιν   verb, pres. act. subjunc. 3 pers. pl.
   {5.B.2} . . . . id.
G3342 **μεταξύ**   (1) adv. with ὁ in the sense *the next,*
   the next after (because *between* the present and
   the one after that), Acts 13:42, ἐν τῷ μεταξύ
   (supply χρόνῳ), *meantime, meanwhile,* John
   4:31; (2) prep. with gen., *between;* μεταξὺ
   σοῦ καὶ αὐτοῦ μόνου, *privately* (Aram.
   idiom), Matt 18:15; μεταξὺ ἀλλήλων, *in*
   their mutual intercourse, Rom 2:15.
μεταξύ   adv., prep. . . . . μεταξύ G3342
μεταπεμπόμενος   vbl., pres. mid./pass. ptc. nom.
   sg. masc. {6.A.1} . . . . μεταπέμπω G3343
G3343 **μεταπέμπω**   *I send for, summon.*
μεταπεμφθείς   vbl., aor. pass. ptc. nom. sg. masc.
   {6.A.1.a} . . . . μεταπέμπω G3343
μετάπεμψαι   verb, aor. mid. impv. 2 pers. sg.
   {5.D.1} . . . . id.
μεταπεμψάμενος   vbl., aor. mid. ptc. nom. sg.
   masc. {6.A.1.b} . . . . id.
μεταπέμψασθαι   vbl., aor. mid. inf. {6.B.1} . . . . id.
μεταπέμψηται   verb, aor. mid. subjunc. 3 pers.
   sg. {5.B.1} . . . . id.
μετασταθῶ   verb, aor. pass. subjunc. 1 pers. sg.
   {5.B.3} . . . . μεθίστημι G3179
μεταστήσας   vbl., aor. act. ptc. nom. sg. masc.
   {6.A.3}. . . . . id.
μεταστραφήσεται   verb, ²fut. pass. indic. 3 pers.
   sg. {5.A.1.d}. . . . . μεταστρέφω G3344
μεταστραφήτω   verb, ²aor. pass. impv. 3 pers.
   sg. {5.D.1} . . . . id.
G3344 **μεταστρέφω**   *I turn, change.*
μεταστρέψαι   vbl., aor. act. inf.
   {6.B.1} . . . . μεταστρέφω G3344
μετασχηματίζεται   verb, pres. mid. indic. 3 pers.
   sg. {5.A.1.d}. . . . . μετασχηματίζω G3345
μετασχηματιζόμενοι   vbl., pres. mid. ptc.
   nom. pl. masc. {6.A.1} . . . . id.
μετασχηματίζονται   verb, pres. pass. indic.
   3 pers. pl. {5.A.1.d} . . . . id.
G3345 **μετασχηματίζω**   *I change the outward appear-*
   ance (the dress, the form of presentation) of
   something; *I transfer by a fiction, adapt.*
μετασχηματίσει   verb, fut. act. indic. 3 pers. sg.
   {5.A.1.a} . . . . μετασχηματίζω G3345

μετατιθεμένης   vbl., pres. pass. ptc. gen. sg. fem.
   {6.A.3}. . . . . μετατίθημι G3346
μετατιθέντες   vbl., pres. act. ptc. nom. pl.
   masc. {6.A.3} . . . . id.
μετατίθεσθε   verb, pres. mid./pass. indic.
   2 pers. pl. {5.A.3.a} . . . . id.
G3346 **μετατίθημι**   (1) *I transfer,* Acts 7:16; Heb 11:5;
   mid. *I go over* to another party, *I desert,* Gal
   1:6; (2) *I change,* Heb 7:12.
μετατραπήτω   verb, ²aor. pass. impv. 3 pers. sg.
   {5.D.1} . . . . μετατρέπω G3344†‡
G3344†‡ **μετατρέπω**   *I turn, change.* Var. for μεταστρέφω, James 4:9.
μετέβη   verb, ²aor. act. indic. 3 pers. sg.
   {5.A.1.b} . . . . μεταβαίνω G3327
μετέθηκεν   verb, aor. act. indic. 3 pers. sg.
   {5.A.3.b} . . . . μετατίθημι G3346
μετεκαλέσατο   verb, aor. mid. indic. 3 pers. sg.
   {5.A.1} . . . . μετακαλέω G3333
μεταλάμβανον   verb, impf. act. indic. 3 pers. pl.
   {5.A.1.b} . . . . μεταλαμβάνω G3335
μετεμελήθητε   verb, aor. pass. indic. 2 pers. pl.
   {5.A.1.b} . . . . μεταμέλομαι G3338
μετεμελόμην   verb, impf. mid./pass. indic.
   1 pers. sg. {5.A.1.e} . . . . id.
μετεμορφώθη   verb, aor. pass. indic. 3 pers. sg.
   {5.A.1} . . . . μεταμορφόω G3339
μετενόησαν   verb, aor. act. indic. 3 pers. pl.
   {5.A.1} . . . . μετανοέω G3340
μετενόησεν   verb, aor. act. indic. 3 pers. sg.
   {5.A.1} . . . . id.
G3347 **μετέπειτα**   adv., *thereafter.*
μετέπειτα   adv. . . . . μετέπειτα G3347
μετεπέμψασθε   verb, aor. mid. indic. 2 pers. pl.
   {5.A.1.e} . . . . μεταπέμπω G3343
μετεπέμψατο   verb, aor. mid. indic. 3 pers. sg.
   {5.A.1.e} . . . . id.
μετέστησεν   verb, aor. act. indic. 3 pers. sg.
   {5.A.3.b} . . . . μεθίστημι G3179
μετέσχε   verb, ²aor. act. indic. 3 pers. sg.
   {5.A.1.b} . . . . μετέχω G3348
μετέσχεν   verb, ²aor. act. indic. 3 pers. sg.
   {5.A.1.b} . . . . id.
μετέσχηκεν   verb, perf. act. indic. 3 pers. sg.
   {5.A.1.c} . . . . id.
μετεσχημάτισα   verb, aor. act. indic. 1 pers. sg.
   {5.A.1.b} . . . . μετασχηματίζω G3345
μετετέθη   verb, aor. pass. indic. 3 pers. sg.
   {5.A.1} . . . . μετατίθημι G3346
μετετέθησαν   verb, aor. pass. indic. 3 pers. pl.
   {5.A.1} . . . . id.
μετέχειν   vbl., pres. act. inf. {6.B.1}. . . μετέχω G3348
μετέχομεν   verb, pres. act. indic. 1 pers. pl.
   {5.A.1.a} . . . . id.
μετέχουσιν   verb, pres. act. indic. 3 pers. pl.
   {5.A.1.a} . . . . id.
G3348 **μετέχω**   *I have a share of, I participate in, I*
   share.
μετέχω   verb, pres. act. indic. 1 pers. sg.
   {5.A.1.a} . . . . μετέχω G3348

μετέχων   vbl., pres. act. ptc. nom. sg. masc.
{6.A.1}............................. id.

μετεωρίζεσθε   verb, pres. mid./pass. impv. 2 pers.
pl. {5.D.1} ....μετεωρίζομαι G3349

G3349 **μετεωρίζομαι**   *I am μετέωρος, i.e., suspended in midair, anxious,* Luke 12:29.

μετήλλαξαν   verb, aor. act. indic. 3 pers. pl.
{5.A.1.b} .... μεταλλάσσω G3337

μετῆρεν   verb, aor. act. indic. 3 pers. sg.
{5.A.1.b} .... μεταίρω G3332

G3350 **μετοικεσία**, -ας, ἡ   *transportation, deportation,* followed by gen. of reference, Βαβυλῶνος.

μετοικεσίαν   noun, acc. sg. fem. {2.A}. μετοικεσία G3350

μετοικεσίας   noun, gen. sg. fem. {2.A}........ id.

G3351 **μετοικίζω**   *I transport.*

μετοικιῶ   verb, fut. act. indic. 1 pers. sg.
{5.A.2}......................μετοικίζω G3351

G3352 **μετοχή**, -ῆς, ἡ   *sharing, partnership.*

μετοχή   noun, nom. sg. fem. {2.A} .... μετοχή G3352

μέτοχοι   adj., nom. pl. masc. {3.C} .....μέτοχος G3353

μετόχοις   adj., dat. pl. masc. {3.C} .... id.

G3353 **μέτοχος**, -ου, ὁ   *a sharer, partner;* with gen. *in something.*

μετόχους   adj., acc. pl. masc. {3.C} ......μέτοχος G3353

μετρεῖτε   verb, pres. act. indic. 2 pers. pl.
{5.A.2} .... μετρέω G3354

G3354 **μετρέω**   *I measure.*

μετρηθήσεται   verb, fut. pass. indic. 3 pers. sg.
{5.A.1} .... μετρέω G3354

μετρήσῃ   verb, aor. act. subjunc. 3 pers. sg. {5.B.1} id.

μετρήσῃς   verb, aor. act. subjunc. 2 pers. sg.
{5.B.1} .... id.

μέτρησον   verb, aor. act. impv. 2 pers. sg. {5.D.1} id.

μετρητάς   noun, acc. pl. masc. {2.A} ... μετρητής G3355

G3355 **μετρητής**, -οῦ, ὁ   *a measure,* about 39.39 liters or 8¾ gallons.

μετριοπαθεῖν   vbl., pres. act. inf.
{6.B.2} .... μετριοπαθέω G3356

G3356 **μετριοπαθέω**   *I feel moderately,* with particular reference to displeasure at men's sin.

G3357 **μετρίως**   adv., *moderately;* οὐ μετρίως, *greatly, exceedingly.*

μετρίως   adv. {3.F} ....μετρίως G3357

G3358 **μέτρον**, -ου, τό   *a measure,* whether lineal (e.g., Rev 21:15) or cubic (e.g., Luke 6:38); ἐκ μέτρου (Aram. idiom?), *in scanty measure.*

μέτρον   noun, acc. sg. neut. {2.B} .... μέτρον G3358

μέτρου   noun, gen. sg. neut. {2.B}............ id.

μετροῦντες   vbl., pres. act. ptc. nom. pl. masc.
{6.A.2} .... μετρέω G3354

μέτρῳ   noun, dat. sg. neut. {2.B}........ μέτρον G3358

μετῴκισεν   verb, aor. act. indic. 3 pers. sg.
{5.A.1.b} ....μετοικίζω G3351

G3359 **μέτωπον**, -ου, τό   *forehead.*

μέτωπον   noun, acc. sg. neut. {2.B} ..... μέτωπον G3359

μετώπου   noun, gen. sg. neut. {2.B} .... id.

μετώπων   noun, gen. pl. neut. {2.B} .... id.

G3360 **μέχρι**, μέχρις   conj. with or without οὗ, the ἄν (ἐάν) being omitted in NT examples, with aor.

subjunc., *until . . . shall have . . . ;* prep. with gen., *as far as; until.*

μέχρι   conj., prep....................μέχρι G3360

μέχρις   adv. .... id.

G3361 **μή**   negative particle, *not, that . . . not (lest),* etc., used generally, instead of οὐ, the negative of fact (expressed by the indic.), where there is some indefiniteness about the action or occurrence referred to (expressed by other moods), either because it is in the future, or because it is in an interrog. clause (a feature of everyday language), or because it is in an indef. rel., or a cond., opt., or final clause, etc. Sometimes with indic. to be translated by *perhaps,* Luke 11:35; Col 2:8 (cf. Heb 3:12); Gal 4:11 (but also with subjunc. as in classical Gk., Matt 25:9, var.). οὐ μή, (1) with indic. fut. or, far more often, with subjunc. aor., in a statement, a very emphatic negative, *assuredly not.* It occurs for the most part in passages coming from the OT and sayings of Christ (both from Semitic originals), where words of decisive tone are esp. in place. In this constr. the prohibition refers to the future, "do not" (in future), as contrasted with μὴ ποίει, meaning "desist from"; the latter is sometimes durative; (2) with subjunc. aor. in interrog. clause, *not,* Luke 18:7; John 18:11. μή ποτε, see μήποτε; μή που, see μήπου.

μή   part., neg., interrog. ....μή G3361

G3378‡ **μὴ οὐκ**   *is it not that?* (interrog. and neg.).

μήγε   part., neg. ....γε G1065

μηδ᾽   conj., neg.. .... μηδέ G3366

G3365 **μηδαμῶς**   adv., *not at all.*

μηδαμῶς   adv. {3.F} ....μηδαμῶς G3365

G3366 **μηδέ**   *nor . . . either,* generally after a preceding μή.

μηδέ   conj., neg. .... μηδέ G3366

G3367 **μηδείς** (μηθείς), μηδεμία, μηδέν   (1) adj., *no,* in agreement with nouns; (2) each gender used as a noun, *no person, nothing.* Its use with respect to that of οὐδείς corresponds to that of μή with respect to that of οὐ. See also μηδέν; (also another Hellenistic orthography μηθείς, Acts 27:33); neut. sg. μηδέν as adv., *not at all, in no way.*

μηδείς   adj., nom. sg. masc. {3.D}........μηδείς G3367

μηδεμίαν   adj., acc. sg. fem. {3.D} .... id.

μηδέν   adj., acc. sg. neut. {3.D} .... id.

μηδέν   adj., nom. sg. neut. {3.D} .... id.

μηδένα   adj., acc. sg. masc. {3.D} .... id.

μηδενί   adj., dat. sg. masc. {3.D} .... id.

μηδενί   adj., dat. sg. neut. {3.D} .... id.

μηδενός   adj., gen. sg. neut. {3.D}............ id.

G3368 **μηδέποτε**   adv., *not at any time.*

μηδέποτε   adv., neg............... μηδέποτε G3368

G3369 **μηδέπω**   adv., *not yet.*

μηδέπω   adv., neg. .... μηδέπω G3369

Μῆδοι   noun prop., nom. pl. masc. {2.B; 2.D}.....................Μῆδος G3370

G3370 **Μῆδος**, -ου, ὁ   *a Mede, a Median,* from east of
Assyria.
μηθέν   adj., acc. sg. neut. {3.D} . . . . .μηδείς G3367
G3371 **μηκέτι**   adv., *no longer.*
μηκέτι   adv., neg. . . . . .μηκέτι G3371
G3372 **μῆκος**, -ους, τό   *length.*
μῆκος   noun, nom. sg. neut. {2.C} . . . . μῆκος G3372
μηκύνηται   verb, pres. mid./pass. subjunc. 3 pers.
sg. {5.B.1} . . . . .μηκύνω G3373
G3373 **μηκύνω**   *I lengthen.*
μηλωταῖς   noun, dat. pl. fem. {2.A} . . . . .μηλωτή G3374
G3374 **μηλωτή**, -ῆς, ἡ   *sheep's* (sometimes *pig's*) *hide,
sheepskin.*
μήν   noun, nom. sg. masc. {2.C} . . . . .μήν² G3376
μήν   part. . . . . .μήν¹ G3375
G3375 **μήν**¹   part., expressing emphasis, mostly in the
formulae of oaths, *assuredly, in very truth.*
G3376 **μήν**², μηνός, ὁ   noun, *a* (lunar) *month.*
μῆνα   noun, acc. sg. masc. {2.C} . . . . .μήν² G3376
μῆνας   noun, acc. pl. masc. {2.C} . . . . id.
μηνί   noun, dat. sg. masc. {2.C} . . . . id.
μηνυθείσης   vbl., aor. pass. ptc. gen. sg. fem.
{6.A.1.a} . . . . .μηνύω G3377
μηνύσαντα   vbl., aor. act. ptc. acc. sg. masc.
{6.A.1.a} . . . . id.
μηνύσῃ   verb, aor. act. subjunc. 3 pers. sg.
{5.B.1} . . . . id.
G3377 **μηνύω**   (1) *I reveal, make known;* in a law
court, *I lay information, I inform,* John 11:57;
Acts 23:30; (2) *I make known, I point out,* Luke
20:37; 1 Cor 10:28.
G3379 **μήποτε**   *lest at any time, lest;* then weakened,
whether perhaps, whether at all; in a principal
clause, *perhaps* (= μή ποτε).
μήποτε   part. neg., interrog., conj. . . . . . . .μήποτε G3379
G3380 **μήπω**   adv., *not yet.*
μήπω   adv., neg. . . . . .μήπω G3380
G3381 **μήπως**   *lest in any way* (= μή πως).
μήπως   conj. {3.F} . . . . .μήπως G3381
μηρόν   noun, acc. sg. masc. {2.B} . . . . μηρός G3382
G3382 **μηρός**, -οῦ, ὁ   *thigh.*
G3383 **μήτε**   (= μή τε) *nor;* μήτε . . . μήτε, *neither . . .
nor,* sometimes also oftener than twice (e.g.,
Jas 5:12).
μήτε   conj., neg. . . . . μήτε G3383
μητέρα   noun, acc. sg. fem. {2.C} . . . . μήτηρ G3384
μητέρας   noun, acc. pl. fem. {2.C} . . . . id.
μητηρ   noun, nom. sg. fem. {2.C} . . . . id.
G3384 **μήτηρ**, τρος, ἡ   *a mother;* sometimes also of
one who is *as a mother,* who takes the place of
a mother, Mark 3:34, 35, etc.; John 19:27; Rom
16:13; Gal 4:26; 1 Tim 5:2; Rev 17:5.
μήτηρ   noun, nom. sg. fem. {2.C} . . . . μήτηρ G3384
G3385 **μήτι**   (1) with εἰ; thus εἰ μήτι = εἰ μή, *if not,
unless,* Luke 9:13; εἰ μήτι ἄν, *unless in a given
case,* 1 Cor 7:5; (2) in questions, expecting a
negative answer, cf. Matt 7:16, *can it be that*
suggesting impossibility (= μή, strengthened
by the addition of the acc. neut. of τις as adv.).
μήτι   part. . . . . .μήτι G3385

G3386 **μήτιγε**   *not to mention, let alone* (= μήτι
and γε).
μήτιγε   part. . . . . .μήτιγε G3386
G3387 **μήτις**   *whether any* (= μή τις).
G3388 **μήτρα**, -ας, ἡ   *the womb.*
μητραλῴαις   noun, dat. pl. masc.
{2.A} . . . . .μητρολῴας G3389
μήτραν   noun, acc. sg. fem. {2.A} . . . . .μήτρα G3388
μήτρας   noun, gen. sg. fem. {2.A} . . . . id.
μητρί   noun, dat. sg. fem. {2.C} . . . . μήτηρ G3384
μητρολῴαις   noun, dat. pl. masc. {2.A}μητρολῴας G3389
G3389 **μητρολῴας** (μητραλῴας), -ου, ὁ   *a person
who murders his mother, a matricide.*
G3390 **μητρόπολις**   *capital city.*
μητρόπολις   noun, nom. sg. fem. {2.C}μητρόπολις G3390
μητρός   noun, gen. sg. fem. {2.C} . . . . μήτηρ G3384
μία   adj., nom. sg. fem. {3.D} . . . . εἷς G1520
μιᾷ   adj., dat. sg. fem. {3.D} . . . . id.
μιαίνουσι   verb, pres. act. indic. 3 pers. pl.
{5.A.1.a} . . . . μιαίνω G3392
μιαίνουσιν   verb, pres. act. indic. 3 pers. pl.
{5.A.1.a} . . . . id.
G3392 **μιαίνω**   met. *I stain, pollute, defile.*
μίαν   adj., acc. sg. fem. {3.D} . . . . εἷς G1520
μιανθῶσι   verb, aor. pass. subjunc. 3 pers. pl.
{5.B.1} . . . . μιαίνω G3392
μιανθῶσιν   verb, aor. pass. subjunc. 3 pers. pl.
{5.B.1} . . . . id.
μιᾶς   adj., gen. sg. fem. {3.D} . . . . εἷς G1520
G3393 **μίασμα**, -ατος, τό   *a pollution, a defilement.*
μιάσματα   noun, acc. pl. neut. {2.C} . . . . . μίασμα G3393
G3394 **μιασμός**, -οῦ, ὁ   *pollution, defilement.*
μιασμοῦ   noun, gen. sg. masc. {2.B} . . . . . μιασμός G3394
G3395 **μίγμα** (μεῖγμα), -ατος, τό   *a mixture.*
μίγμα   noun, acc. sg. neut. {2.C} . . . . .μίγμα G3395
G3396 **μίγνυμι**   *I mix.*
μικρά   adj., nom. sg. fem. {3.A} . . . . . . .μικρός G3398
μικράν   adj., acc. sg. fem. {3.A} . . . . id.
μικροί   adj., nom. pl. masc. {3.A} . . . . id.
μικροί   adj., voc. pl. masc. {3.A} . . . . id.
μικροῖς   adj., dat. pl. masc. {3.A} . . . . id.
μικρόν   adj., acc. sg. masc. {3.A} . . . . id.
μικρόν   adj., acc. sg. neut. {3.A} . . . . id.
μικρόν   adj., nom. sg. neut. {3.A} . . . . id.
μικρόν   adj., voc. sg. neut. {3.A} . . . . id.
G3397 **μικρόν**   neut. subs. of μικρός, *a short while;*
adv., *for a short while.*
G3398 **μικρός**, -ά, -όν   (1) *small;* superl. μικρότερος, *smallest,* in Mark 15:40 possibly
junior; (2) of time, *short.* Adv. μικρόν, neut.
sg. of μικρός, as adv. or noun, *a little,* both of
space and of time as well as of size, degree; in
John 14:19, etc., understand ἐστιν or ἔσται
after μικρόν.
μικρός   adj., nom. sg. masc. {3.A} . . . . .μικρός G3398
μικρότερον   adj. comp., nom. sg. neut. {3.A;
3.G} . . . . id.
μικρότερος   adj. comp., nom. sg. masc. {3.A;
3.G} . . . . id.
μικροῦ   adj., gen. sg. masc. {3.A} . . . . id.

μικρούς   adj., acc. pl. masc. {3.A} . . . . id.
μικρῷ   adj., dat. sg. masc. {3.A} . . . . id.
μικρῶν   adj., gen. pl. masc. {3.A} . . . . id.
μικρῶν   adj., gen. pl. neut. {3.A} . . . . id.
Μίλητον   noun prop., acc. sg. fem. {2.B;
    2.D} . . . . Μίλητος G3399

G3399 **Μίλητος**, -ου, ἡ   *Miletus*, a city on the coast of
  the Roman province Asia.
Μιλήτου   noun prop., gen. sg. fem. {2.B;
    2.D} . . . . Μίλητος G3399
Μιλήτῳ   noun prop., dat. sg. fem. {2.B; 2.D} . . . id.

G3400 **μίλιον**, -ου, τό   *a Roman mile*, measuring
  1478.5 meters (Lat. *milium, a thousand double
  paces*).
μίλιον   noun, acc. sg. neut. {2.B} . . . . μίλιον G3400
μιμεῖσθαι   vbl., pres. mid./pass. inf.
    {6.B.2} . . . . μιμέομαι G3401
μιμεῖσθε   verb, pres. mid./pass. impv. 2 pers. pl.
    {5.D.2} . . . . id.

G3401 **μιμέομαι**   *I imitate.*
μιμηταί   noun, nom. pl. masc. {2.A} . . . . μιμητής G3402

G3402 **μιμητής**, -οῦ, ὁ   *an imitator.*
μιμνήσκεσθε   verb, pres. mid./pass. impv. 2 pers.
  pl. {5.D.1} . . . . μιμνήσκομαι G3403
μιμνήσκεσθε   verb, pres. mid./pass. impv.
  2 pers. pl. {5.D.1} . . . . id.
μιμνήσκη   verb, pres. mid./pass. indic. 2 pers.
  sg. {5.A.1.d} . . . . id.
μιμνήσκη   verb, pres. mid./pass. indic. 2 pers.
  sg. {5.A.1.d} . . . . id.

G3403 **μιμνήσκομαι**   mid. and pass., *I remember;* the
  pass. forms sometimes have pass. sense, from
  act. μιμνήσκω, *I call to mind, I recall, I mention,* Acts 10:31; Rev 16:19.
μιμοῦ   verb, pres. mid./pass. impv. 2 pers. sg.
    {5.D.2} . . . . μιμέομαι G3401
μισεῖ   verb, pres. act. indic. 3 pers. sg. {5.A.2} μισέω G3404
μισεῖν   vbl., pres. act. inf. {6.B.2} . . . . id.
μισεῖς   verb, pres. act. indic. 2 pers. sg. {5.A.2} . . id.

G3404 **μισέω**   *I hate.*
μισῇ   verb, pres. act. subjunc. 3 pers. sg.
    {5.B.2} . . . . μισέω G3404
μισήσει   verb, fut. act. indic. 3 pers. sg. {5.A.1} . id.
μισήσεις   verb, fut. act. indic. 2 pers. sg. {5.A.1}. id.
μισήσουσι   verb, fut. act. indic. 3 pers. pl.
    {5.A.1} . . . . id.
μισήσουσιν   verb, fut. act. indic. 3 pers. pl.
    {5.A.1} . . . . id.
μισήσωσιν   verb, aor. act. subjunc. 3 pers. pl.
    {5.B.1} . . . . id.

G3405 **μισθαποδοσία**, -ας, ἡ   (lit. *repayment of price*
  or *payment of price due*), *reward,* Heb 10:35;
  11:26; in the sense, *due punishment,* Heb 2:2.
μισθαποδοσίαν   noun, acc. sg. fem.
    {2.A} . . . . μισθαποδοσία G3405

G3406 **μισθαποδότης**, -ου, ὁ   *a rewarder* (see
  μισθαποδοσία).
μισθαποδότης   noun, nom. sg. masc.
    {2.A} . . . . μισθαποδότης G3406
μίσθιοι   adj., nom. pl. masc. {3.A} . . . . . . μίσθιος G3407

G3407 **μίσθιος**, -ου, ὁ   *a paid worker, a hired servant,
  a hireling* (contrasted with a slave).
μισθίων   adj., gen. pl. masc. {3.A} . . . . . . μίσθιος G3407
μισθόν   noun, acc. sg. masc. {2.B} . . . . . . .μισθός G3408

G3408 **μισθός**, -οῦ, ὁ   (1) *pay, wages, salary;* (2)
  reward, recompense.
μισθός   noun, nom. sg. masc. {2.B} . . . . . . .μισθός G3408
μισθοῦ   noun, gen. sg. masc. {2.B} . . . . id.

G3409 **μισθόω**   mid. *I hire, engage for myself.*

G3410 **μίσθωμα**, -ατος, τό   *a rented apartment* or *flat.*
μισθώματι   noun, dat. sg. neut. {2.C} . . .μίσθωμα G3410
μισθώσασθαι   vbl., aor. mid. inf. {6.B.1} . . μισθόω G3409

G3411 **μισθωτός**, -ή, -όν   *hired, engaged* for wages;
  subs., *a hired man.*
μισθωτός   adj., nom. sg. masc. {2.B}. . . . μισθωτός G3411
μισθωτῶν   adj., gen. pl. masc. {2.B} . . . . id.
μισούμενοι   vbl., pres. pass. ptc. nom. pl. masc.
    {6.A.2} . . . . μισέω G3404
μισοῦντας   vbl., pres. act. ptc. acc. pl. masc.
    {6.A.2} . . . . id.
μισοῦντες   vbl., pres. act. ptc. nom. pl. masc.
    {6.A.2} . . . . id.
μισούντων   vbl., pres. act. ptc. gen. pl. masc.
    {6.A.2} . . . . id.
μισοῦσιν   vbl., pres. act. ptc. dat. pl. masc.
    {6.A.2} . . . . id.
μισῶ   verb, pres. act. indic. 1 pers. sg. {5.A.2} . . . id.
μισῶν   vbl., pres. act. ptc. nom. sg. masc. {6.A.2} id.

G3412 **Μιτυλήνη** (Μυτιλήνη), -ης, ἡ   *Mitylene,* the
  capital of the island of Lesbos in the northern
  Aegean sea.
Μιτυλήνην   noun prop., acc. sg. fem. {2.A;
    2.D} . . . . .Μιτυλήνη G3412

G3413 **Μιχαήλ**, ὁ   *Michael,* an archangel.
Μιχαήλ   noun prop. . . . . .Μιχαήλ G3413

G3414 **μνᾶ**, -ᾶς, ἡ   *a mina,* a Semitic word for the
  Gk. money unit worth about one hundred
  δραχμαί.
μνᾶ   noun, nom. sg. fem. {2.A} . . . . μνᾶ G3414
μνᾶν   noun, acc. sg. fem. {2.A} . . . . id.

G3415 **μνάομαι**   *I woo* or *court for my bride.* Var. for
  μνηστεύω, Luke 1:27.
μνᾶς   noun, acc. pl. fem. {2.A} . . . . μνᾶ G3414

G3416 **Μνάσων**, -ωνος, ὁ   *Mnason,* an early Christian, native of Cyprus, resident at a place
  between Caesarea and Jerusalem.
Μνάσωνι   noun prop., dat. sg. masc. {2.C;
    2.D} . . . . .Μνάσων G3416

G3417 **μνεία**, -ας, ἡ   *remembrance, recollection, mention; commemoration,* Rom 12:13 (var.).
μνεία   noun, dat. sg. fem. {2.A} . . . . .μνεία G3417
μνείαν   noun, acc. sg. fem. {2.A} . . . . id.

G3418 **μνῆμα**, -ατος, τό   *a tomb, monument.*
μνῆμα   noun, acc. sg. neut. {2.C} . . . . . . .μνῆμα G3418
μνῆμα   noun, nom. sg. neut. {2.C} . . . . id.
μνήμασιν   noun, dat. pl. neut. {2.C} . . . . id.
μνήματα   noun, acc. pl. neut. {2.C} . . . . id.
μνήματι   noun, dat. sg. neut. {2.C}. . . . . id.
μνημεῖα   noun, acc. pl. neut. {2.B} . . . μνημεῖον G3419
μνημεῖα   noun, nom. pl. neut. {2.B} . . . . id.

μνημείοις   noun, dat. pl. neut. {2.B} . . . . id.

G3419 **μνημεῖον**, -ου, τό   *a tomb, monument.*

μνημεῖον   noun, acc. sg. neut. {2.B} . . . . μνημεῖον G3419

μνημεῖον   noun, nom. sg. neut. {2.B} . . . . id.

μνημείου   noun, gen. sg. neut. {2.B} . . . . id.

μνημείῳ   noun, dat. sg. neut. {2.B} . . . . id.

μνημείων   noun, gen. pl. neut. {2.B} . . . . id.

G3420 **μνήμη**, -ης, ἡ   *memory, or mention.*

μνήμην   noun, acc. sg. fem. {2.A} . . . . μνήμη G3420

μνημόνευε   verb, pres. act. impv. 2 pers. sg.
{5.D.1} . . . . μνημονεύω G3421

μνημονεύει   verb, pres. act. indic. 3 pers. sg.
{5.A.1.a} . . . . id.

μνημονεύειν   vbl., pres. act. inf. {6.B.1} . . . . id.

μνημονεύετε   verb, pres. act. impv. 2 pers. pl.
{5.D.1} . . . . id.

μνημονεύετε   verb, pres. act. indic. 2 pers. pl.
{5.A.1.a} . . . . id.

μνημονεύητε   verb, pres. act. subjunc. 2 pers.
pl. {5.B.1} . . . . id.

μνημονεύοντες   vbl., pres. act. ptc. nom. pl.
masc. {6.A.1} . . . . id.

G3421 **μνημονεύω**   *I remember; I hold in remembrance; I make mention of,* Heb 11:22.

μνημονεύωμεν   verb, pres. act. subjunc. 1 pers. pl.
{5.B.1} . . . . μνημονεύω G3421

G3422 **μνημόσυνον**, -ου, τό   *reminder, memorial; a
remembrance offering,* Acts 10:4.

μνημόσυνον   noun, acc. sg. neut.
{2.B} . . . . μνημόσυνον G3422

μνησθῆναι   vbl., aor. pass. inf.
{6.B.1} . . . . μιμνήσκομαι G3403

μνησθῇς   verb, aor. pass. subjunc. 2 pers. sg.
{5.B.1} . . . . id.

μνησθήσομαι   verb, fut. pass. indic. 1 pers. sg.
{5.A.1.d} . . . . id.

μνήσθητε   verb, aor. pass. impv. 2 pers. pl.
{5.D.1} . . . . id.

μνήσθητι   verb, aor. pass. impv. 2 pers. sg.
{5.D.1} . . . . id.

μνησθῶ   verb, aor. pass. subjunc. 1 pers. sg.
{5.B.1} . . . . id.

μνηστευθείσης   vbl., aor. pass. ptc. gen. sg. fem.
{6.A.1.a} . . . . μνηστεύω G3423

G3423 **μνηστεύω**   *I betroth.*

G3424† **μογγιλάλος**, -ον   *speaking with a hoarse voice.*
Var. for μογιλάλος, Mark 7:32.

μογγιλάλον   adj., acc. sg. masc. {3.C}. μογγιλάλον G3424†

μογιλάλον   adj., acc. sg. masc. {3.C} . . . . id.

G3424 **μογιλάλος**, -ον   *dumb* (lit. speaking with
difficulty).

G3425 **μόγις**   adv., *with difficulty; scarcely, hardly.*

μόγις   adv. . . . . μόγις G3425

μόδιον   noun, acc. sg. masc. {2.B} . . . . μόδιος G3426

G3426 **μόδιος**, -ου, ὁ   *a dry measure, the chief corn
unit, nearly two English gallons* (Lat. *modius*).

μοι   pron. pers., 1 pers. dat. sg. {4.A} . . . . ἐγώ G1473

μοί   pron. pers., 1 pers. dat. sg. {4.A} . . . . id.

μοιχαλίδα   noun, acc. sg. fem. {2.C} . . . . μοιχαλίς G3428

μοιχαλίδες   noun, voc. pl. fem. {2.C} . . . . id.

μοιχαλίδι   noun, dat. sg. fem. {2.C} . . . . id.

μοιχαλίδος   noun, gen. sg. fem. {2.C} . . . . id.

G3428 **μοιχαλίς**, -ίδος, ἡ   (1) *an adulteress* (i.e., a
married woman who commits adultery), Rom
7:3; 2 Pet 2:14; (2) Heb., extended to those who
worship any other than the true God (Yahweh).

μοιχαλίς   noun, nom. sg. fem. {2.C} . . . . μοιχαλίς G3428

μοιχᾶσθαι   vbl., pres. mid./pass. inf.
{6.B.2} . . . . μοιχάω G3429

μοιχᾶται   verb, pres. mid./pass. indic. 3 pers.
sg. {5.A.2} . . . . id.

G3429 **μοιχάω**   *I commit adultery; pass., be caused
to commit adultery* (not only of a married
woman but of a married man; see Matt 19:9,
var.; Mark 10:11).

G3430 **μοιχεία**, -ας, ἡ   *adultery.*

μοιχεία   noun, nom. sg. fem. {2.A} . . . . . μοιχεία G3430

μοιχείᾳ   noun, dat. sg. fem. {2.A} . . . . id.

μοιχεῖαι   noun, nom. pl. fem. {2.A} . . . . id.

μοιχεύει   verb, pres. act. indic. 3 pers. sg.
{5.A.1.a} . . . . μοιχεύω G3431

μοιχεύειν   vbl., pres. act. inf. {6.B.1} . . . . id.

μοιχεύεις   verb, pres. act. indic. 2 pers. sg.
{5.A.1.a} . . . . id.

μοιχευθῆναι   vbl., aor. pass. inf. {6.B.1} . . . . . id.

μοιχευομένη   vbl., pres. pass. ptc. nom. sg.
fem. {6.A.1} . . . . id.

μοιχελυομένην   vbl., pres. pass. ptc. acc. sg.
fem. {6.A.1} . . . . id.

μοιχεύοντας   vbl., pres. act. ptc. acc. pl. masc.
{6.A.1} . . . . id.

μοιχεύσεις   verb, fut. act. indic. 2 pers. sg.
{5.A.1.a} . . . . id.

μοιχεύσῃς   verb, aor. act. subjunc. 2 pers. sg.
{5.B.1} . . . . id.

G3431 **μοιχεύω**   *I commit adultery* (of a man with a
married woman, but also (Luke 16:18) of a
married man).

μοιχοί   noun, nom. pl. masc. {2.B} . . . . μοιχός G3432

μοιχοί   noun, voc. pl. masc. {2.B} . . . . id.

G3432 **μοιχός**, -οῦ, ὁ   *an adulterer,* i.e., a man who is
guilty with a married woman.

μοιχούς   noun, acc. pl. masc. {2.B} . . . . μοιχός G3432

G3433 **μόλις**   adv., *with difficulty, hardly.*

μόλις   adv. . . . . μόλις G3433

G3434 **Μολόχ**, ὁ   *Moloch,* a god worshipped by several
Semitic peoples (Heb., name is properly an
appellation = king).

Μολόχ   noun prop. . . . . Μολόχ G3434

Μόλοχ   noun prop. . . . . id.

μολύνεται   verb, pres. pass. indic. 3 pers. sg.
{5.A.1.d} . . . . μολύνω G3435

G3435 **μολύνω**   *I soil, stain, pollute,* lit. and morally.

G3436 **μολυσμός**, -οῦ, ὁ   *staining, contamination,
pollution.*

μολυσμοῦ   noun, gen. sg. masc. {2.B} . . μολυσμός G3436

G3437 **μομφή**, -ῆς, ἡ   (lit. *blame, fault finding*), a
complaint, fault.

μομφήν   noun, acc. sg. fem. {2.A} . . . . μομφή G3437

μόνα   adj., acc. pl. neut. {3.A} . . . . μόνος G3441 μοναί   noun, nom. pl. fem. {2.A} . . . . μονή G3438

μόνας   adj., acc. pl. fem. {3.A} . . . . μόνος G3441

G3438   **μονή**, -ῆς, ἡ   (1) abstr., μονήν ποιεῖσθαι, *to stay, to dwell,* John 14:23; (2) concr., *lodging, dwelling place, room.*

μόνην   adj., acc. sg. fem. {3.A} . . . . μόνος G3441

μονήν   noun, acc. sg. fem. {2.A} . . . . μονή G3438

μονογενῆ   adj., acc. sg. masc. {3.E} . . . . μονογενής G3439

G3439   **μονογενής**, -ές   *only-born, only,* of children.

μονογενής   adj., nom. sg. fem. {3.E} . . . μονογενής G3439

μονογενής   adj., nom. sg. masc. {3.E} . . . . id.

μονογενοῦς   adj., gen. sg. masc. {3.E} . . . . id.

μόνοι   adj., nom. pl. masc. {3.A} . . . . μόνος G3441

μόνοις   adj., dat. pl. masc. {3.A} . . . . id.

μόνον   adj., acc. sg. masc. {3.A} . . . . id.

μόνον   adj., acc. sg. neut. {3.A} . . . . id.

μόνον   adv. {3.F} . . . . id.

G3441   **μόνος**, -η, -ον   *alone;* κατὰ μόνας = κατ᾽ ἰδίαν, *by himself, alone;* sg. neut. μόνον as adv., *only.*

μόνος   adj., nom. sg. masc. {3.A} . . . . μόνος G3441

μόνου   adj., gen. sg. masc. {3.A} . . . . id.

μόνους   adj., acc. pl. masc. {3.A} . . . . id.

μονόφθαλμον   adj., acc. sg. masc. {3.C} . . . . μονόφθαλμος G3442

G3442   **μονόφθαλμος**, -ον   *one-eyed, with one eye only.*

G3443   **μονόω**   *I leave alone (solitary).*

μόνῳ   adj., dat. sg. masc. {3.A} . . . . μόνος G3441

G3444   **μορφή**, -ῆς, ἡ   *form,* implying essential character as well as outline. It suggests unchangeableness, as contrasted with σχῆμα (= figure, fashion). In Phil 2:6 the reference is to the preincarnate Christ with divine attributes.

μορφῇ   noun, dat. sg. fem. {2.A} . . . . μορφή G3444

μορφήν   noun, acc. sg. fem. {2.A} . . . . id.

G3445   **μορφόω**   *I form, shape* (of the development of the embryo into the fully formed child).

μορφωθῇ   verb, aor. pass. subjunc. 3 pers. sg. {5.B.1} . . . . μορφόω G3445

μόρφωσιν   noun, acc. sg. fem. {2.C} . . . μόρφωσις G3446

G3446   **μόρφωσις**, -εως, ἡ   a mere *form, outline.*

μόσχον   noun, acc. sg. masc. {2.B} . . . . . . μόσχος G3448

G3447   **μοσχοποιέω**   *I make* a model of *a calf.*

G3448   **μόσχος**, -ου, ὁ   *a calf.*

μόσχῳ   noun, dat. sg. masc. {2.B} . . . . μόσχος G3448

μόσχων   noun, gen. pl. masc. {2.B} . . . . id.

μου   pron. pers., 1 pers. gen. sg. {4.A} . . . . ἐγώ G1473

μού   pron. pers., 1 pers. gen. sg. {4.A} . . . . id.

G3451   **μουσικός**, -οῦ, ὁ   *a musician,* but probably in some narrower sense in Rev 18:22.

μουσικῶν   adj., gen. pl. masc. {3.A} . . . . μουσικός G3451

μόχθον   noun, acc. sg. masc. {2.B} . . . . . . .μόχθος G3449‡

G3449‡   **μόχθος**, -ου, ὁ   *struggle, hardship,* involved in continued *labors.*

μόχθῳ   noun, dat. sg. masc. {2.B} . . . . .μόχθος G3449‡

G3452   **μυελός**, -οῦ, ὁ   *marrow.*

μυελῶν   noun, gen. pl. masc. {2.B} . . . . . . μυελός G3452

G3453   **μυέω**   (*I initiate* into the Mysteries), hence, *I habituate.*

μύθοις   noun, dat. pl. masc. {2.B} . . . . μῦθος G3454

G3454   **μῦθος**, -ου, ὁ   *an idle tale, fable, fanciful story.*

μύθους   noun, acc. pl. masc. {2.B} . . . . μῦθος G3454

G3455   **μυκάομαι**   *I roar.*

μυκᾶται   verb, pres. mid./pass. indic. 3 pers. sg. {5.A.2} . . . . .μυκάομαι G3455

μυκτηρίζεται   verb, pres. pass. indic. 3 pers. sg. {5.A.1.d} . . . . μυκτηρίζω G3456

G3456   **μυκτηρίζω**   (properly, *I turn up the nose* as a sign of contempt), *I sneer at, disdain.*

G3457   **μυλικός**, -ή, -όν   *belonging to a mill.*

μυλικός   adj., nom. sg. masc. {3.A} . . . . . .μυλικός G3457

μύλινον   adj., acc. sg. masc. {3.A} . . . . . .μύλινος G3458†

G3458†   **μύλινος**, -η, -ον   *a millstone.* Var. for μύλος, Rev 18:21.

μύλον   noun, acc. sg. masc. {2.B} . . . . μύλος G3458

G3458   **μύλος**, -ου, ὁ   *a mill.*

μύλος   noun, nom. sg. masc. {2.B} . . . . μύλος G3458

μύλου   noun, gen. sg. masc. {2.B} . . . . id.

μύλῳ   noun, dat. sg. masc. {2.B} . . . . id.

G3459   **μυλών**, -ῶνος, ὁ   *a mill-house.*

μύλωνι   noun, dat. sg. masc. {2.C} . . . . . . .μυλών G3459

G3460   **Μύρα** (Μύρρα), -ων, τό   *Myra,* a port in Lycia, southwest Asia Minor.

μύρα   noun, acc. pl. neut. {2.B} . . . . μύρον G3464

Μύρα   noun prop., acc. pl. neut. {2.B; 2.D} . . Μύρα G3460

μυριάδας   noun, acc. pl. fem. {2.C} . . . . . μυριάς G3461

μυριάδες   noun, nom. pl. fem. {2.C} . . . . id.

μυριάδων   noun, gen. pl. fem. {2.C} . . . . id.

G3461   **μυριάς**, -άδος, ἡ   a group of *ten thousand, a ten thousand.*

μυριάσιν   noun, dat. pl. fem. {2.C} . . . . . μυριάς G3461

G3462   **μυρίζω**   *I anoint.*

G3463   **μυρίος**, -α, -ον   pl. *ten thousand; innumerable, countless.*

μυρίους   adj., acc. pl. masc. {3.A} . . . . . .μυρίος G3463

μυρίσαι   vbl., aor. act. inf. {6.B.1} . . . . μυρίζω G3462

μυρίων   adj., gen. pl. neut. {3.A} . . . . .μυρίος G3463

G3464   **μύρον**, -ου, τό   *anointing oil; ointment* (a Semitic word).

μύρον   noun, acc. sg. neut. {2.B} . . . . μύρον G3464

μύρον   noun, nom. sg. neut. {2.B} . . . . id.

μύρον   noun, gen. sg. neut. {2.B} . . . . id.

Μύρρα   noun prop., acc. pl. neut. {2.B; 2.D}. Μύρα G3460

μύρῳ   noun, dat. sg. neut. {2.B} . . . . μύρον G3464

G3465   **Μυσία**, -ας, ἡ   *Mysia,* a country in the northwest of the Roman province Asia (and of Asia Minor).

Μυσίαν   noun prop., acc. sg. fem. {2.A; 2.D} . . . . .Μυσία G3465

μυστήρια   noun, acc. pl. neut. {2.B} . . . . μυστήριον G3466

G3466   **μυστήριον**, -ου, τό   *a secret,* Mark 4:11 and parallels; also (1) a symbol containing a *secret* meaning, Rev 17:5, cf. Eph 5:32; (2) the meaning of such a symbol, Rev 1:20; 17:7; (3) as the counterpart of ἀποκάλυψις, *secret* to be revealed, *the secret purpose* of God in His dealings with man, *a Divine secret,* esp. the inclusion of the Gentiles as well as the Jews in the scope of the Messiah's beneficent reign; (4) the sum of the Christian faith, 1 Tim 3:9, 16.

μυστήριον   noun, acc. sg. neut. {2.B}. . μυστήριον G3466
μυστήριον   noun, nom. sg. neut. {2.B}. . . . . . . id.
μυστηρίου   noun, gen. sg. neut. {2.B} . . . . id.
μυστηρίῳ   noun, dat. sg. neut. {2.B} . . . . id.
μυστηρίων   noun, gen. pl. neut. {2.B} . . . . id.
G3467 **μυωπάζω**   I half close the eyes, I blink.
μυωπάζων   vbl., pres. act. ptc. nom. sg. masc.
    {6.A.1}. μυωπάζω G3467
μώλωπι   noun, dat. sg. masc. {2.C}. . . . . . μώλωψ G3468
G3468 **μώλωψ**, -ωπος, ὁ   a welt or bruise left on the
    body by scourging.
G3469 **μωμάομαι**   I calumniate, slander.
μωμηθῇ   verb, aor. pass. subjunc. 3 pers. sg.
    {5.B.1}. . . . . .μωμάομαι G3469
μωμήσηται   verb, aor. mid. subjunc. 3 pers. sg.
    {5.B.1} . . . . id.
μῶμοι   noun, nom. pl. masc. {2.B} . . . . μῶμος G3470
G3470 **μῶμος**, -ου, ὁ   a blemish (a "Hebraic" sense pecu-
    liar to biblical Gk.; the classical sense is blame).
μωρά   adj., acc. pl. neut. {3.A} . . . . μωρός G3474
μωραί   adj., nom. pl. fem. {3.A} . . . . id.
G3471 **μωραίνω**   (1) I make foolish, I turn to foolish-
    ness; (2) I taint, and thus make useless, Matt
    5:13; Luke 14:34 (from μωρός).
μωρανθῇ   verb, aor. pass. subjunc. 3 pers. sg.
    {5.B.1} . . . . .μωραίνω G3471
μωράς   adj., acc. pl. fem. {3.A} . . . . μωρός G3474
μωρέ   adj., voc. sg. masc. {3.A} . . . . id.
G3472 **μωρία**, -ας, ἡ   foolishness.
μωρία   noun, nom. sg. fem. {2.A}. . . . . μωρία G3472
μωρίαν   noun, acc. sg. fem. {2.A}. . . . . id.
μωρίας   noun, gen. sg. fem. {2.A}. . . . . id.

μωροί   adj., nom. pl. masc. {3.A} . . . . μωρός G3474
μωροί   adj., voc. pl. masc. {3.A} . . . . id.
G3473 **μωρολογία**, -ας, ἡ   foolish talking.
μωρολογία   noun, nom. sg. fem. {2.A}. μωρολογία G3473
μωρόν   adj., nom. sg. neut. {3.A} . . . . μωρός G3474
G3474 **μωρός**, -ά, -όν   (1) adj., foolish; (2) noun, a fool.
μωρός   adj., nom. sg. masc. {3.A} . . . . μωρός G3474
μωρῷ   adj., dat. sg. masc. {3.A}. . . . . id.
Μωσέα   noun prop., acc. sg. masc. {2.A;
    2.D}. Μωϋσῆς G3475
Μωσεῖ   noun prop., dat. sg. masc. {2.A; 2.D} . . . id.
Μωσέως   noun prop., gen. sg. masc. {2.C; 2.D} . id.
Μωσῆ   noun prop., dat. sg. masc. {2.A; 2.D}. . . . id.
Μωσῆν   noun prop., acc. sg. masc. {2.A; 2.D}. . . . id.
Μωσῆς   noun prop., nom. sg. masc. {2.A; 2.D}. . . id.
Μωυσέα   noun prop., acc. sg. masc. {2.A; 2.D}. . . id.
Μωϋσέα   noun prop., acc. sg. masc. {2.A; 2.D}. . . id.
Μωυσεῖ   noun prop., dat. sg. masc. {2.A; 2.D} . . id.
Μωϋσεῖ   noun prop., dat. sg. masc. {2.A; 2.D} . . id.
Μωυσέως   noun prop., gen. sg. masc. {2.C; 2.D} id.
Μωϋσέως   noun prop., gen. sg. masc. {2.C; 2.D} id.
Μωυσῆ   noun prop., dat. sg. masc. {2.A; 2.D} . . id.
Μωϋσῆ   noun prop., dat. sg. masc. {2.A; 2.D} . id.
Μωυσῆν   noun prop., acc. sg. masc. {2.A; 2.D} . id.
Μωϋσῆν   noun prop., acc. sg. masc. {2.A; 2.D} . id.
Μωϋσῆς   noun prop., nom. sg. masc. {2.A; 2.D} id.
G3475 **Μωϋσῆς** (Μωσῆς), -έως, ὁ   Moses, the
    lawgiver of the Hebrews, thus regarded as the
    author of the Pentateuch, where the laws are
    preserved (cf. 2 Cor 3:15, etc.).
Μωϋσῆς   noun prop., nom. sg. masc. {2.A;
    2.D}. . . . . Μωϋσῆς G3475

N ν

G3476 **Ναασσών**, ὁ   Naasson, son of Aminadab and
    father of Salmon (Sala), and one of the ances-
    tors of Jesus (Heb.).
Ναασσών   noun prop. . . . . .Ναασσών G3476
G3477 **Ναγγαί**, ὁ   Naggai, one of the ancestors of Jesus
    (Heb.).
Ναγγαί   noun prop. . . . . Ναγγαί G3477
G3478 **Ναζαρά** (Ναζαρέθ), ἡ   Nazareth, a city of
    Galilee, where Jesus lived before His ministry
    (various spellings, not declined).
Ναζαρά   noun prop. . . . . Ναζαρά G3478
Ναζαρέθ   noun prop. . . . . id.
Ναζαρέτ   noun prop. . . . . id.
Ναζαρηνέ   adj. prop., voc. sg. masc.
    {3.A}. . . . . Ναζαρηνός G3479
Ναζαρηνόν   adj. prop., acc. sg. masc. {3.A} . . . . id.
G3479 **Ναζαρηνός**, -οῦ, ὁ   of Nazareth, a Nazarene.
Ναζαρηνός   adj. prop., nom. sg. masc.
    {3.A}. . . . . Ναζαρηνός G3479
Ναζαρηνοῦ   adj. prop., gen. sg. masc. {3.A} . . . id.
Ναζωραῖον   noun prop., acc. sg. masc. {2.B;
    2.D}. . . . . .Ναζωραῖος G3480

Ναζωραῖος   noun prop., nom. sg. masc. {2.B;
    2.D}. . . . . id.
G3480 **Ναζωραῖος**, -ου, ὁ   commonly interpreted
    to mean, of Nazareth, Nazarene, the ω being
    nearer to the Syr. form Natsoreth.
Ναζωραῖος   noun prop., nom. sg. masc. {2.B;
    2.D}. . . . . .Ναζωραῖος G3480
Ναζωραίου   noun prop., gen. sg. masc. {2.B;
    2.D}. . . . . id.
Ναζωραίων   noun prop., gen. pl. masc. {2.B;
    2.D}. . . . . id.
G3481 **Ναθάμ**, ὁ   Nathan, son of David, and an ances-
    tor of Jesus (Heb.).
Ναθάμ   noun prop. . . . . Ναθάμ G3481
Ναθάν   noun prop. . . . . id.
G3482 **Ναθαναήλ**, ὁ   Nathanael, of Cana in Galilee,
    an early disciple.
Ναθαναήλ   noun prop. . . . . Ναθαναήλ G3482
G3483 **ναί**   yes, sometimes made a subs. by prefixing
    the article τό.
ναί   part. . . . . .ναί G3483
Ναιμάν   noun prop. . . . . .Νεεμάν G3497

Ναίν   noun prop. Ναῖν *G3484*

G3484 **Ναῖν**, ἡ   *Nain,* a city southwest of the Sea of Galilee.

Ναῖν   noun prop. Ναῖν *G3484*

ναοῖς   noun, dat. pl. masc. {2.B} . . . . ναός *G3485*

ναόν   noun, acc. sg. masc. {2.B} . . . . id.

G3485 **ναός**, -οῦ, ὁ   *a temple, a shrine,* that part of the temple where the god himself resides (contrast ἱερόν); so also figuratively.

ναός   noun, nom. sg. masc. {2.B} . . . . ναός *G3485*

ναοῦ   noun, gen. sg. masc. {2.B} . . . . id.

G3486 **Ναούμ**, ὁ   *Naum, Nahum,* an ancestor of Jesus (Heb.).

Ναούμ   noun prop. . . . . Ναούμ *G3486*

ναούς   noun, acc. pl. masc. {2.B} . . . . ναός *G3485*

G3487 **νάρδος**, -ου, ἡ   *spikenard,* a perfume made originally from the *Nardo-stachys Jatamansi* growing on the Himalayas (Heb., borrowed into Persian and Sanskrit).

νάρδου   noun, gen. sg. fem. {2.B} . . . . νάρδος *G3487*

G3488 **Νάρκισσος**, -ου, ὁ   *Narcissus,* a resident in Rome in Nero's time.

Ναρκίσσου   noun prop., gen. sg. masc. {2.B; 2.D} . . . . Νάρκισσος *G3488*

G3489 **ναυαγέω**   (1) *I am shipwrecked;* so (2) figuratively, *I come to ruin.*

G3490 **ναύκληρος**, -ου, ὁ   *a captain (master)* of a ship.

ναυκλήρῳ   noun, dat. sg. masc. {2.B} . ναύκληρος *G3490*

ναῦν   noun, acc. sg. fem. {2.C} . . . . ναῦς *G3491*

G3491 **ναῦς**, acc. ναῦν, ἡ   *a ship, a vessel,* Acts 27:41 only (literary, almost obsolete, rare in the vernacular; see πλοῖον).

ναῦται   noun, nom. pl. masc. {2.A} . . . . . ναύτης *G3492*

G3492 **ναύτης**, -ου, ὁ   *a sailor.*

ναυτῶν   noun, gen. pl. masc. {2.A} . . . . . . ναύτης *G3492*

G3493 **Ναχώρ**, ὁ   *Nahor,* one of the ancestors of Jesus (Heb.).

Ναχώρ   noun prop. . . . . Ναχώρ *G3493*

ναῷ   noun, dat. sg. masc. {2.B} . . . . ναός *G3485*

νέαν   adj., acc. sg. fem. {3.A} . . . . .νέος *G3501*

νεανίαν   noun, acc. sg. masc. {2.A} . . . . . νεανίας *G3494*

G3494 **νεανίας**, -ου, ὁ   *a young man, a man in his prime* (used even of a man of 40).

νεανίας   noun, nom. sg. masc. {2.A} . . . . νεανίας *G3494*

νεανίου   noun, gen. sg. masc. {2.A} . . . . id.

νεανίσκε   noun, voc. sg. masc. {2.B} . . νεανίσκος *G3495*

νεανίσκοι   noun, nom. pl. masc. {2.B} . . . . id.

νεανίσκοι   noun, voc. pl. masc. {2.B} . . . . id.

νεανίσκον   noun, acc. sg. masc. {2.B} . . . . id.

G3495 **νεανίσκος**, -ου, ὁ   *a youth.*

νεανίσκος   noun, nom. sg. masc. {2.B} νεανίσκος *G3495*

Νεάπολιν   noun prop., acc. sg. fem. {2.C; 2.D} . . . . Νεάπολις *G3496*

G3496 **Νεάπολις**   *Neopolis,* a port city of Philippi in the Roman province of Macedonia. Var. spelling of Νέα Πόλις, Acts 16:11.

νέας   adj., acc. pl. fem. {3.A} . . . . .νέος *G3501*

νέας   adj., gen. sg. fem. {3.A} . . . . id.

G3497 **Νεεμάν** (Ναιμάν)   *Naaman,* commander in chief of the army of a king of Syria in the ninth c. B.C. (2 Kgs 5).

Νεεμάν   noun prop. . . . . Νεεμάν *G3497*

νεκρά   adj., nom. sg. fem. {3.A} . . . . .νεκρός *G3498*

νεκράν   adj., acc. sg. fem. {3.A} . . . . id.

νεκροί   adj., nom. pl. masc. {3.A} . . . . id.

νεκροῖς   adj., dat. pl. masc. {3.A} . . . . id.

νεκρόν   adj., acc. sg. masc. {3.A} . . . . id.

νεκρόν   adj., nom. sg. neut. {3.A} . . . . id.

G3498 **νεκρός**, -ά, -όν   (1) adj., *dead, lifeless;* hence met.; (2) noun, *a dead body, a corpse,* ἐκ (τῶν) νεκρῶν, *from among the dead.*

νεκρός   adj., nom. sg. masc. {3.A} . . . . .νεκρός *G3498*

νεκροῦ   adj., gen. sg. masc. {3.A} . . . . id.

νεκρούς   adj., acc. pl. masc. {3.A} . . . . id.

G3499 **νεκρόω**   lit. and met. *I make (cause) to be dead; I make as dead.*

νεκρῶν   adj., gen. pl. masc. {3.A} . . . . .νεκρός *G3498*

νεκρῶν   adj., gen. pl. neut. {3.A} . . . . id.

νεκρώσατε   verb, aor. act. impv. 2 pers. pl. {5.D.1} . . . . νεκρόω *G3499*

νέκρωσιν   noun, acc. sg. fem. {2.C} . . . . . .νέκρωσις *G3500*

G3500 **νέκρωσις**, -εως, ἡ   (1) *putting to death,* 2 Cor 4:10; (2) *dead* or *lifeless condition,* Rom 4:19.

νενεκρωμένον   vbl., perf. pass. ptc. acc. sg. neut. {6.A.2} . . . . νεκρόω *G3499*

νενεκρωμένου   vbl., perf. pass. ptc. gen. sg. masc. {6.A.2} . . . . id.

νενίκηκα   verb, perf. act. indic. 1 pers. sg. {5.A.1} . . . . νικάω *G3528*

νενικήκατε   verb, perf. act. indic. 2 pers. pl. {5.A.1} . . . . id.

νενομοθέτηται   verb, perf. pass. indic. 3 pers. sg. {5.A.1} . . . . νομοθετέω *G3549*

νενομοθέτητο   verb, plu. pass. indic. 3 pers. sg. {5.A.1} . . . . id.

νεομηνίας   noun, gen. sg. fem. {2.A} . . . νουμηνία *G3561*

νέον   adj., acc. sg. masc. {3.A} . . . . .νέος *G3501*

νέον   adj., nom. sg. neut. {3.A} . . . . id.

G3501 **νέος**, -α, -ον   (1) *young;* (2) *new, fresh;* Νέα Πόλις, *Neapolis, New City,* the harbor town of Philippi.

νέος   adj., nom. sg. masc. {3.A} . . . . .νέος *G3501*

G3502 **νεοσσός** (νοσσός), -οῦ, ὁ   *a nestling, a young bird, a young one.*

νεοσσούς   noun, acc. pl. masc. {2.B} . . . . νεοσσός *G3502*

G3503 **νεότης**, -ητος, ἡ   *youth, youthfulness.*

νεότητος   noun, gen. sg. fem. {2.C} . . . . . . .νεότης *G3503*

νεόφυτον   adj., acc. sg. masc. {3.C} . . . . νεόφυτος *G3504*

G3504 **νεόφυτος**, -ον   (lit. *newly planted*), *newly converted* to Christianity.

G3505 **Νέρων**, -ωνος, ὁ   *Nero,* a Roman emperor.

Νερῶνι   noun prop., dat. sg. masc. {2.C; 2.D} . . . . .Νέρων *G3505*

νεύει   verb, pres. act. indic. 3 pers. sg. {5.A.1.a} . . . . νεύω *G3506*

νεύσαντος   vbl., aor. act. ptc. gen. sg. masc. {6.A.1.a} . . . . id.

G3506 **νεύω**   *I nod, make a sign.*

νεφέλαι   noun, nom. pl. fem. {2.A} . . . . . νεφέλη *G3507*

νεφέλαις   noun, dat. pl. fem. {2.A} . . . . id.

G3507 **νεφέλη**, -ης, ἡ   *a cloud.*

νεφέλη   noun, nom. sg. fem. {2.A} . . . . νεφέλη *G3507*

νεφέλη   noun, dat. sg. fem. {2.A} . . . . id.

νεφέλην   noun, acc. sg. fem. {2.A} . . . . id.

νεφέλης   noun, gen. sg. fem. {2.A} . . . . id.

νεφελῶν   noun, gen. pl. fem. {2.A} . . . . id.

Νεφθαλείμ   noun prop. . . . . Νεφθαλίμ *G3508*

G3508 **Νεφθαλίμ**, ὁ   *Naphtali, son of Jacob, founder of a tribe which occupied territory.*

Νεφθαλίμ   noun prop. . . . . Νεφθαλίμ *G3508*

G3509 **νέφος**, -ους, τό   (lit. *a cloud*), hence, *a dense crowd.*

νέφος   noun, acc. sg. neut. {2.C} . . . . νέφος *G3509*

G3510 **νεφρός**, -οῦ, ὁ   *a kidney* (as a general emotional centre).

νεφρούς   noun, acc. pl. masc. {2.B} . . . . . . νεφρός *G3510*

νεωκόρον   noun, acc. sg. masc. {2.B} . . . νεωκόρος *G3511*

G3511 **νεωκόρος**, -ου, ὁ   (lit. *temple sweeper*), *temple warden;* an honorary title.

νεωτέρας   adj. comp., acc. pl. fem. {3.A; 3.G} . . νέος *G3501*

νεωτερικάς   adj. comp., acc. pl. fem. {3.A; 3.G} . . . . νεωτερικός *G3512*

G3512 **νεωτερικός**, -ή, -όν   *associated with youth (younger men), youthful.*

νεώτεροι   adj. comp., nom. pl. masc. {3.A; 3.G} . . . . νέος *G3501*

νεώτεροι   adj. comp., voc. pl. masc. {3.A; 3.G} . νέος *G3501*

νεώτερος   adj. comp., nom. sg. masc. {3.A; 3.G} . id.

νεωτέρους   adj. comp., acc. pl. masc. {3.A; 3.G} . id.

G3513 **νή**   *by,* with an acc. of adjuration.

νή   part. . . . . νή *G3513*

νήθει   verb, pres. act. indic. 3 pers. sg. {5.A.1.a} . . . . νήθω *G3514*

νήθουσιν   verb, pres. act. indic. 3 pers. pl. {5.A.1.a} . . . . id.

G3514 **νήθω**   *I spin* (a vulgar and late form of νέω).

νηπιάζετε   verb, pres. act. impv. 2 pers. pl. {5.D.1} . . . . νηπιάζω *G3515*

G3515 **νηπιάζω**   *I am childish (infantile).*

νήπιοι   adj., nom. pl. masc. {3.A} . . . . νήπιος *G3516*

νηπίοις   adj., dat. pl. masc. {3.A} . . . . id.

G3516 **νήπιος**, -α, -ον   *an infant, a child.*

νήπιος   adj., nom. sg. masc. {3.A}. . . . . . . νήπιος *G3516*

νηπίου   adj., gen. sg. masc. {3.A} . . . . id.

νηπίων   adj., gen. pl. masc. {3.A} . . . . id.

Νηρέα   noun prop., acc. sg. masc. {2.C; 2.D}. . . . . Νηρεύς *G3517*

Νηρεί   noun prop. . . . . Νηρί *G3518*

G3517 **Νηρεύς**, -έως, ὁ   *Nereus,* a Christian in Rome.

G3518 **Νηρί**, ὁ   *Neri,* an ancestor of Jesus (Heb.).

Νηρί   noun prop. Νηρί *G3518*

G3519 **νησίον**, -ου, τό   *a little island, an islet.*

νησίον   noun, acc. sg. neut. {2.B} . . . . νησίον *G3519*

νῆσον   noun, acc. sg. fem. {2.B} . . . . νῆσος *G3520*

G3520 **νῆσος**, -ου, ἡ   *an island.*

νῆσος   noun, nom. sg. fem. {2.B} . . . . νῆσος *G3520*

νήσου   noun, gen. sg. fem. {2.B} . . . . id.

G3521 **νηστεία**, -ας, ἡ   *fasting.*

νηστεία   noun, dat. sg. fem. {2.A} . . . . . νηστεία *G3521*

νηστείαις   noun, dat. pl. fem. {2.A} . . . . id.

νηστείαν   noun, acc. sg. fem. {2.A} . . . . id.

νήστεις   adj., acc. pl. masc. {3.A} . . . . νῆστις *G3523*

νηστειῶν   noun, gen. pl. fem. {2.A} . . . . νηστεία *G3521*

νηστεύειν   vbl., pres. act. inf. {6.B.1} . . . νηστεύω *G3522*

νηστεύητε   verb, pres. act. subjunc. 2 pers. pl. {5.B.1} . . . . id.

νηστεύομεν   verb, pres. act. indic. 1 pers. pl. {5.A.1.a} . . . . id.

νηστεύοντες   vbl., pres. act. ptc. nom. pl. masc. {6.A.1} . . . . id.

νηστευόντων   vbl., pres. act. ptc. gen. pl. masc. {6.A.1} . . . . id.

νηστεύουσι   verb, pres. act. indic. 3 pers. pl. {5.A.1.a} . . . . id.

νηστεύουσιν   verb, pres. act. indic. 3 pers. pl. {5.A.1.a} . . . . id.

νηστεῦσαι   vbl., aor. act. inf. {6.B.1} . . . . id.

νηστεύσαντες   vbl., aor. act. ptc. nom. pl. masc. {6.A.1.a} . . . . id.

νηστεύσας   vbl., aor. act. ptc. nom. sg. masc. {6.A.1.a} . . . . id.

νηστεύσουσιν   verb, fut. act. indic. 3 pers. pl. {5.A.1.a} . . . . id.

G3522 **νηστεύω**   *I fast.*

νηστεύω   verb, pres. act. indic. 1 pers. sg. {5.A.1.a} . . . . νηστεύω *G3522*

νηστεύων   vbl., pres. act. ptc. nom. sg. masc. {6.A.1} . . . . id.

G3523 **νῆστις**, -ιδος, acc. pl. νήστεις, ὁ and ἡ   *fasting, without food.*

νήσῳ   noun, dat. sg. fem. {2.B} . . . . νῆσος *G3520*

νηφάλεον   adj., acc. sg. masc. {3.A} . . . . νηφάλιος *G3524*

νηφαλέους   adj., acc. pl. masc. {3.A} . . . . id.

νηφάλιον   adj., acc. sg. masc. {2.B} . . . . id.

G3524 **νηφάλιος**, -α, -ον   *sober, not intoxicated* (with wine).

νηφαλίους   adj., acc. pl. masc. {3.A} . . . νηφάλιος *G3524*

νῆφε   verb, pres. act. impv. 2 pers. sg. {5.D.1}

νήφοντες   vbl., pres. act. ptc. nom. pl. masc. {6.A.1} . . . . id.

G3525 **νήφω**   (lit. *I am sober*), *I am calm (vigilant).*

νήφωμεν   verb, pres. act. subjunc. 1 pers. pl. {5.B.1} . . . . νήφω *G3525*

νήψατε   verb, aor. act. impv. 2 pers. pl. {5.D.1} . . id.

G3526 **Νίγερ**, ὁ   *Niger,* another name of Symeon, a Christian at Antioch.

Νίγερ   noun prop. . . . . Νίγερ *G3526*

νίκα   verb, pres. act. impv. 2 pers. sg. {5.D.2} νικάω *G3528*

νικᾷ   verb, pres. act. indic. 3 pers. sg. {5.A.2} . . . id.

Νικάνορα   noun prop., acc. sg. masc. {2.C; 2.D}. . . . . Νικάνωρ *G3527*

G3527 **Νικάνωρ**, -ορος, ὁ   *Nicanor,* one of the original seven "deacons" in the church at Jerusalem.

G3528 **νικάω**   *I conquer* (transferred from battle to other conflicts).

G3529 **νίκη**, -ης, ἡ   *victory.*

νίκη   noun, nom. sg. fem. {2.A} . . . . νίκη *G3529*

νικῆσαι   vbl., aor. act. inf. {6.B.1}. . . . . νικάω *G3528*
νικήσασα   vbl., aor. act. ptc. nom. sg. fem.
     {6.A.2}. . . . . id.
νικήσει   verb, fut. act. indic. 3 pers. sg. {5.A.1}. . id.
νικήσεις   verb, fut. act. indic. 2 pers. sg. {5.A.1}. id.
νικήσῃ   verb, aor. act. subjunc. 3 pers. sg. {5.B.1} id.
νικήσῃς   verb, aor. act. subjunc. 2 pers. sg.
     {5.B.1}. . . . . id.
G3530 **Νικόδημος**, -ου, ὁ   *Nicodemus*, a rich Jew-
     ish follower of Jesus, and member of the
     Sanhedrin.
Νικόδημος   noun prop., nom. sg. masc. {2.B;
     2.D}. . . . . Νικόδημος *G3530*
G3531 **Νικολαΐτης**, -ου, ὁ   *a Nicolaitan, a follower of
     Nicolaus* (a heretic at Ephesus).
Νικολαϊτῶν   noun prop., gen. pl. masc. {2.A;
     2.D}. . . . . Νικολαΐτης *G3531*
Νικόλαον   noun prop., acc. sg. masc. {2.B;
     2.D}. . . . . Νικόλαος *G3532*
G3532 **Νικόλαος**, -ου, ὁ   *Nicolaus,* a Jewish proselyte
     of Antioch, one of the original seven "dea-
     cons" in the church at Jerusalem.
Νικοπόλεως   noun prop., gen. sg. fem. {2.C;
     2.D}. . . . . .Νικόπολις *G3533*
Νικόπολιν   noun prop., acc. sg. fem. {2.C; 2.D} . id.
G3533 **Νικόπολις**, -εως, ἡ   *Nicopolis,* probably the
     city near Actium in Epirus, northwest Greece.
G3534 **νῖκος**, -ους, τό   *victory* (a later variety of νίκη,
     dating from about the middle of first c. B.C.).
νῖκος   noun, acc. sg. neut. {2.C} . . . . .νῖκος *G3534*
νῖκος   noun, nom. sg. neut. {2.C} . . . . id.
νικῶ   verb, pres. pass. impv. 2 pers. sg.
     {5.D.2}. . . . . νικάω *G3528*
νικῶν   vbl., pres. act. ptc. nom. sg. masc. {6.A.2} id.
νικῶντας   vbl., pres. act. ptc. acc. pl. masc.
     {6.A.2}. . . . . id.
νικῶντι   vbl., pres. act. ptc. dat. sg. masc. {6.A.2} id.
Νινευεῖται   noun prop., nom. pl. masc. {2.A;
     2.D}. . . . . .Νινευΐτης *G3536*
Νινευείταις   noun prop., dat. pl. masc. {2.A;
     2.D}. . . . . id.
G3535 **Νινευΐ** (Νινευή)   *Nineveh,* the capital of the
     Assyrian Empire.
Νινευΐ   noun prop. .Νινευΐ *G3535*
Νινευΐται   noun prop., nom. pl. masc. {2.A;
     2.D}. . . . . .Νινευΐτης *G3536*
Νινευΐταις   noun prop., dat. pl. masc. {2.A; 2.D} id.
Νινευΐταις   noun prop., dat. pl. masc. {2.A; 2.D} id.
G3536 **Νινευΐτης**, -ου, ὁ   *a Ninevite, an inhabitant
     of Nineveh* or *Ninus,* a city on the Tigris in
     Assyria.
νίπτειν   vbl., pres. act. inf. {6.B.1}. . . . . νίπτω *G3538*
νίπτεις   verb, pres. act. indic. 2 pers. sg. {5.A.1.a} id.
G3537 **νιπτήρ**, -ῆρος, ὁ   *a basin.*
νιπτῆρα   noun, acc. sg. masc. {2.C} . . . . . .νιπτήρ *G3537*
νίπτονται   verb, pres. mid. indic. 3 pers. pl.
     {5.A.1.d} . . . . νίπτω *G3538*
G3538 **νίπτω**   *I wash;* mid. *I wash my own* (hands,
     etc.).
νίψαι   verb, aor. mid. impv. 2 pers. sg. {5.D.1}νίπτω *G3538*

νιψάμενος   vbl., aor. mid. ptc. nom. sg. masc.
     {6.A.1.b} . . . . id.
νίψασθαι   vbl., aor. mid. inf. {6.B.1}. . . . . id.
νίψῃς   verb, aor. act. subjunc. 2 pers. sg. {5.B.1} . id.
νίψω   verb, aor. act. subjunc. 1 pers. sg. {5.B.1} . . id.
νίψωνται   verb, aor. mid. subjunc. 3 pers. pl.
     {5.B.1}. . . . . id.
νόει   verb, pres. act. impv. 2 pers. sg. {5.D.2}. . νοέω *G3539*
νοεῖτε   verb, pres. act. indic. 2 pers. pl. {5.A.2}. . id.
νοείτω   verb, pres. act. impv. 3 pers. sg. {5.D.2} . id.
G3539 **νοέω**   *I understand, conceive, apprehend;* aor.
     possibly *realize,* John 12:40; Eph 3:4.
G3540 **νόημα**, -ατος, τό   *a thought; a design.*
νόημα   noun, acc. sg. neut. {2.C} . . . . .νόημα *G3540*
νοήματα   noun, acc. pl. neut. {2.C} . . . . id.
νοήματα   noun, nom. pl. neut. {2.C} . . . . id.
νοῆσαι   vbl., aor. act. inf. {6.B.1} . . . . νοέω *G3539*
νοήσωσι   verb, aor. act. subjunc. 3 pers. pl.
     {5.B.1}. . . . . id.
νοήσωσιν   verb, aor. act. subjunc. 3 pers. pl.
     {5.B.1}. . . . . id.
νόθοι   adj., nom. pl. masc. {3.A}. . . . . νόθος *G3541*
G3541 **νόθος**, -η, -ον   *a bastard, an illegitimate son.*
νοΐ   noun, dat. sg. masc. {2.C}. . . . . νοῦς *G3563*
G3542 **νομή**, -ῆς, ἡ   (1) *pasture;* (2) ἔχειν νομήν, *to
     spread,* 2 Tim 2:17.
νομήν   noun, acc. sg. fem. {2.A}. . . . . νομή *G3542*
νομίζει   verb, pres. act. indic. 3 pers. sg.
     {5.A.1.a} . . . . νομίζω *G3543*
νομίζειν   vbl., pres. act. inf. {6.B.1}. . . . . id.
νομίζοντες   vbl., pres. act. ptc. nom. pl. masc.
     {6.A.1}. . . . . id.
νομιζόντων   vbl., pres. act. ptc. gen. pl. masc.
     {6.A.1}. . . . . id.
G3543 **νομίζω**   *I think, suppose.*
νομίζω   verb, pres. act. indic. 1 pers. sg.
     {5.A.1.a} . . . . νομίζω *G3543*
νομίζων   vbl., pres. act. ptc. nom. sg. masc.
     {6.A.1}. . . . . id.
νομικάς   adj., acc. pl. fem. {3.A}. . . . . .νομικός *G3544*
νομικοί   adj., nom. pl. masc. {3.A} . . . . id.
νομικοῖς   adj., dat. pl. masc. {3.A} . . . . id.
νομικόν   adj., acc. sg. masc. {3.A}. . . . . id.
G3544 **νομικός**, -ή, -όν   (1) adj., *connected with law,
     about law,* Titus 3:9; (2) noun, *a lawyer, one
     learned in the Law* (i.e., in the Gospels), *one
     learned in the OT scriptures* (like γραμμα-
     τεύς), *a scribe; a jurist,* Titus 3:13.
νομικός   adj., nom. sg. masc. {3.A}. . . . . . .νομικός *G3544*
νομικούς   adj., acc. pl. masc. {3.A}. . . . . id.
νομικῶν   adj., gen. pl. masc. {3.A} . . . . id.
G3545 **νομίμως**   adv., *in a legitimate way, according to
     law and regulation.*
νομίμως   adv. {3.F} . . . . νομίμως *G3545*
νομίσαντες   vbl., aor. act. ptc. nom. pl. masc.
     {6.A.1.a} . . . . νομίζω *G3543*
νομίσητε   verb, aor. act. subjunc. 2 pers. pl.
     {5.B.1}. . . . . id.
G3546 **νόμισμα**, -ατος, τό   *a coin.*
νόμισμα   noun, acc. sg. neut. {2.C} . . . . . νόμισμα *G3546*

νομοδιδάσκαλοι   noun, nom. pl. masc.
   {2.B} . . . . νομοδιδάσκαλος G3547

G3547 **νομοδιδάσκαλος**, -ου, ὁ   (1) *a teacher of the Law, one learned in the Law* (i.e., the OT), = γραμματεύς, νομικός; (2) *a teacher of laws,* probably with reference to heretics of ascetic tendency, 1 Tim 1:7.

νομοδιδάσκαλος   noun, nom. sg. masc.
   {2.B} . . . . νομοδιδάσκαλος G3547

G3548 **νομοθεσία**, -ας, ἡ   *legislation* (at Sinai), *enactment of the Law.*

νομοθεσία   noun, nom. sg. fem. {2.A} . νομοθεσία G3548

G3549 **νομοθετέω**   (1) *I ordain, lay down, give the sanction of law to, enact,* Heb 8:6; (2) *I base legally, I regulate, I direct.*

G3550 **νομοθέτης**, -ου, ὁ   *a legislator.*

νομοθέτης   noun, nom. sg. masc. {2.A}   νομοθέτης G3550
νόμον   noun, acc. sg. masc. {2.B} . . . . νόμος G3551

G3551 **νόμος**, -ου, ὁ   (1) *the Law,* and so sometimes = the body of moral and ceremonial enactments forming the basis of Judaism; esp. as set forth in the OT; *the Old Testament;* but also ὁ νόμος καὶ οἱ προφῆται, Matt 7:12, etc., as a description of the content of the OT, though as strictly interpreted the phrase excludes the "writings" (namely Pss, Prov, Job, Song, Ruth, Eccl, Esth, Dan, Ezra, Neh, Chron); (2) *power to legislate, a sense of law, something with legislative authority,* e.g., Rom 7:23; 8:2; Gal 6:2; (3) *a law, an ordinance,* Rom 7:2; Jas 1:25; 2:8.

νόμος   noun, nom. sg. masc. {2.B} . . . . νόμος G3551
νόμου   noun, gen. sg. masc. {2.B} . . . . id.
νόμους   noun, acc. pl. masc. {2.B} . . . . id.
νόμῳ   noun, dat. sg. masc. {2.B} . . . . id.
νοός   noun, gen. sg. masc. {2.C} . . . . νοῦς G3563
νοοῦμεν   verb, pres. act. indic. 1 pers. pl. {5.A.2} νοέω G3539
νοούμενα   vbl., pres. pass. ptc. nom. pl. neut.
   {6.A.2} . . . . id.
νοοῦντες   vbl., pres. act. ptc. nom. pl. masc.
   {6.A.2} . . . . id.

G3552 **νοσέω**   *I am sick,* i.e., (by implication of a diseased appetite) *I hanker after.*

G3553 **νόσημα**, -ατος, τό   *a disease, a trouble.*

νοσήματι   noun, dat. sg. neut. {2.C} . . . . . νόσημα G3553
νόσοις   noun, dat. pl. fem. {2.B} . . . . νόσος G3554
νόσον   noun, acc. sg. fem. {2.B} . . . . id.

G3554 **νόσος**, -ου, ἡ   *a disease, a malady.*

νόσους   noun, acc. pl. fem. {2.B} . . . . νόσος G3554

G3555 **νοσσιά**, -ᾶς, ἡ   *a nestling, a young bird in the nest* (syncopated from νεοσσιά).

νοσσιά   noun, acc. pl. neut. {2.B} . . . . . . νοσσίον G3556
νοσσιάν   noun, acc. sg. fem. {2.A} . . . . . . νοσσιά G3555

G3556 **νοσσίον**, -ου, τό   *a nestling, a young bird in the nest;* cf. νοσσιά.

νοσσούς   noun, acc. pl. masc. {2.B} . . . . νεοσσός G3502
νοσφιζομένους   vbl., pres. mid. ptc. acc. pl. masc.
   {6.A.1} . . . . νοσφίζω G3557

G3557 **νοσφίζω**   mid. *I separate for myself, I set apart for myself, I annex, appropriate for my own benefit, purloin, peculate.*

νοσφίσασθαι   vbl., aor. mid. inf. {6.B.1} . νοσφίζω G3557
νόσων   noun, gen. pl. fem. {2.B} . . . . νόσος G3554
νοσῶν   vbl., pres. act. ptc. nom. sg. masc.
   {6.A.2} . . . . νοσέω G3552
νότον   noun, acc. sg. masc. {2.B} . . . . νότος G3558

G3558 **νότος**, -ου, ὁ   *the south wind;* hence, *the south.*

νότου   noun, gen. sg. masc. {2.B} . . . . νότος G3558

G3559 **νουθεσία**, -ας, ἡ   *a warning, admonition.*

νουθεσίᾳ   noun, dat. sg. fem. {2.A} . . . . νουθεσία G3559
νουθεσίαν   noun, acc. sg. fem. {2.A} . . . . id.
νουθετεῖν   vbl., pres. act. inf. {6.B.2} . . . νουθετέω G3560
νουθετεῖτε   verb, pres. act. impv. 2 pers. pl. {5.D.2} id.

G3560 **νουθετέω**   *I admonish, warn.*

νουθετοῦντας   vbl., pres. act. ptc. acc. pl. masc.
   {6.A.2} . . . . νουθετέω G3560
νουθετοῦντες   vbl., pres. act. ptc. nom. pl.
   masc. {6.A.2} . . . . id.
νουθετῶ   verb, pres. act. indic. 1 pers. sg. {5.A.2} id.
νουθετῶν   vbl., pres. act. ptc. nom. sg. masc.
   {6.A.2} . . . . id.

G3561 **νουμηνία** (νεομηνία), -ας, ἡ   *a new moon.*

νουμηνίας   noun, gen. sg. fem. {2.A} . . . νουμηνία G3561
νοῦν   noun, acc. sg. masc. {2.C} . . . . νοῦς G3563

G3562 **νουνεχῶς**   adv., *reasonably, sensibly.*

νουνεχῶς   adv. {3.F} . . . . νουνεχῶς G3562

G3563 **νοῦς**, νοός, ὁ   *the intellectual faculty* of the natural man, applicable to God or Christ (Rom 11:34; 1 Cor 2:16), employed in practical judgment, capable of being good or evil, and of being regenerated; *the mind, the reason, the reasoning faculty* (a non-Semitic Gk. term, meaning in Plato *reason, intuition,* sometimes in the LXX taking the place of the commoner καρδία as a rendering of Heb. *lēb*).

νοῦς   noun, nom. sg. masc. {2.C} . . . . νοῦς G3563
νύκτα   noun, acc. sg. fem. {2.C} . . . . νύξ G3571
νύκτας   noun, acc. pl. fem. {2.C} . . . . id.
νυκτί   noun, dat. sg. fem. {2.C} . . . . id.
νυκτός   noun, gen. sg. fem. {2.C} . . . . id.

G3564 **Νύμφα** (Νυμφᾶς)   *Nympha,* a woman's name, a pet form of Νυμφόδωρος, Nymphas, Nymphodorus (if we read Νύμφαν and αὐτῆς in Col 4:15, as we probably should); or Νυμφᾶν, the acc. of the masc. name Νυμφᾶς.

Νύμφαν   noun prop., acc. sg. masc. {2.A;
   2.D} . . . . Νύμφα G3564
Νύμφαν   noun prop., acc. sg. fem. {2.A; 2.D} . . . id.

G3565 **νύμφη**, -ης, ἡ   (1) *a bride;* hence, in the symbolism of Rev, the New Jerusalem, the Lamb's Bride; (2) *a daughter-in-law,* Matt 10:35; Luke 12:53.

νύμφη   noun, nom. sg. fem. {2.A} . . . . νύμφη G3565
νύμφην   noun, acc. sg. fem. {2.A} . . . . id.
νύμφης   noun, gen. sg. fem. {2.A} . . . . id.
νυμφίον   noun, acc. sg. masc. {2.B} . . . . νυμφίος G3566

G3566 **νυμφίος**, -ου, ὁ   *a bridegroom;* name applied to the Messiah, Mark 2:19, 20 and parallels.

νυμφίος   noun, nom. sg. masc. {2.B} . . . . νυμφίος G3566
νυμφίου   noun, gen. sg. masc. {2.B} . . . . id.

G3567 **νυμφών**, -ῶνος, ὁ   *a wedding chamber;* οἱ υἱοὶ νυμφῶνος (a Semitism), *the wedding guests,* the Messiah being spoken of as bridegroom, Mark 2:19 and parallels, cf. νυμφίος.

νυμφών   noun, nom. sg. masc. {2.C} . . . . .νυμφών G3567

νυμφῶνος   noun, gen. sg. masc. {2.C} . . . . id.

G3568 **νῦν**, adv.   *now, at present,* sometimes with article preceding, τὸ νῦν, τὰ νῦν, governed at times by preps., ἀπό, ἕως, ἄχρι.

νῦν   adv. . . . . νῦν G3568

G3570 **νυνί**, adv.   *now* (orig. a more emphatic νῦν).

νυνί   adv. . . . . .νυνί G3570

G3571 **νύξ**, νυκτός, ἡ   (1) *night;* νυκτός, διὰ νυκτός, *by night, sometime during the night,* see also ἡμέρα; (2) met. 1 Thess 5:5, etc.

νύξ   noun, nom. sg. fem. {2.C} . . . . νύξ G3571

G3572 **νύσσω**   *I prick.*

νυστάζει   verb, pres. act. indic. 3 pers. sg. {5.A.1.a} . . . . .νυστάζω G3573

G3573 **νυστάζω**   *I sleep, slumber;* met. 2 Pet 2:3.

νυστάξει   verb, fut. act. indic. 3 pers. sg. {5.A.1.a} . . . . .νυστάζω G3573

G3574 **νυχθήμερον**, -ου, τό   *a night and a day* (not necessarily more than the latter part of a night and the earlier part of the succeeding day).

νυχθήμερον   noun, acc. sg. neut. {2.B} . . . . νυχθήμερον G3574

G3575 **Νῶε**, ὁ   *Noah* (Heb.).

Νῶε   noun prop. . . . . Νῶε G3575

νωθροί   adj., nom. pl. masc. {3.A} . . . . . . νωθρός G3576

G3576 **νωθρός**, -ά, -όν   (1) *blunt, dull;* (2) hence spiritually, *sluggish, remiss, slack.*

νῶτον   noun, acc. sg. masc. {2.B} . . . . νῶτος G3577

G3577 **νῶτος**, -ου, ὁ   *the back.*

Ξ ξ

ξέναις   adj., dat. pl. fem. {3.A} . . . . .ξένος G3581

G3578 **ξενία**, -ας, ἡ   *a lodging,* or rather, abstr., *hospitality.*

ξενίαν   noun, acc. sg. fem. {2.A}. . . . . .ξενία G3578

ξενίζεσθε   verb, pres. pass. impv. 2 pers. pl. {5.D.1}. . . . . .ξενίζω G3579

ξενίζεται   verb, pres. pass. indic. 3 pers. sg. {5.A.1.d} . . . . id.

ξενίζοντα   vbl., pres. act. ptc. acc. pl. neut. {6.A.1}. . . . . id.

ξενίζονται   verb, pres. pass. indic. 3 pers. pl. {5.A.1.d} . . . . id.

G3579 **ξενίζω**   (1) *I entertain* a stranger; (2) *I startle, bewilder,* Acts 17:20; 1 Pet 4:4, 12.

ξενίσαντες   vbl., aor. act. ptc. nom. pl. masc. {6.A.1.a} . . . . .ξενίζω G3579

ξενισθῶμεν   verb, aor. pass. subjunc. 1 pers. pl. {5.B.1}. . . . . id.

G3580 **ξενοδοχέω**   *I receive (entertain) strangers.*

ξένοι   adj., nom. pl. masc. {3.A} . . . . .ξένος G3581

ξένοις   adj., dat. pl. masc. {3.A} . . . . id.

ξένον   adj., acc. sg. masc. {3.A}. . . . . id.

G3581 **ξένος**, -η, -ον   (1) adj., *foreign,* Acts 17:18; *strange, unusual,* Heb 13:9; 1 Pet 4:12; (2) noun, *a stranger, a foreigner* (either one belonging to another com munity in the same country, or to another country); *a resident alien,* without city rights, Acts 17:21; Eph 2:19; Heb 11:13; with gen. *a stranger to,* Eph 2:12; *a host (guest) friend,* the word indicating the reciprocal relationship, which was a sacred one, Rom 16:23.

ξένος   adj., nom. sg. masc. {3.A}. . . . . .ξένος G3581

ξένου   adj., gen. sg. neut. {3.A}. . . . . id.

ξένους   adj., acc. pl. masc. {3.A}. . . . . id.

ξένων   adj., gen. pl. neut. {3.A}. . . . . id.

G3582 **ξέστης**, -ου, ὁ   properly a Roman dry measure, rather less than a pint; referred to rather as a household *utensil* than as a measure (Lat. *sextarius*).

ξεστῶν   noun, gen. pl. masc. {2.A} . . . . . . .ξέστης G3582

ξηρά   adj., nom. sg. fem. {3.A} . . . . ξηρός G3584

ξηραίνεται   verb, pres. pass. indic. 3 pers. sg. {5.A.1.d} . . . . ξηραίνω G3583

G3583 **ξηραίνω**   *I dry up; parch.*

ξηράν   adj., acc. sg. fem. {3.A} . . . . ξηρός G3584

ξηρᾶς   adj., gen. sg. fem. {3.A} . . . . id.

G3584 **ξηρός**, -ά, -όν   *dry;* ἡ ξηρά, *dry land,* as opposed to sea, etc.; *dried up, withered, parched;* in generalizing neut., Luke 23:31.

ξηρῷ   adj., dat. sg. neut. {3.A}. . . . . ξηρός G3584

ξηρῶν   adj., gen. pl. masc. {3.A}. . . . . id.

ξύλα   noun, acc. pl. neut. {2.B} . . . . ξύλον G3586

ξύλινα   adj., acc. pl. neut. {3.A} . . . . .ξύλινος G3585

ξύλινα   adj., nom. pl. neut. {3.A} . . . . id.

G3585 **ξύλινος**, -η, -ον   *made of wood.*

G3586 **ξύλον**, -ου, τό   *wood, a piece of wood;* hence, *a club, a staff,* Mark 14:43, 48 and parallels; *the trunk of a tree,* used to support the crossbar of a cross in crucifixion, Acts 5:30, etc.; *a tree,* Luke 23:31, ζωῆς, the fruit of which gives life, Rev 2:7; 22:2, 14, 19.

ξύλον   noun, acc. sg. neut. {2.B}. . . . . .ξύλον G3586

ξύλον   noun, nom. sg. neut. {2.B}. . . . . id.

ξύλου   noun, gen. sg. neut. {2.B} . . . . id.

ξύλῳ   noun, dat. sg. neut. {2.B} . . . . id.

ξύλων   noun, gen. pl. neut. {2.B} . . . . id.

ξυρᾶσθαι   vbl., pres. mid./pass. inf. {6.B.2} .ξυράω G3587

G3587 **ξυράω**   *I shave,* mid. and pass. *I have* my head *shaved.*

ξυρήσονται   verb, fut. mid. indic. 3 pers. pl. {5.A.1}. . . . . .ξυράω G3587

ξυρήσωνται   verb, aor. mid. subjunc. 3 pers. pl. {5.B.1}. . . . . id.

O o

o   art., nom. sg. masc. {1} . . . . ὁ G3588

G3588 ὁ, ἡ, τό   the def. article, by which the following word is defined more precisely or exactly
than it would be (but it is often omitted, for
example, after a prep., even where a definite
place is intended, cf. ἐν οἴκῳ, *in the house,*
Mark 2:1, ἐν ἀγορᾷ, *in the marketplace,* Luke
7:32, ἐν συναγωγῇ, *in church,* John 6:59;
18:20). It is thus found (1) with common
nouns (e.g., ὁ ἀγρός, *the field;* cf. ἀγρός, *a*
field; in Titus 2:13 the absence of τοῦ before
σωτῆρος shows that Christ Jesus is our great
God and Savior), and (2) sometimes also
with proper nouns, where it was equivalent to
pointing out a man, and was popular in origin;
(3) with the voc., commonest where translated
from Semitic; (4) with adjectives, e.g., ὁ
ἄλλος, *the other* (ἄλλος, *another*), ὁ αὐτός,
the same (αὐτός, *he, self*), ὁ πᾶς, πᾶς ὁ, *the*
whole (πᾶς, *every*); (4) with numerals, e.g., ὁ
εἷς *the* one (εἷς, *one*), ὁ πρῶτος, *the first, the*
former (πρῶτος, *first*); (5) with participles,
e.g., τοῖς καθημένοις, *those seated,* Matt 4:16,
cf. instances where a ptc. may be regarded as
understood, e.g., Σαῦλος ὁ καὶ Παῦλος,
Saul who was also called Paul, Saul, otherwise
Paul, Acts 13:9; (6) with the inf., making it
a subs., and so capable of being governed by
preps.; see below also; (7) with advs., e.g., τὸ
πέραν, *the other side* (πέραν, *beyond*), τὸ
νῦν, τὰ νῦν; (8) with interjections, e.g., τὸ
ἀμήν, ἡ οὐαί; (9) with a clause or phrase,
e.g., τὸ οὐ φονεύσεις, *the command, "you*
shall do no murder," Matt 19:18. The gen. sg.
neut. τοῦ with the inf. is used in three special
ways (like ἵνα): (a) as in classical Gk., indicating purpose, final, telic, *in order that* (never in
Paul); (b) indicating consequence, epexegetic,
so that, so as to, with the result that, e.g., Rom
1:24; 7:3; 8:12; 1 Cor 10:13; Rev 12:7; (c)
introducing a noun clause, indicating content,
in no way different from τό, Matt 21:32; Luke
17:1; Acts 10:25; Jas 5:17. Orig. a dem. pron.,
as in τοῦ γένος ἐσμέν, *we are descended from*
Him, Acts 17:28, cf. ὁ μέν . . . ὁ δέ (ἄλλος
δέ), *the one . . . the other.* But in the following
phrases some word is understood, ὁ τινός,
the son of so and so, cf. Matt 4:21, ἡ τινός, *the*
daughter (wife) of so and so, ἐν τοῖς τινός, *in*
the house of so and so, Luke 2:49.

ὁ   art., nom. sg. masc. {1} . . . . ὁ G3588
ὅ   art., nom. sg. masc. {1} . . . . id.
ὅ   pron. rel., acc. sg. neut. {4.C} . . . . ὅς G3739
ὅ   pron. rel., nom. sg. neut. {4.C} . . . . id.

G3603‡ ὅ ἐστι(ν)   *which is.*
ὀγδόη   adj., dat. sg. fem. {3.A} . . . . .ὄγδοος G3590

G3589 ὀγδοήκοντα   *eighty.*
ὀγδοήκοντα   adj. num. . . . . ὀγδοήκοντα G3589
ὄγδοον   adj., acc. sg. masc. {3.A} . . . . .ὄγδοος G3590

G3590 ὄγδοος, -η, -ον   *eighth.*
ὄγδοος   adj., nom. sg. masc. {3.A} . . . . ὄγδοος G3590
ὄγκον   noun, acc. sg. masc. {2.B} . . . . .ὄγκος G3591

G3591 ὄγκος, -ου, ὁ   (properly *bulk, mass*), hence, *a*
burden.

G3592 ὅδε, ἥδε, τόδε   *this here, this;* also as pron.
ὅδε   pron. dem., nom. sg. masc. {4.B} . . . . .ὅδε G3592

G3593 ὁδεύω   *I am on a journey.*
ὁδεύων   vbl., pres. act. ptc. nom. sg. masc.
   {6.A.1} . . . . ὁδεύω G3593
ὁδηγεῖ   verb, pres. act. indic. 3 pers. sg.
   {5.A.2} . . . . ὁδηγέω G3594
ὁδηγεῖν   vbl., pres. act. inf. {6.B.2} . . . . id.

G3594 ὁδηγέω   *I lead, guide.*
ὁδηγῇ   verb, pres. act. subjunc. 3 pers. sg.
   {5.B.2} . . . . ὁδηγέω G3594
ὁδηγήσει   verb, fut. act. indic. 3 pers. sg. {5.A.1} id.
ὁδηγήσῃ   verb, aor. act. subjunc. 3 pers. sg. {5.B.1} id.
ὁδηγοί   noun, nom. pl. masc. {2.B} . . . . . . .ὁδηγός G3595
ὁδηγοί   noun, voc. pl. masc. {2.B} . . . . id.
ὁδηγόν   noun, acc. sg. masc. {2.B} . . . . id.

G3595 ὁδηγός, -οῦ, ὁ   *a guide.*
ὁδηγοῦ   noun, gen. sg. masc. {2.B} . . . . . . .ὁδηγός G3595
ὁδοί   noun, nom. pl. fem. {2.B} . . . . ὁδός G3598

G3596 ὁδοιπορέω   *I am on a journey, I journey.*

G3597 ὁδοιπορία, -ας, ἡ   *journeying, traveling, travel.*
ὁδοιπορίαις   noun, dat. pl. fem. {2.A} . .ὁδοιπορία G3597
ὁδοιπορίας   noun, gen. sg. fem. {2.A} . . . . id.
ὁδοιπορούντων   vbl., pres. act. ptc. gen. pl. masc.
   {6.A.2} . . . . ὁδοιπορέω G3596
ὁδοῖς   noun, dat. pl. fem. {2.B} . . . . ὁδός G3598
ὁδόν   noun, acc. sg. fem. {2.B} . . . . id.
ὀδόντα   noun, acc. sg. masc. {2.C} . . . . ὀδούς G3599
ὀδόντας   noun, acc. pl. masc. {2.C} . . . . id.
ὀδόντες   noun, nom. pl. masc. {2.C} . . . . id.
ὀδόντος   noun, gen. sg. masc. {2.C} . . . . id.
ὀδόντων   noun, gen. pl. masc. {2.C} . . . . id.

G3598 ὁδός, -οῦ, ἡ   (1) *a road;* (2) *a journey;* hence
met., *a way of life, a course of conduct,* and ἡ
ὁδός, *the way* of life, Christianity, Acts 9:2, etc.
ὁδός   noun, nom. sg. fem. {2.B} . . . . ὁδός G3598
ὁδοῦ   noun, gen. sg. fem. {2.B} . . . . id.

G3599 ὀδούς, ὀδόντος, ὁ   *a tooth.*
ὀδούς   noun, acc. pl. fem. {2.B} . . . . ὁδός G3598
ὀδύναις   noun, dat. pl. fem. {2.A} . . . . ὀδύνη G3601
ὀδυνᾶσαι   verb, pres. pass. indic. 2 pers. sg.
   {5.A.2} . . . . ὀδυνάω G3600

G3600 ὀδυνάω   pass. *I suffer acute pain,* physical or
mental.

G3601 ὀδύνη, -ης, ἡ   *acute mental pain.*
ὀδύνη   noun, nom. sg. fem. {2.A} . . . . ὀδύνη G3601
ὀδυνῶμαι   verb, pres. pass. indic. 1 pers. sg.
   {5.A.2} . . . . ὀδυνάω G3600

ὀδυνώμενοι vbl., pres. pass. ptc. nom. pl.
masc. {6.A.2}. . . . . id.
ὀδυρμόν noun, acc. sg. masc. {2.B} . . . . . ὀδυρμός G3602
G3602 ὀδυρμός, -οῦ, ὁ mourning, grieving.
ὀδυρμός noun, nom. sg. masc. {2.B} . . . ὀδυρμός G3602
ὁδῷ noun, dat. sg. fem. {2.B} . . . . ὁδός G3598
ὁδῶν noun, gen. pl. fem. {2.B} . . . . id.
ὄζει verb, pres. act. indic. 3 pers. sg. {5.A.1.a} . ὄζω G3605
Ὀζείαν noun prop., acc. sg. masc. {2.A;
2.D}. . . . . Ὀζίας G3604
Ὀζείας noun prop., nom. sg. masc. {2.A; 2.D}. . id.
Ὀζίαν noun prop., acc. sg. masc. {2.A; 2.D} . . . id.
G3604 Ὀζίας, -ου, ὁ Uzziah, son of Joram and father
of Joatham, and king of Judah from about 785
to 746 B.C., an ancestor of Jesus (Heb.).
Ὀζίας noun prop., nom. sg. masc. {2.A;
2.D}. . . . . Ὀζίας G3604
G3605 ὄζω intrans., I smell, am fetid.
G3606 ὅθεν adv., (1) local, whence, from which place;
(2) inferential, wherefore.
ὅθεν adv. correl. {4.D} . . . . ὅθεν G3606
G3607 ὀθόνη, -ης, ἡ a sheet, made of fine linen (a
word of Semitic origin).
ὀθόνην noun, acc. sg. fem. {2.A} . . . . ὀθόνη G3607
ὀθόνια noun, acc. pl. neut. {2.B} . . . . . . .ὀθόνιον G3608
ὀθονίοις noun, dat. pl. neut. {2.B}. . . . . id.
G3608 ὀθόνιον, -ου, τό a bandage, a wrapping (see
ὀθόνη).
ὀθονίων noun, gen. pl. neut. {2.B}. . . . . .ὀθόνιον G3608
οἱ art., nom. pl. masc. {1}. . . . . ὁ G3588
οἵ art., nom. pl. masc. {1}. . . . . id.
οἵ pron. rel., nom. pl. masc. {4.C}. . . . . .ὅς G3739
οἷα pron. correl., acc. pl. neut. {4.D} . . . . . . .οἷος G3634
οἵα pron. correl., nom. sg. fem. {4.D}. . . . . id.
οἷα pron. correl., acc. pl. neut. {4.D} . . . . id.
οἷα pron. correl., nom. pl. neut. {4.D} . . . . id.
οἶδα verb, ²perf. act. indic. 1 pers. sg. {5.A.1.c} εἴδω G1492
οἴδαμεν verb, ²perf. act. indic. 1 pers. pl.
{5.A.1.c} . . . . id.
οἶδας verb, ²perf. act. indic. 2 pers. sg. {5.A.1.c}. id.
οἴδασι verb, ²perf. act. indic. 3 pers. pl. {5.A.1.c}id.
οἴδασιν verb, ²perf. act. indic. 3 pers. pl.
{5.A.1.c} . . . . id.
οἴδατε verb, ²perf. act. indic. 2 pers. pl. {5.A.1.c}id.
οἶδε verb, ²perf. act. indic. 3 pers. sg. {5.A.1.c}. . id.
οἶδεν verb, ²perf. act. indic. 3 pers. sg. {5.A.1.c}. id.
οἰέσθω verb, pres. mid./pass. impv. 3 pers. sg.
{5.D.1}. . . . . .οἴομαι G3633
οἰκεῖ verb, pres. act. indic. 3 pers. sg. {5.A.2} .οἰκέω G3611
οἰκειακοί adj., nom. pl. masc. {3.A} . . . . οἰκιακός G3615
οἰκειακούς adj., acc. pl. masc. {3.C} . . . . id.
οἰκεῖν vbl., pres. act. inf. {6.B.2}. . . . . .οἰκέω G3611
οἰκεῖοι adj., nom. pl. masc. {3.A}. . . . . . . οἰκεῖος G3609
G3609 οἰκεῖος, -ου, ὁ (from οἶκος, household, family), of one's family, intimate, 1 Tim 5:8; hence
met.
οἰκείους adj., acc. pl. masc. {3.A} . . . . . οἰκεῖος G3609
οἰκείων adj., gen. pl. masc. {3.A} . . . . id.
οἰκέται noun, nom. pl. masc. {2.A} . . . . . . οἰκέτης G3610
οἰκέται noun, voc. pl. masc. {2.A} . . . . . . οἰκέτης G3610

G2322†‡ οἰκετεία, -ας, ἡ a household of slaves. Var. for
θεραπεία, Matt 24:45.
οἰκετείας noun, gen. sg. fem. {2.A} . . . . οἰκετεία G2322†‡
οἰκέτην noun, acc. sg. masc. {2.A}. . . . . . οἰκέτης G3610
G3610 οἰκέτης, -ου, ὁ a household slave, a slave.
οἰκέτης noun, nom. sg. masc. {2.A}. . . . . οἰκέτης G3610
οἰκέτου noun, gen. sg. masc. {2.A} . . . . id.
οἰκετῶν noun, gen. pl. masc. {2.A} . . . . id.
G3611 οἰκέω I dwell, lit. and met.; with acc. I inhabit.
G3612 οἴκημα, -ατος, τό a prison (euphemism for
δεσμωτήριον).
οἰκήματι noun, dat. sg. neut. {2.C} . . . . . οἴκημα G3612
G3613 οἰκητήριον, -ου, τό a dwelling place, lit. and
met.
οἰκητήριον noun, acc. sg. neut. {2.B} .οἰκητήριον G3613
G3614 οἰκία, -ας, ἡ a house (strictly the whole house,
see οἶκος); of Heaven, John 14:2; also met.
property, belongings, Mark 12:40 and parallels;
household, John 4:53; of the body, 2 Cor 5:1, 2.
οἰκία noun, dat. sg. fem. {2.A}. . . . . .οἰκία G3614
οἰκία noun, nom. sg. fem. {2.A}. . . . . id.
οἰκία noun, dat. sg. fem. {2.A}. . . . . id.
οἰκιακοί noun, nom. pl. masc. {2.B} . . . . οἰκιακός G3615
G3615 οἰκιακός, -οῦ, ὁ a member of one's household.
οἰκιακούς noun, acc. pl. masc. {2.B} . . . . οἰκιακός G3615
οἰκίαν noun, acc. sg. fem. {2.A}. . . . . .οἰκία G3614
οἰκίας noun, acc. pl. fem. {2.A}. . . . . id.
οἰκίας noun, gen. sg. fem. {2.A}. . . . . id.
οἰκιῶν noun, gen. pl. fem. {2.A} . . . . id.
οἰκοδεσποτεῖν vbl., pres. act. inf.
{6.B.2} . . . . οἰκοδεσποτέω G3616
G3616 οἰκοδεσποτέω I am master/mistress of a house.
οἰκοδεσπότῃ noun, dat. sg. masc.
{2.A} . . . . .οἰκοδεσπότης G3617
οἰκοδεσπότην noun, acc. sg. masc. {2.A} . . . . . id.
G3617 οἰκοδεσπότης, -ου, ὁ a master of a house, a
head of a house.
οἰκοδεσπότης noun, nom. sg. masc.
{2.A} . . . . .οἰκοδεσπότης G3617
οἰκοδεσπότου noun, gen. sg. masc. {2.A} . . . . . id.
οἰκοδομαί noun, nom. pl. fem. {2.A} . . οἰκοδομή G3619
οἰκοδομάς noun, acc. pl. fem. {2.A} . . . . id.
οἰκοδομεῖ verb, pres. act. indic. 3 pers. sg.
{5.A.2}. . . . . οἰκοδομέω G3618
οἰκοδομεῖν vbl., pres. act. inf. {6.B.2} . . . . id.
οἰκοδομεῖσθε verb, pres. pass. indic. 2 pers. pl.
{5.A.2}. . . . . id.
οἰκοδομεῖται verb, pres. pass. indic. 3 pers. sg.
{5.A.2}. . . . . id.
οἰκοδομεῖτε verb, pres. act. impv. 2 pers. pl.
{5.D.2}. . . . . id.
οἰκοδομεῖτε verb, pres. act. indic. 2 pers. pl.
{5.A.2}. . . . . id.
G3618 οἰκοδομέω I build (a house); hence met.
G3619 οἰκοδομή, -ῆς, ἡ (1) abstr., building, the operation (process) of building, sometimes transi-
tional, without being strictly concr., 1 Cor 3:9;
2 Cor 5:1; Eph 2:21; 4:12, 16, 29 (here perhaps =
improvement); (2) met. upbuilding, edification;
(3) concr., a building, Mark 13:1, 2; Matt 24:1.

οἰκοδομή   noun, nom. sg. fem. {2.A} . . . οἰκοδομή G3619
οἰκοδομήθη   verb, aor. pass. indic. 3 pers. sg.
    {5.A.1}. . . . . οἰκοδομέω G3618
οἰκοδομηθήσεται   verb, fut. pass. indic.
    3 pers. sg. {5.A.1}. . . . . id.
οἰκοδομήν   noun, acc. sg. fem. {2.A} . . . οἰκοδομή G3619
οἰκοδομῆς   noun, gen. sg. fem. {2.A}. . . . . id.
οἰκοδομῆσαι   vbl., aor. act. inf. {6.B.1} οἰκοδομέω G3618
οἰκοδομήσαντι   vbl., aor. act. ptc. dat. sg.
    masc. {6.A.2}. . . . . id.
οἰκοδόμησεν   verb, aor. act. indic. 3 pers. sg.
    {5.A.1}. . . . . id.
οἰκοδομήσετε   verb, fut. act. indic. 2 pers. pl.
    {5.A.1}. . . . . id.
οἰκοδομῆσθαι   vbl., perf. pass. inf. {6.B.1}. . . . id.
οἰκοδομήσω   verb, fut. act. indic. 1 pers. sg.
    {5.A.1}. . . . . id.
G3620   **οἰκοδομία**, -ας, ἡ   *building* (the process or the
    product), fig., *edification*. Var. for οἰκονομία
    in 1 Tim 1:4.
οἰκοδομίαν   noun, acc. sg. fem. {2.A} . .οἰκοδομία G3620
G3618†‡   **οἰκοδόμος**, -ου, ὁ   *a house builder, a builder.*
    Var. for οἰκοδομέω, Acts 4:11.
οἰκοδομούμεναι   vbl., pres. pass. ptc. nom. pl.
    fem. {6.A.2}. . . . . οἰκοδομέω G3618
οἰκοδομουμένη   vbl., pres. pass. ptc. nom. sg.
    fem. {6.A.2}. . . . . id.
οἰκοδομοῦντες   vbl., pres. act. ptc. nom. pl.
    masc. {6.A.2}. . . . . id.
οἰκοδομοῦντι   vbl., pres. act. ptc. dat. sg. masc.
    {6.A.2}. . . . . id.
οἰκοδομούντων   vbl., pres. act. ptc. gen. pl.
    masc. {6.A.2}. . . . . id.
οἰκοδομῶ   verb, pres. act. indic. 1 pers. sg.
    {5.A.2}. . . . . id.
οἰκοδομῶ   verb, pres. act. subjunc. 1 pers. sg.
    {5.B.2}. . . . . id.
οἰκοδόμων   noun, gen. pl. masc. {2.B} οἰκοδόμος G3618†‡
οἰκοδομῶν   vbl., pres. act. ptc. nom. sg. masc.
    {6.A.2}. . . . . οἰκοδομέω G3618
οἴκοις   noun, dat. pl. masc. {2.B} . . . . .οἶκος G3624
οἶκον   noun, acc. sg. masc. {2.B}. . . . . id.
οἰκονομεῖν   vbl., pres. act. inf. {6.B.2} . οἰκονομέω G3621
G3621   **οἰκονομέω**   *I am a steward, I do the work* of a
    steward.
G3622   **οἰκονομία**, -ας, ἡ   *household management,*
    stewardship, the office of a steward; hence met.
    of any position of trust or the duties of that
    position, *provision, arrangement, dispensa-*
    tion (even God being sometimes regarded as
    steward).
οἰκονομία   noun, nom. sg. fem. {2.A} . οἰκονομία G3622
οἰκονομίαν   noun, acc. sg. fem. {2.A} . . . . id.
οἰκονομίας   noun, gen. sg. fem. {2.A} . . . . id.
οἰκονόμοι   noun, nom. pl. masc. {2.B} οἰκονόμος G3623
οἰκονόμοις   noun, dat. pl. masc. {2.B} . . . . id.
οἰκονόμον   noun, acc. sg. masc. {2.B} . . . . id.
G3623   **οἰκονόμος**, -ου, ὁ   (1) *a steward* (commonly a
    superior slave of tried character, who looked

after the accounts of a household; hence met.
1 Cor 4:1, 2; Titus 1:7; 1 Pet 4:10; (2) apparently, *City Steward* or *Treasurer,* Rom 16:23;
(3) perhaps not to be separated from (1), *a*
guardian, a legal guardian, Gal 4:2. In any case
he manages the property of the "infant" till the
age of 25, perhaps.
οἰκονόμος   noun, nom. sg. masc. {2.B} οἰκονόμος G3623
οἰκονόμους   noun, acc. pl. masc. {2.B} . . . . id.
G3624   **οἶκος**, -ου, ὁ   (1) *a house,* the material building
    (strictly *a set of rooms,* see οἰκία); οἶκος τοῦ
    θεοῦ, the Temple at Jerusalem, Mark 2:26, etc.
    (referred to in Matt 23:38); (2) hence met., *a*
    household, family; οἶκος Ἰσραήλ, Ἰακώβ,
    Δαυίδ (Hebraic, note the omission of the
    article).
οἶκος   noun, nom. sg. masc. {2.B}. . . . . .οἶκος G3624
οἶκος   noun, voc. sg. masc. {2.B} . . . . .οἶκος G3624
οἴκου   noun, gen. sg. masc. {2.B} . . . . id.
G3625   **οἰκουμένη**, -ης, ἡ   (properly pres. pass. ptc.
    of οἰκέω, with γῆ understood, *the land that is*
    being inhabited, the land in a state of habita-
    tion), *the inhabited world,* i.e., *the Roman*
    world, for all outside it was regarded as of no
    account.
οἰκουμένη   noun, nom. sg. fem. {2.A} . οἰκουμένη G3625
οἰκουμένη   noun, dat. sg. fem. {2.A} . . . . id.
οἰκουμένην   noun, acc. sg. fem. {2.A} . . . . id.
οἰκουμένης   noun, gen. sg. fem. {2.A} . . . . id.
οἰκουργούς   adj., acc. pl. fem. {3.C} . . . . οἰκουρός G3626
G3626   **οἰκουρός** (οἰκουργός), -όν   *staying at home; a*
    housekeeper, a house worker, Titus 2:5.
οἰκουρούς   adj., acc. pl. fem. {3.C}. . . . . οἰκουρός G3626
οἴκους   noun, acc. pl. masc. {2.B}. . . . . .οἶκος G3624
οἰκοῦσα   vbl., pres. act. ptc. nom. sg. fem.
    {6.A.2}. . . . . .οἰκέω G3611
οἰκτειρήσω   verb, fut. act. indic. 1 pers. sg.
    {5.A.1.a} . . . . οἰκτείρω G3627
G3627   **οἰκτείρω** (οἰκτίρω)   *I pity.*
οἰκτείρω   verb, pres. act. subjunc. 1 pers. sg.
    {5.B.1} . . . . οἰκτείρω G3627
οἰκτιρήσω   verb, fut. act. indic. 1 pers. sg.
    {5.A.1.a} . . . . id.
οἰκτιρμοί   noun, nom. pl. masc. {2.B} . οἰκτιρμός G3628
οἰκτίρμονες   adj., nom. pl. masc. {3.E}. οἰκτίρμων G3629
G3628   **οἰκτιρμός**, -οῦ, ὁ   *pity, mercy;* the frequency
    of the pl. is due to Hebric influence (the cor-
    responding Heb. word has the same meaning
    in the pl.).
οἰκτιρμοῦ   noun, gen. sg. masc. {2.B}. . . οἰκτιρμός G3628
G3629   **οἰκτίρμων**, -ον   *pitiful, merciful.*
οἰκτίρμων   adj., nom. sg. masc. {3.E} . .οἰκτίρμων G3629
οἰκτιρμῶν   noun, gen. pl. masc. {2.B}. . . οἰκτιρμός G3628
οἰκτίρω   verb, pres. act. subjunc. 1 pers. sg.
    {5.B.1} . . . . .οἰκτείρω G3627
οἴκῳ   noun, dat. sg. masc. {2.B} . . . . .οἶκος G3624
οἴκων   noun, gen. pl. masc. {2.B} . . . . .οἶκος G3624
οἰκῶν   vbl., pres. act. ptc. nom. sg. masc.
    {6.A.2}. . . . . .οἰκέω G3611

οἶμαι   verb, pres. mid./pass. indic. 1 pers. sg.
    {5.A.1.d} . . . . .οἴομαι *G3633*
οἶνον   noun, acc. sg. masc. {2.B} . . . . .οἶνος *G3631*
G3630 **οἰνοπότης**, -ου, ὁ   *an excessive wine drinker.*
    οἰνοπότης   noun, nom. sg. masc. {2.A} .οἰνοπότης *G3630*
G3631 **οἶνος**, -ου, ὁ   *wine;* met. Rev (except 6:6;
    18:13), where almost otiose.
    οἶνος   noun, nom. sg. masc. {2.B} . . . . .οἶνος *G3631*
    οἴνου   noun, gen. sg. masc. {2.B} . . . . id.
G3632 **οἰνοφλυγία**, -ας, ἡ   *drunkenness,* steeping of
    oneself in wine.
    οἰνοφλυγίαις   noun, dat. pl. fem. {2.A}οἰνοφλυγία *G3632*
    οἴνῳ   noun, dat. sg. masc. {2.B} . . . . .οἶνος *G3631*
    οἶοι   pron. correl., nom. pl. masc. {4.D} . . . . . .οἷος *G3634*
G3633 **οἴομαι** (οἶμαι)   *I think;* with inf. the underly-
    ing idea is that of purpose, Phil 1:17.
    οἰόμενοι   vbl., pres. mid./pass. ptc. nom. pl. masc.
    {6.A.1} . . . . .οἴομαι *G3633*
    οἶον   pron. correl., acc. sg. masc. {4.D} . . . . . .οἷος *G3634*
    οἶον   pron. correl., nom. sg. neut. {4.D} . . . . id.
G3634 **οἷος**, -α, -ον   rel. and indir. interrog., *such as, of*
    what kind (character); οὐχ οἷον δὲ ὅτι, Rom
    9:6, is equivalent to a strong negative, *not of*
    course (lit. *it is not so that*). Properly correla-
    tive to τοιοῦτος, the combined expression
    meaning *of such a kind as,* 1 Cor 15:48; by
    itself.
    οἷος   pron. correl., nom. sg. masc. {4.D} . . . . . .οἷος *G3634*
    οἵου   pron. correl., gen. sg. neut. {4.D} . . . . id.
    οἵους   pron. correl., acc. pl. masc. {4.D} . . . . id.
    οἷς   pron. rel., dat. pl. masc. {4.C} . . . . .ὅς *G3739*
    οἷς   pron. rel., dat. pl. neut. {4.C} . . . . id.
    οἴσει   verb, fut. act. indic. 3 pers. sg. {5.A.1.a} φέρω *G5342*
    οἴσουσι   verb, fut. act. indic. 3 pers. pl. {5.A.1.a} id.
    οἴσουσιν   verb, fut. act. indic. 3 pers. pl.
    {5.A.1.a} . . . . id.
    οἵτινες   pron. indef. rel., nom. pl. masc. {4.C} ὅστις *G3748*
G3635 **ὀκνέω**   *I shrink (from), I hesitate, I am afraid.*
    ὀκνηρέ   adj., voc. sg. masc. {3.A} . . . . ὀκνηρός *G3636*
    ὀκνηροί   adj., nom. pl. masc. {3.A} . . . . id.
    ὀκνηρόν   adj., nom. sg. neut. {3.A} . . . . id.
G3636 **ὀκνηρός**, -ά, -όν   *timid; slothful;* ἐμοὶ οὐκ
    ὀκνηρόν, a kind of epistolary formula, *I do*
    not hesitate.
    ὀκνῆσαι   vbl., aor. act. inf. {6.B.1} . . . . ὀκνέω *G3635*
    ὀκνήσῃς   verb, aor. act. subjunc. 2 pers. sg.
    {5.B.1} . . . . id.
G3637 **ὀκταήμερος**, -ον   *eight days old.*
    ὀκταήμερος   adj., nom. sg. masc.
    {3.C} . . . . ὀκταήμερος *G3637*
G3638 **ὀκτώ**   *eight.*
    ὀκτώ   adj. num.. ὀκτώ *G3638*
    ὄλεθρον   noun, acc. sg. masc. {2.B} . . . . . ὄλεθρος *G3639*
G3639 **ὄλεθρος**, -ου, ὁ   *ruin, doom, destruction.*
    ὄλεθρος   noun, nom. sg. masc. {2.B} . . . . ὄλεθρος *G3639*
    ὅλη   adj., nom. sg. fem. {3.A} . . . . ὅλος *G3650*
    ὅλη   adj., dat. sg. fem. {3.A} . . . . id.
    ὅλῃ   adj., nom. sg. fem. {3.A} . . . . id.
    ὅλην   adj., acc. sg. fem. {3.A} . . . . id.
    ὅλης   adj., gen. sg. fem. {3.A} . . . . id.

ὀλίγα   adj., acc. pl. neut. {3.A} . . . . ὀλίγος *G3641*
ὀλίγαι   adj., nom. pl. fem. {3.A} . . . . id.
ὀλίγας   adj., acc. pl. fem. {3.A} . . . . id.
ὀλίγην   adj., acc. sg. fem. {3.A} . . . . id.
ὀλίγης   adj., gen. sg. fem. {3.A} . . . . id.
ὀλίγοι   adj., nom. pl. masc. {3.A} . . . . id.
ὀλίγοις   adj., dat. pl. masc. {3.A} . . . . id.
ὀλίγον   adj., acc. sg. masc. {3.A} . . . . id.
ὀλίγον   adj., acc. sg. neut. {3.A} . . . . id.
ὀλίγον   adj., nom. sg. neut. {3.A} . . . . id.
ὀλίγον   adv. {3.F} . . . . id.
ὀλιγόπιστε   adj., voc. sg. masc. {3.C} . ὀλιγόπιστος *G3640*
G570†‡ **ὀλιγοπιστία**, -ας, ἡ   *smallness of belief (faith).*
    Var. of ἀπιστία, Matt 17:20.
    ὀλιγοπιστίαν   noun, acc. sg. fem.
    {2.A} . . . . ὀλιγοπιστία *G570†‡*
    ὀλιγόπιστοι   adj., voc. pl. masc. {3.C} ὀλιγόπιστος *G3640*
G3640 **ὀλιγόπιστος**, -ον   *of little faith (belief).*
G3641 **ὀλίγος** (ὀλίγος), -η, -ον   (1) esp. in the pl.,
    few; (2) in the sg., *small;* hence, of time, *short,*
    of degree, *light, slight, little;* πρὸς ὀλίγον, *to*
    a slight degree, 1 Tim 4:8, *for a short time,* Jas
    4:14; ἐν ὀλίγῳ, *in brief compass, in brief, in*
    few words, briefly (cf. 1 Pet 5:12), Eph 3:3; Acts
    26:28 (perhaps = *in very short time*); ὀλίγον
    (acc. neut.), adverbially, of space, *a little,* Mark
    1:19; Luke 5:3, of time, *for a short (little) time,*
    Mark 6:31; 1 Pet 1:6 (but more probably, *to a*
    little amount), 5:10; Rev 17:10.
    ὀλίγος   adj., nom. sg. masc. {3.A} . . . . ὀλίγος *G3641*
    ὀλίγου   adj., gen. sg. masc. {3.A} . . . . id.
G3642 **ὀλιγόψυχος**, -ον   *pusillanimous, of small*
    courage.
    ὀλιγοψύχους   adj., acc. pl. masc. {3.C} ὀλιγόψυχος *G3642*
    ὀλίγῳ   adj., dat. sg. masc. {3.A} . . . . ὀλίγος *G3641*
    ὀλίγῳ   adj., dat. sg. neut. {3.A} . . . . id.
    ὀλίγων   adj., gen. pl. masc. {3.A} . . . . id.
    ὀλίγων   adj., gen. pl. neut. {3.A} . . . . id.
    ὀλιγώρει   verb, pres. act. impv. 2 pers. sg.
    {5.D.2} . . . . ὀλιγωρέω *G3643*
G3643 **ὀλιγωρέω**   *I hold in low esteem, I make light* of.
G3689†‡ **ὀλίγως**   adv., *slightly, just.* Var. for ὄντως, 2 Pet
    2:18.
    ὀλίγως   adv. {3.F} . . . . ὀλίγως *G3689†‡*
G3644 **ὀλοθρευτής**, -οῦ, ὁ   *the destroying angel* (cf.
    Num 16:41ff.).
    ὀλοθρευτοῦ   noun, gen. sg. masc.
    {2.A} . . . . ὀλοθρευτής *G3644*
G3645 **ὀλοθρεύω**   ὁ ὀλοθρεύων, *the Destroyer,*
    the destroying angel (cf. Exod 12:23, and
    ὀλοθρευτής).
    ὀλοθρεύων   vbl., pres. act. ptc. nom. sg. masc.
    {6.A.1} . . . . .ὀλοθρεύω *G3645*
G3646 **ὁλοκαύτωμα**, -ατος, τό   *a burnt offering.*
    ὁλοκαυτώματα   noun, acc. pl. neut.
    {2.C} . . . . ὁλοκαύτωμα *G3646*
    ὁλοκαυτωμάτων   noun, gen. pl. neut. {2.C} . . . id.
G3647 **ὁλοκληρία**, -ας, ἡ   *perfect (unimpaired) health.*
    ὁλοκληρίαν   noun, acc. sg. fem. {2.A}. ὁλοκληρία *G3647*
    ὁλόκληροι   adj., nom. pl. masc. {3.C} . ὁλόκληρος *G3648*

ὁλόκληρον   adj., nom. sg. neut. {3.C} . . . . id.

G3648   **ὁλόκληρος**, -ον   *complete* (in every part), *entire, whole* (properly a word of Gk. ritual, of either victim for sacrifice or priest, *free from bodily defect*).

ὀλολύζοντες   vbl., pres. act. ptc. nom. pl. masc. {6.A.1} . . . . ὀλολύζω G3649

G3649   **ὀλολύζω**   *I howl* (onomatopoeic).

ὅλον   adj., acc. sg. masc. {3.A} . . . . ὅλος G3650

ὅλον   adj., acc. sg. neut. {3.A} . . . . id.

ὅλον   adj., nom. sg. neut. {3.A} . . . . id.

G3650   **ὅλος**, -η, -ον   *whole, all;* δι᾽ ὅλου, *throughout, for its whole extent, quite, entirely,* John 19:23.

ὅλος   adj., nom. sg. masc. {3.A} . . . . ὅλος G3650

ὁλοτελεῖς   adj., acc. pl. masc. {3.E} . . . . . ὁλοτελής G3651

G3651   **ὁλοτελής**, -ές   *complete, rounded off.*

ὅλου   adj., gen. sg. masc. {3.A} . . . . ὅλος G3650

ὅλου   adj., gen. sg. neut. {3.A} . . . . id.

ὅλους   adj., acc. pl. masc. {3.A} . . . . id.

Ὀλυμπᾶν   noun prop., acc. sg. masc. {2.A; 2.D} . . . . Ὀλυμπᾶς G3652

G3652   **Ὀλυμπᾶς**, -ᾶ, ὁ   *Olympas,* a Christian man in Rome (probably a pet form of Ὀλυμπιόδωρος).

G3653   **ὄλυνθος**, -ου, ὁ   *an unripe fig.*

ὀλύνθους   noun, acc. pl. masc. {2.B} . . . . ὄλυνθος G3653

ὅλῳ   adj., dat. sg. masc. {3.A} . . . . ὅλος G3650

ὅλῳ   adj., dat. sg. neut. {3.A} . . . . id.

G3654   **ὅλως**   adv., (1) *entirely, altogether, at all;* (2) *actually,* 1 Cor 5:1; *absolutely,* 1 Cor 6:7; 15:29.

ὅλως   adv. {3.F} . . . . ὅλως G3654

G3655   **ὄμβρος**, -ου, ὁ   *a rainstorm.*

ὄμβρος   noun, nom. sg. masc. {2.B} . . . . . . ὄμβρος G3655

G2442†‡   **ὁμείρομαι**   *I long for.* Var. for ἱμείρομαι, 1 Thess 2:8.

ὁμειρόμενοι   vbl., pres. mid./pass. ptc. nom. pl. masc. {6.A.1} . . . . ὁμείρομαι G2442†‡

ὁμιλεῖν   vbl., pres. act. inf. {6.B.2} . . . . . . ὁμιλέω G3656

G3656   **ὁμιλέω**   *I consort with, associate with, commune with;* particularly, *I talk (converse) with,* Acts 20:11.

ὁμιλήσας   vbl., aor. act. ptc. nom. sg. masc. {6.A.2} . . . . ὁμιλέω G3656

G3657   **ὁμιλία**, -ας, ἡ   *intercourse, companionship, conversation.*

ὁμιλίαι   noun, nom. pl. fem. {2.A} . . . . ὁμιλία G3657

G3658   **ὅμιλος**, -ου, ὁ   *a crowd, throng* (var. in Rev 18:17).

ὅμιλος   noun, nom. sg. masc. {2.B} . . . . . . ὅμιλος G3658

ὁμίχλαι   noun, nom. pl. fem. {2.A} . . . . ὁμίχλη G3507†‡

G3507†‡   **ὁμίχλη**, -ης, ἡ   *a mist, fog.* Var. for νεφέλη, 2 Pet 2:17.

G3659   **ὄμμα**, -ατος, τό   *an eye.*

ὄμματα   noun, acc. pl. neut. {2.C} . . . . ὄμμα G3659

ὀμμάτων   noun, gen. pl. neut. {2.C} . . . . id.

ὀμνύει   verb, pres. act. indic. 3 pers. sg. {5.A.1.a} . . . . ὀμνύω G3660

ὀμνύειν   vbl., pres. act. inf. {6.B.1} . . . . id.

ὀμνύετε   verb, pres. act. impv. 2 pers. pl. {5.D.1} id.

ὀμνύναι   vbl., pres. act. inf. {6.B.1} . . . . id.

ὀμνύουσι   verb, pres. act. indic. 3 pers. pl. {5.A.1.a} . . . . id.

ὀμνύουσιν   verb, pres. act. indic. 3 pers. pl. {5.A.1.a} . . . . id.

G3660   **ὀμνύω** (ὄμνυμι)   *I swear, I take an oath;* sometimes with cog. acc. or with dat.; with acc., or with κατά with gen., of the power invoked or appealed to, *by,* Jas 5:12; Heb 6:13, 16.

G3661   **ὁμοθυμαδόν**   adv., *with one mind, with one accord.*

ὁμοθυμαδόν   adv. . . . . ὁμοθυμαδόν G3661

ὅμοια   adj., acc. pl. neut. {3.A} . . . . ὅμοιος G3664

ὅμοια   adj., nom. pl. neut. {3.A} . . . . id.

ὅμοια   adj., acc. pl. neut. {3.A} . . . . id.

ὁμοία   adj., nom. pl. fem. {3.A} . . . . id.

ὁμοία   adj., nom. sg. fem. {3.A} . . . . id.

ὁμοιάζει   verb, pres. act. indic. 3 pers. sg. {5.A.1.a} . . . . ὁμοιάζω G3662

G3662   **ὁμοιάζω**   *I am like.*

ὅμοιαι   adj., nom. pl. fem. {3.A} . . . . ὅμοιος G3664

ὁμοίας   adj., acc. pl. fem. {3.A} . . . . id.

ὅμοιοι   adj., nom. pl. masc. {3.A} . . . . id.

ὅμοιον   adj., acc. sg. masc. {3.A} . . . . id.

ὅμοιον   adj., acc. sg. neut. {3.A} . . . . id.

ὅμοιον   adj., nom. sg. neut. {3.A} . . . . id.

ὁμοιοπαθεῖς   adj., nom. pl. masc. {3.E} . . . . ὁμοιοπαθής G3663

G3663   **ὁμοιοπαθής**, -ές   *of like feelings,* almost, *of like nature.*

ὁμοιοπαθής   adj., nom. sg. masc. {3.E} . . . . ὁμοιοπαθής G3663

G3664   **ὅμοιος**, -α, -ον   *like.*

ὅμοιος   adj., nom. sg. masc. {3.A} . . . . ὅμοιος G3664

G3665   **ὁμοιότης**, -ητος, ἡ   *resemblance;* understand ἡμῶν in Heb 4:15; cf. 7:15.

ὁμοιότητα   noun, acc. sg. fem. {2.C} . . . . ὁμοιότης G3665

G3666   **ὁμοιόω**   *I make like, liken; I compare.*

ὁμοιωθέντες   vbl., aor. pass. ptc. nom. pl. masc. {6.A.1.a.} . . . . ὁμοιόω G3666

ὁμοιωθῆναι   vbl., aor. pass. inf. {6.B.1} . . . . id.

ὁμοιωθήσεται   verb, fut. pass. indic. 3 pers. sg. {5.A.1} . . . . id.

ὁμοιωθῆτε   verb, aor. pass. subjunc. 2 pers. pl. {5.B.1} . . . . id.

G3667   **ὁμοίωμα**, -ατος, τό   (orig., *a thing made like something else*), *likeness,* or rather *form.*

ὁμοιώματα   noun, nom. pl. neut. {2.C} . . ὁμοίωμα G3667

ὁμοιώματι   noun, dat. sg. neut. {2.C} . . . . id.

G3668   **ὁμοίως**   adv., *in a similar way, similarly, in the same way.*

ὁμοίως   adv. {3.F} . . . . ὁμοίως G3668

ὁμοίωσιν   noun, acc. sg. fem. {2.C} . . . . ὁμοίωσις G3669

G3669   **ὁμοίωσις**, -εως, ἡ   *making like; likeness* (cf. Gen. 1:26).

ὁμοιώσω   verb, fut. act. indic. 1 pers. sg. {5.A.1} . . . . ὁμοιόω G3666

ὁμοιώσωμεν   verb, aor. act. subjunc. 1 pers. pl. {5.B.1} . . . . id.

ὁμολογεῖ   verb, pres. act. indic. 3 pers. sg. {5.A.2} . . . . ὁμολογέω G3670

ὁμολογεῖται   verb, pres. pass. indic. 3 pers. sg.
{5.A.2}. . . . . id.
G3670 **ὁμολογέω**   (orig., *I agree with the statement* of
another), (1) *I promise*, Matt 14:7; Acts 7:17;
(2) *I confess*; (3) *I publicly declare*, cf. 1 John
2:23, 4:3, sometimes with the Aram. and Syr.
constr., ἐν with dat. equivalent to an acc., Matt
10:32; Luke 12:8, of confessing allegiance to
Jesus before an earthly law court; with cog.
acc. 1 Tim 6:12; (4) a Hebraism, *I praise,
celebrate*, Heb 13:15 (cf. ἐξομολογέομαι).
ὁμολογήσαντες   vbl., aor. act. ptc. nom. pl. masc.
{6.A.2}. . . . . ὁμολογέω G3670
ὁμολογήσει   verb, fut. act. indic. 3 pers. sg.
{5.A.1}. . . . . id.
ὁμολογήσῃ   verb, aor. act. subjunc. 3 pers. sg.
{5.B.1}. . . . . id.
ὁμολογήσῃς   verb, aor. act. subjunc. 2 pers. sg.
{5.B.1}. . . . . id.
ὁμολογήσω   verb, fut. act. indic. 1 pers. sg.
{5.A.1}. . . . . id.
G3671 **ὁμολογία**, -ας, ἡ   *a confession* (the act rather
than the contents or substance) of faith in
Christ; 1 Tim 6:12 refers either to that at
baptism or to that at ordination; 1 Tim 6:13
is referred by Pelagius to John 18:37, not
inappropriately.
ὁμολογίαν   noun, acc. sg. fem. {2.A} . . . ὁμολογία G3671
ὁμολογίας   noun, gen. sg. fem. {2.A} . . . . id.
G3672 **ὁμολογουμένως**   adv., *admittedly*.
ὁμολογουμένως   adv. {3.F} . . . . ὁμολογουμένως G3672
ὁμολογοῦντες   vbl., pres. act. ptc. nom. pl. masc.
{6.A.2}. . . . . ὁμολογέω G3670
ὁμολογούντων   vbl., pres. act. ptc. gen. pl.
masc. {6.A.2}. . . . . id.
ὁμολογούντων   vbl., pres. act. ptc. gen. pl.
neut. {6.A.2} . . . . id.
ὁμολογοῦσι   verb, pres. act. indic. 3 pers. pl.
{5.A.2}. . . . . id.
ὁμολογοῦσιν   verb, pres. act. indic. 3 pers. pl.
{5.A.2}. . . . . id.
ὁμολογῶ   verb, pres. act. indic. 1 pers. sg. {5.A.2}id.
ὁμολογῶμεν   verb, pres. act. subjunc. 1 pers. pl.
{5.B.2}. . . . . id.
ὁμολογῶν   vbl., pres. act. ptc. nom. sg. masc.
{6.A.2}. . . . . id.
ὀμόσαι   vbl., aor. act. inf. {6.B.1} . . . . ὀμνύω G3660
ὀμόσας   vbl., aor. act. ptc. nom. sg. masc.
{6.A.1.a} . . . . id.
ὀμόσῃ   verb, aor. act. subjunc. 3 pers. sg. {5.B.1} id.
ὀμόσῃς   verb, aor. act. subjunc. 2 pers. sg. {5.B.1}id.
ὁμότεχνον   adj., acc. sg. masc. {3.C} . . ὁμότεχνος G3673
G3673 **ὁμότεχνος**, -ον   *of the same trade*.
G3674 **ὁμοῦ**   adv., *together*.
ὁμοῦ   adv. {3.F} . . . . ὁμοῦ G3674
ὁμόφρονες   adj., nom. pl. masc. {3.E}. . . .ὁμόφρων G3675
G3675 **ὁμόφρων**, -ον   *of one mind (intent, purpose)*.
G3676 **ὅμως**   adv., *nevertheless*.
ὅμως   adv. {3.F} . . . . ὅμως G3676
ὄν   vbl., pres. ptc. nom. sg. neut. {7.C.1} . . . . . . εἰμί G1510

ὄν   pron. rel., acc. sg. masc. {4.C} . . . . .ὅς G3739
ὀναίμην   verb, [2]aor. mid. opt. 1 pers. sg.
{5.C.3}. . . . . ὀνίνημι G3685
G3677 **ὄναρ**, τό   *a dream*.
ὄναρ   noun {2.C} . . . . ὄναρ G3677
G3678 **ὀνάριον**, -ου, τό   *a donkey* (a conversational
diminutive).
ὀνάριον   noun, acc. sg. neut. {2.B} . . . . . ὀνάριον G3678
ὀνειδίζειν   vbl., pres. act. inf. {6.B.1} . . . . ὀνειδίζω G3679
ὀνειδίζεσθε   verb, pres. pass. indic. 2 pers. pl.
{5.A.1.d} . . . . id.
ὀνειδιζόμεθα   verb, pres. pass. indic. 1 pers. pl.
{5.A.1.d} . . . . id.
ὀνειδίζοντος   vbl., pres. act. ptc. gen. sg. masc.
{6.A.1}. . . . . id.
ὀνειδιζόντων   vbl., pres. act. ptc. gen. pl. masc.
{6.A.1}. . . . . id.
G3679 **ὀνειδίζω**   *I reproach*.
ὀνειδισμοί   noun, nom. pl. masc. {2.B} ὀνειδισμός G3680
ὀνειδισμοῖς   noun, dat. pl. masc. {2.B}. . . . . . . id.
ὀνειδισμόν   noun, acc. sg. masc. {2.B}. . . . . . . id.
G3680 **ὀνειδισμός**, -οῦ, ὁ   *a reproaching, a reproach*.
ὀνειδίσωσι   verb, aor. act. subjunc. 3 pers. pl.
{5.B.1}. . . . . ὀνειδίζω G3679
ὀνειδίσωσιν   verb, aor. act. subjunc. 3 pers. pl.
{5.B.1}. . . . . id.
G3681 **ὄνειδος**, -ους, τό   *a reproach*.
ὄνειδος   noun, acc. sg. neut. {2.C} . . . . ὄνειδος G3681
Ὀνήσιμον   noun prop., acc. sg. masc. {2.B;
2.D}. . . . . .Ὀνήσιμος G3682
G3682 **Ὀνήσιμος**, -ου, ὁ   *Onesimus*, a slave of Philemon, a Christian of Colossae (orig. adj., *useful*,
hence the play upon words in Phlm 10, 11,
and very common as slave name).
Ὀνησίμου   noun prop., gen. sg. masc. {2.B;
2.D}. . . . . .Ὀνήσιμος G3682
Ὀνησίμῳ   noun prop., dat. sg. masc. {2.B; 2.D} . id.
G3683 **Ὀνησίφορος**, -ου, ὁ   *Onesiphorus*, a Christian
of the province of Asia. (An Onesiphorus,
probably intended to be the same person,
comes into the *Acts of Paul*).
Ὀνησιφόρου   noun prop., gen. sg. masc. {2.B;
2.D}. . . . . Ὀνησίφορος G3683
G3684 **ὀνικός**, -ή, -όν   *connected with a donkey*;
μύλος ὀνικός, an upper millstone so heavy
that it requires a donkey to turn it (in contrast
to the ordinary hand mill).
ὀνικός   adj., nom. sg. masc. {3.A}. . . . . ὀνικός G3684
G3685 **ὀνίνημι**   trans., *I profit*; pass. with gen. *I have
joy of*.
G3686 **ὄνομα**, -ατος, τό   (1) *a name*; but (2) according to Heb. notions, the name is something in-
separable from the person to whom it belongs,
something of his essence, and therefore in the
case of the God specially sacred, it is often
used Hebraistically in the sense of *person,
personality, power, authority, character* (cf. Acts
1:15; Rev 3:4; 11:13); in some passages it is in
consequence best left untranslated altogether;
εἰς τὸ ὄνομά τινος is a vernacular phrase,

however (see #4); (3) *a title of rank (dignity),*
Eph 1:21; Phil 2:9; (4) *account, reason, pretext,*
Mark 9:41; 1 Pet 4:16; similarly εἰς ὄνομα,
Matt 10:41, 42 = *as;* (5) *reputation,* Rev 3:1.
Adv. τοὔνομα (from τὸ ὄνομα), *by name.*

ὄνομα   noun, acc. sg. neut. {2.C} . . . . ὄνομα *G3686*
ὄνομα   noun, nom. sg. neut. {2.C} . . . . id.
ὀνομάζειν   vbl., pres. act. inf. {6.B.1} . . . . ὀνομάζω *G3687*
ὀνομαζέσθω   verb, pres. pass. impv. 3 pers. sg.
  {5.D.1} . . . . id.
ὀνομάζεται   verb, pres. pass. indic. 3 pers. sg.
  {5.A.1.d} . . . . id.
ὀνομαζόμενος   vbl., pres. pass. ptc. nom. sg.
  masc. {6.A.1} . . . . id.
ὀνομαζομένου   vbl., pres. pass. ptc. gen. sg.
  neut. {6.A.1} . . . . id.
G3687 **ὀνομάζω**   *I name, give a name to.*
ὀνομάζων   vbl., pres. act. ptc. nom. sg. masc.
  {6.A.1} . . . . ὀνομάζω *G3687*
ὀνόματα   noun, acc. pl. neut. {2.C} . . . . ὄνομα *G3686*
ὀνόματα   noun, nom. pl. neut. {2.C} . . . . id.
ὀνόματι   noun, dat. sg. neut. {2.C} . . . . id.
ὀνόματος   noun, gen. sg. neut. {2.C} . . . . id.
ὀνομάτων   noun, gen. pl. neut. {2.C} . . . . id.
ὄνον   noun, acc. sg. fem. {2.B} . . . . ὄνος *G3688*
ὄνον   noun, acc. sg. masc. {2.B} . . . . id.
G3688 **ὄνος**, -ου, ὁ and ἡ   *a donkey.*
ὄνος   noun, nom. sg. masc. {2.B} . . . . ὄνος *G3688*
ὄνου   noun, gen. sg. fem. {2.B} . . . . id.
ὄνπερ   pron. rel., acc. sg. masc. {4.C} . . . . ὅσπερ *G3746*
ὄντα   vbl., pres. ptc. acc. pl. neut. {7.C.1} . . . εἰμί *G1510*
ὄντα   vbl., pres. ptc. acc. sg. masc. {7.C.1} . . . . . id.
ὄντα   vbl., pres. ptc. nom. pl. neut. {7.C.1} . . . . . id.
ὄντας   vbl., pres. ptc. acc. pl. masc. {7.C.1} . . . . . id.
ὄντες   vbl., pres. ptc. nom. pl. masc. {7.C.1} . . . . id.
ὄντι   vbl., pres. ptc. dat. sg. masc. {7.C.1} . . . . . . id.
ὄντος   vbl., pres. ptc. gen. sg. masc. {7.C.1} . . . . . id.
ὄντος   vbl., pres. ptc. gen. sg. neut. {7.C.1} . . . . . id.
ὄντων   vbl., pres. ptc. gen. pl. masc. {7.C.1} . . . . . id.
ὄντων   vbl., pres. ptc. gen. pl. neut. {7.C.1} . . . . . id.
G3689 **ὄντως**   adv., *really, actually.*
ὄντως   adv. {3.F} . . . . ὄντως *G3689*
ὀξεῖα   adj., nom. sg. fem. {3.D} . . . . ὀξύς *G3691*
ὀξεῖαν   adj., acc. sg. fem. {3.D} . . . . id.
ὀξεῖς   adj., nom. pl. masc. {3.D} . . . . id.
G3690 **ὄξος**, -ους, τό   *vinegar of wine* (Num 6:3), *vinegar,*
  the drink of field laborers and private soldiers.
ὄξος   noun, acc. sg. neut. {2.C} . . . . ὄξος *G3690*
ὄξους   noun, gen. sg. neut. {2.C} . . . . id.
ὀξύ   adj., acc. sg. neut. {3.D} . . . . ὀξύς *G3691*
G3691 **ὀξύς**, -εῖα, -ύ   (1) *sharp;* (2) *swift, express,* Rom
  3:15.
ὀπαῖς   noun, dat. pl. fem. {2.A} . . . . ὀπή *G3692*
G3692 **ὀπή**, -ῆς, ἡ   *a crevice* (in a rock); *a cave.*
ὀπῆς   noun, gen. sg. fem. {2.A} . . . . ὀπή *G3692*
G3693 **ὄπισθεν**   adv. and prep. with gen., *behind;* in
  Rev 5:1 the reverse (outer) side of the papyrus
  roll, where the fibers are vertical, is referred
  to; this was seldom written on, and only from
  motives of economy.

ὄπισθεν   adv. . . . . ὄπισθεν *G3693*
G3694 **ὀπίσω**   adv. and prep. with gen. *behind; after;*
  εἰς τὰ ὀπίσω (Mark 13:16) = ὀπίσω (Matt
  24:18), cf. Luke 9:62.
ὀπίσω   adv., prep. . . . . ὀπίσω *G3694*
ὅπλα   noun, acc. pl. neut. {2.B} . . . . ὅπλον *G3696*
ὅπλα   noun, nom. pl. neut. {2.B} . . . . id.
G3695 **ὁπλίζω**   trans., *I arm;* mid. *I arm myself;* esp. of
  defensive armor (breastplate, shield, etc.).
ὁπλίσασθε   verb, aor. mid. impv. 2 pers. pl.
  {5.D.1} . . . . ὁπλίζω *G3695*
G3696 **ὅπλον**, -ου, τό   esp. pl. ὅπλα, *defensive armor*
  (Rom 13:12), but also *offensive armor, weap-*
  ons, arms (John 18:3); sometimes met.
ὅπλων   noun, gen. pl. neut. {2.B} . . . . ὅπλον *G3696*
ὁποίαν   pron. correl., acc. sg. fem. {3.A} . . ὁποῖος *G3697*
ὁποῖοι   pron. correl., nom. pl. masc. {4.D} . . . . id.
ὁποῖον   pron. correl., nom. sg. neut. {4.D} . . . . id.
G3697 **ὁποῖος**, -α, -ον   correl. and indir. interrog.
  pron., corresponding to τοιοῦτος, *of which*
  kind; of what kind, what sort of. This word was
  dying out in NT times.
ὁποῖος   pron. correl., nom. sg. masc. {4.D} . . ὁποῖος *G3697*
G3698 **ὁπότε**   adv., *when* (in classical Gk. *whenever*),
  Luke 6:3 (var. ὅτε).
ὁπότε   adv. correl. {4.D} . . . . ὁπότε *G3698*
G3699 **ὅπου**   adv., *where,* also *to what place;* ὅπου ἄν
  (ἐάν), *wherever,* also *to whatever place.*
ὅπου   adv. correl. {4.D} . . . . ὅπου *G3699*
G3700 **ὀπτάνομαι**   *I appear, I am seen (by), I let myself*
  be seen (by).
ὀπτανόμενος   vbl., pres. mid./pass. ptc. nom. sg.
  masc. {6.A.1} . . . . ὀπτάνομαι *G3700*
G3701 **ὀπτασία**, -ας, ἡ   *a vision; an appearance.*
ὀπτασία   noun, dat. sg. fem. {2.A} . . . . . ὀπτασία *G3701*
ὀπτασίαν   noun, acc. sg. fem. {2.A} . . . . id.
ὀπτασίας   noun, acc. pl. fem. {2.A} . . . . id.
G3702 **ὀπτός**, -ή, -όν   *broiled.*
ὀπτοῦ   adj., gen. sg. masc. {3.A} . . . . ὀπτός *G3702*
G3703 **ὀπώρα**, -ας, ἡ   *autumn;* hence, *fruit.*
ὀπώρα   noun, nom. sg. fem. {2.A} . . . . ὀπώρα *G3703*
G3704 **ὅπως**   adv., *how;* conj., *in order that; that* (esp.
  after ἐρωτάω), with the subjunc., with or
  without ἄν.
ὅπως   adv. correl., conj. {4.D} . . . . ὅπως *G3704*
ὅρα   verb, pres. act. impv. 2 pers. sg. {5.D.2} . . ὁράω *G3708*
ὁρᾷ   verb, pres. act. indic. 3 pers. sg. {5.A.2} . . . . id.
G3705 **ὅραμα**, -ατος, τό   (lit., *something seen*), *a sight,*
  a vision.
ὅραμα   noun, acc. sg. neut. {2.C} . . . . ὅραμα *G3705*
ὅραμα   noun, nom. sg. neut. {2.C} . . . . id.
ὁράματι   noun, dat. sg. neut. {2.C} . . . . id.
ὁράματος   noun, gen. sg. neut. {2.C} . . . . id.
ὁράσει   noun, dat. sg. fem. {2.C} . . . . ὅρασις *G3706*
ὁράσεις   noun, acc. pl. fem. {2.C} . . . . id.
G3706 **ὅρασις**, -εως, ἡ   *a sight, a vision;* ὁράσει, *in*
  appearance, Rev 4:3.
ὅρασις   noun, nom. sg. fem. {2.C} . . . . ὅρασις *G3706*
ὁρατά   adj., nom. pl. neut. {3.A} . . . . ὁρατός *G3707*
ὁρᾶτε   verb, pres. act. impv. 2 pers. pl. {5.D.2} ὁράω *G3708*

ὁρᾶτε   verb, pres. act. indic. 2 pers. pl. {5.A.2} .. id.

G3707 ὁρατός, -ή, -όν   to be seen, visible.

G3708 ὁράω   I see; hence, I experience (Luke 3:6, etc.).
Aor. εἶδα (¹aor.) or εἶδον (²aor.), I saw. The
semitic interjections ἴδε and ἰδού, behold! are
orig. ²aor. imperatives. ὅρα (or ὁρᾶτε) μή,
see that you do not . . . , beware of doing so
and so; beware lest. ἰδὼν εἶδον, a Hebraism,
I truly saw.

G3709 ὀργή, -ῆς, ἡ   anger, wrath, passion; the settled
feeling of anger (cf. Eph 4:31), particularly, τοῦ
θεοῦ, of God, the hostility to sin; ἡ μέλλουσα
(ἐρχομένη) ὀργή also refers to the divine
wrath, and has a definite eschatological reference; occasionally also without epithet, of the
divine wrath, e.g., Rom 3:5; 5:9; 9:22; 13:5;
1 Thess 2:16.
ὀργή   noun, nom. sg. fem. {2.A} . . . . ὀργή G3709
ὀργῇ   noun, dat. sg. fem. {2.A} . . . . id.
ὀργήν   noun, acc. sg. fem. {2.A} . . . . id.
ὀργῆς   noun, gen. sg. fem. {2.A} . . . . id.
ὀργίζεσθε   verb, pres. mid./pass. impv. 2 pers. pl.
{5.D.1} . . . . .ὀργίζω G3710
ὀργιζόμενος   vbl., pres. mid./pass. ptc. nom.
sg. masc. {6.A.1} . . . . id.

G3710 ὀργίζω   pass., I am angry.
ὀργίλον   adj., acc. sg. masc. {3.A} . . . . .ὀργίλος G3711

G3711 ὀργίλος, -η, -ον   irascible.
ὀργισθείς   vbl., aor. pass. ptc. nom. sg. masc.
{6.A.1.a} . . . . .ὀργίζω G3710

G3712 ὀργυιά, -ᾶς, ἡ   a fathom (six feet).
ὀργυιάς   noun, acc. pl. fem. {2.A} . . . . .ὀργυιά G3712
ὀρέγεται   verb, pres. mid. indic. 3 pers. sg.
{5.A.1.d} . . . . ὀρέγω G3713
ὀρεγόμενοι   vbl., pres. mid. ptc. nom. pl. masc.
{6.A.1} . . . . id.
ὀρέγονται   verb, pres. mid. indic. 3 pers. pl.
{5.A.1.d} . . . . id.

G3713 ὀρέγω   mid. I hanker after, I seek (long) for, I am
eager for, I aspire to.
ὄρει   noun, dat. sg. neut. {2.C} . . . . ὄρος G3735
ὀρεινῇ   adj., dat. sg. fem. {3.A} . . . . .ὀρεινός G3714
ὀρεινήν   adj., acc. sg. fem. {3.A} . . . . id.

G3714 ὀρεινός, -ή, -όν, ἡ   hilly, mountainous; ἡ
ὀρεινή (supply γῆν), the mountain (mountainous) country (region), the highlands.
ὀρέξει   noun, dat. sg. fem. {2.C} . . . . .ὄρεξις G3715

G3715 ὄρεξις, -εως, ἡ   eagerness, strong desire.
ὄρεσι   noun, dat. pl. neut. {2.C} . . . . .ὄρος G3735
ὄρεσιν   noun, dat. pl. neut. {2.C} . . . . id.
ὀρέων   noun, gen. pl. neut. {2.C} . . . . id.
ὄρη   noun, acc. pl. neut. {2.C} . . . . id.
ὄρη   noun, nom. pl. neut. {2.C} . . . . id.
ὀρθάς   adj., acc. pl. fem. {3.A} . . . . ὀρθός G3717

G3716 ὀρθοποδέω   (strictly, I am an ὀρθόπους, a
man with straight feet, and therefore πρός
= with reference to; but it is possible that we
ought to take it) I go straight, πρός, to.
ὀρθοποδοῦσι   verb, pres. act. indic. 3 pers. pl.
{5.A.2} . . . . .ὀρθοποδέω G3716

ὀρθοποδοῦσιν   verb, pres. act. indic. 3 pers. pl.
{5.A.2} . . . . id.

G3717 ὀρθός, -ή, -όν   straight, erect (perhaps with
reference to recovery of health), Acts 14:10;
met. that goes in the right direction, Heb 12:13.
ὀρθός   adj., nom. sg. masc. {3.A} . . . . ὀρθός G3717

G3718 ὀρθοτομέω   perhaps, I cut (or carve) according
to rule (and thus, I define according to the
norm of the Gospel); if the metaphor be from
drawing furrows (understanding τὴν γῆν),
then it may be, I cultivate, I am occupied with.
ὀρθοτομοῦντα   vbl., pres. act. ptc. acc. sg. masc.
{6.A.2} . . . . .ὀρθοτομέω G3718
ὄρθριαι   adj., nom. pl. fem. {3.A} . . . . .ὄρθριος G3721

G3719 ὀρθρίζω   I rise early, I come in the morning.
ὀρθριναί   adj., nom. pl. fem. {3.A} . . . . .ὀρθρινός G3720

G3720 ὀρθρινός, -ή, -όν   belonging to the morning;
hence, equivalent to adv., in the morning, early.
Later spelling of ὄρθριος.
ὀρθρινός   adj., nom. sg. masc. {3.A} . . . .ὀρθρινός G3720

G3721 ὄρθριος, -ή, -ον   belonging to the morning;
hence, equivalent to adv., in the morning, early.
ὄρθρον   noun, acc. sg. masc. {2.B} . . . . . . ὄρθρος G3722

G3722 ὄρθρος, -ου, ὁ   dawn, early morning, daybreak.
ὄρθρου   noun, gen. sg. masc. {2.B} . . . . . . ὄρθρος G3722

G3723 ὀρθῶς   adv., rightly.
ὀρθῶς   adv. {3.F} .ὀρθῶς G3723
ὅρια   noun, acc. pl. neut. {2.B} . . . . .ὅριον G3725
ὁρίζει   verb, pres. act. indic. 3 pers. sg.
{5.A.1.a} . . . . ὁρίζω G3724

G3724 ὁρίζω   (lit. I bound, I fix a limit); hence, I
fix, determine, define; I fix upon, appoint,
designate.
ὀρινῇ   adj., dat. sg. fem. {3.A} . . . . .ὀρεινός G3714
ὀρινήν   adj., acc. sg. fem. {3.A} . . . . id.
ὁρίοις   noun, dat. pl. neut. {2.B} . . . . .ὅριον G3725

G3725 ὅριον, -ου, τό   pl. ὅρια, territory, district.
ὁρίσας   vbl., aor. act. ptc. nom. sg. masc.
{6.A.1.a} . . . . ὁρίζω G3724
ὁρισθέντος   vbl., aor. pass. ptc. gen. sg. masc.
{6.A.1.a} . . . . id.
ὁρίων   noun, gen. pl. neut. {2.B} . . . . .ὅριον G3725
ὁρκίζομεν   verb, pres. act. indic. 1 pers. pl.
{5.A.1.a} . . . . ὁρκίζω G3726
ὁρκίζομεν   verb, pres. act. indic. 1 pers. pl.
{5.A.1.a} . . . . id.

G3726 ὁρκίζω   I adjure, with double acc., of the one
adjured and of the one in the name of whom
he is adjured.
ὁρκίζω   verb, pres. act. indic. 1 pers. sg.
{5.A.1.a} . . . . ὁρκίζω G3726
ὅρκον   noun, acc. sg. masc. {2.B} . . . . .ὅρκος G3727

G3727 ὅρκος, -ου, ὁ   an oath (see ὀμνύω).
ὅρκος   noun, nom. sg. masc. {2.B} . . . . ὅρκος G3727
ὅρκου   noun, gen. sg. masc. {2.B} . . . . id.
ὅρκους   noun, acc. pl. masc. {2.B} . . . . id.
ὅρκῳ   noun, dat. sg. masc. {2.B} . . . . id.

G3728 ὁρκωμοσία, -ας, ἡ   the swearing of an oath, the
taking of an oath.
ὁρκωμοσίας   noun, gen. sg. fem. {2.A}ὁρκωμοσία G3728

G3729 **ὁρμάω**   *I rush.*

G3730 **ὁρμή**, -ῆς, ἡ   *a sudden movement, an impulse,*
   communicated by the hand, Jas 3:4; *inclina-*
   tion, hostile *intention, instigation.*
   ὁρμή   noun, nom. sg. fem. {2.A} . . . . ὁρμή G3730

G3731 **ὅρμημα**, -ατος, τό   *a mighty impulse (impetus).*
   ὁρμήματι   noun, dat. sg. neut. {2.C} . . . . .ὅρμημα G3731
   ὄρνεα   noun, nom. pl. neut. {2.B} . . . . ὄρνεον G3732
   ὀρνέοις   noun, dat. pl. neut. {2.B} . . . . id.

G3732 **ὄρνεον**, -ου, τό   (orig., *a little bird*), *a bird.*
   ὀρνέου   noun, gen. sg. neut. {2.B} . . . . ὄρνεον G3732

G3733 **ὄρνις**, -ιθος, ἡ   *a bird;* fem., *a hen.*
   ὄρνις   noun, nom. sg. fem. {2.C} . . . . ὄρνις G3733

G3734 **ὁροθεσία**, -ας, ἡ   (orig., *a laying down* or *fixing*
   of a boundary), *a boundary.*
   ὁροθεσίας   noun, acc. pl. fem. {2.A} . . . ὁροθεσία G3734

G3735 **ὄρος**, -ους, τό   *a mountain.*
   ὄρος   noun, acc. sg. neut. {2.C} . . . . ὄρος G3735
   ὄρος   noun, nom. sg. neut. {2.C} . . . . id.
   ὄρους   noun, gen. sg. neut. {2.C} . . . . id.

G3736 **ὀρύσσω**   *I dig.*

G3737 **ὀρφανός**, -ή, -όν   *orphaned; an orphan;* hence,
   friendless, John 14:18.
   ὀρφανούς   adj., acc. pl. masc. {3.A} . . . . . ὀρφανός G3737

G3738 **ὀρχέομαι**   *I dance.*
   ὀρχησαμένης   vbl., aor. mid. ptc. gen. sg. fem.
   {6.A.2} . . . . ὀρχέομαι G3738
   ὁρῶ   verb, pres. act. indic. 1 pers. sg. {5.A.2} . .ὁράω G3708
   ὁρῶμεν   verb, pres. act. indic. 1 pers. pl. {5.A.2} . id.
   ὁρῶν   vbl., pres. act. ptc. nom. sg. masc. {6.A.2} . id.
   ὁρῶντες   vbl., pres. act. ptc. nom. pl. masc.
   {6.A.2} . . . . id.
   ὁρῶσαι   vbl., pres. act. ptc. nom. pl. fem. {6.A.2} id.

G3739 **ὅς, ἥ, ὅ**   rel. pron., *who, which;* ὃς ἂν (ἐάν)
   with subjunc., *whosoever;* ὅς is some times
   equal to the classical ὅστις, Matt 10:26; 24:2;
   Luke 12:2; Acts 19:35, etc.; it is frequently
   attracted into the case of its antecedent, the
   latter being sometimes omitted; sometimes
   the attraction is inverse, i.e., the antecedent
   is attracted into the case of the rel., e.g., Matt
   21:42; Luke 12:48; Acts 10:36; 1 Cor 10:16;
   sometimes the dem. pron. is pleonastically
   added in the rel. clause (a colloquial Gk. use)
   the frequency of which is probably suggested by Semitic usage, e.g., Mark 1:7; 7:25
   (cf. 13:19); Luke 3:16; John 1:27; Acts 15:17;
   1 Pet 2:24 (var.); Rev 3:8; 7:2, 9; 13:8, 12; 20:8
   (either a Heb. or an Aram. source is generally
   presumed); ὃς μέν . . . ὃς δέ, *the one . . . the*
   other, or *one . . . another;* ἀφ᾽ οὗ, ἀφ᾽ ἧς, *since*
   (where ἡμέρας or ὥρας can be supplied)
   2 Pet 3:4; ὅ ἐστιν can introduce rel. clauses
   containing interpretations, whatever be the
   gender and number of the antecedent, e.g.,
   Mark 12:42; 15:22; ἐν ᾧ, *in that, because,* Rom
   2:1; 8:3; Heb 2:18; *wherefore,* Heb 6:17; *as*
   long as, while, Mark 2:19; Luke 5:34; John 5:7;
   until, Luke 19:13 (= εἰς ὅ) ἐφ᾽ ᾧ, see ἐπί; ἐφ᾽
   ὃ πάρει, *to the task for which you have come,*

Matt 26:50 (a command, not a question);
ἄχρι, ἕως, μέχρις οὗ (lit. *up to the point at*
which), *until;* ἀνθ᾽ ὧν, οὗ εἵνεκεν, οὗ χάριν,
on account of which, wherefore; ὅ, as cog. acc.,
Rom 6:10; Gal 2:20.
   ὅς   pron. rel., nom. sg. masc. {4.C} . . . . .ὅς G3739
   ὅσα   adj. correl., acc. pl. neut. {4.D} . . . . . ὅσος G3745
   ὅσα   adj. correl., nom. pl. neut. {4.D} . . . . id.
   ὅσαι   adj. correl., nom. pl. fem. {4.D} . . . . id.

G3740 **ὁσάκις**   adv., always with ἐάν and subjunc., *as*
   often as, as many times as.
   ὁσάκις   adv. . . . . ὁσάκις G3740
   ὅσας   adj. correl., acc. pl. fem. {4.D} . . . . . . ὅσος G3745
   ὅσια   adj., acc. pl. neut. {3.A} . . . . ὅσιος G3741
   ὅσιον   adj., acc. sg. masc. {3.A} . . . . id.

G3741 **ὅσιος**, -α, -ον   (1) *holy, pious* (implying the
   right relation to God); τὰ ὅσια, *the pieties, the*
   pious deeds, Acts 13:34; (2) ὁ ὅσιος, *the Holy*
   One, i.e., the Messiah. (Heb. *hāsîd* means not
   only *godly, pious,* but also *beloved of Yahweh*).
   ὅσιος   adj., nom. sg. masc. {3.A} . . . . .ὅσιος G3741
   ὅσιος   adj., voc. sg. masc. {3.A} . . . . id.

G3742 **ὁσιότης**, -ητος, ἡ   *holiness, piety.*
   ὁσιότητι   noun, dat. sg. fem. {2.C} . . . . . . ὁσιότης G3742
   ὁσίους   adj., acc. pl. fem. {3.A} . . . . .ὅσιος G3741

G3743 **ὁσίως**   adv., *religiously, piously.*
   ὁσίως   adv. {3.F} . . . . ὁσίως G3743

G3744 **ὀσμή**, -ῆς, ἡ   *odor;* generally met. in connection with εὐωδίας (from OT), originally of
   the sweet smelling odor of sacrifice, and then
   widely used.
   ὀσμή   noun, nom. sg. fem. {2.A} . . . . .ὀσμή G3744
   ὀσμήν   noun, acc. sg. fem. {2.A} . . . . id.
   ὀσμῆς   noun, gen. sg. fem. {2.A} . . . . id.
   ὅσοι   adj. correl., nom. pl. masc. {4.D} . . . . ὅσος G3745
   ὅσον   adj. correl., acc. sg. masc. {4.D} . . . . id.
   ὅσον   adj. correl., acc. sg. neut. {4.D} . . . . id.
   ὅσον   adj. correl., nom. sg. neut. {4.D} . . . . id.

G3745 **ὅσος**, -η, -ον   rel. and indir. interrog. adj. (orig.
   correlative to τοσοῦτος, cf. Heb 10:25), *as*
   great as; how great; of time, *as long as,* Mark
   2:19; ὅσος ἐάν (ἄν) generalizes, *however*
   great, pl. *as many as;* ὅσοι = πάντες οἵ, *how*
   many, as many as; ἐφ᾽ ὅσον, *as long as,* e.g.,
   Matt 9:15; *to the degree that, inasmuch as,* e.g.,
   Matt 25:40; Rom 11:13; καθ᾽ ὅσον, *in propor-*
   tion as, Heb 3:3; 7:20; 9:27; ὅσον ὅσον, *a little*
   (cf. Eng. *so so*).
   ὅσους   adj. correl., acc. pl. masc. {4.D} . . . . . ὅσος G3745

G3746 **ὅσπερ**, ἥπερ, ὅπερ   *just the one who, which*
   indeed (= ὅς περ, etc.).
   ὀστέα   noun, acc. pl. neut. {2.B} . . . . ὀστέον G3747

G3747 **ὀστέον** (ὀστοῦν), -έου (οῦ), τό   *a bone.*
   ὀστέων   noun, gen. pl. neut. {2.B} . . . . . . ὀστέον G3747

G3748 **ὅστις**, ἥτις, ὅ τι   either generic, *who,* as other
   like persons, *which,* as other like things, or
   essential, *who,* by his/her very nature, *which,*
   by its very nature. Rare except in the nom.
   There is a tendency (seen in the Ionic dialect
   and also in colloquial Gk.) to weaken ὅστις

to the sense of ὅς, cf. Matt 27:62; Luke 2:4; 10:42, but examples are very rare; ὅστις ἄν (ἐάν) = ἐάν τις, with subjunc., *whosoever* (it is doubtful whether the ἄν should be omitted, cf. Matt 10:33; Jas 2:10); ὅ, τι, short for τί ὅ, τι (= τί γέγονεν ὅτι, John 14:22), *why*, Mark 2:16 (var.); 9:11, 28 (var.); John 8:25 (but in this passage ὅτι can be read, "do you reproach me *that* . . . "); examples of τί ὅ, τι (or ὅτι) are Mark 2:16 (var.), Luke 2:49; ἕως ὅτου, *until* the time at *which, until.*

ὅστις   pron. indef. rel., nom. sg. masc. {4.C} . . ὅστις G3748
ὀστοῦν   noun, nom. sg. neut. {2.B} . . . . . . ὀστέον G3747
ὀστράκινα   adj., nom. pl. neut. {3.A} . ὀστράκινος G3749
ὀστρακίνοις   adj., dat. pl. neut. {3.A} . . . . id.

G3749 **ὀστράκινος**, -η, -ον   *made of pottery, of earthenware.*

G3750 **ὄσφρησις**, -εως, ἡ   *sense of smell.*
ὄσφρησις   noun, nom. sg. fem. {2.C} . . . ὄσφρησις G3750
ὀσφύας   noun, acc. pl. fem. {2.C} . . . . ὀσφῦς G3751
ὀσφύες   noun, nom. pl. fem. {2.C} . . . . id.
ὀσφύϊ   noun, dat. sg. fem. {2.C} . . . . id.
ὀσφύν   noun, acc. sg. fem. {2.C} . . . . id.
ὀσφύος   noun, gen. sg. fem. {2.C} . . . . id.

G3751 **ὀσφῦς**, -ύος, ἡ   sg. and pl., *the loins, the middle,* mentioned in two connections, first as the quarter from which comes the male seed (Hebraism Acts 2:30, etc.), and second as the part of the body round which the girdle is placed, when the flowing robes are girt higher with a view to travel or work (cf. Luke 12:35); hence also met., 1 Pet 1:13 (the negation of mental slackness is referred to).

ὅσῳ   pron. correl., dat. sg. neut. {4.D} . . . . . . ὅσος G3745
ὅσων   pron. correl., gen. pl. neut. {4.D} . . . . id.

G3752 **ὅταν**   *whenever, as often as,* followed by the indic., in case of repeated events in the past (thus it is incorrectly used = *when* in Rev 8:1, etc.), but also like ἐάν with pres. and fut. indic., usually with variations in the reading, Mark 11:25; 13:7; Luke 11:2; 13:28; John 7:27; followed by subjunc., where frequency in the future is referred to, the subjunc. pres. being strictly equivalent to the Lat. pres. subjunc. or fut. indic. (conative, continuous, or iterative), while the subjunc. aor. (punctiliar) corresponds to the fut. perf. indic. in Mark 11:19, perhaps *when.*

ὅταν   conj. . . . . ὅταν G3752

G3753 **ὅτε**   *when, at which time,* used esp. with all tenses of the indic.; only once with subjunc., *the time when,* Luke 13:35 (var.).
ὅτε   adv. correl. {4.D} . . . . ὅτε G3753

G3754 **ὅτι**   most often, either (1) *because, for;* or, (2) after a verb or other word of saying (perhaps under influence of Aram. in Mark) or thinking, *that,* introducing a noun clause; (3) an ellipsis of δῆλον in 1 Tim 6:7; 1 John 3:20; (4) so ὡς ὅτι pleonastically, 2 Cor 5:19; 11:21; 2 Thess 2:2, where the expressions

are equivalent to ὡς with the ptc.; (5) ὅτι sometimes also introduces a piece of direct speech, e.g., John 10:36, and so perhaps in Mark 2:16; 9:11, 28; John 8:25 (see under ὅστις); (6) ὅτι with inf., Acts 27:10, is due to forgetfulness; (7) οὐχ ὅτι = οὐ λέγω ὅτι, *not that,* John 6:46; 7:22; 2 Cor 1:24; Phil 4:11, etc., with which cf. οὐχ οἷον ὅτι, *it is not so that, it is by no means the case that,* Rom 9:6. A Hebraistic weakening of the force of causal ὅτι is seen in Matt 8:27; Mark 1:27 (var.); 4:41; Luke 4:36; 8:25; John 2:18 (14:22); Heb 2:6, etc. In Mark 8:24 ὅτι is a mistranslation of an Aram. word which should have been rendered οὕς. ὅτι orig. a development of ὅ, τι, neut. of ὅστις.

ὅτι   conj. . . . . ὅτι G3754

G3755 **ὅτου**   gen. form of ὅστις used in fixed prep. phrases ἀφ᾽ ὅτου, *from which time,* and ἕως ὅτου and μέχρις ὅτου, *until.*

ὅτου   pron. rel., gen. sg. neut. {4.C} . . . . ὅτου G3755

G3756 **οὐ**, οὐκ, οὐχ   *not,* the proper negative for a denial of a fact, used generally with the indic., as μή is with other moods, but sometimes with the ptc., it being closely related to the indic. and coming also under the rule that οὐ negatives a single word rather than a clause; οὐ with fut. indic. in a question is equivalent to an impv.; for οὐχ ὅτι see ὅτι; οὐ . . . πᾶς is Heb. = οὐδείς, Luke 1:37, etc.; for οὐ μή see under μή. Regularly οὐκ before smooth breathings and οὐχ before rough breathings. Accented form οὔ, *no!* (interj. or neg. reply).

οὐ   part., neg. . . . . οὐ G3756
οὔ   part., neg. . . . . id.

G3757 **οὗ**   rel. adv., *where;* also *to the place where.*
οὗ   adv. . . . . οὗ G3757
οὗ   pron. rel., gen. sg. masc. {4.C} . . . . ὅς G3739
οὗ   pron. rel., gen. sg. neut. {4.C} . . . . id.

G3364‡ **οὐ μή**   *not at all, in no way* (a double neg. strengthening the denial; from οὐ and μή).

G3758 **οὐά**   an interj. expressing real or ironical wonder.
οὐά   interj. . . . . οὐά G3758

G3759 **οὐαί**   interj., *woe,* with dat. or acc., sometimes in Rev made a noun, ἡ οὐαί (= ἡ κραυγὴ οὐαί?); expresses rather a statement than a wish or imprecation, *distress comes (will come) upon.*
οὐαί   interj. . . . . οὐαί G3759
οὐδ᾽   conj., neg. . . . . οὐδέ G3761

G3760 **οὐδαμῶς**   adv., *in no way, in no respect, not at all.*
οὐδαμῶς   adv. {3.F} . . . . οὐδαμῶς G3760

G3761 **οὐδέ**   conj., *and not, neither, nor; not even; not . . . either.*
οὐδέ   conj., neg. . . . . οὐδέ G3761

G3762 **οὐδείς** (οὐθείς), οὐδεμία, οὐδέν   adj. and subs., *no; no one* (masc. or fem.), *nothing* (neut.).

οὐδείς   adj., nom. sg. masc. {3.D} . . . . οὐδείς *G3762*
οὐδεμία   adj., nom. sg. fem. {3.D} . . . . id.
οὐδεμίαν   adj., acc. sg. fem. {3.D} . . . . id.
οὐδέν   adj., acc. sg. neut. {3.D} . . . . id.
οὐδέν   adj., nom. sg. neut. {3.D} . . . . id.
οὐδένα   adj., acc. sg. masc. {3.D} . . . . id.
οὐδενί   adj., dat. sg. masc. {3.D} . . . . id.
οὐδενί   adj., dat. sg. neut. {3.D} . . . . id.
οὐδενός   adj., gen. sg. masc. {3.D} . . . . id.
οὐδενός   adj., gen. sg. neut. {3.D} . . . . id.

G3763 **οὐδέποτε**   adv., *not at any time, never.*
οὐδέποτε   adv., neg. . . . . οὐδέποτε *G3763*

G3764 **οὐδέπω**   adv., *not yet either, not yet, not as yet, never before.*
οὐδέπω   adv., neg. . . . . οὐδέπω *G3764*
οὐθέν   adj., acc. sg. neut. {3.D} . . . . οὐδείς *G3762*
οὐθέν   adj., nom. sg. neut. {3.D} . . . . id.
οὐθενός   adj., gen. sg. masc. {3.D} . . . . id.
οὐθενός   adj., gen. sg. neut. {3.D} . . . . id.
οὐκ   part., neg. οὐ *G3756*
οὐκ   part., neg. . . . . id.

G3765 **οὐκέτι**   adv., *no longer, no more.*
οὐκέτι   adv., neg. . . . . οὐκέτι *G3765*

G3766 **οὐκοῦν**   interrog. adv., *so then?*
οὐκοῦν   adv., neg., interrog. . . . . οὐκοῦν *G3766*

G3767 **οὖν**   adv. or conj., *therefore,* properly in causal connection, but also freely of a mere temp. connection, continuing a narrative, *then,* for example, in the combined expression μέν οὖν (see under μέν); it sometimes indicates the return to the narrative after some digression, John 4:45; 6:24; 1 Cor 8:4; 11:20; ἄρα οὖν is a strengthened οὖν.
οὖν   adv., conj. . . . . οὖν *G3767*

G3768 **οὔπω**   adv., *not yet.*
οὔπω   adv., neg. . . . . οὔπω *G3768*

G3769 **οὐρά**, -ᾶς, ἡ   *a tail.*
οὐρά   noun, nom. sg. fem. {2.A} . . . . οὐρά *G3769*
οὐραί   noun, nom. pl. fem. {2.A} . . . . id.
οὐραῖς   noun, dat. pl. fem. {2.A} . . . . id.
οὐρανέ   noun, voc. sg. masc. {2.B} . . . . οὐρανός *G3772*

G3770 **οὐράνιος**, -ον   *in heaven, belonging to heaven, heavenly, from heaven.*
οὐράνιος   adj., nom. sg. masc. {3.C} . . . οὐράνιος *G3770*
οὐρανίου   adj., gen. sg. fem. {3.C} . . . . id.
οὐρανίῳ   adj., dat. sg. fem. {3.C} . . . . id.

G3771 **οὐρανόθεν**   adv., *from heaven, from the sky.*
οὐρανόθεν   adv. . . . . οὐρανόθεν *G3771*
οὐρανοί   noun, nom. pl. masc. {2.B} . . . . οὐρανός *G3772*
οὐρανοί   noun, voc. pl. masc. {2.B} . . . . id.
οὐρανοῖς   noun, dat. pl. masc. {2.B} . . . . id.
οὐρανόν   noun, acc. sg. masc. {2.B} . . . . id.

G3772 **οὐρανός**, -οῦ, ὁ   *the sky, the heaven;* as later Jewish cosmology conceived of a series of heavens one above the other (sometimes three, sometimes seven), the pl. is sometimes used, where we should use the sg., and numbers are even attached to individual strata (e.g., 2 Cor 12:2). Heaven was conceived as the special realm and abode of the Deity, hence

the word is constantly used in connection with Him, and almost as equivalent to the divine name; cf. the practical equivalence of ἡ βασιλεία τῶν οὐρανῶν, the kingdom (rule) *from heaven,* of *divine* origin, a phrase which may be in origin purely eschatological (so Matthew) with ἡ βασιλεία τοῦ θεοῦ, God Himself being the ruler, Matt 12:28; 19:24 (var.); 21:31, 43; Mark; Luke; Paul.
οὐρανός   noun, nom. sg. masc. {2.B} . . . . οὐρανός *G3772*
οὐρανοῦ   noun, gen. sg. masc. {2.B} . . . . id.
οὐρανούς   noun, acc. pl. masc. {2.B} . . . . id.
οὐρανῷ   noun, dat. sg. masc. {2.B} . . . . id.
οὐρανῶν   noun, gen. pl. masc. {2.B} . . . . id.
οὐράς   noun, acc. pl. fem. {2.A} . . . . οὐρά *G3769*
Οὐρβανόν   noun prop., acc. sg. masc. {2.B; 2.D} . . . . Οὐρβανός *G3773*

G3773 **Οὐρβανός**, -οῦ, ὁ   *Urbanus,* a Christian in Rome, fellow worker of Paul.

G3774 **Οὐρίας**, -ου, ὁ   *Uriah,* husband of Bathsheba, the mother of Solomon (Heb.).
Οὐρίου   noun prop., gen. sg. masc. {2.A; 2.D} . . . . Οὐρίας *G3774*
οὕς   pron. rel., acc. pl. masc. {4.C} . . . . ὅς *G3739*

G3775 **οὖς**, ὠτός, τό   *an ear.*
οὖς   noun, acc. sg. neut. {2.C} . . . . οὖς *G3775*
οὖς   noun, nom. sg. neut. {2.C} . . . . id.
οὖσα   vbl., pres. ptc. nom. sg. fem. {7.C.1} . . . . εἰμί *G1510*
οὖσαι   vbl., pres. ptc. nom. pl. fem. {7.C.1} . . . . . id.
οὖσαν   vbl., pres. ptc. acc. sg. fem. {7.C.1} . . . . . id.
οὔση   vbl., pres. ptc. dat. sg. fem. {7.C.1} . . . . . . id.
οὔσης   vbl., pres. ptc. gen. sg. fem. {7.C.1} . . . . . id.
οὖσι   vbl., pres. ptc. dat. pl. masc. {7.C.1} . . . . . id.

G3776 **οὐσία**, -ας, ἡ   *property.*
οὐσίαν   noun, acc. sg. fem. {2.A} . . . . οὐσία *G3776*
οὐσίας   noun, gen. sg. fem. {2.A} . . . . id.
οὖσιν   vbl., pres. ptc. dat. pl. masc. {7.C.1} . . . . εἰμί *G1510*
οὐσῶν   vbl., pres. ptc. gen. pl. fem. {7.C.1} . . . . . id.

G3777 **οὔτε**   adv., οὔτε . . . οὔτε, *neither . . . nor;* οὐ . . . οὔτε . . . οὔτε, *not . . . neither . . . nor;* sometimes the other clause is positive, e.g., John 4:11; 3 John 10.
οὔτε   conj., neg. οὔτε *G3777*
οὗτοι   pron. dem., nom. pl. masc. {4.B} . . . . οὗτος *G3778*

G3778 **οὗτος**, αὕτη, τοῦτο   dem. adj. and pron., *this; he, her, it;* αὕτη (Hebraistic) = τοῦτο, Matt 21:42; τοῦτ᾽ ἔστιν, *which means, meaning, actually, in reality* (cf. 1 Pet 3:20); ἐκ τούτου, *for this reason,* John 6:66 (possibly, *from that time onwards),*19:12, *by this mark, by this means,* 1 John 4:6; ἐν τούτῳ, *for this reason,* John 16:30; Acts 24:16, *by this mark, by this means,* 1 John 3:19; ἐπὶ τούτῳ, *meantime,* John 4:27; τούτου χάριν, *on this account;* κατὰ ταῦτα, *in the same way,* Luke 6:23 (var.), 17:30 (var.); καὶ τοῦτο, *and that too; especially;* καὶ ταῦτα, *and indeed.* A special sense = *as it is called,* Heb 9:11.
οὗτος   pron. dem., nom. sg. masc. {4.B} . . . . οὗτος *G3778*
οὕτω   adv. {3.F} . . . . οὕτως *G3779*

G3779 **οὕτως** (οὕτω) adv., *in this way (manner), thus, so, under these circumstances;* used sometimes with εἶναι, γίνεσθαι, where a form of τοιοῦτος would be expected (cf. ἔχω), Matt 1:18; 19:10, etc.

οὕτως adv. {3.F}. . . . . οὕτως G3779
οὐχ part., neg. . . . . οὐ G3756

G3780 **οὐχί** *not; no, not so,* a more emphatic form of οὐ (οὐκ, οὐχ), also used in a question, expecting a positive answer.

οὐχί part., interrog. .οὐχί G3780
οὐχί part., neg. . . . . id.
ὀφειλάς noun, acc. pl. fem. {2.A} . . . . . . ὀφειλή G3782
ὀφείλει verb, pres. act. indic. 3 pers. sg.
{5.A.1.a} . . . . ὀφείλω G3784
ὀφείλεις verb, pres. act. indic. 2 pers. sg.
{5.A.1.a} . . . . id.
ὀφειλέται noun, nom. pl. masc. {2.A} . .ὀφειλέτης G3781
ὀφειλέταις noun, dat. pl. masc. {2.A} . . . . id.
ὀφείλετε verb, pres. act. impv. 2 pers. pl.
{5.D.1} . . . . ὀφείλω G3784
ὀφείλετε verb, pres. act. indic. 2 pers. pl.
{5.A.1.a} . . . . id.

G3781 **ὀφειλέτης**, -ου, ὁ (1) *a debtor, one who owes, one who is indebted;* (2) *one who has sinned against* another (an Aramaism, see ὀφείλημα), *a sinner,* Luke 13:4.

ὀφειλέτης noun, nom. sg. masc. {2.A}. .ὀφειλέτης G3781

G3782 **ὀφειλή**, -ῆς, ἡ *a debt, what is owing (due);* the mutual obligation of married life, 1 Cor 7:3.

G3783 **ὀφείλημα**, -ατος, τό (1) *a debt;* (2) in Aram. the same word indicates a debt and a sin; hence, *a sin* (probably as that for which we owe reparation to God or to another person).

ὀφείλημα noun, acc. sg. neut. {2.C} . . . ὀφείλημα G3783
ὀφειλήματα noun, acc. pl. neut. {2.C} . . . . id.
ὀφειλήν noun, acc. sg. fem. {2.A} . . . . ὀφειλή G3782
ὀφείλομεν verb, pres. act. indic. 1 pers. pl.
{5.A.1.a} . . . . ὀφείλω G3784
ὀφειλομένην vbl., pres. pass. ptc. acc. sg. fem.
{6.A.1} . . . . id.
ὀφειλόμενον vbl., pres. pass. ptc. acc. sg. neut.
{6.A.1} . . . . id.
ὀφείλοντες vbl., pres. act. ptc. nom. pl. masc.
{6.A.1} . . . . id.
ὀφείλοντι vbl., pres. act. ptc. dat. sg. masc. {6.A.1} id.
ὀφείλουσι verb, pres. act. indic. 3 pers. pl.
{5.A.1.a} . . . . id.
ὀφείλουσιν verb, pres. act. indic. 3 pers. pl.
{5.A.1.a} . . . . id.

G3784 **ὀφείλω** *I owe;* with inf. *I ought.* Aor. ptc. ὄφελον, *I would that.*

ὄφεις noun, acc. pl. masc. {2.C} . . . . .ὄφις G3789
ὄφεις noun, nom. pl. masc. {2.C}. . . . . id.
ὄφεις noun, voc. pl. masc. {2.C}. . . . . id.
ὄφελον interj. ὀφείλω G3784
ὄφελον verb, ²aor. act. ptc. nom. sg. neut.
{6.A.1.a} . . . . id.

G3785 **ὄφελον** *I ought (wish),* i.e., (interj.) *oh that!* (form of ὀφείλω).

G3786 **ὄφελος**, -ους, τό *advantage, gain.*

ὄφελος noun, nom. sg. neut. {2.C}. . . . . . ὄφελος G3786
ὄφεσιν noun, dat. pl. masc. {2.C}. . . . . .ὄφις G3789
ὄφεων noun, gen. pl. masc. {2.C}. . . . . id.
ὄφεως noun, gen. sg. masc. {2.C}. . . . . id.
ὀφθαλμοδουλείαις noun, dat. pl. fem.
{2.A} . . . . .ὀφθαλμοδουλία G3787
ὀφθαλμοδουλείαν noun, acc. sg. fem. {2.A} . . id.

G3787 **ὀφθαλμοδουλία** (-εία), -ας, ἡ *eye-service,* service performed solely to impress one served.

ὀφθαλμοδουλία noun, dat. sg. fem.
{2.A} . . . . .ὀφθαλμοδουλία G3787
ὀφθαλμοδουλίαις noun, dat. pl. fem. {2.A} . . . id.
ὀφθαλμοδουλίαν noun, acc. sg. fem. {2.A} . . . id.
ὀφθαλμοί noun, nom. pl. masc. {2.B} . .ὀφθαλμός G3788
ὀφθαλμοῖς noun, dat. pl. masc. {2.B} . . . . id.
ὀφθαλμόν noun, acc. sg. masc. {2.B}. . . . . id.

G3788 **ὀφθαλμός**, -οῦ, ὁ (1) *an eye;* (2) ὀφθαλμὸς πονηρός (a Semitic idiom), *envy, ill will,* Matt 20:15; Mark 7:22; (3) met. "the mind's *eye,*" Eph 1:18.

ὀφθαλμός noun, nom. sg. masc. {2.B} . .ὀφθαλμός G3788
ὀφθαλμοῦ noun, gen. sg. masc. {2.B} . . . . id.
ὀφθαλμούς noun, acc. pl. masc. {2.B} . . . . id.
ὀφθαλμῷ noun, dat. sg. masc. {2.B} . . . . id.
ὀφθαλμῶν noun, gen. pl. masc. {2.B} . . . . id.
ὀφθείς vbl., aor. pass. ptc. nom. sg. masc.
{6.A.1.a.} . . . . .ὁράω G3708
ὀφθέντες vbl., aor. pass. ptc. nom. pl. masc.
{6.A.1.a.} . . . . id.
ὀφθέντος vbl., aor. pass. ptc. gen. sg. masc.
{6.A.1.a.} . . . . id.
ὀφθήσεται verb, fut. pass. indic. 3 pers. sg.
{5.A.1} . . . . id.
ὀφθήσομαι verb, fut. pass. indic. 1 pers. sg.
{5.A.1} . . . . id.
ὄφιν noun, acc. sg. masc. {2.C} . . . . .ὄφις G3789

G3789 **ὄφις**, -εως, ὁ *a serpent.*

ὄφις noun, nom. sg. masc. {2.C} . . . . .ὄφις G3789
ὀφρύος noun, gen. sg. fem. {2.C}. . . . . ὀφρῦς G3790

G3790 **ὀφρῦς**, -ύος, ἡ (properly *the brow*); hence, *the brow, a ridge* (of a mountain).

G3791 **ὀχλέω** *I trouble, torment, worry.*

ὄχλοι noun, nom. pl. masc. {2.B}. . . . . . . ὄχλος G3793
ὄχλοις noun, dat. pl. masc. {2.B}. . . . . id.
ὄχλον noun, acc. sg. masc. {2.B} . . . . id.

G3792 **ὀχλοποιέω** *I gather a crowd.*

ὀχλοποιήσαντες vbl., aor. act. ptc. nom. pl. masc.
{6.A.2}. ὀχλοποιέω G3792

G3793 **ὄχλος**, -ου, ὁ *a crowd* of men, *a mob, a multitude;* the pl. much affected by Matthew (Semitism?) does not differ in meaning from the sg. (cf. 4:25).

ὄχλος noun, nom. sg. masc. {2.B} . . . . ὄχλος G3793
ὄχλου noun, gen. sg. masc. {2.B}. . . . . id.
ὀχλούμενοι vbl., pres. pass. ptc. nom. pl. masc.
{6.A.2}. . . . . ὀχλέω G3791
ὀχλουμένους vbl., pres. pass. ptc. acc. pl.
masc. {6.A.2} . . . . id.

ὄχλους   noun, acc. pl. masc. {2.B} . . . . ὄχλος G3793

ὄχλῳ   noun, dat. sg. masc. {2.B} . . . . id.

ὄχλων   noun, gen. pl. masc. {2.B} . . . . id.

G3794 **ὀχύρωμα**, -ατος, τό   *a bulwark, a bastion;*
hence, met.

ὀχυρωμάτων   noun, gen. pl. neut. {2.C} ὀχύρωμα G3794

ὀψάρια   noun, acc. pl. neut. {2.B} . . . . . ὀψάριον G3795

G3795 **ὀψάριον**, -ου, τό   *a relish* (conversational
diminutive of ὄψον, *seasoning,* esp. *fish,* taken
as a relish with bread); then esp., *a fish.*

ὀψάριον   noun, acc. sg. neut. {2.B} . . . . ὀψάριον G3795

ὀψαρίων   noun, gen. pl. neut. {2.B} . . . . id.

G3796 **ὀψέ**   adv., *late;* prep. with gen., either *late on* or
after.

ὀψέ   adv., prep. . . . . ὀψέ G3796

ὄψει   verb, fut. mid. indic. 2 pers. sg. {5.A.1} . ὁράω G3708

ὄψεσθε   verb, fut. mid. indic. 2 pers. pl. {5.A.1} . id.

ὄψεται   verb, fut. mid. indic. 3 pers. sg. {5.A.1} . id.

ὄψῃ   verb, fut. mid. indic. 2 pers. sg. {5.A.1} . . . . id.

ὄψησθε   verb, aor. mid. subjunc. 2 pers. pl.
{5.B.1} . . . . id.

ὀψία   adj., nom. sg. fem. {3.A} . . . . ὄψιος G3798

ὀψίας   adj., gen. sg. fem. {3.A} . . . . id.

ὄψιμον   adj., acc. sg. masc. {3.A} . . . . ὄψιμος G3797

G3797 **ὄψιμος**, -ου, ὁ   *late* in the year (opp. to
πρόϊμος).

ὄψιν   noun, acc. sg. fem. {2.C} . . . . ὄψις G3799

G3798 **ὄψιος**, -α, -ον   *late,* Mark 11:11 (var.). Fem.
subs. ὀψία, *early evening,* of a period never
earlier than sunset.

G3799 **ὄψις**, -εως, ἡ   (1) *the face;* (2) *the features, the
outward appearance,* John 7:24.

ὄψις   noun, nom. sg. fem. {2.C} . . . . ὄψις G3799

ὄψομαι   verb, fut. mid. indic. 1 pers. sg.
{5.A.1} . . . . ὁράω G3708

ὀψόμεθα   verb, fut. mid. indic. 1 pers. pl. {5.A.1} id.

ὄψονται   verb, fut. mid. indic. 3 pers. pl. {5.A.1} id.

ὀψώνια   noun, nom. pl. neut. {2.B} . . . . ὀψώνιον G3800

ὀψωνίοις   noun, dat. pl. neut. {2.B} . . . . id.

G3800 **ὀψώνιον**, -ου, τό   esp. pl. ὀψώνια, (*rations,*
then) soldier's *pay,* Luke 3:14; cf. 1 Cor 9:7;
pay, wages, salary, reward in general, Rom
6:23; 2 Cor 11:8; *charges,* 1 Cor 9:7.

ὀψώνιον   noun, acc. sg. neut. {2.B} . . . . ὀψώνιον G3800

Π π

παγίδα   noun, acc. sg. fem. {2.C} . . . . παγίς G3803

παγιδεύσωσιν   verb, aor. act. subjunc. 3 pers. pl.
{5.B.1} . . . . παγιδεύω G3802

G3802 **παγιδεύω**   *I ensnare, I entrap.*

παγίδος   noun, gen. sg. fem. {2.C} . . . . παγίς G3803

G3803 **παγίς**, -ίδος, ἡ   *a snare* (esp. for catching birds;
perhaps a net thrown over one); hence, met.,
of moral snares.

παγίς   noun, nom. sg. fem. {2.C} . . . . παγίς G3803

Πάγον   noun prop., acc. sg. masc. {2.B; 2.D} Ἄρειος
Πάγος G697

Πάγου   noun prop., gen. sg. masc. {2.B; 2.D} . . . id.

πάθει   noun, dat. sg. neut. {2.C} . . . . πάθος G3806

παθεῖν   vbl., ²aor. act. inf. {6.B.1} . . . . πάσχω G3958

πάθη   noun, acc. pl. neut. {2.C} . . . . πάθος G3806

πάθῃ   verb, ²aor. act. subjunc. 3 pers. sg.
{5.B.1} . . . . πάσχω G3958

G3804 **πάθημα**, -ατος, τό   properly colorless, *an experience;* but most commonly, *an evil experience,
evil treatment, suffering,* e.g., τὰ εἰς Χριστὸν
παθήματα, the sufferings destined for Messiah,
1 Pet 1:11.

πάθημα   noun, acc. sg. neut. {2.C} . . . . . πάθημα G3804

παθήμασι   noun, dat. pl. neut. {2.C} . . . . id.

παθήμασιν   noun, dat. pl. neut. {2.C} . . . . id.

παθήματα   noun, acc. pl. neut. {2.C} . . . . id.

παθήματα   noun, nom. pl. neut. {2.C} . . . . id.

παθημάτων   noun, gen. pl. neut. {2.C} . . . . . . id.

G3805 **παθητός**, -ή, -όν   *capable of suffering.*

παθητός   adj., nom. sg. masc. {3.A} . . . . . παθητός G3805

παθόντας   vbl., ²aor. act. ptc. acc. pl. masc.
{6.A.1.a} . . . . πάσχω G3958

παθόντος   vbl., ²aor. act. ptc. gen. sg. masc.
{6.A.1.a} . . . . id.

G3806 **πάθος**, -ους, τό   (properly *experience, feeling,*
hence) *passion, lustfulness, lust* (as a state or
condition).

πάθος   noun, acc. sg. neut. {2.C} . . . . πάθος G3806

παθοῦσα   vbl., ²aor. act. ptc. nom. sg. fem.
{6.A.1.a} . . . . πάσχω G3958

παθών   vbl., ²aor. act. ptc. nom. sg. masc.
{6.A.1.a} . . . . id.

παῖδα   noun, acc. sg. masc. {2.C} . . . . παῖς G3816

παιδαγωγόν   noun, acc. sg. masc.
{2.B} . . . . παιδαγωγός G3807

G3807 **παιδαγωγός**, -οῦ, ὁ   *a boy leader,* a slave or
freed man who attends and guards a boy to
and from (sometimes also in) school, and
looks after his moral character esp., *a tutor.*

παιδαγωγός   noun, nom. sg. masc.
{2.B} . . . . παιδαγωγός G3807

παιδαγωγούς   noun, acc. pl. masc. {2.B} . . . . . . id.

παιδαρίοις   noun, dat. pl. neut. {2.B} . . παιδάριον G3808

G3808 **παιδάριον**, -ου, τό   either *a boy* or *a slave*
(formerly a diminutive).

παιδάριον   noun, nom. sg. neut. {2.B} . παιδάριον G3808

παῖδας   noun, acc. pl. masc. {2.C} . . . . παῖς G3816

G3809 **παιδεία**, -ας, ἡ   *discipline.*

παιδεία   noun, nom. sg. fem. {2.A} . . . . . . παιδεία G3809

παιδείᾳ   noun, dat. sg. fem. {2.A} . . . . id.

παιδείαν   noun, acc. sg. fem. {2.A} . . . . id.

παιδείας   noun, gen. sg. fem. {2.A} . . . . id.

παιδεύει   verb, pres. act. indic. 3 pers. sg.
{5.A.1.a} . . . . παιδεύω G3811

παιδευθῶσι verb, aor. pass. subjunc. 3 pers. pl.
{5.B.1}................................. id.
παιδευθῶσιν verb, aor. pass. subjunc. 3 pers.
pl. {5.B.1}.............................. id.
παιδευόμεθα verb, pres. pass. indic. 1 pers. pl.
{5.A.1.d}............................. id.
παιδευόμενοι vbl., pres. pass. ptc. nom. pl.
masc. {6.A.1}.......................... id.
παιδεύοντα vbl., pres. act. ptc. acc. sg. masc.
{6.A.1}.............................. id.
παιδεύουσα vbl., pres. act. ptc. nom. sg. fem.
{6.A.1}.............................. id.
παιδεύσας vbl., aor. act. ptc. nom. sg. masc.
{6.A.1.a} .... id.
παιδευτάς noun, acc. pl. masc. {2.A} ..παιδευτής G3810
παιδευτήν noun, acc. sg. masc. {2.A} .... id.
G3810 **παιδευτής**, -οῦ, ὁ one who disciplines, a
trainer; almost a chastiser, Heb 12:9.
G3811 **παιδεύω** (1) I discipline, educate, train; (2)
more severely, I chastise.
παιδεύω verb, pres. act. indic. 1 pers. sg.
{5.A.1.a} .... παιδεύω G3811
παιδία noun, acc. pl. neut. {2.B} ....παιδίον G3813
παιδία noun, nom. pl. neut. {2.B} .... id.
παιδία noun, voc. pl. neut. {2.B} .... id.
G3812 **παιδιόθεν** adv., from childhood, from early
boyhood.
παιδιόθεν adv................... παιδιόθεν G3812
παιδίοις noun, dat. pl. neut. {2.B} ....παιδίον G3813
G3813 **παιδίον**, -ου, τό (1) a little boy, a child (from
birth onwards); hence affectionately, of those
grown up; (2) a slave (cf. the use of boy in
parts of Africa), Luke 11:7.
παιδίον noun, acc. sg. neut. {2.B} ....παιδίον G3813
παιδίον noun, nom. sg. neut. {2.B} .... id.
παιδίον noun, voc. sg. neut. {2.B} .... id.
παιδίου noun, gen. sg. neut. {2.B}.......... id.
παιδίσκας noun, acc. pl. fem. {2.A} ...παιδίσκη G3814
G3814 **παιδίσκη**, -ης, ἡ a female slave, a maidser-
vant, a maid.
παιδίσκη noun, nom. sg. fem. {2.A} ...παιδίσκη G3814
παιδίσκην noun, acc. sg. fem. {2.A} .... id.
παιδίσκης noun, gen. sg. fem. {2.A} .... id.
παιδισκῶν noun, gen. pl. fem. {2.A} .... id.
παιδίων noun, gen. pl. neut. {2.B}.......παιδίον G3813
παιδός noun, gen. sg. fem. {2.C} ....παῖς G3816
παιδός noun, gen. sg. masc. {2.C} .... id.
παίδων noun, gen. pl. masc. {2.C}.......... id.
παίζειν vbl., pres. act. inf. {6.B.1} ....παίζω G3815
G3815 **παίζω** I play, I sport (includes singing and
dancing).
G3816 **παῖς**, παιδός, ὁ and ἡ (1) a male child, a boy;
(2) a male slave, a servant (cf. παιδίον); thus
a servant of God, esp. as a title of the Messiah
(from Isa 41–53) Acts 4:27, 30; (3) a female
child, a girl, Luke 8:51, 54.
παῖς noun, nom. sg. fem. {2.C} ....παῖς G3816
παῖς noun, nom. sg. masc. {2.C} .... id.
παῖς noun, voc. sg. fem. {2.C} .... id.

παίσας vbl., aor. act. ptc. nom. sg. masc.
{6.A.1.a} .... παίω G3817
παίσῃ verb, aor. act. subjunc. 3 pers. sg. {5.B.1}. id.
παισίν noun, dat. pl. masc. {2.C}..........παῖς G3816
G3817 **παίω** I strike.
Πακατιανῆς adj. prop., gen. sg. fem.
{3.A}.......................Πακατιανός G3818
G3818 **Πακατιανός**, -ή, -όν of Pacatian, a part of
Phrygia.
G3819 **πάλαι** adv., long ago, almost weakened to
already in Mark 15:44.
πάλαι adv........................ πάλαι G3819
παλαιά adj., acc. pl. neut. {3.A}....... παλαιός G3820
παλαιά adj., nom. sg. fem. {3.A} .... id.
παλαιᾷ adj., dat. sg. fem. {3.A} .... id.
παλαιάν adj., acc. sg. fem. {3.A} .... id.
παλαιᾶς adj., gen. sg. fem. {3.A} .... id.
παλαιόν adj., acc. sg. masc. {3.A} .... id.
παλαιόν adj., acc. sg. neut. {3.A} .... id.
G3820 **παλαιός**, -ά, -όν old; ὁ παλαιὸς ἄνθρωπος
(perhaps Hebraism), one's former character
(personality). The word and its derivatives bear
a derogatory sense.
παλαιός adj., nom. sg. masc. {3.A} ..... παλαιός G3820
G3821 **παλαιότης**, -ητος, ἡ oldness.
παλαιότητι noun, dat. sg. fem. {2.C} . παλαιότης G3821
παλαιοῦ adj., gen. sg. neut. {3.A} ...... παλαιός G3820
παλαιούμενα vbl., pres. pass. ptc. acc. pl. neut.
{6.A.2}.......................παλαιόω G3822
παλαιούμενον vbl., pres. pass. ptc. nom. sg.
neut. {6.A.2} .... id.
παλαιούς adj., acc. pl. masc. {3.A} ..... παλαιός G3820
G3822 **παλαιόω** I make old, I antiquate; I wear out; I
treat as past, Heb 8:13; pass. I fall to the past,
Heb 8:13.
παλαιῷ adj., dat. sg. neut. {3.A} .... παλαιός G3820
παλαιωθήσονται verb, fut. pass. indic. 3 pers. pl.
{5.A.1}.......................παλαιόω G3822
G3823 **πάλη**, -ης, ἡ wrestling, a wrestling bout; hence,
a struggle, a conflict.
πάλη noun, nom. sg. fem. {2.A}...........πάλη G3823
G3824 **παλιγγενεσία** (παλινγενεσία), -ας, ἡ (1)
rebirth, an eschatological term (used by
Pythagoreans and Stoics, found in Josephus
of the rebirth of the fatherland after the exile,
and in Philo of the rebirth of the earth after
the flood), in Matt 19:28 for the current
conception of the Messianic renewal of the
world or of the people Israel; (2) rebirth of
the individual life following on or typified in
baptism, Titus 3:5.
παλιγγενεσίᾳ noun, dat. sg. fem.
{2.A} ....παλιγγενεσία G3824
παλιγγενεσίας noun, gen. sg. fem. {2.A}..... id.
G3825 **πάλιν** adv., again, properly of a return over the
same course in the reverse direction, but also
used of a repetition of the same journey in
the same direction; it may also be used of any
number of times; in Mark 15:13 perhaps an
unsuitable mistranslation of an Aram. word of

much wider signification, *further, thereupon;*
εἰς τὸ πάλιν = πάλιν, 2 Cor 13:2.

πάλιν   adv. . . . . πάλιν *G3825*

παλιγγενεσία   noun, dat. sg. fem.
{2.A} . . . . παλιγγενεσία *G3824*

παλιγγενεσίας   noun, gen. sg. fem. {2.A} . . . . . id.

G3826 **παμπληθεί**   adv., *all together* (in unison); lit.,
with the whole crowd.

παμπληθεί   adv. . . . . παμπληθεί *G3826*

παμπόλλου   adj., gen. sg. masc. {3.A} . . πάμπολυς *G3827*

G3827 **πάμπολυς** (παμπόλλη, πάμπολυ)   *very great.*

G3828 **Παμφυλία,** -ας, ἡ   *Pamphylia,* a Roman province on the south coast of Asia Minor.

Παμφυλίαν   noun prop., acc. sg. fem. {2.A;
2.D} . . . . Παμφυλία *G3828*

Παμφυλίας   noun prop., gen. sg. fem. {2.A; 2.D} id.

πᾶν   adj., acc. sg. neut. {3.D} . . . . πᾶς *G3956*

πᾶν   adj., nom. sg. neut. {3.D} . . . . id.

πανδοχεῖ   noun, dat. sg. masc. {2.C} . . πανδοχεύς *G3830*

G3829 **πανδοχεῖον,** -ου, τό   *an inn, khan, hotel.*

πανδοχεῖον   noun, acc. sg. neut. {2.B} πανδοχεῖον *G3829*

G3830 **πανδοχεύς,** -έως, ὁ   *an innkeeper, landlord,*
hotel manager.

πανηγύρει   noun, dat. sg. fem. {2.C} . . πανήγυρις *G3831*

G3831 **πανήγυρις,** -εως, ἡ   *a festival assembly.*

G3832 **πανοικεί** (πανοικί)   adv., *with all (his)*
household.

πανοικεί   adv. . . . . πανοικεί *G3832*

πανοικί   adv. . . . . id.

G3833 **πανοπλία,** -ας, ἡ   *armor.*

πανοπλίαν   noun, acc. sg. fem. {2.A} . . πανοπλία *G3833*

G3834 **πανουργία,** -ας, ἡ   (1) *cleverness,* usually with
the idea that it is evil; (2) *cunning, craftiness,*
Luke 20:23.

πανουργίᾳ   noun, dat. sg. fem. {2.A} . . πανουργία *G3834*

πανουργίαν   noun, acc. sg. fem. {2.A} . . . . id.

G3835 **πανοῦργος,** -ον   *crafty* (playfully used).

πανοῦργος   adj., nom. sg. masc. {2.B} . πανοῦργος *G3835*

πανπληθεί   adv. . . . . παμπληθεί *G3826*

πάντα   adj., acc. pl. neut. {3.D} . . . . πᾶς *G3956*

πάντα   adj., acc. sg. masc. {3.D} . . . . id.

πάντα   adj., nom. pl. neut. {3.D} . . . . id.

πάντα   adj., voc. sg. neut. {3.D} . . . . id.

πάντας   adj., acc. pl. masc. {3.D} . . . . id.

G3837†‡ πανταχῇ   *everywhere.* Var. for πανταχοῦ, Acts
21:28.

πανταχῇ   adv. . . . . πανταχῇ *G3837†‡*

G3836 **πανταχόθεν**   adv. *from every direction.* Var. for
πάντοθεν in Mark 1:45.

πανταχόθεν   adv. . . . . πανταχόθεν *G3836*

G3837 **πανταχοῦ**   adv., *everywhere.* = var. πανταχῇ
(Acts 21:28).

πανταχοῦ   adv. . . . . πανταχοῦ *G3837*

παντελές   adj., acc. sg. neut. {3.E} . . . . παντελής *G3838*

G3838 **παντελής,** -ές   εἰς τὸ παντελές, *utterly, at*
all, Luke 13:11; in Heb 7:25 either *entirely,* or,
more probably, *forever, finally.*

πάντες   adj., nom. pl. masc. {3.D} . . . . πᾶς *G3956*

πάντες   adj., voc. pl. masc. {3.D} . . . . id.

G3839 **πάντη**   adv., *in every way.*

πάντη   adv. . . . . πάντη *G3839*

παντί   adj., dat. sg. masc. {3.D} . . . . πᾶς *G3956*

παντί   adj., dat. sg. neut. {3.D} . . . . id.

G3840 **πάντοθεν**   adv., *from all sides, from all quarters;*
on all sides.

πάντοθεν   adv. . . . . πάντοθεν *G3840*

παντοκράτορος   noun, gen. sg. masc.
{2.C} .παντοκράτωρ *G3841*

G3841 **παντοκράτωρ,** -ορος, ὁ   *ruler of all, ruler*
of the universe; the LXX introduced κύριος
(θεὸς) παντοκράτωρ as a translation of *Lord*
of Hosts.

παντοκράτωρ   noun, nom. sg. masc.
{2.C} .παντοκράτωρ *G3841*

παντοκράτωρ   noun, voc. sg. masc. {2.C} . . . . . id.

παντός   adj., gen. sg. masc. {3.D} . . . . πᾶς *G3956*

παντός   adj., gen. sg. neut. {3.D} . . . . id.

G3842 **πάντοτε**   adv., *at all times, always.*

πάντοτε   adv. . . . . πάντοτε *G3842*

πάντων   adj., gen. pl. masc. {3.D} . . . . πᾶς *G3956*

πάντων   adj., gen. pl. neut. {3.D} . . . . id.

G3843 **πάντως,** *entirely; in any case;* (after a negative) *at all; assuredly, to be sure.*

πάντως   adv. {3.F} . . . . πάντως *G3843*

παρ᾿   prep. . . . . .παρά *G3844*

G3844 **παρά**   prep. (1) with acc. *by, beside, near,* without difference between "where?" (properly
παρὰ τίνι) and "to what place?"; not with
persons; (*not in accordance with,* opp. κατά)
against, contrary to, Rom 1:26; 11:24; 2 Cor
8:3 *(over); differently from,* Gal 1:8 (cf. 1 Cor
3:11); *more than,* sometimes with comp., Luke
13:2, 4; Rom 1:25; 12:3; 14:5; *less,* 2 Cor 11:24;
οὐ παρὰ τοῦτο . . . , *this is no reason that*
etc., 1 Cor 12:15; (2) with gen. *from the side of,*
from, only with persons; οἱ παρ᾿ αὐτοῦ, *his*
family, his relations, Mark 3:21 (in papyri generally = *his agents, his representatives*), τὰ παρ᾿
ἑαυτῆς, *her money, her wealth,* Mark 5:26, cf.
Luke 10:7; Phil 4:18; (3) with dat. *by, beside,*
answering the question "where?" with the
exception of John 19:25 only of persons, not of
immediate proximity, but *in the house of* any
one, Luke 19:7; John 1:39; Acts 10:6, *among* a
people, Rev 2:13; *in the eyes of,* e.g., παρὰ τῷ
θεῷ, *in the judgment of,* Rom 12:16, etc.

παρά   prep. . . . . .παρά *G3844*

παραβαίνετε   verb, pres. act. indic. 2 pers. pl.
{5.A.1.a} . . . . παραβαίνω *G3845*

παραβαίνουσι   verb, pres. act. indic. 3 pers. pl.
{5.A.1.a} . . . . id.

παραβαίνουσιν   verb, pres. act. indic. 3 pers.
pl. {5.A.1.a} . . . . id.

G3845 **παραβαίνω**   (1) *I fall away, take a false step,*
Acts 1:25; (2) *I overstep, transgress.*

παραβαίνων   vbl., pres. act. ptc. nom. sg. masc.
{6.A.1} . . . . παραβαίνω *G3845*

G3846 **παραβάλλω**   *I cross over, I strike across.*

παραβάλωμεν   verb, ²aor. act. subjunc. 1 pers. pl.
{5.B.1} .παραβάλλω *G3846*

παραβάσει noun, dat. sg. fem. {2.C}. .παράβασις *G3847*
παραβάσεων noun, gen. pl. fem. {2.C}. . . . . . id.
παραβάσεως noun, gen. sg. fem. {2.C}. . . . . . id.
G3847 **παράβασις**, -εως, ἡ *transgression; a*
    transgression.
παράβασις noun, nom. sg. fem. {2.C}. παράβασις *G3847*
παραβάται noun, nom. pl. masc.
    {2.A} . . . . .παραβάτης *G3848*
παραβάτην noun, acc. sg. masc. {2.A} . . . . . . id.
G3848 **παραβάτης**, -ου, ὁ *a transgressor, a law*
    breaker (lit. *an overstepper*).
παραβάτης noun, nom. sg. masc.
    {2.A} . . . . .παραβάτης *G3848*
G3849 **παραβιάζομαι** *I urge, press.*
παραβολαῖς noun, dat. pl. fem. {2.A}. παραβολή *G3850*
παραβολάς noun, acc. pl. fem. {2.A} . . . . id.
παραβολευσάμενος vbl., aor. mid. ptc. nom. sg.
    masc. {6.A.1.b} . . . . παραβολεύομαι *G3851*†‡
G3850 **παραβολή**, -ῆς, ἡ *a similitude, allegory, parable,*
    emblematic allusion; in Heb 11:19 ἐν = *as.*
παραβολή noun, nom. sg. fem. {2.A}. παραβολή *G3850*
παραβολῇ noun, dat. sg. fem. {2.A} . . . . id.
παραβολήν noun, acc. sg. fem. {2.A} . . . . id.
παραβολῆς noun, gen. sg. fem. {2.A} . . . . id.
G3851†‡ **παραβολεύομαι** *I risk, I expose myself to*
    danger. Var. for παραβουλεύομαι, Phil 2:30.
G3851 **παραβουλεύομαι** *I am careless, I have no*
    concern (w. dat.).
παραβουλευσάμενος vbl., aor. mid. ptc. nom. sg.
    masc. {6.A.1.b} . . . . παραβουλεύομαι *G3851*
παραγγείλαντες vbl., aor. act. ptc. nom. pl. masc.
    {6.A.1.a} . . . . .παραγγέλλω *G3853*
παραγγείλας vbl., aor. act. ptc. nom. sg. masc.
    {6.A.1.a} . . . . id.
παραγγείλῃς verb, aor. act. subjunc. 2 pers. sg.
    {5.B.1} . . . . id.
G3852 **παραγγελία**, -ας, ἡ *a command, an injunc-*
    tion; a precept, rule of living, 1 Thess 4:2.
παραγγελίᾳ noun, dat. sg. fem. {2.A} παραγγελία *G3852*
παραγγελίαν noun, acc. sg. fem. {2.A} . . . . . . id.
παραγγελίας noun, acc. pl. fem. {2.A} . . . . . . id.
παραγγελίας noun, gen. sg. fem. {2.A} . . . . . . id.
παράγγελλε verb, pres. act. impv. 2 pers. sg.
    {5.D.1} .παραγγέλλω *G3853*
παραγγέλλει verb, pres. act. indic. 3 pers. sg.
    {5.A.1.a} . . . . id.
παραγγέλλειν vbl., pres. act. inf. {6.B.1} . . . . . . id.
παραγγέλλομεν verb, pres. act. indic. 1 pers.
    pl. {5.A.1.a} . . . . id.
G3853 **παραγγέλλω** *I command, I charge;* παραγ-
    γελίᾳ παραγγέλλειν (Hebraism), *to charge*
    strictly, Acts 5:28.
παραγγέλλω verb, pres. act. indic. 1 pers. sg.
    {5.A.1.a} . . . . .παραγγέλλω *G3853*
παραγγέλλων vbl., pres. act. ptc. nom. sg.
    masc. {6.A.1} . . . . id.
παράγει verb, pres. act. indic. 3 pers. sg.
    {5.A.1.a} .παράγω *G3855*
παραγενόμενοι vbl., ²aor. mid. ptc. nom. pl. masc.
    {6.A.1.b} . . . . παραγίνομαι *G3854*

παραγενόμενον vbl., ²aor. mid. ptc. acc. sg.
    masc. {6.A.1.b} . . . . id.
παραγενόμενος vbl., ²aor. mid. ptc. nom. sg.
    masc. {6.A.1.b} . . . . id.
παραγενομένου vbl., ²aor. mid. ptc. gen. sg.
    masc. {6.A.1.b} . . . . id.
παραγενομένους vbl., ²aor. mid. ptc. acc. pl.
    masc. {6.A.1.b} . . . . id.
παραγένωμαι verb, ²aor. mid. subjunc. 1 pers.
    sg. {5.B.1} . . . . id.
παραγένωνται verb, ²aor. mid. subjunc.
    3 pers. pl. {5.B.1} . . . . id.
παράγεται verb, pres. mid./pass. indic. 3 pers. sg.
    {5.A.1.d} .παράγω *G3855*
παραγίνεται verb, pres. mid./pass. indic. 3 pers.
    sg. {5.A.1.d}. . . . . παραγίνομαι *G3854*
G3854 **παραγίνομαι** (1) *I come on the scene, I appear,*
    I come; (2) with words expressing destination,
    I present myself at, I arrive at, I reach.
παράγοντα vbl., pres. act. ptc. acc. sg. masc.
    {6.A.1} . . . . .παράγω *G3855*
παράγοντι vbl., pres. act. ptc. dat. sg. masc.
    {6.A.1} . . . . id.
G3855 **παράγω** (1) *I pass by,* Matt 20:30; Mark 15:21,
    etc.; (2) *I vanish, disappear,* 1 Cor 7:31, in
    which sense the pass. is used, 1 John 2:8, 17
    (the verb being originally trans.); (3) *I depart,*
    Matt 9:9, 27 (var. in both passages, and there-
    fore this meaning is questionable); (4) almost,
    I walk, Mark 1:16; 2:14; 15:21(?).
παράγων vbl., pres. act. ptc. nom. sg. masc.
    {6.A.1} . . . . .παράγω *G3855*
παραδεδομένοι vbl., perf. pass. ptc. nom. pl.
    masc. {6.A.3} . . . . παραδίδωμι *G3860*
παραδέδοται verb, perf. pass. indic. 3 pers. sg.
    {5.A.1} . . . . id.
παραδεδώκεισαν verb, plu. act. indic. 3 pers.
    pl. {5.A.1} . . . . id.
παραδεδωκόσι vbl., perf. act. ptc. dat. pl.
    masc. {6.A.3}. . . . . id.
παραδεδωκόσιν vbl., perf. act. ptc. dat. pl.
    masc. {6.A.3} . . . . id.
παραδειγματίζοντας vbl., pres. act. ptc. acc. pl.
    masc. {6.A.1} . . . . παραδειγματίζω *G3856*
G3856 **παραδειγματίζω** *I put to open shame.*
παραδειγματίσαι vbl., aor. act. inf.
    {6.B.1} . . . . παραδειγματίζω *G3856*
παράδεισον noun, acc. sg. masc. {2.B}. παράδεισος *G3857*
G3857 **παράδεισος**, -ου, ὁ *paradise* (lit. *an enclosed*
    orchard or *garden with fruit trees*), a quarter of
    heaven conceived by the later Jews to be in or
    just above the "third heaven".
παραδείσου noun, gen. sg. masc.
    {2.B} . . . . παράδεισος *G3857*
παραδείσῳ noun, dat. sg. masc. {2.B} . . . . id.
παραδέξονται verb, fut. mid. indic. 3 pers. pl.
    {5.A.1.d} . . . . παραδέχομαι *G3858*
παραδέχεσθαι vbl., pres. mid./pass. inf. {6.B.1} id.
παραδέχεται verb, pres. mid./pass. indic.
    3 pers. sg. {5.A.1.d} . . . . id.

G3858 **παραδέχομαι**   *I receive (welcome) favorably.*
παραδέχονται   verb, pres. mid./pass. indic. 3 pers.
pl. {5.A.1.d}................ παραδέχομαι G3858
παραδέχου   verb, pres. mid./pass. impv. 2 pers.
sg. {5.D.1} .... id.
παραδιατριβαί   noun, nom. pl. fem.
{2.A} .... παραδιατριβή G3859
G3859 **παραδιατριβή**, -ῆς, ἡ   *perpetual wrangling.*
παραδιδόμεθα   verb, pres. pass. indic. 1 pers. pl.
{5.A.3.a} .... παραδίδωμι G3860
παραδιδόναι   vbl., pres. act. inf. {6.B.3}...... id.
παραδιδόντα   vbl., pres. act. ptc. acc. sg. masc.
{6.A.3}............................ id.
παραδιδόντες   vbl., pres. act. ptc. nom. pl.
masc. {6.A.3}....................... id.
παραδιδόντος   vbl., pres. act. ptc. gen. sg.
masc. {6.A.3}....................... id.
παραδίδοσθαι   vbl., pres. pass. inf. {6.B.3} .... id.
παραδίδοται   verb, pres. pass. indic. 3 pers. sg.
{5.A.3.a} .... id.
παραδιδούς   vbl., pres. act. ptc. nom. sg. masc.
{6.A.3}............................ id.
παραδιδῷ   verb, pres. act. subjunc. 3 pers. sg.
{5.B.3} .... id.
G3860 **παραδίδωμι**   *I hand over, I pledge; I hand
down, deliver; I betray.*
παραδίδως   verb, pres. act. indic. 2 pers. sg.
{5.A.3.a} .... παραδίδωμι G3860
παραδιδῶσιν   verb, pres. act. subjunc. 3 pers.
pl. {5.B.3}.......................... id.
παραδοθείς   vbl., aor. pass. ptc. nom. sg. masc.
{6.A.3}............................ id.
παραδοθείσῃ   vbl., aor. pass. ptc. dat. sg. fem.
{6.A.3}............................ id.
παραδοθείσης   vbl., aor. pass. ptc. gen. sg. fem.
{6.A.3}............................ id.
παραδοθῆναι   vbl., aor. pass. inf. {6.B.1}...... id.
παραδοθήσεσθε   verb, fut. pass. indic. 2 pers.
pl. {5.A.1} .... id.
παραδοθήσεται   verb, fut. pass. indic. 3 pers.
sg. {5.A.1} .... id.
παραδοθῶ   verb, aor. pass. subjunc. 1 pers. sg.
{5.B.3} .... id.
παραδοῖ   verb, ²aor. act. subjunc. 3 pers. sg.
{5.B.3} .... id.
παραδόντος   vbl., ²aor. act. ptc. gen. sg. masc.
{6.A.3}............................ id.
παράδοξα   adj., acc. pl. neut. {3.C} ...παράδοξος G3861
G3861 **παράδοξος**, -ον   *unexpected;* hence, *wonderful.*
παραδόσει   noun, dat. sg. fem. {2.C} .. παράδοσις G3862
παραδόσεις   noun, acc. pl. fem. {2.C} .... id.
παραδόσεων   noun, gen. pl. fem. {2.C} .... id.
παραδόσιν   noun, acc. sg. fem. {2.C} .... id.
G3862 **παράδοσις**, -εως, ἡ   orig. abstr., *handing over,*
generally concr., *that which is handed down, a
tradition* (whether of written or of oral teaching).
παραδοῦναι   vbl., ²aor. act. inf.
{6.B.3} .... παραδίδωμι G3860
παραδούς   vbl., ²aor. act. ptc. nom. sg. masc.
{6.A.3}............................ id.

παραδῶ   verb, ²aor. act. subjunc. 1 pers. sg.
{5.B.3} .... id.
παραδῷ   verb, ²aor. act. subjunc. 3 pers. sg.
{5.B.3} .... id.
παραδώσει   verb, fut. act. indic. 3 pers. sg.
{5.A.1}............................ id.
παραδώσιν   verb, ²aor. act. subjunc. 3 pers. pl.
{5.B.3} .... id.
παραδώσουσι   verb, fut. act. indic. 3 pers. pl.
{5.A.1}............................ id.
παραδώσουσιν   verb, fut. act. indic. 3 pers. pl.
{5.A.1}............................ id.
παραδώσω   verb, fut. act. indic. 1 pers. sg. {5.A.1}. id.
παραδώσων   vbl., fut. act. ptc. nom. sg. masc.
{6.A.3}............................ id.
παραζηλοῦμεν   verb, pres. act. indic. 1 pers. pl.
{5.A.2}..................... παραζηλόω G3863
G3863 **παραζηλόω**   *I make jealous, I provoke to
jealousy.*
παραζηλῶσαι   vbl., aor. act. inf.
{6.B.1} .... παραζηλόω G3863
παραζηλώσω   verb, aor. act. subjunc. 1 pers.
sg. {5.B.1} .... id.
παραζηλώσω   verb, fut. act. indic. 1 pers. sg.
{5.A.1}............................ id.
παραθαλασσίαν   adj., acc. sg. fem.
{3.C} .... παραθαλάσσιος G3864
G3864 **παραθαλάσσιος**, -α, -ον   *by the sea (lake), on
the coast.*
παραθεῖναι   vbl., ²aor. act. inf. {6.B.3} παρατίθημι G3908
G3865 **παραθεωρέω**   *I look past, overlook, neglect.*
G3866 **παραθήκη**, -ης, ἡ   *a deposit* (properly of
money or valuables deposited with a friend for
safekeeping, while the owner is abroad). 1 Tim
6:20; 2 Tim 1:14,
παραθήκην   noun, acc. sg. fem. {2.A} . παραθήκη G3866
παραθήσομαι   verb, fut. mid. indic. 1 pers. sg.
{5.A.1}..................... παρατίθημι G3908
παραθήσω   verb, fut. act. indic. 1 pers. sg.
{5.A.1}............................ id.
παράθου   verb, ²aor. mid. impv. 2 pers. sg.
{5.D.3} .... id.
παραθῶσι   verb, ²aor. act. subjunc. 3 pers. pl.
{5.B.3} .... id.
παραθῶσιν   verb, ²aor. act. subjunc. 3 pers. pl.
{5.B.3} .... id.
G3867 **παραινέω**   *I admonish, advise.*
παραινῶ   verb, pres. act. indic. 1 pers. sg.
{5.A.2}..................... παραινέω G3867
παραιτεῖσθαι   vbl., pres. mid./pass. inf.
{6.B.2} .... παραιτέομαι G3868
G3868 **παραιτέομαι**   (1) *I beg* from another, Mark
15:6 (var.), Heb 12:19 (cf. 2); (2) *I beg off from,
I seek to turn away* (from myself) *by entreaty;*
hence, *I give an excuse, I excuse myself, I beg
to be excused,* Luke 14:18, 19; Heb 12:25; *I
decline, refuse, object to,* Acts 25:11; 1 Tim 4:7;
5:11; 2 Tim 2:23; Titus 3:10.
παραιτησάμενοι   vbl., aor. mid. ptc. nom. pl.
masc. {6.A.2} .... παραιτέομαι G3868

παραιτήσησθε   verb, aor. mid. subjunc. 2 pers.
    pl. {5.B.1}. . . . . id.
παραιτοῦ   verb, pres. mid./pass. impv. 2 pers.
    sg. {5.D.2} . . . . id.
παραιτοῦμαι   verb, pres. mid./pass. indic.
    1 pers. sg. {5.A.2}. id.
G3869† **παρακαθέζομαι**   *I sit down beside.* Var. for
    παρακαθίζω, Luke 10:39.
παρακαθεσθεῖσα   vbl., aor. pass. ptc. nom. sg.
    fem. {6.A.1.a}. . . . . παρακαθέζομαι G3869†
G3869 **παρακαθίζω**   *I sit down beside.*
παρακαθίσασα   vbl., aor. act. ptc. nom. sg. fem.
    {6.A.1.a} . . . . παρακαθέζομαι G3869†
παρακάλει   verb, pres. act. impv. 2 pers. sg.
    {5.D.2}. παρακαλέω G3870
παρακαλεῖ   verb, pres. act. indic. 3 pers. sg.
    {5.A.2}. . . . . id.
παρακαλεῖν   vbl., pres. act. inf. {6.B.2} . . . . . . id.
παρακαλεῖσθε   verb, pres. pass. impv. 2 pers.
    pl. {5.D.2} . . . . id.
παρακαλεῖται   verb, pres. pass. indic. 3 pers.
    sg. {5.A.2} . . . . id.
παρακαλεῖτε   verb, pres. act. impv. 2 pers. pl.
    {5.D.2} . . . . id.
παρακαλέσαι   vbl., aor. act. inf. {6.B.1} . . . . id.
παρακαλέσαι   verb, aor. act. opt. 3 pers. sg.
    {5.C.1} . . . . id.
παρακαλέσας   vbl., aor. act. ptc. nom. sg.
    masc. {6.A.2} . . . . id.
παρακαλέσῃ   verb, aor. act. subjunc. 3 pers.
    sg. {5.B.1} . . . . id.
παρακάλεσον   verb, aor. act. impv. 2 pers. sg.
    {5.D.1}. . . . . id.
G3870 **παρακαλέω**   (1) *I ask, beseech;* (2) *I exhort;* (3)
    I comfort.
παρακαλούμεθα   verb, pres. pass. indic. 1 pers. pl.
    {5.A.2} . . . . παρακαλέω G3870
παρακαλοῦμεν   verb, pres. act. indic. 1 pers.
    pl. {5.A.2} . . . . id.
παρακαλοῦντες   vbl., pres. act. ptc. nom. pl.
    masc. {6.A.2} . . . . id.
παρακαλοῦντος   vbl., pres. act. ptc. gen. sg.
    masc. {6.A.2} . . . . id.
παρακαλοῦσιν   verb, pres. act. indic. 3 pers.
    pl. {5.A.2} . . . . id.
G3871 **παρακαλύπτω**   *I conceal, veil.*
παρακαλῶ   verb, pres. act. indic. 1 pers. sg.
    {5.A.2}. παρακαλέω G3870
παρακαλῶν   vbl., pres. act. ptc. nom. sg. masc.
    {6.A.2}. . . . . id.
παρακαλῶνται   verb, pres. pass. subjunc.
    3 pers. pl. {5.B.2} . . . . id.
G3872 **παρακαταθήκη**, -ης, ἡ   *a deposit* (properly of
    money or valuables deposited with a friend for
    safekeeping, while the owner is abroad). Var.
    for παραθήκη, 1 Tim 6:20; 2 Tim 1:14.
παρακαταθήκην   noun, acc. sg. fem.
    {2.A} . . . . παρακαταθήκη G3872
G3873 **παράκειμαι**   *I rest with.*

παράκειται   verb, pres. mid./pass. indic. 3 pers. sg.
    {5.A.3.a} . . . . παράκειμαι G3873
παρακεκαλυμμένον   vbl., perf. pass. ptc. nom. sg.
    neut. {6.A.1.b}. . . . . παρακαλύπτω G3871
παρακεκλήμεθα   verb, perf. pass. indic. 1 pers. pl.
    {5.A.1} . . . . παρακαλέω G3870
παρακεχειμακότι   vbl., perf. act. ptc. dat. sg. masc.
    {6.A.1.a} . . . . .παραχειμάζω G3914
παρακεχειμακότι   vbl., perf. act. ptc. dat. sg.
    neut. {6.A.1.a} . . . . id.
παρακληθῆναι   vbl., aor. pass. inf.
    {6.B.1} . . . . παρακαλέω G3870
παρακληθήσονται   verb, fut. pass. indic.
    3 pers. pl. {5.A.1} . . . . id.
παρακληθῶσιν   verb, aor. pass. subjunc.
    3 pers. pl. {5.B.1} . . . . id.
παρακλήσει   noun, dat. sg. fem. {2.C}παράκλησις G3874
παρακλήσεως   noun, gen. sg. fem. {2.C} . . . . . . id.
παράκλησιν   noun, acc. sg. fem. {2.C}. . . . . id.
G3874 **παράκλησις**, -εως, ἡ   *an appeal,* which accord-
    ing to circumstances may be either hortatory,
    exhortation, or consolatory, *consolation;* in Luke
    2:25 it seems to have a quasi-technical sense,
    with reference to the coming of the Messiah.
παράκλησις   noun, nom. sg. fem.
    {2.C} . . . . παράκλησις G3874
παράκλητον   noun, acc. sg. masc.
    {2.B} . . . . .παράκλητος G3875
G3875 **παράκλητος**, -ου, ὁ   *helper; consoler* (corre-
    sponding to the name Menahem given to the
    Messiah); orig. pass. in sense, *one called in* for
    support, *one summoned* as support, but this
    idea drops into the background; in the techni-
    cal legal sense it never occurs, but in writings
    prior to the NT has the general sense, *one
    who speaks in favor of another, an intercessor,
    helper;* it tends thus to have an act. sense, and
    was borrowed by Heb. and Aram.
παράκλητος   noun, nom. sg. masc.
    {2.B} . . . . .παράκλητος G3875
G3876 **παρακοή**, -ῆς, ἡ   *disobedience.*
παρακοή   noun, nom. sg. fem. {2.A} . . . παρακοή G3876
παρακοήν   noun, acc. sg. fem. {2.A} . . . . id.
παρακοῆς   noun, gen. sg. fem. {2.A} . . . . id.
G3877 **παρακολουθέω**   *I accompany, follow closely,*
    both lit. and met., *I investigate; I result* Mark
    16:17 (var.).
παρακολουθήσει   verb, fut. act. indic. 3 pers. sg.
    {5.A.1} . . . . παρακολουθέω G3877
παρακούσας   vbl., aor. act. ptc. nom. sg. masc.
    {6.A.1.a} . . . . παρακούω G3878
παρακούσῃ   verb, aor. act. subjunc. 3 pers. sg.
    {5.B.1} . . . . id.
G3878 **παρακούω**   (1) *I hear carelessly* or *incidentally,*
    or *I pretend not to hear,* Mark 5:36; (2) *I refuse
    to hear; I disobey.*
G3879 **παρακύπτω**   *I stretch forward the head to catch
    a glimpse* (esp. through a window or door,
    sometimes inwards, oftener outwards; fig. it

implies a rapid, hasty, and cursory glance), *I look, peep, peer in (at); I look down.*

παρακύψαι   vbl., aor. act. inf. {6.B.1}. παρακύπτω *G3879*

παρακύψας   vbl., aor. act. ptc. nom. sg. masc. {6.A.1.a} . . . . id.

παράλαβε   verb, ²aor. act. impv. 2 pers. sg. {5.D.1}. . . . . .παραλαμβάνω *G3880*

παραλαβεῖν   vbl., ²aor. act. inf. {6.B.1}. . . . . id.

παραλαβόντα   vbl., ²aor. act. ptc. acc. sg. masc. {6.A.1.a}. . . . . id.

παραλαβόντες   vbl., ²aor. act. ptc. nom. pl. masc. {6.A.1.a}. . . . . id.

παραλαβών   vbl., ²aor. act. ptc. nom. sg. masc. {6.A.1.a} . . . . id.

παραλαμβάνει   verb, pres. act. indic. 3 pers. sg. {5.A.1.a} . . . . id.

παραλαμβάνεται   verb, pres. pass. indic. 3 pers. sg. {5.A.1.d} . . . . id.

παραλαμβάνοντες   vbl., pres. act. ptc. nom. pl. masc. {6.A.1} . . . . id.

παραλαμβάνουσιν   verb, pres. act. indic. 3 pers. pl. {5.A.1.a} . . . . id.

G3880 **παραλαμβάνω**   *I take* from, *I receive* from, or, *I take* to, *I receive* (apparently not used of money, see ἀπέχω); *I take with* me.

G3881 **παραλέγομαι**   *I coast along, sail along.*

παραλεγόμενοι   vbl., pres. mid./pass. ptc. nom. pl. masc. {6.A.1}. . . . . παραλέγομαι *G3881*

παραλελυμένα   vbl., perf. pass. ptc. acc. pl. neut. {6.A.1.b} . . . . παραλύω *G3886*

παραλελυμένοι   vbl., perf. pass. ptc. nom. pl. masc. {6.A.1.b} . . . . id.

παραλελυμένος   vbl., perf. pass. ptc. nom. sg. masc. {6.A.1.b} . . . . id.

παραλελυμένῳ   vbl., perf. pass. ptc. dat. sg. masc. {6.A.1.b} . . . . id.

παραλημφθήσεται   verb, fut. pass. indic. 3 pers. sg. {5.A.1.d}. . . . . .παραλαμβάνω *G3880*

παραλήμψομαι   verb, fut. mid. indic. 1 pers. sg. {5.A.1.d}. . . . . id.

παραληφθήσεται   verb, fut. pass. indic. 3 pers. sg. {5.A.1.d}. . . . . id.

παραλήψομαι   verb, fut. mid. indic. 1 pers. sg. {5.A.1.d} . . . . id.

G3882 **παράλιος**, -ον   *on the seacoast, on the seaboard;* ἡ παράλιος (supply χώρα), *the coast country.*

παραλίου   adj., gen. sg. fem. {3.C}. . . . . παράλιος *G3882*

G3883 **παραλλαγή**, -ῆς, ἡ   *a variation;* hence, *a periodic change* of a heavenly body.

παραλλαγή   noun, nom. sg. fem. {2.A} . . . . παραλλαγή *G3883*

παραλογίζηται   verb, pres. mid./pass. subjunc. 3 pers. sg. {5.B.1} . . . . παραλογίζομαι *G3884*

G3884 **παραλογίζομαι**   *I deceive, beguile.*

παραλογιζόμενοι   vbl., pres. mid./pass. ptc. nom. pl. masc. {6.A.1} . . . . παραλογίζομαι *G3884*

παραλυτικόν   adj., acc. sg. masc. {3.C} . . . . παραλυτικός *G3885*

G3885 **παραλυτικός**, -οῦ, ὁ   *a paralytic,* a more colloquial word than παραλελυμένος, the medical term (cf. Luke 5:24).

παραλυτικός   adj., nom. sg. masc. {3.C} . . . . παραλυτικός *G3885*

παραλυτικούς   adj., acc. pl. masc. {3.C} . . . . . . id.

παραλυτικῷ   adj., dat. sg. masc. {3.C} . . . . id.

G3886 **παραλύω**   pass., παραλελυμένος, *one who has become loosened (unstrung), one whose power of movement has gone, paralyzed, a paralytic.*

παραμείνας   vbl., aor. act. ptc. nom. sg. masc. {6.A.1.a} . . . . παραμένω *G3887*

παραμένειν   vbl., pres. act. inf. {6.B.1}. . . . . . . id.

παραμενῶ   verb, fut. act. indic. 1 pers. sg. {5.A.2}. . . . . id.

G3887 **παραμένω**   *I remain beside, I stand by;* hence equivalent to, *I serve* (as a free man), cf. perhaps Phil 1:25; Jas 1:25; *I remain in* office, Heb 7:23; *I persevere* in the law, Jas 1:25.

παραμυθεῖσθε   verb, pres. mid./pass. impv. 2 pers. pl. {5.D.2} . . . . .παραμυθέομαι *G3888*

G3888 **παραμυθέομαι**   *I encourage, comfort, console.*

παραμυθήσωνται   verb, aor. mid. subjunc. 3 pers. pl. {5.B.1}. . . . . .παραμυθέομαι *G3888*

G3889 **παραμυθία**, -ας, ἡ   *encouragement, comfort, consolation.*

παραμυθίαν   noun, acc. sg. fem. {2.A} παραμυθία *G3889*

G3890 **παραμύθιον**, -ου, τό   *consolation.*

παραμύθιον   noun, nom. sg. neut. {2.B} . . . . .παραμύθιον *G3890*

παραμυθούμενοι   vbl., pres. mid./pass. ptc. nom. pl. masc. {6.A.2} . . . . .παραμυθέομαι *G3888*

G3891 **παρανομέω**   *I contravene a statute (law).*

G3892 **παρανομία**, -ας, ἡ   *a breach of a statute (law).*

παρανομίας   noun, acc. sg. fem. {2.A} παρανομία *G3892*

παρανομῶν   vbl., pres. act. ptc. nom. sg. masc. {6.A.2}. . . . . παρανομέω *G3891*

παραπεσόντας   vbl., ²aor. act. ptc. acc. pl. masc. {6.A.1.a} . . . . .παραπίπτω *G3895*

G3893 **παραπικραίνω**   absol. *I embitter, provoke, irritate.*

G3894 **παραπικρασμός**, -οῦ, ὁ   *embitterment, provocation, irritation.*

παραπικρασμῷ   noun, dat. sg. masc. {2.B} . . . . .παραπικρασμός *G3894*

G3895 **παραπίπτω**   *I fall back* (into the unbelieving and godless ways of the old time).

παραπλεῦσαι   vbl., aor. act. inf. {6.B.1} παραπλέω *G3896*

G3896 **παραπλέω**   *I sail past* (without stopping there).

παραπλήσιον   adv. . . . . .παραπλήσιος *G3897*

G3897 **παραπλήσιος**, -ία, -ιον   *coming near, resembling, similar;* neut. sg. adv. παραπλήσιον, *nearly.*

G3898 **παραπλησίως**   adv., *correspondingly, in like manner.*

παραπλησίως   adv. {3.F} . . . . παραπλησίως *G3898*

παραπορεύεσθαι   vbl., pres. mid./pass. inf. {6.B.1} .παραπορεύομαι *G3899*

G3899 **παραπορεύομαι**   *I go past,* Mark 11:20; 15:29
(= Matt 27:39); *I go,* apparently a colloquial or
incorrect use, Mark 2:23 (var.); 9:30 (var.).
παραπορευόμενοι   vbl., pres. mid./pass. ptc. nom.
pl. masc. {6.A.1} . . . . παραπορεύομαι *G3899*

G3900 **παράπτωμα**, -ατος, τό   *a falling away, a lapse,*
a slip, a false step, a trespass.
παράπτωμα   noun, nom. sg. neut.
{2.C} . . . . παράπτωμα *G3900*
παραπτώμασι   noun, dat. pl. neut. {2.C} . . . . . id.
παραπτώμασιν   noun, dat. pl. neut. {2.C} . . . . id.
παραπτώματα   noun, acc. pl. neut. {2.C} . . . . . id.
παραπτώματι   noun, dat. sg. neut. {2.C} . . . . . id.
παραπτώματος   noun, gen. sg. neut. {2.C} . . . id.
παραπτωμάτων   noun, gen. pl. neut. {2.C} . . . id.

G3901 **παραρρέω**   (lit. *I flow past, I glide past,* hence)
I am lost, I perish, or merely, *I drift away (I fall*
away) from duty (or *the way of salvation*).
παραρρυῶμεν   verb, ²aor. pass. subjunc. 1 pers. pl.
{5.B.1} . . . . παραρρέω *G3901*
παραρυῶμεν   verb, ²aor. pass. subjunc. 1 pers.
pl. {5.B.1} . . . . id.

G3902 **παράσημος**, -ον   *a figurehead.*
παρασήμῳ   adj., dat. sg. neut. {3.C} . . παράσημος *G3902*
παρασκευαζόντων   vbl., pres. act. ptc. gen. pl.
masc. {6.A.1} . . . . παρασκευάζω *G3903*

G3903 **παρασκευάζω**   *I prepare;* mid. *I prepare, make*
preparations, 1 Cor 14:8.
παρασκευάσεται   verb, fut. mid. indic. 3 pers. sg.
{5.A.1.d} . . . . παρασκευάζω *G3903*

G3904 **παρασκευή**, -ῆς, ἡ   *the day of preparation, the*
day before the Sabbath, Friday.
παρασκευή   noun, nom. sg. fem. {2.A}παρασκευή *G3904*
παρασκευήν   noun, acc. sg. fem. {2.A} . . . . id.
παρασκευῆς   noun, gen. sg. fem. {2.A} . . . . id.
παραστῆναι   vbl., ²aor. act. inf. {6.B.3} παρίστημι *G3936*
παραστῆσαι   vbl., aor. act. inf. {6.B.3} . . . . id.
παραστήσατε   verb, aor. act. impv. 2 pers. pl.
{5.D.3} . . . . id.
παραστήσει   verb, fut. act. indic. 3 pers. sg.
{5.A.1} . . . . id.
παραστήσῃ   verb, aor. act. subjunc. 3 pers. sg.
{5.B.3} . . . . id.
παραστησόμεθα   verb, fut. mid. indic. 1 pers.
pl. {5.A.1} . . . . id.
παραστήσωμεν   verb, aor. act. subjunc. 1 pers.
pl. {5.B.3} . . . . id.
παραστῆτε   verb, ²aor. act. subjunc. 2 pers. pl.
{5.B.3} . . . . id.
παρασχών   vbl., ²aor. act. ptc. nom. sg. masc.
{6.A.1.a} . . . . παρέχω *G3930*

G3905 **παρατείνω**   *I prolong.*
παρατηρεῖσθε   verb, pres. mid. indic. 2 pers. pl.
{5.A.2} . . . . παρατηρέω *G3906*

G3906 **παρατηρέω**   act. and mid. (1) *I watch carefully,*
keep my eye on (as a cat does a mouse); absol.
I watch my opportunity, Luke 20:20; (2) *I*
observe, keep, Gal 4:10.
παρατηρήσαντες   vbl., aor. act. ptc. nom. pl.
masc. {6.A.2} . . . . παρατηρέω *G3906*

παρατηρήσεως   noun, gen. sg. fem.
{2.C} . . . . παρατήρησις *G3907*

G3907 **παρατήρησις**, -εως, ἡ   *a watching* for.
παρατηρούμενοι   vbl., pres. mid. ptc. nom. pl.
masc. {6.A.2} . . . . παρατηρέω *G3906*
παρατίθεμαι   verb, pres. mid. indic. 1 pers. sg.
{5.A.3.a} . . . . παρατίθημι *G3908*
παρατιθέμενα   vbl., pres. pass. ptc. acc. pl.
neut. {6.A.3} . . . . id.
παρατιθέμενον   vbl., pres. pass. ptc. acc. sg.
neut. {6.A.3} . . . . id.
παρατιθέμενος   vbl., pres. mid. ptc. nom. sg.
masc. {6.A.3} . . . . id.
παρατιθέναι   vbl., pres. act. inf. {6.B.3} . . . . . . id.
παρατιθέσθωσαν   verb, pres. mid./pass. impv.
3 pers. pl. {5.D.3} . . . . id.

G3908 **παρατίθημι**   (1) *I set* (esp. a meal) *before,*
I serve; (2) act., and mid., *I deposit* with, *I*
entrust to.
παρατιθῶσιν   verb, pres. act. subjunc. 3 pers. pl.
{5.B.3} . . . . παρατίθημι *G3908*
παρατυγχάνοντας   vbl., pres. act. ptc. acc. pl.
masc. {6.A.1} . . . . παρατυγχάνω *G3909*

G3909 **παρατυγχάνω**   *I come by chance, I am by*
chance in a certain place.

G3910 **παραυτίκα**   adv. with force of adj., *present,*
immediate.
παραυτίκα   adv. {3.F} . . . . παραυτίκα *G3910*
παραφέρεσθε   verb, pres. pass. impv. 2 pers. pl.
{5.D.1} . . . . παραφέρω *G3911*
παραφερόμεναι   vbl., pres. pass. ptc. nom. pl.
fem. {6.A.1} . . . . id.

G3911 **παραφέρω**   *I turn aside, I cause (suffer) to*
pass by, Mark 14:36; Luke 22:42; *I carry away,*
remove, lit. or met.

G3912 **παραφρονέω**   *I am out of my senses.*

G3913 **παραφρονία**, -ας, ἡ   *madness.*
παραφρονίαν   noun, acc. sg. fem.
{2.A} . . . . .παραφρονία *G3913*
παραφρονῶν   vbl., pres. act. ptc. nom. sg. masc.
{6.A.2} . . . . παραφρονέω *G3912*

G3914 **παραχειμάζω**   *I spend the winter, I winter.*
παραχειμάσαι   vbl., aor. act. inf.
{6.B.1} .παραχειμάζω *G3914*

G3915 **παραχειμασία**, -ας, ἡ   *spending the winter,*
wintering.
παραχειμασίαν   noun, acc. sg. fem.
{2.A} . . . . .παραχειμασία *G3915*
παραχειμάσω   verb, fut. act. indic. 1 pers. sg.
{5.A.1.a} . . . . .παραχειμάζω *G3914*

G3916 **παραχρῆμα**   adv., *immediately.*
παραχρῆμα   adv. . . . . παραχρῆμα *G3916*
παρδάλει   noun, dat. sg. fem. {2.C} . . . . πάρδαλις *G3917*

G3917 **πάρδαλις**, -εως, ἡ   *a leopard.*
παρεβάλομεν   verb, ²aor. act. indic. 1 pers. pl.
{5.A.1.b} . . . . παραβάλλω *G3846*
παρέβη   verb, ²aor. act. indic. 3 pers. sg.
{5.A.1.b} . . . . παραβαίνω *G3845*
παρεβιάσαντο   verb, aor. mid. indic. 3 pers. pl.
{5.A.1.e} . . . . .παραβιάζομαι *G3849*

παρεβιάσατο   verb, aor. mid. indic. 3 pers. sg.
{5.A.1.e} . . . . id.
παρεγένετο   verb, ²aor. mid. indic. 3 pers. sg.
{5.A.1.e} . . . . παραγίνομαι G3854
παρεγενόμην   verb, ²aor. mid. indic. 1 pers. sg.
{5.A.1.e} . . . . id.
παρεγένοντο   verb, ²aor. mid. indic. 3 pers. pl.
{5.A.1.e} . . . . id.
παρεγίνοντο   verb, impf. mid. indic. 3 pers. pl.
{5.A.1.e} . . . . id.
παρεδέχθησαν   verb, aor. pass. indic. 3 pers. pl.
{5.A.1.b} . . . . παραδέχομαι G3858
παρεδίδετο   verb, impf. pass. indic. 3 pers. sg.
{5.A.3.a} . . . . παραδίδωμι G3860
παρεδίδοσαν   verb, impf. act. indic. 3 pers. pl.
{5.A.3.a} . . . . id.
παρεδίδοτο   verb, impf. pass. indic. 3 pers. sg.
{5.A.3.a} . . . . id.
παρεδίδου   verb, impf. act. indic. 3 pers. sg.
{5.A.3.a} . . . . id.
παρεδίδουν   verb, impf. act. indic. 3 pers. pl.
{5.A.3.a} . . . . id.
παρεδόθη   verb, aor. pass. indic. 3 pers. sg.
{5.A.1} . . . . id.
παρεδόθην   verb, aor. pass. indic. 1 pers. sg.
{5.A.1} . . . . id.
παρεδόθητε   verb, aor. pass. indic. 2 pers. pl.
{5.A.1} . . . . id.
παρέδοσαν   verb, ²aor. act. indic. 3 pers. pl.
{5.A.3.b} . . . . id.
παρεδρεύοντες   vbl., pres. act. ptc. nom. pl. masc.
{6.A.1} . . . . παρεδρεύω G4332†‡
G4332†‡ παρεδρεύω, I have my seat beside, I attend. Var.
for προσεδρεύω, 1 Cor. 9:13.
παρέδωκα   verb, aor. act. indic. 1 pers. sg.
{5.A.3.b} . . . . παραδίδωμι G3860
παρεδώκαμεν   verb, aor. act. indic. 1 pers. pl.
{5.A.3.b} . . . . id.
παρέδωκαν   verb, aor. act. indic. 3 pers. pl.
{5.A.3.b} . . . . id.
παρέδωκας   verb, aor. act. indic. 2 pers. sg.
{5.A.3.b} . . . . id.
παρεδώκατε   verb, aor. act. indic. 2 pers. pl.
{5.A.3.b} . . . . id.
παρέδωκε   verb, aor. act. indic. 3 pers. sg.
{5.A.3.b} . . . . id.
παρέδωκεν   verb, aor. act. indic. 3 pers. sg.
{5.A.3.b} . . . . id.
παρέθεντο   verb, ²aor. mid. indic. 3 pers. pl.
{5.A.3.b} . . . . παρατίθημι G3908
παρεθεωροῦντο   verb, impf. pass. indic. 3 pers. pl.
{5.A.2} . . . . παραθεωρέω G3865
παρέθηκαν   verb, aor. act. indic. 3 pers. pl.
{5.A.3.b} . . . . παρατίθημι G3908
παρέθηκε   verb, aor. act. indic. 3 pers. sg.
{5.A.3.b} . . . . id.
παρέθηκεν   verb, aor. act. indic. 3 pers. sg.
{5.A.3.b} . . . . id.
πάρει   verb, pres. act. indic. 2 pers. sg.
{7.A} . . . . .πάρειμι G3918

παρειμένας   vbl., perf. pass. ptc. acc. pl. fem.
{6.A.3} . . . . παρίημι G3935
G3918 πάρειμι (from εἰμί)   I am present; I have come,
arrived (hence with εἰς, πρός).
παρεῖναι   vbl., pres. act. inf. {7.C.2} . . . . .πάρειμι G3918
παρεῖναι   vbl., ²aor. act. inf. {6.B.3} . . . . παρίημι G3935
G3919 παρεισάγω   I introduce from the side.
G3920 παρείσακτος, -ον   introduced (imported) from
the side.
παρεισάκτους   adj., acc. pl. masc.
{3.C} . . . . παρείσακτος G3920
παρεισάξουσιν   verb, fut. act. indic. 3 pers. pl.
{5.A.1.a} . . . . παρεισάγω G3919
G3921 παρεισδύω (παρεισδύνω)   I creep in.
παρεισεδύησαν   verb, ²aor. pass. indic. 3 pers. pl.
{5.A.1.e} . . . . παρεισδύω G3921
παρεισέδυσαν   verb, aor. act. indic. 3 pers. pl.
{5.A.1.b} . . . . id.
παρεισενέγκαντες   vbl., aor. act. ptc. nom. pl.
masc. {6.A.1.a} . . . . .παρεισφέρω G3923
G3922 παρεισέρχομαι   I come in from the side.
παρεισῆλθεν   verb, ²aor. act. indic. 3 pers. sg.
{5.A.1.b} . . . . παρεισέρχομαι G3922
παρεισῆλθον   verb, ²aor. act. indic. 3 pers. pl.
{5.A.1.b} . . . . id.
πάρεισιν   verb, pres. act. indic. 3 pers. pl.
{7.A} . . . . .πάρειμι G3918
παρειστήκεισαν   verb, plu. act. indic. 3 pers. pl.
{5.A.1} . . . . παρίστημι G3936
G3923 παρεισφέρω   I bring in (import) from the side, I
smuggle.
παρεῖχαν   verb, impf. act. indic. 3 pers. pl.
{5.A.1.b} . . . . .παρέχω G3930
παρεῖχε   verb, impf. act. indic. 3 pers. sg.
{5.A.1.b} . . . . id.
παρεῖχεν   verb, impf. act. indic. 3 pers. sg.
{5.A.1.b} . . . . id.
παρείχετο   verb, impf. mid. indic. 3 pers. sg.
{5.A.1.e} . . . . id.
παρεῖχον   verb, impf. act. indic. 3 pers. pl.
{5.A.1.b} . . . . id.
παρεκάλει   verb, impf. act. indic. 3 pers. sg.
{5.A.2} . . . . παρακαλέω G3870
παρεκάλεσα   verb, aor. act. indic. 1 pers. sg.
{5.A.1} . . . . id.
παρεκάλεσαν   verb, aor. act. indic. 3 pers. pl.
{5.A.1} . . . . id.
παρεκάλεσας   verb, aor. act. indic. 2 pers. sg.
{5.A.1} . . . . id.
παρεκάλεσε   verb, aor. act. indic. 3 pers. sg. {5.A.1} . id.
παρεκάλεσεν   verb, aor. act. indic. 3 pers. sg.
{5.A.1} . . . . id.
παρεκαλοῦμεν   verb, impf. act. indic. 1 pers.
pl. {5.A.2} . . . . id.
παρεκάλουν   verb, impf. act. indic. 3 pers. pl.
{5.A.2} . . . . id.
παρεκλήθη   verb, aor. pass. indic. 3 pers. sg.
{5.A.1} . . . . id.
παρεκλήθημεν   verb, aor. pass. indic. 1 pers.
pl. {5.A.1} . . . . id.

παρεκλήθησαν   verb, aor. pass. indic. 3 pers.
pl. {5.A.1} . . . . id.
G3924 **παρεκτός**   (1) adv. used as adj., *outside, without, left over;* (2) prep., *apart from.*
παρεκτός   adv., prep. . . . . παρεκτός G3924
παρέκυψεν   verb, aor. act. indic. 3 pers. sg.
{5.A.1.b} . . . . παρακύπτω G3879
παρέλαβε   verb, ²aor. act. indic. 3 pers. sg.
{5.A.1.b} .παραλαμβάνω G3880
παρέλαβεν   verb, ²aor. act. indic. 3 pers. sg.
{5.A.1.b} . . . . id.
παρέλαβες   verb, ²aor. act. indic. 2 pers. sg.
{5.A.1.b} . . . . id.
παρελάβετε   verb, ²aor. act. indic. 2 pers. pl.
{5.A.1.b} . . . . id.
παρέλαβον   verb, ²aor. act. indic. 1 pers. sg.
{5.A.1.b} . . . . id.
παρέλαβον   verb, ²aor. act. indic. 3 pers. pl.
{5.A.1.b} . . . . id.
παρελάβοσαν   verb, ²aor. act. indic. 3 pers. pl.
{5.A.1.b} . . . . id.
παρελέγοντο   verb, impf. mid./pass. indic. 3 pers.
pl. {5.A.1.e} . . . . παραλέγομαι G3881
παρελεύσεται   verb, fut. mid. indic. 3 pers. sg.
{5.A.1.d} . . . . παρέρχομαι G3928
παρελεύσονται   verb, fut. mid. indic. 3 pers.
pl. {5.A.1.d} . . . . id.
παρεληλυθέναι   vbl., ²perf. act. inf. {6.B.1} . . . . id.
παρεληλυθώς   vbl., ²perf. act. ptc. nom. sg.
masc. {6.A.1} . . . . id.
παρελθάτω   verb, ²aor. act. impv. 3 pers. sg.
{5.D.1} . . . . id.
παρελθεῖν   vbl., ²aor. act. inf. {6.B.1} . . . . id.
παρελθέτω   verb, ²aor. act. impv. 3 pers. sg.
{5.D.1} . . . . id.
παρέλθη   verb, ²aor. act. subjunc. 3 pers. sg.
{5.B.1} . . . . id.
παρελθόντες   vbl., ²aor. act. ptc. nom. pl. masc.
{6.A.1.a} . . . . id.
παρελθών   vbl., ²aor. act. ptc. nom. sg. masc.
{6.A.1.a} . . . . id.
παρέλθωσι   verb, ²aor. act. subjunc. 3 pers. pl.
{5.B.1} . . . . id.
παρέλθωσιν   verb, ²aor. act. subjunc. 3 pers. pl.
{5.B.1} . . . . id.
G4016†‡ **παρεμβάλλω**   *I throw (raise) up beside.* Var. for
περιβάλλω, Luke 19:43.
παρεμβαλοῦσιν   verb, fut. act. indic. 3 pers. pl.
{5.A.2} . . . . παρεμβάλλω G4016†‡
παρεμβολάς   noun, acc. pl. fem. {2.A} παρεμβολή G3925
G3925 **παρεμβολή**, -ῆς, ἡ   *a camp,* either a fixed
camp, occupied possibly for centuries, *a fort,
castle,* like that at Jerusalem, or a marching
camp, according to context; hence, *the army*
occupying such, Heb 11:34.
παρεμβολήν   noun, acc. sg. fem. {2.A} παρεμβολή G3925
παρεμβολῆς   noun, gen. sg. fem. {2.A} . . . . id.
παρένεγκε   verb, ²aor. act. impv. 2 pers. sg.
{5.D.1} . . . . παραφέρω G3911
παρενεγκεῖν   vbl., ²aor. act. inf. {6.B.1} . . . . id.

παρενοχλεῖν   vbl., pres. act. inf.
{6.B.2} . . . . .παρενοχλέω G3926
G3926 **παρενοχλέω**   *I trouble,* or perhaps, *I trouble
further.*
παρέξει   verb, fut. act. indic. 3 pers. sg.
{5.A.1.a} . . . . παρέχω G3930
παρέξη   verb, fut. mid. indic. 2 pers. sg.
{5.A.1.d} . . . . id.
παρεπίδημοι   adj., nom. pl. masc.
{3.C} . . . . παρεπίδημος G3927
παρεπιδήμοις   adj., dat. pl. masc. {3.C} . . . . . . id.
G3927 **παρεπίδημος**, -ου, ὁ   *a stranger* settled in a
town or region for a time without making it
his permanent residence, *a sojourner;* so in a
spiritual sense of those who are on the earth
for a time, whose real home is heaven.
παρεπιδήμους   adj., acc. pl. masc.
{3.C} . . . . παρεπίδημος G3927
παρεπίκραναν   verb, aor. act. indic. 3 pers. pl.
{5.A.1.b} . . . . παραπικραίνω G3893
παρεπορεύοντο   verb, impf. mid./pass. indic.
3 pers. pl. {5.A.1.e} . . . . παραπορεύομαι G3899
παρέρχεσθε   verb, pres. mid./pass. indic. 2 pers. pl.
{5.A.1.d} . . . . παρέρχομαι G3928
παρέρχεται   verb, pres. mid./pass. indic.
3 pers. sg. {5.A.1.d} . . . . id.
G3928 **παρέρχομαι**   trans. and intrans., *I pass by,
I pass;* sometimes practically, *I pass out of
sight, I disappear;* with acc. (cf. παραβαίνω)
I transgress; intrans., *I approach, come up to,*
Luke 12:37; 17:7; Acts 24:7 (var.).
πάρεσιν   noun, acc. sg. fem. {2.C} . . . . . .πάρεσις G3929
G3929 **πάρεσις**, -εως, ἡ   *overlooking, suspension,
remission* of punishment for (from παρίημι).
παρεσκευασμένοι   vbl., perf. mid./pass. ptc. nom.
pl. masc. {6.A.1.b} . . . . παρασκευάζω G3903
παρεσκεύασται   verb, perf. mid./pass. indic.
3 pers. sg. {5.A.1.f} . . . . id.
πάρεσμεν   verb, pres. act. indic. 1 pers. pl.
{7.A} . . . . .πάρειμι G3918
παρέσται   verb, fut. mid. indic. 3 pers. sg. {7.A} . . id.
πάρεστε   verb, pres. act. indic. 2 pers. pl. {7.A}. . id.
παρέστη   verb, ²aor. act. indic. 3 pers. sg.
{5.A.3.b} . . . . παρίστημι G3936
παρέστηκεν   verb, perf. act. indic. 3 pers. sg.
{5.A.1} . . . . id.
παρεστηκόσιν   vbl., perf. act. ptc. dat. pl.
masc. {6.A.3} . . . . id.
παρεστηκότων   vbl., perf. act. ptc. gen. pl.
masc. {6.A.3} . . . . id.
παρεστηκώς   vbl., perf. act. ptc. nom. sg. masc.
{6.A.3} . . . . id.
παρέστησαν   verb, aor. act. indic. 3 pers. pl.
{5.A.3.b} . . . . id.
παρεστήσατε   verb, aor. act. indic. 2 pers. pl.
{5.A.3.b} . . . . id.
παρέστησεν   verb, aor. act. indic. 3 pers. sg.
{5.A.3.b} . . . . id.
πάρεστι   verb, pres. act. indic. 3 pers. sg.
{7.A} . . . . .πάρειμι G3918

πάρεστιν   verb, pres. act. indic. 3 pers. sg. {7.a} . id.
παρεστῶσιν   vbl., ²perf. act. ptc. dat. pl. masc.
     {6.A.3}. . . . . παρίστημι *G3936*
παρεστῶτα   vbl., ²perf. act. ptc. acc. sg. masc.
     {6.A.3}. . . . . id.
παρεστῶτες   vbl., ²perf. act. ptc. nom. pl. masc.
     {6.A.3}. . . . . id.
παρέσχον   verb, ²aor. act. indic. 3 pers. pl.
     {5.A.1.b} . . . . .παρέχω *G3930*
παρέτεινε   verb, impf. act. indic. 3 pers. sg.
     {5.A.1.b} . . . . παρατείνω *G3905*
παρέτεινεν   verb, impf. act. indic. 3 pers. sg.
     {5.A.1.b} . . . . id.
παρετήρουν   verb, impf. act. indic. 3 pers. pl.
     {5.A.2}. . . . . παρατηρέω *G3906*
παρετηροῦντο   verb, impf. mid. indic. 3 pers.
     pl. {5.A.2} . . . . id.
πάρεχε   verb, pres. act. impv. 2 pers. sg.
     {5.D.1}. . . . . .παρέχω *G3930*
παρέχειν   vbl., pres. act. inf. {6.B.1} . . . . id.
παρέχεσθε   verb, pres. mid. impv. 2 pers. pl.
     {5.D.1}. . . . . id.
παρέχετε   verb, pres. act. indic. 2 pers. pl.
     {5.A.1.a} . . . . id.
παρεχέτω   verb, pres. act. impv. 3 pers. sg. {5.D.1}. id.
παρεχόμενος   vbl., pres. mid. ptc. nom. sg.
     masc. {6.A.1}. . . . . id.
παρέχοντι   vbl., pres. act. ptc. dat. sg. masc.
     {6.A.1}. . . . . id.
παρέχουσι   verb, pres. act. indic. 3 pers. pl.
     {5.A.1.a} . . . . id.
παρέχουσιν   verb, pres. act. indic. 3 pers. pl.
     {5.A.1.a} . . . . id.
G3930 **παρέχω**   act. and mid. *I offer, provide, confer, af-*
     ford, give, bring, show, cause; κόπους (κόπον)
     τινί παρέχειν, *to cause one trouble.*
παρηγγείλαμεν   verb, aor. act. indic. 1 pers. pl.
     {5.A.1.b} . . . . παραγγέλλω *G3853*
παρήγγειλαν   verb, aor. act. indic. 3 pers. pl.
     {5.A.1.b} . . . . id.
παρήγγειλε   verb, aor. act. indic. 3 pers. sg.
     {5.A.1.b} . . . . id.
παρήγγειλεν   verb, aor. act. indic. 3 pers. sg.
     {5.A.1.b} . . . . id.
παρήγγελλεν   verb, impf. act. indic. 3 pers. sg.
     {5.A.1.b} . . . . id.
παρηγγέλλομεν   verb, impf. act. indic. 1 pers.
     pl. {5.A.1.b} . . . . id.
παρηγγελμένα   vbl., perf. pass. ptc. acc. pl.
     neut. {6.A.1.b} . . . . id.
παρῆγεν   verb, impf. act. indic. 3 pers. sg.
     {5.A.1.b} . . . . .παράγω *G3855*
G3931 **παρηγορία**, -ας, ἡ   *a consolation.*
παρηγορία   noun, nom. sg. fem. {2.A}. παρηγορία *G3931*
παρηκολούθηκας   verb, perf. act. indic. 2 pers. sg.
     {5.A.1}. . . . . παρακολουθέω *G3877*
παρηκολουθηκότι   vbl., perf. act. ptc. dat. sg.
     masc. {6.A.2}. . . . . id.
παρηκολούθησας   verb, aor. act. indic. 2 pers.
     sg. {5.A.1} . . . . id.

παρῆλθε   verb, ²aor. act. indic. 3 pers. sg.
     {5.A.1.b} . . . . παρέρχομαι *G3928*
παρῆλθεν   verb, ²aor. act. indic. 3 pers. sg.
     {5.A.1.b} . . . . id.
παρῆλθον   verb, ²aor. act. indic. 1 pers. sg.
     {5.A.1.b} . . . . id.
παρήνει   verb, impf. act. indic. 3 pers. sg.
     {5.A.2}. . . . . παραινέω *G3867*
παρῆσαν   verb, impf. act. indic. 3 pers. pl.
     {7.A} . . . . .πάρειμι *G3918*
παρητημένον   vbl., perf. pass. ptc. acc. sg. masc.
     {6.A.2}. . . . . παραιτέομαι *G3868*
παρητήσαντο   verb, aor. mid. indic. 3 pers. pl.
     {5.A.1} . . . . id.
παρητοῦντο   verb, impf. mid./pass. indic.
     3 pers. pl. {5.A.2}. . . . . id.
G3932 **παρθενία**, -ας, ἡ   *maidenhood, virginity.*
παρθενίας   noun, gen. sg. fem. {2.A}. . . παρθενία *G3932*
παρθένοι   noun, nom. pl. fem. {2.B} . . . παρθένος *G3933*
παρθένοι   noun, nom. pl. masc. {2.B}. . . παρθένος *G3933*
παρθένοις   noun, dat. pl. fem. {2.B}. . . . . id.
παρθένον   noun, acc. sg. fem. {2.B} . . . . id.
G3933 **παρθένος**, -ου, ἡ   *a maiden, a virgin;* hence
     (Rev 14:4), extended to men who have not
     known women; in 1 Cor 7:25–38, the word
     must have its usual sense, and refer to women
     living in merely spiritual wedlock with men.
     In Matt 1:23 παρθένος is an inaccurate trans-
     lation (due to LXX) of a Heb. word in Isa 7:14
     meaning *a female adolescent, a young woman*
     of marriageable age, whether married or not,
     rightly translated by Theodotion and Aquila
     νεᾶνις.
παρθένος   noun, nom. sg. fem. {2.B} . . . παρθένος *G3933*
παρθένου   noun, gen. sg. fem. {2.B}. . . . . id.
παρθένων   noun, gen. pl. fem. {2.B}. . . . . id.
Πάρθοι   noun prop., nom. pl. masc. {2.B;
     2.D} . . . . Πάρθος *G3934*
G3934 **Πάρθος**, -ου, ὁ   pl., *Parthians,* inhabitants of
     the country beyond the eastern boundary of
     the Roman Empire between the Caspian Sea
     and the Persian Gulf.
G3935 **παρίημι**   (1) *I let pass, neglect, omit,* Luke
     11:42; (2) *I slacken, weary,* Heb 12:12.
παριστάνετε   verb, pres. act. impv. 2 pers. pl.
     {5.D.3}. . . . . παρίστημι *G3936*
παριστάνετε   verb, pres. act. indic. 2 pers. pl.
     {5.A.3.a} . . . . id.
παριστήκεισαν   verb, plu. act. indic. 3 pers. pl.
     {5.A.1}. . . . . id.
G3936 **παρίστημι** (παριστάνω)   (1) in the trans.
     tenses, *I cause to come to and stand beside; I*
     bring; I present, offer, commend; I introduce
     (one person to another); *I prove by argument,*
     Acts 24:13; (2) in the intrans. tenses, *I come*
     up to and stand by, sometimes with the idea of
     thus providing support (cf. 2 Tim 4:17).
παρίστησι   verb, pres. act. indic. 3 pers. sg.
     {5.A.3.a} . . . . παρίστημι *G3936*

παρίστησιν   verb, pres. act. indic. 3 pers. sg.
{5.A.3.a} . . . . id.

Παρμενᾶν   noun prop., acc. sg. masc. {2.A;
2.D} . . . . .Παρμενᾶς *G3937*

G3937 **Παρμενᾶς**, -ᾶ, acc. ᾶν, ὁ   *Parmenas,* one of
the original seven "deacons" at Jerusalem (a
pet form of Παρμενίδης).

G3938 **πάροδος**, -ου, ἡ   *way-by, passage.*
παρόδῳ   noun, dat. sg. fem. {2.B} . . . . . . πάροδος *G3938*
παροικεῖς   verb, pres. act. indic. 2 pers. sg.
{5.A.2} . . . . παροικέω *G3939*

G3939 **παροικέω**   *I sojourn (in),* as a resident stranger.

G3940 **παροικία**, -ας, ἡ   *a sojourn* in a foreign city
or land; so also in the spiritual sense (cf.
παρεπίδημος), 1 Pet 1:17.
παροικία   noun, dat. sg. fem. {2.A} . . . . παροικία *G3940*
παροικίας   noun, gen. sg. fem. {2.A} . . . . id.
πάροικοι   adj., nom. pl. masc. {3.C} . . . . πάροικος *G3941*
πάροικον   adj., nom. sg. neut. {3.C} . . . . id.

G3941 **πάροικος**, -ον, ὁ   adj. and noun, *a stranger,
sojourner,* in a land not his own, *a non-citizen,*
with limited rights; so, met., of the Christian
resident on the earth, whose real home is in
heaven, Eph 2:19; 1 Pet 2:11; (= μέτοικος).
πάροικος   adj., nom. sg. masc. {3.C} . . . πάροικος *G3941*
παροίκους   adj., acc. pl. masc. {3.C} . . . . id.

G3942 **παροιμία**, -ας, ἡ   *a veiled speech* in which particularly high thoughts are concealed, *a cryptic
saying, an allegory; a proverb,* 2 Pet 2:22 (from
παρά and οἶμος, *beside the common way*).
παροιμίαις   noun, dat. pl. fem. {2.A} . . . παροιμία *G3942*
παροιμίαν   noun, acc. sg. fem. {2.A} . . . . id.
παροιμίας   noun, gen. sg. fem. {2.A} . . . . id.
πάροινον   adj., acc. sg. masc. {3.C} . . . . πάροινος *G3943*

G3943 **πάροινος**, -ου, ὁ   *one given too much to wine,
an excessive drinker.*

G3944 **παροίχομαι**   *I have passed.*
παρόμοια   adj., acc. pl. neut. {3.C} . . . . παρόμοιος *G3946*
παρομοιάζετε   verb, pres. act. indic. 2 pers. pl.
{5.A.1.a} . . . . .παρομοιάζω *G3945*

G3945 **παρομοιάζω**   *I resemble.*

G3946 **παρόμοιος**, -ον   *like, similar.*
παρόν   vbl., pres. act. ptc. acc. sg. neut.
{7.C.1} . . . . .πάρειμι *G3918*
παρόντες   vbl., pres. act. ptc. nom. pl. masc.
{7.C.1} . . . . id.
παρόντος   vbl., pres. act. ptc. gen. sg. neut. {7.C.1} id.
παροξύνεται   verb, pres. pass. indic. 3 pers. sg.
{5.A.1.d} . . . . .παροξύνω *G3947*

G3947 **παροξύνω**   *I arouse to anger, I provoke.*
παροξυσμόν   noun, acc. sg. masc.
{2.B} . . . . .παροξυσμός *G3948*

G3948 **παροξυσμός**, -οῦ, ὁ   (1) *irritation of mind,
sharp feeling, indignation;* (2) *spurring, incite-
ment,* Heb 10:24.
παροξυσμός   noun, nom. sg. masc.
{2.B} . . . . .παροξυσμός *G3948*
παροργίζετε   verb, pres. act. impv. 2 pers. pl.
{5.D.1} . . . . παροργίζω *G3949*

G3949 **παροργίζω**   *I provoke to anger.*

G3950 **παροργισμός**, -οῦ, ὁ   (generally, an act of *provocation,* hence) *the state of feeling provocation,
wrath.*
παροργισμῷ   noun, dat. sg. masc.
{2.B} . . . . παροργισμός *G3950*
παροργιῶ   verb, fut. act. indic. 1 pers. sg.
{5.A.2} . . . . παροργίζω *G3949*

G3951 **παροτρύνω**   *I urge on.*
παροῦση   vbl., pres. act. ptc. dat. sg. fem.
{7.C.1} . . . . .πάρειμι *G3918*

G3952 **παρουσία**, -ας, ἡ   (in ordinary Gk. = *presence;
arrival;* also, technical term with reference to
the visit of a king or some other official, *a royal
visit*), (1) *presence,* as opposed to "absence,"
1 Cor 16:17; 2 Cor 7:6, 7 (cf. 10:10); Phil 1:26;
2:12; (2) a technical eschatological term,
representing a word used by Jesus Himself, *the
presence, coming, arrival, advent* of the glorified Messiah, to be followed by a permanent
residence with His people (so, in 2 Thess 2:9,
of that of the Lawless One).
παρουσία   noun, nom. sg. fem. {2.A} . .παρουσία *G3952*
παρουσίᾳ   noun, dat. sg. fem. {2.A} . . . . id.
παρουσίαν   noun, acc. sg. fem. {2.A} . . . . id.
παρουσίας   noun, gen. sg. fem. {2.A} . . . . id.
παροῦσιν   vbl., pres. act. ptc. dat. pl. neut.
{7.C.1} . . . . .πάρειμι *G3918*
παροψίδος   noun, gen. sg. fem. {2.C} . . . . παροψίς *G3953*

G3953 **παροψίς**, -ίδος, ἡ   *a bowl, dish.*

G3954 **παρρησία**, -ας, ἡ   *boldness, freedom, liberty,*
shown esp. *in speech;* ἐν παρρησίᾳ, μετὰ
παρρησίας, *quite openly* (opp. to "secretly").
παρρησία   noun, nom. sg. fem. {2.A} . .παρρησία *G3954*
παρρησίᾳ   noun, dat. sg. fem. {2.A} . . . . id.
παρρησιάζεσθαι   vbl., pres. mid./pass. inf.
{6.B.1} . . . . .παρρησιάζομαι *G3955*

G3955 **παρρησιάζομαι**   *I speak boldly, I am bold of
speech.*
παρρησιαζόμενοι   vbl., pres. mid./pass. ptc. nom.
pl. masc. {6.A.1} . . . . .παρρησιάζομαι *G3955*
παρρησιαζόμενος   vbl., pres. mid./pass. ptc.
nom. sg. masc. {6.A.1} . . . . id.
παρρησίαν   noun, acc. sg. fem. {2.A} . .παρρησία *G3954*
παρρησίας   noun, gen. sg. fem. {2.A} . . . . id.
παρρησιασάμενοι   vbl., aor. mid. ptc. nom. pl.
masc. {6.A.1.b} . . . . .παρρησιάζομαι *G3955*
παρρησιάσωμαι   verb, aor. mid. subjunc.
1 pers. sg. {5.B.1} . . . . id.
παρῴκησεν   verb, aor. act. indic. 3 pers. sg.
{5.A.1} . . . . παροικέω *G3939*
παρών   vbl., pres. act. ptc. nom. sg. masc.
{7.C.1} . . . . .πάρειμι *G3918*
παρωξύνετο   verb, impf. pass. indic. 3 pers. sg.
{5.A.1.e} . . . . .παροξύνω *G3947*
παρώτρυναν   verb, aor. act. indic. 3 pers. pl.
{5.A.1.b} . . . . παροτρύνω *G3951*
παρῳχημέναις   vbl., perf. mid./pass. ptc. dat. pl.
fem. {6.A.1.b} . . . . .παροίχομαι *G3944*

G3956 **πᾶς, πᾶσα, πᾶν**, gen. παντός, πάσης,
παντός   (1) adj. (a) in the sg. without the

article, *every, every kind of;* (b) in the sg. with the article preceding or following, *the whole, all the;* (c) in the pl. without the article, *all;* (d) in the pl. with the article following, *all the;* (2) pron. (a) masc. *every one,* neut. *everything;* (b) πάντες, *all, everybody,* πάντα, *all things;* (c) οὐ πᾶς, etc., *not all,* i.e., *only some,* e.g., Matt 19:11; John 13:10; Rom 10:16, but also (like πᾶς . . . οὐ) Hebraistic, esp. when words intervene between οὐ and πᾶς, etc. (translation Gk.), = *none, no,* Matt 24:22; Mark 13:20; Luke 1:37; Acts 20:25; Rom 3:20; Gal 2:16; 2 Pet 1:20; 1 John 2:21; Rev 7:16; 21:27; 22:3; πάντες οὐ = οὐ πάντες, 1 Cor 15:51; (3) with preps. (a) διὰ παντός, *continually, continuously, always;* (b) κατὰ πάντα, *in everything, in every respect,* Acts 3:22; 17:22, etc.

πᾶς   adj., nom. sg. masc. {3.D} . . . . πᾶς *G3956*
πᾶς   adj., voc. sg. masc. {3.D} . . . . id.
πᾶσα   adj., nom. sg. fem. {3.D} . . . . id.
πᾶσαι   adj., nom. pl. fem. {3.D} . . . . id.
πάσαις   adj., dat. pl. fem. {3.D} . . . . id.
πᾶσαν   adj., acc. sg. fem. {3.D} . . . . id.
πάσας   adj., acc. pl. fem. {3.D} . . . . id.
πάσῃ   adj., dat. sg. fem. {3.D} . . . . id.
πάσης   adj., gen. sg. fem. {3.D} . . . . id.
πᾶσι   adj., dat. pl. masc. {3.D} . . . . id.
πᾶσι   adj., dat. pl. neut. {3.D} . . . . id.
πᾶσιν   adj., dat. pl. masc. {3.D} . . . . id.
πᾶσιν   adj., dat. pl. masc. {3.D} . . . . id.
πᾶσιν   adj., dat. pl. neut. {3.D} . . . . id.

G3957 **πάσχα**, τό   *the feast of Passover, the paschal meal,* which took place on the night of full moon after the spring equinox, i.e., the night between 14th and 15th Nisan. On the afternoon of 14th Nisan before sunset the *paschal lamb,* also called τὸ πάσχα (so met., 1 Cor 5:7), was sacrificed (Heb., Aram.).
πάσχα   Aram. . . . . πάσχα *G3957*
πάσχει   verb, pres. act. indic. 3 pers. sg. {5.A.1.a} . . . . πάσχω *G3958*
πάσχειν   vbl., pres. act. inf. {6.B.1} . . . . id.
πάσχετε   verb, pres. act. indic. 2 pers. pl. {5.A.1.a} . . . . id.
πασχέτω   verb, pres. act. impv. 3 pers. sg. {5.D.1} id.
πάσχοιτε   verb, pres. act. opt. 2 pers. pl. {5.C.1} . id.
πάσχομεν   verb, pres. act. indic. 1 pers. pl. {5.A.1.a} . . . . id.
πάσχοντες   vbl., pres. act. ptc. nom. pl. masc. {6.A.1}. . . . . id.

G3958 **πάσχω**   *I am acted upon* in a certain way, *I experience* certain treatment, e.g., Matt 17:15 (var.); hence (by a development from the original use), *I experience ill treatment, etc., I suffer,* e.g., Matt 17:12.
πάσχω   verb, pres. act. indic. 1 pers. sg. {5.A.1.a} . . . . πάσχω *G3958*
πάσχων   vbl., pres. act. ptc. nom. sg. masc. {6.A.1}. . . . . id.
πασῶν   adj., gen. pl. fem. {3.D} . . . . πᾶς *G3956*

πατάξαι   vbl., aor. act. inf. {6.B.1} . . . . . πατάσσω *G3960*
πατάξας   vbl., aor. act. ptc. nom. sg. masc. {6.A.1.a} . . . . id.
πατάξῃ   verb, aor. act. subjunc. 3 pers. sg. {5.B.1} . . . . id.
πατάξομεν   verb, fut. act. indic. 1 pers. pl. {5.A.1.a} . . . . id.
πατάξω   verb, fut. act. indic. 1 pers. sg. {5.A.1.a} id.

G3959 **Πάταρα**, -ων, τό   *Patara,* a town on the coast of the Roman province Lycia.
Πάταρα   noun prop., acc. pl. neut. {2.B; 2.D}. . . . . Πάταρα *G3959*
πατάσσῃ   verb, pres. act. subjunc. 3 pers. sg. {5.B.1}. . . . . πατάσσω *G3960*

G3960 **πατάσσω**   *I strike* (as, with a sword).
πατεῖ   verb, pres. act. indic. 3 pers. sg. {5.A.2} . . . . πατέω *G3961*
πατεῖν   vbl., pres. act. inf. {6.B.2} . . . . id.
πάτερ   noun, voc. sg. masc. {2.C} . . . . πατήρ *G3962*
πατέρα   noun, acc. sg. masc. {2.C} . . . . id.
πατέρας   noun, acc. pl. masc. {2.C} . . . . id.
πατέρες   noun, nom. pl. masc. {2.C} . . . . id.
πατέρες   noun, voc. pl. masc. {2.C} . . . . id.
πατέρων   noun, gen. pl. masc. {2.C} . . . . id.

G3961 **πατέω**   trans. and intrans., *I tread; I trample upon.*

G3962 **πατήρ**, πατρός, ὁ   (1) *father* in the strict sense, e.g., Matt 2:22; (2) any male *ancestor,* e.g., Matt 3:9; (3) *The Father,* used of God as the creator of all beings (cf. Eph 3:14, 15), the fountain and origin of all life, and, among other beings, of our Lord Jesus Christ, who is in a special sense ὁ υἱός, *the Son,* of the Father (cf. esp. John). He is sometimes spoken of as the Heavenly Father, the Father in the Heavens (e.g., Matt 5:16), as distinguished from earthly fathers. Other epithets, such as τῆς δόξης, τῶν οἰκτιρμῶν, τῶν φώτων, are attached to the Name, some of them under the influence of Heb., expressing not only that He is the author of these signs or qualities, but that they bear a likeness to Him; thus πατὴρ τῆς δόξης = *glorious Father.*
πατήρ   noun, nom. sg. masc. {2.C}. . . . . . . πατήρ *G3962*
πατήσουσι   verb, fut. act. indic. 3 pers. pl. {5.A.1}. πατέω *G3961*
πατήσουσιν   verb, fut. act. indic. 3 pers. pl. {5.A.1}. id.

G3963 **Πάτμος**, -ου, ὁ   *Patmos,* a small rocky island in the Aegean sea, southwest of Ephesus.
Πάτμῳ   noun prop., dat. sg. fem. {2.B; 2.D} Πάτμος *G3963*
πατουμένη   vbl., pres. pass. ptc. nom. sg. fem. {6.A.2}. πατέω *G3961*
πατραλῴαις   noun, dat. pl. masc. {2.A}. . . . . πατρολῴας *G3964‡*
πατράσιν   noun, dat. pl. masc. {2.C} . . . . . . πατήρ *G3962*
πατρί   noun, dat. sg. masc. {2.C} . . . . id.

G3965 **πατριά**, -ᾶς, ἡ   a group of persons united by descent from a common father or ancestor, *a family, a tribe.*

πατριά   noun, nom. sg. fem. {2.A} . . . . . . πατριά G3965

πατριαί   noun, nom. pl. fem. {2.A} . . . . id.

πατριάρχαι   noun, nom. pl. masc.
{2.A} . . . . πατριάρχης G3966

πατριάρχας   noun, acc. pl. masc. {2.A} . . . . . . id.

G3966 **πατριάρχης**, -ου, ὁ   a ruler of a family (or
tribe), given as an honorary title to David
(Acts 2:29) as ancestor of the race of Jewish
kings.

πατριάρχης   noun, nom. sg. masc.
{2.A} . . . . πατριάρχης G3966

πατριάρχου   noun, gen. sg. masc. {2.A} . . . . . . id.

πατριᾶς   noun, gen. sg. fem. {2.A} . . . . . . πατριά G3965

πατρίδα   noun, acc. sg. fem. {2.C} . . . . πατρίς G3968

πατρίδι   noun, dat. sg. fem. {2.C} . . . . id.

G3967 **πατρικός**, -ή, -όν   belonging to the fathers
(ancestors).

πατρικῶν   adj., gen. pl. fem. {3.A} . . . . . πατρικός G3967

G3968 **πατρίς**, -ίδος, ἡ   native city, native town, native
place.

Πατροβᾶν   noun prop., acc. sg. masc. {2.A;
2.D} . . . . Πατροβᾶς G3969

Πατρόβαν   noun prop., acc. sg. masc. {2.A; 2.D} id.

G3969 **Πατροβᾶς**, -ᾶ, ὁ   Patrobas, a Christian in
Rome.

πατρολῴαις   noun, dat. pl. masc.
{2.A} . . . . πατρολῴας G3964‡

G3964‡ **πατρολῴας** (πατραλῴας), -ου, ὁ   a parricide,
a murderer of one's father.

G3970 **πατροπαράδοτος**, -ον   handed down by (from)
one's ancestors, inherited.

πατροπαραδότου   adj., gen. sg. fem.
{3.C} . . . . πατροπαράδοτος G3970

πατρός   noun, gen. sg. masc. {2.C} . . . . πατήρ G3962

πατρῴοις   adj., dat. pl. neut. {3.A} . . . . . πατρῷος G3971

G3971 **πατρῷος**, -α, -ον   belonging to ancestors,
ancestral.

πατρῴου   adj., gen. sg. masc. {3.A} . . . . πατρῷος G3971

πατρῴῳ   adj., dat. sg. masc. {3.A} . . . . id.

παύεται   verb, pres. mid. indic. 3 pers. sg.
{5.A.1.d} . . . . παύω G3973

Παῦλε   noun prop., voc. sg. masc. {2.B;
2.D} . . . . Παῦλος G3972

Παῦλον   noun prop., acc. sg. masc. {2.B; 2.D} . . id.

G3972 **Παῦλος**, -ου, ὁ   Paulus, Paul, (1) the third part
(cognomen) of the full Roman name of the
Apostle, the other two parts of which (Gaius
Iulius?) are now unknown; (2) the third part
(cognomen) of the full name of the proconsul
of Cyprus, the first part of which seems to be
unknown, Acts 13:7.

Παῦλος   noun prop., nom. sg. masc. {2.B;
2.D} . . . . Παῦλος G3972

Παύλου   noun prop., gen. sg. masc. {2.B; 2.D} . . id.

Παύλῳ   noun prop., dat. sg. masc. {2.B; 2.D} . . . id.

παύομαι   verb, pres. mid. indic. 1 pers. sg.
{5.A.1.d} . . . . παύω G3973

παυόμεθα   verb, pres. mid. indic. 1 pers. pl.
{5.A.1.d} . . . . id.

παύσασθαι   vbl., aor. mid. inf. {6.B.1} . . . . id.

παυσάτω   verb, aor. act. impv. 3 pers. sg. {5.D.1} id.

παύσῃ   verb, fut. mid. indic. 2 pers. sg. {5.A.1.d} id.

παύσονται   verb, fut. mid. indic. 3 pers. pl.
{5.A.1.d} . . . . id.

G3973 **παύω**   (1) act. I cause to cease, 1 Pet 3:10; (2)
mid. I cease.

G3974 **Πάφος**, -ου, ἡ   Paphos, a city at the western
end of Cyprus.

Πάφου   noun prop., gen. sg. fem. {2.B; 2.D} . Πάφος G3974

G3975 **παχύνω**   I thicken; used with καρδία, of
obtuseness of mind, it has become obtuse.

πέδαις   noun, dat. pl. fem. {2.A} . . . . πέδη G3976

πέδας   noun, acc. pl. fem. {2.A} . . . . id.

G3976 **πέδη**, -ης, ἡ   a fetter.

G3977 **πεδινός**, -ή, -όν   level, low-lying.

πεδινοῦ   adj., gen. sg. masc. {3.A} . . . . πεδινός G3977

πεζεύειν   vbl., pres. act. inf. {6.B.1} . . . . . πεζεύω G3978

G3978 **πεζεύω**   I go by land.

G3979 **πεζῇ**   adv. on foot or by land.

πεζῇ   adv. . . . . πεζῇ G3979

πειθαρχεῖν   vbl., pres. act. inf. {6.B.2} . πειθαρχέω G3980

G3980 **πειθαρχέω**   I obey one in authority.

πειθαρχήσαντας   vbl., aor. act. ptc. acc. pl. masc.
{6.A.2} . . . . πειθαρχέω G3980

πειθαρχοῦσιν   vbl., pres. act. ptc. dat. pl. masc.
{6.A.2} . . . . id.

πείθεις   verb, pres. act. indic. 2 pers. sg.
{5.A.1.a} . . . . πείθω G3982

πείθεσθαι   vbl., pres. pass. inf. {6.B.1} . . . . id.

πείθεσθε   verb, pres. mid./pass. impv. 2 pers. pl.
{5.D.1} . . . . id.

πειθοῖ   noun, dat. sg. fem. {2.C} . . . . πειθώ G3981†‡

πειθοῖς   adj., dat. pl. masc. {3.A} . . . . πειθός G3981

πείθομαι   verb, pres. pass. indic. 1 pers. sg.
{5.A.1.d} . . . . πείθω G3982

πειθόμεθα   verb, pres. pass. indic. 1 pers. pl.
{5.A.1.d} . . . . id.

πείθομεν   verb, pres. act. indic. 1 pers. pl.
{5.A.1.a} . . . . id.

πειθομένοις   vbl., pres. mid./pass. ptc. dat. pl.
masc. {6.A.1} . . . . id.

πειθομένου   vbl., pres. pass. ptc. gen. sg. masc.
{6.A.1} . . . . id.

G3981 **πειθός** (πιθός), -ή, -όν   persuasive.

G3982 **πείθω**   (1) I urge, I apply persuasion, I seek to
persuade, I exercise suasion; (2) ²perf. and
plup., I trust, ἐπί, in; (3) mid. or pass. I am
persuaded (I admit suasion to myself); hence, I
believe; hence also, with dat., I obey.

G3981†‡ **πειθώ**, -οῦς, ἡ (dat. sg. πειθοῖ)   persuasiveness.
Var. for πειθός, 1 Cor 2:4.

πείθω   verb, pres. act. indic. 1 pers. sg.
{5.A.1.a} . . . . πείθω G3982

πείθων   vbl., pres. act. ptc. nom. sg. masc.
{6.A.1} . . . . id.

Πειλᾶτον   noun prop., acc. sg. masc. {2.B;
2.D} . . . . Πιλᾶτος G4091

Πειλᾶτος   noun prop., nom. sg. masc. {2.B; 2.D} id.

Πειλάτου   noun prop., gen. sg. masc. {2.B; 2.D} id.

Πειλάτῳ   noun prop., dat. sg. masc. {2.B; 2.D} . . id.

πεῖν   vbl., ²aor. act. inf. {6.B.1}. . . . . πίνω *G4095*

πεινᾷ   verb, pres. act. indic. 3 pers. sg.
{5.A.2}. . . . . πεινάω *G3983*

πεινᾷ   verb, pres. act. subjunc. 3 pers. sg. {5.B.2} id.

πεινᾶν   vbl., pres. act. inf. {6.B.2} . . . . id.

πεινᾷν   vbl., pres. act. inf. {6.B.2} . . . . id.

πεινάσετε   verb, fut. act. indic. 2 pers. pl. {5.A.1} id.

πεινάσῃ   verb, aor. act. subjunc. 3 pers. sg.
{5.B.1} . . . . id.

πεινάσουσιν   verb, fut. act. indic. 3 pers. pl.
{5.A.1}. . . . . id.

G3983 **πεινάω**   *I hunger,* either lit. or met.; with acc. *I hunger for.*

πεινῶμεν   verb, pres. act. indic. 1 pers. pl.
{5.A.2}. . . . . πεινάω *G3983*

πεινῶντα   vbl., pres. act. ptc. acc. sg. masc.
{6.A.2}. . . . . id.

πεινῶντας   vbl., pres. act. ptc. acc. pl. masc.
{6.A.2}. . . . . id.

πεινῶντες   vbl., pres. act. ptc. nom. pl. masc.
{6.A.2}. . . . . id.

G3984 **πεῖρα**, -ας, ἡ   *an attempt, a trial;* πεῖραν λαμβάνειν, *to have experience of.*

πειράζει   verb, pres. act. indic. 3 pers. sg.
{5.A.1.a} . . . . πειράζω *G3985*

πειράζεται   verb, pres. pass. indic. 3 pers. sg.
{5.A.1.d} . . . . id.

πειράζετε   verb, pres. act. impv. 2 pers. pl.
{5.D.1}. . . . . id.

πειράζετε   verb, pres. act. indic. 2 pers. pl.
{5.A.1.a} . . . . id.

πειράζῃ   verb, pres. act. subjunc. 3 pers. sg.
{5.B.1} . . . . id.

πειράζομαι   verb, pres. pass. indic. 1 pers. sg.
{5.A.1.d} . . . . id.

πειραζομένοις   vbl., pres. pass. ptc. dat. pl.
masc. {6.A.1} . . . . id.

πειραζόμενος   vbl., pres. pass. ptc. nom. sg.
masc. {6.A.1} . . . . id.

πειράζοντες   vbl., pres. act. ptc. nom. pl. masc.
{6.A.1}. . . . . id.

G3985 **πειράζω**   (1) *I make trial of, try, test, explore;* God *tests* man by means of suffering or in some other way, man *tests* God by seeking how far it is possible to go on disobeying Him, without provoking his anger; (2) a secondary neutral or evil sense, *I tempt,* Matt 4:1; Mark 1:13; Luke 4:2; 1 Cor 7:5; Jas 1:13 (second occurrence), 14; if trial fails, the result is moral evil; the agency of Satan is interposed, the same process being carried on for God's good purpose and Satan's evil purpose; thus ὁ πειράζων comes to indicate the intermediary, *the Tempter,* Matt 4:3; 1 Thess 3:5; (3) with inf. *I try, attempt.*

πειράζων   vbl., pres. act. ptc. nom. sg. masc.
{6.A.1}. . . . . πειράζω *G3985*

πεῖραν   noun, acc. sg. fem. {2.A} . . . . πεῖρα *G3984*

πειράσαι   vbl., aor. act. inf. {6.B.1} . . . . . πειράζω *G3985*

πειρασθείς   vbl., aor. pass. ptc. nom. sg. masc.
{6.A.1.a} . . . . id.

πειρασθῆναι   vbl., aor. pass. inf. {6.B.1} . . . . . id.

πειρασθῇς   verb, aor. pass. subjunc. 2 pers. sg.
{5.B.1} . . . . id.

πειρασθῆτε   verb, aor. pass. subjunc. 2 pers. pl.
{5.B.1} . . . . id.

πειρασμοῖς   noun, dat. pl. masc. {2.B} πειρασμός *G3986*

πειρασμόν   noun, acc. sg. masc. {2.B} . . . . id.

G3986 **πειρασμός**, -οῦ, ὁ   (1) *trial, probation, testing, being tried;* (2) *temptation,* Mark 14:38 and parallels, Matt 6:13; Luke 4:13; (3) in Gal 4:14 the reading τὸν πειρασμόν (without ὑμῶν or other addition) has been taken, on the analogy of modern popular Gk. usage, *the devil, the demonic power* as the cause of the Apostle's infirmity. (From πειράζω, q.v.).

πειρασμός   noun, nom. sg. masc. {2.B} πειρασμός *G3986*

πειρασμοῦ   noun, gen. sg. masc. {2.B} . . . . id.

πειρασμῷ   noun, dat. sg. masc. {2.B} . . . . id.

πειρασμῶν   noun, gen. pl. masc. {2.B} . . . . id.

G3987 **πειράω**   mid. or pass., *I try, attempt.*

πείσαντες   vbl., aor. act. ptc. nom. pl. masc.
{6.A.1.a} . . . . .πείθω *G3982*

πείσας   vbl., aor. act. ptc. nom. sg. masc. {6.A.1.a} . id.

πεισθέντες   vbl., aor. pass. ptc. nom. pl. masc.
{6.A.1.a} . . . . id.

πεισθῇς   verb, aor. pass. subjunc. 2 pers. sg.
{5.B.1} . . . . id.

πεισθήσονται   verb, fut. pass. indic. 3 pers. pl.
{5.A.1.d} . . . . id.

G3988 **πεισμονή**, -ῆς, ἡ   *persuasion,* both *the act of persuasion* and *the being persuaded.*

πεισμονή   noun, nom. sg. fem. {2.A} . . . πεισμονή *G3988*

πείσομεν   verb, fut. act. indic. 1 pers. pl.
{5.A.1.a} . . . . .πείθω *G3982*

πελάγει   noun, dat. sg. neut. {2.C} . . . . . . πέλαγος *G3989*

G3989 **πέλαγος**, -ους, τό   *the open sea;* in Matt 18:6 the use of the two words for sea produces a more impressive effect.

πέλαγος   noun, acc. sg. neut. {2.C} . . . . . πέλαγος *G3989*

G3990 **πελεκίζω**   *I behead* with an axe.

πέμπει   verb, pres. act. indic. 3 pers. sg.
{5.A.1.a} . . . . .πέμπω *G3992*

πέμπειν   vbl., pres. act. inf. {6.B.1} . . . . id.

πεμπομένοις   vbl., pres. pass. ptc. dat. pl. masc.
{6.A.1}. . . . . id.

πέμποντα   vbl., pres. act. ptc. acc. sg. masc.
{6.A.1}. . . . . id.

πέμπτην   adj., acc. sg. fem. {3.A} . . . . . . .πέμπτος *G3991*

G3991 **πέμπτος**, -η, -ον   *fifth.*

πέμπτος   adj., nom. sg. masc. {3.A}. . . . . .πέμπτος *G3991*

G3992 **πέμπω**   *I send.*

πέμπω   verb, pres. act. indic. 1 pers. sg.
{5.A.1.a} . . . . .πέμπω *G3992*

πεμφθέντες   vbl., aor. pass. ptc. nom. pl. masc.
{6.A.1.a} . . . . id.

πέμψαι   vbl., aor. act. inf. {6.B.1} . . . . id.

πέμψαντα   vbl., aor. act. ptc. acc. sg. masc.
{6.A.1.a} . . . . id.

πέμψαντες   vbl., aor. act. ptc. nom. pl. masc.
{6.A.1.a} . . . . id.

πέμψαντι   vbl., aor. act. ptc. dat. sg. masc.
  {6.A.1.a} . . . . id.
πέμψαντος   vbl., aor. act. ptc. gen. sg. masc.
  {6.A.1.a} . . . . id.
πέμψας   vbl., aor. act. ptc. nom. sg. masc.
  {6.A.1.a} . . . . id.
πέμψασιν   vbl., aor. act. ptc. dat. pl. masc.
  {6.A.1.a} . . . . id.
πέμψει   verb, fut. act. indic. 3 pers. sg. {5.A.1.a} . id.
πέμψης   verb, aor. act. subjunc. 2 pers. sg. {5.B.1}id.
πέμψον   verb, aor. act. impv. 2 pers. sg. {5.D.1}. . id.
πέμψουσιν   verb, fut. act. indic. 3 pers. pl.
  {5.A.1.a} . . . . id.
πέμψω   verb, fut. act. indic. 1 pers. sg. {5.A.1.a} . id.
πέμψω   verb, aor. act. subjunc. 1 pers. sg. {5.B.1} id.
G3993 **πένης**, -ητος, ὁ   *a poor person.*
πένησιν   noun, dat. pl. masc. {2.C} . . . . πένης G3993
πενθεῖν   vbl., pres. act. inf. {6.B.2} . . . . . . πενθέω G3996
G3994 **πενθερά**, -ᾶς, ἡ   *a mother-in-law.*
πενθερά   noun, nom. sg. fem. {2.A} . . . . πενθερά G3994
πενθεράν   noun, acc. sg. fem. {2.A} . . . . id.
πενθερᾶς   noun, gen. sg. fem. {2.A} . . . . id.
G3995 **πενθερός**, -οῦ, ὁ   *a father-in-law.*
πενθερός   noun, nom. sg. masc. {2.B} . . .πενθερός G3995
G3996 **πενθέω**   *I mourn.*
πενθήσατε   verb, aor. act. impv. 2 pers. pl.
  {5.D.1} . . . . πενθέω G3996
πενθήσετε   verb, fut. act. indic. 2 pers. pl. {5.A.1} . id.
πενθήσουσιν   verb, fut. act. indic. 3 pers. pl.
  {5.A.1} . . . . id.
πενθήσω   verb, aor. act. subjunc. 1 pers. sg.
  {5.B.1} . . . . id.
G3997 **πένθος**, -ους, τό   *mourning, sorrow.*
πένθος   noun, acc. sg. neut. {2.C} . . . . .πένθος G3997
πένθος   noun, nom. sg. neut. {2.C} . . . . id.
πενθοῦντες   vbl., pres. act. ptc. nom. pl. masc.
  {6.A.2} . . . . πενθέω G3996
πενθοῦσι   vbl., pres. act. ptc. dat. pl. masc. {6.A.2}. id.
πενθοῦσιν   verb, pres. act. indic. 3 pers. pl. {5.A.2}. id.
πενθοῦσιν   vbl., pres. act. ptc. dat. pl. masc.
  {6.A.2} . . . . id.
πενιχράν   adj., acc. sg. fem. {3.A} . . . . . . πενιχρός G3998
G3998 **πενιχρός**, -ά, -όν   *poor.*
G3999 **πεντάκις**   adv., *five times.*
πεντάκις   adv. . . . . .πεντάκις G3999
G4000 **πεντακισχίλιοι**, -αι, -α   *five thousand.*
πεντακισχίλιοι   adj. num., nom. pl. masc.
  {3.A} . . . . πεντακισχίλιοι G4000
πεντακισχιλίους   adj. num., acc. pl. masc. {3.A} id.
πεντακισχιλίων   adj. num., gen. pl. masc. {3.A} id.
πεντακόσια   adj. num., acc. pl. neut.
  {3.A} . . . . πεντακόσιοι G4001
G4001 **πεντακόσιοι**, -αι, -α   *five hundred.*
πεντακοσίοις   adj. num., dat. pl. masc.
  {3.A} . . . . πεντακόσιοι G4001
G4002 **πέντε**   *five.*
πέντε   adj. num. . . . . .πέντε G4002
G4003 **πεντεκαιδέκατος**, -η, -ον   *fifteenth.*
πεντεκαιδεκάτῳ   adj., dat. sg. neut.
  {3.A} . . . . πεντεκαιδέκατος G4003

G4004 **πεντήκοντα**   *fifty.*
πεντήκοντα   adj. num.. . . . . πεντήκοντα G4004
G4005 **πεντηκοστή**, -ῆς, ἡ   (orig. supply ἡμέρα; lit.
  the fiftieth day from 14th Nisan, the date of the
  Passover Feast), *Pentecost,* a Feast of the Jews,
  Whitsuntide.
πεντηκοστῆς   noun, gen. sg. fem.
  {2.A} . . . . πεντηκοστή G4005
πεπαιδευμένος   vbl., perf. pass. ptc. nom. sg. masc.
  {6.A.1.b} . . . . παιδεύω G3811
πεπαλαίωκε   verb, perf. act. indic. 3 pers. sg.
  {5.A.1}. . . . . .παλαιόω G3822
πεπαλαίωκεν   verb, perf. act. indic. 3 pers. sg.
  {5.A.1} . . . . id.
πέπαυται   verb, perf. mid./pass. indic. 3 pers. sg.
  {5.A.1.f}. . . . . .παύω G3973
πεπειραμένον   vbl., perf. pass. ptc. acc. sg. masc.
  {6.A.2} . . . . πειράω G3987
πεπειρασμένον   vbl., perf. pass. ptc. acc. sg. masc.
  {6.A.1.b} . . . . πειράζω G3985
πέπεισμαι   verb, perf. pass. indic. 1 pers. sg.
  {5.A.1.f}. . . . . .πείθω G3982
πεπείσμεθα   verb, perf. pass. indic. 1 pers. pl.
  {5.A.1.f} . . . . id.
πεπεισμένος   vbl., perf. pass. ptc. nom. sg.
  masc. {6.A.1.b} . . . . id.
πεπελεκισμένων   vbl., perf. pass. ptc. gen. pl.
  masc. {6.A.1.b} . . . . .πελεκίζω G3990
πεπιεσμένον   vbl., perf. pass. ptc. acc. sg. neut.
  {6.A.1.b} .πιέζω G4085
πεπίστευκα   verb, perf. act. indic. 1 pers. sg.
  {5.A.1.c} . . . . πιστεύω G4100
πεπιστεύκαμεν   verb, perf. act. indic. 1 pers.
  pl. {5.A.1.c} . . . . id.
πεπίστευκας   verb, perf. act. indic. 2 pers. sg.
  {5.A.1.c} . . . . id.
πεπιστεύκασιν   verb, perf. act. indic. 3 pers.
  pl. {5.A.1.c} . . . . id.
πεπιστεύκατε   verb, perf. act. indic. 2 pers. pl.
  {5.A.1.c} . . . . id.
πεπιστεύκεισαν   verb, plu. act. indic. 3 pers.
  pl. {5.A.1.b} . . . . id.
πεπίστευκεν   verb, perf. act. indic. 3 pers. sg.
  {5.A.1.c} . . . . id.
πεπιστευκόσι   vbl., perf. act. ptc. dat. pl. masc.
  {6.A.1.a} . . . . id.
πεπιστευκόσιν   vbl., perf. act. ptc. dat. pl.
  masc. {6.A.1.a}. . . . . id.
πεπιστευκότας   vbl., perf. act. ptc. acc. pl.
  masc. {6.A.1.a}. . . . . id.
πεπιστευκότες   vbl., perf. act. ptc. nom. pl.
  masc. {6.A.1.a}. . . . . id.
πεπιστευκότων   vbl., perf. act. ptc. gen. pl.
  masc. {6.A.1.a}. . . . . id.
πεπιστευκότων   vbl., perf. act. ptc. gen. pl.
  neut. {6.A.1.a} . . . . id.
πεπιστευκώς   vbl., perf. act. ptc. nom. sg. masc.
  {6.A.1.a} . . . . id.
πεπίστευμαι   verb, perf. pass. indic. 1 pers. sg.
  {5.A.1.f}. . . . . id.

πεπλανημένοις   vbl., perf. pass. ptc. dat. pl. neut.
{6.A.2}. . . . . πλανάω *G4105*
πεπλάνησθε   verb, perf. pass. indic. 2 pers. pl.
{5.A.1}. . . . . id.
πεπλάτυνται   verb, perf. pass. indic. 3 pers. sg.
{5.A.1.f}. . . . . πλατύνω *G4115*
πεπληροφορημένοι   vbl., perf. pass. ptc. nom. pl.
masc. {6.A.2}. . . . . πληροφορέω *G4135*
πεπληροφορημένων   vbl., perf. pass. ptc. gen.
pl. neut. {6.A.2}. id.
πεπληρώκατε   verb, perf. act. indic. 2 pers. pl.
{5.A.1}. . . . . πληρόω *G4137*
πεπλήρωκε   verb, perf. act. indic. 3 pers. sg.
{5.A.1}. . . . . id.
πεπλήρωκεν   verb, perf. act. indic. 3 pers. sg.
{5.A.1}. . . . . id.
πεπληρωκέναι   vbl., perf. act. inf. {6.B.1}. . . . . . id.
πεπλήρωμαι   verb, perf. pass. indic. 1 pers. sg.
{5.A.1}. . . . . id.
πεπληρωμένα   vbl., perf. pass. ptc. acc. pl.
neut. {6.A.2} . . . . id.
πεπληρωμένη   vbl., perf. pass. ptc. nom. sg.
fem. {6.A.2}. . . . . id.
πεπληρωμένην   vbl., perf. pass. ptc. acc. sg.
fem. {6.A.2}. . . . . id.
πεπληρωμένοι   vbl., perf. pass. ptc. nom. pl.
masc. {6.A.2}. . . . . id.
πεπληρωμένους   vbl., perf. pass. ptc. acc. pl.
masc. {6.A.2}. . . . . id.
πεπλήρωται   verb, perf. pass. indic. 3 pers. sg.
{5.A.1} . . . . id.
πεπλούτηκα   verb, perf. act. indic. 1 pers. sg.
{5.A.1}. . . . . πλουτέω *G4147*
πεποίηκα   verb, perf. act. indic. 1 pers. sg.
{5.A.1}. . . . . ποιέω *G4160*
πεποιήκαμεν   verb, perf. act. indic. 1 pers. pl.
{5.A.1}. . . . . id.
πεποιήκατε   verb, perf. act. indic. 2 pers. pl.
{5.A.1}. . . . . id.
πεποίηκε   verb, perf. act. indic. 3 pers. sg.
{5.A.1}. . . . . id.
πεποιήκεισαν   verb, plu. act. indic. 3 pers. pl.
{5.A.1}. . . . . id.
πεποίηκεν   verb, perf. act. indic. 3 pers. sg.
{5.A.1}. . . . . id.
πεποιηκέναι   vbl., perf. act. inf. {6.B.1} . . . . . . id.
πεποιηκόσι   vbl., perf. act. ptc. dat. pl. masc.
{6.A.2}. . . . . id.
πεποιηκόσιν   vbl., perf. act. ptc. dat. pl. masc.
{6.A.2}. . . . . id.
πεποιηκότες   vbl., perf. act. ptc. nom. pl. masc.
{6.A.2}. . . . . id.
πεποιηκότος   vbl., perf. act. ptc. gen. sg. masc.
{6.A.2}. . . . . id.
πεποιηκώς   vbl., perf. act. ptc. nom. sg. masc.
{6.A.2}. . . . . id.
πεποιημένων   vbl., perf. pass. ptc. gen. pl.
masc. {6.A.2}. . . . . id.
πεποιημένων   vbl., perf. pass. ptc. gen. pl. neut.
{6.A.2}. . . . . id.

πέποιθα   verb, ²perf. act. indic. 1 pers. sg.
{5.A.1.c}. . . . . πείθω *G3982*
πεποίθαμεν   verb, ²perf. act. indic. 1 pers. pl.
{5.A.1.c}. . . . . id.
πέποιθας   verb, ²perf. act. indic. 2 pers. sg.
{5.A.1.c}. . . . . id.
πέποιθεν   verb, ²perf. act. indic. 3 pers. sg. {5.A.1.c} id.
πεποιθέναι   vbl., ²perf. act. inf. {6.B.1}. . . . . id.
πεποιθήσει   noun, dat. sg. fem. {2.C}. .πεποίθησις *G4006*
πεποίθησιν   noun, acc. sg. fem. {2.C} . . . . id.
G4006 **πεποίθησις**, -εως, ἡ   *confidence, trust.*
πεποιθότας   vbl., ²perf. act. ptc. acc. pl. masc.
{6.A.1}. . . . . πείθω *G3982*
πεποιθότες   vbl., ²perf. act. ptc. nom. pl. masc.
{6.A.1}. . . . . id.
πεποιθώς   vbl., ²perf. act. ptc. nom. sg. masc.
{6.A.1}. . . . . id.
πεπολίτευμαι   verb, perf. mid./pass. indic. 1 pers.
sg. {5.A.1.f}. . . . . πολιτεύομαι *G4176*
πεπόνθασιν   verb, ²perf. act. indic. 3 pers. pl.
{5.A.1.c}. . . . . πάσχω *G3958*
πέπονθεν   verb, ²perf. act. indic. 3 pers. sg.
{5.A.1.c}. . . . . id.
πεπορευμένους   vbl., perf. mid./pass. ptc. acc. pl.
masc. {6.A.1.b}. . . . . πορεύομαι *G4198*
πεπότικε   verb, perf. act. indic. 3 pers. sg.
{5.A.1.c}. . . . . ποτίζω *G4222*
πεπότικεν   verb, perf. act. indic. 3 pers. sg.
{5.A.1.c}. . . . . id.
πεπραγμένον   vbl., perf. pass. ptc. nom. sg. neut.
{6.A.1.b}. . . . . πράσσω *G4238*
πέπρακε   verb, perf. act. indic. 3 pers. sg.
{5.A.1.c}. . . . . πιπράσκω *G4097*
πέπρακεν   verb, perf. act. indic. 3 pers. sg.
{5.A.1.c}. . . . . id.
πεπραμένος   vbl., perf. pass. ptc. nom. sg.
masc. {6.A.1.b}. . . . . id.
πέπραχα   verb, perf. act. indic. 1 pers. sg.
{5.A.1.c}. . . . . πράσσω *G4238*
πεπραχέναι   vbl., perf. act. inf. {6.B.1}. . . . . id.
πέπτωκαν   verb, perf. act. indic. 3 pers. pl.
{5.A.1.c} . . . . πίπτω *G4098*
πέπτωκας   verb, perf. act. indic. 2 pers. sg.
{5.A.1.c}. . . . . id.
πεπτώκασιν   verb, perf. act. indic. 3 pers. pl.
{5.A.1.c}. . . . . id.
πέπτωκες   verb, perf. act. indic. 2 pers. sg.
{5.A.1.c}. . . . . id.
πεπτωκότα   vbl., perf. act. ptc. acc. sg. masc.
{6.A.1.a}. . . . . id.
πεπτωκυῖαν   vbl., perf. act. ptc. acc. sg. fem.
{6.A.1.a}. . . . . id.
πεπυρωμένα   vbl., perf. pass. ptc. acc. pl. neut.
{6.A.2}. . . . . πυρόω *G4448*
πεπυρωμένης   vbl., perf. pass. ptc. gen. sg. fem.
{6.A.2}. . . . . id.
πεπυρωμένοι   vbl., perf. pass. ptc. nom. pl.
masc. {6.A.2}. . . . . id.
πεπυρωμένον   vbl., perf. pass. ptc. acc. sg.
neut. {6.A.2} . . . . id.

πέπωκαν   verb, perf. act. indic. 3 pers. pl.
{5.A.1.c} . . . . πίνω G4095
πέπωκε   verb, perf. act. indic. 3 pers. sg. {5.A.1.c}id.
πεπώρωκεν   verb, perf. act. indic. 3 pers. sg.
{5.A.1} . . . . πωρόω G4456
πεπωρωμένη   vbl., perf. pass. ptc. nom. sg.
fem. {6.A.2} . . . . id.
πεπωρωμένην   vbl., perf. pass. ptc. acc. sg.
fem. {6.A.2} . . . . id.
G2087†‡ **περαιτέρω**   adv., *further, beyond.* Var. for περὶ
ἑτέρων, Acts 13:39.
περαιτέρω   adv. comp. {3.F; 3.G} . . . . περαιτέρω G2087†‡
G4008 **πέραν**   adv., *beyond, on the other side;* τὸ
πέραν, as subs., *the other side, the country
beyond;* prep. with gen., *beyond, on the other
side of, across;* sometimes elliptically used,
πέραν = (ἀπὸ) τῆς πέραν, Mark 3:8 (Matt
4:25), πέραν = τῆς πέραν, Mark 10:1.
πέραν   adv., prep. . . . . πέραν G4008
G4009 **πέρας,** -ατος, τό   (1) *a boundary, limit;* (2) *an
end,* Heb 6:16.
πέρας   noun, nom. sg. neut. {2.C} . . . . πέρας G4009
πέρατα   noun, acc. pl. neut. {2.C} . . . . id.
περάτων   noun, gen. pl. neut. {2.C} . . . . id.
Πέργαμον   noun prop., acc. sg. fem. {2.B;
2.D} . . . . Πέργαμος G4010
G4010 **Πέργαμος** (Πέργαμον), -ου, ἡ (τό)   *Pergamum,* an important city of the Roman
province Asia.
Περγάμῳ   noun prop., dat. sg. fem. {2.B;
2.D} . . . . Πέργαμος G4010
G4011 **Πέργη,** -ης, ἡ   *Perga,* a city on the river Cestrus
in the Roman province Pamphylia.
Πέργη   noun prop., dat. sg. fem. {2.A; 2.D} . . Πέργη G4011
Πέργην   noun prop., acc. sg. fem. {2.A; 2.D} . . . . id.
Πέργης   noun prop., gen. sg. fem. {2.A; 2.D} . . . id.
G4012 **περί**   prep. (1) with gen., most often, *concerning, about* (in such phrases as "to speak, know,
care, etc., about"); at the beginning of a clause,
with regard to, e.g., 1 Cor 7:1; *on account of* (w.
κρίνεσθαι, ἐνκαλεῖν, ἐρωτᾶν, etc.), whence
it often passes into the meaning *for* and
becomes identical with ὑπέρ, e.g., Matt 26:28;
1 Cor 1:13 (ὑπέρ is nearly always a textual
variant in such cases); so with verbs of feeling
(= ἐπί with acc. or dat.), *over;* περί αὐτοῦ,
with him, Luke 2:27, seems incorrect (= περὶ
αὐτόν, αὐτῷ, ἐν αὐτῷ); (2) with acc., local
and temp., *about,* οἱ περὶ αὐτόν Mark 4:10;
Luke 22:49, *his disciples,* but οἱ περὶ Παῦλον,
Acts 13:13, *Paul and his company* (according
to the classical idiom); used to indicate the
circumstances of the action or of the effort,
e.g., with ἐπιθυμίαι, Mark 4:19; Paul in his
later epistles uses it = *concerning, touching,*
e.g., Phil 2:23.
περί   prep. . . . . περί G4012
περιάγειν   vbl., pres. act. inf. {6.B.1} . . . . περιάγω G4013
περιάγετε   verb, pres. act. indic. 2 pers. pl.
{5.A.1.a} . . . . id.

G4013 **περιάγω**   (1) trans., (a) *I carry about;* (b) *I go
about;* (2) intrans., *I go about.*
περιάγων   vbl., pres. act. ptc. nom. sg. masc.
{6.A.1} . . . . περιάγω G4013
περιαιρεῖται   verb, pres. pass. indic. 3 pers. sg.
{5.A.2} . . . . περιαιρέω G4014
G4014 **περιαιρέω**   (1) *I strip off, I strip from, I take
away;* (2) *I cast off, cut adrift,* Acts 27:40; in
Acts 28:13, if the text be right, the word must
be rendered in the same way, *I cast off, I cast
loose.*
G681†‡ **περιάπτω**   *I kindle.* Var. for ἅπτω, Luke 22:55.
G4015 **περιαστράπτω**   *I flash (gleam) around* like
lightning.
περιαστράψαι   vbl., aor. act. inf.
{6.B.1} . . . . περιαστράπτω G4015
περιαψάντων   vbl., aor. act. ptc. gen. pl. masc.
{6.A.1.a} . . . . περιάπτω G681†‡
περιβαλεῖται   verb, fut. mid. indic. 3 pers. sg.
{5.A.2} . . . . περιβάλλω G4016
περιβάλῃ   verb, ²aor. mid. subjunc. 2 pers. sg.
{5.B.1} . . . . id.
περιβάληται   verb, ²aor. mid. subjunc. 3 pers.
sg. {5.B.1} . . . . id.
G4016 **περιβάλλω**   *I cast around,* Luke 19:43 (var.); *I
wrap* a garment *about, I put on;* hence mid., *I
put on* to myself, *I clothe myself, I dress.*
περιβαλοῦ   verb, ²aor. mid. impv. 2 pers. sg.
{5.D.1} . . . . περιβάλλω G4016
περιβαλοῦσιν   verb, fut. act. indic. 3 pers. pl.
{5.A.2} . . . . id.
περιβαλώμεθα   verb, ²aor. mid. subjunc.
1 pers. pl. {5.B.1} . . . . id.
περιβαλών   vbl., ²aor. act. ptc. nom. sg. masc.
{6.A.1.a} . . . . id.
περιβεβλημένη   vbl., perf. mid./pass. ptc.
nom. sg. fem. {6.A.1.b} . . . . id.
περιβεβλημένοι   vbl., perf. mid./pass. ptc.
nom. pl. masc. {6.A.1.b} . . . . id.
περιβεβλημένον   vbl., perf. mid./pass. ptc. acc.
sg. masc. {6.A.1.b} . . . . id.
περιβεβλημένος   vbl., perf. mid./pass. ptc.
nom. sg. masc. {6.A.1.b} . . . . id.
περιβεβλημένους   vbl., perf. mid./pass. ptc.
acc. pl. masc. {6.A.1.b} . . . . id.
G4017 **περιβλέπω**   mid. *I look around (myself) for,
look for, survey.*
περιβλεψάμενοι   vbl., aor. mid. ptc. nom. pl.
masc. {6.A.1.b} . . . . περιβλέπω G4017
περιβλεψάμενος   vbl., aor. mid. ptc. nom. sg.
masc. {6.A.1.b} . . . . id.
G4018 **περιβόλαιον,** -ου, τό   *a wrapper, mantle.*
περιβόλαιον   noun, acc. sg. neut.
{2.B} . . . . περιβόλαιον G4018
περιβολαίου   noun, gen. sg. neut. {2.B} . . . . . . id.
G4019 **περιδέω**   *I bind (tie) around.*
περιδραμόντες   vbl., ²aor. act. ptc. nom. pl. masc.
{6.A.1.a} . . . . περιτρέχω G4063
περιεβάλετε   verb, ²aor. act. indic. 2 pers. pl.
{5.A.1.b} . . . . περιβάλλω G4016

περιεβάλετο   verb, ²aor. mid. indic. 3 pers. sg.
   {5.A.1.e} . . . . id.
περιεβάλομεν   verb, ²aor. act. indic. 1 pers. pl.
   {5.A.1.b} . . . . id.
περιέβαλον   verb, ²aor. act. indic. 3 pers. pl.
   {5.A.1.b} . . . . id.
περιεβλέπετο   verb, impf. mid. indic. 3 pers. sg.
   {5.A.1.e} . . . . περιβλέπω G4017
περιεδέδετο   verb, plu. pass. indic. 3 pers. sg.
   {5.A.1} . . . . περιδέω G4019
περιέδραμον   verb, aor. act. indic. 3 pers. pl.
   {5.A.1.b} . . . . .περιτρέχω G4063
περιεζωσμέναι   vbl., perf. mid./pass. ptc. nom. pl.
   fem. {6.A.3} . . . . .περιζώννυμι G4024
περιεζωσμένοι   vbl., perf. mid./pass. ptc. nom.
   pl. masc. {6.A.3} . . . . id.
περιεζωσμένον   vbl., perf. mid./pass. ptc. acc.
   sg. masc. {6.A.3} . . . . id.
περιέθηκαν   verb, aor. act. indic. 3 pers. pl.
   {5.A.3.b} . . . . περιτίθημι G4060
περιέθηκε   verb, aor. act. indic. 3 pers. sg. {5.A.3.b} .id.
περιέθηκεν   verb, aor. act. indic. 3 pers. sg.
   {5.A.3.b} . . . . id.
περιέκρυβεν   verb, impf. act. indic. 3 pers. sg.
   {5.A.1.b} . . . . περικρύβω G4032
περιέλαμψεν   verb, aor. act. indic. 3 pers. sg.
   {5.A.1.b} . . . . περιλάμπω G4034
περιελεῖν   vbl., ²aor. act. inf. {6.B.1} . . . .περιαιρέω G4014
περιελθόντες   vbl., ²aor. act. ptc. nom. pl. masc.
   {6.A.1.a} . . . . περιέρχομαι G4022
περιελόντες   vbl., ²aor. act. ptc. nom. pl. masc.
   {6.A.2} .περιαιρέω G4014
περιεπάτει   verb, impf. act. indic. 3 pers. sg.
   {5.A.2} . . . . .περιπατέω G4043
περιεπάτεις   verb, impf. act. indic. 2 pers. sg.
   {5.A.2} . . . . id.
περιεπατήσαμεν   verb, aor. act. indic. 1 pers.
   pl. {5.A.1} . . . . id.
περιεπατήσατε   verb, aor. act. indic. 2 pers. pl.
   {5.A.1} . . . . id.
περιεπάτησε   verb, aor. act. indic. 3 pers. sg.
   {5.A.1} . . . . id.
περιεπάτησεν   verb, aor. act. indic. 3 pers. sg.
   {5.A.1} . . . . id.
περιεπάτουν   verb, impf. act. indic. 3 pers. pl.
   {5.A.2} . . . . id.
περιέπειραν   verb, aor. act. indic. 3 pers. pl.
   {5.A.1.b} . . . . περιπείρω G4044
περιέπεσεν   verb, ²aor. act. indic. 3 pers. sg.
   {5.A.1.b} . . . . περιπίπτω G4045
περιεποιήσατο   verb, aor. mid. indic. 3 pers. sg.
   {5.A.1} . . . . περιποιέω G4046
περίεργα   adj., acc. pl. neut. {3.C} . . . . . περίεργος G4021
G4020 **περιεργάζομαι**   *I am active around, I am a*
   busybody.
περιεργαζομένους   vbl., pres. mid./pass. ptc. acc.
   pl. masc. {6.A.1} . . . . περιεργάζομαι G4020
περίεργοι   adj., nom. pl. fem. {3.C} . . . . . περίεργος G4021
G4021 **περίεργος**, -ον, ὁ   (1) *inquisitive, prying, a*
   busybody; (2) *curious, magical,* Acts 19:19.

G4022 **περιέρχομαι**   intrans. and trans., (1) *I go*
   round, I move about (περιερχόμενοι, *strol-*
   ing, Acts 19:13); (2) *I make a circuit, tack,* Acts
   28:13 (var.).
περιερχόμεναι   vbl., pres. mid./pass. ptc. nom. pl.
   fem. {6.A.1} . . . . περιέρχομαι G4022
περιερχομένων   vbl., pres. mid./pass. ptc. gen.
   pl. masc. {6.A.1} . . . . id.
περιεσπᾶτο   verb, impf. pass. indic. 3 pers. sg.
   {5.A.2} . . . . περισπάω G4049
περιέστησαν   verb, ²aor. act. indic. 3 pers. pl.
   {5.A.3.b} . . . . περιΐστημι G4026
περιεστῶτα   vbl., ²perf. act. ptc. acc. sg. masc.
   {6.A.3} . . . . id.
περιέσχεν   verb, ²aor. act. indic. 3 pers. sg.
   {5.A.1.b} . . . . .περιέχω G4023
περιέτεμεν   verb, ²aor. act. indic. 3 pers. sg.
   {5.A.1.b} . . . . .περιτέμνω G4059
περιετμήθητε   verb, aor. pass. indic. 2 pers. pl.
   {5.A.1.b} . . . . id.
περιέχει   verb, pres. act. indic. 3 pers. sg.
   {5.A.1.a} .περιέχω G4023
περιέχουσαν   vbl., pres. act. ptc. acc. sg. fem.
   {6.A.1} . . . . id.
G4023 **περιέχω**   (1) *I contain* (of a book *containing*
   subject matter); hence, impers., *it stands (has*
   its content) thus, 1 Pet 2:6; (2) *I encompass,*
   surround; I get hold of, seize.
G4024 **περιζώννυμι**   *I gird round;* mid. *I gird myself,*
   generally for active work or travel.
περίζωσαι   verb, aor. mid. impv. 2 pers. sg.
   {5.D.3} . . . . .περιζώννυμι G4024
περιζωσάμενοι   vbl., aor. mid. ptc. nom. pl.
   masc. {6.A.3} . . . . id.
περιζωσάμενος   vbl., aor. mid. ptc. nom. sg.
   masc. {6.A.3} . . . . id.
περιζώσεται   verb, fut. mid. indic. 3 pers. sg.
   {5.A.1} . . . . id.
περιῆγε   verb, impf. act. indic. 3 pers. sg.
   {5.A.1.b} . . . . περιάγω G4013
περιῆγεν   verb, impf. act. indic. 3 pers. sg.
   {5.A.1.b} . . . . id.
περιῆλθον   verb, ²aor. act. indic. 3 pers. pl.
   {5.A.1.b} . . . . περιέρχομαι G4022
περιηρεῖτο   verb, impf. pass. indic. 3 pers. sg.
   {5.A.1} . . . . περιαιρέω G4014
περιήστραψεν   verb, aor. act. indic. 3 pers. sg.
   {5.A.1.b} . . . . περιαστράπτω G4015
περιθείς   vbl., ²aor. act. ptc. nom. sg. masc.
   {6.A.3} . . . . περιτίθημι G4060
περιθέντες   vbl., ²aor. act. ptc. nom. pl. masc.
   {6.A.3} . . . . id.
περιθέσεως   noun, gen. sg. fem. {2.C} . . . περίθεσις G4025
G4025 **περίθεσις**, -εως, ἡ   *a putting around* (or *on*).
περιΐστασο   verb, pres. mid. impv. 2 pers. sg.
   {5.D.3} . . . . περιΐστημι G4026
περιΐστασο   verb, pres. mid. impv. 2 pers. sg.
   {5.D.3} . . . . id.
G4026 **περιΐστημι**   (1) in intrans. tenses, *I surround;*
   (2) *I stand clear of, avoid,* 2 Tim 2:16; Titus 3:9.

G4027 **περικάθαρμα**, -ατος, τό   *a rinsing* of a dirty
vessel.
περικαθάρματα   noun, nom. pl. neut.
{2.C} . . . . .περικάθαρμα G4027
περικαλύπτειν   vbl., pres. act. inf.
{6.B.1} . . . . .περικαλύπτω G4028

G4028 **περικαλύπτω**   *I veil round, I cover over; I*
conceal.
περικαλύψαντες   vbl., aor. act. ptc. nom. pl. masc.
{6.A.1.a} .περικαλύπτω G4028

G4029 **περίκειμαι**   *I am placed around* something; *I*
have had something *placed around* me, Acts
28:20; Heb 5:2.
περίκειμαι   verb, pres. mid./pass. indic. 1 pers. sg.
{5.A.3.a} . . . . .περίκειμαι G4029
περικείμενον   vbl., pres. mid./pass. ptc. acc. sg.
neut. {6.A.3} . . . . id.
περίκειται   verb, pres. mid./pass. indic. 3 pers.
sg. {5.A.3.a} . . . . id.
περικεκαλυμμένην   vbl., perf. pass. ptc. acc. sg.
fem. {6.A.1.b} . . . . .περικαλύπτω G4028

G4030 **περικεφαλαία**, -ας, ἡ   *a helmet.*
περικεφαλαίαν   noun, acc. sg. fem.
{2.A} . . . . .περικεφαλαία G4030
περικρατεῖς   adj., nom. pl. masc. {3.E}.περικρατής G4031

G4031 **περικρατής**, -ές   *mastering, gaining control*
over.

G4032 **περικρύβω**   *I conceal, hide (entirely,* by putting
something *around* it).

G4033 **περικυκλόω**   *I encircle, invest.*
περικυκλώσουσι   verb, fut. act. indic. 3 pers. pl.
{5.A.1} . . . . .περικυκλόω G4033
περικυκλώσουσιν   verb, fut. act. indic. 3 pers.
pl. {5.A.1} . . . . id.

G4034 **περιλάμπω**   *I shine around.*
περιλάμψαν   vbl., aor. act. ptc. acc. sg. neut.
{6.A.1.a} . . . . .περιλάμπω G4034
περιλειπόμενοι   vbl., pres. pass. ptc. nom. pl.
masc. {6.A.1} . . . . περιλείπω G4035

G4035 **περιλείπω**   pass. *I am left behind, remain.*
περίλυπον   adj., acc. sg. masc. {3.C} . . . .περίλυπος G4036

G4036 **περίλυπος**, -ον   *deeply pained (grieved).*
περίλυπος   adj., nom. sg. fem. {3.C} . . . .περίλυπος G4036
περίλυπος   adj., nom. sg. masc. {3.C} . . . . id.
περιμένειν   vbl., pres. act. inf. {6.B.1} . . . περιμένω G4037

G4037 **περιμένω**   *I await* the happening of something.

G4038 **πέριξ**   adv., *around, all around, in the vicinity.*
πέριξ   adv. . . . . .πέριξ G4038

G4039 **περιοικέω**   *I dwell around (near).*
περίοικοι   adj., nom. pl. masc. {3.C} . . . περίοικος G4040

G4040 **περίοικος**, -ον, ὁ   *neighboring; a neighbor.*
περιοικοῦντας   vbl., pres. act. ptc. acc. pl. masc.
{6.A.2} . . . . .περιοικέω G4039
περιούσιον   adj., acc. sg. masc. {3.C} . .περιούσιος G4041

G4041 **περιούσιος**, -ον   *of (for) one's own (special,*
private) possession.

G4042 **περιοχή**, -ῆς, ἡ   *a clause, sentence, short*
passage.
περιοχή   noun, nom. sg. fem. {2.A} . . . . . περιοχή G4042

περιπάτει   verb, pres. act. impv. 2 pers. sg.
{5.D.2} . . . . .περιπατέω G4043
περιπατεῖ   verb, pres. act. indic. 3 pers. sg.
{5.A.2} . . . . id.
περιπατεῖ   verb, pres. act. indic. 3 pers. sg.
{5.A.2} . . . . id.
περιπατεῖν   vbl., pres. act. inf. {6.B.2} . . . . id.
περιπατεῖς   verb, pres. act. indic. 2 pers. sg.
{5.A.2} . . . . id.
περιπατεῖτε   verb, pres. act. impv. 2 pers. pl.
{5.D.2} . . . . id.
περιπατεῖτε   verb, pres. act. indic. 2 pers. pl.
{5.A.2} . . . . id.
περιπατείτω   verb, pres. act. impv. 3 pers. sg.
{5.D.2} . . . . id.

G4043 **περιπατέω**   (1) *I walk;* (2) hence Hebraistically
in an ethical sense, *I conduct my life, I live.*
περιπατῇ   verb, pres. act. subjunc. 3 pers. sg.
{5.B.2} . . . . .περιπατέω G4043
περιπατῆσαι   vbl., aor. act. inf. {6.B.1} . . . . id.
περιπατήσαντες   vbl., aor. act. ptc. nom. pl.
masc. {6.A.2} . . . . id.
περιπατήσει   verb, fut. act. indic. 3 pers. sg.
{5.A.1} . . . . id.
περιπατήσῃ   verb, aor. act. subjunc. 3 pers. sg.
{5.B.1} . . . . id.
περιπατήσουσι   verb, fut. act. indic. 3 pers. pl.
{5.A.1} . . . . id.
περιπατήσουσιν   verb, fut. act. indic. 3 pers.
pl. {5.A.1} . . . . id.
περιπατήσωμεν   verb, aor. act. subjunc. 1 pers.
pl. {5.B.1} . . . . id.
περιπατῆτε   verb, pres. act. subjunc. 2 pers. pl.
{5.B.2} . . . . id.
περιπατοῦμεν   verb, pres. act. indic. 1 pers. pl.
{5.A.2} . . . . id.
περιπατοῦντα   vbl., pres. act. ptc. acc. pl. neut.
{6.A.2} . . . . id.
περιπατοῦντα   vbl., pres. act. ptc. acc. sg.
masc. {6.A.2} . . . . id.
περιπατοῦντας   vbl., pres. act. ptc. acc. pl.
masc. {6.A.2} . . . . id.
περιπατοῦντες   vbl., pres. act. ptc. nom. pl.
masc. {6.A.2} . . . . id.
περιπατοῦντι   vbl., pres. act. ptc. dat. sg. masc.
{6.A.2} . . . . id.
περιπατοῦντος   vbl., pres. act. ptc. gen. sg.
masc. {6.A.2} . . . . id.
περιπατοῦσι   verb, pres. act. indic. 3 pers. pl.
{5.A.2} . . . . id.
περιπατοῦσιν   verb, pres. act. indic. 3 pers. pl.
{5.A.2} . . . . id.
περιπατοῦσιν   vbl., pres. act. ptc. dat. pl. masc.
{6.A.2} . . . . id.
περιπατῶμεν   verb, pres. act. subjunc. 1 pers.
pl. {5.B.2} . . . . id.
περιπατῶν   vbl., pres. act. ptc. nom. sg. masc.
{6.A.2} . . . . id.

G4044 **περιπείρω**   *I pierce round about (on all sides).*

περιπεπατήκει   verb, plu. act. indic. 3 pers. sg.
{5.A.1} . . . . περιπατέω G4043
περιπέσητε   verb, ²aor. act. subjunc. 2 pers. pl.
{5.B.1} . . . . .περιπίπτω G4045
περιπεσόντες   vbl., ²aor. act. ptc. nom. pl.
masc. {6.A.1.a} . . . . id.

G4045   **περιπίπτω**   *I fall into, I fall in with, I meet with,*
I come upon accidentally, I chance upon, I light
upon.

G4046   **περιποιέω**   mid. *I acquire (gain) for myself;* in
Luke 17:33 perhaps, *I preserve alive.*
περιποιήσασθαι   vbl., aor. mid. inf.
{6.B.1} . . . . .περιποιέω G4046
περιποιήσεως   noun, gen. sg. fem.
{2.C} . . . . περιποίησις G4047
περιποίησιν   noun, acc. sg. fem. {2.C} . . . . id.

G4047   **περιποίησις**, -εως, ἡ   *acquiring, obtaining, pos-*
sessing, possession, ownership.
περιποιοῦνται   verb, pres. mid. indic. 3 pers. pl.
{5.A.2} . . . . .περιποιέω G4046

G4048   **περιρήγνυμι** (περιρρήγνυμι)   *I rend all*
round, I tear of.
περιρήξαντες   vbl., aor. act. ptc. nom. pl. masc.
{6.A.3} . . . . .περιρήγνυμι G4048
περιρρήξαντες   vbl., aor. act. ptc. nom. pl.
masc. {6.A.3} . . . . id.

G4049   **περισπάω**   *I distract, trouble greatly.*

G4050   **περισσεία**, -ας, ἡ   *surplus, superabundance,*
superfluity.
περισσεία   noun, nom. sg. fem. {2.A} . .περισσεία G4050
περισσείαν   noun, acc. sg. fem. {2.A} . . . . . . id.
περισσεύει   verb, pres. act. indic. 3 pers. sg.
{5.A.1.a} . . . . περισσεύω G4052
περισσεύειν   vbl., pres. act. inf. {6.B.1} . . . id.
περισσεύετε   verb, pres. act. indic. 2 pers. pl.
{5.A.1.a} . . . . id.
περισσεύη   verb, pres. act. subjunc. 3 pers. sg.
{5.B.1} . . . . id.
περισσεύητε   verb, pres. act. subjunc. 2 pers.
pl. {5.B.1} . . . . id.
περισσευθήσεται   verb, fut. pass. indic. 3 pers.
sg. {5.A.1.d} . . . . id.

G4051   **περίσσευμα**, -ατος, τό   *what is in excess;*
overflow, superabundance, superfluity.
περίσσευμα   noun, nom. sg. neut.
{2.C} . . . . περίσσευμα G4051
περισσεύματα   noun, acc. pl. neut. {2.C} . . . . . id.
περισσεύματος   noun, gen. sg. neut. {2.C} . . . . id.
περισσεύομεν   verb, pres. act. indic. 1 pers. pl.
{5.A.1.a} . . . . περισσεύω G4052
περισσεῦον   vbl., pres. act. ptc. acc. sg. neut.
{6.A.1} . . . . id.
περισσεύονται   verb, pres. mid. indic. 3 pers.
pl. {5.A.1.d} . . . . id.
περισσεύοντες   vbl., pres. act. ptc. nom. pl.
masc. {6.A.1} . . . . id.
περισσεύοντος   vbl., pres. act. ptc. gen. sg.
neut. {6.A.1} . . . . id.

περισσεύουσα   vbl., pres. act. ptc. nom. sg.
fem. {6.A.1} . . . . id.
περισσεύουσιν   verb, pres. act. indic. 3 pers.
pl. {5.A.1.a} . . . . id.
περισσεῦσαι   verb, aor. act. opt. 3 pers. sg.
{5.C.1} . . . . id.
περισσεῦσαι   vbl., aor. act. inf. {6.B.1} . . . . . . id.
περισσεῦσαν   vbl., aor. act. ptc. nom. sg. neut.
{6.A.1.a} . . . . id.
περισσεύσαντα   vbl., aor. act. ptc. acc. pl.
neut. {6.A.1.a} . . . . id.
περισσεύσῃ   verb, aor. act. subjunc. 3 pers. sg.
{5.B.1} . . . . id.

G4052   **περισσεύω**   (1) intrans., *I exceed the ordinary*
(the necessary), I abound, I overflow; I am left
over; hence met.; (2) trans., *I cause to abound,*
Matt 13:12; Luke 15:17; 2 Cor 4:15(?); 9:8; Eph
1:8; 1 Thess 3:12.
περισσεύω   verb, pres. act. indic. 1 pers. sg.
{5.A.1.a} . . . . περισσεύω G4052
περισσόν   adj., acc. sg. neut. {3.A} . . . . .περισσός G4053
περισσόν   adj., nom. sg. neut. {3.A} . . . . id.

G4053   **περισσός**, -ή, -όν   adj. and adv., *over and*
above, excessive, abundant, overflowing; super-
fluous. Practically a synonym for πλείων (cf.
Matt 5:37), esp. in the comp. περισσότερος;
ἐκ περισσοῦ, *superabundantly, exceedingly.*
περισσοτέρᾳ   adj. comp., dat. sg. fem. {3.A;
3.G} . . . . .περισσότερος G4055
περισσοτέραν   adj. comp., acc. sg. fem. {3.A;
3.G} . . . . id.
περισσότερον   adj. comp., acc. sg. masc. {3.A;
3.G} . . . . id.
περισσότερον   adj. comp., acc. sg. neut. {3.A;
3.G} . . . . id.
περισσότερον   adj. comp., nom. sg. neut. {3.A;
3.G} . . . . id.
περισσότερον   adv. comp. {3.F; 3.G} . . . . id.

G4055   **περισσότερος**, -α, -ον   *superabundantly,*
exceedingly.
περισσοτέρως   adv. comp. {3.F; 3.G} . . . περισσῶς G4057
περισσοῦ   adj., gen. sg. neut. {3.A} . . . . .περισσός G4053

G4057   **περισσῶς**   adv., *exceedingly,* so perhaps Acts
26:11; but usually *more* (cf. περισσός), with
reference to what precedes.
περισσῶς   adv. {3.F} . . . . περισσῶς G4057

G4058   **περιστερά**, -ᾶς, ἡ   *a dove.*
περιστεραί   noun, nom. pl. fem. {2.A} . .περιστερά G4058
περιστεράν   noun, acc. sg. fem. {2.A} . . . . . . id.
περιστεράς   noun, acc. pl. fem. {2.A} . . . . id.
περιστερῶν   noun, gen. pl. fem. {2.A} . . . . . . id.
περιτεμεῖν   vbl., ²aor. act. inf. {6.B.1} . . .περιτέμνω G4059
περιτέμνειν   vbl., pres. act. inf. {6.B.1} . . . . . . id.
περιτέμνεσθαι   vbl., pres. pass. inf. {6.B.1} . . . . id.
περιτεμνέσθω   verb, pres. pass. impv. 3 pers.
sg. {5.D.1} . . . . id.
περιτέμνετε   verb, pres. act. indic. 2 pers. pl.
{5.A.1.a} . . . . id.

περιτέμνησθε   verb, pres. pass. subjunc. 2 pers.
pl. {5.B.1}. . . . . id.
περιτεμνόμενοι   vbl., pres. pass. ptc. nom. pl.
masc. {6.A.1}. . . . . id.
περιτεμνομένῳ   vbl., pres. pass. ptc. dat. sg.
masc. {6.A.1}. . . . . id.
G4059 **περιτέμνω**   *I cut round* the foreskin, *I circumcise.*
περιτετμημένοι   vbl., perf. pass. ptc. nom. pl.
masc. {6.A.1.b}. . . . . .περιτέμνω G4059
περιτετμημένος   vbl., perf. pass. ptc. nom. sg.
masc. {6.A.1.b}. id.
περιτιθέασιν   verb, pres. act. indic. 3 pers. pl.
{5.A.3.a} . . . . περιτίθημι G4060
περιτίθεμεν   verb, pres. act. indic. 1 pers. pl.
{5.A.3.a} . . . . id.
G4060 **περιτίθημι**   *I place around; I put about (upon), I clothe with.*
περιτμηθῆναι   vbl., aor. pass. inf.
{6.B.1} . . . . .περιτέμνω G4059
περιτμηθῆτε   verb, aor. pass. subjunc. 2 pers.
pl. {5.B.1}. . . . . id.
G4061 **περιτομή**, -ῆς, ἡ   *circumcision* (see πε-
ριτέμνω); οἱ ἐκ περιτομῆς, *the party of circumcision, the party advocating circumci-sion,* the rigorist Christian Jews; sometimes met. (as in OT), of that *chastening* of the heart (mind) which leads to heartier service to God, e.g., Rom 2:29.
περιτομή   noun, nom. sg. fem. {2.A} . . . .περιτομή G4061
περιτομῇ   noun, dat. sg. fem. {2.A} . . . . id.
περιτομήν   noun, acc. sg. fem. {2.A} . . . . id.
περιτομῆς   noun, gen. sg. fem. {2.A} . . . . id.
περιτρέπει   verb, pres. act. indic. 3 pers. sg.
{5.A.1.a} . . . . .περιτρέπω G4062
G4062 **περιτρέπω**   *I turn round, I turn, change.*
G4063 **περιτρέχω**   *I run around, I run about (in).*
περιφέρειν   vbl., pres. act. inf. {6.B.1}. . . περιφέρω G4064
περιφέρεσθε   verb, pres. pass. impv. 2 pers. pl.
{5.D.1}. . . . . id.
περιφερόμεναι   vbl., pres. pass. ptc. nom. pl.
fem. {6.A.1}. . . . . id.
περιφερόμενοι   vbl., pres. pass. ptc. nom. pl.
masc. {6.A.1}. . . . . id.
περιφέροντες   vbl., pres. act. ptc. nom. pl.
masc. {6.A.1}. . . . . id.
G4064 **περιφέρω**   *I carry around (about); I swing round,* Eph 4:14.
περιφρονείτω   verb, pres. act. impv. 3 pers. sg.
{5.D.2}. . . . . περιφρονέω G4065
G4065 **περιφρονέω**   *I lightly esteem; I despise.*
περίχωρον   adj., acc. sg. fem. {3.C}. . . . .περίχωρος G4066
G4066 **περίχωρος**, -ου, ἡ   *neighboring;* ἡ περίχωρος
(supply γῆ), *the neighboring country, the neigh-borhood, surroundings.*
περίχωρος   adj., nom. sg. fem. {3.C}. . . .περίχωρος G4066
περιχώρου   adj., gen. sg. fem. {3.C} . . . . id.
περιχώρῳ   adj., dat. sg. fem. {3.C} . . . . id.
G4067 **περίψημα**, -ατος, τό   *that which is scraped off round* anything, *a scraping.*

περίψημα   noun, nom. sg. neut. {2.C} . . περίψημα G4067
περπερεύεται   verb, pres. mid./pass. indic. 3 pers.
sg. {5.A.1.d}. . . . . περπερεύομαι G4068
G4068 **περπερεύομαι**   *I show myself off; I am boastful (a braggart).*
Περσίδα   noun prop., acc. sg. fem. {2.C; 2.D}. . . . . Περσίς G4069
G4069 **Περσίς**, -ίδος, ἡ   *Persis,* name of a Christian lady in Rome.
G4070 **πέρυσι**   adv., *the previous year, last year.*
πέρυσι   adv. . . . . .πέρυσι G4070
πέσατε   verb, ²aor. act. impv. 2 pers. pl.
{5.D.1}. . . . . πίπτω G4098
πεσεῖν   vbl., ²aor. act. inf. {6.B.1} . . . . id.
πεσεῖται   verb, fut. mid. indic. 3 pers. sg. {5.A.2} id.
πέσετε   verb, ²aor. act. impv. 2 pers. pl. {5.D.1} . . id.
πέσῃ   verb, ²aor. act. subjunc. 3 pers. sg. {5.B.1} . id.
πέσητε   verb, ²aor. act. subjunc. 2 pers. pl. {5.B.1}id.
πεσόν   vbl., ²aor. act. ptc. nom. sg. neut. {6.A.1.a}id.
πεσόντα   vbl., ²aor. act. ptc. acc. sg. masc.
{6.A.1.a} . . . . id.
πεσόντας   vbl., ²aor. act. ptc. acc. pl. masc.
{6.A.1.a} . . . . id.
πεσόντες   vbl., ²aor. act. ptc. nom. pl. masc.
{6.A.1.a} . . . . id.
πεσοῦνται   verb, fut. mid. indic. 3 pers. pl.
{5.A.2}. . . . . id.
πεσών   vbl., ²aor. act. ptc. nom. sg. masc.
{6.A.1.a} . . . . id.
πέσωσι   verb, ²aor. act. subjunc. 3 pers. pl.
{5.B.1}. . . . . id.
πέσωσιν   verb, ²aor. act. subjunc. 3 pers. pl.
{5.B.1}. . . . . id.
πετεινά   noun, acc. pl. neut. {2.B}. . . . . . πετεινόν G4071
πετεινά   noun, nom. pl. neut. {2.B} . . . . id.
G4071 **πετεινόν**, -οῦ, τό   *a bird.*
πετεινῶν   noun, gen. pl. neut. {2.B} . . . . . πετεινόν G4071
πέτηται   verb, pres. mid./pass. subjunc. 3 pers. sg.
{5.B.1}. . . . . .πέτομαι G4072
G4072 **πέτομαι**   *I fly.*
πετομένοις   vbl., pres. mid./pass. ptc. dat. pl. neut.
{6.A.1}. .πέτομαι G4072
πετόμενον   vbl., pres. mid./pass. ptc. acc. sg.
masc. {6.A.1}. . . . . id.
πετομένου   vbl., pres. mid./pass. ptc. gen. sg.
masc. {6.A.1}. . . . . id.
πετομένῳ   vbl., pres. mid./pass. ptc. dat. sg.
masc. {6.A.1}. . . . . id.
G4073 **πέτρα**, -ας, ἡ   *rock, solid rock, native rock,* ris-
ing up through the earth, which trips up the traveler, Rom 9:33; 1 Pet 2:8; in Matt 16:18, of such faith as Peter has just shown; in 1 Cor 10:4, allegorically interpreted.
πέτρα   noun, nom. sg. fem. {2.A} . . . . πέτρα G4073
πέτρᾳ   noun, dat. sg. fem. {2.A} . . . . id.
πέτραι   noun, nom. pl. fem. {2.A}. . . . . id.
πέτραις   noun, dat. pl. fem. {2.A} . . . . id.
πέτραν   noun, acc. sg. fem. {2.A} . . . . id.
πέτρας   noun, acc. pl. fem. {2.A} . . . . id.
πέτρας   noun, gen. sg. fem. {2.A} . . . . id.

Πέτρε   noun prop., voc. sg. masc. {2.B; 2.D} Πέτρος *G4074*
Πέτρον   noun prop., acc. sg. masc. {2.B; 2.D} . . . id.
G4074 **Πέτρος**, -ου, ὁ   *Peter* (a Gk. name meaning
    "rock," a translation of the Aram. name Κηφᾶς,
    given to Symeon (Simon) by our Lord).
Πέτρος   noun prop., nom. sg. masc. {2.B;
    2.D} . . . . Πέτρος *G4074*
Πέτρου   noun prop., gen. sg. masc. {2.B; 2.D} . . id.
Πέτρῳ   noun prop., dat. sg. masc. {2.B; 2.D} . . . . id.
πετρῶδες   adj., acc. sg. neut. {3.E} . . . . . πετρώδης *G4075*
πετρώδη   adj., acc. pl. neut. {3.E} . . . . id.
G4075 **πετρώδης**, -ους, τό   *rocky.*
πετωμένοις   vbl., pres. mid./pass. ptc. dat. pl. neut.
    {6.A.1} . . . . .πέτομαι *G4072*
πετώμενον   vbl., pres. mid./pass. ptc. acc. sg.
    masc. {6.A.1} . . . . id.
πετωμένου   vbl., pres. mid./pass. ptc. gen. sg.
    masc. {6.A.1} . . . . id.
πετωμένῳ   vbl., pres. mid./pass. ptc. dat. sg.
    masc. {6.A.1} . . . . id.
πεφανερώμεθα   verb, perf. pass. indic. 1 pers. pl.
    {5.A.1} . . . . φανερόω *G5319*
πεφανερῶσθαι   vbl., perf. pass. inf. {6.B.1} . . . id.
πεφανέρωται   verb, perf. pass. indic. 3 pers. sg.
    {5.A.1} . . . . id.
πεφιλήκατε   verb, perf. act. indic. 2 pers. pl.
    {5.A.1} . . . . φιλέω *G5368*
πεφίμωσο   verb, perf. pass. impv. 2 pers. sg.
    {5.D.1} . . . . φιμόω *G5392*
πεφορτισμένοι   vbl., perf. pass. ptc. nom. pl. masc.
    {6.A.1.b} . . . . φορτίζω *G5412*
πεφορτισμένοι   vbl., perf. pass. ptc. voc. pl.
    masc. {6.A.1.b} . . . . id.
πεφυσιωμένοι   vbl., perf. pass. ptc. nom. pl. masc.
    {6.A.2} . . . . φυσιόω *G5448*
πεφυσιωμένων   vbl., perf. pass. ptc. gen. pl.
    masc. {6.A.2} . . . . id.
πεφυτευμένην   vbl., perf. pass. ptc. acc. sg. fem.
    {6.A.1.b} . . . . φυτεύω *G5452*
πεφωτισμένους   vbl., perf. pass. ptc. acc. pl. masc.
    {6.A.1.b} . . . . φωτίζω *G5461*
πηγαί   noun, nom. pl. fem. {2.A} . . . . πηγή *G4077*
G4076 **πήγανον**, -ου, τό   *rue*, a plant used for flavor-
    ing, garnishing dishes, etc.
πήγανον   noun, acc. sg. neut. {2.B} . . . . . πήγανον *G4076*
πηγάς   noun, acc. pl. fem. {2.A} . . . . πηγή *G4077*
G4077 **πηγή**, -ῆς, ἡ   *a spring, a fountain; a well*, John
    4:6.
πηγή   noun, nom. sg. fem. {2.A} . . . . πηγή *G4077*
πηγῇ   noun, dat. sg. fem. {2.A} . . . . id.
πηγῆς   noun, gen. sg. fem. {2.A} . . . . id.
G4078 **πήγνυμι**   *I fix, pitch; I erect.*
G4079 **πηδάλιον**, -ου, τό   *a helm, rudder.*
πηδαλίου   noun, gen. sg. neut. {2.B} . . . πηδάλιον *G4079*
πηδαλίων   noun, gen. pl. neut. {2.B} . . . . id.
πηλίκοις   pron. correl. interrog., dat. pl. neut.
    {4.D} . . . . πηλίκος *G4080*
G4080 **πηλίκος**, -η, -ον   *how large, how great.*
πηλίκος   pron. correl. interrog., nom. sg. masc.
    {4.D} . . . . πηλίκος *G4080*

πηλόν   noun, acc. sg. masc. {2.B} . . . . πηλός *G4081*
G4081 **πηλός**, -οῦ, ὁ   *mud; clay.*
πηλοῦ   noun, gen. sg. masc. {2.B} . . . . πηλός *G4081*
G4082 **πήρα**, -ας, ἡ   *a bag* (to hold food, etc.), *a wal-
    let, a traveling bag*, perhaps esp. *a collecting bag*
    (such as beggar-priests of pagan cults carried).
πήραν   noun, acc. sg. fem. {2.A} . . . . .πήρα *G4082*
πήρας   noun, gen. sg. fem. {2.A} . . . . id.
πῆχυν   noun, acc. sg. masc. {2.C} . . . . πῆχυς *G4083*
G4083 **πῆχυς**, -εως, ὁ   *the forearm; hence, a cubit,*
    about a foot and a half; used as a measurement
    of time in Matt 6:27 (Luke 12:25), to indicate
    any extension.
πηχῶν   noun, gen. pl. masc. {2.C} . . . . πῆχυς *G4083*
G4084 **πιάζω**   *I take hold of, seize, apprehend, catch,
    arrest, grasp* (a Doric form; contrast πιέζω).
πιάσαι   vbl., aor. act. inf. {6.B.1} . . . . πιάζω *G4084*
πιάσας   vbl., aor. act. ptc. nom. sg. masc.
    {6.A.1.a} . . . . id.
πιάσωσιν   verb, aor. act. subjunc. 3 pers. pl.
    {5.B.1} . . . . id.
πίε   verb, ²aor. act. impv. 2 pers. sg. {5.D.1} . . . πίνω *G4095*
G4085 **πιέζω**   *I press down.*
πιεῖν   vbl., ²aor. act. inf. {6.B.1} . . . . πίνω *G4095*
πίεσαι   verb, fut. mid. indic. 2 pers. sg. {5.A.1.d} id.
πίεσθε   verb, fut. mid. indic. 2 pers. pl. {5.A.1.d} id.
πίεται   verb, fut. mid. indic. 3 pers. sg. {5.A.1.d}. id.
πίετε   verb, ²aor. act. impv. 2 pers. pl. {5.D.1} . . . id.
πίη   verb, ²aor. act. subjunc. 3 pers. sg. {5.B.1}. . . id.
πίητε   verb, ²aor. act. subjunc. 2 pers. pl. {5.B.1} . id.
G4086 **πιθανολογία**, -ας, ἡ   *persuasive speech.*
πιθανολογίᾳ   noun, dat. sg. fem.
    {2.A} .πιθανολογία *G4086*
πιθοῖς   adj., dat. pl. masc. {3.A} . . . . πειθός *G3981*
πικραίνεσθε   verb, pres. pass. impv. 2 pers. pl.
    {5.D.1} . . . . πικραίνω *G4087*
G4087 **πικραίνω**   *I make bitter (tart., sour)*; mid. *I am
    embittered, I show quick temper.*
πικρανεῖ   verb, fut. act. indic. 3 pers. sg.
    {5.A.2} . . . . πικραίνω *G4087*
G4088 **πικρία**, -ας, ἡ   *bitterness, sourness;* hence met.,
    an embittered (resentful) spirit, which refuses
    reconciliation, Eph 4:31.
πικρία   noun, nom. sg. fem. {2.A} . . . . πικρία *G4088*
πικρίας   noun, gen. sg. fem. {2.A} . . . . id.
πικρόν   adj., acc. sg. masc. {3.A} . . . . .πικρός *G4089*
πικρόν   adj., acc. sg. neut. {3.A} . . . . id.
G4089 **πικρός**, -ά, -όν   *bitter*, lit. and met.
G4090 **πικρῶς**   adv., *bitterly.*
πικρῶς   adv. {3.F} . . . . πικρῶς *G4090*
Πιλάτον   noun prop., acc. sg. masc. {2.B;
    2.D} . . . . Πιλᾶτος *G4091*
Πιλᾶτον   noun prop., acc. sg. masc. {2.B; 2.D} . . id.
Πιλᾶτος   noun prop., nom. sg. masc. {2.B; 2.D} . id.
G4091 **Πιλᾶτος** (Πειλᾶτος), -ου, ὁ   *Pilatus, Pilate,*
    the third name (cognomen) of the procurator
    of Judaea, whose first name (praenomen) is
    unknown.
Πιλᾶτος   noun prop., nom. sg. masc. {2.B;
    2.D} . . . . Πιλᾶτος *G4091*

Πιλάτου   noun prop., gen. sg. masc. {2.B; 2.D} . id.
Πιλάτῳ   noun prop., dat. sg. masc. {2.B; 2.D}. . . id.
πίμπρασθαι   vbl., pres. pass. inf. {6.B.3} . .πίμπρημι *G4092*
G4092 **πίμπρημι**   *I cause to swell; pass., I become
  inflamed, I am swollen.*
πίνακι   noun, dat. sg. masc. {2.C}. . . . . .πίναξ *G4094*
G4093 **πινακίδιον**, -ου, τό   *a little* waxed *tablet*, on
  which to write with iron pen.
πινακίδιον   noun, acc. sg. neut. {2.B}. . πινακίδιον *G4093*
πίνακος   noun, gen. sg. masc. {2.C}. . . . . . . .πίναξ *G4094*
G4094 **πίναξ**, -ακος, ἡ   *a flat dish.*
πίνει   verb, pres. act. indic. 3 pers. sg. {5.A.1.a} πίνω *G4095*
πίνειν   vbl., pres. act. inf. {6.B.1}. . . . . id.
πίνετε   verb, pres. act. indic. 2 pers. pl. {5.A.1.a}. id.
πινέτω   verb, pres. act. impv. 3 pers. sg. {5.D.1} . id.
πίνῃ   verb, pres. act. subjunc. 3 pers. sg. {5.B.1} . id.
πίνητε   verb, pres. act. subjunc. 2 pers. pl. {5.B.1} id.
πίνοντες   vbl., pres. act. ptc. nom. pl. masc.
  {6.A.1}. . . . . id.
πίνουσιν   verb, pres. act. indic. 3 pers. pl.
  {5.A.1.a} . . . . id.
G4095 **πίνω**   *I drink.*
πίνω   verb, pres. act. indic. 1 pers. sg. {5.A.1.a} πίνω *G4095*
πίνω   verb, pres. act. subjunc. 1 pers. sg. {5.B.1} . id.
πίνων   vbl., pres. act. ptc. nom. sg. masc. {6.A.1} id.
G4096 **πιότης**, -ητος, ἡ   *fatness.*
πιότητος   noun, gen. sg. fem. {2.C} . . . . . .πιότης *G4096*
πιοῦσα   vbl., ²aor. act. ptc. nom. sg. fem.
  {6.A.1.a} . . . . πίνω *G4095*
πιπρασκομένων   vbl., pres. pass. ptc. gen. pl. neut.
  {6.A.1}. . . . . .πιπράσκω *G4097*
G4097 **πιπράσκω**   *I sell.*
πίπτει   verb, pres. act. indic. 3 pers. sg.
  {5.A.1.a} . . . . πίπτω *G4098*
πίπτοντες   vbl., pres. act. ptc. nom. pl. masc.
  {6.A.1}. . . . . id.
πιπτόντων   vbl., pres. act. ptc. gen. pl. neut.
  {6.A.1}. . . . . id.
G4098 **πίπτω**   *I fall.*
G4099 **Πισιδία**, -ας, ἡ   *Pisidia*, a country of Asia
  Minor, being the southwestern part of the
  Roman province Galatia.
πισιδίαν   adj., acc. sg. fem. {3.A} . . . . . . Πισίδιος *G4099†*
Πισιδίαν   noun prop., acc. sg. fem. {2.A; 2.D} . . id.
Πισιδίας   noun prop., gen. sg. fem. {2.A; 2.D} . . id.
G4099† Πισίδιος, -α, -ον, *Pisidian*, or rather, *near
  Pisidia.* Var. for Πισιδία, Acts 13:14.
πιστά   adj., acc. pl. neut. {3.A} . . . . .πιστός *G4103*
πιστάς   adj., acc. pl. fem. {3.A}. . . . . id.
πιστέ   adj., voc. sg. masc. {3.A}. . . . . id.
πίστει   noun, dat. sg. fem. {2.C} . . . . .πίστις *G4102*
πίστευε   verb, pres. act. impv. 2 pers. sg.
  {5.D.1}. πιστεύω *G4100*
πιστεύει   verb, pres. act. indic. 3 pers. sg.
  {5.A.1.a} . . . . id.
πιστεύειν   vbl., pres. act. inf. {6.B.1}. . . . . id.
πιστεύεις   verb, pres. act. indic. 2 pers. sg.
  {5.A.1.a} . . . . id.
πιστεύεται   verb, pres. pass. indic. 3 pers. sg.
  {5.A.1.d} . . . . id.

πιστεύετε   verb, pres. act. impv. 2 pers. pl.
  {5.D.1}. . . . . id.
πιστεύετε   verb, pres. act. indic. 2 pers. pl.
  {5.A.1.a} . . . . id.
πιστεύῃ   verb, pres. act. subjunc. 3 pers. sg.
  {5.B.1} . . . . id.
πιστεύητε   verb, pres. act. subjunc. 2 pers. pl.
  {5.B.1} . . . . id.
πιστευθῆναι   vbl., aor. pass. inf. {6.B.1}. . . . . . id.
πιστεύομεν   verb, pres. act. indic. 1 pers. pl.
  {5.A.1.a} . . . . id.
πιστεύοντα   vbl., pres. act. ptc. acc. sg. masc.
  {6.A.1}. . . . . id.
πιστεύοντας   vbl., pres. act. ptc. acc. pl. masc.
  {6.A.1}. . . . . id.
πιστεύοντες   vbl., pres. act. ptc. nom. pl. masc.
  {6.A.1}. . . . . id.
πιστεύοντι   vbl., pres. act. ptc. dat. sg. masc.
  {6.A.1}. . . . . id.
πιστευόντων   vbl., pres. act. ptc. gen. pl. masc.
  {6.A.1}. . . . . id.
πιστεύουσι   verb, pres. act. indic. 3 pers. pl.
  {5.A.1.a} . . . . id.
πιστεύουσι   vbl., pres. act. ptc. dat. pl. masc.
  {6.A.1}. . . . . id.
πιστεύουσιν   verb, pres. act. indic. 3 pers. pl.
  {5.A.1.a} . . . . id.
πιστεύουσιν   vbl., pres. act. ptc. dat. pl. masc.
  {6.A.1}. . . . . id.
πιστεῦσαι   vbl., aor. act. inf. {6.B.1} . . . . id.
πιστεύσαντας   vbl., aor. act. ptc. acc. pl. masc.
  {6.A.1.a} . . . . id.
πιστεύσαντες   vbl., aor. act. ptc. nom. pl. masc.
  {6.A.1.a} . . . . id.
πιστευσάντων   vbl., aor. act. ptc. gen. pl. masc.
  {6.A.1.a} . . . . id.
πιστεύσας   vbl., aor. act. ptc. nom. sg. masc.
  {6.A.1.a} . . . . id.
πιστεύσασα   vbl., aor. act. ptc. nom. sg. fem.
  {6.A.1.a} . . . . id.
πιστεύσασι   vbl., aor. act. ptc. dat. pl. masc.
  {6.A.1.a} . . . . id.
πιστεύσασιν   vbl., aor. act. ptc. dat. pl. masc.
  {6.A.1.a} . . . . id.
πιστεύσατε   verb, aor. act. impv. 2 pers. pl.
  {5.D.1}. . . . . id.
πιστεύσει   verb, fut. act. indic. 3 pers. sg.
  {5.A.1.a} . . . . id.
πιστεύσετε   verb, fut. act. indic. 2 pers. pl.
  {5.A.1.a} . . . . id.
πιστεύσῃ   verb, aor. act. subjunc. 3 pers. sg.
  {5.B.1} . . . . id.
πιστεύσῃς   verb, aor. act. subjunc. 2 pers. sg.
  {5.B.1} . . . . id.
πιστεύσητε   verb, aor. act. subjunc. 2 pers. pl.
  {5.B.1} . . . . id.
πιστεύσομεν   verb, fut. act. indic. 1 pers. pl.
  {5.A.1.a} . . . . id.
πίστευσον   verb, aor. act. impv. 2 pers. sg.
  {5.D.1}. . . . . id.

πιστευσόντων   vbl., fut. act. ptc. gen. pl. masc.
{6.A.1.a} . . . . id.

πιστεύσουσιν   verb, fut. act. indic. 3 pers. pl.
{5.A.1.a} . . . . id.

πιστεύσω   verb, aor. act. subjunc. 1 pers. sg.
{5.B.1} . . . . id.

πιστεύσω   verb, fut. act. indic. 1 pers. sg.
{5.A.1.a} . . . . id.

πιστεύσωμεν   verb, aor. act. subjunc. 1 pers. pl.
{5.B.1} . . . . id.

πιστεύσωσι   verb, aor. act. subjunc. 3 pers. pl.
{5.B.1} . . . . id.

πιστεύσωσιν   verb, aor. act. subjunc. 3 pers. pl.
{5.B.1} . . . . id.

G4100 **πιστεύω**   (1) *I believe,* with various constructions; with dat., *I believe* a person, or a statement made by a person (to be true); εἰς (ἐπί)
with acc., ἐν (ἐπί) with dat., *I place (repose)
my trust* on either God or the Messiah, *I rely*
on them, *I commit my life* to them, *I believe in,
I believe on, I cast myself upon* them as stable
and trustworthy, with energy of faith; ἐν is
sometimes = *in the sphere of,* Mark 1:15 (cf.
Rom 1:9; 2 Cor 8:18; 10:14; 1 Thess 3:2, etc.);
(2) with acc. and dat., *I entrust* (so in pass.
constr., 1 Thess 2:4; 1 Tim 1:11).

πιστεύω   verb, pres. act. indic. 1 pers. sg.
{5.A.1.a} . . . . πιστεύω *G4100*

πιστεύων   vbl., pres. act. ptc. nom. sg. masc.
{6.A.1} . . . . id.

πίστεως   noun, gen. sg. fem. {2.C} . . . . πίστις *G4102*

πιστή   adj., nom. sg. fem. {3.A} . . . . πιστός *G4103*

πιστήν   adj., acc. sg. fem. {3.A} . . . . id.

πιστῆς   adj., gen. sg. fem. {3.A} . . . . id.

πιστικῆς   adj., gen. sg. fem. {3.A} . . . . πιστικός *G4101*

G4101 **πιστικός**, -ή, -όν   probably = *genuine, pure.*

πίστιν   noun, acc. sg. fem. {2.C} . . . . πίστις *G4102*

G4102 **πίστις**, -εως, ἡ   (1) *faith, belief, trust,* generally
of the leaning of the entire human personality
upon God or the Messiah in absolute trust and
confidence in His power, wisdom, and goodness. The older meaning, *intellectual conviction* of certain truths, is often present. (In the
shorter reading of Eph 1:15, εἰς = *among*); (2)
with the article, *the faith* (in Luke 18:8 perhaps
the necessary faith or *the faith that perseveres*),
the Christian faith, Acts 6:7; 13:8; 16:5; 24:24;
Gal 1:23; 3:23; 6:10; Eph 4:13; Jude 3, 20, etc.;
(3) as a psychological faculty, Heb 11:1; (4)
integrity, faithfulness, trustworthiness, loyalty,
Matt 23:23; Rom 1:17(?); Gal 5:22; 2 Tim 4:7;
(5) *a guarantee,* Acts 17:31.

πίστις   noun, nom. sg. fem. {2.C} . . . . πίστις *G4102*

πιστοί   adj., nom. pl. masc. {3.A} . . . . πιστός *G4103*

πιστοῖς   adj., dat. pl. masc. {3.A} . . . . id.

πιστόν   adj., acc. sg. masc. {3.A} . . . . id.

πιστόν   adj., acc. sg. neut. {3.A} . . . . id.

πιστόν   adj., nom. sg. neut. {3.A} . . . . id.

G4103 **πιστός**, -ή, -όν   *faithful, trusty, trustworthy,
reliable;* οἱ πιστοί, *the Christians.*

πιστός   adj., nom. sg. masc. {3.A} . . . . πιστός *G4103*

πιστοῦ   adj., gen. sg. masc. {3.A} . . . . id.

πιστούς   adj., acc. pl. masc. {3.A} . . . . id.

G4104 **πιστόω**   *I make sure, I convince, I give assurance
to;* pass. *I show myself faithful, I am convinced.*

πιστῷ   adj., dat. sg. masc. {3.A} . . . . πιστός *G4103*

πιστῶν   adj., gen. pl. masc. {3.A} . . . . id.

πίω   verb, ²aor. act. subjunc. 1 pers. sg. {5.B.1}   πίνω *G4095*

πίωμεν   verb, ²aor. act. subjunc. 1 pers. pl. {5.B.1}id.

πιών   vbl., ²aor. act. ptc. nom. sg. masc. {6.A.1.a} id.

πίωσιν   verb, ²aor. act. subjunc. 3 pers. pl. {5.B.1}id.

πλάκες   noun, nom. pl. fem. {2.C} . . . . πλάξ *G4109*

πλανᾷ   verb, pres. act. indic. 3 pers. sg.
{5.A.2} . . . . πλανάω *G4105*

πλανᾷ   verb, pres. act. subjunc. 3 pers. sg. {5.B.2}id.

πλανᾶσθαι   vbl., pres. pass. inf. {6.B.2} . . . . id.

πλανᾶσθε   verb, pres. pass. impv. 2 pers. pl.
{5.D.2} . . . . id.

πλανᾶσθε   verb, pres. pass. indic. 2 pers. pl.
{5.A.2} . . . . id.

πλανάτω   verb, pres. act. impv. 3 pers. sg.
{5.D.2} . . . . id.

G4105 **πλανάω**   (1) *I cause to wander;* hence, in the
moral sense, *I cause to err;* (2) pass. *I wander;*
hence, *I err.*

G4106 **πλάνη**, -ης, ἡ   *wandering from the way,* and
so met., *error* (perhaps sometimes actively,
deceit).

πλάνη   noun, nom. sg. fem. {2.A} . . . . πλάνη *G4106*

πλάνη   noun, dat. sg. fem. {2.A} . . . . id.

πλανηθῇ   verb, aor. pass. subjunc. 3 pers. sg.
{5.B.1} . . . . πλανάω *G4105*

πλανηθῆτε   verb, aor. pass. subjunc. 2 pers. pl.
{5.B.1} . . . . id.

πλάνης   noun, gen. sg. fem. {2.A} . . . . πλάνη *G4106*

πλανῆσαι   vbl., aor. act. inf. {6.B.1} . . . . πλανάω *G4105*

πλανήσῃ   verb, aor. act. subjunc. 3 pers. sg.
{5.B.1} . . . . id.

πλανήσουσι   verb, fut. act. indic. 3 pers. pl.
{5.A.1} . . . . id.

πλανήσουσιν   verb, fut. act. indic. 3 pers. pl.
{5.A.1} . . . . id.

πλανῆται   noun, nom. pl. masc. {2.A} . . πλανήτης *G4107*

G4107 **πλανήτης**, -ου, ὁ   *wandering* (probably of
shooting stars).

πλάνοι   adj., nom. pl. masc. {3.A} . . . . . . πλάνος *G4108*

πλάνοις   adj., dat. pl. neut. {3.A} . . . . id.

G4108 **πλάνος**, -ον   adj., *misleading, deceiving;* as subs.
a deceiver.

πλάνος   adj., nom. sg. masc. {3.A} . . . . πλάνος *G4108*

πλανῶμεν   verb, pres. act. indic. 1 pers. pl.
{5.A.2} . . . . πλανάω *G4105*

πλανώμενα   vbl., pres. pass. ptc. nom. pl. neut.
{6.A.2} . . . . id.

πλανώμενοι   vbl., pres. pass. ptc. nom. pl.
masc. {6.A.2} . . . . id.

πλανωμένοις   vbl., pres. pass. ptc. dat. pl.
masc. {6.A.2} . . . . id.

πλανώμενον   vbl., pres. pass. ptc. acc. sg. neut.
{6.A.2} . . . . id.

πλανῶν vbl., pres. act. ptc. nom. sg. masc.
{6.A.2}. . . . . id.
πλανῶνται verb, pres. pass. indic. 3 pers. pl.
{5.A.2}. . . . . id.
πλανῶντες vbl., pres. act. ptc. nom. pl. masc.
{6.A.2}. . . . . id.
πλανώντων vbl., pres. act. ptc. gen. pl. masc.
{6.A.2}. . . . . id.
G4109 **πλάξ**, πλακός, ἡ *a tablet.*
πλαξί noun, dat. pl. fem. {2.C}. . . . . πλάξ G4109
πλαξίν noun, dat. pl. fem. {2.C} . . . . id.
πλάσαντι vbl., aor. act. ptc. dat. sg. masc.
{6.A.1.a}. . . . . πλάσσω G4111
G4110 **πλάσμα**, -ατος, τό *a molded thing; a created*
thing, a creature.
πλάσμα noun, nom. sg. neut. {2.C}. . . . .πλάσμα G4110
G4111 **πλάσσω** *I mold* out of clay; *I create.*
πλαστοῖς adj., dat. pl. masc. {3.A}. . . . . .πλαστός G4112
G4112 **πλαστός**, -ή, -όν *made up, fictitious.*
G4113 **πλατεῖα**, -ας, ἡ *a public square* (supply ὁδός);
generally taken as *an open street, a street.*
πλατεῖα adj., nom. sg. fem. {3.D} . . . . πλατύς G4116
πλατεῖα noun, nom. sg. fem. {2.A} . . . . . πλατεῖα G4113
πλατείαις noun, dat. pl. fem. {2.A} . . . . id.
πλατείας noun, acc. pl. fem. {2.A}. . . . . id.
πλατείας noun, gen. sg. fem. {2.A} . . . . id.
πλατειῶν noun, gen. pl. fem. {2.A} . . . . id.
G4114 **πλάτος**, -ους, τό *breadth.*
πλάτος noun, acc. sg. neut. {2.C}. . . . . . . πλάτος G4114
πλάτος noun, nom. sg. neut. {2.C} . . . . id.
πλατύνθητε verb, aor. pass. impv. 2 pers. pl.
{5.D.1}. . . . . .πλατύνω G4115
πλατύνουσι verb, pres. act. indic. 3 pers. pl.
{5.A.1.a} . . . . id.
πλατύνουσιν verb, pres. act. indic. 3 pers. pl.
{5.A.1.a} . . . . id.
G4115 **πλατύνω** *I broaden, I make broad;* met., of the
growth of tenderness and love, 2 Cor 6:11, 13.
G4116 **πλατύς**, -εῖα, -ύ *broad.*
G4117 **πλέγμα**, -ατος, τό *plaiting, braiding, dressing*
the hair.
πλέγμασιν noun, dat. pl. neut. {2.C} . . . . .πλέγμα G4117
πλεῖν vbl., pres. act. inf. {6.B.2} . . . . πλέω G4126
πλεῖον adj. comp., acc. sg. neut. {3.E; 3.G} . πλείων G4119
πλεῖον adj. comp., nom. sg. neut. {3.E; 3.G}. . . . id.
πλείονα adj. comp., acc. pl. neut. {3.E; 3.G} . . . . id.
πλείονα adj. comp., acc. sg. fem. {3.E; 3.G} . . . . id.
πλείονα adj. comp., acc. sg. masc. {3.E; 3.G} . . . id.
πλείονας adj. comp., acc. pl. fem. {3.E; 3.G} . . . id.
πλείονας adj. comp., acc. pl. masc. {3.E; 3.G} . . id.
πλείονες adj. comp., nom. pl. masc. {3.E; 3.G} . id.
πλείονος adj. comp., gen. sg. fem. {3.E; 3.G} . . . id.
πλειόνων adj. comp., gen. pl. masc. {3.E; 3.G}. . . id.
πλειόνων adj. comp., gen. pl. neut. {3.E; 3.G} . . . id.
πλείοσι adj. comp., dat. pl. masc. {3.E; 3.G}. . . . id.
πλείοσιν adj. comp., dat. pl. masc. {3.E; 3.G} . . . id.
πλείους adj. comp., acc. pl. fem. {3.E; 3.G} . . . . id.
πλείους adj. comp., nom. pl. fem. {3.E; 3.G} . . . id.
πλείους adj. comp., nom. pl. masc. {3.E; 3.G} . . id.
πλεῖσται adj. superl., nom. pl. fem. {3.E}. πλεῖστος G4118

πλεῖστον adj. superl., acc. sg. neut. {3.E} . . . . . id.
πλεῖστον adv. {3.F; 3.G} . . . . id.
G4118 **πλεῖστος**, -η, -ον superl. of πολύς, *very large;*
pl. *very many (numerous);* adv. τὸ πλεῖστον,
at the most, 1 Cor 14:27.
πλεῖστος adj. superl., nom. sg. masc.
{3.B} . . . . .πλεῖστος G4118
πλείω adj. comp., acc. pl. neut. {3.E; 3.G}. . πλείων G4119
G4119 **πλείων**, πλεῖον (πλέον) gen. ονος comp. of
πολύς, *larger; more; a considerable number*
of, Acts 21:10, etc.; οἱ πλείονες, *the majority,*
1 Cor 15:6; as adv., ἐπὶ πλεῖον, *more, to a*
greater extent.
G4120 **πλέκω** *I plait.*
πλέξαντες vbl., aor. act. ptc. nom. pl. masc.
{6.A.1.a} . . . . πλέκω G4120
πλέον adj. comp., acc. sg. neut. {3.E; 3.G} . πλείων G4119
πλέον adv. comp. {3.F; 3.G} . . . . πλείων G4119
πλέον vbl., pres. act. ptc. acc. sg. neut. {6.A.2} πλέω G4126
πλεονάζει verb, pres. act. indic. 3 pers. sg.
{5.A.1.a} . . . . .πλεονάζω G4121
πλεονάζοντα vbl., pres. act. ptc. acc. sg. masc.
{6.A.1} . . . . id.
πλεονάζοντα vbl., pres. act. ptc. nom. pl. neut.
{6.A.1} . . . . id.
G4121 **πλεονάζω** (1) intrans., *I abound, I increase;* (2)
trans., *I make to abound, I cause to increase,*
1 Thess 3:12.
πλεονάσαι verb, aor. act. opt. 3 pers. sg.
{5.C.1} . . . . .πλεονάζω G4121
πλεονάσασα vbl., aor. act. ptc. nom. sg. fem.
{6.A.1.a} . . . . id.
πλεονάσῃ verb, aor. act. subjunc. 3 pers. sg.
{5.B.1} . . . . id.
πλεονέκται noun, nom. pl. masc.
{2.A} . . . . .πλεονέκτης G4123
πλεονέκταις noun, dat. pl. masc. {2.A} . . . . . . id.
πλεονεκτεῖν vbl., pres. act. inf. {6.B.2} πλεονεκτέω G4122
G4122 **πλεονεκτέω** *I take advantage of, I overreach, I*
defraud (sometimes with reference to adultery
and the injury thus done to the husband).
πλεονεκτηθῶμεν verb, aor. pass. subjunc. 1 pers.
pl. {5.B.1}. . . . . πλεονεκτέω G4122
G4123 **πλεονέκτης**, -ου, ὁ *a greedy, covetous, rapa-*
cious, acquisitive, self-aggrandizing person; a
defrauder, one who tramples on the rights of
others.
πλεονέκτης noun, nom. sg. masc.
{2.A} . . . . .πλεονέκτης G4123
G4124 **πλεονεξία**, -ας, ἡ *covetousness, greediness,*
rapacity, entire disregard of the rights of others,
a word act. in meaning and wide in scope.
πλεονεξία noun, nom. sg. fem. {2.A} . .πλεονεξία G4124
πλεονεξίᾳ noun, dat. sg. fem. {2.A}. . . . . id.
πλεονεξίαι noun, nom. pl. fem. {2.A} . . . . id.
πλεονεξίαις noun, dat. pl. fem. {2.A} . . . . id.
πλεονεξίαν noun, acc. sg. fem. {2.A} . . . . id.
πλεονεξίας noun, gen. sg. fem. {2.A} . . . . id.
πλέοντας vbl., pres. act. ptc. acc. pl. masc.
{6.A.2}. . . . . πλέω G4126

πλεόντων   vbl., pres. act. ptc. gen. pl. masc.
{6.A.2} . . . . id.

G4125 **πλευρά**, -ᾶς, ἡ   *a side* of a human being.
πλευράν   noun, acc. sg. fem. {2.A} . . . . . . πλευρά G4125

G4126 **πλέω**   *I travel by sea, I sail, voyage.*
πλέων   vbl., pres. act. ptc. nom. sg. masc.
{6.A.2} . . . . πλέω G4126
πληγαί   noun, nom. pl. fem. {2.A} . . . . πληγή G4127
πληγαῖς   noun, dat. pl. fem. {2.A} . . . . id.
πληγάς   noun, acc. pl. fem. {2.A} . . . . id.

G4127 **πληγή**, -ῆς, ἡ   *a blow,* esp., caused by the lash,
a stripe, a stroke.
πληγή   noun, nom. sg. fem. {2.A} . . . . πληγή G4127
πληγῇ   noun, dat. sg. fem. {2.A} . . . . id.
πληγήν   noun, acc. sg. fem. {2.A} . . . . id.
πληγῆς   noun, gen. sg. fem. {2.A} . . . . id.
πληγῶν   noun, gen. pl. fem. {2.A} . . . . id.
πλήθει   noun, dat. sg. neut. {2.C} . . . . πλῆθος G4128
πλήθη   noun, nom. pl. neut. {2.C} . . . . id.

G4128 **πλῆθος**, -ους, τό   *a multitude, a crowd, a large
number.*
πλῆθος   noun, acc. sg. neut. {2.C} . . . . πλῆθος G4128
πλῆθος   noun, nom. sg. neut. {2.C} . . . . id.
πλήθους   noun, gen. sg. neut. {2.C} . . . . id.
πληθῦναι   verb, aor. act. opt. 3 pers. sg.
{5.C.1} . . . . πληθύνω G4129
πληθυνεῖ   verb, fut. act. indic. 3 pers. sg. {5.A.2} id.
πληθυνθείη   verb, aor. pass. opt. 3 pers. sg.
{5.C.1} . . . . id.
πληθυνθῆναι   vbl., aor. pass. inf. {6.B.1} . . . . . id.
πληθυνόντων   vbl., pres. act. ptc. gen. pl.
masc. {6.A.1} . . . . id.
πληθυνῶ   verb, fut. act. indic. 1 pers. sg. {5.A.2} id.

G4129 **πληθύνω**   (1) trans., *I multiply, I increase;* (2)
intrans., *I multiply, I go on increasing,* Acts 6:1.
πληθύνων   vbl., pres. act. ptc. nom. sg. masc.
{6.A.1} . . . . πληθύνω G4129

G4130‡ **πίμπλημι**   alt. form πλήθω, *I fill, I fulfill.*
πλήκτην   noun, acc. sg. masc. {2.A} . . . . . πλήκτης G4131

G4131 **πλήκτης**, -ου, ὁ   *a striker; a pugnacious person.*

G4132 **πλήμμυρα**, -ης, ἡ   *a flooding, flood.*
πλημμύρας   noun, gen. sg. fem. {2.A} . πλήμμυρα G4132
πλημμύρης   noun, gen. sg. fem. {2.A} . . . . . . id.

G4133 **πλήν**   (1) conj., (a) *however, nevertheless,* Matt
26:39 (Luke 22:42); Matt 11:22, 24; 26:64, etc.;
(b) *but,* Luke 12:31; 23:28; (c) πλὴν ὅτι, *except
that, save that,* Acts 20:23; (d) *only, in any case,*
ending the discussion and calling special attention to the essential, esp. in Paul, e.g., 1 Cor
11:11; Eph 5:33; (2) prep. with gen., *except,
apart from.*
πλήν   conj., prep. . . . . πλήν G4133
πλήρεις   adj., acc. pl. fem. {3.E} . . . . . . πλήρης G4134
πλήρεις   adj., acc. pl. masc. {3.E} . . . . id.
πλήρεις   adj., nom. pl. masc. {3.E} . . . . id.
πλήρη   adj., acc. sg. masc. {3.E} . . . . id.

G4134 **πλήρης**, -ες   *full* (sometimes, from about the
beginning of our era, indeclinable, and used
for any case sg. or pl., a usage perhaps derived
from commercial life; e.g., Mark 4:28?; John

1:14, where πλήρης agrees with δόξαν, and
there should be no parenthesis, Acts 6:5, var.).
πλήρης   adj., acc. sg. masc. {3.E} . . . . πλήρης G4134
πλήρης   adj., nom. sg. fem. {3.E} . . . . id.
πλήρης   adj., nom. sg. masc. {3.E} . . . . id.
πλήρης   adj., voc. sg. masc. {3.E} . . . . id.
πληροῖς   verb, pres. act. subjunc. 2 pers. sg.
{5.B.2} . . . . πληρόω G4137
πληρούμενον   vbl., pres. pass. ptc. nom. sg.
neut. {6.A.2} . . . . id.
πληρουμένου   vbl., pres. mid. ptc. gen. sg.
masc. {6.A.2} . . . . id.
πληροῦν   vbl., pres. act. inf. {6.B.2} . . . . id.
πληροῦσθε   verb, pres. pass. impv. 2 pers. pl.
{5.D.2} . . . . id.
πληροῦται   verb, pres. pass. indic. 3 pers. sg.
{5.A.2} . . . . id.
πληροφορείσθω   verb, pres. pass. impv. 3 pers. sg.
{5.D.2} . . . . πληροφορέω G4135

G4135 **πληροφορέω**   (lit. *I carry full*), (1) *I complete,
carry out fully,* 2 Tim 4:5, 17; Luke 1:1(?); (2) *I
fully convince,* Rom 4:21; 14:5; perhaps *I satisfy
fully,* Col 4:12; (3) *I fully believe,* Luke 1:1(?).
πληροφορηθείς   vbl., aor. pass. ptc. nom. sg. masc.
{6.A.1.a.} . . . . πληροφορέω G4135
πληροφορηθῇ   verb, aor. pass. subjunc. 3 pers.
sg. {5.B.1} . . . . id.
πληροφόρησον   verb, aor. act. impv. 2 pers. sg.
{5.D.1} . . . . id.

G4136 **πληροφορία**, -ας, ἡ   *full assurance, conviction
(confidence).*
πληροφορία   noun, dat. sg. fem. {2.A} . πληροφορία G4136
πληροφορίαν   noun, acc. sg. fem. {2.A} . . . . . id.
πληροφορίας   noun, gen. sg. fem. {2.A} . . . . . id.

G4137 **πληρόω**   (1) *I fill, I fill up,* e.g., Luke 2:40; 3:5;
John 12:3; (2) much oftener, *I fill up to the full,
I fulfill, I give fullness (completion) to, I accomplish, carry out,* of prophecies or other statements which are absolutely and completely
confirmed by reality (actual occurrence), or
of duties; *I preach fully,* Rom 15:19, cf. Col
1:25; in Eph 1:23 the Messiah *is being fulfilled
(completed)* by the Church.
πληρωθείσης   vbl., aor. pass. ptc. gen. sg. fem.
{6.A.1.a.} . . . . πληρόω G4137
πληρωθέντων   vbl., aor. pass. ptc. gen. pl. neut.
{6.A.1.a.} . . . . id.
πληρωθῇ   verb, aor. pass. subjunc. 3 pers. sg.
{5.B.1} . . . . id.
πληρωθῆναι   vbl., aor. pass. inf. {6.B.1} . . . . . . id.
πληρωθήσεται   verb, fut. pass. indic. 3 pers.
sg. {5.A.1} . . . . id.
πληρωθήσονται   verb, fut. pass. indic. 3 pers.
pl. {5.A.1} . . . . id.
πληρωθῆτε   verb, aor. pass. subjunc. 2 pers. pl.
{5.B.1} . . . . id.
πληρωθῶ   verb, aor. pass. subjunc. 1 pers. sg.
{5.B.1} . . . . id.
πληρωθῶσι   verb, aor. pass. subjunc. 3 pers. pl.
{5.B.1} . . . . id.

πληρωθῶσιν   verb, aor. pass. subjunc. 3 pers.
  pl. {5.B.1}. . . . . id.
G4138 **πλήρωμα**, -ατος, τό   (1) *a fill, fullness; full
  complement; supply, supplement,* Mark 2:21;
  Matt 9:16; (2) *fullness, filling, fulfillment,
  completion.* (Indicates the result of the activity
  denoted by πληρόω.).
πλήρωμα   noun, acc. sg. neut. {2.C}. . . . πλήρωμα G4138
πλήρωμα   noun, nom. sg. neut. {2.C}. . . . . id.
πληρώματα   noun, acc. pl. neut. {2.C}. . . . . . . id.
πληρώματι   noun, dat. sg. neut. {2.C} . . . . id.
πληρώματος   noun, gen. sg. neut. {2.C}. . . . . . id.
πληρώσαι   verb, aor. act. opt. 3 pers. sg.
  {5.C.1}. . . . . .πληρόω G4137
πληρώσαι   vbl., aor. act. inf. {6.B.1} . . . . id.
πληρώσαντες   vbl., aor. act. ptc. nom. pl. masc.
  {6.A.2}. . . . . id.
πληρώσατε   verb, aor. act. impv. 2 pers. pl.
  {5.D.1}. . . . . id.
πληρώσει   verb, fut. act. indic. 3 pers. sg. {5.A.1} id.
πληρώσεις   verb, fut. act. indic. 2 pers. sg.
  {5.A.1}. . . . . id.
πληρώσῃ   verb, aor. act. subjunc. 3 pers. sg.
  {5.B.1} . . . . id.
πληρώσονται   verb, fut. mid. indic. 3 pers. pl.
  {5.A.1}. . . . . id.
πληρώσωσιν   verb, aor. act. subjunc. 3 pers. pl.
  {5.B.1} . . . . id.
πλήσαντες   vbl., aor. act. ptc. nom. pl. masc.
  {6.A.1.a} . . . . πίμπλημι G4130‡
πλήσας   vbl., aor. act. ptc. nom. sg. masc.
  {6.A.1.a} . . . . id.
πλησθείς   vbl., aor. pass. ptc. nom. sg. masc.
  {6.A.1.a} . . . . id.
πλησθῆναι   vbl., aor. pass. inf. {6.B.1} . . . . id.
πλησθῇς   verb, aor. pass. subjunc. 2 pers. sg.
  {5.B.1} . . . . id.
πλησθήσεται   verb, fut. pass. indic. 3 pers. sg.
  {5.A.1.d} . . . . id.
G4139 **πλησίον**   adv. and prep. with gen., *near* (John
  4:5), used as adj. and (esp. with article ὁ)
  noun, *neighboring, neighborly; a neighbor.*
πλησίον   adv. {3.F}. . . . . πλησίον G4139
G4140 **πλησμονή**, -ῆς, ἡ   *repletion, satiety.*
πλησμονήν   noun, acc. sg. fem. {2.A} . .πλησμονή G4140
G4141 **πλήσσω**   *I strike.*
πλοῖα   noun, acc. pl. neut. {2.B}. . . . . πλοῖον G4143
πλοῖα   noun, nom. pl. neut. {2.B}. . . . . id.
πλοιάρια   noun, acc. pl. neut. {2.B} . . . .πλοιάριον G4142
πλοιάρια   noun, nom. pl. neut. {2.B} . . . . id.
G4142 **πλοιάριον**, -ου, τό   (lit., *a little boat,* hence) *a
  boat.*
πλοιάριον   noun, acc. sg. neut. {2.B} . . .πλοιάριον G4142
πλοιάριον   noun, nom. sg. neut. {2.B} . . . . id.
πλοιαρίῳ   noun, dat. sg. neut. {2.B}. . . . . id.
G4143 **πλοῖον**, -ου, τό   *a boat;* hence, *a ship* (the old
  word ναῦς having become almost obsolete),
  Acts 20:13, etc.
πλοῖον   noun, acc. sg. neut. {2.B} . . . . πλοῖον G4143
πλοῖον   noun, nom. sg. neut. {2.B}. . . . . id.

πλοίου   noun, gen. sg. neut. {2.B}. . . . . id.
πλοίῳ   noun, dat. sg. neut. {2.B}. . . . . id.
πλοίων   noun, gen. pl. neut. {2.B}. . . . . id.
πλοός   noun, gen. sg. masc. {2.B} . . . . πλόος G4144
G4144 **πλόος** (πλοῦς), ὁ   *a voyage.*
πλοῦν   noun, acc. sg. masc. {2.B} . . . . πλόος G4144
πλούσιοι   adj., nom. pl. masc. {3.A}. . . . πλούσιος G4145
πλούσιοι   adj., voc. pl. masc. {3.A}. . . . . id.
πλουσίοις   adj., dat. pl. masc. {3.A} . . . . id.
πλούσιον   adj., acc. sg. masc. {3.A} . . . . id.
G4145 **πλούσιος**, -α, -ον   *rich, wealthy;* hence, met., of
  other than material wealth.
πλούσιος   adj., nom. sg. masc. {3.A} . . . πλούσιος G4145
πλουσίου   adj., gen. sg. masc. {3.A} . . . . id.
πλουσίους   adj., acc. pl. masc. {3.A} . . . . id.
G4146 **πλουσίως**   adv., *richly; lavishly.*
πλουσίως   adv. {3.F}. . . . . πλουσίως G4146
πλουτεῖν   vbl., pres. act. inf. {6.B.2} . . . . . πλουτέω G4147
G4147 **πλουτέω**   *I am rich (wealthy);* with εἰς and acc.
  the person on whom the wealth is lavished is
  indicated; with ἐν, *I abound in,* 1 Tim 6:18.
πλουτήσαντες   vbl., aor. act. ptc. nom. pl. masc.
  {6.A.2}. . . . . πλουτέω G4147
πλουτήσῃς   verb, aor. act. subjunc. 2 pers. sg.
  {5.B.1} . . . . id.
πλουτήσητε   verb, aor. act. subjunc. 2 pers. pl.
  {5.B.1} . . . . id.
πλουτιζόμενοι   vbl., pres. pass. ptc. nom. pl. masc.
  {6.A.1}. . . . . πλουτίζω G4148
πλουτίζοντες   vbl., pres. act. ptc. nom. pl.
  masc. {6.A.1}. . . . . id.
G4148 **πλουτίζω**   *I enrich.*
πλοῦτον   noun, acc. sg. masc. {2.B} . . . . . πλοῦτος G4149
G4149 **πλοῦτος**, -ου, ὁ and τό   *wealth,* material or
  spiritual.
πλοῦτος   noun, acc. sg. neut. {2.B}. . . . . . . πλοῦτος G4149
πλοῦτος   noun, nom. sg. masc. {2.B} . . . . id.
πλοῦτος   noun, nom. sg. neut. {2.B}. . . . . id.
πλούτου   noun, gen. sg. masc. {2.B}. . . . . id.
πλουτοῦντας   vbl., pres. act. ptc. acc. pl. masc.
  {6.A.2}. . . . . πλουτέω G4147
πλουτῶν   vbl., pres. act. ptc. nom. sg. masc.
  {6.A.2}. . . . . id.
πλύνοντες   vbl., pres. act. ptc. nom. pl. masc.
  {6.A.1}. . . . . .πλύνω G4150
G4150 **πλύνω**   *I wash.*
πνέῃ   verb, pres. act. subjunc. 3 pers. sg.
  {5.B.2}. . . . . πνέω G4154
πνεῖ   verb, pres. act. indic. 3 pers. sg. {5.A.2}. . . . id.
πνέοντα   vbl., pres. act. ptc. acc. sg. masc.
  {6.A.2}. . . . . id.
πνέοντος   vbl., pres. act. ptc. gen. sg. masc.
  {6.A.2}. . . . . id.
πνεούσῃ   vbl., pres. act. ptc. dat. sg. fem. {6.A.2} id.
G4151 **πνεῦμα**, -ατος, τό   (from πνέω, has as its
  earliest meanings *breath* and *wind,* and it is
  from the former that the characteristic use
  is derived), (1) *wind,* John 3:8; Heb 1:7; (2)
  breath, what distinguishes a living from a dead
  body, the life principle, Matt 27:50; Luke 8:55;

23:46; John 6:63; 19:30; Acts 7:59; 2 Thess 2:8; Jas 2:26; Rev 11:11; 13:15; (3) the breath was often in early times identified with the life or soul itself. Heb. employed three words for the breath-soul, *nefesh, ruah, neshamah,* of which the first and second are the more important, indicating respectively the personal soul and the invading spirit. (1) *Nefesh,* orig. *breath,* (a) refers predominantly to the emotional life; (b) is a strong pers. or refl. pron.; or (c) is equivalent to *person.* (2) *Ruah,* orig. *wind,* indicates also esp., (a) supernatural influences acting on man from without; (b) the normal breath-soul, the principle of life (like *nefesh*) or of its energies, directly derived from the wind at the bidding of God; (c) the resultant psychical life, like *nefesh,* "heart.," the inner life in general. It is distinguished from *nefesh* by its association with Yahweh. Normal human nature was regarded as animated by the same divine *ruah* to which its highest inspiration is due. In the Gk. OT *nefesh* is represented by ψυχή (q.v.) and *ruah* by πνεῦμα (a purely Hebraistic usage of the word). In the NT πνεῦμα refers nearly always to supernatural influences. Sometimes it is employed of the *higher nature* in man, e.g., Rom 1:9, and is hardly to be distinguished from the result of the influence of the divine πνεῦμα. Some times, e.g., Rom 8:16; 2 Cor 7:1, it denotes a normal element in human nature. But the Christian is essentially the product of the divine πνεῦμα, which is mediated to us by the Messiah. Parallel to the divine πνεῦμα are the unclean, evil spirits, the spirits of dem., etc., which act in a corresponding way on the spirit of man. πνεῦμα ἅγιον, *holy breath, spirit of holiness,* adopted originally from Isa 63:10–11; Ps 51:11, practically synonymous with πνεῦμα θεοῦ, etc., gradually tends to become personalized. The first step in the process is reached by affixing the def. article and making it τὸ Πνεῦμα τὸ Ἅγιον (τὸ Ἅγιον Πνεῦμα). Each operation of *the* Holy Spirit is most commonly represented as due to *a* holy spirit.

πνεῦμα   noun, acc. sg. neut. {2.C} . . . . . . πνεῦμα *G4151*
πνεῦμα   noun, nom. sg. neut. {2.C} . . . . id.
πνεύμασι   noun, dat. pl. neut. {2.C} . . . . id.
πνεύμασιν   noun, dat. pl. neut. {2.C} . . . . id.
πνεύματα   noun, acc. pl. neut. {2.C} . . . . id.
πνεύματα   noun, nom. pl. neut. {2.C} . . . . id.
πνεύματι   noun, dat. sg. neut. {2.C} . . . . id.
πνευματικά   adj., acc. pl. neut. {3.A} .πνευματικός *G4152*
πνευματικαῖς   adj., dat. pl. fem. {3.A} . . . . id.
πνευματικάς   adj., acc. pl. fem. {3.A} . . . . id.
πνευματικῇ   adj., dat. sg. fem. {3.A} . . . . id.
πνευματικῆς   adj., gen. sg. fem. {3.A} . . . . id.
πνευματικοί   adj., nom. pl. masc. {3.A} . . . . . . id.
πνευματικοῖς   adj., dat. pl. masc. {3.A} . . . . . . id.
πνευματικοῖς   adj., dat. pl. neut. {3.A} . . . . id.
πνευματικόν   adj., acc. sg. neut. {3.A} . . . . id.

πνευματικόν   adj., nom. sg. neut. {3.A} . . . . . . id.
G4152 **πνευματικός**, -ή, -όν   *having the characteristics of* πνεῦμα, *spiritual,* with general reference to the higher nature of man as directly in touch with and influenced by the divine, but sometimes (like πνεῦμα) associated with the demonic world, τὰ πνευματικὰ τῆς πονηρίας, *the spiritual hosts of evil,* Eph 6:12; *supernatural,* 1 Cor 10:3.
πνευματικός   adj., nom. sg. masc. {3.A} . . . . .πνευματικός *G4152*
πνευματικῶν   adj., gen. pl. neut. {3.A} . . . . id.
G4153 **πνευματικῶς**   adv., *spiritually, in a spiritual way; from a spiritual point of view.*
πνευματικῶς   adv. {3.F} . . . . πνευματικῶς *G4153*
πνεύματος   noun, gen. sg. neut. {2.C} . . . . πνεῦμα *G4151*
πνευμάτων   noun, gen. pl. neut. {2.C} . . . . id.
G4154 **πνέω**   *I blow;* τῇ πνεούσῃ (supply αὔρα, *breeze*).
G4155 **πνίγω**   *I choke, throttle, strangle;* hence, *I drown,* Mark 5:13.
πνικτόν   adj., acc. sg. neut. {3.A} . . . . πνικτός *G4156*
G4156 **πνικτός**, -ή, -όν   *strangled* (i.e., killed without letting out the blood).
πνικτοῦ   adj., gen. sg. neut. {3.A} . . . . πνικτός *G4156*
πνικτῶν   adj., gen. pl. neut. {3.A} . . . . id.
G4157 **πνοή**, -ῆς, ἡ   (1) *breath,* Acts 17:25; (2) *gust, breeze, wind,* Acts 2:2.
πνοήν   noun, acc. sg. fem. {2.A} . . . . πνοή *G4157*
πνοῆς   noun, gen. sg. fem. {2.A} . . . . id.
πόδα   noun, acc. sg. masc. {2.C} . . . . πούς *G4228*
πόδας   noun, acc. pl. masc. {2.C} . . . . id.
πόδες   noun, nom. pl. masc. {2.C} . . . . id.
ποδήρη   adj., acc. sg. masc. {3.E} . . . . ποδήρης *G4158*
G4158 **ποδήρης**, -ους, ὁ   *a tunic* or *robe reaching the feet* (properly an adj. in the expression χιτὼν ποδήρης).
ποδός   noun, gen. sg. masc. {2.C} . . . . πούς *G4228*
ποδῶν   noun, gen. pl. masc. {2.C} . . . . id.
G4159 **πόθεν**   interrog. adv., *whence? from what place?* also indir. interrog.; hence, *how?* e.g., Mark 12:37; John 1:48.
πόθεν   adv. correl. interrog. {4.D} . . . . πόθεν *G4159*
ποία   pron. correl. interrog., acc. pl. neut. {4.D} . . . . .ποῖος *G4169*
ποία   pron. correl. interrog., nom. sg. fem. {4.D} id.
ποῖα   pron. correl. interrog., acc. pl. neut. {4.D} . id.
ποίᾳ   pron. correl. interrog., dat. sg. fem. {4.D} . id.
ποίαν   pron. correl. interrog., acc. sg. fem. {4.D} id.
ποίας   pron. correl. interrog., acc. pl. fem. {4.D} id.
ποίας   pron. correl. interrog., gen. sg. fem. {4.D} id.
ποίει   verb, pres. act. impv. 2 pers. sg. {5.D.2} ποιέω *G4160*
ποιεῖ   verb, pres. act. indic. 3 pers. sg. {5.A.2} . . . id.
ποιεῖν   vbl., pres. act. inf. {6.B.2} . . . . id.
ποιεῖς   verb, pres. act. indic. 2 pers. sg. {5.A.2} . . id.
ποιεῖσθαι   vbl., pres. mid./pass. inf. {6.B.2} . . . . id.
ποιεῖσθε   verb, pres. mid. impv. 2 pers. pl. {5.A.2} . . . . id.
ποιεῖται   verb, pres. mid. indic. 3 pers. sg. {5.A.2} . . . . id.

ποιεῖτε   verb, pres. act. impv. 2 pers. pl. {5.D.2} . id.

ποιεῖτε   verb, pres. act. indic. 2 pers. pl. {5.A.2} . id.

ποιείτω   verb, pres. act. impv. 3 pers. sg. {5.D.2}. id.

G4160 **ποιέω**   (1) *I make, manufacture, construct;* (2) *I do, act, cause;* μετά τινος (Hebraistic idiom), *on some one's behalf,* Luke 1:72; Acts 14:27, etc.; with an obj. indicating time, *I spend,* e.g., Jas 4:13; ὁδὸν ποιεῖν, Mark 2:23 (var.), which ought to mean *to construct (pave) a road,* is incorrectly used for ὁδὸν ποιεῖσθαι (cf. μνείαν ποιεῖσθαι, Eph 1:16), *to journey* (cf. Luke 13:22); with καλῶς, see under καλῶς.

ποιῇ   verb, pres. act. subjunc. 3 pers. sg. {5.B.2} . . . . ποιέω G4160

G4161 **ποίημα**, -ατος, τό   (concr.), *creation, workmanship, handiwork;* pl. *pieces of work.*

ποίημα   noun, nom. sg. neut. {2.C} . . . . . . ποίημα G4161

ποιήμασι   noun, dat. pl. neut. {2.C} . . . . id.

ποιήμασιν   noun, dat. pl. neut. {2.C} . . . . id.

ποιῇς   verb, pres. act. subjunc. 2 pers. sg. {5.B.2} . . . . ποιέω G4160

ποιῆσαι   vbl., aor. act. inf. {6.B.1} . . . . id.

ποιήσαιεν   verb, aor. act. opt. 3 pers. pl. {5.C.1}. id.

ποιησάμενοι   vbl., aor. mid. ptc. nom. pl. masc. {6.A.2} . . . . id.

ποιησάμενος   vbl., aor. mid. ptc. nom. sg. masc. {6.A.2} . . . . id.

ποιήσαντα   vbl., aor. act. ptc. acc. sg. masc. {6.A.2} . . . . id.

ποιήσαντες   vbl., aor. act. ptc. nom. pl. masc. {6.A.2} . . . . id.

ποιήσαντι   vbl., aor. act. ptc. dat. sg. masc. {6.A.2} . . . . id.

ποιήσας   vbl., aor. act. ptc. nom. sg. masc. {6.A.2} . . . . id.

ποιήσασαν   vbl., aor. act. ptc. acc. sg. fem. {6.A.2} . . . . id.

ποιήσασθαι   vbl., aor. mid. inf. {6.B.1} . . . . . . id.

ποιήσατε   verb, aor. act. impv. 2 pers. pl. {5.D.1} id.

ποιησάτω   verb, aor. act. impv. 3 pers. sg. {5.D.1} . . . . id.

ποιήσει   noun, dat. sg. fem. {2.C} . . . . . . ποίησις G4162

ποιήσει   verb, fut. act. indic. 3 pers. sg. {5.A.1} . . . . ποιέω G4160

ποιήσειαν   verb, aor. act. opt. 3 pers. pl. {5.C.1}. id.

ποιήσεις   verb, fut. act. indic. 2 pers. sg. {5.A.1}. id.

ποιήσετε   verb, fut. act. indic. 2 pers. pl. {5.A.1}. id.

ποιήσῃ   verb, aor. act. subjunc. 3 pers. sg. {5.B.1}id.

ποιήσῃς   verb, aor. act. subjunc. 2 pers. sg. {5.B.1} . . . . id.

ποιήσητε   verb, aor. act. subjunc. 2 pers. pl. {5.B.1} . . . . id.

G4162 **ποίησις**, -εως, ἡ   *doing.*

ποιησόμεθα   verb, fut. mid. indic. 1 pers. pl. {5.A.1} . . . . ποιέω G4160

ποιήσομεν   verb, fut. act. indic. 1 pers. pl. {5.A.1} . . . . id.

ποιήσον   verb, aor. act. impv. 2 pers. sg. {5.D.1}. id.

ποιήσουσιν   verb, fut. act. indic. 3 pers. pl. {5.A.1} . . . . id.

ποιήσω   verb, fut. act. indic. 1 pers. sg. {5.A.1} . . id.

ποιήσω   verb, aor. act. subjunc. 1 pers. sg. {5.B.1} . . . . id.

ποιήσωμεν   verb, aor. act. subjunc. 1 pers. pl. {5.B.1} . . . . id.

ποιήσων   vbl., fut. act. ptc. nom. sg. masc. {6.A.2} . . . . id.

ποιήσωσι   verb, aor. act. subjunc. 3 pers. pl. {5.B.1} . . . . id.

ποιήσωσιν   verb, aor. act. subjunc. 3 pers. pl. {5.B.1} . . . . id.

ποιηταί   noun, nom. pl. masc. {2.A} . . . . . ποιητής G4163

ποιῆτε   verb, pres. act. subjunc. 2 pers. pl. {5.B.2} . . . . ποιέω G4160

G4163 **ποιητής**, -οῦ, ὁ   (1) *a "maker," a poet,* Acts 17:28 (the reference is to Epimenides' *Minos*); (2) *a doer, a carrier out.*

ποιητής   noun, nom. sg. masc. {2.A} . . . . ποιητής G4163

ποιητῶν   noun, gen. pl. masc. {2.A} . . . . id.

ποικίλαις   adj., dat. pl. fem. {3.A} . . . . . . ποικίλος G4164

ποικίλης   adj., gen. sg. fem. {3.A} . . . . id.

ποικίλοις   adj., dat. pl. masc. {3.A} . . . . id.

G4164 **ποικίλος**, -η, -ον   *multicolored, parti-colored;* hence, *varied, various* (plurality as well as difference seems sometimes to be suggested).

ποίμαινε   verb, pres. act. impv. 2 pers. sg. {5.D.1} . . . . ποιμαίνω G4165

ποιμαίνει   verb, pres. act. indic. 3 pers. sg. {5.A.1.a} . . . . id.

ποιμαίνειν   vbl., pres. act. inf. {6.B.1} . . . . . . id.

ποιμαίνοντα   vbl., pres. act. ptc. acc. sg. masc. {6.A.1} . . . . id.

ποιμαίνοντες   vbl., pres. act. ptc. nom. pl. masc. {6.A.1} . . . . id.

G4165 **ποιμαίνω**   *I shepherd, I tend, I herd;* hence, *I rule.*

ποιμάνατε   verb, aor. act. impv. 2 pers. pl. {5.D.1} . . . . ποιμαίνω G4165

ποιμανεῖ   verb, fut. act. indic. 3 pers. sg. {5.A.2} id.

ποιμένα   noun, acc. sg. masc. {2.C} . . . . . . ποιμήν G4166

ποιμένας   noun, acc. pl. masc. {2.C} . . . . id.

ποιμένες   noun, nom. pl. masc. {2.C} . . . . id.

ποιμένων   noun, gen. pl. masc. {2.C} . . . . id.

G4166 **ποιμήν**, -ένος, ὁ   *a shepherd;* hence met., of the feeder, protector, and *ruler* of a flock of men.

ποιμήν   noun, nom. sg. masc. {2.C} . . . . . . ποιμήν G4166

G4167 **ποίμνη**, -ης, ἡ   *a flock; herd* (of goats perhaps, in 1 Cor 9:7).

ποίμνη   noun, nom. sg. fem. {2.A} . . . . ποίμνη G4167

ποίμνην   noun, acc. sg. fem. {2.A} . . . . id.

ποίμνης   noun, gen. sg. fem. {2.A} . . . . id.

G4168 **ποίμνιον**, -ου, τό   *a little flock;* hence, of men.

ποίμνιον   noun, acc. sg. neut. {2.B} . . . . . ποίμνιον G4168

ποίμνιον   noun, nom. sg. neut. {2.B} . . . . id.

ποίμνιον   noun, voc. sg. neut. {2.B} . . . . id.

ποιμνίου   noun, gen. sg. neut. {2.B} . . . . id.

ποιμνίῳ   noun, dat. sg. neut. {2.B} . . . . id.

ποῖον   pron. correl. interrog., acc. sg. masc. {4.D} . . . . ποῖος G4169

ποῖον   pron. correl. interrog., acc. sg. neut. {4.D} id.

ποῖον   pron. correl. interrog., nom. sg. neut.
{4.D}. . . . . id.

G4169 **ποῖος**, -α, -ον   properly direct interrog., *of what sort?*, then often weakened to *what?* simply; also indir. interrog.; ποίας (local gen., supply ὁδοῦ), *by what way.*

ποίου   pron. correl. interrog., gen. sg. masc.
{4.D}. . . . . .ποῖος G4169

ποιοῦμαι   verb, pres. mid. indic. 1 pers. sg.
{5.A.2}. ποιέω G4160

ποιοῦμεν   verb, pres. act. indic. 1 pers. pl.
{5.A.2}. . . . . id.

ποιούμενοι   vbl., pres. mid. ptc. nom. pl. masc.
{6.A.2}. . . . . id.

ποιούμενος   vbl., pres. mid. ptc. nom. sg. masc.
{6.A.2}. . . . . id.

ποιοῦν   vbl., pres. act. ptc. nom. sg. neut. {6.A.2} id.

ποιοῦντα   vbl., pres. act. ptc. acc. sg. masc.
{6.A.2}. . . . . id.

ποιοῦντα   vbl., pres. act. ptc. nom. pl. neut.
{6.A.2}. . . . . id.

ποιοῦνται   verb, pres. mid. indic. 3 pers. pl.
{5.A.2}. . . . . id.

ποιοῦντας   vbl., pres. act. ptc. acc. pl. masc.
{6.A.2}. . . . . id.

ποιοῦντες   vbl., pres. act. ptc. nom. pl. masc.
{6.A.2}. . . . . id.

ποιοῦντι   vbl., pres. act. ptc. dat. sg. masc.
{6.A.2}. . . . . id.

ποιοῦντι   vbl., pres. act. ptc. dat. sg. neut.
{6.A.2}. . . . . id.

ποιοῦντος   vbl., pres. act. ptc. gen. sg. masc.
{6.A.2}. . . . . id.

ποιοῦσι   verb, pres. act. indic. 3 pers. pl. {5.A.2} id.

ποιοῦσιν   verb, pres. act. indic. 3 pers. pl.
{5.A.2}. . . . . id.

ποιοῦσιν   vbl., pres. act. ptc. dat. pl. masc.
{6.A.2}. . . . . id.

ποιῶ   verb, pres. act. indic. 1 pers. sg. {5.A.2}. . . id.

ποιῶ   verb, pres. act. subjunc. 1 pers. sg. {5.B.2} . id.

ποίῳ   pron. correl. interrog., dat. sg. masc.
{4.D}. . . . . .ποῖος G4169

ποίῳ   pron. correl. interrog., dat. sg. neut. {4.D} . id.

ποιῶμεν   verb, pres. act. subjunc. 1 pers. pl.
{5.B.2}. ποιέω G4160

ποιῶν   vbl., pres. act. ptc. nom. sg. masc. {6.A.2} id.

ποιῶσι   verb, pres. act. subjunc. 3 pers. pl.
{5.B.2}. . . . . id.

ποιῶσιν   verb, pres. act. subjunc. 3 pers. pl.
{5.B.2}. . . . . id.

πόλει   noun, dat. sg. fem. {2.C}. . . . . .πόλις G4172

πόλεις   noun, acc. pl. fem. {2.C}. . . . . id.

πόλεις   noun, nom. pl. fem. {2.C}. . . . . id.

πολεμεῖ   verb, pres. act. indic. 3 pers. sg.
{5.A.2}. πολεμέω G4170

πολεμεῖτε   verb, pres. act. indic. 2 pers. pl. {5.A.2}. id.

G4170 **πολεμέω**   *I war, carry on war.*

πολεμῆσαι   vbl., aor. act. inf. {6.B.1} . . . . πολεμέω G4170

πολεμήσουσι   verb, fut. act. indic. 3 pers. pl.
{5.A.1}. . . . . id.

πολεμήσουσιν   verb, fut. act. indic. 3 pers. pl.
{5.A.1}. . . . . id.

πολεμήσω   verb, fut. act. indic. 1 pers. sg.
{5.A.1}. . . . . id.

πόλεμοι   noun, nom. pl. masc. {2.B}. . . . πόλεμος G4171

πόλεμον   noun, acc. sg. masc. {2.B} . . . . id.

G4171 **πόλεμος**, -ου, ὁ   *a war;* also, *a battle,* Luke 14:31, etc.

πόλεμος   noun, nom. sg. masc. {2.B} . . . . πόλεμος G4171

πολέμους   noun, acc. pl. masc. {2.B}. . . . . id.

πολέμῳ   noun, dat. sg. masc. {2.B}. . . . . id.

πολέμων   noun, gen. pl. masc. {2.B}. . . . . id.

πόλεσιν   noun, dat. pl. fem. {2.C}. . . . . .πόλις G4172

πόλεων   noun, gen. pl. fem. {2.C}. . . . . id.

πόλεως   noun, gen. sg. fem. {2.C}. . . . . id.

πόλιν   noun, acc. sg. fem. {2.C} . . . . id.

G4172 **πόλις**, -εως, ἡ   strictly *a free city, city-state* of the Gk. (particularly the Athenian) type, comprising not only the city in the mod. sense, but territory (often considerable) around it. The word is used rather of the citizens than of the locality (cf. the examples below). Its constitution commonly consisted of an ἐκκλησία (assembly of free citizens) and a βουλή (an advisory and deliberative council, in NT times a mere honorary corporation). Examples are: Matt 8:34; 12:25; Mark 1:33; ἡ ἀγία πόλις (cf. Ἱερο- in Ἱεροσόλυμα), *the holy city,* i.e., Jerusalem, as containing the temple of Yahweh.

πόλις   noun, nom. sg. fem. {2.C}. . . . . .πόλις G4172

πόλις   noun, voc. sg. fem. {2.C}. . . . . id.

πολῖται   noun, nom. pl. masc. {2.A}. . . . . .πολίτης G4177

πολιτάρχας   noun, acc. pl. masc. {2.A}πολιτάρχης G4173

G4173 **πολιτάρχης**, -ου, ὁ   *a politarch, a city magistrate* (a special, characteristically Macedonian, title of the chief magistrates, five or six in number, of Thessalonica and a few other cities).

G4174 **πολιτεία**, -ας, ἡ   (1) *commonwealth, polity; citizen body,* Eph 2:12; (2) (the Roman) *citizenship, citizen's rights, franchise,* Acts 22:28.

πολιτείαν   noun, acc. sg. fem. {2.A}. . . . . πολιτεία G4174

πολιτείας   noun, gen. sg. fem. {2.A}. . . . . id.

πολιτεύεσθε   verb, pres. mid./pass. impv. 2 pers. pl. {5.D.1} . . . . .πολιτεύομαι G4176

G4175 **πολίτευμα**, -ατος, τό   (properly, *that which one does as citizen*), *the constitution; citizenship, franchise; the state, the community, the commonwealth.* The word sometimes means *a colony* of foreigners, whose organization is a miniature copy of the πολιτεία at home, and this gives excellent sense in Phil 3:20.

πολίτευμα   noun, nom. sg. neut. {2.C}. πολίτευμα G4175

G4176 **πολιτεύομαι**   (a characteristic Gk. idea), *I live the life of a citizen; I live as a member of a* (citizen) *body; I fulfill corporate duties;* in Phil 1:27 some take simply of *manner of life.*

πολίτην   noun, acc. sg. masc. {2.A} . . . . . .πολίτης G4177

G4177 **πολίτης**, -ου, ὁ   *a citizen; a fellow citizen,* Luke 19:14; Heb 8:11.

πολίτης   noun, nom. sg. masc. {2.A} . . . . .πολίτης *G4177*
πολιτῶν   noun, gen. pl. masc. {2.A} . . . . id.
πολλά   adj., acc. pl. neut. {3.B} . . . . πολύς *G4183*
πολλά   adj., nom. pl. neut. {3.B} . . . . id.
πολλαί   adj., nom. pl. fem. {3.B} . . . . id.
πολλαῖς   adj., dat. pl. fem. {3.B} . . . . id.
G4178 **πολλάκις**   adv., *often, frequently.*
πολλάκις   adv. . . . . πολλάκις *G4178*
πολλαπλασίονα   adj., acc. pl. neut.
    {3.E} . . . . πολλαπλασίων *G4179*
G4179 **πολλαπλασίων**, -ον   *manifold, many times*
    over.
πολλάς   adj., acc. pl. fem. {3.B} . . . . πολύς *G4183*
πολλή   adj., nom. sg. fem. {3.B} . . . . id.
πολλῇ   adj., dat. sg. fem. {3.B} . . . . id.
πολλήν   adj., acc. sg. fem. {3.B} . . . . id.
πολλῆς   adj., gen. sg. fem. {3.B} . . . . id.
πολλοί   adj., nom. pl. masc. {3.B} . . . . id.
πολλοῖς   adj., dat. pl. masc. {3.B} . . . . id.
πολλοῖς   adj., dat. pl. neut. {3.B} . . . . id.
πολλοῦ   adj., gen. sg. masc. {3.B} . . . . id.
πολλοῦ   adj., gen. sg. neut. {3.B} . . . . id.
πολλούς   adj., acc. pl. masc. {3.B} . . . . id.
πολλῷ   adj., dat. sg. masc. {3.B} . . . . id.
πολλῷ   adj., dat. sg. neut. {3.B} . . . . id.
πολλῶν   adj., gen. pl. fem. {3.B} . . . . id.
πολλῶν   adj., gen. pl. masc. {3.B} . . . . id.
πολλῶν   adj., gen. pl. neut. {3.B} . . . . id.
πολύ   adj., acc. sg. neut. {3.B} . . . . id.
πολύ   adj., nom. sg. neut. {3.B} . . . . id.
G4180 **πολυλογία**, -ας, ἡ   *much speaking, loquacious-*
    ness, volubility.
πολυλογία   noun, dat. sg. fem. {2.A} . . πολυλογία *G4180*
G4181 **πολυμερῶς**   adv., *in many portions* (one at one
    time, another at another, and so on).
πολυμερῶς   adv. {3.F} . . . . πολυμερῶς *G4181*
πολύν   adj., acc. sg. masc. {3.B} . . . . πολύς *G4183*
G4182 **πολυποίκιλος**, -ον   *much varied, very varied.*
πολυποίκιλος   adj., nom. sg. fem.
    {3.C} . . . . .πολυποίκιλος *G4182*
G4183 **πολύς**, πολλή, πολύ, gen. πολλοῦ,
    πολλῆς   a word indicating quantity and
    number, not size, sg. *much,* pl. *many;* οἱ
    πολλοί, *the majority;* πολλῷ, before a
    comp., *much;* πολλά, as adv., *much* (often
    in Mark, an exact translation of Aram.), like
    the more regular πολύ; πολλοῦ, *for much,*
    at a great price, Matt 26:9; with sg. words
    indicating time, *long* is the most suitable
    Eng. rendering; πολλάς (supply πληγάς),
    Luke 12:47. The καί following, Acts 25:7, is
    superfluous according to our idiom. Comp.
    πλείων and superl. πλεῖστος.
πολύς   adj., nom. sg. masc. {3.B} . . . . πολύς *G4183*
G4184 **πολύσπλαγχνος**, -οῦ ον   *full of tender feeling*
    (a Hebraistic idiom, the bowels, σπλάγχνα,
    being regarded as the seat of compassion and
    pity, etc.).
πολύσπλαγχνος   adj., nom. sg. masc.
    {3.C} . . . . .πολύσπλαγχνος *G4184*

πολυτελεῖ   adj., dat. sg. masc. {3.E} . . . πολυτελής *G4185*
πολυτελές   adj., nom. sg. neut. {3.E} . . . . id.
G4185 **πολυτελής**, -ές   *expensive, costly;* hence, *pre-*
    cious, valuable, 1 Pet 3:4.
πολυτελοῦς   adj., gen. sg. fem. {3.E} . . πολυτελής *G4185*
πολύτιμον   adj., acc. sg. masc. {3.C}. . .πολύτιμος *G4186*
G4186 **πολύτιμος**, -ον   *costly, expensive;* hence, *valu-*
    able, precious, 1 Pet 1:7.
πολυτιμότερον   adj. comp., nom. sg. neut. {3.C;
    3.G} . . . . .πολύτιμος *G4186*
πολυτίμου   adj., gen. sg. fem. {3.C} . . . . id.
G4187 **πολυτρόπως**   adv., *in many ways, under many*
    aspects (with reference probably to different
    laws or injunctions).
πολυτρόπως   adv. {3.F} . . . . .πολυτρόπως *G4187*
G4188 **πόμα**, -ατος, τό   *drink.*
πόμα   noun, acc. sg. neut. {2.C} . . . . πόμα *G4188*
πόμασι   noun, dat. pl. neut. {2.C}. . . . . id.
πόμασιν   noun, dat. pl. neut. {2.C} . . . . id.
πονηρά   adj., acc. pl. neut. {3.A}. . . . . . . πονηρός *G4190*
πονηρά   adj., nom. pl. neut. {3.A} . . . . id.
πονηρά   adj., nom. sg. fem. {3.A} . . . . id.
πονηρᾷ   adj., dat. sg. fem. {3.A} . . . . id.
πονηραί   adj., nom. pl. fem. {3.A} . . . . id.
πονηρᾶς   adj., gen. sg. fem. {3.A} . . . . id.
πονηρέ   adj., voc. sg. masc. {3.A} . . . . id.
G4189 **πονηρία**, -ας, ἡ   the active exercise of vicious
    propensity, *malignity, wickedness;* pl. *iniquities,*
    Mark 7:22; Acts 3:26.
πονηρία   noun, dat. sg. fem. {2.A} . . . . . . πονηρία *G4189*
πονηρίαι   noun, nom. pl. fem. {2.A} . . . . id.
πονηρίαν   noun, acc. sg. fem. {2.A} . . . . id.
πονηρίας   noun, gen. sg. fem. {2.A} . . . . id.
πονηριῶν   noun, gen. pl. fem. {2.A} . . . . id.
πονηροί   adj., nom. pl. masc. {3.A} . . . . πονηρός *G4190*
πονηροῖς   adj., dat. pl. masc. {3.A} . . . . id.
πονηροῖς   adj., dat. pl. neut. {3.A} . . . . id.
πονηρόν   adj., acc. sg. masc. {3.A} . . . . id.
πονηρόν   adj., acc. sg. neut. {3.A}. . . . . id.
πονηρόν   adj., nom. sg. neut. {3.A} . . . . id.
G4190 **πονηρός**, -ά, -όν   *evil, wicked, malicious,* par-
    ticularly as active; esp. ὁ πονηρός (even Matt
    6:13; Luke 11:4 var., according to the almost
    unanimous opinion of the early Church), *the*
    evil one, i.e., Satan, the devil (a Hebraism);
    many passages like these, being in the oblique
    cases, are unfortunately ambiguous, but Matt
    13:19; 1 John 2:13, 14; 5:18 are absolutely
    certain examples of the masc., and in many
    other passages there is a strong probability;
    τὸ πονηρόν, *the evil* in the world, *all that is*
    wicked, e.g., Rom 12:9.
πονηρός   adj., nom. sg. masc. {3.A} . . . . . πονηρός *G4190*
πονηρότερα   adj. comp., acc. pl. neut. {3.A; 3.G} id.
G4191 **πονηρότερος**   *more evil* (comp.).
πονηροῦ   adj., gen. sg. masc. {3.A}. . . . . πονηρός *G4190*
πονηροῦ   adj., gen. sg. neut. {3.A} . . . . id.
πονηρούς   adj., acc. pl. masc. {3.A} . . . . id.
πονηρῷ   adj., dat. sg. masc. {3.A} . . . . id.
πονηρῷ   adj., dat. sg. neut. {3.A} . . . . id.

πονηρῶν adj., gen. pl. masc. {3.A} . . . . id.
πονηρῶν adj., gen. pl. neut. {3.A} . . . . id.
πόνον noun, acc. sg. masc. {2.B} . . . . πόνος G4192
G4192 **πόνος**, -ου, ὁ *labor, toil; trouble.*
πόνος noun, nom. sg. masc. {2.B} . . . . πόνος G4192
πόνου noun, gen. sg. masc. {2.B} . . . . id.
Ποντικόν adj. prop., acc. sg. masc. {3.A} Ποντικός G4193
G4193 **Ποντικός**, -ή, -όν *belonging to Pontus* (q.v.).
G4194 **Πόντιος**, -ου, ὁ *Pontius,* the second or gentile
  name of Pilate.
Πόντιος noun prop., nom. sg. masc. {2.B;
  2.D} . . . . Πόντιος G4194
Ποντίου noun prop., gen. sg. masc. {2.B; 2.D} . . id.
Ποντίῳ noun prop., dat. sg. masc. {2.B; 2.D} . . . id.
Πόντον noun prop., acc. sg. masc. {2.B;
  2.D} . . . . Πόντος G4195
G4195 **Πόντος**, -ου, ὁ *Pontus,* a Roman province in
  the north of Asia Minor, bordering on the
  Black Sea, governed along with Bithynia.
Πόντου noun prop., gen. sg. masc. {2.B;
  2.D} . . . . Πόντος G4195
πόνων noun, gen. pl. masc. {2.B} . . . . πόνος G4192
G4196 **Πόπλιος**, -ου, ὁ *Publius,* a governor of Malta
  (the Gk. form of the Lat. name; originally the
  same in form as the Gk. form).
Ποπλίου noun prop., gen. sg. masc. {2.B;
  2.D} . . . . Πόπλιος G4196
Ποπλίῳ noun prop., dat. sg. masc. {2.B; 2.D} . . . id.
G4197 **πορεία**, -ας, ἡ *a journey.*
πορείαις noun, dat. pl. fem. {2.A} . . . . . . πορεία G4197
πορείαν noun, acc. sg. fem. {2.A} . . . . id.
πορεύεσθαι vbl., pres. mid./pass. inf.
  {6.B.1} . . . . πορεύομαι G4198
πορεύεσθε verb, pres. mid./pass. impv. 2 pers.
  pl. {5.D.1} . . . . id.
πορεύεται verb, pres. mid./pass. indic. 3 pers.
  sg. {5.A.1.d} . . . . id.
πορευθείς vbl., aor. pass. ptc. nom. sg. masc.
  {6.A.1.a} . . . . id.
πορευθεῖσα vbl., aor. pass. ptc. nom. sg. fem.
  {6.A.1.a} . . . . id.
πορευθεῖσαι vbl., aor. pass. ptc. nom. pl. fem.
  {6.A.1.a} . . . . id.
πορευθέντα vbl., aor. pass. ptc. acc. sg. masc.
  {6.A.1.a} . . . . id.
πορευθέντες vbl., aor. pass. ptc. nom. pl. masc.
  {6.A.1.a} . . . . id.
πορευθέντι vbl., aor. pass. ptc. dat. sg. masc.
  {6.A.1.a} . . . . id.
πορευθῇ verb, aor. pass. subjunc. 3 pers. sg.
  {5.B.1} . . . . id.
πορευθῆναι vbl., aor. pass. inf. {6.B.1} . . . . . . id.
πορεύθητε verb, aor. pass. impv. 2 pers. pl.
  {5.D.1} . . . . id.
πορευθῆτε verb, aor. pass. subjunc. 2 pers. pl.
  {5.B.1} . . . . id.
πορευθῆτε verb, aor. pass. subjunc. 2 pers. pl.
  {5.B.1} . . . . id.
πορεύθητι verb, aor. pass. impv. 2 pers. sg.
  {5.D.1} . . . . id.

πορευθῶ verb, aor. pass. subjunc. 1 pers. sg.
  {5.B.1} . . . . id.
πορευθῶσιν verb, aor. pass. subjunc. 3 pers.
  pl. {5.B.1} . . . . id.
G4198 **πορεύομαι** *I travel, journey;* sometimes weakened to the sense, *I go; I depart* this life, *I die,*
  Luke 13:33(?); 22:22; Hebraistic, of manner of
  life, 1 Pet 4:3, etc.
πορεύομαι verb, pres. mid./pass. indic. 1 pers. sg.
  {5.A.1.d} . . . . πορεύομαι G4198
πορευόμεναι vbl., pres. mid./pass. ptc. nom.
  pl. fem. {6.A.1} . . . . id.
πορευομένη vbl., pres. mid./pass. ptc. nom.
  sg. fem. {6.A.1} . . . . id.
πορευόμενοι vbl., pres. mid./pass. ptc. nom.
  pl. masc. {6.A.1} . . . . id.
πορευομένοις vbl., pres. mid./pass. ptc. dat.
  pl. masc. {6.A.1} . . . . id.
πορευόμενον vbl., pres. mid./pass. ptc. acc. sg.
  masc. {6.A.1} . . . . id.
πορευόμενον vbl., pres. mid./pass. ptc. nom.
  sg. neut. {6.A.1} . . . . id.
πορευόμενος vbl., pres. mid./pass. ptc. nom.
  sg. masc. {6.A.1} . . . . id.
πορευομένου vbl., pres. mid./pass. ptc. gen.
  sg. masc. {6.A.1} . . . . id.
πορευομένους vbl., pres. mid./pass. ptc. acc.
  pl. masc. {6.A.1} . . . . id.
πορευομένῳ vbl., pres. mid./pass. ptc. dat. sg.
  masc. {6.A.1} . . . . id.
πορευομένων vbl., pres. mid./pass. ptc. gen.
  pl. fem. {6.A.1} . . . . id.
πορευομένων vbl., pres. mid./pass. ptc. gen.
  pl. masc. {6.A.1} . . . . id.
πορεύου verb, pres. mid./pass. impv. 2 pers.
  sg. {5.D.1} . . . . id.
πορεύσεται verb, fut. mid. indic. 3 pers. sg.
  {5.A.1.d} . . . . id.
πορεύσῃ verb, fut. mid. indic. 2 pers. sg.
  {5.A.1.d} . . . . id.
πορεύσομαι verb, fut. mid. indic. 1 pers. sg.
  {5.A.1.d} . . . . id.
πορευσόμεθα verb, fut. mid. indic. 1 pers. pl.
  {5.A.1.d} . . . . id.
πορεύσονται verb, fut. mid. indic. 3 pers. pl.
  {5.A.1.d} . . . . id.
πορευσώμεθα verb, aor. mid. subjunc. 1 pers.
  pl. {5.B.1} . . . . id.
πορεύωμαι verb, pres. mid./pass. subjunc.
  1 pers. sg. {5.B.1} . . . . id.
G4199 **πορθέω** *I devastate, lay waste;* hence, *I bring
  destruction upon, I destroy.*
πορθήσας vbl., aor. act. ptc. nom. sg. masc.
  {6.A.2} . . . . πορθέω G4199
πορισμόν noun, acc. sg. masc. {2.B} . . . πορισμός G4200
G4200 **πορισμός**, -οῦ, ὁ *a means of gain, a way of
  making a living, a livelihood, a living.*
πορισμός noun, nom. sg. masc. {2.B} . . πορισμός G4200
Πόρκιον noun prop., acc. sg. masc. {2.B;
  2.D} . . . . Πόρκιος G4201

G4201 **Πόρκιος**, -ου, ὁ   *Porcius,* the middle (gentile) name of the pro curator Festus.

πόρναι   noun, nom. pl. fem. {2.A} . . . . πόρνη G4204

G4202 **πορνεία**, -ας, ἡ   *fornication,* the practice of consorting with πόρναι or πόρνοι, habitual *immorality.*

πορνεία   noun, nom. sg. fem. {2.A} . . . . πορνεία G4202
πορνείᾳ   noun, dat. sg. fem. {2.A} . . . . id.
πορνεῖαι   noun, nom. pl. fem. {2.A} . . . . id.
πορνείαν   noun, acc. sg. fem. {2.A} . . . . id.
πορνείας   noun, acc. pl. fem. {2.A} . . . . id.
πορνείας   noun, gen. sg. fem. {2.A} . . . . id.
πορνεῦσαι   vbl., aor. act. inf. {6.B.1} . . . . πορνεύω G4203
πορνεύσαντες   vbl., aor. act. ptc. nom. pl. masc. {6.A.1.a} . . . . id.

G4203 **πορνεύω**   *I practice fornication,* esp. of men con sorting with πόρναι.

πορνεύωμεν   verb, pres. act. subjunc. 1 pers. pl. {5.B.1} . . . . πορνεύω G4203
πορνεύων   vbl., pres. act. ptc. nom. sg. masc. {6.A.1} . . . . id.

G4204 **πόρνη**, -ης, ἡ   *a prostitute.*

πόρνη   noun, nom. sg. fem. {2.A} . . . . πόρνη G4204
πόρνῃ   noun, dat. sg. fem. {2.A} . . . . id.
πόρνην   noun, acc. sg. fem. {2.A} . . . . id.
πόρνης   noun, gen. sg. fem. {2.A} . . . . id.
πόρνοι   noun, nom. pl. masc. {2.B} . . . . . . πόρνος G4205
πόρνοις   noun, dat. pl. masc. {2.B} . . . . id.

G4205 **πόρνος**, -ου, ὁ   *a male prostitute;* the weaker sense, one who consorts with πόρναι, *a forni- cator,* is generally adopted for NT.

πόρνος   noun, nom. sg. masc. {2.B} . . . . . . πόρνος G4205
πόρνους   noun, acc. sg. masc. {2.B} . . . . id.
πορνῶν   noun, gen. pl. fem. {2.A} . . . . πόρνη G4204

G4206 **πόρρω**   adv., *far, at a distance;* comp. adv. πορρώτερον *farther.*

πόρρω   adv. . . . . πόρρω G4206

G4207 **πόρρωθεν**   adv., *from a long distance,* Heb 11:13; hence (cf. ἔξωθεν), *at a long distance, far away,* Luke 17:12.

πόρρωθεν   adv. . . . . πόρρωθεν G4207
πορρώτερον   adv. comp. {3.F; 3.G} . . . . πόρρω G4206
πορρωτέρω   adv. comp. {3.F; 3.G} . . . . id.

G4208 **πορρωτέρω**   adv., *farther,* i.e., *a greater distance* (comp.).

G4209 **πορφύρα**, -ας, ἡ   *a purple robe, purple; a red colored cloak,* such as common soldiers wore, Mark 15:17, 20.

πορφύρα   noun, dat. sg. fem. {2.A} . . . . . πορφύρα G4209
πορφύραν   noun, acc. sg. fem. {2.A} . . . . id.
πορφύρας   noun, gen. sg. fem. {2.A} . . . . id.

G4211 **πορφυρόπωλις**, -ιδος, ἡ   a woman *dealer in purple dyed* garments.

πορφυρόπωλις   noun, nom. sg. fem. {2.C} . . . . πορφυρόπωλις G4211
πορφυροῦ   adj., gen. sg. neut. {3.A} . . πορφυροῦς G4210‡
πορφυροῦν   adj., acc. sg. neut. {3.A} . . . . id.

G4210‡ **πορφυροῦς**, -ᾶ, -οῦν   *dyed with purple,* Rev 17:4; 18:16; *dyed scarlet,* John 19:2, 5 (see πορφύρα).

πόσα   pron. correl. interrog., acc. pl. neut. {4.D} . . . . πόσος G4214
πόσαι   pron. correl. interrog., nom. pl. fem. {4.D} . . . . id.

G4212 **ποσάκις**   adv., *how many times?, how often?.*

ποσάκις   adv. interrog. . . . . ποσάκις G4212
πόσας   pron. correl. interrog., acc. pl. fem. {4.D} . . . . πόσος G4214
πόσει   noun, dat. sg. fem. {2.C} . . . . πόσις G4213
πόσην   pron. correl. interrog., acc. sg. fem. {4.D} . . . . πόσος G4214
ποσί   noun, dat. pl. masc. {2.C} . . . . πούς G4228
ποσίν   noun, dat. pl. masc. {2.C} . . . . id.

G4213 **πόσις**, -εως, ἡ   *drinking;* hence, concr., *drink,* as perhaps in all NT passages (certainly in John 6:55).

πόσις   noun, nom. sg. fem. {2.C} . . . . πόσις G4213
πόσοι   pron. correl. interrog., nom. pl. masc. {4.D} . . . . πόσος G4214
πόσον   pron. correl. interrog., acc. sg. neut. {4.D} . . . . id.
πόσον   pron. correl. interrog., nom. sg. neut. {4.D} . . . . id.

G4214 **πόσος**, -η, -ον   *how great?, how large?;* in pl., *how many?;* πόσῳ, before comp. (cf. Matt 12:12), *by how much?, how much?.*

πόσος   pron. correl. interrog., nom. sg. masc. {4.D} . . . . πόσος G4214
πόσους   pron. correl. interrog., acc. pl. masc. {4.D} . . . . id.
πόσῳ   pron. correl. interrog., dat. sg. neut. {4.D} id.
πόσων   pron. correl. interrog., gen. pl. fem. {4.D} id.
πόσων   pron. correl. interrog., gen. pl. neut. {4.D} . . . . id.
ποταμοί   noun, nom. pl. masc. {2.B} . . . . ποταμός G4215
ποταμόν   noun, acc. sg. masc. {2.B} . . . . id.

G4215 **ποταμός**, -οῦ, ὁ   *a river.*

ποταμός   noun, nom. sg. masc. {2.B} . . . . ποταμός G4215
ποταμοῦ   noun, gen. sg. masc. {2.B} . . . . id.
ποταμούς   noun, acc. pl. masc. {2.B} . . . . id.
ποταμοφόρητον   adj., acc. sg. fem. {3.C} . . . . ποταμοφόρητος G4216

G4216 **ποταμοφόρητος**, -ον   *river-borne, carried off by a river.*

ποταμῷ   noun, dat. sg. masc. {2.B} . . . . . . ποταμός G4215
ποταμῶν   noun, gen. pl. masc. {2.B} . . . . id.
ποταπαί   pron. interrog., nom. pl. fem. {3.A} . . . . ποταπός G4217
ποταπή   pron. interrog., nom. sg. fem. {3.A} . . . id.
ποταπήν   pron. interrog., acc. sg. fem. {3.A} . . . id.
ποταποί   pron. interrog., nom. pl. masc. {3.A} . . id.

G4217 **ποταπός**, -ή, -όν   (*from what country?, in what country born?,* and then) *of what sort?, how fashioned?* (hence, practically, *how great?,* 1 John 3:1).

ποταπός   pron. interrog., nom. sg. masc. {3.A} . . . . ποταπός G4217
ποταπούς   pron. interrog., acc. pl. masc. {3.A} . . id.
ποτε   adv. indef. correl. {4.D} . . . . ποτέ G4218

G4219‡ **πότε** interrog. adv., *at what time?, when?;* ἕως πότε, *till what time?, till when?, how long?* Also in indir. interrog. clauses.

πότε adv. correl. interrog. {4.D} . . . . πότε *G4219‡*

G4218 **ποτέ** indef. temp. particle, *at any time, ever, at some time; at one time,* esp. with past tenses; for μή ποτε, see μήποτε.

ποτέ adv. correl., part. {4.D} . . . . .ποτέ *G4218*

G4220 **πότερον** part., *whether.*

πότερον part. interrog. . . . . πότερον *G4220*

G4221 **ποτήριον**, -ου, τό   *a cup.*

ποτήριον noun, acc. sg. neut. {2.B} . . . . ποτήριον *G4221*
ποτήριον noun, nom. sg. neut. {2.B} . . . . id.
ποτηρίου noun, gen. sg. neut. {2.B} . . . . id.
ποτηρίῳ noun, dat. sg. neut. {2.B} . . . . id.
ποτηρίων noun, gen. pl. neut. {2.B} . . . . id.
πότιζε verb, pres. act. impv. 2 pers. sg. {5.D.1} . . . . ποτίζω *G4222*
ποτίζει verb, pres. act. indic. 3 pers. sg. {5.A.1.a}id.

G4222 **ποτίζω**   *I cause to drink, I make to drink, I give drink to.*

ποτίζων vbl., pres. act. ptc. nom. sg. masc. {6.A.1} . . . . ποτίζω *G4222*

G4223 **Ποτίολοι**, -ων, ὁ   *Puteoli* (now Pozzuoli), the great harbor for traffic with Alexandria, etc., on the Bay of Naples.

Ποτιόλους noun prop., acc. pl. masc. {2.B; 2.D} .Ποτίολοι *G4223*
ποτίσῃ verb, aor. act. subjunc. 3 pers. sg. {5.B.1} . . . . ποτίζω *G4222*
πότοις noun, dat. pl. masc. {2.B} . . . . πότος *G4224*

G4224 **πότος**, -ου, ὁ   *a drinking bout.*

που adv. correl. {4.D} . . . . πού *G4225*

G4225 **πού** adv., (1) *anywhere,* Acts 27:29; *somewhere,* Heb 2:6, etc.; (2) *about,* Rom 4:19; for δή που and μή που, see also δήπου, μήπου.

πού adv. correl. {4.D} . . . . πού *G4225*

G4226 **ποῦ** interrog. adv., *where?;* also used (for the obsolete ποῖ) in the sense, *to what place?.*

ποῦ adv. correl. interrog. {4.D} . . . . ποῦ *G4226*

G4227 **Πούδης**, -εντος, ὁ   *Pudens,* a Christian man in Rome (Lat.).

Πούδης noun prop., nom. sg. masc. {2.A; 2.D} . . . . .Πούδης *G4227*

G4228 **πούς**, ποδός, ὁ   *a* (human) *foot.*

πούς noun, nom. sg. masc. {2.C} . . . . πούς *G4228*

G4229 **πρᾶγμα**, -ατος, τό   (1) *a deed, action;* (2) used more vaguely, *a matter, an affair;* πρᾶγμα ἔχειν πρός τινα, *to have something against one, to have ground for a lawsuit against one,* 1 Cor 6:1; ἐν τῷ πράγματι, *in the matter in hand* (i.e., *sins of the flesh*), rather than generically, *in business,* 1 Thess 4:6.

πρᾶγμα noun, acc. sg. neut. {2.C} . . . . . . πρᾶγμα *G4229*
πρᾶγμα noun, nom. sg. neut. {2.C} . . . . id.

G4230 **πραγματεία**, -ῶν, ἡ   *business, business transaction;* pl., *affairs, pursuits.*

πραγματείαις noun, dat. pl. fem. {2.A} . . . . πραγματεία *G4230*

G4231 **πραγματεύομαι**   *I do business, I trade.*

πραγματεύσασθαι vbl., aor. mid. inf. {6.B.1} . . . . πραγματεύομαι *G4231*
πραγματεύσασθε verb, aor. mid. impv. 2 pers. pl. {5.D.1} . . . . id.
πράγματι noun, dat. sg. neut. {2.C} . . . . . πρᾶγμα *G4229*
πραγματίαις noun, dat. pl. fem. {2.A} πραγματεία *G4230*
πράγματος noun, gen. sg. neut. {2.C} . . . . πρᾶγμα *G4229*
πραγμάτων noun, gen. pl. neut. {2.C} . . . . id.
πραεῖς adj., nom. pl. masc. {3.D} . . . . πραΰς *G4239*
πραεῖς adj., nom. pl. masc. {3.D} . . . . id.
πραέος adj., gen. sg. neut. {3.D} . . . . id.
πραέως adj., gen. sg. neut. {3.D} . . . . id.
πραθέν vbl., aor. pass. ptc. nom. sg. neut. {6.A.1.a} . . . . πιπράσκω *G4097*
πραθῆναι vbl., aor. pass. inf. {6.B.1} . . . . id.

G4232 **πραιτώριον**, -ου, τό   (1) *the official residence of the procurator,* which in Jerusalem was the palace of Herod on the west side of the city; (2) pers., *the imperial guard, the praetorian guard,* or perhaps, *the law officers of the Crown,* Phil 1:13 (from Lat. *praetorium,* meaning orig., *the quarters* (residence) *of the general*).

πραιτώριον noun, acc. sg. neut. {2.B} πραιτώριον *G4232*
πραιτώριον noun, nom. sg. neut. {2.B} . . . . . . id.
πραιτωρίῳ noun, dat. sg. neut. {2.B} . . . . id.
πράκτορι noun, dat. sg. masc. {2.C} . . . πράκτωρ *G4233*

G4233 **πράκτωρ**, -ορος, ὁ   (usually, *a collector of revenue,* but in Luke) *an officer* (usher) *of the court.*

πράκτωρ noun, nom. sg. masc. {2.C} . . . πράκτωρ *G4233*
πρᾶξαι vbl., aor. act. inf. {6.B.1} . . . . πράσσω *G4238*
πράξαντες vbl., aor. act. ptc. nom. pl. masc. {6.A.1.a} . . . . id.
πραξάντων vbl., aor. act. ptc. gen. pl. masc. {6.A.1.a} . . . . id.
πράξας vbl., aor. act. ptc. nom. sg. masc. {6.A.1.a} . . . . id.
πράξει noun, dat. sg. fem. {2.C} . . . . .πρᾶξις *G4234*
πράξεις noun, acc. pl. fem. {2.C} . . . . id.
πράξεσιν noun, dat. pl. fem. {2.C} . . . . id.
πράξετε verb, fut. act. indic. 2 pers. pl. {5.A.1.a} . . . . πράσσω *G4238*
πράξῃς verb, aor. act. subjunc. 2 pers. sg. {5.B.1}id.
πρᾶξιν noun, acc. sg. fem. {2.C} . . . . .πρᾶξις *G4234*

G4234 **πρᾶξις**, -εως, ἡ   (1) abstr., *conduct; function,* Rom 12:4; (2) concr., in pl. *doings, deeds.*

G4235 **πρᾶος** alt. form of πραΰς; *gentle,* i.e., *humble.*

πρᾶος adj., nom. sg. masc. {3.D} . . . . πραΰς *G4239*

G4236 **πραότης** alt. form of πραΰτης; *gentleness;* by implication, *humility.*

πραότης noun, nom. sg. fem. {2.C} . . . . πραΰτης *G4240*
πραότητα noun, acc. sg. fem. {2.C} . . . . id.
πραότητι noun, dat. sg. fem. {2.C} . . . . id.
πραότητος noun, gen. sg. fem. {2.C} . . . . id.

G4237 **πρασιά**, -ᾶς, ἡ   *a vegetable* or *flower bed;* πρασιαὶ πρασιαί, colloquial type of phrase, *like vegetable* or *flower beds,* referring to the rectangular arrangement of the groups.

πρασιαί noun, nom. pl. fem. {2.A} . . . . . πρασιά *G4237*

πράσσει   verb, pres. act. indic. 3 pers. sg.
{5.A.1.a} . . . . πράσσω *G4238*
πράσσειν   vbl., pres. act. inf. {6.B.1}. . . . . id.
πράσσεις   verb, pres. act. indic. 2 pers. sg.
{5.A.1.a} . . . . id.
πράσσετε   verb, pres. act. impv. 2 pers. pl.
{5.D.1}. . . . . id.
πράσσῃς   verb, pres. act. subjunc. 2 pers. sg.
{5.B.1} . . . . id.
πράσσοντας   vbl., pres. act. ptc. acc. pl. masc.
{6.A.1}. . . . . id.
πράσσοντες   vbl., pres. act. ptc. nom. pl. masc.
{6.A.1}. . . . . id.
πράσσοντι   vbl., pres. act. ptc. dat. sg. masc.
{6.A.1}. . . . . id.
πράσσουσι   verb, pres. act. indic. 3 pers. pl.
{5.A.1.a} . . . . id.
πράσσουσι   vbl., pres. act. ptc. dat. pl. masc.
{6.A.1}. . . . . id.
πράσσουσιν   verb, pres. act. indic. 3 pers. pl.
{5.A.1.a} . . . . id.
πράσσουσιν   vbl., pres. act. ptc. dat. pl. masc.
{6.A.1}. . . . . id.
G4238 **πράσσω**   (referring rather to the purpose, mo-
tive of an action than to the actual doing), (1)
trans., *I act, do;* (2) trans., *I exact, extort,* Luke
3:13; 19:23; (3) intrans., *I fare;* εὖ πράξετε,
you shall fare well, Acts 15:29, τί πράσσω,
how I fare, Eph 6:21.
πράσσω   verb, pres. act. indic. 1 pers. sg.
{5.A.1.a} . . . . πράσσω *G4238*
πράσσων   vbl., pres. act. ptc. nom. sg. masc.
{6.A.1}. . . . . id.
πράττειν   vbl., pres. act. inf. {6.B.1} . . . . id.
πράττουσι   verb, pres. act. indic. 3 pers. pl.
{5.A.1.a} . . . . id.
G4240†‡ **πραϋπαθία** (πραϋπάθεια), -ας, ἡ   *meekness*
(gentleness) of spirit. Var. for πραΰτης, 1 Tim.
6:11.
πραϋπαθίαν   noun, acc. sg. fem.
{2.A} . . . . πραϋπαθία *G4240†‡*
G4239 **πραΰς**, πραεῖα, πραΰ   *meek, gentle.*
πραΰς   adj., nom. sg. masc. {3.D} . . . . πραΰς *G4239*
G4240 **πραΰτης** (πραότης), -ητος, ἡ   *meekness,*
gentleness.
πραΰτης   noun, nom. sg. fem. {2.C} . . . . . πραΰτης *G4240*
πραΰτητα   noun, acc. sg. fem. {2.C} . . . . id.
πραΰτητι   noun, dat. sg. fem. {2.C} . . . . id.
πραΰτητι   noun, dat. sg. fem. {2.C} . . . . id.
πραΰτητος   noun, gen. sg. fem. {2.C}. . . . . id.
πραΰτητος   noun, gen. sg. fem. {2.C}. . . . . id.
πρέπει   verb, pres. act. indic. 3 pers. sg.
{5.A.1.a} . . . . πρέπω *G4241*
πρέπον   vbl., pres. act. ptc. nom. sg. neut. {6.A.1} id.
G4241 **πρέπω**   *I suit;* generally impers., or with neut.
pron. as subj., πρέπει = πρέπον ἐστίν, *it is*
becoming, it is fitting.
G4242 **πρεσβεία**, -ας, ἡ   *an embassy, delegation.*
πρεσβείαν   noun, acc. sg. fem. {2.A} . . . πρεσβεία *G4242*

πρεσβεύομεν   verb, pres. act. indic. 1 pers. pl.
{5.A.1.a} . . . . πρεσβεύω *G4243*
G4243 **πρεσβεύω**   *I am an ambassador* (esp., *I am on*
embassy to the Emperor).
πρεσβεύω   verb, pres. act. indic. 1 pers. sg.
{5.A.1.a} . . . . πρεσβεύω *G4243*
πρεσβύτας   noun, acc. pl. masc. {2.A} . πρεσβύτης *G4246*
πρεσβυτέρας   adj. comp., acc. pl. fem. {3.A;
3.G} . . . . πρεσβύτερος *G4245*
G4244 **πρεσβυτέριον**, -ου, τό   (1) amongst the Jews,
a college of elders, who supervised the worship,
etc., of the synagogue; hence, *the Sanhedrin* at
Jerusalem; (2) the Christian analogue, *a college*
of elders of a particular church.
πρεσβυτέριον   noun, nom. sg. neut.
{2.B} . . . . .πρεσβυτέριον *G4244*
πρεσβυτερίου   noun, gen. sg. neut. {2.B}. . . . . id.
πρεσβύτεροι   adj. comp., nom. pl. masc. {3.A;
3.G} . . . . πρεσβύτερος *G4245*
πρεσβύτεροι   adj. comp., voc. pl. masc. {3.A;
3.G} . . . . id.
πρεσβυτέροις   adj. comp., dat. pl. masc. {3.A;
3.G} . . . . id.
G4245 **πρεσβύτερος**, -α, -ον   (1) of age simply, *the*
elder of two, Luke 15:25; *old, aged,* Acts 2:17;
1 Tim 5:1; pl. our (their, etc.) *ancestors,* Matt
15:2; Mark 7:3, 5; Heb 11:2; (2) a title of honor
applied among the Jews to various classes of
dignitary, because such offices were originally
conferred on the old, e.g., *a member of the*
Sanhedrin, Matt 16:21, etc.; τοῦ Ἰσραήλ, Acts
4:8; τῶν Ἰουδαίων, Acts 25:15; τοῦ λαοῦ,
Matt 21:23; etc.; *magistrates* of a particular
city, Luke 7:3; (3) among the Christians, *an*
elder of a congregation or church, Acts 11:30,
etc., τῆς ἐκκλησίας, Acts 20:17; Jas 5:14, one
of whom was commonly appointed ἐπίσκοπος; hence the two words are practically
identical in meaning, the former indicating
status, the latter function; (4) *an elder* of the
twenty-four in the heavenly assembly, Rev 4:4,
etc. (The title was applied in Egypt (a) to hold-
ers of a communal office in civil life, who were
responsible for the peace of the village, and
received a small salary, (b) to priests of pagan
temples.).
πρεσβύτερος   adj. comp., nom. sg. masc. {3.A;
3.G} . . . . πρεσβύτερος *G4245*
πρεσβυτέρου   adj. comp., gen. sg. masc. {3.A;
3.G} . . . . id.
πρεσβυτέρους   adj. comp., acc. pl. masc. {3.A;
3.G} . . . . id.
πρεσβυτέρῳ   adj. comp., dat. sg. masc. {3.A;
3.G} . . . . id.
πρεσβυτέρων   adj. comp., gen. pl. masc. {3.A;
3.G} . . . . id.
G4246 **πρεσβύτης**, -ου, ὁ   *an old man.*
πρεσβύτης   noun, nom. sg. masc. {2.A} πρεσβύτης *G4246*
πρεσβύτιδας   noun, acc. pl. fem. {2.C}. .πρεσβῦτις *G4247*
G4247 **πρεσβῦτις**, -ιδος, ἡ   *an old woman.*

G4248 **πρηνής**, -ές gen. οῦς   *swollen up, inflamed* (a
  medical term, denoting a disease, and corresponding to πίμπρημι, q.v.).
  πρηνής   adj., nom. sg. masc. {3.E} . . . . πρηνής G4248
G4249 **πρίζω**   *I saw, I saw through.*
G4250 **πρίν**   used either with or without ἤ *(than)* and
  with the inf. following (once with ἄν and
  subjunc., Luke 2:26, once with the opt., Acts
  25:16), *before.*
  πρίν   adv. . . . . .πρίν G4250
G4251 **Πρίσκα**, -ης, ἡ   *Prisca,* a Roman lady, probably
  of good birth, wife of the Jewish Christian
  Aquila. (The var. form Πρίσκιλλα, *Priscilla,* is
  a diminutive and more familiar form.)
  Πρίσκα   noun prop., nom. sg. fem. {2.A;
  2.D}. . . . . .Πρίσκα G4251
  Πρίσκαν   noun prop., acc. sg. fem. {2.A; 2.D} . . id.
  Πρίσκιλλα   noun prop., nom. sg. fem. {2.A;
  2.D}. . . . . id.
G4252 **Πρίσκιλλα**, -ης, ἡ   *Priscilla* (i.e., *little Prisca*),
  a Chr. woman; dimin. of Πρίσκα.
  Πρίσκιλλαν   noun prop., acc. sg. fem. {2.A;
  2.D}. . . . . .Πρίσκα G4251
G4253 **πρό**   prep. with gen., (1) of place, *before, in
  front of;* (2) of time, *before, earlier than;* found
  even with article and the inf. = πρίν; πρὸ ἓξ
  ἡμερῶν τοῦ πάσχα, *six days before,* etc., John
  12:1, πρὸ ἐτῶν δεκατεσσάρων, *fourteen
  years before,* 2 Cor 12:2.
  πρό   prep. . . . . πρό G4253
  προαγαγεῖν   vbl., ²aor. act. inf. {6.B.1} . . . προάγω G4254
  προαγαγών   vbl., ²aor. act. ptc. nom. sg. masc.
  {6.A.1.a} . . . . id.
  προάγει   verb, pres. act. indic. 3 pers. sg.
  {5.A.1.a} . . . . id.
  προάγειν   vbl., pres. act. inf. {6.B.1} . . . . . . id.
  προάγοντες   vbl., pres. act. ptc. nom. pl. masc.
  {6.A.1}. . . . . id.
  προαγούσαι   vbl., pres. act. ptc. nom. pl. fem.
  {6.A.1}. . . . . id.
  προαγούσας   vbl., pres. act. ptc. acc. pl. fem.
  {6.A.1}. . . . . id.
  προαγούσης   vbl., pres. act. ptc. gen. sg. fem.
  {6.A.1}. . . . . id.
  προάγουσιν   verb, pres. act. indic. 3 pers. pl.
  {5.A.1.a} . . . . id.
G4254 **προάγω**   (1) trans., *I lead forth,* Acts 16:30;
  in the judicial sense, into court, Acts 12:6,
  with ἐπί with gen. of the person who is to try
  the case, Acts 25:26; (2) intrans. and trans.,
  I precede, I go before; so pres. ptc. *preceding,
  previous,* Heb 7:18; *I lead forwards* to a definite
  goal, 1 Tim 1:18; (3) intrans., *I go too far,*
  2 John 9.
  προάγων   vbl., pres. act. ptc. nom. sg. masc.
  {6.A.1}. . . . . .προάγω G4254
  προαιρεῖται   verb, pres. mid./pass. indic. 3 pers.
  sg. {5.A.2} . . . . προαιρέω G4255
G4255 **προαιρέω**   mid. *I choose (for myself)
  deliberately.*

G4256 **προαιτιάομαι**   *I make a prior accusation.*
G4257 **προακούω**   *I hear beforehand.*
G4258 **προαμαρτάνω**   *I sin previously.*
  προάξω   verb, fut. act. indic. 1 pers. sg.
  {5.A.1.a} . . . . .προάγω G4254
G4259 **προαύλιον**, -ου, τό   *a forecourt,* a courtyard in
  the front part of a building.
  προαύλιον   noun, acc. sg. neut. {2.B} . . προαύλιον G4259
G4260 **προβαίνω**   *I go forward, move forward, advance;* met. *I advance* (in years), Luke 1:7, 18;
  2:36.
G4261 **προβάλλω**   (1) trans., *I put forward;* (2) *I put
  forth shoots, I sprout, burst into leaf,* Luke
  21:30.
  προβαλόντων   vbl., ²aor. act. ptc. gen. pl. masc.
  {6.A.1.a} . . . . προβάλλω G4261
  προβάλωσιν   verb, ²aor. act. subjunc. 3 pers. pl.
  {5.B.1} . . . . id.
  προβάς   vbl., ²aor. act. ptc. nom. sg. masc.
  {6.A.1.a} . . . . προβαίνω G4260
  πρόβατα   noun, acc. pl. neut. {2.B} . . . . πρόβατον G4263
  πρόβατα   noun, nom. pl. neut. {2.B} . . . . id.
  προβάτια   noun, acc. pl. neut. {2.B} . . προβάτιον G4263†‡
  προβατικῇ   adj., dat. sg. fem. {3.A} . . προβατικός G4262
G4262 **προβατικός**, -ή, -όν   *connected with sheep;*
  προβατικῇ (supply πύλη) *the Sheep Gate* of
  Jerusalem; if κολυμβήθρα be read, προβατικῇ agrees with it.
G4263†‡ **προβάτιον**, -ου, τό   lit. *a little sheep* (the
  diminutive form of πρόβατον used to express
  tender affection). Var. for πρόβατον, John
  10:3; 21:16–17.
G4263 **πρόβατον**, -ου, τό   *a sheep.*
  πρόβατον   noun, acc. sg. neut. {2.B} . . . πρόβατον G4263
  πρόβατον   noun, nom. sg. neut. {2.B} . . . . id.
  προβάτου   noun, gen. sg. neut. {2.B} . . . . id.
  προβάτων   noun, gen. pl. neut. {2.B} . . . . id.
  προβεβηκότες   vbl., perf. act. ptc. nom. pl. masc.
  {6.A.1.a} . . . . προβαίνω G4260
  προβεβηκυῖα   vbl., perf. act. ptc. nom. sg. fem.
  {6.A.1.a} . . . . id.
G4264 **προβιβάζω**   *I instruct.*
  προβιβασθεῖσα   vbl., aor. pass. ptc. nom. sg. fem.
  {6.A.1.a} . . . . προβιβάζω G4264
G4265 **προβλέπω**   mid. *I provide* (something for
  someone).
  προβλεψαμένου   vbl., aor. mid. ptc. gen. sg. masc.
  {6.A.1.b} .προβλέπω G4265
  προγεγονότων   vbl., ²perf. act. ptc. gen. pl. neut.
  {6.A.1.a} .προγίνομαι G4266
  προγεγραμμένοι   vbl., perf. pass. ptc. nom. pl.
  masc. {6.A.1.b} . . . . .προγράφω G4270
G4266 **προγίνομαι**   *I happen (come about) previously.*
  προγινώσκοντες   vbl., pres. act. ptc. nom. pl.
  masc. {6.A.1} . . . . .προγινώσκω G4267
G4267 **προγινώσκω**   (properly, *I get to know (I learn)
  beforehand*), (1) *I know previously;* (2) *I designate before* (to a position or function), 1 Pet
  1:20.
  προγνώσει   noun, dat. sg. fem. {2.C} . . πρόγνωσις G4268

πρόγνωσιν   noun, acc. sg. fem. {2.C} . . . . id.

G4268 **πρόγνωσις**, -εως, ἡ   *foreknowledge.*

προγόνοις   noun, dat. pl. masc. {2.B} . . . πρόγονος G4269

G4269 **πρόγονος**, -ου, ὁ or ἡ   *an ancestor.*

προγόνων   noun, gen. pl. masc. {2.B} . . . πρόγονος G4269

G4270 **προγράφω**   (1) *I write previously (aforetime),* Rom 15:4; Jude 4; *I write above (already),* Eph 3:3; (2) *I evidently portray* or *I placard, advertise,* Gal 3:1.

πρόδηλα   adj., nom. pl. neut. {3.C} . . . . πρόδηλος G4271

πρόδηλοι   adj., nom. pl. fem. {3.C} . . . . id.

πρόδηλον   adj., nom. sg. neut. {3.C} . . . . id.

G4271 **πρόδηλος**, -ον   *perfectly clear (evident).*

G4272 **προδίδωμι**   *I give previously.*

προδόται   noun, nom. pl. masc. {2.A} . . προδότης G4273

G4273 **προδότης**, -ου, ὁ   (1) *a betrayer;* (2) *traitorous, treacherous,* 2 Tim 3:4.

προδότης   noun, nom. sg. masc. {2.A} . . προδότης G4273

προδραμών   vbl., ²aor. act. ptc. nom. sg. masc. {6.A.1.a} . . . . προτρέχω G4390

G4274 **πρόδρομος**, -ου, ὁ   *a forerunner.*

πρόδρομος   adj., nom. sg. masc. {3.C} . πρόδρομος G4274

προεβίβασαν   verb, aor. act. indic. 3 pers. pl. {5.A.1.b} . . . . προβιβάζω G4264

προέγνω   verb, ²aor. act. indic. 3 pers. sg. {5.A.1.b} . . . . προγινώσκω G4267

προεγνωσμένου   vbl., perf. pass. ptc. gen. sg. masc. {6.A.1.b} . . . . id.

προεγράφη   verb, ²aor. pass. indic. 3 pers. sg. {5.A.1.e} . . . . προγράφω G4270

προέγραψα   verb, aor. act. indic. 1 pers. sg. {5.A.1.b} . . . . id.

προέδραμε   verb, ²aor. act. indic. 3 pers. sg. {5.A.1.b} . . . . προτρέχω G4390

προέδραμεν   verb, ²aor. act. indic. 3 pers. sg. {5.A.1.b} . . . . id.

προέδωκεν   verb, aor. act. indic. 3 pers. sg. {5.A.3.b} . . . . προδίδωμι G4272

προεθέμην   verb, ²aor. mid. indic. 1 pers. sg. {5.A.3.b} . . . . προτίθημι G4388

προέθετο   verb, ²aor. mid. indic. 3 pers. sg. {5.A.3.b} . . . . id.

G4275 **προεῖδον**   aor. act. of προοράω, *I foresaw, I saw previously.*

προείπαμεν   verb, ²aor. act. indic. 1 pers. pl. {5.A.1.b} . . . . προλέγω G4302

προεῖπε   verb, ²aor. act. indic. 3 pers. sg. {5.A.1.b} . . . . id.

προεῖπεν   verb, ²aor. act. indic. 3 pers. sg. {5.A.1.b} . . . . id.

προείπομεν   verb, ²aor. act. indic. 1 pers. pl. {5.A.1.b} . . . . id.

G4277‡ **προεῖπον**   aor. act. from προλέγω, *I said beforehand (previously).*

προεῖπον   verb, ²aor. act. indic. 1 pers. sg. {5.A.1.b} . . . . προλέγω G4302

προείρηκα   verb, perf. act. indic. 1 pers. sg. {5.A.1.c} . . . . id.

προειρήκαμεν   verb, perf. act. indic. 1 pers. pl. {5.A.1.c} . . . . id.

προείρηκεν   verb, perf. act. indic. 3 pers. sg. {5.A.1.c} . . . . id.

προειρηκέναι   vbl., perf. act. inf. {6.B.1} . . . . . id.

προειρημένων   vbl., perf. pass. ptc. gen. pl. masc. {6.A.1.b} . . . . id.

προειρημένων   vbl., perf. pass. ptc. gen. pl. neut. {6.A.1.b} . . . . id.

προείρηται   verb, perf. pass. indic. 3 pers. sg. {5.A.1.f} . . . . id.

προέκοπτε   verb, impf. act. indic. 3 pers. sg. {5.A.1.b} . . . . προκόπτω G4298

προέκοπτεν   verb, impf. act. indic. 3 pers. sg. {5.A.1.b} . . . . id.

προέκοπτον   verb, impf. act. indic. 1 pers. sg. {5.A.1.b} . . . . id.

προέκοψεν   verb, aor. act. indic. 3 pers. sg. {5.A.1.b} . . . . id.

προέλαβε   verb, ²aor. act. indic. 3 pers. sg. {5.A.1.b} . . . . προλαμβάνω G4301

προέλαβεν   verb, ²aor. act. indic. 3 pers. sg. {5.A.1.b} . . . . id.

προελέγομεν   verb, impf. act. indic. 1 pers. pl. {5.A.1.b} . . . . προλέγω G4302

προελεύσεται   verb, fut. mid. indic. 3 pers. sg. {5.A.1.d} . . . . προέρχομαι G4281

προελθόντες   vbl., ²aor. act. ptc. nom. pl. masc. {6.A.1.a} . . . . id.

προελθών   vbl., ²aor. act. ptc. nom. sg. masc. {6.A.1.a} . . . . id.

προέλθωσιν   verb, ²aor. act. subjunc. 3 pers. pl. {5.B.1} . . . . id.

G4276 **προελπίζω**   *I hope before another, I am the first to hope.*

G4278 **προενάρχομαι**   *I begin earlier (previously).*

προενήρξασθε   verb, aor. mid. indic. 2 pers. pl. {5.A.1.e} . . . . προενάρχομαι G4278

προενήρξατο   verb, aor. mid. indic. 3 pers. sg. {5.A.1.e} . . . . id.

G4279 **προεπαγγέλλω**   mid. *I promise beforehand.*

προέπεμπον   verb, impf. act. indic. 3 pers. pl. {5.A.1.b} . . . . προπέμπω G4311

προεπηγγείλατο   verb, aor. mid. indic. 3 pers. sg. {5.A.1.e} . . . . προεπαγγέλλω G4279

προεπηγγελμένην   vbl., perf. mid./pass. ptc. acc. sg. fem. {6.A.1.b} . . . . id.

G4281 **προέρχομαι**   (1) intrans., *I go in front (before);* sometimes with acc. of distance covered, Acts 12:10; (2) trans., *I precede,* Mark 6:33; Luke 22:47.

G4280‡ **προερῶ**   fut. of προοράω.

προεστῶτες   vbl., ²perf. act. ptc. nom. pl. masc. {6.A.3} . . . . προΐστημι G4291

προέτειναν   verb, aor. act. indic. 3 pers. pl. {5.A.1.b} . . . . προτείνω G4385

προέτεινεν   verb, aor. act. indic. 3 pers. sg. {5.A.1.b} . . . . id.

G4282 **προετοιμάζω**   *I prepare beforehand.*

G4283 **προευαγγελίζομαι**   *I proclaim the good news beforehand.*

προευηγγελίσατο   verb, aor. mid. indic. 3 pers. sg.
{5.A.1.e} . . . . .προευαγγελίζομαι G4283
προεφήτευον   verb, impf. act. indic. 3 pers. pl.
{5.A.1.b} . . . . .προφητεύω G4395
προεφητεύσαμεν   verb, aor. act. indic. 1 pers.
pl. {5.A.1.b} . . . . id.
προεφήτευσαν   verb, aor. act. indic. 3 pers. pl.
{5.A.1.b} . . . . id.
προεφήτευσε   verb, aor. act. indic. 3 pers. sg.
{5.A.1.b} . . . . id.
προεφήτευσεν   verb, aor. act. indic. 3 pers. sg.
{5.A.1.b} . . . . id.
προέφθασεν   verb, aor. act. indic. 3 pers. sg.
{5.A.1.b} . . . . προφθάνω G4399
προεχειρίσατο   verb, aor. mid. indic. 3 pers. sg.
{5.A.1.e} . . . . .προχειρίζω G4400
προεχόμεθα   verb, pres. mid./pass. indic. 1 pers.
pl. {5.A.1.d} . . . . προέχω G4284
G4284 προέχω   *I excel, surpass; pass.* in Rom 3:9.
προεωρακότες   vbl., perf. act. ptc. nom. pl. masc.
{6.A.2} .προοράω G4308
προήγαγον   verb, ²aor. act. indic. 1 pers. sg.
{5.A.1.b} . . . . προάγω G4254
προῆγεν   verb, impf. act. indic. 3 pers. sg. {5.A.1.b} id.
G4285 προηγέομαι   *I lead in front, I give a lead to.*
προηγούμενοι   vbl., pres. mid./pass. ptc. nom. pl.
masc. {6.A.2} . . . . προηγέομαι G4285
προηκούσατε   verb, aor. act. indic. 2 pers. pl.
{5.A.1.b} . . . . προακούω G4257
προῆλθον   verb, ²aor. act. indic. 3 pers. pl.
{5.A.1.b} . . . . προέρχομαι G4281
προηλπικότας   vbl., perf. act. ptc. acc. pl. masc.
{6.A.1.a} . . . . προελπίζω G4276
προημαρτηκόσι   vbl., perf. act. ptc. dat. pl. masc.
{6.A.1.a} . . . . προαμαρτάνω G4258
προημαρτηκόσιν   vbl., perf. act. ptc. dat. pl.
masc. {6.A.1.a} . . . . id.
προημαρτηκότων   vbl., perf. act. ptc. gen. pl.
masc. {6.A.1.a} . . . . id.
προῄρηται   verb, perf. mid. indic. 3 pers. sg.
{5.A.1} . . . . προαιρέω G4255
προήρχετο   verb, impf. mid./pass. indic. 3 pers. sg.
{5.A.1.e} . . . . προέρχομαι G4281
προητιασάμεθα   verb, aor. mid. indic. 1 pers. pl.
{5.A.1} . . . . .προαιτιάομαι G4256
προητοίμασεν   verb, aor. act. indic. 3 pers. sg.
{5.A.1.b} . . . . προετοιμάζω G4282
προθέσει   noun, dat. sg. fem. {2.C} . . . . .πρόθεσις G4286
προθέσεως   noun, gen. sg. fem. {2.C} . . . . id.
πρόθεσιν   noun, acc. sg. fem. {2.C} . . . . id.
G4286 πρόθεσις, -εως, ἡ   (1) οἱ ἄρτοι τῆς
προθέσεως, lit. *the loaves of the laying out*
(*before* God), i.e., *the loaves laid out,* Graecized
in Heb 9:2, ἡ πρόθεσις τῶν ἄρτων (Heb.);
(2) *deliberate purpose (plan, scheme).*
πρόθεσις   noun, nom. sg. fem. {2.C} . . . .πρόθεσις G4286
G4287 προθεσμία, -ας, ἡ   *a term* (or *age, date*) *previously indicated (fixed, laid down).*
προθεσμίας   noun, gen. sg. fem. {2.A} . προθεσμία G4287
G4288 προθυμία, -ας, ἡ   *eagerness, zeal, enthusiasm.*

προθυμία   noun, nom. sg. fem. {2.A} . . . προθυμία G4288
προθυμίαν   noun, acc. sg. fem. {2.A} . . . . id.
προθυμίας   noun, gen. sg. fem. {2.A} . . . . id.
πρόθυμον   adj., nom. sg. neut. {3.C} . . . πρόθυμος G4289
G4289 πρόθυμος, -ον   *eager;* in Rom 1:15 τὸ κατ᾽
ἐμὲ πρόθυμον may be = ἡ ἐμὲ προθυμία,
my good will, but perhaps it is better to
read πρόθυμος (supply εἰμί) with some
authorities.
G4290 προθύμως   adv., *eagerly.*
προθύμως   adv. {3.F} . . . . .προθύμως G4290
προϊδοῦσα   vbl., ²aor. act. ptc. nom. sg. fem.
{6.A.2} .προοράω G4308
προιδών   vbl., ²aor. act. ptc. nom. sg. masc.
{6.A.2} . . . . id.
προϊδών   vbl., ²aor. act. ptc. nom. sg. masc.
{6.A.2} . . . . id.
πρόϊμον   adj., acc. sg. masc. {3.C} . . . . . . πρώϊμος G4406
προϊστάμενοι   vbl., pres. mid. ptc. nom. pl. masc.
{6.A.3} .προΐστημι G4291
προϊστάμενον   vbl., pres. mid. ptc. acc. sg.
masc. {6.A.3} . . . . id.
προϊστάμενος   vbl., pres. mid. ptc. nom. sg.
masc. {6.A.3} . . . . id.
προϊσταμένους   vbl., pres. mid. ptc. acc. pl.
masc. {6.A.3} . . . . id.
προΐστασθαι   vbl., pres. mid. inf. {6.B.3} . . . . . id.
G4291 προΐστημι   in intrans. tenses, *I take up a
position (stand) in front; I take the lead, I rule;*
hence, with gen. *I lead, supervise, manage;* also
I practice, exercise a calling or profession.
G4292 προκαλέω   mid. *I call forth, challenge.*
προκαλούμενοι   vbl., pres. mid. ptc. nom. pl.
masc. {6.A.2} . . . . .προκαλέω G4292
προκαταγγείλαντας   vbl., aor. act. ptc. acc. pl.
masc. {6.A.1.a} . . . . .προκαταγγέλλω G4293
G4293 προκαταγγέλλω   *I announce beforehand.*
G4294 προκαταρτίζω   *I prepare (arrange) beforehand.*
προκαταρτίσωσι   verb, aor. act. subjunc. 3 pers.
pl. {5.B.1} . . . . προκαταρτίζω G4294
προκαταρτίσωσιν   verb, aor. act. subjunc.
3 pers. pl. {5.B.1} . . . . id.
προκατήγγειλαν   verb, aor. act. indic. 3 pers. pl.
{5.A.1.b} . . . . προκαταγγέλλω G4293
προκατήγγειλε   verb, aor. act. indic. 3 pers. sg.
{5.A.1.b} . . . . id.
προκατήγγειλεν   verb, aor. act. indic. 3 pers.
sg. {5.A.1.b} . . . . id.
προκατηγγελμένην   vbl., perf. pass. ptc. acc.
sg. fem. {6.A.1.b} . . . . id.
G4295 πρόκειμαι   *I am set (placed, put) before, I am
already there.*
προκειμένης   vbl., pres. mid./pass. ptc. gen. sg.
fem. {6.A.3} . . . . .πρόκειμαι G4295
προκείμενον   vbl., pres. mid./pass. ptc. acc. sg.
masc. {6.A.3} . . . . id.
πρόκεινται   verb, pres. mid./pass. indic. 3 pers.
pl. {5.A.3.a} . . . . id.
πρόκειται   verb, pres. mid./pass. indic. 3 pers.
sg. {5.A.3.a} . . . . id.

προκεκηρυγμένον   vbl., perf. pass. ptc. acc. sg. masc. {6.A.1.b} . . . . προκηρύσσω *G4296*

προκεκυρωμένην   vbl., perf. pass. ptc. acc. sg. fem. {6.A.2} . . . . .προκυρόω *G4300*

προκεχειρισμένον   vbl., perf. mid./pass. ptc. acc. sg. masc. {6.A.1.b} . . . . .προχειρίζω *G4400*

προκεχειροτονημένοις   vbl., perf. pass. ptc. dat. pl. masc. {6.A.2} . . . . προχειροτονέω *G4401*

προκηρύξαντος   vbl., aor. act. ptc. gen. sg. masc. {6.A.1.a} . . . . προκηρύσσω *G4296*

G4296 **προκηρύσσω**   *I proclaim previously.*

G4297 **προκοπή**, -ῆς, ἡ   *progress, advance.*
προκοπή   noun, nom. sg. fem. {2.A} . . . . προκοπή *G4297*
προκοπήν   noun, acc. sg. fem. {2.A} . . . . id.

G4298 **προκόπτω**   *I advance, progress, make progress* (originally of the pioneer cutting his way through brushwood).
προκόψουσιν   verb, fut. act. indic. 3 pers. pl. {5.A.1.a} . . . . προκόπτω *G4298*

G4299 **πρόκριμα**, -ατος, τό   *prejudgment* (favorable or unfavorable).
προκρίματος   noun, gen. sg. neut. {2.C}   πρόκριμα *G4299*

G4300 **προκυρόω**   *I make valid beforehand.*
προλαμβάνει   verb, pres. act. indic. 3 pers. sg. {5.A.1.a} . . . . προλαμβάνω *G4301*

G4301 **προλαμβάνω**   (1) *I take before* another (perhaps); *I am in a hurry to take, I take eagerly, I seize,* 1 Cor 11:21; (2) προέλαβεν μυρίσαι, *has by anticipation anointed* (perhaps an Aramaism), Mark 14:8; (3) *I catch, capture, overtake* (*before* he can escape).

G4302 **προλέγω**   *I tell* (say) *beforehand, I predict.* ²aor. προεῖπον; perf. προείρηκα.
προλέγω   verb, pres. act. indic. 1 pers. sg. {5.A.1.a} . . . . προλέγω *G4302*
προλημφθῇ   verb, aor. pass. subjunc. 3 pers. sg. {5.B.1} . . . . προλαμβάνω *G4301*
προληφθῇ   verb, aor. pass. subjunc. 3 pers. sg. {5.B.1} . . . . id.

G4303 **προμαρτύρομαι**   *I call* (God) *beforehand to witness.*
προμαρτυρόμενον   vbl., pres. mid./pass. ptc. nom. sg. neut. {6.A.1} . . . . προμαρτύρομαι *G4303*
προμελετᾶν   vbl., pres. act. inf. {6.B.2} . . . . προμελετάω *G4304*
προμελετᾶν   vbl., pres. act. inf. {6.B.2} . . . . id.

G4304 **προμελετάω**   *I practice beforehand, I prepare, I get up.*
προμεριμνᾶτε   verb, pres. act. impv. 2 pers. pl. {5.D.2} . . . . προμεριμνάω *G4305*

G4305 **προμεριμνάω**   *I am anxious beforehand.*
προνοεῖ   verb, pres. act. indic. 3 pers. sg. {5.A.2} . . . . προνοέω *G4306*

G4306 **προνοέω**   act. and mid., *I take thought for beforehand, I provide for.*

G4307 **πρόνοια**, -ας, ἡ   *forethought, foresight;* πρόνοιαν ποιοῦμαι = προνοέω.
πρόνοιαν   noun, acc. sg. fem. {2.A} . . . . πρόνοια *G4307*
προνοίας   noun, gen. sg. fem. {2.A} . . . . id.

προνοοῦμεν   verb, pres. act. indic. 1 pers. pl. {5.A.2} . . . . προνοέω *G4306*
προνοούμενοι   vbl., pres. mid. ptc. nom. pl. masc. {6.A.2} . . . . id.

G4308 **προοράω**   *I see beforehand, I foresee, I see previously,* Acts 21:29; mid. *I pay regard to, set before me,* Acts 2:25. ²aor., προεῖδον.

G4309 **προορίζω**   *I foreordain* (lit. *I bound* or *limit beforehand*).
προορίσας   vbl., aor. act. ptc. nom. sg. masc. {6.A.1.a} . . . . προορίζω *G4309*
προορισθέντες   vbl., aor. pass. ptc. nom. pl. masc. {6.A.1.a} . . . . id.
προωρώμην   verb, impf. mid. indic. 1 pers. sg. {5.A.2} . . . . .προοράω *G4308*
προπαθόντες   vbl., ²aor. act. ptc. nom. pl. masc. {6.A.1.a} . . . . προπάσχω *G4310*

G4310 **προπάσχω**   *I suffer previously.*
προπάτορα   noun, acc. sg. masc. {2.C}προπάτωρ *G3962†‡*

G3962†‡ **προπάτωρ**, -ορος, ὁ   *a forefather.* Var. for πατήρ, Rom. 4:1.
προπεμπόντων   vbl., pres. act. ptc. gen. pl. masc. {6.A.1} . . . . .προπέμπω *G4311*

G4311 **προπέμπω**   (1) *I send in front* (forth, forward), *set forward, start on their way* (in Titus 3:13, of being provided with necessaries for the journey); (2) *I convoy, I escort on* (his, etc.) *way,* as a mark of affection and respect, Acts 15:3; 20:38; 21:5; Rom 15:24; 3 John 6.
προπεμφθέντες   vbl., aor. pass. ptc. nom. pl. masc. {6.A.1.a} . . . . .προπέμπω *G4311*
προπεμφθῆναι   vbl., aor. pass. inf. {6.B.1} . . . . . id.
προπέμψας   vbl., aor. act. ptc. nom. sg. masc. {6.A.1.a} . . . . id.
προπέμψατε   verb, aor. act. impv. 2 pers. pl. {5.D.1} . . . . id.
προπέμψητε   verb, aor. act. subjunc. 2 pers. pl. {5.B.1} . . . . id.
πρόπεμψον   verb, aor. act. impv. 2 pers. sg. {5.D.1} . . . . id.
προπετεῖς   adj., nom. pl. masc. {3.E} . . . προπετής *G4312*
προπετές   adj., acc. sg. neut. {3.E} . . . . id.

G4312 **προπετής**, -ές, gen. οὖς   *impulsive, rash, reckless* (of thoughtless haste).

G4313 **προπορεύομαι**   *I journey in front, I go before.*
προπορεύσῃ   verb, fut. mid. indic. 2 pers. sg. {5.A.1.d} . . . . προπορεύομαι *G4313*
προπορεύσονται   verb, fut. mid. indic. 3 pers. pl. {5.A.1.d} . . . . id.

G4314 **πρός**   prep. (1) with gen., *on the side of, in the interests of, for* (literary), Acts 27:34; (2) with dat., *close to, close by, near, at*; (3) with acc. (of persons, places, things), (a) *to,* with verbs of coming, sending, bringing, saying; (b) *near,* after the verb "to be," etc. (instead of παρά τινι); (c) *near,* instead of παρά, Acts 5:10, *into the house of,* Acts 11:3; (d) of time, *near,* Luke 24:29; *for* (a time), and no longer, Luke 8:13; John 5:35; Heb 12:10, etc.; (e) of hostile or friendly relations, *with,* μάχεσθαι, εἰρήνην ἔχειν, etc.; τί πρὸς ἡμᾶς; *what have we to do with it?* Matt 27:4; John 21:22; *with reference to, of,* Mark 12:12; cf. 10:5; Matt 19:8; Luke 12:41; 18:1; 20:19; John 13:28, etc.; (f) with ἀγαθός, ὠφέλιμος, δυνατός, etc., *for,* 2 Cor 10:4; Eph 4:29; 1 Tim 4:8, where it indicates also the destination, purpose, result, e.g., Luke 14:32; 19:42; John 4:35; 11:4 (cf. John 5:16, 17); Acts 3:10; (g) *in conformity with, according to,* Luke 12:47; 1 Cor 12:7; 2 Cor 5:10; *with respect to,* Heb 1:7, 8; (h) *in comparison with,* Rom 8:18.

πρός   prep. .... πρός *G4314*

G4315 **προσάββατον**, -ου, τό *the day before the Sabbath,* i.e., from 6:00 p.m. on Thursday to 6:00 p.m. on Friday.

προσάββατον noun, nom. sg. neut.
{2.B} .... προσάββατον *G4315*
προσάγαγε verb, ²aor. act. impv. 2 pers. sg.
{5.D.1} .... προσάγω *G4317*
προσαγαγεῖν vbl., ²aor. act. inf. {6.B.1} .... id.
προσαγάγῃ verb, ²aor. act. subjunc. 3 pers. sg.
{5.B.1} .... id.
προσαγαγόντες vbl., ²aor. act. ptc. nom. pl.
masc. {6.A.1.a} .... id.
προσάγειν vbl., pres. act. inf. {6.B.1} .... id.
προσαγορευθείς vbl., aor. pass. ptc. nom. sg.
masc. {6.A.1.a} .... προσαγορεύω *G4316*

G4316 **προσαγορεύω** *I designate as* by addressing by a certain title; *I recognize as.*

G4317 **προσάγω** (1) *I lead to, I bring to;* characteristically, *I bring* a subj. *into the presence of* a king, *I present to, I introduce,* 1 Pet 3:18; (2) intrans., *I approach,* Acts 27:27 (var.).

G4318 **προσαγωγή**, -ῆς, ἡ *access, entrée,* or perhaps a metaphor from the concr. sense *landing stage.*

προσαγωγήν noun, acc. sg. fem. {2.A} προσαγωγή *G4318*

G4319 **προσαιτέω** *I beg, I am a beggar.*

G4319† **προσαίτης**, -ου, ὁ *a beggar.* Var. for προσαιτέω, Mark 10:46; John 9:8.

προσαίτης noun, nom. sg. masc.
{2.A} .... προσαίτης *G4319†*
προσαιτῶν vbl., pres. act. ptc. nom. sg. masc.
{6.A.2} .... προσαιτέω *G4319*

G4320 **προσαναβαίνω** *I go up to, I come up to.*

προσανάβηθι verb, ²aor. act. impv. 2 pers. sg.
{5.D.1} .... προσαναβαίνω *G4320*

G4321 **προσαναλόω** (προσαναλίσκω) *I spend in addition.*

προσαναλώσασα vbl., aor. act. ptc. nom. sg. fem.
{6.A.2} .... προσαναλόω *G4321*
προσαναπληροῦσα vbl., pres. act. ptc. nom. sg.
fem. {6.A.2} .... προσαναπληρόω *G4322*

G4322 **προσαναπληρόω** *I fill up by adding, make up, supply.*

G4323 **προσανατίθημι** mid. (1) *I add, contribute;* (2) *I consult with, turn (have recourse) to.*

προσανεθέμην verb, ²aor. mid. indic. 1 pers. sg.
{5.A.3.b} .... προσανατίθημι *G4323*
προσανέθεντο verb, ²aor. mid. indic. 3 pers.
pl. {5.A.3.b} .... id.

προσανεπλήρωσαν verb, aor. act. indic. 3 pers.
pl. {5.A.1} .... προσαναπληρόω *G4322*

G4324 **προσαπειλέω** mid. *I threaten further, in addition.*

προσαπειλησάμενοι vbl., aor. mid. ptc. nom. pl.
masc. {6.A.2} .... προσαπειλέω *G4324*

G4325 **προσδαπανάω** *I spend in addition.*

προσδαπανήσῃς verb, aor. act. subjunc. 2 pers.
sg. {5.B.1} .... προσδαπανάω *G4325*
προσδεξάμενοι vbl., aor. mid. ptc. nom. pl. masc.
{6.A.1.b} .... προσδέχομαι *G4327*
προσδέξησθε verb, aor. mid. subjunc. 2 pers.
pl. {5.B.1} .... id.

G4326 **προσδέομαι** *I need (have need of) something additional.*

προσδεόμενος vbl., pres. mid./pass. ptc. nom. sg.
masc. {6.A.2} .... προσδέομαι *G4326*
προσδέχεσθε verb, pres. mid./pass. impv. 2 pers.
pl. {5.D.1} .... προσδέχομαι *G4327*
προσδέχεται verb, pres. mid./pass. indic.
3 pers. sg. {5.A.1.d} .... id.

G4327 **προσδέχομαι** (1) *I await, expect;* (2) *I receive, welcome* (orig. *to* my house), e.g., Luke 15:2; Rom 16:2; Phil 2:29; (3) *I accept,* Acts 24:15.

προσδεχόμενοι vbl., pres. mid./pass. ptc. nom. pl.
masc. {6.A.1} .... προσδέχομαι *G4327*
προσδεχομένοις vbl., pres. mid./pass. ptc. dat.
pl. masc. {6.A.1} .... id.
προσδεχομένῳ vbl., pres. mid./pass. ptc.
nom. sg. masc. {6.A.1} .... id.
προσδέχονται verb, pres. mid./pass. indic.
3 pers. pl. {5.A.1.d} .... id.
προσδοκᾷ verb, pres. act. indic. 3 pers. sg.
{5.A.2} .... προσδοκάω *G4328*

G4328 **προσδοκάω** *I expect, wait for, await.*

G4329 **προσδοκία**, -ας, ἡ *expectation, waiting.*

προσδοκίας noun, gen. sg. fem. {2.A} προσδοκία *G4329*
προσδοκῶμεν verb, pres. act. indic. 1 pers. pl.
{5.A.2} .... προσδοκάω *G4328*
προσδοκῶν vbl., pres. act. ptc. nom. sg. masc.
{6.A.2} .... id.
προσδοκῶντας vbl., pres. act. ptc. acc. pl.
masc. {6.A.2} .... id.
προσδοκῶντες vbl., pres. act. ptc. nom. pl.
masc. {6.A.2} .... id.
προσδοκῶντος vbl., pres. act. ptc. gen. sg.
masc. {6.A.2} .... id.
προσδοκώντων vbl., pres. act. ptc. gen. pl.
masc. {6.A.2} .... id.
προσδραμών vbl., ²aor. act. ptc. nom. sg. masc.
{6.A.1.a} .... προστρέχω *G4370*

G4330 **προσεάω** *I permit* to go straight *onwards.*

G4331 **προσεγγίζω** *I come near to, I approach.*

προσεγγίσαι vbl., aor. act. inf. {6.B.1} προσεγγίζω *G4331*
προσεδέξασθε verb, aor. mid. indic. 2 pers. pl.
{5.A.1.e} .... προσδέχομαι *G4327*
προσεδέχετο verb, impf. mid./pass. indic.
3 pers. sg. {5.A.1.e} .... id.
προσεδόκων verb, impf. act. indic. 3 pers. pl.
{5.A.2} .... προσδοκάω *G4328*

προσεδρεύοντες   vbl., pres. act. ptc. nom. pl.
    masc. {6.A.1}. . . . . .προσεδρεύω *G4332*
G4332 **προσεδρεύω**   *I serve, I wait upon.*
προσέθετο   verb, ²aor. mid. indic. 3 pers. sg.
    {5.A.3.b} . . . . .προστίθημι *G4369*
προσέθηκε   verb, aor. act. indic. 3 pers. sg.
    {5.A.3.b} . . . . id.
προσέθηκεν   verb, aor. act. indic. 3 pers. sg.
    {5.A.3.b} . . . . id.
προσειργάσατο   verb, aor. mid. indic. 3 pers. sg.
    {5.A.1.e} . . . . προσεργάζομαι *G4333*
προσεῖχον   verb, impf. act. indic. 3 pers. pl.
    {5.A.1.b} . . . . προσέχω *G4337*
προσεκαλέσατο   verb, aor. mid. indic. 3 pers. sg.
    {5.A.1}. . . . . προσκαλέω *G4341*
προσεκλήθη   verb, aor. pass. indic. 3 pers. sg.
    {5.A.1}. . . . . id.
προσεκληρώθησαν   verb, aor. pass. indic. 3 pers.
    pl. {5.A.1} . . . . προσκληρόω *G4345*
προσεκλίθη   verb, aor. pass. indic. 3 pers. sg.
    {5.A.1.b} . . . . .προσκλίνω *G4347*†‡
προσεκολλήθη   verb, aor. pass. indic. 3 pers. sg.
    {5.A.1} . . . . προσκολλάω *G4347*
προσέκοψαν   verb, aor. act. indic. 3 pers. pl.
    {5.A.1.b} . . . . .προσκόπτω *G4350*
προσεκύλισε   verb, aor. act. indic. 3 pers. sg.
    {5.A.1.b} . . . . .προσκυλίω *G4351*
προσεκύλισεν   verb, aor. act. indic. 3 pers. sg.
    {5.A.1.b} . . . . id.
προσεκύνει   verb, impf. act. indic. 3 pers. sg.
    {5.A.2} . . . . .προσκυνέω *G4352*
προσεκύνησαν   verb, aor. act. indic. 3 pers. pl.
    {5.A.1}. . . . . id.
προσεκύνησεν   verb, aor. act. indic. 3 pers. sg.
    {5.A.1}. . . . . id.
προσεκύνουν   verb, impf. act. indic. 3 pers. pl.
    {5.A.2}. . . . . id.
προσελάβετο   verb, ²aor. mid. indic. 3 pers. sg.
    {5.A.1.e} . . . . προσλαμβάνω *G4355*
προσελάβοντο   verb, ²aor. mid. indic. 3 pers.
    pl. {5.A.1.e} . . . . id.
προσεληλύθατε   verb, ²perf. act. indic. 2 pers.
    {5.A.1.c} . . . . προσέρχομαι *G4334*
πρόσελθε   verb, ²aor. act. impv. 2 pers. sg. {5.D.1} id.
προσελθόντες   vbl., ²aor. act. ptc. nom. pl.
    masc. {6.A.1.a}. id.
προσελθόντων   vbl., ²aor. act. ptc. gen. pl.
    masc. {6.A.1.a}. id.
προσελθοῦσα   vbl., ²aor. act. ptc. nom. sg. fem.
    {6.A.1.a} . . . . id.
προσελθοῦσαι   vbl., ²aor. act. ptc. nom. pl.
    fem. {6.A.1.a}. . . . . id.
προσελθών   vbl., ²aor. act. ptc. nom. sg. masc.
    {6.A.1.a} . . . . id.
προσενέγκαι   vbl., ²aor. act. inf. {6.B.1} .προσφέρω *G4374*
προσενέγκας   vbl., aor. act. ptc. nom. sg. masc.
    {6.A.1.a} . . . . id.
προσένεγκε   verb, ²aor. act. impv. 2 pers. sg.
    {5.D.1}. . . . . id.

προσενέγκῃ   verb, aor. act. subjunc. 3 pers. sg.
    {5.B.1} . . . . id.
προσένεγκον   verb, ²aor. act. impv. 2 pers. sg.
    {5.D.1}. . . . . id.
προσενεχθείς   vbl., aor. pass. ptc. nom. sg.
    masc. {6.A.1.a}. id.
προσενήνοχεν   verb, ²perf. act. indic. 3 pers.
    sg. {5.A.1.c} . . . . id.
προσέπεσαν   verb, aor. act. indic. 3 pers. pl.
    {5.A.1.b} . . . . προσπίπτω *G4363*
προσέπεσε   verb, ²aor. act. indic. 3 pers. sg.
    {5.A.1.b} . . . . id.
προσέπεσεν   verb, ²aor. act. indic. 3 pers. sg.
    {5.A.1.b} . . . . id.
προσέπεσον   verb, ²aor. act. indic. 3 pers. pl.
    {5.A.1.b} . . . . id.
προσέπιπτεν   verb, impf. act. indic. 3 pers. sg.
    {5.A.1.b} . . . . id.
προσέπιπτον   verb, impf. act. indic. 3 pers. pl.
    {5.A.1.b} . . . . id.
προσεποιεῖτο   verb, impf. mid. indic. 3 pers. sg.
    {5.A.2} . . . . προσποιέω *G4364*
προσεποιήσατο   verb, aor. mid. indic. 3 pers.
    sg. {5.A.1} . . . . id.
G4333 **προσεργάζομαι**   *I produce in addition, I gain.*
προσέρηξεν   verb, aor. act. indic. 3 pers. sg.
    {5.A.3.b} . . . . προσρήσσω *G4366*
προσέρρηξεν   verb, aor. act. indic. 3 pers. sg.
    {5.A.3.b} . . . . id.
προσέρχεσθαι   vbl., pres. mid./pass. inf.
    {6.B.1} . . . . προσέρχομαι *G4334*
προσέρχεται   verb, pres. mid./pass. indic.
    3 pers. sg. {5.A.1.d} . . . . id.
G4334 **προσέρχομαι**   *I come up to, I come to; I come*
    near (to), I approach; I consent (to), 1 Tim 6:3.
προσερχόμενοι   vbl., pres. mid./pass. ptc. nom. pl.
    masc. {6.A.1}. . . . . προσέρχομαι *G4334*
προσερχόμενον   vbl., pres. mid./pass. ptc. acc.
    sg. masc. {6.A.1} . . . . id.
προσερχομένου   vbl., pres. mid./pass. ptc. gen.
    sg. masc. {6.A.1} . . . . id.
προσερχομένους   vbl., pres. mid./pass. ptc.
    acc. pl. masc. {6.A.1} . . . . id.
προσέρχονται   verb, pres. mid./pass. indic.
    3 pers. pl. {5.A.1.d} . . . . id.
προσερχώμεθα   verb, pres. mid./pass. subjunc.
    1 pers. pl. {5.B.1} . . . . id.
προσέσχηκε   verb, perf. act. indic. 3 pers. sg.
    {5.A.1.c} . . . . προσέχω *G4337*
προσέσχηκεν   verb, perf. act. indic. 3 pers. sg.
    {5.A.1.c} . . . . id.
προσέταξε   verb, aor. act. indic. 3 pers. sg.
    {5.A.1.b} . . . . προστάσσω *G4367*
προσέταξεν   verb, aor. act. indic. 3 pers. sg.
    {5.A.1.b} . . . . id.
προσετέθη   verb, aor. pass. indic. 3 pers. sg.
    {5.A.1}. . . . . προστίθημι *G4369*
προσετέθησαν   verb, aor. pass. indic. 3 pers.
    pl. {5.A.1} . . . . id.

προσετίθει   verb, impf. act. indic. 3 pers. sg.
{5.A.3.a} . . . . id.
προσετίθεντο   verb, impf. pass. indic. 3 pers.
pl. {5.A.3.a} . . . . id.
πρόσευξαι   verb, aor. mid. impv. 2 pers. sg.
{5.D.1} . . . . προσεύχομαι *G4336*
προσευξάμενοι   vbl., aor. mid. ptc. nom. pl.
masc. {6.A.1.b} . . . . id.
προσευξάμενος   vbl., aor. mid. ptc. nom. sg.
masc. {6.A.1.b} . . . . id.
προσεύξασθαι   vbl., aor. mid. inf. {6.B.1} . . . . . id.
προσευξάσθωσαν   verb, aor. mid. impv.
3 pers. pl. {5.D.1} . . . . id.
προσεύξηται   verb, aor. mid. subjunc. 3 pers.
sg. {5.B.1} . . . . id.
προσεύξομαι   verb, fut. mid. indic. 1 pers. sg.
{5.A.1.d} . . . . id.
προσευξόμεθα   verb, fut. mid. indic. 1 pers. pl.
{5.A.1.d} . . . . id.
προσεύξωμαι   verb, aor. mid. subjunc. 1 pers.
sg. {5.B.1} . . . . id.
προσευξώμεθα   verb, aor. mid. subjunc. 1 pers.
pl. {5.B.1} . . . . id.
προσευχαί   noun, nom. pl. fem. {2.A} . . προσευχή *G4335*
προσευχαῖς   noun, dat. pl. fem. {2.A} . . . . id.
προσευχάς   noun, acc. pl. fem. {2.A} . . . . id.
προσεύχεσθαι   vbl., pres. mid./pass. inf.
{6.B.1} . . . . προσεύχομαι *G4336*
προσεύχεσθε   verb, pres. mid./pass. impv.
2 pers. pl. {5.D.1} . . . . id.
προσεύχεσθε   verb, pres. mid./pass. indic.
2 pers. pl. {5.A.1.d} . . . . id.
προσευχέσθω   verb, pres. mid./pass. impv.
3 pers. sg. {5.D.1} . . . . id.
προσεύχεται   verb, pres. mid./pass. indic.
3 pers. sg. {5.A.1.d} . . . . id.

G4335 **προσευχή**, -ῆς, ἡ   (1) *prayer* (to God); τοῦ
θεοῦ, *to God,* Luke 6:12; (2) *a place for prayer,*
Acts 16:13 (used by Jews, perhaps where there
was no synagogue).
προσευχή   noun, nom. sg. fem. {2.A} . . προσευχή *G4335*
προσευχῇ   noun, dat. sg. fem. {2.A} . . . . id.
προσεύχῃ   verb, pres. mid./pass. subjunc. 2 pers.
sg. {5.B.1} . . . . προσεύχομαι *G4336*
προσευχήν   noun, acc. sg. fem. {2.A} . . . προσευχή *G4335*
προσευχῆς   noun, gen. sg. fem. {2.A} . . . . id.
προσεύχησθε   verb, pres. mid./pass. subjunc.
2 pers. pl. {5.B.1} . . . . προσεύχομαι *G4336*

G4336 **προσεύχομαι**   *I pray;* with acc., *I pray for;*
sometimes with Hebraistic tautology, προ-
σευχῇ or διὰ προσευχῆς is added.
προσεύχομαι   verb, pres. mid./pass. indic. 1 pers.
sg. {5.A.1.d} . . . . προσεύχομαι *G4336*
προσευχόμεθα   verb, pres. mid./pass. indic.
1 pers. pl. {5.A.1.d} . . . . id.
προσευχομένη   vbl., pres. mid./pass. ptc. nom.
sg. fem. {6.A.1} . . . . id.
προσευχόμενοι   vbl., pres. mid./pass. ptc.
nom. pl. masc. {6.A.1} . . . . id.

προσευχόμενον   vbl., pres. mid./pass. ptc. acc.
sg. masc. {6.A.1} . . . . id.
προσευχόμενον   vbl., pres. mid./pass. ptc.
nom. sg. neut. {6.A.1} . . . . id.
προσευχόμενος   vbl., pres. mid./pass. ptc.
nom. sg. masc. {6.A.1} . . . . id.
προσευχομένου   vbl., pres. mid./pass. ptc. gen.
sg. masc. {6.A.1} . . . . id.
προσεύχονται   verb, pres. mid./pass. indic.
3 pers. pl. {5.A.1.d} . . . . id.
προσεύχωμαι   verb, pres. mid./pass. subjunc.
1 pers. sg. {5.B.1} . . . . id.
προσευχῶν   noun, gen. pl. fem. {2.A} . . προσευχή *G4335*
προσέφερεν   verb, impf. act. indic. 3 pers. sg.
{5.A.1.b} . . . . προσφέρω *G4374*
προσέφερον   verb, impf. act. indic. 3 pers. pl.
{5.A.1.b} . . . . id.
προσεφώνει   verb, impf. act. indic. 3 pers. sg.
{5.A.2} . . . . προσφωνέω *G4377*
προσεφώνησε   verb, aor. act. indic. 3 pers. sg.
{5.A.1} . . . . id.
προσεφώνησεν   verb, aor. act. indic. 3 pers. sg.
{5.A.1} . . . . id.
πρόσεχε   verb, pres. act. impv. 2 pers. sg.
{5.D.1} . . . . προσέχω *G4337*
προσέχειν   vbl., pres. act. inf. {6.B.1} . . . . id.
προσέχετε   verb, pres. act. impv. 2 pers. pl.
{5.D.1} . . . . id.
προσέχοντας   vbl., pres. act. ptc. acc. pl. masc.
{6.A.1} . . . . id.
προσέχοντες   vbl., pres. act. ptc. nom. pl. masc.
{6.A.1} . . . . id.

G4337 **προσέχω**   (1) *I attend to, pay attention to,* with
dat., Acts 8:6; 16:14, etc. (τὸν νοῦν was originally added, *I direct the mind*), cf. (3); (2) with
ἐμαυτῷ, or absol., *I attend to myself, I pay attention for myself,* Hebraism for *I am cautious,
I beware, I take care for (of) myself,* Luke 17:3;
Acts 5:35, with ἀπό governing the thing *of*
which one has to beware, Matt 7:15; Luke 12:1,
etc.; so with μή, *lest;* (3) supply ἐμαυτόν, *I
attach myself to, I join,* Acts 8:10; 1 Tim 4:1;
I devote myself to (by way of enjoyment or of
work), 1 Tim 1:4; 3:8; 4:13; Titus 1:14; Heb
7:13.
προσεῶντος   vbl., pres. act. ptc. gen. sg. masc.
{6.A.2} . . . . προσεάω *G4330*
προσῆλθαν   verb, ²aor. act. indic. 3 pers. pl.
{5.A.1.b} . . . . προσέρχομαι *G4334*
προσῆλθε   verb, ²aor. act. indic. 3 pers. sg.
{5.A.1.b} . . . . id.
προσῆλθεν   verb, ²aor. act. indic. 3 pers. sg.
{5.A.1.b} . . . . id.
προσῆλθον   verb, ²aor. act. indic. 3 pers. pl.
{5.A.1.b} . . . . id.

G4338 **προσηλόω**   *I nail to.*
προσήλυτοι   noun, nom. pl. masc.
{2.B} . . . . προσήλυτος *G4339*
προσήλυτον   noun, acc. sg. masc. {2.B} . . . . id.

G4339 **προσήλυτος**, -ου, ὁ   (lit. *that has come to*), *a proselyte*, i.e., a non-Jew, who has been circumcised and has adopted the Jews' religion.
προσηλύτων   noun, gen. pl. masc.
{2.B} . . . . προσήλυτος G4339
προσηλώσας   vbl., aor. act. ptc. nom. sg. masc.
{6.A.2}. . . . . προσηλόω G4338
προσήνεγκα   verb, aor. act. indic. 1 pers. sg.
{5.A.1.b} . . . . .προσφέρω G4374
προσήνεγκαν   verb, aor. act. indic. 3 pers. pl.
{5.A.1.b} . . . . id.
προσηνέγκατε   verb, aor. act. indic. 2 pers. pl.
{5.A.1.b} . . . . id.
προσήνεγκε   verb, aor. act. indic. 3 pers. sg.
{5.A.1.b} . . . . id.
προσήνεγκεν   verb, aor. act. indic. 3 pers. sg.
{5.A.1.b} . . . . id.
προσηνέχθη   verb, aor. pass. indic. 3 pers. sg.
{5.A.1.b} . . . . id.
προσηνέχθησαν   verb, aor. pass. indic. 3 pers.
pl. {5.A.1.b} . . . . id.
προσηργάσατο   verb, aor. mid. indic. 3 pers. sg.
{5.A.1.e} . . . . προσεργάζομαι G4333
προσήρχοντο   verb, impf. mid./pass. indic. 3 pers.
pl. {5.A.1.e} . . . . προσέρχομαι G4334
προσηυξάμεθα   verb, aor. mid. indic. 1 pers. pl.
{5.A.1.e} . . . . προσεύχομαι G4336
προσηύξαντο   verb, aor. mid. indic. 3 pers. pl.
{5.A.1.e} . . . . id.
προσηύξατο   verb, aor. mid. indic. 3 pers. sg.
{5.A.1.e} . . . . id.
προσηύχετο   verb, impf. mid./pass. indic.
3 pers. sg. {5.A.1.e} . . . . id.
προσήχθη   verb, aor. pass. indic. 3 pers. sg.
{5.A.1.b} . . . . .προσάγω G4317
προσθεῖναι   vbl., ²aor. act. inf. {6.B.3} .προστίθημι G4369
προσθείς   vbl., ²aor. act. ptc. nom. sg. masc.
{6.A.3}. . . . . id.
πρόσθες   verb, ²aor. act. impv. 2 pers. sg. {5.D.3} id.
πρόσκαιρα   adj., nom. pl. neut. {3.C} πρόσκαιρος G4340
πρόσκαιροι   adj., nom. pl. masc. {3.C}. . . . . id.
πρόσκαιρον   adj., acc. sg. fem. {3.C} . . . . id.
G4340 **πρόσκαιρος**, -ον   *for an occasion, transitory.*
πρόσκαιρος   adj., nom. sg. masc. {3.C} πρόσκαιρος G4340
προσκαλεῖται   verb, pres. mid./pass. indic. 3 pers.
sg. {5.A.2} . . . . προσκαλέω G4341
προσκαλεσάμενοι   vbl., aor. mid. ptc. nom. pl.
masc. {6.A.2}. . . . . id.
προσκαλεσάμενος   vbl., aor. mid. ptc. nom.
sg. masc. {6.A.2} . . . . id.
προσκαλεσάσθω   verb, aor. mid. impv. 3 pers.
sg. {5.D.1} . . . . id.
προσκαλέσηται   verb, aor. mid. subjunc.
3 pers. sg. {5.B.1} . . . . id.
G4341 **προσκαλέω**   mid. *I call to myself, I summon, invite.*
προσκαρτερεῖτε   verb, pres. act. impv. 2 pers. pl.
{5.D.2}. .προσκαρτερέω G4342
G4342 **προσκαρτερέω**   (1) *I continue all the time, I continue steadfast, I persist,* either of remaining

in a place, or of persisting in a certain course of action; (2) *I attach myself assiduously to,* Acts 8:13; 10:7; (3) with a lifeless subj., *I continue near (at hand),* Mark 3:9.
προσκαρτερῇ   verb, pres. act. subjunc. 3 pers. sg.
{5.B.2} .προσκαρτερέω G4342
προσκαρτερήσει   noun, dat. sg. fem.
{2.C} . . . . προσκαρτέρησις G4343
G4343 **προσκαρτέρησις**, -εως, ἡ   *constant attendance, persistence, perseverance, constancy.*
προσκαρτερήσομεν   verb, fut. act. indic. 1 pers.
pl. {5.A.1} . . . . .προσκαρτερέω G4342
προσκαρτεροῦντες   vbl., pres. act. ptc. nom.
pl. masc. {6.A.2} . . . . id.
προσκαρτερούντων   vbl., pres. act. ptc. gen.
pl. masc. {6.A.2} . . . . id.
προσκαρτερῶν   vbl., pres. act. ptc. nom. sg.
masc. {6.A.2}. . . . . id.
προσκέκλημαι   verb, perf. mid./pass. indic. 1 pers.
sg. {5.A.1} . . . . προσκαλέω G4341
προσκέκληται   verb, perf. mid./pass. indic.
3 pers. sg. {5.A.1}. . . . . id.
G4344 **προσκεφάλαιον**, -ου, τό   *a pillow* or *a cushion.*
προσκεφάλαιον   noun, acc. sg. neut.
{2.B} .προσκεφάλαιον G4344
G4345 **προσκληρόω**   *I allot (assign) to* (as disciples), Acts 17:4, where, if the pass. has a mid. force, we may translate, *threw in their lot with.*
πρόσκλησιν   noun, acc. sg. fem. {2.C} .πρόσκλισις G4346
G4347†‡ **προσκλίνω**   mid. *I attach myself to, follow.* Var. for προσκολλάω, Acts 5:36.
πρόσκλισιν   noun, acc. sg. fem. {2.C} .πρόσκλισις G4346
G4346 **πρόσκλισις**, -εως, ἡ   *inclination;* possibly, *taking sides, party spirit.*
G4347 **προσκολλάω**   *I join (unite) closely* (lit. *I glue one thing to another*); fut. pass. probably as mid., *I cleave (to).*
προσκολληθήσεται   verb, fut. pass. indic. 3 pers.
sg. {5.A.1} . . . . προσκολλάω G4347
G4348 **πρόσκομμα**, -ατος, τό   (lit. *striking against,* generally in the Hebraistic gen., after λίθος, a stone or loose boulder in the way, *against* which the traveler may *strike* his foot), *an obstacle, a cause of stumbling; stumbling;* hence esp. met.
πρόσκομμα   noun, acc. sg. neut. {2.C} πρόσκομμα G4348
πρόσκομμα   noun, nom. sg. neut. {2.C}. . . . . . id.
προσκόμματος   noun, gen. sg. neut. {2.C}. . . . . id.
G4349 **προσκοπή**, -ῆς, ἡ   *causing of stumbling* (met.).
προσκοπήν   noun, acc. sg. fem. {2.A} . .προσκοπή G4349
προσκόπτει   verb, pres. act. indic. 3 pers. sg.
{5.A.1.a} . . . . .προσκόπτω G4350
προσκόπτουσι   verb, pres. act. indic. 3 pers. pl.
{5.A.1.a} . . . . id.
προσκόπτουσιν   verb, pres. act. indic. 3 pers.
pl. {5.A.1.a} . . . . id.
G4350 **προσκόπτω**   *I strike against;* intrans., Matt 7:27, etc., also absol., *I stumble,* John 11:9, 10; Rom 14:21; *I stumble at,* 1 Pet 2:8. Sometimes met. (cf. πρόσκομμα).

προσκόψης   verb, aor. act. subjunc. 2 pers. sg.
{5.B.1} . . . . .προσκόπτω G4350
προσκυλίσας   vbl., aor. act. ptc. nom. sg. masc.
{6.A.1.a} . . . . .προσκυλίω G4351
G4351 **προσκυλίω**   I roll to (up to).
προσκυνεῖ   verb, pres. act. indic. 3 pers. sg.
{5.A.2} . . . . .προσκυνέω G4352
προσκυνεῖν   vbl., pres. act. inf. {6.B.2} . . . . id.
προσκυνεῖτε   verb, pres. act. indic. 2 pers. pl.
{5.A.2} . . . . id.
G4352 **προσκυνέω**   I go down on my knees to; I do
obeisance to; I worship.
προσκυνῆσαι   vbl., aor. act. inf. {6.B.1}προσκυνέω G4352
προσκυνήσαντες   vbl., aor. act. ptc. nom. pl.
masc. {6.A.2} . . . . id.
προσκυνήσατε   verb, aor. act. impv. 2 pers. pl.
{5.D.1} . . . . id.
προσκυνησάτωσαν   verb, aor. act. impv.
3 pers. pl. {5.D.1} . . . . id.
προσκυνήσει   verb, fut. act. indic. 3 pers. sg.
{5.A.1} . . . . id.
προσκυνήσεις   verb, fut. act. indic. 2 pers. sg.
{5.A.1} . . . . id.
προσκυνήσετε   verb, fut. act. indic. 2 pers. pl.
{5.A.1} . . . . id.
προσκυνήσῃς   verb, aor. act. subjunc. 2 pers.
sg. {5.B.1} . . . . id.
προσκύνησον   verb, aor. act. impv. 2 pers. sg.
{5.D.1} . . . . id.
προσκυνήσουσι   verb, fut. act. indic. 3 pers.
pl. {5.A.1} . . . . id.
προσκυνήσουσιν   verb, fut. act. indic. 3 pers.
pl. {5.A.1} . . . . id.
προσκυνήσω   verb, aor. act. subjunc. 1 pers. sg.
{5.B.1} . . . . id.
προσκυνήσων   vbl., fut. act. ptc. nom. sg.
masc. {6.A.2} . . . . id.
προσκυνήσωσι   verb, aor. act. subjunc. 3 pers.
pl. {5.B.1} . . . . id.
προσκυνήσωσιν   verb, aor. act. subjunc.
3 pers. pl. {5.B.1} . . . . id.
προσκυνηταί   noun, nom. pl. masc.
{2.A} . . . . προσκυνητής G4353
G4353 **προσκυνητής**, -οῦ, ὁ   a worshipper.
προσκυνοῦμεν   verb, pres. act. indic. 1 pers. pl.
{5.A.2} . . . . .προσκυνέω G4352
προσκυνοῦντας   vbl., pres. act. ptc. acc. pl.
masc. {6.A.2} . . . . id.
προσκυνοῦντες   vbl., pres. act. ptc. nom. pl.
masc. {6.A.2} . . . . id.
προσκυνοῦσα   vbl., pres. act. ptc. nom. sg.
fem. {6.A.2} . . . . id.
προσκυνοῦσι   verb, pres. act. indic. 3 pers. pl.
{5.A.2} . . . . id.
προσλαβεῖν   vbl., 2aor. act. inf.
{6.B.1} . . . . .προσλαμβάνω G4355
προσλαβόμενοι   vbl., 2aor. mid. ptc. nom. pl.
masc. {6.A.1.b} . . . . id.
προσλαβόμενος   vbl., 2aor. mid. ptc. nom. sg.
masc. {6.A.1.b} . . . . id.

προσλαβοῦ   verb, 2aor. mid. impv. 2 pers. sg.
{5.D.1} . . . . id.
G4354 **προσλαλέω**   I speak to.
προσλαλῆσαι   vbl., aor. act. inf.
{6.B.1} . . . . .προσλαλέω G4354
προσλαλοῦντες   vbl., pres. act. ptc. nom. pl.
masc. {6.A.2} . . . . id.
προσλαμβάνεσθε   verb, pres. mid. impv. 2 pers.
pl. {5.D.1} . . . . .προσλαμβάνω G4355
G4355 **προσλαμβάνω**   mid. (1) I take to myself; (2) I
take aside, take along Mark 8:32; Matt 16:22;
Acts 17:5; 18:26; (3) I welcome, Acts 28:2; Rom
14:1, etc.
G4356 **πρόσλημψις**, -εως, ἡ   taking to one's self; assumption into God's favor.
πρόσλημψις   noun, nom. sg. fem.
{2.C} . . . . .πρόσλημψις G4356
πρόσληψις   noun, nom. sg. fem. {2.C} . . . . id.
προσμεῖναι   vbl., aor. act. inf. {6.B.1} . . .προσμένω G4357
προσμείνας   vbl., aor. act. ptc. nom. sg. masc.
{6.A.1.a} . . . . id.
προσμένει   verb, pres. act. indic. 3 pers. sg.
{5.A.1.a} . . . . id.
προσμένειν   vbl., pres. act. inf. {6.B.1} . . . . id.
προσμένουσι   verb, pres. act. indic. 3 pers. pl.
{5.A.1.a} . . . . id.
προσμένουσιν   verb, pres. act. indic. 3 pers. pl.
{5.A.1.a} . . . . id.
G4357 **προσμένω**   I remain; with dat., I abide in, I
remain in, I persist in.
G4358 **προσορμίζω**   pass. I am brought into harbor, I
anchor at a place.
προσοφείλεις   verb, pres. act. indic. 2 pers. sg.
{5.A.1.a} . . . . .προσοφείλω G4359
G4359 **προσοφείλω**   I owe besides (in addition).
G4360 **προσοχθίζω**   I entertain anger (disgust,
abhorrence).
G4361 **πρόσπεινος**, -ον   either inclined to hunger or
very hungry.
πρόσπεινος   adj., nom. sg. masc. {3.C}.πρόσπεινος G4361
προσπεσοῦσα   vbl., 2aor. act. ptc. nom. sg. fem.
{6.A.1.a} . . . . .προσπίπτω G4363
G4362 **προσπήγνυμι**   I fix to anything.
προσπήξαντες   vbl., aor. act. ptc. nom. pl. masc.
{6.A.3} . . . . προσπήγνυμι G4362
G4363 **προσπίπτω**   I fall upon; I fall at (beside).
G4364 **προσποιέω**   mid. (1) I pretend; (2) I take notice.
προσποιούμενος   vbl., pres. mid./pass. ptc. nom.
sg. masc. {6.A.2} . . . . .προσποιέω G4364
G4365 **προσπορεύομαι**   I come to.
προσπορεύονται   verb, pres. mid./pass. indic.
3 pers. pl. {5.A.1.d} . . . . .προσπορεύομαι G4365
G4366 **προσρήσσω** (προσρήγνυμι)   I burst upon,
break in pieces.
G4367 **προστάσσω**   (1) I instruct, command; (2) I appoint, Acts 17:26. Cf. προτάσσω.
G4368 **προστάτις**, -ιδος, ἡ   protectress, patroness,
helper (a development of the political sense
of προστάτης, a political sponsor of resident
aliens).

προστάτις   noun, nom. sg. fem. {2.C} . .προστάτις G4368
προστεθῆναι   vbl., aor. pass. inf.
   {6.B.1} . . . . .προστίθημι G4369
προστεθήσεται   verb, fut. pass. indic. 3 pers.
   sg. {5.A.1} . . . . id.
προστεταγμένα   vbl., perf. pass. ptc. acc. pl. neut.
   {6.A.1.b} . . . . προστάσσω G4367
προστεταγμένους   vbl., perf. pass. ptc. acc. pl.
   masc. {6.A.1.b} . . . . id.
προστῆναι   vbl., ²aor. act. inf. {6.B.3} . . .προΐστημι G4291
G4369 **προστίθημι**   I place (put) to, I add; mid. with
   inf. (perhaps a Hebraistic idiom), best translated by representing the verb in the inf. by
   the indic., and adding the word besides, etc.,
   thus: προσέθετο πέμψαι, besides (in addition,
   further) he sent, Luke 20:11.
προστρέχοντες   vbl., pres. act. ptc. nom. pl. masc.
   {6.A.1} . . . . προστρέχω G4370
G4370 **προστρέχω**   I run (run up) to a person.
G4371 **προσφάγιον**, -ου, τό   a relish, delicacy, or tidbit
   eaten with bread (commonly it would be fish).
προσφάγιον   noun, acc. sg. neut. {2.B}προσφάγιον G4371
πρόσφατον   adj., acc. sg. fem. {3.C} . . .πρόσφατος G4372
G4372 **πρόσφατος**, -ον   (from πρός and the root of
   φόνος, therefore orig. newly slaughtered, fresh-
   killed), now for the first time made, new.
G4373 **προσφάτως**   adv., freshly, recently.
προσφάτως   adv. {3.F} . . . . .προσφάτως G4373
πρόσφερε   verb, pres. act. impv. 2 pers. sg.
   {5.D.1} . . . . .προσφέρω G4374
προσφέρει   verb, pres. act. indic. 3 pers. sg.
   {5.A.1.a} . . . . id.
προσφέρειν   vbl., pres. act. inf. {6.B.1} . . . . id.
προσφέρεται   verb, pres. pass. indic. 3 pers. sg.
   {5.A.1.d} . . . . id.
προσφέρῃ   verb, pres. act. subjunc. 3 pers. sg.
   {5.B.1} . . . . id.
προσφέρῃς   verb, pres. act. subjunc. 2 pers. sg.
   {5.B.1} . . . . id.
προσφερόμεναι   vbl., pres. pass. ptc. nom. pl.
   fem. {6.A.1} . . . . id.
προσφέρονται   verb, pres. pass. indic. 3 pers.
   pl. {5.A.1.d} . . . . id.
προσφέροντες   vbl., pres. act. ptc. nom. pl.
   masc. {6.A.1} . . . . id.
προσφερόντων   vbl., pres. act. ptc. gen. pl.
   masc. {6.A.1} . . . . id.
προσφέρουσιν   verb, pres. act. indic. 3 pers. pl.
   {5.A.1.a} . . . . id.
προσφέρουσιν   vbl., pres. act. ptc. dat. pl.
   masc. {6.A.1} . . . . id.
G4374 **προσφέρω**   (1) I bring to; (2) characteristically,
   I offer (of gifts, sacrifices, etc.).
προσφέρων   vbl., pres. act. ptc. nom. sg. masc.
   {6.A.1} . . . . .προσφέρω G4374
προσφέρωσιν   verb, pres. act. subjunc. 3 pers.
   pl. {5.B.1} . . . . id.
προσφιλῆ   adj., nom. pl. neut. {3.E} . . . προσφιλής G4375
G4375 **προσφιλής**, -ές   lovable, amiable.
G4376 **προσφορά**, -ᾶς, ἡ   an offering (esp. to God).

προσφορά   noun, nom. sg. fem. {2.A} . .προσφορά G4376
προσφορᾷ   noun, dat. sg. fem. {2.A} . . . . id.
προσφοράν   noun, acc. sg. fem. {2.A} . . . . id.
προσφοράς   noun, acc. pl. fem. {2.A}. . . . . id.
προσφορᾶς   noun, gen. sg. fem. {2.A} . . . . id.
G4377 **προσφωνέω**   w. acc. I call, I summon; with dat.
   I call (out) to; I address, I give a speech to, Acts
   22:2, cf. absol. Acts 21:40.
προσφωνοῦντα   vbl., pres. act. ptc. nom. pl. neut.
   {6.A.2} . . . . προσφωνέω G4377
προσφωνοῦσι   vbl., pres. act. ptc. dat. pl. neut.
   {6.A.2} . . . . id.
προσφωνοῦσιν   vbl., pres. act. ptc. dat. pl.
   neut. {6.A.2} . . . . id.
πρόσχυσιν   noun, acc. sg. fem. {2.C} . . πρόσχυσις G4378
G4378 **πρόσχυσις**, -εως, ἡ   pouring upon the altar (as
   was done in later times, not in that of Moses).
προσψαύετε   verb, pres. act. indic. 2 pers. pl.
   {5.A.1.a} . . . . προσψαύω G4379
G4379 **προσψαύω**   I touch, handle.
πρόσωπα   noun, acc. pl. neut. {2.B} . . . πρόσωπον G4383
πρόσωπα   noun, nom. pl. neut. {2.B} . . . . id.
προσωπολημπτεῖτε   verb, pres. act. indic. 2 pers.
   pl. {5.A.2} . . . . προσωπολημπτέω G4380
G4380 **προσωπολημπτέω**   I favor specially (from προσωπολήμπτης, Hebraistic, later than LXX).
G4381 **προσωπολήμπτης**, -ου, ὁ   a special favorer
   of one more than of another, a respecter of
   persons (from πρόσωπον and λαμβάνειν,
   Hebraistic, later than LXX; see under the
   latter).
προσωπολήμπτης   noun, nom. sg. masc.
   {2.A} . . . . προσωπολήμπτης G4381
G4382 **προσωπολημψία**, -ας, ἡ   favoritism, partiality
   (a Hebraistic expression, later than LXX).
προσωπολημψία   noun, nom. sg. fem.
   {2.A} . . . . .προσωπολημψία G4382
προσωπολημψίαις   noun, dat. pl. fem. {2.A} . . id.
προσωποληπτεῖτε   verb, pres. act. indic. 2 pers. pl.
   {5.A.2} . . . . προσωπολημπτέω G4380
προσωπολήπτης   noun, nom. sg. masc.
   {2.A} . . . . προσωπολήμπτης G4381
προσωποληψία   noun, nom. sg. fem.
   {2.A} . . . . .προσωπολημψία G4382
προσωποληψίαις   noun, dat. pl. fem. {2.A}. . . . id.
G4383 **πρόσωπον**, -ου, τό   (1) the human face; often
   Hebraistically otiose, e.g., πρὸ προσώπου σου
   practically = πρὸ σοῦ, Matt 11:10; πρόσωπον
   πρὸς πρόσωπον (Hebraistic), face to face; (2)
   hence applied to God, from His having been
   originally conceived as in human form, presence (cf. Acts 5:41); (3) appearance, outward
   aspect (Matt 16:3), Luke 12:56, etc.; surface,
   Luke 21:35; (4) for the practically synonymous
   Hebraistic expressions βλέπειν εἰς πρόσωπον, θαυμάζειν πρόσωπον, λαμβάνειν
   πρόσωπον, to show special favor to, see under
   λαμβάνω; (5) by Hebraistic pleonasm (cf. (1)
   above), πρὸ προσώπου τῆς εἰσόδου αὐτοῦ,
   before his entrance, Acts 13:24; (6) person in a

rather loose sense as a possessor of dignity or honor; *pride,* Jas 1:11.

πρόσωπον   noun, acc. sg. neut. {2.B} . . πρόσωπον G4383

πρόσωπον   noun, nom. sg. neut. {2.B} . . . . id.

προσώπου   noun, gen. sg. neut. {2.B} . . . . id.

προσώπῳ   noun, dat. sg. neut. {2.B} . . . . id.

προσώπων   noun, gen. pl. neut. {2.B} . . . . id.

προσωρμίσθησαν   verb, aor. pass. indic. 3 pers. pl.
    {5.A.1.b} . . . . προσορμίζω G4358

προσώχθισα   verb, aor. act. indic. 1 pers. sg.
    {5.A.1.b} . . . . προσοχθίζω G4360

προσώχθισε   verb, aor. act. indic. 3 pers. sg.
    {5.A.1.b} . . . . id.

προσώχθισεν   verb, aor. act. indic. 3 pers. sg.
    {5.A.1.b} . . . . id.

G4384 **προτάσσω**   *I prearrange, appoint beforehand.*
    Var. for προστάσσω, Acts 17:26.

G4385 **προτείνω**   *I stretch forward, I put into a tense posture.*

προτέραν   adj. comp., acc. sg. fem. {3.A;
    3.G} . . . . πρότερος G4387

G4386 **πρότερον**   adv., *earlier, in former times* (see πρότερος).

πρότερον   adj. comp., acc. sg. masc. {3.A;
    3.G} . . . . πρότερος G4387

πρότερον   adj. comp., acc. sg. neut. {3.A; 3.G} . . id.

πρότερον   adj. comp., nom. sg. neut. {3.A; 3.G} . id.

πρότερον   adv. comp. {3.F; 3.G} . . . . id.

G4387 **πρότερος,** -α, -ον   *first of two, former, previous, earlier* (becoming replaced by πρῶτος); acc. as adv. (τὸ) πρότερον, *on the former of two occasions,* e.g., Gal 4:13; *on a previous occasion; at first, formerly, previously,* sometimes used practically as an adj., as the latter was dying out (see πρῶτος), 1 Tim 1:13.

προτεταγμένους   vbl., perf. pass. ptc. acc. pl. masc.
    {6.A.1.b} . . . . προτάσσω G4384

G4388 **προτίθημι**   mid. (1) *I add (to);* (2) *I set before myself, I purpose openly;* but perhaps, (3) *I offer, I provide.*

G4389 **προτρέπω**   mid. *I encourage, urge forward.*

G4390 **προτρέχω**   *I run forward.*

προτρεψάμενοι   vbl., aor. mid. ptc. nom. pl. masc.
    {6.A.1.b} . . . . προτρέπω G4389

G4391 **προϋπάρχω**   *I am (previously), I exist before, I have been already.*

προυπῆρχεν   verb, impf. act. indic. 3 pers. sg.
    {5.A.1.b} . . . . προϋπάρχω G4391

προϋπῆρχεν   verb, impf. act. indic. 3 pers. sg.
    {5.A.1.b} . . . . id.

προϋπῆρχον   verb, impf. act. indic. 3 pers. pl.
    {5.A.1.b} . . . . id.

προφάσει   noun, dat. sg. fem. {2.C} . . . . πρόφασις G4392

προφάσιν   noun, acc. sg. fem. {2.C} . . . . id.

G4392 **πρόφασις,** -εως, ἡ   *ostensible reason* for which a thing is done (i.e., commonly, the false reason), *pretence; excuse, pretext;* προφάσει, *under color, under pretence.*

προφέρει   verb, pres. act. indic. 3 pers. sg.
    {5.A.1.a} . . . . προφέρω G4393

G4393 **προφέρω**   *I bring forth (out), produce.*

προφῆται   noun, nom. pl. masc. {2.A} . . προφήτης G4396

προφῆται   noun, voc. pl. masc. {2.A} . . . . id.

προφήταις   noun, dat. pl. masc. {2.A} . . . . id.

προφήτας   noun, acc. pl. masc. {2.A} . . . . id.

G4394 **προφητεία,** -ας, ἡ   the quality or action of a προφήτης, *declaration* of the will of God, whether with special reference to the future, in which case it may be translated *prophecy,* or not.

προφητεία   noun, nom. sg. fem. {2.A} . προφητεία G4394

προφητείᾳ   noun, dat. sg. fem. {2.A} . . . . id.

προφητεῖαι   noun, nom. pl. fem. {2.A} . . . . id.

προφητείαν   noun, acc. sg. fem. {2.A} . . . . id.

προφητείας   noun, acc. pl. fem. {2.A} . . . . id.

προφητείας   noun, gen. sg. fem. {2.A} . . . . id.

προφητεύειν   vbl., pres. act. inf. {6.B.1} προφητεύω G4395

προφητεύητε   verb, pres. act. subjunc. 2 pers.
    pl. {5.B.1} . . . . id.

προφητεύομεν   verb, pres. act. indic. 1 pers. pl.
    {5.A.1.a} . . . . id.

προφητεύουσα   vbl., pres. act. ptc. nom. sg.
    fem. {6.A.1} . . . . id.

προφητεύουσαι   vbl., pres. act. ptc. nom. pl.
    fem. {6.A.1} . . . . id.

προφητεῦσαι   vbl., aor. act. inf. {6.B.1} . . . . . . id.

προφητεύσαντες   vbl., aor. act. ptc. nom. pl.
    masc. {6.A.1.a} . . . . id.

προφήτευσον   verb, aor. act. impv. 2 pers. sg.
    {5.D.1} . . . . id.

προφητεύσουσι   verb, fut. act. indic. 3 pers. pl.
    {5.A.1.a} . . . . id.

προφητεύσουσιν   verb, fut. act. indic. 3 pers.
    pl. {5.A.1.a} . . . . id.

G4395 **προφητεύω**   *I do the duty of a προφήτης, I declare* the will of God, sometimes with regard to what is to happen in the future, in which case it may be rendered, *I prophesy.*

προφητεύων   vbl., pres. act. ptc. nom. sg. masc.
    {6.A.1} . . . . προφητεύω G4395

προφητεύωσιν   verb, pres. act. subjunc. 3 pers.
    pl. {5.B.1} . . . . id.

προφήτῃ   noun, dat. sg. masc. {2.A} . . . . προφήτης G4396

προφήτην   noun, acc. sg. masc. {2.A} . . . . id.

G4396 **προφήτης,** -ου, ὁ   a man specially endowed to *tell forth (declare)* the will of God in speech, whether as touching the present or as regards the future, *a prophet;* the adoption of a literary form as seen in the prophetical books of the OT is a later stage of a prophet's activity; Epimenides is so styled (in Titus 1:12), perhaps as related to the Cretans in the same way as the prophets of Israel were to Israel.

προφήτης   noun, nom. sg. masc. {2.A} . . προφήτης G4396

προφητικόν   adj., acc. sg. masc. {3.A} προφητικός G4397

G4397 **προφητικός,** -ή, -όν   belonging to a προφήτης or to προφῆται, *prophetic.*

προφητικῶν   adj., gen. pl. fem. {3.A} . προφητικός G4397

προφῆτιν   noun, acc. sg. fem. {2.C} . . . προφῆτις G4398

G4398 **προφῆτις,** -ιδος, ἡ   *a prophetess.*

προφῆτις   noun, nom. sg. fem. {2.C} . . .προφῆτις *G4398*
προφήτου   noun, gen. sg. masc. {2.A} . προφήτης *G4396*
προφητῶν   noun, gen. pl. masc. {2.A} . . . . id.

G4399 **προφθάνω**   *I anticipate, I forestall.*

G4400 **προχειρίζω**   *mid., I appoint, elect* (for an important duty).
προχειρίσασθαι   vbl., aor. mid. inf.
   {6.B.1} . . . . .προχειρίζω *G4400*

G4401 **προχειροτονέω**   *I appoint beforehand.*
Πρόχορον   noun prop., acc. sg. masc. {2.B;
   2.D} . . . . .Πρόχορος *G4402*

G4402 **Πρόχορος**, -ου, ὁ   *Prochorus,* one of the seven original "deacons" at Jerusalem.
προώρισε   verb, aor. act. indic. 3 pers. sg.
   {5.A.1.b} .προορίζω *G4309*
προώρισεν   verb, aor. act. indic. 3 pers. sg.
   {5.A.1.b} . . . . id.
προωρώμην   verb, impf. mid. indic. 1 pers. sg.
   {5.A.2} . . . . .προοράω *G4308*

G4403 **πρύμνα**, -ης, ἡ   *the stern* of a ship.
πρύμνα   noun, nom. sg. fem. {2.A} . . . . .πρύμνα *G4403*
πρύμνη   noun, dat. sg. fem. {2.A} . . . . id.
πρύμνης   noun, gen. sg. fem. {2.A} . . . . id.
πρωΐ   adv. . . . . πρωΐ *G4404*

G4404 **πρωΐ**   adv., *early, in the morning* (in John 20:1, even of the period before dawn).
πρωΐ   adv. . . . . πρωΐ *G4404*

G4405 **πρωΐα**, -ας, ἡ   *early morning.*
πρωΐα   noun, nom. sg. fem. {2.A} . . . . πρωΐα *G4405*
πρωΐας   noun, gen. sg. fem. {2.A} . . . . id.
πρωΐας   noun, gen. sg. fem. {2.A} . . . . id.
πρωΐμον   adj., acc. sg. masc. {3.C} . . . . πρωΐμος *G4406*

G4406 **πρωΐμος** (πρόϊμος), -ου, ὁ   *early* in the year (understand ὑετός or some other word meaning *rain*); reference is to that beginning in October; opposed to ὄψιμος. Πρόϊμος is the preferred spelling, from πρό, not from πρωΐ. Cf. πρωϊνός.
πρωϊνόν   adj., acc. sg. masc. {3.A} . . . . . πρωϊνός *G4407*
πρωϊνόν   adj., acc. sg. masc. {3.A} . . . . id.
πρωϊνός   adj., nom. sg. masc. {3.A} . . . . id.

G4407 **πρωϊνός**, -ή, -όν   *belonging to the morning, morning;* opp. ἑσπερινός (from πρωΐ).
πρωϊνός   adj., nom. sg. masc. {3.A} . . . . . πρωϊνός *G4407*

G4408 **πρῷρα**, -ης, ἡ   *the prow, bow, forward part* of a ship.
πρῷρα   noun, nom. sg. fem. {2.A} . . . . .πρῷρα *G4408*
πρῷρα   noun, nom. sg. fem. {2.A} . . . . id.
πρῴρας   noun, gen. sg. fem. {2.A} . . . . id.
πρῴρας   noun, gen. sg. fem. {2.A} . . . . id.
πρῴρης   noun, gen. sg. fem. {2.A} . . . . id.
πρῶτα   adj. superl., acc. pl. neut. {3.A} . . . . πρῶτος *G4413*
πρῶτα   adj. superl., nom. pl. neut. {3.A} . . . . . . id.

G4409 **πρωτεύω**   *I hold the first (chief) place, I am the head.*
πρωτεύων   vbl., pres. act. ptc. nom. sg. masc.
   {6.A.1} . . . . .πρωτεύω *G4409*
πρώτη   adj. superl., nom. sg. fem. {3.A} . . . πρῶτος *G4413*
πρώτῃ   adj. superl., dat. sg. fem. {3.A} . . . . . . id.
πρώτην   adj. superl., acc. sg. fem. {3.A} . . . . . . id.

πρώτης   adj. superl., gen. sg. fem. {3.A} . . . . . . id.
πρῶτοι   adj. superl., nom. pl. masc. {3.A} . . . . . id.
πρώτοις   adj. superl., dat. pl. masc. {3.A} . . . . . id.
πρώτοις   adj. superl., dat. pl. neut. {3.A} . . . . . id.

G4410 **πρωτοκαθεδρία**, -ας, ἡ   *the chief (most honorable) seat (chair, stall).*
πρωτοκαθεδρίαν   noun, acc. sg. fem.
   {2.A} . . . . .πρωτοκαθεδρία *G4410*
πρωτοκαθεδρίας   noun, acc. pl. fem. {2.A} . . . . id.

G4411 **πρωτοκλισία**, -ας, ἡ   *the chief (most honorable) reclining place* on the dining couches at a dinner table.
πρωτοκλισίαν   noun, acc. sg. fem.
   {2.A} . . . . πρωτοκλισία *G4411*
πρωτοκλισίας   noun, acc. pl. fem. {2.A} . . . . id.
πρῶτον   adj. superl., acc. sg. masc. {3.A} . . πρῶτος *G4413*
πρῶτον   adj. superl., acc. sg. neut. {3.A} . . . . . id.
πρῶτον   adj. superl., nom. sg. neut. {3.A} . . . . . id.

G4412 **πρῶτον**   adv., *in the first place, first;* τὸ πρῶτον, *at first, at the beginning.*
πρῶτον   adv. superl. . . . . .πρῶτον *G4412*

G4413 **πρῶτος**, -η, -ον   *first* (of time, then of status), strictly of more than two, being a superl., but also used where there are two elements only, as πρότερος, the true comp., was dying out in NT times, Acts 1:1; Heb 8:7, 13; 9:1, 2, 6, 8, etc.; οἱ πρῶτοι, *the chief men,* Mark 6:21; Luke 19:47, etc., cf. ὁ πρῶτος, an official title, equivalent to *the governor,* Acts 28:7; πρῶτος μου, John 1:15, 30, either = πρότερός μου, *earlier than I* (cf. 15:18), or, with μου as possessive gen., *my chief, my lord.* See adv. πρῶτον.
πρῶτος   adj. superl., nom. sg. masc. {3.A} . πρῶτος *G4413*
πρωτοστάτην   noun, acc. sg. masc.
   {2.A} .πρωτοστάτης *G4414*

G4414 **πρωτοστάτης**, -ου, ὁ   *one who stands in the front rank,* hence, *a leader, ringleader.*
πρωτότοκα   adj., acc. pl. neut. {3.C} . πρωτότοκος *G4416*

G4415 **πρωτοτόκια**, -ων, τό   pl. *one's rights as firstborn.*
πρωτοτόκια   noun, acc. pl. neut. {2.B}πρωτοτόκια *G4415*
πρωτότοκος   adj., acc. sg. masc. {3.C}πρωτότοκος *G4416*

G4416 **πρωτότοκος**, -ον   *firstborn, earliest born, eldest.*
πρωτότοκος   adj., nom. sg. masc.
   {3.C} .πρωτότοκος *G4416*
πρωτοτόκων   adj., gen. pl. masc. {3.C} . . . . id.
πρώτου   adj. superl., gen. sg. masc. {3.A} . . πρῶτος *G4413*
πρώτου   adj. superl., gen. sg. neut. {3.A} . . . . . id.
πρώτους   adj. superl., acc. pl. masc. {3.A} . . . . . id.
πρώτῳ   adj. superl., dat. sg. masc. {3.A} . . . . . id.
πρώτῳ   adj. superl., dat. sg. neut. {3.A} . . . . . . id.
πρώτων   adj. superl., gen. pl. fem. {3.A} . . . . . . id.
πρώτων   adj. superl., gen. pl. masc. {3.A} . . . . . id.
πρώτων   adj. superl., gen. pl. neut. {3.A} . . . . . . id.

G4412†‡ **πρώτως**   adv., *for the first time.* Var. for πρῶτον, Acts 11:26.
πρώτως   adv. superl. {3.F} . . . . .πρώτως *G4412†‡*
πταίει   verb, pres. act. indic. 3 pers. sg.
   {5.A.1.a} . . . . πταίω *G4417*

πταίομεν   verb, pres. act. indic. 1 pers. pl.
{5.A.1.a} . . . . id.
πταίσει   verb, fut. act. indic. 3 pers. sg. {5.A.1.a} id.
πταίσῃ   verb, aor. act. subjunc. 3 pers. sg. {5.B.1} id.
πταίσητε   verb, aor. act. subjunc. 2 pers. pl.
{5.B.1} . . . . id.

G4417 πταίω   of incipient falling, *I trip, stumble,* lit. or met.

G4418 πτέρνα, -ης, ἡ   *heel.*
πτέρναν   noun, acc. sg. fem. {2.A} . . . . πτέρνα G4418
πτέρυγας   noun, acc. pl. fem. {2.C} . . . . . . .πτέρυξ G4420
πτέρυγες   noun, nom. pl. fem. {2.C} . . . . id.

G4419 πτερύγιον, -ου, τό   *the gable, roof projection of the temple roof, pinnacle;* or possibly (see ἱερόν), *the wall* surrounding the temple precinct.
πτερύγιον   noun, acc. sg. neut. {2.B} . . . πτερύγιον G4419
πτερύγων   noun, gen. pl. fem. {2.C} . . . . . .πτέρυξ G4420

G4420 πτέρυξ, -υγος, ἡ   *a wing.*

G4421 πτηνός, -ή, -όν, τό   *winged;* hence as neut. subs., *a bird.*
πτηνῶν   adj., gen. pl. neut. {3.A} . . . . πτηνός G4421

G4422 πτοέω   *I scare, I strike with panic.*
πτοηθέντες   vbl., aor. pass. ptc. nom. pl. masc.
{6.A.1.a.} . . . . πτοέω G4422
πτοηθῆτε   verb, aor. pass. subjunc. 2 pers. pl.
{5.B.1} . . . . id.
πτόησιν   noun, acc. sg. fem. {2.C} . . . . . .πτόησις G4423

G4423 πτόησις, -εως, ἡ   *fear, terror* (or other violent excitement).
Πτολεμαΐδα   noun prop., acc. sg. fem. {2.C; 2.D} . . . . Πτολεμαΐς G4424

G4424 Πτολεμαΐς, ΐδος, ἡ   *Ptolemais,* a coast city of Phoenicia, midway between Tyre and Caesarea.
πτύξας   vbl., aor. act. ptc. nom. sg. masc.
{6.A.1.a} . . . . .πτύσσω G4428

G4425 πτύον, -ου, τό   *a winnowing fan,* a simple wooden pitchfork.
πτύον   noun, nom. sg. neut. {2.B} . . . . πτύον G4425
πτυρόμενοι   vbl., pres. pass. ptc. nom. pl. masc.
{6.A.1} . . . . .πτύρω G4426

G4426 πτύρω   *I frighten, terrify.*
πτύσας   vbl., aor. act. ptc. nom. sg. masc.
{6.A.1.a} . . . . πτύω G4429

G4427 πτύσμα, -ατος, τό   *spittle.*
πτύσματος   noun, gen. sg. neut. {2.C} . . . .πτύσμα G4427

G4428 πτύσσω   *I roll up, close.*

G4429 πτύω   *I spit.*

G4430 πτῶμα, -ατος, τό   *a corpse.*
πτῶμα   noun, acc. sg. neut. {2.C} . . . . πτῶμα G4430
πτῶμα   noun, nom. sg. neut. {2.C} . . . . id.
πτώματα   noun, acc. pl. neut. {2.C} . . . . id.
πτώματα   noun, nom. pl. neut. {2.C} . . . . id.
πτῶσιν   noun, acc. sg. fem. {2.C} . . . . .πτῶσις G4431

G4431 πτῶσις, -εως, ἡ   *falling, fall.*
πτῶσις   noun, nom. sg. fem. {2.C} . . . . . . .πτῶσις G4431
πτωχά   adj., acc. pl. neut. {3.A} . . . . .πτωχός G4434

G4432 πτωχεία, -ας, ἡ   (strictly *beggary,* but rather merely) *poverty.*

πτωχεία   noun, nom. sg. fem. {2.A} . . . . . πτωχεία G4432
πτωχείᾳ   noun, dat. sg. fem. {2.A} . . . . id.
πτωχείαν   noun, acc. sg. fem. {2.A} . . . . id.

G4433 πτωχεύω   *I live the life of a poor man.*
πτωχή   adj., nom. sg. fem. {3.A} . . . . πτωχός G4434
πτωχοί   adj., nom. pl. masc. {3.A}. . . . . id.
πτωχοί   adj., voc. pl. masc. {3.A}. . . . . id.
πτωχοῖς   adj., dat. pl. masc. {3.A} . . . . id.
πτωχόν   adj., acc. sg. masc. {3.A} . . . . id.

G4434 πτωχός, -ή, -όν   (strictly *a beggar;* weakened afterwards), *poor; a poor man;* met. (Matt 5:3; Luke 6:20; Rev 3:17), not of those who are poor in material things, but of the humble devout persons, who feel the need of God's help.
πτωχός   adj., nom. sg. masc. {3.A} . . . . πτωχός G4434
πτωχούς   adj., acc. pl. masc. {3.A} . . . . id.
πτωχῷ   adj., dat. sg. masc. {3.A} . . . . id.
πτωχῶν   adj., gen. pl. masc. {3.A}. . . . . id.

G4435 πυγμή, -ῆς, ἡ   *the fist;* meaning of Mark 7:3 (var.) still uncertain ("turning the closed fist of one hand about the hollow of the other," or "as far as the elbow," or paraphrased by "diligently," "carefully").
πυγμῇ   noun, dat. sg. fem. {2.A} . . . . πυγμή G4435
πυθέσθαι   vbl., ²aor. mid. inf. {6.B.1} . πυνθάνομαι G4441
πυθόμενος   vbl., ²aor. mid. ptc. nom. sg. masc.
{6.A.1.b} . . . . id.

G4436 πύθων, -ωνος, ὁ   *a ventriloquist* (the utterance being supposed to be due to the presence of a πύθων or familiar spirit within the body of the speaker).
πύθωνα   noun, acc. sg. masc. {2.C} . . . . . . .πύθων G4436
πύθωνος   noun, gen. sg. masc. {2.C} . . . . id.
πυκνά   adj., acc. pl. neut. {3.A}. . . . . πυκνός G4437
πυκνάς   adj., acc. pl. fem. {3.A} . . . . id.

G4437 πυκνός, -ή, -όν   (spissus, *thick;* hence) *frequent;* acc. pl. neut. πυκνά as adv., *frequently, often* (cf. regular comp. of adv., Acts 24:26).
πυκνότερον   adj. comp., acc. sg. neut. {3.A; 3.G}. . . . . πυκνός G4437
πυκνότερον   adj. comp., nom. sg. neut. {3.A; 3.G}. . . . . id.
πυκνότερον   adv. comp. {3.F; 3.G} . . . . id.

G4438 πυκτεύω   *I am a boxer, I box.*
πυκτεύω   verb, pres. act. indic. 1 pers. sg.
{5.A.1.a} . . . . πυκτεύω G4438
πύλαι   noun, nom. pl. fem. {2.A} . . . . πύλη G4439
πύλας   noun, acc. pl. fem. {2.A} . . . . id.

G4439 πύλη, -ης, ἡ   *a gate.*
πύλη   noun, nom. sg. fem. {2.A}. . . . . πύλη G4439
πύλῃ   noun, dat. sg. fem. {2.A} . . . . id.
πύλην   noun, acc. sg. fem. {2.A} . . . . id.
πύλης   noun, gen. sg. fem. {2.A} . . . . id.

G4440 πυλών, -ῶνος, ὁ   *entrance passage, gateway; gate* (properly, *the passage which led from the street through the front part of the house to the inner court,* closed by a heavy πύλη at the streetward end).
πυλῶνα   noun, acc. sg. masc. {2.C} . . . . . . .πυλῶν G4440

πυλῶνας   noun, acc. pl. masc. {2.C}. . . . . id.
πυλῶνες   noun, nom. pl. masc. {2.C}. . . . . id.
πυλῶνος   noun, gen. sg. masc. {2.C} . . . . id.
πυλώνων   noun, gen. pl. masc. {2.C} . . . . id.
πυλῶσιν   noun, dat. pl. masc. {2.C} . . . . id.
πυνθάνεσθαι   vbl., pres. mid./pass. inf.
    {6.B.1}. πυνθάνομαι G4441
G4441 **πυνθάνομαι** I enquire.
    πυνθάνομαι   verb, pres. mid./pass. indic. 1 pers.
    sg. {5.A.1.d}. . . . . πυνθάνομαι G4441
G4442 **πῦρ**, -ός, τό fire; a fire, both lit., and met., and
    eschatologically (as an instrument of punish-
    ment in the conception of later Judaism,
    the fire of the Divine wrath which burns in
    Gehenna).
    πῦρ   noun, acc. sg. neut. {2.C}. . . . . πῦρ G4442
    πῦρ   noun, nom. sg. neut. {2.C} . . . . id.
G4443 **πυρά**, -ᾶς, ἡ a fire.
    πυράν   noun, acc. sg. fem. {2.A}. . . . . πυρά G4443
    πύργον   noun, acc. sg. masc. {2.B} . . . . . . πύργος G4444
G4444 **πύργος**, -ου, ὁ a tower.
    πύργος   noun, nom. sg. masc. {2.B} . . . . . . πύργος G4444
    πυρέσσουσα   vbl., pres. act. ptc. nom. sg. fem.
    {6.A.1}. . . . . πυρέσσω G4445
    πυρέσσουσαν   vbl., pres. act. ptc. acc. sg. fem.
    {6.A.1}. . . . . id.
G4445 **πυρέσσω** I have fever, I suffer from fever.
    πυρετοῖς   noun, dat. pl. masc. {2.B} . . . . . πυρετός G4446
G4446 **πυρετός**, -οῦ, ὁ a fever; medical writers use the
    pl. (Acts 28:8), where we should use the sg.,
    because of recurring attacks of fever.
    πυρετός   noun, nom. sg. masc. {2.B} . . . . πυρετός G4446
    πυρετῷ   noun, dat. sg. masc. {2.B} . . . . id.
    πυρί   noun, dat. sg. neut. {2.C} . . . . πῦρ G4442
G4447 **πύρινος**, -η, -ον as of fire, i.e., probably, fire
    colored.
    πυρίνους   adj., acc. pl. masc. {3.A}. . . . . . πύρινος G4447
    πυρός   noun, gen. sg. neut. {2.C} . . . . πῦρ G4442
    πυροῦμαι   verb, pres. pass. indic. 1 pers. sg.
    {5.A.2}. . . . . πυρόω G4448
    πυρούμενοι   vbl., pres. pass. ptc. nom. pl.
    masc. {6.A.2}. . . . . id.
    πυροῦσθαι   vbl., pres. pass. inf. {6.B.2} . . . . id.
G4448 **πυρόω** (1) I equip with fire, Eph 6:16 (of flam-
    ing darts), I refine by fire, Rev 1:15; 3:18, I burn
    with fire, I fire, 2 Pet 3:12; (2) mid. or pass.
    met., of strong passion or feeling, I burn with
    fleshly lust, 1 Cor 7:9; I blaze with anger, 2 Cor
    11:29.
    πυρράζει   verb, pres. act. indic. 3 pers. sg.
    {5.A.1.a} . . . . πυρράζω G4449
G4449 **πυρράζω** I am red (ruddy).
G4450 **πυρρός**, -ά, -όν red. As prop. name, Πύρρος,
    -ου, ὁ, Pyrrhus, father of the Christian Sopater
    of Beroea.
    πυρρός   adj., nom. sg. masc. {3.A} . . . . . . πυρρός G4450
    Πύρρου   noun prop., gen. sg. masc. {2.B; 2.D} . . id.
    πυρώσει   noun, dat. sg. fem. {2.C} . . . . . πύρωσις G4451
    πυρώσεως   noun, gen. sg. fem. {2.C} . . . . id.

G4451 **πύρωσις**, -εως, ἡ (1) burning; (2) met. trial as
    it were by fire, fiery test, 1 Pet 4:12.
    πωλεῖ   verb, pres. act. indic. 3 pers. sg.
    {5.A.2}. . . . . πωλέω G4453
    πωλεῖται   verb, pres. pass. indic. 3 pers. sg.
    {5.A.2}. . . . . id.
G4453 **πωλέω** (I advertise, put up for sale), I sell.
    πωλῆσαι   vbl., aor. act. inf. {6.B.1} . . . . πωλέω G4453
    πωλήσας   vbl., aor. act. ptc. nom. sg. masc.
    {6.A.2}. . . . . id.
    πωλήσατε   verb, aor. act. impv. 2 pers. pl.
    {5.D.1}. . . . . id.
    πωλησάτω   verb, aor. act. impv. 3 pers. sg.
    {5.D.1}. . . . . id.
    πωλήσει   verb, fut. act. indic. 3 pers. sg. {5.A.1} . id.
    πώλησον   verb, aor. act. impv. 2 pers. sg. {5.D.1} id.
    πῶλον   noun, acc. sg. masc. {2.B}. . . . . . . πῶλος G4454
G4454 **πῶλος**, -ου, ὁ (the young of various animals,
    hence particularly) the foal (colt) of a donkey.
    πωλούμενον   vbl., pres. pass. ptc. acc. sg. neut.
    {6.A.2}. . . . . πωλέω G4453
    πωλοῦνται   verb, pres. pass. indic. 3 pers. pl.
    {5.A.2}. . . . . id.
    πωλοῦντας   vbl., pres. act. ptc. acc. pl. masc.
    {6.A.2}. . . . . id.
    πωλοῦντες   vbl., pres. act. ptc. nom. pl. masc.
    {6.A.2}. . . . . id.
    πωλούντων   vbl., pres. act. ptc. gen. pl. masc.
    {6.A.2}. . . . . id.
    πωλοῦσιν   vbl., pres. act. ptc. dat. pl. masc.
    {6.A.2}. . . . . id.
G4455 **πώποτε** adv., ever yet, yet at any time, only used
    after a negative word.
    πώποτε   adv. . . . . πώποτε G4455
G4456 **πωρόω** (from πῶρος, a kind of marble, then,
    a bony formation on the joints, and a callus or
    ossification uniting two portions of a fractured
    bone; thus πωρόω, I petrify and I cover with
    a callus, and I deaden, I dull) I make (render)
    obtuse (dull, dead); I bind (intellectually or
    morally).
    πωρώσει   noun, dat. sg. fem. {2.C} . . . . . πώρωσις G4457
    πώρωσιν   noun, acc. sg. fem. {2.C}. . . . . id.
G4457 **πώρωσις**, -εως, ἡ (orig., petrifaction, hard-
    ness; then the result of this, as met. applied
    to organs of feeling), insensibility, numb-
    ness, obtuseness, dulling of the faculty of
    perception, deadness; intellectual (moral)
    blindness.
    πώρωσις   noun, nom. sg. fem. {2.C} . . . . πώρωσις G4457
G4458 **πώς** indef. part., enclitic, in some way, in any
    way; εἴ πως, if in any way; see μήπως.
    πώς   part. . . . . πώς G4458
G4459 **πῶς** interrog. part., (1) how?, in what manner?,
    also in indir. interrog.; πῶς γάρ . . . why,
    how . . . ; (2) = ὡς, ὅτι, that (variant readings
    sometimes occur), Matt 12:4; Mark 12:26, 41;
    Luke 6:4; 14:7; Acts 11:13; 1 Thess 1:9.
    πῶς   part., interrog. . . . . πῶς G4459

Ρ ρ

G4460 **Ῥαάβ**, ἡ   *Rahab,* a Canaanite woman, who rescued the Hebrew spies at Jericho, by tradition wife of Salmon (Matt 1:4, 5) (Heb.).

Ῥαάβ   noun prop. . . . . Ῥαάβ G4460
ῥαββεί   Heb.. ῥαββί G4461

G4461 **ῥαββί** (ῥαββεί)   *teacher, sir, rabbi;* lit. "my master," a title given by pupils to their teacher (Aram.).

ῥαββί   Heb. . . . . ῥαββί G4461
ῥαββονί   Aram. . . . . ῥαββουνί G4462
ῥαββουνεί   Aram. . . . . id.
ῥαββουνι   Aram. . . . . id.
ῥαββουνι   Aram. . . . . id.

G4462 **ῥαββουνί** (ῥαββονί), ῥαββουνεί)   *my master, my teacher* (Aram., a fuller form of ῥαββί).

ῥαββουνί   Aram. . . . . ῥαββουνί G4462
ῥαβδίζειν   vbl., pres. act. inf. {6.B.1} . . . ῥαβδίζω G4463

G4463 **ῥαβδίζω**   *I flog (beat) with a rod (staff),* a Roman punishment.

ῥάβδον   noun, acc. sg. fem. {2.B} . . . . ῥάβδος G4464

G4464 **ῥάβδος**, -ου, ἡ   *a staff, rod.*

ῥάβδος   noun, nom. sg. fem. {2.B} . . . . . . ῥάβδος G4464
ῥάβδου   noun, gen. sg. fem. {2.B} . . . . id.
ῥάβδους   noun, acc. pl. fem. {2.B} . . . . id.
ῥαβδοῦχοι   noun, nom. pl. masc. {2.B} ῥαβδοῦχος G4465

G4465 **ῥαβδοῦχος**, -ου, ὁ   (lit. *a rod holder, holder of rods*), *a lictor, an attendant (orderly),* of certain Roman magistrates, *a tipstaff.*

ῥαβδούχους   noun, acc. pl. masc. {2.B} ῥαβδοῦχος G4465
ῥάβδῳ   noun, dat. sg. fem. {2.B} . . . . ῥάβδος G4464

G4466 **Ῥαγαύ**, ὁ   *Reu,* an ancestor of Jesus (Heb.).

Ῥαγαύ   noun prop.. . . . . .Ῥαγαύ G4466
Ῥαγαῦ   noun prop.. . . . . id.

G4467 **ῥαδιούργημα**, -ατος, τό   *a moral wrong, a crime.*

ῥαδιούργημα   noun, nom. sg. neut.
{2.C} . . . . ῥαδιούργημα G4467

G4468 **ῥαδιουργία**, -ας, ἡ   (*ease in working; so unscrupulousness*); hence, *fraud, wickedness.*

ῥαδιουργίας   noun, gen. sg. fem. {2.A}ῥαδιουργία G4468
ῥαιδῶν   noun, gen. pl. fem. {2.A} . . . . ῥέδη G4480
Ῥαιφάν   noun prop.. . . . . .Ῥεμφάν G4481

G4469 **ῥακά** (ῥαχά)   *empty, foolish, fool* (Aram.).

ῥακά   Aram. . . . . ῥακά G4469

G4470 **ῥάκος**, -ους, τό   *a piece of cloth.*

ῥάκους   noun, gen. sg. neut. {2.C} . . . . ῥάκος G4470

G4471 **Ῥαμά**, ἡ   *Rama,* a place in Ephraim, two hours north of Jerusalem.

Ῥαμά   noun prop. . . . . .Ῥαμά G4471
Ῥαμά   noun prop. id.
ῥαντίζουσα   vbl., pres. act. ptc. nom. sg. fem.
{6.A.1} . . . . ῥαντίζω G4472

G4472 **ῥαντίζω**   (1) *I sprinkle* and thus *purify;* (2) mid. *I sprinkle* (i.e., *purify*) *myself,* Mark 7:4.

ῥαντισμόν   noun, acc. sg. masc. {2.B} . ῥαντισμός G4473

G4473 **ῥαντισμός**, -οῦ, ὁ   *sprinkling,* as a symbolic purification (cf. Exod 24:6–8).

ῥαντισμοῦ   noun, gen. sg. masc. {2.B}. ῥαντισμός G4473
ῥαντίσωνται   verb, aor. mid. subjunc. 3 pers. pl.
{5.B.1} . . . . ῥαντίζω G4472
ῥαπίζει   verb, pres. act. indic. 3 pers. sg.
{5.A.1.a} . . . . ῥαπίζω G4474

G4474 **ῥαπίζω**   *I slap, strike.*

ῥαπίσει   verb, fut. act. indic. 3 pers. sg.
{5.A.1.a} . . . . ῥαπίζω G4474

G4475 **ῥάπισμα**, -ατος, τό   *a slap, a blow on the cheek with the open hand.*

ῥάπισμα   noun, acc. sg. neut. {2.C} . . . . ῥάπισμα G4475
ῥαπίσμασιν   noun, dat. pl. neut. {2.C}. . . . . . . id.
ῥαπίσματα   noun, acc. pl. neut. {2.C} . . . . . . id.
ῥαφίδος   noun, gen. sg. fem. {2.C} . . . . . . ῥαφίς G4476

G4476 **ῥαφίς**, -ίδος, ἡ   *a sewing needle.*

G4477 **Ῥαχάβ**, ἡ   another spelling of Ῥαάβ (Heb.).

Ῥαχάβ   noun prop. . . . . Ῥαχάβ G4477

G4478 **Ῥαχήλ**, ἡ   *Rachel,* younger wife of the patriarch Jacob (Heb.).

Ῥαχήλ   noun prop. . . . . .Ῥαχήλ G4478

G4479 **Ῥεβέκκα**, -ας, ἡ   *Rebecca,* wife of the patriarch Isaac (Heb.).

Ῥεβέκκα   noun prop., nom. sg. fem. {2.A;
2.D} . . . . .Ῥεβέκκα G4479

G4480 **ῥέδη**, -ης, ἡ   *a carriage* (cf. *reda,* a word of Keltic origin).

ῥεδῶν   noun, gen. pl. fem. {2.A} . . . . ῥέδη G4480

G4481 **Ῥεμφάν** (Ῥαιφάν, Ῥεφάν, Ῥομφά, Ῥομφάν)   *Remphan, etc.,* a foreign deity, perhaps a corruption of the Assyrian name for the planet Saturn (= Chiun, Amos 5:26).

Ῥεμφάν   noun prop.. . . . . .Ῥεμφάν G4481
ῥεραντισμένοι   vbl., perf. pass. ptc. nom. pl. masc.
{6.A.1.b} . . . . ῥαντίζω G4472
ῥεραντισμένοι   vbl., perf. pass. ptc. nom. pl.
masc. {6.A.1.b} . . . . id.
ῥεραντισμένον   vbl., perf. pass. ptc. acc. sg.
neut. {6.A.1.b} . . . . id.
ῥεύσουσιν   verb, fut. act. indic. 3 pers. pl.
{5.A.1} . . . . ῥέω G4482

G4482 **ῥέω**   *I flow.*

G4484 **Ῥήγιον**, -ου, τό   *Regium,* a city in the southwest corner of Italy opposite Sicily (mod. Reggio).

Ῥήγιον   noun prop., acc. sg. neut. {2.B; 2.D}Ῥήγιον G4484

G4485 **ῥῆγμα**, -ατος, τό   *a breaking up, collapse.*

ῥῆγμα   noun, nom. sg. neut. {2.C} . . . . . . ῥῆγμα G4485

G4486 **ῥήγνυμι** (ῥήσσω)   (1) *I break; I rend, tear;* in Mark 9:18; Luke 9:42, it either = σπαράσσω, of convulsions, or *I throw on the ground;* (2) intrans., *I break forth into joy,* Gal 4:27.

ῥήγνυνται   verb, pres. pass. indic. 3 pers. pl.
{5.A.3.a} . . . . ῥήγνυμι G4486
ῥηθείς   vbl., aor. pass. ptc. nom. sg. masc.
{6.A.1.a.} . . . . ἐρέω G2046

ῥηθέν   vbl., aor. pass. ptc. acc. sg. neut. {6.A.1.a.} id.
ῥηθέν   vbl., aor. pass. ptc. nom. sg. neut. {6.A.1.a.} id.

G4487 ῥῆμα, -ατος, τό   (1) *a spoken word, an utter-ance*, the concr. expression of λόγος; hence, perhaps Hebraistic; (2) a subject as spoken about, a subject of speech, *a matter, a thing, a fact,* Matt 18:16; Luke 1:37; 2:15, etc.; (3) in a solemn sense, of a divine *word,* Luke 3:2; Eph 6:17, etc.; (4) the Christian *teaching, the gospel,* 1 Pet 1:25 (twice, the first of which is the promise to deliver Israel; cf. Rom 10:8ff.); (5) the Christian *confession,* "Jesus is Lord," which leads to salvation, and precedes baptism, Eph 5:26, cf. Rom 10:9; 1 Cor 12:3; Phil 2:11.

ῥῆμα   noun, acc. sg. neut. {2.C} . . . . .ῥῆμα G4487
ῥῆμα   noun, nom. sg. neut. {2.C} . . . . id.
ῥήμασι   noun, dat. pl. neut. {2.C} . . . . id.
ῥήμασιν   noun, dat. pl. neut. {2.C} . . . . id.
ῥήματα   noun, acc. pl. neut. {2.C} . . . . id.
ῥήματα   noun, nom. pl. neut. {2.C} . . . . id.
ῥήματι   noun, dat. sg. neut. {2.C} . . . . id.
ῥήματος   noun, gen. sg. neut. {2.C} . . . . id.
ῥημάτων   noun, gen. pl. neut. {2.C} . . . . id.
ῥήξει   verb, fut. act. indic. 3 pers. sg.
    {5.A.1} . . . . .ῥήγνυμι G4486
ῥῆξον   verb, aor. act. impv. 2 pers. sg. {5.D.3} . . . id.
ῥήξωσιν   verb, aor. act. subjunc. 3 pers. pl.
    {5.B.3} . . . . id.

G4488 Ῥησά, ὁ   *Resa,* an ancestor of Jesus (Heb.).
Ῥησά   noun prop. . . . . .Ῥησά G4488
ῥήσσει   verb, pres. act. indic. 3 pers. sg.
    {5.A.3.a} .ῥήγνυμι G4486
ῥήτορος   noun, gen. sg. masc. {2.C} . . . . . .ῥήτωρ G4489

G4489 ῥήτωρ, -ορος, ὁ   *a rhetorician, a professional public speaker;* hence, *a barrister,* acting as counsel for the prosecution.

G4490 ῥητῶς   adv., *in so many words, expressly, explicitly.*
ῥητῶς   adv. {3.F} . . . . .ῥητῶς G4490

G4491 ῥίζα, -ης, ἡ   *a root;* hence met., *a source.*
ῥίζα   noun, nom. sg. fem. {2.A} . . . . .ῥίζα G4491
ῥίζαν   noun, acc. sg. fem. {2.A} . . . . id.
ῥίζης   noun, gen. sg. fem. {2.A} . . . . id.

G4492 ῥιζόω   *I root, I fix by the root.*
ῥιζῶν   noun, gen. pl. fem. {2.A} . . . . .ῥίζα G4491

G4493 ῥιπή, -ῆς, ἡ   *a glance* (indicating instanta-neousness), *flash of an eye.*
ῥιπῇ   noun, dat. sg. fem. {2.A} . . . . .ῥιπή G4493
ῥιπιζομένῳ   vbl., pres. pass. ptc. dat. sg. masc.
    {6.A.1} . . . . .ῥιπίζω G4494

G4494 ῥιπίζω   *I raise* with the wind (from ῥιπίς, *a fire fan*; hence, *I fan* either a fire or a person).
ῥιπτόντων   vbl., pres. act. ptc. gen. pl. masc.
    {6.A.2} . . . . .ῥίπτω G4496
ῥιπτούντων   vbl., pres. act. ptc. gen. pl. masc.
    {6.A.2} . . . . id.

G4496 ῥίπτω (ῥιπτέω)   *I throw, cast; I shake, toss;* ἐρριμμένοι, *sunk powerless,* Matt 9:36; in Acts 22:23, *I toss about,* a sign of excitement and uncontrollable rage.

ῥῖψαν   vbl., aor. act. ptc. nom. sg. neut.
    {6.A.1.a} . . . . .ῥίπτω G4496
ῥῖψαν   vbl., aor. act. ptc. nom. sg. neut. {6.A.1.a} id.
ῥίψαντες   vbl., aor. act. ptc. nom. pl. masc.
    {6.A.1.a} . . . . id.
ῥίψας   vbl., aor. act. ptc. nom. sg. masc. {6.A.1.a} id.

G4497 Ῥοβοάμ, ὁ   *Rehoboam,* son of Solomon, and King of Israel (Heb.).
Ῥοβοάμ   noun prop. . . . . .Ῥοβοάμ G4497

G4498 Ῥόδη, -ης, ἡ   *Rhoda* (lit. *Rose*), a maidser-vant in the house of John Mark's mother at Jerusalem.
Ῥόδη   noun prop., nom. sg. fem. {2.A; 2.D} . .Ῥόδη G4498
Ῥόδον   noun prop., acc. sg. fem. {2.B; 2.D} . .Ῥόδος G4499

G4499 Ῥόδος, -ου, ἡ   *Rhodes,* an island in the Aegean sea, southwest of Asia Minor.

G4500 ῥοιζηδόν   adv., *with thunderous crash (roar);* properly expressing the whizzing sound pro-duced by rapid motion through the air.
ῥοιζηδόν   adv. {3.F} . . . . .ῥοιζηδόν G4500
Ῥομφά   noun prop. . . . . .Ῥεμφάν G4481

G4501 ῥομφαία, -ας, ἡ   *a sword, scimitar* (properly a long Thracian sword); met. in Luke 2:35 of acute suffering.
ῥομφαία   noun, nom. sg. fem. {2.A} . . . . .ῥομφαία G4501
ῥομφαίᾳ   noun, dat. sg. fem. {2.A} . . . . id.
ῥομφαίαν   noun, acc. sg. fem. {2.A} . . . . id.

G4502 Ῥουβήν, ὁ   *Reuben,* eldest son of the patriarch Jacob and founder of a tribe (Heb.).
Ῥουβήν   noun prop. . . . . .Ῥουβήν G4502
Ῥουβίμ   noun prop. id.

G4503 Ῥούθ, ἡ   *Ruth,* wife of Boaz and mother of Obed (Heb.).
Ῥούθ   noun prop. . . . . .Ῥούθ G4503
Ῥοῦφον   noun prop., acc. sg. masc. {2.B; 2.D} Ῥοῦφος G4504

G4504 Ῥοῦφος, -ου, ὁ   *Rufus,* a Christian man in Rome (Rom 16:3), probably to be identified with the brother of Alexander and son of Simon of Cyrene mentioned in Mark 15:21.
Ῥούφου   noun prop., gen. sg. masc. {2.B;
    2.D} . . . . .Ῥοῦφος G4504
ῥύεσθαι   vbl., pres. mid./pass. inf. {6.B.1} . ῥύομαι G4506
ῥύεται   verb, pres. mid./pass. indic. 3 pers. sg.
    {5.A.1.d} . . . . id.
ῥύμαις   noun, dat. pl. fem. {2.A} . . . . .ῥύμη G4505
ῥύμας   noun, acc. pl. fem. {2.A} . . . . id.

G4505 ῥύμη, -ης, ἡ   *a street* or *lane* in a town or city.
ῥύμην   noun, acc. sg. fem. {2.A} . . . . .ῥύμη G4505

G4506 ῥύομαι   *I rescue* (from danger or destruction).
ῥυόμενον   vbl., pres. mid./pass. ptc. acc. sg. masc.
    {6.A.1} . . . . .ῥύομαι G4506
ῥυόμενος   vbl., pres. mid./pass. ptc. nom. sg.
    masc. {6.A.1} . . . . id.
ῥυπανθήτω   verb, aor. pass. impv. 3 pers. sg.
    {5.D.1} . . . . .ῥυπόω G4510
ῥυπαρᾷ   adj., dat. sg. fem. {3.A} . . . . . . .ῥυπαρός G4508
ῥυπαρευθήτω   verb, aor. pass. impv. 3 pers. sg.
    {5.D.1} . . . . .ῥυπόω G4510

G4507 ῥυπαρία, -ας, ἡ   *defilement.*
ῥυπαρίαν   noun, acc. sg. fem. {2.A} . . . . .ῥυπαρία G4507

G4508 **ῥυπαρός**, -ά, -όν   *shabby, soiled;* hence morally,
  filthy, corrupt, sinful, Rev 22:11.
  ῥυπαρός adj., nom. sg. masc. {3.A} . . . . . ῥυπαρός G4508
G4509 **ῥύπος**, -ου, ὁ   *filth, dirt.*
  ῥύπου noun, gen. sg. masc. {2.B} . . . . ῥύπος G4509
G4510 **ῥυπόω** (ῥυπαρεύω, ῥυπαίνω)   *I make dirty,*
  I stain; mid. and pass., *I am filthy* (morally), *I*
  am stained (by sin).
  ῥυπῶν vbl., pres. act. ptc. nom. sg. masc.
  {6.A.2} . . . . ῥυπόω G4510
  ῥυπωσάτω verb, aor. act. impv. 3 pers. sg.
  {5.D.1} . . . . id.
  ῥῦσαι verb, aor. mid. impv. 2 pers. sg.
  {5.D.1} . . . . ῥύομαι G4506
  ῥυσάσθω verb, aor. mid. impv. 3 pers. sg.
  {5.D.1} . . . . id.
  ῥύσει noun, dat. sg. fem. {2.C} . . . . ῥύσις G4511
  ῥύσεται verb, fut. mid. indic. 3 pers. sg.
  {5.A.1.d} . . . . ῥύομαι G4506
  ῥυσθέντας vbl., aor. pass. ptc. acc. pl. masc.
  {6.A.1.a} . . . . id.
  ῥυσθῶ verb, aor. pass. subjunc. 1 pers. sg.
  {5.B.1} . . . . id.
  ῥυσθῶμεν verb, aor. pass. subjunc. 1 pers. pl.
  {5.B.1} . . . . id.
G4511 **ῥύσις**, -εως, ἡ   *flowing;* ῥύσις αἵματος,
  hemorrhage.

ῥύσις noun, nom. sg. fem. {2.C} . . . . ῥύσις G4511
ῥυτίδα noun, acc. sg. fem. {2.C} . . . . ῥυτίς G4512
G4512 **ῥυτίς**, -ίδος, ἡ   *a wrinkle* of age.
  Ῥωμαϊκοῖς adj. prop., dat. pl. neut.
  {3.A} . . . . Ῥωμαϊκός G4513
G4513 **Ῥωμαϊκός**, -ή, -όν   *Roman* (language), *Latin.*
  Ῥωμαῖοι adj. prop., nom. pl. masc. {3.A} Ῥωμαῖος G4514
  Ῥωμαίοις adj. prop., dat. pl. masc. {3.A} . . . . . id.
  Ῥωμαῖον adj. prop., acc. sg. masc. {3.A} . . . . . id.
G4514 **Ῥωμαῖος**, -ου, ὁ   *Roman; a Roman;* the pl.,
  according to context, suggests either the impe-
  rial people (e.g., John 11:48) or citizens of the
  Roman Empire (e.g., Acts 16:21).
  Ῥωμαῖος adj. prop., nom. sg. masc. {3.A} Ῥωμαῖος G4514
  Ῥωμαίους adj. prop., acc. pl. masc. {3.A} . . . . . id.
G4515 **Ῥωμαϊστί**   adv., *in the Latin language.*
  Ῥωμαϊστί adv. prop. . . . . Ῥωμαϊστί G4515
  Ῥωμαίων adj. prop., gen. pl. masc.
  {3.A} . . . . Ῥωμαῖος G4514
G4516 **Ῥώμη**, -ης, ἡ   *Rome,* the famous city on the
  Tiber, the capital of the Roman Empire.
  Ῥώμη noun prop., dat. sg. fem. {2.A; 2.D} . . Ῥώμη G4516
  Ῥώμην noun prop., acc. sg. fem. {2.A; 2.D} . . . . id.
  Ῥώμης noun prop., gen. sg. fem. {2.A; 2.D} . . . . id.
G4517 **ῥώννυμι**   *I make strong;* perf. mid. impv., a
  formula of correspondence, at the end of a
  letter, ἔρρωσο, ἔρρωσθε, *farewell.*

Σ ς

σά pron. posses, 2 pers. sg. acc. pl. neut. {4.H} . σός G4674
σά pron. posses, 2 pers. sg. nom. pl. neut. {4.H} . id.
σαβαχθανεί Aram. . . . . σαβαχθάνι G4518
σαβαχθανι Aram. . . . . id.
σαβαχθανί Aram. . . . . id.
G4518 **σαβαχθάνι** (σαβαχθάνει)   *thou hast forsaken*
  (Aram.).
G4519 **Σαβαώθ**   (Lord of) *Sabaoth, hosts, armies*
  (Heb.).
  σαβαώθ Heb. . . . . Σαβαώθ G4519
  σάββασι noun, dat. pl. neut. {2.B} . . . . σάββατον G4521
  σάββασιν noun, dat. pl. neut. {2.B} . . . . id.
  σάββατα noun, acc. pl. neut. {2.B} . . . . id.
G4520 **σαββατισμός**, -οῦ, ὁ   *a resting* as on the
  Sabbath.
  σαββατισμός noun, nom. sg. masc.
  {2.B} . . . . σαββατισμός G4520
G4521 **σάββατον**, -ου, τό   sg. and pl., *the Sabbath,* a
  night and day which lasted from about 6:00
  p.m. on Friday till about 6:00 p.m. on Saturday
  (Semitic); πρώτη (μία) (τῶν) σαββάτων or
  (τοῦ) σαββάτου), *Sunday, the first day after*
  the Sabbath, the day following the Sabbath, i.e.,
  from about 6:00 p.m. on Saturday till about
  6:00 p.m. on Sunday (Heb.).
  σάββατον noun, acc. sg. neut. {2.B} . . . σάββατον G4521
  σάββατον noun, nom. sg. neut. {2.B} . . . . id.

σαββάτου noun, gen. sg. neut. {2.B} . . . . id.
σαββάτῳ noun, dat. sg. neut. {2.B} . . . . id.
σαββάτων noun, gen. pl. neut. {2.B} . . . . id.
G4522 **σαγήνη**   *a fishing net.*
  σαγήνη noun, dat. sg. fem. {2.A} . . . . . . σαγήνη G4522
  Σαδδουκαῖοι noun prop., nom. pl. masc. {2.B;
  2.D} . . . . Σαδδουκαῖος G4523
G4523 **Σαδδουκαῖος**, -ου, ὁ   *a Sadducee, a Zadokite*
  priest, a member of the aristocratic party
  among the Jews, from whom the high priests
  were almost invariably chosen.
  Σαδδουκαίους noun prop., acc. pl. masc. {2.B;
  2.D} . . . . Σαδδουκαῖος G4523
  Σαδδουκαίων noun prop., gen. pl. masc. {2.B;
  2.D} . . . . id.
G4524 **Σαδώκ**, ὁ   *Zadok,* an ancestor of Jesus (Heb.).
  Σαδώκ noun prop. . . . . Σαδώκ G4524
  σαίνεσθαι vbl., pres. pass. inf. {6.B.1} . . . . σαίνω G4525
G4525 **σαίνω**   *I draw aside, allure* from the right
  path (properly of dogs, *I wag the tail, fawn;*
  then met. *I fawn upon, beguile*), 1 Thess 3:3.
  (Perhaps the var. σιαίνεσθαι, *to be disturbed*
  (troubled), ought to be read instead.)
G4526 **σάκκος**, -ου, ὁ   *sackcloth, sacking,* a rough
  mourning dress held together by string, and
  hanging on the bare body (a Semitic word).
  σάκκος noun, nom. sg. masc. {2.B} . . . . . . σάκκος G4526

σάκκους   noun, acc. pl. masc. {2.B} . . . . id.

σάκκῳ   noun, dat. sg. masc. {2.B} . . . . id.

G4527 **Σαλά**, ὁ   *Sala,* the name of two of the ancestors of Jesus (var. in Luke 3:32) (Heb.).

Σαλά   noun prop. . . . . .Σαλά G4527

G4528 **Σαλαθιήλ**, ὁ   *Salathiel,* son of Jechonias and father (according to one tradition) of Zerubbabel (Heb.).

Σαλαθιήλ   noun prop. . . . . .Σαλαθιήλ G4528

Σαλαμῖνι   noun prop., dat. sg. fem. {2.C; 2.D} . . . . Σαλαμίς G4529

G4529 **Σαλαμίς**, ῖνος, ἡ   *Salamis,* a city at the eastern end of Cyprus.

G4530 **Σαλείμ** (Σαλίμ), ὁ   *Salim,* a place eight Roman miles south of Scythopolis in the extreme north of Samaria.

Σαλείμ   noun prop. Σαλείμ G4530

σαλευθῆναι   vbl., aor. pass. inf. {6.B.1} . . .σαλεύω G4531

σαλευθήσονται   verb, fut. pass. indic. 3 pers. pl. {5.A.1.d} . . . . id.

σαλευθῶ   verb, aor. pass. subjunc. 1 pers. sg. {5.B.1} . . . . id.

σαλευόμενα   vbl., pres. pass. ptc. nom. pl. neut. {6.A.1} . . . . id.

σαλευόμενον   vbl., pres. pass. ptc. acc. sg. masc. {6.A.1} . . . . id.

σαλευομένων   vbl., pres. pass. ptc. gen. pl. neut. {6.A.1} . . . . id.

σαλεύοντες   vbl., pres. act. ptc. nom. pl. masc. {6.A.1} . . . . id.

σαλεῦσαι   vbl., aor. act. inf. {6.B.1} . . . . id.

G4531 **σαλεύω**   *I shake,* lit., and met.; *I dislodge.*

G4532 **Σαλήμ**, ἡ   *Salem,* doubtless identical with Jerusalem.

Σαλήμ   noun prop. .Σαλήμ G4532

G4533 **Σαλμών**, ὁ   *Salmon,* son of Naasson and father of Boaz; var. in Luke 3:32.

Σαλμών   noun prop. . . . . .Σαλμών G4533

G4534 **Σαλμώνη**, -ης, ἡ   *Salmone,* a promontory on the east of Crete.

Σαλμώνην   noun prop., acc. sg. fem. {2.A; 2.D} . . . . Σαλμώνη G4534

G4535 **σάλος**, -ου, ὁ   *a rough sea, surf.*

σάλου   noun, gen. sg. masc. {2.B} . . . . σάλος G4535

σάλπιγγα   noun, acc. sg. fem. {2.C} . . . . . σάλπιγξ G4536

σάλπιγγας   noun, acc. pl. fem. {2.C} . . . . id.

σάλπιγγες   noun, nom. pl. fem. {2.C} . . . . id.

σάλπιγγι   noun, dat. sg. fem. {2.C} . . . . id.

σάλπιγγος   noun, gen. sg. fem. {2.C} . . . . id.

G4536 **σάλπιγξ**, -ιγγος, ἡ   *a bugle, a war trumpet,* used for signals and commands; hence in eschatological passage as signal for Judgment or Resurrection.

σάλπιγξ   noun, nom. sg. fem. {2.C} . . . . . σάλπιγξ G4536

σαλπίζειν   vbl., pres. act. inf. {6.B.1} . . . . σαλπίζω G4537

G4537 **σαλπίζω**   *I sound the bugle, I give a blast of the bugle;* the subj. is sometimes omitted, so that the word becomes practically impers.

σαλπίσει   verb, fut. act. indic. 3 pers. sg. {5.A.1.a} . . . . σαλπίζω G4537

σαλπίσῃς   verb, aor. act. subjunc. 2 pers. sg. {5.B.1} . . . . id.

G4538 **σαλπιστής**, -οῦ, ὁ   *a bugler, trumpeter.*

σαλπιστῶν   noun, gen. pl. masc. {2.A} σαλπιστής G4538

σαλπίσωσι   verb, aor. act. subjunc. 3 pers. pl. {5.B.1} . . . . σαλπίζω G4537

σαλπίσωσιν   verb, aor. act. subjunc. 3 pers. pl. {5.B.1} . . . . id.

G4539 **Σαλώμη**, -ης, ἡ   *Salome,* wife of Zebedee and mother of James and John, the disciples.

Σαλώμη   noun prop., nom. sg. fem. {2.A; 2.D} . . . . Σαλώμη G4539

G4540 **Σαμάρεια**, -ας, ἡ   *Samaria,* a small district of Palestine, bounded by Galilee on the north, and by Judaea on the south, and taking its name from the city of Samaria, the ancient capital of the kingdom of (northern) Israel.

Σαμάρεια   noun prop., nom. sg. fem. {2.A; 2.D} . . . . Σαμάρεια G4540

Σαμαρείᾳ   noun prop., dat. sg. fem. {2.A; 2.D} . . id.

Σαμάρειαν   noun prop., acc. sg. fem. {2.A; 2.D} id.

Σαμαρείας   noun prop., gen. sg. fem. {2.A; 2.D} id.

Σαμαρεῖται   noun prop., nom. pl. masc. {2.A; 2.D} . . . . Σαμαρίτης G4541

Σαμαρείταις   noun prop., dat. pl. masc. {2.A; 2.D} . . . . id.

Σαμαρείτης   noun prop., nom. sg. masc. {2.A; 2.D} . . . . id.

Σαμαρείτιδος   noun prop., gen. sg. fem. {2.C; 2.D} . . . . .Σαμαρῖτις G4542

Σαμαρεῖτις   noun prop., nom. sg. fem. {2.C; 2.D} . . . . id.

Σαμαρειτῶν   noun prop., gen. pl. masc. {2.A; 2.D} . . . . Σαμαρίτης G4541

Σαμαρία   noun prop., nom. sg. fem. {2.A; 2.D} . . . . Σαμάρεια G4540

Σαμαρίᾳ   noun prop., dat. sg. fem. {2.A; 2.D} . id.

Σαμαρίαν   noun prop., acc. sg. fem. {2.A; 2.D} . id.

Σαμαρίας   noun prop., gen. sg. fem. {2.A; 2.D} . id.

Σαμαρῖται   noun prop., nom. pl. masc. {2.A; 2.D} . . . . Σαμαρίτης G4541

Σαμαρίταις   noun prop., dat. pl. masc. {2.A; 2.D} . . . . id.

G4541 **Σαμαρίτης**, -ου, ὁ   *a Samaritan, an inhabitant of Samaria.*

Σαμαρίτης   noun prop., nom. sg. masc. {2.A; 2.D} . . . . Σαμαρίτης G4541

Σαμαρίτιδος   noun prop., gen. sg. fem. {2.C; 2.D} . . . . .Σαμαρῖτις G4542

G4542 **Σαμαρῖτις**, -ιδος, ἡ   *a Samaritan woman.*

Σαμαρῖτις   noun prop., nom. sg. fem. {2.C; 2.D} . . . . .Σαμαρῖτις G4542

Σαμαριτῶν   noun prop., gen. pl. masc. {2.A; 2.D} . . . . Σαμαρίτης G4541

G4543 **Σαμοθράκη**, -ης, ἡ   *Samothrace,* an island south of the province of Thrace.

Σαμοθράκην   noun prop., acc. sg. fem. {2.A; 2.D} . . . . Σαμοθράκη G4543

Σάμον   noun prop., acc. sg. fem. {2.B; 2.D} . . Σάμος G4544

G4544 **Σάμος**, -ου, ἡ   *Samos*, an island in the Aegean
        sea off the coast of Asia Minor, near Ephesus
        and Miletus.

G4545 **Σαμουήλ**, ὁ   *Samuel*, an OT prophet (Heb.).
        Σαμουήλ   noun prop.. . . . . Σαμουήλ G4545

G4546 **Σαμψών**, ὁ   *Samson*, one of the Judges of Israel
        (Heb.).
        Σαμψών   noun prop. . . . . Σαμψών G4546
        σανδάλια   noun, acc. pl. neut. {2.B}. . . σανδάλιον G4547

G4547 **σανδάλιον**, -ου, τό   *a sandal, an open work
        shoe, a shoe.*

G4548 **σανίς**, -ίδος, ἡ   *a plank, board.*
        σανίσιν   noun, dat. pl. fem. {2.C}. . . . . .σανίς G4548

G4549 **Σαούλ**, ὁ   (1) *Saul*, the first king of Israel, Acts
        13:21; (2) *Saul*, the Heb. name of the Apostle
        to the Gentiles (see Σαῦλος).
        Σαούλ   noun prop.. . . . . .Σαούλ G4549
        σαπρά   adj., acc. pl. neut. {3.A} . . . . σαπρός G4550
        σαπρόν   adj., acc. sg. masc. {3.A} . . . . id.
        σαπρόν   adj., acc. sg. neut. {3.A} . . . . id.
        σαπρόν   adj., nom. sg. neut. {3.A} . . . . id.

G4550 **σαπρός**, -ά, -όν   *crumbling, decayed, decaying,
        rotten*; hence, *old and worn out, stale, worth-
        less*; met. *corrupt*, Eph 4:29.
        σαπρός   adj., nom. sg. masc. {3.A} . . . . . . σαπρός G4550
        Σαπφείρη   noun prop., dat. sg. fem. {2.A;
            2.D}. .Σάπφιρα G4551
        σάπφειρος   noun, nom. sg. fem. {2.B} . . σάπφιρος G4552

G4551 **Σάπφιρα** (Σαπφείρη), -ης, ἡ   *Sapphira*, wife of
        Ananias, an early Christian (perhaps from an
        Aram. word meaning *beautiful*).
        Σαπφίρη   noun prop., dat. sg. fem. {2.A;
            2.D}. .Σάπφιρα G4551

G4552 **σάπφιρος** (σάπφειρος), -ου, ἡ   *a sapphire;
        lapis lazuli* (Semitic).
        σάπφιρος   noun, nom. sg. fem. {2.B} . . . σάπφιρος G4552
        Σάραπτα   noun prop., acc. pl. neut. {2.B;
            2.D}. .Σάρεπτα G4558

G4553 **σαργάνη**, -ης, ἡ   *a mat basket*, a large basket of
        flexible material closed by sewing and usually
        employed to hold slices of salt fish (raisins and
        figs are also mentioned).
        σαργάνῃ   noun, dat. sg. fem. {2.A}. . . . . σαργάνη G4553

G4554 **Σάρδεις**, -εων, ἡ   *Sardis*, an ancient city of
        Lydia in the province of Asia.
        Σάρδεις   noun prop., acc. pl. fem. {2.C; 2.D} .Σάρδεις G4554
        Σάρδεσιν   noun prop., dat. pl. fem. {2.C; 2.D} . . id.

G4555 **σάρδινος**   Alt. form of σάρδιον.
        σαρδίνῳ   noun, dat. sg. masc. {2.B} . . . . σάρδινος G4555

G4556 **σάρδιον**, -ου, τό   *sardius, sard*, a quartz of a
        deep red color.
        σάρδιον   noun, nom. sg. neut. {2.B}. . . . . σάρδιον G4556
        σάρδιος   noun, nom. sg. masc. {2.B} . . . . id.
        σαρδίῳ   noun, dat. sg. neut. {2.B}. . . . . id.

G4557 **σαρδόνυξ**, -υχος, ὁ   *sardonyx.*
        σαρδόνυξ   noun, nom. sg. masc. {2.C}. .σαρδόνυξ G4557

G4558 **Σάρεπτα**, -ων, τό   *Sarepta*, a town in the dis-
        trict of Sidon in Phoenicia.
        Σάρεπτα   noun prop., acc. pl. neut. {2.B;
            2.D}. .Σάρεπτα G4558

σάρκα   noun, acc. sg. fem. {2.C} . . . . σάρξ G4561
σάρκας   noun, acc. pl. fem. {2.C} . . . . id.
σαρκί   noun, dat. sg. fem. {2.C} . . . . id.
σαρκικά   adj., acc. pl. neut. {3.A} . . . . . σαρκικός G4559
σαρκικά   adj., nom. pl. neut. {3.A} . . . . id.
σαρκικῇ   adj., dat. sg. fem. {3.A} . . . . id.
σαρκικῆς   adj., gen. sg. fem. {3.A} . . . . id.
σαρκικοί   adj., nom. pl. masc. {3.A} . . . . id.
σαρκικοῖς   adj., dat. pl. masc. {3.A} . . . . id.
σαρκικοῖς   adj., dat. pl. neut. {3.A}. . . . . id.

G4559 **σαρκικός**, -ή, -όν   generally ethical, *belonging
        to σάρξ* (q.v.), belonging to the natural life of
        man as a creature of flesh, *with the characteris-
        tics of σάρξ, fleshly, unspiritual, carnal.*
        σαρκικός   adj., nom. sg. masc. {3.A} . . . σαρκικός G4559
        σαρκικῶν   adj., gen. pl. fem. {3.A} . . . . id.
        σαρκίναις   adj., dat. pl. fem. {3.A} . . . . σάρκινος G4560
        σαρκίνης   adj., gen. sg. fem. {3.A} . . . . id.
        σαρκίνοις   adj., dat. pl. masc. {3.A} . . . . id.

G4560 **σάρκινος**, -η, -ον   material, *made of flesh,
        consisting of flesh.*
        σάρκινος   adj., nom. sg. masc. {3.A} . . . σάρκινος G4560
        σαρκός   noun, gen. sg. fem. {2.C}. . . . . .σάρξ G4561
        σαρκῶν   noun, gen. pl. fem. {2.C} . . . . id.

G4561 **σάρξ**, σαρκός, ἡ   (in general used Hebra-
        istically), (1) *flesh,* all the solid part of the
        body of man or beast except the bones, pl.
        (Hebraistic), e.g., Luke 24:39 (var.), Rev 17:16;
        σὰρξ καὶ αἷμα, a Hebraistic periphrasis for
        human nature, a human being; (2) hence, the
        substance (material) of the body, *the body;*
        μία σάρξ, *one body,* of husband and wife; it
        is contrasted some times with πνεῦμα, some-
        times with ψυχή; (3) (Hebraistic) *mankind,
        humanity* as such, without any necessary
        connotation of frailty, e.g., Rom 3:20; 1 Cor
        1:29; Gal 2:16; (4) *the animal (sensuous) nature*
        of man, the sphere of present existence, e.g.,
        John 1:13; Rom 9:3; 1 Cor 10:18; Heb 12:9;
        (5) in reference to fleshly (physical) weakness,
        helplessness, 1 Cor 15:50 (corruptible); 2 Cor
        4:11 (mortal); 7:5; 10:3; Eph 6:12; intellectual
        weakness, Rom 6:19; Gal 1:16; Col 2:18; cf.
        also 2 Cor 11:18; Gal 6:12, 13; Phil 3:3, 4; (6)
        in an ethical sense, characteristic of Paul,
        applied to part of human nature, generally as
        ruling instead of being, as it ought to be, in
        subjection; the two aspects are, (a) a general
        relation is implied between *the flesh* and sin,
        Rom 7:5; 8:3–9, 12, 13; 2 Cor 10:2; Gal 4:29;
        Col 2:11, 13; (b) *the flesh* is in some sense
        active in the production of evil, its desires (or
        lusts) are evil; in the physical nature it is the
        immediate enemy of the higher life, e.g., Rom
        7:7–25; 8:12; 13:14; Gal 5:13, 16, 17, 19, 24;
        Eph 2:3; Col 2:23.
        σάρξ   noun, nom. sg. fem. {2.C} . . . . σάρξ G4561
        σαροῖ   verb, pres. act. indic. 3 pers. sg. {5.A.2} .σαρόω G4563

G4562 **Σαρούχ** (Σερούχ), ὁ   *Saruch* (Seruch), an
        ancestor of Jesus (Heb.).

Σαρούχ   noun prop. . . . . Σαρούχ *G4562*

G4563 **σαρόω** *I sweep.*

G4564 **Σάρρα**, -ας, ἡ *Sarah, wife of Abraham* (Heb.).
Σάρρα noun prop., nom. sg. fem. {2.A; 2.D}Σάρρα *G4564*
Σάρρᾳ noun prop., dat. sg. fem. {2.A; 2.D} . . . . id.
Σάρρας noun prop., gen. sg. fem. {2.A; 2.D} . . . id.

G4565 **Σαρών** (Σαρρών), -ῶνος, ὁ *Sharon,* the mari-
time plain between Carmel and Joppa.
Σαρῶνα noun prop., acc. sg. masc. {2.C;
2.D} . . . . .Σαρών *G4565*
Σαρωνᾶν noun prop., acc. sg. masc. {2.C; 2.D} . id.
σάτα noun, acc. pl. neut. {2.B} . . . . σάτον *G4568*

G4566 **Σατάν**, ὁ Shortened spelling of Σατανᾶς.
Σατᾶν noun prop. . . . . Σατάν *G4566*
Σατανᾶ noun prop., gen. sg. masc. {2.A;
2.D} . . . . .Σατανᾶς *G4567*
Σατανᾶ noun prop., voc. sg. masc. {2.A; 2.D} . . id.
Σατανᾷ noun prop., dat. sg. masc. {2.A; 2.D} . . id.
Σατανᾶν noun prop., acc. sg. masc. {2.A; 2.D} . . id.

G4567 **Σατανᾶς**, -ᾶ, ὁ *the enemy, Satan, the devil, the
chief of the evil spirits* (Aram., lit. *adversary*),
both with and without the article, a representation of the word which is also translated ὁ
διάβολος.
Σατανᾶς noun prop., nom. sg. masc. {2.A;
2.D} . . . . .Σατανᾶς *G4567*

G4568 **σάτον**, -ου, τό a large measure equivalent to
nearly three English gallons (Aram.).
Σαῦλον noun prop., acc. sg. masc. {2.B;
2.D} . . . . .Σαῦλος *G4569*

G4569 **Σαῦλος**, -ου, ὁ the Graecized form of the Heb.
name Σαούλ of the Apostle to the Gentiles.
Σαῦλος noun prop., nom. sg. masc. {2.B;
2.D} . . . . .Σαῦλος *G4569*
Σαύλου noun prop., gen. sg. masc. {2.B; 2.D} . . id.
Σαύλῳ noun prop., dat. sg. masc. {2.B; 2.D} . . . id.
σαυτόν pron. refl., 2 pers. acc. sg. masc.
{4.F} . . . . .σεαυτοῦ *G4572*

G4570 **σβέννυμι** *I extinguish, put out;* met. 1 Thess
5:19.
σβέννυνται verb, pres. pass. indic. 3 pers. pl.
{5.A.3.a} . . . . σβέννυμι *G4570*
σβέννυται verb, pres. pass. indic. 3 pers. sg.
{5.A.3.a} . . . . id.
σβέννυτε verb, pres. act. impv. 2 pers. pl.
{5.D.3} . . . . id.
σβέσαι vbl., aor. act. inf. {6.B.3} . . . . id.
σβέσει verb, fut. act. indic. 3 pers. sg. {5.A.1} . id.
σε pron. pers., 2 pers. acc. sg. {4.A} . . . . σύ *G4771*
σέ pron. pers., 2 pers. acc. sg. {4.A} . . . . id.
σεαυτόν pron. refl., 2 pers. acc. sg. masc.
{4.F} . . . . .σεαυτοῦ *G4572*

G4572 **σεαυτοῦ**, -ῆς *of thyself (yourself).*
σεαυτοῦ pron. refl., 2 pers. gen. sg. masc.
{4.F} . . . . .σεαυτοῦ *G4572*
σεαυτῷ pron. refl., 2 pers. dat. sg. masc. {4.F} . . id.

G4573 **σεβάζομαι** *I reverence, worship.*

G4574 **σέβασμα**, -ατος, τό *an object of worship, a
thing worshipped.*
σέβασμα noun, acc. sg. neut. {2.C} . . . . .σέβασμα *G4574*

σεβάσματα noun, acc. pl. neut. {2.C} . . . . id.
Σεβαστῆς adj. prop., gen. sg. fem. {3.A} σεβαστός *G4575*
Σεβαστόν adj. prop., acc. sg. masc. {3.A} . . . . . id.

G4575 **σεβαστός**, -ή, -όν *revered, august;* ὁ Σεβαστός, *Augustus* (official Gk. equivalent),
the name meaning "worthy to be reverenced
(worshipped)," given to Octavian by the Senate in January, 27 B.C., and retained by most of
his successors, e.g., by Nero, to whom it refers
in Acts 25:21, 25, where it is of course used by
non-Christians; in Acts 27:1 σπεῖρα Σεβαστή
is the official equivalent of a *cohors Augusta*
(a *cohors I Augusta* had its head quarters in
Batanaea in northeast Palestine).
Σεβαστοῦ adj. prop., gen. sg. masc.
{3.A} . . . . σεβαστός *G4575*
σέβεσθαι vbl., pres. mid./pass. inf. {6.B.1}. . . σέβω *G4576*
σέβεται verb, pres. mid./pass. indic. 3 pers. sg.
{5.A.1.d} . . . . id.
σεβομένας vbl., pres. mid./pass. ptc. acc. pl.
fem. {6.A.1} . . . . id.
σεβομένη vbl., pres. mid./pass. ptc. nom. sg.
fem. {6.A.1} . . . . id.
σεβομένοις vbl., pres. mid./pass. ptc. dat. pl.
masc. {6.A.1} . . . . id.
σεβομένου vbl., pres. mid./pass. ptc. gen. sg.
masc. {6.A.1} . . . . id.
σεβομένων vbl., pres. mid./pass. ptc. gen. pl.
masc. {6.A.1} . . . . id.
σέβονται verb, pres. mid./pass. indic. 3 pers.
pl. {5.A.1.d} . . . . id.

G4576 **σέβω** mid., *I reverence, worship* generally in
Acts of god-fearing, uncircumcised Gentiles
who joined the Jewish synagogues (contrast
Acts 13:43).
σειομένη vbl., pres. pass. ptc. nom. sg. fem.
{6.A.1} . . . . σείω *G4579*

G4577 **σειρά**, -ᾶς, ἡ *a chain, cord, fetter.*
σειραῖς noun, dat. pl. fem. {2.A} . . . . σειρά *G4577*
σειροῖς noun, dat. pl. masc. {2.B} . . . . σιρός *G4577‡*
σεισμοί noun, nom. pl. masc. {2.B} . . . . . . .σεισμός *G4578*
σεισμόν noun, acc. sg. masc. {2.B} . . . . id.

G4578 **σεισμός**, -οῦ, ὁ *an earthquake.*
σεισμός noun, nom. sg. masc. {2.B} . . . . .σεισμός *G4578*
σεισμῷ noun, dat. sg. masc. {2.B} . . . . id.
σείσω verb, fut. act. indic. 1 pers. sg. {5.A.1.a} σείω *G4579*

G4579 **σείω** *I shake.*
σείω verb, pres. act. indic. 1 pers. sg. {5.A.1.a} σείω *G4579*

G4580 **Σεκοῦνδος**, -ου, ὁ *Secundus,* a Christian of
Thessalonica (Lat.).
Σεκοῦνδος noun prop., nom. sg. masc. {2.B;
2.D} . . . . Σεκοῦνδος *G4580*
Σέκουνδος noun prop., nom. sg. masc. {2.B;
2.D} . . . . id.

G4581 **Σελεύκεια**, -ας, ἡ *Seleucia,* on the Syrian
coast, the harbor of Syrian Antioch.
Σελεύκειαν noun prop., acc. sg. fem. {2.A;
2.D} . . . . .Σελεύκεια *G4581*
Σελευκίαν noun prop., acc. sg. fem. {2.A; 2.D} . id.

G4582 **σελήνη**, -ης, ἡ *the moon.*

σελήνη   noun, nom. sg. fem. {2.A}. . . . . . σελήνη G4582
σελήνη   noun, dat. sg. fem. {2.A}. . . . . id.
σελήνης   noun, gen. sg. fem. {2.A}. . . . . id.
σεληνιάζεται   verb, pres. mid./pass. indic. 3 pers.
   sg. {5.A.1.d}. . . . . σεληνιάζομαι G4583
G4583 **σεληνιάζομαι**   I bring under the influence
   of the moon; pass. I am epileptic (the state of
   an epileptic being attributed to σελήνη or
   moon).
σεληνιαζομένους   vbl., pres. mid./pass. ptc. acc.
   pl. masc. {6.A.1} . . . . σεληνιάζομαι G4583
Σεμεείν   noun prop. . . . . .Σεμεΐν G4584
Σεμεΐ   noun prop. . . . . id.
G4584 **Σεμεΐν**, ὁ   Semein, an ancestor of Jesus (Heb.).
Σεμεΐν   noun prop. . . . . .Σεμεΐν G4584
Σεμευ   noun prop. . . . . id.
σεμίδαλιν   noun, acc. sg. fem. {2.C}. . . .σεμίδαλις G4585
G4585 **σεμίδαλις**, -εως, ἡ   the finest wheaten meal.
σεμνά   adj., nom. pl. neut. {3.A}. . . . . σεμνός G4586
σεμνάς   adj., acc. pl. fem. {3.A} . . . . id.
G4586 **σεμνός**, -ή, -όν   grave, worthy of respect.
G4587 **σεμνότης**, -ητος, ἡ   gravity, dignified behavior.
σεμνότητα   noun, acc. sg. fem. {2.C} . . . . σεμνότης G4587
σεμνότητι   noun, dat. sg. fem. {2.C}. . . . . id.
σεμνότητος   noun, gen. sg. fem. {2.C} . . . . id.
σεμνούς   adj., acc. pl. masc. {3.A} . . . . σεμνός G4586
G4588 **Σέργιος**, -ου, ὁ   Sergius, the middle (gentile)
   name of the pro consul of Cyprus.
Σεργίῳ   noun prop., dat. sg. masc. {2.B; 2.D} . Σέργιος G4588
Σεροὺχ   noun prop. . . . . .Σαρούχ G4562
σεσαλευμένον   vbl., perf. pass. ptc. acc. sg. neut.
   {6.A.1.b} . . . . .σαλεύω G4531
σεσαρωμένον   vbl., perf. pass. ptc. acc. sg. masc.
   {6.A.2}. . . . . .σαρόω G4563
σέσηπε   verb, ²perf. act. indic. 3 pers. sg.
   {5.A.1.c} . . . . .σήπω G4595
σέσηπεν   verb, ²perf. act. indic. 3 pers. sg.
   {5.A.1.c} . . . . id.
σεσιγημένου   vbl., perf. pass. ptc. gen. sg. neut.
   {6.A.2}. . . . . σιγάω G4601
σεσοφισμένοις   vbl., perf. pass. ptc. dat. pl. masc.
   {6.A.1.b} . . . . .σοφίζω G4679
σέσωκε   verb, perf. act. indic. 3 pers. sg.
   {5.A.1.c} . . . . .σῴζω G4982
σέσωκεν   verb, perf. act. indic. 3 pers. sg.
   {5.A.1.c} . . . . id.
σεσωρευμένα   vbl., perf. pass. ptc. acc. pl. neut.
   {6.A.1.b} . . . . .σωρεύω G4987
σεσωσμένοι   vbl., perf. pass. ptc. nom. pl. masc.
   {6.A.1.b} . . . . .σῴζω G4982
σεσωσμένοι   vbl., perf. pass. ptc. nom. pl.
   masc. {6.A.1.b} . . . . id.
σέσωσται   verb, perf. pass. indic. 3 pers. sg.
   {5.A.1.f}. . . . . id.
σέσωται   verb, perf. pass. indic. 3 pers. sg.
   {5.A.1.f}. . . . . id.
σῇ   pron. posses, 2 pers. sg. dat. sg. fem. {4.H} . σός G4674
G4589 **Σήθ**, ὁ   Seth, third son of Adam (Heb.).
Σήθ   noun prop. .Σήθ G4589

G4590 **Σήμ**, ὁ   Shem, a son of Noah (Heb.).
Σήμ   noun prop. .Σήμ G4590
G4591 **σημαίνω**   I indicate by a word; I point out in
   a letter (by letter), Acts 25:27 (a technical
   term for the speech of a communicator of an
   oracle).
σημαίνων   vbl., pres. act. ptc. nom. sg. masc.
   {6.A.1}. . . . . .σημαίνω G4591
σημᾶναι   vbl., aor. act. inf. {6.B.1} . . . . id.
σημεῖα   noun, acc. pl. neut. {2.B}. . . . . . σημεῖον G4592
σημεῖα   noun, nom. pl. neut. {2.B}. . . . . id.
σημείοις   noun, dat. pl. neut. {2.B}. . . . . id.
G4592 **σημεῖον**, -ου, τό   a sign, an outward (visible)
   indication of secret power or truth; a miracle
   regarded from that point of view.
σημεῖον   noun, acc. sg. neut. {2.B}. . . . . . σημεῖον G4592
σημεῖον   noun, nom. sg. neut. {2.B}. . . . . id.
σημειοῦσθε   verb, pres. mid. impv. 2 pers. pl.
   {5.A.2}. . . . . σημειόω G4593
G4593 **σημειόω**   mid. I mark (notify) for myself, I take
   note of; hence, with an idea of disapprobation
   added.
σημείων   noun, gen. pl. neut. {2.B} . . . . . σημεῖον G4592
G4594 **σήμερον**   adv. today, this day; ἡ σήμερον
   (supply ἡμέρα), noun, today, this day.
σήμερον   adv. .σήμερον G4594
σήν   pron. posses, 2 pers. sg. acc. sg. fem. {4.H} σός G4674
G4595 **σήπω**   trans., I cause to rot; ²perf. σέσηπα, I
   have rotted, I am rotten.
G4596 **σηρικός** (σιρικός), -ή, -όν   silken; neut. subs.,
   silk fabrics or garments (from Σῆρες, the Chi-
   nese, from whose country silk was obtained).
σηρικοῦ   adj., gen. sg. neut. {3.A} . . . . . σηρικός G4596
G4597 **σής**, σητός, ὁ   a moth.
σής   noun, nom. sg. masc. {2.A} . . . . σής G4597
σής   pron. posses, 2 pers. sg. gen. sg. fem. {4.H} σός G4674
σητόβρωτα   adj., nom. pl. neut. {3.C} σητόβρωτος G4598
G4598 **σητόβρωτος**, -ον   moth-eaten.
G4599 **σθενόω**   I strengthen.
σθενώσαι   verb, aor. act. opt. 3 pers. sg.
   {5.C.1}. . . . . .σθενόω G4599
σθενώσει   verb, fut. act. indic. 3 pers. sg. {5.A.1} id.
σιαγόνα   noun, acc. sg. fem. {2.C} . . . . . . σιαγών G4600
G4600 **σιαγών**, -όνος, ἡ   a cheek.
σιγᾶν   vbl., pres. act. inf. {6.B.2} . . . . σιγάω G4601
σιγᾶν   vbl., pres. act. inf. {6.B.2} . . . . id.
σιγάτω   verb, pres. act. impv. 3 pers. sg. {5.D.2} . id.
σιγάτωσαν   verb, pres. act. impv. 3 pers. pl.
   {5.D.2}. . . . . id.
G4601 **σιγάω**   I am silent.
G4602 **σιγή**, -ῆς, ἡ   silence.
σιγή   noun, nom. sg. fem. {2.A} . . . . .σιγή G4602
σιγῆς   noun, gen. sg. fem. {2.A} . . . . id.
σιγῆσαι   vbl., aor. act. inf. {6.B.1} . . . . . . σιγάω G4601
σιγήσῃ   verb, aor. act. subjunc. 3 pers. sg. {5.B.1} id.
σιδηρᾷ   adj., dat. sg. fem. {3.A} . . . . . .σιδηροῦς G4603‡
σιδηρᾶν   adj., acc. sg. fem. {3.A} . . . . id.
G4604 **σίδηρος**, -ου, ὁ   iron.
σιδήρου   noun, gen. sg. masc. {2.B} . . . . . σίδηρος G4604

G4603‡ **σιδηροῦς**, -ᾶ, -οῦν   *made of iron.*
σιδηροῦς   adj., acc. pl. masc. {3.A}. . . . .σιδηροῦς G4603‡

G4605 **Σιδών**, -ῶνος, ἡ   *Sidon,* a great coast city of Phoenicia; in Mark 7:31 perhaps an error for *Saidan* = Bethsaida.
Σιδῶνα   noun prop., acc. sg. fem. {2.C; 2.D}.   Σιδών G4605
Σιδῶνι   noun prop., dat. sg. fem. {2.C; 2.D} . . . . id.
Σιδωνίας   noun prop., gen. sg. fem. {2.B; 2.D}. . . . . .Σιδώνιος G4606
Σιδωνίοις   adj. prop., dat. pl. fem. {3.A}. . . . . . id.
Σιδωνίοις   adj. prop., dat. pl. masc. {3.A}. . . . . . id.

G4606 **Σιδώνιος**, -α, -ον   *belonging to Sidon, Sidonian;* hence, as subs., *a Sidonian;* ἡ Σιδωνία (supply χώρα), *the region* or *territory of Sidon,* Luke 4:26.
Σιδῶνος   noun prop., gen. sg. fem. {2.C; 2.D} Σιδών G4605

G4607 **σικάριος**, -ου, ὁ   *an assassin, a murderer* (from Lat. *sica,* a stiletto); with reference to a fanatical Jewish political faction, accustomed to assassinate their opponents.
σικαρίων   noun, gen. pl. masc. {2.B} . . . .σικάριος G4607

G4608 **σίκερα**, τό   *an intoxicating drink, a strong fruit wine* (Aram.).
σίκερα   noun, indecl. . . . . σίκερα G4608
Σίλα   noun prop., dat. sg. masc. {2.A; 2.D} . . Σίλας G4609
Σιλᾷ   noun prop., dat. sg. masc. {2.A; 2.D} . . . . . id.
Σίλαν   noun prop., acc. sg. masc. {2.A; 2.D} . . . . id.
Σίλαν   noun prop., acc. sg. masc. {2.A; 2.D} . . . . id.
Σίλας   noun prop., nom. sg. masc. {2.A; 2.D} . . . id.

G4609 **Σίλας** (Σιλᾶς), -ᾶ, ὁ   *Silas,* a Jewish prophet and evangelist, a Roman citizen and a helper of Paul. The name is generally regarded as a pet form (used in Acts only) of Σιλουανός, and Silas is in consequence identified with him.
Σίλας   noun prop., nom. sg. masc. {2.A; 2.D} Σίλας G4609

G4610 **Σιλουανός** (Σιλβανός), -οῦ, ὁ   *Silvanus* (Lat., *Siluanus*); *probably the same person as* Σιλᾶς.
Σιλουανός   noun prop., nom. sg. masc. {2.B; 2.D}. Σιλουανός G4610
Σιλουανοῦ   noun prop., gen. sg. masc. {2.B; 2.D}. . . . . id.

G4611 **Σιλωάμ**, ὁ   *Siloam,* a spring (the only spring) within the walls, in the southeast corner of Jerusalem. The name is Aram. and really a subs. (= *discharge* or *gushing forth* of water).
Σιλωάμ   noun prop. . . . . .Σιλωάμ G4611
σιμικίνθια   noun, acc. pl. neut. {2.B} . σιμικίνθιον G4612

G4612 **σιμικίνθιον**, -ου, τό   *an* artisan's *working apron* (Lat., *semicinctium*).

G4613 **Σίμων**, -ωνος, ὁ   *Simon,* (1) the Apostle, son of Jonas (John) and brother of Andrew; (2) the Cananaean (former Zealot), one of the disciples; (3) a brother of Jesus; (4) a Pharisee, a former leper, at Bethany; (5) a native of Cyrene, Mark 15:21; Matt 27:32; Luke 23:26; (6) father of Judas Iscariot; (7) Simon Magus, a sorcerer in Samaria; (8) a tanner at Joppa. (See also Συμεών.).
Σίμων   noun prop., nom. sg. masc. {2.C; 2.D}Σίμων G4613

Σίμων   noun prop., voc. sg. masc. {2.C; 2.D}. . . . id.
Σίμωνα   noun prop., acc. sg. masc. {2.C; 2.D}. . . id.
Σίμωνι   noun prop., dat. sg. masc. {2.C; 2.D} . . . id.
Σίμωνος   noun prop., gen. sg. masc. {2.C; 2.D}. . id.
Σινᾶ   noun prop. . . . . Σινᾶ G4614

G4614 **Σινᾶ**   *Sinai,* a mountain in Arabia; according to Hebrew allegorical methods of interpretation identified with Hagar, concubine of Abraham, Gal 4:25 (Arabic *hadjar* = *rock, stone,* and thus comes the equation Hagar = Sinai).
Σινᾶ   noun prop. . . . . Σινᾶ G4614
σινάπεως   noun, gen. sg. neut. {2.C} . . . . . .σίναπι G4615

G4615 **σίναπι**, -εως, τό   *mustard.*
σινδόνα   noun, acc. sg. fem. {2.C} . . . . . . σινδών G4616
σινδόνι   noun, dat. sg. fem. {2.C}. . . . . id.

G4616 **σινδών**, -όνος, ἡ   *a fine light dress* worn over the under clothing, or *a nightgown,* or *a sheet* hastily seized (Semitic), Mark 14:51; of the grave clothes of Jesus, probably *a piece of unused linen,* Mark 15:46, etc.

G4617 **σινιάζω**   *I sift, winnow.*
σινιάσαι   vbl., aor. act. inf. {6.B.1} . . . . . . σινιάζω G4617
σιρικοῦ   adj., gen. sg. neut. {3.A} . . . . σηρικός G4596

G4577†‡ **σιρός** (σειρός), -οῦ, ὁ   *a pit* (properly a pit, excavation for the storage of grain). Var. for σειρά, 2 Pet 2:4.
σῖτα   noun, acc. pl. neut. {2.B} . . . . .σῖτος G4621
σιτευτόν   adj., acc. sg. masc. {3.A} . . . . . σιτευτός G4618

G4618 **σιτευτός**, -ή, -όν   *fed up* (with grain), *fattened.*
σιτία   noun, acc. pl. neut. {2.B}. . . . . σιτίον G4621†‡

G4621†‡ σιτίον, -ου, τό   *food made of corn, bread.* Var. for σῖτος, Acts 7:12.
σιτιστά   adj., nom. pl. neut. {3.A}. . . . . . σιτιστός G4619

G4619 **σιτιστός**, -ή, -όν   the same in meaning as the much commoner σιτευτός.

G4620 **σιτομέτριον**, -ου, τό   *measure of corn, portion of corn, allowance of corn.*
σιτομέτριον   noun, acc. sg. neut. {2.B} . . . . .σιτομέτριον G4620
σῖτον   noun, acc. sg. masc. {2.B}. . . . . .σῖτος G4621

G4621 **σῖτος**, -ου, ὁ   *corn.*
σίτου   noun, gen. sg. masc. {2.B} . . . . .σῖτος G4621

G4622 **Σιών**, ἡ   *Zion,* the mountain on which the Davidic citadel of Jerusalem was built, and thus the center of the life of the people Israel.
Σιών   noun prop. . . . . Σιών G4622
σιώπα   verb, pres. act. impv. 2 pers. sg. {5.D.2}. . . . . .σιωπάω G4623

G4623 **σιωπάω**   *I keep silence, I am silent.*
σιωπήσῃ   verb, aor. act. subjunc. 3 pers. sg. {5.B.1} . . . . .σιωπάω G4623
σιωπήσῃς   verb, aor. act. subjunc. 2 pers. sg. {5.B.1} . . . . id.
σιωπήσουσιν   verb, fut. act. indic. 3 pers. pl. {5.A.1} . . . . id.
σιωπήσωσιν   verb, aor. act. subjunc. 3 pers. pl. {5.B.1} . . . . id.
σιωπῶν   vbl., pres. act. ptc. nom. sg. masc. {6.A.2}. . . . . id.
σκάνδαλα   noun, acc. pl. neut. {2.B} . .σκάνδαλον G4625

σκανδαλίζει   verb, pres. act. indic. 3 pers. sg.
{5.A.1.a} .σκανδαλίζω G4624
σκανδαλίζεται   verb, pres. pass. indic. 3 pers.
sg. {5.A.1.d} . . . . id.
σκανδαλίζῃ   verb, pres. act. subjunc. 3 pers.
sg. {5.B.1} . . . . id.
σκανδαλίζονται   verb, pres. pass. indic.
3 pers. pl. {5.A.1.d} . . . . id.

G4624 **σκανδαλίζω**   *I put a stumbling block in the*
way of, I cause to stumble, I set a trap for (in
the moral sphere); a Hebraistic, biblical word.
σκανδαλίσῃ   verb, aor. act. subjunc. 3 pers. sg.
{5.B.1} . . . . .σκανδαλίζω G4624
σκανδαλισθῇ   verb, aor. pass. subjunc. 3 pers.
sg. {5.B.1} . . . . id.
σκανδαλισθήσεσθε   verb, fut. pass. indic.
2 pers. pl. {5.A.1.d} . . . . id.
σκανδαλισθήσομαι   verb, fut. pass. indic.
1 pers. sg. {5.A.1.d} . . . . id.
σκανδαλισθήσονται   verb, fut. pass. indic.
3 pers. pl. {5.A.1.d} . . . . id.
σκανδαλισθῆτε   verb, aor. pass. subjunc.
2 pers. pl. {5.B.1} . . . . id.
σκανδαλίσω   verb, aor. act. subjunc. 1 pers. sg.
{5.B.1} . . . . id.
σκανδαλίσωμεν   verb, aor. act. subjunc.
1 pers. pl. {5.B.1} . . . . id.

G4625 **σκάνδαλον**, -ου, τό   (1) *stumbling, cause*
of stumbling (in the moral sphere); πέτρα
σκανδάλου (Isa 8:14), *the native rock* rising up through the earth, *which trips up* the
traveler, hence, of Jesus the Messiah, to the
Jews who refused him; (2) *some person* (Matt
13:41; 16:23) or *thing which leads one to sin;* a
Hebraistic, biblical word.
σκάνδαλον   noun, acc. sg. neut. {2.B} .σκάνδαλον G4625
σκάνδαλον   noun, nom. sg. neut. {2.B} . . . . id.
σκανδάλου   noun, gen. sg. neut. {2.B} . . . . id.
σκανδάλων   noun, gen. pl. neut. {2.B} . . . . id.
σκάπτειν   vbl., pres. act. inf. {6.B.1} . . . . .σκάπτω G4626

G4626 **σκάπτω**   *I dig.*

G4627 **σκάφη**, -ης, ἡ   *a small boat,* towed behind.
σκάφην   noun, acc. sg. fem. {2.A} . . . . .σκάφη G4627
σκάφης   noun, gen. sg. fem. {2.A} . . . . id.
σκάψω   verb, aor. act. subjunc. 1 pers. sg.
{5.B.1} . . . . .σκάπτω G4626
σκέλη   noun, acc. pl. neut. {2.C} . . . . . . σκέλος G4628
σκέλη   noun, nom. pl. neut. {2.C} . . . . id.

G4628 **σκέλος**, -ους, τό   *a leg.*

G4629 **σκέπασμα**, -ατος, τό   strictly *roofing, shelter,*
but with special reference to *clothing.*
σκεπάσματα   noun, acc. pl. neut. {2.C} .σκέπασμα G4629
Σκευᾶ   noun prop., gen. sg. masc. {2.A;
2.D} . . . . Σκευᾶς G4630

G4630 **Σκευᾶς**, -ᾶ, ὁ   *Sceva,* an inhabitant of Ephesus.
σκεύει   noun, dat. sg. neut. {2.C} . . . . . . σκεῦος G4632
σκεύεσιν   noun, dat. pl. neut. {2.C} . . . . id.

G4631 **σκευή**, -ῆς, ἡ   *tackle* (a collective noun).
σκεύη   noun, acc. pl. neut. {2.C} . . . . σκεῦος G4632
σκεύη   noun, nom. pl. neut. {2.C} . . . . id.

σκευήν   noun, acc. sg. fem. {2.A} . . . . σκευή G4631

G4632 **σκεῦος**, -ους, τό   (1) *a vessel,* generally of
earthenware, e.g., John 19:29; τὰ σκεύη,
utensils, goods and chattels, effects, property;
(2) met. of persons, e.g., of Paul as chosen
repository of the power of Jesus (Hebraistic),
Acts 9:15; either of one's own body as the case
enclosing the soul, or of one's wife, 1 Thess 4:4
(cf. 1 Pet 3:7); (3) *tackle, furniture* of a ship,
Acts 27:17.
σκεῦος   noun, acc. sg. neut. {2.C} . . . . σκεῦος G4632
σκεῦος   noun, nom. sg. neut. {2.C} . . . . id.
σκηναῖς   noun, dat. pl. fem. {2.A} . . . . σκηνή G4633
σκηνάς   noun, acc. pl. fem. {2.A} . . . . id.
σκήνει   noun, dat. sg. neut. {2.C} . . . . . σκῆνος G4636

G4633 **σκηνή**, -ῆς, ἡ   *a tent; a hut;* usually with
reference to the temporary abode of Yahweh,
which preceded the Temple; ἡ σκηνὴ τοῦ
μαρτυρίου, *the tent as a witness to the*
covenant between God and His people; in Heb
9 the two parts of the one σκηνή, separated
from one another by the curtain, are each
called σκηνή.
σκηνή   noun, nom. sg. fem. {2.A} . . . . .σκηνή G4633
σκηνῇ   noun, dat. sg. fem. {2.A} . . . . id.
σκηνήν   noun, acc. sg. fem. {2.A} . . . . id.
σκηνῆς   noun, gen. sg. fem. {2.A} . . . . id.

G4634 **σκηνοπηγία**, -ας, ἡ   *the Feast of Tabernacles*
(lit. *of booth building*), sometimes called
ἑορτὴ (τῶν) σκηνῶν or ἑορτὴ (τῆς) σκηνο-
πηγίας, the great festival of the Jews, held in
October, originally the Feast of Ingathering.
σκηνοπηγία   noun, nom. sg. fem.
{2.A} . . . . σκηνοπηγία G4634
σκηνοποιοί   noun, nom. pl. masc.
{2.B} . . . . σκηνοποιός G4635

G4635 **σκηνοποιός**, -οῦ, ὁ   *a tentmaker.*

G4636 **σκῆνος**, -ους, τό   *a tent;* so met. (used in
Pythagorean philosophy) of the body as the
temporary dwelling place of the soul.
σκηνοῦντας   vbl., pres. act. ptc. acc. pl. masc.
{6.A.2} . . . . .σκηνόω G4637
σκηνοῦντες   vbl., pres. act. ptc. nom. pl. masc.
{6.A.2} . . . . id.
σκήνους   noun, gen. sg. neut. {2.C} . . . . . . σκῆνος G4636

G4637 **σκηνόω**   *I dwell as in a tent, I encamp.*

G4638 **σκήνωμα**, -ατος, τό   *a tent,* really a humble
word for the permanent building aimed at,
Acts 7:46; of the body as the temporary abode
of the soul.
σκήνωμα   noun, acc. sg. neut. {2.C} . . . . σκήνωμα G4638
σκηνώματι   noun, dat. sg. neut. {2.C} . . . . . id.
σκηνώματος   noun, gen. sg. neut. {2.C} . . . . . . id.
σκηνώσει   verb, fut. act. indic. 3 pers. sg.
{5.A.1} . . . . .σκηνόω G4637

G4639 **σκιά**, -ᾶς, ἡ   *a shadow, darkness, shade;* contrasted with the body casting the shadow, and
used met. somewhat like *a pale reflection,* Col
2:17; Heb 8:5; 10:1.
σκιά   noun, nom. sg. fem. {2.A} . . . . σκιά G4639

σκιᾷ   noun, dat. sg. fem. {2.A} . . . . id.

σκιάν   noun, acc. sg. fem. {2.A} . . . . id.

G4640 **σκιρτάω**   I leap, bound, jump.

σκιρτήσατε   verb, aor. act. impv. 2 pers. pl.
{5.D.1} . . . . σκιρτάω G4640

G4641 **σκληροκαρδία**, -ας, ἡ   stiffness, stubbornness,
unyieldingness, obduracy Hebraistic, from
σκληρός and καρδία, as the seat of the will).

σκληροκαρδίαν   noun, acc. sg. fem.
{2.A} . . . . σκληροκαρδία G4641

σκληρόν   adj., nom. sg. neut. {3.A} . . . . . σκληρός G4642

G4642 **σκληρός**, -ά, -όν   (properly hard), (1) strong,
Jas 3:4; (2) met. harsh, rough; almost = dangerous, Acts 26:14.

σκληρός   adj., nom. sg. masc. {3.A} . . . . . σκληρός G4642

G4643 **σκληρότης**, -ητος, ἡ   obstinacy.

σκληρότητα   noun, acc. sg. fem. {2.C}. σκληρότης G4643

σκληροτράχηλοι   adj., voc. pl. masc.
{3.C} . . . . σκληροτράχηλος G4644

G4644 **σκληροτράχηλος**, -ον   stiff-necked, stubborn.

σκληρύνει   verb, pres. act. indic. 3 pers. sg.
{5.A.1.a} . . . . σκληρύνω G4645

σκληρύνητε   verb, pres. act. subjunc. 2 pers. pl.
{5.B.1} . . . . id.

σκληρυνθῇ   verb, aor. pass. subjunc. 3 pers. sg.
{5.B.1} . . . . id.

G4645 **σκληρύνω**   I make unyielding.

σκληρῶν   adj., gen. pl. masc. {3.A}. . . . . . σκληρός G4642

σκληρῶν   adj., gen. pl. neut. {3.A} . . . . id.

σκολιά   adj., nom. pl. neut. {3.A} . . . . σκολιός G4646

σκολιᾶς   adj., gen. sg. fem. {3.A} . . . . id.

σκολιοῖς   adj., dat. pl. masc. {3.A} . . . . id.

G4646 **σκολιός**, -ά, -όν   crooked; hence met., perverse,
of turning off from the truth, crooked in
nature.

G4647 **σκόλοψ**, -οπος, ὁ   orig., a stake; but commonly
in NT times a thorn; a splinter; met. referring
to some physical trouble.

σκόλοψ   noun, nom. sg. masc. {2.C} . . . . σκόλοψ G4647

σκόπει   verb, pres. act. impv. 2 pers. sg.
{5.D.2} . . . . σκοπέω G4648

σκοπεῖν   vbl., pres. act. inf. {6.B.2} . . . . id.

σκοπεῖτε   verb, pres. act. impv. 2 pers. pl. {5.D.2} id.

G4648 **σκοπέω**   I look upon, I gaze upon, watch.

σκοπόν   noun, acc. sg. masc. {2.B} . . . . . . σκοπός G4649

G4649 **σκοπός**, -οῦ, ὁ   a mark to be aimed at (e.g., by
an archer).

σκοποῦντες   vbl., pres. act. ptc. nom. pl. masc.
{6.A.2} . . . . σκοπέω G4648

σκοπούντων   vbl., pres. act. ptc. gen. pl. masc.
{6.A.2} . . . . id.

σκοπῶν   vbl., pres. act. ptc. nom. sg. masc.
{6.A.2} . . . . id.

σκορπίζει   verb, pres. act. indic. 3 pers. sg.
{5.A.1.a} . . . . σκορπίζω G4650

G4650 **σκορπίζω**   I scatter.

σκορπίοι   noun, nom. pl. masc. {2.B}. . . σκορπίος G4651

σκορπίοις   noun, dat. pl. masc. {2.B} . . . . id.

σκορπίον   noun, acc. sg. masc. {2.B} . . . . id.

G4651 **σκορπίος**, -ου, ὁ   a scorpion.

σκορπίου   noun, gen. sg. masc. {2.B}. . . σκορπίος G4651

σκορπισθῆτε   verb, aor. pass. subjunc. 2 pers. pl.
{5.B.1} . . . . σκορπίζω G4650

σκορπίων   noun, gen. pl. masc. {2.B}. . . σκορπίος G4651

σκότει   noun, dat. sg. neut. {2.C} . . . . σκότος G4655

σκοτεινόν   adj., acc. sg. neut. {3.A} . . . σκοτεινός G4652

σκοτεινόν   adj., nom. sg. neut. {3.A} . . . . id.

G4652 **σκοτεινός**, -ή, -όν   dark.

G4653 **σκοτία**, -ας, ἡ   darkness; hence met. of ignorance and sin.

σκοτία   noun, nom. sg. fem. {2.A} . . . . σκοτία G4653

σκοτίᾳ   noun, dat. sg. fem. {2.A} . . . . id.

σκοτίας   noun, gen. sg. fem. {2.A} . . . . id.

G4654 **σκοτίζω**   I darken, esp. of an eclipse of the sun,
cf. Luke 23:45 (var.); met. of blindness, Rom
11:10, ignorance, Rom 1:21.

σκοτινόν   adj., acc. sg. neut. {3.A} . . . . σκοτεινός G4652

σκοτινόν   adj., nom. sg. neut. {3.A} . . . . id.

σκοτισθῇ   verb, aor. pass. subjunc. 3 pers. sg.
{5.B.1} . . . . σκοτίζω G4654

σκοτισθήσεται   verb, fut. pass. indic. 3 pers.
sg. {5.A.1.d} . . . . id.

σκοτισθήτωσαν   verb, aor. pass. impv. 3 pers.
pl. {5.D.1} . . . . id.

G4655 **σκότος**, -ους, τό   darkness; frequent in the
conceptions of Jewish eschatology, Matt 8:12;
22:13; 25:30; met. of the darkness of ignorance
and sin, Luke 1:79; John 3:19, etc.

σκότος   noun, acc. sg. neut. {2.C} . . . . σκότος G4655

σκότος   noun, nom. sg. neut. {2.C}. . . . . id.

σκότους   noun, gen. sg. neut. {2.C} . . . . id.

G4656 **σκοτόω**   I darken, lit. or met.

σκότῳ   noun, dat. sg. masc. {2.B} . . . . . . σκότος G4655

σκύβαλα   noun, acc. pl. neut. {2.B} . . . σκύβαλον G4657

G4657 **σκύβαλον**, -ου, τό   sweepings, refuse, esp. dirt,
dung (popularly used of the human skeleton).

G4658 **Σκύθης**, -ου, ὁ   a Scythian, an uncivilized
inhabitant of northeast Europe.

Σκύθης   noun prop., nom. sg. masc. {2.A;
2.D} . . . . Σκύθης G4658

σκυθρωποί   adj., nom. pl. masc. {3.C} . σκυθρωπός G4659

G4659 **σκυθρωπός**, -ή, -όν   with downcast countenance; sad-faced; gloomy.

σκῦλα   noun, acc. pl. neut. {2.B} . . . . σκῦλον G4661

σκύλλε   verb, pres. act. impv. 2 pers. sg.
{5.D.1} . . . . σκύλλω G4660

σκύλλεις   verb, pres. act. indic. 2 pers. sg.
{5.A.1.a} . . . . id.

σκύλλου   verb, pres. pass. impv. 2 pers. sg.
{5.D.1} . . . . id.

G4660 **σκύλλω**   (orig., I flay, skin), (1) I tire out by
hunting; I distress, Matt 9:36; (2) (a slang usage
in origin) I worry, trouble.

G4661 **σκῦλον**, -ου, τό   pl., booty, spoils.

G4662 **σκωληκόβρωτος**, -ον   eaten by worms.

σκωληκόβρωτος   adj., nom. sg. masc.
{3.C} . . . . σκωληκόβρωτος G4662

G4663 **σκώληξ**, -ηκος, ὁ   a worm.

σκώληξ   noun, nom. sg. masc. {2.C} . . . . σκώληξ G4663

G4664 **σμαράγδινος**, -η, -ον   of an emerald.

σμαραγδίνῳ   adj., dat. sg. masc.
{3.A} . . . . σμαράγδινος G4664

σμαραγδίνων   adj., gen. pl. masc. {3.A} . . . . . . id.

G4665 **σμάραγδος**, -ου, ὁ   *an emerald.*

σμάραγδος   noun, nom. sg. masc. {2.B}σμάραγδος G4665

G4666 **σμύρνα**, -ης, ἡ   *myrrh* (= **μύρρα**), a fragrant
gum-resin from the Arabian Balsamodendron
Myrrhae.

G4667 **Σμύρνα**, -ης, ἡ   *Smyrna,* a great port of the
Roman province Asia.

G4668 **Σμυρναῖος**, -α, -ον   *Smyrnaean, coming from
Smyrna.*

Σμυρναίων   noun prop., gen. pl. masc. {2.B;
2.D} . . . . Σμυρναῖος G4668

σμύρναν   noun, acc. sg. fem. {2.A} . . . . . σμύρνα G4666

Σμύρναν   noun prop., acc. sg. fem. {2.A;
2.D} . . . . Σμύρναν G4667

Σμύρνῃ   noun prop., dat. sg. fem. {2.A; 2.D} . . . id.

σμύρνης   noun, gen. sg. fem. {2.A} . . . . . . σμύρνα G4666

G4669 **σμυρνίζω**   *I spice with myrrh.*

G4670 **Σόδομα**, -ων, τό   *Sodom,* a city submerged by
the Dead Sea.

Σόδομα   noun prop., nom. pl. neut. {2.B;
2.D} . . . . Σόδομα G4670

Σοδόμοις   noun prop., dat. pl. neut. {2.B; 2.D} . . id.

Σοδόμων   noun prop., gen. pl. neut. {2.B; 2.D} . . id.

σοι   pron. pers., 2 pers. dat. sg. {4.A} . . . . σύ G4771

σοι   pron. posses, 2 pers. sg. nom. pl. masc.
{4.H} . . . . σός G4674

σοί   pron. pers., 2 pers. dat. sg. {4.A} . . . . σύ G4771

σοί   pron. posses, 2 pers. sg. nom. pl. masc. {4.H} σός G4674

G4672 **Σολομών**, -ῶνος (ῶντος), ὁ   *Solomon,* son of
David, King of Israel, and Bathsheba (oldest
form Σαλωμών, next oldest Σαλομών).

Σολομών   noun prop., nom. sg. masc. {2.C;
2.D} . . . . Σολομών G4672

Σολομῶν   noun prop., nom. sg. masc. {2.C; 2.D} id.

Σολομῶνα   noun prop., acc. sg. masc. {2.C; 2.D} id.

Σολομῶνος   noun prop., gen. sg. masc. {2.C;
2.D} . . . . id.

Σολομῶντα   noun prop., acc. sg. masc. {2.C;
2.D} . . . . id.

Σολομῶντος   noun prop., gen. sg. masc. {2.C;
2.D} . . . . id.

σόν   pron. posses, 2 pers. sg. acc. sg. neut. {4.H} σός G4674

σόν   pron. posses, 2 pers. sg. nom. sg. neut. {4.H}id.

G4673 **σορός**, -οῦ, ἡ   *a bier.*

σοροῦ   noun, gen. sg. fem. {2.B} . . . . σορός G4673

G4674 **σός**, σή, σόν   *your, yours;* neut. subs., τὰ σά,
your property.

σός   pron. posses, 2 pers. sg. nom. sg. masc.
{4.H} . . . . σός G4674

σου   pron. pers., 2 pers. gen. sg. {4.A} . . . . σύ G4771

σού   pron. pers., 2 pers. gen. sg. {4.A} . . . . id.

σοῦ   pron. pers., 2 pers. gen. sg. {4.A} . . . . id.

σουδάρια   noun, acc. pl. neut. {2.B} . . σουδάριον G4676

G4676 **σουδάριον**, -ου, τό   *a handkerchief* (Lat., borrowed by Gk., and thence by Aram.).

σουδάριον   noun, acc. sg. neut. {2.B} . . σουδάριον G4676

σουδαρίῳ   noun, dat. sg. neut. {2.B} . . . . id.

σούς   pron. posses, 2 pers. sg. acc. pl. masc.
{4.H} . . . . σός G4674

G4677 **Σουσάννα**, -ης, ἡ   *Susannah,* a woman of the
retinue of Jesus.

Σουσάννα   noun prop., nom. sg. fem. {2.A;
2.D} . . . . Σουσάννα G4677

G4678 **σοφία**, -ας, ἡ   *wisdom,* the highest intellectual gift, of comprehensive insight into the
ways and purposes of God; sometimes, e.g.,
Acts 6:3; 1 Cor 6:5; Jas 1:5, *practical wisdom,*
that endowment of heart and mind which is
needed for the right conduct of life.

σοφία   noun, nom. sg. fem. {2.A} . . . . σοφία G4678

σοφίᾳ   noun, dat. sg. fem. {2.A} . . . . id.

σοφίαν   noun, acc. sg. fem. {2.A} . . . . id.

σοφίας   noun, gen. sg. fem. {2.A} . . . . id.

G4679 **σοφίζω**   *I make wise;* σεσοφισμένος, *fictitious,*
2 Pet 1:16.

σοφίσαι   vbl., aor. act. inf. {6.B.1} . . . . σοφίζω G4679

σοφοί   adj., nom. pl. masc. {3.A} . . . . . σοφός G4680

σοφοῖς   adj., dat. pl. masc. {3.A} . . . . id.

G4680 **σοφός**, -ή, -όν   *wise; skilled, an expert, a man of
learning* (Hebraism), Matt 11:25; 1 Cor 3:10,
etc.

σοφός   adj., nom. sg. masc. {3.A} . . . . σοφός G4680

σοφούς   adj., acc. pl. masc. {3.A} . . . . id.

σοφῷ   adj., dat. sg. masc. {3.A} . . . . id.

σοφῶν   adj., gen. pl. masc. {3.A} . . . . id.

σοφώτερον   adj. comp., nom. sg. neut. {3.A;
3.G} . . . . id.

G4681 **Σπανία**, -ας, ἡ   *Spain,* roughly coextensive
with the mod. country of the name (Lat.
Hispania).

Σπανίαν   noun prop., acc. sg. fem. {2.A;
2.D} . . . . Σπανία G4681

σπαράξαν   vbl., aor. act. ptc. nom. sg. neut.
{6.A.1.a} . . . . σπαράσσω G4682

σπαράξας   vbl., aor. act. ptc. nom. sg. masc.
{6.A.1.a} . . . . id.

σπαράσσει   verb, pres. act. indic. 3 pers. sg.
{5.A.1.a} . . . . id.

G4682 **σπαράσσω**   *I throw* on the ground.

G4683 **σπαργανόω**   *I swathe.*

σπαρείς   vbl., ²aor. pass. ptc. nom. sg. masc.
{6.A.1.a} . . . . σπείρω G4687

σπαρέντες   vbl., ²aor. pass. ptc. nom. pl. masc.
{6.A.1.a} . . . . id.

σπαρῇ   verb, ²aor. pass. subjunc. 3 pers. sg.
{5.B.1} . . . . id.

σπασάμενος   vbl., aor. mid. ptc. nom. sg. masc.
{6.A.2} . . . . σπάω G4685

G4684 **σπαταλάω**   *I live voluptuously* or *luxuriously.*

σπαταλῶσα   vbl., pres. act. ptc. nom. sg. fem.
{6.A.2} . . . . σπαταλάω G4684

G4685 **σπάω**   mid. *I draw my* (sword).

G4686 **σπεῖρα**, -ης, ἡ   *a cohort,* i.e., about 600 infantry, under the command of a tribune.

σπεῖρα   noun, nom. sg. fem. {2.A} . . . . σπεῖρα G4686

σπεῖραι   vbl., aor. act. inf. {6.B.1} . . . . σπείρω G4687
σπεῖραν   noun, acc. sg. fem. {2.A} . . . . . . σπεῖρα G4686
σπείραντι   vbl., aor. act. ptc. dat. sg. masc.
    {6.A.1.a} . . . . σπείρω G4687
σπείραντος   vbl., aor. act. ptc. gen. sg. masc.
    {6.A.1.a} . . . . id.
σπείρας   vbl., aor. act. ptc. nom. sg. masc.
    {6.A.1.a} . . . . id.
σπείρει   verb, pres. act. indic. 3 pers. sg.
    {5.A.1.a} . . . . id.
σπείρειν   vbl., pres. act. inf. {6.B.1} . . . . id.
σπείρεις   verb, pres. act. indic. 2 pers. sg.
    {5.A.1.a} . . . . id.
σπείρεται   verb, pres. pass. indic. 3 pers. sg.
    {5.A.1.d} . . . . id.
σπείρῃ   verb, pres. act. subjunc. 3 pers. sg.
    {5.B.1} . . . . id.
σπείρης   noun, gen. sg. fem. {2.A} . . . . . . σπεῖρα G4686
σπειρόμενοι   vbl., pres. pass. ptc. nom. pl. masc.
    {6.A.1} . . . . σπείρω G4687
σπείροντι   vbl., pres. act. ptc. dat. sg. masc.
    {6.A.1} . . . . id.
σπείροντος   vbl., pres. act. ptc. gen. sg. masc.
    {6.A.1} . . . . id.
σπείρουσιν   verb, pres. act. indic. 3 pers. pl.
    {5.A.1.a} . . . . id.
G4687   **σπείρω**   *I sow,* lit. or met.
σπείρων   vbl., pres. act. ptc. nom. sg. masc.
    {6.A.1} . . . . σπείρω G4687
σπεκουλάτορα   noun, acc. sg. masc.
    {2.C} . . . . σπεκουλάτωρ G4688
G4688   **σπεκουλάτωρ**, -ορος, ὁ   *a scout; a courier;*
    also *an executioner* (Lat.).
σπεκουλάτωρα   noun, acc. sg. masc.
    {2.C} . . . . σπεκουλάτωρ G4688
σπένδομαι   verb, pres. pass. indic. 1 pers. sg.
    {5.A.1.d} . . . . σπένδω G4689
G4689   **σπένδω**   *I pour out* an offering of wine to a god;
    hence pass. met., of the *outpouring* of one's life
    blood in service and suffering.
G4690   **σπέρμα**, -ατος, τό   (1) *seed,* commonly of cere-
    als; (2) *offspring, descendants,* in the animal
    kingdom (frequent in Heb.).
σπέρμα   noun, acc. sg. neut. {2.C} . . . . . . σπέρμα G4690
σπέρμα   noun, nom. sg. neut. {2.C} . . . . id.
σπέρμασιν   noun, dat. pl. neut. {2.C} . . . . id.
σπέρματι   noun, dat. sg. neut. {2.C} . . . . id.
σπέρματος   noun, gen. sg. neut. {2.C} . . . . id.
σπερμάτων   noun, gen. pl. neut. {2.C} . . . . id.
G4691   **σπερμολόγος**, -ου, ὁ   (from σπέρμα and
    λέγω; a slang term in Acts, used properly
    of a bird *picking up seeds;* hence) *a parasite,*
    hanger on; (also of one who *picks up scraps* of
    information and retails them at secondhand), ·
    an ignorant plagiarist.
σπερμολόγος   adj., nom. sg. masc.
    {3.C} . . . . σπερμολόγος G4691
σπεύδοντας   vbl., pres. act. ptc. acc. pl. masc.
    {6.A.1} . . . . σπεύδω G4692
G4692   **σπεύδω**   *I hasten, hurry.*

σπεύσαντες   vbl., aor. act. ptc. nom. pl. masc.
    {6.A.1.a} . . . . σπεύδω G4692
σπεύσας   vbl., aor. act. ptc. nom. sg. masc.
    {6.A.1.a} . . . . id.
σπεῦσον   verb, aor. act. impv. 2 pers. sg. {5.D.1}. id.
σπήλαια   noun, acc. pl. neut. {2.B} . . . . σπήλαιον G4693
σπηλαίοις   noun, dat. pl. neut. {2.B} . . . . id.
G4693   **σπήλαιον**, -ου, τό   *a cave* (esp. as inhabited).
σπήλαιον   noun, acc. sg. neut. {2.B} . . . σπήλαιον G4693
σπήλαιον   noun, nom. sg. neut. {2.B} . . . . id.
σπιλάδες   noun, nom. pl. fem. {2.C} . . . . . σπιλάς G4694
G4694   **σπιλάς**, -άδος, ἡ   adjectivally used with ἄνε-
    μος understood, *a dirty, foul* (lit.), *miry wind,*
    perhaps of its effect on the water.
σπίλοι   noun, nom. pl. masc. {2.B} . . . . . . .σπίλος G4696
σπίλον   noun, acc. sg. masc. {2.B} . . . . id.
σπῖλον   noun, acc. sg. masc. {2.B} . . . . id.
G4696   **σπίλος**, -ου, ὁ   *a spot* of disfigurement.
σπιλοῦσα   vbl., pres. act. ptc. nom. sg. fem.
    {6.A.2} . . . . σπιλόω G4695‡
G4695‡   **σπιλόω**   *I stain,* lit. or met.
σπλάγχνα   noun, acc. pl. neut. {2.B} . . σπλάγχνον G4698
σπλάγχνα   noun, nom. pl. neut. {2.B} . . . . id.
G4697   **σπλαγχνίζομαι**   *I am filled with pity, I have*
    sympathy (Hebraism).
σπλαγχνίζομαι   verb, pres. mid./pass. indic.
    1 pers. sg. {5.A.1.d} . . . . σπλαγχνίζομαι G4697
σπλαγχνισθείς   vbl., aor. pass. ptc. nom. sg.
    masc. {6.A.1.a}. id.
σπλάγχνοις   noun, dat. pl. neut. {2.B} . σπλάγχνον G4698
G4698   **σπλάγχνον**, -ου, τό   (alt. fem. form σπλάγχνα
    in Phil 2:1, if text be genuine), usually pl.
    σπλάγχνα, *the nobler viscera, heart.,* etc., and
    esp., Hebraistically, as the seat of certain feel-
    ings, or from the observed effect of emotion
    on them, *compassion* and *pity.*
σπόγγον   noun, acc. sg. masc. {2.B} . . . .σπόγγος G4699
G4699   **σπόγγος**, -ου, ὁ   *a sponge.*
G4700   **σποδός**, -οῦ, ἡ   *ashes.*
σποδός   noun, nom. sg. fem. {2.B} . . . . . . σποδός G4700
σποδῷ   noun, dat. sg. fem. {2.B} . . . . id.
G4701   **σπορά**, -ᾶς, ἡ   *seed* (individual or collective).
σπορᾶς   noun, gen. sg. fem. {2.A} . . . . .σπορά G4701
G4702   **σπόριμος**, -ου, τό   *sown;* pl. subs., τὰ
    σπόριμα, *the crops.*
σπορίμων   adj., gen. pl. masc. {3.A} . . . σπόριμος G4702
σπορίμων   adj., gen. pl. neut. {3.A} . . . σπόριμος G4702
σπόρον   noun, acc. sg. masc. {2.B} . . . . . . σπόρος G4703
G4703   **σπόρος**, -ου, ὁ   *seed.*
σπόρος   noun, nom. sg. masc. {2.B} . . . . . . σπόρος G4703
σπουδάζοντες   vbl., pres. act. ptc. nom. pl. masc.
    {6.A.1}. . . . . σπουδάζω G4704
G4704   **σπουδάζω**   *I hasten; I am eager (zealous).*
σπουδαῖον   adj., acc. sg. masc. {3.A} . . σπουδαῖος G4705
G4705   **σπουδαῖος**, -α, -ον   *eager, zealous; earnest.*
σπουδαιότερον   adj. comp., acc. sg. masc. {3.A;
    3.G}. . . . . σπουδαῖος G4705
G4706   **σπουδαιότερον**   adv., *more earnestly*
    than others), i.e., *very promptly* (neut. of
    σπουδαιότερος).

σπουδαιότερος   adj. comp., nom. sg. masc. {3.A; 3.G}. . . . . σπουδαῖος *G4705*

G4707 **σπουδαιότερος**, -α, -ον   *more prompt, more earnest* (comp. form of σπουδαῖος).

G4708 **σπουδαιοτέρως**   adv. *very eagerly, very earnestly* (comp. form of σπουδαῖος).

σπουδαιοτέρως   adv. comp. {3.F; 3.G}. . . . . σπουδαιοτέρως *G4708*

G4709 **σπουδαίως**   adv., *eagerly, zealously; earnestly.*

σπουδαίως   adv. {3.F}. . . . . σπουδαίως *G4709*

σπουδάσατε   verb, aor. act. impv. 2 pers. pl. {5.D.1}. . . . . σπουδάζω *G4704*

σπούδασον   verb, aor. act. impv. 2 pers. sg. {5.D.1}. . . . . id.

σπουδάσω   verb, fut. act. indic. 1 pers. sg. {5.A.1.a}. . . . . id.

σπουδάσωμεν   verb, aor. act. subjunc. 1 pers. pl. {5.B.1}. id.

G4710 **σπουδή**, -ῆς, ἡ   *haste; eagerness, zeal; carefulness, care, anxiety; diligence, earnestness* (characteristically in connection with religion).

σπουδῇ   noun, dat. sg. fem. {2.A}. . . . . . . σπουδή *G4710*

σπουδήν   noun, acc. sg. fem. {2.A}. . . . . id.

σπουδῆς   noun, gen. sg. fem. {2.A}. . . . . id.

σπυρίδας   noun, acc. pl. fem. {2.C} . . . . . σπυρίς *G4711*

σπυρίδι   noun, dat. sg. fem. {2.C}. . . . . id.

σπυρίδων   noun, gen. pl. fem. {2.C}. . . . . id.

G4711 **σπυρίς** (σφυρίς), -ίδος, ἡ   a flexible mat *basket* made of rushes and such like, and used to carry either fish or eatables generally, *a fish basket, a fisherman's basket.*

G4712 **στάδιον**, -ου, ὁ   *a stadium;* pl. *a stade* (a measurement of distance about 1/8 mile).

σταδίους   noun, acc. pl. masc. {2.B}. . . . . στάδιον *G4712*

σταδίῳ   noun, dat. sg. neut. {2.B}. . . . . id.

σταδίων   noun, gen. pl. masc. {2.B}. . . . . id.

σταθείς   vbl., aor. pass. ptc. nom. sg. masc. {6.A.3}. . . . . ἵστημι *G2476*

σταθέντα   vbl., aor. pass. ptc. acc. sg. masc. {6.A.3}. . . . . id.

σταθέντες   vbl., aor. pass. ptc. nom. pl. masc. {6.A.3}. . . . . id.

σταθῇ   verb, aor. pass. subjunc. 3 pers. sg. {5.B.3}. . . . . id.

σταθῆναι   vbl., aor. pass. inf. {6.B.1} . . . . id.

σταθήσεσθε   verb, fut. pass. indic. 2 pers. pl. {5.A.1}. . . . . id.

σταθήσεται   verb, fut. pass. indic. 3 pers. sg. {5.A.1}. . . . . id.

σταθῆτε   verb, aor. pass. subjunc. 2 pers. pl. {5.B.3}. . . . . id.

G4713 **στάμνος**, -ου, ἡ   *an earthenware pot (jar).*

στάμνος   noun, nom. sg. fem. {2.B} . . . . στάμνος *G4713*

στάντος   vbl., ²aor. act. ptc. gen. sg. masc. {6.A.3}. . . . . ἵστημι *G2476*

στάς   vbl., ²aor. act. ptc. nom. sg. masc. {6.A.3}. . id.

στᾶσα   vbl., ²aor. act. ptc. nom. sg. fem. {6.A.3} . id.

στάσει   noun, dat. sg. fem. {2.C} . . . . στάσις *G4714*

στάσεις   noun, acc. pl. fem. {2.C}. . . . . id.

στάσεως   noun, gen. sg. fem. {2.C}. . . . . id.

G4955†‡ **στασιαστής**, -οῦ, ὁ   *a revolutionary.* Var. for συστασιαστής, Mark 15:7.

στασιαστῶν   noun, gen. pl. masc. {2.A}. . . . . στασιαστής *G4955†‡*

στάσιν   noun, acc. sg. fem. {2.C} . . . . στάσις *G4714*

G4714 **στάσις**, -εως, ἡ   (1) *faction, sedition, discord; disturbance, upheaval, revolution, riot;* (2) in the more original but much rarer meaning, *standing, position, place,* Heb 9:8.

στάσις   noun, nom. sg. fem. {2.C}. . . . . . στάσις *G4714*

G4715 **στατήρ**, -ῆρος, ὁ   *a stater,* i.e., four drachmae (see δραχμή), the temple tax for two persons.

στατῆρα   noun, acc. sg. masc. {2.C}. . . . . . στατήρ *G4715*

σταυρόν   noun, acc. sg. masc. {2.B} . . . . σταυρός *G4716*

G4716 **σταυρός**, -οῦ, ὁ   *a cross,* strictly the transverse beam, which was placed at the top of the vertical part, thus forming a capital T. It was this transverse beam that was carried by the criminal; *the crucifixion* of Jesus.

σταυρός   noun, nom. sg. masc. {2.B} . . . . σταυρός *G4716*

σταυροῦ   noun, gen. sg. masc. {2.B} . . . . id.

σταύρου   verb, pres. act. impv. 2 pers. sg. {5.D.2}. . . . . σταυρόω *G4717*

σταυροῦνται   verb, pres. pass. indic. 3 pers. pl. {5.A.2}. . . . . id.

σταυροῦσι   verb, pres. act. indic. 3 pers. pl. {5.A.2}. . . . . id.

σταυροῦσιν   verb, pres. act. indic. 3 pers. pl. {5.A.2}. . . . . id.

G4717 **σταυρόω**   *I crucify;* hence met., Gal 6:14.

σταυρῷ   noun, dat. sg. masc. {2.B} . . . . . σταυρός *G4716*

σταυρωθῇ   verb, aor. pass. subjunc. 3 pers. sg. {5.B.1}. σταυρόω *G4717*

σταυρωθῆναι   vbl., aor. pass. inf. {6.B.1} . . . . . id.

σταυρωθήτω   verb, aor. pass. impv. 3 pers. sg. {5.D.1}. . . . . id.

σταυρῶσαι   vbl., aor. act. inf. {6.B.1} . . . . id.

σταυρώσαντες   vbl., aor. act. ptc. nom. pl. masc. {6.A.2}. . . . . id.

σταυρώσατε   verb, aor. act. impv. 2 pers. pl. {5.D.1}. . . . . id.

σταυρώσετε   verb, fut. act. indic. 2 pers. pl. {5.A.1}. . . . . id.

σταύρωσον   verb, aor. act. impv. 2 pers. sg. {5.D.1}. . . . . id.

σταυρώσω   verb, aor. act. subjunc. 1 pers. sg. {5.A.1}. . . . . id.

σταυρώσω   verb, fut. act. indic. 1 pers. sg. {5.A.1}. . . . . id.

σταυρώσωσιν   verb, aor. act. subjunc. 3 pers. pl. {5.B.1}. . . . . id.

σταφυλαί   noun, nom. pl. fem. {2.A} . . . σταφυλή *G4718*

σταφυλάς   noun, acc. pl. fem. {2.A}. . . . . id.

G4718 **σταφυλή**, -ῆς, ἡ   *a grape.*

σταφυλή   noun, nom. sg. fem. {2.A} . . . σταφυλή *G4718*

σταφυλήν   noun, acc. sg. fem. {2.A}. . . . . id.

στάχυας   noun, acc. pl. masc. {2.C} . . . . στάχυς *G4719*

στάχυϊ   noun, dat. sg. masc. {2.C}. . . . . id.

Στάχυν   noun prop., acc. sg. masc. {2.C; 2.D}. . . . . Στάχυς *G4720*

στάχυν   noun, acc. sg. masc. {2.C} . . . . . .   στάχυς G4719
G4719 **στάχυς**, -voς, ὁ   an ear (spike) of corn.
G4720 **Στάχυς**, -voς, ὁ   a Christian man at Rome.
στέγει   verb, pres. act. indic. 3 pers. sg.
   {5.A.1.a} . . . .   στέγω G4722
G4721 **στέγη**, -ης, ἡ   a roof (orig. poetical); in Mark
   2:4 perhaps of thatch.
στέγην   noun, acc. sg. fem. {2.A} . . . . .στέγη G4721
στέγομεν   verb, pres. act. indic. 1 pers. pl.
   {5.A.1.a} . . . .   στέγω G4722
στέγοντες   vbl., pres. act. ptc. nom. pl. masc.
   {6.A.1}. . . . . id.
G4722 **στέγω**   (1) I roof over, cover; hence, I conceal,
   hide, but not in NT; (2) I keep out (weather);
   hence, I keep close, put up with, endure patiently, bear up under.
στέγων   vbl., pres. act. ptc. nom. sg. masc.
   {6.A.1}. . . . .   στέγω G4722
G4723 **στεῖρα**, -ας, ἡ   a barren (childless) woman.
στεῖρα   noun, nom. sg. fem. {2.A} . . . . . . .στεῖρα G4723
στεῖρα   noun, voc. sg. fem. {2.A} . . . . id.
στεῖρα   noun, dat. sg. fem. {2.A} . . . . id.
στεῖραι   noun, nom. pl. fem. {2.A}. . . . . id.
στέλλεσθαι   vbl., pres. mid. inf. {6.B.1} . . .   στέλλω G4724
στελλόμενοι   vbl., pres. mid. ptc. nom. pl.
   masc. {6.A.1}. . . . . id.
G4724 **στέλλω**   (orig., I set, place; hence, I bring
   together. make compact; then, I restrain, check),
   mid. I draw (shrink) back from anything.
G4725 **στέμμα**, -ατος, τό   (from στέφω, I wreathe), a
   garland.
στέμματα   noun, acc. pl. neut. {2.C} . . . . .   στέμμα G4725
στεναγμοῖς   noun, dat. pl. masc. {2.B} . στεναγμός G4726
G4726 **στεναγμός**, -οῦ, ὁ   a groan.
στεναγμοῦ   noun, gen. sg. masc. {2.B} . στεναγμός G4726
στενάζετε   verb, pres. act. impv. 2 pers. pl.
   {5.D.1}. . . . .   στενάζω G4727
στενάζομεν   verb, pres. act. indic. 1 pers. pl.
   {5.A.1.a} . . . . id.
στενάζοντες   vbl., pres. act. ptc. nom. pl. masc.
   {6.A.1}. . . . . id.
G4727 **στενάζω**   I groan.
στενή   adj., nom. sg. fem. {3.A} . . . . .στενός G4728
στενῆς   adj., gen. sg. fem. {3.A} . . . . id.
G4728 **στενός**, -ή, -όν   narrow.
στενοχωρεῖσθε   verb, pres. pass. indic. 2 pers. pl.
   {5.A.2}. . . . .   στενοχωρέω G4729
G4729 **στενοχωρέω**   I press upon, cramp, restrain
   (στενός and χῶρος, cf. Eng. colloquial, I keep
   someone in a tight place).
G4730 **στενοχωρία**, -ας, ἡ   (lit. confinement in a narrow space), restriction, restraint; anguish, great
   trouble.
στενοχωρία   noun, nom. sg. fem.
   {2.A} . . . .   στενοχωρία G4730
στενοχωρίαις   noun, dat. pl. fem. {2.A}. . . . . . id.
στενοχωρούμενοι   vbl., pres. pass. ptc. nom. pl.
   masc. {6.A.2}. . . . .   στενοχωρέω G4729
στερεά   adj., nom. pl. neut. {3.A} . . . . . . .στερεός G4731
στερεᾶς   adj., gen. sg. fem. {3.A} . . . . id.

στερεοί   adj., nom. pl. masc. {3.A} . . . . id.
G4731 **στερεός**, -ά, -όν   solid; firm, lit. or met.
στερεός   adj., nom. sg. masc. {3.A} . . . . . .στερεός G4731
G4732 **στερεόω**   I make firm, or solid; met., Acts 16:5.
G4733 **στερέωμα**, -ατος, τό   firm foundation, bulwark
   (probably a military metaphor).
στερέωμα   noun, acc. sg. neut. {2.C} . . .   στερέωμα G4733
Στεφανᾶ   noun prop., gen. sg. masc. {2.A;
   2.D}. . . . .   Στεφανᾶς G4734
G4734 **Στεφανᾶς**, -ᾶ, ὁ   Stephanas, a Corinthian
   Christian (a pet form of Στεφανηφόρος).
στέφανοι   noun, nom. pl. masc. {2.B} . .   στέφανος G4735
στέφανον   noun, acc. sg. masc. {2.B} . . .   στέφανος G4735
Στέφανον   noun prop., acc. sg. masc. {2.B;
   2.D}. . . . .   Στέφανος G4736
G4735 **στέφανος**, -ου, ὁ   a garland, wreath, chaplet,
   crown, generally as the Greek victor's crown or
   chaplet, of perishable leaves (1 Cor 9:25), won
   in athletic and other con tests, and familiar
   to the Jews for generations; ὁ στέφανος τῆς
   ζωῆς (Jas 1:12; Rev 2:10), the crown (reward),
   which is life.
G4736 **Στέφανος**, -ου, ὁ   Stephen, one of the seven
   original "deacons" at Jerusalem, and the first
   martyr.
στέφανος   noun, nom. sg. masc. {2.B} . .   στέφανος G4735
Στέφανος   noun prop., nom. sg. masc. {2.B;
   2.D}. . . . .   Στέφανος G4736
Στεφάνου   noun prop., gen. sg. masc. {2.B; 2.D} id.
στεφάνους   noun, acc. pl. masc. {2.B} . .   στέφανος G4735
στεφανοῦται   verb, pres. pass. indic. 3 pers. sg.
   {5.A.2}. . . . . .στεφανόω G4737
G4737 **στεφανόω**   I wreathe, crown as victor, 2 Tim
   2:5, hence met.
Στεφάνῳ   noun prop., dat. sg. masc. {2.B;
   2.D}. . . . .   Στέφανος G4736
στήθη   noun, acc. pl. neut. {2.C}. . . . .   στῆθος G4738
στῆθι   verb, ²aor. act. impv. 2 pers. sg.
   {5.D.3}. . . . . .ἵστημι G2476
G4738 **στῆθος**, -ους, τό   the breast.
στῆθος   noun, acc. sg. neut. {2.C} . . . .   στῆθος G4738
στήκει   verb, pres. act. indic. 3 pers. sg.
   {5.A.1.a} . . . . .στήκω G4739
στήκετε   verb, pres. act. impv. 2 pers. pl. {5.D.1}. id.
στήκετε   verb, pres. act. indic. 2 pers. pl.
   {5.A.1.a} . . . . id.
στήκητε   verb, pres. act. subjunc. 2 pers. pl.
   {5.B.1} . . . . id.
στήκοντες   vbl., pres. act. ptc. nom. pl. masc.
   {6.A.1}. . . . . id.
G4739 **στήκω**   I stand; I remain standing, stand firm,
   lit. or met. (form arising from the need for
   an act. form present in the intrans. sense, cf.
   ἵστημι).
στῆναι   vbl., ²aor. act. inf. {6.B.3} . . . . .ἵστημι G2476
G4740 **στηριγμός**, -οῦ, ὁ   support.
στηριγμοῦ   noun, gen. sg. masc. {2.B} . .στηριγμός G4740
G4741 **στηρίζω**   (1) I fix firmly, Luke 16:26; τὸ
   πρόσωπον (Hebraism) I direct myself
   towards, I have my face turned steadfastly,

Luke 9:51; (2) generally met. *I buttress, prop., support; I strengthen, establish.*

στηρίζων   vbl., pres. act. ptc. nom. sg. masc. {6.A.1}. . . . . στηρίζω *G4741*

στηρίξαι   verb, aor. act. opt. 3 pers. sg. {5.C.1}. . id.

στηρίξαι   vbl., aor. act. inf. {6.B.1}. . . . . id.

στηρίξατε   verb, aor. act. impv. 2 pers. pl. {5.D.1}. . . . . id.

στηρίξει   verb, fut. act. indic. 3 pers. sg. {5.A.1.a} . . . . id.

στήριξον   verb, aor. act. impv. 2 pers. sg. {5.D.1} id.

στήρισον   verb, aor. act. impv. 2 pers. sg. {5.D.1} id.

στηριχθῆναι   vbl., aor. pass. inf. {6.B.1}. . . . . . id.

στῆσαι   vbl., aor. act. inf. {6.B.3} . . . . ἵστημι *G2476*

στήσαντες   vbl., aor. act. ptc. nom. pl. masc. {6.A.3}. . . . . id.

στήσει   verb, fut. act. indic. 3 pers. sg. {5.A.1} . . id.

στήσῃ   verb, aor. act. subjunc. 3 pers. sg. {5.B.3} id.

στήσῃς   verb, aor. act. subjunc. 2 pers. sg. {5.B.3}id.

στήσητε   verb, aor. act. subjunc. 2 pers. pl. {5.B.3} . . . . id.

στήσονται   verb, fut. mid. indic. 3 pers. pl. {5.A.1}. . . . . id.

στῆτε   verb, ²aor. act. impv. 2 pers. pl. {5.D.3}. . . id.

στῆτε   verb, ²aor. act. subjunc. 2 pers. pl. {5.B.3}. id.

στιβάδας   noun, acc. pl. fem. {2.C} . . . . . στοιβάς *G4746*

G4742 **στίγμα**, -ατος, τό   properly, *a brand* burned into, or *the mark* of a cut made in, the skin of a slave; in Gal 6:17 τὰ στίγματα are the *marks* or *scars*, due to the lictor's rods at Pisidian Antioch and the stones at Lystra, *marking* Paul as the slave of Jesus.

στίγματα   noun, acc. pl. neut. {2.C} . . . . . . στίγμα *G4742*

G4743 **στιγμή**, -ῆς, ἡ   (lit. *a pricking*), *an instant, a moment.*

στιγμῇ   noun, dat. sg. fem. {2.A}. . . . . στιγμή *G4743*

στίλβοντα   vbl., pres. act. ptc. nom. pl. neut. {6.A.1}. . . . . στίλβω *G4744*

G4744 **στίλβω**   *I gleam, flash.*

G4745 **στοά**, -ᾶς, ἡ   *a portico, colonnade, porch;* that "of Solomon" was on the east side of the Temple.

στοᾷ   noun, dat. sg. fem. {2.A}. . . . . στοά *G4745*

στοάς   noun, acc. pl. fem. {2.A} . . . . id.

στοιβάδας   noun, acc. pl. fem. {2.C} . . . . . στοιβάς *G4746*

G4746 **στοιβάς** (στιβάς), -άδος, ἡ   *a wisp (bundle)* of brushwood, twigs or other light growth.

Στοϊκῶν   adj. prop., gen. pl. masc. {3.A}. . Στωϊκός *G4770*

στοιχεῖα   noun, acc. pl. neut. {2.B} . . . . στοιχεῖον *G4747*

στοιχεῖα   noun, nom. pl. neut. {2.B} . . . . . id.

στοιχεῖν   vbl., pres. act. inf. {6.B.2} . . . . . στοιχέω *G4748*

G4747 **στοιχεῖον**, -ου, τό   (1) pl. *the heavenly bodies,* 2 Pet 3:10, 12; (2) *a rudiment, an element, a rudimentary principle, an elementary rule* (but in Gal 4:3 there is much to be said for taking the word in the sense of *spirit, demon,* possibly also in #1); pl., (physical) *elements, basic principles.*

στοιχεῖς   verb, pres. act. indic. 2 pers. sg. {5.A.2}. . . . . στοιχέω *G4748*

στοιχείων   noun, gen. pl. neut. {2.B} . . . στοιχεῖον *G4747*

G4748 **στοιχέω**   *I walk* (properly, in a straight line, in rank).

στοιχήσουσιν   verb, fut. act. indic. 3 pers. pl. {5.A.1}. . . . . στοιχέω *G4748*

στοιχοῦσι   vbl., pres. act. ptc. dat. pl. masc. {6.A.2}. . . . . id.

στοιχοῦσιν   vbl., pres. act. ptc. dat. pl. masc. {6.A.2}. . . . . id.

στοιχῶμεν   verb, pres. act. subjunc. 1 pers. pl. {5.B.2}. . . . . id.

στολαί   noun, nom. pl. fem. {2.A} . . . . στολή *G4749*

στολαῖς   noun, dat. pl. fem. {2.A}. . . . . id.

στολάς   noun, acc. pl. fem. {2.A} . . . . id.

G4749 **στολή**, -ῆς, ἡ   *a long robe,* worn by the upper classes in the east.

στολή   noun, nom. sg. fem. {2.A}. . . . . στολή *G4749*

στολήν   noun, acc. sg. fem. {2.A}. . . . . id.

G4750 **στόμα**, -ατος, τό   *the mouth,* esp. as an organ of speech in man and God; the sword has a mouth *(edge),* because it *drinks* blood, Luke 21:24; Heb 11:34; στόμα πρὸς στόμα (cf. πρόσωπον πρὸς πρόσωπον), *by word of mouth,* practically, *face to face.*

στόμα   noun, acc. sg. neut. {2.C} . . . . στόμα *G4750*

στόμα   noun, nom. sg. neut. {2.C} . . . . id.

στόματα   noun, acc. pl. neut. {2.C}. . . . . id.

στόματι   noun, dat. sg. neut. {2.C}. . . . . id.

στόματος   noun, gen. sg. neut. {2.C}. . . . . . . id.

στομάτων   noun, gen. pl. neut. {2.C}. . . . . . . id.

στόμαχον   noun, acc. sg. masc. {2.B} . . . στόμαχος *G4751*

G4751 **στόμαχος**, -ου, ὁ   *the stomach.*

G4752 **στρατεία**, -ας, ἡ   *military service,* used met.

στρατείαν   noun, acc. sg. fem. {2.A} . . . στρατεία *G4752*

στρατείας   noun, gen. sg. fem. {2.A} . . . . . . id.

στρατεύεται   verb, pres. mid. indic. 3 pers. pl. {5.A.1.d} . . . . στρατεύω *G4754*

στρατεύῃ   verb, pres. mid. subjunc. 2 pers. sg. {5.B.1} . . . . id.

G4753 **στράτευμα**, -ατος, τό   *an army, a body of soldiers.*

στράτευμα   noun, acc. sg. neut. {2.C} . στράτευμα *G4753*

στρατεύμασιν   noun, dat. pl. neut. {2.C}. . . . . . id.

στρατεύματα   noun, acc. pl. neut. {2.C}. . . . . . id.

στρατεύματα   noun, nom. pl. neut. {2.C} . . . . . id.

στρατεύματι   noun, dat. sg. neut. {2.C} . . . . . . id.

στρατεύματος   noun, gen. sg. neut. {2.C}. . . . . id.

στρατευμάτων   noun, gen. pl. neut. {2.C} . . . . id.

στρατευόμεθα   verb, pres. mid. indic. 1 pers. pl. {5.A.1.d} . . . . στρατεύω *G4754*

στρατευόμενοι   vbl., pres. mid. ptc. nom. pl. masc. {6.A.1}. id.

στρατευόμενος   vbl., pres. mid. ptc. nom. sg. masc. {6.A.1}. id.

στρατευομένων   vbl., pres. mid. ptc. gen. pl. fem. {6.A.1}. . . . . id.

στρατεύονται   verb, pres. mid. indic. 3 pers. pl. {5.A.1.d}. . . . . id.

G4754 **στρατεύω**   mid., *I serve in the army, I am in the army, I am a soldier* (whether on active service

or not); hence met., *I make war, I take up war,*
e.g., 1 Pet 2:11.

στρατηγοί   noun, nom. pl. masc. {2.B}. στρατηγός *G4755*
στρατηγοῖς   noun, dat. pl. masc. {2.B} . . . . id.

G4755 **στρατηγός**, -οῦ, ὁ   (1) in Jerusalem, ὁ στρα-
τηγὸς τοῦ ἱεροῦ, *the commandant of the
temple,* a priest, next in rank to the high priest,
and commander of the priests and Levites
who guarded the temple, Acts 4:1; 5:24, 26;
under him were the στρατηγοί, *captains of
the temple guards,* Luke 22:4 (var.), 52; (2)
at Philippi, a Roman "colonia," a *praetor* or
a duumvir, a chief magistrate of the "colonia"
Acts 16 (there were probably two of them).

στρατηγός   noun, nom. sg. masc. {2.B} στρατηγός *G4755*
στρατηγούς   noun, acc. pl. masc. {2.B} . . . . id.

G4756 **στρατιά**, -ᾶς, ἡ   *an army.*
στρατιᾷ   noun, dat. sg. fem. {2.A} . . . . . . στρατιά *G4756*
στρατιᾶς   noun, gen. sg. fem. {2.A} . . . . id.
στρατιῶται   noun, nom. pl. masc. {2.A} .στρατιώτης *G4757*
στρατιώταις   noun, dat. pl. masc. {2.A} . . . . id.
στρατιώτας   noun, acc. pl. masc. {2.A} . . . . id.
στρατιώτῃ   noun, dat. sg. masc. {2.A} . . . . id.
στρατιώτην   noun, acc. sg. masc. {2.A} . . . . id.

G4757 **στρατιώτης**, -ου, ὁ   *a soldier;* hence (perhaps
under the influence of the language of the
Mysteries and that of philosophy), the worshipper as *the soldier* of his God, cf. 2 Tim 2:3.

στρατιώτης   noun, nom. sg. masc.
     {2.A} . . . . στρατιώτης *G4757*
στρατιωτῶν   noun, gen. pl. masc. {2.A} . . . . . . id.

G4758 **στρατολογέω**   trans., *I enroll in the army.*
στρατολογήσαντι   vbl., aor. act. ptc. dat. sg. masc.
     {6.A.2} . . . . στρατολογέω *G4758*
στρατοπεδάρχῃ   noun, dat. sg. masc.
     {2.A} . . . . .στρατοπεδάρχης *G4759*

G4759 **στρατοπεδάρχης**, -ου, ὁ   *the chief of the camp,
the commander of the corps* connected with the
commissariat, custody of prisoners, etc., which
was on detached duty.

G4760 **στρατόπεδον**, -ου, τό   *a camp.*
στρατοπέδων   noun, gen. pl. neut.
     {2.B} . . . . στρατόπεδον *G4760*
στραφείς   vbl., ²aor. pass. ptc. nom. sg. masc.
     {6.A.1.a} . . . . στρέφω *G4762*
στραφεῖσα   vbl., ²aor. pass. ptc. nom. sg. fem.
     {6.A.1.a} . . . . id.
στραφέντες   vbl., ²aor. pass. ptc. nom. pl. masc.
     {6.A.1.a} . . . . id.
στραφῆτε   verb, ²aor. pass. subjunc. 2 pers. pl.
     {5.B.1} . . . . id.
στραφῶσιν   verb, ²aor. pass. subjunc. 3 pers. pl.
     {5.B.1} . . . . id.
στρεβλοῦσιν   verb, pres. act. indic. 3 pers. pl.
     {5.A.2} . . . . στρεβλόω *G4761*

G4761 **στρεβλόω**   (lit. *I twist, warp, stretch on the
rack),* hence met., *I twist, strain.*
στρέφειν   vbl., pres. act. inf. {6.B.1} . . . . . στρέφω *G4762*
στρεφόμεθα   verb, pres. pass. indic. 1 pers. pl.
     {5.A.1.d} . . . . id.

G4762 **στρέφω**   trans., *I turn;* hence, *I bring back(?),*
Matt 27:3; *I change,* Rev 11:6; act. intrans.,
Acts 7:42; mid. and pass. intrans., *I turn,* also
met. *I change.*
στρέψον   verb, aor. act. impv. 2 pers. sg.
     {5.D.1} . . . . στρέφω *G4762*
στρηνιάσαντες   vbl., aor. act. ptc. nom. pl. masc.
     {6.A.2} . . . . στρηνιάω *G4763*

G4763 **στρηνιάω**   *I am wanton, I wanton.*

G4764 **στρῆνος**, -ους, τό   *wantonness, luxury.*
στρήνους   noun, gen. sg. neut. {2.C} . . . . στρῆνος *G4764*
στρουθία   noun, nom. pl. neut. {2.B}. . στρουθίον *G4765*

G4765 **στρουθίον**, -ου, τό   *a sparrow,* the cheapest of
all birds for food.
στρουθίων   noun, gen. pl. neut. {2.B} . στρουθίον *G4765*

G4766 **στρώννυμι** (στρωννύω)   *I spread out, strew;*
in Mark 14:15; Luke 22:12 of the dining
couches with the cushions ready for diners, cf.
Acts 9:34 of *making* one's *bed.*
στρῶσον   verb, aor. act. impv. 2 pers. sg.
     {5.D.3} . . . . στρώννυμι *G4766*
στυγητοί   adj., nom. pl. masc. {3.A} . . . .στυγητός *G4767*

G4767 **στυγητός**, -ή, -όν   *hated, hateful.*

G4768 **στυγνάζω**   (1) *I am sad,* Mark 10:22; (2) *I am
dull (over cast),* Matt 16:3.
στυγνάζων   vbl., pres. act. ptc. nom. sg. masc.
     {6.A.1} . . . . στυγνάζω *G4768*
στυγνάσας   vbl., aor. act. ptc. nom. sg. masc.
     {6.A.1.a} . . . . id.
στῦλοι   noun, nom. pl. masc. {2.B}. . . . . . στῦλος *G4769*
στῦλοι   noun, nom. pl. masc. {2.B}. . . . . id.
στῦλον   noun, acc. sg. masc. {2.B} . . . . id.
στῦλον   noun, acc. sg. masc. {2.B} . . . . id.

G4769 **στῦλος**, -ου, ὁ   *a pillar* for supporting an
entablature or other structure; hence met.
στῦλος   noun, nom. sg. masc. {2.B} . . . . . . στῦλος *G4769*

G4770 **Στωϊκός** (Στοϊκός)   *a Stoic,* a member of one
of the two leading schools of philosophy (from
στοιά, στοά, because of the original place of
meeting).
Στωικῶν   adj. prop., gen. pl. masc. {3.A} . Στωϊκός *G4770*
Στωϊκῶν   adj. prop., gen. pl. masc. {3.A} . . . . . . id.

G4771 **σύ**, σοῦ (σου)   ὑμεῖς, *you;* τί ἡμῖν (ἐμοὶ)
καὶ σοί; Matt 8:29, etc., *what have we (I) to do
with you?* but in John 2:4 it is probable that we
ought to translate, *what have you and I to do
with it? what concern is it of ours? never mind!*
note the order ἡμῖν καὶ ὑμῖν (Matt 25:9), as
in Lat.; for καθ᾽ ὑμᾶς, see κατά.
σύ   pron. pers., 2 pers. nom. sg. {4.A} . . . . σύ *G4771*

G4772 **συγγένεια**, -ας, ἡ   collective, all the συγγενεῖς,
kindred, kin, relations.
συγγενείᾳ   noun, dat. sg. fem. {2.A} . . . . συγγένεια *G4772*
συγγένειαν   noun, acc. sg. fem. {2.A} . . . . id.
συγγενείας   noun, gen. sg. fem. {2.A} . . . . id.
συγγενεῖς   adj., acc. pl. masc. {3.E} . . . .συγγενής *G4773*
συγγενεῖς   adj., nom. pl. masc. {3.E}. . . . . id.
συγγενέσι   adj., dat. pl. masc. {3.E}. . . . . id.
συγγενέσιν   adj., dat. pl. masc. {3.E}. . . . . id.
συγγενεῦσιν   adj., dat. pl. masc. {3.E} . . . . id.

συγγενῆ adj., acc. sg. masc. {3.E} . . . . id.

G4773 **συγγενής**, -οῦς, ὁ   *a relation, relative, kinsman;* in Rom 9:3 the term is wide enough to include all Hebrews; in Rom 16:7, 11, 21 the reference may be narrower, to fellow members of the same (Jewish) tribe (φυλή) in the city of Tarsus.

συγγενής adj., nom. sg. fem. {3.E} . . . . .συγγενής *G4773*

συγγενής adj., nom. sg. masc. {3.E} . . . . id.

G4773† **συγγενίς**, -ίδος, ἡ   *a kinswoman.* Var. for συγγενής, Luke 1:36.

συγγενίς noun, nom. sg. fem. {2.C} . . . **συγγενίς** *G4773†*

συγγενῶν adj., gen. pl. masc. {3.E}. . . . . id.

G4774 **συγγνώμη**, -ης, ἡ   *indulgence, allowance* for circumstances.

συγγνώμην noun, acc. sg. fem. {2.A} . . . συγγνώμη *G4774*

G4775 **συγκάθημαι**   *I am sitting (seated) with;* in Acts 26:30, perhaps to be compared with Eng. *assessor.*

συγκαθήμενοι vbl., pres. mid./pass. ptc. nom. pl. masc. {6.A.3} . . . . .συγκάθημαι *G4775*

συγκαθήμενος vbl., pres. mid./pass. ptc. nom. sg. masc. {6.A.3} . . . . id.

G4776 **συγκαθίζω**   (1) trans., *I cause to sit along with;* (2) intrans., *I sit in company (together).*

συγκαθισάντων vbl., aor. act. ptc. gen. pl. masc. {6.A.1.a} . . . . συγκαθίζω *G4776*

G4777 **συγκακοπαθέω**   *I am ill treated along with, I take my share of suffering* (in 2 Tim 1:8 the dat. is not governed by σύν, but = *for the benefit of*).

συγκακοπάθησον verb, aor. act. impv. 2 pers. sg. {5.D.1} . . . . συγκακοπαθέω *G4777*

συγκακουχεῖσθαι vbl., pres. mid./pass. inf. {6.B.2} . . . . .συγκακουχέομαι *G4778*

G4778 **συγκακουχέομαι** pass. *I suffer mistreatment with.*

συγκαλεῖ verb, pres. act. indic. 3 pers. sg. {5.A.2} .συγκαλέω *G4779*

συγκαλεῖται verb, pres. mid. indic. 3 pers. sg. {5.A.2} . . . . id.

συγκαλεσάμενος vbl., aor. mid. ptc. nom. sg. masc. {6.A.2} . . . . id.

συγκαλέσασθαι vbl., aor. mid. inf. {6.B.1} . . . . id.

G4779 **συγκαλέω**   *I call together, invite, summon;* mid. *I call together to myself.*

συγκαλοῦσιν verb, pres. act. indic. 3 pers. pl. {5.A.2} .συγκαλέω *G4779*

G4780 **συγκαλύπτω**   *I veil (cover) completely.*

G4781 **συγκάμπτω**   *I bend low, I cause to stoop low.*

σύγκαμψον verb, aor. act. impv. 2 pers. sg. {5.D.1} .συγκάμπτω *G4781*

G4782 **συγκαταβαίνω**   *I come down along with (together).*

συγκαταβάντες vbl., ²aor. act. ptc. nom. pl. masc. {6.A.1.a} . . . . .συγκαταβαίνω *G4782*

G4783 **συγκατάθεσις**, -εως, ἡ   *agreement, union.*

συγκατάθεσις noun, nom. sg. fem. {2.C} . . . . συγκατάθεσις *G4783*

συγκατατεθειμένος vbl., perf. mid./pass. ptc. nom. sg. masc. {6.A.3} . . . . συγκατατίθημι *G4784*

G4784 **συγκατατίθημι** mid. *I find myself in agreement with; I agree with.*

G4785 **συγκαταψηφίζομαι** pass. *I am chosen together with; I am numbered (reckoned) along with.*

συγκατεψηφίσθη verb, aor. pass. indic. 3 pers. sg. {5.A.1.b} . . . . .συγκαταψηφίζομαι *G4785*

συγκεκαλυμμένον vbl., perf. pass. ptc. nom. sg. neut. {6.A.1.b} . . . . .συγκαλύπτω *G4780*

συγκεκερασμένους vbl., perf. pass. ptc. acc. pl. masc. {6.A.3} . . . . .συγκεράννυμι *G4786*

συγκεκλεισμένοι vbl., perf. pass. ptc. nom. pl. masc. {6.A.1.b} . . . . .συγκλείω *G4788*

συγκεκραμένος vbl., perf. pass. ptc. nom. sg. masc. {6.A.3} . . . . .συγκεράννυμι *G4786*

συγκεκραμένους vbl., perf. pass. ptc. acc. pl. masc. {6.A.3} . . . . id.

G4786 **συγκεράννυμι**   (1) *I mix together, compound,* 1 Cor 12:24; (2) pass. with dat. of instrument (πίστει), *I agree with,* Heb 4:2 (reading acc. pl.).

συγκεχυμένη vbl., perf. pass. ptc. nom. sg. fem. {6.A.2} . . . . συγχέω *G4797*

συγκέχυται verb, perf. pass. indic. 3 pers. sg. {5.A.1} . . . . id.

G4787 **συγκινέω**   *I stir violently.*

συγκλειόμενοι vbl., pres. pass. ptc. nom. pl. masc. {6.A.1} . . . . .συγκλείω *G4788*

G4788 **συγκλείω**   *I shut together; I enclose, I shut in on all sides,* e.g., Rom 11:32.

συγκληρονόμα adj., acc. pl. neut. {3.C} . . . . .συγκληρονόμος *G4789*

συγκληρονόμοι adj., nom. pl. masc. {3.C} . . . . id.

συγκληρονόμοις adj., dat. pl. masc. {3.C}. . . . . id.

G4789 **συγκληρονόμος**, -ον   *a joint heir, a fellow heir.*

συγκληρονόμων adj., gen. pl. masc. {3.C} . . . . .συγκληρονόμος *G4789*

συγκοινωνεῖτε verb, pres. act. impv. 2 pers. pl. {5.D.2} . . . . .συγκοινωνέω *G4790*

G4790 **συγκοινωνέω**   *I have partnership in, I share in* (with others).

συγκοινωνήσαντες vbl., aor. act. ptc. nom. pl. masc. {6.A.2} . . . . .συγκοινωνέω *G4790*

συγκοινωνήσητε verb, aor. act. subjunc. 2 pers. pl. {5.B.1} . . . . id.

G4791 **συγκοινωνός**, -οῦ, ὁ   *a fellow sharer* (in), *a joint partaker* (of).

συγκοινωνός noun, nom. sg. masc. {2.B} . . . . συγκοινωνός *G4791*

συγκοινωνούς noun, acc. pl. masc. {2.B} . . . . . id.

G4792 **συγκομίζω**   *I carry (convey) together,* i.e., to burial; or *I take up* for burial; hence, *I bury;* perhaps, however, *I get back, recover* (the συν- expressig the collecting of the mangled remains).

συγκρῖναι vbl., aor. act. inf. {6.B.1} . . . . συγκρίνω *G4793*

συγκρίνοντες vbl., pres. act. ptc. nom. pl. masc. {6.A.1} . . . . id.

G4793 **συγκρίνω**   *I compare.*

συγκύπτουσα vbl., pres. act. ptc. nom. sg. fem. {6.A.1} . . . . .συγκύπτω *G4794*

G4794 **συγκύπτω**   *I am bent double, bent in two, bowed down.*

G4795 **συγκυρία**, -ας, ἡ   *coincidence, chance.*
συγκυρίαν   noun, acc. sg. fem. {2.A} . . . συγκυρία G4795
συγχαίρει   verb, pres. act. indic. 3 pers. sg. {5.A.1.a} . . . . συγχαίρω G4796
συγχαίρετε   verb, pres. act. impv. 2 pers. pl. {5.D.1} . . . . id.

G4796 **συγχαίρω**   act. and pass. *I rejoice with;* perhaps *I congratulate.*
συγχαίρω   verb, pres. act. indic. 1 pers. sg. {5.A.1.a} . . . . συγχαίρω G4796
συγχάρητε   verb, ²aor. pass. impv. 2 pers. pl. {5.D.1} . . . . id.

G4797 **συγχέω** (συγχύννω, συγχύνω)   *I confuse, confound, trouble.*

G4798 **συγχράομαι**   *I associate with, have friendly dealings with.*
συγχρῶνται   verb, pres. mid./pass. indic. 3 pers. pl. {5.A.2} . . . . συγχράομαι G4798
συγχύννεται   verb, pres. pass. indic. 3 pers. sg. {5.A.2} . . . . συγχέω G4797
συγχύσεως   noun, gen. sg. fem. {2.C} . . σύγχυσις G4799

G4799 **σύγχυσις**, -εως, ἡ   *confusion, disturbance.*

G4800 **συζάω**   *I live along with (in company with).*

G4801 **συζεύγνυμι**   *I yoke (harness) together, join.*
συζῆν   vbl., pres. act. inf. {6.B.2} . . . . συζάω G4800
συζῆν   vbl., pres. act. inf. {6.B.2} . . . . id.
συζήσομεν   verb, fut. act. indic. 1 pers. pl. {5.A.1} . . . . id.
συζητεῖν   vbl., pres. act. inf. {6.B.2} . . . . συζητέω G4802
συζητεῖτε   verb, pres. act. indic. 2 pers. pl. {5.A.2} . . . . id.

G4802 **συζητέω**   (lit. *I seek in company*), *I discuss, debate, dispute.*
συζητήσεως   noun, gen. sg. fem. {2.C}   συζήτησις G4803
συζήτησιν   noun, acc. sg. fem. {2.C} . . . . id.

G4803 **συζήτησις**, -εως, ἡ   *discussion, debate.*

G4804 **συζητητής**, -οῦ, ὁ   *a discusser, debater.*
συζητητής   noun, nom. sg. masc. {2.A} συζητητής G4804
συζητοῦντας   vbl., pres. act. ptc. acc. pl. masc. {6.A.2} . . . . συζητέω G4802
συζητοῦντες   vbl., pres. act. ptc. nom. pl. masc. {6.A.2} . . . . id.
συζητούντων   vbl., pres. act. ptc. gen. pl. masc. {6.A.2} . . . . id.
σύζυγε   adj., voc. sg. masc. {3.C} . . . . σύζυγος G4805

G4805 **σύζυγος**, -ου, ὁ   *yokefellow, companion, colleague* (perhaps a proper name).

G4806 **συζωοποιέω**   *I make living along with.*
σῦκα   noun, acc. pl. neut. {2.B} . . . . σῦκον G4810

G4807 **συκάμινος**, -ου, ἡ   *the black mulberry tree* (a Semitic word).
συκαμίνῳ   noun, dat. sg. fem. {2.B} . . συκάμινος G4807
συκῇ   noun, dat. sg. fem. {2.A} . . . . συκῆ G4808

G4808 **συκῆ**, -ῆς, ἡ   *a fig tree.*
συκῆ   noun, nom. sg. fem. {2.A} . . . . συκῆ G4808
συκῆν   noun, acc. sg. fem. {2.A} . . . . id.
συκῆς   noun, gen. sg. fem. {2.A} . . . . id.

G4809 **συκομορέα**, -ας, ἡ   *a sycamore tree.*

συκομορέαν   noun, acc. sg. fem. {2.A} συκομορέα G4809
συκομωραίαν   noun, acc. sg. fem. {2.A} . . . . . id.

G4810 **σῦκον**, -ου, τό   *a fig.*

G4811 **συκοφαντέω**   *I accuse falsely.*
συκοφαντήσητε   verb, aor. act. subjunc. 2 pers. pl. {5.B.1} . . . . συκοφαντέω G4811
σύκων   noun, gen. pl. neut. {2.B} . . . . σῦκον G4810

G4812 **συλαγωγέω**   *I take away from as booty (plunder), I rob.*
συλαγωγῶν   vbl., pres. act. ptc. nom. sg. masc. {6.A.2} . . . . συλαγωγέω G4812

G4813 **συλάω**   *I rob.*
συλλαβεῖν   vbl., ²aor. act. inf. {6.B.1} συλλαμβάνω G4815
συλλαβέσθαι   vbl., ²aor. mid. inf. {6.B.1} . . . . . id.
συλλαβόμενοι   vbl., ²aor. mid. ptc. nom. pl. masc. {6.A.1.b} . . . . id.
συλλαβόντες   vbl., ²aor. act. ptc. nom. pl. masc. {6.A.1.a} . . . . id.
συλλαβοῦσα   vbl., ²aor. act. ptc. nom. sg. fem. {6.A.1.a} . . . . id.
συλλαβοῦσι   vbl., ²aor. act. ptc. dat. pl. masc. {6.A.1.a} . . . . id.
συλλαβοῦσιν   vbl., ²aor. act. ptc. dat. pl. masc. {6.A.1.a} . . . . id.

G4814 **συλλαλέω**   *I speak together* (with).
συλλαλήσας   vbl., aor. act. ptc. nom. sg. masc. {6.A.2} . . . . συλλαλέω G4814
συλλαλοῦντες   vbl., pres. act. ptc. nom. pl. masc. {6.A.2} . . . . id.
συλλαμβάνου   verb, pres. mid. impv. 2 pers. sg. {5.D.1} . . . . συλλαμβάνω G4815

G4815 **συλλαμβάνω**   (1) act. and mid., *I arrest, catch, capture;* (2) *I conceive* (a child), cf. met. Jas 1:15; (3) mid. *I lend a hand to, I help,* Luke 5:7; Phil 4:3.
συλλέγεται   verb, pres. pass. indic. 3 pers. sg. {5.A.1.d} . . . . συλλέγω G4816
συλλέγοντες   vbl., pres. act. ptc. nom. pl. masc. {6.A.1} . . . . id.
συλλέγουσι   verb, pres. act. indic. 3 pers. pl. {5.A.1.a} . . . . id.
συλλέγουσιν   verb, pres. act. indic. 3 pers. pl. {5.A.1.a} . . . . id.

G4816 **συλλέγω**   *I collect, gather together.*
συλλέξατε   verb, aor. act. impv. 2 pers. pl. {5.D.1} . . . . συλλέγω G4816
συλλέξομεν   verb, fut. act. indic. 1 pers. pl. {5.A.1.a} . . . . id.
συλλέξουσιν   verb, fut. act. indic. 3 pers. pl. {5.A.1.a} . . . . id.
συλλέξωμεν   verb, aor. act. subjunc. 1 pers. pl. {5.B.1} . . . . id.
συλλημφθέντα   vbl., aor. pass. ptc. acc. sg. masc. {6.A.1.a} . . . . συλλαμβάνω G4815
συλλημφθῆναι   vbl., aor. pass. inf. {6.B.1} . . . . . id.
συλλήμψη   verb, fut. mid. indic. 2 pers. sg. {5.A.1.d} . . . . id.
συλληφθέντα   vbl., aor. pass. ptc. acc. sg. masc. {6.A.1.a} . . . . id.
συλληφθῆναι   vbl., aor. pass. inf. {6.B.1} . . . . . id.

συλλήψη   verb, fut. mid. indic. 2 pers. sg.
{5.A.1.d} . . . . id.

G4817 **συλλογίζομαι**   *I reason together* with others.

G4818 **συλλυπέω**   pass. *I am greatly pained (grieved)*
with.
συλλυπούμενος   vbl., pres. mid./pass. ptc. nom.
sg. masc. {6.A.2} . . . . .συλλυπέω G4818
συμβαίνειν   vbl., pres. act. inf. {6.B.1} . .συμβαίνω G4819
συμβαίνοντος   vbl., pres. act. ptc. gen. sg.
neut. {6.A.1} . . . . id.

G4819 **συμβαίνω**   w. neut. subj. or impers., *I happen,*
occur; it happens.
συμβαλεῖν   vbl., ²aor. act. inf. {6.B.1} . . συμβάλλω G4820
συμβάλλουσα   vbl., pres. act. ptc. nom. sg.
fem. {6.A.1} . . . . id.

G4820 **συμβάλλω**   (1) with λόγους expressed or
understood, *I engage in discussion with,* Luke
11:53 (var.); Acts 4:15; 17:18; (2) *I reflect, pon-*
der, Luke 2:19; (3) *I meet with, I fall in with,*
Acts 20:14; in hostile sense, *I enter into conflict*
with, attack, Luke 14:31; (4) mid. *I contribute*
to, benefit.
συμβάντων   vbl., ²aor. act. ptc. gen. pl. masc.
{6.A.1.a} .συμβαίνω G4819
συμβασιλεύσομεν   verb, fut. act. indic. 1 pers. pl.
{5.A.1.a} . . . . συμβασιλεύω G4821
συμβασιλεύσωμεν   verb, aor. act. subjunc.
1 pers. pl. {5.B.1} . . . . id.

G4821 **συμβασιλεύω**   *I reign along with (together*
with) another, *I am a king with,* in met. sense.
συμβέβηκε   verb, perf. act. indic. 3 pers. sg.
{5.A.1.c} . . . . .συμβαίνω G4819
συμβέβηκεν   verb, ²perf. act. indic. 3 pers. sg.
{5.A.1.c} . . . . id.
συμβεβηκότι   vbl., perf. act. ptc. dat. sg. neut.
{6.A.1.a} . . . . id.
συμβεβηκότων   vbl., perf. act. ptc. gen. pl.
neut. {6.A.1.a} . . . . id.
συμβιβαζόμενον   vbl., pres. pass. ptc. nom. sg.
neut. {6.A.1} . . . . .συμβιβάζω G4822
συμβιβάζοντες   vbl., pres. act. ptc. nom. pl.
masc. {6.A.1} . . . . id.

G4822 **συμβιβάζω**   (1) *I bring together, join, unite,*
Eph 4:16; Col 2:19; (2) *I put together, compare,*
examine closely, hence, *I consider, conclude,*
Acts 16:10; *I deduce, prove,* Acts 9:22; (3) *I*
teach, instruct (a biblical sense, translation
Gk.), Acts 19:33 (var.), 1 Cor 2:16; Col 2:2.
συμβιβάζων   vbl., pres. act. ptc. nom. sg. masc.
{6.A.1} . . . . .συμβιβάζω G4822
συμβιβάσει   verb, fut. act. indic. 3 pers. sg.
{5.A.1.a} . . . . id.
συμβιβασθέντες   vbl., aor. pass. ptc. nom. pl.
masc. {6.A.1.a}. . . . . id.
συμβιβασθέντων   vbl., aor. pass. ptc. gen. pl.
masc. {6.A.1.a}. . . . . id.
συμβουλεύσας   vbl., aor. act. ptc. nom. sg. masc.
{6.A.1.a} . . . . συμβουλεύω G4823

G4823 **συμβουλεύω**   act. *I advise;* mid. συμβου-
λευόμεθα, *we counsel one another.*

συμβουλεύω   verb, pres. act. indic. 1 pers. sg.
{5.A.1.a} . . . . συμβουλεύω G4823

G4824 **συμβούλιον**, -ου, τό   (1) *a body of advisers*
(assessors) in a court, *a council,* Acts 25:12; (2)
abstr., *consultation, counsel, advice; resolution,*
decree; διδόναι (Aramaism) Mark 3:6.
συμβούλιον   noun, acc. sg. neut.
{2.B} . . . . .συμβούλιον G4824
συμβουλίου   noun, gen. sg. neut. {2.B} . . . . . . id.

G4825 **σύμβουλος**, -ου, ὁ   *an adviser.*
σύμβουλος   noun, nom. sg. masc.
{2.B} . . . . .σύμβουλος G4825

G4826 **Συμεών**, ὁ   *Symeon,* (1) the patriarch, son of
Jacob and founder of a tribe, Rev 7:7; (2) an
ancestor of Jesus, Luke 3:30; (3) an inhabitant
of Jerusalem, who blessed the babe Jesus, Luke
2:25, 34; (4) an Antiochian Christian, also called
Niger, Acts 13:1; (5) a form of the Heb. name of
Peter the Apostle, Acts 15:14; 2 Pet 1:1 (var.).
Συμεών   noun prop. . . . . .Συμεών G4826
συμμαθηταῖς   noun, dat. pl. masc.
{2.A} . . . . .συμμαθητής G4827

G4827 **συμμαθητής**, -οῦ, ὁ   *a fellow disciple, a fellow*
scholar.
συμμαρτυρεῖ   verb, pres. act. indic. 3 pers. sg.
{5.A.2} . . . . συμμαρτυρέω G4828

G4828 **συμμαρτυρέω**   *I join in giving evidence (bear-*
ing witness) with.
συμμαρτυροῦμαι   verb, pres. mid./pass. indic.
1 pers. sg. {5.A.2}. . . . . συμμαρτυρέω G4828
συμμαρτυρούσης   vbl., pres. act. ptc. gen. sg.
fem. {6.A.2} . . . . id.
συμμερίζονται   verb, pres. mid./pass. indic.
3 pers. pl. {5.A.1.d} . . . . συμμερίζω G4829

G4829 **συμμερίζω**   *I cause to share with* (in the sacrifices); mid. *I share with* (w. dat.).
συμμέτοχα   adj., acc. pl. neut. {3.C} . . συμμέτοχος G4830
συμμέτοχοι   adj., nom. pl. masc. {3.C}. . . . . . . id.

G4830 **συμμέτοχος**, -ου, ὁ   *a fellow sharer, a partner.*
συμμιμηταί   noun, nom. pl. masc.
{2.A} . . . . συμμιμητής G4831

G4831 **συμμιμητής**, -οῦ, ὁ   *a joint imitator, an imita-*
tor along (together) with others.
συμμορφιζόμενος   vbl., pres. pass. ptc. nom. sg.
masc. {6.A.1} . . . . συμμορφίζω G4833†‡

G4833†‡ **συμμορφίζω**   lit. *I cause to share the form* (see
μορφή) *of another,* hence, συμμορφιζόμενος
= *being made to share the experience of.* Var.
for συμμορφόω, Phil 3:10.
σύμμορφον   adj., acc. sg. neut. {3.C} . .σύμμορφος G4832

G4832 **σύμμορφος**, -ον   *sharing the form* of another.
συμμορφούμενος   vbl., pres. pass. ptc. nom. sg.
masc. {6.A.2}. . . . . συμμορφόω G4833
συμμόρφους   adj., acc. pl. masc. {3.C} .σύμμορφος G4832

G4833 **συμμορφόω**   *to take on the same form, to con-*
form to.
συμπαθεῖς   adj., nom. pl. masc. {3.C} . .συμπαθής G4835

G4834 **συμπαθέω**   *I suffer along with.*

G4835 **συμπαθής**, -ές   *sharing the experiences* of
others.

συμπαθῆσαι   vbl., aor. act. inf. {6.B.1}. συμπαθέω *G4834*
συμπαραγενόμενοι   vbl., ²aor. mid. ptc. nom. pl.
    masc. {6.A.1.b} . . . . .συμπαραγίνομαι *G4836*
G4836 **συμπαραγίνομαι**   *I arrive along with.*
G4837 **συμπαρακαλέω**   *I cheer (encourage) along with;*
    pass., receive encouragement together with.
συμπαρακληθῆναι   vbl., aor. pass. inf.
    {6.B.1} . . . . .συμπαρακαλέω *G4837*
συμπαραλαβεῖν   vbl., ²aor. act. inf.
    {6.B.1} . . . . συμπαραλαμβάνω *G4838*
συμπαραλαβόντες   vbl., ²aor. act. ptc. nom.
    pl. masc. {6.A.1.a} . . . . id.
συμπαραλαβών   vbl., ²aor. act. ptc. nom. sg.
    masc. {6.A.1.a}. . . . . id.
συμπαραλαμβάνειν   vbl., pres. act. inf. {6.B.1} id.
G4838 **συμπαραλαμβάνω**   *I take along with me* (as
    helper).
συμπαραμενῶ   verb, fut. act. indic. 1 pers. sg.
    {5.A.2}. . . . . συμπαραμένω *G4839*
G4839 **συμπαραμένω**   *I remain and help someone.*
συμπαρεγένετο   verb, ²aor. mid. indic. 3 pers. sg.
    {5.A.1.e} . . . . .συμπαραγίνομαι *G4836*
G4840 **συμπάρειμι** (from εἰμί)   *I am present (here)*
    along with.
συμπαρόντες   vbl., pres. act. ptc. nom. pl. masc.
    {7.A.1}. . . . . συμπάρειμι *G4840*
συμπάσχει   verb, pres. act. indic. 3 pers. sg.
    {5.A.1.a} . . . . συμπάσχω *G4841*
συμπάσχομεν   verb, pres. act. indic. 1 pers. pl.
    {5.A.1.a} . . . . id.
G4841 **συμπάσχω**   *I suffer together.*
G4842 **συμπέμπω**   *I send along with.*
συμπεριλαβών   vbl., ²aor. act. ptc. nom. sg. masc.
    {6.A.1.a} . . . . συμπεριλαμβάνω *G4843*
G4843 **συμπεριλαμβάνω**   *I embrace closely.*
G4844 **συμπίνω**   *I drink* (wine) *along with.*
G4098†‡ **συμπίπτω**   *I fall together, I fall in, I collapse.*
    Var. for πίπτω, Luke 6:49.
συμπληροῦσθαι   vbl., pres. pass. inf.
    {6.B.2} . . . . συμπληρόω *G4845*
G4845 **συμπληρόω**   (1) *I fill up,* hence pass., by an
    idiom analogous to Eng., συνεπληροῦντο,
    Luke 8:23, *they were filling up* (where it was re-
    ally the ship that was filling up); (2) *I complete*
    (Hebraistic), of the coming to an end of an
    interval of days before some event (in Acts 2:1
    the day of the event may be partly included).
συμπνίγει   verb, pres. act. indic. 3 pers. sg.
    {5.A.1.a} . . . . συμπνίγω *G4846*
συμπνίγονται   verb, pres. pass. indic. 3 pers.
    pl. {5.A.1.d} . . . . id.
συμπνίγουσι   verb, pres. act. indic. 3 pers. pl.
    {5.A.1.a} . . . . id.
συμπνίγουσιν   verb, pres. act. indic. 3 pers. pl.
    {5.A.1.a} . . . . id.
G4846 **συμπνίγω**   met. *I choke utterly;* in Luke 8:42 by
    exaggeration (possibly slang), of *pressing very*
    hard upon, hustling, in a crowd (cf. the more
    correct συνθλίβω).

συμπολῖται   noun, nom. pl. masc.
    {2.A} . . . . συμπολίτης *G4847*
G4847 **συμπολίτης**, -ου, ὁ   *a fellow citizen.*
G4848 **συμπορεύομαι**   *I journey with, I go with; I go*
    together.
συμπορεύονται   verb, pres. mid./pass. indic.
    3 pers. pl. {5.A.1.d} . . . . .συμπορεύομαι *G4848*
συμπόσια   noun, acc. pl. neut. {2.B} . . συμπόσιον *G4849*
G4849 **συμπόσιον**, -ου, τό   properly *a drinking bout,*
    following dinner; συμπόσια συμπόσια (col-
    loquial), *in companies of diners.*
G4850 **συμπρεσβύτερος**, -ου, ὁ   *a fellow elder.*
συμπρεσβύτερος   noun, nom. sg. masc.
    {2.B} . . . . συμπρεσβύτερος *G4850*
συμφέρει   verb, pres. act. indic. 3 pers. sg.
    {5.A.1.a} . . . . .συμφέρω *G4851*
συμφέρον   vbl., pres. act. ptc. acc. sg. neut.
    {6.A.1}. . . . . id.
συμφέρον   vbl., pres. act. ptc. nom. sg. neut.
    {6.A.1}. . . . . id.
συμφερόντων   vbl., pres. act. ptc. gen. pl. neut.
    {6.A.1}. . . . . id.
G4851 **συμφέρω**   (1) trans., *I collect, bring together,*
    Acts 19:19; (2) intrans. and generally impers.,
    συμφέρει, *it is an advantage, it is expedient*
    (beneficial); συμφέρον (supply ἐστίν), 2 Cor
    12:1 = συμφέρει; τὸ συμφέρον, as subs.
G4852 **σύμφημι**   *I express agreement with, I agree with.*
σύμφημι   verb, pres. act. indic. 1 pers. sg.
    {5.A.3.a} . . . . σύμφημι *G4852*
σύμφορον   adj., acc. sg. neut. {3.C} . . σύμφορος *G4851†‡*
G4851†‡ **σύμφορος**, -ου, τό   *a benefit, advantage.* Var.
    for συμφέρω, 1 Cor 7:35; 10:33.
συμφυεῖσαι   vbl., ²aor. pass. ptc. nom. pl. fem.
    {6.A.1.a} . . . . συμφύω *G4855*
G4853 **συμφυλέτης**, -ου, ὁ   *a fellow tribesman, one*
    of the same tribe, doubtless with reference
    to Jews in Thessalonica, all enrolled in one
    city-tribe.
συμφυλετῶν   noun, gen. pl. masc.
    {2.A} . . . . .συμφυλέτης *G4853*
σύμφυτοι   adj., nom. pl. masc. {3.C} . . .σύμφυτος *G4854*
G4854 **σύμφυτος**   *grown along with, vitally one with,*
    united with.
G4855 **συμφύω**   *I grow up together with* (another),
    ²aor. pass. as act.
συμφωνεῖ   verb, pres. act. indic. 3 pers. sg.
    {5.A.2}. . . . . συμφωνέω *G4856*
G4856 **συμφωνέω**   (first of a harmony of voices, then)
    I harmonize with, I agree with; of more than
    one, *we agree together;* pass. impers. *it is agreed*
    upon among (possibly a Latinism, *conuenit*
    inter), Acts 5:9.
συμφωνήσας   vbl., aor. act. ptc. nom. sg. masc.
    {6.A.2} . . . . συμφωνέω *G4856*
συμφωνήσει   verb, fut. act. indic. 3 pers. sg.
    {5.A.1} . . . . id.
G4857 **συμφώνησις**, -εως, ἡ   *harmony, agreement.*
συμφώνησις   noun, nom. sg. fem.
    {2.C} . . . . .συμφώνησις *G4857*

συμφωνήσωσιν verb, aor. act. subjunc. 3 pers. pl.
{5.B.1}. . . . . συμφωνέω G4856

G4858 **συμφωνία**, -ας, ἡ *bagpipes* (cf. Dan 3:5), but
perhaps *music, symphony.*
συμφωνίας noun, gen. sg. fem. {2.A} . .συμφωνία G4858

G4859 **σύμφωνος**, -ον, τό *agreeing;* neut. subs., *agreement;* ἐκ συμφώνου *by agreement.*
συμφώνου adj., gen. sg. neut. {3.C}. . . .σύμφωνος G4859
συμφωνοῦσιν verb, pres. act. indic. 3 pers. pl.
{5.A.2}. . . . . συμφωνέω G4856

G4860 **συμψηφίζω** *I calculate together, I reckon up.*
σύμψυχοι adj., nom. pl. masc. {3.C} . . .σύμψυχος G4861

G4861 **σύμψυχος**, -ον *one in feeling with* others, *sharing the feelings of* others.

G4862 **σύν** prep. with dat., *with* (Gk. allows either the
sense *plus* or the sense *including*).
σύν prep. . . . . σύν G4862
συναγαγεῖν vbl., ²aor. act. inf. {6.B.1} . . . .συνάγω G4863
συναγάγετε verb, ²aor. act. impv. 2 pers. pl.
{5.D.1}. . . . . id.
συναγάγῃ verb, ²aor. act. subjunc. 3 pers. sg.
{5.B.1}. . . . . id.
συναγαγόντες vbl., ²aor. act. ptc. nom. pl.
masc. {6.A.1.a}. . . . . id.
συναγαγούσῃ vbl., ²aor. act. ptc. dat. sg. fem.
{6.A.1.a} . . . . id.
συναγαγών vbl., ²aor. act. ptc. nom. sg. masc.
{6.A.1.a} . . . . id.
συνάγει verb, pres. act. indic. 3 pers. sg. {5.A.1.a}. id.
συνάγεις verb, pres. act. indic. 2 pers. sg.
{5.A.1.a} . . . . id.
συνάγεσθε verb, pres. pass. impv. 2 pers. pl.
{5.D.1}. . . . . id.
συνάγεται verb, pres. pass. indic. 3 pers. sg.
{5.A.1.d} . . . . id.
συνάγετε verb, pres. act. impv. 2 pers. pl. {5.D.1} id.
συνάγονται verb, pres. pass. indic. 3 pers. pl.
{5.A.1.d} . . . . id.
συνάγουσιν verb, pres. act. indic. 3 pers. pl.
{5.A.1.a} . . . . id.

G4863 **συνάγω** *I gather together, collect, assemble,*
persons or things; συναγαγὼν πάντα implies
the converting of the goods into money, *having sold all of,* Luke 15:13.
συνάγω verb, pres. act. indic. 1 pers. sg.
{5.A.1.a} . . . . .συνάγω G4863
συναγωγαῖς noun, dat. pl. fem. {2.A} . .συναγωγή G4864
συναγωγάς noun, acc. pl. fem. {2.A}. . . . . id.

G4864 **συναγωγή**, -ῆς, ἡ (in origin abstr., *a leading* or
bringing together, convening an assembly, then
concr., *a religious meeting*), *a meeting (assembly), a place of meeting (assembly),* particularly
of Jews for the reading of scripture and for
worship, *a synagogue.* In certain passages it is
doubtful whether the congregation (e.g., John
6:59; 18:20) or the place of meeting (e.g., Jas
2:2) is particularly intended, but the sense is
not seriously affected by the doubt. In the OT
συναγωγή and ἐκκλησία are practically synonymous, but in ordinary Christian writings

the former is rarely used, and seemingly only
of communities of Jews or Jewish Christians
(e.g., Jas 2:2, where it is probably the building).
συναγωγή noun, nom. sg. fem. {2.A} . .συναγωγή G4864
συναγωγῇ noun, dat. sg. fem. {2.A}. . . . . id.
συναγωγήν noun, acc. sg. fem. {2.A}. . . . . id.
συναγωγῆς noun, gen. sg. fem. {2.A} . . . . id.
συναγωγῶν noun, gen. pl. fem. {2.A} . . . . id.
συνάγων vbl., pres. act. ptc. nom. sg. masc.
{6.A.1}. . . . . .συνάγω G4863

G4865 **συναγωνίζομαι** *I struggle (contend) in company with.*
συναγωνίσασθαι vbl., aor. mid. inf.
{6.B.1}. . . . . .συναγωνίζομαι G4865

G4866 **συναθλέω** *I compete together with* others,
originally of athletic contests, and then met.
συναθλοῦντες vbl., pres. act. ptc. nom. pl. masc.
{6.A.2}. .συναθλέω G4866

G4867 **συναθροίζω** trans., *I gather together, assemble.*
συναθροίσας vbl., aor. act. ptc. nom. sg. masc.
{6.A.1.a} . . . . .συναθροίζω G4867
συναίρει verb, pres. act. indic. 3 pers. sg.
{5.A.1.a} .συναίρω G4868
συναίρειν vbl., pres. act. inf. {6.B.1} . . . . id.

G4868 **συναίρω** w. λόγον, *I compare (settle) accounts,
make a reckoning.*

G4869 **συναιχμάλωτος**, -ου, ὁ *a fellow captive, a
fellow prisoner, a companion in chains.*
συναιχμάλωτος noun, nom. sg. masc.
{3.C} . . . . .συναιχμάλωτος G4869
συναιχμαλώτους noun, acc. pl. masc. {3.C} . . id.

G4870 **συνακολουθέω** *I accompany.*
συνακολουθῆσαι vbl., aor. act. inf.
{6.B.1} . . . . .συνακολουθέω G4870
συνακολουθήσασαι vbl., aor. act. ptc. nom.
pl. fem. {6.A.2} . . . . id.
συνακολουθοῦσαι vbl., pres. act. ptc. nom.
pl. fem. {6.A.2} . . . . id.
συναλιζόμενος vbl., pres. mid./pass. ptc. nom. sg.
masc. {6.A.1}. . . . . .συναλίζω G4871

G4871 **συναλίζω** *I have table fellowship with, I share
a common meal with* (as from σύν and ἅλς,
"salt"); or *I gather together* (as from σύν and
ἁλής, "crowded").

G4900†‡ **συναλλάσσω** *I attempt (seek) to reconcile.* Var.
for συνελαύνω, Acts 7:26.

G4872 **συναναβαίνω** *I go up with.*
συναναβᾶσαι vbl., ²aor. act. ptc. nom. pl. fem.
{6.A.1.a} . . . . .συναναβαίνω G4872
συναναβᾶσιν vbl., ²aor. act. ptc. dat. pl. masc.
{6.A.1.a} . . . . id.

G4873 **συνανάκειμαι** *I recline at* (dinner) *table with.*
συνανάκειμενοι vbl., pres. mid./pass. ptc. nom.
pl. masc. {6.A.3} . . . . .συνανάκειμαι G4873
συνανακειμένοις vbl., pres. mid./pass. ptc.
dat. pl. masc. {6.A.3} . . . . id.
συνανακειμένους vbl., pres. mid./pass. ptc.
acc. pl. masc. {6.A.3} . . . . id.
συνανακειμένων vbl., pres. mid./pass. ptc.
gen. pl. masc. {6.A.3}. . . . . id.

G4874 **συναναμίγνυμι** mid. *I associate intimately with.*
συναναμίγνυσθαι vbl., pres. mid. inf.
{6.B.3} . . . . συναναμίγνυμι *G4874*
συναναμίγνυσθε verb, pres. mid. impv.
2 pers. pl. {5.D.3} . . . . id.
G4875 **συναναπαύομαι** *I rest along with.*
συναναπαύσωμαι verb, aor. mid. subjunc. 1 pers.
sg. {5.B.1} . . . . συναναπαύομαι *G4875*
συνανέκειντο verb, impf. mid./pass. indic. 3 pers.
pl. {5.A.3.a} . . . . συνανάκειμαι *G4873*
G4876 **συναντάω** *I meet, encounter; in* Acts 20:22,
with in animate subj.
συναντήσας vbl., aor. act. ptc. nom. sg. masc.
{6.A.2} . . . . συναντάω *G4876*
συναντήσει verb, fut. act. indic. 3 pers. sg.
{5.A.1} . . . . id.
συνάντησιν noun, acc. sg. fem. {2.C} συνάντησις *G4877*
G4877 **συνάντησις, -εως, ἡ** *a meeting.*
συναντήσοντα vbl., fut. act. ptc. acc. pl. neut.
{6.A.2} . . . . συναντάω *G4876*
συναντιλάβηται verb, ²aor. mid. subjunc. 3 pers.
sg. {5.B.1} . . . . .συναντιλαμβάνομαι *G4878*
συναντιλαμβάνεται verb, pres. mid./pass.
indic. 3 pers. sg. {5.A.1.d} . . . . id.
G4878 **συναντιλαμβάνομαι** *I lend a hand along with, I take interest in* (a thing) *along with* (others), *I assist jointly* to perform some task, *I cooperate with, I take my share in.*
συνάξει verb, fut. act. indic. 3 pers. sg.
{5.A.1.a} . . . . .συνάγω *G4863*
συνάξω verb, fut. act. indic. 1 pers. sg. {5.A.1.a} id.
συναπαγόμενοι vbl., pres. mid. ptc. nom. pl.
masc. {6.A.1} . . . . συναπάγω *G4879*
G4879 **συναπάγω** *I lead away with, I carry along with* (in good or bad sense according to context);
mid. with dat., *I condescend to,* Rom 12:16.
συναπαχθέντες vbl., aor. pass. ptc. nom. pl. masc.
{6.A.1.a} . . . . συναπάγω *G4879*
συναπεθάνομεν verb, ²aor. act. indic. 1 pers. pl.
{5.A.1.b} . . . . .συναποθνήσκω *G4880*
συναπέστειλα verb, aor. act. indic. 1 pers.
{5.A.1.b} . . . . συναποστέλλω *G4882*
συναπήχθη verb, aor. pass. indic. 3 pers. sg.
{5.A.1.b} . . . . συναπάγω *G4879*
συναποθανεῖν vbl., ²aor. act. inf.
{6.B.1} . . . . .συναποθνήσκω *G4880*
G4880 **συναποθνήσκω** *I die along with, I die together* (with others).
G4881 **συναπόλλυμι** pass. *I am destroyed, perish along with.*
G4882 **συναποστέλλω** *I send away in some one's company.*
συναπώλετο verb, ²aor. mid. indic. 3 pers. sg.
{5.A.3.b} . . . . .συναπόλλυμι *G4881*
συνάραι vbl., aor. act. inf. {6.B.1} . . . . . .συναίρω *G4868*
G4883 **συναρμολογέω** *I fit together* (by means of all the elaborate preparatory processes necessary); an architectural term, from ἁρμός meaning "the side of a stone," and λογεῖν

added by analogy with λιθολόγος without its proper force.
συναρμολογουμένη vbl., pres. pass. ptc. nom. sg.
fem. {6.A.2} . . . . .συναρμολογέω *G4883*
συναρμολογούμενον vbl., pres. pass. ptc.
nom. sg. neut. {6.A.2} . . . . id.
G4884 **συναρπάζω** *I keep a firm grip of.*
συναρπάσαντες vbl., aor. act. ptc. nom. pl. masc.
{6.A.1.a} . . . . συναρπάζω *G4884*
συναρπασθέντος vbl., aor. pass. ptc. gen. sg.
neut. {6.A.1.a} . . . . id.
συναυξάνεσθαι vbl., pres. pass. inf.
{6.B.1} . . . . συναυξάνω *G4885*
G4885 **συναυξάνω** *I make to increase (grow) together; pass. grow together.*
συναχθέντες vbl., aor. pass. ptc. nom. pl. masc.
{6.A.1.a} .συνάγω *G4863*
συναχθέντων vbl., aor. pass. ptc. gen. pl.
masc. {6.A.1.a} . . . . id.
συναχθῆναι vbl., aor. pass. inf. {6.B.1} . . . . . . id.
συναχθήσεται verb, fut. pass. indic. 3 pers.
sg. {5.A.1.d} . . . . id.
συναχθήσονται verb, fut. pass. indic. 3 pers.
pl. {5.A.1.d} . . . . id.
συνάχθητε verb, aor. pass. impv. 2 pers. pl.
{5.D.1} . . . . id.
συνβαλεῖν vbl., ²aor. act. inf. {6.B.1} . . συμβάλλω *G4820*
συνβάλλουσα vbl., pres. act. ptc. nom. sg.
fem. {6.A.1} . . . . id.
συνβασιλεύσομεν verb, fut. act. indic. 1 pers. pl.
{5.A.1.a} . . . . συμβασιλεύω *G4821*
συνβασιλεύσωμεν verb, aor. act. subjunc.
1 pers. pl. {5.B.1} . . . . id.
συνβιβαζόμενον vbl., pres. pass. ptc. nom. sg.
neut. {6.A.1} . . . . .συμβιβάζω *G4822*
συνβιβάζοντες vbl., pres. act. ptc. nom.
masc. {6.A.1} . . . . id.
συνβιβάζων vbl., pres. act. ptc. nom. sg. masc.
{6.A.1} . . . . id.
συνβιβάσει verb, fut. act. indic. 3 pers. sg.
{5.A.1.a} . . . . id.
συνβιβασθέντες vbl., aor. pass. ptc. nom. pl.
masc. {6.A.1.a} . . . . id.
συνγνώμην noun, acc. sg. fem. {2.A} . .συγγνώμη *G4774*
συνδεδεμένοι vbl., perf. pass. ptc. nom. pl. masc.
{6.A.2} . . . . συνδέω *G4887*
σύνδεσμον noun, acc. sg. masc. {2.B} . σύνδεσμος *G4886*
G4886 **σύνδεσμος, -ου, ὁ** *a binding together, a means of holding together, a bond,* lit. and met.; in Acts 8:23 the man is *in* (εἰς = ἐν) the grip of ἀδικία.
σύνδεσμος noun, nom. sg. masc. {2.B} σύνδεσμος *G4886*
συνδέσμῳ noun, dat. sg. masc. {2.B} . . . . id.
συνδέσμων noun, gen. pl. masc. {2.B} . . . . id.
G4887 **συνδέω** *I bind along with another; pass.* συνδεδεμένοι, *fellow captives.*
G4888 **συνδοξάζω** *I glorify along with.*
συνδοξασθῶμεν verb, aor. pass. subjunc. 1 pers.
pl. {5.B.1} . . . . .συνδοξάζω *G4888*
σύνδουλοι noun, nom. pl. masc. {2.B} σύνδουλος *G4889*

σύνδουλον   noun, acc. sg. masc. {2.B} . . . . id.

G4889 **σύνδουλος**, -ου, ὁ   *a fellow slave,* either of an earthly master, or of the glorified Lord.

σύνδουλος   noun, nom. sg. masc. {2.B}σύνδουλος G4889

συνδούλου   noun, gen. sg. masc. {2.B} . . . . . . id.

συνδούλους   noun, acc. pl. masc. {2.B} . . . . . . id.

συνδούλων   noun, gen. pl. masc. {2.B} . . . . . . id.

G4890 **συνδρομή**, -ῆς, ἡ   *a running together, a tumultuous concourse.*

συνδρομή   noun, nom. sg. fem. {2.A} . .συνδρομή G4890

συνέβαινεν   verb, impf. act. indic. 3 pers. sg. {5.A.1.b} .συμβαίνω G4819

συνέβαινον   verb, impf. act. indic. 3 pers. pl. {5.A.1.b} . . . . id.

συνέβαλεν   verb, ²aor. act. indic. 3 pers. sg. {5.A.1.b} . . . . συμβάλλω G4820

συνεβάλετο   verb, ²aor. mid. indic. 3 pers. sg. {5.A.1.e} . . . . id.

συνέβαλλεν   verb, impf. act. indic. 3 pers. sg. {5.A.1.b} . . . . id.

συνέβαλλον   verb, impf. act. indic. 3 pers. pl. {5.A.1.b} . . . . id.

συνέβαλον   verb, ²aor. act. indic. 3 pers. pl. {5.A.1.b} . . . . id.

συνέβη   verb, ²aor. act. indic. 3 pers. sg. {5.A.1.b} . . . . .συμβαίνω G4819

συνεβίβασαν   verb, aor. act. indic. 3 pers. pl. {5.A.1.b} .συμβιβάζω G4822

συνεβουλεύσαντο   verb, aor. mid. indic. 3 pers. pl. {5.A.1.e} . . . . συμβουλεύω G4823

G4891 **συνεγείρω**   *I raise along with* the Messiah (from the dead, or from a dead spiritual state).

συνέδραμε   verb, ²aor. act. indic. 3 pers. sg. {5.A.1.b} . . . . συντρέχω G4936

συνέδραμεν   verb, ²aor. act. indic. 3 pers. sg. {5.A.1.b} . . . . id.

συνέδραμον   verb, ²aor. act. indic. 3 pers. pl. {5.A.1.b} . . . . id.

συνέδρια   noun, acc. pl. neut. {2.B; 2.D}συνέδριον G4892

G4892 **συνέδριον** (Συνέδριον), -ου, τό   *a council* of leading Jews, Mark 13:9; Matt 10:17, but elsewhere *the Jewish council at Jerusalem, the Sanhedrin, the High Court, the Senate,* composed of seventy one members comprising members of high priestly families, Pharisees learned in the law, and a lay element of Elders.

συνέδριον   noun, acc. sg. neut. {2.B; 2.D} . . . . .συνέδριον G4892

συνέδριον   noun, nom. sg. neut. {2.B; 2.D} . . . . id.

συνεδρίου   noun, gen. sg. neut. {2.B; 2.D} . . . . . id.

συνεδρίῳ   noun, dat. sg. neut. {2.B; 2.D} . . . . . id.

συνέζευξεν   verb, aor. act. indic. 3 pers. sg. {5.A.3.b} . . . . συζεύγνυμι G4801

συνεζήτει   verb, impf. act. indic. 3 pers. sg. {5.A.2} . . . . συζητέω G4802

συνεζωοποίησε   verb, aor. act. indic. 3 pers. sg. {5.A.1} . . . . συζωοποιέω G4806

συνεζωοποίησεν   verb, aor. act. indic. 3 pers. sg. {5.A.1} . . . . id.

συνεζῳοποίησεν   verb, aor. act. indic. 3 pers. sg. {5.A.1} . . . . id.

συνέθεντο   verb, ²aor. mid. indic. 3 pers. pl. {5.A.3.b} . . . . .συντίθημι G4934

συνέθλιβον   verb, impf. act. indic. 3 pers. pl. {5.A.1.b} . . . . συνθλίβω G4918

συνειδήσει   noun, dat. sg. fem. {2.C} . .συνείδησις G4893

συνειδήσεσιν   noun, dat. pl. fem. {2.C} . . . . . . id.

συνειδήσεως   noun, gen. sg. fem. {2.C} . . . . . . id.

συνείδησιν   noun, acc. sg. fem. {2.C} . . . . id.

G4893 **συνείδησις**, -εως, ἡ   (orig., *consciousness,* e.g., 1 Pet 2:19, where θεοῦ is obj. gen., but through the influence of the Stoic terminology) *conscience,* the innate power to discern what is good, an abiding consciousness bearing witness concerning a man's conduct.

συνείδησις   noun, nom. sg. fem. {2.C}.συνείδησις G4893

συνειδυίας   vbl., ²perf. act. ptc. gen. sg. fem. {6.A.1.a} . . . . συνείδω G4894

συνειδυίης   vbl., ²perf. act. ptc. gen. sg. fem. {6.A.1.a} . . . . id.

G4894 **συνείδω** (συνοῖδα, συνεῖδον)   Obsolete present tense of the ²perf. form συνοῖδα, 1. *share knowledge with;* 2. *to know within oneself* (Acts 5:2; 1 Cor 4:4); and (2) the form συνεῖδον, ²aor. of συνοράω, *I understand, I become aware of* (Acts 12:12; 14:6).

συνείληφεν   verb, ²perf. act. indic. 3 pers. sg. {5.A.1.c} . . . . συλλαμβάνω G4815

συνειληφυῖα   vbl., ²perf. act. ptc. nom. sg. fem. {6.A.1.a} . . . . id.

G4895 **σύνειμι**¹ (from εἰμί)   *I am with, I am in company with, I join with.*

G4896 **σύνειμι**² (from εἶμι)   *I come together,* Luke 8:4.

συνείπετο   verb, impf. mid./pass. indic. 3 pers. sg. {5.A.1.e} . . . . συνέπομαι G4902

G4897 **συνεισέρχομαι**   *I go in with, I enter with.*

συνεισῆλθε   verb, ²aor. act. indic. 3 pers. sg. {5.A.1.b} . . . . συνεισέρχομαι G4897

συνεισῆλθεν   verb, ²aor. act. indic. 3 pers. sg. {5.A.1.b} . . . . id.

συνείχετο   verb, impf. pass. indic. 3 pers. sg. {5.A.1.e} . . . . συνέχω G4912

συνείχοντο   verb, impf. pass. indic. 3 pers. pl. {5.A.1.e} . . . . id.

συνεκάθισεν   verb, aor. act. indic. 3 pers. sg. {5.A.1.b} . . . . συγκαθίζω G4776

συνεκάλεσαν   verb, aor. act. indic. 3 pers. sg. {5.A.1} . . . . συγκαλέω G4779

G4898 **συνέκδημος**, -ου, ὁ   *a traveling companion.*

συνέκδημος   noun, nom. sg. masc. {2.B} . . . . συνέκδημος G4898

συνεκδήμους   noun, acc. pl. masc. {2.B} . . . . . . id.

συνεκέρασε   verb, aor. act. indic. 3 pers. sg. {5.A.3.b} . . . . συγκεράννυμι G4786

συνεκέρασεν   verb, aor. act. indic. 3 pers. sg. {5.A.3.b} . . . . id.

συνεκίνησαν   verb, aor. act. indic. 3 pers. pl. {5.A.1} . . . . συγκινέω G4787

συνέκλεισαν   verb, aor. act. indic. 3 pers. pl.
{5.A.1.b} . . . . συγκλείω *G4788*
συνέκλεισε   verb, aor. act. indic. 3 pers. sg.
{5.A.1.b} . . . . id.
συνέκλεισεν   verb, aor. act. indic. 3 pers. sg.
{5.A.1.b} . . . . id.
συνεκλεκτη   adj., nom. sg. fem. {3.C} συνεκλεκτός *G4899*
συνεκλεκτή   adj., nom. sg. fem. {3.C} . . . . id.
G4899 **συνεκλεκτός,** -ή, -όν   *fellow-chosen, fellow-elect,* understand ἐκκλησία.
συνεκόμισαν   verb, aor. act. indic. 3 pers. pl.
{5.A.1.b} . . . . συγκομίζω *G4792*
συνέλαβεν   verb, [2]aor. act. indic. 3 pers. sg.
{5.A.1.b} . . . . συλλαμβάνω *G4815*
συνέλαβον   verb, [2]aor. act. indic. 3 pers. pl.
{5.A.1.b} . . . . id.
συνελάλησε   verb, aor. act. indic. 3 pers. sg.
{5.A.1} . . . . συλλαλέω *G4814*
συνελάλησεν   verb, aor. act. indic. 3 pers. sg.
{5.A.1} . . . . id.
συνελάλουν   verb, impf. act. indic. 3 pers. pl.
{5.A.2} . . . . id.
G4900 **συνελαύνω**   *to drive, to force.*
συνέλεξαν   verb, aor. act. indic. 3 pers. pl.
{5.A.1.b} . . . . συλλέγω *G4816*
συνεληλύθεισαν   verb, plu. act. indic. 3 pers. pl.
{5.A.1.b} . . . . συνέρχομαι *G4905*
συνεληλυθότας   vbl., [2]perf. act. ptc. acc. pl.
masc. {6.A.1.a} . . . . id.
συνεληλυθυῖαι   vbl., [2]perf. act. ptc. nom. pl.
fem. {6.A.1.a} . . . . id.
συνελθεῖν   vbl., [2]aor. act. inf. {6.B.1} . . . . id.
συνέλθη   verb, [2]aor. act. subjunc. 3 pers. sg.
{5.B.1} . . . . id.
συνελθόντα   vbl., [2]aor. act. ptc. acc. sg. masc.
{6.A.1.a} . . . . id.
συνελθόντας   vbl., [2]aor. act. ptc. acc. pl. masc.
{6.A.1.a} . . . . id.
συνελθόντες   vbl., [2]aor. act. ptc. nom. pl. masc.
{6.A.1.a} . . . . id.
συνελθόντων   vbl., [2]aor. act. ptc. gen. pl. masc.
{6.A.1.a} . . . . id.
συνελθούσαις   vbl., [2]aor. act. ptc. dat. pl. fem.
{6.A.1.a} . . . . id.
συνελογίσαντο   verb, aor. mid. indic. 3 pers. pl.
{5.A.1.e} . . . . συλλογίζομαι *G4817*
συνενέγκαντες   vbl., [2]aor. act. ptc. nom. pl. masc.
{6.A.1.a} . . . . .συμφέρω *G4851*
συνέξουσι   verb, fut. act. indic. 3 pers. pl.
{5.A.1.a} . . . . συνέχω *G4912*
συνέξουσιν   verb, fut. act. indic. 3 pers. pl.
{5.A.1.a} . . . . id.
συνεπαθήσατε   verb, aor. act. indic. 2 pers. pl.
{5.A.1} . . . . συμπαθέω *G4834*
συνεπέθεντο   verb, [2]aor. mid. indic. 3 pers. pl.
{5.A.3.b} . . . . .συνεπιτίθημι *G4934†‡*
συνεπέμψαμεν   verb, aor. act. indic. 1 pers. pl.
{5.A.1.b} . . . . συμπέμπω *G4842*
συνέπεσεν   verb, [2]aor. act. indic. 3 pers. sg.
{5.A.1.b} . . . . .συμπίπτω *G4098†‡*

συνεπέστη   verb, [2]aor. act. indic. 3 pers. sg.
{5.A.3.b} . . . . συνεφίστημι *G4911*
G4901 **συνεπιμαρτυρέω**   *I add my testimony to that already given.*
συνεπιμαρτυροῦντος   vbl., pres. act. ptc. gen. sg.
masc. {6.A.2} . . . . .συνεπιμαρτυρέω *G4901*
συνεπίομεν   verb, [2]aor. act. indic. 1 pers. pl.
{5.A.1.b} . . . . συμπίνω *G4844*
G4934†‡ συνεπιτίθημι   mid. *I join in the charge,* lit. *I join in attacking.* Var. for συντίθημι, Acts 24:9.
συνεπληροῦντο   verb, impf. pass. indic. 3 pers. pl.
{5.A.2} . . . . συμπληρόω *G4845*
συνέπνιγον   verb, impf. act. indic. 3 pers. pl.
{5.A.1.b} . . . . συμπνίγω *G4846*
συνέπνιξαν   verb, aor. act. indic. 3 pers. pl.
{5.A.1.b} . . . . id.
G4902 **συνέπομαι**   *I accompany.*
συνεπορεύετο   verb, impf. mid./pass. indic. 3 pers.
sg. {5.A.1.e} . . . . .συμπορεύομαι *G4848*
συνεπορεύοντο   verb, impf. mid./pass. indic.
3 pers. pl. {5.A.1.e} . . . . id.
συνεργεῖ   verb, pres. act. indic. 3 pers. sg.
{5.A.2} . . . . συνεργέω *G4903*
G4903 **συνεργέω**   *I work along with, I cooperate with.*
συνεργοί   adj., nom. pl. masc. {3.C} . . . . συνεργός *G4904*
συνεργόν   adj., acc. sg. masc. {3.C} . . . . id.
G4904 **συνεργός,** -οῦ, ὁ   *a fellow worker.*
συνεργός   adj., nom. sg. masc. {3.C} . . . . συνεργός *G4904*
συνεργοῦντες   vbl., pres. act. ptc. nom. pl. masc.
{6.A.2} . . . . συνεργέω *G4903*
συνεργοῦντι   vbl., pres. act. ptc. dat. sg. masc.
{6.A.2} . . . . id.
συνεργοῦντος   vbl., pres. act. ptc. gen. sg.
masc. {6.A.2} . . . . id.
συνεργούς   adj., acc. pl. masc. {3.C} . . . . συνεργός *G4904*
συνεργῷ   adj., dat. sg. masc. {3.C} . . . . id.
συνεργῶν   adj., gen. pl. masc. {3.C} . . . . id.
συνέρχεσθε   verb, pres. mid./pass. indic. 2 pers. pl.
{5.A.1.d} . . . . συνέρχομαι *G4905*
συνέρχεται   verb, pres. mid./pass. indic.
3 pers. sg. {5.A.1.d} . . . . id.
συνέρχησθε   verb, pres. mid./pass. subjunc.
2 pers. pl. {5.B.1} . . . . id.
G4905 **συνέρχομαι**   *I go along with, I accompany; I come (meet) together* with others, αὐτῷ in Mark 14:53 being = πρὸς αὐτόν; *have sexual intercourse,* Matt 1:18.
συνερχόμενοι   vbl., pres. mid./pass. ptc. nom. pl.
masc. {6.A.1} . . . . συνέρχομαι *G4905*
συνερχομένων   vbl., pres. mid./pass. ptc. gen.
pl. masc. {6.A.1} . . . . id.
συνέρχονται   verb, pres. mid./pass. indic.
3 pers. pl. {5.A.1.d} . . . . id.
συνέσει   noun, dat. sg. fem. {2.C} . . . . . . .σύνεσις *G4907*
συνέσεως   noun, gen. sg. fem. {2.C}. . . . . id.
συνεσθίει   verb, pres. act. indic. 3 pers. sg.
{5.A.1.a} . . . . συνεσθίω *G4906*
συνεσθίειν   vbl., pres. act. inf. {6.B.1} . . . . id.
G4906 **συνεσθίω**   *I eat in company with.*
σύνεσιν   noun, acc. sg. fem. {2.C} . . . . . . .σύνεσις *G4907*

G4907 **σύνεσις**, -εως, ἡ   *practical discernment, intelligence, understanding.*

συνεσπάραξεν   verb, aor. act. indic. 3 pers. sg.
{5.A.1.b} . . . . συσπαράσσω G4952

συνεσταλμένος   vbl., perf. pass. ptc. nom. sg.
masc. {6.A.1.b} . . . . σνστέλλω G4958

συνεσταυρώθη   verb, aor. pass. indic. 3 pers. sg.
{5.A.1} . . . . σνσταυρόω G4957

συνεσταύρωμαι   verb, perf. pass. indic. 1 pers.
sg. {5.A.1} . . . . id.

συνεσταυρωμένοι   vbl., perf. pass. ptc. nom.
pl. masc. {6.A.2} . . . . id.

συνέστειλαν   verb, aor. act. indic. 3 pers. pl.
{5.A.1.b} . . . . σνστέλλω G4958

συνέστηκε   verb, perf. act. indic. 3 pers. sg.
{5.A.1} . . . . σννίστημι G4921

συνέστηκεν   verb, perf. act. indic. 3 pers. sg.
{5.A.1} . . . . id.

συνεστήσατε   verb, aor. act. indic. 2 pers. pl.
{5.A.3.b} . . . . id.

συνεστῶσα   vbl., ²perf. act. ptc. nom. sg. fem.
{6.A.3} . . . . id.

συνεστῶτας   vbl., ²perf. act. ptc. acc. pl. masc.
{6.A.3} . . . . id.

συνέσχον   verb, ²aor. act. indic. 3 pers. pl.
{5.A.1.b} . . . . συνέχω G4912

συνέταξε   verb, aor. act. indic. 3 pers. sg.
{5.A.1.b} . . . . σνντάσσω G4929

συνέταξεν   verb, aor. act. indic. 3 pers. sg.
{5.A.1.b} . . . . id.

συνετάφημεν   verb, ²aor. pass. indic. 1 pers. pl.
{5.A.1.e} . . . . σνυθάπτω G4916

σύνετε   verb, ²aor. act. impv. 2 pers. pl.
{5.D.3} . . . . συνίημι G4920

συνετέθειντο   verb, plu. mid. indic. 3 pers. pl.
{5.A.1} . . . . σνντίθημι G4934

συνετέλεσεν   verb, aor. act. indic. 3 pers. sg.
{5.A.1} . . . . σνντελέω G4931

συνετήρει   verb, impf. act. indic. 3 pers. sg.
{5.A.2} . . . . σνντηρέω G4933

G4908 **συνετός**, -ή, -όν   (lit. *one who can put things
together,* from συνίημι), *intelligent;* in Matt
11:25; Luke 10:21 it doubtless refers to Pharisees learned in the law.

συνετῷ   adj., dat. sg. masc. {3.C} . . . . . . συνετός G4908

συνετῶν   adj., gen. pl. masc. {3.C} . . . . id.

συνευδοκεῖ   verb, pres. act. indic. 3 pers. sg.
{5.A.2} . . . . συνευδοκέω G4909

συνευδοκεῖτε   verb, pres. act. indic. 2 pers. pl.
{5.A.2} . . . . id.

G4909 **συνευδοκέω**   *I entirely approve of.*

συνευδοκοῦσι   verb, pres. act. indic. 3 pers. pl.
{5.A.2} . . . . συνευδοκέω G4909

συνευδοκοῦσιν   verb, pres. act. indic. 3 pers.
pl. {5.A.2} . . . . id.

συνευδοκῶν   vbl., pres. act. ptc. nom. sg. masc.
{6.A.2} . . . . id.

G4910 **συνευωχέομαι**   *I feast along with.*

συνευωχούμενοι   vbl., pres. mid./pass. ptc. nom.
pl. masc. {6.A.2} . . . . συνευωχέομαι G4910

συνέφαγεν   verb, ²aor. act. indic. 3 pers. sg.
{5.A.1.b} . . . . σννεσθίω G4906

συνέφαγες   verb, ²aor. act. indic. 2 pers. sg.
{5.A.1.b} . . . . id.

συνεφάγομεν   verb, ²aor. act. indic. 1 pers. pl.
{5.A.1.b} . . . . id.

G4911 **συνεφίστημι**   pl., *(the multitude) rose up
together, set upon together,* ²aor. intrans.

συνεφωνήθη   verb, aor. pass. indic. 3 pers. sg.
{5.A.1} . . . . σνμφωνέω G4856

συνεφώνησας   verb, aor. act. indic. 2 pers. sg.
{5.A.1} . . . . id.

συνέχαιρον   verb, impf. act. indic. 3 pers. pl.
{5.A.1.b} . . . . συγχαίρω G4796

συνέχει   verb, pres. act. indic. 3 pers. sg.
{5.A.1.a} . . . . συνέχω G4912

συνέχεον   verb, impf. act. indic. 3 pers. pl.
{5.A.2} . . . . συγχέω G4797

συνέχομαι   verb, pres. pass. indic. 1 pers. sg.
{5.A.1.d} . . . . συνέχω G4912

συνεχομένη   vbl., pres. pass. ptc. nom. sg. fem.
{6.A.1} . . . . id.

συνεχόμενον   vbl., pres. pass. ptc. acc. sg.
masc. {6.A.1} . . . . id.

συνεχομένους   vbl., pres. pass. ptc. acc. pl.
masc. {6.A.1} . . . . id.

συνέχοντες   vbl., pres. act. ptc. nom. pl. masc.
{6.A.1} . . . . id.

συνέχουσι   verb, pres. act. indic. 3 pers. pl.
{5.A.1.a} . . . . id.

συνέχουσιν   verb, pres. act. indic. 3 pers. pl.
{5.A.1.a} . . . . id.

συνεχύθη   verb, aor. pass. indic. 3 pers. sg.
{5.A.1} . . . . συγχέω G4797

συνέχυνε   verb, impf. act. indic. 3 pers. sg.
{5.A.2} . . . . id.

συνέχυνεν   verb, impf. act. indic. 3 pers. sg.
{5.A.2} . . . . id.

συνέχυννεν   verb, impf. act. indic. 3 pers. sg.
{5.A.2} . . . . id.

G4912 **συνέχω**   (1) *I hold together,* hence, *I restrain; I
close,* Acts 7:57; *I press from every side,* Luke
8:45; 19:43; (2) *I hold seized, I have in charge,*
Luke 22:63, so pass. met. *I am pressed,* Acts
18:5; esp. in pass. with datives, *I am seized
(by), I am afflicted (by), I am suffering (from),*
e.g., Matt 4:24; Luke 8:37; *I urge, impel, compel,* Luke 12:50; 2 Cor 5:14; Phil 1:23.

συνεψήφισαν   verb, aor. act. indic. 3 pers. pl.
{5.A.1.b} . . . . σνμψηφίζω G4860

συνζῆν   vbl., pres. act. inf. {6.B.2} . . . . συζάω G4800

συνζήσομεν   verb, fut. act. indic. 1 pers. pl.
{5.A.1} . . . . id.

συνζητεῖν   vbl., pres. act. inf. {6.B.2} . . . . συζητέω G4802

συνζητεῖτε   verb, pres. act. indic. 2 pers. pl.
{5.A.2} . . . . id.

συνζητητής   noun, nom. sg. masc.
{2.A} . . . . συζητητής G4804

συνζητοῦντας   vbl., pres. act. ptc. acc. pl. masc.
{6.A.2} . . . . συζητέω G4802

συνζητοῦντες vbl., pres. act. ptc. nom. pl.
masc. {6.A.2} . . . . id.
συνζητούντων vbl., pres. act. ptc. gen. pl.
masc. {6.A.2} . . . . id.
σύνζυγε adj., voc. sg. masc. {3.C} . . . . . . σύζυγος G4805
συνήγαγεν verb, ²aor. act. indic. 3 pers. sg.
{5.A.1.b} . . . . .συνάγω G4863
συνηγάγετε verb, ²aor. act. indic. 2 pers. pl.
{5.A.1.b} . . . . id.
συνηγάγομεν verb, ²aor. act. indic. 1 pers. pl.
{5.A.1.b} . . . . id.
συνήγαγον verb, ²aor. act. indic. 3 pers. pl.
{5.A.1.b} . . . . id.
συνήγειρε verb, aor. act. indic. 3 pers. sg.
{5.A.1.b} . . . . .συνεγείρω G4891
συνήγειρεν verb, aor. act. indic. 3 pers. sg.
{5.A.1.b} . . . . id.
συνηγέρθητε verb, aor. pass. indic. 2 pers. pl.
{5.A.1.b} . . . . id.
συνηγμένα vbl., perf. pass. ptc. acc. pl. neut.
{6.A.1.b} . . . . .συνάγω G4863
συνηγμένοι vbl., perf. pass. ptc. nom. pl. masc.
{6.A.1.b} . . . . id.
συνηγμένων vbl., perf. pass. ptc. gen. pl. masc.
{6.A.1.b} . . . . id.
G4913 **συνήδομαι** I delight in.
συνήδομαι verb, pres. mid./pass. indic. 1 pers. sg.
{5.A.1.d} . . . . συνήδομαι G4913
G4914 **συνήθεια**, -ας, ἡ custom, habit; with gen. ha-
bituation to, intercourse with, familiarity with,
1 Cor 8:7.
συνήθεια noun, nom. sg. fem. {2.A} . . . συνήθεια G4914
συνηθείᾳ noun, dat. sg. fem. {2.A} . . . . id.
συνήθειαν noun, acc. sg. fem. {2.A} . . . . id.
συνήθλησαν verb, aor. act. indic. 3 pers. pl.
{5.A.1} . . . . .συναθλέω G4866
συνηθροισμένοι vbl., perf. pass. ptc. nom. pl.
masc. {6.A.1.b} . . . . .συναθροίζω G4867
συνηθροισμένους vbl., perf. pass. ptc. acc. pl.
masc. {6.A.1.b} . . . . id.
συνῆκαν verb, aor. act. indic. 3 pers. pl.
{5.A.3.b} . . . . .συνίημι G4920
συνήκατε verb, aor. act. indic. 2 pers. pl.
{5.A.3.b} . . . . id.
συνηκολούθει verb, impf. act. indic. 3 pers. sg.
{5.A.2} . . . . συνακολουθέω G4870
συνήλασεν verb, aor. act. indic. 3 pers. sg.
{5.A.1.b} . . . . συνελαύνω G4900
συνῆλθαν verb, ²aor. act. indic. 3 pers. pl.
{5.A.1.b} . . . . συνέρχομαι G4905
συνῆλθε verb, ²aor. act. indic. 3 pers. sg.
{5.A.1.b} . . . . id.
συνῆλθεν verb, ²aor. act. indic. 3 pers. sg.
{5.A.1.b} . . . . id.
συνῆλθον verb, ²aor. act. indic. 3 pers. pl.
{5.A.1.b} . . . . id.
συνηλικιώτας noun, acc. pl. masc.
{2.A} . . . . συνηλικιώτης G4915
G4915 **συνηλικιώτης**, -ου, ὁ a contemporary, one of
the same age.

συνήλλασσεν verb, impf. act. indic. 3 pers. sg.
{5.A.1.b} . . . . συναλλάσσω G4900†‡
συνήντησεν verb, aor. act. indic. 3 pers. sg.
{5.A.1} . . . . συναντάω G4876
συνήργει verb, impf. act. indic. 3 pers. sg.
{5.A.2} . . . . συνεργέω G4903
συνηρπάκει verb, plu. act. indic. 3 pers. sg.
{5.A.1.b} . . . . συναρπάζω G4884
συνήρπασαν verb, aor. act. indic. 3 pers. pl.
{5.A.1.b} . . . . id.
συνήρχετο verb, impf. mid./pass. indic. 3 pers. sg.
{5.A.1.e} . . . . συνέρχομαι G4905
συνήρχοντο verb, impf. mid./pass. indic.
3 pers. pl. {5.A.1.e} . . . . id.
συνῆσαν verb, impf. act. indic. 3 pers. pl.
{7.A} . . . . σύνειμι¹ G4895
συνήσθιεν verb, impf. act. indic. 3 pers. sg.
{5.A.1.b} . . . . συνεσθίω G4906
συνήσουσι verb, fut. act. indic. 3 pers. pl.
{5.A.1} . . . . .συνίημι G4920
συνήσουσιν verb, fut. act. indic. 3 pers. pl.
{5.A.1} . . . . id.
συνῆτε verb, ²aor. act. subjunc. 2 pers. pl.
{5.B.3} . . . . id.
συνήχθη verb, aor. pass. indic. 3 pers. sg.
{5.A.1.b} . . . . .συνάγω G4863
συνήχθησαν verb, aor. pass. indic. 3 pers. pl.
{5.A.1.b} . . . . id.
G4916 **συνθάπτω** I bury along with.
συνθλασθήσεται verb, fut. pass. indic. 3 pers. sg.
{5.A.1} . . . . .συνθλάω G4917
G4917 **συνθλάω** I break in pieces, break completely.
συνθλίβοντα vbl., pres. act. ptc. acc. sg. masc.
{6.A.1} . . . . .συνθλίβω G4918
G4918 **συνθλίβω** I press closely upon, hustle.
συνθρύπτοντες vbl., pres. act. ptc. nom. pl. masc.
{6.A.1} . . . . .συνθρύπτω G4919
G4919 **συνθρύπτω** (lit. I crush to pieces), I weaken
thoroughly, unman.
συνιᾶσιν verb, pres. act. indic. 3 pers. pl.
{5.A.3.a} . . . . .συνίημι G4920
συνιδόντες vbl., ²aor. act. ptc. nom. pl. masc.
{6.A.1.a} . . . . συνείδω G4894
συνιδών vbl., ²aor. act. ptc. nom. sg. masc.
{6.A.1.a} . . . . id.
συνιείς vbl., pres. act. ptc. nom. sg. masc.
{6.A.3} . . . . .συνίημι G4920
συνιέναι vbl., pres. act. inf. {6.B.3} . . . . id.
συνιέντες vbl., pres. act. ptc. nom. pl. masc.
{6.A.3} . . . . id.
συνιέντος vbl., pres. act. ptc. gen. sg. masc.
{6.A.3} . . . . id.
συνίετε verb, pres. act. impv. 2 pers. pl. {5.D.3} . id.
συνίετε verb, pres. act. indic. 2 pers. pl.
{5.A.3.a} . . . . id.
G4920 **συνίημι** I understand; I have understanding.
συνιόντος vbl., pres. act. ptc. gen. sg. masc.
{7.C.1} . . . . σύνειμι² G4896
συνίουσι verb, pres. act. indic. 3 pers. pl.
{5.A.3.a} . . . . .συνίημι G4920

συνιοῦσιν   verb, pres. act. indic. 3 pers. pl.
  {5.A.2}. . . . . id.
συνίουσιν   verb, pres. act. indic. 3 pers. pl.
  {5.A.3.a}. . . . . id.
συνιστάνειν   vbl., pres. act. inf. {6.B.3} .συνίστημι *G4921*
συνιστάνομεν   verb, pres. act. indic. 1 pers. pl.
  {5.A.3.a} . . . . id.
συνιστάνοντες   vbl., pres. act. ptc. nom. pl.
  masc. {6.A.3}. . . . . id.
συνιστανόντων   vbl., pres. act. ptc. gen. pl.
  masc. {6.A.3}. . . . . id.
συνιστάντες   vbl., pres. act. ptc. nom. pl. masc.
  {6.A.3}. . . . . id.
συνιστάνω   verb, pres. act. indic. 1 pers. sg.
  {5.A.3.a} . . . . id.
συνιστάνων   vbl., pres. act. ptc. nom. sg. masc.
  {6.A.3}. . . . . id.
συνίστασθαι   vbl., pres. pass. inf. {6.B.3} . . . . id.
G4921 **συνίστημι** (συνιστάνω)   (1) trans., (a) *I
  recommend, commend, introduce*, Rom 16:1;
  2 Cor 3:1; 4:2; 5:12; 6:4; 10:12, 18; 12:11; (b) *I
  demonstrate, show, prove*, Rom 3:5; 5:8; 2 Cor
  7:11; Gal 2:18; (2) intrans. (pres. mid. and
  perf. act.), (a) *I stand with (by)*, Luke 9:32; (b)
  I consist, I am held together, Col 1:17; 2 Pet 3:5.
συνίστημι   verb, pres. act. indic. 1 pers. sg.
  {5.A.3.a} .συνίστημι *G4921*
συνίστησι   verb, pres. act. indic. 3 pers. sg.
  {5.A.3.a} . . . . id.
συνίστησιν   verb, pres. act. indic. 3 pers. sg.
  {5.A.3.a} . . . . id.
συνιστῶν   vbl., pres. act. ptc. nom. sg. masc.
  {6.A.3}. . . . . id.
συνιστῶντες   vbl., pres. act. ptc. nom. pl. masc.
  {6.A.3}. . . . . id.
συνιών   vbl., pres. act. ptc. nom. sg. masc.
  {6.A.3}. . . . . .συνίημι *G4920*
συνιῶν   vbl., pres. act. ptc. nom. sg. masc.
  {6.A.3}. . . . . id.
συνίων   vbl., pres. act. ptc. nom. sg. masc.
  {6.A.3}. . . . . id.
συνιῶσι   verb, pres. act. subjunc. 3 pers. pl.
  {5.B.3}. . . . . id.
συνιῶσιν   verb, pres. act. subjunc. 3 pers. pl.
  {5.B.3}. . . . . id.
συνίωσιν   verb, pres. act. subjunc. 3 pers. pl.
  {5.B.3}. . . . . id.
συνκαθήμενοι   vbl., pres. mid./pass. ptc. nom. pl.
  masc. {6.A.3}. . . . . συγκάθημαι *G4775*
συνκαθήμενος   vbl., pres. mid./pass. ptc. nom.
  sg. masc. {6.A.3} . . . . id.
συνκαθισάντων   vbl., aor. act. ptc. gen. pl. masc.
  {6.A.1.a} . . . . συγκαθίζω *G4776*
συνκακοπάθησον   verb, aor. act. impv. 2 pers. sg.
  {5.D.1}. . . . . συγκακοπαθέω *G4777*
συνκακουχεῖσθαι   vbl., pres. mid./pass. inf.
  {6.B.2} . . . . συγκακουχέομαι *G4778*
συνκαλεῖ   verb, pres. act. indic. 3 pers. sg.
  {5.A.2}. . . . . .συγκαλέω *G4779*

συνκαλεσάμενος   vbl., aor. mid. ptc. nom. sg.
  masc. {6.A.2}. . . . . id.
συνκαλέσασθαι   vbl., aor. mid. inf. {6.B.1}. . . . id.
συνκαλοῦσιν   verb, pres. act. indic. 3 pers. pl.
  {5.A.2}. . . . . id.
σύνκαμψον   verb, aor. act. impv. 2 pers. sg.
  {5.D.1}. .συγκάμπτω *G4781*
συνκαταβάντες   vbl., ²aor. act. ptc. nom. pl. masc.
  {6.A.1.a} . . . . .συγκαταβαίνω *G4782*
συνκατάθεσις   noun, nom. sg. fem.
  {2.C} . . . . συγκατάθεσις *G4783*
συνκατατεθειμένος   vbl., perf. mid./pass. ptc.
  nom. sg. masc. {6.A.3}. . . . . . . συγκατατίθημι *G4784*
συνκατεψηφίσθη   verb, aor. pass. indic. 3 pers. sg.
  {5.A.1.b}. . . . . .συγκαταψηφίζομαι *G4785*
συνκεκερασμένους   vbl., perf. pass. ptc. acc. pl.
  masc. {6.A.3}. . . . . .συγκεράννυμι *G4786*
συνκεχυμένη   vbl., perf. pass. ptc. nom. sg. fem.
  {6.A.2}. .συγχέω *G4797*
συνκλειόμενοι   vbl., pres. pass. ptc. nom. pl. masc.
  {6.A.1}. . . . . .συγκλείω *G4788*
συνκληρονόμα   adj., acc. pl. neut.
  {3.C} . . . . .συγκληρονόμος *G4789*
συνκληρονόμοι   adj., nom. pl. masc. {3.C} . . . . id.
συνκληρονόμων   adj., gen. pl. masc. {3.C} . . . . id.
συνκοινωνεῖτε   verb, pres. act. impv. 2 pers. pl.
  {5.D.2}. . . . . .συγκοινωνέω *G4790*
συνκοινωνήσαντες   vbl., aor. act. ptc. nom.
  pl. masc. {6.A.2} . . . . id.
συνκοινωνήσητε   verb, aor. act. subjunc.
  2 pers. pl. {5.B.1} . . . . id.
συνκοινωνός   noun, nom. sg. masc.
  {2.B} . . . . συγκοινωνός *G4791*
συνκοινωνούς   noun, acc. pl. masc. {2.B} . . . . id.
συνκρῖναι   vbl., aor. act. inf. {6.B.1}. . . συγκρίνω *G4793*
συνκρίνοντες   vbl., pres. act. ptc. nom. pl.
  masc. {6.A.1}. . . . . id.
συνκύπτουσα   vbl., pres. act. ptc. nom. sg. fem.
  {6.A.1}. .συγκύπτω *G4794*
συνλαλήσας   vbl., aor. act. ptc. nom. sg. masc.
  {6.A.2}. .συλλαλέω *G4814*
συνλαλοῦντες   vbl., pres. act. ptc. nom. pl.
  masc. {6.A.2}. . . . . id.
συνλαμβάνου   verb, pres. mid. impv. 2 pers. sg.
  {5.D.1}. . . . . .συλλαμβάνω *G4815*
συνλυπούμενος   vbl., pres. mid./pass. ptc. nom.
  sg. masc. {6.A.2} . . . . .συλλυπέω *G4818*
συνμαθηταῖς   noun, dat. pl. masc.
  {2.A} .συμμαθητής *G4827*
συνμαρτυρεῖ   verb, pres. act. indic. 3 pers. sg.
  {5.A.2}. . . . . .συμμαρτυρέω *G4828*
συνμαρτυρούσης   vbl., pres. act. ptc. gen. sg.
  fem. {6.A.2}. . . . . id.
συνμερίζονται   verb, pres. mid./pass. indic.
  3 pers. pl. {5.A.1.d} . . . . .συμμερίζω *G4829*
συνμέτοχα   adj., acc. pl. neut. {3.C} . . συμμέτοχος *G4830*
συνμέτοχοι   adj., nom. pl. masc. {3.C}. . . . . . id.
συνμιμηταί   noun, nom. pl. masc.
  {2.A} .συμμιμητής *G4831*

συνοδεύοντες   vbl., pres. act. ptc. nom. pl. masc.
   {6.A.1}. .συνοδεύω G4922
G4922 **συνοδεύω**   *I journey (travel) along with.*
G4923 **συνοδία**, -ας, ἡ   *a traveling company, caravan.*
   συνοδίᾳ   noun, dat. sg. fem. {2.A}. . . . . . συνοδία G4923
   σύνοιδα   verb, ²perf. act. indic. 1 pers. sg.
   {5.A.1.c}. . . . . συνείδω G4894
G4924 **συνοικέω**   *I cohabit with, live in wedlock with.*
   συνοικοδομεῖσθε   verb, pres. pass. indic. 2 pers.
   pl. {5.A.2}. . . . . συνοικοδομέω G4925
G4925 **συνοικοδομέω**   met. *I build together.*
   συνοικοῦντες   vbl., pres. act. ptc. nom. pl. masc.
   {6.A.2}. . . . . συνοικέω G4924
G4926 **συνομιλέω**   *I talk with.*
   συνομιλῶν   vbl., pres. act. ptc. nom. sg. masc.
   {6.A.2}. . . . . .συνομιλέω G4926
G4927 **συνομορέω**   *I am contiguous with, I am next door to.*
   συνομοροῦσα   vbl., pres. act. ptc. nom. sg. fem.
   {6.A.2}. . . . . .συνομορέω G4927
   συνόντων   vbl., pres. act. ptc. gen. pl. masc.
   {7.C.1}. σύνειμι¹ G4895
G4928 **συνοχή**, -ῆς, ἡ   (lit. *compression;* then *narrow- ness*), met. *anxiety.*
   συνοχή   noun, nom. sg. fem. {2.A}. . . . . .συνοχή G4928
   συνοχῆς   noun, gen. sg. fem. {2.A}. . . . . id.
   συνπαθῆσαι   vbl., aor. act. inf. {6.B.1}. συμπαθέω G4834
   συνπαραγενόμενοι   vbl., ²aor. mid. ptc. nom. pl.
   masc. {6.A.1.b}. . . . . .συμπαραγίνομαι G4836
   συνπαρακληθῆναι   vbl., aor. pass. inf.
   {6.B.1}. . . . . .συμπαρακαλέω G4837
   συνπαραλαβεῖν   vbl., ²aor. act. inf.
   {6.B.1}. . . . . .συμπαραλαμβάνω G4838
   συνπαραλαβόντες   vbl., ²aor. act. ptc. nom. pl.
   masc. {6.A.1.a}. . . . . id.
   συνπαραλαβών   vbl., ²aor. act. ptc. nom. sg.
   masc. {6.A.1.a}. . . . . id.
   συνπαραλαμβάνειν   vbl., pres. act. inf. {6.B.1}. id.
   συνπαρόντες   vbl., pres. act. ptc. nom. pl. masc.
   {7.C.1}. . . . . συμπάρειμι G4840
   συνπάσχει   verb, pres. act. indic. 3 pers. sg.
   {5.A.1.a}. . . . . συμπάσχω G4841
   συνπάσχομεν   verb, pres. act. indic. 1 pers. pl.
   {5.A.1.a}. . . . . id.
   συνπεριλαβών   vbl., ²aor. act. ptc. nom. sg. masc.
   {6.A.1.a}. . . . . .συμπεριλαμβάνω G4843
   συνπληροῦσθαι   vbl., pres. pass. inf.
   {6.B.2}. . . . . .συμπληρόω G4845
   συνπνίγει   verb, pres. act. indic. 3 pers. sg.
   {5.A.1.a}. . . . . .συμπνίγω G4846
   συνπνίγονται   verb, pres. pass. indic. 3 pers.
   pl. {5.A.1.d}. . . . . id.
   συνπνίγουσιν   verb, pres. act. indic. 3 pers. pl.
   {5.A.1.a}. . . . . id.
   συνπολῖται   noun, nom. pl. masc.
   {2.A}. . . . . συμπολίτης G4847
   συνπορεύονται   verb, pres. mid./pass. indic.
   3 pers. pl. {5.A.1.d}. . . . . συμπορεύομαι G4848
   συνπρεσβύτερος   noun, nom. sg. masc.
   {2.B}. . . . . συμπρεσβύτερος G4850

συνσταυρωθέντες   vbl., aor. pass. ptc. nom. pl.
   masc. {6.A.1.a.}. . . . . συσταυρόω G4957
   συνσταυρωθέντος   vbl., aor. pass. ptc. gen. sg.
   masc. {6.A.1.a.}. . . . . id.
   συνστενάζει   verb, pres. act. indic. 3 pers. sg.
   {5.A.1.a}. . . . . .συστενάζω G4959
   συνστοιχεῖ   verb, pres. act. indic. 3 pers. sg.
   {5.A.2}. . . . . συστοιχέω G4960
   συνστρατιώτη   noun, dat. sg. masc.
   {2.A}. . . . . .συστρατιώτης G4961
   συνστρατιώτην   noun, acc. sg. masc. {2.A}. . . . id.
   συνσχηματίζεσθε   verb, pres. mid./pass. impv.
   2 pers. pl. {5.D.1}. . . . . .συσχηματίζω G4964
   συνσχηματιζόμενοι   vbl., pres. mid./pass. ptc.
   nom. pl. masc. {6.A.1}. . . . . id.
   σύνσωμα   adj., acc. pl. neut. {3.C}. . . σύσσωμος G4954
G4929 **συντάσσω**   *I direct, instruct, command.*
   συνταφέντες   vbl., ²aor. pass. ptc. nom. pl. masc.
   {6.A.1.a}. . . . . .συνθάπτω G4916
G4930 **συντέλεια**, -ας, ἡ   w. αἰῶνος, a characteristic expression of Jewish apocalyptic, *conclusion, consummation, end* of the present period of time.
   συντέλεια   noun, nom. sg. fem. {2.A}. .συντέλεια G4930
   συντελείᾳ   noun, dat. sg. fem. {2.A}. . . . . . . id.
   συντελείας   noun, gen. sg. fem. {2.A}. . . . . . . id.
   συντελεῖσθαι   vbl., pres. pass. inf.
   {6.B.2}. . . . . συντελέω G4931
   συντελέσας   vbl., aor. act. ptc. nom. sg. masc.
   {6.A.2}. . . . . id.
   συντελεσθεισῶν   vbl., aor. pass. ptc. gen. pl.
   fem. {6.A.1.a.}. id.
   συντελέσω   verb, fut. act. indic. 1 pers. sg.
   {5.A.1}. . . . . id.
G4931 **συντελέω**   *I bring to an end, complete, finish, exhaust; I accomplish, fulfill, bring to pass.*
   συντελῶν   vbl., pres. act. ptc. nom. sg. masc.
   {6.A.2}. . . . . συντελέω G4931
G4932 **συντέμνω**   *I cut down;* hence, *I contract, limit, restrict* the scope of.
   συντέμνων   vbl., pres. act. ptc. nom. sg. masc.
   {6.A.1}. . . . . .συντέμνω G4932
   συντετμημένον   vbl., perf. pass. ptc. acc. sg.
   masc. {6.A.1.b}. . . . . id.
   συντετριμμένον   vbl., perf. pass. ptc. acc. sg. masc.
   {6.A.1.b}. . . . . .συντρίβω G4937
   συντετριμμένους   vbl., perf. pass. ptc. acc. sg.
   masc. {6.A.1.b}. . . . . id.
   συντετρίφθαι   vbl., perf. pass. inf. {6.B.1}. . . . . id.
   συντετρῖφθαι   vbl., perf. pass. inf. {6.B.1}. . . . . id.
G4933 **συντηρέω**   *I keep safe.*
   συντηροῦνται   verb, pres. pass. indic. 3 pers. pl.
   {5.A.2}. . . . . συντηρέω G4933
G4934 **συντίθημι**   mid. and pass. *I make a compact (agreement) with (together), I covenant with, I agree.*
G4935 **συντόμως**   adv., *briefly.*
   συντόμως   adv. {3.F}. . . . . συντόμως G4935
   συντρεχόντων   vbl., pres. act. ptc. gen. pl. masc.
   {6.A.1}. . . . . συντρέχω G4936

G4936 **συντρέχω** *I run (rush) together,* lit. or met.
συντρίβεται verb, pres. pass. indic. 3 pers. sg.
{5.A.1.d} . . . . συντρίβω G4937
συντριβήσεται verb, ²fut. pass. indic. 3 pers.
sg. {5.A.1.d} . . . . id.
συντρῖβον vbl., pres. act. ptc. nom. sg. neut.
{6.A.1} . . . . id.

G4937 **συντρίβω** (1) *I break; I bruise;* (2) *I trample upon,*
crush, Rom 16:20; *I maul,* Luke 9:39; (3) met.
pass. *I am stunned, crushed,* Luke 4:18 (var.).

G4938 **σύντριμμα**, -ατος, τό *destruction, ruin.*
σύντριμμα noun, nom. sg. neut. {2.C} σύντριμμα G4938
συντρίψασα vbl., aor. act. ptc. nom. sg. fem.
{6.A.1.a} . . . . συντρίβω G4937
συντρίψει verb, fut. act. indic. 3 pers. sg.
{5.A.1.a} . . . . id.

G4939 **σύντροφος**, -ου, ὁ *foster brother;* such is the
lit. rendering, but it would appear to be a
court title, and might there fore be translated *a*
courtier.
σύντροφος adj., nom. sg. masc. {3.C} . σύντροφος G4939

G4940 **συντυγχάνω** *I encounter, come up with, come*
close to.
συντυχεῖν vbl., ²aor. act. inf. {6.B.1} . συντυγχάνω G4940

G4941 **Συντύχη**, -ης, ἡ *Syntyche,* a woman member
of the church at Philippi.
Συντύχην noun prop., acc. sg. fem. {2.A;
2.D} . . . . Συντύχη G4941
συνυπεκρίθησαν verb, aor. pass. indic. 3 pers. pl.
{5.A.1.b} . . . . συνυποκρίνομαι G4942

G4942 **συνυποκρίνομαι** pass. *I dissemble along with.*

G4943 **συνυπουργέω** *I cooperate in a subordinate*
capacity.
συνυπουργούντων vbl., pres. act. ptc. gen. pl.
masc. {6.A.2} . . . . συνυπουργέω G4943
σύνφημι verb, pres. act. indic. 1 pers. sg.
{5.A.3.a} . . . . σύμφημι G4852
συνφυεῖσαι vbl., ²aor. pass. ptc. nom. pl. fem.
{6.A.1.a} . . . . συμφύω G4855
συνχαίρει verb, pres. act. indic. 3 pers. sg.
{5.A.1.a} . . . . συγχαίρω G4796
συνχαίρετε verb, pres. act. impv. 2 pers. pl.
{5.D.1} . . . . id.
συνχαίρω verb, pres. act. indic. 1 pers. sg.
{5.A.1.a} . . . . id.
συνχάρητε verb, ²aor. pass. impv. 2 pers. pl.
{5.D.1} . . . . id.
συνχρῶνται verb, pres. mid./pass. indic. 3 pers.
pl. {5.A.2} . . . . συγχράομαι G4798
συνχύννεται verb, pres. pass. indic. 3 pers. sg.
{5.A.2} . . . . συγχέω G4797
σύνψυχοι adj., nom. pl. masc. {3.C} . . σύμψυχος G4861
συνωδίνει verb, pres. act. indic. 3 pers. sg.
{5.A.1.a} . . . . συνωδίνω G4944

G4944 **συνωδίνω** *I unite in suffering travail (birth*
pangs, severe pain).

G4945 **συνωμοσία**, -ας, ἡ *a conspiracy, plot.*
συνωμοσίαν noun, acc. sg. fem. {2.A} συνωμοσία G4945
συνῶσι verb, ²aor. act. subjunc. 3 pers. pl.
{5.B.3} . . . . συνίημι G4920

συνῶσιν verb, ²aor. act. subjunc. 3 pers. pl.
{5.B.3} . . . . id.

G4946 **Συράκουσαι**, -ῶν, ἡ *Syracuse,* in east Sicily
(pl. because originally, as in many similar
cases, both a citadel and a settlement in the
valley).
Συρακούσας noun prop., acc. pl. fem. {2.A;
2.D} . . . . Συράκουσαι G4946
Συραφοινίκισσα noun prop., nom. sg. fem. {2.A;
2.D} . . . . Συροφοινίκισσα G4949
σύρει verb, pres. act. indic. 3 pers. sg.
{5.A.1.a} . . . . σύρω G4951

G4947 **Συρία**, -ας, ἡ *Syria,* a great Roman imperial
province, united with Cilicia.
Συρίαν noun prop., acc. sg. fem. {2.A; 2.D} . Συρία G4947
Συρίας noun prop., gen. sg. fem. {2.A; 2.D} . . . id.
σύροντες vbl., pres. act. ptc. nom. pl. masc.
{6.A.1} . . . . σύρω G4951

G4948 **Σύρος**, -ου, ὁ *Syrian,* belonging to Syria.
Σύρος noun prop., nom. sg. masc. {2.B; 2.D} Σύρος G4948

G4949 **Συροφοινίκισσα**, -ης, ἡ *Syro-Phoenician,* i.e.,
Phoenician (of Syria, in contrast to Carthage
and its territory in N. Africa).
Συροφοινίκισσα noun prop., nom. sg. fem. {2.A;
2.D} . . . . Συροφοινίκισσα G4949
Συροφοίνισσα noun prop., nom. sg. fem.
{2.A; 2.D} . . . . id.
Σύρτην noun prop., acc. sg. fem. {2.C; 2.D} Σύρτις G4950
Σύρτιν noun prop., acc. sg. fem. {2.C; 2.D} . . . . id.

G4950 **Σύρτις**, -εως, ἡ *Syrtis,* a shifting sandbar
feared by mariners off the coast of N. Africa.

G4951 **σύρω** *I drag, pull, draw.*
σύρων vbl., pres. act. ptc. nom. sg. masc.
{6.A.1} . . . . σύρω G4951

G4952 **συσπαράσσω** *I throw violently* on the ground.

G4953 **σύσσημον**, -ου, ἡ *a signal agreed upon* between two parties.
σύσσημον noun, acc. sg. neut. {2.B} . . σύσσημον G4953
σύσσωμα adj., acc. pl. neut. {3.C} . . . . σύσσωμος G4954

G4954 **σύσσωμος**, -ον *sharing in a body;* it has been
taken as *fellow slave* (see σῶμα).

G4955 **συστασιαστής** *a fellow insurgent, a*
co-revolutionary.
συστασιαστῶν noun, gen. pl. masc.
{2.A} . . . . συστασιαστής G4955

G4956 **συστατικός**, -ή, -όν *recommending,*
introducing.
συστατικῶν adj., gen. pl. fem. {3.C} . συστατικός G4956
συστατικῶν adj., gen. pl. masc. {3.C} . . . . id.

G4957 **συσταυρόω** *I crucify along with,* lit. or met.
συσταυρωθέντες vbl., aor. pass. ptc. nom. pl.
masc. {6.A.1.a.} . . . . συσταυρόω G4957
συσταυρωθέντος vbl., aor. pass. ptc. gen. sg.
masc. {6.A.1.a.} . . . . id.

G4958 **συστέλλω** (1) *I wrap round, swathe* in a sort
of winding sheet, or possibly, *I lay out,* Acts
5:6; (2) *I con tract, compress;* hence, *I shorten,*
1 Cor 7:29.
συστενάζει verb, pres. act. indic. 3 pers. sg.
{5.A.1.a} . . . . συστενάζω G4959

G4959 **συστενάζω**   *I groan together.*
συστοιχεῖ   verb, pres. act. indic. 3 pers. sg.
   {5.A.2}. . . . . συστοιχέω G4960
G4960 **συστοιχέω**   (properly a military term, *I keep in line* or *file*), *I correspond exactly to.*
συστρατιώτῃ   noun, dat. sg. masc.
   {2.A} . . . . συστρατιώτης G4961
συστρατιώτην   noun, acc. sg. masc. {2.A} . . . . . id.
G4961 **συστρατιώτης**, -ου, ὁ   *a fellow soldier, comrade in arms.*
συστρεφομένων   vbl., pres. pass. ptc. gen. pl.
   masc. {6.A.1}. . . . . .συστρέφω G4962
G4962 **συστρέφω**   (1) trans., *I gather together, collect,* Acts 28:3; (2) mid. either, *I press together* (about one) or *I stroll.*
συστρέψαντος   vbl., aor. act. ptc. gen. sg. masc.
   {6.A.1.a} . . . . .συστρέφω G4962
G4963 **συστροφή**, -ῆς, ἡ   *a crowding together;* hence, *a seditious meeting,* Acts 19:40; *a conspiracy,* Acts 23:12.
συστροφήν   noun, acc. sg. fem. {2.A} . .συστροφή G4963
συστροφῆς   noun, gen. sg. fem. {2.A} . . . . id.
συσχηματίζεσθαι   vbl., pres. mid. inf.
   {6.B.1} .συσχηματίζω G4964
συσχηματίζεσθε   verb, pres. mid./pass. impv.
   2 pers. pl. {5.D.1}. . . . . id.
συσχηματιζόμενοι   vbl., pres. mid./pass. ptc.
   nom. pl. masc. {6.A.1} . . . . id.
G4964 **συσχηματίζω**   mid. *I fashion myself in agreement with, I conform myself outwardly to.*
G4965 **Συχάρ**, ἡ   *Sychar,* a "city" of Samaria.
Συχάρ   noun prop. .Συχάρ G4965
G4966 **Συχέμ**   *Shechem* (later *Neapolis,* from which mod. *Nablus*), a city of Samaria.
Συχέμ   noun prop. .Συχέμ G4966
G4967 **σφαγή**, -ῆς, ἡ   *slaughter, sacrifice* (of an animal); πρόβατον σφαγῆς (Hebraism), *a sheep destined for sacrifice.*
σφαγήν   noun, acc. sg. fem. {2.A}. . . . . σφαγή G4967
σφαγῆς   noun, gen. sg. fem. {2.A}. . . . . id.
σφάγια   noun, acc. pl. neut. {2.B} . . . . . . σφάγιον G4968
G4968 **σφάγιον**, -ου, τό   *a sacrifice* (of an animal).
G4969 **σφάζω**   *I slaughter; I sacrifice.*
σφάξουσιν   verb, fut. act. indic. 3 pers. pl.
   {5.A.1.a} . . . . .σφάζω G4969
σφάξωσι   verb, aor. act. subjunc. 3 pers. pl.
   {5.B.1} . . . . id.
σφάξωσιν   verb, aor. act. subjunc. 3 pers. pl.
   {5.B.1} . . . . id.
G4970 **σφόδρα**   adv., *greatly, exceedingly, very much.*
σφόδρα   adv. . . . . .σφόδρα G4970
G4971 **σφοδρῶς**   adv., *exceedingly.*
σφοδρῶς   adv. {3.F} . . . . σφοδρῶς G4971
σφραγῖδα   noun, acc. sg. fem. {2.C} . . . . . σφραγίς G4973
σφραγῖδας   noun, acc. pl. fem. {2.C} . . . . id.
σφραγίδων   noun, gen. pl. fem. {2.C} . . . . id.
G4972 **σφραγίζω**   (1) *I seal* and thus close, for guardianship or protection, Matt 27:66; Rev 20:3; (2) *I conceal,* Rev 10:4; 22:10; (3) *I mark* with the impress of the signet ring, lit. or met.; (4)

I confirm, make un doubted, John 3:33; 6:27; mid. Rom 15:28 (cf. under #1).
G4973 **σφραγίς**, ῖδος, ἡ   *a seal,* a means not merely of attestation but also of closing, so that a cabinet, document, etc., could not be opened without breaking the seals.
σφραγίς   noun, nom. sg. fem. {2.C} . . . . . σφραγίς G4973
σφραγισάμενος   vbl., aor. mid. ptc. nom. sg. masc.
   {6.A.1.b} . . . . .σφραγίζω G4972
σφραγίσαντες   vbl., aor. act. ptc. nom. pl.
   masc. {6.A.1.a}. . . . . id.
σφραγίσεται   verb, fut. mid. indic. 3 pers. sg.
   {5.A.1.d} . . . . id.
σφραγίσῃς   verb, aor. act. subjunc. 2 pers. sg.
   {5.B.1} . . . . id.
σφραγῖσιν   noun, dat. pl. fem. {2.C}. . . . . σφραγίς G4973
σφράγισον   verb, aor. act. impv. 2 pers. sg.
   {5.D.1}. . . . . .σφραγίζω G4972
σφραγίσωμεν   verb, aor. act. subjunc. 1 pers.
   pl. {5.B.1}. . . . . id.
σφυδρά   noun, nom. pl. neut. {2.B} . . . σφυδρόν G4974
G4974 **σφυδρόν** (σφυρόν), -οῦ, τό   *an ankle (bone).*
σφυρά   noun, nom. pl. neut. {2.B} . . . . . σφυδρόν G4974
σφυρίδας   noun, acc. pl. fem. {2.C} . . . . . .σπυρίς G4711
σφυρίδι   noun, dat. sg. fem. {2.C}. . . . . id.
σφυρίδων   noun, gen. pl. fem. {2.C}. . . . . id.
G4975 **σχεδόν**   adv., *almost, nearly.*
σχεδόν   adv. . . . . .σχεδόν G4975
G4976 **σχῆμα**, -ατος, τό   *the* outward (changeable) *fashion (form).*
σχῆμα   noun, nom. sg. neut. {2.C} . . . . . . .σχῆμα G4976
σχήματι   noun, dat. sg. neut. {2.C}. . . . . id.
σχῆτε   verb, ²aor. act. subjunc. 2 pers. pl. {5.B.1}ἔχω G2192
σχίζει   verb, pres. act. indic. 3 pers. sg.
   {5.A.1.a} . . . . .σχίζω G4977
σχιζομένους   vbl., pres. pass. ptc. acc. pl. masc.
   {6.A.1}. . . . . id.
G4977 **σχίζω**   *I cleave, split;* (of cloth) *I rend, tear;* of a crowd, *I divide* (sharply) *into two parties.*
σχίσας   vbl., aor. act. ptc. nom. sg. masc.
   {6.A.1.a} . . . . .σχίζω G4977
σχίσει   verb, fut. act. indic. 3 pers. sg. {5.A.1.a} . id.
G4978 **σχίσμα**, -ατος, τό   *a cleavage, cleft, split, rent;* so met., *a division* in a crowd, due to difference of opinion, *a party division.*
σχίσμα   noun, nom. sg. neut. {2.C} . . . . . σχίσμα G4978
σχίσματα   noun, acc. pl. neut. {2.C} . . . . id.
σχίσματα   noun, nom. pl. neut. {2.C} . . . . id.
σχίσωμεν   verb, aor. act. subjunc. 1 pers. pl.
   {5.B.1} . . . . .σχίζω G4977
σχοινία   noun, acc. pl. neut. {2.B} . . . . . .σχοινίον G4979
G4979 **σχοινίον**, -ου, τό   *a rope; a cable, hawser.*
σχοινίων   noun, gen. pl. neut. {2.B} . . . . .σχοινίον G4979
σχολάζητε   verb, pres. act. subjunc. 2 pers. pl.
   {5.B.1} . . . . .σχολάζω G4980
σχολάζοντα   vbl., pres. act. ptc. acc. sg. masc.
   {6.A.1}. . . . . id.
G4980 **σχολάζω**   (1) *I have leisure,* with dat. for, 1 Cor 7:5; (2) *I stand empty,* of a house, Matt 12:44; Luke 11:25 (var.).

σχολάσητε   verb, aor. act. subjunc. 2 pers. pl.
{5.B.1} . . . . σχολάζω *G4980*

G4981 **σχολή**, -ῆς, ἡ   *a school,* or *lecture hall.*
σχολῇ   noun, dat. sg. fem. {2.A} . . . . σχολή *G4981*
σχῶ   verb, ²aor. act. subjunc. 1 pers. sg. {5.B.1} . ἔχω *G2192*
σχῶμεν   verb, ²aor. act. subjunc. 1 pers. pl. {5.B.1}. id.
σχῶσιν   verb, ²aor. act. subjunc. 3 pers. pl. {5.B.1}. id.
σῷ   pron. posses, 2 pers. sg. dat. sg. masc. {4.H} σός *G4674*
σῷ   pron. posses, 2 pers. sg. dat. sg. neut. {4.H}. . id.
σῴζει   verb, pres. act. indic. 3 pers. sg.
{5.A.1.a} . . . . σῴζω *G4982*
σῴζειν   vbl., pres. act. inf. {6.B.1} . . . . id.
σῴζεσθαι   vbl., pres. pass. inf. {6.B.1} . . . . id.
σῴζεσθε   verb, pres. pass. indic. 2 pers. pl.
{5.A.1.d} . . . . id.
σῴζεται   verb, pres. pass. indic. 3 pers. sg.
{5.A.1.d} . . . . id.
σῴζετε   verb, pres. act. impv. 2 pers. pl. {5.D.1} . id.
σῳζόμενοι   vbl., pres. pass. ptc. nom. pl. masc.
{6.A.1} . . . . id.
σῳζομένοις   vbl., pres. pass. ptc. dat. pl. masc.
{6.A.1} . . . . id.
σῳζομένους   vbl., pres. pass. ptc. acc. pl. masc.
{6.A.1} . . . . id.
σῳζομένων   vbl., pres. pass. ptc. gen. pl. masc.
{6.A.1} . . . . id.

G4982 **σῴζω**   (1) *I save, rescue* a life from death, e.g.,
Matt 8:25, a person from grave illness (and
thus restore to health), e.g., Matt 9:21; (2)
thus specially, of God and His Messiah, *I save,
rescue, preserve,* from spiritual death (cf. Heb
5:7) or spiritual disease, i.e., from sin and its
effects; the process is regarded as complete
on God's part by the sacrifice of Jesus (e.g.,
Eph 2:5), but as progressive in our experience (1 Cor 1:18) or only to be realized in
the future after acknowledgement of sin and
expressed trust in Jesus.
σωθῇ   verb, aor. pass. subjunc. 3 pers. sg.
{5.B.1} . . . . σῴζω *G4982*
σωθῆναι   vbl., aor. pass. inf. {6.B.1} . . . . id.
σωθήσεται   verb, fut. pass. indic. 3 pers. sg.
{5.A.1.d} . . . . id.
σωθήσῃ   verb, fut. pass. indic. 2 pers. sg.
{5.A.1.d} . . . . id.
σωθήσομαι   verb, fut. pass. indic. 1 pers. sg.
{5.A.1.d} . . . . id.
σωθησόμεθα   verb, fut. pass. indic. 1 pers. pl.
{5.A.1.d} . . . . id.
σώθητε   verb, aor. pass. impv. 2 pers. pl. {5.D.1}. id.
σωθῆτε   verb, aor. pass. subjunc. 2 pers. pl.
{5.B.1} . . . . id.
σωθῶ   verb, aor. pass. subjunc. 1 pers. sg. {5.B.1} id.
σωθῶσι   verb, aor. pass. subjunc. 3 pers. pl.
{5.B.1} . . . . id.
σωθῶσιν   verb, aor. pass. subjunc. 3 pers. pl.
{5.B.1} . . . . id.

G4983 **σῶμα**, -ατος, τό   (1) *the* human *body,* alive or
dead (e.g., Matt 27:58); *the physical nature,*
and thus in Gk. thought distinguished from

πνεῦμα (e.g., 1 Cor 5:3) or ψυχή (e.g., 1 Thess
5:23); Hebraistic genitives (= adjs.) ἁμαρτίας,
σαρκός, sometimes follow; (2) figuratively,
the Church is *the Body* of the Messiah who is
the Head (e.g., Eph 1:23); (3) *a slave,* as a mere
body and nothing more, Rev 18:13.
σῶμα   noun, acc. sg. neut. {2.C} . . . . σῶμα *G4983*
σῶμα   noun, nom. sg. neut. {2.C} . . . . id.
σώματα   noun, acc. pl. neut. {2.C} . . . . id.
σώματα   noun, nom. pl. neut. {2.C} . . . . id.
σώματι   noun, dat. sg. neut. {2.C} . . . . id.
σωματικὴ   adj., nom. sg. fem. {3.A} . . σωματικός *G4984*

G4984 **σωματικός**, -ή, -όν   (1) *bodily,* hence, almost =
visible, tangible, Luke 3:22; (2) *bodily, physical,*
contrasted with "mental," "spiritual," 1 Tim
4:8.
σωματικῷ   adj., dat. sg. neut. {3.A} . . . σωματικός *G4984*

G4985 **σωματικῶς**   adv., *bodily, in a bodily way,*
almost = visibly.
σωματικῶς   adv. {3.F} . . . . σωματικῶς *G4985*
σώματος   noun, gen. sg. neut. {2.C} . . . . σῶμα *G4983*
σωμάτων   noun, gen. pl. neut. {2.C} . . . . id.

G4986 **Σώπατρος**, -ου, ὁ   *Sopater,* son of Pyrrhus, and
a Christian of Berea in Macedonia (a pet form
of Σωσίπατρος).
Σώπατρος   noun prop., nom. sg. masc. {2.B;
2.D} . . . . Σώπατρος *G4986*
σωρεύσεις   verb, fut. act. indic. 2 pers. sg.
{5.A.1.a} . . . . σωρεύω *G4987*

G4987 **σωρεύω**   *I heap;* with acc. and dat., *I overwhelm*
someone with something, 2 Tim 3:6.
σῶσαι   vbl., aor. act. inf. {6.B.1} . . . . σῴζω *G4982*
σώσαντος   vbl., aor. act. ptc. gen. sg. masc.
{6.A.1.a} . . . . id.
σώσας   vbl., aor. act. ptc. nom. sg. masc.
{6.A.1.a} . . . . id.
σωσάτω   verb, aor. act. impv. 3 pers. sg. {5.D.1} . id.
σώσει   verb, fut. act. indic. 3 pers. sg. {5.A.1.a} . id.
σώσεις   verb, fut. act. indic. 2 pers. sg. {5.A.1.a} . id.
Σωσθένην   noun prop., acc. sg. masc. {2.A;
2.D} . . . . Σωσθένης *G4988*

G4988 **Σωσθένης**, -ους, ὁ   *Sosthenes,* the ruler of the
synagogue at Corinth (Acts 18:17), probably
to be identified with the Christian of 1 Cor
1:1.
Σωσθένης   noun prop., nom. sg. masc. {2.A;
2.D} . . . . Σωσθένης *G4988*

G4989 **Σωσίπατρος**, -ου, ὁ   *Sosipater,* a Christian at
Rome.
Σωσίπατρος   noun prop., nom. sg. masc. {2.B;
2.D} . . . . Σωσίπατρος *G4989*
σῶσον   verb, aor. act. impv. 2 pers. sg. {5.D.1} σῴζω *G4982*
σώσω   verb, aor. act. subjunc. 1 pers. sg. {5.B.1} . id.
σώσω   verb, fut. act. indic. 1 pers. sg. {5.B.1} . . . id.
σώσων   vbl., fut. act. ptc. nom. sg. masc.
{6.A.1.a} . . . . id.

G4990 **σωτήρ**, -ῆρος, ὁ   *savior, rescuer, preserver,* a
term applied to (the) God and to the Mes-
siah with respect to the human race and sin
and its consequences (a word familiar to the

Graeco-Roman world as a constant epithet of kings like the Ptolemies and of the Roman emperors, esp. in the phrase ὁ σωτὴρ τοῦ κόσμου, connoting probably *preserver* from the enemies of the nation or the empire, and thus *a maintainer* of life and prosperity; cf. John 4:42; 1 John 4:14).

σωτήρ   noun, nom. sg. masc. {2.C} . . . . . . σωτήρ *G4990*
σωτῆρα   noun, acc. sg. masc. {2.C} . . . . id.
σωτῆρι   noun, dat. sg. masc. {2.C} . . . . id.

G4991 **σωτηρία**, -ας, ἡ   *the salvation* to be wrought by the Messiah for the Jews, the release from the foreign yoke in particular and the recovery of independence (cf. John 4:22); in purely Christian terminology, far fuller in content, including complete *recovery of health* from the disease of sin, *release* from captivity to it (in extrabiblical language it has a reference generally to *bodily health, welfare*; cf. Acts 27:34; Heb 11:7; esp. as recovered after illness, but also to *deliverance* from every calamity, *victory* over enemies).

σωτηρία   noun, nom. sg. fem. {2.A}. . . . σωτηρία *G4991*
σωτηρίαν   noun, acc. sg. fem. {2.A}. . . . . id.
σωτηρίας   noun, gen. sg. fem. {2.A}. . . . . id.
σωτήρια   adj., acc. sg. neut. {3.C}. . . . σωτήριος *G4992*
σωτήριον   adj., nom. sg. neut. {3.C}. . . . . id.

G4992 **σωτήριος**, -ον   *bringing salvation, fraught with salvation;* neut. subs. σωτήριον, *the Messianic salvation* in the wide sense (properly that which produces σωτηρία, a sacrifice or gift dedicated to bring salvation, or to give thanks for salvation; cf. σωτηρία).

σωτήριος   adj., nom. sg. fem. {3.C} . . . . σωτήριος *G4992*
σωτηρίου   adj., gen. sg. neut. {3.C} . . . . id.
σωτῆρος   noun, gen. sg. masc. {2.C} . . . . . σωτήρ *G4990*
σώφρονα   adj., acc. sg. masc. {3.E} . . . . . σώφρων *G4998*
σώφρονας   adj., acc. pl. fem. {3.E} . . . . id.
σώφρονας   adj., acc. pl. masc. {3.E} . . . . id.
σωφρονεῖν   vbl., pres. act. inf. {6.B.2} . σωφρονέω *G4993*

G4993 **σωφρονέω**   (1) *I am in my senses,* Mark 5:15 (Luke 8:35); (2) *I am sober-minded, I am orderly* and *restrained* in all the relations of life.

σωφρονήσατε   verb, aor. act. impv. 2 pers. pl. {5.D.1}. σωφρονέω *G4993*

G4994 **σωφρονίζω**   (lit. *I make* σώφρων), hence, *I admonish, warn.*

σωφρονίζωσι   verb, pres. act. subjunc. 3 pers. pl. {5.B.1}. . . . . σωφρονίζω *G4994*
σωφρονίζωσιν   verb, pres. act. subjunc. 3 pers. pl. {5.B.1}. . . . . id.

G4995 **σωφρονισμός**, -οῦ, ὁ   *self-discipline.*

σωφρονισμοῦ   noun, gen. sg. masc. {2.B} . . . . σωφρονισμός *G4995*
σωφρονοῦμεν   verb, pres. act. indic. 1 pers. pl. {5.A.2}. . . . . σωφρονέω *G4993*
σωφρονοῦντα   vbl., pres. act. ptc. acc. sg. masc. {6.A.2}. . . . . id.

G4996 **σωφρόνως**   adv., *sober-mindedly.*

σωφρόνως   adv. {3.F} . . . . σωφρόνως *G4996*

G4997 **σωφροσύνη**, -ης, ἡ   *sound sense, sober-mindedness.*

σωφροσύνης   noun, gen. sg. fem. {2.A} . . . . σωφροσύνη *G4997*

G4998 **σώφρων**, -ον   *sober-minded, prudent* (from σῶς, *safe, sound,* and φρήν, *the mind*).

Τ τ

τά   art., acc. pl. neut. {1} . . . . ὁ *G3588*
τά   art., nom. pl. neut. {1} . . . . id.
Ταβειθά   noun prop. . . . . Ταβιθά *G5000*

G4999 **Ταβέρναι**, -ῶν, -αί   *inns, taverns;* Τρεῖς Ταβέρναι, *Three Taverns,* the name of a village or town on the Appian Way, about thirty-three miles from Rome (Lat. *Tres Tabernae*).

Ταβερνῶν   noun prop., gen. pl. fem. {2.A; 2.D}. . . . . Ταβέρναι *G4999*
Ταβηθά   noun prop. . . . . Ταβιθά *G5000*

G5000 **Ταβιθά**, ἡ   *Tabitha,* a Christian woman at Joppa.

Ταβιθά   noun prop. . . . . Ταβιθά *G5000*

G5001 **τάγμα**, -ατος, τό   *rank; division* (a military term).

τάγματι   noun, dat. sg. neut. {2.C} . . . . τάγμα *G5001*
τάδε   pron. dem., acc. pl. neut. {4.B}. . . . . ὅδε *G3592*
ταῖς   art., dat. pl. fem. {1} . . . . ὁ *G3588*
τακτῇ   adj., dat. sg. fem. {3.A}. . . . . τακτός *G5002*

G5002 **τακτός**, -ή, -όν   *appointed, arranged.*

G5003 **ταλαιπωρέω**   *I am wretched (afflicted, in distress).*

ταλαιπωρήσατε   verb, aor. act. impv. 2 pers. pl. {5.D.1}. . . . . ταλαιπωρέω *G5003*

G5004 **ταλαιπωρία**, -ας, ἡ   *wretchedness, distress, misery.*

ταλαιπωρία   noun, nom. sg. fem. {2.A}. ταλαιπωρία *G5004*
ταλαιπωρίαις   noun, dat. pl. fem. {2.A} . . . . . . id.

G5005 **ταλαίπωρος**, -ον   *wretched, miserable.*

ταλαίπωρος   adj., nom. sg. masc. {3.C} . . . . ταλαίπωρος *G5005*
τάλαντα   noun, acc. pl. neut. {2.B}. . . . τάλαντον *G5007*
ταλαντιαία   adj., nom. sg. fem. {3.A} ταλαντιαῖος *G5006*

G5006 **ταλαντιαῖος**, -α, -ον   *a talent in weight* or size. (But ἀγῶνες ταλαντιαῖοι are games where the value of the prizes amounted to a talent.).

G5007 **τάλαντον**, -ου, τό   *a talent,* i.e., a talent weight (see ταλαντιαῖος) of silver, both the weight and the value being different in different coun-

tries and at different times. A common value
was 6000 *denarii.*

τάλαντον   noun, acc. sg. neut. {2.B}. . . . τάλαντον *G5007*
ταλάντων   noun, gen. pl. neut. {2.B} . . . . id.
ταλειθά   Aram. . . . . ταλιθά *G5008*
ταλιθα   Aram. . . . . id.

G5008 **ταλιθά**   *maiden* (Aram.).

ταλιθά   Aram. . . . . ταλιθά *G5008*
ταμείοις   noun, dat. pl. neut. {2.B} . . . . . .ταμεῖον *G5009*

G5009 **ταμεῖον**, -ου, τό   *an office, a private room;*
also *a store,* Luke 12:24 (being derived from
ταμίας, "a steward"); syncopated from ταμιεῖον, and first appearing in syncopated form
in first cent. after Christ.

ταμεῖον   noun, acc. sg. neut. {2.B} . . . . .ταμεῖον *G5009*
ταμεῖον   noun, nom. sg. neut. {2.B} . . . . id.
ταμιεῖον   noun, acc. sg. neut. {2.B} . . . . id.
τανῦν   adv. comp.. . . . . νῦν *G3568*

G3569‡ **τανῦν**   = τὰ νῦν (from neut. pl. of ὁ and νῦν),
lit. *the things now,* i.e., (adv.) *for the present.*

ταξάμενοι   vbl., aor. mid. ptc. nom. pl. masc.
{6.A.1.b} . . . . .τάσσω *G5021*
τάξει   noun, dat. sg. fem. {2.C}. . . . . .τάξις *G5010*
τάξιν   noun, acc. sg. fem. {2.C}. . . . . id.

G5010 **τάξις**, -εως, ἡ   (1) *appointed order,* Luke 1:8;
regulation, rule, per haps *office,* Heb 5:6, etc.;
(2) *right order,* 1 Cor 14:40, *orderly attitude,*
Col 2:5.

ταπεινοῖς   adj., dat. pl. masc. {3.A} . . . .ταπεινός *G5011*
ταπεινοῖς   adj., dat. pl. neut. {3.A} . . . . id.

G5011 **ταπεινός**, -ή, -όν   *of low estate, poor* (and thus
despised by the mass of mankind); also *poor
in spirit, meek,* a notion often combined by the
Jews with the previous.

ταπεινός   adj., nom. sg. masc. {3.A} . . . . .ταπεινός *G5011*
ταπεινούς   adj., acc. pl. masc. {3.A} . . . . id.
ταπεινοῦσθαι   vbl., pres. pass. inf.
{6.B.2} . . . . .ταπεινόω *G5013*
ταπεινόφρονες   adj., nom. pl. masc.
{3.E} .ταπεινόφρων *G5391†‡*

G5012 **ταπεινοφροσύνη**, -ης, ἡ   *meekness; lowliness,
humility.*

ταπεινοφροσύνη   noun, dat. sg. fem.
{2.A} . . . . .ταπεινοφροσύνη *G5012*
ταπεινοφροσύνην   noun, acc. sg. fem. {2.A}. . . id.
ταπεινοφροσύνης   noun, gen. sg. fem. {2.A} . . id.

G5391†‡ **ταπεινόφρων**, -ον, gen. ονος   *meek minded;
humble minded.* Var. for φιλόφρων, 1 Pet 3:8.

G5013 **ταπεινόω**   lit. *I make low, I lower,* Luke 3:5;
generally met. *I humble.*

ταπεινωθήσεται   verb, fut. pass. indic. 3 pers. sg.
{5.A.1} . . . . .ταπεινόω *G5013*
ταπεινώθητε   verb, aor. pass. impv. 2 pers. pl.
{5.D.1} . . . . id.
ταπεινῶν   vbl., pres. act. ptc. nom. sg. masc.
{6.A.2} . . . . id.
ταπεινώσει   noun, dat. sg. fem. {2.C}. .ταπείνωσις *G5014*
ταπεινώσει   verb, fut. act. indic. 3 pers. sg.
{5.A.1} . . . . .ταπεινόω *G5013*

ταπεινώσεως   noun, gen. sg. fem.
{2.C} . . . . .ταπείνωσις *G5014*
ταπεινώση   verb, aor. act. subjunc. 3 pers. sg.
{5.B.1} . . . . .ταπεινόω *G5013*
ταπείνωσιν   noun, acc. sg. fem. {2.C} .ταπείνωσις *G5014*

G5014 **ταπείνωσις**, -εως, ἡ   *a being brought low,* Acts
8:33; Jas 1:10; *meekness; humility.*

ταρασσέσθω   verb, pres. pass. impv. 3 pers. sg.
{5.D.1} . . . . .ταράσσω *G5015*
ταράσσοντες   vbl., pres. act. ptc. nom. pl.
masc. {6.A.1} . . . . id.

G5015 **ταράσσω**   *I disturb, trouble.*

ταράσσων   vbl., pres. act. ptc. nom. sg. masc.
{6.A.1} . . . . .ταράσσω *G5015*
ταραχαί   noun, nom. pl. fem. {2.A} . . . . .ταραχή *G5016*

G5016 **ταραχή**, -ῆς, ἡ   *disturbing, ruffling.*

ταραχήν   noun, acc. sg. fem. {2.A}. . . . . .ταραχή *G5016*
ταραχθῇ   verb, aor. pass. subjunc. 3 pers. sg.
{5.B.1} . . . . .ταράσσω *G5015*
ταραχθῆτε   verb, aor. pass. subjunc. 2 pers. pl.
{5.B.1} . . . . id.

G5017 **τάραχος**, -ου, ὁ   *disturbance.*

τάραχος   noun, nom. sg. masc. {2.B} . . . . τάραχος *G5017*
Ταρσέα   noun prop., acc. sg. masc. {2.C;
2.D}. . . . . .Ταρσεύς *G5018*

G5018 **Ταρσεύς**, -έως, ὁ   *belonging to Tarsus, a
Tarsian.*

Ταρσεύς   noun prop., nom. sg. masc. {2.C;
2.D}. . . . . .Ταρσεύς *G5018*
Ταρσόν   noun prop., acc. sg. fem. {2.B;
2.D}. . . . . .Ταρσός *G5019*

G5019 **Ταρσός**, -οῦ, ἡ   *Tarsus,* the capital of the
Roman province Cilicia.

Ταρσῷ   noun prop., dat. sg. fem. {2.B; 2.D} Ταρσός *G5019*

G5020 **ταρταρόω**   *I send to Tartarus* (Tartarus being
in the Greek view a place of punishment
under the earth, to which, for example, the
Titans were sent).

ταρταρώσας   vbl., aor. act. ptc. nom. sg. masc.
{6.A.2} . . . . .ταρταρόω *G5020*
τάς   art., acc. pl. fem. {1} . . . . ὁ *G3588*
τασσόμενος   vbl., pres. pass. ptc. nom. sg. masc.
{6.A.1} . . . . .τάσσω *G5021*

G5021 **τάσσω**   (1) *I put in its place, assign, fix,* Matt
8:9 (var.), Luke 7:8; Acts 13:48; 22:10; Rom
13:1; 1 Cor 16:15; (2) *I order,* with acc. and inf.
Acts 15:2; mid. *I order* by virtue of my power
(authority), Matt 28:16; with pl. subj., *we fix
upon* among ourselves, Acts 28:23.

ταῦροι   noun, nom. pl. masc. {2.B} . . . . . . ταῦρος *G5022*

G5022 **ταῦρος**, -ου, ὁ   *a bull; an ox.*

ταύρους   noun, acc. pl. masc. {2.B} . . . . . . ταῦρος *G5022*
ταύρων   noun, gen. pl. masc. {2.B}. . . . . id.

G5024 **ταὐτά**   adv., *in the same way* (crasis form of τὰ
αὐτά, neut. pl. forms of ὁ and αὐτός).

ταὐτά   art + pron. pers., acc. pl. neut. {4.B} . . αὐτός *G846*
ταῦτα   pron. dem., acc. pl. neut. {4.B} . . . . οὗτος *G3778*
ταῦτα   pron. dem., nom. pl. neut. {4.B} . . . . . . id.
ταύταις   pron. dem., dat. pl. fem. {4.B} . . . . . . id.

ταύτας   pron. dem., acc. pl. fem. {4.B} . . . . .id.
ταύτῃ   pron. dem., dat. sg. fem. {4.B} . . . . id.
ταύτην   pron. dem., acc. sg. fem. {4.B} . . . . id.
ταύτης   pron. dem., gen. sg. fem. {4.B} . . . . id.
G5027 **ταφή**, -ῆς, ἡ *burial.*
ταφήν   noun, acc. sg. fem. {2.A} . . . . ταφή G5027
τάφοις   noun, dat. pl. masc. {2.B} . . . . τάφος G5028
τάφον   noun, acc. sg. masc. {2.B} . . . . id.
G5028 **τάφος**, -ου, ὁ *a tomb;* sepulchral *monument.*
τάφος   noun, nom. sg. masc. {2.B} . . . . τάφος G5028
τάφου   noun, gen. sg. masc. {2.B} . . . . id.
τάφους   noun, acc. pl. masc. {2.B} . . . . id.
G5029 **τάχα** adv., *perhaps.*
τάχα   adv. {3.F} . . . . τάχα G5029
τάχει   noun, dat. sg. neut. {2.C} . . . . τάχος G5034
τάχειον   adv. comp. {3.F; 3.G} . . . . .τάχιον G5032
G5030 **ταχέως** adv., *quickly, swiftly, speedily;* comp.
    τάχιον (more) quickly; superl. *τάχιστα.*
ταχέως   adv. {3.F} . . . . ταχέως G5030
ταχινή   adj., nom. sg. fem. {3.A} . . . . . . .ταχινός G5031
ταχινήν   adj., acc. sg. fem. {3.A} . . . . id.
G5031 **ταχινός**, -ή, -όν *speedy,* possibly *sudden.*
G5032 **τάχιον** (τάχειον) adv., *(more) quickly* (comp.
    of ταχέως).
τάχιον   adv. comp. {3.F; 3.G} . . . . .τάχιον G5032
G5033 **τάχιστα** adv., superl. of ταχέως, ὡς τάχιστα,
    as quickly as possible.
τάχιστα   adv. super {3.F; 3.G} . . . . τάχιστα G5033
G5034 **τάχος**, -ους, τό *quickness;* ἐν τάχει, adverbi-
    ally, *speedily, quickly.*
G5035 **ταχύ** adv., *quickly, speedily* (neut. of ταχύς, as
    adv.).
ταχύ   adv. {3.F; 3.G} . . . . ταχύ G5035
G5036 **ταχύς**, -εῖα, -ύ *quick.*
ταχύς   adj., nom. sg. masc. {3.D} . . . . ταχύς G5036
τε   part. . . . . .τέ G5037
G5037 **τέ** *and,* an enclitic connective particle, weaker
    in force than καί, to which it is related as Lat.
    que to *et (ac, atque);* τε . . . τε, τε . . . δέ, *both*
    . . . *and.*
τεθέαμαι   verb, perf. mid./pass. indic. 1 pers. sg.
    {5.A.1} . . . . θεάομαι G2300
τεθεάμεθα   verb, perf. mid./pass. indic. 1 pers.
    pl. {5.A.1} . . . . id.
τεθέαται   verb, perf. mid./pass. indic. 3 pers.
    sg. . . . . θεάομαι G2300
τέθεικα   verb, perf. act. indic. 1 pers. sg.
    {5.A.1} . . . . .τίθημι G5087
τεθείκατε   verb, perf. act. indic. 2 pers. pl.
    {5.A.1} . . . . id.
τεθεικώς   vbl., perf. act. ptc. nom. sg. masc.
    {6.A.3} . . . . id.
τεθειμένος   vbl., perf. pass. ptc. nom. sg. masc.
    {6.A.3} . . . . id.
τέθειται   verb, perf. pass. indic. 3 pers. sg.
    {5.A.1} . . . . id.
τεθεμελιωμένοι   vbl., perf. pass. ptc. nom. pl.
    masc. {6.A.2} . . . . θεμελιόω G2311
τεθεμελίωτο   verb, plu. pass. indic. 3 pers. sg.
    {5.A.1} . . . . id.

τεθεραπευμέναι   vbl., perf. pass. ptc. nom. pl. fem.
    {6.A.1.b} . . . . θεραπεύω G2323
τεθεραπευμένον   vbl., perf. pass. ptc. acc. sg.
    masc. {6.A.1.b} . . . . id.
τεθεραπευμένῳ   vbl., perf. pass. ptc. dat. sg.
    masc. {6.A.1.b} . . . . id.
τεθῇ   verb, aor. pass. subjunc. 3 pers. sg.
    {5.B.3} . . . . .τίθημι G5087
τεθῆναι   vbl., aor. pass. inf. {6.B.1} . . . . id.
τεθησαυρισμένοι   vbl., perf. pass. ptc. nom. pl.
    masc. {6.A.1.b} . . . . .θησαυρίζω G2343
τεθλιμμένη   vbl., perf. pass. ptc. nom. sg. fem.
    {6.A.1.b} . . . . θλίβω G2346
τεθνάναι   vbl., ²perf. act. inf. {6.B.1} . . . .θνῄσκω G2348
τεθνήκασι   verb, perf. act. indic. 3 pers. pl.
    {5.A.1.c} . . . . id.
τεθνήκασιν   verb, perf. act. indic. 3 pers. pl.
    {5.A.1.c} . . . . id.
τέθνηκε   verb, perf. act. indic. 3 pers. sg.
    {5.A.1.c} . . . . id.
τέθνηκεν   verb, perf. act. indic. 3 pers. sg.
    {5.A.1.c} . . . . id.
τεθνηκέναι   vbl., perf. act. inf. {6.B.1} . . . . id.
τεθνηκότα   vbl., perf. act. ptc. acc. sg. masc.
    {6.A.1.a} . . . . id.
τεθνηκότος   vbl., perf. act. ptc. gen. sg. masc.
    {6.A.1.a} . . . . id.
τεθνηκώς   vbl., perf. act. ptc. nom. sg. masc.
    {6.A.1.a} . . . . id.
τεθραμμένος   vbl., perf. pass. ptc. nom. sg. masc.
    {6.A.1.b} . . . . τρέφω G5142
τεθραυσμένους   vbl., perf. pass. ptc. acc. pl. masc.
    {6.A.1.b} . . . . θραύω G2352
τεθυμένα   vbl., perf. pass. ptc. nom. pl. neut.
    {6.A.1.b} . . . . θύω G2380
τεθῶσιν   verb, aor. pass. subjunc. 3 pers. pl.
    {5.B.3} . . . . .τίθημι G5087
τείχη   noun, nom. pl. neut. {2.C} . . . . τεῖχος G5038
G5038 **τεῖχος**, -ους, τό *a wall,* esp. *the wall* of a city.
τεῖχος   noun, acc. sg. neut. {2.C} . . . . τεῖχος G5038
τεῖχος   noun, nom. sg. neut. {2.C} . . . . id.
τείχους   noun, gen. sg. neut. {2.C} . . . . id.
τεκεῖν   vbl., ²aor. act. inf. {6.B.1} . . . . .τίκτω G5088
τέκῃ   verb, ²aor. act. subjunc. 3 pers. sg. {5.B.1} . . id.
τεκμηρίοις   noun, dat. pl. neut. {2.B} . . . τεκμήριον G5039
G5039 **τεκμήριον**, -ου, τό *an infallible proof,* a piece
    of certain (convincing) evidence.
τέκνα   noun, acc. pl. neut. {2.B} . . . . .τέκνον G5043
τέκνα   noun, nom. pl. neut. {2.B} . . . . id.
τέκνα   noun, voc. pl. neut. {2.B} . . . . id.
τεκνία   noun, voc. pl. neut. {2.B} . . . . τεκνίον G5040
G5040 **τεκνίον**, -ου, τό *little child* (a diminutive
    form, suggesting affection, applied to grown
    up persons).
τεκνογονεῖν   vbl., pres. act. inf. {6.B.2}.τεκνογονέω G5041
G5041 **τεκνογονέω** *I bear a child (children), become a
    mother.*
G5042 **τεκνογονία**, -ας, ἡ *childbearing; motherhood.*
τεκνογονίας   noun, gen. sg. fem. {2.A}. τεκνογονία G5042
τέκνοις   noun, dat. pl. neut. {2.B} . . . . .τέκνον G5043

G5043 **τέκνον**, -ου, τό   (1) *a child,* used affectionately also of grown up persons; (2) met. (Hebraistic, cf. υἱός) with gen., of those who show qualities like that expressed by the gen.; σοφίας, cf. Luke 7:35, those who draw from wisdom the impulses which mold their lives, and are as it were its representatives to others in speech and acts, *those who show* wisdom, φωτός Eph 5:8, ὑπακοῆς 1 Pet 1:14, τέκνα θεοῦ, *of godlike nature, of godly nature.*

τέκνον   noun, acc. sg. neut. {2.B} . . . . .τέκνον G5043

τέκνον   noun, nom. sg. neut. {2.B} . . . . id.

τέκνον   noun, voc. sg. neut. {2.B} . . . . id.

G5044 **τεκνοτροφέω**   *I bring up children.*

τέκνου   noun, gen. sg. neut. {2.B} . . . . .τέκνον G5043

τέκνῳ   noun, dat. sg. neut. {2.B} . . . . id.

τέκνων   noun, gen. pl. neut. {2.B} . . . . id.

τέκτονος   noun, gen. sg. masc. {2.C} . . . . . τέκτων G5045

G5045 **τέκτων**, -ονος, ὁ   *a worker in wood, a carpenter.*

τέκτων   noun, nom. sg. masc. {2.C} . . . . . τέκτων G5045

τελεῖ   verb, pres. act. indic. 3 pers. sg. {5.A.2} τελέω G5055

τελεία   adj., nom. sg. fem. {3.A} . . . . τέλειος G5046

τέλειοι   adj., nom. pl. masc. {3.A} . . . . id.

τελείοις   adj., dat. pl. masc. {3.A} . . . . id.

τέλειον   adj., acc. sg. masc. {3.A} . . . . id.

τέλειον   adj., acc. sg. neut. {3.A} . . . . id.

τέλειον   adj., nom. sg. neut. {3.A} . . . . id.

G5046 **τέλειος**, -α, -ον   (1) *full grown, mature, complete,* having reached its utmost development, e.g., Eph 4:13; Heb 5:14; (2) *completely good* (simply), Jas 1:4; (3) *completely operative,* Jas 1:17; (4) *perfect,* as dealing with universal principles, Jas 1:25; (5) *perfect* in character, Matt 5:48; Jas 3:2, etc. (from τέλος, *final end*).

τέλειος   adj., nom. sg. masc. {3.A} . . . . . . τέλειος G5046

τελειοτέρας   adj. comp., gen. sg. fem. {3.A; 3.G} id.

G5047 **τελειότης**, -ητος, ἡ   moral *completeness* (*perfection*).

τελειότητα   noun, acc. sg. fem. {2.C} . . . τελειότης G5047

τελειότητος   noun, gen. sg. fem. {2.C} . . . . id.

τελειοῦμαι   verb, pres. pass. indic. 1 pers. sg. {5.A.2} . . . . .τελειόω G5048

τελειοῦται   verb, pres. pass. indic. 3 pers. sg. {5.A.2} . . . . id.

G5048 **τελειόω**   (1) *I bring to completion, I complete;* of persons, *I bring to ethical* or *spiritual maturity* (*completeness*); *I fulfill,* John 19:28.

τελεῖται   verb, pres. pass. indic. 3 pers. sg. {5.A.2} . . . . τελέω G5055

τελεῖτε   verb, pres. act. indic. 2 pers. pl. {5.A.2} . id.

τελειωθείς   vbl., aor. pass. ptc. nom. sg. masc. {6.A.1.a.} . . . . .τελειόω G5048

τελειωθῇ   verb, aor. pass. subjunc. 3 pers. sg. {5.B.1} . . . . id.

τελειωθήσεται   verb, fut. pass. indic. 3 pers. sg. {5.A.1} . . . . id.

τελειωθῶσι   verb, aor. pass. subjunc. 3 pers. pl. {5.B.1} . . . . id.

τελειωθῶσιν   verb, aor. pass. subjunc. 3 pers. pl. {5.B.1} . . . . id.

τελείων   adj., gen. pl. masc. {3.A} . . . . τέλειος G5046

G5049 **τελείως**   adv., *perfectly, absolutely,* with νήφοντες, 1 Pet 1:13.

τελείως   adv. {3.F} . . . . τελείως G5049

τελειῶσαι   vbl., aor. act. inf. {6.B.1} . . . . .τελειόω G5048

τελειωσάντων   vbl., aor. act. ptc. gen. pl. masc. {6.A.2} . . . . id.

τελειώσας   vbl., aor. act. ptc. nom. sg. masc. {6.A.2} . . . . id.

G5050 **τελείωσις**, -εως, ἡ   *a bringing to completion* (*perfection, fulfillment*).

τελείωσις   noun, nom. sg. fem. {2.C} . . . τελείωσις G5050

τελειώσω   verb, aor. act. subjunc. 1 pers. sg. {5.B.1} . . . . .τελειόω G5048

τελειωτήν   noun, acc. sg. masc. {2.A} . . τελειωτής G5051

G5051 **τελειωτής**, -οῦ, ὁ   *a completer, perfecter.*

τελέσητε   verb, aor. act. subjunc. 2 pers. pl. {5.B.1} . . . . τελέω G5055

τελεσθῇ   verb, aor. pass. subjunc. 3 pers. sg. {5.B.1}. id.

τελεσθῆναι   vbl., aor. pass. inf. {6.B.1} . . . . id.

τελεσθήσεται   verb, fut. pass. indic. 3 pers. sg. {5.A.1} . . . . id.

τελεσθήσονται   verb, fut. pass. indic. 3 pers. pl. {5.A.1} . . . . id.

τελεσθῶσιν   verb, aor. pass. subjunc. 3 pers. pl. {5.B.1} . . . . id.

G5052 **τελεσφορέω**   *I bring* (fruit) *to maturity.*

τελεσφοροῦσι   verb, pres. act. indic. 3 pers. pl. {5.A.2} . . . . τελεσφορέω G5052

τελεσφοροῦσιν   verb, pres. act. indic. 3 pers. pl. {5.A.2} . . . . id.

τελέσωσι   verb, aor. act. subjunc. 3 pers. pl. {5.B.1} . . . . τελέω G5055

τελέσωσιν   verb, aor. act. subjunc. 3 pers. pl. {5.B.1} . . . . id.

τελευτᾷ   verb, pres. act. indic. 3 pers. sg. {5.A.2} . . . . τελευτάω G5053

τελευτᾶν   vbl., pres. act. inf. {6.B.2} . . . . id.

τελευτᾶν   vbl., pres. act. inf. {6.B.2} . . . . id.

τελευτάτω   verb, pres. act. impv. 3 pers. sg. {5.D.2} . . . . id.

G5053 **τελευτάω**   *I die* (lit. *I end*).

G5054 **τελευτή**, -ῆς, ἡ   *death* (lit. *end*).

τελευτῆς   noun, gen. sg. fem. {2.A} . . . . . .τελευτή G5054

τελευτήσαντος   vbl., aor. act. ptc. gen. sg. masc. {6.A.2} . . . . τελευτάω G5053

τελευτῶν   vbl., pres. act. ptc. nom. sg. masc. {6.A.2} . . . . id.

G5055 **τελέω**   (1) *I end, complete, accomplish, finish;* (2) *I fulfill;* (3) in Gal 5:16, possibly *I perform;* (4) of taxes, dues, *I pay,* Matt 17:24; Rom 13:6.

τέλη   noun, acc. pl. neut. {2.C} . . . . .τέλος G5056

τέλη   noun, nom. pl. neut. {2.C} . . . . id.

G5056 **τέλος**, -ους, τό   (1) sg. *the end, the final end* of anything; εἰς τέλος, *continually,* Luke 18:5; (2) *the result, the culmination,* e.g., 1 Pet 1:9; (3) *fulfillment,* Luke 22:37; (4) esp. pl. *revenues, dues,* Matt 17:25, also sg. Rom 13:7; of the spiritual *revenues* of the ages, 1 Cor 10:11.

τέλος   noun, acc. sg. neut. {2.C} . . . . .τέλος G5056

τέλος   noun, nom. sg. neut. {2.C} . . . . id.
τέλους   noun, gen. sg. neut. {2.C} . . . . id.
τελοῦσα   vbl., pres. act. ptc. nom. sg. fem.
    {6.A.2} . . . . τελέω G5055
τελῶναι   noun, nom. pl. masc. {2.A} . . . . τελώνης G5057
τελώνην   noun, acc. sg. masc. {2.A} . . . . id.
G5057   **τελώνης**, -ου, ὁ   *collector (receiver) of customs,*
    tax gatherer, revenue official, of any rank, but
    esp. of Jews of the lower rank, who collected
    revenue for the Roman overlord, detested
    by their fellow countrymen and practically
    identified with ἁμαρτωλοί.
τελώνης   noun, nom. sg. masc. {2.A} . . . . τελώνης G5057
G5058   **τελώνιον**, -ου, τό   *a revenue office, a*
    custom-house.
τελώνιον   noun, acc. sg. neut. {2.B} . . . . τελώνιον G5058
τελωνῶν   noun, gen. pl. masc. {2.A} . . . . τελώνης G5057
τέξεται   verb, fut. mid. indic. 3 pers. sg.
    {5.A.1.d} . . . . .τίκτω G5088
τέξῃ   verb, fut. mid. indic. 2 pers. sg. {5.A.1.d} . . id.
G5059   **τέρας**, -ατος, τό   *a prodigy, an extraordinary*
    occurrence (appearance, act), a startling
    portent.
τέρασι   noun, dat. pl. neut. {2.C} . . . . .τέρας G5059
τέρασιν   noun, dat. pl. neut. {2.C} . . . . id.
τέρατα   noun, acc. pl. neut. {2.C} . . . . id.
τέρατα   noun, nom. pl. neut. {2.C} . . . . id.
τεράτων   noun, gen. pl. neut. {2.C} . . . . id.
G5060   **Τέρτιος**, -ου, ὁ   *Tertius,* a Roman(?) Christian,
    who wrote the Epistle to the Romans at Paul's
    dictation (Lat.).
Τέρτιος   noun prop., nom. sg. masc. {2.B;
    2.D} . . . . .Τέρτιος G5060
G5061   **Τέρτυλλος**, -ου, ὁ   *Tertullus,* a barrister acting as
    professional prosecutor of Paul at Caesarea (Lat.).
Τέρτυλλος   noun prop., nom. sg. masc. {2.B;
    2.D} . . . . Τέρτυλλος G5061
Τερτύλλου   noun prop., gen. sg. masc. {2.B;
    2.D} . . . . id.
τέσσαρα   adj. num., acc. pl. neut. {3.E} . τέσσαρες G5064
τέσσαρα   adj. num., nom. pl. neut. {3.E} . . . . . . id.
G5062   **τεσσαράκοντα** (τεσσεράκοντα)   *forty.*
τεσσαράκοντα   adj. num. . . . . . . .τεσσαράκοντα G5062
τεσσαρακονταετῆ   adj., acc. sg. masc.
    {3.E} . . . . .τεσσαρακονταετής G5063
G5063   **τεσσαρακονταετής** (τεσσερακονταετής),
    -ές   *of forty years, forty years long.*
τεσσαρακονταετής   adj., nom. sg. masc.
    {3.E} . . . . .τεσσαρακονταετής G5063
τέσσαρας   adj. num., acc. pl. fem. {3.E} . τέσσαρες G5064
τέσσαρας   adj. num., acc. pl. masc. {3.E} . . . . . . id.
G5064   **τέσσαρες** (τέσσερες), τέσσαρα   *four.*
τέσσαρες   adj. num., nom. pl. fem. {3.E} τέσσαρες G5064
τέσσαρες   adj. num., nom. pl. masc. {3.E} . . . . . id.
τεσσαρεσκαιδεκάτη   adj., nom. sg. fem.
    {3.A} . . . . τεσσαρεσκαιδέκατος G5065
τεσσαρεσκαιδεκάτην   adj., acc. sg. fem. {3.A} . id.
G5065   **τεσσαρεσκαιδέκατος**, -η, -ον   *fourteenth.*
τέσσαρσι   adj. num., dat. pl. fem. {3.E} . τέσσαρες G5064
τέσσαρσι   adj. num., dat. pl. neut. {3.E} . . . . . . id.

τέσσαρσιν   adj. num., dat. pl. fem. {3.E} . . . . . id.
τέσσαρσιν   adj. num., dat. pl. masc. {3.E} . . . . . id.
τέσσαρσιν   adj. num., dat. pl. neut. {3.E}. . . . . . id.
τεσσάρων   adj. num., gen. pl. masc. {3.E} . . . . id.
τεσσάρων   adj. num., gen. pl. neut. {3.E} . . . . . id.
τέσσερα   adj. num., acc. pl. neut. {3.E} . . . . . . id.
τέσσερα   adj. num., nom. pl. neut. {3.E}. . . . . . id.
τεσσεράκοντα   adj. num. . . . . . . .τεσσαράκοντα G5062
τεσσερακονταετῆ   adj., acc. sg. masc.
    {3.E} . . . . .τεσσαρακονταετής G5063
τεσσερακονταετής   adj., nom. sg. masc. {3.E} . id.
τεταγμέναι   vbl., perf. pass. ptc. nom. pl. fem.
    {6.A.1.b} . . . . .τάσσω G5021
τεταγμένοι   vbl., perf. pass. ptc. nom. pl. masc.
    {6.A.1.b} . . . . id.
τέτακται   verb, perf. pass. indic. 3 pers. sg.
    {5.A.1.f}. . . . . id.
τεταραγμένοι   vbl., perf. pass. ptc. nom. pl. masc.
    {6.A.1.b} . . . . ταράσσω G5015
τετάρακται   verb, perf. pass. indic. 3 pers. sg.
    {5.A.1.f}. . . . . id.
G5066   **τεταρταῖος**, -α, -ον   *of the fourth day* (Gk.
    idiom often personalizes such adjs.), *four days*
    since he died.
τεταρταῖος   adj., nom. sg. masc. {3.A} . τεταρταῖος G5066
τετάρτη   adj., dat. sg. fem. {3.A} . . . . . . .τέταρτος G5067
τετάρτην   adj., acc. sg. fem. {3.A}. . . . . id.
τετάρτης   adj., gen. sg. fem. {3.A} . . . . id.
τέταρτον   adj., acc. sg. neut. {3.A} . . . . id.
τέταρτον   adj., nom. sg. neut. {3.A} . . . . id.
G5067   **τέταρτος**, -η, -ον   *fourth.*
τέταρτος   adj., nom. sg. masc. {3.A} . . . . .τέταρτος G5067
τετάρτου   adj., gen. sg. neut. {3.A} . . . . id.
τεταχέναι   vbl., perf. act. inf. {6.B.1} . . . . . .τάσσω G5021
τετελείωκεν   verb, perf. act. indic. 3 pers. sg.
    {5.A.1} . . . . .τελειόω G5048
τετελείωμαι   verb, perf. pass. indic. 1 pers. sg.
    {5.A.1} . . . . id.
τετελειωμένη   vbl., perf. pass. ptc. nom. sg.
    fem. {6.A.2} . . . . id.
τετελειωμένοι   vbl., perf. pass. ptc. nom. pl.
    masc. {6.A.2} . . . . id.
τετελειωμένον   vbl., perf. pass. ptc. acc. sg.
    masc. {6.A.2} . . . . id.
τετελειωμένων   vbl., perf. pass. ptc. gen. pl.
    masc. {6.A.2} . . . . id.
τετελείωται   verb, perf. pass. indic. 3 pers. sg.
    {5.A.1} . . . . id.
τετέλεκα   verb, perf. act. indic. 1 pers. sg.
    {5.A.1} . . . . .τελέω G5055
τετέλεσται   verb, perf. pass. indic. 3 pers. sg.
    {5.A.1} . . . . id.
τετελευτηκότος   vbl., perf. act. ptc. gen. sg. masc.
    {6.A.2} . . . . τελευτάω G5053
τέτευχε   verb, ²perf. act. indic. 3 pers. sg.
    {5.A.1.c} .τυγχάνω G5177
τετήρηκα   verb, perf. act. indic. 1 pers. sg.
    {5.A.1} . . . . .τηρέω G5083
τετήρηκαν   verb, perf. act. indic. 3 pers. pl.
    {5.A.1} . . . . id.

τετήρηκας   verb, perf. act. indic. 2 pers. sg.
{5.A.1} . . . . id.
τετηρήκασι   verb, perf. act. indic. 3 pers. pl.
{5.A.1} . . . . id.
τετηρήκασιν   verb, perf. act. indic. 3 pers. pl.
{5.A.1} . . . . id.
τετήρηκεν   verb, perf. act. indic. 3 pers. sg. {5.A.1} id.
τετηρημένην   vbl., perf. pass. ptc. acc. sg. fem.
{6.A.2} . . . . id.
τετηρημένοις   vbl., perf. pass. ptc. dat. pl.
masc. {6.A.2} . . . . id.
τετηρημένους   vbl., perf. pass. ptc. acc. pl.
masc. {6.A.2} . . . . id.
τετήρηται   verb, perf. pass. indic. 3 pers. sg.
{5.A.1} . . . . id.
τετιμημένου   vbl., perf. pass. ptc. gen. sg. masc.
{6.A.2} . . . . τιμάω G5091
τετραάρχης   noun, nom. sg. masc.
{2.A} . . . . τετράρχης G5076
τετραάρχου   noun, gen. sg. masc. {2.A} . . . . id.
τετρααρχοῦντος   vbl., pres. act. ptc. gen. sg. masc.
{6.A.2} . . . . τετραρχέω G5075
G5068 **τετράγωνος**, -ον   with four corners, square.
τετράγωνος   adj., nom. sg. fem. {3.C}   τετράγωνος G5068
τετραδίοις   noun, dat. pl. neut. {2.B} . . τετράδιον G5069
G5069 **τετράδιον**, -ου, τό   a quaternion, a group of
four soldiers.
G5070 **τετρακισχίλιοι**, -αι, -α   four thousand.
τετρακισχίλιοι   adj., nom. pl. masc.
{3.A} .τετρακισχίλιοι G5070
τετρακισχιλίους   adj., acc. pl. masc. {3.A} . . . . id.
τετρακισχιλίων   adj., gen. pl. masc. {3.A} . . . . id.
τετρακόσια   adj., acc. pl. neut. {3.A} . τετρακόσιοι G5071
G5071 **τετρακόσιοι**, -αι, -α   four hundred.
τετρακοσίοις   adj., dat. pl. neut. {3.A}τετρακόσιοι G5071
τετρακοσίων   adj., gen. pl. masc. {3.A} . . . . id.
τετράμηνον   adj., nom. sg. neut. {3.C} τετράμηνος G5072
G5072 **τετράμηνος**, -ου, ἡ   adj., of four months (understand χρόνος); hence, four months.
τετράμηνος   adj., nom. sg. masc. {3.C}τετράμηνος G5072
τετραπλοῦν   adj., acc. sg. neut. {3.C} . τετραπλοῦς G5073
G5073 **τετραπλοῦς**, -ῆ, -οῦν   fourfold, four times as
much.
τετράποδα   adj., acc. pl. neut. {3.E} . . . τετράπους G5074
τετράποδα   adj., nom. pl. neut. {3.E} . . . . id.
τετραπόδων   adj., gen. pl. neut. {3.E} . . . . id.
G5074 **τετράπους**, πουν, gen. ποδος   four footed; a
quadruped.
G5075 **τετραρχέω** (τετρααρχέω)   I rule as tetrarch.
G5076 **τετράρχης** (τετραάρχης), -ου, ὁ   a tetrarch,
i.e., the ruler of a fourth part of a territory di-
vided into four parts for efficient government,
a division sometimes found in the Roman
east.
τετράρχης   noun, nom. sg. masc. {2.A} τετράρχης G5076
τετράρχου   noun, gen. sg. masc. {2.A} . . . . id.
τετραρχοῦντος   vbl., pres. act. ptc. gen. sg. masc.
{6.A.2} . . . . τετραρχέω G5075
τετραυματισμένους   vbl., perf. pass. ptc. acc. pl.
masc. {6.A.1.b} . . . . τραυματίζω G5135

τετραχηλισμένα   vbl., perf. pass. ptc. nom. pl.
neut. {6.A.1.b} . . . . τραχηλίζω G5136
τετύφλωκεν   verb, perf. act. indic. 3 pers. sg.
{5.A.1} . . . . τυφλόω G5186
τετυφωμένοι   vbl., perf. pass. ptc. nom. pl. masc.
{6.A.2} . . . . τυφόω G5187
τετύφωται   verb, perf. pass. indic. 3 pers. sg.
{5.A.1} . . . . id.
τέτυχεν   verb, ²perf. act. indic. 3 pers. sg.
{5.A.1.c} . . . . τυγχάνω G5177
G5077 **τεφρόω**   I cover with, or I convert into, ashes.
τεφρώσας   vbl., aor. act. ptc. nom. sg. masc.
{6.A.2} . . . . τεφρόω G5077
τεχθείς   vbl., aor. pass. ptc. nom. sg. masc.
{6.A.1.a} . . . . τίκτω G5088
G5078 **τέχνη**, -ης, ἡ   art., handicraft, trade.
τέχνη   noun, dat. sg. fem. {2.A} . . . . τέχνη G5078
τέχνην   noun, acc. sg. fem. {2.A} . . . . id.
τέχνης   noun, gen. sg. fem. {2.A} . . . . id.
τεχνῖται   noun, nom. pl. masc. {2.A} . . . . τεχνίτης G5079
τεχνίταις   noun, dat. pl. masc. {2.A} . . . . id.
G5079 **τεχνίτης**, -ου, ὁ   a craftsman, an artisan; with
gen. a designer, Heb 11:10.
τεχνίτης   noun, nom. sg. masc. {2.A} . . . . τεχνίτης G5079
τῇ   art., dat. sg. fem. {1} . . . . ὁ G3588
τῇδε   pron. dem., dat. sg. fem. {4.B} . . . . .ὅδε G3592
τήκεται   verb, pres. pass. indic. 3 pers. sg.
{5.A.1.d} . . . . τήκω G5080
G5080 **τήκω**   pass. intrans., I melt.
G5081 **τηλαυγῶς**   adv., clearly from afar, clearly.
τηλαυγῶς   adv. {3.F} . . . . τηλαυγῶς G5081
τηλικαῦτα   pron. correl., nom. pl. neut.
{4.D} . . . . .τηλικοῦτος G5082
τηλικαύτης   pron. correl., gen. sg. fem. {4.D} . id.
G5082 **τηλικοῦτος**, -αύτη, -οῦτο   so large, so great.
τηλικοῦτος   pron. correl., nom. sg. masc.
{4.D} . . . . .τηλικοῦτος G5082
τηλικούτου   pron. correl., gen. sg. masc. {4.D} . id.
τήν   art., acc. sg. fem. {1} . . . . ὁ G3588
τήνδε   pron. dem., acc. sg. fem. {4.B} . . . . .ὅδε G3592
τήρει   verb, pres. act. impv. 2 pers. sg. {5.D.2}τηρέω G5083
τηρεῖ   verb, pres. act. indic. 3 pers. sg. {5.A.2}. . . id.
τηρεῖν   vbl., pres. act. inf. {6.B.2} . . . . id.
τηρεῖσθαι   vbl., pres. pass. inf. {6.B.2} . . . . id.
τηρεῖτε   verb, pres. act. impv. 2 pers. pl. {5.D.2} . id.
G5083 **τηρέω**   (1) lit. I watch, observe; (2) I guard,
preserve, keep, protect; (3) of commandments
and regulations, I observe, keep, obey.
τηρῇ   verb, pres. act. subjunc. 3 pers. sg.
{5.B.2} . . . . τηρέω G5083
τηρηθείη   verb, aor. pass. opt. 3 pers. sg. {5.C.1} id.
τηρηθῆναι   vbl., aor. pass. inf. {6.B.1} . . . . id.
τηρῆσαι   vbl., aor. act. inf. {6.B.1} . . . . id.
τηρήσαντας   vbl., aor. act. ptc. acc. pl. masc.
{6.A.2} . . . . id.
τηρήσατε   verb, aor. act. impv. 2 pers. pl. {5.D.1} id.
τηρήσει   noun, dat. sg. fem. {2.C} . . . . . τήρησις G5084
τηρήσει   verb, fut. act. indic. 3 pers. sg.
{5.A.1} . . . . τηρέω G5083
τηρήσετε   verb, fut. act. indic. 2 pers. pl. {5.A.1} id.

τηρήσῃ   verb, aor. act. subjunc. 3 pers. sg.
{5.B.1} . . . . id.
τηρήσῃς   verb, aor. act. subjunc. 2 pers. sg.
{5.B.1} . . . . id.
τηρήσητε   verb, aor. act. subjunc. 2 pers. pl.
{5.B.1} . . . . id.
τήρησιν   noun, acc. sg. fem. {2.C} . . . . . τήρησις G5084
G5084 **τήρησις**, -εως, ἡ   (1) *a keeping, an observance,*
1 Cor 7:19; (2) *a place of custody.*
τήρησις   noun, nom. sg. fem. {2.C} . . . . τήρησις G5084
τήρησον   verb, aor. act. impv. 2 pers. sg.
{5.D.1} . . . . τηρέω G5083
τηρήσουσιν   verb, fut. act. indic. 3 pers. pl.
{5.A.1} . . . . id.
τηρήσω   verb, fut. act. indic. 1 pers. sg. {5.A.1} . id.
τηροῦμεν   verb, pres. act. indic. 1 pers. pl.
{5.A.2} . . . . id.
τηρούμενοι   vbl., pres. pass. ptc. nom. pl.
masc. {6.A.2} . . . . id.
τηρουμένους   vbl., pres. pass. ptc. acc. pl.
masc. {6.A.2} . . . . id.
τηροῦντες   vbl., pres. act. ptc. nom. pl. masc.
{6.A.2} . . . . id.
τηρούντων   vbl., pres. act. ptc. gen. pl. masc.
{6.A.2} . . . . id.
τηρῶ   verb, pres. act. indic. 1 pers. sg. {5.A.2} . . . id.
τηρῶμεν   verb, pres. act. subjunc. 1 pers. pl.
{5.B.2} . . . . id.
τηρῶν   vbl., pres. act. ptc. nom. sg. masc. {6.A.2} id.
τῆς   art., gen. sg. fem. {1} . . . . ὁ G3588
τι   pron. indef., acc. sg. neut. {4.E} . . . . τις G5100
τι   pron. indef., nom. sg. neut. {4.E}
τί   pron. interrog., acc. sg. neut. {4.E} . . . . . τίς G5101
τί   pron. interrog., nom. sg. neut. {4.E} . . . . . . id.
Τιβεριάδος   noun prop., gen. sg. fem. {2.C;
2.D} . . . . Τιβεριάς G5085
G5085 **Τιβεριάς**, -άδος, ἡ   *Tiberias,* a town in Galilee
on the western border of the sea called after it.
G5086 **Τιβέριος**, -ου, ὁ   *Tiberius,* the second Roman
emperor (died 37 A.D.).
Τιβερίου   noun prop., gen. sg. masc. {2.B;
2.D} . . . . Τιβέριος G5086
τιθέασιν   verb, pres. act. indic. 3 pers. pl.
{5.A.3.a} . . . . τίθημι G5087
τιθείς   vbl., pres. act. ptc. nom. sg. masc. {6.A.3}. id.
τιθέναι   vbl., pres. act. inf. {6.B.3} . . . . id.
τιθέντες   vbl., pres. act. ptc. nom. pl. masc.
{6.A.3} . . . . id.
τίθεται   verb, pres. pass. indic. 3 pers. sg.
{5.A.3.a} . . . . id.
τιθέτω   verb, pres. act. impv. 3 pers. sg. {5.D.3} . . id.
G5087 **τίθημι**   *I place, put, set forth;* sometimes with
two accusatives, the second in the pred., e.g.,
πατέρα πολλῶν ἐθνῶν τέθεικά σε, Rom
4:17, *I have made you a father,* etc.; τίθημι
γόνατα, *I kneel;* τίθεμαι εἰς ὦτα, ἐν καρδίᾳ,
I put into my ears, into my mind, i.e., *attend to,*
e.g., Luke 1:66; 9:44; τίθημι ψυχήν, e.g., John
10:11 etc., for the synoptic and usual δίδωμι, *I
give up my life, I offer up my life.*

τίθημι   verb, pres. act. indic. 1 pers. sg.
{5.A.3.a} . . . . τίθημι G5087
τίθησι   verb, pres. act. indic. 3 pers. sg. {5.A.3.a} id.
τίθησιν   verb, pres. act. indic. 3 pers. sg.
{5.A.3.a} . . . . id.
τίκτει   verb, pres. act. indic. 3 pers. sg.
{5.A.1.a} . . . . τίκτω G5088
τίκτῃ   verb, pres. act. subjunc. 3 pers. sg. {5.B.1}. id.
τίκτουσα   vbl., pres. act. ptc. nom. sg. fem.
{6.A.1} . . . . id.
G5088 **τίκτω**   (of a woman), *I bear, give birth to, bring
forth;* hence, met., of the earth, Heb 6:7, of evil
desire, Jas 1:15.
τίλλειν   vbl., pres. act. inf. {6.B.1} . . . . τίλλω G5089
τίλλοντες   vbl., pres. act. ptc. nom. pl. masc.
{6.A.1} . . . . id.
G5089 **τίλλω**   *I pluck, pull, pick.*
τίμα   verb, pres. act. impv. 2 pers. sg. {5.D.2} τιμάω G5091
τιμᾷ   verb, pres. act. indic. 3 pers. sg. {5.A.2} . . . id.
G5090 **Τιμαῖος**, -ου, ὁ   *Timaeus,* father of the blind
beggar Bartimaeus.
Τιμαίου   noun prop., gen. sg. masc. {2.B;
2.D} . . . . Τιμαῖος G5090
τιμαῖς   noun, dat. pl. fem. {2.A} . . . . τιμή G5092
τιμάς   noun, acc. pl. fem. {2.A} . . . . id.
τιμᾶτε   verb, pres. act. impv. 2 pers. pl.
{5.D.2} . . . . τιμάω G5091
G5091 **τιμάω**   *I honor, give honor to.*
G5092 **τιμή**, -ῆς, ἡ   (1) *honor,* e.g., John 4:44; (2) *price,*
e.g., Matt 27:6.
τιμή   noun, nom. sg. fem. {2.A} . . . . τιμή G5092
τιμῇ   noun, dat. sg. fem. {2.A} . . . . id.
τιμήν   noun, acc. sg. fem. {2.A} . . . . id.
τιμῆς   noun, gen. sg. fem. {2.A} . . . . id.
τιμήσατε   verb, aor. act. impv. 2 pers. pl.
{5.D.1} . . . . τιμάω G5091
τιμήσει   verb, fut. act. indic. 3 pers. sg. {5.A.1} . . id.
τιμήσῃ   verb, aor. act. subjunc. 3 pers. sg. {5.B.1} id.
τίμια   adj., acc. pl. neut. {3.A} . . . . τίμιος G5093
τίμια   adj., nom. pl. neut. {3.A} . . . . id.
τιμίαν   adj., acc. sg. fem. {3.A} . . . . id.
τίμιον   adj., acc. sg. masc. {3.A} . . . . id.
G5093 **τίμιος**, -α, -ον   *precious, valuable,* in the lit.
sense (of money value), e.g., Rev 17:4, and
also, e.g., Acts 5:34, in an extended sense.
τίμιος   adj., nom. sg. masc. {3.A} . . . . τίμιος G5093
G5094 **τιμιότης**, -ητος, ἡ   *preciousness.*
τιμιότητος   noun, gen. sg. fem. {2.C} . . . . τιμιότης G5094
τιμίου   adj., gen. sg. masc. {3.A} . . . . τίμιος G5093
τιμίους   adj., acc. pl. masc. {3.A} . . . . id.
τιμίῳ   adj., dat. sg. masc. {3.A} . . . . id.
τιμίῳ   adj., dat. sg. neut. {3.A} . . . . id.
τιμιωτάτου   adj. superl., gen. sg. neut. {3.A} . . . id.
τιμιωτάτῳ   adj. superl., dat. sg. masc. {3.A} . . . . id.
τιμιώτερον   adj. comp., nom. sg. neut. {3.A; 3.G}id.
Τιμόθεε   noun prop., voc. sg. masc. {2.B;
2.D} . . . . Τιμόθεος G5095
Τιμόθεον   noun prop., acc. sg. masc. {2.B; 2.D} . id.
G5095 **Τιμόθεος**, -ου, ὁ   *Timothy,* a Christian of Lystra, helper of Paul.

Τιμόθεος   noun prop., nom. sg. masc. {2.B;
    2.D}. . . . . .Τιμόθεος *G5095*
Τιμοθέου   noun prop., gen. sg. masc. {2.B; 2.D} . id.
Τιμοθέῳ   noun prop., dat. sg. masc. {2.B; 2.D} . . id.
τιμῶ   verb, pres. act. indic. 1 pers. sg. {5.A.2} τιμάω *G5091*
τιμῶν   vbl., pres. act. ptc. nom. sg. masc. {6.A.2} id.
G5096 **Τίμων**, -ωνος, ὁ   *Timon*, one of the seven
    original "deacons" at Jerusalem.
Τίμωνα   noun prop., acc. sg. masc. {2.C;
    2.D}. . . . . Τίμων *G5096*
G5097 **τιμωρέω**   *I punish.*
τιμωρηθῶσιν   verb, aor. pass. subjunc. 3 pers. pl.
    {5.B.1}. . . . . τιμωρέω *G5097*
G5098 **τιμωρία**, -ας, ἡ   (deserved) *punishment.*
τιμωρίας   noun, gen. sg. fem. {2.A} . . . . .τιμωρία *G5098*
τιμωρῶν   vbl., pres. act. ptc. nom. sg. masc.
    {6.A.2}. . . . . τιμωρέω *G5097*
τιμῶσι   verb, pres. act. indic. 3 pers. pl.
    {5.A.2}. . . . . τιμάω *G5091*
τιμῶσι   verb, pres. act. subjunc. 3 pers. pl. {5.B.2}id.
τιμῶσιν   verb, pres. act. indic. 3 pers. pl. {5.A.2} id.
τιμῶσιν   verb, pres. act. subjunc. 3 pers. pl.
    {5.B.2}. . . . . id.
τινα   pron. indef., acc. pl. neut. {4.E} . . . . . . τις *G5100*
τινα   pron. indef., acc. sg. fem. {4.E} . . . . id.
τινα   pron. indef., acc. sg. masc. {4.E} . . . . . . id.
τινα   pron. indef., nom. pl. neut. {4.E} . . . . . . id.
τίνα   pron. interrog., acc. sg. masc. {4.E} . . . . . τίς *G5101*
τίνα   pron. interrog., acc. sg. fem. {4.E} . . . . . . id.
τίνα   pron. interrog., nom. pl. neut. {4.E} . . . . . id.
τινά   pron. indef., acc. sg. fem. {4.E} . . . . τις *G5100*
τινά   pron. indef., acc. sg. masc. {4.E} . . . . id.
τινας   pron. indef., acc. pl. fem. {4.E} . . . . id.
τινας   pron. indef., acc. pl. masc. {4.E} . . . . . . id.
τίνας   pron. interrog., acc. pl. fem. {4.E} . . . . . τίς *G5101*
τίνας   pron. interrog., acc. pl. masc. {4.E} . . . . . id.
τινάς   pron. indef., acc. pl. fem. {4.E} . . . . τις *G5100*
τινάς   pron. indef., acc. pl. masc. {4.E} . . . . . . id.
τινες   pron. indef., nom. pl. fem. {4.E} . . . . . . id.
τινες   pron. indef., nom. pl. masc. {4.E} . . . . . . id.
τίνες   pron. interrog., nom. pl. masc. {4.E} . . . . τίς *G5101*
τινές   pron. indef., nom. pl. masc. {4.E} . . . . . . τις *G5100*
τινι   pron. indef., dat. sg. fem. {4.E} . . . . id.
τινι   pron. indef., dat. sg. masc. {4.E} . . . . id.
τινι   pron. indef., dat. sg. neut. {4.E} . . . . id.
τίνι   pron. interrog., dat. sg. masc. {4.E} . . . . . τίς *G5101*
τίνι   pron. interrog., dat. sg. neut. {4.E}. . . . . . id.
τινί   pron. indef., dat. sg. fem. {4.E} . . . . τις *G5100*
τινί   pron. indef., dat. sg. masc. {4.E} . . . . id.
τινος   pron. indef., gen. sg. fem. {4.E}. . . . . . . id.
τινος   pron. indef., gen. sg. masc. {4.E} . . . . . . id.
τινος   pron. indef., gen. sg. neut. {4.E} . . . . . . id.
τίνος   pron. interrog., gen. sg. masc. {4.E} . . . . τίς *G5101*
τίνος   pron. interrog., gen. sg. neut. {4.E} . . . . . id.
τινός   pron. indef., gen. sg. neut. {4.E} . . . . . . τις *G5100*
G5099 **τίνω**   *I pay.*
τινων   pron. indef., gen. pl. masc. {4.E}. . . . . . τις *G5100*
τινων   pron. indef., gen. pl. neut. {4.E} . . . . . . id.
τίνων   pron. interrog., gen. pl. masc. {4.E} . . . . τίς *G5101*
τίνων   pron. interrog., gen. pl. neut. {4.E} . . . . . id.

τινῶν   pron. indef., gen. pl. fem. {4.E}. . . . . . . τις *G5100*
τινῶν   pron. indef., gen. pl. masc. {4.E}. . . . . . id.
G5100 **τις**, τι, gen. τινός   enclitic indef. pron. and adj.,
    (1) *someone, anyone, something, any thing;* (2)
    a (an), a certain, any, some; (3) special uses,
    (a) softening the metaphor, *so to speak, a sort
    of,* ἀπαρχήν τινα, Jas 1:18; (b) with numbers,
    making indef., *about,* but τινας δύο, *a certain
    two,* Acts 23:23 (cf. Luke 22:50; John 11:49);
    (c) with adjs., strengthening, Heb 10:27, cf.
    Acts 5:36; 8:9; (d) τι, *something special,* Gal
    2:6; 6:3. Sometimes unexpressed, where it
    would be expected (Hebraism?), John 7:40;
    16:17; Acts 19:33; 21:16, etc.
τις   pron. indef., nom. sg. fem. {4.E} . . . . τις *G5100*
τις   pron. indef., nom. sg. masc. {4.E} . . . . id.
G5101 **τίς**, τί, gen. τίνος   interrog. pron. and (some-
    times) adj., *who? what? which?* (usually of
    more than two, but sometimes = πότερος,
    of two only, e.g., Matt 21:31); (1) τί = *what
    reward?* Matt 19:27; τί neut. as pred. to ταῦτα,
    e.g., Luke 15:26; Acts 17:20 (var.); John
    6:9 (what use are they?); τί ἄρα ὁ Πέτρος
    ἐγένετο, *what then had happened to Peter,*
    Acts 12:18, τί ἄρα τὸ παιδίον τοῦτο ἔσται;
    Luke 1:66; Acts 5:24 (τί in pred.), abbrevi-
    ated, οὗτος δὲ τί; *what will become of him?*
    John 21:21; (2) adverbially = *why?* Matt 6:28;
    Luke 2:48; Acts 14:15, like διὰ τί and ἵνα τί
    (supply γένηται), as well as τί ὅ, τι (ὅτι) = τί
    γέγονεν ὅτι (or δι᾿ ὅ,τι) (cf. John 14:22); (3)
    (Hebraistic) *how,* Matt 7:14 (var.); Luke 12:49;
    1 Cor 7:16; (4) τί πρὸς ἡμᾶς (supply ἐστιν);
    what have we to do with it? Matt 27:4, cf. John
    21:22; 1 Cor 5:12 (see also under σύ); (5) τί
    γάρ; *what does it matter?* or *what difference
    does it make?* Rom 3:3; Phil 1:18; (6) τί οὖν
    (supply ἐροῦμεν?); Rom 6:15; (7) masc. ἐγώ
    τίς ἤμην; Acts 11:17; (8) double interrog.,
    τίς τί ἄρη, Mark 15:24, τίς τί *(what each)*
    διεπραγματεύσατο, Luke 19:15 (var.). Some
    times τίς is confused with the rel. ὅστις, ὅς,
    which is rather a sign of illiteracy, Matt 10:19;
    Luke 17:8; Acts 13:25 (according to one punc-
    tuation); Jas 3:13 (if read as one sentence).
    In Luke 11:5, 11, τίς (= εἴ τις, cf. Phil 2:1) is
    non-Gk. and Semitic.
τίς   pron. interrog., nom. sg. fem. {4.E}. . . . . . . τίς *G5101*
τίς   pron. interrog., nom. sg. masc. {4.E}. . . . . . id.
τισι   pron. indef., dat. pl. masc. {4.E} . . . . τις *G5100*
τίσι   pron. interrog., dat. pl. masc. {4.E} . . . . . . τίς *G5101*
τισί   pron. indef., dat. pl. masc. {4.E} . . . . τις *G5100*
τισιν   pron. indef., dat. pl. masc. {4.E} . . . . id.
τίσιν   pron. interrog., dat. pl. masc. {4.E} . . . . . τίς *G5101*
τισίν   pron. indef., dat. pl. masc. {4.E} . . . . τις *G5100*
τίσουσιν   verb, fut. act. indic. 3 pers. pl.
    {5.A.1.a} . . . . .τίνω *G5099*
G5103‡ **Τίτιος**, ου, ὁ   *Titius.* Var. for Τίτος, Acts 18:7.
Τιτίου   noun prop., gen. sg. masc. {2.B;
    2.D}. . . . . Τίτιος *G5103‡*

τίτλον   noun, acc. sg. masc. {2.B} . . . . τίτλος G5102
G5102 **τίτλος**, -ου, ὁ   *an inscription* (Lat., *titulus*).
Τίτον   noun prop., acc. sg. masc. {2.B; 2.D} . . Τίτος G5103
G5103 **Τίτος**, -ου, ὁ   *Titus*, a Greek Christian, helper
of Paul, perhaps also brother of Luke.
Τίτος   noun prop., nom. sg. masc. {2.B; 2.D} . Τίτος G5103
Τίτου   noun prop., gen. sg. masc. {2.B; 2.D} . . . . id.
Τίτῳ   noun prop., dat. sg. masc. {2.B; 2.D} . . . . . id.
τό   art., acc. sg. neut. {1} . . . . ὁ G3588
τό   art., nom. sg. neut. {1} . . . . id.
τοι   part. . . . . τοί G5104
G5104 **τοί**   enclitic particle, *truly, surely, furthermore.*
τοιᾶσδε   pron. correl., gen. sg. fem. {4.D} . . τοιόσδε G5107
τοιαῦτα   pron. correl., acc. pl. neut. {4.D} τοιοῦτος G5108
τοιαῦται   pron. correl., nom. pl. fem. {4.D} . . . . id.
τοιαύταις   pron. correl., dat. pl. fem. {4.D} . . . . id.
τοιαύτας   pron. correl., acc. pl. fem. {4.D} . . . . id.
τοιαύτη   pron. correl., nom. sg. fem. {4.D} . . . . id.
τοιαύτην   pron. correl., acc. sg. fem. {4.D} . . . . id.
G5105 **τοιγαροῦν**   *accordingly, wherefore.*
τοιγαροῦν   part. τοιγαροῦν G5105
G5106 **τοίνυν**   *so.*
τοίνυν   part. . . . . τοίνυν G5106
G5107 **τοιόσδε**, -άδε, -όνδε, gen. -οῦδε, -ᾶσδε,
-οῦδε   *of such character, to the following
effect.*
τοιοῦτο   pron. correl., acc. sg. neut. {4.D} τοιοῦτος G5108
τοιοῦτοι   pron. correl., nom. pl. masc. {4.D} . . id.
τοιούτοις   pron. correl., dat. pl. masc. {4.D} . . . id.
τοιούτοις   pron. correl., dat. pl. neut. {4.D} . . . . id.
τοιοῦτον   pron. correl., acc. sg. masc. {4.D} . . . id.
τοιοῦτον   pron. correl., acc. sg. neut. {4.D} . . . id.
G5108 **τοιοῦτος**, -αύτη, -οῦτον   *of such a kind (character), such.*
τοιοῦτος   pron. correl., nom. sg. masc.
{4.D} . . . . τοιοῦτος G5108
τοιούτου   pron. correl., gen. sg. masc. {4.D} . . . id.
τοιούτους   pron. correl., acc. pl. masc. {4.D} . . . id.
τοιούτῳ   pron. correl., dat. sg. masc. {4.D} . . . . id.
τοιούτων   pron. correl., gen. pl. masc. {4.D} . . . id.
τοιούτων   pron. correl., gen. pl. neut. {4.D} . . . . id.
τοῖς   art., dat. pl. masc. {1} . . . . ὁ G3588
τοῖς   art., dat. pl. neut. {1} . . . . id.
τοῖχε   noun, voc. sg. masc. {2.B} . . . . τοῖχος G5109
G5109 **τοῖχος**, -ου, ὁ   *a wall.*
G5110 **τόκος**, -ου, ὁ   (from τίκτω), *interest* on money
loaned.
τόκῳ   noun, dat. sg. masc. {2.B} . . . . τόκος G5110
τολμᾷ   verb, pres. act. indic. 3 pers. sg.
{5.A.2} . . . . τολμάω G5111
τολμᾷ   verb, pres. act. subjunc. 3 pers. sg. {5.B.2} id.
τολμᾶν   vbl., pres. act. inf. {6.B.2} . . . . id.
τολμᾶν   vbl., pres. act. inf. {6.B.2} . . . . id.
G5111 **τολμάω**   (1) *I have courage, I dare, I have the
hardihood;* (2) *I take courage,* Mark 15:43; (3) *I
submit to,* Rom 5:7.
G5112 **τολμηρός**, -ά, -όν   *bold, courageous, audacious;*
comp. adv. τολμηροτέρως or τολμηρότε-
ρον, *rather boldly.*

τολμηρότερον   adv. comp. {3.F; 3.G} . . . τολμηρός G5112
τολμηροτέρως   adv. comp. {3.F; 3.G} . . . . id.
τολμῆσαι   vbl., aor. act. inf. {6.B.1} . . . . . τολμάω G5111
τολμήσας   vbl., aor. act. ptc. nom. sg. masc.
{6.A.2} . . . . id.
τολμήσω   verb, fut. act. indic. 1 pers. sg. {5.A.1} id.
τολμηταί   noun, nom. pl. masc. {2.A} . . τολμητής G5113
G5113 **τολμητής**, -οῦ, ὁ   *a shameless and headstrong
man.*
τολμῶ   verb, pres. act. indic. 1 pers. sg.
{5.A.2} . . . . τολμάω G5111
τολμῶμεν   verb, pres. act. indic. 1 pers. pl.
{5.A.2} . . . . id.
G5114 **τομός**, -ή, -όν   *cutting, with cutting power.*
τομώτερος   adj. comp., nom. sg. masc. {3.A;
3.G} . . . . τομός G5114
τόν   art., acc. sg. masc. {1} . . . . ὁ G3588
G5115 **τόξον**, -ου, τό   *a bow* (and arrows).
τόξον   noun, acc. sg. neut. {2.B} . . . . τόξον G5115
G5116 **τοπάζιον**, -ου, τό   *a topaz.*
τοπάζιον   noun, nom. sg. neut. {2.B} . . . τοπάζιον G5116
τόποις   noun, dat. pl. masc. {2.B} . . . . τόπος G5117
τόπον   noun, acc. sg. masc. {2.B} . . . . id.
G5117 **τόπος**, -ου, ὁ   (1) *a place;* κατὰ τόπους,
in various places, Mark 13:8, etc., διδόναι
τόπον, *to make room for, give place to,* Luke
14:9, etc.; (2) met. *an opportunity,* Acts 25:16;
Rom 15:23; Eph 4:27; Heb 12:17.
τόπος   noun, nom. sg. masc. {2.B} . . . . τόπος G5117
τόπου   noun, gen. sg. masc. {2.B} . . . . id.
τόπους   noun, acc. pl. masc. {2.B} . . . . id.
τόπῳ   noun, dat. sg. masc. {2.B} . . . . id.
τόπων   noun, gen. pl. masc. {2.B} . . . . id.
τοσαῦτα   pron. correl., acc. pl. neut.
{4.D} . . . . τοσοῦτος G5118
τοσαῦτα   pron. correl., nom. pl. neut. {4.D} . . . id.
τοσαύτην   pron. correl., acc. sg. fem. {4.D} . . . id.
τοσοῦτο   pron. correl., acc. sg. neut. {4.D} . . . . id.
τοσοῦτοι   pron. correl., nom. pl. masc. {4.D} . . id.
τοσοῦτον   pron. correl., acc. sg. masc. {4.D} . . id.
τοσοῦτον   pron. correl., acc. sg. neut. {4.D} . . . id.
τοσοῦτον   pron. correl., nom. sg. neut. {4.D} . . id.
G5118 **τοσοῦτος**, -αύτη, -οῦτον   (1) *so great, so
large;* (2) of time, *so long,* pl. *so many;* (3)
τοσούτου, *at such and such a price,* Acts 5:8.
τοσοῦτος   pron. correl., nom. sg. masc.
{4.D} . . . . τοσοῦτος G5118
τοσούτου   pron. correl., gen. sg. neut. {4.D} . . . id.
τοσούτους   pron. correl., acc. pl. masc. {4.D} . . id.
τοσούτῳ   pron. correl., dat. sg. masc. {4.D} . . . . id.
τοσούτῳ   pron. correl., dat. sg. neut. {4.D} . . . . id.
τοσούτων   pron. correl., gen. pl. masc. {4.D} . . . id.
G5119 **τότε**   adv., *then, at that time;* ὁ τότε κόσμος,
the world of that day, 2 Pet 3:6; ἀπὸ τότε, *from
that time, thence forward,* Matt 4:17, etc.; very
often in Matt representing Heb. *waw* consecu-
tive, and thus simply continuing the narrative.
τότε   adv. correl. {4.D} . . . . τότε G5119
τοῦ   art., gen. sg. masc. {1} . . . . ὁ G3588

τοῦ   art., gen. sg. neut. {1}. . . . . id.

G5121 τοὐναντίον   *on the contrary, on the other hand* (crasis form of the gen. sg. of ὁ and ἐναντίον).

τοὐναντίον   art + adv. {1} . . . . .τοὐναντίον G5121

G5122 τοὔνομα   *named, whose name is* (crasis form of the neut. sg. of ὁ and ὄνομα).

τοὔνομα   art + noun {1, 2.C} . . . . ὄνομα G3686

τούς   art., acc. pl. masc. {1}. . . . . ὁ G3588

τοῦτ'   pron. dem., nom. sg. neut. {4.B} . . . . οὗτος G3778

G5123 τουτέστι(ν)   *that is (to say), in other words* (= τοῦτ' ἔστιν, from neut. sg. of οὗτος and the 3 pers. sg. of εἰμί).

τοῦτο   pron. dem., acc. sg. neut. {4.B} . . . . οὗτος G3778

τοῦτο   pron. dem., nom. sg. neut. {4.B} . . . . id.

τούτοις   pron. dem., dat. pl. masc. {4.B}. . . . . . . id.

τούτοις   pron. dem., dat. pl. neut. {4.B} . . . . id.

τοῦτον   pron. dem., acc. sg. masc. {4.B} . . . . id.

τούτου   pron. dem., gen. sg. masc. {4.B}. . . . . . . id.

τούτου   pron. dem., gen. sg. neut. {4.B} . . . . id.

τούτους   pron. dem., acc. pl. masc. {4.B} . . . . . . id.

τούτῳ   pron. dem., dat. sg. masc. {4.B} . . . . id.

τούτῳ   pron. dem., dat. sg. neut. {4.B} . . . . id.

τούτων   pron. dem., gen. pl. fem. {4.B}. . . . . . . id.

τούτων   pron. dem., gen. pl. masc. {4.B}. . . . . . id.

τούτων   pron. dem., gen. pl. neut. {4.B}. . . . . . . id.

G5131 τράγος, -ου, ὁ   *a goat.*

τράγων   noun, gen. pl. masc. {2.B} . . . . . . .τράγος G5131

G5132 τράπεζα, -ης, ἡ   *a table.*

τράπεζα   noun, nom. sg. fem. {2.A} . . . . τράπεζα G5132

τραπέζαις   noun, dat. pl. fem. {2.A} . . . . id.

τράπεζαν   noun, acc. sg. fem. {2.A} . . . . id.

τραπέζας   noun, acc. pl. fem. {2.A} . . . . id.

τραπεζείταις   noun, dat. pl. masc. {2.A} . . . . .τραπεζίτης G5133

τραπέζης   noun, gen. sg. fem. {2.A} . . . . τράπεζα G5132

τραπεζίταις   noun, dat. pl. masc. {2.A}τραπεζίτης G5133

G5133 τραπεζίτης, -ου, ὁ   *a moneychanger, a banker* (from τράπεζα, moneychanger's *table*).

G5134 τραῦμα, -ατος, τό   *a wound.*

τραύματα   noun, acc. pl. neut. {2.C} . . . . .τραῦμα G5134

G5135 τραυματίζω   *I wound.*

τραυματίσαντες   vbl., aor. act. ptc. nom. pl. masc. {6.A.1.a} . . . . τραυματίζω G5135

τραχεῖαι   adj., nom. pl. fem. {3.D} . . . . . . τραχύς G5138

τραχεῖς   adj., acc. pl. masc. {3.D} . . . . id.

G5136 τραχηλίζω   τετραχηλισμένα, *open, manifest* (from τράχηλος).

τράχηλον   noun, acc. sg. masc. {2.B} . . . τράχηλος G5137

G5137 τράχηλος, -ου, ὁ   *the neck;* τὸν ἑαυτῶν τράχηλον ὑποθεῖναι, *to lay down their own necks,* i.e., *to risk their own lives.*

G5138 τραχύς, -εῖα, -ύ   *rough.*

Τραχωνίτιδος   noun prop., gen. sg. fem. {2.C; 2.D}. .Τραχωνῖτις G5139

G5139 Τραχωνῖτις, -ιδος, ἡ   *Trachonitis, belonging to Trachon,* adj. applied to a hilly region (inhabited by a nomad tribe), considerably to the south of Damascus, called also Iturea.

G5140 τρεῖς, τρία, gen. τριῶν, dat. τρισίν   *three;* μετὰ τρεῖς ἡμέρας = τῇ τρίτῃ ἡμέρᾳ.

τρεῖς   adj. num., acc. pl. fem. {3.E} . . . . τρεῖς G5140

τρεῖς   adj. num., acc. pl. masc. {3.E} . . . . id.

τρεῖς   adj. num., nom. pl. fem. {3.E} . . . . id.

τρεῖς   adj. num., nom. pl. masc. {3.E} . . . . id.

τρέμουσα   vbl., pres. act. ptc. nom. sg. fem. {6.A.1}. . . . . τρέμω G5141

τρέμουσι   verb, pres. act. indic. 3 pers. pl. {5.A.1.a} . . . . id.

τρέμουσιν   verb, pres. act. indic. 3 pers. pl. {5.A.1.a} . . . . id.

G5141 τρέμω   *I tremble.*

τρέμων   vbl., pres. act. ptc. nom. sg. masc. {6.A.1}. . . . . τρέμω G5141

τρέφει   verb, pres. act. indic. 3 pers. sg. {5.A.1.a} . . . . .τρέφω G5142

τρέφεσθαι   vbl., pres. pass. inf. {6.B.1}. . . . . id.

τρέφεται   verb, pres. pass. indic. 3 pers. sg. {5.A.1.d} . . . . id.

τρέφηται   verb, pres. pass. subjunc. 3 pers. sg. {5.B.1} . . . . id.

G5142 τρέφω   (1) *I nourish, feed;* (2) *I bring up,* Luke 4:16; (2) met., Jas 5:5.

τρέφωσιν   verb, pres. act. subjunc. 3 pers. pl. {5.B.1} . . . . .τρέφω G5142

τρέχει   verb, pres. act. indic. 3 pers. sg. {5.A.1.a} . . . . .τρέχω G5143

τρέχετε   verb, pres. act. impv. 2 pers. pl. {5.D.1} . id.

τρέχῃ   verb, pres. act. subjunc. 3 pers. sg. {5.B.1} id.

τρέχοντες   vbl., pres. act. ptc. nom. pl. masc. {6.A.1}. . . . . id.

τρέχοντος   vbl., pres. act. ptc. gen. sg. masc. {6.A.1}. . . . . id.

τρεχόντων   vbl., pres. act. ptc. gen. pl. masc. {6.A.1}. . . . . id.

τρέχουσιν   verb, pres. act. indic. 3 pers. pl. {5.A.1.a} . . . . id.

G5143 τρέχω   (1) *I run;* sometimes with acc. of the course, Heb 12:1; (2) met., e.g., Gal 2:2.

τρέχω   verb, pres. act. indic. 1 pers. sg. {5.A.1.a} . . . . .τρέχω G5143

τρέχω   verb, pres. act. subjunc. 1 pers. sg. {5.B.1} id.

τρέχωμεν   verb, pres. act. subjunc. 1 pers. pl. {5.B.1} . . . . id.

G5169†‡ τρῆμα, -ατος, τό   *an opening, a hole* (perhaps a favorite term of medical writers); τρῆμα ῥαφίδος, *eye of a needle.* Var. for τρύπημα, Matt 19:24; Luke 18:25.

τρήματος   noun, gen. sg. neut. {2.C} . . . . .τρῆμα G5169†‡

τρία   adj., acc. pl. neut. {3.E} . . . . τρεῖς G5140

τρία   adj., nom. pl. neut. {3.E}. . . . . id.

G5144 τριάκοντα   *thirty.*

τριάκοντα   adj. num. . . . . τριάκοντα G5144

G5145 τριακόσιοι, -αι, -α   *three hundred.*

τριακοσίων   adj. num., gen. pl. masc. {3.A} . . . . τριακόσιοι G5145

τριακοσίων   adj. num., gen. pl. neut. {3.A} . . . . id.

G5146 τρίβολος, -ου, ὁ   *a thistle.*

τριβόλους   noun, acc. pl. masc. {2.B}. . . . τρίβολος G5146
τριβόλων   noun, gen. pl. masc. {2.B} . . . . id.

G5147 **τρίβος**, -ου, ἡ   *a path, track.*
τρίβους   noun, acc. pl. fem. {2.B} . . . . τρίβος G5147

G5148 **τριετία**, -ας, ἡ   *a period of three years, three
years.*
τριετίαν   noun, acc. sg. fem. {2.A} . . . . . . τριετία G5148
τρίζει   verb, pres. act. indic. 3 pers. sg.
{5.A.1.a} . . . . .τρίζω G5149

G5149 **τρίζω**   *I grind, crunch.*
τρίμηνον   adj., acc. sg. neut. {3.C} . . . . .τρίμηνος G5150

G5150 **τρίμηνος**, -η, -ον   *lasting three months;* acc.
neut. as adv. *for three months.*

G5151 **τρίς**   adv., *thrice, three times.*
τρίς   adv.. . . . . τρίς G5151
τρισί   adj. num., dat. pl. masc. {3.E} . . . . τρεῖς G5140
τρισίν   adj. num., dat. pl. fem. {3.E} . . . . id.
τρισίν   adj. num., dat. pl. masc. {3.E} . . . . id.

G5152 **τρίστεγον**, -ου, τό   *the third floor* (it is uncertain whether the ground floor was counted or
not in this enumeration; if so, we should have
to translate, *the second floor*).
τριστέγου   noun, gen. sg. neut. {2.B} . . . τρίστεγον G5152
τρισχίλιαι   adj., nom. pl. fem. {3.A}. . .τρισχίλιοι G5153

G5153 **τρισχίλιοι**, -αι, -α   *three thousand.*
τρίτη   adj., nom. sg. fem. {3.A} . . . . τρίτος G5154
τρίτῃ   adj., dat. sg. fem. {3.A} . . . . id.
τρίτην   adj., acc. sg. fem. {3.A} . . . . id.
τρίτης   adj., gen. sg. fem. {3.A} . . . . id.
τρίτον   adj., acc. sg. masc. {3.A} . . . . id.
τρίτον   adj., acc. sg. neut. {3.A}. . . . . id.
τρίτον   adj., nom. sg. neut. {3.A} . . . . id.
τρίτον   adv. {3.F} . . . . id.

G5154 **τρίτος**, -η, -ον   *third;* ἐκ τρίτου, *a third time;*
τῇ τρίτῃ ἡμέρᾳ (according to the ancient
method of counting), *on the third day, two
days after, on the next day but one, on the
day after tomorrow;* acc. neut. τρίτον as adv.
(generally with def. article), (1) *the third time;*
(2) *thirdly, in the third place,* 1 Cor 12:28.
τρίτος   adj., nom. sg. masc. {3.A} . . . . τρίτος G5154
τρίτου   adj., gen. sg. masc. {3.A}. . . . . id.
τρίτου   adj., gen. sg. neut. {3.A} . . . . id.
τρίχα   noun, acc. sg. fem. {2.C}. . . . . θρίξ G2359
τρίχας   noun, acc. pl. fem. {2.C}. . . . . id.
τρίχες   noun, nom. pl. fem. {2.C} . . . . id.

G5155 **τρίχινος**, -η, -ον   *made of hair.*
τρίχινος   adj., nom. sg. masc. {3.A} . . . . . τρίχινος G5155
τριχῶν   noun, gen. pl. fem. {2.C} . . . . .θρίξ G2359
τριῶν   adj. num., gen. pl. fem. {3.E} . . . . τρεῖς G5140
τριῶν   adj. num., gen. pl. masc. {3.E} . . . . id.

G5156 **τρόμος**, -ου, ὁ   *trembling.*
τρόμος   noun, nom. sg. masc. {2.B} . . . . . . τρόμος G5156
τρόμου   noun, gen. sg. masc. {2.B}. . . . . id.
τρόμῳ   noun, dat. sg. masc. {2.B} . . . . id.

G5157 **τροπή**, -ῆς, ἡ   (1) any *change* undergone by any
object; (2) hence, referring to night and day,
or the waxing and waning of the moon, the
solstice, etc.

τροπῆς   noun, gen. sg. fem. {2.A} . . . . τροπή G5157
τρόπον   noun, acc. sg. masc. {2.B} . . . . . . τρόπος G5158

G5158 **τρόπος**, -ου, ὁ   (1) *manner, way;* (2) often
acc. as adv. ὃν τρόπον, *in the way in which,
as* (also with κατά, etc.); (3) *manner of life,*
Heb 13:5.
τρόπος   noun, nom. sg. masc. {2.B} . . . . . τρόπος G5158

G5159 **τροποφορέω**   *I bear (endure) the ways (disposition) of* (var.).
τρόπῳ   noun, dat. sg. masc. {2.B} . . . . τρόπος G5158
τροφάς   noun, acc. pl. fem. {2.A} . . . . τροφή G5160

G5160 **τροφή**, -ῆς, ἡ   *nourishment, food, sustenance.*
τροφή   noun, nom. sg. fem. {2.A}. . . . . τροφή G5160
τροφήν   noun, acc. sg. fem. {2.A} . . . . id.
τροφῆς   noun, gen. sg. fem. {2.A} . . . . id.
Τρόφιμον   noun prop., acc. sg. masc. {2.B;
2.D}. . . . . Τρόφιμος G5161

G5161 **Τρόφιμος**, -ου, ὁ   *Trophimus,* a Christian of
Ephesus in Asia.
Τρόφιμος   noun prop., nom. sg. masc. {2.B;
2.D}. . . . . Τρόφιμος G5161

G5162 **τροφός**, -οῦ, ἡ   *a nurse* (and thus of a mother
who suckles her own children).
τροφός   noun, nom. sg. fem. {2.B} . . . . τροφός G5162

G5163 **τροχιά**, -ᾶς, ἡ   *(a track);* hence, *a road.*
τροχιάς   noun, acc. pl. fem. {2.A}. . . . . . . .τροχιά G5163
τροχόν   noun, acc. sg. masc. {2.B} . . . . τροχός G5164

G5164 **τροχός**, -οῦ, ὁ   *(a wheel);* hence, *the chariot
wheel* of man as he advances on the way of life,
following his appointed course.
τρυβλίον   noun, acc. sg. neut. {2.B} . . . . .τρύβλιον G5165

G5165 **τρύβλιον**, -ου, τό   *a dish.*
τρύβλιον   noun, acc. sg. neut. {2.B} . . . . .τρύβλιον G5165
τρυβλίῳ   noun, dat. sg. neut. {2.B} . . . . id.

G5166 **τρυγάω**   *I gather* (always of *grapes,* τρύξ).
τρύγησον   verb, aor. act. impv. 2 pers. sg.
{5.D.1}. . . . . .τρυγάω G5166
τρυγόνων   noun, gen. pl. fem. {2.C} . . . . . τρυγών G5167

G5167 **τρυγών**, -όνος, ἡ   *a turtledove.*
τρυγῶσι   verb, pres. act. indic. 3 pers. pl.
{5.A.2}. . . . . .τρυγάω G5166
τρυγῶσιν   verb, pres. act. indic. 3 pers. pl.
{5.A.2}. . . . . id.

G5168 **τρυμαλιά**, -ᾶς, ἡ   (1) *an opening, hole;* (2) *an
eye* of needle.
τρυμαλιᾶς   noun, gen. sg. fem. {2.A}. . . τρυμαλιά G5168

G5169 **τρύπημα**, -ατος, τό   (1) *a hole;* (2) *an eye of a
needle.*
τρυπήματος   noun, gen. sg. neut. {2.C} . .τρύπημα G5169

G5170 **Τρύφαινα**, -ης, ἡ   *Tryphaena,* a Christian
woman in Rome.
Τρύφαιναν   noun prop., acc. sg. fem. {2.A;
2.D}. . . . . Τρύφαινα G5170

G5171 **τρυφάω**   *I live a luxurious life.*

G5172 **τρυφή**, -ῆς, ἡ   *luxury.*
τρυφῇ   noun, dat. sg. fem. {2.A} . . . . τρυφή G5172
τρυφήν   noun, acc. sg. fem. {2.A} . . . . id.

G5173 **Τρυφῶσα**, -ης, ἡ   *Tryphosa,* a Christian woman
in Rome, perhaps a sister of Tryphaena.

Τρυφῶσαν   noun prop., acc. sg. fem. {2.A;
  2.D}. . . . . Τρυφῶσα G5173
Τρωάδα   noun prop., acc. sg. fem. {2.C; 2.D}Τρωάς G5174
Τρωάδα   noun prop., acc. sg. fem. {2.C; 2.D} . . . id.
Τρωάδι   noun prop., dat. sg. fem. {2.C; 2.D}. . . . id.
Τρωάδος   noun prop., gen. sg. fem. {2.C; 2.D} . . id.
Τρῳάδος   noun prop., gen. sg. fem. {2.C; 2.D} . . id.
G5174 **Τρῳάς**, -άδος, ἡ   *Troas*, a harbor city of Mysia.
τρώγοντες   vbl., pres. act. ptc. nom. pl. masc.
  {6.A.1}. . . . . τρώγω G5176
Τρωγυλίῳ   noun prop., dat. sg. neut.
  {2.B; 2.D}. . . . . Τρωγύλλιον G5175
G5175 **Τρωγύλλιον**, -ου, τό   *Trogyllium*, a promontory somewhat to the south of Ephesus.
Τρωγυλλίῳ   noun prop., dat. sg. neut. {2.B;
  2.D}. . . . . Τρωγύλλιον G5175
G5176 **τρώγω**   (orig., *I munch, I eat audibly*), *I eat.*
  (This word was displacing ἐσθίω in ordinary
  use.).
τρώγων   vbl., pres. act. ptc. nom. sg. masc.
  {6.A.1}. . . . . τρώγω G5176
τυγχάνοντα   vbl., pres. act. ptc. acc. sg. masc.
  {6.A.1}. . . . . τυγχάνω G5177
τυγχάνοντες   vbl., pres. act. ptc. nom. pl. masc.
  {6.A.1}. . . . . id.
G5177 **τυγχάνω**   (1) with gen., *I obtain*; (2) absol., *I
  chance, happen*; (3) τυχόν, *ordinary, everyday*,
  Acts 19:11; 28:2; (4) εἰ τύχοι (lit. *if it should
  happen*), *it may chance*; (5) old acc. absol.,
  belonging to impers. verbs, τυχόν, *perhaps.*
G5178 **τυμπανίζω**   *I break on the wheel* (from τύμπα-
  νον, "drum" used in worship, then "imple-
  ment of torture").
G5179†‡ **τυπικῶς**   adv., either *by way of example*, or
  typically, prefiguratively. Var. for τύπος, 1 Cor
  10:11.
τυπικῶς   adv. {3.F}. . . . . τυπικῶς G5179†‡
τύποι   noun, nom. pl. masc. {2.B}. . . . . τύπος G5179
τύπον   noun, acc. sg. masc. {2.B} . . . . id.
G5179 **τύπος**, -ου, ὁ   (1) *a figure; a copy, image*; (2) *a
  pattern, model*; (3) *a type*, prefiguring something or somebody (orig., *the mark of a blow*,
  cf. John 20:25; then *a stamp struck by a die*).
τύπος   noun, nom. sg. masc. {2.B} . . . . τύπος G5179
τύπους   noun, acc. pl. masc. {2.B} . . . . id.
τύπτειν   vbl., pres. act. inf. {6.B.1} . . . . τύπτω G5180
τύπτεσθαι   vbl., pres. pass. inf. {6.B.1} . . . . . . id.
τύπτοντες   vbl., pres. act. ptc. nom. pl. masc.
  {6.A.1}. . . . . id.
τύπτοντι   vbl., pres. act. ptc. dat. sg. masc.
  {6.A.1}. . . . . id.
G5180 **τύπτω**   *I strike.*
G5181 **Τύραννος**, -ου, ὁ   *Tyrannus* an inhabitant of
  Ephesus, probably a rhetorician.
Τυράννου   noun prop., gen. sg. masc. {2.B;
  2.D}. . . . . Τύραννος G5181
τυρβάζῃ   verb, pres. pass. indic. 2 pers. sg.
  {5.A.1.d}. . . . . τυρβάζω G5182
G5182 **τυρβάζω**   mid. *trouble oneself*, or pass. *be
  troubled, agitated.*

Τυρίοις   noun prop., dat. pl. masc. {2.B;
  2.D}. . . . . Τύριος G5183
G5183 **Τύριος**, -ου, ὁ   *a Tyrian, an inhabitant of Tyre.*
Τύρον   noun prop., acc. sg. fem. {2.B; 2.D}. . Τύρος G5184
G5184 **Τύρος**, -ου, ἡ   *Tyre*, an ancient city, the capital
  of Phoenicia.
Τύρου   noun prop., gen. sg. fem. {2.B; 2.D} . Τύρος G5184
Τύρῳ   noun prop., dat. sg. fem. {2.B; 2.D}. . . . . id.
τυφλέ   adj., voc. sg. masc. {3.A} . . . . τυφλός G5185
τυφλοί   adj., nom. pl. masc. {3.A}. . . . . id.
τυφλοί   adj., voc. pl. masc. {3.A} . . . . id.
τυφλοῖς   adj., dat. pl. masc. {3.A} . . . . id.
τυφλόν   adj., acc. sg. masc. {3.A} . . . . id.
G5185 **τυφλός**, -ή, -όν   *blind*, either lit. or met.
τυφλός   adj., nom. sg. masc. {3.A} . . . . τυφλός G5185
τυφλοῦ   adj., gen. sg. masc. {3.A} . . . . id.
τυφλούς   adj., acc. pl. masc. {3.A} . . . . id.
G5186 **τυφλόω**   *I blind, make blind*, lit. or met.
τυφλῷ   adj., dat. sg. masc. {3.A} . . . . τυφλός G5185
τυφλῶν   adj., gen. pl. masc. {3.A} . . . . id.
τυφόμενον   vbl., pres. pass. ptc. acc. sg. neut.
  {6.A.1}. . . . . τύφω G5188
G5187 **τυφόω**   pass. (1) *I am puffed up, haughty*; (2) *I
  am blinded, foolish.*
G5188 **τύφω**   pass. intrans., *I smoke.*
τυφωθείς   vbl., aor. pass. ptc. nom. sg. masc.
  {6.A.1.a.}. . . . . τυφόω G5187
G5189 **τυφωνικός**, -ή, -όν   (from τυφώς, *a vehement
  wind*); τυφωνικὸς ἄνεμος, *a heavy eddying
  squall.*
τυφωνικός   adj., nom. sg. masc. {3.A} . τυφωνικός G5189
τυχεῖν   vbl., ²aor. act. inf. {6.B.1}. . . . . . . τυγχάνω G5177
Τυχικόν   noun prop., acc. sg. masc. {2.B;
  2.D}. . . . . Τυχικός G5190
Τύχικον   noun prop., acc. sg. masc. {2.B; 2.D} . . id.
G5190 **Τυχικός** (Τύχικος), -οῦ, ὁ   *Tychicus*, a Christian of the Roman province Asia.
Τυχικός   noun prop., nom. sg. masc. {2.B;
  2.D}. . . . . Τυχικός G5190
Τύχικος   noun prop., nom. sg. masc. {2.B; 2.D} . . id.
Τυχικοῦ   noun prop., gen. sg. masc. {2.B; 2.D} . . id.
τύχοι   verb, ²aor. act. opt. 3 pers. sg.
  {5.C.1}. . . . . τυγχάνω G5177
τυχόν   vbl., ²aor. act. ptc. acc. sg. neut. {6.A.1.a} . id.
τυχοῦσαν   vbl., ²aor. act. ptc. acc. sg. fem.
  {6.A.1.a} . . . . id.
τυχούσας   vbl., ²aor. act. ptc. acc. pl. fem.
  {6.A.1.a} . . . . id.
τυχών   vbl., ²aor. act. ptc. nom. sg. masc.
  {6.A.1.a}. . . . . id.
τύχωσι   verb, ²aor. act. subjunc. 3 pers. pl. {5.B.1}id.
τύχωσιν   verb, ²aor. act. subjunc. 3 pers. pl. {5.B.1}. id.
τῷ   art., dat. sg. masc. {1} . . . . ὁ G3588
τῷ   art., dat. sg. neut. {1}. . . . . id.
τῶν   art., gen. pl. fem. {1} . . . . id.
τῶν   art., gen. pl. masc. {1} . . . . id.
τῶν   art., gen. pl. neut. {1} . . . . id.
τῶν   art., gen. pl. fem. {1} . . . . id.
τῶν   art., gen. pl. masc. {1} . . . . id.
τῶν   art., gen. pl. neut. {1}. . . . . id.

Υ υ

G5191 **ὑακίνθινος**, -η, -ον   *of the color of the marta-*
gon lily, i.e., of a dusky red color.
ὑακινθίνους adj., acc. pl. masc. {3.A} . ὑακίνθινος G5191

G5192 **ὑάκινθος**, -ου, ὁ   *a sapphire* of dusky red color
like the martagon lily.
ὑάκινθος noun, nom. sg. masc. {2.B} . . .ὑάκινθος G5192
ὑαλίνη adj., nom. sg. fem. {3.A} . . . . ὑάλινος G5193
ὑαλίνην adj., acc. sg. fem. {3.A} . . . . id.

G5193 **ὑάλινος**, -η, -ον *glassy, transparent as glass.*

G5194 **ὕαλος**, -ου, ἡ *glass.*
ὕαλος noun, nom. sg. masc. {2.B} . . . . ὕαλος G5194
ὑάλῳ noun, dat. sg. masc. {2.B} . . . . id.
ὕβρεσιν noun, dat. pl. fem. {2.C} . . . . .ὕβρις G5196
ὕβρεως noun, gen. sg. fem. {2.C} . . . . id.
ὑβρίζεις verb, pres. act. indic. 2 pers. sg.
{5.A.1.a} . . . . ὑβρίζω G5195

G5195 **ὑβρίζω** *I treat insolently (outrageously), I*
insult.
ὕβριν noun, acc. sg. fem. {2.C} . . . . .ὕβρις G5196

G5196 **ὕβρις**, -εως, ἡ (1) *wanton insult, outrage,* 2 Cor
12:10; (2) *injury, loss,* due to the sea.
ὑβρίσαι vbl., aor. act. inf. {6.B.1} . . . . ὑβρίζω G5195
ὕβρισαν verb, aor. act. indic. 3 pers. pl.
{5.A.1.b} . . . . id.
ὑβρισθέντες vbl., aor. pass. ptc. nom. pl. masc.
{6.A.1.a} . . . . id.
ὑβρισθήσεται verb, fut. pass. indic. 3 pers. sg.
{5.A.1.d} . . . . id.
ὑβριστάς noun, acc. pl. masc. {2.A} . . . ὑβριστής G5197
ὑβριστήν noun, acc. sg. masc. {2.A} . . . . id.

G5197 **ὑβριστής**, -οῦ, ὁ noun as adj., *insolent, insult-*
ing, outrageous.
ὑγιαίνειν vbl., pres. act. inf. {6.B.1} . . . . .ὑγιαίνω G5198
ὑγιαίνοντα vbl., pres. act. ptc. acc. sg. masc.
{6.A.1} . . . . id.
ὑγιαίνοντας vbl., pres. act. ptc. acc. pl. masc.
{6.A.1} . . . . id.
ὑγιαίνοντες vbl., pres. act. ptc. nom. pl. masc.
{6.A.1} . . . . id.
ὑγιαινόντων vbl., pres. act. ptc. gen. pl. masc.
{6.A.1} . . . . id.
ὑγιαινούσῃ vbl., pres. act. ptc. dat. sg. fem.
{6.A.1} . . . . id.
ὑγιαινούσης vbl., pres. act. ptc. gen. sg. fem.
{6.A.1} . . . . id.
ὑγιαίνουσι vbl., pres. act. ptc. dat. pl. masc.
{6.A.1} . . . . id.
ὑγιαίνουσιν vbl., pres. act. ptc. dat. pl. masc.
{6.A.1} . . . . id.

G5198 **ὑγιαίνω** (1) *I am in* (good) *health, I am*
healthy (well); (2) hence met. in connection with words and teaching, *I am right,*
reasonable.
ὑγιαίνωσιν verb, pres. act. subjunc. 3 pers. pl.
{5.B.1} . . . . .ὑγιαίνω G5198
ὑγιεῖς adj., acc. pl. masc. {3.E} . . . . ὑγιής G5199

ὑγιῆ adj., acc. sg. masc. {3.E} . . . . id.

G5199 **ὑγιής**, -ές, acc. ὑγιῆ (1) *whole, in health,*
sound; (2) *restored to health;* (3) met.
reasonable.
ὑγιής adj., nom. sg. fem. {3.E} . . . . ὑγιής G5199
ὑγιής adj., nom. sg. masc. {3.E} . . . . id.

G5200 **ὑγρός**, -ά, -όν *moist, full of sap.*
ὑγρῷ adj., dat. sg. neut. {3.A} . . . . .ὑγρός G5200
ὕδασιν noun, dat. pl. neut. {2.C} . . . . ὕδωρ G5204
ὕδατα noun, acc. pl. neut. {2.C} . . . . id.
ὕδατα noun, nom. pl. neut. {2.C} . . . . id.
ὕδατι noun, dat. sg. neut. {2.C} . . . . id.
ὕδατος noun, gen. sg. neut. {2.C} . . . . id.
ὑδάτων noun, gen. pl. neut. {2.C} . . . . id.

G5201 **ὑδρία**, -ας, ἡ *a water pot* (hence, of any pot).
ὑδρίαι noun, nom. pl. fem. {2.A} . . . . ὑδρία G5201
ὑδρίαν noun, acc. sg. fem. {2.A} . . . . id.
ὑδρίας noun, acc. pl. fem. {2.A} . . . . id.
ὑδροποτει verb, pres. act. impv. 2 pers. sg.
{5.D.2} . . . . .ὑδροποτέω G5202

G5202 **ὑδροποτέω** *I drink water* (alone, not mixed
with wine).

G5203 **ὑδρωπικός**, -ή, -όν *afflicted with dropsy,*
edema.
ὑδρωπικός adj., nom. sg. masc. {3.A} . ὑδρωπικός G5203

G5204 **ὕδωρ**, ὕδατος, τό *water;* ὕδωρ ζῶν, ζωῆς
(Hebraistic gen.), *flowing water* (as opposed to
stagnant), John 4:10, etc.
ὕδωρ noun, acc. sg. neut. {2.C} . . . . ὕδωρ G5204
ὕδωρ noun, nom. sg. neut. {2.C} . . . . id.
ὕελος noun, nom. sg. masc. {2.B} . . . . ὕαλος G5194
ὑέλῳ noun, dat. sg. masc. {2.B} . . . . id.
ὑετόν noun, acc. sg. masc. {2.B} . . . . .ὑετός G5205

G5205 **ὑετός**, -οῦ, ὁ (1) *a shower of rain;* (2) *rain.*
ὑετός noun, nom. sg. masc. {2.B} . . . . .ὑετός G5205
ὑετούς noun, acc. pl. masc. {2.B} . . . . id.
υἱέ noun, voc. sg. masc. {2.B} . . . . .υἱός G5207

G5206 **υἱοθεσία**, -ας, ἡ *adoption.*
υἱοθεσία noun, nom. sg. fem. {2.A} . . . .υἱοθεσία G5206
υἱοθεσίαν noun, acc. sg. fem. {2.A} . . . . id.
υἱοθεσίας noun, gen. sg. fem. {2.A} . . . . id.
υἱοί noun, nom. pl. masc. {2.B} . . . . .υἱός G5207
υἱοί noun, voc. pl. masc. {2.B} . . . . id.
υἱοῖς noun, dat. pl. masc. {2.B} . . . . id.
υἱόν noun, acc. sg. masc. {2.B} . . . . id.

G5207 **υἱός**, -οῦ, ὁ (1) *a son* in the ordinary sense,
with this difference, that one must keep in
mind the greater solidarity of the family in
ancient times and the greater ease in identifying father and son thence arising; also *a male*
descendant, Matt 1:1, etc.; (2) in special senses:
(a) with a gen. of the Deity, θεοῦ, ὑψίστου,
εὐλογητοῦ ("sons of God" in Job 1:6, etc.,
rendered by ἄγγελοι "angels," are members of
the heavenly court gathered round Yahweh,
and all men could be called "sons of God" as

having been created by Him), rarely of a class of human beings, and in such cases only of those who perfectly perform God's will, those in and through whom His will is made known and who are thus like Him, e.g., Matt 5:9; (b) generally of Jesus, who as *God's Son* in an unique sense, as specially united with Him, is the Messiah, God's representative on earth, by whom His will is perfectly performed, and thus at times as it were identified with Him, Mark 1:11, etc.; (c) ὁ υἱὸς τοῦ ἀνθρώπου (lit. *the Son of the Man,* an Aram. expression, originally equivalent to ὁ ἄνθρωπος, cf. Mark 3:28; Rev 1:13, *the man, the human being,* simply) at some stage become a Messianic title (cf. Dan 7:13 and *Parables of Enoch* for the growth in the use of the expression), used by Jesus Himself, representing the whole human race in the one Man, *the Son of Man,* who has to suffer but will be glorified, Mark 8:29, 31–32; Matt 16:13, 27–28, cf. Luke 9:18, 22–23, etc.; (d) a similar Hebraism with genitives indicating qualities, etc., ἀπειθείας, ἀπωλείας, γεέννης (cf. also διαβόλου), used of persons who so perfectly exemplify these qualities, etc., that they can be spoken of as having a family likeness to them (cf. τέκνον).

υἱός   noun, nom. sg. masc. {2.B} . . . . .υἱός G5207
υἱοῦ   noun, gen. sg. masc. {2.B} . . . . id.
υἱούς   noun, acc. pl. masc. {2.B} . . . . id.
υἱῷ   noun, dat. sg. masc. {2.B} . . . . id.
υἱῶν   noun, gen. pl. masc. {2.B} . . . . id.

G5208   **ὕλη**, -ης, ἡ   *wood, timber, brushwood.*
ὕλην   noun, acc. sg. fem. {2.A} . . . . .ὕλη G5208
ὑμᾶς   pron. pers., 2 pers. acc. pl. {4.A} . . . . .σύ G4771
ὑμεῖς   pron. pers., 2 pers. nom. pl. {4.A}. . . . . . . id.

G5211   Ὑμέναιος, -ου, ὁ   *Hymenaeus,* a backsliding
Christian.
Ὑμέναιος   noun prop., nom. sg. masc. {2.B;
2.D}. .Ὑμέναιος G5211
ὑμετέρα   pron. posses, 2 pers. pl. nom. sg. fem.
{4.H} . . . . .ὑμέτερος G5212
ὑμετέρᾳ   pron. posses, 2 pers. pl. dat. sg. fem.
{4.H} . . . . id.
ὑμετέραν   pron. posses, 2 pers. pl. acc. sg. fem.
{4.H} . . . . id.
ὑμετέρας   pron. posses, 2 pers. pl. gen. sg. fem.
{4.H} . . . . id.
ὑμέτερον   pron. posses, 2 pers. pl. acc. sg.
masc. {4.H} . . . . id.
ὑμέτερον   pron. posses, 2 pers. pl. acc. sg. neut.
{4.H} . . . . id.

G5212   **ὑμέτερος**, -α, -ον   *your.*
ὑμέτερος   pron. posses, 2 pers. pl. nom. sg. masc.
{4.H} .ὑμέτερος G5212
ὑμετέρῳ   pron. posses, 2 pers. pl. dat. sg. masc.
{4.H} . . . . id.
ὑμετέρῳ   pron. posses, 2 pers. pl. dat. sg. neut.
{4.H} . . . . id.

ὑμῖν   pron. pers., 2 pers. dat. pl. {4.A} . . . . .σύ G4771

G5214   **ὑμνέω**   (1) intrans., *I sing a hymn;* (2) trans., *I
praise in a hymn.*
ὑμνήσαντες   vbl., aor. act. ptc. nom. pl. masc.
{6.A.2}. .ὑμνέω G5214
ὑμνήσω   verb, fut. act. indic. 1 pers. sg. {5.A.1} . id.
ὕμνοις   noun, dat. pl. masc. {2.B} . . . . .ὕμνος G5215

G5215   **ὕμνος**, -ου, ὁ   *a hymn,* esp. of praise to God.
ὕμνουν   verb, impf. act. indic. 3 pers. pl.
{5.A.2}. .ὑμνέω G5214
ὑμῶν   pron. pers., 2 pers. gen. pl. {4.A}. . . . . . .σύ G4771
ὑπ᾽   prep. . . . . .ὑπό G5259
ὕπαγε   verb, pres. act. impv. 2 pers. sg.
{5.D.1} . . . . .ὑπάγω G5217
ὑπάγει   verb, pres. act. indic. 3 pers. sg. {5.A.1.a} id.
ὑπάγειν   vbl., pres. act. inf. {6.B.1} . . . . id.
ὑπάγεις   verb, pres. act. indic. 2 pers. sg.
{5.A.1.a} . . . . id.
ὑπάγετε   verb, pres. act. impv. 2 pers. pl. {5.D.1}. id.
ὑπάγῃ   verb, pres. act. subjunc. 3 pers. sg. {5.B.1} id.
ὑπάγητε   verb, pres. act. subjunc. 2 pers. pl.
{5.B.1} . . . . id.
ὑπάγοντας   vbl., pres. act. ptc. acc. pl. masc.
{6.A.1} . . . . id.
ὑπάγοντες   vbl., pres. act. ptc. nom. pl. masc.
{6.A.1} . . . . id.

G5217   **ὑπάγω**   (1) *I go away, withdraw, depart;* (2) *I
depart this life,* Matt 26:24.
ὑπάγω   verb, pres. act. indic. 1 pers. sg.
{5.A.1.a} .ὑπάγω G5217

G5218   **ὑπακοή**, -ῆς, ἡ   *obedience.*
ὑπακοή   noun, nom. sg. fem. {2.A} . . . . .ὑπακοή G5218
ὑπακοῇ   noun, dat. sg. fem. {2.A} . . . . id.
ὑπακοήν   noun, acc. sg. fem. {2.A} . . . . id.
ὑπακοῆς   noun, gen. sg. fem. {2.A} . . . . id.
ὑπακούει   verb, pres. act. indic. 3 pers. sg.
{5.A.1.a} . . . . .ὑπακούω G5219
ὑπακούειν   vbl., pres. act. inf. {6.B.1}. . . . . id.
ὑπακούετε   verb, pres. act. impv. 2 pers. pl.
{5.D.1} . . . . id.
ὑπακούετε   verb, pres. act. indic. 2 pers. pl.
{5.A.1.a} . . . . id.
ὑπακούουσι   vbl., pres. act. ptc. dat. pl. masc.
{6.A.1} . . . . id.
ὑπακούουσιν   vbl., pres. act. ptc. dat. pl. masc.
{6.A.1} . . . . id.
ὑπακούουσιν   verb, pres. act. indic. 3 pers. pl.
{5.A.1.a} . . . . id.
ὑπακοῦσαι   vbl., aor. act. inf. {6.B.1} . . . . id.

G5219   **ὑπακούω**   *I obey;* with inf., Heb 11:8.
G5220   **ὕπανδρος**, -ον   *under the authority of a
husband.*
ὕπανδρος   adj., nom. sg. fem. {3.C} . . . .ὕπανδρος G5220
G5221   **ὑπαντάω**   *I meet.*
ὑπαντῆσαι   vbl., aor. act. inf. {6.B.1} . .ὑπαντάω G5221
ὑπάντησιν   noun, acc. sg. fem. {2.C} . .ὑπάντησις G5222
G5222   **ὑπάντησις**, -εως, ἡ   *a meeting, the act of
meeting.*
ὑπάρξεις   noun, acc. pl. fem. {2.C} . . . . . .ὕπαρξις G5223

ὕπαρξιν   noun, acc. sg. fem. {2.C} . . . . id.

G5223 **ὕπαρξις, -εως, ἡ** *a possession,* generally of *personal property.*

ὑπάρχει   verb, pres. act. indic. 3 pers. sg.
{5.A.1.a} . . . . .ὑπάρχω G5225

ὑπάρχειν   vbl., pres. act. inf. {6.B.1} . . . . id.

ὑπάρχοντα   vbl., pres. act. ptc. acc. pl. neut.
{6.A.1} . . . . id.

ὑπάρχοντα   vbl., pres. act. ptc. acc. sg. masc.
{6.A.1} . . . . id.

ὑπάρχοντα   vbl., pres. act. ptc. nom. pl. neut.
{6.A.1} . . . . id.

G5224 **ὑπάρχοντα, τά** one's *property* or *possessions* (neut. pl. of pres. act. ptc. as subs.).

ὑπάρχοντας   vbl., pres. act. ptc. acc. pl. masc.
{6.A.1} . . . . .ὑπάρχω G5225

ὑπάρχοντες   vbl., pres. act. ptc. nom. pl. masc.
{6.A.1} . . . . id.

ὑπάρχοντος   vbl., pres. act. ptc. gen. sg. masc.
{6.A.1} . . . . id.

ὑπάρχοντος   vbl., pres. act. ptc. gen. sg. neut.
{6.A.1} . . . . id.

ὑπαρχόντων   vbl., pres. act. ptc. gen. pl. neut.
{6.A.1} . . . . id.

ὑπαρχούσης   vbl., pres. act. ptc. gen. sg. fem.
{6.A.1} . . . . id.

ὑπάρχουσι   verb, pres. act. indic. 3 pers. pl.
{5.A.1.a} . . . . id.

ὑπάρχουσιν   verb, pres. act. indic. 3 pers. pl.
{5.A.1.a} . . . . id.

ὑπάρχουσιν   vbl., pres. act. ptc. dat. pl. neut.
{6.A.1} . . . . id.

G5225 **ὑπάρχω** (1) *I am,* denoting originally a state or condition still subsisting in contrast to what is temporary or accidental; (2) τὰ ὑπάρχοντα, *one's belongings, possessions, personal property.*

ὑπάρχων   vbl., pres. act. ptc. nom. sg. masc.
{6.A.1} . . . . .ὑπάρχω G5225

ὑπάρχωσι   verb, pres. act. subjunc. 3 pers. pl.
{5.B.1} . . . . id.

ὑπάρχωσιν   verb, pres. act. subjunc. 3 pers. pl.
{5.B.1} . . . . id.

ὑπέβαλον   verb, ²aor. act. indic. 3 pers. pl.
{5.A.1.b} . . . . ὑποβάλλω G5260

ὑπέδειξα   verb, aor. act. indic. 1 pers. sg.
{5.A.3.b} . . . . .ὑποδείκνυμι G5263

ὑπέδειξεν   verb, aor. act. indic. 3 pers. sg.
{5.A.3.b} . . . . id.

ὑπεδέξατο   verb, aor. mid. indic. 3 pers. sg.
{5.A.1.e} . . . . ὑποδέχομαι G5264

ὑπέθηκαν   verb, aor. act. indic. 3 pers. pl.
{5.A.3.b} . . . . .ὑποτίθημι G5294

ὑπείκετε   verb, pres. act. impv. 2 pers. pl.
{5.D.1} . . . . .ὑπείκω G5226

G5226 **ὑπείκω** *I yield, submit.*

ὑπέλαβεν   verb, ²aor. act. indic. 3 pers. sg.
{5.A.1.b} . . . . ὑπολαμβάνω G5274

ὑπελείφθην   verb, aor. pass. indic. 1 pers. sg.
{5.A.1.b} . . . . ὑπολείπω G5275

ὑπέμειναν   verb, aor. act. indic. 3 pers. pl.
{5.A.1.b} . . . . ὑπομένω G5278

ὑπεμείνατε   verb, aor. act. indic. 2 pers. pl.
{5.A.1.b} . . . . id.

ὑπέμεινε   verb, aor. act. indic. 3 pers. sg.
{5.A.1.b} . . . . id.

ὑπέμεινεν   verb, aor. act. indic. 3 pers. sg.
{5.A.1.b} . . . . id.

ὑπέμενον   verb, impf. act. indic. 3 pers. pl.
{5.A.1.b} . . . . id.

ὑπεμνήσθη   verb, aor. pass. indic. 3 pers. sg.
{5.A.1.b} . . . . ὑπομιμνήσκω G5279

ὑπεναντίον   adj., nom. sg. neut. {3.A} .ὑπεναντίος G5227

G5227 **ὑπεναντίος, -α, -ον** (1) *opposing, hostile;* (2) subs., *adversary,* Heb 10:27.

ὑπεναντίους   adj., acc. pl. masc. {3.A} .ὑπεναντίος G5227

ὑπενεγκεῖν   vbl., ²aor. act. inf. {6.B.1} . . . .ὑποφέρω G5297

ὑπενόουν   verb, impf. act. indic. 1 pers. sg.
{5.A.2} . . . . .ὑπονοέω G5282

ὑπενόουν   verb, impf. act. indic. 3 pers. pl.
{5.A.2} . . . . id.

ὑπεπλεύσαμεν   verb, aor. act. indic. 1 pers. pl.
{5.A.1} . . . . .ὑποπλέω G5284

G5228 **ὑπέρ** (1) prep. with gen., (a) *for, on behalf of, for the sake of* (opp. to κατά, e.g., Mark 9:40), as agent of, Phlm 13; perhaps, *in memory of,* 1 Cor 15:29; (b) colorlessly, *concerning, about, as to,* John 1:30; 2 Cor 8:23; 12:8; Phil 1:7; 4:10; 2 Thess 2:1; (c) perhaps elsewhere of the goal one wants to reach, *with a view to,* 2 Cor 1:6; Phil 2:13; (2) prep. with acc., (a) *over, beyond,* indicating excess; (b) with the comp., *than,* Luke 16:8; John 12:43 (var.); Acts 20:35 (var.); Heb 4:12, and in compound expressions given below; (3) adv., *more* (than they), an ancient use.

ὑπέρ   prep. . . . . ὑπέρ G5228

ὑπεραιρόμενος   vbl., pres. mid./pass. ptc. nom. sg.
masc. {6.A.1} . . . . .ὑπεραίρω G5229

G5229 **ὑπεραίρω** (1) lit. *I raise beyond;* (2) pass. met., *I am exceedingly uplifted.*

ὑπεραίρωμαι   verb, pres. pass. subjunc. 1 pers. sg.
{5.B.1} . . . . .ὑπεραίρω G5229

G5230 **ὑπέρακμος, -ον** of doubtful meaning; probably *of excessive* sexual *vigor* (of the man), rather than *past the bloom of youth* (of the woman).

ὑπέρακμος   adj., nom. sg. fem. {3.C} . ὑπέρακμος G5230

ὑπέρακμος   adj., nom. sg. masc. {3.C} . . . . id.

G5231 **ὑπεράνω** prep. with gen., *far above.*

ὑπεράνω   adv., prep. . . . . .ὑπεράνω G5231

ὑπεραυξάνει   verb, pres. act. indic. 3 pers. sg.
{5.A.1.a} . . . . ὑπεραυξάνω G5232

G5232 **ὑπεραυξάνω** intrans., *I grow exceedingly.*

ὑπερβαίνειν   vbl., pres. act. inf. {6.B.1} ὑπερβαίνω G5233

G5233 **ὑπερβαίνω** intrans., *I transgress.*

ὑπερβάλλον   vbl., pres. act. ptc. acc. sg. neut.
{6.A.1} . . . . .ὑπερβάλλω G5235

ὑπερβάλλον   vbl., pres. act. ptc. nom. sg. neut.
{6.A.1} . . . . id.

ὑπερβάλλοντα   vbl., pres. act. ptc. acc. sg.
  masc. {6.A.1} . . . . id.

G5234 **ὑπερβαλλόντως**   adv., *exceedingly.*
  ὑπερβαλλόντως   adv. {3.F} . . . . ὑπερβαλλόντως G5234
  ὑπερβάλλουσαν   vbl., pres. act. ptc. acc. sg. fem.
  {6.A.1} . . . . ὑπερβάλλω G5235
  ὑπερβαλλούσης   vbl., pres. act. ptc. gen. sg.
  fem. {6.A.1} . . . . id.

G5235 **ὑπερβάλλω**   (1) intrans. with gen., *I exceed,*
  surpass; (2) pres. ptc., absol., *excessive,*
  extraordinary.

G5236 **ὑπερβολή**, -ῆς, ἡ   (1) *excess, abundance;* (2)
  καθ᾽ ὑπερβολήν, *superlatively, exceedingly,*
  beyond measure.
  ὑπερβολή   noun, nom. sg. fem. {2.A} . . . ὑπερβολή G5236
  ὑπερβολῇ   noun, dat. sg. fem. {2.A} . . . . id.
  ὑπερβολήν   noun, acc. sg. fem. {2.A} . . . . id.

G5237 **ὑπερεῖδον**   ²aor. of ὑπεροράω, *I look past,*
  overlook, pretend not to see.

G5238 **ὑπερέκεινα**   adv. *beyond;* τὰ ὑπερέκεινα, *the*
  places beyond.
  ὑπερέκεινα   adv. {3.F} . . . . ὑπερέκεινα G5238

G4053†‡ **ὑπερεκπερισσοῦ**   adv., *most exceedingly,*
  beyond all measure; with gen. of comparison,
  exceedingly more than, Var. for περισσός, Eph
  3:20.
  ὑπερεκπερισσοῦ   adv. {3.F} . . . ὑπερεκπερισσοῦ G4053†‡
  ὑπερεκτείνομεν   verb, pres. act. indic. 1 pers. pl.
  {5.A.1.a} . . . . ὑπερεκτείνω G5239

G5239 **ὑπερεκτείνω**   trans., *I stretch beyond the mea-*
  sure assigned to me.
  ὑπερεκχυννόμενον   vbl., pres. pass. ptc. acc. sg.
  neut. {6.A.1} . . . . ὑπερεκχύννω G5240

G5240 **ὑπερεκχύννω** (ὑπερεκχύνω)   *I pour out so*
  that it overflows.
  ὑπερεκχυνόμενον   vbl., pres. pass. ptc. acc. sg.
  neut. {6.A.1} . . . . ὑπερεκχύννω G5240
  ὑπερεντυγχάνει   verb, pres. act. indic. 3 pers. sg.
  {5.A.1.a} . . . . ὑπερεντυγχάνω G5241

G5241 **ὑπερεντυγχάνω**   *I supplicate on behalf of.*
  ὑπερεπερίσσευσεν   verb, aor. act. indic. 3 pers. sg.
  {5.A.1.b} . . . . ὑπερπερισσεύω G5248
  ὑπερεπλεόνασε   verb, aor. act. indic. 3 pers. sg.
  {5.A.1.b} . . . . ὑπερπλεονάζω G5250
  ὑπερεπλεόνασεν   verb, aor. act. indic. 3 pers.
  sg. {5.A.1.b} . . . . id.
  ὑπερέχον   vbl., pres. act. ptc. acc. sg. neut.
  {6.A.1} . . . . ὑπερέχω G5242
  ὑπερέχοντας   vbl., pres. act. ptc. acc. pl. masc.
  {6.A.1} . . . . id.
  ὑπερέχοντι   vbl., pres. act. ptc. dat. sg. masc.
  {6.A.1} . . . . id.
  ὑπερέχουσα   vbl., pres. act. ptc. nom. sg. fem.
  {6.A.1} . . . . id.
  ὑπερεχούσαις   vbl., pres. act. ptc. dat. pl. fem.
  {6.A.1} . . . . id.

G5242 **ὑπερέχω**   absol. or with gen. or with acc., (1) *I*
  am superior, I am supreme; (2) *I surpass.*

G5243 **ὑπερηφανία**, -ας, ἡ   *haughtiness, arrogance.*

ὑπερηφανία   noun, nom. sg. fem.
  {2.A} . . . . ὑπερηφανία G5243
  ὑπερήφανοι   adj., nom. pl. masc.
  {3.C} . . . . ὑπερήφανος G5244
  ὑπερηφάνοις   adj., dat. pl. masc. {3.C} . . . . id.

G5244 **ὑπερήφανος**, -ον   *haughty, disdainful,*
  arrogant.
  ὑπερηφάνους   adj., acc. pl. masc.
  {3.C} . . . . ὑπερήφανος G5244
  ὑπεριδών   vbl., aor. act. ptc. nom. sg. masc.
  {6.A.2} . . . . ὑπερεῖδον G5237

G3029†‡ **ὑπερλίαν**   adv. used as adj., *exceedingly,*
  extremely (lit. *more than very much*); οἱ
  ὑπερλίαν ἀπόστολοι, in irony, *the super-*
  apostles. Var. for λίαν, 2 Cor 11:5; 12:11.
  ὑπερλίαν   adv. . . . . ὑπερλίαν G3029†‡

G5245 **ὑπερνικάω**   (1) *I score a heavy victory;* (2) *I am*
  more than a conqueror.
  ὑπερνικῶμεν   verb, pres. act. indic. 1 pers. pl.
  {5.A.2} . . . . ὑπερνικάω G5245
  ὑπέρογκα   adj., acc. pl. neut. {3.C} . . . . ὑπέρογκος G5246

G5246 **ὑπέρογκος**, -ον   (lit. *of great* or *excessive bulk*),
  arrogant.

G5247 **ὑπεροχή**, -ῆς, ἡ   (1) *superiority,* 1 Cor 2:1; (2) *a*
  position of superiority, 1 Tim 2:2.
  ὑπεροχῇ   noun, dat. sg. fem. {2.A} . . . . . ὑπεροχή G5247
  ὑπεροχήν   noun, acc. sg. fem. {2.A} . . . . id.
  ὑπερπερισσεύομαι   verb, pres. mid./pass. indic.
  1 pers. sg. {5.A.1.d} . . . . ὑπερπερισσεύω G5248

G5248 **ὑπερπερισσεύω**   (1) intrans., *I abound exceed-*
  ingly; (2) mid. as act. *I overflow.*

G5249 **ὑπερπερισσῶς**   adv., *most exceedingly.*
  ὑπερπερισσῶς   adv. {3.F} . . . . ὑπερπερισσῶς G5249

G5250 **ὑπερπλεονάζω**   *I abound exceedingly, I am*
  exceedingly abundant.

G5251 **ὑπερυψόω**   *I elevate greatly (exceedingly).*
  ὑπερύψωσε   verb, aor. act. indic. 3 pers. sg.
  {5.A.1} . . . . ὑπερυψόω G5251
  ὑπερύψωσεν   verb, aor. act. indic. 3 pers. sg.
  {5.A.1} . . . . id.
  ὑπερφρονεῖν   vbl., pres. act. inf.
  {6.B.2} . . . . ὑπερφρονέω G5252

G5252 **ὑπερφρονέω**   *I have high notions.*

G5253 **ὑπερῷον**, -ου, τό   *an upper room, an upstairs*
  room.
  ὑπερῷον   noun, acc. sg. neut. {2.B} . . . . . ὑπερῷον G5253
  ὑπερῴῳ   noun, dat. sg. neut. {2.B} . . . . id.
  ὑπεστειλάμην   verb, aor. mid. indic. 1 pers. sg.
  {5.A.1.e} . . . . ὑποστέλλω G5288
  ὑπέστελλε   verb, impf. act. indic. 3 pers. sg.
  {5.A.1.b} . . . . id.
  ὑπέστελλεν   verb, impf. act. indic. 3 pers. sg.
  {5.A.1.b} . . . . id.
  ὑπέστρεφον   verb, impf. act. indic. 3 pers. pl.
  {5.A.1.b} . . . . ὑποστρέφω G5290
  ὑπέστρεψα   verb, aor. act. indic. 1 pers. sg.
  {5.A.1.b} . . . . id.
  ὑπέστρεψαν   verb, aor. act. indic. 3 pers. pl.
  {5.A.1.b} . . . . id.

ὑπέστρεψε   verb, aor. act. indic. 3 pers. sg.
{5.A.1.b} . . . . id.
ὑπέστρεψεν   verb, aor. act. indic. 3 pers. sg.
{5.A.1.b} . . . . id.
ὑπεστρώννυον   verb, impf. act. indic. 3 pers. pl.
{5.A.1.b} . . . . ὑποστρωννύω G5291
ὑπετάγη   verb, ²aor. pass. indic. 3 pers. sg.
{5.A.1.e} . . . . ὑποτάσσω G5293
ὑπετάγησαν   verb, ²aor. pass. indic. 3 pers. pl.
{5.A.1.e} . . . . id.
ὑπέταξας   verb, aor. act. indic. 2 pers. sg.
{5.A.1.b} . . . . id.
ὑπέταξε   verb, aor. act. indic. 3 pers. sg. {5.A.1.b}id.
ὑπέταξεν   verb, aor. act. indic. 3 pers. sg.
{5.A.1.b} . . . . id.
ὑπέχουσαι   vbl., pres. act. ptc. nom. pl. fem.
{6.A.1} . . . . ὑπέχω G5254
G5254 **ὑπέχω**   I undergo.
ὑπεχώρησε   verb, aor. act. indic. 3 pers. sg.
{5.A.1} . . . . ὑποχωρέω G5298
ὑπεχώρησεν   verb, aor. act. indic. 3 pers. sg.
{5.A.1} . . . . id.
ὑπῆγον   verb, impf. act. indic. 3 pers. pl.
{5.A.1.b} . . . . ὑπάγω G5217
ὑπήκοοι   adj., nom. pl. masc. {3.C} . . . . ὑπήκοος G5255
G5255 **ὑπήκοος**, -ον   obedient.
ὑπήκοος   adj., nom. sg. masc. {3.C} . . . . ὑπήκοος G5255
ὑπήκουεν   verb, impf. act. indic. 3 pers. sg.
{5.A.1.b} . . . . ὑπακούω G5219
ὑπήκουον   verb, impf. act. indic. 3 pers. pl.
{5.A.1.b} . . . . id.
ὑπήκουσαν   verb, aor. act. indic. 3 pers. pl.
{5.A.1.b} . . . . id.
ὑπηκούσατε   verb, aor. act. indic. 2 pers. pl.
{5.A.1.b} . . . . id.
ὑπήκουσε   verb, aor. act. indic. 3 pers. sg.
{5.A.1.b} . . . . id.
ὑπήκουσεν   verb, aor. act. indic. 3 pers. sg.
{5.A.1.b} . . . . id.
ὑπήνεγκα   verb, aor. act. indic. 1 pers. sg.
{5.A.1.b} . . . . ὑποφέρω G5297
ὑπήντησαν   verb, aor. act. indic. 3 pers. pl.
{5.A.1} . . . . ὑπαντάω G5221
ὑπήντησεν   verb, aor. act. indic. 3 pers. sg.
{5.A.1} . . . . id.
ὑπηρέται   noun, nom. pl. masc. {2.A} . . ὑπηρέτης G5257
ὑπηρέταις   noun, dat. pl. masc. {2.A} . . . . id.
ὑπηρέτας   noun, acc. pl. masc. {2.A} . . . . id.
ὑπηρετεῖν   vbl., pres. act. inf. {6.B.2} . . . ὑπηρετέω G5256
G5256 **ὑπηρετέω**   I serve, minister to.
ὑπηρέτῃ   noun, dat. sg. masc. {2.A} . . . . ὑπηρέτης G5257
ὑπηρέτην   noun, acc. sg. masc. {2.A} . . . . id.
G5257 **ὑπηρέτης**, -ου, ὁ   a servant, an attendant.
ὑπηρέτησαν   verb, aor. act. indic. 3 pers. pl.
{5.A.1} . . . . ὑπηρετέω G5256
ὑπηρετήσας   vbl., aor. act. ptc. nom. sg. masc.
{6.A.2} . . . . id.
ὑπηρετῶν   noun, gen. pl. masc. {2.A} . . ὑπηρέτης G5257
ὑπῆρχε   verb, impf. act. indic. 3 pers. sg.
{5.A.1.b} . . . . ὑπάρχω G5225

ὑπῆρχεν   verb, impf. act. indic. 3 pers. sg.
{5.A.1.b} . . . . id.
ὑπῆρχον   verb, impf. act. indic. 3 pers. pl.
{5.A.1.b} . . . . id.
G5258 **ὕπνος**, -ου, ὁ   sleep.
ὕπνου   noun, gen. sg. masc. {2.B} . . . . ὕπνος G5258
ὕπνῳ   noun, dat. sg. masc. {2.B} . . . . id.
G5259 **ὑπό**   prep. (1) with gen., by, esp. of a person
as the original author (contrast διά), with a
verb pass. or quasi-pass. (cf. Rev 6:8); (2) with
acc., (a) both lit. and met., under, after a verb
of motion, and so answering the question
"to what place?" (b) both lit. and met., after
a verb of rest, and so answering the question
"where?" (c) of time, about, Acts 5:21.
ὑπό   prep. . . . . ὑπό G5259
G5260 **ὑποβάλλω**   I suborn.
ὑπογραμμόν   noun, acc. sg. masc.
{2.B} . . . . ὑπογραμμός G5261
G5261 **ὑπογραμμός**, -οῦ, ὁ   (properly a piece of cal-
ligraphy, a copy, for children to imitate, hence)
a model, a type to be followed.
ὑποδέδεκται   verb, perf. mid./pass. indic. 3 pers.
sg. {5.A.1.f} . . . . ὑποδέχομαι G5264
ὑποδεδεμένους   vbl., perf. mid./pass. ptc. acc. pl.
masc. {6.A.2} . . . . ὑποδέω G5265
G5262 **ὑπόδειγμα**, -ατος, τό   (1) a sign, image of
something, Heb 8:5; 9:23; (2) an example,
given for imitation.
ὑπόδειγμα   noun, acc. sg. neut. {2.C} . . ὑπόδειγμα G5262
ὑποδείγματα   noun, acc. pl. neut. {2.C} . . . . . . id.
ὑποδείγματι   noun, dat. sg. neut. {2.C} . . . . . . id.
G5263 **ὑποδείκνυμι**   (1) I point out, show; (2) hence, I
advise, warn, Matt 3:7; Luke 3:7.
ὑποδείξω   verb, fut. act. indic. 1 pers. sg.
{5.A.1} . . . . ὑποδείκνυμι G5263
ὑποδεξαμένη   vbl., aor. mid. ptc. nom. sg. fem.
{6.A.1.b} . . . . ὑποδέχομαι G5264
G5264 **ὑποδέχομαι**   I receive under my roof, I welcome
to my house, I entertain hospitably.
G5265 **ὑποδέω**   (lit. I bind under), mid. I put on (my
feet).
G5266 **ὑπόδημα**, -ατος, τό   a shoe (cf. ὑποδέω).
ὑπόδημα   noun, acc. sg. neut. {2.C} . . . . ὑπόδημα G5266
ὑποδήματα   noun, acc. pl. neut. {2.C} . . . . id.
ὑποδήματος   noun, gen. sg. neut. {2.C} . . . . . . id.
ὑποδημάτων   noun, gen. pl. neut. {2.C} . . . . . . id.
ὑπόδησαι   verb, aor. mid. impv. 2 pers. sg.
{5.D.1} . . . . ὑποδέω G5265
ὑποδησάμενοι   vbl., aor. mid. ptc. nom. pl.
masc. {6.A.2} . . . . id.
G5267 **ὑπόδικος**, -ον   (a forensic word), liable to
(brought under) the judgment of, answerable to.
ὑπόδικος   adj., nom. sg. masc. {3.C} . . . . ὑπόδικος G5267
ὑποδραμόντες   vbl., ²aor. act. ptc. nom. pl. masc.
{6.A.1.a} . . . . ὑποτρέχω G5295
G5268 **ὑποζύγιον**, -ου, τό   a beast of burden, either a
donkey or a mule.
ὑποζύγιον   noun, nom. sg. neut. {2.B} . ὑποζύγιον G5268
ὑποζυγίου   noun, gen. sg. neut. {2.B} . . . . id.

G5269 **ὑποζώννυμι**   *I undergird, frap,* i.e., I fasten cables
vertically round the hull of the ship to prevent
the timbers from straining or giving way.
ὑποζωννύντες   vbl., pres. act. ptc. nom. pl. masc.
{6.A.3} . . . . .ὑποζώννυμι G5269

G5270 **ὑποκάτω**   prep. with gen., *underneath.*
ὑποκάτω   adv., prep. . . . . .ὑποκάτω G5270

G5271 **ὑποκρίνομαι**   *I act the part, pretend.*
ὑποκρινομένους   vbl., pres. mid./pass. ptc. acc. pl.
masc. {6.A.1} . . . . ὑποκρίνομαι G5271
ὑποκρίσει   noun, dat. sg. fem. {2.C} . . . .ὑπόκρισις G5272
ὑποκρίσεις   noun, acc. pl. fem. {2.C} . . . . id.
ὑποκρίσεως   noun, gen. sg. fem. {2.C} . . . . id.
ὑπόκρισιν   noun, acc. sg. fem. {2.C} . . . . id.

G5272 **ὑπόκρισις**, -εως, ἡ   (*acting a part,* properly),
hypocrisy, pose.
ὑπόκρισις   noun, nom. sg. fem. {2.C} . . .ὑπόκρισις G5272
ὑποκριτά   noun, voc. sg. masc. {2.A} . . .ὑποκριτής G5273
ὑποκριταί   noun, nom. pl. masc. {2.A} . . . . id.
ὑποκριταί   noun, voc. pl. masc. {2.A} . . . . id.

G5273 **ὑποκριτής**, -οῦ, ὁ   (properly *an actor*), *a*
hypocrite, one who outwardly plays the part of
a religious man to perfection, but is inwardly
alien to the spirit of true religion.
ὑποκριτῶν   noun, gen. pl. masc. {2.A} . .ὑποκριτής G5273
ὑπολαβών   vbl., ²aor. act. ptc. nom. sg. masc.
{6.A.1.a} . . . . .ὑπολαμβάνω G5274
ὑπολαμβάνειν   vbl., pres. act. inf. {6.B.1} . . . . . id.
ὑπολαμβάνετε   verb, pres. act. indic. 2 pers. pl.
{5.A.1.a} . . . . id.

G5274 **ὑπολαμβάνω**   (1) *I receive from beneath, I take*
up, Acts 1:9; (2) *I welcome, entertain,* 3 John
8; (3) *I catch up* in speech, by answering or
contradicting or supplementing, Luke 10:30;
(4) *I suppose, imagine.*
ὑπολαμβάνω   verb, pres. act. indic. 1 pers. sg.
{5.A.1.a} . . . . .ὑπολαμβάνω G5274

G2640†‡ **ὑπόλειμμα**, -ατος, τό   a remnant. Var. for
κατάλειμμα.
ὑπόλειμμα   noun, nom. sg. neut. {2.C}. ὑπόλειμμα G2640†‡

G5275 **ὑπολείπω**   *I leave behind.*

G5276 **ὑπολήνιον**, -ου, τό   *a winepress,* probably the
lower (ὑπο-) trough, smaller but deeper than
the ληνός proper, both being cut out of the
solid rock.
ὑπολήνιον   noun, acc. sg. neut. {2.B} . . ὑπολήνιον G5276
ὑπόλιμμα   noun, nom. sg. neut. {2.C} ὑπόλειμμα G2640†‡

G5277 **ὑπολιμπάνω**   Ionic form of ὑπολείπω.
ὑπολιμπάνων   vbl., pres. act. ptc. nom. sg. masc.
{6.A.1} .ὑπολιμπάνω G5277
ὑπομείναντας   vbl., aor. act. ptc. acc. pl. masc.
{6.A.1.a} .ὑπομένω G5278
ὑπομείνας   vbl., aor. act. ptc. nom. sg. masc.
{6.A.1.a} . . . . id.
ὑπομεμενηκότα   vbl., perf. act. ptc. acc. sg.
masc. {6.A.1.a} . . . . id.
ὑπομένει   verb, pres. act. indic. 3 pers. sg. {5.A.1.a} . id.
ὑπομενεῖτε   verb, fut. act. indic. 2 pers. pl. {5.A.2} . id.
ὑπομένετε   verb, pres. act. indic. 2 pers. pl.
{5.A.1.a} . . . . id.

ὑπομένομεν   verb, pres. act. indic. 1 pers. pl.
{5.A.1.a} . . . . id.
ὑπομένοντας   vbl., pres. act. ptc. acc. pl. masc.
{6.A.1} . . . . id.
ὑπομένοντες   vbl., pres. act. ptc. nom. pl.
masc. {6.A.1} . . . . id.

G5278 **ὑπομένω**   (1) *I remain behind,* Luke 2:43; Acts
17:14; (2) absol., *I stand my ground, I show*
endurance, Matt 10:22, etc.; with τῇ θλίψει,
Rom 12:12, *in persecution, amid persecution,*
with εἰς = ἐν, Heb 12:7; (3) trans., *I endure,*
bear up against.
ὑπομένω   verb, pres. act. indic. 1 pers. sg.
{5.A.1.a} .ὑπομένω G5278
ὑπομίμνησκε   verb, pres. act. impv. 2 pers. sg.
{5.D.1} . . . . ὑπομιμνήσκω G5279
ὑπομίμνησκε   verb, pres. act. impv. 2 pers. sg.
{5.D.1} . . . . id.
ὑπομιμνήσκειν   vbl., pres. act. inf. {6.B.1} . . . . id.
ὑπομιμνήσκειν   vbl., pres. act. inf. {6.B.1} . . . . id.

G5279 **ὑπομιμνήσκω**   (1) *I remind;* (2) pass. practically *I remember,* Luke 22:61.
ὑπομνῆσαι   vbl., aor. act. inf.
{6.B.1} . . . . ὑπομιμνήσκω G5279
ὑπομνήσει   noun, dat. sg. fem. {2.C} . . ὑπόμνησις G5280
ὑπομνήσει   verb, fut. act. indic. 3 pers. sg.
{5.A.1.a} . . . . ὑπομιμνήσκω G5279
ὑπόμνησιν   noun, acc. sg. fem. {2.C} . . ὑπόμνησις G5280

G5280 **ὑπόμνησις**, -εως, ἡ   *remembrance, recollection.*
ὑπομνήσω   verb, fut. act. indic. 1 pers. sg.
{5.A.1.a} . . . . ὑπομιμνήσκω G5279

G5281 **ὑπομονή**, -ῆς, ἡ   *steadfast endurance,* the
virtue shown by martyrs.
ὑπομονή   noun, nom. sg. fem. {2.A} . . . .ὑπομονή G5281
ὑπομονῇ   noun, dat. sg. fem. {2.A} . . . . id.
ὑπομονήν   noun, acc. sg. fem. {2.A} . . . . id.
ὑπομονῆς   noun, gen. sg. fem. {2.A} . . . . id.
ὑπονοεῖτε   verb, pres. act. indic. 2 pers. pl.
{5.A.2} . . . . .ὑπονοέω G5282

G5282 **ὑπονοέω**   *I suppose.*

G5283 **ὑπόνοια**, -ας, ἡ   *a supposition, suspicion.*
ὑπόνοιαι   noun, nom. pl. fem. {2.A} . . . .ὑπόνοια G5283
ὑποπιάζῃ   verb, pres. act. subjunc. 3 pers. sg.
{5.B.1} . . . . .ὑπωπιάζω G5299
ὑποπιάζω   verb, pres. act. indic. 1 pers. sg.
{5.A.1} . . . . id.

G5284 **ὑποπλέω**   *I sail under the lee of (close to).*
ὑποπνεύσαντος   vbl., aor. act. ptc. gen. sg. masc.
{6.A.2} . . . . .ὑποπνέω G5285

G5285 **ὑποπνέω**   *I blow moderately (gently).*

G5286 **ὑποπόδιον**, -ου, τό   *a footstool* (of the con-
quering king placing his foot on the neck of
the conquered).
ὑποπόδιον   noun, acc. sg. neut. {2.B} . . ὑποπόδιον G5286
ὑποπόδιον   noun, nom. sg. neut. {2.B} . . . . id.
ὑποστάσει   noun, dat. sg. fem. {2.C} . . ὑπόστασις G5287
ὑποστάσεως   noun, gen. sg. fem. {2.C} . . . . . . id.

G5287 **ὑπόστασις**, -εως, ἡ   (lit. *an underlying*), (1)
confidence, assurance; (2) *a giving substance*
(or *reality*) *to,* or *a guaranteeing,* Heb 11:1

(where possibly *title deed* is the sense); (3)
substance, reality, Heb 1:3.
ὑπόστασις   noun, nom. sg. fem. {2.C}. ὑπόστασις G5287
ὑποστείληται   verb, aor. mid. subjunc. 3 pers. sg.
 {5.B.1} . . . . .ὑποστέλλω G5288
G5288 **ὑποστέλλω**   (1) act. trans., *I withdraw,* Gal
 2:12; (2) mid. trans., *I keep back,* Acts 20:20;
 (3) intrans., *I withdraw,* Heb 10:38; (4) with
 inf. and answering negative, *I shrink from, I
 shun,* Acts 20:27.
G5289 **ὑποστολή,** -ῆς, ἡ   (1) *withdrawal;* (2) *shrinking.*
ὑποστολῆς   noun, gen. sg. fem. {2.A} . . ὑποστολή G5289
ὑπόστρεφε   verb, pres. act. impv. 2 pers. sg.
 {5.D.1} . . . . .ὑποστρέφω G5290
ὑποστρέφειν   vbl., pres. act. inf. {6.B.1} . . . . . . id.
ὑποστρέφοντι   vbl., pres. act. ptc. dat. sg.
 masc. {6.A.1} . . . . id.
G5290 **ὑποστρέφω**   (1) intrans., *I return;* (2) met., *I
 withdraw,* 2 Pet 2:21.
ὑποστρέφων   vbl., pres. act. ptc. nom. sg. masc.
 {6.A.1} . . . . .ὑποστρέφω G5290
ὑποστρέψαι   vbl., aor. act. inf. {6.B.1} . . . . id.
ὑποστρέψαντες   vbl., aor. act. ptc. nom. pl.
 masc. {6.A.1.a} . . . . id.
ὑποστρέψαντι   vbl., aor. act. ptc. dat. sg. masc.
 {6.A.1.a} . . . . id.
ὑποστρέψας   vbl., aor. act. ptc. nom. sg. masc.
 {6.A.1.a} . . . . id.
ὑποστρέψασαι   vbl., aor. act. ptc. nom. pl.
 fem. {6.A.1.a} . . . . id.
ὑποστρέψω   verb, fut. act. indic. 1 pers. sg.
 {5.A.1.a} . . . . id.
G5291 **ὑποστρωννύω** (ὑποστρώννυμι)   trans., *I
 spread underneath.*
ὑποταγέντων   vbl., ²aor. pass. ptc. gen. pl. masc.
 {6.A.1.a} . . . . ὑποτάσσω G5293
G5292 **ὑποταγή,** -ῆς, ἡ   *subordination, subjection,
 submission.*
ὑποταγῇ   noun, dat. sg. fem. {2.A} . . . . . ὑποταγή G5292
ὑποταγῇ   verb, ²aor. pass. subjunc. 3 pers. sg.
 {5.B.1} . . . . ὑποτάσσω G5293
ὑποταγήσεται   verb, ²fut. pass. indic. 3 pers.
 sg. {5.A.1.d} . . . . id.
ὑποταγησόμεθα   verb, ²fut. pass. indic. 1 pers.
 pl. {5.A.1.d} . . . . id.
ὑποτάγητε   verb, ²aor. pass. impv. 2 pers. pl. {5.D.1} id.
ὑποτάξαι   vbl., aor. act. inf. {6.B.1} . . . . id.
ὑποτάξαντα   vbl., aor. act. ptc. acc. sg. masc.
 {6.A.1.a} . . . . id.
ὑποτάξαντι   vbl., aor. act. ptc. dat. sg. masc.
 {6.A.1.a} . . . . id.
ὑποτάξαντος   vbl., aor. act. ptc. gen. sg. masc.
 {6.A.1.a} . . . . id.
ὑποτάσσεσθαι   vbl., pres. mid./pass. inf. {6.B.1} id.
ὑποτάσσεσθε   verb, pres. mid./pass. impv.
 2 pers. pl. {5.D.1} . . . . id.
ὑποτασσέσθω   verb, pres. mid./pass. impv.
 3 pers. sg. {5.D.1} . . . . id.
ὑποτασσέσθωσαν   verb, pres. pass. impv.
 3 pers. pl. {5.D.1} . . . . id.

ὑποτάσσεται   verb, pres. pass. indic. 3 pers. sg.
 {5.A.1.d} . . . . id.
ὑποτάσσησθε   verb, pres. pass. subjunc.
 2 pers. pl. {5.B.1} . . . . id.
ὑποτασσόμεναι   vbl., pres. pass. ptc. nom. pl.
 fem. {6.A.1} . . . . id.
ὑποτασσομένας   vbl., pres. pass. ptc. acc. pl.
 fem. {6.A.1} . . . . id.
ὑποτασσόμενοι   vbl., pres. pass. ptc. nom. pl.
 masc. {6.A.1} . . . . id.
ὑποτασσόμενος   vbl., pres. pass. ptc. nom. sg.
 masc. {6.A.1} . . . . id.
G5293 **ὑποτάσσω**   (1) *I subject, I put into subjection*
 (lit. *I put in a lower rank, I rank under,* a military term); (2) mid. and pass., *I subordinate
 myself, I put myself into subjection, I submit.*
ὑποτεταγμένα   vbl., perf. pass. ptc. acc. pl. neut.
 {6.A.1.b} . . . . ὑποτάσσω G5293
ὑποτέτακται   verb, perf. pass. indic. 3 pers. sg.
 {5.A.1.f} . . . . id.
ὑποτιθέμενος   vbl., pres. mid. ptc. nom. sg. masc.
 {6.A.3} . . . . ὑποτίθημι G5294
G5294 **ὑποτίθημι**   (1) *I place (put) under* some danger,
 I expose; (2) mid. *I suggest, advise.*
G5295 **ὑποτρέχω**   *I run before a wind under the lee of.*
ὑποτύπωσιν   noun, acc. sg. fem. {2.C}ὑποτύπωσις G5296
G5296 **ὑποτύπωσις,** -εως, ἡ   *a figurative representation,* serving as *an example.*
ὑποφέρει   verb, pres. act. indic. 3 pers. sg.
 {5.A.1.a} . . . . ὑποφέρω G5297
G5297 **ὑποφέρω**   *I endure, suffer.*
G5298 **ὑποχωρέω**   *I withdraw.*
ὑποχωρῶν   vbl., pres. act. ptc. nom. sg. masc.
 {6.A.2} . . . . ὑποχωρέω G5298
ὑπωπιάζῃ   verb, pres. act. subjunc. 3 pers. sg.
 {5.B.1} . . . . .ὑπωπιάζω G5299
G5299 **ὑπωπιάζω**   (1) *I strike under the eye, bruise*
 (from ὑπώπιον, which is from ὑπό and ὤψ,
 "that part of the face under the eyes"); (2)
 hence, *I treat severely,* 1 Cor 9:27, *I molest,
 annoy, harass, worry, exhaust,* Luke 18:5.
ὑπωπιάζω   verb, pres. act. indic. 1 pers. sg.
 {5.A.1.a} . . . . .ὑπωπιάζω G5299
G5300 **ὗς,** ὑός, ἡ   *a sow.*
ὗς   noun, nom. sg. fem. {2.C} . . . . ὗς G5300
G5301 **ὕσσωπος,** -ου, ὁ, ἡ, and τό   *hyssop.* In John 19:29
 ὑσσώπῳ is a graphic error for ὑσσῷ, *pike.*
ὑσσώπου   noun, gen. sg. fem. {2.B} . . . . .ὕσσωπος G5301
ὑσσώπου   noun, gen. sg. masc. {2.B} . . . . id.
ὑσσώπῳ   noun, dat. sg. fem. {2.B} . . . . id.
ὑσσώπῳ   noun, dat. sg. masc. {2.B} . . . . id.
ὑστερεῖ   verb, pres. act. indic. 3 pers. sg.
 {5.A.2} . . . . ὑστερέω G5302
ὑστερεῖσθαι   vbl., pres. pass. inf. {6.B.2} . . . . . . id.
G5302 **ὑστερέω**   (1) act. intrans., (a) *I come late, I am
 late,* Heb 4:1; (b) *I am left behind in the race
 for, I have no part in,* with ἀπό and the gen.
 of the end, Heb 12:15; (c) *I fall short, I am
 inferior,* Matt 19:20; 1 Cor 12:24 (var.); 2 Cor
 11:5; 12:11; (d) *I am wanting (to),* Mark 10:21

(var.); John 2:3; (e) *I am without,* with gen.,
Luke 22:35; (2) pass., (a) *I suffer from want,*
absol., or with gen., or with ἐν and dat.; (b) *I
am worse off* (for honor), 1 Cor 8:8.
ὑστερηθείς vbl., aor. pass. ptc. nom. sg. masc.
{6.A.1.a.} . . . . ὑστερέω G5302
ὑστερήθητε verb, aor. pass. indic. 2 pers. pl.
{5.A.1.b} . . . . id.
ὑστερηκέναι vbl., perf. act. inf. {6.B.1} . . . . . . id.
G5303 **ὑστέρημα**, -ατος, τό (1) *that which is lacking,*
of things or persons; (2) *want, poverty,* Luke
21:4; 2 Cor 8:14; 9:12; 11:9.
ὑστέρημα noun, acc. sg. neut. {2.C} . . . ὑστέρημα G5303
ὑστερήματα noun, acc. pl. neut. {2.C} . . . . id.
ὑστερήματος noun, gen. sg. neut. {2.C} . . . . . . id.
ὑστέρησα verb, aor. act. indic. 1 pers. sg.
{5.A.1} . . . . ὑστερέω G5302
ὑστερήσαντος vbl., aor. act. ptc. gen. sg.
masc. {6.A.2} . . . . id.
ὑστερήσατε verb, aor. act. indic. 2 pers. pl. {5.A.1} id.
ὑστερήσεως noun, gen. sg. fem. {2.C} . . ὑστέρησις G5304
ὑστέρησιν noun, acc. sg. fem. {2.C} . . . . id.
G5304 **ὑστέρησις**, -εως, ἡ *poverty, want.*
ὑστέροις adj. comp., dat. pl. masc. {3.A;
3.G} . . . . ὕστερος G5306
ὕστερον adv. comp. {3.F; 3.G} . . . . id.
G5306 **ὕστερος**, -α, -ον (1) comp., *latter;* (2) neut.
sg. as adv., (a) comp., *later, afterwards, in the
second place;* (b) superl., *last, latest, finally;*
ὕστερον πάντων, *last of all.*
ὕστερος adj. comp., nom. sg. masc. {3.A;
3.G} . . . . ὕστερος G5306
ὑστερούμεθα verb, pres. pass. indic. 1 pers. pl.
{5.A.2} . . . . ὑστερέω G5302
ὑστερούμενοι vbl., pres. pass. ptc. nom. pl.
masc. {6.A.2} . . . . id.
ὑστερουμένῳ vbl., pres. pass. ptc. dat. sg.
neut. {6.A.2} . . . . id.
ὑστεροῦνται verb, pres. pass. indic. 3 pers. pl.
{5.A.2} . . . . id.
ὑστεροῦντι vbl., pres. act. ptc. dat. sg. neut. {6.A.2} id.
ὑστερῶ verb, pres. act. indic. 1 pers. sg. {5.A.2}. id.
ὑστερῶν vbl., pres. act. ptc. nom. sg. masc. {6.A.2} id.
ὑφ’ prep. . . . . ὑπό G5259
G5307 **ὑφαντός**, -ή, -όν *woven.*
ὑφαντός adj., nom. sg. masc. {3.A} . . . . . ὑφαντός G5307
ὕψει noun, dat. sg. neut. {2.C} . . . . ὕψος G5311
ὑψηλά adj., acc. pl. neut. {3.A} . . . . .ὑψηλός G5308
ὑψηλοῖς adj., dat. pl. masc. {3.A} . . . . id.
ὑψηλοῖς adj., dat. pl. neut. {3.A} . . . . id.
ὑψηλόν adj., acc. sg. neut. {3.A} . . . . id.

ὑψηλόν adj., nom. sg. neut. {3.A} . . . . id.
G5308 **ὑψηλός**, -ή, -όν (1) lit. *high, lofty;* (2) met.
μετὰ βραχίονος ὑψηλοῦ (Hebraistic), of
God; (3) with φρονεῖν, of haughtiness, arrogance, boasting.
ὑψηλότερος adj. comp., nom. sg. masc. {3.A;
3.G} . . . . .ὑψηλός G5308
ὑψηλοῦ adj., gen. sg. masc. {3.A} . . . . id.
ὑψηλοφρόνει verb, pres. act. impv. 2 pers. sg.
{5.D.2} . . . . ὑψηλοφρονέω G5309
ὑψηλοφρονεῖν vbl., pres. act. inf. {6.B.2} . . . . . id.
G5309 **ὑψηλοφρονέω** *I am haughty (arrogant).*
ὑψίστοις adj. superl., dat. pl. neut. {3.A} . ὕψιστος G5310
G5310 **ὕψιστος**, -η, -ον *highest,* always as epithet
either of God, or of the region where He lives.
ὕψιστος adj. superl., nom. sg. masc. {3.A} ὕψιστος G5310
ὑψίστου adj. superl., gen. sg. masc. {3.A} . . . . . id.
G5311 **ὕψος**, -ους, τό (1) *height;* (2) *heaven,* Luke
1:78; 24:49; Eph 4:8; (3) met. spiritual *height.*
ὕψος noun, acc. sg. neut. {2.C} . . . . ὕψος G5311
ὕψος noun, nom. sg. neut. {2.C} . . . . id.
ὕψους noun, gen. sg. neut. {2.C} . . . . id.
G5312 **ὑψόω** *I raise to a height, I lift up, I exalt,* usually
met.
ὑψωθείς vbl., aor. pass. ptc. nom. sg. masc.
{6.A.1.a.} . . . . .ὑψόω G5312
ὑψωθεῖσα vbl., aor. pass. ptc. nom. sg. fem.
{6.A.1.a.} . . . . id.
ὑψωθῆναι vbl., aor. pass. inf. {6.B.1} . . . . id.
ὑψωθήσεται verb, fut. pass. indic. 3 pers. sg.
{5.A.1} . . . . id.
ὑψωθήσῃ verb, fut. pass. indic. 2 pers. sg.
{5.A.1} . . . . id.
ὑψωθῆτε verb, aor. pass. subjunc. 2 pers. pl.
{5.B.1} . . . . id.
ὑψωθῶ verb, aor. pass. subjunc. 1 pers. sg.
{5.B.1} . . . . id.
G5313 **ὕψωμα**, -ατος, τό (1) *height,* Rom 8:39; (2)
loftiness, haughtiness, (self-) exaltation, 2 Cor
10:5 (but including concr. as well as abstr.,
whatever is lofty, etc.).
ὕψωμα noun, acc. sg. neut. {2.C} . . . . ὕψωμα G5313
ὕψωμα noun, nom. sg. neut. {2.C} . . . . id.
ὑψῶν vbl., pres. act. ptc. nom. sg. masc.
{6.A.2} . . . . .ὑψόω G5312
ὕψωσε verb, aor. act. indic. 3 pers. sg. {5.A.1} . . id.
ὑψώσει verb, fut. act. indic. 3 pers. sg. {5.A.1} . . id.
ὕψωσεν verb, aor. act. indic. 3 pers. sg. {5.A.1} . id.
ὑψώσῃ verb, aor. act. subjunc. 3 pers. sg. {5.B.1} id.
ὑψώσητε verb, aor. act. subjunc. 2 pers. pl.
{5.B.1} . . . . id.

Φ φ

φάγε verb, ²aor. act. impv. 2 pers. sg. {5.D.1} ἐσθίω G2068
φαγεῖν vbl., ²aor. act. inf. {6.B.1} . . . . id.
φάγεσαι verb, fut. mid. indic. 2 pers. sg.
{5.A.1.d} . . . . id.

φάγεται verb, fut. mid. indic. 3 pers. sg.
{5.A.1.d} . . . . id.
φάγετε verb, ²aor. act. impv. 2 pers. pl. {5.D.1} . . id.
φάγῃ verb, ²aor. act. subjunc. 3 pers. sg. {5.B.1} . id.

φάγῃς   verb, ²aor. act. subjunc. 2 pers. sg. {5.B.1} id.

φάγητε   verb, ²aor. act. subjunc. 2 pers. pl. {5.B.1}id.

φάγοι   verb, ²aor. act. opt. 3 pers. sg. {5.C.1} . . . . id.

φάγονται   verb, fut. mid. indic. 3 pers. pl.
{5.A.1.d} . . . . id.

φαγόντες   vbl., ²aor. act. ptc. nom. pl. masc.
{6.A.1.a} . . . . id.

G5314   **φάγος**, -ου, ὁ   *a glutton, gourmand.*

φάγος   noun, nom. sg. masc. {2.B} . . . . φάγος *G5314*

φάγω   verb, ²aor. act. subjunc. 1 pers. sg.
{5.B.1} . . . . ἐσθίω *G2068*

φάγωμεν   verb, ²aor. act. subjunc. 1 pers. pl.
{5.B.1} . . . . id.

φάγωσι   verb, ²aor. act. subjunc. 3 pers. pl.
{5.B.1} . . . . id.

φάγωσιν   verb, ²aor. act. subjunc. 3 pers. pl.
{5.B.1} . . . . id.

φαιλόνην   noun, acc. sg. masc. {2.A} . . . . φελόνης *G5341*

φαίνει   verb, pres. act. indic. 3 pers. sg.
{5.A.1.a} . . . . φαίνω *G5316*

φαίνεσθε   verb, pres. mid./pass. indic. 2 pers.
pl. {5.A.1.d} . . . . id.

φαίνεται   verb, pres. mid./pass. indic. 3 pers.
sg. {5.A.1.d} . . . . id.

φαίνῃ   verb, pres. act. subjunc. 3 pers. sg. {5.B.1} id.

φαινομένη   vbl., pres. mid./pass. ptc. nom. sg.
fem. {6.A.1} . . . . id.

φαινομένου   vbl., pres. mid./pass. ptc. gen. sg.
masc. {6.A.1} . . . . id.

φαινομένων   vbl., pres. mid./pass. ptc. gen. pl.
neut. {6.A.1} . . . . id.

φαίνονται   verb, pres. mid./pass. indic. 3 pers.
pl. {5.A.1.d} . . . . id.

φαίνοντι   vbl., pres. mid./pass. ptc. dat. sg.
masc. {6.A.1} . . . . id.

G5316   **φαίνω**   (1) act. *I shine, I shed light;* (2) pass.,
(a) *I shine;* (b) *I become visible, I appear,* cf.
ἐφάνη, impers., Matt 9:33; (c) *I become clear,
appear, show myself* as, Matt 6:5, 16, 18; 23:27;
Rom 7:13; 2 Cor 13:7; 1 Pet 4:18; (d) of the
mind and judgment (= δοκεῖ), Mark 14:64;
Luke 24:11.

φαίνων   vbl., pres. act. ptc. nom. sg. masc.
{6.A.1} . . . . φαίνω *G5316*

φαίνωσιν   verb, pres. act. subjunc. 3 pers. pl.
{5.B.1} . . . . id.

Φάλεγ   noun prop. . . . . Φάλεκ *G5317*

Φαλέκ   noun prop. . . . . id.

G5317   **Φάλεκ** (Φάλεγ), ὁ   *Phalek,* son of Eber, and
one of the ancestors of Jesus (Heb.).

Φάλεκ   noun prop. . . . . Φάλεκ *G5317*

φανεῖται   verb, fut. mid. indic. 3 pers. sg.
{5.A.2} . . . . φαίνω *G5316*

φανερά   adj., nom. pl. neut. {3.A} . . . . . . φανερός *G5318*

φανερά   adj., nom. sg. fem. {3.A} . . . . id.

φανεροί   adj., nom. pl. masc. {3.A} . . . . id.

φανερόν   adj., acc. sg. masc. {3.A} . . . . id.

φανερόν   adj., acc. sg. neut. {3.A} . . . . id.

φανερόν   adj., nom. sg. neut. {3.A} . . . . id.

G5318   **φανερός**, -ά, -όν   (1) *clear, visible* (as opposed
to "hidden," "secret"); (2) εἰς θανερὸν ἐλθεῖν,
*to come into the open, to appear before the
public,* Mark 4:22; Luke 8:17, ἐν τῷ φανερῷ,
in public.

φανερούμενοι   vbl., pres. pass. ptc. nom. pl. masc.
{6.A.2} . . . . φανερόω *G5319*

φανερούμενον   vbl., pres. pass. ptc. nom. sg.
neut. {6.A.2} . . . . id.

φανεροῦντι   vbl., pres. act. ptc. dat. sg. masc.
{6.A.2} . . . . id.

φανερούς   adj., acc. pl. masc. {3.A} . . . . . φανερός *G5318*

φανεροῦται   verb, pres. pass. indic. 3 pers. sg.
{5.A.2} . . . . φανερόω *G5319*

G5319   **φανερόω**   *I make clear (visible, manifest).*

φανερῷ   adj., dat. sg. neut. {3.A} . . . . . . φανερός *G5318*

φανερωθεῖσαν   vbl., aor. pass. ptc. acc. sg. fem.
{6.A.1.a.} . . . . φανερόω *G5319*

φανερωθέντες   vbl., aor. pass. ptc. nom. pl.
masc. {6.A.1.a.} . . . . id.

φανερωθέντος   vbl., aor. pass. ptc. gen. sg.
masc. {6.A.1.a.} . . . . id.

φανερωθῇ   verb, aor. pass. subjunc. 3 pers. sg.
{5.B.1} . . . . id.

φανερωθῆναι   vbl., aor. pass. inf. {6.B.1} . . . . . id.

φανερωθήσεσθε   verb, fut. pass. indic. 2 pers.
pl. {5.A.1} . . . . id.

φανερωθῶσιν   verb, aor. pass. subjunc. 3 pers.
pl. {5.B.1} . . . . id.

G5320   **φανερῶς**   adv., *openly, overtly.*

φανερῶς   adv. {3.F} . . . . φανερῶς *G5320*

φανερώσαντες   vbl., aor. act. ptc. nom. pl. masc.
{6.A.2} . . . . φανερόω *G5319*

φανερώσει   noun, dat. sg. fem. {2.C} . . φανέρωσις *G5321*

φανερώσει   verb, fut. act. indic. 3 pers. sg.
{5.A.1} . . . . φανερόω *G5319*

G5321   **φανέρωσις**, -εως, ἡ   *a showing forth,* with obj.
gen.

φανέρωσις   noun, nom. sg. fem. {2.C} . φανέρωσις *G5321*

φανέρωσον   verb, aor. act. impv. 2 pers. sg.
{5.D.1} . . . . φανερόω *G5319*

φανερώσω   verb, aor. act. subjunc. 1 pers. sg.
{5.B.1} . . . . id.

φάνῃ   verb, ²aor. act. subjunc. 3 pers. sg.
{5.B.1} . . . . φαίνω *G5316*

φάνῃ   verb, ²aor. pass. subjunc. 3 pers. sg. {5.B.1} id.

φανῇ   verb, ²aor. pass. subjunc. 3 pers. sg. {5.B.1} id.

φανῇς   verb, ²aor. pass. subjunc. 2 pers. sg.
{5.B.1} . . . . id.

φανήσεται   verb, ²fut. pass. indic. 3 pers. sg.
{5.A.1.d} . . . . id.

G5322   **φανός**, -οῦ, ὁ   *(a light, a torch);* then, *a lantern.*

G5323   **Φανουήλ**, ὁ   *Phanuel,* father of Anna the
prophetess.

Φανουήλ   noun prop. . . . . Φανουήλ *G5323*

φανταζόμενον   vbl., pres. pass. ptc. nom. sg. neut.
{6.A.1} . . . . φαντάζω *G5324*

G5324   **φαντάζω**   *I make to appear;* τὸ φανταζόμενον, *the appearance.*

G5325   **φαντασία**, -ας, ἡ   *show, display.*

φαντασίας   noun, gen. sg. fem. {2.A} . . . . φαντασία G5325
G5326   **φάντασμα**, -ατος, τό   (1) *an appearance;* (2)
     hence, *a ghost, a spirit.*
     φάντασμα   noun, nom. sg. neut. {2.C}.   φάντασμα G5326
     φανῶμεν   verb, ²aor. pass. subjunc. 1 pers. pl.
       {5.B.1} . . . . φαίνω G5316
     φανῶν   noun, gen. pl. masc. {2.B}. . . . . φανός G5322
     φανῶσι   verb, ²aor. pass. subjunc. 3 pers. pl.
       {5.B.1} . . . . φαίνω G5316
     φανῶσιν   verb, ²aor. pass. subjunc. 3 pers. pl.
       {5.B.1} . . . . id.
G5327   **φάραγξ**, -αγγος, ἡ   *a hollow place, a hollow, a*
     valley.
     φάραγξ   noun, nom. sg. fem. {2.C} . . . . . . φάραγξ G5327
G5328   **Φαραώ**, ὁ   *Pharaoh,* a king of Egypt, properly a
     dynastic title (cf. Decebalus in Dacia, Candace
     in Ethiopia), but, though sometimes preceded
     by the def. article, probably everywhere under
     stood as a proper name.
     Φαραώ   noun prop. . . . . Φαραώ G5328
     Φαρές   noun prop. Φάρες G5329
G5329   **Φάρες**, ὁ   *Phares,* son of Judah and one of the
     ancestors of Jesus (Heb.).
     Φάρες   noun prop. Φάρες G5329
     Φαρισαῖε   noun prop., voc. sg. masc. {2.B;
       2.D} . . . . Φαρισαῖος G5330
     Φαρισαῖοι   noun prop., nom. pl. masc. {2.B;
       2.D} . . . . id.
     Φαρισαῖοι   noun prop., voc. pl. masc. {2.B; 2.D} id.
     Φαρισαίοις   noun prop., dat. pl. masc. {2.B;
       2.D} . . . . id.
G5330   **Φαρισαῖος**, -ου, ὁ   (lit. a Separatist, a Purist),
     a Pharisee, a member of the strict religious
     legalistic party in Judaism after the exile.
     Φαρισαῖος   noun prop., nom. sg. masc. {2.B;
       2.D} . . . . Φαρισαῖος G5330
     Φαρισαίου   noun prop., gen. sg. masc. {2.B;
       2.D} . . . . id.
     Φαρισαίους   noun prop., acc. pl. masc. {2.B;
       2.D} . . . . id.
     Φαρισαίων   noun prop., gen. pl. masc. {2.B; 2.D} . id.
G5331   **φαρμακεία**, -ας, ἡ   (1) *the practice of drugging,*
     drugging; (2) hence, esp., from the use of mys-
     terious liquids, *sorcery, witchcraft,* inextricably
     combined with idolatry.
     φαρμακεία   noun, nom. sg. fem. {2.A}. φαρμακεία G5331
     φαρμακείᾳ   noun, dat. sg. fem. {2.A} . . . . id.
     φαρμακειῶν   noun, gen. pl. fem. {2.A} . . . . id.
G5332   **φαρμακεύς**, -έως, ὁ   *a sorcerer, magician* (cf.
     φάρμακος).
     φαρμακεῦσι   noun, dat. pl. masc. {2.C}φαρμακεύς G5332
     φαρμακία   noun, nom. sg. fem. {2.A} . φαρμακεία G5331
     φαρμακίᾳ   noun, dat. sg. fem. {2.A} . . . . id.
     φαρμακοί   noun, nom. pl. masc. {2.B} . φάρμακος G5333
     φάρμακοι   noun, nom. pl. masc. {2.B} . . . . id.
     φαρμακοῖς   noun, dat. pl. masc. {2.B} . . . . id.
     φαρμάκοις   noun, dat. pl. masc. {2.B} . . . . id.
G5331†‡   **φάρμακον**, -ου, τό   (1) *a drug;* (2) hence, pl.,
     of those used in sorcery, and thus *sorcery.* Var.
     for φαρμακεία G5331 (Rev 9:21).

G5333   **φάρμακος**, -ου, ὁ   *a sorcerer, magician* (cf.
     φαρμακία).
     φαρμάκων   noun, gen. pl. neut. {2.B}   φάρμακον G5331†‡
     φασί   verb, pres. act. indic. 3 pers. pl. {5.A.3.a} φημί G5346
     φασίν   verb, pres. act. indic. 3 pers. pl. {5.A.3.a}. id.
G5334   **φάσις**, -εως, ἡ   *information* (from φαίνω).
     φάσις   noun, nom. sg. fem. {2.C} . . . . φάσις G5334
     φάσκοντας   vbl., pres. act. ptc. acc. pl. masc.
       {6.A.1} . . . . φάσκω G5335
     φάσκοντες   vbl., pres. act. ptc. nom. pl. masc.
       {6.A.1} . . . . id.
G5335   **φάσκω**   *I say,* either *I say frequently,* or *I allege.*
G5336   **φάτνη**, -ης, ἡ   *a manger, a feeding trough.*
     φάτνη   noun, dat. sg. fem. {2.A} . . . . φάτνη G5336
     φάτνης   noun, gen. sg. fem. {2.A}. . . . . id.
     φαῦλα   adj., acc. pl. neut. {3.A} . . . . φαῦλος G5337
     φαῦλον   adj., acc. sg. neut. {3.A} . . . . id.
     φαῦλον   adj., nom. sg. neut. {3.A} . . . . id.
G5337   **φαῦλος**, -η, -ον   *worthless, low, paltry,* implying
     not so much what is evil as the limited and pal-
     try qualities belonging to a low order of things.
G5338   **φέγγος**, -ους, τό   *a light, ray, beam.*
     φέγγος   noun, acc. sg. neut. {2.C} . . . . φέγγος G5338
G5339   **φείδομαι**   *I spare,* I exempt from punishment
     or injury (death).
     φείδομαι   verb, pres. mid./pass. indic. 1 pers. sg.
       {5.A.1.d} . . . . φείδομαι G5339
     φειδόμενοι   vbl., pres. mid./pass. ptc. nom. pl.
       masc. {6.A.1} . . . . id.
     φειδόμενος   vbl., pres. mid./pass. ptc. nom. sg.
       masc. {6.A.1} . . . . id.
G5340   **φειδομένως**   adv., *sparingly.*
     φειδομένως   adv. {3.F} . . . . φειδομένως G5340
     φείσεται   verb, fut. mid. indic. 3 pers. sg.
       {5.A.1.d} . . . . φείδομαι G5339
     φείσηται   verb, aor. mid. subjunc. 3 pers. sg.
       {5.B.1} . . . . id.
     φείσομαι   verb, fut. mid. indic. 1 pers. sg.
       {5.A.1.d} . . . . id.
     φελόνην   noun, acc. sg. masc. {2.A} . . . . . φελόνης G5341
G5341   **φελόνης** (φαιλόνης), -ου, ὁ   *a mantle, cloak;* a
     metathesis from φαινόλης.
     φέρε   verb, pres. act. impv. 2 pers. sg. {5.D.1} . φέρω G5342
     φέρει   verb, pres. act. indic. 3 pers. sg. {5.A.1.a} . id.
     φέρειν   vbl., pres. act. inf. {6.B.1} . . . . id.
     φέρεσθαι   vbl., pres. pass. inf. {6.B.1} . . . . id.
     φέρετε   verb, pres. act. impv. 2 pers. pl. {5.D.1} . id.
     φέρετε   verb, pres. act. indic. 2 pers. pl. {5.A.1.a} id.
     φέρῃ   verb, pres. act. subjunc. 3 pers. sg. {5.B.1} . id.
     φέρητε   verb, pres. act. subjunc. 2 pers. pl.
       {5.B.1} . . . . id.
     φερομένην   vbl., pres. pass. ptc. acc. sg. fem.
       {6.A.1} . . . . id.
     φερομένης   vbl., pres. pass. ptc. gen. sg. fem.
       {6.A.1} . . . . id.
     φερόμενοι   vbl., pres. pass. ptc. nom. pl. masc.
       {6.A.1} . . . . id.
     φέρον   vbl., pres. act. ptc. acc. sg. neut. {6.A.1} . . id.
     φέροντες   vbl., pres. act. ptc. nom. pl. masc.
       {6.A.1} . . . . id.

φέρουσαι   vbl., pres. act. ptc. nom. pl. fem.
    {6.A.1}............................... id.
φέρουσαν   vbl., pres. act. ptc. acc. sg. fem.
    {6.A.1}............................... id.
φέρουσι   verb, pres. act. indic. 3 pers. pl.
    {5.A.1.a} .... id.
φέρουσιν   verb, pres. act. indic. 3 pers. pl.
    {5.A.1.a} .... id.
G5342 **φέρω**   (1) *I carry, bear, bring;* (2) *I conduct, lead,*
    both trans. and intrans.; (3) perhaps, *I make*
    publicly known, Heb 9:16.
φερώμεθα   verb, pres. pass. subjunc. 1 pers. pl.
    {5.B.1}........................... φέρω G5342
φέρων   vbl., pres. act. ptc. nom. sg. masc. {6.A.1} id.
φεῦγε   verb, pres. act. impv. 2 pers. sg.
    {5.D.1}.......................... φεύγω G5343
φεύγει   verb, pres. act. indic. 3 pers. sg. {5.A.1.a} id.
φεύγετε   verb, pres. act. impv. 2 pers. pl. {5.D.1} . id.
φευγέτωσαν   verb, pres. act. impv. 3 pers. pl.
    {5.D.1}.............................. id.
G5343 **φεύγω**   (1) *I flee;* (2) *I escape.*
φεύξεται   verb, fut. mid. indic. 3 pers. sg.
    {5.A.1.d} .... φεύγω G5343
φεύξονται   verb, fut. mid. indic. 3 pers. pl.
    {5.A.1.d} .... id.
Φήλικα   noun prop., acc. sg. masc. {2.C;
    2.D}........................... Φῆλιξ G5344
Φήλικι   noun prop., dat. sg. masc. {2.C; 2.D} . . . id.
Φήλικος   noun prop., gen. sg. masc. {2.C; 2.D} . id.
G5344 **Φῆλιξ**, -ικος, ὁ   *Felix,* third name of (Marcus)
    Antonius Felix, procurator of the Roman
    province Judaea from an uncertain date (be-
    fore 52 A.D.?) till 59 A.D. (Lat.).
Φῆλιξ   noun prop., nom. sg. masc. {2.C; 2.D}Φῆλιξ G5344
Φῆλιξ   noun prop., voc. sg. masc. {2.C; 2.D} . . . id.
G5345 **φήμη**, -ης, ἡ   *a report, a rumor.*
φήμη   noun, nom. sg. fem. {2.A} .... φήμη G5345
φημι   verb, pres. act. indic. 1 pers. sg. {5.A.3.a} φημί G5346
G5346 **φημί**   *I say.*
φημί   verb, pres. act. indic. 1 pers. sg. {5.A.3.a} φημί G5346
φησι   verb, pres. act. indic. 3 pers. sg. {5.A.3.a} . . id.
φησί   verb, pres. act. indic. 3 pers. sg. {5.A.3.a} . id.
φησιν   verb, pres. act. indic. 3 pers. sg. {5.A.3.a}. id.
φησίν   verb, pres. act. indic. 3 pers. sg. {5.A.3.a}. id.
Φῆστε   noun prop., voc. sg. masc. {2.B;
    2.D}......................... Φῆστος G5347
Φῆστον   noun prop., acc. sg. masc. {2.B; 2.D} . . id.
G5347 **Φῆστος**, -ου, ὁ   Porcius *Festus,* procurator of
    the Roman province Judaea from 59 A.D.
    (Lat.).
Φῆστος   noun prop., nom. sg. masc. {2.B;
    2.D}......................... Φῆστος G5347
Φήστου   noun prop., gen. sg. masc. {2.B; 2.D} . . id.
Φήστῳ   noun prop., dat. sg. masc. {2.B; 2.D} . . . id.
G5348 **φθάνω**   (1) *I anticipate, I precede,* 1 Thess 4:15;
    (2) *I come, I arrive.*
φθαρῇ   verb, ²aor. pass. subjunc. 3 pers. sg.
    {5.B.1} .... φθείρω G5351
φθαρήσονται   verb, ²fut. pass. indic. 3 pers. pl.
    {5.A.1.d} .... id.

φθαρτῆς   adj., gen. sg. fem. {3.A} ...... φθαρτός G5349
φθαρτοῖς   adj., dat. pl. neut. {3.A} .... id.
φθαρτόν   adj., acc. sg. masc. {3.A} .... id.
φθαρτόν   adj., acc. sg. neut. {3.A}. .... id.
φθαρτόν   adj., nom. sg. neut. {3.A} .... id.
G5349 **φθαρτός**, -ή, -όν   *perishable.*
φθαρτοῦ   adj., gen. sg. masc. {3.A} ...... φθαρτός G5349
φθάσωμεν   verb, aor. act. subjunc. 1 pers. pl.
    {5.B.1}.........................φθάνω G5348
φθέγγεσθαι   vbl., pres. mid./pass. inf.
    {6.B.1} ....φθέγγομαι G5350
G5350 **φθέγγομαι**   *I utter* (a word), *I open the mouth*
    in speech.
φθεγγόμενοι   vbl., pres. mid. ptc. nom. pl. masc.
    {6.A.1}.......................φθέγγομαι G5350
φθεγξάμενον   vbl., aor. mid. ptc. nom. sg. neut.
    {6.A.1.b} .... id.
φθείρει   verb, pres. act. indic. 3 pers. sg.
    {5.A.1.a} .... φθείρω G5351
φθειρόμενον   vbl., pres. pass. ptc. acc. sg. masc.
    {6.A.1}............................. id.
φθείρονται   verb, pres. pass. indic. 3 pers. pl.
    {5.A.1.d} .... id.
φθείρουσιν   verb, pres. act. indic. 3 pers. pl.
    {5.A.1.a} .... id.
G5351 **φθείρω**   (1) lit., (a) *I destroy, I waste;* (b) *I*
    damage, injure (in being); (2) usually met., (a)
    I corrupt morally, I deprave, injure (in charac-
    ter); (b) *I seduce,* 2 Cor 11:3.
φθερεῖ   verb, fut. act. indic. 3 pers. sg.
    {5.A.2} .... φθείρω G5351
φθινοπωρινά   adj., nom. pl. neut.
    {3.A} .... φθινοπωρινός G5352
G5352 **φθινοπωρινός**, -ή, -όν   *autumnal, in autumn,*
    when fruit is expected (derived from τὸ
    φθινόπωρον, which itself = φθίνουσα
    ὀπώρα, "the concluding portion of the
    ὀπώρα").
φθόγγοις   noun, dat. pl. masc. {2.B} ...... φθόγγος G5353
G5353 **φθόγγος**, -ου, ὁ   (1) *a measured harmoni-*
    ous sound, of voice or instrument; (2) *an*
    utterance.
φθόγγος   noun, nom. sg. masc. {2.B} ......φθόγγος G5353
G5354 **φθονέω**   *I envy.*
φθόνοι   noun, nom. pl. masc. {2.B} ...... φθόνος G5355
φθόνον   noun, acc. sg. masc. {2.B} .... id.
G5355 **φθόνος**, -ου, ὁ   *envy, grudge;* pl. where related
    to various advantages.
φθόνος   noun, nom. sg. masc. {2.B} ...... φθόνος G5355
φθόνου   noun, gen. sg. masc. {2.B}. .... id.
φθονοῦντες   vbl., pres. act. ptc. nom. pl. masc.
    {6.A.2}........................ φθονέω G5354
φθόνους   noun, acc. pl. masc. {2.B} ...... φθόνος G5355
φθόνῳ   noun, dat. sg. masc. {2.B} .... id.
G5356 **φθορά**, -ᾶς, ἡ   *rottenness, perishableness, cor-*
    ruption, decay, decomposition.
φθορά   noun, nom. sg. fem. {2.A}........ φθορά G5356
φθορᾷ   noun, dat. sg. fem. {2.A}. .... id.
φθοράν   noun, acc. sg. fem. {2.A}. .... id.
φθορᾶς   noun, gen. sg. fem. {2.A}. .... id.

φιάλας   noun, acc. pl. fem. {2.A} . . . . φιάλη G5357

G5357 **φιάλη**, -ης, ἡ   (1) strictly *a wine cup,* much like a modern champagne glass in shape; (2) hence, *a cup.*

φιάλην   noun, acc. sg. fem. {2.A} . . . . φιάλη G5357

φιλάγαθον   adj., acc. sg. masc. {3.C} . . φιλάγαθος G5358

G5358 **φιλάγαθος**, -ον   *loving what is good.*

G5360 **φιλαδελφία**, -ας, ἡ   (1) *love of brothers* for each other; (2) hence, *love of the brethren, love of fellow Christians,* all being sons of the same Father in a special sense.

G5359‡ **Φιλαδέλφεια** (Φιλαδελφία), -ας, ἡ   *Philadelphia,* a city of the Roman province Asia.

Φιλαδελφείᾳ   noun prop., dat. sg. fem. {2.A; 2.D} . . . . .Φιλαδέλφεια G5359‡

Φιλαδέλφειαν   noun prop., acc. sg. fem. {2.A; 2.D} . . . . id.

φιλαδελφία   noun, nom. sg. fem. {2.A} . . . . φιλαδελφία G5360

φιλαδελφίᾳ   noun, dat. sg. fem. {2.A} φιλαδελφία G5360

Φιλαδελφίᾳ   noun prop., dat. sg. fem. {2.A; 2.D} . . . . Φιλαδέλφεια G5359‡

φιλαδελφίαν   noun, acc. sg. fem. {2.A} . . . . φιλαδελφία G5360

Φιλαδελφίαν   noun prop., acc. sg. fem. {2.A; 2.D} . . . . Φιλαδέλφεια G5359‡

φιλαδελφίας   noun, gen. sg. fem. {2.A} . . . . φιλαδελφία G5360

φιλάδελφοι   adj., nom. pl. masc. {3.C} φιλάδελφος G5361

G5361 **φιλάδελφος**, -ον   *loving one's brothers (fellow Christians).*

G5362 **φίλανδρος**   *loving one's husband.*

φιλάνδρους   adj., acc. pl. fem. {3.C} . . . φίλανδρος G5362

G5363 **φιλανθρωπία**, -ας, ἡ   (1) *love of (for) mankind;* (2) *humanity, kindness,* Acts 28:2.

φιλανθρωπία   noun, nom. sg. fem. {2.A} .φιλανθρωπία G5363

φιλανθρωπίαν   noun, acc. sg. fem. {2.A}. . . . . . id.

G5364 **φιλανθρώπως**   adv., *kindly.*

φιλανθρώπως   adv. {3.F} . . . . . . .φιλανθρώπως G5364

G5365 **φιλαργυρία**, -ας, ἡ   *love of money.*

φιλαργυρία   noun, nom. sg. fem. {2.A} . . . . φιλαργυρία G5365

φιλάργυροι   adj., nom. pl. masc. {3.C} φιλάργυρος G5366

G5366 **φιλάργυρος**, -ον   *loving money.*

φίλας   adj., acc. pl. fem. {2.B} . . . . .φίλος G5384

φίλαυτοι   adj., nom. pl. masc. {3.C} . . . . φίλαυτος G5367

G5367 **φίλαυτος**, -ον   *loving self.*

φίλε   adj., voc. sg. masc. {2.B} . . . . .φίλος G5384

φιλεῖ   verb, pres. act. indic. 3 pers. sg. {5.A.2} φιλέω G5368

φιλεῖς   verb, pres. act. indic. 2 pers. sg. {5.A.2} . . id.

G5368 **φιλέω**   (1) *I love,* of friendship (contrast ἔραμαι, of passionate love, and ἀγαπάω, of reverential love); (2) *I kiss,* Mark 14:44; Matt 26:48; Luke 22:47.

φιλήδονοι   adj., nom. pl. masc. {3.C} . . φιλήδονος G5369

G5369 **φιλήδονος**, -ον   *loving* (sensuous) *pleasure.*

G5370 **φίλημα**, -ατος, τό   *a kiss.*

φίλημα   noun, acc. sg. neut. {2.C} . . . . . . φίλημα G5370

φιλήματι   noun, dat. sg. neut. {2.C} . . . . id.

Φιλήμονα   noun prop., acc. sg. masc. {2.C; 2.D}. . . . . .Φιλήμων G5371

Φιλήμονι   noun prop., dat. sg. masc. {2.C; 2.D} . id.

G5371 **Φιλήμων**, -ονος, ὁ   *Philemon,* a Christian man of Colossae.

φιλῆσαι   vbl., aor. act. inf. {6.B.1}. . . . . φιλέω G5368

φιλήσω   verb, aor. act. subjunc. 1 pers. sg. {5.B.1} id.

Φιλητός   noun prop., nom. sg. masc. {2.B; 2.D} . . . . .Φίλητος G5372

G5372 **Φίλητος**, -ου, ὁ   *Philetus,* a backsliding Christian at Rome.

Φίλητος   noun prop., nom. sg. masc. {2.B; 2.D} . . . . .Φίλητος G5372

G5373 **φιλία**, -ας, ἡ   *friendship.*

φιλία   noun, nom. sg. fem. {2.A} . . . . .φιλία G5373

Φίλιππε   noun prop., voc. sg. masc. {2.B; 2.D} . . . . .Φίλιππος G5376

Φιλιππήσιοι   noun prop., voc. pl. masc. {2.B; 2.D} . . . . .Φιλιππήσιος G5374

G5374 **Φιλιππήσιος**, -ου, ὁ   *a Philippian, an inhabitant of Philippi.*

Φιλιππησίους   noun prop., acc. pl. masc. {2.B; 2.D} . . . . .Φιλιππήσιος G5374

G5375 **Φίλιπποι**, -ων, οἱ   *Philippi,* a great city of the Roman province Macedonia.

Φιλίπποις   noun prop., dat. pl. masc. {2.B; 2.D} . . . . .Φίλιπποι G5375

Φίλιππον   noun prop., acc. sg. masc. {2.B; 2.D} . . . . .Φίλιππος G5376

G5376 **Φίλιππος**, -ου, ὁ   *Philip* (a Gk. name); (1) one of the twelve disciples of Jesus; (2) tetrarch of the region of Iturea and Trachonitis region, half brother of Herod Antipas, tetrarch of Galilee; perhaps another half brother is intended in Mark 6:17 and parallels; (3) one of the seven original "deacons" at Jerusalem and a missionary, Acts 6:5; 8:5–40; 21:8.

Φίλιππος   noun prop., nom. sg. masc. {2.B; 2.D} . . . . .Φίλιππος G5376

Φιλίππου   noun prop., gen. sg. masc. {2.B; 2.D}. id.

Φιλίππους   noun prop., acc. pl. masc. {2.B; 2.D} . . . . .Φίλιπποι G5375

Φιλίππῳ   noun prop., dat. sg. masc. {2.B; 2.D} . . . . .Φίλιππος G5376

Φιλίππων   noun prop., gen. pl. masc. {2.B; 2.D} . . . . .Φίλιπποι G5375

φιλόθεοι   adj., nom. pl. masc. {3.C} . . . .φιλόθεος G5377

G5377 **φιλόθεος**, -ον   *loving God.*

φίλοι   adj., nom. pl. masc. {3.A} . . . . .φίλος G5384

φίλοις   adj., dat. pl. masc. {3.A} . . . . id.

Φιλόλογον   noun prop., acc. sg. masc. {2.B; 2.D} . . . . Φιλόλογος G5378

G5378 **Φιλόλογος**, -ου, ὁ   *Philologus,* a Roman Christian.

φίλον   adj., acc. sg. masc. {3.A} . . . . .φίλος G5384

G5379 **φιλονεικία**, -ας, ἡ   *emulation, rivalry* (see φιλόνεικος).

φιλονεικία   noun, nom. sg. fem. {2.A} . φιλονεικία G5379

G5380 **φιλόνεικος**, -ον   *contentious* (φίλος and νεῖκη or νίκη, *victory*).

φιλόνεικος   adj., nom. sg. masc. {3.C} . φιλόνεικος G5380

G5381 **φιλοξενία**, -ας, ἡ   (1) *love to foreigners;* (2) *entertainment of strangers.*

φιλοξενίαν   noun, acc. sg. fem. {2.A} . . . φιλοξενία G5381

φιλοξενίας   noun, gen. sg. fem. {2.A} . . . . id.

φιλόξενοι   adj., nom. pl. masc. {3.C} . . .φιλόξενος G5382

φιλόξενον   adj., acc. sg. masc. {3.C} . . . . id.

G5382 **φιλόξενος**, -ον   (1) *friendly to foreigners;* (2) *hospitable.*

G5383 **φιλοπρωτεύω**   *I love the first (chief) place.*

φιλοπρωτεύων   vbl., pres. act. ptc. nom. sg. masc.
{6.A.1} . . . . φιλοπρωτεύω G5383

G5384 **φίλος**, -η, -ον   (1) *friendly;* (2) subs. *a friend* (masc. or fem.).

φίλος   adj., nom. sg. masc. {3.A} . . . . .φίλος G5384

G5385 **φιλοσοφία**, -ας, ἡ   *philosophy,* in a bad sense, and perhaps identified with ἀπάτη.

φιλοσοφίας   noun, gen. sg. fem. {2.A} . φιλοσοφία G5385

G5386 **φιλόσοφος**, -ου, ὁ   *a philosopher.*

φιλοσόφων   noun, gen. pl. masc. {2.B}. φιλόσοφος G5386

φιλόστοργοι   adj., nom. pl. masc.
{3.C} . . . . φιλόστοργος G5387

G5387 **φιλόστοργος**, -ον   *loving warmly (strongly).*

G5388 **φιλότεκνος**, -ον   *loving one's children.*

φιλοτέκνους   adj., acc. pl. fem. {3.C} . . φιλότεκνος G5388

φιλοτιμεῖσθαι   vbl., pres. mid./pass. inf.
{6.B.2} . . . . φιλοτιμέομαι G5389

G5389 **φιλοτιμέομαι**   (earlier, *I am ambitious;* then, *I act with public spirit*); now, *I am zealous, I strive eagerly.*

φιλοτιμούμεθα   verb, pres. mid./pass. indic.
1 pers. pl. {5.A.2} . . . . φιλοτιμέομαι G5389

φιλοτιμούμενον   vbl., pres. mid./pass. ptc. acc.
sg. masc. {6.A.2} . . . . id.

φιλοῦντας   vbl., pres. act. ptc. acc. pl. masc.
{6.A.2} . . . . φιλέω G5368

φιλούντων   vbl., pres. act. ptc. gen. pl. masc.
{6.A.2} . . . . id.

φίλους   adj., acc. pl. masc. {3.A} . . . . .φίλος G5384

φιλοῦσι   verb, pres. act. indic. 3 pers. pl.
{5.A.2} . . . . φιλέω G5368

φιλοῦσιν   verb, pres. act. indic. 3 pers. pl.
{5.A.2} . . . . id.

φιλόφρονες   adj., nom. pl. masc. {3.E} . .φιλόφρων G5391

G5390 **φιλοφρόνως**   adv., *with friendly thoughtfulness.*

φιλοφρόνως   adv. {3.F} . . . . φιλοφρόνως G5390

G5391 **φιλόφρων**   *friendly, kind.*

φιλῶ   verb, pres. act. indic. 1 pers. sg. {5.A.2} φιλέω G5368

φιλῶ   verb, pres. act. subjunc. 1 pers. sg. {5.B.2} . id.

φίλων   adj., gen. pl. masc. {3.A} . . . . .φίλος G5384

φιλῶν   vbl., pres. act. ptc. nom. sg. masc.
{6.A.2} . . . . φιλέω G5368

φιμοῖν   vbl., pres. act. inf. {6.B.2} . . . . φιμόω G5392

φιμοῦν   vbl., pres. act. inf. {6.B.2} . . . . id.

G5392 **φιμόω**   (1) *I muzzle;* (2) hence, probably originally a slang use, *I silence,* φιμώθητι, *be quiet!* Mark 1:25, etc.

φιμώθητι   verb, aor. pass. impv. 2 pers. sg.
{5.D.1} . . . . φιμόω G5392

φιμώσεις   verb, fut. act. indic. 2 pers. sg. {5.A.1} id.

Φλέγοντα   noun prop., acc. sg. masc. {2.C;
2.D} . . . . .Φλέγων G5393

G5393 **Φλέγων**, -οντος, ὁ   *Phlegon,* a Roman Christian man.

φλόγα   noun, acc. sg. fem. {2.C} . . . . φλόξ G5395

φλογί   noun, dat. sg. fem. {2.C} . . . . id.

φλογιζομένη   vbl., pres. pass. ptc. nom. sg. fem.
{6.A.1} . . . . φλογίζω G5394

φλογίζουσα   vbl., pres. act. ptc. nom. sg. fem.
{6.A.1} . . . . id.

G5394 **φλογίζω**   *I set on fire.*

φλογός   noun, gen. sg. fem. {2.C} . . . . φλόξ G5395

G5395 **φλόξ**, φλογός, ἡ   (1) *a flame;* (2) πυρός (Hebraistic), *a fiery flame;* (3) spiritualized, 2 Thess 1:8.

φλόξ   noun, nom. sg. fem. {2.C} . . . . φλόξ G5395

G5396 **φλυαρέω**   w. acc. *I chatter (gossip) against.*

φλύαροι   adj., nom. pl. fem. {3.C} . . . . . φλύαρος G5397

G5397 **φλύαρος**, -ον   *chattering, gossiping.*

φλυαρῶν   vbl., pres. act. ptc. nom. sg. masc.
{6.A.2} . . . . .φλυαρέω G5396

φοβεῖσθαι   vbl., pres. mid./pass. inf. {6.B.2}. φοβέω G5399

φοβεῖσθε   verb, pres. mid./pass. impv. 2 pers.
pl. {5.D.2} . . . . id.

φοβερά   adj., nom. sg. fem. {3.A} . . . . φοβερός G5398

φοβερόν   adj., nom. sg. neut. {3.A} . . . . id.

G5398 **φοβερός**, -ά, -όν   *fearful, terrible.*

G5399 **φοβέω**   pass., *I fear, dread, reverence,* absol. or with acc. or with inf.; also with cog. acc. φόβον, πτόησιν, *I fear greatly;* with ἀπό and gen. (Hebraism), *I am afraid of,* Matt 10:28 (Luke 12:4); with μή and conjunctive, *I fear lest, I fear that.*

φοβῇ   verb, pres. mid./pass. indic. 2 pers. sg.
{5.A.2} . . . . φοβέω G5399

φοβηθείς   vbl., aor. pass. ptc. nom. sg. masc.
{6.A.1.a.} . . . . id.

φοβηθεῖσα   vbl., aor. pass. ptc. nom. sg. fem.
{6.A.1.a.} . . . . id.

φοβηθέντες   vbl., aor. pass. ptc. nom. pl. masc.
{6.A.1.a.} . . . . id.

φοβηθῇ   verb, aor. pass. subjunc. 3 pers. sg.
{5.B.1} . . . . id.

φοβηθῇς   verb, aor. pass. subjunc. 2 pers. sg.
{5.B.1} . . . . id.

φοβηθήσομαι   verb, fut. pass. indic. 1 pers. sg.
{5.A.1} . . . . id.

φοβήθητε   verb, aor. pass. impv. 2 pers. pl.
{5.D.1} . . . . id.

φοβηθῆτε   verb, aor. pass. subjunc. 2 pers. pl.
{5.B.1} . . . . id.

φόβηθρα   noun, nom. pl. neut. {2.B} . . . φόβητρον G5400

φοβηθῶμεν   verb, aor. pass. subjunc. 1 pers. pl.
{5.B.1} . . . . φοβέω G5399

φοβῆται   verb, pres. mid./pass. subjunc. 3 pers.
sg. {5.B.2} . . . . id.

φόβητρα   noun, nom. pl. neut. {2.B} . . . φόβητρον G5400

G5400 **φόβητρον** (φόβηθρον), -ου, τό   *an instrument of terror, an object of fear, a bugbear.*

φόβοι   noun, nom. pl. masc. {2.B} . . . . φόβος G5401 φόβον   noun, acc. sg. masc. {2.B} . . . . id.

G5401 **φόβος**, -ου, ὁ   *fear, terror,* often fear on the
reverential side, in reference to God, and such
as inspires cautious dealing towards men, cf.
1 Pet 1:17.

φόβος   noun, nom. sg. masc. {2.B} . . . . φόβος G5401

φόβου   noun, gen. sg. masc. {2.B} . . . . φόβος G5401

φοβοῦ   verb, pres. mid./pass. impv. 2 pers. sg.
{5.D.2} . . . . φοβέω G5399

φοβοῦμαι   verb, pres. mid./pass. indic. 1 pers.
sg. {5.A.2} . . . . id.

φοβούμεθα   verb, pres. mid./pass. indic. 1 pers.
pl. {5.A.2} . . . . id.

φοβούμεναι   vbl., pres. mid./pass. ptc. nom. pl.
fem. {6.A.2} . . . . id.

φοβούμενοι   vbl., pres. mid./pass. ptc. nom. pl.
masc. {6.A.2} . . . . id.

φοβουμένοις   vbl., pres. mid./pass. ptc. dat. pl.
masc. {6.A.2} . . . . id.

φοβούμενος   vbl., pres. mid./pass. ptc. nom. sg.
masc. {6.A.2} . . . . id.

φόβῳ   noun, dat. sg. masc. {2.B} . . . . φόβος G5401

G5402 **Φοίβη**, -ης, ἡ   *Phoebe,* a leading Christian
woman in the church at Cenchrea.

Φοίβην   noun prop., acc. sg. fem. {2.A; 2.D}. Φοίβη G5402

Φοίβης   noun prop., gen. sg. fem. {2.A; 2.D} . . id.

Φοίνικα   noun prop., acc. sg. masc. {2.C;
2.D} . . . . Φοῖνιξ G5405

φοίνικας   noun, acc. pl. masc. {2.C} . . . . . φοῖνιξ G5404

φοίνικες   noun, nom. pl. masc. {2.C} . . . . id.

G5403 **Φοινίκη**, -ης, ἡ   *Phoenicia,* a northern coast
strip of the Roman province Syria.

Φοινίκην   noun prop., acc. sg. fem. {2.A;
2.D} . . . . Φοινίκη G5403

Φοινίκης   noun prop., gen. sg. fem. {2.A; 2.D} . . id.

φοινίκων   noun, gen. pl. masc. {2.C} . . . . . . φοῖνιξ G5404

G5404 **φοῖνιξ**, -ικος, ὁ   (1) *a palm tree,* John 12:13; (2)
a branch of a palm tree, a palm, Rev 7:9.

G5405 **Φοῖνιξ**, -ικος, ὁ   *Phoenix* (perhaps modern
Lutro), a bay on the south coast of Crete.

φονέα   noun, acc. sg. masc. {2.C} . . . . φονεύς G5406

φονεῖς   noun, acc. pl. masc. {2.C} . . . . id.

φονεῖς   noun, nom. pl. masc. {2.C} . . . . id.

φονεύεις   verb, pres. act. indic. 2 pers. sg.
{5.A.1.a} . . . . φονεύω G5407

φονεύετε   verb, pres. act. indic. 2 pers. pl.
{5.A.1.a} . . . . id.

G5406 **φονεύς**, -έως, ὁ   *a murderer.*

φονεύς   noun, nom. sg. masc. {2.C} . . . . . φονεύς G5406

φονευσάντων   vbl., aor. act. ptc. gen. pl. masc.
{6.A.1.a} . . . . φονεύω G5407

φονεύσεις   verb, fut. act. indic. 2 pers. sg.
{5.A.1.a} . . . . id.

φονεύσῃ   verb, aor. act. subjunc. 3 pers. sg. {5.B.1} id.

φονεύσῃς   verb, aor. act. subjunc. 2 pers. sg.
{5.B.1} . . . . id.

φονεῦσι   noun, dat. pl. masc. {2.C} . . . . . . φονεύς G5406

φονεῦσιν   noun, dat. pl. masc. {2.C} . . . . id.

G5407 **φονεύω**   (1) with acc. *I murder;* (2) absol. *I
commit murder.*

φόνοι   noun, nom. pl. masc. {2.B} . . . . φόνος G5408

φόνον   noun, acc. sg. masc. {2.B} . . . . id.

G5408 **φόνος**, -ου, ὁ   *murder.*

φόνου   noun, gen. sg. masc. {2.B} . . . . φόνος G5408

φόνῳ   noun, dat. sg. masc. {2.B} . . . . id.

φόνων   noun, gen. pl. masc. {2.B} . . . . id.

φορεῖ   verb, pres. act. indic. 3 pers. sg.
{5.A.2} . . . . φορέω G5409

φορέσομεν   verb, fut. act. indic. 1 pers. pl.
{5.A.1} . . . . id.

φορέσωμεν   verb, aor. act. subjunc. 1 pers. pl.
{5.B.1} . . . . id.

G5409 **φορέω**   (1) *I carry;* (2) hence, very often, *I wear.*

G5410 **φόρον**, -ου, τό   *Forum, Market, Market Town*
(Lat., *Forum*), Ἀππίου φόρον, *Appian Forum*
(Acts 28:15).

φόρον   noun, acc. sg. masc. {2.B} . . . . φόρος G5411

G5411 **φόρος**, -ου, ὁ   *tribute, war tax.*

Φόρου   noun prop., gen. sg. neut. {2.B; 2.D}. φόρον G5410

φοροῦντα   vbl., pres. act. ptc. acc. sg. masc.
{6.A.2} . . . . φορέω G5409

φοροῦντες   vbl., pres. act. ptc. nom. pl. masc.
{6.A.2} . . . . id.

φόρους   noun, acc. pl. masc. {2.B} . . . . φόρος G5411

φορτία   noun, acc. pl. neut. {2.B} . . . . φορτίον G5413

φορτίζετε   verb, pres. act. indic. 2 pers. pl.
{5.A.1.a} . . . . φορτίζω G5412

G5412 **φορτίζω**   *I load, burden.*

φορτίοις   noun, dat. pl. neut. {2.B} . . . . . . φορτίον G5413

G5413 **φορτίον**, -ου, τό   (1) *a burden;* (2) *a cargo,* Acts
27:10.

φορτίον   noun, acc. sg. neut. {2.B} . . . . . . φορτίον G5413

φορτίον   noun, nom. sg. neut. {2.B} . . . . id.

φορτίου   noun, gen. sg. neut. {2.B} . . . . id.

G5414 **φόρτος**   *a burden, cargo.* Var. for φορτίον.

φόρτου   noun, gen. sg. masc. {2.B} . . . . . . φόρτος G5414

G5415 **Φορτουνᾶτος**, -ου, ὁ   *Fortunatus,* a Christian
of Corinth (Lat.).

Φορτουνάτου   noun prop., gen. sg. masc. {2.B;
2.D} . . . . Φορτουνᾶτος G5415

φορῶν   vbl., pres. act. ptc. nom. sg. masc.
{6.A.2} . . . . φορέω G5409

Φουρτουνάτου   noun prop., gen. sg. masc. {2.B;
2.D} . . . . Φορτουνᾶτος G5415

G5416 **φραγέλλιον**, -ου, τό   *a lash* (by dissimilation
from Lat., *flagellum*).

φραγέλλιον   noun, acc. sg. neut. {2.B} φραγέλλιον G5416

G5417 **φραγελλόω**   *I lash, flog* (Lat., *flagello*).

φραγελλώσας   vbl., aor. act. ptc. nom. sg. masc.
{6.A.2} . . . . φραγελλόω G5417

φραγῇ   verb, ²aor. pass. subjunc. 3 pers. sg.
{5.B.1} . . . . φράσσω G5420

φραγήσεται   verb, ²fut. pass. indic. 3 pers. sg.
{5.A.1.d} . . . . id.

φραγμόν   noun, acc. sg. masc. {2.B} . . . . . φραγμός G5418

G5418 **φραγμός**, -οῦ, ὁ   (1) *a hedge, a fence, a parti-
tion;* (2) hence, *a path* bounded by hedges or
fences, Luke 14:23.

φραγμοῦ   noun, gen. sg. masc. {2.B} . . . . . φραγμός G5418

φραγμούς   noun, acc. pl. masc. {2.B} . . . . id.

G5419 **φράζω** *I explain, I interpret.*
φράσον verb, aor. act. impv. 2 pers. sg. {5.D.1}. φράζω G5419
G5420 **φράσσω** *I stop, close.*
G5421 **φρέαρ**, -ατος, τό (1) *a well;* (2) hence, transferred, *a pit, a shaft,* Rev 9:1, 2.
φρέαρ noun, acc. sg. neut. {2.C} . . . . φρέαρ G5421
φρέαρ noun, nom. sg. neut. {2.C} . . . . id.
φρέατος noun, gen. sg. neut. {2.C} . . . . id.
φρεναπατᾷ verb, pres. act. indic. 3 pers. sg.
{5.A.2} . . . . φρεναπατάω G5422
φρεναπάται noun, nom. pl. masc.
{2.A} . . . . φρεναπάτης G5423
G5422 **φρεναπατάω** (lit. *I deceive the mind*), *I deceive.*
G5423 **φρεναπάτης**, -ου, ὁ (1) *a deceiver;* (2) *deceiving* (see φρεναπατάω).
φρεσί noun, dat. pl. fem. {2.C} . . . . φρήν G5424
φρεσίν noun, dat. pl. fem. {2.C} . . . . id.
G5424 **φρήν**, φρενός, ἡ *the mind.*
φρίσσουσι verb, pres. act. indic. 3 pers. pl.
{5.A.1.a} . . . . φρίσσω G5425
φρίσσουσιν verb, pres. act. indic. 3 pers. pl.
{5.A.1.a} . . . . id.
G5425 **φρίσσω** *I feel awe* (used properly of the standing of the hair on end with fear).
φρόνει verb, pres. act. impv. 2 pers. sg.
{5.D.2} . . . . φρονέω G5426
φρονεῖ verb, pres. act. indic. 3 pers. sg. {5.A.2} . id.
φρονεῖν vbl., pres. act. inf. {6.B.2} . . . . id.
φρονεῖς verb, pres. act. indic. 2 pers. sg. {5.A.2} id.
φρονείσθω verb, pres. pass. impv. 3 pers. sg.
{5.D.2} . . . . id.
φρονεῖτε verb, pres. act. impv. 2 pers. pl. {5.D.2} id.
φρονεῖτε verb, pres. act. indic. 2 pers. pl. {5.A.2} id.
G5426 **φρονέω** (1) with acc. *I have in my mind, I think of, I set my mind upon,* suggesting my moral interest, thought, and study, and not a mere unreflecting opinion; (2) intrans., *I think, I cherish a habit of thought.*
G5427 **φρόνημα**, -ατος, τό *an object of thought* (or *endeavor*).
φρόνημα noun, nom. sg. neut. {2.C} . . . . φρόνημα G5427
φρονήσει noun, dat. sg. fem. {2.C} . . . . φρόνησις G5428
φρονήσετε verb, fut. act. indic. 2 pers. pl.
{5.A.1} . . . . φρονέω G5426
G5428 **φρόνησις**, -εως, ἡ *understanding,* which leads to right action.
φρονῆτε verb, pres. act. subjunc. 2 pers. pl.
{5.B.2} . . . . φρονέω G5426
φρόνιμοι adj., nom. pl. fem. {3.C} . . . . φρόνιμος G5429
φρόνιμοι adj., nom. pl. masc. {3.C} . . . . id.
φρονίμοις adj., dat. pl. fem. {3.C} . . . . id.
φρονίμοις adj., dat. pl. masc. {3.C} . . . . id.
G5429 **φρόνιμος**, -ον *sensible, prudent.*
φρόνιμος adj., nom. sg. masc. {3.C} . . . φρόνιμος G5429
φρονίμῳ adj., dat. sg. masc. {3.C} . . . . id.
G5430 **φρονίμως** adv., *wisely, sensibly, prudently.*
φρονίμως adv. {3.F} . . . . φρονίμως G5430
φρονιμώτεροι adj. comp., nom. pl. masc. {3.C;
3.G} . . . . φρόνιμος G5429

φρονοῦντες vbl., pres. act. ptc. nom. pl. masc.
{6.A.2} . . . . φρονέω G5426
φρονοῦσιν verb, pres. act. indic. 3 pers. pl.
{5.A.2} . . . . id.
G5431 **φροντίζω** *I am careful, I take care.*
φροντίζωσι verb, pres. act. subjunc. 3 pers. pl.
{5.B.1} . . . . φροντίζω G5431
φροντίζωσιν verb, pres. act. subjunc. 3 pers.
pl. {5.B.1} . . . . id.
φρονῶμεν verb, pres. act. subjunc. 1 pers. pl.
{5.B.2} . . . . φρονέω G5426
φρονῶν vbl., pres. act. ptc. nom. sg. masc.
{6.A.2} . . . . id.
G5432 **φρουρέω** *I guard,* or rather *I garrison,* lit. and met.
φρουρήσει verb, fut. act. indic. 3 pers. sg.
{5.A.1} . . . . φρουρέω G5432
φρουρουμένους vbl., pres. pass. ptc. acc. pl.
masc. {6.A.2} . . . . id.
G5433 **φρυάσσω** *I roar, rage* (properly, of the snorting and neighing of a high-spirited horse).
G5434 **φρύγανον**, -ου, τό *brushwood, copse.*
φρυγάνων noun, gen. pl. neut. {2.B} . . . φρύγανον G5434
G5435 **Φρυγία**, -ας, ἡ *Phrygia,* an ethnic district in Asia Minor, the northwestern part of which was in the Roman province Asia, and the southeastern part in the Roman province Galatia; in Acts 16:6 φρυγίαν is adj.
Φρυγίαν noun prop., acc. sg. fem. {2.A;
2.D} . . . . Φρυγία G5435
Φρυγίας noun prop., gen. sg. fem. {2.A; 2.D} . . id.
φυγεῖν vbl., ²aor. act. inf. {6.B.1} . . . . . . φεύγω G5343
Φύγελλος noun prop., nom. sg. masc. {2.B;
2.D} . . . . Φύγελος G5436
G5436 **Φύγελος**, -ου, ὁ *Phygelus,* a Christian of the Roman province Asia who deserted Paul.
Φύγελος noun prop., nom. sg. masc. {2.B;
2.D} . . . . Φύγελος G5436
G5437 **φυγή**, -ῆς, ἡ *flight.*
φυγή noun, nom. sg. fem. {2.A} . . . . φυγή G5437
φύγητε verb, ²aor. act. subjunc. 2 pers. pl.
{5.B.1} . . . . φεύγω G5343
φυέν vbl., ²aor. pass. ptc. nom. sg. neut.
{6.A.1.a} . . . . φύω G5453
φυλαί noun, nom. pl. fem. {2.A} . . . . φυλή G5443
φυλαῖς noun, dat. pl. fem. {2.A} . . . . id.
φυλακαῖς noun, dat. pl. fem. {2.A} . . . . . . φυλακή G5438
φύλακας noun, acc. pl. masc. {2.C} . . . . . . φύλαξ G5441
φυλακάς noun, acc. pl. fem. {2.A} . . . . φυλακή G5438
φύλακες noun, nom. pl. masc. {2.C} . . . . . . φύλαξ G5441
G5438 **φυλακή**, -ῆς, ἡ (1) abstr., *guardianship, guard,* in cog. acc., Luke 2:8; Acts 12:6; (2) *a guard,* Acts 12:10; (3) much commoner, *a prison;* hence, *the place of confinement* of the spirits of the dead, 1 Pet 3:19; (4) as a division of the night, (a) perhaps according to the old Jewish system by which there were three divisions, Luke 12:38; (b) according to the Roman system, popularized in Judaea, by which there were four, Mark 6:48 (cf. 13:35), Matt 14:25; 24:43.

φυλακή   noun, nom. sg. fem. {2.A} . . . . .φυλακή G5438
φυλακῇ   noun, dat. sg. fem. {2.A}. . . . . .id.
φυλακήν   noun, acc. sg. fem. {2.A} . . . . id.
φυλακῆς   noun, gen. sg. fem. {2.A} . . . . id.
G5439 φυλακίζω   *I put in prison, I imprison.*
   φυλακίζων   vbl., pres. act. ptc. nom. sg. masc.
    {6.A.1}. . . . . .φυλακίζω G5439
   φυλακτήρια   noun, acc. pl. neut.
    {2.B} . . . . .φυλακτήριον G5440
G5440 φυλακτήριον, -ου, τό   *a phylactery, an amulet,*
   a parchment capsule containing little parchment rolls with the Heb. texts, Exod 13:1–10,
   11–16; Deut 6:4–9; 11:13–21, affixed to the left
   upper arm or the forehead of men at morning
   prayer, and regarded as a protection (hence
   the name) against evil spirits.
G5441 φύλαξ, -ακος, ὁ   *a guard* (for one person).
   φυλάξαι   vbl., aor. act. inf. {6.B.1} . . . . . φυλάσσω G5442
   φυλάξατε   verb, aor. act. impv. 2 pers. pl. {5.D.1}id.
   φυλάξει   verb, fut. act. indic. 3 pers. sg. {5.A.1.a}id.
   φυλάξῃ   verb, aor. act. subjunc. 3 pers. sg. {5.B.1}   id.
   φυλάξῃς   verb, aor. act. subjunc. 2 pers. sg.
    {5.B.1} . . . . id.
   φύλαξον   verb, aor. act. impv. 2 pers. sg. {5.D.1}   id.
   φυλάς   noun, acc. pl. fem. {2.A}. . . . . .φυλή G5443
   φυλάσσειν   vbl., pres. act. inf. {6.B.1} . . φυλάσσω G5442
   φυλάσσεσθαι   vbl., pres. mid. inf. {6.B.1} . . . . . id.
   φυλάσσεσθε   verb, pres. mid. impv. 2 pers. pl.
    {5.D.1}. . . . . id.
   φυλάσσῃ   verb, pres. act. subjunc. 3 pers. sg.
    {5.B.1} . . . . id.
   φυλασσόμενος   vbl., pres. pass. ptc. nom. sg.
    masc. {6.A.1}. . . . . id.
   φυλάσσοντες   vbl., pres. act. ptc. nom. pl.
    masc. {6.A.1}. . . . . id.
   φυλάσσοντι   vbl., pres. act. ptc. dat. sg. masc.
    {6.A.1}. . . . . id.
   φυλάσσου   verb, pres. mid. impv. 2 pers. sg.
    {5.D.1}. . . . . id.
   φυλάσσουσιν   verb, pres. act. indic.3 pers. pl.
    {5.A.1.a} . . . . id.
G5442 φυλάσσω   (1) *I guard, protect,* with pers. or
   other concr. obj., or (Luke 2:8) cog. acc.; mid. *I*
   am on my guard, Luke 12:15; (2) act. and mid.,
   of customs or regulations, *I keep, I observe.*
   φυλάσσων   vbl., pres. act. ptc. nom. sg. masc.
    {6.A.1}. . . . . φυλάσσω G5442
G5443 φυλή, -ῆς, ἡ   *a tribe,* esp. one of the twelve
   tribes of Israel, and perhaps (by analogy) of
   Christendom, Jas 1:1.
   φυλήν   noun, acc. sg. fem. {2.A}. . . . . .φυλή G5443
   φυλῆς   noun, gen. sg. fem. {2.A}. . . . . id.
   φύλλα   noun, acc. pl. neut. {2.B} . . . . φύλλον G5444
   φύλλα   noun, nom. pl. neut. {2.B} . . . . id.
G5444 φύλλον, -ου, τό   *a leaf* of a tree.
   φυλῶν   noun, gen. pl. fem. {2.A} . . . . φυλή G5443
   φύουσα   vbl., pres. act. ptc. nom. sg. fem.
    {6.A.1}. . . . . .φύω G5453
G5445 φύραμα, -ατος, τό   (1) *a mixture;* (2) hence lit.
   or met., *a lump, a mass.*

φύραμα   noun, acc. sg. neut. {2.C}. . . . . . φύραμα G5445
φύραμα   noun, nom. sg. neut. {2.C}. . . . . id.
φυράματος   noun, gen. sg. neut. {2.C}. . . . . id.
φύσει   noun, dat. sg. fem. {2.C} . . . . φύσις G5449
φύσεως   noun, gen. sg. fem. {2.C} . . . . id.
φυσικά   adj., nom. pl. neut. {3.A}. . . . . . φυσικός G5446
φυσικήν   adj., acc. sg. fem. {3.A} . . . . id.
G5446 φυσικός, -ή, -όν   (1) *natural;* (2) φυσικά,
   2 Pet 2:12, *creatures of instinct.*
G5447 φυσικῶς   adv., *by instinct.*
   φυσικῶς   adv. {3.F}. . . . . φυσικῶς G5447
   φύσιν   noun, acc. sg. fem. {2.C} . . . . φύσις G5449
   φυσιοῖ   verb, pres. act. indic. 3 pers. sg.
    {5.A.2}. . . . . φυσιόω G5448
   φυσιούμενος   vbl., pres. pass. ptc. nom. sg.
    masc. {6.A.2}. . . . . id.
   φυσιοῦσθε   verb, pres. pass. subjunc. 2 pers. pl.
    {5.B.2}. . . . . id.
   φυσιοῦται   verb, pres. pass. indic. 3 pers. sg.
    {5.A.2}. . . . . id.
G5448 φυσιόω   (lit. *I inflate*), met. *I puff up,* with
   anger, conceit, etc.
G5449 φύσις, -εως, ἡ   *nature, inherent nature,* in NT
   nonmoral, neither good nor bad; φύσει, *by*
   nature, in myself (itself, etc.).
   φύσις   noun, nom. sg. fem. {2.C} . . . . φύσις G5449
   φυσιώσεις   noun, nom. pl. fem. {2.C} . . φυσίωσις G5450
G5450 φυσίωσις, -εως, ἡ   *a puffing up* (due to conceit).
G5451 φυτεία, -ας, ἡ   (lit. *planting*), *a plant.*
   φυτεία   noun, nom. sg. fem. {2.A} . . . . . . .φυτεία G5451
   φυτεύει   verb, pres. act. indic. 3 pers. sg.
    {5.A.1.a} . . . . φυτεύω G5452
   φυτεύθητι   verb, aor. pass. impv. 2 pers. sg.
    {5.D.1}. . . . . id.
G5452 φυτεύω   *I plant.*
   φυτεύων   vbl., pres. act. ptc. nom. sg. masc.
    {6.A.1}. . . . . φυτεύω G5452
G5453 φύω   *I grow, I grow up.*
G5454 φωλεός, -οῦ, ὁ   *a hole* in the earth.
   φωλεούς   noun, acc. pl. masc. {2.B} . . . . . . φωλεός G5454
   φωναί   noun, nom. pl. fem. {2.A}. . . . . .φωνή G5456
   φωναῖς   noun, dat. pl. fem. {2.A} . . . . id.
   φωνάς   noun, acc. pl. fem. {2.A} . . . . id.
   φώνει   verb, pres. act. impv. 2 pers. sg.
    {5.D.2}. . . . . .φωνέω G5455
   φωνεῖ   verb, pres. act. indic. 3 pers. sg. {5.A.2} . . id.
   φωνεῖτε   verb, pres. act. indic. 2 pers. pl. {5.A.2}. id.
G5455 φωνέω   *I give forth a sound,* hence; (1) of a
   cock, *I crow;* (2) of men, *I shout;* (3) trans.,
   (a) *I call* (to myself), *I summon, I invite,* Luke
   14:12; (b) *I address,* John 13:13.
G5456 φωνή, -ῆς, ἡ   (1) *a sound;* (2) hence, *a voice.*
   φωνή   noun, nom. sg. fem. {2.A} . . . . .φωνή G5456
   φωνῇ   noun, dat. sg. fem. {2.A}. . . . . id.
   φωνηθῆναι   vbl., aor. pass. inf. {6.B.1} . . . . .φωνέω G5455
   φωνήν   noun, acc. sg. fem. {2.A}. . . . . .φωνή G5456
   φωνῆς   noun, gen. sg. fem. {2.A} . . . . id.
   φωνῆσαι   vbl., aor. act. inf. {6.B.1} . . . . . .φωνέω G5455
   φωνῆσαν   vbl., aor. act. ptc. nom. sg. neut.
    {6.A.2}. . . . . id.

φωνήσαντες   vbl., aor. act. ptc. nom. pl. masc.
{6.A.2} . . . . id.
φωνήσας   vbl., aor. act. ptc. nom. sg. masc.
{6.A.2} . . . . id.
φωνήσατε   verb, aor. act. impv. 2 pers. pl.
{5.D.1} . . . . id.
φωνήσει   verb, fut. act. indic. 3 pers. sg. {5.A.1} . id.
φωνήσῃ   verb, aor. act. subjunc. 3 pers. sg.
{5.B.1} . . . . id.
φώνησον   verb, aor. act. impv. 2 pers. sg. {5.D.1} id.
φωνοῦντες   vbl., pres. act. ptc. nom. pl. masc.
{6.A.2} . . . . id.
φωνοῦσι   verb, pres. act. indic. 3 pers. pl. {5.A.2} id.
φωνοῦσιν   verb, pres. act. indic. 3 pers. pl. {5.A.2} id.
φωνῶν   noun, gen. pl. fem. {2.A} . . . . φωνή G5456
G5457 **φῶς**, φωτός, τό   (1) *a light*, particularly *the light* of the sun, but also *the heavenly bodies* specially, Jas 1:17; (2) as indispensable to life, it comes to be associated with life (cf. John 1:4), and as universal beneficence, with God and the Messiah (cf. John 1:8; 8:12), etc. (cf. John 12:36; Eph 5:8); (3) τὸ φῶς, *the (bright) fire*, Mark 14:54; Luke 22:56.
φῶς   noun, acc. sg. neut. {2.C} . . . . φῶς G5457
φῶς   noun, nom. sg. neut. {2.C} . . . . id.
G5458 **φωστήρ**, -ῆρος, ὁ   (1) *a light*, perhaps *a sun*, Rev 21:11; (2) *a star*, Phil 2:15.
φωστήρ   noun, nom. sg. masc. {2.C} . . . . . φωστήρ G5458
φωστῆρες   noun, nom. pl. masc. {2.C} . . . . id.
G5459 **φωσφόρος**, -ου, ὁ   *the day star* (lit. *light-bringing*, Lat. *lucifer*, probably the planet Venus).
φωσφόρος   adj., nom. sg. masc. {3.C} . . . φωσφόρος G5459

φῶτα   noun, acc. pl. neut. {2.C} . . . . φῶς G5457
φωτεινή   adj., nom. sg. fem. {3.A} . . . . . φωτεινός G5460
φωτεινόν   adj., nom. sg. neut. {3.A} . . . . id.
G5460 **φωτεινός**, -ή, -όν   *shining, brilliant*.
φωτί   noun, dat. sg. neut. {2.C} . . . . φῶς G5457
φωτιεῖ   verb, fut. act. indic. 3 pers. sg.
{5.A.2} . . . . φωτίζω G5461
φωτίζει   verb, pres. act. indic. 3 pers. sg.
{5.A.1.a} . . . . id.
φωτίζῃ   verb, pres. act. subjunc. 3 pers. sg.
{5.B.1} . . . . id.
G5461 **φωτίζω**   (1) *I shed light upon, I enlighten* (of the public disclosure of what has been kept secret); pass. with acc. Eph 1:18; (2) *I bring to light*, Eph 3:9; (3) φωτισθέντες, *having received enlightenment*, having had experience of God's grace in conversion, Heb 6:4; 10:32.
φωτινή   adj., nom. sg. fem. {3.A} . . . . . . φωτεινός G5460
φωτινόν   adj., nom. sg. neut. {3.A} . . . . id.
φωτίσαι   vbl., aor. act. inf. {6.B.1} . . . . φωτίζω G5461
φωτίσαντος   vbl., aor. act. ptc. gen. sg. masc.
{6.A.1.a} . . . . id.
φωτίσει   verb, fut. act. indic. 3 pers. sg. {5.A.1.a} id.
φωτισθέντας   vbl., aor. pass. ptc. acc. pl. masc.
{6.A.1.a} . . . . id.
φωτισθέντες   vbl., aor. pass. ptc. nom. pl. masc.
{6.A.1.a} . . . . id.
φωτισμόν   noun, acc. sg. masc. {2.B} . . . φωτισμός G5462
G5462 **φωτισμός**, -οῦ, ὁ   (1) act. *enlightening*, 2 Cor 4:4; (2) pass. *enlightenment*, 2 Cor 4:6.
φωτός   noun, gen. sg. neut. {2.C} . . . . φῶς G5457
φώτων   noun, gen. pl. neut. {2.C} . . . . id.

Χ χ

χαῖρε   verb, pres. act. impv. 2 pers. sg. {5.D.1} χαίρω G5463
χαίρει   verb, pres. act. indic. 3 pers. sg. {5.A.1.a} id.
χαίρειν   vbl., pres. act. inf. {6.B.1} . . . . id.
χαίρετε   verb, pres. act. impv. 2 pers. pl. {5.D.1} . id.
χαίρῃ   verb, pres. act. subjunc. 3 pers. sg. {5.B.1} id.
χαίρομεν   verb, pres. act. indic. 1 pers. pl.
{5.A.1.a} . . . . id.
χαίροντες   vbl., pres. act. ptc. nom. pl. masc.
{6.A.1} . . . . id.
χαιρόντων   vbl., pres. act. ptc. gen. pl. masc.
{6.A.1} . . . . id.
χαίρουσιν   verb, pres. act. indic. 3 pers. pl.
{5.A.1.a} . . . . id.
G5463 **χαίρω**   (1) *I rejoice*, with cog. acc. or with dat., *I rejoice exceedingly*; (2) in the impv., χαῖρε, χαίρετε, a greeting, *farewell*, Christianized in Phil 3:1; 4:4 by the addition ἐν κυρίῳ (and generally mistranslated), cf. χαίρειν, impv. inf., e.g., Acts 15:23 (cf. 2 John 10); (3) *hail!* Mark 15:18; Matt 27:29.
χαίρω   verb, pres. act. indic. 1 pers. sg.
{5.A.1.a} . . . . χαίρω G5463

χαίρωμεν   verb, pres. act. subjunc. 1 pers. pl.
{5.B.1} . . . . id.
χαίρων   vbl., pres. act. ptc. nom. sg. masc. {6.A.1} id.
G5464 **χάλαζα**, -ης, ἡ   *hail*.
χάλαζα   noun, nom. sg. fem. {2.A} . . . . . χάλαζα G5464
χαλάζης   noun, gen. sg. fem. {2.A} . . . . id.
χαλάσαντες   vbl., aor. act. ptc. nom. pl. masc.
{6.A.2} . . . . χαλάω G5465
χαλασάντων   vbl., aor. act. ptc. gen. pl. masc.
{6.A.2} . . . . id.
χαλάσατε   verb, aor. act. impv. 2 pers. pl. {5.D.1} id.
χαλάσω   verb, fut. act. indic. 1 pers. sg. {5.A.1} . id.
G5465 **χαλάω**   *I slacken*.
G5466 **Χαλδαῖος**, -ου, ὁ   *a Chaldean*, one living in southern Armenia.
Χαλδαίων   noun prop., gen. pl. masc. {2.B; 2.D} . . . . Χαλδαῖος G5466
χαλεποί   adj., nom. pl. masc. {3.A} . . . . . χαλεπός G5467
G5467 **χαλεπός**, -ή, -όν   (1) *hard, difficult*, 2 Tim 3:1; (2) *difficult to restrain, dangerous*, Matt 8:28.
G5468 **χαλιναγωγέω**   *I bridle*, met. *I keep in check, restrain*.

χαλιναγωγῆσαι   vbl., aor. act. inf.
   {6.B.1} . . . . χαλιναγωγέω G5468
χαλιναγωγῶν   vbl., pres. act. ptc. nom. sg.
   masc. {6.A.2} . . . . id.
G5469 **χαλινός**, -οῦ, ὁ   a bridle.
χαλινούς   noun, acc. pl. masc. {2.B} . . . .χαλινός G5469
χαλινῶν   noun, gen. pl. masc. {2.B} . . . . id.
χαλκᾶ   adj., acc. pl. neut. {3.A} . . . . χαλκοῦς G5470‡
G5471 **χαλκεύς**, -έως, ὁ   a worker in bronze, a smith.
χαλκεύς   noun, nom. sg. masc. {2.C} . . . . χαλκεύς G5471
G5472 **χαλκηδών**, -όνος, ὁ   a chalcedony, a small
   stone of various colors.
χαλκηδών   noun, nom. sg. masc. {2.C} . χαλκηδών G5472
G5473 **χαλκίον**, -ου, τό   a bronze vessel.
χαλκίων   noun, gen. pl. neut. {2.B} . . . . . . χαλκίον G5473
G5474 **χαλκολίβανον**, -ου, τό, or -ος, -ου, ὁ   brass,
   bronze; a word of uncertain signification,
   translated aeramentum turinum (incense
   bronze) in certain Old Latin authorities, and
   orichalcum (= ὀρείχαλκος, mountain bronze)
   in the Vulgate; the latter was understood to be
   a mixture of gold and copper.
χαλκολιβάνῳ   noun, dat. sg. neut.
   {2.B} . . . . χαλκολίβανον G5474
χαλκόν   noun, acc. sg. masc. {2.B} . . . . . χαλκός G5475
G5475 **χαλκός**, -οῦ, ὁ   (1) copper or bronze; (2) hence,
   a copper coin; (3) copper money, Mark 6:8
   (Matt 10:9); Mark 12:41.
χαλκός   noun, nom. sg. masc. {2.B} . . . . . . χαλκός G5475
χαλκοῦ   noun, gen. sg. masc. {2.B} . . . . id.
G5470‡ **χαλκοῦς**, -ῆ, -οῦν   made of copper, brass, or
   bronze
χαλῶσι   verb, pres. act. indic. 3 pers. pl.
   {5.A.2} . . . . χαλάω G5465
χαλῶσιν   verb, pres. act. indic. 3 pers. pl. {5.A.2} id.
G5476 **χαμαί**   adv., on the ground.
χαμαί   adv. . . . . χαμαί G5476
Χανάαν   noun prop. . . . . Χανάαν G5477
G5477 **Χανάαν**, ἡ   Canaan, the whole of Palestine
   (Acts 13:19) or Palestine west of the river
   Jordan (Acts 7:11).
Χανάαν   noun prop. . . . . Χανάαν G5477
Χαναναία   adj. prop., nom. sg. fem.
   {3.A} . . . . Χαναναῖος G5478
G5478 **Χαναναῖος**, -α, -ον   Canaanite, a biblical and
   archaic name for Phoenician.
G5479 **χαρά**, -ᾶς, ἡ   (1) joy; (2) delight.
χαρά   noun, nom. sg. fem. {2.A} . . . . χαρά G5479
χαρά   noun, voc. sg. fem. {2.A} . . . . id.
χαρᾷ   noun, dat. sg. fem. {2.A} . . . . id.
G5480 **χάραγμα**, -ατος, τό   (1) an engraved work,
   Acts 17:29; (2) an inscription engraved, a
   stamp.
χάραγμα   noun, acc. sg. neut. {2.C} . . . . χάραγμα G5480
χαράγματα   noun, acc. pl. neut. {2.C} . . . . id.
χαράγματι   noun, dat. sg. neut. {2.C} . . . . id.
χαράγματος   noun, gen. sg. neut. {2.C} . . . . id.
χάρακα   noun, acc. sg. masc. {2.C} . . . . . . χάραξ G5482
G5481 **χαρακτήρ**, -ῆρος, ὁ   a representation.
χαρακτήρ   noun, nom. sg. masc. {2.C} . χαρακτήρ G5481

χαράν   noun, acc. sg. fem. {2.A} . . . . χαρά G5479
G5482 **χάραξ**, -ακος, ὁ   a mound, rampart.
χαρᾶς   noun, gen. sg. fem. {2.A} . . . . χαρά G5479
χαρῆναι   vbl., ²aor. pass. inf. {6.B.1} . . . . . . χαίρω G5463
χαρήσεται   verb, ²fut. pass. indic. 3 pers. sg.
   {5.A.1.d} . . . . id.
χαρήσομαι   verb, ²fut. pass. indic. 1 pers. sg.
   {5.A.1.d} . . . . id.
χαρήσονται   verb, ²fut. pass. indic. 3 pers. pl.
   {5.A.1.d} . . . . id.
χάρητε   verb, ²aor. pass. impv. 2 pers. pl. {5.D.1} id.
χαρῆτε   verb, ²aor. pass. subjunc. 2 pers. pl.
   {5.B.1} . . . . id.
χαρίζεσθαι   vbl., pres. mid./pass. inf.
   {6.B.1} . . . . .χαρίζομαι G5483
χαρίζεσθε   verb, pres. mid./pass. indic. 2 pers.
   pl. {5.A.1.d} . . . . id.
G5483 **χαρίζομαι**   (1) I graciously confer, Luke 7:21,
   etc.; (2) I pardon, forgive, 2 Cor 2:7, 10; 12:13;
   Eph 4:32; Col 2:13; 3:13; (3) I show kindness to,
   Gal 3:18.
χαριζόμενοι   vbl., pres. mid./pass. ptc. nom. pl.
   masc. {6.A.1} . . . . .χαρίζομαι G5483
G5484 **χάριν**   acc. sg. of χάρις, used as prep. with
   gen., often standing after the word it governs,
   for the sake of; by reason of, on account of.
χάριν   adv. and prep. . . . . χάριν G5484
χάριν   noun, acc. sg. fem. {2.C} . . . . .χάρις G5485
G5485 **χάρις**, -ιτος, ἡ   (1) grace, as a gift or blessing
   brought to man by Jesus Christ, John 1:14, 16,
   17; (2) favor, as in LXX, i.e., Luke 1:30; 2:40,
   52; Acts 2:47, etc.; (3) gratitude, Luke 6:32–34;
   17:9; thanks, e.g., in χάρις τῷ θεῷ and ἔχειν
   χάριν (to thank); (4) a favor, Acts 24:27; 25:3,
   9; (5) a new Christian sense, often with a defining gen., of the divine favor, grace, the free-
   ness and universality of which are shown in
   the inclusion of the Gentiles within the scope
   of the love and care of the God of the Jews.
   Paul, as the apostle to the Gentiles, and the
   proclaimer of the universal Gospel, naturally
   makes most use of this term (but cf. also Acts
   13:43; 14:26, etc.), e.g., 1 Cor 3:10; 15:10; 1 Cor
   1:4; 2 Cor 6:1; grace was given to him for his
   ministry to them, and to them through his
   ministry. (In early Gk. literature, gracefulness,
   graciousness; favor; a favor; gratitude; χάριν
   as above; in LXX esp. of the favor which an
   inferior finds in the eyes of his superior).
χάρις   noun, nom. sg. fem. {2.C} . . . . .χάρις G5485
χαρισάμενος   vbl., aor. mid. ptc. nom. sg. masc.
   {6.A.1.b} .χαρίζομαι G5483
χαρίσασθαι   vbl., aor. mid. inf. {6.B.1} . . . . id.
χαρίσασθε   verb, aor. mid. impv. 2 pers. pl.
   {5.D.1} . . . . id.
χαρίσεται   verb, fut. mid. indic. 3 pers. sg.
   {5.A.1.d} . . . . id.
χαρισθέντα   vbl., aor. pass. ptc. acc. pl. neut.
   {6.A.1.a} . . . . id.
χαρισθῆναι   vbl., aor. pass. inf. {6.B.1} . . . . id.

χαρισθήσομαι   verb, fut. pass. indic. 1 pers. sg.
    {5.A.1.d} . . . . id.

G5486 **χάρισμα**, -ατος, τό   *a free (gracious) gift, a gift,*
    an endowment, esp. from God.
    χάρισμα   noun, acc. sg. neut. {2.C} . . . . . χάρισμα G5486
    χάρισμα   noun, nom. sg. neut. {2.C} . . . . id.
    χαρίσματα   noun, acc. pl. neut. {2.C} . . . . id.
    χαρίσματα   noun, nom. pl. neut. {2.C} . . . . . . id.
    χαρίσματι   noun, dat. sg. neut. {2.C} . . . . id.
    χαρίσματος   noun, gen. sg. neut. {2.C} . . . . . . id.
    χαρισμάτων   noun, gen. pl. neut. {2.C} . . . . . . id.
    χάριτα   noun, acc. sg. fem. {2.C} . . . . χάρις G5485
    χάριτας   noun, acc. pl. fem. {2.C} . . . . id.
    χάριτι   noun, dat. sg. fem. {2.C} . . . . id.
    χάριτος   noun, gen. sg. fem. {2.C} . . . . id.

G5487 **χαριτόω**   *I endue with grace* (properly, *I endow*
    with χάρις, *the divine favor*); in Eph 1:6 fol-
    lowed by cog. acc. (gen.).
    χαροῦσιν   verb, fut. act. indic. 3 pers. pl.
    {5.A.2} . . . . χαίρω G5463

G5488 **Χαρράν**, ἡ   *Haran,* identical with Carrae, in
    Mesopotamia.
    Χαρράν   noun prop. . . . . Χαρράν G5488

G5489 **χάρτης**, -ου, ὁ   *papyrus, paper.*
    χάρτου   noun, gen. sg. masc. {2.A} . . . . . χάρτης G5489

G5490 **χάσμα**, -ατος, τό   (from χαίνω, *I yawn*), *an*
    intervening space, a chasm.
    χάσμα   noun, nom. sg. neut. {2.C} . . . . χάσμα G5490
    χείλεσι   noun, dat. pl. neut. {2.C} . . . . χεῖλος G5491
    χείλεσιν   noun, dat. pl. neut. {2.C} . . . . id.
    χειλέων   noun, gen. pl. neut. {2.C} . . . . id.
    χείλη   noun, acc. pl. neut. {2.C} . . . . id.

G5491 **χεῖλος**, -ους, τό   (1) *a lip;* (2) hence, *the edge,*
    Heb 11:12.
    χεῖλος   noun, acc. sg. neut. {2.C} . . . . χεῖλος G5491
    χειμαζομένων   vbl., pres. pass. ptc. gen. pl. masc.
    {6.A.1} . . . . χειμάζω G5492

G5492 **χειμάζω**   pass. *I am exposed to bad weather, I*
    am in the grip of a storm.

G5493 **χείμαρρος** (χειμάρρους), -ου, ὁ   *a winter*
    torrent.
    χειμάρρου   noun, gen. sg. masc. {2.B} . χείμαρρος G5493

G5494 **χειμών**, -ῶνος, ὁ   (1) *winter;* (2) *stormy*
    weather, Matt 16:3; Acts 27:20.
    χειμών   noun, nom. sg. masc. {2.C} . . . . . χειμών G5494
    χειμῶνος   noun, gen. sg. masc. {2.C} . . . . id.

G5495 **χείρ**, χειρός, ἡ   (1) *a hand;* (2) used also with
    reference to God, meaning, His power in ac-
    tion, Luke 1:66; 1 Pet 5:6, etc.; (3) διὰ χειρός
    (χειρῶν), *by the instrumentality of;* and so
    also ἐν χειρί (Hebraistic), Acts 7:35.
    χείρ   noun, nom. sg. fem. {2.C} . . . . χείρ G5495
    χεῖρα   noun, acc. sg. fem. {2.C} . . . . id.

G5496 **χειραγωγέω**   *I lead by the hand.*

G5497 **χειραγωγός**, -οῦ, ὁ   *one who leads* a helpless
    person *by the hand.*
    χειραγωγούμενος   vbl., pres. pass. ptc. nom. sg.
    masc. {6.A.2} . . . . χειραγωγέω G5496
    χειραγωγοῦντες   vbl., pres. act. ptc. nom. pl.
    masc. {6.A.2} . . . . id.

χειραγωγούς   noun, acc. pl. masc.
    {2.B} . . . . χειραγωγός G5497
χεῖρας   noun, acc. pl. fem. {2.C} . . . . χείρ G5495
χεῖρες   noun, nom. pl. fem. {2.C} . . . . id.
χειρί   noun, dat. sg. fem. {2.C} . . . . id.

G5498 **χειρόγραφον**, -ου, τό   properly, *a signature,*
    hence, as a term of a court of justice, (1) *a*
    bill, bond, certificate of debt; or (2) any *written*
    obligation or *agreement.*
    χειρόγραφον   noun, acc. sg. neut.
    {2.B} . . . . χειρόγραφον G5498
    χεῖρον   adj. comp., acc. sg. neut. {3.E; 3.G}. χείρων G5501
    χεῖρον   adj. comp., nom. sg. neut. {3.E; 3.G}. . . . id.
    χείρονα   adj. comp., nom. pl. neut. {3.E; 3.G} . . id.
    χείρονος   adj. comp., gen. sg. fem. {3.E; 3.G} . . . id.
    χειροποίητα   adj., acc. pl. neut.
    {3.C} . . . . χειροποίητος G5499
    χειροποιήτοις   adj., dat. pl. masc. {3.C} . . . . . . id.
    χειροποίητον   adj., acc. sg. masc. {3.C} . . . . . . id.

G5499 **χειροποίητος**, -ον   *made by hand, handmade.*
    χειροποιήτου   adj., gen. sg. fem.
    {3.C} . . . . χειροποίητος G5499
    χειρός   noun, gen. sg. fem. {2.C} . . . . χείρ G5495

G5500 **χειροτονέω**   *I elect* (lit. *I stretch out the hand,*
    thus expressing agreement with a motion,
    then, *I* popularly *elect by show of hands.*
    χειροτονηθείς   vbl., aor. pass. ptc. nom. sg. masc.
    {6.A.1.a.} . . . . χειροτονέω G5500
    χειροτονηθέντα   vbl., aor. pass. ptc. acc. sg.
    masc. {6.A.1.a.} . . . . id.
    χειροτονήσαντες   vbl., aor. act. ptc. nom. pl.
    masc. {6.A.2} . . . . id.

G5501 **χείρων**, -ον, gen. ονος   comp., *worse;* ἐπὶ τὸ
    χεῖρον, *to the (a) worse result (degree).*
    χείρων   adj., nom. sg. fem. {3.E} . . . . χείρων G5501
    χείρων   adj., nom. sg. masc. {3.E} . . . . id.
    χειρῶν   adj., nom. sg. fem. {3.E} . . . . id.
    χειρῶν   adj., nom. sg. masc. {3.E} . . . . id.
    χειρῶν   noun, gen. pl. fem. {2.C} . . . . χείρ G5495

G5502 **Χερούβ**, pl. Χερουβίν (-βείν, -βίμ, -βείμ,),
    τό   *cherub,* pl. *cherubim,* two golden figures
    of winged animals over the mercy seat (and
    the ark) in the Jewish tabernacle (χερουβίν/-
    είν is Aram., while -ίμ/-είμ is Heb.).
    Χερουβείν   noun prop. . . . . Χερούβ G5502
    Χερουβίμ   noun prop. . . . . id.
    Χερουβίν   noun prop. . . . . id.
    χερσί   noun, dat. pl. fem. {2.C} . . . . χείρ G5495
    χερσίν   noun, dat. pl. fem. {2.C} . . . . id.

G5503 **χήρα**, -ας, ἡ   *a widow.*
    χήρα   noun, nom. sg. fem. {2.A} . . . . χήρα G5503
    χῆραι   noun, nom. pl. fem. {2.A} . . . . id.
    χήραις   noun, dat. pl. fem. {2.A} . . . . id.
    χήραν   noun, acc. sg. fem. {2.A} . . . . id.
    χήρας   noun, acc. pl. fem. {2.A} . . . . id.
    χηρῶν   noun, gen. pl. fem. {2.A} . . . . id.

G5504 **χθές**   adv., *yesterday.*
    χθές   adv. . . . . χθές G5504
    χίλια   adj. num., acc. pl. neut. {3.A} . . . . . . χίλιοι G5507
    χίλια   adj. num., nom. pl. neut. {3.A} . . . . id.

χιλιάδες   noun, nom. pl. fem. {2.C} . . . . . χιλιάς G5505‡
χιλιάδων   noun, gen. pl. fem. {2.C} . . . . id.
χιλίαρχοι   noun, nom. pl. masc. {2.B} . . χιλίαρχος G5506
χιλιάρχοις   noun, dat. pl. masc. {2.B} . . . . id.
χιλίαρχον   noun, acc. sg. masc. {2.B} . . . . id.
G5506 **χιλίαρχος**, -ου, ὁ   (lit. *a ruler of a thousand*),
    a tribune, a Roman officer commanding a
    cohort, i.e., about a thousand men), *a colonel.*
χιλίαρχος   noun, nom. sg. masc. {2.B} . . χιλίαρχος G5506
χιλιάρχῳ   noun, dat. sg. masc. {2.B} . . . . id.
χιλιάρχων   noun, gen. pl. masc. {2.B} . . . . id.
G5505‡ **χιλιάς**, -άδος, ἡ   *a thousand*, looked upon as a
    unit.
χιλίας   adj. num., acc. pl. fem. {3.A} . . . . . . χίλιοι G5507
χιλιάσιν   noun, dat. pl. fem. {2.C} . . . . . χιλιάς G5505‡
G5507 **χίλιοι**, -αι, -α   *one thousand, a thousand.*
χιλίων   adj. num., gen. pl. masc. {3.A} . . . . χίλιοι G5507
G5508 **Χίος**, -ου, ἡ   *Chios* (mod. Scio), an important
    island in the Aegean Sea, off the west central
    coast of Asia Minor.
Χίου   noun prop., gen. sg. fem. {2.B; 2.D} . . . . Χίος G5508
G5509 **χιτών**, -ῶνος, ὁ   *a tunic, an undergarment* (a
    Semitic word).
χιτών   noun, nom. sg. masc. {2.C} . . . . χιτών G5509
χιτῶνα   noun, acc. sg. masc. {2.C} . . . . id.
χιτῶνας   noun, acc. pl. masc. {2.C} . . . . id.
G5510 **χιών**, -όνος, ἡ   *snow.*
χιών   noun, nom. sg. fem. {2.C} . . . . χιών G5510
χλαμύδα   noun, acc. sg. fem. {2.C} . . . . . χλαμύς G5511
G5511 **χλαμύς**, -ύδος, ἡ   *a cloak.*
χλευάζοντες   vbl., pres. act. ptc. nom. pl. masc.
    {6.A.1} . . . . χλευάζω G5512
G5512 **χλευάζω**   *I scoff* by gesture and word.
G5513 **χλιαρός**, -ά, -όν   *lukewarm, tepid.*
χλιαρός   adj., nom. sg. masc. {3.A} . . . . χλιαρός G5513
G5514 **Χλόη**, -ης, ἡ   *Chloe*, a woman, probably with
    business connections either in Corinth or in
    Ephesus or in both.
Χλόης   noun prop., gen. sg. fem. {2.A; 2.D} . . Χλόη G5514
χλωρόν   adj., acc. sg. neut. {3.A} . . . . χλωρός G5515
G5515 **χλωρός**, -ά, -όν   *of the color of grass, green* or
    yellow, as the case may be (from χλόη).
χλωρός   adj., nom. sg. masc. {3.A} . . . . . . χλωρός G5515
χλωρῷ   adj., dat. sg. masc. {3.A} . . . . id.
G5516 **χ´ξ´ς´**   666 (letters of the Greek alphabet used as
    numbers, denoting respectively 600, 60 and 6).
χοϊκοί   adj., nom. pl. masc. {3.A} . . . . χοϊκός G5517
G5517 **χοϊκός**, -ή, -όν   *made of earth (dust)* and with
    the quality attaching to this origin (from
    χοῦς).
χοϊκός   adj., nom. sg. masc. {3.A} . . . . χοϊκός G5517
χοϊκοῦ   adj., gen. sg. masc. {3.A} . . . . id.
χοίνικες   noun, nom. pl. fem. {2.C} . . . . . . χοῖνιξ G5518
G5518 **χοῖνιξ**, -ικος, ἡ   a Greek dry *measure*, equiva-
    lent to 1.92 pints.
χοῖνιξ   noun, nom. sg. fem. {2.C} . . . . . . χοῖνιξ G5518
χοῖροι   noun, nom. pl. masc. {2.B} . . . . . . χοῖρος G5519
G5519 **χοῖρος**, -ου, ὁ   *a pig.*
χοίρους   noun, acc. pl. masc. {2.B} . . . . χοῖρος G5519
χοίρων   noun, gen. pl. masc. {2.B} . . . . id.

χολᾶτε   verb, pres. act. indic. 2 pers. pl.
    {5.A.2} . . . . χολάω G5520
G5520 **χολάω**   *I am angry with.*
G5521 **χολή**, -ῆς, ἡ   (1) *gall, bile*, Matt 27:34; (2) met.
    bitterness, i.e., intense malignity. In LXX it
    represents three Heb. words, meaning respec-
    tively, (1) *gall, bile;* (2) *wormwood;* (3) *poison.*
χολήν   noun, acc. sg. fem. {2.A} . . . . χολή G5521
χολῆς   noun, gen. sg. fem. {2.A} . . . . id.
G5522 **χόος** (χοῦς), acc. χοῦν, ὁ   *dust.*
Χοραζείν   noun prop. . . . . Χοραζίν G5523
G5523 **Χοραζίν**, ἡ   *Chorazin*, probably the pres-
    ent Keρâze, ruins northwest of Tell-hum
    (Capernaum?).
Χοραζίν   noun prop. . . . . Χοραζίν G5523
χορηγεῖ   verb, pres. act. indic. 3 pers. sg.
    {5.A.2} . . . . χορηγέω G5524
G5524 **χορηγέω**   *I supply* (with lavish hand).
χορηγῆσαι   verb, aor. act. opt. 3 pers. sg.
    {5.C.1} . . . . χορηγέω G5524
χορηγήσει   verb, fut. act. indic. 3 pers. sg.
    {5.A.1} . . . . id.
G5525 **χορός**, -οῦ, ὁ   *dancing.*
χορτάζεσθαι   vbl., pres. pass. inf. {6.B.1} . χορτάζω G5526
χορτάζεσθε   verb, pres. mid./pass. impv.
    2 pers. pl. {5.D.1} . . . . id.
G5526 **χορτάζω**   (from χόρτος, in earlier Gk. of feed-
    ing animals), *I feed to the full, I satisfy with
    food.*
χορτάσαι   vbl., aor. act. inf. {6.B.1} . . . . . χορτάζω G5526
χορτασθῆναι   vbl., aor. pass. inf. {6.B.1} . . . . . id.
χορτασθήσεσθε   verb, fut. pass. indic. 2 pers.
    pl. {5.A.1.d} . . . . id.
χορτασθήσονται   verb, fut. pass. indic. 3 pers.
    pl. {5.A.1.d} . . . . id.
G5527 **χόρτασμα**, -ατος, τό   *food, sustenance, corn*
    for man as well as beast.
χορτάσματα   noun, acc. pl. neut. {2.C} . χόρτασμα G5527
χόρτον   noun, acc. sg. masc. {2.B} . . . . χόρτος G5528
G5528 **χόρτος**, -ου, ὁ   *grass, hay*, such grass or herbage
    as makes fodder.
χόρτος   noun, nom. sg. masc. {2.B} . . . . . . χόρτος G5528
χόρτου   noun, gen. sg. masc. {2.B} . . . . id.
χόρτους   noun, acc. pl. masc. {2.B} . . . . id.
χόρτῳ   noun, dat. sg. masc. {2.B} . . . . id.
χορῶν   noun, gen. pl. masc. {2.B} . . . . χορός G5525
Χουζᾶ   noun prop., gen. sg. masc. {2.A;
    2.D} . . . . Χουζᾶς G5529
G5529 **Χουζᾶς**, -ᾶ, ὁ   *Chuza*, a steward of Herod
    Antipas.
χοῦν   noun, acc. sg. masc. {2.B} . . . . χόος G5522
G5530 **χράομαι**   *I use, employ* (from χρή, "necessity,"
    properly, "I make for myself what is necessary
    with something"); in 1 Cor 7:21 perhaps un-
    derstand τῇ ἐλευθερίᾳ; with persons, *I treat*,
    Acts 27:3.
G5531 **χράω**   *I lend.*
G5532 **χρεία**, -ας, ἡ   (1) *need;* (2) any special *occasion*
    or *matter in hand*, Acts 6:3; Eph 4:29(?).
χρεία   noun, nom. sg. fem. {2.A} . . . . χρεία G5532

χρείαις   noun, dat. pl. fem. {2.A} . . . . id.
χρείαν   noun, acc. sg. fem. {2.A} . . . . id.
χρείας   noun, acc. pl. fem. {2.A} . . . . id.
χρείας   noun, gen. sg. fem. {2.A} . . . . id.
χρεοφειλέται   noun, nom. pl. masc.
   {2.A} . . . . χρεοφειλέτης G5533
G5533 **χρεοφειλέτης** (χρεωφειλέτης), -ου, ὁ   *a*
   debtor.
χρεοφειλετῶν   noun, gen. pl. masc.
   {2.A} . . . . χρεοφειλέτης G5533
χρεοφιλετῶν   noun, nom. pl. masc. {2.A} . . . . . id.
χρεοφιλετῶν   noun, gen. pl. masc. {2.A} . . . . . id.
χρεωφειλέται   noun, nom. pl. masc. {2.A} . . . . id.
χρεωφειλετῶν   noun, gen. pl. masc. {2.A} . . . . . id.
G5534 **χρή**   *it is fitting, it is necessary* (it is congruous
   to a law or standard); the word is somewhat
   vague.
χρή   verb, pres. act. indic. 3 pers. sg. . . . . χρή G5534
χρήζει   verb, pres. act. indic. 3 pers. sg.
   {5.A.1.a} . . . . χρήζω G5535
χρήζετε   verb, pres. act. indic. 2 pers. pl.
   {5.A.1.a} . . . . id.
χρήζῃ   verb, pres. act. subjunc. 3 pers. sg. {5.B.1} id.
χρήζομεν   verb, pres. act. indic. 1 pers. pl.
   {5.A.1.a} . . . . id.
G5535 **χρήζω**   *I need, have need.*
G5536 **χρῆμα**, -ατος, τό   (1) pl. *property, possessions,*
   riches; (2) sg. *the money got, the proceeds,* Acts
   4:37.
χρῆμα   noun, acc. sg. neut. {2.C} . . . . χρῆμα G5536
χρήμασιν   noun, dat. pl. neut. {2.C} . . . . id.
χρήματα   noun, acc. pl. neut. {2.C} . . . . id.
χρήματα   noun, nom. pl. neut. {2.C} . . . . id.
χρηματίζοντα   vbl., pres. act. ptc. acc. sg. masc.
   {6.A.1} . . . . χρηματίζω G5537
G5537 **χρηματίζω**   (orig., *I transact business*), (1) act.,
   of God, *I warn,* Heb 12:25; pass. *I am warned*
   by God (properly in response to an inquiry as
   to one's duty), Matt 2:12, 22; Luke 2:26; Acts
   10:22; Heb 8:5; 11:7; (2) *(I take a name from*
   my public business), hence, *I receive a name, I*
   am publicly called . . . , Acts 11:26; Rom 7:3.
χρηματίσαι   vbl., aor. act. inf. {6.B.1}   χρηματίζω G5537
χρηματίσει   verb, fut. act. indic. 3 pers. sg.
   {5.A.1.a} . . . . id.
χρηματισθείς   vbl., aor. pass. ptc. nom. sg.
   masc. {6.A.1.a} . . . . id.
χρηματισθέντες   vbl., aor. pass. ptc. nom. pl.
   masc. {6.A.1.a} . . . . id.
G5538 **χρηματισμός**, -οῦ, ὁ   *a response of God* (to an
   inquiry as to one's duty), *an oracle.*
χρηματισμός   noun, nom. sg. masc.
   {2.B} . . . . χρηματισμός G5538
χρημάτων   noun, gen. pl. neut. {2.C} . . . . . χρῆμα G5536
χρῆσαι   verb, aor. mid. impv. 2 pers. sg.
   {5.D.1} . . . . χράομαι G5530
χρησάμενος   vbl., aor. mid. ptc. nom. sg. masc.
   {6.A.2} . . . . id.
χρήσθ᾽   adj., acc. pl. neut. {3.A} . . . . χρηστός G5543
χρήσιμον   adj., acc. sg. neut. {3.A} . . . . χρήσιμος G5539

G5539 **χρήσιμος**, -η, -ον   (1) *useful;* (2) neut. subs.
   profit, value.
χρῆσιν   noun, acc. sg. fem. {2.C} . . . . χρῆσις G5540
G5540 **χρῆσις**, -εως, ἡ   *usage, use.*
χρῆσον   verb, aor. act. impv. 2 pers. sg.
   {5.D.1} . . . . χράω G5531
χρηστά   adj., acc. pl. neut. {3.A} . . . . χρηστός G5543
χρηστεύεται   verb, pres. mid./pass. indic. 3 pers.
   sg. {5.A.1.d} . . . . χρηστεύομαι G5541
G5541 **χρηστεύομαι**   *I play the part of a kind person*
   (full of service to others).
χρηστοί   adj., nom. pl. masc. {3.A} . . . . . χρηστός G5543
G5542 **χρηστολογία**, -ας, ἡ   *affectation of kind speech,*
   with insinuating tone.
χρηστολογίας   noun, gen. sg. fem.
   {2.A} . . . . χρηστολογία G5542
χρηστόν   adj., nom. sg. neut. {3.A} . . . . . χρηστός G5543
G5543 **χρηστός**, -ή, -όν   (1) *good;* (2) hence, *comfort-*
   able, kindly, not pressing, Matt 11:30; (3)
   often has the idea of *kind;* subs. τὸ χρηστόν,
   kindness.
χρηστός   adj., nom. sg. masc. {3.A} . . . . . χρηστός G5543
χρηστότερος   adj. comp., nom. sg. masc. {3.A;
   3.G} . . . . id.
G5544 **χρηστότης**, -ητος, ἡ   *kindness, kindliness* (see
   χρηστός).
χρηστότης   noun, nom. sg. fem. {2.C} . χρηστότης G5544
χρηστότητα   noun, acc. sg. fem. {2.C} . . . . id.
χρηστότητι   noun, dat. sg. fem. {2.C} . . . . id.
χρηστότητος   noun, gen. sg. fem. {2.C} . . . . . . id.
χρήσωμαι   verb, aor. mid. subjunc. 1 pers. sg.
   {5.B.1} . . . . χράομαι G5530
χρῆται   verb, pres. mid./pass. subjunc. 3 pers.
   sg. {5.B.2} . . . . id.
χρίσας   vbl., aor. act. ptc. nom. sg. masc.
   {6.A.1.a} . . . . χρίω G5548
χρῖσμα   noun, acc. sg. neut. {2.C} . . . . . . χρῖσμα G5545
χρῖσμα   noun, nom. sg. neut. {2.C} . . . . id.
G5545 **χρῖσμα**, -ατος, τό   *anointing,* referring to the
   gift of holy spirit.
χρῖσμα   noun, acc. sg. neut. {2.C} . . . . χρῖσμα G5545
χρῖσμα   noun, nom. sg. neut. {2.C} . . . . id.
Χριστέ   noun prop., voc. sg. masc. {2.B;
   2.D} . . . . Χριστός G5547
Χριστιανόν   noun prop., acc. sg. masc. {2.B;
   2.D} . . . . Χριστιανός G5546
G5546 **Χριστιανός**, -οῦ, ὁ   *Christian, a follower of*
   Christ. See Χριστός. The formation is Lat.,
   and indicates either *partisan of Christ* or
   more exactly *soldier of Christ* (cf. Fimbriani,
   Caesariani, Pompeiani).
Χριστιανός   noun prop., nom. sg. masc. {2.B;
   2.D} . . . . Χριστιανός G5546
Χριστιανούς   noun prop., acc. pl. masc. {2.B;
   2.D} . . . . id.
Χριστόν   noun prop., acc. sg. masc. {2.B;
   2.D} . . . . Χριστός G5547
Χριστος   noun prop., nom. sg. masc. {2.B; 2.D} . id.
G5547 **Χριστός**, -οῦ, ὁ   (a rare verbal from χρίω, "*I*
   anoint," and therefore *anointed,* ὁ Χριστός

being an epithet used at first practically in the sense of *the king,* anointing being the outward sign of his appointment to kingship, cf. 1 Sam 10:1; 12:3; 15:1 and often), (1) ὁ Χριστός, *the anointed, the Messiah* (the Aram. equivalent of ὁ Χριστός, John 1:41, *the expected king* of Israel, to be appointed by God as his vicegerent. In NT this epithet is, therefore, attached (either prefixed or affixed) to (ὁ) = Ἰησοῦς, *Jesus,* recognized by his followers as the expected Messiah; the epithet with or without article is also found alone referring to Jesus; (2) gradually it tends to lose the meaning it originally had and to become merely a proper name, *Christ.* By many the curious word was confused with χρηστός, "good," which as a proper name was often a slave name, and thus Χριστιανοί became Χρηστιανοί, confusion being due to the fact that the two words were pronounced alike.

Χριστός   noun prop., nom. sg. masc. {2.B; 2.D}. Χριστός G5547
Χριστοῦ   noun prop., gen. sg. masc. {2.B; 2.D}. . id.
Χριστῷ   noun prop., dat. sg. masc. {2.B; 2.D}. . . id.

G5548 **χρίω**   *I anoint,* to the kingly office, used generally with regard to dedication to Messiahship, etc.
χρονιεῖ   verb, fut. act. indic. 3 pers. sg. {5.A.2}. χρονίζω G5549
χρονίζει   verb, pres. act. indic. 3 pers. sg. {5.A.1.a}. . . . . id.
χρονίζειν   vbl., pres. act. inf. {6.B.1}. . . . . id.
χρονίζοντος   vbl., pres. act. ptc. gen. sg. masc. {6.A.1}. . . . . id.

G5549 **χρονίζω**   *I delay.*
χρονίσει   verb, fut. act. indic. 3 pers. sg. {5.A.1.a}. . . . . χρονίζω G5549
χρόνοις   noun, dat. pl. masc. {2.B}. . . . . . χρόνος G5550
χρόνον   noun, acc. sg. masc. {2.B}. . . . . id.

G5550 **χρόνος**, -ου, ὁ   (1) *time;* (2) *a time, period* (instrumental in Luke 8:27; Rom 16:25); (3) locative, πολλοῖς χρόνοις, *oftentimes,* Luke 8:29.
χρόνος   noun, nom. sg. masc. {2.B} . . . . . χρόνος G5550

G5551 **χρονοτριβέω**   *I waste time.*
χρονοτριβῆσαι   vbl., aor. act. inf. {6.B.1}. . . . . χρονοτριβέω G5551
χρόνου   noun, gen. sg. masc. {2.B}. . . . . . χρόνος G5550
χρόνους   noun, acc. pl. masc. {2.B} . . . . id.
χρόνῳ   noun, dat. sg. masc. {2.B} . . . . id.
χρόνων   noun, gen. pl. masc. {2.B}. . . . . id.
χρυσᾶ   adj., acc. pl. neut. {3.A}. . . . . . . χρύσεος G5552
χρυσᾶ   adj., nom. pl. neut. {3.A} . . . . id.
χρυσᾶν   adj., acc. sg. fem. {3.A} . . . . id.
χρυσᾶς   adj., acc. pl. fem. {3.A} . . . . id.

G5552 **χρύσεος** (χρυσοῦς), -ῆ, -οῦν   *made of gold, golden.*
χρυσῆ   adj., nom. sg. fem. {3.A}. . . . . . . χρύσεος G5552
χρυσῆν   adj., acc. sg. fem. {3.A} . . . . id.

G5553 **χρυσίον**, -ου, τό   (1) *gold;* (2) pl. *gold (golden) ornaments,* 1 Pet 3:3.

χρυσίον   noun, acc. sg. neut. {2.B}. . . . . . χρυσίον G5553
χρυσίον   noun, nom. sg. neut. {2.B}. . . . . id.
χρυσίου   noun, gen. sg. neut. {2.B} . . . . id.
χρυσίῳ   noun, dat. sg. neut. {2.B}. . . . . id.
χρυσίων   noun, gen. pl. neut. {2.B} . . . . id.

G5554 **χρυσοδακτύλιος**, -ον   *with (wearing) a* (one or more) *gold ring(s)* on the finger(s).
χρυσοδακτύλιος   adj., nom. sg. masc. {3.C}. . . . . χρυσοδακτύλιος G5554
χρυσοῖ   adj., nom. pl. masc. {3.A}. . . . . χρύσεος G5552

G5555 **χρυσόλιθος**, -ου, ὁ   a sparkling gem, of gold-yellow color, possibly our *topaz,* almost certainly not our *chrysolite.*
χρυσόλιθος   noun, nom. sg. masc. {2.B} . . . . χρυσόλιθος G5555
χρυσόν   noun, acc. sg. masc. {2.B}. . . . . . χρυσός G5557

G5556 **χρυσόπρασος**, -ου, ὁ   a precious stone of leek-green color, which sparkled golden yellow, from India, perhaps *fluorite,* certainly not *chrysoprase.*
χρυσόπρασος   noun, nom. sg. masc. {2.B} . . . . χρυσόπρασος G5556

G5557 **χρυσός**, -οῦ, ὁ   *gold.*
χρυσός   noun, nom. sg. masc. {2.B} . . . . . . χρυσός G5557
χρυσοῦ   adj., gen. sg. neut. {3.A} . . . . . . χρύσεος G5552
χρυσοῦ   noun, gen. sg. masc. {2.B}. . . . . . χρυσός G5557
χρυσοῦν   adj., acc. sg. masc. {3.A}. . . . . . χρύσεος G5552
χρυσοῦν   adj., acc. sg. neut. {3.A} . . . . id.
χρυσοῦς   adj., acc. pl. masc. {3.A} . . . . id.

G5558 **χρυσόω**   *I adorn with gold, I overlay with gold.*
χρυσῷ   noun, dat. sg. masc. {2.B} . . . . . . χρυσός G5557
χρυσῶν   adj., gen. pl. fem. {3.A}. . . . . . χρύσεος G5552
χρῶ   verb, pres. mid./pass. impv. 2 pers. sg. {5.D.2}. . . . . χράομαι G5530
χρώμεθα   verb, pres. mid./pass. indic. 1 pers. pl. {5.A.2}. . . . . id.
χρώμενοι   vbl., pres. mid./pass. ptc. nom. pl. masc. {6.A.2}. id.

G5559 **χρώς**, χρωτός, ὁ   *skin.*
χρωτός   noun, gen. sg. masc. {2.C}. . . . . . . χρώς G5559
χωλοί   adj., nom. pl. masc. {3.A} . . . . χωλός G5560
χωλόν   adj., acc. sg. masc. {3.A} . . . . id.
χωλόν   adj., nom. sg. neut. {3.A}. . . . . id.

G5560 **χωλός**, -ή, -όν   *lame;* generalizing neut., Heb 12:13.
χωλός   adj., nom. sg. masc. {3.A} . . . . χωλός G5560
χωλοῦ   adj., gen. pl. masc. {3.A}. . . . . id.
χωλούς   adj., acc. pl. masc. {3.A}. . . . . id.
χωλῶν   adj., gen. pl. masc. {3.A}. . . . . id.

G5561 **χώρα**, -ας, ἡ   (1) strictly used, *a region,* a great geographical (and sometimes administrative) division of a province, e.g., Acts 16:6; 18:23, but often more loosely, *country, district;* (2) hence met., e.g., Matt 4:16; (3) sometimes almost *a field,* John 4:35; Jas 5:4.
χώρα   noun, nom. sg. fem. {2.A} . . . . .χώρα G5561
χώρα   noun, dat. sg. fem. {2.A}. . . . . id.
Χωραζίν   noun prop.. . . . . Χοραζίν G5523
χώραις   noun, dat. pl. fem. {2.A} . . . . .χώρα G5561
χώραν   noun, acc. sg. fem. {2.A}. . . . . id.

χώρας   noun, acc. pl. fem. {2.A} . . . . id.

χώρας   noun, gen. sg. fem. {2.A} . . . . id.

χωρεῖ   verb, pres. act. indic. 3 pers. sg.
{5.A.2}. . . . . χωρέω *G5562*

χωρεῖν   vbl., pres. act. inf. {6.B.2} . . . . id.

χωρείτω   verb, pres. act. impv. 3 pers. sg. {5.D.2} id.

G5562 **χωρέω**   (1) intrans., (a) *I go away, I withdraw, I come,* lit. and met., Matt 15:17; 2 Pet 3:9; (b) *I have room, find room,* John 8:37; (2) trans., (a) *I contain, am capable of receiving, hold, grasp,* Mark 2:2; Matt 19:11; etc.; (b) *I make room for (I give a place to) someone in my heart,* *I take into* my heart., 2 Cor 7:2.

χωρῆσαι   vbl., aor. act. inf. {6.B.1} . . . . χωρέω *G5562*

χωρήσατε   verb, aor. act. impv. 2 pers. pl. {5.D.1} id.

χωρήσειν   vbl., fut. act. inf. {6.B.1}. . . . . id.

χωρία   noun, nom. pl. neut. {2.B} . . . . χωρίον *G5564*

χωρίζεσθαι   vbl., pres. pass. inf. {6.B.1} . . . χωρίζω *G5563*

χωριζέσθω   verb, pres. pass. impv. 3 pers. sg.
{5.D.1}. . . . . id.

χωρίζεται   verb, pres. mid./pass. indic. 3 pers.
sg. {5.A.1.d}. . . . . id.

χωριζέτω   verb, pres. act. impv. 3 pers. sg.
{5.D.1}. . . . . id.

G5563 **χωρίζω**   (1) act. trans., *I separate, I put apart;* (2) mid. or pass. *I separate myself, I depart.*

G5564 **χωρίον**, -ου, τό   (1) *a place;* (2) *a piece of land, a field,* enclosed (diminutive of χώρα or χῶρος).

χωρίον   noun, acc. sg. neut. {2.B} . . . . χωρίον *G5564*

χωρίου   noun, gen. sg. neut. {2.B} . . . . id.

G5565 **χωρίς**   (1) adv., *separately, apart, by itself;* (2) prep. with gen., *apart from, separate from, without.*

χωρίς   adv., prep. .χωρίς *G5565*

χωρίσαι   vbl., aor. act. inf. {6.B.1}. . . . . χωρίζω *G5563*

χωρίσει   verb, fut. act. indic. 3 pers. sg. {5.A.1.a} id.

χωρισθείς   vbl., aor. pass. ptc. nom. sg. masc.
{6.A.1.a} . . . . id.

χωρισθῇ   verb, aor. pass. subjunc. 3 pers. sg.
{5.B.1} . . . . id.

χωρισθῆναι   vbl., aor. pass. inf. {6.B.1} . . . . id.

χωρίων   noun, gen. pl. neut. {2.B} . . . . . . χωρίον *G5564*

χῶρον   noun, acc. sg. masc. {2.B} . . . . χῶρος *G5566*

G5566 **χῶρος**, -ου, ὁ   *the northwest wind,* and so, the quarter of the sky from which it comes, *northwest* (Lat., *caurus, corus*).

χωροῦσαι   vbl., pres. act. ptc. nom. pl. fem.
{6.A.2} . . . . .χωρέω *G5562*

χωροῦσι   verb, pres. act. indic. 3 pers. pl. {5.A.2} id.

χωροῦσιν   verb, pres. act. indic. 3 pers. pl.
{5.A.2}. . . . . id.

Ψ ψ

ψαλλέτω   verb, pres. act. impv. 3 pers. sg.
{5.D.1}. . . . . ψάλλω *G5567*

ψάλλοντες   vbl., pres. act. ptc. nom. pl. masc.
{6.A.1}. . . . . id.

G5567 **ψάλλω**   *I play on the harp* (or other stringed instrument).

ψαλμοῖς   noun, dat. pl. masc. {2.B} . . . . . .ψαλμός *G5568*

ψαλμόν   noun, acc. sg. masc. {2.B}. . . . . id.

G5568 **ψαλμός**, -οῦ, ὁ   *a psalm,* i.e., a song of praise, etc., to God, with an accompaniment on the harp.

ψαλμῷ   noun, dat. sg. masc. {2.B} . . . . . . .ψαλμός *G5568*

ψαλμῶν   noun, gen. pl. masc. {2.B} . . . . id.

ψαλῶ   verb, fut. act. indic. 1 pers. sg.
{5.A.2}. . . . . ψάλλω *G5567*

ψευδαδέλφοις   noun, dat. pl. masc.
{2.B} . . . . .ψευδάδελφος *G5569*

G5569 **ψευδάδελφος**, -ου, ὁ   *a false brother,* i.e., an unreal (insincere) Christian.

ψευδαδέλφους   noun, acc. pl. masc.
{2.B} . . . . .ψευδάδελφος *G5569*

ψευδαπόστολοι   noun, nom. pl. masc.
{2.B} . . . . .ψευδαπόστολος *G5570*

G5570 **ψευδαπόστολος**, -ου, ὁ   *a false apostle,* i.e., one who has received no commission from Jesus to preach the Gospel, though he pretends to have received it.

ψεύδει   noun, dat. sg. neut. {2.C} . . . . ψεῦδος *G5579*

ψευδεῖς   adj., acc. pl. masc. {3.E} . . . . ψευδής *G5571*

ψεύδεσθε   verb, pres. mid./pass. impv. 2 pers. pl.
{5.D.1}. . . . . ψεύδομαι *G5574*

ψευδέσι   adj., dat. pl. masc. {3.E} . . . . ψευδής *G5571*

ψευδέσιν   adj., dat. pl. masc. {3.E} . . . . id.

G5571 **ψευδής**, -ές   (1) *false;* (2) *untrue* in word, etc.

ψευδοδιδάσκαλοι   noun, nom. pl. masc.
{2.B} . . . . .ψευδοδιδάσκαλος *G5572*

G5572 **ψευδοδιδάσκαλος**, -ου, ὁ   *a teacher of false things.*

G5573 **ψευδολόγος**, -ου, ὁ   (1) *speaking false things, lying;* (2) *a liar.*

ψευδολόγων   adj., gen. pl. masc. {3.C} ψευδολόγος *G5573*

G5574 **ψεύδομαι**   (1) *I speak falsely;* (2) with acc. *I deceive by words,* Acts 5:3.

ψεύδομαι   verb, pres. mid./pass. indic. 1 pers.
{5.A.1.d} . . . . ψεύδομαι *G5574*

ψευδομάρτυρες   noun, nom. pl. masc.
{2.C} . . . . ψευδόμαρτυς *G5575‡*

G5576 **ψευδομαρτυρέω**   *I give (bear) false witness.*

ψευδομαρτυρήσεις   verb, fut. act. indic. 2 pers.
sg. {5.A.1} . . . . ψευδομαρτυρέω *G5576*

ψευδομαρτυρήσῃς   verb, aor. act. subjunc.
2 pers. sg. {5.B.1} . . . . id.

G5577 **ψευδομαρτυρία**, -ας, ἡ   (1) *giving of false evidence;* (2) *false witness.*

ψευδομαρτυρίαι   noun, nom. pl. fem.
{2.A} .ψευδομαρτυρία *G5577*

ψευδομαρτυρίαν   noun, acc. sg. fem. {2.A} . . . id.
ψευδομαρτύρων   noun, gen. pl. masc.
{2.C} . . . . ψευδόμαρτυς G5575‡
G5575‡ **ψευδόμαρτυς**, -υρος, ὁ   *a false witness,* one
who gives untrue evidence.
ψευδόμεθα   verb, pres. mid./pass. indic. 1 pers. pl.
{5.A.1.d} . . . . ψεύδομαι G5574
ψευδόμενοι   vbl., pres. mid./pass. ptc. nom. pl.
masc. {6.A.1} . . . . id.
ψεύδονται   verb, pres. mid./pass. indic. 3 pers.
pl. {5.A.1.d} . . . . id.
ψευδοπροφῆται   noun, nom. pl. masc.
{2.A} . . . . .ψευδοπροφήτης G5578
ψευδοπροφήταις   noun, dat. pl. masc. {2.A} . . . id.
ψευδοπροφήτην   noun, acc. sg. masc. {2.A} . . . id.
G5578 **ψευδοπροφήτης**, -ου, ὁ   *a false (untrue, unau-
thenticated) prophet.*
ψευδοπροφήτης   noun, nom. sg. masc.
{2.A} . . . . .ψευδοπροφήτης G5578
ψευδοπροφήτου   noun, gen. sg. masc. {2.A} . . . id.
ψευδοπροφητῶν   noun, gen. pl. masc. {2.A} . . . id.
G5579 **ψεῦδος**, -ους, τό   (1) *that which is false, falsehood;* (2) *an untruth, a lie;* (2) *lying;* in Rom
1:25 abstr. for concr.
ψεῦδος   noun, acc. sg. neut. {2.C} . . . . ψεῦδος G5579
ψεῦδος   noun, nom. sg. neut. {2.C} . . . . id.
ψεύδους   noun, gen. sg. neut. {2.C} . . . . id.
ψευδόχριστοι   noun, nom. pl. masc.
{2.B} . . . . ψευδόχριστος G5580
G5580 **ψευδόχριστος**, -ου, ὁ   *a false Messiah, a pre-
tended Messiah.*
G5581 **ψευδώνυμος**, -ον   *falsely named.*
ψευδωνύμου   adj., gen. sg. fem. {3.C}ψευδώνυμος G5581
ψεύσασθαι   vbl., aor. mid. inf. {6.B.1} . . ψεύδομαι G5574
G5582 **ψεῦσμα**, -ατος, τό   *a lie.*
ψεύσματι   noun, dat. sg. neut. {2.C} . . . . .ψεῦσμα G5582
ψεῦσται   noun, nom. pl. masc. {2.A} . . . . ψεύστης G5583
ψεύσταις   noun, dat. pl. masc. {2.A} . . . . id.
ψεύστην   noun, acc. sg. masc. {2.A} . . . . id.
G5583 **ψεύστης**, -ου, ὁ   *a liar.*
ψεύστης   noun, nom. sg. masc. {2.A} . . . . ψεύστης G5583
G5584 **ψηλαφάω**   *I touch;* in Heb 12:18 perhaps corrupt; πεφεψαλωμένῳ has been suggested,
burnt to ashes, calcined, volcanic.
ψηλαφήσατε   verb, aor. act. impv. 2 pers. pl.
{5.D.1} . . . . ψηλαφάω G5584
ψηλαφήσειαν   verb, aor. act. opt. 3 pers. pl.
{5.C.1} . . . . id.
ψηλαφωμένῳ   vbl., pres. pass. ptc. dat. sg.
neut. {6.A.2} . . . . id.
ψηφίζει   verb, pres. act. indic. 3 pers. sg.
{5.A.1.a} . . . . ψηφίζω G5585
G5585 **ψηφίζω**   *I count up* (lit. with pebbles).
ψηφισάτω   verb, aor. act. impv. 3 pers. sg.
{5.D.1} . . . . ψηφίζω G5585
ψῆφον   noun, acc. sg. fem. {2.B} . . . . ψῆφος G5586
G5586 **ψῆφος**, -ου, ἡ   (1) *a pebble,* Rev 2:17; (2) hence,
from their use in voting, *a vote.*
ψιθυρισμοί   noun, nom. pl. masc.
{2.B} . . . . ψιθυρισμός G5587

G5587 **ψιθυρισμός**, -οῦ, ὁ   *whispering,* esp. of secret
attacks on a person's character.
ψιθυριστάς   noun, acc. pl. masc. {2.A}ψιθυριστής G5588
G5588 **ψιθυριστής**, -οῦ, ὁ   *a whisperer* (cf.
ψιθυρισμός).
G5589 **ψιχίον**, -ου, τό   *a small crumb.*
ψιχίων   noun, gen. pl. neut. {2.B} . . . . .ψιχίον G5589
ψυγήσεται   verb, ²fut. pass. indic. 3 pers. sg.
{5.A.1.d} . . . . .ψύχω G5594
ψυχαί   noun, nom. pl. fem. {2.A} . . . . .ψυχή G5590
ψυχαῖς   noun, dat. pl. fem. {2.A} . . . . id.
ψυχάς   noun, acc. pl. fem. {2.A} . . . . id.
ψύχει   noun, dat. sg. neut. {2.C} . . . . ψῦχος G5592
G5590 **ψυχή**, -ῆς, ἡ   (1) *life,* without any psychological content, Matt 2:20; John 10:11, 15, 17; Acts
15:26; Rom 11:3; 16:4; 1 Cor 15:45; 2 Cor 1:23;
Phil 2:30; 1 Thess 2:8, etc.; (2) *an individual,* or
as a strong pers. pron. (Hebraistic, cf. *nefesh*),
cf. Mark 8:36 (contrast Luke 9:25); Acts 2:41,
43; 3:23; Rom 2:9; 13:1; 2 Cor 12:15; (3)
psychical, *desire,* Eph 6:6; Phil 1:27; Col 3:23,
cf. also 1 Thess 5:23, where the enumeration
is not systematic. The general use of the word
in the Bible is in the sense of whatever is felt
to belong most essentially to man's life, when
his bodily life has come to be regarded as a
secondary thing. It comes near the modern
conception, *self.* See also ψυχικός. In the LXX
there is, in general, a lack of sharp distinction
between ψυχή (lit. *breath, breath of life* in the
individual), πνεῦμα, and καρδία, though
ψυχή generally refers to appetite and desire;
it is there as a rule a translation of the Heb.
nefesh, one of the words for the "breath-soul,"
the personal soul; in Paul, soul (ψυχή) and
spirit (πνεῦμα) are hardly to be distinguished
(yet cf. 1 Cor 15:45; cf. also πνεῦμα).
ψυχή   noun, nom. sg. fem. {2.A} . . . . .ψυχή G5590
ψυχή   noun, voc. sg. fem. {2.A} . . . . id.
ψυχῇ   noun, dat. sg. fem. {2.A} . . . . id.
ψυχήν   noun, acc. sg. fem. {2.A} . . . . id.
ψυχῆς   noun, gen. sg. fem. {2.A} . . . . id.
ψυχική   adj., nom. sg. fem. {3.A} . . . . . ψυχικός G5591
ψυχικοί   adj., nom. pl. masc. {3.A} . . . . id.
ψυχικόν   adj., nom. sg. neut. {3.A} . . . . id.
G5591 **ψυχικός**, -ή, -όν   *emotional* or *sensuous* (from
ψυχή, in the sense "the principle of life and
the basis of its emotional aspect, animating the
present body of flesh, in contrast to the higher
life").
ψυχικός   adj., nom. sg. masc. {3.A} . . . . ψυχικός G5591
ψύχος   noun, acc. sg. neut. {2.C} . . . . ψῦχος G5592
ψύχος   noun, nom. sg. neut. {2.C} . . . . id.
G5592 **ψῦχος**, -ους, τό   *cold.*
ψῦχος   noun, acc. sg. neut. {2.C} . . . . ψῦχος G5592
ψῦχος   noun, nom. sg. neut. {2.C} . . . . id.
G5593 **ψυχρός**, -ά, -όν   (1) lit., *cold,* neut. *cold water,*
Matt 10:42; (2) met. *cold, frigid, indifferent,
phlegmatic.*
ψυχρός   adj., nom. sg. masc. {3.A} . . . . . . ψυχρός G5593

ψυχροῦ   adj., gen. sg. neut. {3.A} . . . . id.

G5594   **ψύχω**   pass. *I become cold, I am extinguished* (of a flame), met.

ψυχῶν   noun, gen. pl. fem. {2.A} . . . . ψυχή G5590

ψώμιζε   verb, pres. act. impv. 2 pers. sg. {5.D.1} . . . . ψωμίζω G5595

G5595   **ψωμίζω**   (1) *I confer a dole upon,* Rom 12:20; (2) *I dole out.*

G5596   **ψωμίον**, -ου, τό   *a little bit, morsel,* or *crumb* of food.

ψωμίον   noun, acc. sg. neut. {2.B} . . . . ψωμίον G5596

ψωμίσω   verb, aor. act. subjunc. 1 pers. sg. {5.B.1} . . . . ψωμίζω G5595

ψώχοντες   vbl., pres. act. ptc. nom. pl. masc. {6.A.1} . . . . ψώχω G5597

G5597   **ψώχω**   *I rub.*

Ω ω

G5598   **Ω**   the last letter of the Gk. alphabet, *Omega* (at first the long and short o sounds were represented by one letter; when distinguished the short was called οὖ or ὄ μικρόν, the long ὦ or ὦ μέγα).

ω   noun, letter . . . . Ω G5598

ὤ   interj. . . . . ὦ G5599

G5599   **ὦ**   an interj. of address, *O.*

ὦ   interj. . . . . ὦ G5599

ὦ   noun, letter . . . . Ω G5598

ὦ   verb, pres. subjunc. 1 pers. sg. {7.B} . . . . . . εἰμί G1510

ᾧ   pron. rel., dat. sg. masc. {4.C} . . . . ὅς G3739

ᾧ   pron. rel., dat. sg. neut. {4.C} . . . . id.

G5601   **Ὠβήδ** (Ἰωβήδ, Ἰωβήλ)   *Obed,* son of Boaz and Ruth, father of Jesse and grandfather of David (Heb.).

Ὠβήδ   noun prop. Ὠβήδ G5601

ᾠδαῖς   noun, dat. pl. fem. {2.A} . . . . ᾠδή G5603

G5602   **ὧδε**   adv., *here,* both of rest and of motion to *(hither);* τὰ ὧδε, the things here, what is here, what is going on here, the state of affairs here.

ὧδε   adv. . . . . ὧδε G5602

G5603   **ᾠδή**, -ῆς, ἡ   *a song.*

ᾠδήν   noun, acc. sg. fem. {2.A} . . . . ᾠδή G5603

G5604   **ὠδίν**, ῖνος, ἡ   (1) *pangs of childbirth, birth pangs,* 1 Thess 5:3; in Acts 2:24 Death is regarded as in *labor* and his pains as relieved by the birth of the child; (2) hence, of any *sharp sudden pain.*

ὠδίν   noun, nom. sg. fem. {2.C} . . . . ὠδίν G5604

ὠδίνας   noun, acc. pl. fem. {2.C} . . . . id.

ὠδίνουσα   vbl., pres. act. ptc. nom. sg. fem. {6.A.1} . . . . ὠδίνω G5605

G5605   **ὠδίνω**   (1) *I suffer birth pangs,* with acc. of the children that are being born; (2) met., Gal 4:19.

ὠδίνω   verb, pres. act. indic. 1 pers. sg. {5.A.1.a} . . . . ὠδίνω G5605

ὠδίνων   noun, gen. pl. fem. {2.C} . . . . ὠδίν G5604

ᾠκοδομήθη   verb, aor. pass. indic. 3 pers. sg. {5.A.1} . . . . οἰκοδομέω G3618

ᾠκοδόμησε   verb, aor. act. indic. 3 pers. sg. {5.A.1} . . . . id.

ᾠκοδόμησεν   verb, aor. act. indic. 3 pers. sg. {5.A.1} . . . . id.

ᾠκοδόμητο   verb, plu. pass. indic. 3 pers. sg. {5.A.1} . . . . id.

ᾠκοδόμουν   verb, impf. act. indic. 3 pers. pl. {5.A.2} . . . . id.

ὦμεν   verb, pres. subjunc. 1 pers. pl. {7.B} . . . . . εἰμί G1510

ὡμίλει   verb, impf. act. indic. 3 pers. sg. {5.A.2} . . . . ὁμιλέω G3656

ὡμίλουν   verb, impf. act. indic. 3 pers. pl. {5.A.2} . . . . id.

ὡμοιώθη   verb, aor. pass. indic. 3 pers. sg. {5.A.1} . . . . ὁμοιόω G3666

ὡμοιώθημεν   verb, aor. pass. indic. 1 pers. pl. {5.A.1} . . . . id.

ὡμολόγησας   verb, aor. act. indic. 2 pers. sg. {5.A.1} . . . . ὁμολογέω G3670

ὡμολόγησε   verb, aor. act. indic. 3 pers. sg. {5.A.1} . . . . id.

ὡμολόγησεν   verb, aor. act. indic. 3 pers. sg. {5.A.1} . . . . id.

ὡμολόγουν   verb, impf. act. indic. 3 pers. pl. {5.A.2} . . . . id.

G5606   **ὦμος**, -ου, ὁ   *shoulder.*

ὤμοσα   verb, aor. act. indic. 1 pers. sg. {5.A.1.b} . . . . ὀμνύω G3660

ὤμοσε   verb, aor. act. indic. 3 pers. sg. {5.A.1.b} . id.

ὤμοσεν   verb, aor. act. indic. 3 pers. sg. {5.A.1.b} id.

ὤμους   noun, acc. pl. masc. {2.B} . . . . ὦμος G5606

ὤν   vbl., pres. ptc. nom. sg. masc. {7.C.1} . . . . . εἰμί G1510

ὧν   pron. rel., gen. pl. fem. {4.C} . . . . ὅς G3739

ὧν   pron. rel., gen. pl. masc. {4.C} . . . . id.

ὧν   pron. rel., gen. pl. neut. {4.C} . . . . id.

ὠνείδιζον   verb, impf. act. indic. 3 pers. pl. {5.A.1.b} . . . . ὀνειδίζω G3679

ὠνείδισε   verb, aor. act. indic. 3 pers. sg. {5.A.1.b} . . . . id.

ὠνείδισεν   verb, aor. act. indic. 3 pers. sg. {5.A.1.b} . . . . id.

G5608   **ὠνέομαι**   *I buy.*

ὠνήσατο   verb, aor. mid. indic. 3 pers. sg. {5.A.1} . . . . ὠνέομαι G5608

ὠνόμασε   verb, aor. act. indic. 3 pers. sg. {5.A.1.b} . . . . ὀνομάζω G3687

ὠνόμασεν   verb, aor. act. indic. 3 pers. sg. {5.A.1.b} . . . . id.

ὠνομάσθη   verb, aor. pass. indic. 3 pers. sg. {5.A.1.b} . . . . id.

G5609   **ᾠόν**, -οῦ, τό   *an egg.*

ᾠόν   noun, acc. sg. neut. {2.B} . . . . ᾠόν G5609

G5610 ὥρα, -ας, ἡ   (1) *an hour*, i.e., a twelfth part of the period from sunrise to sunset, and thus of constantly changing length; (2) the shortest measurement of time among the ancients; (3) sometimes generally of *time;* ὥρα πολλή, *an advanced period of time, a considerable time,* Mark 6:35; πρὸς ὥραν, *for a* (little) *time.*

ὥρα   noun, nom. sg. fem. {2.A} . . . . .ὥρα *G5610*
ὥρᾳ   noun, dat. sg. fem. {2.A} . . . . id.
ὧραι   noun, nom. pl. fem. {2.A} . . . . id.
ὡραίᾳ   adj., dat. sg. fem. {3.A} . . . . ὡραῖος *G5611*
ὡραίαν   adj., acc. sg. fem. {3.A} . . . . id.
ὡραῖοι   adj., nom. pl. masc. {3.A} . . . . id.

G5611 ὡραῖος, -α, -ον   (lit. *in season*), *beautiful.*

ὥραν   noun, acc. sg. fem. {2.A} . . . . .ὥρα *G5610*
ὥρας   noun, acc. pl. fem. {2.A} . . . . id.
ὥρας   noun, gen. sg. fem. {2.A} . . . . id.
ὠργίσθη   verb, aor. pass. indic. 3 pers. sg. {5.A.1.b} . . . . .ὀργίζω *G3710*
ὠργίσθησαν   verb, aor. pass. indic. 3 pers. pl. {5.A.1.b} . . . . id.
ὤρθριζε   verb, impf. act. indic. 3 pers. sg. {5.A.1.b} . . . . .ὀρθρίζω *G3719*
ὤρθριζεν   verb, impf. act. indic. 3 pers. sg. {5.A.1.b} . . . . id.
ὥρισαν   verb, aor. act. indic. 3 pers. pl. {5.A.1.b} . . . . .ὁρίζω *G3724*
ὥρισε   verb, aor. act. indic. 3 pers. sg. {5.A.1.b} . . id.
ὥρισεν   verb, aor. act. indic. 3 pers. sg. {5.A.1.b} id.
ὡρισμένη   vbl., perf. pass. ptc. dat. sg. fem. {6.A.1.b} . . . . id.
ὡρισμένον   vbl., perf. pass. ptc. acc. sg. neut. {6.A.1.b} . . . . id.
ὡρισμένος   vbl., perf. pass. ptc. nom. sg. masc. {6.A.1.b} . . . . id.
ὥρμησαν   verb, aor. act. indic. 3 pers. pl. {5.A.1} . . . . .ὁρμάω *G3729*
ὥρμησε   verb, aor. act. indic. 3 pers. sg. {5.A.1} . id.
ὥρμησεν   verb, aor. act. indic. 3 pers. sg. {5.A.1} id.
ὤρυξεν   verb, aor. act. indic. 3 pers. sg. {5.A.1.b} . . . . .ὀρύσσω *G3736*

G5612 ὠρύομαι   *I roar.*

ὠρυόμενος   vbl., pres. mid./pass. ptc. nom. sg. masc. {6.A.1} . . . . .ὠρύομαι *G5612*
ὠρχήσασθε   verb, aor. mid. indic. 2 pers. pl. {5.A.1} . . . . .ὀρχέομαι *G3738*
ὠρχήσατο   verb, aor. mid. indic. 3 pers. sg. {5.A.1} . . . . id.
ὡρῶν   noun, gen. pl. fem. {2.A} . . . . .ὥρα *G5610*

G5613 ὡς   adv. and conj., (1) with superl., ὡς τάχιστα, *as quickly as possible*, Acts 17:15; (2) with comp., ambiguous, either *uncommonly . . .* or *very . . .*, Acts 17:22; (3) before numbers, etc., *about;* (4) excl., *how*, e.g., Rom 10:15; (5) often in the pred. (nom. or acc.) *as*, e.g., Matt 14:5; 22:30; Luke 15:19; 2 Cor 10:2; (6) with fut. ptc., *as such who have to . . .* , Heb 13:17; giving a reason, Luke 16:1; 23:4; Acts 3:12, etc.; ptc. sometimes has disappeared, e.g., Col 3:23; (7) with absol. inf., ὡς ἔπος εἰπεῖν, *one might*

almost say, Heb 7:9; (8) = ὥστε, *so as to*, Luke 9:52 (var.); Acts 20:24 (var.); (9) οὐχ ὡς, *not as if*, e.g., Acts 28:19; ὡς ὅτι = ὡς with gen. absol., *as if*; 2 Cor 5:19; 11:21; 2 Thess 2:2; (10) ὡς correlative to οὕτως (with or without καί), *as . . . so;* (11) ὡς introducing a clause can also have something of a causal sense, Matt 6:12 (= Luke 11:4), etc., so, ὡς with preps. often in Hellenistic), cf. Acts 17:14 (var.); Rom 9:32; (12) (it is) *as* (when), without connection, either with what precedes or with what follows, Mark 13:34; (13) after verbs of saying, thinking, etc., *how;* (14) temp., *when, while, as long as*, Luke 1:23; Gal 6:10; etc.; ὡς ἄν, *when*, Rom 15:24; *as soon as*, 1 Cor 11:34; Phil 2:23 (but in 2 Cor 10:9, *as it were*).

ὡς   adv., conj. {4.D} . . . . .ὡς *G5613*
ὧς   adv. conj. {4.D} . . . . id.

G5614 ὡσαννά   a cry of happiness, *hosanna!* (Aram. and Heb., originally a cry for help).

ὡσαννά   Aram. . . . . .ὡσαννά *G5614*

G5615 ὡσαύτως   adv., *in the same way, likewise.*

ὡσαύτως   adv. {3.F} . . . . .ὡσαύτως *G5615*

G5616 ὡσεί   (1) *as if, as it were, like;* (2) with numbers, *about.*

ὡσεί   adv. . . . . .ὡσεί *G5616*
Ὡσηέ   noun prop. . . . . .Ὡσηέ *G5617*

G5617 Ὡσηέ (Ὡσῆε), ὁ   *Hosea,* the OT prophet (Heb.).

Ὡσηέ   noun prop. . . . . .Ὡσηέ *G5617*
ὠσί   noun, dat. pl. neut. {2.C} . . . . .οὖς *G3775*
ὦσι   verb, pres. subjunc. 3 pers. pl. {7.B} . . . . .εἰμί *G1510*
ὠσίν   noun, dat. pl. neut. {2.C} . . . . .οὖς *G3775*
ὦσιν   verb, pres. subjunc. 3 pers. pl. {7.B} . . . .εἰμί *G1510*

G5618 ὥσπερ   *even as, as.*

ὥσπερ   adv. . . . . .ὥσπερ *G5618*

G5619 ὡσπερεί   *even as if, as if* (= ὥσπερ εἰ).

ὡσπερεί   adv. . . . . .ὡσπερεί *G5619*

G5620 ὥστε   (1) with inf., expressing result, *so as to*, Luke 4:29 (var.), 9:52 (var.), 20:20 (var.), etc.; (2) (a) introducing an independent clause, in indic., impv., subjunc. of exhortation, *so that,* John 3:16; Gal 2:13; (b) with result stated merely as a new fact, *consequently, and so, therefore.*

ὥστε   conj. . . . . .ὥστε *G5620*
ὦτα   noun, acc. pl. neut. {2.C} . . . . .οὖς *G3775*
ὦτα   noun, nom. pl. neut. {2.C} . . . . id.

G5621† ὠτάριον, -ου, τό   *an ear.* Var. for ὠτίον, Matt 14:47; John 18:10.

ὠτάριον   noun, acc. sg. neut. {2.B} . . . . .ὠτάριον *G5621†*

G5621 ὠτίον, -ου, τό   *an ear.*

ὠτίον   noun, acc. sg. neut. {2.B} . . . . .ὠτίον *G5621*
ὠτίου   noun, gen. sg. neut. {2.B} . . . . id.
ὤφειλε   verb, impf. act. indic. 3 pers. sg. {5.A.1.b} . . . . .ὀφείλω *G3784*
ὤφειλεν   verb, impf. act. indic. 3 pers. sg. {5.A.1.b} . . . . id.
ὠφείλετε   verb, impf. act. indic. 2 pers. pl. {5.A.1.b} . . . . id.

ὠφείλομεν   verb, impf. act. indic. 1 pers. pl.
{5.A.1.b} . . . . id.

ὤφειλον   verb, impf. act. indic. 1 pers. sg.
{5.A.1.b} . . . . id.

ὠφελεῖ   verb, pres. act. indic. 3 pers. sg.
{5.A.2} . . . . ὠφελέω G5623

G5622 ὠφέλεια, -ας, ἡ   advantage.

ὠφέλεια   noun, nom. sg. fem. {2.A} . . . . . ὠφέλεια G5622

ὠφελείας   noun, gen. sg. fem. {2.A} . . . . id.

ὠφελεῖται   verb, pres. pass. indic. 3 pers. sg.
{5.A.2} . . . . ὠφελέω G5623

ὠφελεῖτε   verb, pres. act. indic. 2 pers. pl. {5.A.2} id.

G5623 ὠφελέω   I help, benefit, do good, am useful (to);
(1) absol. Rom 2:25; (2) with adv. acc. οὐδέν,
in no way, τί, in what way?; (3) generally with
acc. of the person.

ὠφεληθεῖσα   vbl., aor. pass. ptc. nom. sg. fem.
{6.A.2} . . . . ὠφελέω G5623

ὠφεληθῇς   verb, aor. pass. subjunc. 2 pers. sg.
{5.B.1} . . . . id.

ὠφελήθησαν   verb, aor. pass. indic. 3 pers. pl.
{5.A.1} . . . . id.

ὠφεληθήσεται   verb, fut. pass. indic. 3 pers.
sg. {5.A.1} . . . . id.

ὠφελήσει   verb, fut. act. indic. 3 pers. sg. {5.A.1} id.

ὠφέλησεν   verb, aor. act. indic. 3 pers. sg.
{5.A.1} . . . . id.

ὠφελήσω   verb, fut. act. indic. 1 pers. sg. {5.A.1} id.

ὠφελία   noun, nom. sg. fem. {2.A} . . . . . ὠφέλεια G5622

ὠφελίας   noun, gen. sg. fem. {2.A} . . . . id.

ὠφέλιμα   adj., nom. pl. neut. {3.C} . . . . . ὠφέλιμος G5624

G5624 ὠφέλιμος, -ον   beneficial, useful, serviceable.

ὠφέλιμος   adj., nom. sg. fem. {3.C} . . . . ὠφέλιμος G5624

ὠφέλιμος   adj., nom. sg. masc. {3.C} . . . ὠφέλιμος G5624

ὠφελοῦμαι   verb, pres. pass. indic. 1 pers. sg.
{5.A.2} . . . . ὠφελέω G5623

ὤφθη   verb, aor. pass. indic. 3 pers. sg. {5.A.1} ὁράω G3708

ὤφθην   verb, aor. pass. indic. 1 pers. sg. {5.A.1} . id.

ὤφθησαν   verb, aor. pass. indic. 3 pers. pl.
{5.A.1} . . . . id.

Appendix I

Rearrangements to the Strong's Numbering System

Prepared by Mark A. House

Due to refinements in Greek lexicography that have occurred since the Strong's numbering system was developed, the alphabetical arrangement of words in current lexicons does not always match up perfectly with the Strong's numbers. Whenever the alphabetical order of the dictionary entries found in this lexicon vary from the Strong's arrangement, the Strong's numbers are followed by a double dagger symbol [‡]. In such cases, those using Strong's numbers can refer to the following list to locate the dictionary entry they are seeking. See the Features of the Analytical Lexicon section on page ix for further explanation.

Strong's No.	Pg. / Col.	Strong's No.	Pg. / Col.	Strong's No.	Pg. / Col.
G30†‡	5b	G643†‡	140b	G1349†‡	192a
G76†‡	9a	G650†‡	57b	G1424†‡	93a
G90†‡	56b	G681†‡	276b	G1494†‡	179b
G127†‡	78a	G689†‡	49a	G1496‡	102a
G138‡	11a	G693‡	48a	G1499‡	101a
G157‡	12a	G730‡	50a	G1503‡	131a
G294†‡	19b	G782†‡	35a	G1508‡	101a
G344†‡	132a	G886‡	57b	G1509‡	101b
G376†‡	24b	G906†‡	19b	G1512‡	101b
G378†‡	45a	G987†‡	93a	G1513‡	101b
G448†‡	27b	G1081†‡	69b	G1527‡	103b
G450†‡	24b	G1138‡	75b	G1530†‡	110b
G508†‡	21a	G1157‡	75b	G1536‡	101b
G518†‡	5b	G1174‡	77a	G1565†‡	107b
G570†‡	250b	G1176†‡	77a	G1650†‡	114a
G617†‡	23a	G1248†‡	93b	G1701†‡	119a
G621†‡	139b	G1328†‡	147a	G1714‡	119a

Strong's No.	Pg. / Col.	Strong's No.	Pg. / Col.	Strong's No.	Pg. / Col.
G1766‡	120b	G2927†‡	214b	G4240†‡	294a
G1768†‡	122a	G2944†‡	215a	G4263†‡	295b
G1769†‡	122a	G2955†‡	193b	G4277‡	296a
G1782†‡	123a	G2992‡	219a	G4280‡	296b
G1831†‡	106a	G2997‡	217a	G4332†‡	267a
G1856†‡	111b	G3028‡	221b	G4347†‡	302b
G1904†‡	134a	G3029†‡	355b	G4412†‡	306b
G1944†‡	132b	G3166†‡	55b	G4476†‡	62b
G1966‡	133b	G3199‡	231a	G4577†‡	316b
G1999†‡	141a	G3344†‡	235b	G4603‡	316a
G2027†‡	139a	G3362‡	93a	G4621†‡	316b
G2045‡	145b	G3363‡	181b	G4687†‡	141a
G2087†‡	276a	G3364‡	256b	G4695‡	320b
G2095†‡	154a	G3378‡	236b	G4833†‡	327b
G2112†‡	155a	G3395†‡	115b	G4851†‡	328b
G2127†‡	199b	G3449‡	240a	G4867†‡	10a
G2145†‡	156a	G3461†‡	89a	G4900†‡	329b
G2148†‡	156b	G3507†‡	251a	G4934†‡	332b
G2206†‡	162a	G3569‡	341a	G4955†‡	321b
G2214†‡	108a	G3603‡	247a	G5081†‡	79a
G2274†‡	149b	G3618†‡	249a	G5103†‡	347b
G2276‡	171a	G3689†‡	250b	G5169†‡	349b
G2296†‡	108b	G3726†‡	124a	G5179†‡	351a
G2310†‡	174a	G3837†‡	261a	G5182†‡	176b
G2322†‡	248b	G3851†‡	262a	G5331†‡	361a
G2442†‡	251a	G3859†‡	82a	G5359‡	363a
G2509†‡	187a	G3962†‡	298b	G5391†‡	341a
G2640†‡	357a	G3964‡	272a	G5392†‡	205a
G2652†‡	192b	G3981†‡	272b	G5470‡	369a
G2653†‡	192b	G4016†‡	268a	G5504†‡	160b
G2730†‡	201b	G4053†‡	110b	G5505‡	371a
G2735†‡	88b	G4053†‡	355a	G5512†‡	84a
G2736†‡	202a	G4098†‡	328a	G5531†‡	206b
G2744†‡	97a	G4130‡	285a	G5575‡	375a
G2825†‡	208a	G4210‡	292a		
G2857‡	210a	G4219‡	293a		

Appendix II
Glossary of Greek Grammatical Terms
Prepared by Mark A. House

The Analytical Lexicon contains two types of entry—analytical and dictionary. In the analytical entries you will find each word of the Greek NT listed alphabetically and analyzed according to its lexical source word, the part of speech it represents (noun, adjective, verb, etc.), and, where applicable, the grammatical information encoded in the word's inflected form (also referred to as the word's *parsing*). Every part of this information is vital for understanding the grammatical role each word plays in its context and how this affects the word's meaning.

In the dictionary entries you will find each distinct lexical form from the Greek NT with a short listing of its different meanings. Understanding a word's range of definitions sheds light on the possible meanings it can have in various contexts. However, by using the information from the grammatical analysis in the analytical listing, you can gain even deeper insight into how the word functions in its context and the additional nuances that may shape its meaning.

The glossary that follows serves to facilitate the work of grammatical analysis begun by using the Analytical Lexicon. It is designed to be used in conjunction with the *Greek Word Tables* (Appendix III). Words in **bold type** throughout the glossary have separate entries that may be consulted for additional information. Armed with a word's analysis (or parsing), the student can use the glossary to decode each grammatical element for a fuller understanding of how it modifies the word's meaning. Coupled with information from the corresponding dictionary entry, the student can get a deeper appreciation of a word's meaning in its context.

For example, suppose you want to get more information about the word ἀγάπαις, found in Jude 12. From the listing in the Analytical Lexicon you discover that the lexical form is ἀγάπη. The dictionary entry for ἀγάπη reveals that the word means "love" (of various kinds), but the plural form of the word can also mean "love feasts."

Returning to the analytical listing, you discover that the word ἀγάπαις is a *noun* with the parsing: *dative, plural, feminine*. Taking the data from the analytical listing, you may now look up each term in the glossary to discover how that element affects this word's meaning in context. The glossary gives additional information such as the following:

- Ἀγάπη is a *noun,* so it refers to a person, place, or thing. This fits with the possible definitions of "love" and "love feast," both referring to things.

- It is in the *dative case,* adding the meanings of "in," "with," "by," "to," or "for," depending on the context. In Jude 12 the dative noun is used in combination with the preposition ἐν, which clarifies and amplifies the case meaning. Here the meaning of ἐν is "in."

- The *plural number* indicates that more than one "love" is indicated. However, as previously mentioned, the dictionary entry clarified that when the noun is plural, "love feasts" is a possible meaning.

- Because the gender of non-personal nouns is often simply a grammatical convention, the *feminine gender* does not have any special significance here.

Were you to analyze the other words in the immediate context of Jude 12 (a prepositional phrase), you would arrive at the contextual meaning of "in your love feasts." The parsing information from the dictionary entry and the analytical listing has helped expand our understanding of the meaning of the word in at least two distinct ways: 1) it has clarified the meaning of the plural noun ("love feasts" rather than "loves"), and 2) it has revealed the dative noun's connection with the preposition ἐν, which supplies the meaning of "in." Combining the information gleaned from your analysis of both the dictionary and analytical entries, you conclude that the best meaning of ἀγάπαις is "in love feasts."

In using the Analytical Lexicon, some words of caution are in order. Since words are extremely flexible both in terms of their meanings and their grammatical usages in various contexts, a thorough knowledge of Koiné Greek syntax is necessary to gain the fullest understanding of each word's meaning. Consequently, this lexicon is no substitute for the study of the language as a whole and an understanding of the well-established principles of exegesis that guide NT interpreters. Also, since the glossary and word tables in this lexicon contain only basic summaries of Greek grammar, the student desiring a more comprehensive understanding should consult a beginning or advanced Greek grammar.

Glossary

Abstract noun: See **Noun.**

Accusative case: The **case** that typically indicates the **direct object** (cf. the English objective case) of a sentence. Thus in the sentence, "Paul preached the *gospel,*" the word "gospel" is the **verb's** direct object and would typically be in the accusative case. In Greek sentences the direct object may stand before or after the verb, while in English sentences the direct object is typically placed after the verb. The accusative case is also used to indicate the objects of certain **prepositions.** The accusative case has other specialized meanings that must be determined by factors in the context in which it is used. For detailed descriptions of these functions, consult an advanced Greek grammar.

Active voice: A grammatical feature of **verbs** and **verbals** that indicates that the **subject** is the person or thing performing the action. In the sentence, "Peter *healed* the blind man," the verb "healed" is an active verb, indicating that the subject, "Peter," is the one performing the action. A verb's **infix** or **suffix** indicates its **voice**.

Adjectival participle: See **Participle**.

Adjective: A word that further describes, qualifies, or tells about a person or thing. Adjectives often tell *what kind* of person or thing is being described. Instead of merely referring to a man, we might describe a *tall* man. Adjectives include words like *big*, *red*, *happy*, *distant*, and *warm*. A **substantive** adjective is an adjective that acts like a **noun**, referring to someone or something without the use of a noun, such as the word "good" in the sentence, "The *good* sometimes suffer." Most adjectives can be expressed in *comparative* and *superlative* degrees. For example, the comparative degree of the adjective "big" is "bigger," and the superlative degree is "biggest."

Adverb: A word that further describes or qualifies a **verb**. It may tell more about the manner, time, or place in which the action occurs. Some English adverbs end in "-ly," but many do not. Adverbs include words like *quickly, yesterday,* and *there*. Greek adverbs normally have *absolute* forms, meaning that they do not inflect but always occur in the same form. However, like adjectives, adverbs may have *comparative* and *superlative* forms, as in "more quickly" and "most quickly." Some words can function as **adverbs** or **prepositions**, depending on whether they are used with a **noun** (the **prepositional object**). In the sentence, "He walked *around*," the word "around" functions as an adverb, while in the sentence, "He walked *around* the block," it functions as a preposition. See Appendix III, section 3.F, for information on the formation of Greek adverbs.

Adverbial participle: See **Participle**.

Aorist tense: The **tense** of **verbs** that typically indicates *simple* or *undefined* action. In the **indicative mood**, the aorist tense generally represents action that took place in the past from the perspective of the writer. In some contexts, the aorist has a sense similar to the **perfect** tense. For a complete description of the contextual nuances of the aorist, consult an advanced grammar. With **participles**, the aorist tense generally represents action that takes place *prior to* that that of the leading verb of the sentence.

The aorist tense is inflected in two distinct ways—*first* and *second aorist*. These two **inflections** represent differences in form only, not in meaning. See the *Greek Word Tables* (Appendix III) for more on these differences; also see **Aspect** and **Simple aspect**.

Article: A word that serves to indicate the specificity of reference of the **noun** phrase with which it occurs. English has both an indefinite article ("a" or "an"), referring to the noun in a general way, and a definite article ("the"), which refers to a specific person or thing. Greek has only a definite article (ὁ, ἡ, or τό). When the article is not used, the person or thing referred to is often considered indefinite. However, other features in a sentence beside the article can indicate whether or not a noun is definite. The article is inflected for **gender**, **number**, and **case** in agreement with its noun.

Aspect: A feature of the **tense** of a **verb** or **verbal** that represents the *manner* in which the writer conceives of a verb's action as occurring. Many scholars theorize that the Greek tenses can represent three distinct aspects—**simple**, **continuous**, and **stative**.

Augmentation: Past-tense forms (**aorist, imperfect, pluperfect**) of the **indicative verb** are typically augmented. This augmentation can take two forms: 1) For verbs beginning with a consonant, an epsilon with smooth breathing (ἐ) is added to the beginning of the word (e.g., λυ- → ἐλυ-), 2) For verbs beginning with a short vowel or **diphthong**, the vowel or diphthong is lengthened (see the table below). If the initial diphthong contains an iota, it is converted to an iota subscript (e.g., οι → ῳ). For verbs beginning with a long vowel and some verbs beginning with diphthongs, augmentation produces no change. For **compound verbs**, augmentation normally affects the verb root itself rather than the attached preposition, often with the augment replacing the final vowel of the preposition (e.g., ἀπολύ- → ἀπέλυ-).

<table>
<tr><td colspan="9" align="center">VOWEL AUGMENTATION</td></tr>
<tr><td>Short</td><td>α</td><td>ε</td><td>ο</td><td>αι</td><td>ει</td><td>οι</td><td>αυ</td><td>ευ</td></tr>
<tr><td>Long</td><td>η</td><td>η</td><td>ω</td><td>ῃ</td><td>ῃ</td><td>ῳ</td><td>ηυ</td><td>ηυ</td></tr>
</table>

Case: A feature of words that indicates their grammatical relationship to the other words in the sentence. There are five Greek cases: **nominative, accusative, genitive, dative,** and **vocative.** Like **gender**, case is generally indicated by a word's **suffix.** When used in combination with a **preposition**, case helps in identifying which words are objects within the **prepositional phrase.** See also the entries for the individual cases.

Clause: A sentence or portion of a sentence that has its own distinct **verb** or **verbal.** Certain parts of speech, such as **participles** and **relative pronouns**, are closely associated with the clauses they generate.

Compound verb: The prefixing of a **verb** with one or more **prepositions**, resulting in a modified or sometimes completely different meaning. For example, ἀναβλέπω, a **compound verb** consisting of the preposition ἀνά ("up," "again") and βλέπω ("see"), means "to look up" or "to regain one's sight."

Conditional particle: A part of speech used to set up a conditional ("if…then…") statement. The two most common conditional particles are εἰ and ἐάν, both meaning "if." See also **Particle.**

Conjugation: The system of changes a **verb** goes through in the process of **inflection.**

Conjunction: A word that joins sentences, **clauses,** or words together. Some common conjunctions are *and, but,* and *because.* Coordinating conjunctions link items on an equal level, as in, "He preached the gospel *and* healed many." Subordinating conjunctions indicate that one item is subordinate to another, as in, "He left the boat *in order to* walk on land."

Consonant shift: The changes Greek consonants undergo when placed next to other consonants. Three types of changes occur: 1) *Amalgamation:* the combination of two consonants into a double consonant that occurs when the second consonant is the letter σ (e.g., πσ → ψ). 2) *Assimilation:* the conformity of one consonant to the sound characteristics of the other (e.g., κμ → γμ). 3) *Absorption:* the elimination of a consonant in the presence of another consonant (e.g., τσ → σ). The table below illustrates all three of these phenomena.

CONSONANT SHIFT

		Second Consonant			
		μ	σ	τ	σθ
First Consonant	Labial (π, β, φ)	μμ	ψ	πτ	φ
	Guttural (κ, γ, χ)	γμ	ξ	κτ	χθ
	Dental (τ, δ, θ)	σμ	σ	στ	σθ
	Liquid (λ, ρ, ν)	μμ	—	—	θ

Continuous aspect: A feature of the **tense** of a **verb** or **verbal** that represents action as *in progress*—occurring regularly or over a period of time. Continuous aspect is typically represented by the **present** and **imperfect tenses**. In translation, English progressive verbs that include verbal auxiliaries such as "am," "are," "was," or "were" are often used to help bring out the sense of action in progress, as in, "I *am learning* to read Greek" and "Jesus *was going* to Jerusalem." When indicated by contextual factors, continuous tenses may represent the beginning of a process ("Jesus *began to teach*") or a repeated or recurrent action ("Jesus *kept healing*"). See **Aspect**.

Contraction: The merging of vowels or **diphthongs** into a single syllable, which sometimes occurs when a word's **inflection** juxtaposes two vowels. Contraction most commonly occurs with contract verbs having stems ending in α, ε, and ο (see the table below). These **stem** ending vowels contract with the **suffix** vowels or diphthongs to produce new vowels or diphthongs, as shown in the table below. For example, the verb ἀγαπᾷ results from the contraction of the verb stem ἀγαπα- with the suffix -ει. In some cases, the suffix vowel or diphthong simply absorbs the stem vowel and remains unchanged.

VOWEL CONTRACTION

		Suffix Vowel									
		α	αι	ε	ει	η	ῃ	ο	οι	ου	ω
Stem Vowel	α	α	ᾳ	α	ᾳ	α	ᾳ	ω	ῳ	ω	ω
	ε	η	ῃ	ει	ει	η	ῃ	ου	οι	ου	ω
	ο	ω	ῳ	ου	οι	ω	ῳ	ου	οι	ου	ω

Correlative: A pronoun or adverb that corresponds with one or more other words that are often similar in form. For example, the **relative pronoun** οἷος ("of which sort") corresponds to the **interrogative pronoun** ποῖος ("of what sort?"), the **indefinite pronoun** ποιός ("of some sort"), the **demonstrative pronoun** τοῖος ("such a sort"), and the **indefinite relative pronoun** ὁποῖος ("of whatever sort"). See section 4.D of the *Greek Word Tables* (Appendix III).

Crasis: The merger of two words, resulting in the loss (**elision**) of one or more letters. Crasis is indicated by the presence of an apostrophe over a non-initial vowel (or, rarely, **diphthong**). For example, the form κἀγώ is the result of crasis of two words—καὶ ἐγώ. Crasis involves a change in form only, and does not affect the meaning of the words.

Dative case: The **case** most often used to indicate the **indirect object** of a sentence. In English the indirect object is often placed before the direct object, as in the sentence, "I gave you the Bible." Another common way to translate the Greek indirect object is by using a prepositional phrase with "to" or "for," as in "I gave the Bible to you."

There are three general categories of the dative:

1) *Indirect object,* as discussed above.

2) *Instrumental,* used to indicate *the means* by which something is accomplished. When so used, the dative is often translated "with" or "by," as in the word "apostle" in the sentence, "The gospel was proclaimed *by the apostle.*"

3) *Locative,* used to indicate *the location* of a person or thing. In this usage, the dative is often translated "in" or "at," as in the word "Galilee" in the sentence, "Jesus healed the sick *in Galilee.*"

The dative case is also commonly used to indicate the objects of certain **prepositions**. The dative case has other specialized uses and meanings that may be determined by other factors in the context. For detailed descriptions of these functions, consult an advanced Greek grammar.

Declension: The pattern of changes in word **inflection** seen in **nouns**, **pronouns**, and **adjectives**. In Greek there are three major declensions: first, second, and third. See section 2 of the *Greek Word Tables* (Appendix III) for examples.

Definite article: See **Article**.

Demonstrative pronoun: A **pronoun** that points to a person or thing. Greek has two demonstratives—οὗτος ("this") and ἐκεῖνος ("that"). The first refers to people or things close by, while the second refers to people or things that are farther away.

Deponent verb: A **middle-** or **passive-voice verb** that has no **active-voice** form for a particular **tense**, but whose middle or passive form serves the active function for that tense. Verbs indicated as deponent in the analytical lexicon are deponent in the **present tense**, but may or may not be deponent in other tenses. Likewise, a verb that is not deponent in its present-tense form may be deponent in other tenses. Whether or not a verb's individual tenses are deponent can be determined by examining the verb's **principal parts**. Many deponent verbs have lost the distinctive meaning of the middle or passive **voice** and are simply translated as active verbs.

Diphthong: The combination of two vowels to produce a single sound. The Greek diphthongs are αι, αυ, ει, ευ, οι, ου, ηυ, and υι.

Direct object: The person or thing that receives the action of an **active verb**. In the sentence, "The apostle healed the *woman*," the word "woman" is the direct object. See **Accusative case.**

Elision: The dropping off of a short vowel at the end of a word that precedes another word beginning with a vowel. An apostrophe takes the place of the omitted letter. This happens most often with certain prepositions. For example, the phrase κατά αὐτοῦ is written as κατ' αὐτοῦ. Elision is a change in form only, and does not affect the meaning of the words.

Enclitic: A word that attaches closely to the word it follows, often losing its own accent and sometimes causing an extra accent in the previous word. One of the most common enclitics in the NT is the verb ἐστίν, as used in the phrase, οὗτός ἐστιν ὁ υἱός ("this is the son"). See also **Proclitic.**

Feminine gender: See **Gender.**

First person: See **Person.**

Fixed form: An indeclinable word; a word not subject to changes in word **inflection**.

Future perfect tense: See **Perfect tense.**

Future tense: The **tense** of **verbs** that typically represents action that will take place *in the future* from the perspective of the communicator in the **indicative mood**. With **participles** (rarely), the future tense represents action that occurs *subsequent to* that of the leading **verb** of the sentence. The future tense most often represents **simple aspect**, but when indicated by the context, may sometimes represent **continuous aspect**. For other contextual nuances of the future tense, consult an advanced Greek grammar. See also **Aspect.**

Gender: A grammatical feature of Greek **nouns**, **adjectives**, **pronouns**, and **participles** that helps identify them with related words. The three genders are *feminine, masculine*, and *neuter*. A noun's gender, typically indicated by its **suffix**, is a fixed grammatical feature.

Gender can be either grammatical or natural. Words representing genderless objects have *grammatical* gender. For example, the word θάλασσα ("sea" or "lake") is feminine, the word λόγος ("word") is masculine, and the word πλοῖον ("boat") is neuter. For nouns that refer to objects, the grammatical gender of the word may have little to do with natural or biological gender. It is simply one of the linguistic conventions by which the thing is referred.

For words referring to persons or animals, grammatical gender often reflects *natural* gender. Thus ἄνθρωπος ("man") is masculine and γυνή ("woman") is feminine. In the same way, third-person **personal pronouns** take the gender of the person to whom they refer, like "she" and "he" in English.

In some contexts, Greek gender is more specific than English gender. When we say "someone" in English, we may be referring either to a man or a woman, but in Greek the word for "someone" can either be masculine, referring specifically to some male person or (with plurals) generically to both genders; feminine, referring to some female person; or neuter, referring to a thing or concept.

Adjectives derive their gender from the noun they describe. Thus in the phrase ἡ ἀγαθὴ γυνή ("the good woman"), the adjective translated "good" is feminine because it describes the feminine noun translated "woman."

Gender is especially important for adjectives and **pronouns** because it helps identify to which person or thing a word is referring. Greek adjectives used as **substantives** describe an implied person or thing that is not explicitly mentioned. For example, ἡ ἀγαθή means "the good woman." In this case the feminine gender of the adjective tells us that the person described is female.

In many cases, masculine pronouns and adjectives that refer to people are not gender-specific. Though masculine in form, they can refer to or describe groups that include females and males. Feminine pronouns and adjectives that refer to people, however, generally refer to or describe exclusively female groups. Likewise, neuter pronouns and adjectives generally refer to or describe things rather than people. Thus the phrase οἱ πιστεύοντες ("those who believe") would most often refer to a mixed group of male and female believers.

Genitive absolute: An adverbial **participle** in the **genitive case** that has a genetive **subject** distinct from the nominative subject of the main **verb**.

Genitive case: The **case** that expresses that a **noun, pronoun,** or **substantive** further describes or has a special relationship with another noun, pronoun, or substantive. This relationship could represent close association, origin, or possession. The genitive relationship is typically translated by the English word "of," but it may have a variety of other translations as well. Thus in the phrase, ὁ λόγος τοῦ θεοῦ ("the word of God"), the genitive noun translated "God" is related in some special way to the word translated "word." The "word" may be *from* God (origin), it may *belong to* God (possession), or it may be closely associated with God in some other sense (generally indicated by "of").

In English, the possessive relationship is often indicated by ending a word with "apostrophe s" or "s apostrophe." Thus "the word of God" and "God's word" mean roughly the same thing.

The genitive case is also used to indicate the objects of certain **prepositions**. The genitive case has other specialized uses and meanings that may be determined by other factors in the context in which it is used. For detailed descriptions of these functions, consult an advanced Greek grammar.

Gerund: In English grammar, a word constructed from a verb ending in "-ing," which converts verbal action into a **substantive**. For example, in the sentence, "Learning Greek is challenging," the word "learning" is a gerund that serves as the **subject** of the sentence—the thing that is challenging. Like verbs, gerunds can have **direct objects**. In the example just given, "Greek" is the direct object—the thing that is being learned. Though Greek does not have gerunds, **substantive infinitives** and **participles** perform a function very similar to the gerund.

Imperative mood: The **mood** of **verbs** that expresses a strong admonition or command, as in the statement, "Rise up and walk!" The imperative mood is sometimes described as the mood of *command*. **Present-tense** imperatives are normally commands for general or continuous action (e.g., "Trust in the Lord always!"), while **aorist-tense** imperatives are simple commands, usually to begin performance of a given action (e.g., "Rise up!"). See also **Aspect**.

Imperfect tense: The **tense** of **indicative verbs** that indicates continuous or progressive action in the past, as in the sentence, "The disciples *were walking* to Galilee." The **aspect** of the imperfect should be carefully distinguished from that of the **aorist** indicative, which typically represents *simple* or *undefined* past action, as in "The disciples *walked* to Galilee." The imperfect tense can also represent, when indicated by the context, regular or repeated action in the past ("the disciples *used to* walk," or "the disciples *kept walking*"), as well as the inception of a process in the past ("The disciples *began walking*"). For a complete description of various nuances of the imperfect tense, consult an advanced Greek grammar.

Impersonal verb: A **verb** that technically has no **subject**, as in the phrases, "it is necessary" or "it is appropriate."

Indefinite pronoun: A **pronoun** that refers to a person or thing in a *general* rather than a specific way. Common translations include "someone" and "something." The Greek **indefinite pronoun** is τις, τι. The indefinite pronoun should be carefully distinguished from the **interrogative pronoun** τίς, τί ("who?" "what?"), used to raise questions.

Indefinite relative pronoun: The Greek **pronoun** ὅστις, constructed from the **relative pronoun** (ὅς) and the **indefinite pronoun** (τις). It is commonly translated "whoever," "whichever," or "whatever."

Indicative mood: The **mood** of **verbs** that indicates that the action or state of being communicated has actually occurred, is occurring, or will occur, as in the sentences "Paul *wrote* to the Corinthians" and "Jesus *will come* again." The indicative mood is thus sometimes described as the mood of *reality*. The indicative mood is also used with a negative particle to deny the reality of certain states or actions, as in the statement, "Barnabas *was not* an apostle."

Indirect object: A word that indicates the person or thing *to* or *for whom* the action of the **verb** is done, or the person or thing receiving the direct object. For example, in the sentence, "Paul wrote them an epistle," the word "them" is the indirect object—it indicates that Paul wrote an epistle *to* or *for* them. In Greek, indirect objects most often occur in the **dative case**.

Infinitive: A word grammatically constructed from a **verb** that allows the verb's action to be used as a **noun** or **substantive**, thus converting the action into a thing. In English this same function is most often accomplished by using a **gerund**. Another way to translate the infinitive is through the use of the English infinitive, normally preceded by the word "to," as in "to read," "to preach," or "to serve." Thus the sentence "I love *serving*" (using the English **gerund**) means essentially the same thing as "I love *to serve*" (using the English **infinitive**).

There are three main functions of the infinitive:

1) to explain the *purpose* for which the action of the leading verb of the sentence takes place. In the sentence, "Jesus came *to die* for sinners," the infinitive translated "to die" tells why Jesus came.

2) to complete the meaning of certain verbs, or *complementary* infinitive. In a phrase like "We want *to see* Jesus," the infinitive "to see" completes the meaning of the verb "want" by describing what is wanted.

3) to express idioms. Infinitives used with the **article** (articular infinitives) are often used in prepositional phrases. For example, the phrase διὰ τὸ βλέπειν (literally "on account of the seeing") means, "in order to see." See also **Verbal**.

Infix: In Greek word **inflection**, the additions or changes to the middle of a word that affect meaning. For example, the verb form λε-λύ-κα-τε consists of the perfect-tense **prefix** λε (**reduplication**), the verb **stem** λυ, the perfect-tense **infix** κα, and the **suffix** τε.

Inflection: The regular changes a Greek word undergoes that affect its meaning. Inflection occurs through additions or modifications to a word's **prefix**, **infix**, or **suffix**. For example, the word ἄνθρωπος ("man") is made plural by adding the suffix -οι to the end of the word, forming ἄνθρωποι ("men"). The inflection of a word is the primary means by which its morphological features are revealed, including such items as **gender**, **number**, **case**, **tense**, **voice**, and **mood**.

Instrumental case: See **Dative case**.

Interjection: A word used to exclaim or to express a sudden or strong feeling. An interjection is often used with an exclamation point. Examples include ἀμήν (*amen, truly*), ναί (*yes, indeed*), and οὐαί (*woe*).

Interrogative pronoun: A pronoun typically used in a direct or indirect question. The most commonly used interrogative pronoun in the NT is τίς ("who?" "which?"). Other common interrogatives include ποῖος ("of what kind?") and πόσος ("how much?").

Intransitive verb: See **Verb**.

Lexical form: The form of a word used for listing the word in a Greek dictionary or lexicon. For **verbs**, this is normally the present active indicative form first-person singular. For **deponent verbs**, it is the present middle or (occasionally) the passive indicative. For nouns, it is the singular nominative form. For adjectives and (to the extent applicable) pronouns, it is the masculine singular nominative form. Thus for the word ἀνθρώπων, the lexical form is ἄνθρωπος.

Locative case: See **Dative case**.

Masculine gender: See **Gender**.

Middle voice: A grammatical feature of **verbs** and **verbals** that indicates that the **subject** (normally a person) is both acting and receiving, or at least specially participating in, the action of the verb. The subject's participation in the verbal action can take three forms, as suggested by the context: 1) the subject may act *directly* on himself or herself (i.e. reflexive action), as in the sentence, "The traveler *washed herself* in the stream"; 2) the subject may act on himself or herself *indirectly* by doing something in his or her own interest, as in the sentence, "The prophet *prepared* a meal *for himself*"; 3) the subject may involve himself or herself in the action in some special or intensive way, as in the sentence, "The worshipper *himself gathered* the wood for the sacrifice." A verb's **voice** is indicated by its suffix.

Mood: The feature of a **verb's** meaning that portrays how the verbal action is related to reality. There are four Greek moods: **indicative**, **subjunctive**, **optative**, and **imperative**. The moods range in their portrayal of action from what is actually occurring to what is merely desired. See the individual entries for each mood.

Movable nu: The letter *ν* when optionally added at the end of certain inflected forms of words, usually when the word is followed by a vowel or a punctuation mark. An optional form of the verb λύουσι is λύουσιν, which has the same parsing and meaning.

Negative particle: A word that negates the meaning of a phrase or sentence. The most common negative particles are οὐ and μή, both meaning "no" or "not." See **Particle**.

Nominative case: The **case** that typically indicates a **verb's subject** (the *subjective* case in English). Thus in the sentence, "The *apostle* preached the gospel," the noun "apostle" is the verb's subject and would typically be nominative. In Greek sentences the subject may stand before or after the verb, while in English sentences the subject is typically placed before the verb. The nominative case has other specialized uses and meanings that may be determined by other factors in the context in which it is used. For detailed descriptions of these meanings, consult an advanced Greek grammar.

Noun: A word that stands for persons (Paul, woman), places (Galilee, valley), or things (bread, scrolls). A **proper noun** is a name like "Paul" or "Galilee." An **abstract noun** is a noun that refers to a concept or quality, such as "justification" or "goodness." Proper and abstract nouns are often accompanied by the **article** in Greek (e.g., ὁ Παῦλος ["Paul"], ὁ ἀγαθός ["the goodness"]). In these cases, the article is often best left untranslated.

Number: A grammatical feature of a **noun** or **substantive** that indicates whether it is **singular**, referring to one person or thing, or **plural**, referring to more than one person or thing. Like **gender** and **case**, a word's number can be determined from the word's **suffix**. Thus ἄνθρωπος means "a man," while ἄνθρωποι means "men."

Number is also a feature of **verbs** and **verbals**, indicating whether the **subject** is a single person/thing or multiple persons/things. In the sentence, "He healed the blind man," the verb translated "healed" is singular, indicating that there is a single actor—"he." In the sentence, "The Pharisees questioned Jesus," the verb translated "questioned" is plural with the implied subject of "they."

The following table illustrates the function of number with nouns:

NUMBER IN NOUNS	
Singular	Plural
apostle	*apostles*
man	*men*

Object of preposition: See **Preposition**.

Objective case: See **Accusative case**.

Optative mood: The **mood** of **verbs** that indicates that the future occurrence of the action or state of being described by a verb is *possible* but not certain. It is used most often in the NT to represent something wished or prayed for, as in the sentence, "*May the Lord bless* you." The optative mood was fading from use in the first century, and thus optatives are rarely used in the NT.

Paradigm: A table displaying the pattern of changes a word undergoes in **inflection**.

Participle: A word grammatically constructed from a **verb** that allows the verbal action to be used to describe another person or thing in the sentence. While keeping some of its flavor as a verb, a participle also takes on the characteristics of an **adjective**. In English, participles most often end in "-ing," as in the phrase, "the flying angel."

Participles have two common grammatical functions:

1) *Adjectival,* as in the phrase, "the flying angel," the participle "flying" takes the verbal action of flying and uses it to further describe the angel. A *substantive participle* is an adjectival participle that acts like a noun, often translated with "the one who" before the verbal, as in the phrase, "*the one who hates* his brother."

2) *Adverbial,* which provides more information about what is happening or has happened while another event is occurring. That is, while keeping some of its verbal flavor,

a participle may also take on the characteristics of an **adverb**. In such situations, the words "while" or "after" are often used in the English translation. In the sentence, "While sleeping, Peter saw a vision," the phrase "while sleeping" represents a participle that tells what else was happening when Peter saw a vision. Similarly, in the sentence, "After teaching, Jesus healed the sick," the phrase "after teaching" represents a participle that tells what happened just before Jesus began his healing ministry.

Adverbial participles can communicate several other elements of meaning in relation to the main verb of a sentence. They may, for example, explain the *cause, purpose,* or *means* by which the leading action takes place. For a more complete listing of the functions of the adverbial participle, consult an advanced Greek grammar.

A *participial phrase* includes a participle, its **subject**, **direct** and **indirect objects**, and any related modifiers. See also **Verbal**, **Genitive absolute**, and **Periphrastic**.

Particle: A catch-all term for non-inflecting words that do not fit into other grammatical categories. (In older usage, "particle" referred to any small, non-inflecting word, including some **adverbs**, **prepositions**, and **conjunctions**.) Particles can affect the tone of a **clause** or sentence by providing such elements as emphasis, irony, concession, assent, affirmation, or questioning. The most commonly used particle is the **negative particle**.

Passive voice: The voice of **verbs** and **verbals** that indicates that the **subject** is the person or thing *receiving* the verb's action, as in the sentence, "The blind man *was healed* by Jesus." **Voice** is indicated by a word's **infix**, **suffix**, or both.

Perfect tense: The **tense** of **verbs** and **verbals** that indicates a current state of affairs resulting from a past occurrence or activity. As indicated by the context, a perfect verb may especially focus either on the *completion* of the past action or on the *continuation* of the present result or state of the action. Perfect-tense verbs are often translated using the English verbal auxiliaries "has" and "have," as in the sentence, "I *have read* my Bible today."

Perfect **aspect** can also be applied to the past and future. The *pluperfect* tense represents a state of completion that existed in the past resulting from a prior act, as in the sentence, "By the end of the day yesterday I *had spent* all my money." The *future perfect* represents a state of completion that will exist in the future resulting from a prior act, as in the sentence, "By this time tomorrow I *will have arrived* home." The pluperfect and future perfect tenses are rarely used in the NT. See also **Stative aspect**.

Periphrastic: A **participle** used in conjunction with a form of the verb εἰμί ("to be"), as in ἦν περιπατεύων ("he was walking"). Periphrastic constructions are used either to provide an alternative to a difficult mode of expression or to emphasize the **aspect** of the verb **tense** represented by the participle. In the example given, the periphrastic construction emphasizes the ongoing nature of the walking: "he was *in the process* of walking."

PERIPHRASTIC CONSTRUCTIONS

Periphrastic Tense		Form of εἰμί		Ptc. Tense	Example
Pres.	=	Pres.	+	Pres.	εἰμί λύων
Impf.	=	Impf.	+	Pres.	ἤμην λύων
Fut.	=	Fut.	+	Pres.	ἔσομαι λύων
Perf.	=	Pres.	+	Perf.	εἰμί λελυκώς
Plup.	=	Impf.	+	Perf.	ἤμην λελυκώς
Fut. Perf.	=	Fut.	+	Perf.	ἔσομαι λελυκώς

Person: A feature of **verbs** that contains information about the **subject**, indicating whether the subject includes the speaker/writer (first person), is a person or persons being addressed (second person), or is a person or persons being spoken about (third person). A first-person verb is typically translated with the subject "I" or "We," as in "We see the Lord"; a second-person verb with the subject "you," as in "You have eternal life"; and a third-person verb with the subject "he," "she," "it," or "they," as in "He is a disciple. " In Greek a sentence with a third-person verb will often have a stated subject, in which case the implied subject of the verb is not translated, as in "The disciples [they] were amazed." See also **Number**.

The following table summarizes the way person and number work together to represent a verb's implied **subject**:

		Number	
		Singular	Plural
Person	1st	I	We
	2nd	You	You
	3rd	He, She, It	They

Personal pronoun: A **pronoun** used as a substitute to refer to persons or things. Greek personal pronouns are used in three persons: the first (ἐγώ, "I, me, my, we, us, our"), second (σύ, "you, your"), and third (αὐτός, "he, him, his).

Pluperfect tense: See **Perfect tense**.

Plural number: A grammatical feature of nouns, pronouns, and adjectives that indicates that a word represents more than one person or object. Also a feature of **verbs** that indicates that the **subject** consists of more than one person or thing. See **Number**.

Possessive case: See **Genitive case**.

Possessive pronoun: A form of the **personal pronoun** used to express possession or relationship. English possessive pronouns are *my, our, your, his, her, its,* and *their.* In Greek, possession is most often indicted by the personal pronouns in the **genitive case**. Greek also has a set of personal adjectives (ἐμός, σός, ἡμέτερος, ὑμέτερος) used to indicate possession. See **Pronoun**.

Prefix: In Greek word **inflection**, the additions or changes to the beginning of a word that affect meaning. For example, the verb form λε-λύ-κα-τε consists of the perfect-tense **prefix** λε (reduplication), the verb **stem** λυ, the perfect-tense **infix** κα, and the **suffix** τε.

Preposition: A word typically positioned before a **noun** or **substantive**, called the prepositional *object,* to show that noun's relationship to something else in a sentence. Prepositions commonly express *position* (in, under), *direction* (from, toward), *time* (during, after), or *conceptual relationships* (because of, instead of, by means of). The preposition and its *object,* along with any other words modifying the object, form a *prepositional phrase,* such as "around the corner." The case of the prepositional object may alter the meaning of the preposition.

A prepositional phrase may either be adjectival or adverbial. *Adjectival* prepositional phrases tell more about a person or thing, as in the phrase, "the man *in the gray coat.*" *Adverbial* prepositional phrases commonly give more information about the time, location, or manner of the verb's action, as in the sentence, "The child hid *under the bed.*"

Present tense: The **tense** of **verbs** and **verbals** that generally represents *continuous action.* In the **indicative mood**, the present tense generally represents action taking place *at the present time* from the perspective of the communicator. With **participles**, the present tense generally represents action that takes place *simultaneously with* that of the leading verb of the sentence. See also **Aspect**.

Primary-tense suffixes: The suffixes used on Greek primary-tense verbs—present, future, and perfect.

PRIMARY ACTIVE SUFFIXES			
1S	-ω, —	1P	-μεν
2S	-εις, ες	2P	-τε
3S	-ει, ε[ν]	3P	-σι[ν]

PRIMARY MID./PASS. SUFFIXES			
1S	-μαι	1P	-μεθα
2S	-σαι, -η	2P	-σθε
3S	-ται	3P	-νται

Principal parts: The six specific **tense** forms used to illustrate the basis for a verb's pattern of **inflection**. These forms are: 1) present active, 2) future active, 3) aorist active, 4) perfect active, 5) perfect middle/passive, and 6) aorist passive. Thus the principal parts of the regular verb λύω are λύω, λύσω, ἔλυσα, λέλυκα, λέλυμαι, and ἐλύθην. For regular verbs, the principal parts follow predictable patterns of inflection, while the principle parts of irregular verbs must be learned individually.

Proclitic: An unaccented word that attaches closely to the word that follows it. See also **Enclitic.**

Pronoun: A word that stands for or in place of a noun. Rather than repeating nouns over and over again, pronouns allow the communicator to refer to people or things in an indirect way. There are several different types of pronouns, including **demonstrative** (this, that), **indefinite** (someone), **indefinite relative** (whoever), **intensive** (he himself, etc.), **interrogative** (who? what? how much? etc.), **personal** (he, she, it, they), **possessive** (his, her, their), **reciprocal** (one another), **reflexive** (myself, yourself, etc.), and **relative** (who, which).

Proper noun: A **noun** that represents a name like "Paul" or "Galilee." Some proper nouns, especially those derived from Hebrew or Aramaic, are completely or partially *indeclinable,* meaning that they do not fully inflect like normal Greek nouns.

Reciprocal pronoun: A plural **pronoun**, normally the **direct** or **indirect object** of a sentence or the object of a **preposition**, that expresses a mutual action or relationship between the persons or things expressed in a verb's **subject**. In the sentence, "The believers love one another," the pronoun "one another" is a reciprocal pronoun. The Greek reciprocal pronoun is ἀλλήλων ("one another").

Reduplication: The addition of a **prefix** in the formation of certain **verbs**, including the perfect and pluperfect tenses. Reduplication can take two forms: 1) For verbs beginning with a consonant, the initial **stem** consonant is *doubled,* with an epsilon (ε) placed between the two consonants (e.g., λυ- → λελυ-). Some verbs beginning with σ reduplicate with rough breathing (e.g., στα [from ἵστημι] → ἕστηκα). *Aspirated* consonants (those produced by the passage of air; θ, χ, φ) are reduplicated with their unaspirated counterparts (τ, κ, π; e.g., φιλ- → πεφιλ-). 2) For verbs beginning with a vowel, the initial vowel is lengthened as in vowel **augmentation**. For **compound verbs**, reduplication affects the verb **stem** rather than the initial preposition (ἀπολυ- → ἀπολελ-). Several verbs have irregular patterns of reduplication that must be learned individually (e.g., ἔχω → ἔσχηκα).

Many verbs of the -μι conjugation have present-tense stems reduplicated with ι (e.g., δίδωμι). Future and aorist stems of these verbs are not reduplicated, and perfect stems are reduplicated with ε as described above.

Reflexive pronoun: A **pronoun** that, when used as the **direct** or **indirect object** of a sentence or the object of a preposition, refers the action of a **verb** back to the **subject**. In the sentence, "I saw myself in a mirror," the word "myself" is a reflexive pronoun. The Greek reflexive pronouns are ἐμαυτοῦ ("myself"), σεαυτοῦ ("yourself"), and ἑαυτοῦ ("himself, herself, itself").

Reflexive verb: See **Middle voice.**

Relative clause: See **Relative pronoun.**

Relative pronoun: A **pronoun** that introduces a **relative clause**, which is used to further describe a person or thing. Relative pronouns are commonly translated "who," "whom," "what," "that," "which," and "whose," as in the phrase, "The man *whom* Jesus healed." The phrase "whom Jesus healed" is a relative clause introduced by the relative pronoun *whom*. Its function is to tell more about the man being described. Relative pronouns should be distinguished from **interrogative pronouns**, often translated the same way but used strictly to raise questions. The most common relative pronoun is ὅς, ἥ, ὅ. Less common relative pronouns are οἷος ("such, of what sort") and the **indefinite relative pronoun** ὅστις ("who(m) ever, whatever"). The **article** can sometimes function as a relative pronoun as well.

Second person: See **Person**.

Secondary-tense suffixes: The suffixes used on Greek secondary tenses—**imperfect**, **aorist**, and **pluperfect**.

SECONDARY ACTIVE SUFFIXES			
1S	-ν, —	1P	-μεν
2S	-ες	2P	-τε
3S	-ε[ν]	3P	-ν, -σαν

SECONDARY MID./PASS. SUFFIXES			
1S	-μην	1P	-μεθα
2S	-σο, -ου	2P	-σθε
3S	-το	3P	-ντο

Simple aspect: A grammatical feature of a verb's **tense** that represents the action of the **verb** *as a whole*, without describing the internal details of its progression. The Greek tense most closely associated with simple aspect is the **aorist**, although **present** and **future tenses** may also communicate simple aspect when indicated by the context. Simple aspect is sometimes described as *undefined* aspect, since the word *aorist* means "undefined." In English, simple past, present, or future tenses are often used to translate these tenses, as in "Jesus *went* to Jerusalem" or "I *will come* home tomorrow." See **Aspect**.

Singular number: A grammatical feature that indicates that the **noun** or **substantive** refers to a single person or object. Also a feature of **verbs** that indicates that the verb's **subject** consists of a single person or thing. See **Number**.

Stative aspect: A grammatical feature of the **tense** of **verbs** and **verbals** that represents action that occurred sometime prior to a given point in time but that resulted in a *state of being* or a *state of affairs* that continues on from that point in time. Stative aspect is typically represented by the **perfect**, pluperfect, and future perfect tenses. The perfect tense is often translated using the English verbal auxiliaries "has" or "have" with a past tense form of the verb, as in "I *have seen* the light." The implication is not merely that I saw the light at some point in the past, but that the light I saw has had a continuing impact on me. As a result of the *past* action, my *present* status has changed from one who has never seen the light to one who has. See **Aspect**.

Stem: The part of a word that remains unchanged during **inflection**. It is part of the word to which **prefixes**, **infixes**, and **suffixes** are attached.

Subject: With an **active verb**, the person or thing that performs or is associated with the action. In the sentence, "Love never fails," the word "love" is the subject. Greek subjects are typically in the **nominative case**.

Subjective case: See **Nominative case**.

Subjunctive mood: The **mood** of **verbs** that indicates that the action or state of being indicated by the verb will possibly or probably occur in the future. The subjunctive mood is sometimes described as the mood of *potentiality* or *probability*.

There are three common uses of the subjunctive mood:

1) *Conditional* statement, as in the sentence, "If the Lord *should come*, we will travel to Galilee." In this sentence, the phrase "should come" represents a subjunctive verb in which an early arrival is considered a strong possibility.

2) *Purpose* statement, as in the sentence, "I am clearing the table in order that *we may eat*." Here the subjunctive indicates that the eating is probable once the table is cleared.

3) *Exhortation,* as in the sentence, "*Let us pray,*" or in a *prohibition*.

Present-tense subjunctive verbs typically represent ongoing action, while **aorist-tense** subjunctives represent simple action.

Substantive: A word other than a noun that is used like a noun to represent people or things. For example, in the sentence, "The rich have no worries," the adjective "rich" is used substantively to refer to *people* who are rich. In Greek, several types of words can be used as substantives, including **articles**, **adjectives**, **infinitives**, and **participles**.

Suffix: In Greek word **inflection**, the additions or changes to a word's ending that affect meaning. For example, the verb form λε-λύ-κα-τε consists of the perfect-tense **prefix** λε (**reduplication**), the verb **stem** λυ, the perfect-tense **infix** κα, and the **suffix** τε.

Tense: A grammatical feature of **verbs** that indicates the *time* and *manner* of the verb's action or state of being. The time element (past, present, or future) is present only in the **indicative mood** and in a relative sense in **participles**. The manner in which the action is presented as occurring is known as **aspect**.

There are seven tenses in Greek: *present, imperfect, future, aorist, perfect, pluperfect,* and *future perfect*. The pluperfect and future perfect are rarely used in the NT.

Many Greek scholars see a correlation between time and aspect in the Greek tenses. The following table illustrates this relationship as it is commonly understood. The three aspects are shown in the left column, while the three times fill the top row. The seven Greek tenses are shown in italics. Tenses in parentheses represent less common correlations.

The element of time is represented only in the **indicative mood**. In the other **moods**, a verb's tense communicates only its aspect.

GREEK ASPECT AND TENSE

	Past	Present	Future
Simple	*Aorist*	*(Present)*	*Future*
Continuous	*Imperfect*	*Present*	*(Future)*
Stative	*Pluperfect*	*Perfect*	*Future Perfect*

The time element of the tenses functions in a special way with participles. Normally, the aorist participle represents action that occurs *prior to* the action of the leading verb of a sentence and is often represented by including the word "after" in the translation, as in the sentence, "*After eating* a meal, the disciples were full." Present participles typically represent action the occurs *simultaneously with* that of the main verb and is represented by including the word "while" in the translation, as in the sentence, "*While hearing* the apostle preach, many were healed."

Other elements in a sentence may modify or qualify the way a verb represents either aspect or time. To learn more about these features, consult an advanced Greek grammar. See also the entries for individual aspects and tenses.

Third person: See **Person**.

Transitive verb: See **Verb**.

Verb: A word that represents an action (like *run, read,* and *learn*) or asserts that something exists or is coming into existence (like *is, were,* and *become*). In the sentence, "Mary *anointed* Jesus' feet," the word "anointed" is a verb.

Verbs can be either *transitive* or *intransitive*. Transitive verbs are used with a **direct object**, as in "Philip *preached* the word." Intransitive verbs do not take a direct object, as in "He *arose* and *walked.*"

Verbal: A special form of a **verb** that functions as a **noun**, an **adjective**, or an **adverb**. The Greek verbals are the **participle** and the **infinitive**.

Verbal auxiliary: In English grammar, the extra words added to a simple **verb** to form its various **tenses**, **voices**, and **moods**. In the sentence, "I have been entrusted with the gospel," the words "have been" are verbal auxiliaries used to form the perfect passive tense of the English verb "entrust." Greek verbs form tense, voice, and mood by the **inflection** of the verb itself and do not normally have verbal auxiliaries.

Vocative case: The **case** used when another person or thing is addressed directly, as with the name "Peter" in the sentence, "*Peter,* come and follow me!" Often a vocative is indicated in English by placing the word "O" before the noun representing the person or thing, as the word "death" in the sentence, "*O death,* where is your sting?"

Voice: A grammatical feature of **verbs** and **verbals** that indicates the manner in which the verb's **subject** is involved in the verbal action. Greek has three voices: **active**, **passive**, and **middle**, indicating respectively that the subject is the doer of the action, the one acted upon, or the doer that is specially involved in the verb's action. See also **Deponent verb** and entries for individual voices.

Appendix III
Greek Word Tables
Prepared by Mark A. House

The word tables that follow, together with the descriptions that accompany them, serve to aid the student of NT Greek in placing the forms found in the analytical lexicon into the larger scheme of Greek grammar. Rather than attempting a comprehensive treatment of Greek morphology, they provide a succinct overview of the system of NT Greek grammatical forms. Where a relevant word table exists, the entries in the Analytical Lexicon include a reference in curly braces pointing to the appropriate table. Thus in the example below, the reference to "6.B.2" points to the word table in category 6 (Verbals), subdivision B (Infinitives), and section 2 (Contract Verbs).

ἀγαπᾶτε   verb, pres. act. indic. 2 pers. pl. {5.A.2} . . . . .id.

Using the parsing information from the analytical entry, one can locate a form in the appropriate word table (in this case τιμᾶ-τε) that corresponds to the form in the entry (ἀγαπᾶτε). In many cases, the forms in the word tables contain hyphens that separate the stem of the word from any prefixes, infixes, and suffixes that have been added, making it easier to analyze the word being investigated.

The *Greek Word Tables* have been designed for use in conjunction with *Glossary of Greek Grammatical Terms* (Appendix II). Most of the grammatical and morphological terms found in the descriptions below are explained in the various entries of the glossary. For example, students wishing to gain more insight into the meaning of such terms as "article," "declension," "suffix," or "pronoun" (all contained in the following paragraph) should consult the glossary.

1. The Definite Article

Most forms of the definite article ὁ are created by combining the consonant τ with the first- and second-declension adjective suffixes. The NSM, NSF, NPM, and NPF forms of the article begin with rough breathing rather than τ. The NSM form ὁ lacks the characteristic suffix ς, which distinguishes it from the relative pronoun ὅς.

THE DEFINITE ARTICLE

THE DEFINITE ARTICLE

	M	F	N		M	F	N
NS	ὁ	ἡ	τό	NP	οἱ	αἱ	τά
GS	τοῦ	τῆς	τοῦ	GP	τῶν	τῶν	τῶν
DS	τῷ	τῇ	τῷ	DP	τοῖς	ταῖς	τοῖς
AS	τόν	τήν	τό	AP	τούς	τάς	τά

2. Nouns

2.A. First Declension

First-declension nouns have singular suffixes formed with either -α or -η and plural suffixes (except GP) formed with -α. The following inflectional patterns have been observed for singular forms:

1. Nouns whose NSF form ends with -η consistently have singular suffixes with -η (φωνή);

2. Nouns whose NSF form ends with -α and whose stems end in ε, ι, or ρ form their singular suffixes consistently with -α (χρεία);

3. All other nouns having NSF forms ending with -α have -η in their GS and DS forms (δόξ-α);

4. Masculine nouns whose NS form ends in -ας follow pattern 2, except that the GS suffix is -ου (νεανίας);

5. Masculine nouns whose NS form ends in -ης follow pattern 1, except that the GS suffix is -ου (προφήτ-ης). They have a VS suffix of α.

FIRST DECLENSION NOUNS

	1. Fem.	2. Fem.	3. Fem.	4. Masc.	5. Masc.
NS	φων-ή	χρεί-α	δόξ-α	νεανί-ας	προφήτ-ης
GS	φων-ῆς	χρεί-ας	δόξ-ης	νεανί-ου	προφήτ-ου
DS	φων-ῇ	χρεί-ᾳ	δόξ-η	νεανί-ᾳ	προφήτ-η
AS	φων-ήν	χρεί-αν	δόξ-αν	νεανί-αν	προφήτ-ην
VS	φων-ή	χρεί-α	δόξ-α	νεανί-α	προφήτ-α
N/VP	φων-αί	χρεῖ-αι	δόξ-αι	νεανί-αι	προφήτ-αι
GP	φων-ῶν	χρει-ῶν	δοξῶν	νεανι-ῶν	προφητ-ῶν
DP	φων-αῖς	χρεί-αις	δόξ-αις	νεανί-αις	προφήτ-αις
AP	φων-άς	χρεί-ας	δόξ-ας	νεανί-ας	προφήτ-ας

2.B. Second Declension

Most masculine and neuter nouns, and a small number of feminine nouns, inflect according to the second declension. Neuter nouns (δῶρον) differ from masculine nouns (ἄνθρωπος) in their NS, VS, NP, AP, and VP suffixes. Nouns with stems ending in a vowel (ὀστοῦν, stem ὀστε-) normally form by contraction of the stem and suffix vowels (as shown in the parentheses), although many forms do not contract.

SECOND DECLENSION NOUNS

	1. Masc.	2. Neut.	3. Neut., Contracted
NS	ἄνθρωπ-ος	δῶρ-ον	ὀστοῦν (έ-ον)
GS	ἀνθρώπ-ου	δώρ-ου	ὀστοῦ (έ-ου)
DS	ἀνθρώπ-ῳ	δώρ-ῳ	ὀστῷ (έ-ῳ)
AS	ἄνθρωπ-ον	δῶρ-ον	ὀστοῦν (έ-ον)
VS	ἄνθρωπ-ε	δῶρ-ον	ὀστοῦν (έ-ον)
N/VP	ἄνθρωπ-οι	δῶρ-α	ὀστᾶ (έ-α)
GP	ἀνθρώπ-ων	δώρ-ων	ὀστῶν (έ-ων)
DP	ἀνθρώπ-οις	δώρ-οις	ὀστοῖς (έ-οις)
AP	ἀνθρώπ-ους	δῶρ-α	ὀστᾶ (έ-α)

2.C. Third Declension

The formation of third declension nouns varies considerably, depending on the gender of the noun and the final letter of the stem to which the suffixes are attached. In lexical entries for third-declension nouns, the GS form is typically given along with the NS form, since the genitive shows the noun's stem more clearly than does the lexical form. The paradigms below cover the most common patterns, categorized according to the stem ending. For example, the dictionary entry for χάρις has the genitive suffix -ιτος, revealing the full stem to be χαριτ-.

1. Stems ending in various consonants:

   - NS and DP forms result from amalgamation of the final stem consonant and the -σ of the suffix (see **Consonant shift** in the Glossary).

   - Forms whose NS stem ends in ι sometimes have the AS suffix -ν.

2. Stems ending in various vowels:

   - The stem vowel contracts with the suffix connecting vowel (see **Contraction** in the Glossary).

   - Irregular formation in some words results from the presence of half-vowels that are no longer represented in the Greek alphabet.

3. Neuter nouns:

- NS and AS forms are identical.

- NP and AP forms end in -α and are identical. (With γένος, the α has been changed due to contraction with the stem vowel.)

THIRD DECLENSION NOUN SUFFIXES

	M/F	N			M/F	N
NS	-ς	none		NP	-ες	-α
GS	-ος	-ος		GP	-ων	-ων
DS	-ι	-ι		DP	-σι[ν]	-σι[ν]
AS	-α, -ν	none		AP	-ας	-α
VS	various	none		VP	-ες	-α

THIRD DECLENSION NOUNS

1. Consonantal Stems

	Labial	Guttural	Dental	Liquid	Nasal
NS	λίψ	σάρξ	χάρι-ς	ἀνήρ	αἰών
GS	λιβ-ός	σαρκ-ός	χάριτ-ος	ἀνδρ-ός	αἰῶν-ος
DS	λιβ-ί	σαρκ-ί	χάριτ-ι	ἀνδρ-ί	αἰῶν-ι
AS	λίβ-α	σάρκ-α	χάρι-ν	ἄνδρ-α	αἰῶν-α
VS	λίψ	σάρξ	χάρι-ς	ἄνερ	αἰών
N/VP	λίβ-ες	σάρκ-ες	χάριτ-ες	ἄνδρ-ες	αἰῶν-ες
GP	λιβ-ῶν	σαρκ-ῶν	χαρίτ-ων	ἀνδρ-ῶν	αἰών-ων
DP	λι-ψί[ν]	σαρ-ξί[ν]	χάρι-σι[ν]	ἀνδρά-σι[ν]	αἰῶ-σι[ν]
AP	λίβ-ας	σάρκ-ας	χάριτ-ας	ἄνδρ-ας	αἰῶν-ας

2. Vowel Stems

	ε/ι	ε/ευ
NS	πόλι-ς	βασιλε-ύς
GS	πόλε-ως	βασιλέ-ως
DS	πόλε-ι	βασιλε-ῖ
AS	πόλι-ν	βασιλέ-α
VS	πόλι	βασιλεῦ

3. Neuter Nouns

	Dental	Dental (ματ)	ος/ους
NS	φῶς	ὄνομα	γέν-ος
GS	φωτ-ός	ὀνόματ-ος	γέν-ους
DS	φωτ-ί	ὀνόματ-ι	γέν-ει
AS	φῶς	ὄνομα	γέν-ος
VS	φῶς	ὄνομα	γέν-ος

N/VP	πόλε-ις	βασιλε-ῖς	φῶτ-α	ὀνόματ-α	γέν-η
GP	πόλε-ων	βασιλέ-ων	φώτ-ων	ὀνομάτ-ων	γεν-ῶν
DP	πόλε-σι[ν]	βασιλεῦ-σι[ν]	φω-σί[ν]	ὀνόμα-σι[ν]	γέν-εσι[ν]
AP	πόλε-ις	βασιλε-ῖς	φῶτ-α	ὀνόματ-α	γέν-η

2.D. Proper Nouns

Proper nouns are typically capitalized in modern editions of the Greek NT. Many, being transliterations of Hebrew or Aramaic names, have fixed forms that do not inflect (e.g., Ἀβραάμ). Others inflect fully or partially in accordance with the first (e.g., Ἀνανίας), second (e.g., Ἰησοῦς: VSM, GSM, and DSM = Ἰησοῦ; ASM = Ἰησοῦν), or third declension (e.g., Μακεδών: GSM = Μακεδόνος).

3. Adjectives

3.A. First and Second Declension (2/1/2)

3.A.1. Regular adjectives: Most adjectives follow the inflectional pattern of first-declension nouns in their feminine forms and second-declension nouns in their masculine and neuter forms (2/1/2). Feminine singular forms have suffixes with -α or -η, following the rules for first-declension nouns (see section 2.A). Pronominal adjectives—adjectives whose function closely parallels that of personal pronouns and the demonstrative pronouns οὗτος and ἐκεῖνος (sections 4.A and 4.B) form the neuter singular suffix without final –ν (cf. N² below).

2/1/2 Adjectives—Consonantal Stems

	M	F	N	F²	N²
NS	καλ-ός	καλ-ή	καλ-όν	ἁγί-α	ἄλλ-ο
GS	καλ-οῦ	καλ-ῆς	καλ-οῦ	ἁγί-ας	ἄλλ-ου
DS	καλ-ῷ	καλ-ῇ	καλ-ῷ	ἁγί-α	ἄλλ-ῳ
AS	καλ-όν	καλ-ήν	καλ-όν	ἁγί-αν	ἄλλ-ο
VS	καλ-έ	καλ-ή	καλ-όν	ἁγί-α	ἄλλ-ο
N/VP	καλ-οί	καλ-αί	καλ-ά	ἅγι-αι	ἄλλ-α
GP	καλ-ῶν	καλ-ῶν	καλ-ῶν	ἁγί-ων	ἄλλ-ων
DP	καλ-οῖς	καλ-αῖς	καλ-οῖς	ἁγί-αις	ἄλλ-οις
AP	καλ-ούς	καλ-άς	καλ-ά	ἁγί-ας	ἄλλ-α

3.A.2. Adjectives with contraction: A few 2/1/2 adjectives have stems that end in a vowel, resulting in contraction with the suffix vowel (e.g., χρυσοῦς, stem χρυσε-). Sometimes uncontracted forms (shown in parentheses) are also used. Alternate feminine singular forms have -α rather than -η as the suffix vowel.

	M	F	N
		2/1/2 ADJECTIVES—CONTRACTED	
N/VS	χρυσ-οῦς	χρυσ-ῆ	χρυσ-οῦν (έ-ος)
GS	χρυσ-οῦ	χρυσ-ῆς	χρυσ-οῦ (έ-ου)
DS	χρυσ-ῷ	χρυσ-ῇ	χρυσ-ῷ (έ-ῳ)
AS	χρυσ-οῦν	χρυσ-ῆν, ᾶν	χρυσ-οῦν (έ-ον)
N/VP	χρυσ-οῖ	χρυσ-αῖ	χρυσ-ᾶ (έ-οι)
GP	χρυσ-ῶν	χρυσ-ῶν	χρυσ-ῶν (έ-ων)
DP	χρυσ-οῖς	χρυσ-αῖς	χρυσ-οῖς (έ-οις)
AP	χρυσ-οῦς	χρυσ-ᾶς	χρυσ-ᾶ (έ-ους)

3.B. First and Second Declension with Modified Stems (2/1/2)

A few 2/1/2 adjectives have modified NSM, ASM, NSN, ASN, and VSN forms. Feminine singular forms have -α or -η in accordance with the rules for first-declension nouns (see section 2.A).

	M	F	N
		2/1/2 ADJECTIVES—MODIFIED STEMS	
NS	μέγας	μεγάλ-η	μέγα
GS	μεγάλ-ου	μεγάλ-ης	μεγάλ-ου
DS	μεγάλ-ῳ	μεγάλ-ῃ	μεγάλ-ῳ
AS	μέγα-ν	μεγάλ-ην	μέγα
VS	μεγάλ-ε	μεγάλ-η	μέγα
N/VP	μεγάλ-οι	μεγάλ-αι	μεγάλ-α
GP	μεγάλ-ων	μεγάλ-ων	μεγάλ-ων
DP	μεγάλ-οις	μεγάλ-αις	μεγάλ-οις
AP	μεγάλ-ους	μεγάλ-ας	μεγάλ-α

	M	F	N
NS	πολύ-ς	πολλ-ή	πολύ
GS	πολλ-οῦ	πολλ-ῆς	πολλ-οῦ
DS	πολλ-ῷ	πολλ-ῇ	πολλ-ῷ
AS	πολύ-ν	πολλ-ήν	πολ-ύ
VS	πολύ-ς	πολλ-ή	πολύ
N/VP	πολλ-οί	πολλ-αί	πολλ-ά
GP	πολλ-ῶν	πολλ-ῶν	πολλ-ῶν
DP	πολλ-οῖς	πολλ-αῖς	πολλ-οῖς
AP	πολλ-ούς	πολλ-άς	πολλ-α

3.C. Second Declension (2/2)

Some adjectives, including compound (e.g., ἄπιστος) and personal (e.g., ἁμαρτωλός) adjectives, have feminine forms that are identical to their second-declension masculine forms. Otherwise, they inflect like 2/1/2 adjectives (see section 3.A above).

2/2 ADJECTIVES		
	M/F	N
NS	ἄπιστ-ος	ἄπιστ-ον
GS	ἀπίστ-ου	ἀπίστ-ου
DS	ἀπίστ-ῳ	ἀπίστ-ῳ
AS	ἄπιστ-ον	ἄπιστ-ον
VS	ἄπιστ-ε	ἄπιστ-ον
N/VP	ἄπιστ-οι	ἄπιστ-α
GP	ἀπίστ-ων	ἀπίστ-ων
DP	ἀπίστ-οις	ἀπίστ-οις
AP	ἀπίστ-ους	ἄπιστ-α

3.D. First and Third Declension (3/1/3)

3/1/3 adjectives have third-declension masculine and neuter forms (see section 2.C) and first-declension feminine forms (see section 2.A).

3.D.1. Adjectives with stems ending in a consonant: The NS, DP, and all feminine forms of πᾶς result from consonant amalgamation (παντσ → πασ). The inflectional pattern of πᾶς is similar to that of the first aorist (¹aorist) active participle (see section 6.A). For the DPM and DPN forms of both πᾶς and μέλας, the stem consonants -ντ- and -ν- have dropped out in the presence of -σ. The feminine forms of μέλας have a lengthened stem (μελαιν).

	3/1/3 ADJECTIVES		
	M	F	N
NS	πᾶς	πᾶσ-α	πᾶν
GS	παντ-ός	πάσ-ης	παντ-ός
DS	παντ-ί	πάσ-η	παντ-ί
AS	πάντ-α	πᾶσ-αν	πᾶν
NP	πάντ-ες	πᾶσ-αι	πάντ-α
GP	πάντ-ων	πασ-ῶν	πάντ-ων
DP	πᾶσι[ν]	πάσ-αις	πᾶσ-ι[ν]
AP	πάντ-ας	πάσ-ας	πάντ-α
	M	F	N
NS	μέλας	μέλαιν-α	μέλαν
GS	μέλαν-ος	μελαίν-ης	μέλαν-ος
DS	μέλαν-ι	μελαίν-η	μέλαν-ι
AS	μέλαν-α	μέλαιν-αν	μέλαν
NP	μέλαν-ες	μέλαιν-αι	μέλαν-α
GP	μελάν-ων	μελαιν-ῶν	μελάν-ων
DP	μέλασ-ι[ν]	μελαίν-αις	μέλασ-ι[ν]
AP	μέλαν-ας	μελαίν-ας	μέλαν-α

The numeral εἷς (stem, ἑν) follows a similar 3/1/3 pattern. The NSM form results from consonant amalgamation (as show in the parentheses). The distinctive first-declension feminine form is μία.

	THE NUMERAL εἷς		
	M	F	N
NS	εἷς (ἑν-ς)	μί-α	ἕν
GS	ἑν-ός	μι-ᾶς	ἑν-ός
DS	ἑν-ί	μι-ᾷ	ἑν-ί
AS	ἕν-α	μί-αν	ἕν

3.D.2. Adjectives with stems ending in a vowel: In this rare pattern, the stem vowel contracts in some instances with the suffix vowel (see **Contraction** in the Glossary). In the GSM and GSN forms, the contraction pattern is modified by the presence of a half-vowel.

		M	F	N
		3/1/3 ADJECTIVES—CONTRACTED		
NS		ὀξύς	ὀξεῖα	ὀξύ
GS		ὀξέως	ὀξείας	ὀξέως
DS		ὀξεῖ	ὀξείᾳ	ὀξεῖ
AS		ὀξύν	ὀξεῖαν	ὀξύ
NP		ὀξεῖς	ὀξεῖαι	ὀξέα
GP		ὀξέων	ὀξειῶν	ὀξέων
DP		ὀξέσι[ν]	ὀξείαις	ὀξέσι[ν]
AP		ὀξεῖς	ὀξείας	ὀξέα

3.E. Third Declension (3/3)

A small number of adjectives have third-declension forms in all three genders, with identical masculine and feminine forms. Adjectives with stems ending in a consonant show a regular pattern of inflections, while for those with stems ending in a vowel, suffixes form by contraction of the stem vowel and the suffix vowel, as shown in the parentheses (see **Contraction** in the Glossary).

		3/3 ADJECTIVES				
	1. Consonant Stem μείζων (stem μειζον)			2. Vowel Stem ἀληθής (stem ἀληθε)		
	M/F	N		M/F	N	
N/VS	μείζων	μεῖζον	N/VS	ἀληθής	ἀληθές	
GS	μείζον-ος	μεῖζον-ος	GS	ἀληθοῦς (έ-ος)	ἀληθοῦς (έ-ος)	
DS	μείζον-ι	μεῖζον-ι	DS	ἀληθεῖ (έ-ι)	ἀληθεῖ (έ-ι)	
AS	μείζον-α	μεῖζον	AS	ἀληθῆ (έ-α)	ἀληθές	
N/VP	μείζον-ες	μείζον-α	N/VP	ἀληθεῖς (έ-ες)	ἀληθῆ (έ-α)	
GP	μειζόν-ων	μειζόν-ων	GP	ἀληθῶν (έ-ων)	ἀληθῶν (έ-ων)	
DP	μειζόν-οσι[ν]	μειζόν-οσι[ν]	DP	ἀληθέ-σι[ν]	ἀληθέ-σι[ν]	
AP	μείζον-ας	μείζον-α	AP	ἀληθεῖς (έ-ας)	ἀληθῆ (έ-α)	

The third-declension cardinal numerals δύο, τρεῖς, and τέσσαρες also have identical masculine and feminine forms (3/3, plural only). The number δύο inflects only in the DP form. The higher cardinal numerals have fixed forms.

3/3 NUMERALS

	δύο		τρεῖς			τέσσαρες	
	M/F/N		M/F	N		M/F	N
NP	δύο	NP	τρεῖς (ι-ες)	τρί-α	NP	τέσσαρ-ες	τέσσαρ-α
GP	δύο	GP	τρι-ῶν	τρι-ῶν	GP	τεσσάρ-ων	τεσσάρ-ων
DP	δυ-σί[ν]	DP	τρι-σί[ν]	τρι-σί[ν]	DP	τέσσαρ-σι[ν]	τέσσαρ-σι[ν]
AP	δύο	AP	τρεῖς (ι-ας)	τρί-α	AP	τέσσαρ-ας	τέσσαρ-α

3.F. Construction of Adverbs from Adjectives

Some adverbs are constructed from adjectives, while others consist of unique forms unrelated to adjectives. The most common way to form an adverb from an adjective is by adding the -ως suffix to the adjectival stem (ἀγνός → ἀγνῶς). For other adjectives, the neuter singular (e.g., ἀγαθόν) or neuter plural (e.g., ἴσα) form of the adjective (or both, e.g., πολύ / πολλά) may function as an adverb. GS (καθόλου) or DS (δημοσίᾳ) forms of a few adjectives are also used adverbially.

3.G. Formation of Comparative and Superlative Degrees

Most adjectives are capable of forming comparative and superlative degrees. In English this is normally done by adding the suffixes "-er" and "-est" to the adjective, as in "big, bigger, biggest." In Greek there are two different ways of forming comparatives and superlatives:

1. The comparative degree of many adjectives is formed by inserting the infix -τερ- to the adjective stem prior to attaching first- or second-declension suffixes. The infix may be connected to the stem with ο (-οτερ-) or ω (-ωτερ-), or for third-declension nouns, attached directly to the stem or after the addition of εσ (-εστερ-). Adjectives that form their comparative degree with -τερ- tend to form their superlative degree with -τατ-, as illustrated below. Both comparative and superlative forms follow the 2/1/2 pattern of adjective inflection.

DEGREES OF ADJECTIVES—PATTERN 1

Positive	Comparative	Superlative
μικρός (2/1/2) "small"	μικρό-τερ-ος (2/1/2) "smaller"	μικρό-τατ-ος (2/1/2) "smallest"
νεός	νεώ-τερ-ος	νεώ-τατ-ος
ἀκριβής	ἀκριβέσ-τερ-ος	ἀκριβέσ-τατ-ος
δεισιδαίμων	δεισιδαιμον-έσ-τερ-ος	δεισιδαιμον-έσ-τατ-ος

2. For other adjectives, the comparative degree is constructed by the formation of a modified, third-declension (3/3) stem with the suffix -ων or -ιων attached. Thus the comparative degree of the adjective μέγας is μείζων (gen. -ονος). Adjectives that form their comparative degree in this way tend to form their superlative degree with -ιστος, which inflects according to the 2/1/2 pattern.

DEGREES OF ADJECTIVES—PATTERN 2		
Positive	Comparative	Superlative
μέγας (2/1/2)	μείζ-ων (3/3)	μέγ-ιστος (2/1/2)
κρατύς	κρείττ-ων	κράτ-ιστος
πολύς	πλε-ίων	πλε-ῖστος
μικρός	ἐλάσσ-ων	ἐλάχ-ιστος

3. Although adverbs have fixed forms, comparative and superlative degrees can be constructed from the neuter singular of the comparative and neuter plural of the superlative degrees of the adjective.

DEGREES OF ADVERBS			
	Positive	Comparative	Superlative
Adjective	ἐγγύς "near"	ἐγγύ-τερος "nearer"	ἔγγ-ιστος "nearest"
Adverb	ἐγγύς "near(ly)"	ἐγγύ-τερον "more nearly"	ἔγγ-ιστα "most nearly"
Adjective	ταχύς quick	τάχ-ιων quicker	τάχ-ιστος quickest
Adverb	ταχύ quickly	τάχ-ιον more quickly	τάχ-ιστα most quickly

4. Pronouns

4.A. Personal Pronouns

1. The first- and second-person personal pronouns ἐγώ and σύ are similar in inflection. Neither is parsed according to gender. The unaccented forms are enclitic. Accented GS, DS, and AS forms are used for emphasis and following prepositions.

PERSONAL PRONOUNS

First Person		Second Person	
NS	ἐγώ	NS	σύ
GS	μου, ἐμοῦ	GS	σου, σοῦ
DS	μοι, ἐμοί	DS	σοι, σοί
AS	με, ἐμέ	AS	σε, σέ
NP	ἡμεῖς	NP	ὑμεῖς
GP	ἡμῶν	GP	ὑμῶν
DP	ἡμῖν	DP	ὑμῖν
AP	ἡμᾶς	AP	ὑμᾶς

2. The third-person personal pronoun is fully parsed according to case, number, and gender. It uses suffixes identical to those of pronominal adjectives (see section 3.A.1, ἄλλο), with the NSN and ASN forms having the suffix o rather than ον. Beside its pronominal function, αὐτός also may also have an intensifying, reflexive, or identifying force.

PERSONAL PRONOUNS

Third Person/Intensive

	M	F	N		M	F	N
NS	αὐτ-ός	αὐτ-ή	αὐτ-ό	NP	αὐτ-οί	αὐτ-αί	αὐτ-ά
GS	αὐτ-οῦ	αὐτ-ῆς	αὐτ-οῦ	GP	αὐτ-ῶν	αὐτ-ῶν	αὐτ-ῶν
DS	αὐτ-ῷ	αὐτ-ῇ	αὐτ-ῷ	DP	αὐτ-οῖς	αὐτ-αῖς	αὐτ-οῖς
AS	αὐτ-όν	αὐτ-ήν	αὐτ-ό	AP	αὐτ-ούς	αὐτ-άς	αὐτ-ά

4.B. Demonstrative Pronouns

1. The demonstrative pronouns οὗτος and ἐκεῖνος (2/1/2) use suffixes identical to those of pronominal adjectives (see section 3.A.1, ἄλλο). Like the definite article, the NSM, NSF, NPM, and NPF forms of οὗτος begin with rough breathing rather than τ. For the feminine forms of οὗτος (except the genitive plural), the first syllable contains the diphthong αυ rather than ου.

DEMONSTRATIVE PRONOUNS

	Near Demonstrative				Far Demonstrative		
	M	F	N		M	F	N
NS	οὗτ-ος	αὗτ-η	τοῦτ-ο	NS	ἐκεῖν-ος	ἐκείν-η	ἐκεῖν-ο
GS	τούτ-ου	ταύτ-ης	τούτ-ου	GS	ἐκείν-ου	ἐκείν-ης	ἐκείν-ου
DS	τούτ-ῳ	ταύτ-ῃ	τούτ-ῳ	DS	ἐκείν-ῳ	ἐκείν-ῃ	ἐκείν-ῳ
AS	τοῦτ-ον	ταύτ-ην	τοῦτ-ο	AS	ἐκεῖν-ον	ἐκείν-ην	ἐκεῖν-ο
NP	οὗτ-οι	αὗτ-αι	ταῦτ-α	NP	ἐκεῖν-οι	ἐκεῖν-αι	ἐκεῖν-α
GP	τούτ-ων	τούτ-ων	τούτ-ων	GP	ἐκείν-ων-	ἐκείν-ων-	ἐκείν-ων-
DP	τούτ-οις	ταύτ-αις	τούτ-οις	DP	ἐκείν-οις	ἐκείν-αις	ἐκείν-οις
AP	τούτ-ους	ταύτ-ας	ταῦτ-α	AP	ἐκείν-ους	ἐκείν-ας	ἐκεῖν-α

2. The form ταὐτά is the result of crasis—the contraction of the APN article τά and the substantive APN form of αὐτός. It may be distinguished from a similar form of the demonstrative pronoun by the apostrophe above the υ.

3. Two correlative pronouns are constructed from οὗτος: τοιοῦτος ("such") and τηλικοῦτος ("so great"). These have the same inflectional pattern as οὗτος. See section 4.D below.

4. There are three forms of the demonstrative ὅδε in the NT: τήνδε, τῇδε, and τάδε. These inflect like the definite article (see section 1) with the suffix -δε added.

4.C. Relative Pronouns

1. The relative pronoun ὅς forms regularly by adding rough breathing and accenting to the first and second declension adjectival suffixes (2/1/2).

RELATIVE PRONOUN

	M	F	N		M	F	N
NS	ὅς	ἥ	ὅ	NP	οἵ	αἵ	ἅ
GS	οὗ	ἧς	οὗ	GP	ὧν	ὧν	ὧν
DS	ᾧ	ᾗ	ᾧ	DP	οἷς	αἷς	οἷς
AS	ὅν	ἥν	ὅ	AP	οὕς	ἅς	ἅ

2. The indefinite relative pronoun ὅστις is constructed by combining forms of the relative pronoun (above) and the indefinite pronoun (section 4.E below). With the exception of the irregular GSN form ὅτου, it is found in the NT only in the nominative case.

INDEFINITE RELATIVE PRONOUN

	M	F	N
NS	ὅστις	ἥτις	ὅτι
GS			ὅτου
NP	οἵτιν-ες	αἵτιν-ες	ἅτιν-α

4.D. Correlative Pronouns and Adverbs

There are several sets of correlative pronouns and adverbs in the NT. Understanding the correlations between them enables a better grasp of the meaning of each. All the pronouns inflect like the adjective καλός (see section 3.A.1). In the table below, forms in parentheses are lacking in the NT but are found in broader Greek. See **Correlative pronoun** in the Glossary.

CORRELATIVE PRONOUNS

Demonstrative	Interrogative	Indefinite	Relative	Indefinite Relative
(τηλίκος) or τηλικοῦτος "so old/great"	πηλίκος "how old/great?"	πηλίκος "of some age"	ἡλίκος "of which age/size"	(ὁπηλίκος) "of whatever age/size"
τοιόσδε or τοιοῦτος "such kind"	ποῖος "of what kind?"	(ποιός) "of some kind"	οἷος "of which kind"	ὁποῖος "of whatever kind"
(τόσος) or τοσοῦτος "so much" "so many"	πόσος "how much?" "how many?"	ποσός "of some quantity"	ὅσος "as much as" "as many as"	(ὁπόσος) "of whatever size/number"

CORRELATIVE ADVERBS

Demonstrative	Interrogative	Indefinite	Relative	Indefinite Relative
(τόθεν) "thence"	πόθεν "from whence?"	(ποθέν) "from someplace"	ὅθεν "from which place"	(ὁπόθεν) "from where"
τότε "then"	πότε "when?"	ποτέ "at some time"	ὅτε, ὁπότε "at which time"	(ὁπόταν) "whenever"
	ποῦ "where?"	που "somewhere"	ὅπου "at which place"	ὅπου ἄν "wherever"
	πῶς "how?" "in what manner?"		ὥς "as"	

4.E. Indefinite and Interrogative Pronouns

The indefinite and interrogative pronouns τις and τίς, identical except for accent, inflect according to the third declension with identical masculine and feminine forms (3/3). The indefinite pronouns are either unaccented or have the accent on the final syllable, while the interrogatives are always accented over the syllable containing τι. Being third-declension forms with nasal stems, the NSM, NSF, and all DP forms lose the final stem consonant -ν- before suffixes beginning with -σ (e.g., τινσί → τισί).

INDEFINITE AND INTERROGATIVE PRONOUNS					
1. Indefinite Pronoun			2. Interrogative Pronoun		
	M/F	N		M/F	N
NS	τις	τι	NS	τίς	τί
GS	τιν-ός	τιν-ός	GS	τίν-ος	τίν-ος
DS	τιν-ί	τιν-ί	DS	τίν-ι	τίν-ι
AS	τιν-ά	τι	AS	τίν-α	τί
NP	τιν-ές	τιν-ά	NP	τίν-ες	τίν-α
GP	τιν-ῶν	τιν-ῶν	GP	τίν-ων	τίν-ων
DP	τι-σί[ν]	τι-σί[ν]	DP	τί-σι[ν]	τί-σι[ν]
AP	τιν-άς	τιν-ά	AP	τίν-ας	τίν-α

Several additional interrogative pronouns may be found in the second column of section 4.D above.

4.F. Reflexive Pronouns

The first-, second-, and third-person reflexive pronouns follow the inflectional pattern of pronominal adjectives (cf. ἄλλο, 3.A.1). Nominative forms are not used. Neuter forms of first- and second-person pronouns are not found in the NT. Plural forms of the first- and second-person reflexive pronouns are identical with those of the third person. Third person reflexive pronouns sometimes appear in contracted forms that retain the rough breather but lack the initial ε (e.g., αὑτοῦ instead of ἑαυτοῦ).

REFLEXIVE PRONOUNS								
First Person		Second Person		Third Person				
	M	F	M	F	M	F	N	
GS	ἐμαυτ-οῦ	ἐμαυτ-ῆς	σεαυτ-οῦ	σεαυτ-ῆς	ἑαυτ-οῦ	ἑαυτ-ῆς	ἑαυτ-οῦ	
DS	ἐμαυτ-ῷ	ἐμαυτ-ῇ	σεαυτ-ῷ	σεαυτ-ῇ	ἑαυτ-ῷ	ἑαυτ-ῇ	ἑαυτ-ῷ	
AS	ἐμαυτ-όν	ἐμαυτ-ήν	σεαυτ-όν	σεαυτ-ήν	ἑαυτ-όν	ἑαυτ-ήν	ἑαυτ-ό	

REFLEXIVE PRONOUNS, CONT'D

	First Person		Second Person		Third Person		
	M	F	M	F	M	F	N
GP	ἑαυτ-ῶν	ἑαυτ-ῶν	ἑαυτ-ῶν	ἑαυτ-ῶν	ἑαυτ-ῶν	ἑαυτ-ῶν	ἑαυτ-ῶν
DP	ἑαυτ-οῖς	ἑαυτ-αῖς	ἑαυτ-οῖς	ἑαυτ-αῖς	ἑαυτ-οῖς	ἑαυτ-αῖς	ἑαυτ-οῖς
AP	ἑαυτ-ούς	ἑαυτ-άς	ἑαυτ-ούς	ἑαυτ-άς	ἑαυτ-ούς	ἑαυτ-άς	ἑαυτ-ά

4.G. Reciprocal Pronouns

Only plural forms of the reciprocal pronoun (see Reciprocal pronoun in the Glossary) are used. The following forms are found in the NT: ἀλλήλων (GPM), ἀλλήλοις (DPM), and ἀλλήλους (APM).

4.H. Possessive Pronouns

Personal pronouns in the genitive case are commonly used to indicate relationship or ownership. Alternatively, possessive pronouns (or adjectives) may be used. Functioning like adjectives, they take on the case, number, and gender of the noun or substantive they modify. While in older Greek there were possessive pronouns representing all three persons, in the NT only the first and second persons are represented. As with the personal pronoun, the plural forms have roots distinct from the singular forms. All forms inflect like the adjective καλός, except that the feminine singular forms of both plural pronouns inflect like ἀγία (see section 3.A.1).

First Person Singular ("my"):	ἐμός, ή, όν
Second Person Singular ("your"):	σός, ή, όν
First Person Plural ("our"):	ἡμέτερος, ά, όν
Second Person Plural ("your"):	ὑμέτερος, ά, όν

5. Verbs

5.A. Indicative Mood

5.A.1. -ω Conjugation

Most Greek verbs follow the -ω (or thematic) conjugation, having suffixes that include a theme (or linking) vowel and a present active indicative 1S form ending in ω. Deponent tenses in this class have no active forms, with the middle (or rarely the passive) forms having taken over the active function in many cases. The main distinction to be observed with indicative-mood verbs is between primary suffixes, used with present and future tenses, secondary suffixes, used with perfect, aorist, and pluperfect tenses, and perfect suffixes.

5.A.1.a. Primary Active

Primary suffixes are used to form the present and future tenses of the indicative mood (see **Primary-tense suffixes** in the Glossary). Both tenses use identical suffixes, but the future tense is distinguished from the present by the insertion of the infix -σ- between the verb stem and the suffix.

	-ω Verbs—Primary Active Forms	
	1. Pres. Act. Indic.	2. Fut. Act. Indic.
1S	λύ-ω	λύ-σ-ω
2S	λύ-εις	λύ-σ-εις
3S	λύ-ει	λύ-σ-ει
1P	λύ-ομεν	λύ-σ-ομεν
2P	λύ-ετε	λύ-σ-ετε
3P	λύ-ουσι[ν]	λύ-σ-ουσι

5.A.1.b. Secondary Active

Augmentation and secondary suffixes are used to form the imperfect, aorist, and pluperfect tenses of the indicative mood. The first aorist active is formed by the insertion of the infix -σ- between the verb stem and the suffix and the use of the α suffix vowel for all but the 3S suffix. If the -σ- infix is preceded by a consonant, the two consonants undergo amalgamation (see **Consonant shift** in the Glossary). Liquid verbs (i.e., those with stems ending in λ, μ, ν, or ρ) often form the aorist indicative without the -σ- infix (e.g., ἔκρινα, from κρίνω).

Verbs with secondary suffixes also undergo augmentation (see **Augmentation** in the Glossary).

Verbs that form without -σα- are classified as second aorists (e.g., ἔλιπον). These differ from ¹aorists only in their pattern of formation, not in their meaning. Second aorist (²aorist) and imperfect verbs have identical inflection patterns, but the imperfect is built on the present-tense stem, while the ²aorist uses a stem that is distinct from the present-tense stem (cf. the imperfect-tense form ἔλειπον, from λείπω, with the ²aorist ἔλιπον). Alternatively, certain verbs form the ²aorist with α suffixes similar to ¹aorist, but without the σ (e.g., εἶπαν). A handful of verbs (e.g., κατέβην [καταβαίνω] and ἔγνων [γινώσκω]) have athematic ²aorists (forms in which suffixes are attached directly to the verb stem without an intervening connecting vowel) that inflect like the ²aorists of -μι verbs (cf. ἔστην, section 5.A.3.b). Virtually all verbs form the aorist either according to the first or second aorist pattern, not both.

Aorist passive indicatives inflect with secondary active suffixes added to a -θη- infix. Aorist passives that form without the θ are classified as ²aorist passives (e.g., ἐχάρην). These differ from regular aorist passives in form only, not in meaning. There is no correlation between ²aorist actives and ²aorist passives. Aorist passive indicatives are augmented.

Pluperfect active indicatives are formed by adding secondary active suffixes to a -κ- infix followed by the diphthong ει. Pluperfect actives that form without the -κ- are classified as second pluperfects (cf. ἤδ-ει-ν). These differ from regular pluperfects in form only, not in meaning. Like perfects, pluperfects also undergo reduplication and may also be augmented (see **Augmentation** and **Reduplication** in the Glossary).

VERBS—SECONDARY ACTIVE FORMS

	¹Aor. Act. Indic.	¹Aor. Act. Indic. (βλέπω)	Liq. Aor. Indic. (κρίνω)
1S	ἔ-λυ-σα	ἔβλεψ-α	ἔ-κριν-α
2S	ἔ-λυ-σα-ς	ἔβλεψ-ας	ἔ-κριν-ας
3S	ἔ-λυ-σε[ν]	ἔβλεψ-ε[ν]	ἔ-κριν-ε[ν]
1P	ἐ-λύ-σα-μεν	ἐβλέψ-αμεν	ἐ-κρίν-αμεν
2P	ἐ-λύ-σα-τε	ἐβλέψ-ατε	ἐ-κρίν-ατε
3P	ἔ-λυ-σαν	ἔβλεψ-αν	ἔ-κριν-αν

	Impf. Act. Indic.	²Aor. Act. Indic. (λείπω)	Athematic ²Aor. Act. Indic. (γινώσκω)
1S	ἔ-λυ-ον	ἔ-λιπ-ον	ἔ-γνω-ν
2S	ἔ-λυ-ες	ἔ-λιπ-ες	ἔ-γνω-ς
3S	ἔ-λυ-ε[ν]	ἔ-λιπ-ε[ν]	ἔ-γνω
1P	ἐ-λύ-ομεν	ἐ-λίπ-ομεν	ἔ-γνω-μεν
2P	ἐ-λύ-ετε	ἐ-λίπ-ετε	ἔ-γνω-τε
3P	ἔ-λυ-ον	ἔ-λιπ-ον	ἔ-γνω-σαν

	Plu. Act. Indic.	²Plu. Act. Indic. (οἶδα)
1S	[ἐ-]λε-λύ-κει-ν	ἤδ-ει-ν
2S	[ἐ-]λε-λύ-κει-ς	ἤδ-ει-ς
3S	[ἐ-]λε-λύ-κει	ἤδ-ει
1P	[ἐ-]λε-λύ-κει-μεν	ἤδ-ει-μεν
2P	[ἐ-]λε-λύ-κει-τε	ἤδ-ει-τε
3P	[ἐ-]λε-λύ-κει-σαν	ἤδ-ει-σαν

	Aor. Pass. Indic.	²Aor. Pass. Indic. (χαίρω)
1S	ἐ-λύ-θη-ν	ἐ-χάρ-η-ν
2S	ἐ-λύ-θη-ς	ἐ-χάρ-η-ς
3S	ἐ-λύ-θη	ἐ-χάρ-η
1P	ἐ-λύ-θη-μεν	ἐ-χάρ-η-μεν
2P	ἐ-λύ-θη-τε	ἐ-χάρ-η-τε
3P	ἐ-λύ-θη-σαν	ἐ-χάρ-η-σαν

5.A.1.c. Perfect Active

Although the perfect is often considered a primary tense, its active suffixes are somewhat distinctive from the primary suffixes shown in the present and future tenses. All suffixes except 3P are similar to the secondary suffixes of the ¹aorist. However, the -σι suffix of the 3P is closer to the corresponding primary active suffix.

Perfect indicatives are normally formed by adding suffixes to the infix -κ- followed by an α linking vowel. (The 3S form lacks the α.) Verbs that form the perfect without the addition of the infix -κ- are classified as second perfects (e.g., οἶδα). These differ from regular perfects only in form, not in meaning.

Perfect indicatives are also distinguished by the reduplication of the initial stem consonant (λ- → λελ-). For verbs beginning with a vowel or diphthong, reduplication is normally accomplished by the lengthening of the initial vowel, similar to augmentation (see **Augmentation** in the Glossary), while initial diphthongs remain unchanged.

-ω Verbs—Perfect Active Forms		
	Perf. Act. Indic.	²Perf. Act. Indic. (οἶδα)
1S	λέ-λυ-κα	οἶδ-α
2S	λέ-λυ-κα-ς	οἶδ-α-ς
3S	λέ-λυ-κε[ν]	οἶδ-ε[ν]
1P	λε-λύ-κα-μεν	οἶδ-α-μεν
2P	λε-λύ-κα-τε	οἶδ-α-τε
3P	λε-λύ-κα-σι[ν]	οἶδ-ασι

5.A.1.d. Primary Middle and Passive

Primary middle and passive verbs have primary middle suffixes (see **Primary-tenses suffixes** in the Glossary). Since middle and passive forms of the present and perfect tenses are identical, context is required to distinguish the one from the other. The future tense has distinct middle and passive forms. For present and future tenses, the 2S suffix results from the reduction of the 2S suffix -εσαι through the loss of the -σ- and the contraction of the remaining vowels (-εαι → -η).

Future passive forms are constructed from the sixth principal part (aorist passive) and are characterized by the -θη- infix combined with the -σ- infix .

Perfect middle/passive forms (e.g., λέλυμαι) lack the -κα- infix of the perfect active. Suffixes are connected directly to the verb stem without a linking vowel, often resulting in consonant assimilation of amalgamation (e.g., κεκήρυγμαι, from κηρύσσω; see **Consonant shift** in the Glossary). The 3P form is avoided by using a periphrastic construction (e.g., εἰσιν κεκηρυγμένος; see **Periphrastic** in the Glossary).

	Pres. Mid./Pass. Indic.	Fut. Mid. Indic.	Fut. Pass. Indic.
1S	λύ-ομαι	λύ-σ-ομαι	λυ-θήσ-ομαι
2S	λύ-η	λύ-σ-η	λυ-θήσ-η
3S	λύ-εται	λύ-σ-εται	λυ-θήσ-εται
1P	λυ-όμεθα	λυ-σ-όμεθα	λυ-θησ-όμεθα
2P	λύ-εσθε	λύ-σ-εσθε	λυ-θήσ-εσθε
3P	λύ-ονται	λύ-σ-ονται	λυ-θήσ-ονται

-ω Verbs—Primary Middle and Passive Forms

5.A.1.e. Secondary Middle and Passive

Secondary middle and passive indicatives form like secondary actives, but with secondary middle secondary endings, with the exception of the aorist passive, which has secondary active endings (see section 5.A.1.b. for aorist passive forms). Since middle and passive forms of the present, imperfect, and pluperfect tenses are identical, context is required to distinguish the one from the other. For the aorist tense, the 2S suffix -ω results from the reduction of the suffix -ασο through the loss of the -σ- and the contraction of the remaining vowels (-αο → -ω). For ²aorist and imperfect tenses, the 2S suffix results from the reduction of the suffix -εσο through the loss of the -σ- and the contraction of the remaining vowels (-εο → -ου). Liquid verbs (i.e., those with stems ending in λ, μ, ν, or ρ) often form the aorist indicative without the -σ- infix (e.g., ἐκρινάμην, from κρίνω).

Pluperfect middle/passive forms lack the -κει- infix of the pluperfect active. Suffixes are connected directly to the verb stem without a linking vowel, often resulting in consonant amalgamation or assimilation (cf. [ἐ]κεκήρυγμαι, from κηρύσσω; see **Consonant shift** in the Glossary). The 3P form is avoided by using a periphrastic construction (ἦσαν κεκηρυγμένος; see **Periphrastic** in the Glossary).

Secondary Middle and Passive Forms

	¹Aor. Mid. Indic.	²Aor. Mid. Indic. (λείπω)	Liq. Aor. Mid. Indic. (κρίνω)
1S	ἐ-λυ-σά-μην	ἐ-λιπ-όμην	ἐ-κριν-άμην
2S	ἐ-λύ-σω	ἐ-λίπ-ου	ἐ-κρίν-ω
3S	ἐ-λύ-σα-το	ἐ-λίπ-ετο	ἐ-κρίν-ατο
1P	ἐ-λυ-σά-μεθα	ἐ-λιπ-όμεθα	ἐ-κριν-άμεθα
2P	ἐ-λύ-σα-σθε	ἐ-λίπ-εσθε	ἐ-κρίν-ασθε
3P	ἐ-λύ-σα-ντο	ἐ-λίπ-οντο	ἐ-κρίν-αντο

	Impf. Mid./Pass. Indic.	Plu. Mid./Pass. Indic.	Plu. Mid./Pass. Indic. (κηρύσσω)
1S	ἐ-λυ-όμην	[ἐ-]λε-λύ-μην	[ἐ-]κε-κηρύγ-μην
2S	ἐ-λύ-ου	[ἐ-]λέ-λυ-σο	[ἐ-]κε-κήρυξ-ο
3S	ἐ-λύ-ετο	[ἐ-]λέ-λυ-το	[ἐ-]κε-κήρυκ-το
1P	ἐ-λυ-όμεθα	[ἐ-]λε-λύ-μεθα	[ἐ-]κε-κηρύγ-μεθα
2P	ἐ-λύ-εσθε	[ἐ-]λέ-λυ-σθε	[ἐ-]κε-κήρυξ-θε
3P	ἐ-λύ-οντο	[ἐ-]λέ-λυ-ντο	*periphrastic*

5.A.1.f. Perfect Middle/Passive

Perfect middle/passive indicatives (e.g., λέλυμαι) lack the -κα- infix of the perfect active. Instead, suffixes are connected directly to the verb stem without a linking vowel. For verb stems ending in a consonant, this often results in consonant assimilation or amalgamation (e.g., κεκήρυγμαι, from κηρύσσω; see **Consonant shift** in the Glossary). The difficult 3P form is avoided by using a periphrastic construction (e.g., εἰσιν κεκηρυγμένος; see **Periphrastic** in the Glossary).

Perfect Middle and Passive Forms

	Perf. Mid./Pass. Indic.	Perf. Mid./Pass. Indic. (κηρύσσω)
1S	λέ-λυ-μαι	κε-κήρυγ-μαι
2S	λέ-λυ-σαι	κε-κήρυξ-αι
3S	λέ-λυ-ται	κε-κήρυκ-ται
1P	λε-λύ-μεθα	κε-κηρύγ-μεθα
2P	λέ-λυ-σθε	κε-κήρυξ-θε
3P	λέ-λυ-νται	*periphrastic*

5.A.2. Contract, Liquid, and ιζω Verbs

Contract verbs are a special class of the -ω conjugation that use the same suffixes as other -ω verbs, but the suffix linking vowels contract with the verb stem's final vowel, resulting in modified inflections (see **Contraction** in the Glossary). There are three classes of contract verbs, described in terms of the verb's stem vowel: -αω, -εω, and -οω. For the verb τιμάω, for example, the stem ending vowel α contracts with the ο linking vowel of the 1P suffix -ομεν to form the vowel -ω- in the contracted form τιμῶμεν.

Verb contraction occurs only with the present and imperfect tenses. Contract verbs form the other tenses regularly by lengthening the stem vowel and adding suffixes similar to -ω verbs (see section 5.A.1 above). Thus the future of τιμάω is τιμήσω and the [1]aorist is ἐτίμησα. A few contract verbs with an ε stem vowel do not lengthen the vowel in the formation of other tenses. The future of καλέω, for example, is καλέσω.

Many liquid verbs (i.e., verbs with stems ending in λ, μ, ν, or ρ) and several verbs ending with -ιζω also form their future indicatives like -εω contracts (e.g., κρινῶ, from κρίνω, and ἐγγιῶ, from ἐγγίζω).

	CONTRACT VERBS		
	τιμάω	φιλέω	δηλόω
	Pres. Act. Indic.		
1S	τιμῶ	φιλῶ	δηλῶ
2S	τιμᾷ-ς	φιλεῖ-ς	δηλοῖ-ς
3S	τιμᾷ	φιλεῖ	δηλοῖ
1P	τιμῶ-μεν	φιλοῦ-μεν	δηλοῦ-μεν
2P	τιμᾶ-τε	φιλεῖ-τε	δηλοῦ-τε
3P	τιμῶ-σι	φιλοῦ-σι	δηλοῦ-σι
	Pres. Mid./Pass. Indic.		
1S	τιμῶ-μαι	φιλοῦ-μαι	δηλοῦ-μαι
2S	τιμᾷ	φιλῇ	δηλοῖ
3S	τιμᾶ-ται	φιλεῖ-ται	δηλοῦ-ται
1P	τιμώ-μεθα	φιλού-μεθα	δηλού-μεθα
2P	τιμᾶ-σθε	φιλεῖ-σθε	δηλοῦ-σθε
3P	τιμῶ-νται	φιλοῦ-νται	δηλοῦ-νται

Impf. Act. Indic.

1S	ἐ-τίμω-ν	ἐ-φίλου-ν	ἐ-δήλου-ν
2S	ἐ-τίμα-ς	ἐ-φίλει-ς	ἐ-δήλου-ς
3S	ἐ-τίμα	ἐ-φίλει	ἐ-δήλου
1P	ἐ-τιμῶ-μεν	ἐ-φιλοῦ-μεν	ἐ-δηλοῦ-μεν
2P	ἐ-τιμᾶ-τε	ἐ-φιλεῖ-τε	ἐ-δηλοῦ-τε
3P	ἐ-τίμω-ν	ἐ-φίλου-ν	ἐ-δήλου-ν

Impf. Mid./Pass. Indic.

1S	ἐ-τιμώ-μην	ἐ-φιλού-μην	ἐ-δηλού-μην
2S	ἐ-τιμῶ	ἐ-φιλοῦ	ἐ-δηλοῦ
3S	ἐ-τιμᾶ-το	ἐ-φιλεῖ-το	ἐ-δηλοῦ-το
1P	ἐ-τιμώ-μεθα	ἐ-φιλού-μεθα	ἐ-δηλού-μεθα
2P	ἐ-τιμᾶ-σθε	ἐ-φιλεῖ-σθε	ἐ-δηλοῦ-σθε
3P	ἐ-τιμῶ-ντο	ἐ-φιλοῦ-ντο	ἐ-δηλοῦ-ντο

LIQUID AND -ιζω VERBS

	Liq. Fut. Act. Indic. (κρίνω)	Liq. Fut. Mid. Indic. (κρίνω)	Fut. Act. Indic. (ἐγγίζω)	Fut. Mid. Indic. (ἐγγίζω)
1S	κριν-ῶ	κριν-οῦμαι	ἐγγι-ῶ	ἐγγι-οῦμαι
2S	κριν-εῖς	κριν-ῇ	ἐγγι-εῖς	ἐγγι-ῇ
3S	κριν-εῖ	κριν-εῖται	ἐγγι-εῖ	ἐγγι-εῖται
1P	κριν-οῦμεν	κριν-ούμεθα	ἐγγι-οῦμεν	ἐγγι-ούμεθα
2P	κριν-εῖτε	κριν-εῖσθε	ἐγγι-εῖτε	ἐγγι-εῖσθε
3P	κριν-οῦσι[ν]	κριν-οῦνται	ἐγγι-οῦσι[ν]	ἐγγι-οῦνται

5.A.3. -μι Conjugation

Verbs of the -μι (or athematic) conjugation have suffixes that connect directly to the verb stem without a linking vowel. Often this leads to contraction or lengthening of the stem vowel (see **Contraction** and **Vowel length** in the Glossary).

5.A.3.a. Present and Imperfect Indicative

The present- and imperfect-tense stems of many -μι verbs are reduplicated with ι (e.g., διδ) (see **Reduplication** in the Glossary). The 1S (-μι) and 3S (-σι) suffixes differ from verbs of the -ω conjugation. The verb ἀπόλλυμι has alternate singular forms that follow the -ω conjugation.

-μι Conjugation

	δίδω-μι (stem: δο)	τίθη-μι (stem: θε)	ἵστη-μι (stem: στα)	ἀπόλλυ-μι (stem: ἀπολλυ)

Pres. Act. Indic.

1S	δίδω-μι	τίθη-μι	ἵστη-μι	ἀπόλλυ-μι (-ύ-ω)
2S	δίδω-ς	τίθη-ς	ἵστη-ς	ἀπόλλυ-ς (-ύ-εις)
3S	δίδω-σι[ν]	τίθη-σι[ν]	ἵστη-σι[ν]	ἀπόλλυ-σι[ν] (-ύ-ει)
1P	δίδο-μεν	τίθε-μεν	ἵστα-μεν	ἀπόλλυ-μεν (-ύ-ομεν)
2P	δίδο-τε	τίθε-τε	ἵστα-τε	ἀπόλλυ-τε (-ύ-ετε)
3P	διδό-ασι[ν]	τιθέ-ασι[ν]	ἱστᾶ-σι[ν]	ἀπολλύ-ασι[ν] (-ύ-ουσι[ν])

Pres. Mid./Pass. Indic.

1S	δίδο-μαι	τίθε-μαι	ἵστα-μαι	ἀπόλλυ-μαι
2S	δίδο-σαι	τίθε-σαι	ἵστα-σαι	ἀπόλλυ-σαι
3S	δίδο-ται	τίθε-ται	ἵστα-ται	ἀπόλλυ-ται
1P	διδό-μεθα	τιθέ-μεθα	ἱστά-μεθα	ἀπολλύ-μεθα
2P	δίδο-σθε	τίθε-σθε	ἵστα-σθε	ἀπόλλυ-σθε
3P	δίδο-νται	τίθε-νται	ἵστα-νται	ἀπόλλυ-νται

Impf. Act. Indic.

1S	ἐ-δίδου-ν	ἐ-τίθη-ν	ἵστη-ν	ἀπώλλυ-ν (-υ-ον)
2S	ἐ-δίδου-ς	ἐ-τίθει-ς	ἵστη-ς	ἀπώλλυ-ς (-υ-ες)
3S	ἐ-δίδου	ἐ-τίθει	ἵστη	ἀπώλλυ (-υ-ε)
1P	ἐ-δίδο-μεν	ἐ-τίθε-μεν	ἵστα-μεν	ἀπώλλυ-μεν (-υ-ομεν)
2P	ἐ-δίδο-τε	ἐ-τίθε-τε	ἵστα-τε	ἀπώλλυ-τε (-υ-ετε)
3P	ἐ-δίδο-σαν	ἐ-τίθε-σαν	ἵστα-σαν	ἀπώλλυ-σαν (-υ-ον)

Impf. Mid./Pass. Indic.

1S	ἐ-διδό-μην	ἐ-τιθέ-μην	ἱστά-μην	ἀπωλλύ-μην
2S	ἐ-δίδο-σο	ἐ-τίθε-σο	ἵστα-σο	ἀπώλλυ-σο
3S	ἐ-δίδο-το	ἐ-τίθε-το	ἵστα-το	ἀπώλλυ-το
1P	ἐ-διδό-μεθα	ἐ-τιθέ-μεθα	ἱστά-μεθα	ἀπωλλύ-μεθα
2P	ἐ-δίδο-σθε	ἐ-τίθε-σθε	ἵστα-σθε	ἀπώλλυ-σθε
3P	ἐ-δίδο-ντο	ἐ-τίθε-ντο	ἵστα-ντο	ἀπώλλυ-ντο

5.A.3.b. Aorist Indicative

-μι verbs are not reduplicated in the aorist tense as they often are in the present tense. The aorist tense of some verbs (called *kappa aorists*) forms with a -κ- infix rather than -σ- (cf. ἔδωκα and ἔθηκα). Otherwise, they follow [1]aorist inflection. [1]Aorist and κ aorist forms consistently use the lengthened form of the stem vowel. Some -μι verbs have both [1]aorist and [2]aorist active forms. For the verb ἵστημι, the [1]aorist forms are transitive while the [2]aorists are intransitive.

-μι Conjugation		
δίδω-μι (stem: δο)	τίθη-μι (stem: θε)	ἵστη-μι (stem: στα)

	Aor. Act. Indic.		
	κ Aor.	κ Aor.	[1]Aor. (trans)
1S	ἔ-δω-κα	ἔ-θη-κα	ἔ-στη-σα
2S	ἔ-δω-κα-ς	ἔ-θη-κα-ς	ἔ-στη-σα-ς
3S	ἔ-δω-κε[ν]	ἔ-θη-κε[ν]	ἔ-στη-σε[ν]
1P	ἐ-δώ-κα-μεν	ἐ-θή-κα-μεν	ἐ-στή-σα-μεν
2P	ἐ-δώ-κα-τε	ἐ-θή-κα-τε	ἐ-στή-σα-τε
3P	ἔ-δω-κα-ν	ἔ-θη-κα-ν	ἔ-στη-σα-ν

	Aor. Mid. Indic.		
	κ Aor.	κ Aor.	[1]Aor.
1S	ἐ-δω-κά-μην	ἐ-θη-κά-μην	ἐ-στη-σά-μην
2S	ἐ-δώ-κα-σο	ἐ-θή-κα-σο	ἐ-στή-σα-σο
3S	ἐ-δώ-κα-το	ἐ-θή-κα-το	ἐ-στή-σα-το
1P	ἐ-δω-κά-μεθα	ἐ-θη-κά-μεθα	ἐ-στη-σά-μεθα
2P	ἐ-δώ-κα-σθε	ἐ-θή-κα-σθε	ἐ στή-σα-σθε
3P	ἐ-δώ-κα-ντο	ἐ-θή-κα-ντο	ἐ-στή-σα-ντο

	[2]Aor. Act. Indic.		
1S	ἔ-δω-ν	ἔ-θη-ν	ἔ-στη-ν
2S	ἔ-δω-ς	ἔ-θη-ς	ἔ-στη-ς
3S	ἔ-δω	ἔ-θη	ἔ-στη
1P	ἔ-δο-μεν	ἔ-θε-μεν	ἔ-στη-μεν
2P	ἔ-δο-τε	ἔ-θε-τε	ἔ-στη-τε
3P	ἔ-δο-σαν	ἔ-θε-σαν	ἔ-στη-σαν

	-μι Conjugation, cont'd		
		²Aor. Mid. Indic.	
1S	ἐ-δό-μην	ἐ-θέ-μην	ἐ-στά-μην
2S	ἔ-δου	ἔ-θου	ἔ-στω
3S	ἔ-δο-το	ἔ-θε-το	ἔ-στα-το
1P	ἐ-δό-μεθα	ἐ-θέ-μεθα	ἐ-στά-μεθα
2P	ἔ-δο-σθε	ἔ-θε-σθε	ἔ-στα-σθε
3P	ἔ-δο-ντο	ἔ-θε-ντο	ἔ-στα-ντο

5.B. Subjunctive Mood

5.B.1. Regular Verbs

The suffixes for the subjunctive mood are consistent throughout the system of the -ω verb, with forms differing only in terms of their verb stem and accentuation. Primary suffixes have their connecting vowel lengthened either to ω or η, with the ι of the 2S and 3S suffixes becoming a subscript. The 2S form of the present middle/passive subjunctive is the same as the corresponding form in the indicative mood. Aorist passive forms are accented over the suffix vowel.

	Subjunctive Mood—ω Conjugation			
	Pres. Act. (λύω)	¹Aor. Act. (λύω)	²Aor. Act. (λείπω)	Liq. Aor. Act. (κρίνω)
1S	λύ-ω	λύσ-ω	λίπ-ω	κρίν-ω
2S	λύ-η-ς	λύσ-η-ς	λίπ-η-ς	κρίν-ης
3S	λύ-η	λύσ-η	λίπ-η	κρίν-η
1P	λύ-ω-μεν	λύσ-ω-μεν	λίπ-ω-μεν	κρίν-ω-μεν
2P	λύ-η-τε	λύσ-η-τε	λίπ-η-τε	κρίν-η-τε
3P	λύ-ω-σι[ν]	λύσ-ω-σι[ν]	λίπ-ω-σι[ν]	κρίν-ωσι[ν]

	²Perf. Act. (οἶδα)	¹Aor. Pass. (λύω)	²Aor. Pass. (λείπω)
1S	εἰδ-ῶ	λυθ-ῶ	λιπ-ῶ
2S	εἰδ-ῇ-ς	λυθ-ῇ-ς	λιπ-ῇ-ς
3S	εἰδ-ῇ	λυθ-ῇ	λιπ-ῇ
1P	εἰδ-ῶ-μεν	λυθ-ῶ-μεν	λιπ-ῶ-μεν
2P	εἰδ-ῆ-τε	λυθ-ῆ-τε	λιπ-ῆ-τε
3P	εἰδ-ῶ-σι[ν]	λυθ-ῶ-σι[ν]	λιπ-ῶ-σι[ν]

426

	Pres. Mid./Pass. (λύω)	¹Aor. Mid. (λύω)	²Aor. Mid. (λείπω)	Liq. Aor. Mid. (κρίνω)
1S	λύ-ω-μαι	λύσ-ω-μαι	λίπ-ω-μαι	κρίν-ω-μαι
2S	λύ-η	λύσ-η	λίπ-η	κρίν-η
3S	λύ-η-ται	λύσ-η-ται	λίπ-η-ται	κρίν-η-ται
1P	λυ-ώ-μεθα	λυσ-ώ-μεθα	λιπ-ώ-μεθα	κριν-ώ-μεθα
2P	λύ-η-σθε	λύσ-η-σθε	λίπ-η-σθε	κρίν-η-σθε
3P	λύ-ω-νται	λύσ-ω-νται	λίπ-ω-νται	κρίν-ω-νται

5.B.2. Contract Verbs

Contract verbs form the present subjunctive by contraction of the stem ending vowel with the subjunctive suffix (τιμά-ης → τιμᾷς; see **Contraction** in the Glossary).

SUBJUNCTIVE MOOD—CONTRACT VERBS

	τιμάω	φιλέω	δηλόω
		Pres. Act. Subj.	
1S	τιμ-ῶ	φιλ-ῶ	δηλ-ῶ
2S	τιμ-ᾷ-ς	φιλ-ῇ-ς	δηλ-οῖ-ς
3S	τιμ-ᾷ	φιλ-ῇ	δηλοῖ
1P	τιμ-ῶ-μεν	φιλ-ῶ-μεν	δηλ-ῶ-μεν
2P	τιμ-ᾶ-τε	φιλ-ῆ-τε	δηλ-ῶ-τε
3P	τιμ-ῶ-σι[ν]	φιλ-ῶ-σι[ν]	δηλ-ῶ-σι[ν]
		Pres. Mid./Pass. Subj.	
1S	τιμ-ῶ-μαι	φιλ-ῶ-μαι	δηλ-ῶ-μαι
2S	τιμ-ᾷ	φιλ-ῇ	δηλ-οῖ
3S	τιμ-ᾶ-ται	φιλ-ῆ-ται	δηλ-ῶ-ται
1P	τιμ-ώ-μεθα	φιλ-ώ-μεθα	δηλ-ώ-μεθα
2P	τιμ-ᾶ-σθε	φιλ-ῆ-σθε	δηλ-ῶ-σθε
3P	τιμ-ῶ-νται	φιλ-ῶ-νται	δηλ-ῶ-νται

5.B.3. -μι Verbs

-μι verbs form the subjunctive mood by lengthening the stem vowel either to ω or η and adding primary suffixes. Perfect active, perfect middle/passive, and aorist passive forms inflect like -ω verbs (see section 1 above).

	δίδωμι	ἵστημι	τίθημι
		SUBJUNCTIVE MOOD—μι VERBS	
		Pres. Act. Subj.	
1S	διδ-ῶ	ἱστ-ῶ	τιθ-ῶ
2S	διδ-ῷ-ς	ἱστ-ῇ-ς	τιθ-ῇ-ς
3S	διδ-ῷ	ἱστ-ῇ	τιθ-ῇ
1P	διδ-ῶ-μεν	ἱστ-ῶ-μεν	τιθ-ῶ-μεν
2P	διδ-ῶ-τε	ἱστ-ῆ-τε	τιθ-ῆ-τε
3P	διδ-ῶ-σι[ν]	ἱστ-ῶ-σι[ν]	τιθ-ῶ-σι[ν]
		Pres. Mid./Pass. Subj.	
1S	διδῶ-μαι	ἱστ-ῶ-μαι	τιθ-ῶ-μαι
2S	διδῷ	ἱστ-ῇ	τιθ-ῇ
3S	διδῶ-ται	ἱστ-ῆ-ται	τιθ-ῆ-ται
1P	διδώ-μεθα	ἱστ-ώ-μεθα	τιθ-ώ-μεθα
2P	διδῶ-σθε	ἱστ-ῆ-σθε	τιθ-ῆ-σθε
3P	διδῶ-νται	ἱστ-ῶ-νται	τιθ-ῶ-νται
		Aor. Act. Subj.	
1S	δ-ῶ	στ-ῶ	θ-ῶ
2S	δ-ῷ-ς	στ-ῇ-ς	θ-ῇ-ς
3S	δ-ῷ	στ-ῇ	θ-ῇ
1P	δ-ῶ-μεν	στ-ῶ-μεν	θ-ῶ-μεν
2P	δ-ῶ-τε	στ-ῆ-τε	θ-ῆ-τε
3P	δ-ῶ-σι[ν]	στ-ῶ-σι[ν]	θ-ῶ-σι[ν]
		Aor. Mid. Subj.	
1S	δ-ῶ-μαι	στ-ῶ-μαι	θ-ῶ-μαι
2S	δ-ῷ	στ-ῇ	θ-ῇ
3S	δ-ῶ-ται	στ-ῆ-ται	θ-ῆ-ται

1P	δ-ώ-μεθα	στ-ώ-μεθα	θ-ώ-μεθα
2P	δ-ῶ-σθε	στ-ῆ-σθε	θ-ῆ-σθε
3P	δ-ῶ-νται	στ-ῶ-νται	θ-ῶ-νται

5.C. Optative Mood

The optative mood appears in the NT only in the present and aorist tenses. Optative forms are relatively easy to recognize because in each case a diphthong ending in iota (αι, ει, οι) replaces the connecting vowel that links secondary suffixes to the various tense stems. οι is characteristic of the present and ²aorist tenses, αι (preceded by the infix -σ-) of the ¹aorist, and ει (preceded by the infix -θ-) of the aorist passive. As with the indicative mood, ²aorist active and middle forms lack the aorist active tense sign σ. There are no ²aorist passive optatives in the NT.

5.C.1. Regular Verbs

OPTATIVE MOOD—ω VERBS

	Pres. Act. (λύω)	¹Aor. Act. (λύω)	²Aor. Act. (λείπω)	¹Aor. Pass. (λύω)
1S	λύ-οι-μι	λύ-σαι-μι	λίπ-οι-μι	λυ-θεί-ην
2S	λύ-οι-ς	λύ-σαι-ς	λίπ-οι-ς	λυ-θεί-ης
3S	λύ-οι	λύ-σαι	λίπ-οι	λυ-θεί-η
1P	λύ-οι-μεν	λύ-σαι-μεν	λίπ-οι-μεν	λυ-θεί-ημεν
2P	λύ-οι-τε	λύ-σαι-τε	λίπ-οι-τε	λυ-θεί-ητε
3P	λύ-οι-εν	λύ-σαι-εν	λίπ-οι-εν	λυ-θεί-ησαν

	Pres. Mid./Pass. (λύω)	¹Aor. Mid. (λύω)	²Aor. Mid. (λείπω)
1S	λυ-οί-μην	λυ-σαί-μην	λιπ-οί-μην
2S	λύ-οι-ο	λύ-σαι-ο	λίπ-οι-ο
3S	λύ-οι-το	λύ-σαι-το	λίπ-οι-το
1P	λυ-οί-μεθα	λυ-σαί-μεθα	λιπ-οί-μεθα
2P	λύ-οι-σθε	λύ-σαι-σθε	λίπ-οι-σθε
3P	λύ-οι-ντο	λύ-σαι-ντο	λίπ-οι-ντο

5.C.2. Contract Verbs

Contract verbs form present-tense optatives by contraction of the stem vowel with the optative mood infix -οι-. Aorist optatives follow the [1]aorist pattern.

OPTATIVE MOOD—CONTRACT VERBS		
τιμάω	φιλέω	δηλόω

	Pres. Act. Opt.		
1S	τιμ-ῷ-μι	φιλ-οῖ-μι	δηλ-οῖ-μι
2S	τιμ-ῷ-ς	φιλ-οῖ-ς	δηλ-οῖ-ς
3S	τιμ-ῷ	φιλ-οῖ	δηλ-οῖ
1P	τιμ-ῷ-μεν	φιλ-οῖ-μεν	δηλ-οῖ-μεν
2P	τιμ-ῷ-τε	φιλ-οῖ-τε	δηλ-οῖ-τε
3P	τιμ-ῷ-εν	φιλ-οῖ-εν	δηλ-οῖ-εν

	Pres. Mid./Pass. Opt.		
1S	τιμ-ῷ-μην	φιλ-οί-μην	δηλ-οί-μην
2S	τιμ-ῷ-ο	φιλ-οῖ-ο	δηλ-οῖ-ο
3S	τιμ-ῷ-το	φιλ-οῖ-το	δηλ-οῖ-το
1P	τιμ-ῷ-μεθα	φιλ-οί-μεθα	δηλ-οί-μεθα
2P	τιμ-ῷ-σθε	φιλ-οῖ-σθε	δηλ-οῖ-σθε
3P	τιμ-ῷ-ντο	φιλ-οῖ-ντο	δηλ-οῖ-ντο

5.C.3. -μι Verbs

-μι verbs form the optative infix by the combination of the stem vowel with ι, to which is added the secondary suffixes. Aorist optatives are identical to present-tense forms except that they are not reduplicated.

OPTATIVE MOOD—μι VERBS		
δίδωμι (stem: δο)	ἵστημι (stem: στα)	τίθημι (stem: θε)

	Pres. Act. Opt.		
1S	διδ-οί-ην	ἱστ-αί-ην	τιθ-εί-ην
2S	διδ-οί-ης	ἱστ-αί-ης	τιθ-εί-ης
3S	διδ-οί-η	ἱστ-αί-η	τιθ-εί-η

1P	διδ-οί-ημεν	ἱστ-αί-ημεν	τιθ-εί-ημεν
2P	διδ-οί-ητε	ἱστ-αί-ητε	τιθ-εί-ητε
3P	διδ-οί-ησαν	ἱστ-αί-ησαν	τιθ-εί-ησαν

Pres. Mid./Pass. Opt.

1S	διδ-οί-μην	ἱστ-αί-μην	τιθ-εί-μην
2S	διδ-οῖ-ο	ἱστ-αῖ-ο	τιθ-εῖ-ο
3S	διδ-οῖ-το	ἱστ-αῖ-το	τιθ-εῖ-το
1P	διδ-οί-μεθα	ἱστ-αί-μεθα	τιθ-εί-μεθα
2P	διδ-οῖ-σθε	ἱστ-αῖ-σθε	τιθ-εῖ-σθε
3P	διδ-οῖ-ντο	ἱστ-αῖ-ντο	τιθ-εῖ-ντο

Aor. Act. Opt.

1S	δ-οί-ην	στ-αί-ην	θ-εί-ην
2S	δ-οί-ης	στ-αί-ης	θ-εί-ης
3S	δ-οί-η	στ-αί-η	θ-εί-η
1P	δ-οί-ημεν	στ-αί-ημεν	θ-εί-ημεν
2P	δ-οί-ητε	στ-αί-ητε	θ-εί-ητε
3P	δ-οί-ησαν	στ-αί-ησαν	θ-εί-ησαν

Aor. Mid. Opt.

1S	δ-οί-μην	στ-αί-μην	θ-εί-μην
2S	δ-οῖ-ο	στ-αῖ-ο	θ-εῖ-ο
3S	δ-οῖ-το	στ-αῖ-το	θ-εῖ-το
1P	δ-οί-μεθα	στ-αί-μεθα	θ-εί-μεθα
2P	δ-οῖ-σθε	στ-αῖ-σθε	θ-εῖ-σθε
3P	δ-οῖ-ντο	στ-αῖ-ντο	θ-εῖ-ντο

Aor. Pass. Opt.

1S	δο-θεί-ην	στα-θεί-ην	τε-θεί-ην
2S	δο-θεί-ης	στα-θεί-ης	τε-θεί-ης
3S	δο-θεί-η	στα-θεί-η	τε-θεί-η
1P	δο-θεί-ημεν	στα-θεί-ημεν	τε-θεί-ημεν
2P	δο-θεί-ητε	στα-θεί-ητε	τε-θεί-ητε
3P	δο-θεί--ησαν	στα-θεί-ησαν	τε-θεί-ησαν

5.D. *Imperative Mood*

Imperative verbs do not inflect in the first person. 2S forms of both active and middle/passive imperatives vary somewhat, but the other suffixes are quite consistent from tense to tense.

Only three perfect imperative forms are found in the NT: ἴστε (²perf. act. impv. 2P from οἶδα; "Be aware!"), ἔρρωσθε (perf. mid./pass. impv. 2P; "Farewell!"), and πεφίμωσο (perf. mid./pass. impv. 2S; "Be quiet!").

5.D.1. Regular Verbs

	IMPERATIVE MOOD			
	Pres. Act. Impv.	¹Aor. Act. Impv.	²Aor. Act. Impv.	¹Aor. Pass. Impv.
2S	λῦ-ε	λῦ-σον	λίπ-ε	λύ-θη-τι
3S	λυ-έ-τω	λυ-σά-τω	λιπ-έ-τω	λυ-θή-τω
2P	λύ-ε-τε	λύ-σα-τε	λίπ-ε-τε	λύ-θη-τε
3P	λυ-έ-τωσαν	λυ-σά-τωσαν	λιπ-έ-τωσαν	λυ-θή-τωσαν
	Pres. Mid./Pass. Impv.	¹Aor. Mid. Impv.	²Aor. Mid. Impv.	²Aor. Pass. Impv.
2S	λύ-ου	λῦ-σαι	λιπ-οῦ	γράφ-η-τι
3S	λυ-έ-σθω	λυ-σά-σθω	λιπ-έ-σθω	γραφ-ή-τω
2P	λύ-ε-σθε	λύ-σα-σθε	λίπ-ε-σθε	γράφ-η-τε
3P	λύ-ε-σθωσαν	λυ-σά-σθωσαν	λιπ-έ-σθωσαν	γραφ-ή-τωσαν

5.D.2. Contract Verbs

Imperatives undergo contraction only in the present tense. In doing so, they follow the standard rules of contraction (see **Contraction** in the Glossary). The other tenses form imperatives regularly.

		IMPERATIVE MOOD—CONTRACT VERBS		
		τιμάω	φιλέω	δηλόω
			Pres. Act. Impv.	
	2S	τίμα	φίλει	δήλου
	3S	τιμά-τω	φιλεί-τω	δηλού-τω
	2P	τιμᾶ-τε	φιλεῖ-τε	δηλοῦ-τε
	3P	τιμά-τωσαν	φιλεί-τωσαν	δηλού-τωσαν

		Pres. Mid./Pass. Impv.	
2S	τιμῶ	φιλοῦ	δηλοῦ
3S	τιμά-σθω	φιλεί-σθω	δηλού-σθω
2P	τιμᾶ-σθε	φιλεῖ-σθε	δηλοῦ-σθε
3P	τιμά-σθωσαν	φιλεί-σθωσαν	δηλού-σθωσαν

5.D.3. -μι Verbs

Imperatives of -μι verbs are constructed by adding imperative suffixes to the shortened verb stem, with the exception of the aorist active forms of ἵστημι, which have the lengthened stem. For the present active 2S forms, the stem vowel contracts with the suffix vowel, as shown in the parentheses. Aorist active 2S forms are unique.

IMPERATIVE MOOD—μι VERBS

	δίδωμι (stem: δο)	ἵστημι (stem: στα)	τίθημι (stem: θε)
		Pres. Act. Impv.	
2S	δίδου (ο-ε)	ἵστη (α-ε)	τίθει (ε-ε)
3S	διδό-τω	ἱστά-τω	τιθέ-τω
2P	δίδο-τε	ἵστα-τε	τίθε-τε
3P	διδό-τωσαν	ἱστά-τωσαν	τιθέ-τωσαν
		Pres. Mid./Pass. Impv.	
2S	δίδο-σο	ἵστα-σο	τίθε-σο
3S	διδό-σθω	ἱστά-σθω	τιθέ-σθω
2P	δίδο-σθε	ἵστα-σθε	τίθε-σθε
3P	διδό-σθωσαν	ἱστά-σθωσαν	τιθέ-σθωσαν
		Aor. Act. Impv.	
2S	δός	στῆ-θι	θές
3S	δό-τω	στή-τω	θέ-τω
2P	δό-τε	στῆ-τε	θέ-τε
3P	δό-τωσαν	στή-τωσαν	θέ-τωσαν

IMPERATIVE MOOD—μι VERBS		
δίδωμι (stem: δο)	ἵστημι (stem: στα)	τίθημι (stem: θε)
Aor. Mid./Pass. Impv.		

	δίδωμι (stem: δο)	ἵστημι (stem: στα)	τίθημι (stem: θε)
2S	δό-σο	στά-σο	θέ-σο
3S	δό-σθω	στά-σθω	θέ-σθω
2P	δό-σθε	στά-σθε	θέ-σθε
3P	δό-σθωσαν	στά-σθωσαν	θέ-σθωσαν

6. Verbals

Verbals are special forms of verbs that function either as adjectives or nouns. The Greek verbals are the participle and the infinitive.

6.A. Participles

6.A.1. -ω Verbs

6.A.1.a. Active Participles

- Active participles inflect according to the third declension in the masculine and neuter genders and the first declension in the feminine gender (3/1/3).

- Present active participles have the infix -οντ-, except for the DPM and DPN forms, which have the infix -ου- before the 3P suffix -σι.

- [1]Aorist active participles have the aorist-tense infix -σα- before the participial infix -ντ-, while [2]aorist participles are constructed on the [2]aorist stem and inflect like present participles. Liquid aorist participles inflect like [1]aorists, but without the -σ- infix.

- Perfect active participles have reduplicated stems with the perfect-tense infix -κ- followed by the participial infix -οτ- for masculine and neuter forms and -υι- for feminine forms.

- The feminine singular suffixes have either α or η suffix vowels in accordance with the rules for first-declension nouns (see section 2.A).

- Aorist passive participles have active participial suffixes and thus are included in the table below rather than in the middle and passive table.

Appendix III: Greek Word Tables

ACTIVE PARTICIPLES—ω VERBS

Pres. Act. Ptc.

	M	F	N
NS	λύ-ων	λύ-ουσ-α	λῦ-ον
GS	λύ-οντ-ος	λυ-ούσ-ης	λύ-οντ-ος
DS	λύ-οντ-ι	λυ-ούσ-ῃ	λύ-ον-τι
AS	λύ-οντ-α	λύ-ουσ-αν	λῦ-ον
NP	λύ-οντ-ες	λύ-ουσ-αι	λύ-οντ-α
GP	λυ-όντ-ων	λυ-ουσ-ῶν	λυ-όντ-ων
DP	λύ-ου-σι[ν]	λυ-ούσ-αις	λύ-ου-σι[ν]
AP	λύ-οντ-ας	λυ-ούσ-ας	λύ-οντ-α

Fut. Act. Ptc.

	M	F	N
NS	λύσ-ων	λύσ-ουσ-α	λῦσ-ον
GS	λύσ-οντ-ος	λυσ-ούσ-ης	λύσ-οντ-ος
DS	λύσ-οντ-ι	λυσ-ούσ-ῃ	λύσ-ον-τι
AS	λύσ-οντ-α	λύσ-ουσ-αν	λῦσ-ον
NP	λύσ-οντ-ες	λύσ-ουσ-αι	λύσ-οντ-α
GP	λυσ-όντ-ων	λυσ-ουσ-ῶν	λυσ-όντ-ων
DP	λύσ-ου-σι[ν]	λυσ-ούσ-αις	λύσ-ου-σι[ν]
AP	λύσ-οντ-ας	λυσ-ούσ-ας	λύσ-οντ-α

[1]Aor. Act. Ptc.

	M	F	N
NS	λύ-σας	λύ-σασ-α	λύ-σαν
GS	λύ-σαντ-ος	λυ-σάσ-ης	λύ-σαντ-ος
DS	λύ-σαντ-ι	λυ-σάσ-ῃ	λύ-σαντ-ι
AS	λύ-σαντ-α	λυ-σάσ-αν	λύ-σαν
NP	λύ-σαντ-ες	λύ-σασ-αι	λύ-σαντ-α
GP	λυ-σάντ-ων	λυ-σασ-ῶν	λυ-σάντ-ων
DP	λύ-σα-σι[ν]	λυ-σάσ-αις	λύ-σα-σι[ν]
AP	λύ-σαντ-ας	λυ-σάσ-ας	λύ-σαντ-α

Active Participles—ω Verbs, cont'd

Liq. Aor. Act. Ptc. (κρίνω)

	M	F	N
NS	κρίν-ας	κρίν-ασ-α	κρίν-αν
GS	κρίν-αντ-ος	κριν-άσ-ης	κρίν-αντ-ος
DS	κρίν-αντ-ι	κριν-άσ-η	κρίν-αντ-ι
AS	κρίν-αντ-α	κρίν-ασ-αν	κρίν-αν
NP	κρίν-αντ-ες	κρίν-ασ-αι	κρίν-αντ-α
GP	κριν-άντ-ων	κριν-ασ-ῶν	κριν-άντ-ων
DP	κρίν-α-σι[ν]	κριν-άσ-αις	κρίν-α-σι[ν]
AP	κρίν-αντ-ας	κριν-άσ-ας	κρίν-αντ-α

²Aor. Act. Ptc. (λαμβάνω)

	M	F	N
NS	λαβ-ών	λαβ-οῦσ-α	λαβ-όν
GS	λαβ-όντ-ος	λαβ-ούσ-ης	λαβ-όντ-ος
DS	λαβ-όντ-ι	λαβ-ούσ-η	λαβ-όντ-ι
AS	λαβ-όντ-α	λαβ-οῦσ-αν	λαβ-όν
NP	λαβ-όντ-ες	λαβ-οῦσ-αι	λαβ-όντ-α
GP	λαβ-όντ-ων	λαβ-ουσ-ῶν	λαβ-όντ-ων
DP	λαβ-οῦ-σι[ν]	λαβ-ούσ-αις	λαβ-οῦ-σι[ν]
AP	λαβ-όντ-ας	λαβ-ούσ-ας	λαβ-όντ-α

Perf. Act. Ptc.

	M	F	N
NS	λε-λυ-κώς	λε-λυ-κυῖ-α	λε-λυ-κός
GS	λε-λυ-κότ-ος	λε-λυ-κυί-ας	λε-λυ-κότ-ος
DS	λε-λυ-κότι	λε-λυ-κυί-α	λε-λυ-κότ-ι
AS	λε-λυ-κότ-α	λε-λυ-κυῖ-αν	λε-λυ-κός
NP	λε-λυ-κότ-ες	λε-λυ-κυῖ-αι	λε-λυ-κότ-α
GP	λε-λυ-κότ-ων	λε-λυ-κυι-ῶν	λε-λυ-κότ-ων
DP	λε-λυ-κό-σι[ν]	λε-λυ-κυί-αις	λε-λυ-κό-σι[ν]
AP	λε-λυ-κότ-ας	λε-λυ-κυί-ας	λε-λυ-κότ-α

²Perf. Act. Ptc. (οἶδα)

	M	F	N
NS	εἰδ-ώς	εἰδ-υῖ-α	εἰδ-ός
GS	εἰδ-ότ-ος	εἰδ-υί-ας	εἰδ-ότ-ος
DS	εἰδ-ότ-ι	εἰδ-υί-ᾳ	εἰδ-ότ-ι
AS	εἰδ-ότ-α	εἰδ-υῖ-αν	εἰδ-ός
NP	εἰδ-ότ-ες	εἰδ-υῖ-αι	εἰδ-ότ-α
GP	εἰδ-ότ-ων	εἰδ-υι-ῶν	εἰδ-ότ-ων
DP	εἰδ-ό-σι[ν]	εἰδ-υί-αις	εἰδ-ό-σι[ν]
AP	εἰδ-ό-τας	εἰδ-υί-ας	εἰδ-ότ-α

Aor. Pass. Ptc.

	M	F	N
NS	λυ-θείς	λυ-θεῖσ-α	λυ-θέν
GS	λυ-θέντ-ος	λυ-θείσ-ης	λυ-θέντ-ος
DS	λυ-θέντ-ι	λυ-θείσ-ῃ	λυ-θέντ-ι
AS	λυ-θέντ-α	λυ-θεῖσ-αν	λυ-θέν
NP	λυ-θέντ-ες	λυ-θεῖσ-αι	λυ-θέντ-α
GP	λυ-θέντ-ων	λυ-θεισ-ῶν	λυ-θέντ-ων
DP	λυ-θεῖ-σι[ν]	λυ-θείσ-αις	λυ-θεῖ-σι[ν]
AP	λυ-θέντ-ας	λυ-θείσ-ας	λυ-θέντ-α

²Aor. Pass. Ptc. (στρέφω)

	M	F	N
NS	στρεφ-είς	στρεφ-εῖσ-α	στρεφ-έν
GS	στρεφ-έντ-ος	στρεφ-είσ-ης	στρεφ-έντ-ος
DS	στρεφ-έντ-ι	στρεφ-είσ-η	στρεφ-έντ-ι
AS	στρεφ-έντ-α	στρεφ-εῖσ-αν	στρεφ-έν
NP	στρεφ-έντ-ες	στρεφ-εῖσ-αι	στρεφ-έντ-α
GP	στρεφ-έντ-ων	στρεφ-εισ-ῶν	στρεφ-έντ-ων
DP	στρεφ-εῖ-σι[ν]	στρεφ-είσ-αις	στρεφ-εῖ-σι[ν]
AP	στρεφ-έντ-ας	στρεφ-είσ-ας	στρεφ-έντ-α

6.A.1.b. Middle and Passive Participles

Infixes and suffixes are the same for all middle and passive participles. Thus a full paradigm is given only for the present middle/passive participle.

- Middle and passive participles have the infix -μεν- before regular first- and second-declension suffixes (2/1/2, cf. section 3.A.1).

- [1]Aorist active participles have the aorist-tense infix -σα- before the participial infix -ντ-, while [2]aorist participles inflect like present participles, but are constructed on the [2]aorist stem. Liquid aorist participles inflect like [1]aorists, but without the -σ- infix.

- Perfect middle/passive participles have reduplicated stems and lack a connecting vowel between the verb stem and the -μεν- infix.

MIDDLE AND PASSIVE PARTICIPLES—ω VERBS		
Pres. Mid./Pass. Ptc.		
M	F	N
NS λυ-ό-μεν-ος	λυ-ο-μέν-η	λυ-ό-μεν-ον
GS λυ-ο-μέν-ου	λυ-ο-μέν-ης	λυ-ο-μέν-ου
DS λυ-ο-μέν-ῳ	λυ-ο-μέν-η	λυ-ο-μέν-ῳ
AS λυ-ό-μεν-ον	λυ-ο-μέν-ην	λυ-ό-μεν-ον
NP λυ-ό-μεν-οι	λυ-ό-μεν-αι	λυ-ό-μεν-α
GP λυ-ο-μέν-ων	λυ-ο-μέν-ων	λυ-ο-μέν-ων
DP λυ-ο-μέν-οις	λυ-ο-μέν-αις	λυ-ο-μέν-οις
AP λυ-ο-μέν-ους	λυ-ο-μέν-ας	λυ-ό-μεν-α
Fut. Mid. Ptc.		
M	F	N
NS λυσ-ό-μεν-ος	λυσ-ο-μέν-η	λυσ-ό-μεν-ον
. . .		
Liq. Fut. Mid. Ptc.		
M	F	N
NS κριν-ού-μεν-ος	κριν-ου-μέν-η	κριν-ού-μεν-ον
. . .		
[1]Aor. Mid. Ptc.		
M	F	N
NS λυ-σά-μεν-ος	λυ-σα-μέν-η	λυ-σά-μεν-ον
. . .		

438

Liq. Aor. Mid. Ptc.

	M	F	N
NS	κριν-ά-μεν-ος	κριν-α-μέν-η	κριν-ά-μεν-ον

. . .

²Aor. Mid. Ptc. (λαμβάνω)

	M	F	N
NS	λαβ-ό-μεν-ος	λαβ-ο-μέν-η	λαβ-ό-μεν-ον

. . .

Perf. Mid./Pass. Ptc.

	M	F	N
NS	λε-λυ-μέν-ος	λε-λυ-μέν-η	λε-λυ-μέν-ον

. . .

Fut. Pass. Ptc.

	M	F	N
NS	λυ-θησ-ό-μεν-ος	λυ-θησ-ο-μέν-η	λυ-θησ-ό-μεν-ον

. . .

6.A.2. Contract Verbs

Contract verbs form their present-tense participles just as regular -ω verbs, except that the stem vowel contracts with the connecting vowel of the participial suffixes (see **Contraction** in the Glossary). Since the patterns of inflection can be surmised from the -ω verb paradigms, only partial paradigms are given here.

Present Participles—Contract Verbs

Pres. Act. Ptc. (τιμάω)

	M	F	N
NS	τιμ-ῶν	τιμ-ῶσα	τιμ-ῶν
GS	τιμ-ῶντ-ος	τιμ-ώσης	τιμ-ῶντ-ος

. . .

Pres. Act. Ptc. (φιλέω)

	M	F	N
NS	φιλ-ῶν	φιλ-οῦσ-α	φιλ-οῦν
GS	φιλ-οῦντ-ος	φιλ-ούσ-ης	φιλ-οῦντ-ος

. . .

Pres. Act. Ptc. (δηλόω)

	M	F	N
NS	δηλ-ῶν	δηλ-οῦσ-α	δηλ-οῦν
GS	δηλ-οῦντ-ος	δηλ-ούσ-ης	δηλ-οῦντ-ος

. . .

PRESENT PARTICIPLES—CONTRACT VERBS, CONT'D

Pres. Mid./Pass. Ptc.(τιμάω)		
	M	F	N
NS	τιμώ-μεν-ος	τιμω-μέν-η	τιμώ-μεν-ον

. . .

Pres. Mid./Pass. Ptc. (φιλέω)		
	M	F	N
NS	φιλού-μεν-ος	φιλου-μέν-η	φιλού-μεν-ον

. . .

Pres. Mid./Pass. Ptc. (δηλόω)		
	M	F	N
NS	δηλού-μεν-ος	δηλου-μέν-η	δηλού-μεν-ον

. . .

6.A.3 -μι Verbs

-μι verbs form active participles by contraction of the stem vowel with the connecting vowel of the participial suffix (see **Contraction** in the Glossary). Middle and passive participles form like -ω verbs. Aorist participles form like present participles, but without reduplication. Due to their similarity with other forms, only partial paradigms are given here.

PARTICIPLES—μι VERBS

Pres. Act. Ptc.—δίδωμι (stem δο)		
	M	F	N
NS	διδούς	διδοῦσα	διδόν
GS	διδόντος	διδούσης	διδόντος

. . .

Pres. Act. Ptc.—ἵστημι (stem στα)		
	M	F	N
NS	ἱστάς	ἱστᾶσα	ἱστάν
GS	ἱστάντος	ἱστάσης	ἱστάντος

. . .

Pres. Act. Ptc.—τίθημι (stem θε)		
	M	F	N
NS	τιθείς	τιθεῖσα	τιθέν
GS	τιθέντος	τιθείσης	τιθέντος

. . .

Appendix III: Greek Word Tables

Pres. Mid./Pass. Ptc.—δίδωμι (stem δο)

	M	F	N
NS	διδόμενος	διδομένη	διδόμενον

. . .

Pres. Mid./Pass. Ptc.—ἵστημι (stem στα)

	M	F	N
NS	ἱστάμενος	ἱσταμένη	ἱστάμενον

. . .

Pres. Mid./Pass. Ptc.—τίθημι (stem θε)

	M	F	N
NS	τιθέμενος	τιθεμένη	τιθέμενον

. . .

Aor. Act. Ptc.—δίδωμι (stem δο)

	M	F	N
NS	δούς	δοῦσα	δόν
GS	δόντος	δούσης	δόντος

. . .

Aor. Act. Ptc.—ἵστημι (stem στα)

	M	F	N
NS	στάς	στᾶσα	στάν
GS	στάντος	στάσης	στάντος

. . .

Aor. Act. Ptc.—τίθημι (stem θε)

	M	F	N
NS	θείς	θεῖσα	θέν
GS	θέντος	θείσης	θέντος

. . .

Aor. Mid. Ptc.—δίδωμι (stem δο)

	M	F	N
NS	δόμενος	δομένη	δόμενον

. . .

Aor. Mid. Ptc.—ἵστημι (stem στα)

	M	F	N
NS	στάμενος	σταμένη	στάμενον

. . .

PARTICIPLES—μι VERBS, CONT'D		
Aor. Mid. Ptc.—τίθημι (stem θε)		
M	F	N
NS θέμενος	θεμένη	θέμενον

. . .

6.B. Infinitives

6.B.1. Regular Verbs

Infinitives for each tense-voice combination are fixed forms. Present, future, and [2]aorist active infinitives have the suffix -ειν. Middle and future passive forms have –σθαι. [1]Aorist active forms have -αι, and aorist passive forms have -ναι.

INFINITIVES—ω VERBS			
	Active	Middle	Passive
Present	λύ-ειν	λύ-εσθαι	λύ-εσθαι
Future	λύσ-ειν	λύσ-εσθαι	λυ-θήσ-εσθαι
[1]Aorist	λῦσ-αι	λύσ-ασθαι	λυ-θῆ-ναι
Liq. Aorist (κρίνω)	κρῖν-αι	κρίν-ασθαι	κρι-θῆ-ναι
[2]Aorist (λείπω, χαίρω)	λιπ-εῖν	λιπ-έσθαι	χαρ-ῆ-ναι
Perfect	λε-λυκ-έ-ναι	λε-λύ-σθαι	λε-λύ-σθαι
[2]Perfect (οἶδα)	εἰδ-έ-ναι		

6.B.2. Contract Verbs

Present infinitives of contract verbs form by contraction of the stem vowel with the connecting vowel of the infinitive suffix (see **Contraction** in the Glossary).

PRESENT INFINITIVES—CONTRACT VERBS		
Pres. Act. Inf.		
τιμ-ᾶν	φιλ-εῖν	δηλ-οῦν
Pres. Mid./Pass. Inf.		
τιμ-ᾶσθαι	φιλ-εῖσθαι	δηλ-οῦσθαι

6.B.3. -μι Verbs

Active infinitives of -μι verbs have the suffix -ναι, while middle forms have -σθαι. Aorist forms have a lengthened vowel or diphthong in the verb stem and lack reduplication. Perfect infinitives inflect as present infinitives, but are reduplicated with ε rather than ι. Other tenses follow regular inflection patterns.

PRESENT INFINITIVES—μι VERBS		
δίδωμι	ἵστημι	τίθημι
Pres. Act. Inf.		
διδ-ό-ναι	ἱστ-ά-ναι	τιθ-έ-ναι
Pres. Mid./Pass. Inf.		
δίδ-ο-σθαι	ἵστ-α-σθαι	τίθ-ε-σθαι
Aor. Act. Inf.		
δοῦ-ναι	στῆ-ναι	θεῖ-ναι
Aor. Mid. Inf.		
δό-σθαι	στά-σθαι	θέ-σθαι

7. The Verb Εἰμί

Since εἰμί is a verb of being rather than activity, it is not properly parsed according to voice. However, due to their suffixes, the present and imperfect forms of the verb are sometimes parsed as active and the future forms as middle.

7.A. Indicative Mood

The verb εἰμί occurs in only three tenses in the indicative mood—present, imperfect, and future. Although the present indicative 1S takes the form of -μί verb, the forms are irregular enough to warrant separate treatment. The suffixes for the imperfect tense are similar to those of the secondary active -μί verbs (see section 5.A.3.b), except for the 1S suffix -μην, which is similar to the secondary Mid./Pass. suffix. The future tense uses regular middle suffixes (cf. section 5.A.1).

	Εἰμί—INDICATIVE FORMS		
	Pres. Indic.	Impf. Indic.	Fut. Indic.
1S	εἰ-μί	ἤ-μην	ἔσ-ο-μαι
2S	εἶ	ἦ-ς	ἔσ-η
3S	ἐσ-τί[ν]	ἦ-ν	ἔσ-ται
1P	ἐσ-μέν	ἦ-μεν	ἐσ-ό-μεθα
2P	ἐσ-τέ	ἦ-τε	ἔσ-ε-σθε
3P	εἰ-σί[ν]	ἦ-σαν	ἔσ-ο-νται

443

7.B. Other Moods

Only the present tense of εἰμί is used with the non-indicative moods. For the subjunctive mood, the forms are the same as the subjunctive suffixes for λύω, except for accents and breathing marks. The optative forms are the same as the aorist passive optative suffixes for λύω. The imperative forms have the same suffixes as the present active imperative of λύω, except for the 2S form, but they are attached to the stem εσ- (ισ-).

	Εἰμί—OTHER MOODS		
	Pres. Subj.	Pres. Opt.	Pres. Impv.
1S	ὦ	εἴη-ν	—
2S	ᾖ-ς	εἴη-ς	ἴσ-θι
3S	ᾖ	εἴη	ἔσ-τω (or ἤτω)
1P	ὦ-μεν	εἴη-μεν	—
2P	ᾖ-τε	εἴη-τε	ἔσ-τε
3P	ὦ-σι[ν]	εἴη-σαν	ἔσ-τωσαν

7.C. Verbals

Only the present and future tenses of εἰμί are used to form participles and infinitives.

7.C.1. Participles

The forms of the present participle of εἰμί are the same as the participial suffixes for λύω, with accents and breathing marks added. The suffixes of the future participle are the same as the middle/passive participial suffixes for λύω.

	Εἰμί—PARTICIPLES		
	Pres. Ptc.		
	M	F	N
NS	ὤν	οὖσ-α	ὄν
GS	ὄντ-ος	οὔσ-ης	ὄντ-ος
DS	ὄντ-ι	οὔσ-η	ὄντ-ι
AS	ὄντ-α	οὖσ-αν	ὄν
NP	ὄντ-ες	οὖσ-αι	ὄντ-α
GP	ὄντ-ων	οὐσ-ῶν	ὄντ-ων
DP	οὖ-σι[ν]	οὔσ-αις	οὖ-σι[ν]
AP	ὄντ-ας	οὔσ-ας	ὄντ-α

Fut. Ptc.

	M	F	N
NS	ἐσ-ό-μεν-ος	ἐσ-ο-μέν-η	ἐσ-ό-μεν-ον
GS	ἐσ-ο-μέν-ου	ἐσ-ο-μέν-ης	ἐσ-ο-μέν-ου
DS	ἐσ-ο-μέν-ῳ	ἐσ-ο-μέν-ῃ	ἐσ-ο-μέν-ῳ
AS	ἐσ-ό-μεν-ον	ἐσ-ο-μέν-ην	ἐσ-ό-μεν-ον
NP	ἐσ-ό-μεν-οι	ἐσ-ό-μεν-αι	ἐσ-ό-μεν-α
GP	ἐσ-ο-μέν-ων	ἐσ-ο-μέν-ων	ἐσ-ο-μέν-ων
DP	ἐσ-ο-μέν-οις	ἐσ-ο-μέν-αις	ἐσ-ο-μέν-οις
AP	ἐσ-ο-μέν-ους	ἐσ-ο-μέν-ας	ἐσ-ό-μεν-α

7.C.2. Infinitives

The present infinitive of εἰμί is similar to the liquid aorist active infinitive. The future infinitive has the same suffix as the present middle infinitive of λύω (see section 6.B.1).

Εἰμί—Infinitives

Pres.	Fut.
εἶ-ναι	ἔσ-ε-σθαι

Appendix IV
Principal Parts of Common Greek Verbs

Prepared by Mark A. House

The "principal parts" of Greek verbs are the six specific tense forms used to illustrate the basis for each verb's inflection. Most Greek verbs form their principal parts according to regular rules of inflection. The following list includes verbs that occur (or whose compound forms occur) at least thirty times in the Greek NT and whose principal parts are irregular or may be difficult to recognize. Forms beginning with a hyphen occur only in compounds.

Pres Act. (or Depon.)	Fut. Act. (or Depon.)	Aor. Act. (or Depon.)	Perf. Act. (or Depon.)	Perf. Mid./Pass.	Aor. Pass.
ἀγγέλλω	ἀγγελῶ	ἤγγειλα	ἤγγελκα		ἠγγέλην
ἄγω	ἄξω	ἤγαγον		ἦγμαι	ἤχθην
αἴρω	ἀρῶ	ἦρα	ἦρκα	ἦρμαι	ἤρθην
ἀκούω	ἀκούσω	ἤκουσα	ἀκήκοα		ἠκούσθην
ἁμαρτάνω	ἁμαρτήσω	ἡμάρτησα, ἥμαρτον	ἡμάρτηκα		
ἀνοίγω	ἀνοίξω	ἀνέῳξα, ἤνοιξα, ἠνέῳξα	ἀνέῳγα	ἀνέῳγμαι, ἤνοιγμαι, ἠνέῳγμαι	ἀνεῴχθην, ἠνοίχθην, ἠνεῴχθην
ἀποθνήσκω	ἀποθανοῦμαι	ἀπέθανον			
ἀποκρίνομαι		ἀπεκρινάμην			ἀπεκρίθην
ἀποκτείνω, ἀποκτέννω	ἀποκτενῶ	ἀπέκτεινα			ἀπεκτάνθην
ἀπόλλυμι	ἀπολέσω, ἀπολῶ	ἀπώλεσα	ἀπόλωλα		
ἀποστέλλω	ἀποστελῶ	ἀπέστειλα	ἀπέσταλκα	ἀπέσταλμαι	ἀπεστάλην
ἀφίημι	ἀφήσω	ἀφῆκα		ἀφεῖμαι, ἀφέωμαι	ἀφέθην, ἀφείθην
βαίνω	βήσομαι	ἔβην	βέβηκα		ἐβήθην
βάλλω	βαλῶ	ἔβαλον	βέβληκα	βέβλημαι	ἐβλήθην

Pres Act. (or Depon.)	Fut. Act. (or Depon.)	Aor. Act. (or Depon.)	Perf. Act. (or Depon.)	Perf. Mid./Pass.	Aor. Pass.
γίνομαι	γενήσομαι	ἐγενόμην	γέγονα	γεγένημαι	ἐγενήθην
γινώσκω	γνώσομαι	ἔγνων	ἔγνωκα	ἔγνωσμαι	ἐγνώσθην
γράφω	γράψω	ἔγραψα	γέγραφα	γέγραμμαι	ἐγράφην
δείκνυμι, δεικνύω	δείξω	ἔδειξα			ἐδείχθην
εἰμί	ἔσομαι	ἤμην (impf.)			
ἐλπίζω	ἐλπιῶ	ἤλπισα	ἤλπικα		
ἐργάζομαι		ἠργασάμην		εἴργασμαι	
ἔρχομαι	ἐλεύσομαι	ἦλθον	ἐλήλυθα		
ἐσθίω	φάγομαι	ἔφαγον			
εὑρίσκω	εὑρήσω	εὗρον	εὕρηκα		εὑρέθην
ἔχω	ἕξω	ἔσχον	ἔσχηκα		
θέλω	θελήσω	ἠθέλησα			ἠθελήθην
ἵστημι	στήσω	ἔστησα (tr.), ἔστην (intr.)	ἕστηκα	ἕσταμαι	ἐστάθην
καθαρίζω	καθαριῶ	ἐκαθάρισα		κεκαθάρισμαι	ἐκαθαρίσθην
κάθημαι	καθήσομαι				
καθίζω	καθίσω, καθιῶ	ἐκάθισα	κεκάθικα		
καλέω	καλῶ, καλέσω	ἐκάλεσα	κέκληκα	κέκλημαι	ἐκλήθην
κηρύσσω	κηρύξω	ἐκήρυξα		κεκήρυγμαι	ἐκηρύχθην
κλαίω	κλαύσω	ἔκλαυσα			
κράζω	κράξω	ἔκραξα	κέκραγα		
κρίνω	κρινῶ	ἔκρινα	κέκρικα	κέκριμαι	ἐκρίθην
λαμβάνω	λήμψομαι	ἔλαβον	εἴληφα	εἴλημμαι	ἐλημφθην
λέγω	ἐρῶ	εἶπον	εἴρηκα	εἴρημαι	ἐρρέθην, ἐρρήθην
λείπω	-λείψω	ἔλιπον		-λέλειμμαι	-ελείφθην
μέλλω	μελλήσω				
μένω	μενῶ	ἔμεινα	μεμένηκα		
οἶδα	εἰδήσω	ἤδειν			
ὁράω	εἶδον	ἑώρακα			ὤφθην
πάσχω		ἔπαθον	πέπονθα		
πείθω	πείσω	ἔπεισα	πέποιθα	πέπεισμαι	ἐπείσθην
πέμπω	πέμψω	ἔπεμψα	πέπομφα	πέπεμμαι	ἐπέμφθην
πίνω	πίομαι	ἔπιον	πέπωκα		ἐπόθην

Appendix IV: Principal Parts of Common Greek Verbs

PRES ACT. (OR DEPON.)	FUT. ACT. (OR DEPON.)	AOR. ACT. (OR DEPON.)	PERF. ACT. (OR DEPON.)	PERF. MID./PASS.	AOR. PASS.
πίπτω	πεσοῦμαι	ἔπεσον	πέπτωκα		
πράσσω	πράξω	ἔπραξα	πέπραχα	πέπραγμαι	
σπείρω		ἔσπειρα		ἔσπαρμαι	ἐσπάρην
στρέφω	-στρέψω	ἔστρεψα		-εστραμμαι	ἐστράφην
σῴζω	σώσω	ἔσωσα	σέσωκα	σέσῳ(σ)μαι	ἐσώθην
τίθημι	θήσω	ἔθηκα	τέθεικα	τέθειμαι	ἐτέθην
ὑποτάσσω		ὑπέταξα		ὑποτέταγμαι	ὑπετάγη